Global Marketing Management

The Prentice Hall International Series in Marketing
Philip Kotler, Series Editor

Seventh Edition

Global
Marketing
Management

Warren J. Keegan

Lubin School of Business
Pace University, New York City and Westchester
Visiting University Professor, Cranfield University, Bedford, U.K.

Upper Saddle River, New Jersey 07458

Keegan, Warren J.
    Global marketing management / Warren J. Keegan.—7th ed.
      p. cm.
    Includes bibliographical references and index.
    ISBN 0-13-033271-2
    1. Export marketing—Management. 2. Export marketing—Management—Case studies.
 I. Green, Mark C. II. Title.

    HF1416 .K44 1999
    658.8'48—dc21

2001016317

Executive Editor: Whitney Blake
Assistant Editor: Anthony Palmiotto
Editorial Assistant: Melissa Pellerano
Media Project Manager: Cindy Harford
Managing Editor (Production): Gail Steier de Acevedo
Production Editor: Maureen Wilson
Permissions Coordinator: Suzanne Grappi
Associate Director, Manufacturing: Vincent Scelta
Manufacturing Buyer: Natacha St. Hill Moore
Cover Design: Kiwi Design
Cover Illustration/Photo: PhotoDisc
Full-Service Project Management and Composition: Omegatype Typography, Inc.
Printer/Binder: Hamilton Printing Co.

Credits and acknowledgments borrowed from other sources and reproduced, with permission, in this textbook appear on appropriate page within text.

10 9 8 7 6 5 4 3 2
ISBN 0-13-033271-2

To my parents, Donald Rayfield Keegan and Edla Polson Keegan

Brief Contents

Contents

PART III   ANALYZING AND TARGETING GLOBAL MARKET OPPORTUNITIES   143

Cases

Preface

Global Marketing Management, Seventh Edition, traces its ancestry to *Multinational Marketing Management,* a book that broke new ground in the field of international marketing when it was published in 1974. The first edition departed from the traditional export trade focus in the field of international marketing and adopted a strategic approach that reflected the growing importance of multinational corporations, the latest findings of research, and the most advanced experience of practitioners. The book combined text with classroom tested graduate-level cases and was an immediate worldwide success. The objective of each revision has been to not only reflect current practice but to anticipate the direction of development of the field and maintain the book's authoritative position as the leading MBA graduate-level and reference text for practitioners of international marketing.

This revision continues the path-breaking tradition of this book. Every chapter has been completely revised and updated, and a new chapter on global e.marketing has been added. Also included is the completely updated "Global Income and Population for 2000 and Projections to 2010 and 2020" in the Appendix. There are four new cases, and two of the cases that were retained from the previous edition have been revised and updated.

The seventh edition is the most exciting revision in the book's history. Perhaps most significantly, for the first time in modern history, even large population, low-income countries such as China and India appear to have achieved the ability to maintain sustained development and growth that will, if continued, transform these countries from low- or lower-middle to high-income countries. In the meantime, companies in the high-income countries have begun to recognize that they now face formidable competitive challenges from companies located in countries at every stage of development.

World economic integration has proceeded to advance both in the multilateral framework of the World Trade Organization and in regional economic agreements such as NAFTA (The North American Free Trade Agreement) and the EU (European Union). NAFTA links the United States, Canada, and Mexico in a program of economic integration; the EU links the 15 countries of Western Europe; and the member countries of both of these regional agreements are actively exploring expanding the membership of these agreements to other countries in the region: Central and Eastern Europe for the EU, and Central and South America for NAFTA. The two Koreas continue to meet, and the economic linkages in the Pacific basin continue to expand.

The book is organized into six parts: Part I is an introduction to global marketing. Part II covers the major dimensions of the environment of global marketing: economic; social and cultural; and political, legal, and regulatory. Part III is devoted to analyzing and targeting global market opportunities. Part IV focuses on global marketing strategy, and Part V, "Creating Global Marketing Programs," covers the global marketing mix of product, pricing, place, and promotion decisions, and how e.marketing can be integrated into the marketing mix. Part VI, "Managing the Global Marketing Program," concludes the book with a focus on implementation. It addresses the tasks of leading, organizing, and monitoring the global strategy; the future of global marketing; and careers in global marketing.

◆ ACKNOWLEDGMENTS

This edition, like the previous six, reflects the contributions, insights, and labor of many persons. My colleagues, associates, and students at the Lubin School of Business, Pace University, and at many other universities around the world; the fellows and members of the Academy of International Business; and my clients, past and present, have all contributed.

Although many colleagues, students, clients, and others have contributed to this and to previous editions, I especially want to thank Dorothy Minkus-McKenna, who has been invaluable in organizing the material for this edition. The reference librarians at Pace, Anne B. Campbell and Michelle Lang, have been an author's dream come true: No matter how obscure the request, they always get their document. They have a simple rule: "If it's out there, we'll find it."

Hermawan Kartajaya, President of the Asia Pacific Marketing Federation and Chief Service Officer of MarkPlus, Jakarta, has been a knowledgeable and perceptive guide to marketing in Southeast Asia and a great source of insight and creative thinking about the marketing concept and discipline.

Professor Bodo B. Schlegelmilch, Vice-Dean International and Chair of International Marketing and Management, Vienna University of Economics and Business Administration (WU-Wien) and Editor-in-Chief of the *Journal of International Marketing,* my co-author of the new *Global Marketing Management: A European Perspective,* has generously shared his thoughts, experience, and insights for this revision and was especially helpful in contributing to Chapter 16. Mark Green, Professor, Simpson College, my co-author of *Global Marketing,* has generously shared his ongoing research into case examples for this edition.

Pace University has a unique doctoral program that attracts an impressive group of students who have established themselves as leaders in their various fields and organizations, and who work toward their doctorate on a part-time basis while continuing their full-time careers. I have been privileged to teach a seminar in this program and would especially like to acknowledge the many contributions of my doctoral students in my doctoral seminar on global strategic marketing. In particular, I would like to acknowledge Thomas C. Finnerty for preparing the revised "Kodak Versus Fuji" case and for Michael A. Allocca for his preparation of the "Ascom Hasler Mailing System" case. Others who have made special contributions to this revision include Malcolm McDonald, Cranfield University, my co-author for *Marketing Plans that Work,* and colleague at Cranfield; John Stopford, London Business School; Paul D. Ellis, Assistant Professor, The Hong Kong Polytechnic University–Hong Kong, Yang Fu; Joseph Ganitsky, Professor of International Business, Loyola University–New Orleans; Donald Gibson, Professor, Macquarere University; H. Donald Hopkins, Associate Professor, Temple University–Philadelphia; Raj Komaran, National University of Singapore; Hermann Kopp, Professor, Norwegian School of Management; Howard Perlmutter, The Wharton School, Inc.; James A. F. Stoner, Fordham University; Martin Topol, Pace University; Robert Vambery, Pace University; David Zenoff, Zenoff Associates; and Dinker Raval and Bala Subramanian of Morgan State University.

Case studies have always been and continue to be a unique pedagogical tool. I am grateful to all of the case authors who contributed cases to this edition.

- *A.S. Norlight:* Carl Arthus Solberg and Hermann Kopp, The Norwegian School of Management
- *CEAC–China:* Lluis G. Renart and Francisco Pares, Professors, IESE

- *Coca-Cola: Universal Appeal?:* Donna Cristo, Doctoral Student, Pace University
- *The Education of an Expat:* Tom Miller, President, Carl Zeiss, Inc.
- *Euro Disney:* James L. Bauer, Vice President, Chemical Bank
- *The Launch of GSM Cellular in South Africa:* Steve Burgess, Professor, The School of Economic and Business Studies, University of the Witwatersrand, Johannesburg, South Africa
- *Oriflame:* Dominique Zardel, Professor, ESSEC
- *Parker Pen Co.,* Charles J. Anderer
- *Metro Corporation:* Farok J. Contractor, Professor, Rutgers University
- *Nokia and the Cellular Phone Industry:* Jakob Fritz Hansen and Claus Groth-Andersen.

My secretaries, Gail Weldon-Pietrangolare, Victoria Underhill, and Mary O'Connor, have provided constant support and cheerful assistance.

The talented and creative people at Prentice Hall are always a pleasure to work with. I especially want to thank the acquisitions editor, Whitney Blake, and her assistant, Melissa Pellerano, for their support and helpful assistance.

Finally, my greatest debt is to my customers: the faculty who adopt this book and the students and executives who purchase the book to study and learn about how to be a successful player in the exciting world of global marketing. To all of you I say, thank you for your support and inspiration and best wishes for every success in your global marketing programs.

About the Author

◆ DR. WARREN J. KEEGAN

FELLOW, ACADEMY OF INTERNATIONAL BUSINESS

Dr. Keegan is Professor of International Business and Marketing and Director of the Center for Global Business Strategy at the Lubin School of Business of Pace University–New York, and is Visiting Professor, Cranfield University School of Management (UK), CEIBS (China European International Business School)–Shanghai, Wharton Executive Programs, University of Pennsylvania, and ESSEC, Cergy-Pontoise–France. He is the founder of Warren Keegan Associates, Inc., a consulting consortium of experts in global strategy formulation and implementation. The firm is affiliated with Marketing Strategy & Planning, Inc.–New York, and MarkPlus, Indonesia's leading marketing consulting firm. Dr. Keegan is Chairman of the Markplus Global Institute–Singapore.

He wrote the first multinational marketing textbook and is one of the world's leading experts on marketing and global business. He holds B.S. and M.S. degrees in economics from Kansas State University and an MBA and doctorate in marketing and international business from the Harvard Business School. He has held faculty positions at a number of business schools including Columbia, George Washington University, New York University, INSEAD, IMD, and the Stockholm School of Economics.

His experience includes consulting with Boston Consulting Group and Arthur D. Little, marketing planning with the Pontiac Division of General Motors, and Chairman of Douglas A. Edwards, Inc., a New York commercial real estate firm. He is a consultant to a number of global firms. Current or former clients include AT&T, Bertelsmann, Bell Atlantic, General Electric, J. Walter Thompson, PurduePharma, Philips, Reckitt & Colman, Singapore International Airlines, and the Singapore Trade Development Board.

Dr. Keegan is the author or co-author of many books, including *Global Marketing Management: A European Perspective* (Financial Times/Prentice Hall, 2001), *Marketing Plans That Work: Targeting Growth and Profitability* (Butterworth Heinemann, 1997), *Global Marketing* (2nd ed., Prentice Hall, 2000), *Marketing* (2nd ed., Prentice Hall, 1996), *Marketing Sans Frontiers* (InterEditions, 1994), *Advertising Worldwide* (Prentice Hall, 1991), and *Judgments, Choices, and Decisions: Effective Management Through Self-Knowledge* (John Wiley & Sons). He has published numerous articles in leading journals including *Harvard Business Review, Administrative Science Quarterly, Journal of Marketing, Journal of International Business Studies,* and *The Columbia Journal of World Business.*

Dr. Keegan is a former MIT Fellow in Africa, Assistant Secretary, Ministry of Development Planning and Secretary of the Economic Development Commission, Government of Tanzania, consultant with Boston Consulting Group and Arthur D. Little, and Chairman of Douglas A. Edwards, a New York corporate real estate firm.

He is a Lifetime Fellow of the Academy of International Business; Individual Eminent Person (IEP) appointed by Asian Global Business Leaders Society (other awardees include Noel Tichy, Rosabeth Moss Kanter, and Gary Wendt); listed in Marquis Who's

Who in America, 55th and earlier editions; member of the International Advisory Board of École des Hautes Études Commerciales (HEC)–Montreal; Member, Editorial Advisory Board, Cranfield School of Management and Financial Times/Prentice Hall Management Monograph Series, *The International Journal of Medical Marketing;* and is a commissioner of PT Indofood Sukses Makmur (Jakarta). He is a former director of The S.M. Stoller Company, Inc., The Cooper Companies, Inc. (NYSE), Inter-Ad, Inc., American Thermal Corporation, Inc., Halfway Houses of Westchester, Inc., Wainwright House, and The Rye Arts Center.

Global Marketing Management

CHAPTER 1

Introduction to Global Marketing

"The new electronic interdependence re-creates the world in the image of a global village."
—MARSHALL HERBERT MCLUHAN
The Medium Is the Message (1967)

". . . globalization must be taken for granted. There will be only one standard for corporate success: international market share. The winning corporations will win by finding markets all over the world."
—JACK WELCH
CEO, GE (1994)

We live in a global marketplace. As you read this book, you may be sitting in a chair imported from Brazil or at a desk imported from Denmark. You may have purchased these items from IKEA, the Swedish global furniture retailer. The computer on your desk could be a sleek new IBM Thinkpad designed and marketed worldwide by IBM and manufactured in Taiwan by Acer, Inc., or perhaps a Macintosh designed and marketed worldwide by Apple and manufactured in Ireland. Your shoes are likely to be from Italy, and the coffee you are sipping is from Latin America or Africa.

You might be listening to "Mambo # 5" by Lou Bega, a German artist with an Italian father and a Ugandan mother who lives in Munich and is signed by BMG Entertainment, a division of the German headquartered global media company, thanks to your boom box's built-in CD player, the technology for which was developed jointly by two companies—one Japanese and the other Dutch. Your sweater could be the latest fashion from Italy's Benetton. What time is it now? When you check your watch, can you tell where it was made? It may be from Japan, Hong Kong, Singapore, the Philippines, or Switzerland. Welcome to the 21st century. Yesterday's marketing fantasy has become today's reality: A global marketplace has emerged.

Indeed, global marketing is truly global with many innovations returning to their country or region of origin in a new form that expresses the tastes and preferences of global markets. Round one in this cycle was the expansion of U.S. fast-food burger chains to the Philippines. In the Philippines, local competition entered the burger market with products that were more adapted to the local taste than those of the global companies. Next, the latest fast-food craze in California was from Jollibee, a Filipino chain that served up burgers with a taste of the islands: Hamburgers topped with pineapple, and dessert pies filled with mango.

In the past 160 years, a sweeping transformation has profoundly affected the people and industries of many nations. Prior to 1840, students sitting at their desks would not have had any item in their possession that was manufactured more than a few miles from where they lived—with the possible exception of the books they were reading. Some countries—most notably Great Britain—were actively involved in international trade in the mid-19th century. However, since World War II there has been an unparalleled expansion into global markets by companies that previously served only customers located in the home country. Two decades ago, the phrase *global marketing* did not even exist. Today, businesses look to global marketing for the realization of their full commercial potential. That is why you may own some of the products described in the preceding paragraphs, no matter whether you live in Asia-Pacific, Europe, Africa, or North or South America. However, there is another even more critical reason why companies need to take global marketing seriously: survival. A company that fails to become global in outlook risks losing its domestic business to competitors having lower costs, greater experience, and better products.

But what is global marketing? How does it differ from "regular" marketing? Marketing can be defined as a series of activities leading to an exchange transaction between a seller and a buyer at a profit. Marketing activities center on an organization's efforts to satisfy customer wants and needs with products and services that offer competitive value. The marketing mix (product, price, place, and promotion) comprises a contemporary marketer's primary tools. Marketing is a universal discipline as applicable in Australia as it is in Zanzibar.

This book is about global marketing. An organization that engages in global marketing focuses its resources on global market opportunities and threats. One difference between "regular" marketing and "global" marketing is in the scope of activities. A company that engages in global marketing conducts important business activities outside the home-country market. Another difference is that global marketing involves an understanding of specific concepts, considerations, and strategies that must be skillfully applied in conjunction with universal marketing fundamentals to ensure success in global markets. This book concentrates on the major dimensions of global marketing. A brief overview of marketing is presented next, although the author assumes that the reader has completed introductory marketing and international business courses or has equivalent experience.

◆ MARKETING: A UNIVERSAL DISCIPLINE

The foundation for a successful global marketing program is a sound understanding of the marketing discipline. Marketing is the process of focusing the resources and objectives of an organization on environmental opportunities and needs. The first and most fundamental fact about marketing is that it is a universal discipline. Marketing is a set of concepts, tools, theories, practices and procedures, and experience. Together, these elements constitute a teachable and learnable body of knowledge. Although marketing is universal, marketing practice, of course, varies from country to country. Each person is unique, and each country is unique. This reality of differences means that we cannot always directly apply experience from one country to another. If the customers, competitors, channels of distribution, and available media are different, it may be necessary to change our marketing plan.

THE MARKETING CONCEPT

During the past three decades, the concept of marketing has changed dramatically. It has evolved from a focus on the product and on making a "better" product where better was based on internal standards and values. The objective was profit, and the means to achieving the objective was selling, or persuading the potential customer to exchange his or her money for the company's product.

The New Concept of Marketing and the Four Ps

The "new" concept of marketing, which appeared about 1960, shifted the focus of marketing from the product to the customer. The objective was still profit, but the means of achieving the objective expanded to include the entire marketing mix, or the "four Ps" as they became known: product, price, place (channels of distribution), and promotion. For an Asian perspective of marketing, see "The 18 Guiding Principles of the Marketing Company" in the appendix at the end of this chapter.

The Strategic Concept of Marketing

By the 1990s, it was clear that the "new" concept of marketing was outdated and that the times demanded a strategic concept. The strategic concept of marketing, a major evolution in the history of marketing thought, shifted the focus of marketing from the customer or the product to the customer in the context of the broader external environment. Knowing everything there is to know about the customer is not enough. To succeed, marketers must know the customer in a context including the competition, government policy and regulation, and the broader economic, social, and political macro forces that shape the evolution of markets. In global marketing this may mean working closely with home-country government trade negotiators and other officials and industry competitors to gain access to a target-country market.

A revolutionary development in the shift to the strategic concept of marketing is in the marketing objective—from profit to stakeholder benefits. Stakeholders are individuals or groups who have an interest in the activity of a company. They include the employees and management, customers, society, and government, to mention only the most prominent. There is a growing recognition that profits are a reward for performance (defined as satisfying customers in a socially responsible or acceptable way). To compete in today's market, it is necessary to have an employee team committed to continuing innovation and to producing quality products. In other words, marketing must focus on the customer in context and deliver value by creating stakeholder benefits for both customers and employees. This change is a revolutionary idea that is accepted today by a vanguard minority of marketing practitioners.

Profitability is not forgotten in the strategic concept. Indeed, it is a critical means to the end of creating stakeholder benefits. The means of the strategic marketing concept is strategic management, which integrates marketing with the other management functions. One of the tasks of strategic management is to make a profit, which can be a source of funds for investing in the business and for rewarding shareholders and management. Thus, profit is still a critical objective and measure of marketing success, but it is not an end in itself. The aim of marketing is to create value for stakeholders, and the key stakeholder is the customer. If your customer can get greater value from your competitor because your competitor is willing to accept a lower level of profit reward for investors and management, the customer will choose your competitor, and you will be out of business. The spectacular inroads of the "clones" into IBM's PC market illustrate that even the largest and most powerful companies can be challenged by competitors who are more efficient or who are willing to accept lower profit returns.

Finally, the strategic concept of marketing has shifted the focus of marketing from a microeconomics maximization paradigm to a focus of managing strategic partnerships and positioning the firm between vendors and customers in the value chain with the aim

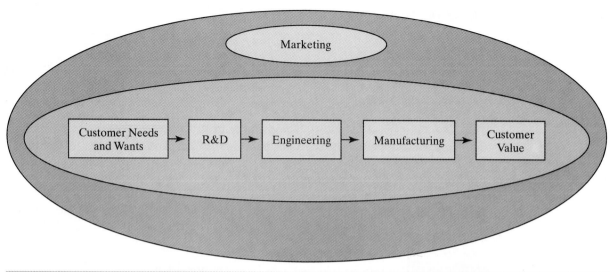

FIGURE 1-1 Boundaryless Marketing

and purpose of creating value for customers. This expanded concept of marketing was termed *boundaryless marketing* by Jack Welch, chairperson and chief executive officer (CEO) of General Electric. The notion of boundaryless marketing is shown in Figure 1-1. Marketing, in addition to being a concept and a philosophy, is a set of activities and a business process. The marketing activities are called the four Ps: product, price, place (distribution), and promotion (or communications). These four Ps can be expanded to five Ps by adding probe (research). The marketing management process is the task of focusing the resources and objectives of the organization on opportunities in the environment. The three basic principles that underlie marketing are discussed next.

◆ THE THREE PRINCIPLES OF MARKETING

The essence of marketing can be summarized in three great principles. The first identifies the purpose and task of marketing, the second the competitive reality of marketing, and the third the principal means for achieving the first two.

CUSTOMER VALUE AND THE VALUE EQUATION

The task of marketing is to create customer value that is greater than the value created by competitors. The value equation, shown in Figure 1-2, is a guide to this task. As suggested in the equation, value for the customer can be increased by expanding or improving product and/or service benefits, by reducing the price, or by a combination of these elements. Companies with a cost advantage can use price as a competitive weapon. Knowledge of the customer combined with innovation and creativity can lead to a total offering that offers superior customer value. If the benefits are strong enough and valued enough by customers, a company does not need to be the low-price competitor to win customers.

COMPETITIVE OR DIFFERENTIAL ADVANTAGE

The second great principle of marketing is competitive advantage. A competitive advantage is a total offer, vis-à-vis relevant competition, that is more attractive to customers. The advantage can exist in any element of the company's offer: the product, the

$$V = \frac{B}{P}$$

where

V = value
B = perceived benefits – perceived costs (for example, switching costs)
P = price

FIGURE 1-2   The Value Equation

price, the advertising and point-of-sale promotion, or the distribution of the product. One of the most powerful strategies for penetrating a new national market is to offer a superior product at a lower price. The price advantage will get immediate customer attention, and, for those customers who purchase the product, the superior quality will make an impression.

FOCUS

The third marketing principle is focus, or the concentration of attention. Focus is required to succeed in the task of creating customer value at a competitive advantage. All great enterprises, large and small, are successful because they have understood and applied this great principle. IBM succeeded and became a great company because it was more clearly focused on customer needs and wants than any other company in the emerging data-processing industry.

One of the reasons IBM found itself in crisis in the early 1990s was that its competitors had become much more clearly focused on customer needs and wants. Dell and Compaq, for example, focused on giving customers computing power at low prices: IBM was offering the same computing power at higher prices.

A clear focus on customer needs and wants and on the competitive offer is required to mobilize the effort needed to maintain a differential advantage. This can be accomplished only by focusing or concentrating resources and efforts on customer needs and wants and on how to deliver a product that will meet those needs and wants.

◆ GLOBAL MARKETING: WHAT IT IS AND WHAT IT IS NOT

The foundation for a successful global marketing program is a sound understanding of the marketing discipline. Marketing is the process of focusing the resources and objectives of an organization on environmental opportunities and needs. The first and most fundamental fact about marketing is that it is a universal discipline. Marketing is a set of concepts, tools, theories, practices and procedures, and experience. Together these elements constitute a teachable and learnable body of knowledge.

Although the marketing discipline is universal, markets and customers are quite differentiated. This means that marketing practice must vary from country to country. Each person is unique, and each country is unique. This reality of differences means that we cannot always directly apply experience from one country to another. If the customers, competitors, channels of distribution, and available media are different, it may be necessary to change our marketing plan.

Companies who don't appreciate this fact will soon learn about it if they transfer irrelevant experience from one country or region to another. Nestlé, for example, sought to transfer its great success with a four-flavor coffee line from Europe to the United States. Its U.S. competitors were delighted: The transfer led to a decline of 1 percent in

U.S. market share![1] An important task in global marketing is learning to recognize the extent to which marketing plans and programs can be extended worldwide, as well as the extent to which they must be adapted.

Much of the controversy about global marketing dates to Professor Theodore Levitt's 1983 seminal article in the *Harvard Business Review,* "The Globalization of Markets." Professor Levitt argued that marketers were confronted with a "homogenous global village." Levitt advised organizations to develop standardized, high-quality world products and market them around the globe using standardized advertising, pricing, and distribution. Some well-publicized failures by Parker Pen and other companies seeking to follow Levitt's advice brought his proposals into question. The business press frequently quoted industry observers who disputed Levitt's views. For example, Carl Spielvogel, chairman and CEO of the Backer Spielvogel Bates Worldwide advertising agency, told *The Wall Street Journal,* "Theodore Levitt's comment about the world becoming homogenized is bunk. There are about two products that lend themselves to global marketing—and one of them is Coca-Cola."[2]

Indeed, it was global marketing that made Coke a worldwide success. However, that success was not based on a total standardization of marketing mix elements. In his book, *The Borderless World,* Kenichi Ohmae explains that Coke's success in Japan could be achieved only by spending a great deal of time and money becoming an insider. That is, the company built a complete local infrastructure with its sales force and vending machine operations. Coke's success in Japan, according to Ohmae, was a function of its ability to achieve "global localization," the ability to be as much of an insider as a local company but still reap the benefits that result from world-scale operations.

What does the phrase *global localization* really mean? In a nutshell, it means a successful global marketer must have the ability to "think globally and act locally." As we will see many times in this book, "global" marketing may include a combination of standard (e.g., the actual product itself) and nonstandard (e.g., distribution or packaging) approaches. A "global product" may be "the same" product everywhere and yet "different." Global marketing requires marketers to behave in a way that is global and local at the same time by responding to similarities and differences in world markets.

As the Coca-Cola Company has demonstrated, the ability to think globally and act locally can be a source of competitive advantage. By adapting sales promotion, distribution, and customer service efforts to local needs, Coke established such strong brand preference that the company claims a 78 percent share of the soft-drink market in Japan. At first, Coca-Cola managers did not understand the Japanese distribution system. However, with considerable investment of time and money, they succeeded in establishing a sales force that was as effective in Japan as it was in the United States. To complement Coke sales, the Japanese unit has created products such as Georgia-brand canned coffee and Lactia, a lactic, noncarbonated soft drink that promotes healthy digestion and quick refreshment expressly for the Japanese market.

Coke is a product embodying marketing mix elements that are both global and local in nature. In this book, we do not propose that global marketing is a "knee-jerk" attempt to impose a totally standardized approach to marketing around the world. A central issue in global marketing is how to tailor the global marketing concept to fit a particular product or business. Finally, it is necessary to understand that global marketing does not mean entering every country in the world. Global marketing does mean widening business horizons to encompass the world when scanning for opportunity and threat. The decision to enter markets outside the home country depends on a company's re-

---

[1] Interview with Raymond Viault, vice chairman of General Mills, Inc.
[2] Joanne Lipman, "Ad Fad: Marketers Turn Sour on Global Sales Pitch Harvard Guru Makes," *The Wall Street Journal,* 12 May 1988, p. 1.

Cola
" ot very, brode

sources, managerial mind-set, and the nature of opportunity and threat. The Coca-Cola Company's soft-drink products are distributed in almost 200 countries; in fact, the theme of a recent annual report was "A Global Business System Dedicated to Customer Service." Coke is the best-known, strongest brand in the world; its enviable global position has resulted in part from the Coca-Cola Company's willingness and ability to back its flagship product with a strong local marketing effort. Although the ubiquitous red-and-white Coca-Cola symbol is available globally, the company also produces over 200 other nonalcoholic beverages to suit local beverage preferences.

A number of other companies have successfully pursued global marketing by creating strong global brands. Philip Morris, for example, has made Marlboro the number-one cigarette brand in the world. In automobiles, DaimlerChrysler has gained global recognition for its Mercedes nameplate as has its competitor, Bayerische Motoren Werke Aktiengesellschaft, Munich for its nameplate BMW automobiles and motorcycles.

However, as shown in Table 1-1, global marketing strategies can also be based on product or system design, product positioning, packaging, distribution, customer service, and sourcing considerations. For example, McDonald's has designed a restaurant system that can be set up virtually anywhere in the world. Like Coca-Cola, McDonald's also customizes its menu offerings in accordance with local eating customs. In Jakarta, Indonesia, for example, McDonald's is upscale dining. It is the place to be and to be seen in Jakarta. Cisco Systems, which makes local area network routers that allow computers to communicate with each other, designs new products that can be programmed to operate under virtually any conditions in the world.[3]

Unilever uses a teddy bear in various world markets to communicate the benefits of the company's fabric softener. Harley-Davidson's motorcycles are positioned around the world as the all-American bike. Gillette uses the same packaging for its flagship Sensor razor everywhere in the world. Italy's Benetton utilizes a sophisticated distribution system to quickly deliver the latest fashions to its worldwide network of stores.

The backbone of Caterpillar's global success is a network of dealers that supports a promise of "24 hour parts and service" anywhere in the world. The success of Honda and Toyota in world markets was initially based on exporting cars from factories in Japan. Now, both companies have invested in manufacturing facilities in the United States and other countries from which they export. In 1994, Honda earned the distinction of being the number-one exporter of cars from the United States by shipping more than 100,000 Accords and Civics to Japan and 35 other countries. Gap focuses its marketing effort on

TABLE 1-1 Examples of Global Marketing	
Global Marketing Strategy	*Company/Home Country*
Brand Name	Coca-Cola (U.S.), Philip Morris (U.S.), DaimlerChrysler (Germany)
Product Design	McDonalds's (U.S.), Toyota (Japan), Ford (U.S.), Cisco Systems (U.S.)
Product positioning	Unilever (Great Britain/Netherlands), Harley-Davidson (U.S.)
Packaging	Gillette (U.S.)
Distribution	Benetton (Italy)
Customer service	Caterpillar (U.S.)
Sourcing	Toyota (Japan), Honda (Japan), Gap (U.S.)

---

[3] Gregory L. Miles, "Tailoring a Global Product," *International Business* (March 1995): 50.

the United States but relies on apparel factories in low-wage countries to supply most of its clothing.

The particular approach to global marketing that a company adopts will depend on industry conditions and its source or sources of competitive advantage. Should Harley-Davidson start manufacturing motorcycles in a low-wage country such as Mexico or China? Will U.S. consumers continue to snap up U.S.-built Toyotas? The answer to these questions is: "It all depends." Because Harley's competitive advantage is based in part on its "Made in the U.S.A." positioning, shifting production outside the United States is not advisable at this time. Toyota's success in the United States is partly attributable to its ability to transfer world-class manufacturing skills to the United States while using advertising to stress that its Camry is built by Americans, with many components purchased in the United States.

Toyota has positioned itself as a global brand independent of any country-of-origin link. A Toyota is a Toyota wherever it is made. The same thing is true for thousands of companies that have successfully positioned their brand independent of country of origin. A Harley-Davidson motorcycle made in China would shock Harley buyers: The brand at this stage of its development is linked to a single country of origin, the United States.

◆ THE IMPORTANCE OF GLOBAL MARKETING

The largest national market in the world, the United States, today represents roughly 25 percent of the total world market for all products and services. Thus, U.S. companies wishing to achieve maximum growth potential must "go global" because nearly 75 percent of world market potential is outside their home country. Coca-Cola is one U.S.-based company that understands this; 68 percent of its 1999 operating income and 62 percent of revenues were generated by its soft-drink business outside North America.

Non-U.S. companies have an even greater motivation to seek market opportunities beyond their own borders; their opportunities include the 276 million people in the United States. For example, even though the dollar value of the home market for Japanese companies is the second largest in the world (after the United States), the market outside Japan is 85 percent of the world potential for Japanese companies. For European countries, the picture is even more dramatic. Even though Germany is the largest single-country market in Europe, 94 percent of the world market potential for German companies is outside of Germany.

Many companies have recognized the importance of conducting business activities outside the home country. Industries that were strictly national in scope only a few years ago are dominated today by a handful of global companies. The rise of the global corporation closely parallels the rise of the national corporation, which emerged from the local and regional corporation in the 1880s and the 1890s in the United States. The auto industry provides a dramatic—and sobering—example. In the first quarter of the 20th century, there were thousands of auto companies in the world and more than 500 in the United States alone. Today, fewer than 20 companies remain worldwide, and only 2 of them are American (Table 1-2). Fortune only tracks 24 automotive companies in its survey of Global 500 companies. In most industries, the companies that will survive and prosper in the this century will be global enterprises. Some companies that do not respond to the challenges and opportunities of globalization will be absorbed by more dynamic enterprises; others will simply disappear.

This fact is illustrated by the stunning announcement of a merger between Daimler-Benz and Chrysler in 1998. This $36 billion dollar deal, the largest industrial takeover in history as of May 1998, underlined the importance of scale and size and scope in the global motor vehicle industry. The combined companies moved from 6th and 15th in the

TABLE 1-2 Total Motor Vehicle and Parts Sales Worldwide (US$ million)

	1998 Sales	*1998 Profits*	*1998 Market Share*
General Motors	$161,315	$2,956	14.5
DaimlerChrysler	154,615	5,656	13.9
Ford Motor	144,416	22,071	13.0
Toyota	99,740	2,787	9.0
Volkswagen	76,307	1,261	6.9
Nissan Motor	51,478	(217)	4.6
Fiat	50,999	692	4.6
Honda Motor	48,748	2,386	4.4
Renault	41,353	1,500	3.7
Peugeot	37,540	539	3.4
BMW	35,887	513	3.2
Robert Bosch	28,610	446	2.6
Mitsubishi Motors	27,480	44	2.5
Volvo	26,773	1,086	2.4
Mazda Motor	16,093	303	1.4
All Other	108,625	2,749	9.9
Total	1,109,949	44,772	100.0

Source: Adapted from *Fortune* Global 500, 2 August 1999, p. F-19.

world to a combined 5th place ranking after GM, Ford, Toyota, and Volkswagen. When you look at the list of the top companies in the world in Table 1-2, you can see that the pressure will build for further combinations and mergers in this industry.

The Japanese auto market is quite fragmented. The market is divided between Toyota (32 percent), Nissan (16 percent), Honda (12 percent), Mitsubishi (11 percent), Mazda (8 percent), Suzuki (8 percent), Daihatsu (5 percent), and others (8 percent).[4] The importance of automobile export sales as a percentage of a country's total production is illustrated in Table 1-3. It is quite clear that not all of these companies will survive, and indeed, Nissan in late 1999 was in serious financial trouble. As Thomas Middelhoff, chairman of Bertelsmann AG, said recently, "There are no German and American companies. There are only successful and unsuccessful companies."[5] Unfortunately, publications such as *Fortune* magazine still like to categorize companies geographically by where their headquarters are located.

Table 1-4 shows 25 of *The Wall Street Journal*'s top 100 companies ranked in terms of market capitalization—that is, the market value of all shares of stock outstanding. Table 1-5 provides a different perspective: the top 25 of *Fortune* magazine's 1998 ranking of the 500 largest service and manufacturing companies by revenues. Comparing the top 10 companies in each table, it is striking to note that, although General Electric has the second highest market value, it ranked 9th in revenues and 2nd in profits. General Motors has the highest revenue but ranks 79th in market value and 42nd in profits. It is interesting to note that only one Japanese company (Nippon Telegraph and Telephone) appears in the top 10 companies in terms of market value but that four Japanese companies (Mitsui, Itochu, Mitsubishi, and Toyota Motor) appear in the top 10 in sales.

---

[4] Haig Simonian, "Can Japan Keep 11 Carmakers?" *The Financial Times,* 22 July 1998, p. 13.
[5] As quoted in "Global Mall," *The Wall Street Journal,* 7 May 1998, p. 1.

TABLE 1-3	Automobile Industry—A Global Perspective, Passenger Car Production 1996 by Country (1,000 units)			
	Production	*Exports*	*Percent*	*Imports*
Japan	7,864	3,232	41	440
United States	6,037	534	9	4,064
Germany	4,540	2,650	58	1,852
France	3,148	2,026	64	1,386
Korea	2,265	1,056	47	16
Spain	1,942	1,543	79	512
United Kingdom	1,686	914	54	—
Italy	1,318	640	49	—
Canada	1,279	872	68	—
Total	30,079	13,448	45	8,270

Source: Japanese Automobile Manufacturers Association in JAPAN 1998, Keizai Koho Center.

TABLE 1-4	The Largest Corporations by Market Value (US$ millions)		
Rank			
1998	*1996*	*Company (Country)*	*Market Value*
1	12	Microsoft (U.S.)	$460,304
2	1	General Electric (U.S.)	370,661
3	16	IBM (U.S.)	233,825
4	19	Wal-Mart (U.S.)	214,719
5		Cisco Systems (U.S.)	205,839
6		Lucent (U.S.)	205,616
7	2	Royal Dutch/Shell (Netherlands/U.K.)	200,735
8	14	Intel (U.S.)	197,818
9	5	Exxon (U.S.)	187,243
10	4	Nippon Telegraph & Telephone (Japan)	186,566
11		AT&T (U.S.)	178,390
12	10	Merck (U.S.)	174,681
13	22[a]	BP Amaco (U.K.)	174,461
14		Citigroup	171,143
15		MCI WorldCom (U.S.)	160,133
16	3	Coca-Cola (U.S.)	153,076
17	30	American International Group (U.S.)	144,987
18	29	Pfizer (U.S.)	142,046
19	31	Bristol-Myers Squibb (U.S.)	139,894
20	13	Johnson & Johnson (U.S.)	131,830
21		Deutsche Telekom (Germany)	126,781
22		Bank of America (U.S.)	126,312
23	7	Toyota Motors (Japan)	119,244
24	15	Procter & Gamble (U.S.)	118,569
25		American Online (U.S.)	117,872

[a] Reflects a merger.

Source: "The World's 100 Largest Public Companies," *The Wall Street Journal,* 28 September 1999, p. R27. Ranked by market value as of June 30, 1999.

TABLE 1-5	The *Fortune* Global 500: Largest Companies by Revenue (US$ Millions)					
Rank						
1999	*1996*	*Company*	*Country*	*Revenues*	*Profits*	*Rank*
1	1	General Motors	U.S.	$161,315	$ 2,956	42
2	—	DaimlerChrysler	Germany	154,615	5,656	9
3	2	Ford Motor	U.S.	144,416	22,071	1
4	11	Wal-Mart Stores	U.S.	139,208	4,430	17
5	3	Mitsui	Japan	109,373	233	338
6	5	Itochu	Japan	108,749	(266.7)	462
7	4	Mitsubishi	Japan	107,184	244	328
8	8	Exxon	U.S.	100,697	6,370	5
9	12	General Electric	U.S.	100,469	9,296	2
10	10	Toyota Motor	Japan	99,740	2,787	47
11	6	Royal Dutch/Shell	Brit./Neth.	93,692	350	296
12	7	Maruben	Japan	93,569	(921)	481
13	9	Sumitomo	Japan	89,021	(102)	444
14	15	IBM	U.S.	81,667	6,328	6
15	—	AXA	France	78,729	1,702	85
16	—	Citigroup	U.S.	76,431	5,807	8
17	23	Volkswagen	Germany	76,307	1,261	114
18	14	Nippon Telephone	Japan	76,119	415	14
19	—	BP Amaco	Britain	68,304	3,260	33
20	13	Nissho Iwai	Japan	67,742	(771)	479
21	14	Nippon Life	Japan	66,300	828	182
22	25	Siemens	Germany	66,038	370	295
23	—	Allianz	Germany	64,875	2,022	68
24	16	Hitachi	Japan	62,405	(2,651)	490
25	—	U.S. Postal Service	U.S.	60,072	550	242

Source: Adapted from *Fortune* Global 500, 2 August 1999, p. F-1.

Table 1-5 also highlights the importance of the automobile industry. The top three companies in the world by revenues are automotive manufacturers. DaimlerChrysler, the result of the merger of Daimler-Benz and Chrysler in 1998, lifted Daimler-Benz from its 1996 ranking of number 20 to number 2. Interestingly, the company is classified as a Germany company despite the importance of the Chrysler business. Wal-Mart, a global retailer, has shown tremendous growth over the past few years. In 1995, it ranked number 12. In 1998, Wal-Mart had jumped to the position of number 4. Also noteworthy is the rise of Citigroup, a diversified financial services company. It ranked number 58 in 1997 but had risen to number 16 in 1998. In the case of DaimlerChrysler and Citigroup, the rise was primarily through acquisitions or mergers as opposed to Wal-Mart's growth, which was primarily through opening new stores. Some of the economic problems Japanese companies have experienced in the mid-1990s are reflected in the companies included. In 1996, 6 of the top 10 companies were Japanese; two years later in 1998, only 4 of the top 10 companies were Japanese. No matter what their position in the *Fortune* Global 500 today, companies must constantly look to the future. Due to changing economic conditions, mergers and acquisitions, and innovation, major shifts can occur. In fact, between 1975 and 1995, 60 percent of the companies on the *Fortune* 500 were replaced.[6]

---

[6] W. Chan Kim and Renèe Mauborgne, "How to Discover the Unknown Market," *The Financial Times,* 6 May 1999, p. 12.

◆ MANAGEMENT ORIENTATIONS

The form and substance of a company's response to global market opportunities depend greatly on management's assumptions or beliefs—both conscious and unconscious—about the nature of the world. The worldview of a company's personnel can be described as ethnocentric, polycentric, regiocentric, and geocentric.[7] Management at a company with a prevailing ethnocentric orientation may consciously make a decision to move in the direction of geocentricism. The orientations—collectively known as the EPRG framework—are summarized in Figure 1-3.

ETHNOCENTRIC ORIENTATION

A person who assumes his or her home country is superior compared to the rest of the world is said to have an ethnocentric orientation. The ethnocentric orientation means company personnel see only similarities in markets and assume the products and practices that succeed in the home country will, due to their demonstrated superiority, be successful anywhere. At some companies, the ethnocentric orientation means that opportunities outside the home country are ignored. Such companies are sometimes called domestic companies. Ethnocentric companies that do conduct business outside the home country can be described as international companies; they adhere to the notion that the products that succeed in the home country are superior and, therefore, can be sold everywhere without adaptation.

In the ethnocentric international company, foreign operations are viewed as being secondary or subordinate to domestic ones. An ethnocentric company operates under the assumption that "tried and true" headquarters' knowledge and organizational capabilities can be applied in other parts of the world. Although this can sometimes work to a company's advantage, valuable managerial knowledge and experience in local markets may go unnoticed. For a manufacturing firm, ethnocentrism means foreign markets are viewed

FIGURE 1-3 Orientation of Management and Companies

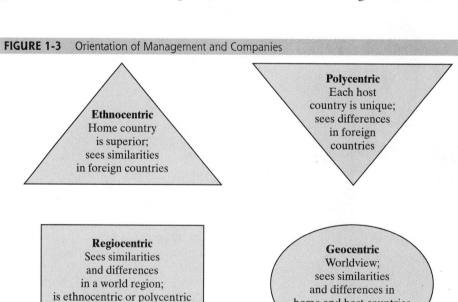

Ethnocentric
Home country
is superior;
sees similarities
in foreign countries

Polycentric
Each host
country is unique;
sees differences
in foreign
countries

Regiocentric
Sees similarities
and differences
in a world region;
is ethnocentric or polycentric
in its view of
the rest of the world

Geocentric
Worldview;
sees similarities
and differences in
home and host countries

---

[7] Adapted from Howard Perlmutter, "The Torturous Evolution of the Multinational Corporation," *Columbia Journal of Business* (January–February 1969).

as a means of disposing of surplus domestic production. Plans for overseas markets are developed utilizing policies and procedures identical to those employed at home. No systematic marketing research is conducted outside the home country, and no major modifications are made to products. Even if consumer needs or wants in international markets differ from those in the home country, those differences are ignored at headquarters.

Nissan's ethnocentric orientation was quite apparent during its first few years of exporting cars and trucks to the United States. Designed for mild Japanese winters, the vehicles were difficult to start in many parts of the United States during the cold winter months. In northern Japan, many car owners would put blankets over the hoods of their cars. Nissan's assumption was that Americans would do the same thing. Until the 1980s, Eli Lilly and Company operated as an ethnocentric company in which activity outside the United States was tightly controlled by headquarters and focused on selling products originally developed for the U.S. market.[8]

Fifty years ago, most business enterprises—and especially those located in a large country such as the United States—could operate quite successfully with an ethnocentric orientation. Today, however, ethnocentrism is one of the biggest internal threats a company faces.

POLYCENTRIC ORIENTATION

The polycentric orientation is the opposite of ethnocentrism. The term *polycentric* describes management's often unconscious belief or assumption that each country in which a company does business is unique. This assumption lays the groundwork for each subsidiary to develop its own unique business and marketing strategies in order to succeed; the term *multinational company* is often used to describe such a structure. Until recently, Citicorp's financial services around the world operated on a polycentric basis. James Bailey, a Citicorp executive, offered this description of the company: "We were like a medieval state. There was the king and his court and they were in charge, right? No. It was the land barons who were in charge. The king and his court might declare this or that, but the land barons went and did their thing."[9] Realizing that the financial services industry is globalizing, CEO John Reed is attempting to achieve a higher degree of integration between Citicorp's operating units. Like Jack Welch at GE, Reed is moving to instill a geocentric orientation throughout his company.

REGIOCENTRIC AND GEOCENTRIC ORIENTATIONS

In a company with a regiocentric orientation, management views regions as unique and seeks to develop an integrated regional strategy. For example, a U.S. company that focuses on the countries included in the North American Free Trade Agreement (NAFTA)—the United States, Canada, and Mexico—has a regiocentric orientation. Similarly, a European company that focuses its attention on the EU or Europe is regiocentric. A company with a geocentric orientation views the entire world as a potential market and strives to develop integrated world market strategies. A company whose management has a regiocentric or geocentric orientation is sometimes known as a global or transnational company.[10]

---

[8] T. W. Malnight, "Globalization of an Ethnocentric Firm: An Evolutionary Perspective," *Strategic Management Journal,* 16, no. 2 (February 1995):125.

[9] Saul Hansell, "Uniting the Feudal Lords at Citicorp," *The New York Times,* 16 January 1994, Sec. 3, p. 1.

[10] Although the definitions provided here are important, to avoid confusion we will use the term *global marketing* when describing the general activities of global companies. Another note of caution is in order: Usage of the terms *international, multinational,* and *global* varies widely. Alert readers of the business press are likely to recognize inconsistencies; usage does not always reflect the definitions provided here. In particular, companies that are (in the view of your author as well as numerous other academics) global are often described as multinational enterprises (abbreviated MNE) or multinational corporations (abbreviated MNC). The United Nations prefers the term *transnational company* rather than *global company.* When we refer to an international company or a multinational, we will do so in a way that maintains the distinctions described in the text.

◆ BOX 1-1 ◆

PHILIPS AND MATSUSHITA: HOW GLOBAL COMPANIES WIN

Until recently, Philips Electronics, headquartered in Eindhoven, the Netherlands, was a classic example of a company with a polycentric orientation. Philips relied on relatively autonomous national organizations (called *NOs* in company parlance) in each country. Each NO developed its own strategy. This approach worked quite well until Philips faced competition from Matsushita and other Japanese consumer electronics companies in which management's orientation was geocentric. The difference in competitive advantage between Philips and its Japanese competition was dramatic.

For example, Matsushita adopted a global strategy that focused its resources on serving a world market for home entertainment products. In television receivers, Matsushita offered European customers two models based on a single chassis. In contrast, Philips's European NOs offered customers seven different models based on four different chassis. If customers had demanded this variety, Philips would have been the stronger competitor. Unfortunately, the product designs created by the NOs were not based on customer preferences. Customers wanted value in the form of quality, features, design—and price. Philips's decision to offer greater design variety was based not on what customers were asking for but, rather, on Philips's structure and strategy. Each major country organization had its own engineering and manufacturing

group. Each country unit had its own design and manufacturing operations. This polycentric, multinational approach was part of Philips's heritage and was attractive to NOs that had grown accustomed to functioning independently. However, the polycentric orientation was irrelevant to consumers, who were looking for value. They were getting more value from Matsushita's global strategy than from Philips's multinational strategy. Why? Matsushita's global strategy created value for consumers by lowering costs and, in turn, prices.

As a multinational company, Philips squandered resources in a duplication of effort that led to greater product variety. Variety entailed higher costs, which were passed on to consumers with no offsetting increase in consumer benefit. It is easy to understand how the right strategy resulted in Matsushita's success in the global consumer electronics industry. Because the Matsushita strategy offered greater customer value, Philips lost market share. Clearly, Philips needed a new company strategy. To meet the Japanese challenge, Philips executives consciously abandoned the polycentric, multinational approach and adopted a more geocentric orientation. A first step in this direction was to create industry groups in the Netherlands responsible for developing global strategies for research and development (R&D), marketing, and manufacturing.

The geocentric orientation represents a synthesis of ethnocentrism and polycentrism; it is a "worldview" that sees similarities and differences in markets and countries and seeks to create a global strategy that is fully responsive to local needs and wants. A regiocentric manager might be said to have a worldview on a regional scale; the world outside the region of interest will be viewed with an ethnocentric or a polycentric orientation, or a combination of the two. Jack Welch's quote at the beginning of this chapter that "globalization must be taken for granted" implies that at least some company managers must have a geocentric orientation. However, some research suggests that many companies are seeking to strengthen their regional competitiveness rather than moving directly to develop global responses to changes in the competitive environment.[11]

The ethnocentric company is centralized in its marketing management, the polycentric company is decentralized, and the regiocentric and geocentric companies are integrated on a regional and global scale, respectively. A crucial difference between the orientations is the underlying assumption for each. The ethnocentric orientation is based on a belief in home-country superiority. The underlying assumption of the polycentric approach is that there are so many differences in cultural, economic, and marketing conditions in the world that it is impossible and futile to attempt to transfer experience across national boundaries.

---

[11] Allen Morrison, David A. Ricks, and Kendall Roth, "Globalization versus Regionalization: Which Way for the Multinational?" *Organizational Dynamics* (Winter 1991): 18.

◆ DRIVING AND RESTRAINING FORCES AFFECTING GLOBAL INTEGRATION AND GLOBAL MARKETING

The remarkable growth of the global economy over the past 50 years has been shaped by the dynamic interplay of various driving and restraining forces. During most of those decades, companies from different parts of the world in different industries achieved great success by pursuing international, multinational, or global strategies. During the 1990s, changes in the business environment have presented a number of challenges to established ways of doing business. Today, the growing importance of global marketing stems from the fact that driving forces have more momentum than the restraining forces. The forces affecting global integration are shown in Figure 1-4.

DRIVING FORCES

Converging market needs and wants, technology advances, pressure to cut costs, pressure to improve quality, improvements in communication and transportation technology, global economic growth, and opportunities for leverage all represent important driving forces; any industry subject to these forces is a candidate for globalization.

Technology

Technology is a universal factor that crosses national and cultural boundaries. Technology is truly "stateless"; there are no cultural boundaries limiting its application. Once a technology is developed, it soon becomes available everywhere in the world. This phenomenon supports Levitt's prediction concerning the emergence of global markets for standardized products. In his landmark *Harvard Business Review* article, Levitt anticipated the communication revolution that has, in fact, become a driving force behind global marketing.[12] Satellite dishes, globe-spanning television networks such as CNN and MTV, and the Internet are just a few of the technological factors underlying the emergence of a true global village. In regional markets such as Europe, the increasing overlap of advertising across national boundaries and the mobility of consumers have created opportunities for marketers to pursue pan-European product positionings.

FIGURE 1-4 Driving and Restraining Forces Affecting Global Integration

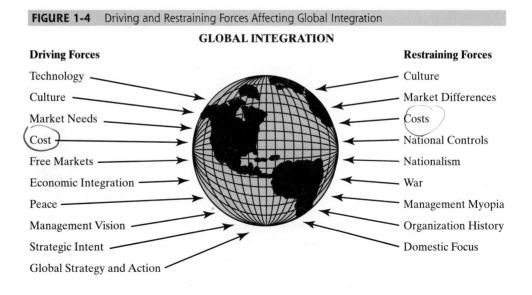

GLOBAL INTEGRATION

Driving Forces	Restraining Forces
Technology	Culture
Culture	Market Differences
Market Needs	Costs
Cost	National Controls
Free Markets	Nationalism
Economic Integration	War
Peace	Management Myopia
Management Vision	Organization History
Strategic Intent	Domestic Focus
Global Strategy and Action	

---

[12] Theodore Levitt, "The Globalization of Markets," *Harvard Business Review* (May–June 1983): 92.

Regional Economic Agreements

A number of multilateral trade agreements have accelerated the pace of global integration. NAFTA is already expanding trade among the United States, Canada, and Mexico. The General Agreement on Tariffs and Trade (GATT), which was ratified by more than 120 nations in 1994, has been replaced by the World Trade Organization to promote and protect free trade, but it has come under attack by developing countries. In Europe, the expanding membership of the European Union is lowering barriers to trade within the region.

Market Needs and Wants

A person studying markets around the world will discover cultural universals as well as cultural differences. The common elements in human nature provide an underlying basis for the opportunity to create and serve global markets. The word *create* is deliberate. Most global markets do not exist in nature: They must be created by marketing effort. For example, no one needs soft drinks, and yet today in some countries per capita soft-drink consumption exceeds the consumption of water. Marketing has driven this change in behavior, and today the soft-drink industry is a truly global one. Evidence is mounting that consumer needs and wants around the world are converging today as never before. This creates an opportunity for global marketing. Multinational companies pursuing strategies of product adaptation run the risk of being overtaken by global competitors that have recognized opportunities to serve global customers.

Marlboro is an example of a successful global brand. Targeted at urban smokers around the world, the brand appeals to the spirit of freedom, independence, and open space symbolized by the image of the cowboy in beautiful, open western settings. The need addressed by Marlboro is universal, and, therefore, the basic appeal and execution of its advertising and positioning are global. Philip Morris, which markets Marlboro, is a global company that discovered years ago how the same basic market need can be met with a global approach.

Transportation and Communication Improvements

The time and cost barriers associated with distance have fallen tremendously over the past 100 years. The jet airplane revolutionized communication by making it possible for people to travel around the world in less than 48 hours. Tourism enables people from many countries to see and experience the newest products being sold abroad. One essential characteristic of the effective global business is face-to-face communication among employees and between the company and its customers. Without modern jet travel, such communication would be difficult to sustain. In the 1990s, new communication technologies such as e-mail, fax, and teleconferencing and videoconferencing allowed managers, executives, and customers to link up electronically from virtually any part of the world for a fraction of the cost of air travel.

A similar revolution has occurred in transportation technology. Physical distribution has declined in terms of cost; the time required for shipment has been greatly reduced as well. A letter from China to New York is now delivered in eight days—faster than domestic mail is delivered within many countries. The per-unit cost of shipping automobiles from Japan and Korea to the United States by specially designed auto-transport ships is less than the cost of overland shipping from Detroit to either U.S. coast.

Product Development Costs

The pressure for globalization is intense when new products require major investments and long periods of development time. The pharmaceuticals industry provides a striking illustration of this driving force. According to the Pharmaceutical Manufacturers Association (PMA), the cost of developing a new drug in 1976 was $54 million; by 1982, the cost had increased to $87 million. By 1993, the cost of developing a new drug had reached $359 million.[13] Such costs must be recovered in the global marketplace, as no single national market is likely to be large enough to support investments of this size. As noted earlier, global marketing does not necessarily mean operating everywhere; in the $200 billion pharmaceutical industry, for example, seven countries account for 75 percent of sales.

Quality

Global marketing strategies can generate greater revenue and greater operating margins, which, in turn, support design and manufacturing quality. A global and a domestic company may each spend 5 percent of sales on research and development, but the global company may have many times the total revenue of the domestic because it serves the world market. It is easy to understand how Nissan, Matsushita, Caterpillar, and other global companies can achieve world-class quality. Global companies "raise the bar" for all competitors in an industry. When a global company establishes a benchmark in quality, competitors must quickly make their own improvements and come up to par. Global competition has forced all companies to improve quality. For truly global products, uniformity can drive down research, engineering, design, and production costs across business functions. Quality, uniformity, and cost reduction were all driving forces behind Ford's development of its "World Car," which is sold in the United States as the Ford Contour and Mercury Mystique and in Europe as the Mondeo.

World Economic Trends

There are three reasons why economic growth has been a driving force in the expansion of the international economy and the growth of global marketing. First, growth has created market opportunities that provide a major incentive for companies to expand globally. At the same time, slow growth in a company's domestic market can signal the need to look abroad for opportunities in nations or regions with high rates of growth.

Second, economic growth has reduced resistance that might otherwise have developed in response to the entry of foreign firms into domestic economies. When a country is growing rapidly, policy makers are likely to look favorably on outsiders. A growing country means growing markets; there is often plenty of opportunity for everyone. It is possible for a "foreign" company to enter a domestic economy and to establish itself without taking business away from local firms. Without economic growth, global enterprises may take business away from domestic ones. Domestic businesses are more likely to seek governmental intervention to protect their local position if markets are not growing. Predictably, the worldwide recession of the early 1990s created pressure in most countries to limit access by foreigners to domestic markets.

The worldwide movement toward deregulation and privatization is another driving force. The trend toward privatization is opening up formerly closed markets significantly; tremendous opportunities are being created as a result. For example, when a nation's telephone company is a state monopoly, it is much easier to require it to buy only from national companies. An independent, private company will be more inclined to look for the best offer, regardless of the nationality of the supplier. Privatization of telephone systems around the world is creating opportunities and threats for every company in the industry.

Leverage

A global company possesses the unique opportunity to develop leverage. Leverage is simply some type of advantage that a company enjoys by virtue of the fact that it conducts business in more than one country. Four important types of leverage are experience transfers, scale economies, resource utilization, and global strategy.

---

[13] PMA figures cited in Malnight, "Globalization of an Ethnocentric Firm," p. 123.

1. *Experience transfers.* A global company can leverage its experience in any market in the world. It can draw on management practices, strategies, products, advertising appeals, or sales or promotional ideas that have been tested in actual markets and apply them in other comparable markets.

   For example, Asea Brown Boveri (ABB), a company with 1,300 operating subsidiaries in 140 countries, has considerable experience with a well-tested management model that it transfers across national boundaries. The Zurich-based company knows that a company's headquarters can be run with a lean staff. When ABB acquired a Finnish company, it reduced the headquarters staff from 880 to 25 between 1986 and 1989. Headquarters staff at a German unit was reduced from 1,600 to 100 between 1988 and 1989. After acquiring Combustion Engineering (a U.S. company producing power plant boilers), ABB knew from experience that the headquarters staff of 800 could be drastically reduced, in spite of the fact that Combustion Engineering had a justification for every one of the headquarters staff positions.

2. *Scale economies.* The global company can take advantage of its greater manufacturing volume to obtain traditional scale advantages within a single factory. Also, finished products can be produced by combining components manufactured in scale-efficient plants in different countries. Japan's giant Matsushita Electric Company is a classic example of global marketing; it achieved scale economies by exporting videocassette recorders (VCRs), televisions, and other consumer electronics products throughout the world from world-scale factories in Japan. The importance of manufacturing scale has diminished somewhat as companies implement flexible manufacturing techniques and invest in factories outside the home country. However, scale economies were a cornerstone of Japanese success in the 1970s and 1980s.

   Leverage from scale economies is not limited to manufacturing. Just as a domestic company can achieve economies in staffing by eliminating duplicate positions after an acquisition, a global company can achieve the same economies on a global scale by centralizing functional activities. The larger scale of the global company also creates opportunities to improve corporate staff competence and quality.

3. *Resource utilization.* A major strength of the global company is its ability to scan the entire world to identify people, money, and raw materials that will enable it to compete most effectively in world markets. This is equally true for established companies and start-ups. For example, British Biotechnology Group, founded in 1986, raised $60 million from investors in the United States, Japan, and Great Britain. For a global company, it is not problematic if the value of the "home" currency rises or falls dramatically, because for this company there really is no such thing as a home currency. The world is full of currencies, and a global company seeks financial resources on the best available terms. In turn, it uses them where there is the greatest opportunity to serve a need at a profit.

4. *Global strategy.* The global company's greatest single advantage can be its global strategy. A global strategy is built on an information system that scans the world business environment to identify opportunities, trends, threats, and resources. When opportunities are identified, the global company adheres to the three principles identified earlier: It leverages its skills and focuses its resources to create superior perceived value for customers and achieve competitive advantage. The global strategy is a design to create a winning offering on a global scale. This takes great discipline, much creativity, and constant effort. The reward is not just success—it is survival.

The Global/Transnational Corporation

The global/transnational corporation, or any business enterprise that pursues global business objectives by linking world resources to world market opportunity, is the organization that has responded to the driving, restraining, and underlying forces in the world. Within the international financial framework and under the umbrella of global peace, the global corporation has taken advantage of the expanding communications technologies to pursue market opportunities and serve needs and wants on a global scale. The global enterprise has both responded to market opportunity and competitive threat by going global and at the same time has been one of the forces driving the world toward greater globalization.

RESTRAINING FORCES

Despite the impact of the driving forces identified earlier, several restraining forces may slow a company's efforts to engage in global marketing. Three important restraining forces are management myopia, organizational culture, and national controls. As we have noted, however, in today's world the driving forces predominate over the restraining forces. That is why the importance of global marketing is steadily growing.

Management Myopia and Organizational Culture

In many cases, management simply ignores opportunities to pursue global marketing. A company that is "nearsighted" and ethnocentric will not expand geographically. Myopia is also a recipe for market disaster if headquarters attempts to dictate when it should listen. Global marketing does not work without a strong local team that can provide information about local market conditions. Executives at Parker Pen once attempted to implement a top-down marketing strategy that ignored experience gained by local market representatives. Costly market failures resulted in Parker's buyout by managers of the former U.K. subsidiary. Eventually, the Gillette Company acquired Parker.

In companies in which subsidiary management "knows it all," there is no room for vision from the top. In companies in which headquarters management is all-knowing, there is no room for local initiative or an in-depth knowledge of local needs and conditions. Executives and managers at successful global companies have learned how to integrate global vision and perspective with local market initiative and input. A striking theme emerged during interviews conducted by the author with executives of successful global companies. That theme was the respect for local initiative and input by headquarters executives, and the corresponding respect for headquarters' vision by local executives.

National Controls and Barriers

Every country protects local enterprise and interests by maintaining control over market access and entry in both low- and high-tech industries and advertising. Such control ranges from a monopoly controlling access to tobacco markets to national government control of broadcast, equipment, and data transmission markets. Today, tariff barriers have been largely removed in the high-income countries, thanks to the World Trade Organization (WTO), NAFTA, and other economic agreements. However, nontariff barriers (NTBs) still make it more difficult for outside companies to succeed in foreign markets. The only way global companies can overcome these barriers is to become "insiders" in every country in which they do business. For example, utility companies in France are notorious for accepting bids from foreign equipment suppliers but, in the end, favoring national suppliers when awarding contracts. When a global company such as ABB acquires or establishes a subsidiary in France, it can receive the same treatment as other local companies. It becomes an "insider."

Global advertising and promotion are also hampered by government regulations. It is illegal in some countries to use comparative advertising. In some countries, such as

Germany, premiums and sweepstakes are illegal. Also working against global advertising is the use of different technical standards around the world. Videotape players in the Americas and Japan use the NTSC standard, whereas in Europe (except for France, which uses SECAM), the PAL system is used.

◆ OUTLINE OF THIS BOOK

The book is divided into four parts. Part I begins with an overview of the external environment, global marketing, and the basic theory of global marketing. Chapters 2 through 4 cover the external environments of global marketing: economic and regional market characteristics, including the location of income and population, patterns of trade and investment, and stages of market development; social and cultural elements; and legal and regulatory dimensions. Part II discusses analyzing and targeting global market opportunities. Chapter 5 discusses the major geographic and consumer markets of the world, and Chapter 6 provides information on marketing information systems and research. Market segmentation, targeting, and positioning are the topics discussed in Chapter 7.

Part III addresses ways a company manages international business and various strategic alliances. Chapter 8 covers the basics of sourcing, importing, and exporting whereas Chapter 9 addresses cooperative and global strategic partnerships. Competitive analysis and strategy are discussed in Chapter 10. Part III is devoted to global considerations pertaining to the marketing mix. The application of product, price, channel, and marketing communications decisions in response to global market opportunities and threats is covered in detail in Chapters 12 through 15. Chapter 16 addresses the implication of Internet marketing and e-commerce.

Part IV consists of Chapters 17 and 18, which describe the managerial dimensions of global marketing: planning, leading, organizing, and controlling and the future of global marketing.

Summary

Global marketing is the process of focusing the resources and objectives of a company on global marketing opportunities. Companies engage in global marketing for two reasons: to take advantage of opportunities for growth and expansion, and to survive. Companies that fail to pursue global opportunities are likely to eventually lose their domestic markets because they will be pushed aside by stronger and more competitive global competitors. This book presents the theory and practice of applying the universal discipline of marketing to the global opportunities found in world markets.

The basic goals of marketing are to create customer value and competitive advantage by maintaining focus. Company management can be classified in terms of its orientation toward the world: ethnocentric, polycentric, regiocentric, and geocentric. An ethnocentric orientation characterizes domestic and international companies; international companies pursue marketing opportunities outside the home market by extending various elements of the marketing mix. A polycentric worldview predominates at a multinational company, where the marketing mix is adapted by country managers operating autonomously. Managers at global and transnational companies are regiocentric or geocentric in their orientation and pursue both extension and adaptation strategies in global markets.

Global marketing's importance today is shaped by the dynamic interplay of several driving and restraining forces. The former include market needs and wants, technology, transportation improvements, costs, quality, global peace, world economic growth, and a recognition of opportunities to develop leverage by operating globally. Restraining forces include market differences, management myopia, organizational culture, and national controls.

Discussion Questions

1. What are the basic goals of marketing? Are these goals relevant to global marketing?
2. What is meant by global localization? Is Coca-Cola a global product? Explain.
3. Describe some of the global marketing strategies available to companies. Give examples of companies using the different strategies.
4. How do the global marketing strategies of Harley-Davidson and Toyota differ?
5. Describe the differences among ethnocentric, polycentric, regiocentric, and geocentric management orientations.
6. Identify and briefly describe some of the forces that have resulted in increased global integration and the growing importance of global marketing.
7. Define leverage, and explain the different types of leverage utilized by companies with global operations.
8. What, in your view, is the future of a company such as Renault? Will it be able to continue as an independent company? Why? Why not?
9. What are some major trends in the world that will affect marketing?

Suggested Readings

Barnet, Richard J., and John Cavanagh. *Global Dreams: Imperial Corporations and the New World Order.* New York: Simon & Schuster, 1994.

Bassiry, G. R., and R. Hrair Dekmejian. "America's Global Companies: A Leadership Profile." *Business Horizons,* 36, no. 1 (January–February 1993): 47–53.

Burgess, Steven M. *The New Marketing.* Halfway House, South Africa: Zebra Press, 1998.

Chen, Zhengyi. "Marketing Globally: Planning and Practice." *Journal of International Marketing,* 7, no. 2 (1999): 96–98.

Halal, William E. "Global Strategic Management in a New World Order." *Business Horizons,* 36 (November–December 1993): 5–10.

Herschell, Gordon Lewis, and Carol Nelson. *Advertising Age Handbook of Advertising.* Chicago: NTC Business Books, 1998.

Johansson, Johny K., and Ikujiro Nonaka. *Relentless, The Japanese Way of Marketing.* New York: HarperBusiness, 1997.

Keegan, Warren J., and Bodo B. Schlegelmilch. *Global Marketing Management: A European Perspective.* New York: Prentice Hall International, 2000.

Khanna, T., and K. Palepu. "Why Focused Strategies May Be Wrong for Emerging Markets." *Harvard Business Review* (July–August 1997): 41–51.

Malnight, T. W. "Globalization of an Ethnocentric Firm: An Evolutionary Perspective." *Strategic Management Journal,* 16 (February 1995): 119–141.

Miles, Gregory L. "Tailoring a Global Product." *International Business* (March 1995): 50–52.

Miller, L. K. *Transnational Corporations: A Selective Bibliography, 1991–1992.* New York: United Nations, 1992.

Ohmae, Kenichi. *The End of the Nation State: The Rise of Regional Economies.* New York: The Free Press, 1995.

Reich, Robert B. *The Work of Nations.* New York: Vintage Books, 1992.

Reid, David McHardy. "Perspectives for International Marketers on the Japanese Market." *Journal of International Marketing,* 3, no. 1 (1995): 63–84.

The 18 Guiding Principles of the Marketing Company

INTRODUCTION

The Marketing Company

Welcome to the global marketplace! Regardless of the size, profit, and market strength, every company on the earth has entered a new era of competition.

The change drivers such as technology, economy, and market conditions have increasingly redefined almost every sector of industries, and the way we do business. The advance of information technology has transformed the marketplace; it has provided industry players a vast array of alternatives to compete more strategically and forcefully.

The dynamic change of economic and social conditions have revolutionized consumer behavior and attitudes. With a dizzying array of product choices in the marketplace, consumers, to the highest degree, have more demanding expectations than ever before. They do not just expect a high-quality product; product quality has become a norm and requirement. This new breed of consumers want high product quality with an affordable price within their convenient reach.

The traditional strategy that brought companies successes will lose the applicability in this new marketplace. The conventional disciplines that guaranteed market leadership during the past years will lose their adaptability. In order to survive in this new marketplace, companies need a new set of strategies and tools. They need a set of guiding principles that will create a sustainable competitive advantage. They need to become a new breed of company: the Marketing Company!

What is the Marketing Company? As you will soon explore the characters of the company in the following pages, it is not just a marketing-oriented company. The Marketing Company is not just a market-driven company. The Marketing Company is an organization that adopts the 18 Guiding Principles of the Marketing Company as its credo—as its guiding values, its principles to compete in the new marketplace. It endures **external and internal change drivers, more demanding customers, and even fiercer competitors.** After all, a new competition needs a different kind of rules and principles to survive and win the race. *Be ready to rewrite your credo or your company will die!*

Principle #1—The Principle of the Company: Marketing Is a Strategic Business Concept

This principle is the first foundation of the Marketing Company. In the chaotic marketplace in the global economy era, the traditional concept of Marketing has lost its adaptability in market competition. As companies are squeezed by external change drivers such as technology, economy, and market—and as they face internal organizational changes within themselves (shareholders, people, and organization culture)—marketing is no longer about selling, advertising, or even 4Ps introduced by Jerome McCarthy.

Marketing should become the *strategic business concept* within corporations. It is no longer functional tasks and responsibilities carried by a department. Marketing is strategic because it should be *formulated by top-level management, long-term oriented, navigate a company's direction,* and *hold the responsibilities of creating loyal business customers (internal, external, and investor customers).*

Al Ries, in his book, *Focus,* says that, "A good Chief Executive Officer should also be a Chief Marketing Officer." David Packard, a cofounder of Hewlett-Packard, once said that "Marketing is too important for a marketing department." Peter Drucker long ago envisioned that: "Business has only two basic functions: marketing and innovation. Marketing and innovation produce results, the rest are cost!"

Admittedly, their statements are definitely true. In other words, they agree with this first principle: *Marketing is a strategic business concept.*

Principle #2—The Principle of the Community: Marketing Is Everyone's Business

This principle is the second foundation of the Marketing Company. Within a Marketing Company, marketing should be adopted as a strategic business concept. In the company, ideally, the organization structure is almost flat and layerless. There is even no marketing department and function in the Marketing Company because marketing is not a department, and marketing as a department is becoming weaker. *Therefore, all departments are marketing departments, and all functions are marketing functions.*

All people within the Marketing Company form a community, called a *marketing community.* So in the community *everyone is a marketer,* meaning that the responsibilities and tasks of acquiring, satisfying, and retaining customers lie on the shoulders of everyone. Regardless of what level and department a person works in, he/she should be involved in the process of retaining customers.

New roles such as Accounting–Marketer, Operations–Marketer, R&D–Marketer, Janitor–Marketer, Maintenance–Marketer, and the like will be emerging as this principle is instilled in the Marketing Company. While their jobs will not be exactly similar, the responsibility to create customer loyalty becomes the central theme of their works.

Thus, everyone led by the Chief Executive Officer (acting as Chief Marketing Officer) of the company, should march in the same direction. They should carry a similar mission: It is the responsibility of everyone to attract, satisfy, and retain customers. *Everyone is a marketer, whatever his/her job description is.*

Principle #3—The Principle of Competition: Marketing War Is About Value War

This principle is the third foundation of the Marketing Company. The Marketing Company does not pursue short-term profits; it creates customer value for long-term relationships. Unfortunately, the company's principle does not parallel with stockholders' short-term orientation in stock exchange institutions. While they rely upon companies' quarterly financial reports to buy and sell stocks, the Marketing Company looks beyond this short-term time frame for result.

The company regards profit as short term and value creation as long term. By continuously and consistently creating customer value, the Marketing Company will generate profits. Hence, profit follows value. This is because marketing war is not merely marketing war. Marketing war is value war.

While value is defined as total get (customer benefits) divided by total give (customer expenses), there are five value-creating formula alternatives to win competition. First, increase benefits and lower expenses. Second, increase benefits and hold expenses constant. Third, hold benefits constant and lower expenses. Fourth, increase benefits significantly and increase expenses. Fifth, lower benefits and significantly lower expenses.

As the value impact among the formula alternatives above varies significantly, the core idea behind the principle remains unchanged: Value is the key to winning and keeping customers. *Therefore, improve customer value to win the marketing war.*

Principle #4—The Principle of Retention: Concentrate on Loyalty, Not Just on Satisfaction

In addition to the three previous founding principles, the Marketing Company concentrates on loyalty, not just on satisfaction.

As marketing war becomes value war and as industry competition becomes value competition, it is inadequate for the Marketing Company to concentrate merely on customer satisfaction. The ultimate objective of the Marketing Company should be customer loyalty.

As we enter the *era of choices,* there is no guarantee that satisfied customers will become loyal customers. Satisfaction has increasingly become a commodity. It is only the process, not the end result. The final goal of the Marketing Company is customer loyalty. *Customer loyalty has become the moving target* every Marketing Company must

pursue to remain competitive. What matters most to the Marketing Company is now *the quality of profit, not just the quantity of profit.* It is already evident that customer attraction activities cost a company much more than a customer retention program; the cost to acquire a new customer will cost more than retaining one good customer. Profits, therefore, should come more from old, existing customers than from new, first-time buyers.

A company's profit record, accordingly, provides an insight on the level of customer loyalty. As customer attraction, customer satisfaction, and customer retention will become an endless process of company survival, the ultimate effort of the Marketing Company should remain clear: *Concentrate on loyalty, not just on satisfaction.*

Principle #5—The Principle of Integration: Concentrate on Differences, Not Just on Averages

The Marketing Company concentrates on differences, not just averages.

In order for the Marketing Company to create the loyal customer base mentioned in the first topping principle, it has to concentrate on customers individually. The principle commands the company to build intimate relationships with customers—intimate enough to learn about customers' needs and wants; close enough to understand customers' expectations. In the chaotic competitive setting, every customer will become unique.

Underlying this principle is a profound fact that *all customers are not created equal.* Many companies are tempted to think that their customers have roughly similar needs and wants. This dangerous assumption, however, will lead them to create mediocre and average offers for their diversified customers.

The principle emphasizes that by no means are customers equal. *They are uniquely different and their needs are distinctively diversified.* In other words, *there are no average customers.* The Marketing Company, as a result, has to integrate itself with customers to create a bonding that produces a vivid picture about customers' needs, wants, and expectations.

There are no average customers. *In order to build customer loyalty, a company has to concentrate on differences, not just on averages.*

Principle #6—The Principle of Anticipation: Concentrate on Proactivity, Not Just on Reactivity

The Marketing Company concentrates on proactivity, not just reactivity.

To fully integrate with customers, as described in the second topping principle, the Marketing Company should be ready for change. It has to be adaptive to the current state of industry. It even should anticipate any change and be proactive in coping with the change.

Stephen Covey, in his landmark book, *The Seven Habits of Highly Effective People,* defines *proactivity* as *responsibility.* In this context, responsibility means the ability of an organization to choose responses within a given circumstance and environment. Between a stimulus and a response, there is a gap. It is the gap of freedom to react, freedom to choose a response.

Thus, to be competitive, a company has to be ready for change in its environment. It has to be able to anticipate change of technology, economy, and markets. It has to have proactivity to operate in an uncertain and unpredictable environment. To be fluid and dynamic operationally, the Marketing Company concentrates on proactivity, not just reactivity. Be a *change agent, change driver,* or even *change surpriser* to your competitors.

Principle #7—The Principle of Brand:
Avoid the Commodity-Like Trap

This is the first value-creating principle of the Marketing Company. To the company, brand is not just a name, nor is it a logo and symbols. Brand is the *value indicator* of the Marketing Company. It is the umbrella that represents the product or service, companies, persons, or even countries. It is determined by the company's new product development, customer satisfaction and retention, and value-chain management.

It is the equity of the firm that adds value to products and services it offers. It is an asset that creates value to consumers by enhancing satisfaction and recognition of quality. With brand, the company is able to liberate itself from the supply–demand curve.

When the firm successfully liberates itself from the supply–demand curve, the price of the firm's offers will not be dependent on the price equilibrium point. The firm, as a result, is able to be the *price maker, not price taker.*

Unfortunately, macroeconomists, to a certain extent, do not realize the power of brand. They view economy from a global perspective and derive numbers from a macro point of view. This ignores the most crucial element of a price driver: brand.

It is brand that determines a price. It is brand that liberates the company to create values for internal customers, external customers, and investor customers. It is brand that indicates a value of the firm's products and services. Therefore, use, build, and protect your brand. *It is the brand that will enable the company to avoid the commodity-like trap.*

Principle #8—The Principle of Service:
Avoid the Business-Category Trap

This is the second value-creating principle of the Marketing Company. To the company, service is not just after-sales service, before-sales service, or even during-sales service. Service is not customer toll-free numbers, maintenance service, or customer service. Service is a *value enhancer* of the Marketing Company. It is the paradigm of the company to create a lasting value to customers through products (small "p") and services (small "s"). Service in this principle refers to service with a big "S," not a small "s." It is the answer to Peter Drucker's question: "What business are

you in?" The only answer to the question is: "We are in the service business!" There is only one business category: service. Why? It is because *service means solution.* Companies must give the true solution to customers.

Whether the company's business is a restaurant, hotel, or shoe manufacturing, the only category for all businesses must become a service business. To become a real service company, a firm has to continuously enhance the small "p" and the small "s." To create a long-lasting value and build relationships with customers, the firm's offers should provide constant value to customers. Therefore, a CEO acting as CMO has the key role between *corporate governance* and *corporate management* to create, maintain, and even develop this sense of service throughout the whole organization.

In this sense, service is a paradigm. It is the spirit of the company. It is the attitude to sustain and win tomorrow's competition. *It is the strategy to avoid the business-category trap.*

Principle #9—The Principle of Process:
Avoid the Function-Orientation Trap

This is the third value-creating principle of the Marketing Company. It refers to the process of creating value to customers. It reflects the product quality, cost, and delivery of a company to customers. It is the *value enabler* of a company.

The principle commands the company to be the captain of supply-chain process. It should manage the supply-chain process, from raw materials to finished products, in a way that would enhance value-creating activities and reduce and eliminate value-eroding activities within the company.

In addition, it requires a firm to be *the hub of network organizations* where it could establish relationships with organizations that have the potential to add value. The renowned term for this is *strategic alliance.* These partnering organizations may be the company's suppliers, customers, or even competitors. Benchmarking, reengineering, outsourcing, merger, and acquisition are examples of strategic actions to improve process.

The value-creating drivers such as brand, service, and process (as the value enabler) should not only create value to external customers and investor customers, but also become the credo of internal customers, who are people. People within the organization should be marketers. They should avoid functional arrogance within the company because everyone holds a similar belief: Customer value is the end result, not titles and job positions in the company. *Brand, service, and process as three value-creating principles are drivers to win the heart share of customers.*

Principle #10—The Principle of Segmentation:
View Your Market Creatively

Another crucial part of a company: marketing strategy. The strategy comprises three elements, namely segmentation, targeting, and positioning. Together they are *drivers to win shares of customers.*

The first element of marketing strategy is Segmentation. A typical definition of segmentation is the process of segmenting or partitioning the market into several segments. However, segmentation to us is about *viewing a market creatively.* It is about mapping a market into several categories by gathering similar behavior of consumers into a segment. It is the *mapping strategy* of a company.

Segmentation is an art to identify and pinpoint opportunity emerging in the markets. At the same time, it is a science to view the market based on *geographic, demographic, psychographic,* and *behavior* variables or even a *segment of one.* Whatever segmentation variables are used, please make sure that each person in a segment has similar behavior, especially in purchasing, using, or servicing the products.

The Marketing Company should be creative enough to view a market from a unique angle. It also has to clearly identify the market from an advanced perspective, using segmentation variables. Segmentation is the first marketing strategy element. It is the initial step that determines the life of the company. *Market opportunities are in the eyes of the beholder. In order to exploit the opportunity arising in the market, that beholder must first view the market creatively.*

Principle #11—The Principle of Targeting: Allocate Your Resources Effectively

The second element of marketing strategy is *targeting.* By the traditional definition, targeting is the process of selecting the right target market for a company's products and services. We, however, define targeting as the strategy to *allocate the company's resources effectively.* Why? Because resources are always limited. It is about how to fit the company within a selected target market segment. Hence, we call it the *fitting strategy of a company.*

There are several criteria used to select an appropriate market segment for the company's resources. The first criterion is market size. The company has to select the market segment that has "good" size to generate expected financial returns. The bigger the market size, the more lucrative the segment is to the company.

The second criterion used to choose market segment is growth. The potential growth of a market segment is a crucial attribute for the company. The better and higher the growth is, the more promising the market segment to the company.

The third criterion is competitive advantage. Competitive advantage is a way to measure whether the company has such strength and expertise to dominate the chosen market segment.

The fourth criterion is competitive situation. The company has to consider the competition intensity within the industry including the number of players, suppliers, and entry barriers. Using these main criteria, the company has to find its "fit" with the right market segment.

Principle #12—The Principle of Positioning: Lead Your Customers Credibly

The third element of marketing strategy is *positioning.* By the traditional definition, positioning is the strategy to occupy the consumers' minds with our company's offerings. In this principle, however, we define positioning as the strategy to *lead the company's customers credibly.* It is about how to establish trustworthiness, confidence, and competence for customers. If the company has those elements, customers will then have the "being" of the company or product within their minds. Therefore, positioning is about the *being strategy* of the company or product in the customers' minds. It is about earning customers' trust to make them willingly follow the company.

Yoram Wind, a marketing strategy professor, defines positioning as *the reason for being.* He advocates that positioning is about defining the company's identity and personality in the customers' minds. As we move toward the era of choices, the company can no longer force customers to buy their products; they no longer can manage the customers. In this era, the company should have credibility in the minds of customers. Because customers cannot be managed, they have to be led. In order to successfully lead customers, companies have to have credibility. So positioning is not just about persuading and creating image in the consumers' minds, it is about earning consumers' trust. It is about *the quest of trustworthiness. It is about creating a being in the consumers' minds and leading them credibly.*

Principle #13—The Principle of Differentiation: Integrate Your Content, Context, and Infrastructure

The first element of marketing tactics is *differentiation.* Traditionally, differentiation is the act of designing a set of meaningful differences in the company's offers. To us, this definition by Philip Kotler is still valid. We define differentiation as "integrating the content, context, and infrastructure of our offers to customers." Different products are the core tactic of the company to support its positioning. Differentiation, therefore, is the *core tactic* of the Marketing Company.

As the first marketing tactic element, differentiation should create a truly different and unique product for customers. The product not only has to be perceived differently by customers (positioning), it has to be really different in content, context, and infrastructure (differentiation).

A company can ideally create a unique offer by concentrating on three aspects of differentiation: *content, context, and infrastructure.* Content (what to offer) is the core benefit of the product itself. Context (how to offer), in addition, refers to the way the company offers the product. Infrastructure (enabler) is the technology, facilities, and people used to create the content and context.

When positioning strategy is not supported by differentiation, the company may overpromise and underdeliver to customers, which could ruin the company's brand and reputation. On the other hand, if the positioning is supported by differentiation, the company will establish *strong brand integrity*. It means the brand image in the consumers' minds is similar to brand identity communicated by companies.

Principle #14—The Principle of Marketing Mix: Integrate Your Offer, Logistics, and Communications

The second element of marketing tactics is *marketing mix*. To many practitioners, this is considered as the whole marketing concept. The 4Ps (product, price, place, promotion), initially introduced by Jerome McCarthy, is often thought of as the complete marketing principle. To us, marketing mix is only an element of marketing tactic. It is also the tip of an iceberg—the most visible part of the company in the market.

The marketing mix, to us, is about *integrating the company's offers, logistics, and communications*. The company's offers, consisting of products and prices, should well be integrated with logistics (including channel distribution) and communications to create a powerful marketing force in the marketplace. Therefore, we call it the *creation tactic* of the company. Why? Because marketing mix has to be the creation of content–context–infrastructure differentiation. There are three types of marketing mix in the market. First is *destructive marketing mix*. It is marketing mix that does not add customer value and does not build company's brand. Second is *me-too marketing mix*. It is marketing mix that often imitates other existing marketing mix from other players in an industry. Third is *creative marketing mix*. It is the marketing mix that supports the marketing strategy (segmentation–targeting–positioning) and other marketing tactic principles (differentiation–selling) of the company and builds marketing value (brand–service–process).

Principle #15—The Principle of Selling: Integrate Your Company, Customers, and Relationships

The last element of marketing tactics is *selling*. The principle of selling does not refer to personal selling at all, nor is it related to the activities of selling products to customers. What we mean by selling is "the tactic to create long-term relationship with customers through company's products." It is the tactic to *integrate company, customers, and relationships*.

After developing marketing strategy and creating marketing mix, the company should be able to generate financial returns through selling. Thus, it is the *capture tactic* of the company. There are three main levels of selling: feature selling, benefit selling, and solution selling. As the choice of products in the marketplace overwhelm customers, companies have to sell solutions to customers, not just features and benefits. There is a relevant framework called *customer bonding* that emphasizes the importance of this principle. In the concept, customers have to go through five steps, from consumers to loyalists, as follows: awareness–identity–relationship–community–advocacy.

Hence, consumers should be made aware of our products and drive them to become advocacies. The principle of

differentiation, marketing mix, and selling are *drivers to win the market share*.

Principle #16—The Principle of Totality: Balance Your Strategy, Tactics, and Value

After focusing on the nine core elements of marketing (segmentation, targeting, positioning, differentiation, marketing mix, selling, brand, service, and process) individually, in the implementation, the Marketing Company should be able to balance those elements operationally as well as strategically. The Marketing Company should be able to balance the strategy, tactic, and value in the implementation. Marketing strategy is about how to win *the mind share*. Marketing tactic is about how to win *the market share*. Marketing value is about how to win *the heart share*. Together, they will win the mind, heart, and market shares.

As the business environment changes dynamically, the strategy, tactic, and value of the company may not be as precise as when it was developed. The maneuvers of competitors, the revolution of technology, and the changes in consumer behavior will require the company to adjust and readjust the strategy, tactic, and value. It demands the company to align strategy, tactic, and value to adapt to the most current business environment. The dynamic business environment will necessitate the company to constantly monitor or review the balance of strategy, tactic, and value; to build the totality of the business. The Marketing Company should also *balance the time allocation* in strategy, tactic, and value activities.

Principle #17—The Principle of Agility: Integrate Your What, Why, and How

To operate in a competitive, dynamic environment, where technology, consumer behavior, and competitor movement change in a chaotic pattern, a company has to be agile to survive. The question, then, is, "What does it take to be agile?"

In this principle, an agile company continually engages in three main activities: First, it constantly monitors the competitors' movement and consumer behavior (what). It has marketing intelligence and information systems to take a picture of the business environment. Second, it continuously uses and analyzes the information gathered from the first activity to get a useful insight about the environment (why). Third, the gathered and analyzed information is incorporated in its strategy and tactic development process (how).

To put it simply, an agile company monitors, scans, and reviews the business environment continually. It analyzes the information and uses it to respond and preempt the competitor movement.

This principle will allow the company to be informed about the changes in the marketplace. This principle will allow the company to be not just a change agent and a change driver, but also a *change surpriser*. A change surpriser is a company who is agile. It is the organization that can balance what, why, and how. Balance your time allocation on what–why–how activities in the implementation.

Principle #18—The Principle of Utility: Integrate Your Present, Future, and Gap

The Marketing Company does not just create profit for today and lose tomorrow. It does not just think about tomorrow and forget about today. The Marketing Company knows exactly the utility to integrate the present, future, and gap.

Together with the principles of totality and agility, utility is *the driver to win the activity share,* which is important, as mentioned by Michael Porter in one of his writings in *Harvard Business Review.* In the implementation, finally, the Marketing Company can successfully balance present activities, future activities, and gap activities.

Present activities are about today's products, which create profit by servicing today's customers. Future activities, meanwhile, are about developing tomorrow's products, which create sustainable growth by servicing tomorrow's different customers.

Gap activities are about enhancing capabilities of the technology and people, internally and externally, or by creating a strategic alliance or merger and acquisition in order to create future's activities.

Living by this principle, the company can maintain its competitiveness today and tomorrow and pursue whatever it lacks (the gap) to stay competitive in the present and future.

FINAL THOUGHT

The Company Making

Throughout this writing, we have learned about the new principles of marketing. It is not just a set of static principles. It is a set of dynamic, guiding principles of the Marketing Company.

The 18 principles are organized around six dimensions—Foundation, Topping, Strategy, Tactic, Value, and Implementation—in which each dimension contains three principles.

Using these principles, a company's transformation from production oriented, selling oriented, marketing oriented, and market driven to a customer-driven company should be clearly guided along the way to become the Marketing Company.

The making of the Marketing Company involves strategic processes and steps as follows: The company should conduct an internal and external marketing audit. The results of the audit will produce what we call CAP (company alignment profile) and CSP (competitive setting profile). The gap between CAP and CSP portrays what the company should do.

In addition, the Marketing Company should adopt the 18 Guiding Principles as the corporate guiding credo and value that determine how it should act and react in the marketplace. The set of principles should become the guidance, culture, and foundation to live by.

Furthermore, the Marketing Company should be navigated by top management or a CEO (Chief Executive Of-ficer) who acts as a CMO (Chief Marketing Officer). How the company behaves in the marketplace—and which direction it should take—must be decided by the top management based on the gap.

One final word: *The Marketing Company is not a destination.* It is not a goal or objective. Becoming the Marketing Company is a *process.* It is the never-ending pursuit of excellence. It is a *moving target* every company should pursue if it wants to survive and become competitive.

The Anatomy of Marketing

Many people who come to the subject of marketing with little or no business experiences think of it as a study of selling. Those who already have extensive professional experience or have undergone intensive academic training regard marketing as marketing mix. We at MarkPlus define marketing with three strategic dimensions: marketing strategy, marketing tactic, and marketing value (STV). The integrated concept of marketing is illustrated in Figure 1A.1.

In the global marketplace of the new millennium, marketing should be redefined to reflect the increasingly intensified competition in almost every sector of industries.

Marketing Strategy: How to Win the Mind Share

Marketing strategy is the first dimension in the marketing concept. Its role is to *win the mind share* of consumers. Because of its strategic importance, it is in the Strategic Business Unit (SBU) level of a company.

The first element of marketing strategy is segmentation. Segmentation is defined as a way to view a market creatively. We call it the *mapping strategy* of a company.

FIGURE 1A.1   Strategy, Tactic, and Value Model

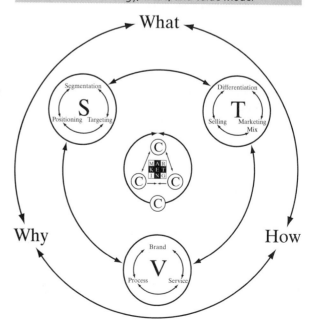

After the market is mapped and segmented into groups of potential customers with similar characteristics and behavior, the company needs to select which segments to enter. This act is called *targeting,* which is the second element of the marketing strategy. Targeting is defined as a way to allocate company's resources effectively—by selecting the right target market. We also define it as a company's *fitting strategy.*

The 18 Guiding Principles of the Marketing Company
Rewrite your credo or your company will die.

1. **The Principle of the Company**   Marketing Is a Strategic Business Concept
2. **The Principle of the Community**   Marketing Is Everyone's Business
3. **The Principle of Competition**   Marketing War Is about Value War
4. **The Principle of Retention**   Concentrate on Loyalty, Not Just on Satisfaction
5. **The Principle of Integration**   Concentrate on Differences, Not Just on Averages
6. **The Principle of Anticipation**   Concentrate on Proactivity, Not Just on Reactivity
7. **The Principle of Brand**   Avoid the Commodity-like Trap
8. **The Principle of Service**   Avoid the Business-Category Trap
9. **The Principle of Process**   Avoid the Function-Orientation Trap
10. **The Principle of Segmentation**   View Your Market Creatively
11. **The Principle of Targeting**   Allocate Your Resources Effectively
12. **The Principle of Positioning**   Lead Your Customers Credibly
13. **The Principle of Differentiation**   Integrate Your Content, Context, and Infrastructure
14. **The Principle of the Marketing Mix**   Integrate Your Offer, Logistics, and Communications
15. **The Principle of Selling**   Integrate Your Company, Customers, and Relationships
16. **The Principle of Totality**   Balance Your Strategy, Tactic, and Value
17. **The Principle of Agility**   Balance Your What, Why, and How
18. **The Principle of Utility**   Balance Your Present, Future, and Gap

The last element of strategy is *positioning.* Positioning is defined as a way to lead customers credibly. We call it the *being strategy* of a company. After mapping the market and fitting the company's resources into its selected market segment, a company has to define its *being* in the mind of the target market—in order to have a credible position in their minds.

Marketing Tactic: How to Win the Market Share

The second dimension of *The STV Model* is marketing tactic. Marketing tactic, because of its role, is regarded as elements to *win the market share.* Whereas marketing strategy is in the SBU level, marketing tactics is in operational level.

The first element of marketing tactic is differentiation. Differentiation is the *core tactic* to differentiate the content, context, and infrastructure of a company's offers to the target markets. Meanwhile, we call marketing mix a *creation tactic,* which integrates a company's offer, logistics, and communications. Selling, furthermore, is the third element of marketing tactic, which we define as the *capture tactic* to generate cash inflows for the company and to integrate the customer and company in a long-term, satisfying relationship.

Marketing Value: How to Win the Heart Share

Marketing value is the last dimension of *The STV Model.* It is the corporate-level responsibility and is intended to *win the heart share* of target markets.

The first element of marketing value is brand. Brand is the *value indicator* of a company, which enables the company to avoid the commodity trap. Service is the second element of marketing. It is the paradigm of a company to always meet or exceed the customers' needs, wants, and expectations. We define it as the *value enhancer* of a company.

The last element of marketing value is process. It is the *value enabler* of a company that enables it to deliver value to customers through the process within and without the firm.

DISCUSSION QUESTIONS

1. What do you think of The 18 Guiding Principles of the Marketing Company? How do these principles compare to the marketing concepts and principles that you learned in your basic marketing course or that you have acquired through your experience as a marketer?
2. Hermawan Kartajaya is an Asian marketer. Do his 18 Guiding Principles apply in your country? Is marketing a universal discipline? Do the marketing concepts, tools, and methods that are used in a home country need to be modified or changed when used in other countries? Explain your answer.
3. What, in your view, are the key principles of marketing? List your principles (no more than six), and explain their importance to marketing success.

◆◆◆ **Part I Case**

Which Company Is Transnational?

Four senior executives of companies operating in many countries speak:

COMPANY A

We are a transnational company. We sell our products in over 80 countries, and we manufacture in 14 countries. Our overseas subsidiaries manage our business in their respective countries. They have complete responsibility for their country operations including strategy formulation. Most of the key executives in our subsidiaries are host-country nationals, although we still rely on home-country persons for the CEO and often the CFO (chief financial officer) slots. Recently, we have divided the world into world regions and the United States. Each of the world regions reports to our world trade organization, which is responsible for all of our business outside the United States.

The overseas companies are responsible for adapting to the unique market preferences that exist in their country or region and are quite autonomous. We are proud of our international reach: We manufacture not only in the United States but also in Europe and the United Kingdom, Latin America, and Australia.

We have done very well in overseas markets, especially in the high-income countries with the exception of Japan. We would like to enter the Japanese market, but let's face it, Japan is a protected country. There is no level playing field, and as you no doubt know, the Japanese have taken advantage of the protection they enjoy in their home country to launch an export drive that has been a curse for us. Our industry and our home country (the United States) has been a principal target of the Japanese, who have taken a real bite out of our market share here in the United States. We are currently lobbying for more protection from Japanese competition.

COMPANY B

We are a unique transnational media company. We do not dominate any particular area, but we have an important presence on three continents in magazines, newspapers, and television. We have a global strategy. We are a global communications and entertainment company. We're in the business of informing people around the world on the widest possible basis. We know how to serve the needs of our customers who are readers, viewers, and advertisers. We transfer people and money across national boundaries, and we know how to acquire and integrate properties as well as how to start up a new business. We started out as Australian, and then the weight of our effort shifted to the United Kingdom and today our main effort is in the United States. We go where the opportunity is because we are market driven.

Sure, there are lots of Australians in the top management of this company, but we started in Australia, and those Aussies know our business and the company from the ground up. Look around and you'll see more and more Americans and Brits taking the top jobs. We stick to English because I don't believe that we could really succeed in foreign print or broadcast. We know English, and so far the English-speaking world is big enough for us. The world is shrinking faster than we all realize, and to be in communications is to be at the center of all change. That's the excitement of what we're doing—and also the importance.

COMPANY C

We're a transnational company. We are committed to being the number-one company in our industry worldwide. We do all of our manufacturing in our home country because we have been able to achieve the lowest cost and the highest quality in the world by keeping all engineering and manufacturing in one location. The constantly rising value of our home currency is forcing us to invest in overseas manufacturing in order to maintain our cost advantage. We are doing this reluctantly but we believe that the essence of being global is dominating markets and we plan to do whatever we must do in order to maintain our position of leadership.

It is true that all of our senior managers at home and in most of our foreign markets are home-country nationals. We feel more comfortable with our own nationals in key jobs because they speak our language and they understand the history and the culture of our company and our country. It would be difficult for an outsider to have this knowledge, which is so important to smooth-working relationships.

COMPANY D

We are a transnational company. We have 24 nationalities represented on our headquarters staff, we manufacture in 28 countries, we market in 92 countries, and we are committed to leadership in our industry. It is true that we are backing off on our commitment to develop business in the Third World. We have found it extremely difficult to increase sales and earnings in the Third World, and we have been criticized for our aggressive marketing in these countries. It is also true that only home-country nationals may own voting shares in our company. So, even though we are global, we do have a home and a history and we respect the traditions and sensibilities of our home country.

We want to maintain our number-one position in Europe, and over time achieve the same position of leadership in our target markets in North America and Japan. We are also keeping a close eye on the developing countries of the world, and whenever we see a country making the move from low income to lower middle, or from lower middle to upper middle, or from upper middle to high income we commit our best effort to expand our positions, or, if we don't have a position, to establish a position. Since our objective is to achieve an undisputed leadership position in our industry, we simply cannot afford not to be in every growing market in the world.

We have always had a European CEO, and this will probably not change. The executives in this company from Europe tend to serve all over the world, whereas the executives from the United States and Japan serve only in their home countries. They are very able and valuable executives, but they lack the necessary perspective of the world required for the top jobs here at headquarters.

DISCUSSION QUESTIONS

1. Which company is transnational?
2. What are the attributes of a transnational company?
3. What is the difference between a domestic, international, multinational, global, and transnational company?
4. At what stage of development is your company and your line of business today? Where should you be?

[handwritten notes:]

regiocentric

Criteria:
→ ethocetic: Centralized, underlying belief of superiority, adaptation of products, standardization — Specific market research no knowledge transfer back

→ polycetic

TIME   QUALITY   MONEY   PEOPLE

→ Build Revenue
→ Cut Costs

CHAPTER 2

The Global Economic Environment

"Free trade, one of the greatest blessings which a government can confer to a people, is in almost every country unpopular."

—LORD MACAULAY, 1800–1859

CHAPTER CONTENTS

The macro dimensions of the environment are economic, social and cultural, political and legal, and technological. Each is important, but perhaps the single most important characteristic of the global market environment is the economic dimension. With money, all things (well, almost all!) are possible. Without money, many things are impossible for the marketer. Luxury products, for example, cannot be sold to low-income consumers. Hypermarkets for food, furniture, or durables require a large base of consumers with the ability to make large purchases of goods and the ability to drive away with those purchases. Sophisticated industrial products require sophisticated industries as buyers.

Today, in contrast to any previous time in the history of the world, there is global economic growth. For the first time in the history of global marketing, markets in every region of the world are potential targets for almost every company from high tech to low tech, across the spectrum of products from basic to luxury. Indeed, the fastest-growing markets, as we shall see, are in countries at earlier stages of development. The economic dimensions of this world market environment are of vital importance. This chapter examines the characteristics of the world economic environment from a marketing perspective.

The global marketer is fortunate in having a substantial body of data available that charts the nature of the environment on a country-by-country basis. Each country has national accounts data, indicating estimates of gross national product, gross domestic product, consumption, investment, government expenditures, and price levels. Also available on a global basis are demographic data indicating the number of people, their distribution by age category, and rates of population growth. National accounts and demographic data do not exhaust the types of economic data available. A single source, *The Statistical Yearbook of the United Nations,* contains global data on agriculture, mining, manufacturing, construction, energy production and consumption, internal and external trade, railroad and air transport, wages and prices, health, housing, education, communication (mail, telegraph, and telephone), and mass communications by book, film, radio, and television. These data are available for all high-income countries. The less developed a country is, the scarcer is the availability of economic data. In the low-income countries of the world, one cannot be certain of obtaining anything more than basic national accounts, and demographic and external trade data. Nevertheless, in considering the world's economic environment, the marketer's problem is not one of an absence of data but rather of an abundance. This chapter will identify the most salient characteristics of the economic environment to provide the framework for further consideration of the elements of a global marketing program.

◆ THE WORLD ECONOMY—AN OVERVIEW

The world economy has changed profoundly since World War II. Perhaps the most fundamental change is the emergence of global markets; responding to new opportunities, global competitors have steadily displaced local ones. Concurrently, the integration of the world economy has increased significantly. Economic integration stood at 10 percent at the beginning of the 20th century; today, it is approximately 50 percent. Integration is particularly striking in two regions, the European Union (formerly the European Community) and the North American Free Trade Area.

Just 40 years ago, the world was far less integrated than it is today. As a young man working in Europe and Africa in the 1960s, the author was struck by how different everything was. There were many companies, many products, and great differentiation. As evidence of the changes that have taken place, consider the automobile. European nameplates such as Renault, Citroën, Peugeot, Morris, Volvo, and others were radically different from the American Chevrolet, Ford, or Plymouth, or Japanese models from Toyota or Nissan. These were local cars built by local companies, mostly destined for local or regional markets. Today, the world car is a reality for Toyota, Nissan, Honda, and Ford. Product changes reflect organizational changes as well: The world's largest automakers have, for the most part, evolved into global companies.

Within the past decade, there have been several remarkable changes in the world economy that hold important implications for business. The likelihood of business success is much greater when plans and strategies are based on the new reality of the changed world economy:

- Capital movements rather than trade have become the driving force of the world economy.
- Production has become "uncoupled" from employment.
- The world economy dominates the scene. The macroeconomics of individual countries no longer control economic outcomes.
- The growth of commerce via the Internet diminishes the importance of national barriers.

The first change is the increased volume of capital movements. The dollar value of world trade is greater than ever before. Trade in goods and services is running at roughly $4 trillion per year, but the London Eurodollar market turns over $400 billion each working day. That totals $100 trillion per year—25 times the dollar value of world trade. In addition, foreign exchange transactions are running at approximately $1 trillion per day worldwide, which is $250 trillion per year—40 times the volume of world trade in goods and services.[1] There is an inescapable conclusion in these data: Global capital movements far exceed the volume of global merchandise and services trade. This explains the bizarre combination of U.S. trade deficits and a continually rising dollar during the first half of the 1980s. Previously, when a country ran a deficit on its trade accounts, its currency would depreciate in value. Today, it is capital movements and trade that determine currency value.

The second change concerns the relationship between productivity and employment. Although employment in manufacturing remains steady or has declined, productivity continues to grow. The pattern is especially clear in American agriculture, where fewer farm employees produce more output. In the United States, manufacturing holds a steady 23 to 24 percent of gross national product (GNP). This is true of all the other major industrial economies as well. Manufacturing is not in decline—it is employment in manufacturing that is in decline.[2] Countries such as the United Kingdom, which have tried to maintain blue-collar employment in manufacturing, have lost both production and jobs for their efforts.

The third major change is the emergence of the world economy as the dominant economic unit. Company executives and national leaders who recognize this have the greatest chance of success. Those who do not recognize this fact will suffer decline and bankruptcy (in business) or overthrow (in politics). The real secret of the economic success of Germany and Japan is the fact that business leaders and policy makers focus on the world economy and world markets; a top priority for government and business in both Japan and Germany has been their competitive position in the world. In contrast, many other countries, including the United States, have focused on domestic objectives and priorities to the exclusion of their global competitive position.

In the 1990s the greatest economic change was the end of the Cold War. The success of the capitalist market system had caused the overthrow of communism as an economic and political system. The overwhelmingly superior performance of the world's market economies has led socialist countries to renounce their ideology. A key policy change in such countries has been the abandonment of futile attempts to manage national economies with a single central plan. The different types of economic systems are contrasted in the next section.

In this new decade, the growth of computer usage and e-commerce is revising the economic landscape. The impact of the Internet and e-commerce is discussed in Chapter 16.

◆ ECONOMIC SYSTEMS

There are three types of economic systems: capitalist, socialist, and mixed. This classification is based on the dominant method of resource allocation: market allocation, command or central plan allocation, and mixed allocation, respectively.

---

[1] Alan C. Shapiro, *Multinational Finance Management,* 3rd ed. (Boston: Allyn & Bacon, 1989):116.
[2] Some companies have cut employment by outsourcing or subcontracting nonmanufacturing activities such as data processing, housekeeping, and food service.

MARKET ALLOCATION

A market allocation system is one that relies on consumers to allocate resources. Consumers "write" the economic plan by deciding what will be produced by whom. The market system is an economic democracy—citizens have the right to vote with their pocketbooks for the goods of their choice. The role of the state in a market economy is to promote competition and ensure consumer protection. The United States, most Western European countries, and Japan—the triad countries that account for three quarters of gross world product—are examples of predominantly market economies. The clear superiority of the market allocation system in delivering the goods and services that people need and want has led to its adoption in many formerly socialist countries.

COMMAND ALLOCATION

In a command allocation system, the state has broad powers to serve the public interest. These include deciding which products to make and how to make them. Consumers are free to spend their money on what is available, but decisions about what is produced and, therefore, what is available are made by state planners. Because demand exceeds supply, the elements of the marketing mix are not used as strategic variables. There is little reliance on product differentiation, advertising, and promotion; distribution is handled by the government to cut out "exploitation" by intermediaries. Three of the most populous countries in the world—China, the former USSR, and India—relied on command allocation systems for decades. All three countries are now engaged in economic reforms directed at shifting to market allocation systems. The prediction made by India's Jawaharlal Nehru nearly a half century ago regarding the imminent demise of capitalism has been refuted. Market reforms and nascent capitalism in many parts of the world are creating opportunities for large-scale investments by global companies. Indeed, Coca-Cola returned to India in 1994, two decades after being forced out by the government. A new law allowing 100 percent foreign ownership of enterprises helped pave the way. By contrast, Cuba stands as one of the last bastions of the command allocation approach.

MIXED SYSTEM

There are, in reality, no pure market or command allocation systems among the world's economies. All market systems have a command sector, and all command systems have a market sector; in other words, they are "mixed." In a market economy, the command allocation sector is the proportion of gross domestic product (GDP) that is taxed and spent by government. For the 24 member countries of the Organization for Economic Cooperation and Development (OECD), this proportion ranges from 32 percent of GDP in the United States to 64 percent in Sweden.[3] In Sweden, therefore, where 64 percent of all expenditures are controlled by government, the economic system is more "command" than "market." The reverse is true in the United States. Similarly, farmers in most socialist countries were traditionally permitted to offer part of their production in a free market. China has given considerable freedom to businesses and individuals in the Guangdong province to operate within a market system. Still, China's private sector constitutes only 1 to 2 percent of national output.[4]

---

[3] *OECD Economic Outlook,* no. 50, December 1991 (Paris: OECD, 1991): 206.
[4] *The Economist,* 8 April 2000, Special Section.

A recent report by the Washington, DC–based Heritage Foundation ranked more than 100 countries by degree of economic freedom. Ten key economic variables were considered: trade policy, taxation policy, government consumption of economic output, monetary policy, capital flows and foreign investment, banking policy, wage and price controls, property rights, regulations, and the black market. The rankings form a continuum from "Free" to "Repressed," with "Mostly Free" and "Mostly Unfree" in between. Hong Kong is ranked number 1 in terms of economic freedom. This status has not changed even though Hong Kong has legally reverted to the People's Republic of China in 1997. Libya, Iraq, and North Korea are ranked lowest.[5] Overall, 57 of the 161 countries listed have expanded economic freedom while 34 countries have curtailed it. The report's findings are reported in Table 2-1.

TABLE 2-1   Index of Economic Freedom, 2000 Rankings

Free	*Mostly Free*		*Mostly Unfree*		*Repressed*
1 Hong Kong	11 Canada	44 Bolivia	74 Cambodia	108 Algeria	139 Burundi
2 Singapore	Chile	Latvia	Mexico	Ivory Coast	Haiti
3 New Zealand	El Salvador	46 Guatemala	Slovak Rep.	110 Brazil	Rwanda
4 Bahrain	Taiwan	Malaysia	Slovenia	Croatia	Syria
Luxembourg	15 Austria	Thailand	Swaziland	Egypt	Tajikistan
U.S.	Netherlands	49 Greece	Tunisia	Ethiopia	144 Equatorial
7 Ireland	17 Argentina	Israel	Uganda	Indonesia	Guinea
8 Australia	Belgium	Morocco	81 Kenya	115 Lesotho	145 Belarus
Switzerland	19 Iceland	Turkey	Qatar	116 Kyrgyz Rep.	Myanmar
U.K.	Japan	53 Belize	Senegal	Nepal	147 Azerbaijan
	U.A.E.	Oman	84 Armenia	Nicaragua	148 Guinea-
	22 Bahamas	Paraguay	Ecuador	Ukraine	Bissau
	Czech Rep.	Poland	Gabon	120 Georgia	Turkmen.
	Estonia	Samoa	Ghana	Malawi	Vietnam
	Finland	58 Costa Rica	Guinea	122 Albania	151 Bosnia
	Germany	Mauritius	89 Mongolia	Cape Verde	Uzbekistan
	27 Denmarck	Philippines	90 Guyana	Kazakstan	153 Angola
	28 Italy	61 Benin	Lebanon	Russia	154 Iran
	Norway	Colombia	Madagascar	126 Bangladesh	155 Laos
	Portugal	Dom. Rep.	Moldava	Chad	156 Congo
	31 Sweden	Jordan	94 Fiji	India	*(Dem. Rep.)*
	Trinidad &	Lithuania	Nigeria	Mauritania	157 Cuba
	Tobago	Mali	Papua New	Mozambique	158 Somalia
	33 South Korea	Namibia	Guinea	Niger	159 Libya
	Panama	South Africa	Romania	Sierra Leone	160 Iraq
	Spain	Sri Lanka	Venezuela	Togo	161 North Korea
	36 Peru	Zambia	99 Honduras	134 Sudan	
	37 Barbados	71 Botswana	100 Bulgaria	Yemen	
	France	Malta	Burkina Faso	136 Congo	
	Jamaica	Saudi Arabia	Cameroon	Suriname	
	Kuwait		China	Zimbabwe	
	41 Cyprus		Djibouti		
	Hungary		Gambia		
	Uruguay		Pakistan		
			Tanzania		

Source: The Wall Street Journal, 30 November 1999, p. A-26.

---

[5] Gerald P. O'Driscoll, Jr., Kim R. Holmes, and Melanie Kirkpatrick, "Economic Freedom Marches On," *The Wall Street Journal,* 30 November 1999, p. A26.

◆ STAGES OF MARKET DEVELOPMENT

Global country markets are at different stages of development. GNP per capita provides a very useful way of grouping these countries. Using GNP as a base, we have divided global markets into four categories. Although the income definition for each of the stages is arbitrary, countries in each of the four categories have similar characteristics. Thus, the stages provide a useful basis for global market segmentation and target marketing. The categories are shown in Table 2-2. For complete information about the economic status of each country and predictions for 2010 and 2020, see *Global Income and Population* in the appendix at the back of this book.

LOW-INCOME COUNTRIES

Low-income countries, also known as preindustrial countries, are those with incomes of less than $786 per capita. They constitute 37 percent of the world population but less than 3 percent of world GNP. The following characteristics are shared by countries at this income level:

1. Limited industrialization and a high percentage of the population engaged in agriculture and subsistence farming
2. High birthrates
3. Low literacy rates
4. Heavy reliance on foreign aid
5. Political instability and unrest
6. Concentration in Africa, south of the Sahara

In general, these countries represent limited markets for all products and are not significant locations for competitive threats. Still, there are exceptions; for example, in Bangladesh, where GNP per capita is $366, a growing garment industry has enjoyed burgeoning exports.

LOWER-MIDDLE-INCOME COUNTRIES

Lower-middle-income countries (also known as less developed countries or LDCs) are those with a GNP per capita of more than $786 and less than $3,125. These countries constitute 39 percent of the world population but only 11 percent of world GNP. These countries are at the early stages of industrialization. Factories supply a growing domes-

TABLE 2-2 Stages of Market Development				
Income Group by Per Capita GNP	*2000 GNP ($ Millions)*	*2000 GNP per Capita ($)*	*% of World GNP*	*2000 Population (Million)*
High-Income Countries (GNP per Capita >$9,656)	24,259	24,722	81	981
Upper-Middle-Income Countries (GNP per Capita >$3,126 but <$9,655)	2,031	4,503	7	451
Lower-Middle-Income Countries (GNP per Capita >$785 but <$3,125)	3,148	1,302	10	2,418
Low-Income Countries (GNP per Capita <$785)	812	356	3	2,284

Source: Warren J. Keegan, *Global Income and Population 2000 Edition: Projections to 2010 and 2020.* Institute for Global Business Strategy, Pace University, New York, NY.

tic market with such items as clothing, batteries, tires, building materials, and packaged foods. These countries are also locations for the production of standardized or mature products such as clothing for export markets.

Consumer markets in these countries are expanding. LDCs represent an increasingly competitive threat as they mobilize their relatively cheap—and often highly motivated—labor to serve target markets in the rest of the world. LDCs have a major competitive advantage in mature, standardized, labor-intensive products such as athletic shoes. Indonesia, the largest country in Southeast Asia, is a good example of an LDC on the move: Despite political problems GNP per capita has risen from $250 in 1985 to $1,176 in 2000. Several factories there produce athletic shoes under contract for Nike.

UPPER-MIDDLE-INCOME COUNTRIES

Upper-middle-income countries, also known as industrializing countries, are those with GNP per capita between $3,126 and $9,655. These countries account for 7 percent of world population and almost 7 percent of world GNP. In these countries, the percentage of population engaged in agriculture drops sharply as people move to the industrial sector and the degree of urbanization increases. Many of the countries in this stage—Malaysia, for example—are rapidly industrializing. They have rising wages and high rates of literacy and advanced education, but they still have significantly lower wage costs than the advanced countries. Countries in this stage of development frequently become formidable competitors and experience rapid, export-driven economic growth.

HIGH-INCOME COUNTRIES

High-income countries, also known as advanced, industrialized, postindustrial, or First World countries, are those with GNP per capita above $9,655. With the exception of a few oil-rich nations, the countries in this category reached their present income level through a process of sustained economic growth. These countries account for only 16 percent of world population but 82 percent of world GNP.

The phrase *postindustrial countries* was first used by Daniel Bell of Harvard to describe the United States, Sweden, and Japan and other advanced, high-income societies. Bell suggests that there is a difference between the industrial and the postindustrial societies that goes beyond mere measures of income. Bell's thesis is that the sources of innovation in postindustrial societies are derived increasingly from the codification of theoretical knowledge rather than from "random" inventions. Other characteristics are the importance of the service sector (more than 50 percent of GNP); the crucial importance of information processing and exchange; and the ascendancy of knowledge over capital as the key strategic resource, of intellectual technology over machine technology, and of scientists and professionals over engineers and semiskilled workers. Other aspects of the postindustrial society are an orientation toward the future and the importance of interpersonal relationships in the functioning of society.

Product and market opportunities in a postindustrial society are more heavily dependent on new products and innovations than in industrial societies. Ownership levels for basic products are extremely high in most households. Organizations seeking to grow often face a difficult task if they attempt to expand share of existing markets. Alternatively, they can endeavor to create new markets. For example, in the 1990s, global companies in a range of communication-related industries were seeking to create new markets for multimedia, interactive forms of electronic communication.

BASKET CASES

A basket case is a country with economic, social, and political problems that are so serious they make the country unattractive for investment and operations. Some basket cases are low-income, no-growth countries, such as Ethiopia and Mozambique, that lurch from one disaster to the next. Others are once growing and successful countries that have become divided by political struggles. The result is civil strife, declining income, and, often, considerable danger to residents. Basket cases embroiled in civil wars are dangerous areas; most companies find it prudent to avoid these countries during active conflict. Most marketers tend to stay away from these countries or do business on a limited basis.

◆ STAGES OF ECONOMIC DEVELOPMENT

The stages of market development based on GNP per capita correspond with the stages of economic development as shown in Table 2-3. Low- and lower-middle-income countries are also referred to as less developed countries or LDCs. The upper-middle-income countries are also called industrializing countries, and high-income countries are referred to as advanced, industrialized, and postindustrial. Note that the shares of world GNP and the GNP per capita data shown in Table 2-3 are based on income in national currency translated into U.S. dollars at year-end exchange rates. They do not reflect the actual purchasing power and standard of living in the different countries.

Some countries are moving up the economic ladder while other countries are stagnating in their economic developments. The "Country Income Category Movement" chart in the Appendix (page 580) shows that Estonia, Peru, and South Africa are moving from the lower-middle category to the upper income category. Another way of looking at changes in economic development is looking at the "big emerging markets" (BEMs). This view was originated by Jeffrey E. Carten in his book, *The Big Ten*. These are markets that have an annual GNP greater than $100 billion, are growing at rates faster than the world average, and are well positioned to move into the next higher income category. Marketers should be cognizant of the tremendous growth potential that exists in these countries and develop plans accordingly.

TABLE 2-3 Stages of Economic Development

Income Group by Per Capita GNP	2000 GNP Per Capita ($)	% of World GNP	2000 Population (Million)	Stage of Economic Development
High-Income Countries (GNP per Capita >$9,656)	24,259	81	981	Advanced, industrialized, postindustrial
Upper-Middle-Income Countries (GNP per Capita >$3,126 but <$9,655)	4,503	7	451	Industrializing
Lower-Middle-Income Countries (GNP per Capita >$785 but <$3,125)	1,302	10	2,418	Less developed (LDC)
Low-Income Countries (GNP per Capita <$785)	356	3	2,284	Preindustrial (LDC)

Source: Warren J. Keegan, *Global Income and Population 2000 Edition: Projections to 2010 and 2020.* Institute for Global Business Strategy, Pace University, New York, NY.

◆ INCOME AND PURCHASING POWER PARITY AROUND THE GLOBE

When a company charts a plan for global market expansion, it often finds that, for most products, income is the single most valuable economic variable. After all, a market can be defined as a group of people willing and able to buy a particular product. For some products, particularly those that have a very low unit cost—cigarettes, for example—population is a more valuable predictor of market potential than income. Nevertheless, for the vast range of industrial and consumer products in international markets today, the single most valuable and important indicator of potential is income.

Ideally, GNP and other measures of national income converted to U.S. dollars should be calculated on the basis of purchasing power parities (i.e., what the currency will buy in the country of issue) or through direct comparisons of actual prices for a given product. This would provide an actual comparison of the standards of living in the countries of the world. Unfortunately, these data are not available in regular statistical reports. Throughout this book we use, instead, conversion of local currency measured at the year-end U.S. dollar foreign exchange rate. The reader must remember that exchange rates equate, at best, the prices of internationally traded goods and services. They often bear little relationship to the prices of those goods and services not traded internationally, which form the bulk of the national product in most countries. Agricultural output and services, in particular, are often priced lower in relation to industrial output in developing countries than in industrial countries. Furthermore, agriculture typically accounts for the largest share of output in developing countries. Thus, the use of exchange rates tends to exaggerate differences in real income between countries at different stages of economic development. Table 2-4 ranks the top 10 countries in terms of 2000 GNP per capita; the last two columns show the rankings adjusted for purchasing power parity (PPP). Although the United States ranks 8th in income, its standard of living—as measured by what money can buy—is second only to Luxembourg.

Beyond the exchange distortion illustrated in Table 2-4, there is the distortion of money itself as an indicator of a nation's welfare and standard of living. The per capita GNP for Brazil and Chile are similar, $4,986 and $5,822, respectively. However, the PPP per capita GNP is quite different, $5,536 and $12,035, respectively. The typical consumer in Chile has more than twice the purchasing power than the Brazilian consumer! A visit

TABLE 2-4	Top 10 Nations Ranked by Per Capita Income and Purchasing Power Parity		
2000 GNP Per Capita Income		**2000 GNP Income Adjusted for Purchasing Power Parity (PPP)**	
1. Luxembourg	$38,587	1. Luxembourg	$35,708
2. Norway	38,070	2. United States	29,953
3. Singapore	36,484	3. Singapore	28,648
4. Switzerland	36,479	4. Norway	25,807
5. Kuwait	35,242	5. Hong Kong	24,602
6. Japan	34,796	6. Switzerland	24,222
7. Denmark	33,894	7. Denmark	23,555
8. United States	20,953	8. Japan	23,353
9. Hong Kong	27,463	9. Belgium	22,765
10. Austria	25,854	10. Austria	21,787

Source: Warren J. Keegan, *Global Income and Population 2000 Edition: Projections to 2010 and 2020.* Institute for Global Business Strategy, Pace University, New York, NY.

to a mud house in Tanzania will reveal many of the things that money can buy: radios, an iron bed frame, a corrugated metal roof, beer and soft drinks, bicycles, shoes, photographs, and razor blades. What Tanzania's per capita income of $244 does not reflect is the fact that instead of utility bills, Tanzanians have the local well and the sun. Instead of nursing homes, tradition and custom ensure that families will take care of the elderly at home. Instead of expensive doctors and hospitals, villagers can turn to witch doctors and healers. In industrialized countries, a significant portion of national income is generated by taking goods and services that would be free in a poor country and putting a price on them. Thus, the standard of living in many countries is often higher than income data might suggest.

With these qualifications in mind, the reader is referred to the table in the Appendix that shows the location of world income and population by region in 2000. The striking fact revealed by these tables is the concentration of income in the "Triad"—the United States and Canada, the European Union (EU), and Japan. The Triad accounted for almost 73 percent of global income but only 13 percent of global population in 2000.

The concentration of wealth in a handful of large, industrialized countries is the most striking characteristic of the global economic environment. The United States is, of course, a colossus in North America. In 2000 it accounted for 90 percent of the region's GNP. In Western Europe, four countries—Germany, France, the United Kingdom, and Italy—accounted for almost 73 percent of Western Europe's GNP. Japan accounted for 62 percent of Asia's GDP; in fact, Japan's GNP alone is nearly twice the size of all other Asia-Pacific country GDPs combined. In Latin America, Argentina, Brazil, and Mexico accounted for 73 percent of LAFTA (Latin America Free Trade Area) GDP.

With the exception of China and Brazil, the top 10 countries in 2000 in terms of total GNP are all located in the Triad (see Table 2-5). The United States, the world's largest economy, is larger than the rest of the world, excluding the 8 other countries in the top 10. No one knows what the future will bring, but an extrapolation of the growth to the year 2020 produces an interesting result, shown in Table 2-6. The United States, Japan, and China occupy the top three positions. China overtakes Germany, France, and the United Kingdom. South Korea and India appear on the list and surpass Spain and Canada. These extrapolation results suggest that China, with its combination of high real-income growth and relatively low population growth, is a strong candidate to become a leading world economic power.

An examination of the distribution of wealth within countries also reveals patterns of income concentration, particularly in the less developed countries outside the former communist bloc. Adelman and Morris found that, in less developed countries,

TABLE 2-5 World GNP Top 10 in 2000	
Country	*GNP (in Millions)*
United States	$8,259,358
Japan	4,427,104
Germany	2,127,086
France	1,446,515
United Kingdom	1,359,764
China	1,179,345
Italy	1,168,771
Brazil	850,852
Canada	602,158
Spain	544,944

TABLE 2-6 Projected World GNP Top 10 in 2020	
Country	*GNP (in Millions)*
United States	$15,809,426
Japan	6,262,992
China	3,962,808
Germany	3,451,622
France	2,428,733
United Kingdom	2,316,692
Italy	1,771,088
Brazil	1,597,467
Korea, Rep.	1,140,994
India	1,114,291

Source: Warren J. Keegan, *Global Income and Population: 2000 Edition: Projections to 2010 and 2020.* Institute for Global Business Strategy, Pace University, New York, NY.

the average share of GNP accruing to the poorest 20 percent of the population was 5.6 percent as compared with 56.0 percent going to the top 20 percent.[6] The income of the bottom 20 percent was about one fourth of what it would have been had income been distributed uniformly throughout the population. This study suggests that the relationship between the share of income at the lowest 20 percent and economic development varies with the level of development. Economic development is associated with increases in the share of the bottom 20 percent only after relatively high levels of socioeconomic development have been attained. At the early stages of the development process, economic development works to the relative disadvantage of the lowest-income groups. Brazil, for example, has become one of the world's most unequal societies, with the top fifth of the country's population earning some 65 percent of national income; the bottom fifth earns less than 3 percent. China is experiencing a similar type of income inequality. The per capita GDP ranges from $250 to $500 in the province of Tibet to over $1,000 in Guangdong, Jiangsu, and other coastal provinces.[7] Unfortunately, a wide degree of income disparity tends to breed political unrest. Throughout the ages, people have spent most of their energy making a living finding food, clothing, and shelter. An old Armenian folk saying, "Making a living is like taking food out of a lion's mouth," captures this reality. Although the problem of poverty has not been eliminated in all the industrialized countries, those countries with homogeneous populations and an advanced collective social conscience have indeed greatly reduced poverty within their borders.

The actual conditions of life for the masses in the richest and the poorest countries were not significantly different in the 1850s. This is in sharp contrast to the conditions today in which the gap between the living standard of the majority in the high-income countries is vastly different than that of the majority in the low-income countries. This growing gap between the richest and the poorest countries is a tremendous incentive to people in poor countries to move to a high-income country to seek economic opportunity and a higher standard of living.

Since 1850, the distribution of population between the industrial and the preindustrial countries has not changed significantly. But between 1850 and 1992, the industrial

---

[6] Irma Adelman and Cynthia Taft Morris, *Comparative Patterns of Economic Development, 1850–1914* (Baltimore: Johns Hopkins University Press, 1988); Irma Adelman and Cynthia Taft Morris, *Economic Growth and Social Equity in Developing Countries* (Stanford, CA: Stanford University Press, 1973).
[7] *The Economist,* 8 April 2000, p. 4 Special Section.

countries' share of world income increased from 39 to 75 percent. During this period, annual compound rates of growth of 2.7 percent in total output and 1.8 percent in per capita output profoundly altered the world's distribution of income. The magnitude of change, as compared with the previous 6,000 years of our civilized existence, is enormous: Over one third of the real income and about two thirds of the industrial output produced by people throughout recorded history were generated in the industrialized countries in the last century. Note that relatively small average annual rates of growth have transformed the economic geography of the world. What the industrial countries have done is to systematize economic growth. Put another way, they have established a process of continuous, gradual change.

One researcher has calculated that India, one of the poorest countries in the world, could reach U.S. income levels by growing at an average rate of 5 to 6 percent in real terms for 40 to 50 years. This is no more than the lifetime of an average Indian, and about half the lifetime of an average American. Japan was the first country with a non-European heritage to achieve high-income status. This was the result of sustained high growth and the ability to acquire knowledge and know-how, first by making copies of products and then by making improvements. As Japan has dramatically demonstrated, this is a potent formula for catching up and achieving economic leadership.

Today, much more than was true 1,000 years ago, wealth and income are concentrated regionally, nationally, and within nations. The implications of this reality are crucial for the global marketer. A company that decides to diversify geographically can accomplish this objective by establishing operations in a handful of national markets.

◆ THE LOCATION OF POPULATION

We have already noted the concentration of 72 percent of world income in the Triad (North America, the EU, and Japan) but only 13 percent of the world population. As shown in Table 2-7, in 2000, the 10 most populous countries in the world accounted for

TABLE 2-7   The 10 Most Populous Countries: 2000 with Projection to 2020

Global Income and Population	2000 Population (Thousands)	% of World Population	Projected Population 2020	2000 GNP (Millions)	Per Capita GNP	% of World GNP
World Total	6,134,466	100.0	8,504,642	30,578,246	—	100.0
1. China	1,268,121	20.7	1,609,796	1,179,345	930	3.9
2. India	1,015,287	16.6	1,464,902	430,096	424	1.4
3. United States	275,746	4.5	326,607	8,259,358	29,953	27.3
4. Indonesia	210,785	3.4	286,706	247,846	1,176	0.7
5. Brazil	170,661	2.8	232,130	850,852	5,535	2.8
6. Russian Federation	146,866	2.4	157,495	342,008	2,329	1.1
7. Pakistan	138,334	2.3	242,669	66,219	479	0.2
8. Bangladesh	129,663	2.1	190,792	47,489	1,501	0.2
9. Nigeria	128,454	2.1	255,338	38,416	299	0.1
10. Japan	127,229	2.1	137,804	4,427,104	34,796	14.6

Source: Warren J. Keegan, *Global Income and Population: 2000 Edition: Projections to 2010 and 2020.* Institute for Global Business Strategy, Pace University, New York, NY.

59 percent of world income, and the 5 largest accounted for 48 percent. The concentration of income in the high-income and large-population countries means that a company can be global—derive a significant proportion of its income from countries at different stages of development—while operating in 10 or fewer countries.

For products whose price is low enough, population is a more important variable than income in determining market potential. Although population is not as concentrated as income, there is, in terms of size of nations, a pattern of considerable concentration. The 10 most populous countries in the world account for roughly 60 percent of the world's population today.

People have inhabited the earth for over 2.5 million years. The number of human beings has been small during most of this period. In Christ's lifetime, there were approximately 300 million people on earth, or roughly one quarter of the number of people on mainland China today. World population increased tremendously during the 18th and 19th centuries, reaching 1 billion by 1850. Between 1850 and 1925, global population had doubled, to 2 billion, and from 1925 to 1960 it had increased to 3 billion. World population is now over 6 billion; at the present rate of growth it will reach 10 billion by the middle of this century. Projections on whether this growth rate will continue or not will have has a dramatic effect on the total future population. Also to consider is that the population is not expanding equally across the globe. Developing countries are expanding much faster than developed countries but the birthrate even in developing countries can vary widely as attitudes toward the number of children, economic development, and diseases change. Simply put, global population will probably double during the lifetime of many students using this textbook (see Figure 2-1).

Generally, there is a negative correlation between population growth rate and income per capita. The lower the income per capita, the higher the rate of population growth and vice versa. In countries such as the United States, Germany, and Japan, the growth rate from 1990 to 1996 was 1 percent or under. Recently, however, some countries in the low-middle and lower-income categories have negative rates of population. These are concentrated in the former republics of the Soviet Union.

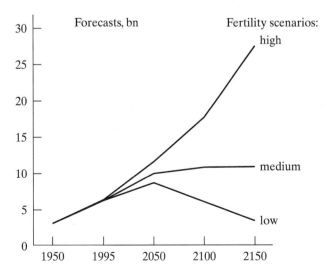

FIGURE 2-1   World Population

Source: United Nations.

◆ MARKETING AND ECONOMIC DEVELOPMENT

An important concern in marketing is whether it has any relevance to the process of economic development. Some people believe the field of marketing is relevant only to the conditions that apply in affluent, industrialized countries where the major problem is one of directing society's resources into ever-changing output or production to satisfy a dynamic marketplace. In the less developed country, the argument goes, the major problem is the allocation of scarce resources toward obvious production needs. Efforts should focus on production and how to increase output, not on customer needs and wants.

Conversely, it can be argued that the marketing process of focusing an organization's resources on environmental opportunities is a process of universal relevance. The role of marketing—to identify people's needs and wants, and to focus individual and organizational efforts to respond to these needs and wants—is the same in both low- and high-income countries. For example, pursuing alternative sources of energy such as wind and solar power is important for two reasons: the lack of coal reserves in many countries, and concerns that overreliance on fossil fuels will contribute to global warming. These concerns have led to the development of solar-powered lanterns that are used in villages in India. Similarly, solar water heaters have been installed in Gaborone, the capital of Botswana, eliminating as much as 40 percent of the energy requirements for thousands of families.

The economics literature places a great deal of emphasis on "the role of marketing in economic development" when marketing is defined as distribution. In his book, *West African Trade,* P. T. Bauer considered the question of the number of traders and their productivity.[8] The number and variety of traders in West Africa had been much criticized by both official and unofficial observers. Traders were condemned as wasteful and said to be responsible for wide margins both in the sale of merchandise and in the purchase of produce. Bauer examined these criticisms and concluded that they stemmed from a misunderstanding. In his view, the West African system economized in capital and used a redundant resource—labor. Therefore, Bauer argued, it was a productive system by rational economic criteria.

A simple example illustrates Bauer's point. A trader buys a pack of cigarettes for 1 shilling and resells them one at a time for 2 cents each, for a total of 2 shillings. Has this person exploited society to the tune of 1 shilling, or has he provided a useful service? In a society in which consumers can afford to smoke only one cigarette at a time, the trader has provided a useful service in substituting labor for capital. In this case, capital would be the accumulation of an inventory of cigarettes by a consumer. The possession of a shilling is the critical first obstacle to this accumulation. However, even if a consumer were able to accumulate a shilling, his standard of living would not allow him to smoke the 20 cigarettes fast enough to prevent them from going stale. Thus, even if he were able to save and accumulate a shilling, he would end up with a package of spoiled cigarettes. The trader in this case, by breaking bulk, serves the useful function of making available a product in a quantity that a consumer can afford and in a condition that is attractive. As income levels rise, the purchaser will smoke more frequently and will be able to buy an entire package of cigarettes. In the process, the amount of local resources consumed by distribution will decline and the standard of living will have risen. Meanwhile, less developed countries in which labor is redundant and cheap and capital is scarce, the availability of this distribution function represents a useful, rational application of society's resources. Moreover, experience in the distributive sector is valuable because it generates a pool of entrepreneurial talent in a society in which alternatives for such training are scarce.

---

[8] Peter T. Bauer, *West Africa Trade* (London: Routledge and K. Paul, 1963).

ECONOMIC RISK

Economic development does not always follow a straight upward path. Even in countries with established governments, radical political change often goes hand in hand with drastic economic change. This has a tremendous effect on consumer purchases and how marketers adapt their efforts in these countries. Depending on the gravity of the economic disorder, stagflation to depression, consumers buy fewer, less expensive but more functional products. This is a signal to marketers to adjust pricing and product design accordingly. Recent examples of cases in which marketers had to implement such changes are the countries affected by the Asian Flu. In Southeast Asia in the late 1990s, the Indonesian rupiah fell more than 70 percent against the U.S. dollar, the Thai baht and Korean won depreciated by 40 to 50 percent, the Malaysian ringgit and Philippine peso lost 40 percent of their value, and the currency in Singapore and Taiwan lost 20 percent as well. Global marketers in the region had to adapt their marketing strategies on a country-by-country basis.[9]

◆ BALANCE OF PAYMENTS

The balance of payments is a record of all of the economic transactions between residents of a country and the rest of the world. The U.S. and Japanese balance-of-payments statistics for the period 1990 to 1993 are shown in Tables 2-8 and 2-9. The format here closely mirrors that used by the International Monetary Fund in its *Balance of Payments Yearbook,* which summarizes economic activity for all the countries of the world.

The balance of payments is divided into a so-called "current" and "capital" account. The current account is a record of all of the recurring trade in merchandise and service, private gifts, and public aid transactions between countries. The capital account is a record of all long-term direct investment, portfolio investment, and other short- and long-term capital flows. The minus signs signify outflows of cash; for example, in Table 2-8, line A2 shows an outflow of $877 billion that represents payment for U.S. merchandise imports. In general, a country accumulates reserves when the net of its current and capital account transactions shows a surplus; it gives up reserves when the net shows a deficit. The important fact to recognize about the overall balance of payments is that it is always in

TABLE 2-8 U.S. Balance of Payments, 1994–1997 (US$ Billions)

	1994	*1995*	*1996*	*1997*
A. Current Account	**–123.21**	**–115.22**	**–135.44**	**–155.38**
1. Goods: Exports FOB	504.45	577.69	613.89	681.27
2. Goods: Imports FOB	–668.59	–749.57	–803.32	–877.28
3. Balance on Goods	–164.14	–171.88	–189.43	–196.01
4. Services: Credit	199.25	217.80	236.71	256.06
5. Services: Debit	–132.45	–141.98	–152.00	–166.09
6. Balance on Goods and Services	–97.34	–96.06	–104.72	–106.04
B. Capital Account	**–.60**	**.10**	**.52**	**.16**
Total A + B	–123.81	–115.12	–134.91	–155.22

Source: Adapted from *Balance of Payments Statistics Yearbook* (Washington, DC: The International Monetary Fund, 1998), p. 852.

[9] Ang Swee Hoon, "Marketing Under Challenging Economic Conditions: Consumer and Business Perspective," *MarkPlus Quarterly* (October–December 1998): 18–31.

TABLE 2-9 Japan Balance of Payments, 1994–1997 (US$ Billions)	1994	1995	1996	1997
A. Current Account	**131.64**	**111.04**	**65.88**	**94.35**
1. Goods: Exports FOB	385.70	428.72	400.28	409.24
2. Goods: Imports FOB	−241.51	−296.93	−316.72	−307.64
3. Balance on Goods	144.19	131.79	83.56	101.60
4. Services: Credit	58.30	65.27	67.72	69.30
5. Services: Debit	−106.36	−122.63	−129.96	−123.45
6. Balance on Goods and Services	96.13	74.43	21.32	47.45
B. Capital Account	**−1.85**	**−2.23**	**−3.29**	**−4.05**
Total A + B	128.41	108.82	62.59	90.30

Source: Adapted from *Balance of Payments Statistics Yearbook* (Washington, DC: The International Monetary Fund, 1998), p. 405.

balance. Imbalances occur in subsets of the overall balance. For example, a commonly reported balance is the merchandise trade balance (line 3 in Tables 2-8 and 2-9).

Tables 2-8 and 2-9 show that, between 1994 and 1997, Japan showed a declining surplus in both its current account and its merchandise trade balances. Conversely, in the same period, the United States showed increasing deficits in both balances. The United States' overall trade deficit has continued to surprise observers, given the dollar's weakness relative to the currencies of trading partners such as Germany and Japan. A comparison of lines 4 and 5 in the two tables shows a bright spot, from the U.S. perspective. Overall, Japan offsets its trade surplus with an outflow of capital, whereas the United States offsets its trade deficit with an inflow of capital. As trading partners, the United States owns an increasing quantity of Japanese products, whereas Japan owns more U.S. land, real estate, and government securities.

◆ TRADE PATTERNS

Since the end of World War II, world merchandise trade has grown faster than world production. In other words, import and export growth has outpaced the rate of increase in GNP. Moreover, since 1983, foreign direct investment has grown five times faster than world trade and 10 times faster than GNP.[10] The structure of world trade is summarized in Figure 2-2. The importance of Europe and Central Eurasia is quite pronounced: They accounted for approximately 60 percent of world exports and imports. Industrialized nations have increased their share of world trade by trading more among themselves and less with the rest of the world.

MERCHANDISE TRADE

Table 2-10 shows trade patterns for the world. In 1994, the dollar value of world trade was approximately $4.1 trillion. Seventy-five percent of world exports were generated by industrialized countries, and 25 percent by developing countries. The European Union accounted for 40 percent, the United States and Canada for 18 percent, and Japan for 9 percent. If the EU were considered a single country, its share of world exports

---

[10]"Who Wants to Be a Giant?" *The Economist,* 24 June 1995, Survey, p. 1.

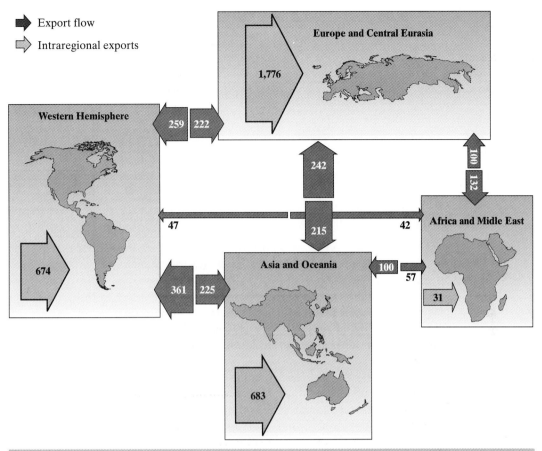

FIGURE 2-2   World Trade in 1997 (US$ in Billions)

Source: Handbook of International Economic Statistics, February 1999, p. 74.

TABLE 2-10 Key U.S. Trade Information				
1998 $ Volume	*Exports: $663 Billion*		*Imports: $912 Billion*	
Partners	Canada	22%	Canada	19%
	Western Europe	21%	Western Europe	18%
	Japan	10%	Japan	14%
	Mexico	10%	Mexico	10%
			China	7%
	Total	63%	Total	68%
Commodities	Capital Goods		Oil and Petroleum Products	
	Automobiles		Machinery	
	Industrial Supplies		Autmobiles	
	Consumer Goods		Consumer Goods	
	Agricultural Products		Industrial Raw Materials	
			Food and Beverages	

Source: The World Factbook, 1999, Central Intelligence Agency.

would be slightly less than that of the United States. Trade growth outside industrialized countries has been slow.

The top 20 exporting and importing countries of the world (as reported by the International Monetary Fund) are shown in Table 2-11. Among Asian exporters, China and South Korea both showed growth exceeding 20 percent from 1993 to 1994, evidence of economic strength. In the Western Hemisphere, Mexico's export growth of 20.73 percent shows the impact of NAFTA; by comparison, in 1992 and 1993 Mexico's exports grew only 9 percent. Perhaps the most surprising statistic in Table 2-11 is the nearly 50 percent increase in Russia's 1994 exports resulting from privatization of major industry sectors and increased emphasis on exports. An illustration of the impact of international trade on a typical student in the United States is illustrated in the box "Measuring the Russian Economy."

SERVICES TRADE

Probably the fastest-growing sector of world trade is trade in services. Services include travel and entertainment; education; business services such as engineering, accounting, and legal services; and payments of royalties and license fees. Unfortunately, the statistics and data on trade in services are not as comprehensive as those for merchandise trade. For example, many countries (especially low-income countries) are lax in enforcing international copyrights, protecting intellectual property, and patent laws. As a result, countries that export service products such as software and video entertainment

TABLE 2-11 Twenty Leading Exporters and Importers in World Merchandise Trade, 1997 (US$ Billions)

Leading Exporters	1997	Percent Change '97/'96	Leading Importers	1997	Percent Change '97/'96
1. United States	762.8	9.0	1. United States	867.0	8.9
2. Germany	482.4	−2.2	2. Germany	438.9	−1.6
3. Japan	464.4	3.6	3. Japan	304.9	−3.1
4. China, P. R.	287.6	12.9	4. United Kingdom	297.5	6.7
5. France	280.9	−1.0	5. France	270.4	3.5
6. United Kingdom	265.2	6.3	6. Netherlands	204.7	2.5
7. Italy	222.4	−1.8	7. Canada	195.2	13.0
8. Canada	220.1	5.8	8. Italy	190.4	3.8
9. Netherlands	171.3	−.005	9. Hong Kong	186.6	11.0
10. Belgium–Luxembourg	143.3	1.1	10. China, P. R.	164.6	5.2
11. Taiwan	135.2	3.6	11. Belgium–Luxembourg	155.2	0.2
12. South Korea	125.0	7.5	12. South Korea	123.2	−4.0
13. Malaysia	115.0	24.0	13. Spain	119.9	3.5
14. Mexico	108.7	16.2	14. Taiwan	103.9	11.3
15. Spain	99.5	3.9	15. Mexico	92.5	25.8
16. Singapore	98.9	1.8	16. Switzerland	87.9	−2.7
17. Switzerland	90.8	−3.9	17. Malaysia	79.3	4.6
18. Sweden	79.1	−1.5	18. Russia	63.6	9.6
19. Russia	82.9	−2.7	19. Brazil	61.2	15.0
20. Saudi Arabia	67.2	7.3	20. Austria	60.6	−3.5

Source: Adapted from International Monetary Fund, *Direction of Trade Statistics* (Washington, DC: IMF, 1998), pp. 2–3.

◆ BOX 2-1 ◆

MEASURING THE RUSSIAN ECONOMY

In today's Russia, average citizens are not the only ones struggling to keep pace with rapid and revolutionary economic change; government statisticians cannot even keep up. The result is that economic information and statistics coming from Russia are inaccurate, inadequate, distorted, and biased.

Russia's main source of economic statistics is an agency called Goskomstat, or the Russian State Statistical Committee. The inherent problem with the statistics generated by Goskomstat is one of original intent: Historically, Goskomstat measured the state economy of the Soviet Union; the purpose of the statistics that are still used for economic measurement today does not exist anymore because of the change from a planned economy to a market economy.

Goskomstat continues to collect data and measure production in the least productive sectors, namely, industries that have not been privatized and farms still owned by the state. If those statistics were somewhat balanced by equivalent numbers from the private sector, Russian GNP might not be so severely underestimated. However, Goskomstat is not at all aggressive about counting the growing private sector in the Russian economy. The growth in Russian joint ventures, retail and service trade, and private banking has been well documented in the press but not by Goskomstat.

The problem of gathering data from start-up businesses in the emerging private sector is compounded by the fact that those enterprises are reluctant to be in-cluded because of potential tax implications. Also, be-cause of inadequate survey techniques, thousands of sole proprietorships, entrepreneurial and barter trade enterprises, as well as informal, black and gray markets are all outside the reach of Goskomstat's reckoning.

Even the data generated from the fading state sector are inadequate because organizations on the government dole are not motivated to report any increased production. Those enterprises could stand to lose government subsidies if production goes up. Ironically, in the Soviet era, managers of state-owned businesses were inclined to inflate production numbers to reach goals set by state planners.

So what is the impact of the skewed numbers put forth by Goskomstat? The faulty numbers create a ripple effect worldwide. Other agencies that rely on this imperfect source for economic data include the World Bank, International Monetary Fund, U.S. Department of Commerce, the Central Intelligence Agency (CIA), plus countless banks and industrial and investment analysts. At the very least, statistics severely understate production, especially in the growing private economy. The estimated amount of underreported production ranges from 25 percent to 60 percent, with most experts estimating a 45 percent undercount to be closest to reality. One consequence for the Russian economy is slowed growth because nervous investors may be reluctant to enter a market depicted by such bleak numbers.

SOURCES: S. Frederick Starr, "The 'Glass Is Half Full' Case For Russia," *The International Economy* (March/April 1995): 46, 46+; Judy Shelton, *The Coming Soviet Crash: Gorbachev's Desperate Pursuit of Credit in Western Financial Markets* (New York: The Free Press, 1989).

suffer a loss of service. According to the Software Publishers Association, annual worldwide losses due to software piracy amount to $8 billion. In China and the countries of the former Soviet Union, more than 95 percent of the personal computer software in use is believed to be pirated.

As shown in Figure 2-3, in 1994, U.S. service exports totaled $195 billion, partially offsetting the merchandise trade deficit. In 1994, the service surplus—service exports minus imports—stood at $60 billion. American Express, Walt Disney, and Texas Instruments are a few of the U.S. companies currently enjoying rapid growth in demand for their services around the world, fueled in part by the weak dollar.[11]

---

[11] Ralph T. King, Jr., "Quiet Boom: U.S. Service Exports Are Growing Rapidly, but Almost Unnoticed," *The Wall Street Journal,* 21 April 1993, p. A1.

GOODS AND SERVICES

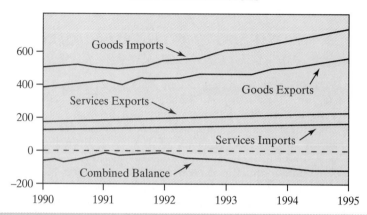

FIGURE 2-3 U.S. Trade Balance on Services and on Merchandise Trade ($ Billions)

Source: Business America (June 1995): 28. U.S. Government Printing Office.

◆ INTERNATIONAL TRADE ALLIANCES

VISIT THE WEB SITES

www.wto.org   www.Caricom.org
www.apecsec.org.sg   www.aei.org
www.iie.org   www.coha.org

Since World War II, there has been a tremendous interest among nations in economic cooperation. This interest has been stimulated by the success of the European Community, which was itself inspired by the U.S. economy. There are many degrees of economic cooperation, ranging from agreement between two or more nations to reductions of barriers to trade, to the full-scale economic integration of two or more national economies. The best-known preferential arrangement of the early 20th century was the British Commonwealth preference system. This system provided a foundation for trade among the United Kingdom, Canada, Australia, New Zealand, India, and certain other former British colonies in Africa, Asia, and the Middle East. The decision by the United Kingdom to join the European Economic Community resulted in the demise of this system and illustrates the constantly evolving nature of international economic cooperation.

The marketing implications of trade alliances may include harmonization of business requirements such as packaging requirements, a common currency that allows consumers to more easily compare pricing across countries, and economic development that leads to more consumers who can afford to buy more products.

DEGREES OF ECONOMIC COOPERATION

There are four degrees of economic cooperation and integration, as illustrated in Table 2-12.

Free Trade Area

A free trade area (FTA) is a group of countries that have agreed to abolish all internal barriers to trade among themselves. Countries that belong to a free trade area can and do maintain independent trade policies with third countries. A system of certificates of origin is used to avoid trade diversion in favor of low-tariff members. The system dis-

	Abolition of Tariffs and Quotas	Common Tariff and Quota System	Removal of Restrictions on Factor Movements	Harmonization of Economic, Social, and Regulatory Policies
Stage of Integration				
Free trade area	Yes	No	No	No
Customs union	Yes	Yes	No	No
Common market	Yes	Yes	Yes	No
Economic union	Yes	Yes	Yes	Yes

TABLE 2-12   Degrees of International Economic Integration

courages importing goods in the member country with the lowest tariff for shipment to countries within the area with higher external tariffs. Customs inspectors police the borders between members. The European Economic Area is an FTA that includes the 15-nation European Union and Norway, Liechtenstein, and Iceland. The Canada–U.S. Free Trade Area formally came into existence in 1989. In 1992, representatives from the United States, Canada, and Mexico concluded negotiations for the North American Free Trade Agreement (NAFTA). The agreement was approved by both houses of the U.S. Congress and became effective on January 1, 1994.

Customs Union

+ Common external barriers

A customs union represents the logical evolution of an FTA. In addition to eliminating the internal barriers to trade, members of a customs union agree to the establishment of common external barriers. The Central American Common Market, Southern Cone Common Market (Mercosur), and the Andean Group are all examples of customs unions.

Common Market

A common market goes beyond the removal of internal barriers to trade and the establishment of common external barriers to the important next stage of eliminating the barriers to the flow of factors (labor and capital) within the market. A common market builds on the elimination of the internal tariff barriers and the establishment of common external barriers. It seeks to coordinate economic and social policy within the market to allow free flow of capital and labor from country to country. Thus, a common market creates an open market not only for goods but also for services and capital.

Economic Union

The full evolution of an economic union would involve the creation of a unified central bank; the use of a single currency; and common policies on agriculture, social services and welfare, regional development, transport, taxation, competition and mergers, construction and building, and so on. A fully developed economic union requires extensive political unity, which makes it similar to a nation. The further integration of nations that were members of fully developed economic unions would be the formation of a central government that would bring together independent political states into a single political framework.

The European Union (EU) is approaching its target of completing most of the steps required to create a full economic union, but major hurdles remain.

◆ THE WORLD TRADE ORGANIZATION AND GATT

The year 1997 marked the 50th anniversary of the GATT, a treaty among 123 nations whose governments agreed, at least in principle, to promote trade among members. GATT was intended to be a multilateral, global initiative, and GATT negotiators did, indeed, succeed in liberalizing world merchandise trade. It was also an organization that had handled 300 trade disputes—many involving food—during its half century of existence. GATT itself had no enforcement power (the losing party in a dispute was entitled to ignore the ruling), and the process of dealing with disputes sometime stretched on for years. Little wonder, then, that some critics referred to GATT as the "general agreement to talk and talk."

The successor to GATT, the World Trade Organization (WTO), came into existence on January 1, 1995. From its base in Geneva, the WTO provides a forum for trade-related negotiations. The WTO's staff of neutral trade experts will also serve as mediators in global trade disputes. The WTO had a Dispute Settlement Body (DSB) that mediates complaints about unfair trade barriers and other issues between WTO member countries. During a 60-day consultation period, parties to a complaint are expected to engage in good-faith negotiations and reach an amicable resolution. Failing that, the complainant can ask the DSB to appoint a three-member panel of trade experts to hear the case behind closed doors. After convening, the panel has 9 months within which to issue its ruling. The DSB is empowered to act on the panel's recommendations. The losing party has the option of turning to a seven-member appellate body. If, after due process, trade policies are found to violate WTO rules, the country is expected to change those policies. If changes are not forthcoming, the WTO can authorize trade sanctions against the loser.

One of the WTO's first major tasks was hosting negotiations on the General Agreement on Trade in Services, in which 76 signatories made binding market access commitments in banking, securities, and insurance. The WTO faced its first real test when representatives from the United States and Japan met in 1995 to try to resolve a dispute over Washington's claims that Japan engaged in unfair trade practices that limited imports of U.S. car parts. The Clinton administration was responding to the fact that one third of the U.S. merchandise trade deficit—$66 billion in 1994 alone—is with Japan. Moreover, cars and auto parts accounted for approximately two thirds of that $66 billion. In the spring of 1995, the United States threatened to slap 100 percent tariffs on 13 models of cars imported from Japan. Japan formally filed a complaint with the WTO to object to the tariffs; although a trade war was narrowly averted at the last moment, trade-related tensions between the two countries continue to simmer. Trade tensions flared up again in 1998 as the United States threatened to slap 100 percent tariffs on European imports such as Italian hams and bed linens. The United States was acting in response to Europe's banana import quota system.[12]

Trade ministers representing the WTO member nations meet annually to work on improving world trade. At the 1996 meeting in Singapore, agreement was reached concerning tariffs on information technology. For the year 2000, zero tariffs are now slated for 500 products, ranging from calculators, fax machines, and CD-ROM drives to computer keyboards and ATM machines. The United States, Canada, and several Asian countries will benefit the most, because they are home to companies that command 80 percent of world trade in high-tech products, compared with a 15 percent share held by Western European companies. The agreement could result in lower prices for businesses and consumers, especially in Asia and Europe, where tariffs had been relatively high.[13] Still, it remains to be seen whether the WTO will live up to expectations regarding additional major policy initiatives on such issues as competition of foreign investment. One problem is that politicians in many countries are resisting the WTO's plans to move swiftly in removing trade barriers. A Norwegian trade group told reporters that the WTO's motto should be, "If you can decide it tomorrow, why decide it today?" Still, as Director General Renato Ruggiero said recently, "Free trade is a process that cannot be stopped."[14]

For detailed information of the Seattle Meeting, visit the Web site: www.wto.org/wto/seattle/mindex_e.htm.

---

[12] Karl Taro Greenfeld, "Banana Wars," *Time,* 8 February 1999, pp. 42–43.

[13] Helene Cooper and Bhushan Bahree, "Nations Agree to Drop Computer Tariffs," *The Wall Street Journal,* 13 December 1996, pp. A2, A6.

[14] Helene Cooper and Bhushan Bahree, "No 'Gatzilla': World's Best Hope for Global Trade Topples Few Barriers," *The Wall Street Journal,* 3 December 1996, p. A8.

◆ REGIONAL ECONOMIC ORGANIZATIONS

In addition to the multilateral initiatives of the World Trade Organization (WTO), countries in each of the world's regions are seeking to lower barriers to trade within their regions. The following section describes the major regional economic cooperation agreements. The trade groups listed next are divided geographically into the European, North American, Asian, South and Latin American, and African and Middle Eastern trade groups.

EUROPEAN TRADE GROUPS

The European Union (EU)

The European Union (formerly known as the European Community [EC]) was established by the Treaty of Rome in 1958. The six original members were Belgium, France, Holland, Italy, Luxembourg, and West Germany. In 1973, Britain, Denmark, and Ireland were admitted, followed by Greece in 1981 and Spain and Portugal in 1986. The three newest members, Finland, Sweden, and Austria joined in 1995. (In 1994, voters in Norway rejected a membership proposal.) Today, the 15 nations of the EU represent 378 million people, a combined GNP of $8.3 trillion, and 28 percent of world GNP. The map in Figure 2-4 shows the EU membership; the lightly shaded countries are the three newest members.

FIGURE 2-4   EU Countries

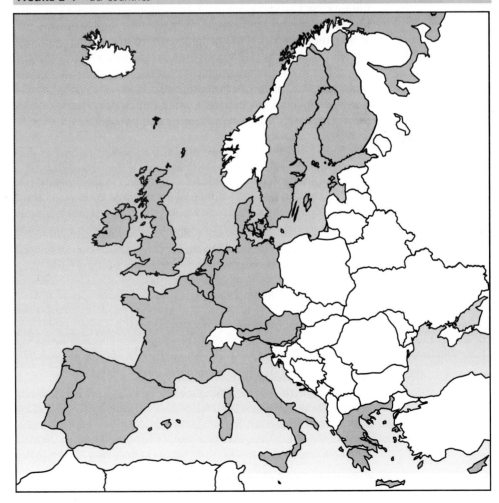

Beginning in 1987, the 12 countries that were EC members at that time set about the difficult task of creating a genuine single market in goods, services, and capital. Completing the single-market program by year-end 1992 was a major EC achievement; the Council of Ministers adopted 282 pieces of legislation and regulations to make the single market a reality. Now, citizens of the 15 countries are able to freely cross borders within the EU.

How have companies responded to the movement in the EU toward a single market? In a series of surveys carried out in 1973, 1983, and 1993, Boddewyn and Grosse found that there was a growing standardization of marketing policies by U.S. firms in the EU from its inception in 1958 to the early 1980s followed by a return to greater adaptation. The obstacles to standardization mentioned by respondents include differences in tastes and habits and national government regulations for consumer products, as well as nationalistic feelings and government regulations for industrial goods. These findings suggest that the EU effort to achieve greater harmonization has some distance to go.[15]

Under provisions of the Maastricht Treaty, the EU is working to create an economic and monetary union (EMU) that will include a European Central Bank and a single European currency. Implementation of the EMU will require working out the extent to which countries sharing a currency need to coordinate taxes and budgets. A single currency would eliminate costs associated with currency conversion and exchange rate uncertainty. It would also make it easier for consumers in the various participating countries to compare pricing of goods and services. Member countries recognize that the use of multiple currencies in the EU is a source of economic "drag" on their economy, but they also realize that the adoption of a single currency would expose the member countries to economic risks that the countries do not face when operating with separate currencies. There is also the realization that having a currency is a key element of national control and in the end is what distinguishes a nation from a subnational unit of political organization. Countries have currencies, and states or provinces do not. Since the EU members adopted a single currency, they no longer can control the inflation and interest rates, the two key levers of monetary policy, which are key tools of any sovereign for controlling its economic destiny. Britain, Denmark, Greece, and Sweden are not currently participating in the single currency, which will not assume a cash form until 2002.

Further EU enlargement has become a major issue with 12 countries having been accepted as applicants. The list of applicants is divided into several categories. *The Economist* estimates that Hungary, Poland, and Cyprus may become full members by 2003; Estonia, Malta, Czech Republic, and Latvia in 2004; Slovenia, Lithuania, and Slovakia in 2005; Bulgaria and Romania in 2008; and Turkey in 2011.[16] In theory, economic development should be the main criteria for entry; however, many political issues are also involved in making the decision for admission into the EU.

The Lomé Convention

The EU maintains an accord with 70 countries in Africa, the Caribbean, and the Pacific (ACP). The Lomé Convention was designed to promote trade and provide poor countries with financial assistance from the European Development Fund. Recently, budget pressures at home have prompted some EU nations to push for cuts in Lomé aid.

European Economic Area

In 1991, after 14 months of negotiations, the European Economic Community and the seven-nation European Free Trade Association (EFTA) reached agreement on the creation of the European Economic Area (EEA) beginning January 1993. Although the

---

[15] Jean J. Boddewyn and Robert Gross, "American Marketing in the European Union: Standardization's Uneven Progress in 1973–1993," *European Journal of Marketing,* 29, no. 12 (1995): 23–43.

[16] "Enlarging the European Union; A New Pace?" *The Economist,* 2 October 1999, pp. 45–55.

goal was to achieve the free movement of goods, services, capital, and labor between the two groups, the EEA is a free trade area, not a customs union with common external tariffs. With Austria, Finland, and Sweden now members of the EU, Norway, Iceland, and Liechtenstein are the sole remnants of the EFTA that are not EU members (Switzerland voted not to be part of the EEA). The EEA is the world's largest trading bloc, with 383 million consumers and $8.5 trillion combined GNP.

Central European Free Trade Association

The transition in Central and Eastern Europe from command to market economies led to the demise, in 1991, of the Council for Mutual Economic Assistance. COMECON (or CMEA, as it was also known) was a group of communist bloc countries allied with the Soviet Union. In the post-COMECON era, a number of proposals for multilateral cooperation have been advanced, including the creation of a successor body to be called the Organization for International Economic Cooperation (OIEC). Ultimately, most proposals were blocked by potential member states whose representatives feared that a membership in a new regional bloc would hinder their chances of joining the EU. In 1992, Hungary, Poland, and Czechoslovakia signed an agreement creating the Central European Free Trade Association (CEFTA). The signatories pledged cooperation in a number of areas, including infrastructure and telecommunications, subregional projects, interenterprise cooperation, and tourism and retail trade.[17] Romania, Slovenia, and the two countries created by the division of Czechoslovakia—Czech Republic and Slovakia—are also CEFTA members (Figure 2-5). Meanwhile, within the Commonwealth of Independent States, formal economic integration between the former Soviet republics is proceeding slowly. In 1995, the governments of Russia and Belarus agreed to form a customs union and remove border posts between their two countries.

NORTH AMERICAN TRADE GROUP

North American Free Trade Agreement

In 1988, the United States signed a free trade agreement with Canada (U.S.–Canada Free Trade Agreement, or CFTA), the scope of which was enlarged in 1993 to include Mexico. The resulting free trade area had a 2000 population of 406.7 million and a gross national product of $9.3 trillion.

All three governments will promote economic growth through expanded trade and investment. The benefits of continental free trade will enable all three countries to meet the economic challenges of the decades to come. The gradual elimination of barriers to the flow of goods, services, and investment, coupled with strong intellectual property rights protection (patents, trademarks, and copyrights), will benefit businesses, workers, farmers, and consumers.

Canada and Mexico rank first and third as the United States' most important trading partners (Japan ranks second). In 1994, the first year of the agreement, U.S. exports to Canada totaled $114.4 billion; U.S. exports to Mexico were $50.8 billion. In 1994, U.S. merchandise imports from Canada totaled $128.9 billion; imports from Mexico amounted to $49.5 billion. The NAFTA countries are shown in Figure 2-6. By 1998, the volume of intra-NAFTA trade had risen considerably. U.S. exports to Canada had increased 37 percent to $156.6 billion and exports to Mexico totaled $78.8 billion, an increase of 55 percent. U.S. imports for 1998 from Canada were $173.3 billion, an increase of 34 percent, while imports from Mexico almost doubled to $94.6 billion, an increase of 91 percent.

---

[17] Bob Jessop, "Regional Economic Blocs, Cross-Border Cooperation, and Local Economic Strategies in Postsocialsm," *American Behavioral Scientist,* 38, no. 5 (March 1995): 689–690.

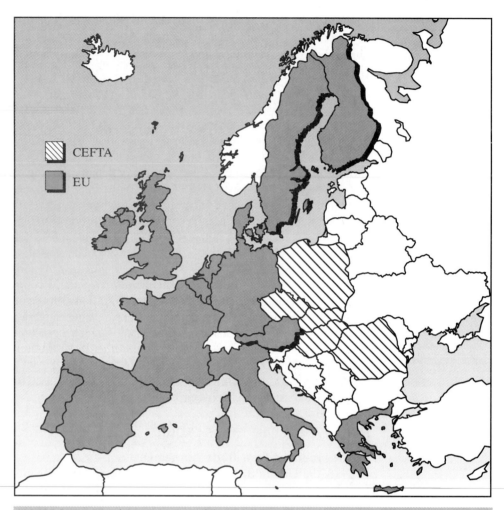

FIGURE 2-5 Central European Free Trade Agreement Countries

ASIAN TRADE GROUPS

Asia–Pacific Economic Cooperation

Each November of each year representatives of 18 countries that border on the Pacific Ocean meet formally to discuss prospects for liberalizing trade. Collectively, the countries that make up the Asia—Pacific Economic Cooperation (APEC) forum account for 38 percent of world population and 52 percent of world GNP. APEC provides a chance for annual discussions by people at various levels: academics and business executives, ministers, and heads of state. Some small Asian countries view APEC as a welcome means of using the United States to counterbalance the dominance of Japan and China in the region. As one expert observed, "Not so long ago, the thought of South Korea or Indonesia, let alone China, having anything to do with even a 'vision' of free trade would have been fantastic."

Much debate among APEC members has centered on whether all trade barriers in Asia can be eliminated, without exception, by the year 2020. It has become apparent that policy makers and farmers in South Korea, China, and Japan still support agricultural subsidies. Agricultural producers in the United States, Canada, and Australia want to sell more food products in Asia. Although the Japanese government took action in 1993 to

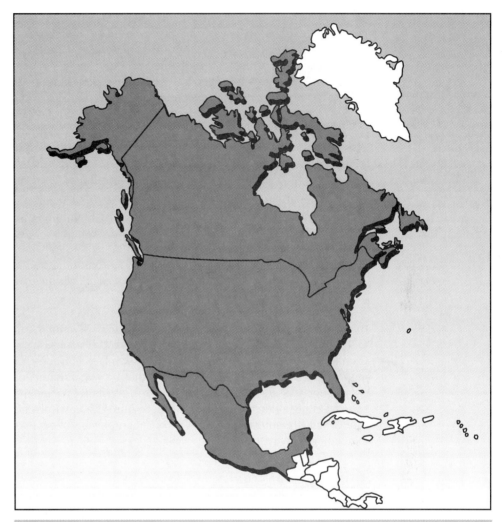

FIGURE 2-6   NAFTA Countries

end an outright ban on imports of foreign rice, market access is still restricted. Australian farmers have worked particularly hard to develop varieties of rice that will appeal to finicky Japanese consumers. Notes a member of an Australian rice growers' cooperative, "Japanese are connoisseurs of rice. If we can sell our product in Japan, we can sell it anywhere. All we need is the market to open up."

Besides agriculture, other divisive issues have been Washington's annual review of China's most-favored-nation trading status and the Clinton administration's firm stand on human rights.

In 1997, the APEC meeting in Vancouver, British Columbia, faced a surprising challenge: the so-called Asian Flu financial crisis that began in Thailand and quickly spread to Malaysia, Indonesia, Korea, and even Japan. This crisis, caused by careless lending and borrowing practices in the private sectors of these countries, led to a crisis in investor confidence in security values, which led to a collapse in prices in equity markets, a major decline in currency values, and a massive increase in exports from countries in the region to the United States. The entire world was caught off guard by this crisis, which underlined the fact that lending and banking practices in the region had become quite "loose" and sloppy. The world realized that the Asian "miracle" had some major deficiencies that needed to be repaired. These repairs presented a challenge to the world economy: how to fix the problems in Asia without spreading the "flu" to the rest of the world. It was clear to economists that as long as the economic leaders of the high-income countries of the world did not allow aggregate demand in their markets to collapse or trade barriers to be imposed, it would be possible for the countries in the Asian region to clean house. This would require ending the traditional close relationship that had existed in many countries between business and government and the establishment of a more rigorous system of private sector responsibility for investment decisions.

Association of Southeast Asian Nations

The Association of Southeast Asian Nations (ASEAN) is an organization for economic, political, social, and cultural cooperation among its 10 member countries: Brunei, Cambodia, Indonesia, Laos, Malaysia, Myanmar, the Philippines, Singapore, Thailand, and Vietnam. ASEAN (pronounced OZZIE-on) was established in 1967 with the signing of the Bangkok Declaration (see Figure 2-7). Vietnam became the first communist nation in the group when it was admitted in 1995. Cambodia and Laos were admitted to ASEAN in 1997. Myanmar joined in 1998. The countries have agreed to eliminate most tariffs by 2010.

The ASEAN group has 495 million people and a GNP of $700 billion. (Please note that economic data are not available for Brunei, Myanmar, and Vietnam.) Per capita GNPs among ASEAN members in 2000 ranged from $36,484 in Singapore to $290 in Cambodia. ASEAN is the United States' sixth largest trading partner. There is a growing realization among ASEAN officials that broad common goals and perceptions are not enough to keep the association alive. A constant problem is the strict need for consensus among all members before proceeding with any form of cooperative effort. Although the 10 countries of ASEAN are geographically close, they have historically been divided in many respects.

FIGURE 2-7 ASEAN Countries

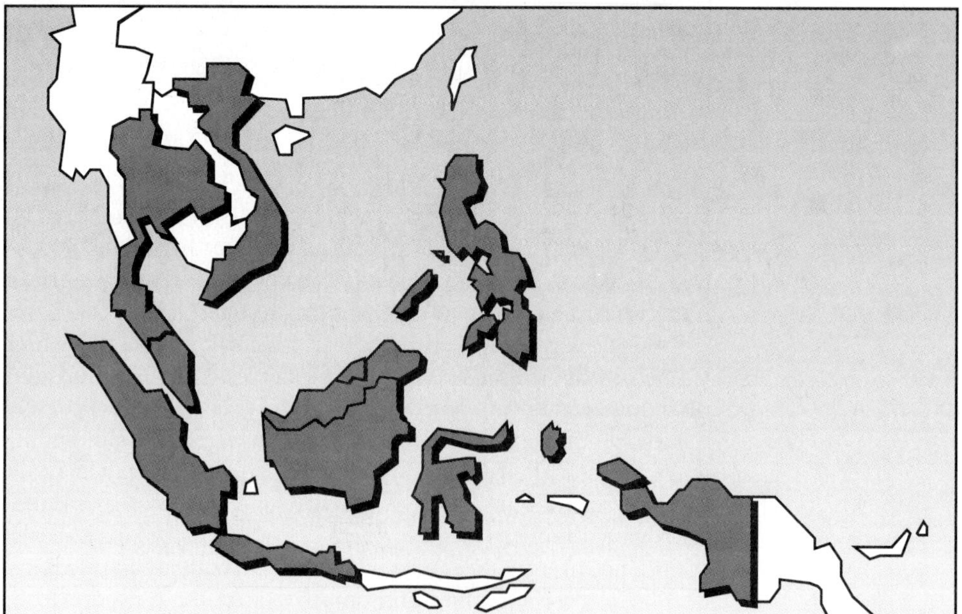

SOUTH AND CENTRAL AMERICAN TRADE GROUPS

Andean Group

The Andean Group (Figure 2-8) was formed in 1969 to accelerate development of its member states—Bolivia, Colombia, Ecuador, Peru, and Venezuela—through economic and social integration. Members agreed to lower tariffs on intragroup trade and work together to decide what products each country should produce. At the same time, foreign goods and companies were kept out as much as possible. One Bolivian described the unfortunate result of this lack of competition in the following way: "We had agreed, 'You buy our overpriced goods and we'll buy yours.' "[18]

In 1988, the group members decided to get a fresh start. Beginning in 1992, the Andean Pact signatories agreed to form Latin America's first operating subregional free trade zone. More than 100 million consumers would be affected by the pact, which abolished all foreign exchange, financial and fiscal incentives, and export subsidies at the end of 1992. Common external tariffs were established, marking the transition to a true customs union. A high-level commission was created to look into any alleged unfair trade practices among countries.

The Andean Group, with a population of only 113 thousand people, accounts for $284 million GNP or $2,513 per capita.

FIGURE 2-8   The Andean Group and Mercosur Countries

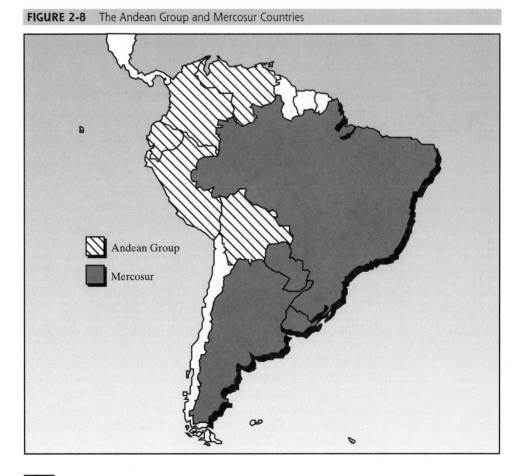

Andean Group

Mercosur

[18] "NAFTA Is Not Alone," *The Economist*, 18 June 1994, pp. 47–48.

Southern Cone Common Market

Argentina, Brazil, Paraguay, and Uruguay (Figure 2-8)—with a combined population of 232 million people, a GNP of $1,332 billion or a per capita GNP of $5,741 in 2000—agreed in 1991 to form a customs union known as the Southern Cone Common Market (in Spanish, Mercado del Sur, or Mercosur). In 1996, Chile became an associate member. Chile chose not to become a full member because it already had lower external tariffs than the rest of Mercosur; full membership would have required raising them. Presently, Chile has been negotiating for membership in NAFTA.

One immediate result of the tariff reform was that prices of many consumer goods fell overnight in Argentina and Brazil. This, in turn, directly impacted commerce in Paraguay, which had long been a low-tariff haven where cigarettes, electronics equipment, and liquor prices were 40 percent lower than in the rest of South America. Historically, bargain seekers—and smugglers—swarmed across the Paraguay border to shop at Ciudad del Este, where annual merchandise sales reached $13 billion in 1994. Now, many Paraguayan entrepreneurs who engaged in "import-export" activities must seek other sources of income.[19]

Much depends on the successful outcome of this experiment in regional cooperation. If Brazil and Argentina can work well together, hopes for an integrated Latin America will rise significantly. Brazil has the largest population, the strongest economy (in terms of both GDP and exports) in Latin America, and the richest reserves of natural resources in the hemisphere; Argentina has the fourth largest population and third largest economy. A major impediment to integration is the lack of economic and political discipline and responsibility, a situation reflected in the volatility of currencies in the Mercosur countries. In Figure 2-8, the Andean Group is shown in light shading, and the Mercosur countries are shown in dark shading.

Caribbean Community and Common Market

The Caribbean Community and Common Market (CARICOM) was formed in 1973 as a movement toward unity in the Caribbean. It replaced the Caribbean Free Trade Association (CARIFTA) founded in 1965. The members are Antigua and Barbuda, the Bahamas, Barbados, Belize, Dominica, Grenada, Guyana, Haiti, Jamaica, Montserrat, Saint Kitts and Nevis, Saint Lucia, Saint Vincent and the Grenadines, Surinam, and Trinidad and Tobago. The population of the entire 15-member Caribbean Community is 14 million. The total population is 112,000 and has a GNP of $209 million or per capita GNP of $1,866.

The Caribbean Community's main activity is economic integration by means of a Caribbean Common Market. CARICOM (Figure 2-9) has created a customs union with common tariffs on imports from third countries, cross-listed stocks on the various exchanges, created a Caribbean Court of Justice to deal with economic issues and trade disputes, and is working toward a common currency.

Central American Integration System (SICA)

Central America is trying to revive its common market, which was set up in the 1960s. It collapsed in 1969 when war broke out between Honduras and El Salvador after a riot at a soccer match between teams from the two countries. The five members—El Salvador, Honduras, Guatemala, Nicaragua, and Costa Rica—decided in 1991 to reestablish the common market by 1994. Efforts to improve regional integration gained momentum with the granting of observer status to Panama. In 1997, with Panama as a member, the group's name was changed to Central American Integration System.

---

[19] Matt Moffett, "Attention, Shoppers! Paraguay's Bargains May Be Going Fast," *The Wall Street Journal,* 30 May 1995, pp. A1, A10.

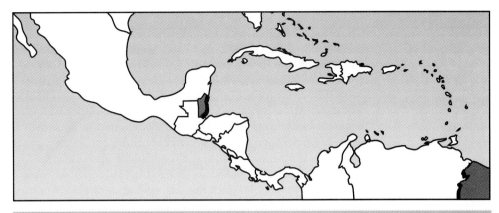

FIGURE 2-9   CARICOM Countries

The Secretariat for Central American Economic Integration (SIECA), headquartered in Guatemala City, is comprised of ministers responsible for economic integration and regional development. SIECA is charged with helping to coordinate the movement toward a Central American common market. It has been serving as secretariat for a group of customs experts who are in the process of revising the Central American Customs Duty. As of 1993, all Central American Common Market (CACM) countries conformed to a common external tariff (CET) of 5 to 20 percent for most goods; many tariffs had previously exceeded 100 percent. There was some resistance to this change; for example, the Costa Rican government had previously benefited from the revenues generated by triple-digit tariffs on automobiles imported from Japan and elsewhere. Lower tariffs are expected to result in improved export prospects for American companies. Common rules of origin were also adopted, allowing for free movement of goods among CACM countries. The CACM group is shown in Figure 2-10. The total population is 37 million and total GNP is $54 million for a per capita GNP of $1,458.

Free Trade Area of the Americas

One of the biggest issues pertaining to trade in the Western Hemisphere is the Free Trade Area of the Americas (FTAA). The idea was formally proposed in 1994 by U.S. President Bill Clinton during a summit of heads of state in Miami. Meeting in Brazil in May 1997, trade ministers from the 34 participating countries agreed to create "preparatory committees" in anticipation of formal talks that would begin in 1998. The Clinton administration was keen to open the region's fast-growing big emerging markets (BEM)

FIGURE 2-10   CACM Countries

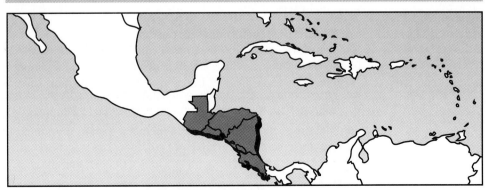

countries to U.S. companies. In particular, the president wanted talks to focus immediately on tariffs and "early harvest" agreements on individual industry sectors, such as information technology. However, the president's bargaining position was weakened by the refusal of Congress to grant him "fast track" authority. Under fast track, the president would be authorized to negotiate trade agreements, which Congress would then have to vote on without making any changes or amendments. Many Latin American countries are frustrated by what they perceive as America's failure to follow through on its promises in the region. As a result, Brazil and its Mercosur partners are advocating a slower, three-stage approach to negotiations. The first stage would include discussions on business facilitation issues such as standardized customs forms and industry deregulation, the second would focus on dispute settlement and rules of origin, and the third would focus on tariffs. When the second Summit of the Americas was held in Santiago, Chile, in April 1998, the FTAA was formally launched. However, it was also clear that fast track authority will be essential to successfully concluding the negotiations. Meanwhile, Mercosur, CARICOM, SICA, and the Andean Community intend to pursue further integration among themselves, as well as with Europe.

AFRICAN AND MIDDLE EASTERN TRADE GROUPS

Economic Community of West African States

The Treaty of Lagos establishing the Economic Community of West African States (ECOWAS) was signed in May 1975 by 16 states, with the object of promoting trade, cooperation, and self-reliance in West Africa. The members are Benin, Burkina Faso, Cape Verde, the Gambia, Ghana, Guinea, Guinea-Bissau, the Ivory Coast, Liberia, Mali, Mauritania, Niger, Nigeria, Senegal, Sierra Leone, and Togo (Figure 2-11). The total population of ECOWAS is 300 million and total GNP is $254 million for a per capita GNP of $846.

In 1980, the member countries agreed to establish a free trade area for unprocessed agricultural products and handicrafts. Tariffs on industrial goods were also to be abolished; however, there were implementation delays. By January 1990, tariffs on 25 items manufactured in ECOWAS member states had been eliminated. The organization installed a computer system to process customs and trade statistics and to calculate the loss of revenue resulting from the liberalization of intercommunity trade. In a move to a common currency, which is unlikely before 2005, an ECOWAS traveler's check was initiated in 1999 for purchase by citizens of the member countries.

East African Cooperation Treaty

During the 1960s and 1970s, efforts to organize the countries of East Africa failed for several reasons. Given the trend toward globalization, a new attempt has been made and the result is that Kenya, Tanzania, and Uganda have signed an agreement forming the East African Cooperation Treaty. Modeled after the EU, it already has a common passport and is working toward a common currency, a regional stock market, and harmonization of laws.

South African Development Coordination Conference

The South African Development Coordination Conference (SADCC) was set up in 1980 by the region's black-ruled states to promote trade and cooperation. The members are Angola, Botswana, Congo, Lesotho, Malawi, Mauritius, Mozambique, Namibia, Seychelles, South Africa, Swaziland, Tanzania, Zambia, and Zimbabwe. The real impediment to trade has been SADCC's poverty. The World Bank indicates that combined 2000 gross national product (GNP) for the 14 member nations amounted to $174 million, a figure that is even lower than the GNP of Denmark. The total population of SADCC is 216 million for a per capita GNP of $805. The ECOWAS and SADCC countries are shown in Figure 2-11.

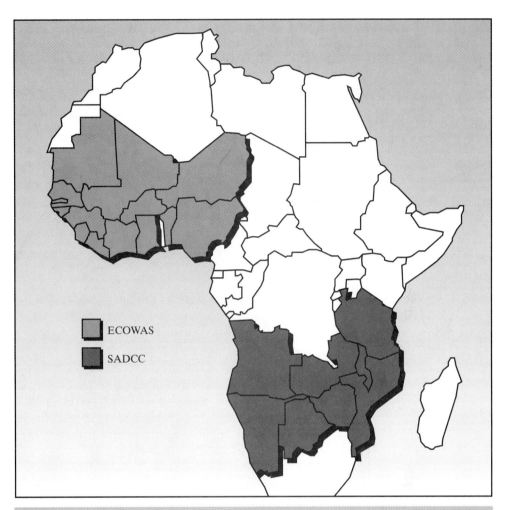

FIGURE 2-11   ECOWAS and SADCC Countries

Cooperation Council for the Arab States of the Gulf

The organization generally known as the Gulf Cooperation Council (GCC) was established in 1981 by six Arab states—Bahrain, Kuwait, Oman, Qatar, Saudi Arabia, and United Arab Emirates (see Figure 2-12). It is difficult to provide GNP numbers for the GCC as economic data are not provided for several of the countries.

The organization provides a means of realizing coordination, integration, and cooperation in all economic, social, and cultural affairs. Gulf finance ministers drew up an economic cooperation agreement covering investment, petroleum, the abolition of customs duties, harmonization of banking regulations, and financial and monetary coordination. GCC committees coordinate trade development in the region, industrial strategy, agricultural policy, and uniform petroleum policies and prices.

Arab Maghreb Union and Arab Cooperation Council

In 1989, two other organizations were established. Today, the Arab Maghreb Union (AMU) consists of Morocco, Algeria, Mauritania, Tunisia, and Libya, and the Arab Cooperation Council (ACC) consists of Egypt, Iraq, Jordan, and Yemen. Many Arabs see their regional groups—the GCC, ACC, and AMU—as embryonic economic communities that will foster the development of inter-Arab trade and investment. The newer

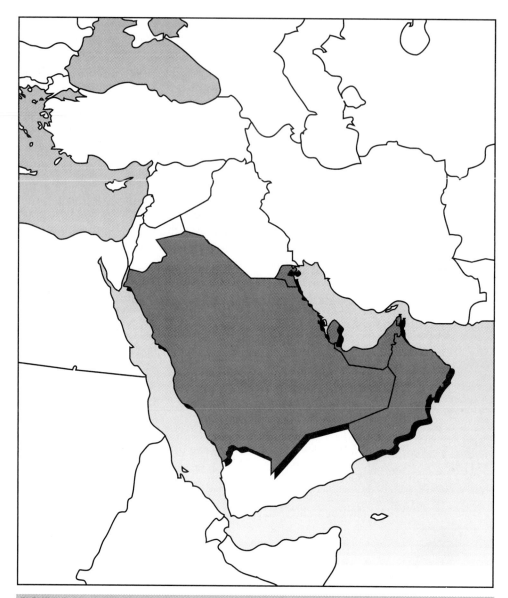

FIGURE 2-12   GCC Countries

organizations are more promising than the Arab League, which consists of 21 member states and a constitution that requires unanimous decisions.[20]

The AMU (without data for Libya) has a population of 78 million and a GNP of $95 billion for a per capita GNP of $1,231. The ACC (without GNP data for Iraq) has a population of 42 million and a GNP of $27 billion or a per capita GNP of $1,523.

Summary

The economic environment is a major determinant of global market potential and opportunity. The world's economies can be categorized as market allocation systems, command allocation systems, and mixed systems. A major trend in recent years has been the

---

[20] "A Survey of the Arab World," *The Economist,* 12 May 1990, pp. 3, 19.

transition toward market economies in many countries that had been centrally controlled. Countries can be categorized in terms of their stage of economic development: low income, lower-middle income, upper-middle income, high income, and basket cases. It is possible to identify distinct stages and formulate general estimates about the type of demand associated with a particular stage of development. For many products, the single most important indicator of market potential is income; therefore, the first step in determining the potential of a country or region is to identify the total and per capita income.

Market potential for a product can be evaluated by determining product saturation levels in light of income levels. In general, it is appropriate to compare the saturation levels of countries or of consumer segments with similar income levels. Balance-of-payments issues are also important economic considerations. The U.S. merchandise trade deficit has passed the $100 billion mark several times in recent years; the United States is, thus, a debtor; Japan enjoys a trade surplus and serves as a creditor nation.

One of the ways of dealing with the complexity of a world with over 200 national markets is to focus on economic cooperation agreements. The EU is bringing down trade barriers in Europe not only between the 15 member countries but also with the countries of Central and Eastern Europe. NAFTA has created a free trade area encompassing Canada, the United States, and Mexico. In the Asia–Pacific region, ASEAN is expanding and eliminating trade barriers in that region. Mercosur, the Andean Group, CACM, and CARICOM are the four economic cooperation agreements in Central and South America.

Discussion Questions ■

1. Explain the differences among a market allocation economic system, a command allocation system, and a mixed system.
2. What are the stages of national market development, and what percentage of world income is found in each of the stages? Why is this information important to marketers?
3. What is the pattern of income distribution in the world today? How do developing country markets compare with high-income country markets in the proportion of income going to the bottom and the top 20 percent of the population?
4. A manufacturer of long-range radios is assessing the world market potential for his products. He asks you if he should consider developing countries as potential markets. How would you advise him?
5. Are income and standard of living the same thing? What is meant by the term *standard of living*?
6. Describe the similarities and differences of a free trade area, a customs union, a common market, and an economic union. Give an example of each.
7. Do you agree or disagree with the time table for acceptance into the EU of the 12 applicant countries? Why or why not?

Suggested Readings ■

Ardrey, William J., Anthony Pecotich, and Clifford J. Schultz. "American Involvement in Vietnam, Part II: Prospects for U.S. Business in a New Era." *Business Horizons,* 38 (March/April 1995): 21–27.

Cellich, Claude. "The Big Ten: The Big Emerging Markets and How They Will Change Our Lives." *Journal of International Marketing,* 6, no. 4 (1998): 94–98.

Drucker, Peter. "Marketing and Economic Development." *Journal of Marketing* (January 1958): 252–259.

Enghold, Christopher. *Doing Business in Asia's Booming "China Triangle."* Upper Saddle River, NJ: Prentice Hall, 1994.

"The European Community," Survey. *The Economist,* 11 July 1992, pp. 5–30.

Galbraith, John Kenneth. *The Nature of Mass Poverty.* Cambridge, MA: Harvard University Press, 1979.

Ganesh, Jaishankar. "Converging Trends Within the European Union: Insights from an Analysis of Diffusion

Patterns." *Journal of International Marketing,* 6, no. 4 (1998): 32–49.

Garten, Jeffery E. *The Big Ten.* New York: BasicBooks, 1997.

Gilder, George F. *Microcosm: The Quantum Revolution in Economics and Technology.* New York: Simon & Schuster, 1989.

Golden, Peggy A., Patricia M. Doney, Denise M. Johnson, and Jerald R. Smith. "The Dynamics of a Marketing Orientation in Transition Economies: A Study of Russian Firms." *Journal of International Marketing,* 3, no. 2 (1995): 29–49.

Isaak, Robert A. *International Political Economy.* Upper Saddle River, NJ: Prentice Hall, 1991.

Johansson, J. K., and M. Hirano. "Japanese Marketing in the Post-Bubble Era." *The International Executive,* 38 (January/February 1996): 33–51.

Kennedy, Paul. *The Rise and Fall of Great Powers.* New York: Random House, 1987.

Porter, Michael E. *The Competitive Advantage of Nations.* New York: The Free Press, 1990.

Prowse, Michael. "Is America in Decline?" *Harvard Business Review* (July–August 1992): 36–37.

Randall, Stephen J., and Herman W. Konrad. "NAFTA in Transition," *Journal of Canadian Studies,* 32, no. 4 (Winter 1998): 168–177.

Reid, David McHardy. "Changes in Japan's Post-Bubble Business Environment: Implications for Foreign-Affiliated Companies." *Journal of International Marketing,* 7, no. 3 (1999): 38–64.

Shapiro, Alan C. *Multinational Finance Management,* 3rd ed. Boston: Allyn & Bacon, 1989.

Shaw, Timothy M., and Julius Emeka Okolo, eds. *The Political Economy of Foreign Policy in ECOWAS.* London: Macmillan/St. Martin's Press, 1994.

Thurow, Lester. *Head to Head: The Coming Economic Battle Among Japan, Europe, and America.* New York: William Morrow and Company, 1992.

Yan, Rick. "To Reach China's Consumers, Adapt to Guo Qing." *Harvard Business Review* (September–October 1994): 66–74.

CHAPTER 3

Social and Cultural Environment

"I believe only in French culture, and regard everything else in Europe which calls itself 'culture' as a misunderstanding. I do not even take the German kind into consideration."

—FRIEDRICH WILHELM NIETZSCHE, 1844–1900

The opening quote by the famous philosopher, Friedrich Nietzsche, is a reminder that culture has always been a source of disagreement and misunderstanding. What does Nietzsche mean when he says "culture"? As you will soon see, the meaning of culture to a global marketer is quite different than it was to Nietzsche who is probably referring to art, literature, and perhaps even music in the preceding quote. All of these elements of "high" and "low" culture are important, but as global marketers know, culture is about much more than art. It is definitely a major influence on what happens in the marketplace.

In Europe, where scones, croissants, and strudels have long been the pride of bakers and pastry chefs, trend-conscious consumers have started gobbling up American-style baked goods. It seems the Europeans are discovering what Americans have known all along: In addition to being tasty, brownies, muffins, and cookies are perfectly suited to on-the-go lifestyles that include snacking while traveling on the metro or riding a bicycle. Also, American baked goods have a shelf life of more than one day, unlike many traditional European baked goods such as fresh cream tarts. European bakers, many of whom regard pastries from across the Atlantic as inferior, had to make some adjustments to accommodate changing taste buds. As Bernard M. Schapiro of Millie's Foods Ltd. in Britain recalls, "It wasn't an easy sell. Here biscuits [cookies] are hard, and you don't find soft cookies. The perception was that it was underbaked."

American companies have also experienced some culture shock. While British consumers snapped up soft, moist Otis Spunkmeyer muffins, the American company's managers soon discovered that the word *spunk* is slang for "semen" in Britain and other countries. After the disc jockey of a national radio show asked on the air, "Who's going to eat a product with a name like that?" the company sent him a free sample. The result was favorable publicity in the form of an on-air endorsement for the goodies. Now some bakeries that sell the muffins put stickers reading "American Muffin" over the offending word. In the final analysis, as Heather McEvoy of the Colorado Cookie Company points out, "A good pastry is a good pastry no matter where it comes from and no matter what country it's sold in. Any company making good pastries will have a market in Europe."

The warm reception in Europe for American baked goods shows that many products can achieve success outside the home-country cultural environment. This chapter focuses on the social and cultural forces that shape and affect individual and corporate behavior in the marketplace. The conceptual orientation of this chapter and this book is that the cultures of the world are characterized by both differences and similarities. Thus, the task of the global marketer is twofold. Marketers must be prepared to recognize and understand the differences between cultures and then incorporate this understanding into the marketing planning process so that appropriate strategies and marketing programs are adapted. At the same time, marketers should take advantage of shared cultural characteristics and avoid unneeded and costly adaptations of the marketing mix.

Another fact about culture is that it constantly changes and evolves. At the beginning of the 20th century, there was a culture of mistrust and ethnocentrism in Europe, which was a fundamental reason for the horror of World War I. At the beginning of the 21st century, the culture of Western Europe embraces the new European Union. The old suspicions and mistrust have been replaced with cooperation and integration. In the 21st century, the convergence of cultures will be enormously accelerated by the rapid expansion of the Internet as a communications, marketing, transaction, and entertainment medium.

Global marketers must recognize and deal with the differences in the social and cultural environments of world markets. This chapter focuses on the important differences in world markets and the equally important similarities that express the fact of cultural universals. To help marketers better understand social and cultural dynamics in the global marketplace, several useful analytical approaches are explained. These include Maslow's hierarchy, Hofstede's cultural typology, the self-reference criterion, and environmental sensitivity. The chapter offers specific examples of the impact of culture and society on the marketing of both industrial and consumer products. The chapter ends with suggested solutions to cross-cultural difficulties and a review of cross-cultural training procedures currently being used in global companies.

◆ BASIC ASPECTS OF SOCIETY AND CULTURE

Anthropologists and sociologists define culture as "ways of living," built up by a group of human beings, which are transmitted from one generation to another. A culture acts out its ways of living in the context of social institutions, including family, educational, religious, governmental, and business institutions. Culture includes both conscious and unconscious values, ideas, attitudes, and symbols that shape human behavior *and that are transmitted from one generation to the next.* In this sense, culture does not include one-time solutions to unique problems, or passing fads and styles. As defined by organizational anthropologist Geert Hofstede, culture is "the collective programming of the mind that distinguishes the members of one category of people from those of another."[1]

---

[1] Geert Hofstede and Michael Harris Bond, "The Confucius Connection: From Cultural Roots to Economic Growth," *Organizational Dynamics* (Spring 1988): 5.

In addition to agreeing that culture is learned, not innate, most anthropologists share two additional views. First, all facets of culture are interrelated: Influence or change one aspect of a culture and everything else is affected. Second, because it is shared by the members of a group, culture defines the boundaries between different groups.[2]

Culture consists of learned responses to recurring situations. The earlier these responses are learned, the more difficult they are to change. Taste and preferences for food and drink, for example, represent learned responses that are highly variable from culture to culture and can have a major impact on consumer behavior. Preference for color is culturally influenced as well. For example, although green is a highly regarded color in Moslem countries, it is associated with disease in some Asian countries. White, usually associated with purity and cleanliness in the West, can signify death in Asian countries. Red is a popular color in most parts of the world (often associated with full flavor, passion, or virility); however, it is poorly received in some African countries.[3] Of course, there is no inherent attribute to any color of the spectrum; all associations and perceptions regarding color arise from culture.

Attitudes toward whole classes of products can also be a function of culture. For example, in the United States consumers have a cultural predisposition for product innovations that have a "gadgetry" quality. Thus, the electric knife, the electric toothbrush, the Water-Pik, and a host of other "labor-saving" small appliances find ready market acceptance even though many are purchased, used for a while, and then quietly put away and never used again. There is unquestionably a smaller predisposition to purchase such products in other developed markets such as Europe.

This difference is a result of cultural differences. As we noted in the last chapter, income levels also influence consumer behavior and attitudes around the world. Indeed, a basic question that must be answered by marketers who want to understand or predict behavior is, "How much do social and cultural factors influence behavior independent of income levels?" Sometimes the influence is strong. For example, U.S. companies introduced fluffy, frosted cake mixes in the United Kingdom where cake is eaten at tea time with the fingers rather than as a dessert with a fork. Green Giant Foods attempted to market corn in Europe where the prevailing attitude is that corn is a grain fed to hogs, not people. In both instances, cultural differences resulted in market failures.

Nevertheless, the demand for convenience foods, luxury consumer products, electronic products, disposable products, and soft drinks in the United States, Europe, Asia, Africa, and the Middle East suggests that most consumer products have broad, almost universal, appeal. As communications continue to shrink the world, more and more products will be marketed and consumed globally. This implies that an important characteristic of culture—that it defines boundaries between people—will not limit the global reach of companies that want to extend their operations globally. This does not suggest, however, that these companies can ignore cultural factors. The fact that there is a global market for a product does not mean that you can approach the market in different countries identically. Cultural sensitivity to differences spells the difference between global success and failure.

THE SEARCH FOR CULTURAL UNIVERSALS

An important quest for the global marketer is to discover cultural universals. A universal is a mode of behavior existing in all cultures. Universal aspects of the cultural environment represent opportunities for global marketers to standardize some or all elements of a marketing program. A partial list of cultural universals, taken from cultural anthropologist

---

[2] Edward T. Hall, *Beyond Culture* (Garden City, NY: Anchor Books, 1977), p. 16.
[3] Richard R. Still and John S. Hill, "Multinational Product Planning: A Meta Market Analysis," *International Marketing Review* (Spring 1985): 60.

George P. Murdock's classic study, includes the following: athletic sports, body adornment, cooking, courtship, dancing, decorative art, education, ethics, etiquette, family feasting, food taboos, language, marriage, mealtime, medicine, mourning, music, property rights, religious rituals, residence rules, status differentiation, and trade.[4] The astute global marketer often discovers that much of the apparent cultural diversity in the world turns out to be different ways of accomplishing the same thing.

Music provides one example of how these universals apply to marketing. Music is part of all cultures, accepted as a form of artistic expression and source of entertainment. However, music is also an art form characterized by widely varying styles. Therefore, although background music can be used effectively in broadcast commercials, the type of music appropriate for a commercial in one part of the world may not be acceptable or effective in another part. A jingle might utilize a bossa nova rhythm for Latin America, a rock rhythm for North America, and "high life" for Africa. Music, then, is a cultural universal that global marketers can adapt to cultural preferences in different countries or regions.

Because music is a cultural universal, it should come as no surprise that the music business is going global. And yet, this does not mean that the world's music is uniform. Table 3-1 shows the share of music in different markets that is local versus "international." As you can see, in countries such as Turkey and China, over 90 percent of all music played is local. Even in the United States 75 percent of music is local. Does this mean that the music business in Turkey is entirely local? Certainly not: The global music companies are in Turkey giving the Turkish people the music that they want and using their know-how and experience about the process of serving music markets: identifying and signing artists and building a repertoire, introducing and promoting artists, recording and packaging and distributing recordings, and so on. Thus, even though the content of the Turkish music market may be largely unique, the process of creating value for customers in Turkey is identical to the process of creating value anywhere. Moreover, the one constant in every market is change, and the clear trend in global music markets is toward new sounds and acts.

The global marketers in the business are always alert toward the potential of extending a successful act across national boundaries. For example, the success of Robyn, a Swedish vocalist who sings in English, first in Sweden and northern Europe established her potential to go beyond these markets. Kadja Nin, a vocalist from Burundi who sings

TABLE 3-1	Top 10 Most Domestic Music Markets (in percent)		
	Domestic	*International Pop*	*Classical*
Turkey	95.7	4.1	0.2
China	92.6	0.5	6.9
Indonesia	87.5	12.5	0.0
Venezuela	85.0	10.0	5.0
Japan	77.2	17.8	5.0
Thailand	77.2	22.4	0.4
United States	75.0	21.0	4.0
Nigeria	70.0	30.0	0.0
Taiwan	70.0	19.9	10.1
Hong Kong	64.9	28.3	6.8

Source: Music Business International, MBI World Report 1996.

---

[4] George P. Murdock, "The Common Denominator of Culture," in *The Science of Man in the World Crisis*, ed. Ralph Linton (New York: Columbia University Press, 1945), p. 145.

in Swahili and French, has been positioned as a new sound, sensuous, and international. Many feel that she has great potential for global markets.

Increasing travel and improving communications mean that many national attitudes toward style in clothing, color, music, food, and drink are converging. The globalization of culture has been capitalized upon, and even significantly accelerated, by companies that have seized opportunities to find customers around the world. Coca-Cola, Pepsi, Levi Strauss, McDonald's, IBM, Heineken, and BMG Entertainment are some of the companies breaking down cultural barriers as they expand into new markets with their products. Similarly, new laws and changing attitudes toward the use of credit are providing huge global opportunities for financial service providers such as American Express, Visa, and MasterCard International. According to one estimate, the volume of global credit card sales surpassed $2 trillion in the year 2000. The credit card companies and on-line marketers had to use communications efforts to persuade large numbers of people to use the cards. There is a great variation in the world in the use of credit and debit cards and cash. Japan is a cash and debit card culture, Europe is more of a check and debit card culture, and the United States is a credit card culture.

THE ANTHROPOLOGIST'S STANDPOINT

As Ruth Benedict points out in her classic *The Chrysanthemum and the Sword,* the way a person thinks, feels, and acts has some relation to his or her experience of the world. It doesn't matter if (normal) actions and opinions are thought of as bizarre by outsiders. Successful global marketers must understand human experience from the local point of view—and become insiders with cultural empathy in the process—if they are to understand the dynamics of markets outside the home country.

Any systematic study of a new geographic market requires a combination of tough-mindedness and generosity. The appreciation of another way of life cannot develop when one is defensive about one's own way of life; it is necessary to be secure in one's own convictions and traditions. In addition, generosity is required to appreciate the integrity and value of other ways of life and points of view—to overcome the prejudices that are a natural result of the human tendency toward ethnocentricity. When people from other countries complain that the (Americans) or (Japanese) or (French) or (British) or (Chinese) and so on are haughty, patronizing, or arrogant, home-country ethnocentricity is probably contributing to the problem. Global marketers need to develop an objective standpoint that recognizes diversity and seeks to understand its origins. There are many paths to the same end in life. The successful global marketer knows this and rejoices in life's rich diversity.

HIGH- AND LOW-CONTEXT CULTURES

Edward T. Hall has suggested the concept of high and low context as a way of understanding different cultural orientations.[5] In a low-context culture, messages are explicit; words carry most of the information in communication. In a high-context culture, less information is contained in the verbal part of a message. Much more information resides in the context of communication, including the background, associations, and basic values of the communicators. In general, high-context cultures function with much less legal paperwork than is deemed essential in low-context cultures. Japan, Saudi Arabia, and other high-context cultures place a great deal of emphasis on a person's values and position or place in society. In such cultures, a business loan is more likely to be based on who you are than on formal analysis of pro forma financial documents. In China, *guanxi* or *kuan-xie* is extremely important. *Guanxi* is roughly translated as "relationships," which

---

[5] See Edward T. Hall, *Beyond Culture* (Garden City, NY: Anchor Press/Doubleday, 1976), and "How Cultures Collide," *Psychology Today* (July 1976): 66–97.

take years to develop. In business and society, *guanxi* is even more important than laws. Chin-ning Chu quotes: "In China, it does not matter how many laws and how much right-eousness are on your side, without Kuan-Xie, you have nothing. Even if you are outside the law and there is no righteousness to your position, if you have the right Kuan-Xie and Ho-Tai (backstage), you can do no wrong."[6] In a low-context culture such as the United States, Switzerland, or Germany, deals are made with much less information about the character, background, and values of the participants. Much more reliance is placed on the words and numbers in the loan application.

In a high-context culture, a person's word is his or her bond. There is less need to anticipate contingencies and provide for external legal sanctions because the culture emphasizes obligations and trust as important values. In these cultures, shared feelings of obligation and honor take the place of impersonal legal sanctions. This helps explain the importance of long and protracted negotiations that never seem to "get to the point." Part of the purpose of negotiating for a person from a high-context culture is to get to know the potential partner.

For example, insisting on competitive bidding can cause complications in low-context cultures. In a high-context culture, the job is given to the person who will do the best work and whom you can trust and control. In a low-context culture, one tries to make the specifications so precise that a builder is forced by the threat of legal sanction to do a good job. According to Hall, a builder in Japan is likely to say, "What has that piece of paper got to do with the situation? If we can't trust each other enough to go ahead without it, why bother?"

Although countries can be classified as high or low context in their overall tendency, there are exceptions to the general tendency. These exceptions are found in subcultures. The United States, for example, is a low-context culture with subcultures that operate in the high-context mode. Charles A. Coombs, senior vice president of the Federal Reserve Bank of New York in charge of foreign exchange operations, provides such an example in his book *The Arena of International Finance*. The world of the central banker, as he describes it, is a "gentleman's" world, that is, a high-context culture. Even during the most hectic days in the foreign exchange markets, a central banker's word is sufficient for him to borrow millions of dollars.

During rioting and political upheavals in France several years ago, the confidence of central bankers in one another was dramatically demonstrated. Except for telephones, all communications between France and the United States were cut off. Consequently, the New York Fed agreed that it would follow instructions received by telephone from the Bank of France for intervening on its behalf in support of the franc. Within eight days the New York Fed had bought more than $50 million of francs without a single written confirmation for any part of the purchase. The Fed was far out on a limb. A couple of weeks later the daughter of the governor of the Bank of France came to New York on personal business. She brought written confirmations with her. "Our legal department heaved a sigh of relief," Coombs remembers. The legal department was operating in a low-context culture, with all the assumptions—that is, everything must be spelled out and confirmed in writing—that go with this culture. The central bankers, who were obviously much more relaxed about the matter, were operating within a high-context subculture in which a person's word is his or her bond. Another high-context subculture in the United States is the Mafia, which has imported the high-context culture of Sicily to the United States and has maintained this culture with language, ritual, and a strong sense of distinct identity.

These examples illustrate the ways of a high-context culture in which there is trust, a sense of fair play, and a widespread acceptance of the rules of the game as it is played. Table 3-2 summarizes some of the ways in which high- and low-context cultures differ.

---

[6] Chin-ning, Chu, *The Asian Mind Game* (New York: Rawson Associates, 1991), p. 199.

TABLE 3-2 High- and Low- Context Cultures		
Factors/Dimensions	*High Context*	*Low Context*
Lawyers	Less important	Very important
A person's word	Is his or her bond	Is not to be relied on; "get it in writing"
Responsibility for organizational error	Taken by highest level	Pushed to lowest level
Space	People breathe on each other	People maintain a bubble of private space and resent intrusions
Time	Polychronic—everything in life must be dealt with in its own time	Monochronic—time is money. Linear—one thing at a time
Negotiations	Are lengthy—a major purpose is to allow the parties to get to know each other	Proceed quickly
Competitive bidding	Infrequent	Common
Country/regional examples	Japan, Middle East	United States, Northern Europe

One of these clearest and most painful instances of a failure of one culture to perceive another culture's motivations and behaviors dates back to the beginnings of World War II. Throughout the war and even to this day, the United States encountered great difficulties in attempting to understand the empire of Japan, its enemy. In response to the obstacles the United States faced, studies of Japanese culture were commissioned, focusing on Japan's history, tradition, national character, social life and customs, family, personality, and mind. The result is such great works as Benedict's *The Chrysanthemum and the Sword*. Since the end of World War II, Japan has emerged as the leading competitor of the United States; thus, the body of studies and publications has continued to grow over the last 50 years, with the focus shifting somewhat from an emphasis on societal and individual values and motivations to business and corporate culture.

It would be easy to get paranoid about the hazards of doing business across cultures, but, in fact, the main obstacle is attitude. If you are sincere and truly want to learn about a culture, you will find that people respond to your sincerity and interest and will help you acquire the knowledge you need to be effective. If you are arrogant and insincere and believe that you are right and "they" are wrong, you can expect a full measure of trouble and misunderstanding. The best antidote to the problem of misperceiving a situation is constant vigilance and an awareness that there are many opportunities to err. This should create an attitude of openness to see what is so. Every global marketer should strive to suspend judgment and simply listen, observe, perceive, and take in the facts, however they may be defined.

COMMUNICATION AND NEGOTIATION

Although English continues to grow in importance as the language of international travel and business, understanding and speaking the language of a country is an invaluable asset in understanding the country's culture. There is an often repeated maxim: You can buy in your home-country language, but you need to learn your customers' language to sell.

The ability to communicate in our own language is, as most us have learned, not an easy task. Whenever languages and culture change, additional communication challenges will present themselves. For example, "yes" and "no" are used in an entirely different way in Japanese than in Western languages. This has caused much confusion and misunderstanding. In English, the answer "yes" or "no" to a question is based on whether the answer is affirmative or negative. In Japanese, this is not so. The answer "yes" or "no" may indicate whether or not the answer affirms or negates the question. For example, in Japanese the question, "Don't you like meat?" would be answered "yes" if the answer is negative, as in, "Yes, I don't like meat." The word *wakarimashita* means both "I understand" and "I agree." To avoid misunderstandings, Westerners must learn to distinguish which interpretation is correct in terms of the entire context of the conversation. The box "A Matter of Culture: Getting Lost in Translation" shows other ways the verbal component of cross-cultural communication can get "lost in translation."

The challenges presented by nonverbal communication are perhaps even more formidable. For example, Westerners doing business in the Middle East must be careful not to reveal the soles of their shoes to hosts or pass documents with the left hand. In Japan, bowing is an important form of nonverbal communication that has many nuances. People who grow up in the West tend to be verbal, whereas those from the East are more nonverbal. Not surprisingly, there is a greater expectation in the East that people will pick up nonverbal cues and understand intuitively without being told.[7] Westerners must pay close attention not only to what they hear but also to what they see when conducting business in such cultures.

SOCIAL BEHAVIOR[8]

There are a number of social behaviors and comments that have different meanings in other cultures. For example, Americans generally consider it impolite to mound food on a plate, make noises when eating, and belch. However, some Chinese feel it is polite to take a portion of every food served and consider it evidence of satisfaction to belch.

Other social behaviors, if not known, will place the international traveler at a disadvantage. For example, in Saudi Arabia, it is an insult to question a host about the health of his spouse, show the soles of one's shoes, or touch or deliver objects with the left hand. In Korea, both hands should be used when passing objects to another person, and it is considered impolite to discuss politics, communism, or Japan. Also in Korea, formal introductions are very important. In both Japan and Korea, ranks and titles are expected to be used in addressing hosts. In the United States, there is not a clear rule on this behavior, except in select fields such as the armed forces or medicine. In Indonesia, it is considered rude to point at another person with a finger. However, one may point with the thumb or gesture with the chin.

When greeting someone, it is appropriate in most countries to shake hands. In some countries the greeting includes a handshake and more. In Japan, a handshake may be followed by a bow, going as low and lasting as long as that of the senior person. In Brazil, Korea, Indonesia, China, and Taiwan, a slight bow is also appropriate.

In some countries, the greeting involves more contact. For instance, in Venezuela, close friends greet each other with a full embrace and a hearty pat on the back; in Indonesia, a social kiss is in vogue, and a touching of first the right then the left cheek as one shakes hands. In Malaysia, close friends grasp with both hands; and in South Africa, blacks shake hands, followed by a clench of each other's thumbs, and another handshake.

In most countries, addressing someone as Mr., Mrs., Miss, or Ms. is acceptable, but this is certainly not universal. Monsieur, Madame, and Mademoiselle are preferred in France, Belgium, and Luxembourg, while Señor, Señora, and Señorita are the norm in Spain and Spanish-speaking Latin America. It is sometimes the case that conversation

---

[7] See Anthony C. diBenedetto, Miriko Tamate, and Rajan Chandran, "Developing Strategy for the Japanese Marketplace," *Journal of Advertising Research* (January–February 1992): 39–48.
[8] Adapted from Gary Bonvillian and William A. Nowlin, "Cultural Awareness: An Essential Element of Doing Business Abroad," *Business Horizons*, 37, no. 6 (November 1994): 44.

◆ BOX 3-1 ◆

A MATTER OF CULTURE: GETTING LOST IN TRANSLATION

The slang rendering of Otis Spunkmeyer's name described at the beginning of this chapter is hardly unique, but it underscores the importance of language and translation for persons and companies doing business across national boundaries. Even in England, many of the terms are different than what are used in the United States. For example,

British Version	American Version
chemist	pharmacist
lorry	truck
nappies	diapers
loo	bathroom
biscuits	cookies
crisps	potato chips
shandy	beer with lemonade

Sometimes translation errors result in bloopers that are harmless but funny. Consider this assortment of hotel signs from around the world translated into English: Paris: "Please leave your values at the front desk"; Japan: "You are invited to take advantage of the chambermaid"; Zurich: "Because of the impropriety of entertaining guests of the opposite sex in the bedroom, it is suggested that the lobby be used for this purpose." Finally, the following sign appeared in a hotel in Romania: "The lift is being fixed for the next day. During that time we regret that you will be unbearable."

In Japan, many consumer packaged goods—including some that are not imported—have English, French, or German on the labels to suggest a stylish image and Western look. A Westerner may wonder, however, what point the copywriters are actually trying to get across. For example, English on the label of City Original Coffee proclaims, "Ease Your Bosoms. This coffee has carefully selected high quality beans and roasted by our all the experience." The intended message: Drinking the coffee provides a relaxing break and "takes a load off your chest." Other products, such as casual wear and sports apparel, are also emblazoned with fractured messages. These words appeared on the back of a jacket: "Vigorous throw up. Go on a journey." A sports bag bore the message, "A drop of sweat is the precious gift for your guts."

Finally, consider the message printed on the cover of a notebook: "Be a man I recommend it with confidence as like a most intelligent stationary of basic design." One expert on "Japanese English" believes messages like these highlight basic differences between Japanese and other languages. Many Western languages lack exact equivalents for the rich variety of Japanese words that convey feelings. This presents difficulties for copywriters trying to render feelings in a language other than Japanese. The message on the black notebook was supposed to convey manliness. As the English-speaking Japanese copywriter explained, "I wanted to say I'm proud to present the product to the consumer because it's got a simple, masculine image." While a Westerner might argue whether the copywriter succeeded, Japanese retailers do not seem at all concerned that the messages are gibberish. As one retailer explained, the point is that a message in English, French, or German can convey hipness and help sell a product. "I don't expect people to *read* it," she said.

SOURCES: Yumiko Ono, "A Little Bad English Goes a Long Way in Japan's Boutiques," *The Wall Street Journal*, 20 May 1992, pp. A1, A6; Charles Goldsmith, "Look See! Anyone Do Read This And It Will Make You Laughable," *The Wall Street Journal*, 19 November 1992, p. B1.

occurs as greetings are exchanged. In Sweden, the greeting is "goddag"; in the Netherlands, it is "pleased to meet you"; in the United Kingdom it's "how do you do"; in Tanzania it is "jambo" and in Israel it is "shalom." Other greetings vary by country. In many countries, men do not shake hands with a woman unless she extends her hand first. In India, women, or a man and a woman, greet each other by placing the palms of their hands together and bowing slightly, and in Mexico simply by a slight bow. In some countries, such as India, it is not advisable for men to touch or talk alone with a woman.

Although many of the social behaviors mentioned vary from the home-country norm, negative judgments should not be made about them. When trying to explain what took so long in closing a deal, home office executives need to understand that drinking tea, socializing, and relationship building are important components in accomplishing corporate international goals.

Intercultural Socialization

In addition to knowing specific courtesies, personal space, language and communication, and social behavioral differences, there are numerous intercultural socialization behaviors that an international business traveler should learn. Knowing a culture means knowing the habits, actions, and reasons behind the behaviors. It is a mistake to make assumptions about what is culturally proper or incorrect based on your own experiences.

For example, in the United States the bathtub and toilet are likely to be in the same room. Some cultures, however, such as that of the Japanese, consider it unhygienic. Other cultures think it unhygienic even to sit on a toilet seat. In many cultures, toilet paper is not the norm. The author remembers his first visit to the toilet of an Indonesian ministry. It was here that he discovered that the Indonesian government in Jakarta does not offer toilet paper to toilet users. This is something that you will not discover in the Intercontinental Hotel in Jakarta.

It is not always necessary for an international business traveler to understand the "whys" of a culture, but it is important to accept them and to abide by them while on foreign soil. Becoming aware of the culture in which you will be visiting or working will pay excellent dividends.

◆ ANALYTICAL APPROACHES TO CULTURAL FACTORS

The reason cultural factors are a challenge to global marketers is that they are hidden from view. Because culture is learned behavior passed on from generation to generation, it is difficult for the inexperienced or untrained outsider to fathom. Becoming a global manager means learning how to let go of cultural assumptions. Failure to do so will hinder accurate understanding of the meaning and significance of the statements and behaviors of business associates from a different culture.

For example, a person from a culture that encourages responsibility and initiative could experience misunderstandings with a client or boss from a culture that encourages bosses to remain in personal control of all activities. Such a boss would expect to be kept advised in detail of a subordinate's actions; the subordinate might be taking initiative on the mistaken assumption that the boss would appreciate a willingness to assume responsibility.

To transcend ethnocentricity and cultural myopia, managers must make the effort to learn and internalize cultural differences. There are several guidelines that will improve the ability to learn about other cultures:

1. The beginning of wisdom is to accept that we will never fully understand ourselves or others. People are far too complex to be "understood." As Carl Jung pointed out, "There are no misunderstandings in nature . . . misunderstandings are found only in the realm of what we call 'understanding.' "[9]
2. Our perceptual systems are extremely limited. We "see" almost nothing. Our nervous systems are organized on the principle of negative feedback. That is, the only time our control system is brought into play is when input signals deviate from what we have learned to expect.
3. We spend most of our energy managing perceptual inputs.
4. When we do not understand the beliefs and values of a particular cultural system and society, things that we observe and experience may seem "bizarre."
5. If we want to be effective in another culture, we must attempt to understand that culture's beliefs, motives, and values. This requires an open attitude that allows us to transcend perceptual limitations based on our own culture.

---

[9] C. G. Jung, *Critique of Psychoanalysis*, Bollingen Series XX (Princeton, NJ: Princeton University Press, 1975), p. 228.

MASLOW'S HIERARCHY OF NEEDS

The late A. H. Maslow developed an extremely useful theory of human motivation that helps explain cultural universals.[10] He hypothesized that people's desires can be arranged into a hierarchy of five needs. As an individual fulfills needs at each level, he or she progresses to higher levels (see Figure 3-1). Once physiological, safety, and social needs have been satisfied, two higher needs become dominant. First is a need for esteem. This is the desire for self-respect, self-esteem, and the esteem of others and is a powerful drive creating demand for status-improving goods. George Zeien, chairman of Gillette Corporation, understands this. Marketers in Gillette's Parker Pen subsidiary assume that shoppers in Malaysia and Singapore wishing to give an upscale gift will buy the same Parker pen as Americans shopping at Neiman Marcus. "We are not going to come out with a special product for Malaysia," Zeien says.[11] In East Africa women who owned bras always wore them with straps exposed to show the world that they owned a bra. In Asia today, young women are taking up smoking—and showing a preference for Western brands—as a symbol of their improved status and increased affluence.

The final stage in the need hierarchy is self-actualization. When all the needs for food, safety, security, friendship, and the esteem of others are satisfied, discontent and restlessness will develop unless one is doing what one is fit for. A musician must make music, an artist must create, a poet must write, a builder must build, and so on. Maslow's hierarchy of needs is, of course, a simplification of complex human behavior. Other researchers have shown that a person's needs do not progress neatly from one stage of a hierarchy to another. For example, an irony of modern times is the emergence of the need for safety in the United States, one of the richest countries in the world. Indeed, the high incidence of violence in the United States may leave Americans with a lower level of satisfaction of this need than in many so-called "poor" countries. Nevertheless, the hierarchy does suggest a way for relating consumption patterns and levels to basic human need-fulfilling behavior. Maslow's model implies that, as countries progress through the stages of economic development, more and more members of society operate at the esteem need level and higher, having satisfied physiological, safety, and social needs. It appears that self-actualization needs begin to affect consumer behavior as well.

For example, there is a tendency among some consumers in high-income countries to reject material objects as status symbols. The automobile is not quite the classic American status symbol it once was, and some consumers are turning away from material possessions. This trend toward rejection of materialism is not, of course, limited to high-income

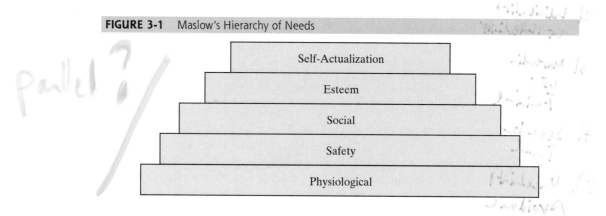

FIGURE 3-1 Maslow's Hierarchy of Needs

Self-Actualization

Esteem

Social

Safety

Physiological

[10] A. H. Maslow, "A Theory of Human Motivation," in *Readings in Managerial Psychology*, eds. Harold J. Levitt and Louis R. Pondy (Chicago: University of Chicago Press, 1964), pp. 6–24.

[11] Louis Uchitelle, "Gillette's World View: One Blade Fits All," *The New York Times*, 3 January, 1994, p. C3.

countries. In India, for example, there is a long tradition of the pursuit of consciousness or self-actualization as a first rather than a final goal in life. And yet, each culture is different. For example, in Germany today, the automobile remains a supreme status symbol. Germans give their automobiles loving care, even going so far as to travel to distant locations on weekends to wash their cars in pure spring water.

Helmut Schütte has proposed a modified hierarchy to explain the needs and wants of Asian consumers (Figure 3-2).[12] While the two lower-level needs are the same as in the traditional hierarchy, the three highest levels emphasize the intricacy and importance of social needs. Affiliation needs are satisfied when an individual in Asia has been accepted by a group. Conformity with group norms becomes a driving force of consumer behavior. For example, when Tamagotchis and other brands of electronic pets were the "in" toy in Japan, every teenager who wanted to fit in bought one (or more). Knowing this, Japanese companies develop local products specifically designed to appeal to teens. The next level is admiration, a higher-level need that can be satisfied through acts within a group that command respect. At the top of the Asian hierarchy is status, the esteem of society as a whole. In part, attainment of high status is character driven. However, the quest for status also leads to luxury badging, a phrase that describes consumers who engage in conspicuous consumption and buy products and brands that others will notice. Support for Schutte's contention that status is the highest-ranking need in the Asian hierarchy can be seen in the geographic breakdown of the $35 billion global luxury goods market. Fully 20 percent of industry sales are to Japan alone, with another 22 percent of sales occurring in the rest of the Asia-Pacific region. Nearly half of all sales revenues of Italy's Gucci Group are generated in Asia.

HOFSTEDE'S CULTURAL TYPOLOGY[13]

Organizational anthropologist Geert Hofstede has argued that the cultures of different nations can be compared in terms of four dimensions. The first, *power distance*, is the extent to which the less powerful members of a society accept—even expect—that power is to be distributed unequally. To paraphrase Orwell, all societies are unequal, but

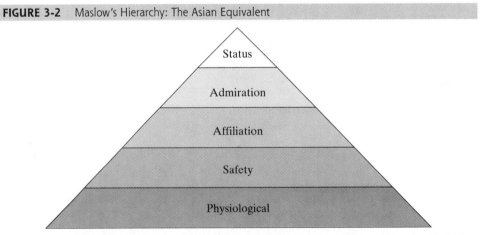

FIGURE 3-2 Maslow's Hierarchy: The Asian Equivalent

Status

Admiration

Affiliation

Safety

Physiological

Source: Hellmut Schütte, "Asian Culture and the Global Consumer," *Financial Times–Mastering Marketing,* Part II, 21 September 1998, p. 2.

---

[12] Helmut Schütte, "Asian Culture and the Global Consumer," *Financial Times-Mastering Marketing,* 21 September 1998, p. 2.

[13] Hofstede and Bond, "The Confucius Connection," pp. 5–21.

some are more unequal than others. The second dimension is a reflection of the degree to which individuals in a society are integrated into groups. In *individualist cultures*, each member of society is primarily concerned with his or her own interest and those of the immediate family. In *collectivist cultures*, all of society's members are integrated into cohesive in-groups. *Masculinity*, the third dimension, describes a society in which men are expected to be assertive, competitive, and concerned with material success, while women fulfill the role of nurturer and are concerned with issues such as the welfare of children. *Femininity,* on the other hand, describes a society in which the social roles of men and women overlap, with neither gender exhibiting overly ambitious or competitive behavior. Hofstede notes that the first three dimensions refer to expected social behavior; the fourth dimension is concerned with, in Hofstede's words, "man's search for Truth." *Uncertainty avoidance* is the extent to which the members of a society are uncomfortable with unclear, ambiguous, or unstructured situations. Some cultures express strong uncertainty avoidance with aggressive, emotional, intolerant behavior; they are characterized by a belief in absolute truth. The manifestation of low uncertainty avoidance is behavior that is more contemplative, relativistic, and tolerant.

Hofstede's research convinced him that, although the four dimensions yielded interesting and useful interpretations, they did not provide any insight into possible cultural bases for economic growth. Hofstede was also disturbed by the fact that the surveys used in the research had been developed by Western social scientists. Because many economists failed to predict the explosive economic development of Japan and the "tigers" (i.e., South Korea, Taiwan, Hong Kong, and Singapore), Hofstede surmised that some cultural dimensions in Asia were eluding the researchers. This methodological problem was remedied by a Chinese Value Survey (CVS) developed by Chinese social scientists. The CVS data supported the first three "social behavior" dimensions of culture identified earlier (i.e., power distance, individualism/collectivism, and masculinity/femininity). Uncertainty avoidance, however, did not show up in the CVS. Instead, the CVS revealed a dimension that had eluded Western researchers. Moreover, this dimension—which Hofstede calls "Confucian Dynamism"—concerns several aspects of culture that appear to be strongly linked to economic growth. Hofstede explains that these dimensions concern "a society's search for virtue" rather than a search for truth. *Persistence* (perseverance) is a general tenacity in the pursuit of a goal. *Ordering relationships* by status reflects the presence of societal hierarchies, and *observing this order* indicates the acceptance of complementary relations. *Thrift* manifests itself in high savings rates. Finally, *a sense of shame* leads to sensitivity in social contacts. Hofstede notes that these values are widely held within the high-performing countries but that the presence of these values by themselves is not sufficient to lead to economic growth. Two other conditions are necessary: the existence of a market and a supportive political context.

THE SELF-REFERENCE CRITERION AND PERCEPTION

As we have shown, a person's perception of market needs is framed by his or her own cultural experience. A framework for systematically reducing perceptual blockage and distortion was developed by James Lee.[14] Lee termed the unconscious reference to one's own cultural values the *self-reference criterion,* or SRC. To address this problem and eliminate or reduce cultural myopia, he proposed a systematic four-step framework.

1. Define the problem or goal in terms of home-country cultural traits, habits, and norms.
2. Define the problem or goal in terms of the host culture, traits, habits, and norms. Make no value judgments.

---

[14] James A. Lee, "Cultural Analysis in Overseas Operations," *Harvard Business Review* (March–April 1966): 106–114.

3. Isolate the SRC influence and examine it carefully to see how it complicates the problem.
4. Redefine the problem without the SRC influence and solve for the host-country market situation.

The lesson that SRC teaches is that a vital, critical skill of the global marketer is unbiased perception, the ability to see what is so in a culture. Although this skill is as valuable at home as it is abroad, it is critical to the global marketer because of the widespread tendency toward ethnocentrism and use of the self-reference criterion. The SRC can be a powerfully negative force in global business, and forgetting to check for it can lead to misunderstanding and failure. While planning Euro Disney, chairman Michael Eisner and other company executives were blindsided by a lethal combination of their own prior success and ethnocentrism. Avoiding the SRC requires a person to suspend assumptions based on prior experience and success and be prepared to acquire new knowledge about human behavior and motivation.

ENVIRONMENTAL SENSITIVITY

Environmental sensitivity is the extent to which products must be adapted to the culture-specific needs of different national markets. A useful approach is to view products on a continuum of environmental sensitivity. At one end of the continuum are environmentally insensitive products that do not require significant adaptation to the environments of various world markets. At the other end of the continuum are products that are highly sensitive to different environmental factors. A company with environmentally insensitive products will spend relatively less time determining the specific and unique conditions of local markets because the product is basically universal. The greater a product's environmental sensitivity, the greater the need for managers to address country-specific economic, regulatory, technological, social, and cultural environmental conditions.

The sensitivity of products can be represented on a two-dimensional scale as shown in Figure 3-3. The horizontal axis shows environmental sensitivity, the vertical axis the degree for product adaptation needed. Any product exhibiting low levels of environmental sensitivity—highly technical products, for example—belongs in the lower left of the figure. Intel has sold over 100 million microprocessors, because a chip is a chip anywhere around the world. Moving to the right on the horizontal axis, the level of sensitivity increases, as does the amount of adaptation. Computers are characterized by low levels of environmental sensitivity but variations in country voltage requirements require some adaptation. In addition, the computer's software documentation should be

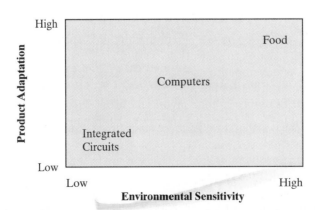

FIGURE 3-3 Environmental Sensitivity Product Adaptation Matrix

◆ BOX 3-2 ◆

A MATTER OF CULTURE: "SINCERELY"

While it may be true that "brevity is the soul of wit," when it comes to signing a business letter, the French go far beyond the simple "Sincerely" that often suffices for anyone writing in English. Following are the top 10 ways to close a business letter in French.

1. *Nous vous prions d'agréer, Monsieur, l'expression de nos sentiments dévoués.*

   Literally: "We beg you to receive, sir, the expression of our devoted sentiments."

2. *Agréez, Monsieur, l'assurance de mes meilleurs sentiments.*

   "Accept, sir, the assurance of my best sentiments."

3. *Je vous prie d'agréer, Monsieur le Directeur, mes meilleures salutations.*

   "I beg you to accept, Mr. Director, my best greetings."

4. *Je vous prie d'agréer, Madame la Directrice, mes meilleures salutations.*

   "I beg you to accept, Ms. Director, my best greetings."

5. *Veuillez, croire, Messieurs, à l'assurance de ma haute considération.*

   "Please believe, Gentlemen, the assurance of my highest consideration."

6. *Recevez, Messieurs, mes sincères salutations.*

   "Receive, Gentlemen, my sincere greetings."

7. *Je vous prie d'agréer, Monsieur, l'expression de mes sentiments les meilleurs.*

   "I beg you to accept, Sir, the expression of my best sentiments."

8. *Je vous prie d'agréer, Mademoiselle, mes respectueuses salutations.*

   "I beg you to accept, Miss, my respectful greetings."

9. *Veuillez agréer, Monsieur, l'expression de mes sentiments distingués.*

   "Please accept, Sir, the expression of my distinguished sentiments."

10. *Je vous prie d'agréer, Messieurs, avec mes remerciements anticipés, l'expression de mes sentiments distingués.*

    "I beg you to accept, Gentlemen, with my anticipated thanks, the expression of my distinguished sentiments."

in the local language. At the upper right of Figure 3-3 are products with high environmental sensitivity. Food, especially food consumed in the home, falls into this category because it is sensitive to climate and culture. McDonald's has achieved great success outside the United States by adapting its menu items to local tastes. Particular food items such as chocolate, however, must be modified for various differences in taste and climate. The consumers in some countries prefer a milk chocolate; others prefer a darker chocolate while other countries in the Tropics have to adjust the formula for their chocolate products to withstand high temperatures.

◆ SOCIAL AND CULTURAL ENVIRONMENTS: IMPACT ON MARKETING INDUSTRIAL PRODUCTS

The various cultural factors described earlier can exert important influences on industrial products marketing around the globe. (See box "Marketing an Industrial Product in Latin America.") They must be recognized in formulating a global marketing plan. Some industrial products may exhibit either low levels of environmental sensitivity, as in the case of computer chips, for example, or high levels, as in the case of turbine generators when "buy national" government policy puts foreign bidders at a disadvantage.

Boeing, the giant U.S.-based aerospace manufacturer, has felt the impact of an unwritten "buy national" policy. Boeing has only one major competitor, Airbus, which is a

♦ BOX 3-3 ♦

MARKETING AN INDUSTRIAL PRODUCT IN LATIN AMERICA

A Latin American republic had decided to modernize one of its communication networks at a cost of several million dollars. Because of its reputation for quality, the government approached American company "Y."

Company management, having been sounded out informally, considered the size of the order and decided to bypass its regular Latin American representative and send its sales manager instead. The following describes what took place.

The sales manager arrived and checked into the leading hotel. He immediately had some difficulty pinning down just who was his business contact. After several days without results, he called at the American embassy where he found the commercial attaché had the necessary up-to-the-minute information. The commercial attaché listened to his story. The attaché realized the sales manager had already made a number of mistakes but, figuring that the Latins were used to American blundering, he reasoned that all was not lost. The attaché informed the sales manager that the Minister of Communications was the key man and that whoever got the nod from him would get the contract. He also briefed the sales manager on methods of conducting business in Latin America and offered some pointers about dealing with the minister.

The attaché's advice ran somewhat as follows:

1. "You don't do business here the way you do in the States; it is necessary to spend much more time. You have to get to know your man and vice versa."
2. "You must meet with him several times before you talk business. I will tell you at what point you can bring up the subject. Take your cues from me." (At this point, our American sales manager made a few observations to himself about "cookie pushers" and wondered how many payrolls had been met by the commercial attaché.)
3. "Take that price list and put it in your pocket. Don't get it out until I tell you to. Down here price is only one of the many things taken into account before closing a deal. In the United States, your past experience will prompt you to act according to a certain set of principles, but many of these principles will not work here. Every time you feel the urge to act or to say something, look at me. Suppress the urge and take your cues from me. This is very important."
4. "Down here people like to do business with men who are somebody. 'Being somebody' means having written a book, lectured at a university, or developed your intellect in some way. The man you are going to see is a poet. He has published several volumes of

poetry. Like many Latin Americans, he prizes poetry highly. You will find that he will spend a good deal of business time quoting his poetry to you, and he will take great pleasure in this."
5. "You will also note that the people here are very proud of their past and of their Spanish blood, but they are also exceedingly proud of their liberation from Spain and their independence. The fact that they are a democracy, that they are free, and also that they are no longer a colony is very, very important to them. They are warm and friendly and enthusiastic if they like you. If they don't, they are cold and withdrawn."
6. "And another thing, time down here means something different. It works in a different way. You know how it is back in the States when a certain type blurts out whatever is on his mind without waiting to see if the situation is right. He is considered an impatient bore and somewhat egocentric. Well, down here you have to wait much, much longer, and I really mean much, *much* longer, before you can begin to talk about the reason for your visit."
7. "There is another point I want to caution you about. At home, the man who sells takes the initiative. Here, *they* tell you when they are ready to do business. But most of all, don't discuss price until you are asked and don't rush things."

THE PITCH

The next day the commercial attaché introduced the sales manager to the Minister of Communications. First, there was a long wait in the outer office while people went in and out. The sales manager looked at his watch, fidgeted, and finally asked whether the minister was really expecting him. The reply he received was scarcely reassuring, "Oh yes, he is expecting you but several things have come up that require his attention. Besides, one gets used to waiting down here." The sales manager irritably replied, "But doesn't he know I flew all the way down here from the United States to see him, and I have spent over a week already of my valuable time trying to find him?" "Yes, I know," was the answer, "but things just move much more slowly here."

At the end of about 30 minutes, the minister emerged from the office, greeted the commercial attaché with a double abrazo, throwing his arms around him and patting him on the back as though they were long-lost brothers. Now, turning and smiling, the minister extended his hand to the sales manager, who, by this time, was feeling rather miffed because he had been kept in the outer office so long.

After what seemed to be an all too short chat, the minister rose, suggesting a well-known cafe where they might meet for dinner the next evening. The sales manager expected, of course, that, considering the nature of their business and the size of the order, he might be taken to the minister's home, not realizing that the Latin American home is reserved for family and very close friends.

Until now, nothing at all had been said about the reason for the sales manager's visit, a fact which bothered him somewhat. The whole setup seemed wrong; nor did he like the idea of wasting another day in town. He told the home office before he left that he would be gone for a week or 10 days at most, and made a mental note that he would clean this order up in three days and enjoy a few days in Acapulco or Mexico City. Now the week had already gone and he would be lucky if he made it home in 10 days.

Voicing his misgivings to the commercial attaché, he wanted to know if the minister really meant business, and if he did, why could they not get together and talk about it? The commercial attaché by now was beginning to show the strain of constantly having to reassure the sales manager. Nevertheless, he tried again: "What you don't realize is that part of the time we were waiting, the minister was rearranging a very tight schedule so that he could spend tomorrow night with you. You see, down here they don't delegate responsibility the way we do in the States. They exercise much tighter control than we do. As a consequence, this man spends up to 15 hours a day at his desk. It may not look like it to you, but I assure you he really means business. He wants to give your company the order; if you play your cards right, you will get it."

The next evening was more of the same. Much conversation about food and music, about many people the sales manager had never heard of. They went to a night club, where the sales manager brightened up and began to think that perhaps he and the minister might have something in common after all. It bothered him, however, that the principal reason for his visit was not even alluded to tangentially. But every time he started to talk about electronics, the commercial attaché would nudge him and proceed to change the subject.

The next meeting was to be held over morning coffee at a café. By now the sales manager was having difficulty hiding his impatience. To make matters worse the minister had a mannerism that he did not like. When they talked he was likely to put his hand on him; he would take hold of his arm and get so close that he nearly spit in his face. Consequently, the sales manager kept trying to dodge and put more distance between himself and the minister.

Following coffee, they walked in a nearby park. The minister expounded on the shrubs, the birds, and the beauties of nature, and at one spot he stopped to point at a statue and said: "There is a statue of the world's greatest hero, the liberator of mankind!" At this point, the worst happened, for the sales manager asked who the statue represented and, when told the name of a famous Latin American patriot, said, "I never heard of him," and walked on. After this meeting, the American sales manager was never able to see the minister again. The order went to a Swedish concern.

DISCUSSION QUESTIONS

1. What impression do you think the sales manager made on the minister?
2. How would you critique the quality of the communication between all parties in this case?
3. Is a high-context culture or a low-context culture at work in this case? Explain your answer.

SOURCE: Adapted from Edward T. Hall, "The Silent Language in Overseas Business," *Harvard Business Review* (May–June 1960): 93–96. © 1960 by the President and Fellows of Harvard College; all rights reserved.

consortium of European companies. Its partners are Aerospatiale SA of France; Dasa, a unit of DaimlerChrysler of Germany; British Aerospace Plc; and Constucciones Aeronauticas SA of Spain. Given that Airbus was only formed in the 1970s, its current market share of 50 percent of the market for commercial planes is phenomenal. Although Boeing has customers in over 145 countries, its share in Europe continues to decline. This decline, in combination with the Asian Flu and many management problems, contributed to a loss of $178 million in 1997.

In a joint venture effort among Russian, Ukrainian, and Norwegian partners, Boeing hired a designer to decorate a facility from which the joint venture partners could watch the launch of the Sea Launch rocket. Unfortunately, the facility was decorated in black, a bad luck color in Russia. Supposedly, "the Russians were furious."[15] Hurriedly, the facility was repainted with a shade of blue to avoid a cultural faux pas.

> **VISIT THE WEB SITES**
> www.boeing.com
> www.airbus.com

◆ SOCIAL AND CULTURAL ENVIRONMENTS: IMPACT ON MARKETING CONSUMER PRODUCTS

Research studies show that, independent of social class and income, culture is a significant influence on consumption behavior and durable goods ownership.[16] Consumer products are more sensitive to cultural difference than are industrial products. Hunger is a basic physiological need in Maslow's hierarchy; everyone needs to eat, but what we want to eat can be strongly influenced by culture. Evidence from the front lines of the marketing wars suggests that food is probably the most sensitive category of consumer products. CPC International failed to win popularity for Knorr dehydrated soups among Americans. The U.S. soup market was dominated by Campbell Soup Company; 90 percent of the soup consumed by households was canned. Knorr was a Swiss company acquired by CPC that had a major share of the European prepared market in which bouillon and dehydrated soups accounted for 80 percent of consumer soup sales. Despite CPC's failure to change the soup-eating habits of Americans, the company has achieved great success as a sauce and gravy product in the United States and as a global marketer; sales outside the United States comprise 63 percent of its revenues from food lines.

At Campbell, by contrast, the figures are reversed: 63 percent of food revenues are generated in the United States, 27 percent from global markets. When the company moved into global markets it discovered that the attitude of homemakers toward food preparation is a cultural factor in marketing prepared foods. Recall that cooking was one of the cultural universals identified by Murdock. However, cooking habits and customs vary from country to country. Campbell's research revealed that Italian housewives devoted approximately 4.5 hours per day to food preparation versus 1 hour a day spent by their U.S. counterparts. The difference reflected cultural norms regarding the kitchen as well as the fact that a higher percentage of U.S. women work outside the home. The differences if anything are increasing. Since 1990, the use of stoves in meal preparation in the U.S. has declined 25 percent while a recent survey shows that over 80 percent of Italian men have a hot meal at home for lunch.

Campbell discovered a strongly negative opinion of convenience food in Italy. A panel of randomly selected Italian housewives was asked: "Would you want your son to marry a canned soup user?" The response to this question was sobering: All but a small fraction of a percent of the respondents answered, "No." Increased incomes as well as product innovations may have an impact on Italian attitudes toward time and convenience, with a corresponding positive effect on the market for convenience foods. Already, taste improvements in frozen pizza have boosted sales in Italy.

Thirst also shows how needs differ from wants. Liquid intake is a universal physiological need. As is the case with food and cooking, however, the particular beverages people *want* to drink can be strongly influenced by culture. Coffee is a beverage category that illustrates the point. In the United Kingdom instant coffee has 90 percent of the total

---

[15] Seanna Browder and Robert McNatt, "Color Boeing Red-Faced," *Business Week*, 5 April 1999, p. 6.
[16] Charles M. Schaninger, Jacques C. Bourgeois, and Christian W. Buss, "French-English Canadian Subcultural Consumption Differences," *Journal of Marketing* (Spring 1985): 82–92.

coffee market as compared with only 15 percent in Sweden. The other European countries fall between these two extreme points. Instant coffee's large share of the British market can be traced to the fact that, in the hot beverage category, Britain has historically been a nation of tea drinkers. Only in recent times have the British been persuaded to take up coffee drinking. Instant coffee is more like tea than ground coffee in its preparation. Not surprisingly, when the British did begin to drink coffee, they opted for instant since its preparation was compatible with past experience. Another reason for the popularity of instant coffee in Britain is the practice of drinking coffee with a large quantity of milk, so that the coffee flavor is masked. Differences in the coffee flavor are thus hidden, so that a "better cup" of coffee is not really important. In Sweden, on the other hand, coffee is the hot beverage of choice. Swedes consume coffee without large quantities of milk; therefore, the coffee flavor is not masked and brewed coffee is preferred.

Soft-drink consumption patterns also show conspicuous differences around the globe. The Coca-Cola Company reports that per capita consumption of its soft-drink products stands at 376 8-ounce servings in the United States, 203 servings in Germany, 95 servings in Italy, and 88 servings in France.[17] Differences in soft-drink consumption are associated in part with much higher per capita consumption of other kinds of beverages in Europe. In France and Italy, for example, 30 to 40 times as much wine is consumed as in America on a per capita basis. The French also prefer mineral water to soft drinks; the converse is true in America, where soft-drink consumption surpasses that of water. Germany far exceeds the United States in per capita consumption of beer. Does culture alone account for the difference between the popularity of soft drinks in Western Europe and the United States? No; in fact, several variables—including culture— are responsible for the differences, as portrayed in the following equation:

$$C = f(A, B, C, D, E, F, G)$$

where

C = consumption of soft drinks
f = function of
A = influences of other beverages' relative prices, quality, and taste
B = advertising expenditure and effectiveness, all beverage categories
C = availability of products in distribution channels
D = cultural elements, tradition, custom, habit
E = availability of raw materials (particularly of water)
F = climatic conditions, temperature, and relative humidity
G = income levels

To be sure, culture affects the demand for soft drinks. Note, however, that it is only one of several variables. Therefore, culture is an influencing rather than a determining factor. If a soft-drink marketer in Western Europe launches an aggressive marketing program (including lower prices, more intensive distribution, and heavy advertising), consumption can be expected to increase. However, it is also clear that any effort to convert Europeans to soft drinks will run up against cultural tradition, custom, and competition from widely available alternative beverages. Culture in this case is a restraining force, but, because culture is changing so rapidly, it is a restraint that can be overcome. For example, Coca-Cola used promotion and a massive sampling effort to increase 1992 unit case volume of Coke Light in Italy by 73 percent over 1991. In Germany, Coke's third largest global market, 1992 unit case volume increased by 6 percent over 1991, despite a recession and dislocations due to unification; unit case volume in the former East Germany grew 20 percent. In France, the 1992 marketing effort focused on availability and

---

[17] The Coca-Cola Company, *1997 Annual Report*, p. 31.

greater consumer acceptance, resulting in a 6 percent increase in unit case volume.[18] Of course, sales of Coca-Cola in McDonald's franchises around the world also impact its growing acceptance.

The penetration of the U.S. beverage market by bottled water producers is another excellent example of the impact of an effective creative strategy on a firmly entrenched cultural tradition. Prior to the 1980s, drinking bottled water was not an important part of U.S. culture. The general attitude in the United States was, "Why pay for something that is free?" Source Perrier SA, the French bottled water firm, decided to take aim at the U.S. market. It hired Bruce Nevin, an experienced American marketing executive, and gave him a free hand to formulate a creative strategy.

Nevin decided to reposition Perrier from an expensive imported bottled water (which no sane, red-blooded American would touch) to a competitively priced, low-calorie beverage in the soft-drink market. To back up this positioning, Nevin launched a major consumer advertising campaign, lowered prices, and moved the product from the gourmet section of the supermarket to the soft-drink section. The strategy boiled down to significant adjustment of three marketing mix elements: price, promotion, and place. Only the product was left unchanged.

The campaign succeeded beyond even the most optimistic expectations, essentially creating an entirely new market. By the mid-1980s, the $2.2 billion bottled water category had become the fastest-growing segment of the U.S. beverage industry. Perrier's annual U.S. sales grew from about $40 million to $800 million, and Perrier commanded 80 percent of the U.S. bottled water market. The success of this strategy was rooted in two indisputable facts: Americans were ready for bottled water, and the tactics were brilliantly executed. The results illustrate how the restraining force of culture can be changed by a creative marketing strategy grounded in market possibilities.[19]

◆ CROSS-CULTURAL COMPLICATIONS AND SUGGESTED SOLUTIONS

Global marketing activities are conducted in an ever-changing environment that blends economic, cultural, and social forces. Stepping out of the global perspective for a moment, we should acknowledge one thing: Even when the parties to a commercial transaction belong to the *same* low-context society—America, for example—and the terms of the deal are spelled out "in black and white," different understandings of the respective obligations of the parties will often occur.

Business relationships between parties of *different* cultures and/or nationalities are subject to additional challenges. Parties from different countries may have trouble coming to contract terms because of differences in the laws governing their respective activities and problems of enforcement across international boundaries. No matter what is stated in a contract, taking another party to court for breach of contract will probably require a suit in the defendant's own home turf, which may be an insurmountable advantage for the home-country participant.

When a party from a high-context culture takes part in a business understanding, the proceedings are likely to be further complicated by very different beliefs about the significance of formal business understandings and the ongoing obligations of all parties. The business environment in many countries outside the triad markets can be characterized by all manner of "hostile" elements: natural and human-induced catastrophes, political problems, foreign exchange inconvertibility, widely fluctuating exchange rates, depressions, and changes in national economic priorities and tariff schedules. One cannot predict precisely how the most carefully laid plans will go awry, only that they will. Mar-

---

[18] The Coca-Cola Company, *1992 Annual Report*, p. 32.

[19] Unfortunately, Perrier's poor handling of a public relations crisis in 1990 led to a 50 percent decrease in U.S. sales of Perrier from which the company has yet to recover.

keting executives and managers with dealings outside the home market must build mutual trust, rapport, and empathy with business contacts; all are required to sustain enduring relationships. Appointing a host-country national to a position as sales representative will not automatically guarantee success. If a corporation constantly shuffles its international staff, it risks impeding the formation of what we might call "high-context subcultures" between home office personnel and host nationals. This diminishes the company's chances of effectively dealing with the business crises that will inevitably occur.

India is an important supplier of crude and processed agricultural and forest products to world markets. Small family-owned enterprises collect, process, and sell these materials. Typically, months before the crop is in, sellers are required to contract with foreign buyers for later delivery of these products. The buyers, in turn, make long-term contractual commitments to their own customers. It is not possible for the Indian firms to hedge reliably by making forward crop purchases; there are no regulated commodity exchanges for these products. Nor do the farmers and forest product collectors have the resources to cover their sales if the crop fails. There are major problems during most growing seasons: Natural disasters or insufficient plantings result in short crops; strikes, protracted power shortages, or the lack of spare parts results in excessive shipment delays and reduced capacity. Business downturns or unexpected changes in required inventory levels may prompt buyers to request—or even insist—that shipments be held back or prices be reduced. Of course, such actions will cause the supplier severe financial hardship. Sometimes the supplier is unable to comply precisely with the terms of the contract and, therefore, provides a substitute order (usually without advance notice). The hope is that the buyer will inadvertently pay before discovering the switch and then reluctantly accept the merchandise with only minor adjustment.

Ongoing business between India and its global customers is, of course, perpetuated by mutual interest, but personal relationships are what make it possible. False rumors, supplier defaults, and customer cancellations are prevalent. Therefore, the greatest importance is assigned to contacts and business associates who can be fully trusted and whose culture-influenced perceptions are understood and predictable. Indian society is at least as ethnically and culturally diverse as that in Europe, and business practices are probably even more varied than in Europe.

TRAINING IN CROSS-CULTURAL COMPETENCY

Language competency and personal relationships are invaluable for the international businessperson. An increasing number of M.B.A. programs require students to learn one or even two foreign languages. Landis Gabel, associate dean for the M.B.A. program at Insead states, "Does one need it [another language]? No. Is it an advantage? Yes."[20] Knowing other languages is a very strong selling point for recruiters who feel that knowing another language allows employees to make immediate contributions on foreign assignments.

On an informal basis, many international business transactions are the result of relations established by foreign students while attending school in another country. One third of a Peace Corps volunteer's training is devoted to learning about ways things are done in the host country (particularly personal relationships). The international businessperson should have comparable preparation and a willingness to at least consider the merits of accommodating to the host culture's ways of doing business.

Samsung, GE, AT&T, and other large companies that are globalizing are taking steps to train managers and sensitize them to other ways of thinking, feeling, and acting. The goal is to improve their ability to deal effectively with customers, suppliers, bosses, and employees from other countries and regions. Managers must learn to question their own

---

[20] Della Bradshaw, "Mastering the Word," *The Financial Times,* 22 March 1999, p. 9.

beliefs, to overcome the SRC, and to adapt the way they communicate, solve problems, and even make decisions. Multicultural managers must learn to question and to reevaluate their feelings concerning such rudimentary management issues as leadership, motivation, and teamwork; this means an examination of some extremely fundamental and personal systems of belief. Lastly, managers must learn to overcome stereotypes they hold regarding individuals of various races and religions from other countries; managers must also diplomatically deal with stereotypes others may have about them.

Samsung Group, South Korea's largest company, recently launched an internationalization campaign. Prior to departing for overseas assignments, managers attend a month-long "boot camp," where the topics range from Western table manners to sexual harassment. Hundreds of promising Samsung junior managers spend a year in Western countries pursuing an unusual assignment: goofing off. Notes one Korean management theorist, "International exposure is important, but you have to develop international taste. You have to do more than visit. You have to goof off at the mall, watch people and develop international tastes." Park Kwang Moo, an employee at Samsung's trading subsidiary, didn't get to spend time in malls: His assignment was to visit the former Soviet Union. He spent his first six months immersed in language study and then traveled to all 15 former Soviet republics. Park's superiors were delighted with the 80-page report he filed upon his return, despite the fact that there was very little in it about business issues per se. A director at the trading company noted that the report was mostly about Russians' drinking habits and idiosyncrasies. "But," he noted, "in 20 years, if this man is representing Samsung in Moscow, he will have friends and he will be able to communicate, and then we will get the payoff."[21]

Another widely used approach to accomplish sensitization is the use of workshops, incorporating case studies, role-playing, and other exercises designed to permit participants to confront a relevant situation, contemplate what their own thoughts and actions would be in such a situation, and analyze and learn from the results. Participants must be able to understand and evaluate their motivations and approaches. Often, role-playing will bring out thoughts and feelings that otherwise might go unexamined or even unacknowledged. A variety of other techniques have been used for cross-cultural training; the common goal is to teach members of one culture ways of interacting effectively in another culture.

Becoming internationally adept and culturally aware should be a goal of any professional who aspires to do business abroad. This generally means a conscious effort in training and professional development by organizations. The Canadian International Development Agency (CIDA) provides an excellent model. CIDA hosts a five day predeparture briefing for Canadians that includes travel information, introduction to the geographical area of the host country, and presentations by a host national or a returnee. Cross-cultural communication, information for family members, and information on skills transfer are also included.[22]

If you cannot attend a formal training and orientation session or program, at the minimum you should take advantage of the written, audio, and visual material available on the country you will be visiting. Brigham Young University publishes a series called Culturegram on more than 140 areas of the world. A Culturegram is a product of native commentary and original, expert analysis. It is a general introduction to the culture of a world area or country.[23]

---

[21] "Sensitivity Kick: Korea's Biggest Firm Teaches Junior Execs Strange Foreign Ways," *The Wall Street Journal*, 30 December 1992, p. A1.
[22] Bonvillian and Nowlin, "Cultural Awareness."
[23] To place an order or to receive a free catalog, call 800-528-6279.

Summary

Culture, a society's "programming of the mind," has both a pervasive and changing influence on each national market environment. Global marketers must recognize the influence of culture on all aspects of life including work habits and consumption of products. Human behavior is a function both of a person's own unique personality and that person's interaction with the collective forces of the particular society and culture in which he or she has lived. A number of concepts can help guide anyone seeking insight into cultural issues. Nations can be classified as high- and low-context cultures; communication and negotiation styles can differ from country to country. Maslow's hierarchy, Hofstede's typology, and the self-reference criterion can provide clues about certain cultural differences and similarities.

Global marketing has played an important—even leading—role in influencing the rate of cultural change around the world. This is particularly true of food, but it includes virtually every industry, particularly in communication and consumer products. The Internet and global television have changed how and what people learn about products. Soap and detergent manufacturers have changed washing habits, the electronics industry has changed entertainment patterns, clothing marketers have changed styles, and so on. Although culture can also affect characteristics of industrial products, it is more important as an influence on the marketing process, particularly in the way business is conducted. Global marketers have learned to rely on people who know and understand local customs and attitudes for marketing expertise. Even so, many persons doing business in a new culture avail themselves of training opportunities to help avoid potential cross-cultural complications.

Discussion Questions

1. What is culture? Is there such a thing as a cultural universal or cultural universals? If your answer is affirmative, give an example of a cultural universal. If it is negative, explain why there is no such thing.
2. Can Hofstede's cultural typologies help marketers better understand cultures outside their home country? If your answer is yes, explain how, and if it is no, explain why not.
3. Explain the self-reference criterion. Go to the library and find examples of product failures that might have been avoided through the application of the SRC.
4. What is the difference between a low-context culture and a high-context culture? Give an example of a country that is an example of each type, and provide evidence for your answer. How does this apply to marketing?
5. Consider the equation $Y = f(A, B, C, D, E, F, G)$, where Y stands for consumption of soft drinks and D is the variable for cultural elements. How would this equation help a soft-drink marketer understand demand for soft drinks in global markets?

Suggested Readings

Abegglen, James C., and George Stalk, Jr. *Kaisha, The Japanese Corporation.* New York: Basic Books, Inc., 1985.

Benedict, Ruth. *The Chrysanthemum and the Sword.* Rutland, VT: Charles E. Tuttle, 1972.

Benedict, Ruth. *Patterns of Culture.* Boston: Houghton Mifflin, 1959.

Dale, Peter N. *The Myth of Japanese Uniqueness.* New York: St. Martin's Press, 1986.

de Tocqueville, Alexis. *Democracy in America.* New York: New American Library, 1956.

Dulek, Ronald E., John S. Fielden, and John S. Hill. "International Communications: An Executive Primer." *Business Horizons,* 34 (January/February 1991): 20–25.

Fields, George. *From Bonsai to Levis*. New York: Mentor, New American Library, 1983, 1985.

Fields, George. *Gucci on the Ginza*. Tokyo and New York: Kodansha International, 1989.

Ford, John B., and Earl D. Honeycutt, Jr. "Japanese National Culture as a Basis for Understanding Japanese Business Practices." *Business Horizons*, 35 (November/December 1992): 27–34.

Guptara, Prabhu. "Multicultural Aspects of Managing Multinationals." *Management Japan*, 26 (Spring 1993): 7–14.

Hagen, E. *On the Theory of Social Change*. Homewood, IL: Dorsey Press, 1962.

Hall, Edward T. *Beyond Culture*. Garden City, NY: Anchor Press Doubleday, 1976.

Hall, Edward T., and Mildred Reed Hall. *Hidden Differences: Doing Business with the Japanese*. New York: Doubleday, 1990.

Harris, Philip R., and Robert T. Moran. *Managing Cultural Differences: High Performance Strategies for a New World of Business,* 3rd ed. Houston: Gulf Publishing Company, 1991.

Hofstede, Geert. "Cultures Constraints in Management Theories." *Academy of Management Executive,* 7, no. 1 (1993): 81–93.

Hofstede, Geert, and Michael Harris Bond. "The Confucius Connection: From Cultural Roots to Economic Growth." *Organizational Dynamics* (Spring 1988): 5–21.

Hofstede, Geert, B. Neuijen, et al. "Measuring Organizational Cultures: A Qualitative and Quantitative Study Across Twenty Cases." *Administrative Science Quarterly* (June 1990): 286–317.

Kaynak, E., O. Kucukemiroglu, et al. "Consumer Preferences for Fast Food Outlets in a Developing Country." *Journal of Euromarketing,* 5, no. 4 (1996): 99–113.

Jacobs, Laurence, Charles Keown, et al. "Cross-Cultural Colour Comparisons—Global Marketers Beware!" *International Marketing Review,* 8, no. 3 (1991): 21–30.

Lin, Carolyn A. "Cultural Differences in Message Strategies: A Comparison Between American and Japanese Commercials." *Journal of Advertising Research*, 33 (July/August 1993): 40–48

Luo, Y., and M. Chen. "Managerial Implications of Guanxi-Based Strategies," *The American Graduate School of International Management*. Working Paper (1996).

McClelland, D. *The Achieving Society*. New York: Van Nostrand, 1961.

Miracle, Gordon E., Kyu Yeol Chang, and Charles R. Taylor, "Culture and Advertising Executions: A Comparison of Selected Characteristics of Korean and U.S. Television Commercials," *International Marketing Review*, 9, no. 4 (1992): 5–17.

Pizam, A. "Life and Tourism in the Year 2050." *International Journal of Hospitality*, 18, no. 4 (1999).

Raval, Dinker, and Bala Subramanian, "International Benchmarking Issues: A Cross-Cultural Perspective." In C. Jayachandran, N. Balasubramanian, and S. M. Dastagir (eds.), *Managing Economic Liberalisation in South Asia* (New Dehli: Macmillan India, 1998).

Reischauer, Edwin O. *The Japanese*. Cambridge, MA: The Belknap Press of Harvard University Press, 1977.

Redondo-Bellon, Ignacio. "The Effects of Bilingualism on the Consumer: The Case of Spain," *European Journal of Marketing*. 33, no. 11/12 (1999).

Reisinger, Yvette, and Lindsay Turner. "A Cultural Analysis of Japanese Tourists: Case for Tourism Marketers." *European Journal of Marketing*, 33, no. 11/12 (1999).

Samuel, S. Nicholas, Elton Li, and Heath McDonald. "The Purchase Behavior of Shanghai Buyers of Processed Food and Beverage Product: Implications for Research on Retail Management." *International Journal of Retail & Distribution Management,* 24, (April 1996): 29.

Schneider, Susan C., and Arnoud De Meyer. "Interpreting and Responding to Strategic Issues: The Impact of National Culture." *Strategic Management Journal,* 12 (May 1991): 307–320.

Stening, Bruce W., and Mitchell R. Hammer. "Cultural Baggage and the Adaption of Expatriate American and Japanese Managers." *Management International Review,* 32 (First Quarter 1992): 77–89.

Usunier, Jean-Claude G. "Business Time Perception and National Cultures: A Comparative Survey." *Management International Review,* 31, (Third Quarter 1991): 197–217.

CHAPTER 4

The Political, Legal, and Regulatory Environments of Global Marketing

"When you are at Rome live in the Roman style; when you are elsewhere live as they live elsewhere."

—St. Ambrose, a.d. 340–397
Advice to St. Augustine

"The global economy in which both managers and policymakers must now operate is not the neat, easily divisible sum of separate national economies. It has its own reality, its own rules, and its own logic."

—Kenichi Ohmae
Author

While governments in many countries are studying environmental issues, particularly recycling, Germany already has a packaging ordinance that has shifted the cost burden for waste material disposal onto industry. The German government hopes the law, known as *Verpackungsverordung,* will create a "closed loop economy." The goal is to force manufacturers to eliminate nonessential materials that cannot be recycled and adopt other innovative approaches to producing and packaging products. Despite the costs associated with compliance, industry appears to be making significant progress toward creating the closed loop economy. Companies are developing new packaging that uses less material and includes more recycled content. More than 1,900 non-German companies are currently participating in the program.

The German packaging law is just one example of the impact that political, legal, and regulatory environments can have on marketing activities. Each of the world's national governments regulates trade and commerce with other countries and attempts to control the access of outside enterprises to national resources. Every country has its own unique legal and regulatory system that impacts the operations and activities of the global enterprise, including the global marketer's ability to address market opportunities. Laws and regulations constrain the cross-border movement of products, services, people, money, and know-how. The global marketer must attempt to comply with each set of national—and in some instances, regional—constraints. These efforts are hampered by the fact that laws and regulations are frequently ambiguous and continually changing.

In this chapter, we consider the basic elements of the political, legal, and regulatory environments of global marketing, including the current issues and some suggested approaches for dealing with those issues. Some specific topics, such as rules for exporting and importing industrial and consumer products, standards for health and safety, and regulations regarding packaging, labeling, advertising, promotion, and the Internet, are covered in later chapters devoted to individual marketing mix elements. The question of ethical issues is also raised.

◆ THE POLITICAL ENVIRONMENT

Global marketing activities take place within the political environment of governmental institutions, political parties, and organizations through which a country's people and rulers exercise power. Any company doing business outside its home country should carefully study the government structure in the target country and analyze salient issues arising from the political environment. These include the governing party's attitude toward sovereignty, political risk, taxes, the threat of equity dilution, and expropriation.

NATION-STATES AND SOVEREIGNTY

Sovereignty can be defined as supreme and independent political authority. A century ago, U.S. Supreme Court Chief Justice Fuller said, "Every sovereign state is bound to respect the independence of every other sovereign state, and the courts in one country will not sit in judgment on the acts of government of another done within its territory." More recently, Richard Stanley offered the following concise description:

A sovereign state was considered free and independent. It regulated trade, managed the flow of people into and out of its boundaries, and exercised undivided jurisdiction over all persons and property within its territory. It had the right, authority, and ability to conduct its domestic affairs without outside interference and to use its international power and influence with full discretion.[1]

Government actions taken in the name of sovereignty occur in the context of two important criteria: a country's stage of development and the political and economic system in place in the country.

Many governments in developing countries exercise control over their nations' economic development by passing protectionist laws and regulations. Their objective is to encourage economic development by protecting emerging or strategic industries. Conversely, when many nations reach advanced stages of economic development, their governments declare that (in theory, at least) any practice or policy that restrains free trade is illegal. Antitrust laws and regulations are established to promote fair competition. Advanced country laws often define and preserve a nation's social order; laws may extend to political, cultural, and even intellectual activities and social conduct. In France, for

---

[1] See *Changing Concepts of Sovereignty: Can the United Nations Keep Pace?* (Muscatine, IA: The Stanley Foundation, 1992), p. 7.

example, laws forbid the use of foreign words such as *le weekend* or *le marketing* in official documents.

Although, as noted in Chapter 2, most of the world's economies combine elements of command and market systems, the sovereign political power of a government in a predominantly command economy reaches quite far into the economic life of a country. By contrast, in a capitalist, market-oriented democracy, that power tends to be much more constrained. A current global phenomenon in both command and market structures is the trend toward privatization, that is, government actions designed to reduce direct governmental involvement in an economy as a supplier of goods and services. In essence, each act of privatization dilutes the command portion of a mixed economic system. The trend is clearly evident in Mexico, where, at one time, the government controlled over 1,000 "parastatals." Most of them have been sold, including the two Mexican airlines, mines, banks, and other enterprises. Privatization in Mexico and elsewhere is evidence that national governments are changing how they exercise sovereign power.

Some observers believe global market integration is eroding national economic sovereignty. Economic consultant Neal Soss notes, "The ultimate resource of a government is power, and we've seen repeatedly that the willpower of governments can be overcome by persistent attacks from the marketplace."[2] Is this a disturbing trend? If the issue is framed in terms of marketing, the concept of the exchange comes to the fore: Nations may be willing to give up sovereignty in return for something of value. If countries can increase their share of world trade and increase national income, perhaps they will be willing to cede some sovereignty. The European Union (EU) countries are giving up individual rights—to set their own product standards, for example—in exchange for improved market access.

POLITICAL RISK

Political risk—the risk of a change in government policy that would adversely impact a company's ability to operate effectively and profitably—can deter a company from investing abroad. When the perceived level of political risk is lower, a country is more likely to attract investment. The level of political risk is inversely proportional to a country's stage of economic development: All other things being equal, the less developed a country, the greater the political risk. The political risk of the triad countries, for example, is quite limited as compared to a country in an earlier stage of development in Africa, Latin America, or Asia.

In the late 1990s changes in Central and Eastern Europe and the dissolution of the Soviet Union clearly demonstrated the risks and opportunities resulting from political upheavals. The current political climate of Eastern Europe is characterized by a high degree of uncertainty in countries such as Belarus and stability in countries such as Estonia. Having thrown off the shackles of communism, Russia and members of the Commonwealth of Independent States (CIS) are subject to substantial political risk; political forces could drastically change the business environment with little advance notice. Because of the potential for such volatility, businesspersons need to stay apprised of the formation and evolution of political parties in Russia, particularly those with an ultra-nationalist (i.e., anti-Western) orientation. Although some companies have concluded that political risk in Russia and the Commonwealth of Independent States is too high to justify investment at present, diligent attention to risk assessment should be ongoing to determine whether the opportunities outweigh the risks.

---

[2] Cited in Karen Pennar, "Is the Nation-State Obsolete in a Global Economy?" *Business Week,* 17 July 1995, p. 80.

◆ BOX 4-1 ◆

NATIONAL CONTROLS CREATE BARRIERS FOR GLOBAL MARKETING

Many countries attempt to exercise control over the transfers of goods, services, money, people, technology, and rights across their borders. Historically, an important control motive was economic: The goal was to generate revenue by levying tariffs and duties. Today, policymakers have additional motives for controlling cross-border flows, including protection of local industry and fostering the development of local enterprise. Such policies are known as protectionism or economic nationalism.

Differing economic and political goals and different value systems are the primary reasons for protectionism. The barriers that exist between the United States and Cuba, for example, exist because of major differences between the values and objectives of the two countries. Many barriers based on different political systems have come down with the end of the Cold War. However, barriers based on different value systems continue. The world's farmers—be they Japanese, European, or American—are committed to getting as much protection as possible from their respective govern-

ments. Because of the political influence of the farm lobby in every country, and in spite of the efforts of trade negotiators to open up agricultural markets, controls on trade in agricultural products continue to distort economic efficiency. Such controls work against the driving forces of economic integration.

The price of protection can be very high for two basic reasons. The first is the cost to consumers: When foreign producers are presented with barriers rather than free access to a market, the result is higher prices for domestic consumers and a reduction in their standard of living. The second cost is the impact on the competitiveness of domestic companies. Companies that are protected from competition may lack the motivation to create and sustain world-class competitive advantage. One of the greatest stimuli to competitiveness is the open market. When a company faces world competition, it must figure out how to serve a niche market better than any company in the world, or it must figure out how to compete in face-to-face competition.

TAXES

It is not uncommon for a company to be incorporated in one place, do business in another, and maintain its corporate headquarters in a third. This type of diverse geographical activity requires special attention to tax laws. Many companies make efforts to minimize their tax liability by shifting the location of income. For example, it has been estimated that tax avoidance by foreign companies doing business in the United States costs the U.S. government several billion dollars each year in lost revenue. In one approach, called earnings stripping, foreign companies reduce earnings by making loans to U.S. affiliates rather than using direct investment to finance U.S. activities. The U.S. subsidiary can deduct the interest it pays on such loans, thereby reducing its tax burden.

There are no universal international laws governing the levy of taxes on companies that do business across national boundaries. To provide fair treatment, many governments have negotiated bilateral tax treaties to provide tax credits for taxes paid abroad. The United States has dozens of such agreements in place. In 1977, the Organization for Economic Cooperation and Development (OECD) passed the Model Double Taxation Convention on Income and Capital to help guide countries in bilateral negotiations. Generally, foreign companies are taxed by the host nation up to the level imposed in the home country, an approach that does not increase the total tax burden to the company.

DILUTION OF EQUITY CONTROL[3]

Political pressure for national control of foreign-owned companies is a part of the environment of global business in lower-income countries. The foremost goal of na-

---

[3] This section is based on Dennis J. Encarnation and Sushil Vachani, "Foreign Ownership: When Hosts Change the Rules," *Harvard Business Review* (September–October 1985): 152–160.

tional governance is to protect the right of national sovereignty, especially in all aspects of domestic business activity. Host-nation governments sometimes attempt to control ownership of foreign-owned companies operating within their borders. In underdeveloped countries, political pressures frequently cause companies to take in local partners.

Legislation that requires companies to dilute their equity is never popular in the boardroom, yet the consequences of such legislation are often surprisingly favorable. Dennis J. Encarnation and Sushil Vachani examined corporate responses to India's 1973 Foreign Exchange Regulation Act (FERA), which restricted foreign equity participation in local projects to 40 percent. The researchers identified four options available to companies faced with the threat of dilution:

1. **Follow the law to the letter.** Colgate-Palmolive (India) took this course, became an Indian company, and maintained its dominant position in a growing market.
2. **Leave the country.** This was IBM's response. After several years of negotiations, IBM concluded that it would lose more in shared control than it would gain from continued operations under the new rules.
3. **Negotiate under the law.** Some companies used the equity dilution requirement to raise funds for growth and diversification. In most cases, this was done by issuing fresh equity to local investors. Ciba-Geigy increased its equity base 27 percent to $17.7 million, for example, and also negotiated an increase in production that doubled the sales of Hindustan Ciba-Geigy.
4. **Take preemptive action.** Some foreign firms initiated defensive strategies well before FERA's passage. These included proactive diversification to take advantage of investment incentives, gradual "Indianization" of the company, and continuously updating technology and maintaining export sales.

Encarnation and Vachani's study offers some important lessons.

1. **First, look at the range of possibilities.** There is no single best solution, and each company should look at itself and at the country situation to decide on strategy.
2. **Companies should use the law to achieve their own objectives.** The experiences of many companies demonstrate that by satisfying government demands, it is possible to take advantage of government concessions, subsidies, and market protection.
3. **Anticipate government policy changes.** Create a win–win situation. Companies that take initiatives are prepared to act when the opportunity arises. It takes time to implement changes; the sooner a company identifies possible government directions and initiatives, the sooner it will be in a position to propose its own plan to help the country achieve its objectives.
4. **Listen to country managers.** Country managers should be encouraged to anticipate government initiatives and to propose company strategy for taking advantage of opportunities created by government policy. Local managers often have the best understanding of the political environment. Experience suggests that they are in the best position to know when issues are arising and how to turn potential adversity into opportunity through creative responses.

The threat of equity dilution has caused some companies to operate in host nations via joint ventures or strategic alliances (see Chapters 8 and 10). These alternatives create special legal problems; there should be clauses in the joint venture or alliance agreement regarding its subsequent dissolution, as well as for the ownership of patents, trademarks, or technology realized from the joint effort, including cross-licensing after dissolution of intellectual property rights developed under joint operations.

EXPROPRIATION

The ultimate threat a government can pose toward a company is expropriation. Expropriation refers to governmental action to dispossess a company or investor. Compensation is generally provided to foreign investors, although not often in the "prompt, effective, and adequate" manner provided for by international standard. Nationalization occurs if ownership of the property or assets in question is transferred to the host government. If no compensation is provided, the action is referred to as confiscation.

Short of outright expropriation or nationalization, the phrase *creeping expropriation* has been applied to severe limitations on economic activities of foreign firms in certain developing countries. These have included limitations on repatriation of profits, dividends, royalties, or technical assistance fees from local investments or technology arrangements. Other issues are increased local content requirements, quotas for hiring local nationals, price controls, and other restrictions affecting return on investment. Global companies have also suffered discriminatory tariffs and nontariff barriers that limit market entry of certain industrial and consumer goods, as well as discriminatory laws on patents and trademarks. Intellectual property restrictions have had the practical effect of eliminating or drastically reducing protection of pharmaceutical products.

When governments expropriate foreign property, there are impediments to action to reclaim that property. For example, according to the U.S. Act of State Doctrine, if the government of a foreign state is involved in a specific act, the U.S. court will not get involved. Representatives of expropriated companies may seek recourse through arbitration at the World Bank Investment Dispute Settlement Center (International Centre for Settlement of Investment Disputes, or ICSID). It is also possible to buy expropriation insurance, either from a private company or the U.S. government's Overseas Private Investment Corporation (OPIC). The expropriation of copper companies operating in Chile in 1970 and 1971 shows the impact that companies can have on their own fate. Companies that strenuously resisted government efforts to introduce home-country nationals into the company management were expropriated outright; other companies that made genuine efforts to follow Chilean guidelines were allowed to remain under joint Chilean–U.S. management.

◆ INTERNATIONAL LAW

International law may be defined as the rules and principles that nation-states consider binding upon themselves. There are two categories of international law: public law, or the law of nations; and international commercial law, which is evolving. International law pertains to trade and other areas that have traditionally been under the jurisdiction of individual nations.

The roots of modern international law can be traced back to the early Middle Ages in Europe and later to the 17th-century Peace of Westphalia. Early international law was concerned with waging war, establishing peace, and other political issues such as diplomatic recognition of new national entities and governments. Elaborate international rules gradually emerged—covering, for example, the status of neutral nations. The creation of laws governing commerce developed on a state-by-state basis, evolving into what is termed the *law of the merchant*. International law still has the function of upholding order, although in a broader sense than dealing with problems arising from war. At first, international law was essentially an amalgam of treaties, covenants, codes, and agreements. As trade grew among nations, order in commercial affairs assumed increasing importance.

Whereas the law had originally dealt only with nations as entities, a growing body of law rejected the idea that only states can be subject to international law.

Paralleling the expanding body of international case law in the 20th century, new international judiciary organizations have contributed to the creation of an established rule of international law. These include the Permanent Court of International Justice (1920–1945); the International Court of Justice (ICJ), the judicial arm of the United Nations, established by article 7 of the United Nations Charter in 1946; and the International Law Commission, established by the United States in 1947. Disputes arising between nations are issues of public international law, and they may be taken before the ICJ located in The Hague, often referred to as the World Court. Article 38 of the ICJ Statute identifies recognized sources of public international law. As described in the supplemental documents to the United Nations Charter, Article 38 of the ICJ Statute (concerns) defines sources of international law:

> The Court, whose function is to decide in accordance with international law such disputes as are submitted to it, shall apply:
>
> a. international conventions, whether general or particular, establishing rules expressly recognized by the contesting states;
> b. international custom, as evidence of a general practice accepted as law;
> c. the general principles of law recognized by civilized nations;
> d. subject to the provisions of Article 59, judicial decisions and the teachings of the most highly qualified publicists of the various nations, as subsidiary means for the determination of rules of law.

What happens if a nation has allowed a case against it to be brought before the ICJ and then refuses to accept a judgment against it? The plaintiff nation can seek recourse through the UN's highest political arm, the United Nations Security Council, which can use its full range of powers to enforce the judgment.

COMMON VERSUS CODE LAW

Private international law is the body of law that applies to interpretations of and disputes arising from commercial transactions between companies of different nations. As noted, laws governing commerce emerged gradually. Forty-nine of the 50 states of the United States, nine of Canada's 10 provinces, and other former English colonies (Australia; New Zealand; India; Hong Kong; the English-speaking former African colonies, for example, with a colonial history) founded their systems on common law. Historically, much of continental Europe was influenced by Roman law and, later, the Napoleonic Code. Asian countries are split: India, Pakistan, Malaysia, Singapore, and Hong Kong—all former British colonies—are common-law jurisdictions. Japan, Korea, Thailand, Indochina, Taiwan, Indonesia, and China are civil-law jurisdictions. Today, the majority of countries have legal systems based on civil-code traditions, although an increasing number of countries are blending concepts, and hybrid systems are emerging. Despite the differences in systems, three distinct forms of laws are common to all nations. Statutory law is codified at the national, federal, or state level; administrative law originates in regulatory bodies and local communities; and case law is the product of the court system.

Under civil or code law, the judicial system is divided into civil, commercial, and criminal law. Thus, commercial law has its own administrative structure. Property rights, for example, are established by a formal registration of the property in commercial courts. Code law uses codified, written norms, which are complemented by court decisions. Common law, on the other hand, is established by tradition and precedents, which are rulings from previous cases; until recently, commercial law was not recognized as a special entity. Differences include the definition of "acts of God"; under common law, this phrase can refer only to floods, storms, and other acts of nature unless expanded by contract. In code-law countries, an "unavoidable interference with performance" can be considered an act of God. In code-law countries, intellectual property rights must be registered, whereas in common-law countries, some—such as trademarks but not patents—are established by prior use.

A significant recent development is the Uniform Commercial Code (UCC), fully adopted by 49 U.S. states, which codifies a body of specifically designed rules covering commercial conduct. (Louisiana has adopted parts of the UCC, but its laws are still heavily influenced by French civil code.) The host country's legal system—that is, common or civil law—directly affects the form a legal business entity will take. In common-law countries, companies are granted the ability to operate by public authority. In civil-law countries, companies are formed by contract between two or more parties who are fully liable for the actions of the company.

◆ SIDESTEPPING LEGAL PROBLEMS: IMPORTANT BUSINESS ISSUES

Clearly, the global legal environment is very dynamic and complex. Therefore, the best course to follow is to get expert legal help. However, the astute, proactive marketer can do a great deal to prevent conflicts from arising in the first place, especially concerning issues such as establishment, jurisdiction, patents and trademarks, antitrust, licensing and trade secrets, and bribery.

The services of counsel are essential for addressing these and other legal issues. The importance of international law firms is growing as national firms realize that to properly serve their clients, they must have a presence in overseas jurisdictions. As in many industries, global consolidation is increasing among international law firms. One forecast is that within a decade, only five to 10 global law firms will exist.[4] Table 4-1 shows the top 10 law firms in the world and the percentage of lawyers outside the home country.

ESTABLISHMENT

Under what conditions can trade be established? To transact business, citizens of one country must be assured that they will be treated fairly in another country. In Western Europe, for example, the creation of the Single Market now assures that citizens from member na-

TABLE 4-1 Top 10 Law Firms in the World			
	Headquarters	*Number of Lawyers*	*Lawyers Outside Home Country (%)*
Baker and Mckenzie	Chicago	2,300	80
Clifford Chance	London	1,795	48
Eversheds	London	1,290	4
Jones, Day, Reavis & Pogue	Cleveland	1,191	10
Skadden, Arps, Slate, Meagher & Flom	New York	1,125	9
Linklaters & Alliance[a]	London	1,116	32
Freshfields	London	1,104	42
Allen & Overy	London	1,089	28
Dibb Lupton Alsop	London	902	1
Morgan, Lewis & Bockius	Philadelphia	901	6

[a] Figures are for Linklaters before it merged with the Alliance.

Source: Legal Business

---

[4] Jean Eaglesham, "A Global Brief," *Financial Times,* 29 April 1999, p. 10.

THE MULTILATERAL AGREEMENT ON INVESTMENT

In 1995, the OECD began talks on a new initiative known as the Multilateral Agreement on Investment (MAI) that will set rules for foreign investment and provide a forum for dispute settlement. In some countries, so-called performance requirements favor local investors over foreigners. For example, foreign companies may be required to obtain some goods and services from local companies rather than the home office. Performance requirements can also take the form of stipulations that a certain number of senior managers must be local nationals or that the foreign company must export a set percentage of its production.

The existence of the MAI negotiations remained largely unknown to the general public until a Canadian consumer rights group obtained the text of MAI and posted it on the Internet. In fact, a large number of consumer and environmentalist action groups have joined in opposition to the agreement. As Mark A. Vallianatos, an international policy analyst at Friends of the Earth, explained:

> Our fear is that MAI will give multinational corporations the opportunity to treat the whole world as their raw pool of natural resources and labor and consumer markets. It may allow them to do everything based on profit motives without environmental considerations providing sensible limits on how they operate. MAI gives new rights to corporations without addressing their responsibilities to workers and the

environment. . . . An MAI that is worth doing should deal with how investments will affect sustainable development, how they will affect workers' rights, and how they will affect excessive resource extraction—those kinds of issues.

Some industry experts downplay MAI's potential to contribute to environmental degradation. R. Garrity Baker, senior director at the Chemical Manufacturers Association, says, "When foreign companies that have better environmental performance come in and invest in a market bring that know-how with them, then over time that know-how kind of trickles down to other companies. Foreign companies set an example that others can learn from." MAI supporters also point out that the agreement allows countries to adopt any measure deemed appropriate to ensure investment is undertaken in a manner that reflects sensitivity to environmental issues. As of mid-1998, prospects for MAI approval in the United States were clouded by disagreements between key Washington agencies that might be affected by the agreement's provisions. The U.S. State Department and Commerce Department are generally supportive, but the Environmental Protection Agency, the U.S. Agency for International Development, and the Justice Department are concerned that MAI will lead to a rash of lawsuits against the United States. At the state level, a number of governors felt that MAI would impinge on state sovereignty.

SOURCES: Bette Hileman, "A Globalization Conundrum." *Chemical & Engineering News,* 20 April 1998, p. 45; "Bye-bye, MAI?" *Financial Times,* 19 February 1998, p. 13.

tions get fair treatment with regard to business and economic activities carried out within the Common Market. The formulation of the governance rules for trade, business, and economic activities in the EU will provide additional substance to international law.

The United States has signed treaties of friendship, commerce, and navigation with more than 40 countries. These agreements provide U.S. citizens the right to nondiscriminatory treatment in trade, the reciprocal right to establish a business, and, particularly, to invest. Commercial treaties provide one with the privilege, not the right, to engage in business activities in other than one's own country. This can create problems for business managers who may still be under the jurisdiction of their own laws even when they are out of their native country. U.S. citizens, for example, are forbidden by the Foreign Corrupt Practices Act to give bribes to an official of a foreign government or political party, even if bribes are customary for conducting business in that country.

JURISDICTION

Company personnel working abroad should understand the extent to which they are subject to the jurisdiction of host-country courts. Employees of foreign companies working in the United States must understand that courts have jurisdiction to the extent that the company can be demonstrated to be "doing business" in the state in which the court sits. The court may examine whether the foreign company maintains an office, solicits business, maintains bank accounts or other property, or has agents or other employees in the state in question. In a recent case, Revlon Inc. sued United Overseas Ltd. (UOL), in U.S. District Court for the Southern District of New York. Revlon charged the British company with breach of contract, contending that UOL had failed to purchase some specialty shampoos as agreed. UOL, claiming lack of jurisdiction, asked the court to dismiss the complaint. Revlon countered with the argument that UOL was, in fact, subject to the court's jurisdiction; Revlon cited the presence of a UOL sign above the entrance to the offices of a New York company in which UOL had a 50 percent ownership interest. The court denied UOL's motion to dismiss.[5]

Normally, all economic activity within a nation is governed by that nation's laws. When a transaction crosses boundaries, which nation's laws apply? If the national laws of country Q pertaining to a simple export transaction differ from those of country P, which country's laws apply to the export contract? Which apply to the letter of credit opened to finance the export transaction? The parties involved must reach agreement on such issues, and the nation whose laws apply should be specified in a jurisdictional clause. There are several alternatives from which to choose: the laws of the domicile or principal place of business of one of the parties, the place where the contract was entered, or the place of performance of the contract. If a dispute arises under such a contract, it must be heard and determined by a neutral party such as a court or an arbitration panel. If the parties fail to specify which nation's laws apply, a fairly complex set of rules governing the "conflict of laws" will be applied by the court or arbitration tribunal. Sometimes, the result will be determined with the help of "the scales of justice," with each party's criteria stacked on different sides of the scale.[6]

INTELLECTUAL PROPERTY: PATENTS AND TRADEMARKS

Patents and trademarks that are protected in one country are not necessarily protected in another, so global marketers must ensure that patents and trademarks are registered in each country where business is conducted. In the United States, where patents, trademarks, and copyrights are registered with the Federal Patent Office, the patent holder retains all rights for the life of the patent even if the product is not produced or sold. Patent and trademark protection in the United States is very good, and American law relies on the precedent of previously decided court cases for guidance.

Companies sometimes find ways to exploit loopholes or other unique opportunities offered by patent and trademark laws in individual nations. In France, designer Yves Saint Laurent was barred from marketing a new luxury perfume called Champagne because French laws allow the name to be applied only to sparkling wines produced in the Champagne region. Saint Laurent proceeded to launch Champagne in the United States, England, Germany, and Belgium; "Champagne" and other geographic names are not protected trademarks in the United States. In France, the perfume is sold without a name.[7] Trademark and copyright infringement is a critical problem in global marketing and one that can take a variety of forms. Counterfeiting is the unauthorized copying and production of a product. An associative counterfeit, or imitation, uses a product name that differs slightly from a well-known brand but is close enough that consumers will as-

---

[5] Joseph Ortego and Josh Kardisch, "Foreign Companies Can Limit the Risk of Being Subject to U.S. Courts," *The National Law Journal*, 17, no. 3, 19 September 1994, p. C2.
[6] For a more extensive development of this point, see Radway, "Legal Dimensions of International Business." In Malcom Warner (ed.) *International Encyclopedia of Business and Management* (London: Thomson, 1996).
[7] Karla Vermeulen, "Champagne Perfume Launched in United States but Barred in France," *Wine Spectator,* 31 October 1994, p. 9.

◆ BOX 4-3 ◆

SOFTWARE PIRACY

In Lebanon, one of the largest retailers of software sells the original Microsoft Office 97 Professional for $200, but it also sells the pirated version for $7. Selling pirated versions is rationalized for the following reasons: (1) Given a per capita GNP of approximately $3,000, the $7 version is certainly more affordable. (2) Islam religion says that no one can own science. Since the software is considered science, it should belong to everyone. (3) Dealers question, given the cost of production, the large price difference. "We know how much profit Microsoft is making." (4) Is the government going to enforce trademark law and, if so, how vigorously?

SOURCE: James Schofield, "Beating Software Piracy Proves to Be No Soft Touch." *Financial Times,* 1 April 1999, p. 7.

---

sociate it with the genuine product. A third type of counterfeiting is piracy, the unauthorized publication or reproduction of copyrighted work. Piracy is particularly damaging to the entertainment and software industries; computer programs, videotapes, cassettes, and compact discs are particularly easy to duplicate illegally. Figure 4-1 shows the percentage of pirated software in select countries. Pirating costs the software industry an estimated $11.4 billion per year.

Of the many separate international patent agreements, the most important is the International Convention for the Protection of Industrial Property. Also known as the Paris Union, the convention dates to 1883 and is now honored by nearly 100 countries. This treaty facilitates multicountry patent registrations by ensuring that, once a company files in a signatory country, it will be afforded a "right of priority" in other countries for one year from the date of the original filing. U.S. companies wishing to obtain foreign patent rights must apply to the Paris Union within one year of filing in the United States or risk a permanent loss of patent rights abroad.[8]

Two other treaties deserve mention. The Patent Cooperation Treaty (PCT) has 39 signatories, including Australia, Brazil, France, Germany, Japan, the Democratic Peoples Republic (North Korea), the Republic of Korea, the Netherlands, Switzerland, the former Soviet Union, and the United States. The members constitute a union that provides certain technical services and cooperates in the filing, searching, and examining of patent applications in all member countries. In 1994, China became an official signatory of the PCT. The European Patent Office administers applications for the European Patent Convention, which is effective in the EU and Switzerland. An applicant can file a single patent application covering all of the convention states; the advantage is that the application will be subject to only one procedure of grant. Whereas national patent laws remain effective under this system, approved patents are effective in all member countries for a period of 20 years from the filing date.

In the United States, trademarks are covered by the Trademark Act of 1946, also known as the Lanham Act. President Reagan signed the Trademark Law Revision Act into law in November 1988. The law makes it easier for companies to register new trademarks; as a result, the number of filings has increased dramatically. Table 4-2 shows that foreign trademark filings in the United States have increased dramatically since 1988. The U.S. Patent and Trademark office has focused efforts recently on improving the patent environment in Japan. After years of discussion, the United States and Japan

---

[8] Franklin R. Root, *Entry Strategies for International Markets* (New York: Lexington Books, 1994), p. 113.

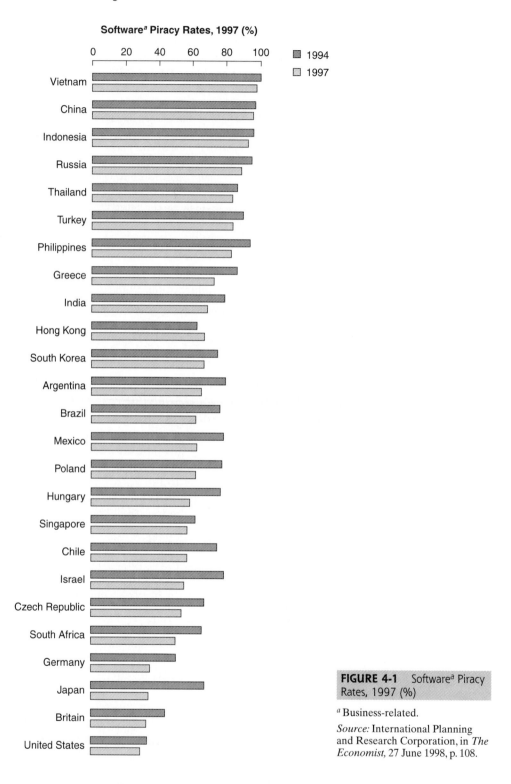

FIGURE 4-1 Software[a] Piracy Rates, 1997 (%)

[a] Business-related.

Source: International Planning and Research Corporation, in *The Economist,* 27 June 1998, p. 108.

have agreed to make changes in their respective systems; Japan has promised to speed up patent examinations, eliminate challenges to patent submissions, and allow patent applications to be filed in English. Effective in 1995, new U.S. patents are granted for a period of 20 years from the filing date. Previously, patents had been valid for a 17-year term effective after being granted. Thus, U.S. patent laws now harmonize with those in

TABLE 4-2	Foreign Company Trademark Filings in the United States for Selected Countries	
Country	*1988*	*1998*
Belgium	111	246
Britain	1,392	2,619
Canada	2,447	4,894
Germany	1,400	2,984
Hong Kong	168	396
Israel	45	438
Japan	1,010	2,231
Mexico	126	693
South Korea	131	372
Total	6,830	14,873

Source: U.S. Patent and Trademark Office.

the EU as well as Japan. Even with the changes, however, patents in Japan are narrower than those in the United States. As a result, companies such as Caterpillar have been unable to protect critical innovations in Japan because products very similar to those made by American companies can be patented without fear of infringement.[9]

VISIT THE WEB SITES

www.uspto.gov for U.S. information

www.european-patent-office.org for information about Europe

ANTITRUST

Antitrust laws are designed to combat restrictive business practices and to encourage competition. American antitrust laws are a legacy of the 19th-century U.S. "trust-busting" era and are intended to maintain free competition by limiting the concentration of economic power. The Sherman Act of 1890 prohibits certain restrictive business practices, including fixing prices, limiting production, allocating markets, or any other scheme designed to limit or avoid competition. The law applies to foreign companies conducting business in the United States and extends to the activities of U.S. companies outside U.S. boundaries as well if the company conduct is deemed to have an effect on U.S. commerce contrary to law. Similar laws are taking on increasing importance outside the United States as well.

The European Commission prohibits agreements and practices that prevent, restrict, and distort competition. The interstate trade clause of the Treaty of Rome applies to trade with third countries, so that a company must be aware of the conduct of its affiliates. The commission also exempts certain cartels from articles 85 and 86 of the treaty in an effort to encourage the growth of important businesses. The intent is to allow European companies to compete on an equal footing with Japanese and U.S. companies.

In some instances, individual country laws in Europe apply to specific marketing mix elements. For example, some countries permit selective or exclusive product distribution. However, community law can take precedence. In one case, Consten, a French company, had exclusive French rights to import and distribute consumer electronics products from the German Grundig Company. Consten sued another French firm, charging the latter with bringing "parallel imports" into France illegally. That is, Consten charged that the competitor bought Grundig products from various foreign suppliers without Consten's

---

[9] John Carey, "Inching toward a Borderless Patent," *Business Week,* 5 September 1994, p. 35.

knowledge and was selling them in France. Although Consten's complaint was upheld by two French courts, the Paris court of appeals suspended the judgment, pending a ruling by the European Commission on whether the Grundig–Consten arrangement violated articles 85 and 86. The commission ruled against Consten on the grounds that "territorial protection proved to be particularly damaging to the realization of the Common Market."[10] The principle being offended was that of the free flow of goods defined in articles 24 to 30 of the Treaty of Rome.

LICENSING AND TRADE SECRETS

Licensing is a contractual agreement in which a licensor allows a licensee to use patents, trademarks, trade secrets, technology, or other intangible assets in return for royalty payments or other forms of compensation (see Chapter 8 for a discussion of licensing as a marketing strategy). In the United States, laws do not regulate the licensing process per se as do technology transfer laws in the EU, Australia, Japan, and many developing countries. The duration of the licensing agreement and the amount of royalties a company can receive are considered a matter of commercial negotiation between licensor and licensee, and there are no government restrictions on remittances of royalties abroad. In many countries, these elements of licensing are regulated by government agencies.

Important considerations in licensing include analysis of what assets a firm may offer for license, how to price the assets, whether to grant only the right to "make" the product or to grant the rights to "use" and to "sell" the product as well. The right to sublicense is another important issue. As with distribution agreements, decisions must also be made regarding exclusive or nonexclusive arrangements and the size of the licensee's territory.

To prevent the licensee from using the licensed technology to compete directly with the licensor, the latter may try to limit the licensee to selling only in its home country. The licensor may also seek to contractually bind the licensee to discontinue use of the technology after the contract has expired. In practice, host government laws, including U.S. and EU antitrust laws, may make such agreements impossible to obtain. Licensing is a potentially dangerous action: It may be instrumental in creating a competitor. Therefore, licensors should be careful to ensure that their own competitive position remains advantageous. This requires constant innovation. There is a simple rule: If you are licensing technology and know-how that are going to remain unchanged, it is only a matter of time before your licensee will become your competitor, not merely with your technology and know-how but with improvements on that technology and know-how. When this happens, you are history.

As noted, licensing agreements can come under antitrust scrutiny. In one recent case, Bayer AG granted an exclusive patent license for a new household insecticide to S. C. Johnson & Sons. The German firm's decision to license was based in part on the time required for Environmental Protection Agency (EPA) approval, which had stretched to three years. Bayer decided it made better business sense to let the American firm deal with regulatory authorities in return for a 5 percent royalty on sales. However, a class action suit was filed against the companies, alleging that the licensing deal would allow Johnson to monopolize the $450 million home insecticide market. Then the U.S. Justice Department stepped in, calling the licensing agreement anticompetitive. In a statement, Anne Bingaman, head of the Justice Department's antitrust unit, said, "The cozy arrangement that Bayer and Johnson maintained is unacceptable in a highly concentrated market." Bayer agreed to offer licenses to any interested company on better terms than the original contract with Johnson. Johnson agreed to notify the U.S. government of any future pending exclusive licensing agreements for household insecticides. If Bayer is

---

[10] Detlev Vagts, *Transnational Business Problems* (Mineola, NY: The Foundation Press, 1986), pp. 285–291.

party to any such agreements, the Justice Department has the right to veto them. Not surprisingly, the reaction from the legal community has been negative. One Washington lawyer who specializes in intellectual property law noted that the case "really attacks traditional licensing practices." As Melvin Jager, president of the Licensing Executives Society, explained, "An exclusive license is a very valuable tool to promote intellectual property and get it out into the marketplace."[11]

What happens if a licensee gains knowledge of the licensor's trade secrets? Trade secrets are confidential information or knowledge that has commercial value, is not in the public domain, and for which steps have been taken to keep it secret. Trade secrets include manufacturing processes, formulas, designs, and customer lists. To prevent disclosure, the licensing of unpatented trade secrets should be linked to confidentiality contracts with each employee who has access to the protected information. In the United States, trade secrets are protected by state law rather than federal statute; most states have adopted the Uniform Trade Secrets Act (UTSA). U.S. law provides trade secret liability against third parties that obtain confidential information through an intermediary. Remedies include damages and other forms of relief.

The 1990s saw widespread improvements in laws pertaining to trade secrets. Several countries adopted trade secret statutes for the first time. Mexico's first statute protecting trade secrets became effective in 1991; China's first trade secret law took effect in 1993. In both countries, the new laws were part of broader revisions of intellectual property laws. Japan and South Korea also amended their intellectual property laws to include trade secrets. Many countries in Central and Eastern Europe have also enacted laws to protect trade secrets. When the North American Free Trade Agreement (NAFTA) became effective in 1994, it marked the first international trade agreement with provisions for protecting trade secrets. This milestone was quickly followed by the Agreement on Trade-Related Aspects of Intellectual Property Rights (TRIPs) that resulted from the Uruguay Round of GATT negotiations. The TRIPs agreement requires signatory countries to protect against acquisition, disclosure, or use of trade secrets "in a manner contrary to honest commercial practices."[12] Despite these formal legal developments, in practice, enforcement is the key issue. Companies transferring trade secrets across borders should apprise themselves not only of the existence of legal protection but also of the risks associated with lax enforcement.

BRIBERY AND CORRUPTION: LEGAL AND ETHICAL ISSUES

History does not record a burst of international outrage when Charles M. Schwab presented a $200,000 diamond and pearl necklace to the mistress of Czar Alexander's nephew. In return for that consideration, Bethlehem Steel won the contract to supply the rails for the trans-Siberian railroad. Today, in the post-Soviet era, Western companies are again being lured by emerging opportunities in Eastern Europe. Here, as in the Middle East and other parts of the world, they are finding that bribery is a way of life and that corruption is widespread. American companies in particular are constrained in their responses to such a situation by U.S. government policies of the post-Watergate age.

The Foreign Corrupt Practices Act[13]

The Foreign Corrupt Practices Act (FCPA) is a legacy of the Watergate scandal during Richard Nixon's presidency. In the course of his investigation, the Watergate Special Prosecutor discovered that more than 300 American companies had made undisclosed

---

[11] Brigid McMenamin, "Eroding Patent Rights," *Forbes* 24 October 1994, p. 92.

[12] Salem M. Katsh and Michael P. Dierks, "Globally, Trade Secrets Laws Are All over the Map," *The National Law Journal,* 17, no. 36, 8 May 1995, p. C12.

[13] Much of the material in this section is adapted from Daniel Pines, "Amending the Foreign Corrupt Practices Act to Include a Private Right of Action," *California Law Review* (January 1994): 185–229.

payments to foreign officials, totaling hundreds of millions of dollars. The act was unanimously passed by Congress and signed into law in 1977. Administered by the Department of Justice and the Securities and Exchange Commission, the act was concerned with disclosure and prohibition. The disclosure part of the act required publicly held companies to institute internal accounting controls that would record all transactions. The prohibition part made it a crime for U.S. corporations to bribe an official of a foreign government or political party to obtain or retain business. Payments to third parties were also prohibited when the company had reason to believe part or all of the money would be channeled to foreign officials.

The American business community immediately began lobbying for changes to the act, complaining that the statute was too vague and so broad in scope that it threatened to severely curtail U.S. business activities abroad. Amendments to the statutes were signed into law in 1988 as part of the Omnibus Trade and Competitiveness Act. Among the changes were exclusions for "grease" payments to low-level officials to cut red tape and expedite "routine governmental actions" such as clearing shipments through customs, securing permits, or getting airport passport clearance to leave a country.

Although several well-known American companies have pleaded guilty to violations of the antibribery provisions, enforcement of the act has generally been lax. Only 23 cases were filed between 1977 and 1988. (In a recent case, a business executive was convicted of giving money and honeymoon airplane tickets to a Nigerian government official in the hopes of securing a contract.[14]) There are stiff penalties for violating the law: Convictions carry severe jail sentences (in excess of one to five years) and heavy fines (in excess of $1 million). Fines cannot be paid or reimbursed by the company, under the theory that individuals commit such crimes. It has also been made clear that the law will not let a person do indirectly (e.g., through an "agent," joint venture partner, or other third party) what it prohibits directly.

Some critics of the FCPA decry it as a regrettable display of moral imperialism. At issue is the extraterritorial sovereignty of U.S. law. It is wrong, according to these critics, to impose U.S. laws, standards, values, and mores on American companies and citizens worldwide. As one legal expert points out, however, this criticism has one fundamental flaw: There is no nation in which the letter of the law condones bribery of government officials. Thus, the standard set by the FCPA is shared by other nations.[15]

A second criticism of the FCPA has been that it put American companies in a difficult position vis-à-vis foreign competitors, especially those in Japan and Europe. Several opinion polls and surveys of the business community have revealed the widespread perception that the act adversely affects American businesses overseas. Some academic researchers have concluded that there is no evidence that the FCPA has negatively affected the export performance of U.S. industry in corrupt countries. However, a Commerce Department report prepared with the help of U.S. intelligence services indicated that in 1994 bribes offered by non-U.S. companies were a factor in 100 business deals valued at $45 billion. Foreign companies prevailed in 80 percent of those deals.[16]

The U.S. government position has been that the best solution to this concern was to lobby other countries to adopt a treaty that would outlaw the practice of bribing foreign government officials. In 1997, 20 years after the United States outlawed bribery of government officials, an antibribery treaty was negotiated in Paris by the 29 members of the OECD. The central provisions of the treaty would force countries to prosecute

---

[14] Katherine Albright and Grace Won, "Foreign Corrupt Practices Act," *American Criminal Law Review* (Spring 1993): 787.

[15] Pines, "Amending the Foreign Corrupt Practices Act," p. 205.

[16] Amy Borrus, "Inside the World of Greased Palms," *Business Week*, 6 November 1995, pp. 36–38.

corporations for paying bribes to foreign government officials in the same way that bribery of its own officials is illegal.[17]

When companies operate abroad in the absence of home-country legal constraints, they face a continuum of choices concerning company ethics. At one extreme, they can maintain home-country ethics worldwide with absolutely no adjustment or adaptation to local practice. At the other extreme, they can abandon any attempt to maintain company ethics and adapt entirely to local conditions and circumstances as they are perceived by company managers in each local environment. Between these extremes, one approach that companies may select is to utilize varying degrees of extension of home-country ethics. Alternatively, they may adapt in varying degrees to local customs and practices.

The existence of bribery as a fact of life in world markets may not change overnight because it is condemned by governments. What should a company do if competitors are offering a bribe? Three alternative courses of action are possible. One is to ignore bribery and act as if it does not exist. Another is to recognize the existence of bribery and evaluate its effect on the customer's purchase decision as if it were just another element of the marketing mix. A third is to inform the competitor that you intend to file bribery charges in his or her home country.

The overall value of a company's offer must be as good as, or better than, the competitor's overall offering, bribe included. It may be possible to offer a lower price, a better product, better distribution, or better advertising to offset the value added by the bribe. The best line of defense is to have a product that is clearly superior to that of the competition. In such a case, a bribe should not sway the purchase decision. Alternatively, clear superiority in service and in local representation may tip the scales.

For a discussion of dumping (the sale of an imported product at a price lower than that normally charged in a domestic market or country of origin), see Chapter 13. The U.S. Congress has designated dumping as an unfair trade practice that results in "injury, destruction, or prevention of the establishment of American industry," so it is both a legal and a pricing issue. One of the major issues before the World Trade Organization is the objection of U.S. trading partners to U.S. antidumping legislation, which is seen as an unfair trade restriction by U.S. trading partners.

◆ CONFLICT RESOLUTION, DISPUTE SETTLEMENT, AND LITIGATION

Countries vary in their approach toward conflict resolution. Table 4-3 shows the number of practicing lawyers per 100,000 population in selected countries. The United States has more lawyers than any other country in the world and is arguably the most litigious nation on earth. In part, this is a reflection of the low-context nature of American culture, a spirit of confrontational competitiveness, and the absence of one important principle of code law: The loser pays all court costs for all parties. The degree of legal cooperation and harmony in the EU is unique and stems in part from the existence of code law as a common bond. Other regional organizations have made far less progress toward harmonization.

Conflicts will inevitably arise in business anywhere, especially when different cultures come together to buy, sell, establish joint ventures, compete, and cooperate in global markets. For American companies, the dispute with a foreign party is frequently in the home-country jurisdiction. The issue can be litigated in the United States, where a company and its attorneys might be said to enjoy "home court" advantage. Litigation in foreign courts, however, becomes vastly more complex. This is due in part to differences in language, legal systems, currencies, and traditional business customs and patterns. In addition,

---

[17] "29 Nations Agree to Outlaw Bribing Foreign Officials," *The New York Times,* 11 November 1997, pp. 1, D–2.

TABLE 4-3 Lawyers: An International Comparison	
Country	*Lawyers per 100,000 People*
United States	290
Australia	242
United Kingdom	141
France	80
Germany	79
Hungary	79
Japan	11
Korea	3

Source: Adapted from Frank B. Cross. "Lawyers, the Economy, and Society," *American Business Law Journal* (Summer 1998): 477+.

problems arise from differences in procedures relating to discovery. In essence, discovery is the process of obtaining evidence to prove claims and determining which evidence may be admissible in which countries under which conditions. A further complication is the fact that judgments handed down in courts in another country may not be enforceable in the home country. For all these reasons, many companies prefer to pursue arbitration before proceeding to litigate.

ALTERNATIVES TO LITIGATION FOR DISPUTE SETTLEMENT[18]

Extrajudicial, alternative approaches often provide a faster, easier, and less expensive way to resolve commercial disputes than litigation. Indeed, alternative approaches have a tradition that is centuries old. Chambers of trade and commerce first began to hear and resolve disputes as trade developed between different tribes or nations. Settlement of modern trade disputes takes various forms and occurs in many locations. Formal arbitration is one means of settling international business disputes outside the courtroom. Arbitration generally involves a hearing of all parties before a three-member panel. The result is usually a decision by which the parties agree in advance to abide. Courts of arbitration have long existed in London and Zurich. For decades, business arbitration has also been promoted through the Paris-based International Chamber of Commerce (ICC). The ICC recently modernized some of its older rules. However, because it is the best-known international business organization, it has the biggest backlog of cases. Thus, the ICC has gained a reputation for being slower, more expensive, and more cumbersome than some alternatives. The United Nations Convention on the Recognition and Enforcement of Foreign Arbitral Awards (also known as the New York Convention) has more than 50 signatories. The New York Convention facilitates arbitration when disputes arise, and signatories agree to abide by decisions reached through arbitration.

Some firms and lawyers, inexperienced in the practice of international commercial arbitration, have used standard "boilerplate" arbitration clauses in contracts that cover merger, severability, choice of law, and other issues. U.S. companies may stipulate the arbitration will take place in the United States; companies in other countries may choose Paris. Arbitration can be a minefield due to the number of the issues that must be addressed. For example, if the parties to a patent licensing agreement agree in the arbitration clause that the validity of the patent cannot be contested, such a provision may not be enforceable in some countries. Which country's laws will be used as the standard for invalidity?

Pursuing such an issue on a country-by-country basis would be inordinately time consuming. In addition, there is the issue of acceptance; by law, U.S. courts must accept

---

[18] This section draws heavily on the work of Radway, "Amending the Foreign Corrupt Practices Act."

an arbitrator's decision in patent disputes; in other countries, however, there is no general rule of acceptance. To reduce delays relating to such issues, one expert suggests drafting arbitration clauses with as much specificity as possible. To the extent possible, for example, patent policies in various countries should be addressed; persons drafting arbitration clauses may also include a provision that all foreign patent issues will be judged according to the standard of home-country law. Another provision could forbid the parties from commencing separate legal actions in other countries. The goal is to help the arbitration tribunal zero in on the express intentions of the parties.[19]

As U.S. involvement in global commerce grew dramatically during the post–World War II period, the American Arbitration Association (AAA) became recognized as a very effective institution within which to resolve disputes. Each year, the AAA uses mediation to help resolve thousands of disputes. The AAA has entered into cooperation agreements with the ICC and other global organizations to promote the use of alternative dispute resolution methods; it serves as the agent to administer arbitration in the United States under ICC auspices. In 1992, the AAA signed a cooperation agreement with the China's Beijing Conciliation Center.

Other agencies for settling disputes include the Swedish Arbitration Institute of the Stockholm Chamber of Commerce. This agency frequently administered disputes between Western and socialist countries and has gained credibility for its even-handed administration. Other alternatives have proliferated in recent years. In addition to those mentioned, active centers for arbitration exist in Vancouver, Hong Kong, Cairo, Kuala Lumpur, Singapore, Buenos Aires, Bogotá, and Mexico City. The World Arbitration Institute was established in New York; in the United Kingdom, the Advisory, Conciliation, and Arbitration Service (ACAS) has achieved great success at handling industrial disputes. The International Council for Commercial Arbitration (ICCA) was established to coordinate the far-flung activities of arbitration organizations. The ICCA meets in different locations around the world every four years.

The United Nations Conference on International Trade Law (UNCITRAL) has also been a significant force in the area of arbitration. UNCITRAL rules have become more or less standard, as many of the organizations named previously have adopted them with some modifications. Many developing countries, for example, long held prejudices against the ICC, AAA, and other organizations in developed countries. Representatives of developing nations assumed that such organizations would be biased in favor of multinational corporations. Developing nations insisted on settlement in national courts, which was unacceptable to the multinational firms. This was especially true in Latin America, where the Calvo Doctrine required disputes arising with foreign investors to be resolved in national courts under national laws. The growing influence of the ICCA and UNCITRAL rules, coupled with the proliferation of regional arbitration centers, has contributed to changing attitudes in developing countries and has resulted in the increased use of arbitration around the world.

◆ THE REGULATORY ENVIRONMENT

The regulatory environment of global marketing consists of a variety of agencies, both governmental and nongovernmental, that enforce laws or set guidelines for conducting business. A number of regulatory agencies (sometimes referred to as "international economic organizations," or IEOs) are identified in Table 4-4 and in "Trade Groups" on page 562 in the Appendix, and are discussed in Chapter 2, "Global Economic Environment."

---

[19] Bruce Londa, "An Agreement to Arbitrate Disputes Isn't the Same in Every Language," *Brandweek,* 18 September 1994, p. 18. See also John M. Allen, Jr. and Bruce G. Merritt, "Drafters of Arbitration Clauses Face a Variety of Unforeseen Perils," *National Law Journal,* 17, no. 33, 17 April 1995, pp. C6–C7.

TABLE 4-4	International Economic Organizations
Abbreviation	*Full Name*
APPA	African Petroleum Producers' Association
ADB	Asian Development Bank
APEC	Asia Pacific Economic Cooperation
ATPC	Association of Tin Producing Countries
CDB	Caribbean Development Bank
CCASG	Cooperation Council for the Arab States of the Gulf
ECLAC	Economic Commission for Latin America and the Caribbean
ECCAS	Economic Community of Central African States
FAO	Food and Agricultural Organization
ICAO	International Civil Aviation Organization
IEA	International Energy Agency
IFC	International Finance Corporation
ITPA	International Tea Promotion Association
IDB	Islamic Development Bank
MIGA	Multilateral Investment Guarantee Agency
UNCTAD	United Nations Conference on Trade and Development
UNIDO	United Nations Industrial Development Organization
UNITAR	United Nations Institute for Training and Research
WACU	West African Customs Union
WHO	World Health Organization
WMO	World Meteorological Organization

These organizations address a wide range of marketing issues, including price control, valuation of imports and exports, trade practices, labeling, food and drug regulations, employment conditions, collective bargaining, advertising content, competitive practices, and so on. The decisions of IEOs are binding and are carried out by the member states.[20]

The influence of regulatory agencies is pervasive, and an understanding of how they operate is essential to protect business interests and advance new programs. For example, in the United States, the International Trade Commission administers the Tariff Act of 1930. Section 337 prohibits "unfair methods of competition" if the effect of this competition is to destroy or substantially injure an industry. To seek relief or defend access to the U.S. market if challenged under this act, a company should retain the services of specialized legal talent, supported by technical expertise in patents and in international marketing. It is useful to call on the assistance of home-country diplomatic staff to assist and support the effort to obtain a favorable ruling.

THE EUROPEAN UNION

The Treaty of Rome established the European Economic Community (EEC), the precursor to the EU. The treaty contains hundreds of articles, several of which are directly applicable to global companies and global marketers. Articles 30 to 36 establish the general policy referred to as "Free Flow of Goods, People, Capital and Technology" among the member states. Articles 85 and 86 contain competition rules, as amended by various directives of the EU Commission. These articles and directives constitute community law, which is somewhat analogous to U.S. federal law.

---

[20] See Sergi A. Voitovich, "Normative Acts of International Economic Organizations in International Law Making," *Journal of World Trade* (August 1990): 21–38.

The European Court of Justice, based in Luxembourg, hears disputes that arise among the 15 EU member nations on trade issues such as mergers, monopolies, and trade barriers. The court is also empowered to resolve conflicts between national law and EU law. In most cases, the latter supersedes national laws of individual European countries. Marketers must be aware, however, that national laws should always be consulted. National laws may be more strict than community law, especially in such areas as competition and antitrust. Community law is intended to harmonize, to the extent possible, national laws to promote the purposes defined in articles 30 to 36. The goal is to bring the "lax" laws of some member states up to designated minimum standards. However, more restrictive positions may still exist in some national laws.

The 1987 Single European Act amended the Treaty of Rome and provided strong impetus for the creation of a Single Market by December 31, 1992. Although technically the target was not completely met, approximately 85 percent of the new recommendations were implemented into national law by most member states by the target date, resulting in substantial harmonization.

One function of the European Union is to harmonize business regulations so as to facilitate business. Rather than conforming to individual country laws, a company now must follow the laws established by the legal arm that apply to all member countries. One law relates to product guarantees and goes into effect on January 1, 2002. The EU countries have agreed to a two-year guarantee on goods purchased. This will quadruple the guarantee period in Austria, Germany, Greece, Portugal, and Spain. In countries with longer guarantee periods (in the United Kingdom it is six years and in France and the Netherlands there are no limits), these time periods may be maintained.[21] Although harmonization is occurring, companies must comply with the laws of the individual countries. Table 4-5 provides some examples.

THE WORLD TRADE ORGANIZATION AND ITS ROLE IN INTERNATIONAL TRADE

In 1948 when 23 countries underlined in the General Agreement on Tariffs and Trade (GATT) their determination to reduce import tariffs, this was considered a milestone in international trade relations. GATT is based on three principles. The first concerns nondiscrimination: Each member country must treat the trade of all other member countries equally. The second principle is open markets, which are encouraged by the GATT through a prohibition of all forms of protection except customs tariffs. Fair trade is the third principle, which prohibits export subsidies on manufactured products and limits the use of export subsidies on primary products. In reality, none of these principles is fully realized as yet, although much progress was made during the Uruguay Round on issues such as nontariff barriers, protection of intellectual property rights, and government subsidies.

TABLE 4-5 Uncommon Laws in the EU	
Italy	Bans all forms of tobacco advertising
Greece	Bans all advertising of toys
Finland	Bans speed as a feature in car advertising
Sweden	Bans television advertising directed at children under age 12
Netherlands	Bans claims about automobile fuel consumption

Source: Adapted from Brandon Mitchener, "Border Crossings," *The Wall Street Journal,* 22 November 1999, p. R41.

---

[21] Michael Smith, "Accord on Product Guarantees," *Financial Times,* 23 March 1999, p. 2.

Another major breakthrough at the Uruguay Round was the establishment of the World Trade Organization (WTO) in 1995, which replaced GATT. In contrast to GATT, which was more loosely organized, WTO as a permanent institution is endowed with much more decision-making power in undecided cases. These extended competencies have become manifest in visible consequences. During its 50 years of existence, only 300 complaints in international trade disputes were filed with GATT; since its installation in 1995, the WTO has already dealt with 200 cases.

◆ ETHICAL ISSUES

Ethics, just as the legal environment, vary around the world. What is acceptable in one country may be considered unethical in another. In addition to the obvious moral questions, companies may suffer when negative publicity is generated. A case in point is the use of child labor or allegations of its use. Nike is well aware of this problem. Nike sources its goods in countries with low wages and poor labor regulations. Although Nike does not directly employ children in its overseas manufacturing, the sourcing agent may. A program has been established by Nike to monitor its suppliers but it is difficult when some locals may argue in favor of child labor. Regarding child labor in Pakistan, "trade bands on goods produced by child labor could have the unintended effect of forcing the children into other paid work at a lower wage"[22] and/or prostitution. The U.S. Department of Labor has many publications on this specific issue.[23]

In order to "do the right thing" but also generate good publicity, companies can take an active approach to ethical issues. Reebok and Levi Strauss have done this by establishing standards that their contractors must follow, and they actively monitor results to ensure that standards are met.[24]

An increasing number of companies are addressing ethical issues. A recent survey of companies in 22 countries found that 78 percent of boards of directors were establishing ethical standards.[25] This is up significantly from 21 percent in 1987. The study also warns that regional differences can hinder effective implementation of any efforts.

Summary

The legal and political environment of global marketing is the set of governmental institutions, political parties, and organizations that are the expression of the people in the nations of the world. In particular, anyone engaged in global marketing should have an overall understanding of the importance of sovereignty to national governments. The political environment varies from country to country, and risk assessment is crucial. It is also important to understand a particular government's actions with respect to taxes, dilution of equity control, and expropriation.

The legal environment consists of laws, courts, attorneys, and legal customs and practices. The countries of the world can be broadly categorized in terms of common-law system or code (civil)-law system. The United States, United Kingdom, and the British Commonwealth countries, which include Canada, Australia, New Zealand, the former British colonies in Africa, and India, are common-law countries; other countries are based on code law. Some of the most important legal issues pertain to establishment, jurisdiction, patents and trademarks, licensing, antitrust, and bribery. When legal conflicts arise, companies can pursue the matter in court or use arbitration.

---

[22] Richard Adams, "Sanctions over Child Labor 'Can Backfire'," *Financial Times,* 31 March 1999, p. 4.

[23] U.S. Department of Labor, "The Apparel Industry and Codes of Conduct: A Solution to the International Child labor Problem?" 1996.

[24] Philip Rosenzweig, "How Should Multinationals Set Global Workplace Standards?" Mastering Global Business Section of *Financial Times,* p. 11.

[25] "Global Ethic Codes," *The Wall Street Journal,* 19 August 1999, p. A1

The regulatory environment consists of agencies, both governmental and non-governmental, that enforce laws or set guidelines for conducting business. Global marketing activities can be affected by a number of international or regional economic organizations; in Europe, for example, the EU makes laws governing member states. The WTO will have broad impact on global marketing activities in the years to come.

Although these three environments are complex, astute marketers plan ahead to avoid situations that might result in conflict, misunderstanding, or outright violation of national laws.

Discussion Questions ▪▪▪

1. What is sovereignty? Why is it an important consideration in the political environment of global marketing?
2. Briefly describe some of the differences that relate to marketing between the legal environment of a country that embraces common law as opposed to a country that observes civil law.
3. Global marketers can avoid legal conflicts by understanding the reasons conflicts arise in the first place. Identify and describe several legal issues that relate to global commerce. What alternatives are available from a marketing perspective?
4. You are a sales representative of a multinational corporation and of American citizenship traveling on business in West Africa. As you are leaving country X, the passport control officer at the airport tells you there will be a passport "processing" delay of one hour. You explain that your plane leaves in 30 minutes, and that the next plane out of the country does not leave for three days. You also explain how valuable your time is (at least $300 an hour) and that it is urgent that you catch the flight you have reserved. The official listens carefully to your appeal and then "suggests" that a contribution of $1,000 would definitely assure your passport clearance priority treatment, and considering how valuable your time is, it is quite a bargain.

   Would you comply with the "suggestion"? Why? Why not? If you would not comply, what would you do?

   If you comply with the suggestion, have you violated any laws? Explain.

   If the official requests $25, have you violated any laws?

5. "See you in court" is one way to respond when legal issues arise. What other approaches are possible?
6. If you were Nike, what would you do to prevent negative publicity regarding reports of unsafe factory conditions?

Suggested Readings ▪▪▪

Albright, Katherine, and Grace Won. "Foreign Corrupt Practices Act." *American Criminal Law Review* (Spring 1993): 787.

Amine, Lyn S. "The Need for Moral Champions in Global Marketing." *European Journal of Marketing,* 30 (May 1996): 81.

Bagley, Jennifer M., Stephanie S. Glickman, and Elizabeth B. Wyatt. "Intellectual Property." *American Criminal Law Review,* 32 (Winter 1995): 457–479.

Basu, K., and A. Chattopadhyay. "Marketing Pharmaceuticals to Developing Nations: Research Issues and a Framework for Public Policy." *Canadian Journal of Administrative Sciences,* 12 (December 1995): 300–313.

Braithwaite, John. "Transnational Regulation of the Pharmaceutical Industry." *Annals of the American Academy of Political & Social Science,* 525 (January 1993): 12–30.

Chukwumerige, Okezie. *Choice of Law in International Commercial Arbitration.* Westport, CT: Quorum Books, 1994.

Clarke, Irvine III. "The Harmonization of Product Country Marking Statutes: Strategic Implications for International Marketers." *Journal of International Marketing,* 7, no. 2 (1999): 81–103.

Epstein, M. J., and M.-J. Roy. *Strategic Learning through Corporate Environmental Management: Implementing the ISO 14001 Standard,* INSEAD's Centre for the Management of Environmental Resources (1997).

Fishbein, Bette K. *Germany, Garbage, and the Green Dot: Challenging the Throwaway Society.* New York: Inform, 1994.

Garg, R., G. Kumra, et al. "Four Opportunities in India's Pharmaceutical Market." *McKinsey Quarterly,* 4 (1996): 132–145.

Gillespie, Kate. "Middle East Response to the U.S. Foreign Corrupt Practices Act." *California Management Review,* 29 (1987): 9–31.

Graham, John L. "The Foreign Corrupt Practice Act: A New Perspective." *Journal of International Business Studies* (Winter 1984): 107–121.

Howell, Llewellyn D. and Brad Chaddick. "An Assessment of Three Approaches to Political Risk," *Columbia Journal of World Business* (Fall 1994): 71–91.

Jacoby, Neil H., Peter Nehmenkis, and Richard Eells. *Bribery and Extortion in World Business.* New York: McMillan, 1977.

Kaikati, Jack, and Wayne A. Label. "The Foreign Anti-bribery Law: Friend or Foe?" *Columbia Journal of World Business* (Spring 1980): 46–51.

Katsh, Salem M., and Michael P. Dierks. "Globally, Trade Secrets Laws Are All Over the Map." *The National Law Journal,* 17 (May 8, 1995): C12–C14.

Nash, Marian Leich. "Contemporary Practice of the United States Relating to International Law." *American Journal of International Law,* 88 (October 1994): 719–765.

Neimanis, G. J. "Business Ethics in the Former Soviet Union: A Report." *Journal of Business Ethics,* 16 (February 1997): 357–362.

Ohmae, K. "Putting Global Logic First." *Harvard Business Review* (January/February 1995): 119–125.

Ohmae, Kenichi. *The Borderless World.* New York: Harper Perennial, 1991.

Ortego, Joseph, and Josh Kardisch. "Foreign Companies Can Limit the Risk of Being Subject to U.S. Courts." *National Law Journal,* 17 (September 19, 1994): C2–C3+.

Pines, Daniel. "Amending the Foreign Corrupt Practices Act to Include a Private Right of Action." *California Law Review* (January 1994): 185–229.

Robock, Stephan H., and Kenneth Simmonds. *International Business and Multinational Enterprises.* Homewood, IL: Irwin, 1989.

Rodgers, Frank A. "The War Is Won, but Peace Is Not." *Vital Speeches of the Day* (May 14, 1991): 430–432.

Root, Franklin R. *Entry Strategies for International Markets.* New York: Lexington Books, 1994.

Samuels, Barbara C. *Managing Risk in Developing Countries: National Demands and Multinational Response.* Princeton, NJ: Princeton University Press, 1990.

Slomanson, William R. *Fundamental Perspectives on International Law.* St. Paul, MN: West Publishing, 1990.

Sohn, Louis B. (ed). *Basic Documents of the United Nations.* Brooklyn: The Foundation Press, 1968.

Spero, Donald M. "Patent Protection or Piracy: A CEO Views Japan." *Harvard Business Review* (September/October 1990): 58–62.

Tancer, Shoshana B. "Strategic Management of Legal Issues in the Evolving Transnational Business," Discussion Paper, Thunderbird Research Center, no. 99-5.

U.S. Department of Labor, *The Apparel Industry and Codes of Conduct: A Solution to the International Child Labor Problem?* Washington, DC: Bureau of International Labor Affairs, 1996.

Vagts, Detlev. *Transnational Business Problems.* Mineola, NY: The Foundation Press, 1986.

Vernon, Raymond. "The World Trade Organization: A New Stage in International Trade and Development." *Harvard International Law Journal,* 36 (Spring 1995): 329–340.

Vogel, David. "The Globalization of Business Ethics: Why America Remains Distinctive." *California Management Review,* 35 (Fall 1992): 30–49.

Voitovich, Sergei A. "Normative Acts of International Economic Organizations in International Law Making." *Journal of World Trade* (August 4, 1990): 21–38.

VISIT THE WEB SITES

www.asiandevbank.org (Asian Development Bank)

www.eiu.com (European Intelligence Unit)

www.prsgroup.com (political risk)

www.beri.com (political risk)

www.icj-cij.org (International Court of Justice)

www.iccwbo.org (International Chamber of Commerce)

www.un.or.at/uncitral (United Nations Conference on International Trade Law)

www.iadb.org (American Arbitration Association)

Euro Disney (A)

Michael Eisner, chairperson of Walt Disney Company, was sitting in his Los Angeles office. It was New Year's Eve 1993, and Eisner had one meeting left before he could go home to celebrate a quiet holiday. The meeting was with yet another group of high-powered consultants from one of the world's most prestigious general management and strategy consulting companies. The consultants had assembled a multidisciplinary team including financial, marketing, and strategic planning experts from the New York and Paris offices. The meeting couldn't wait until after the holidays—the topic, what to do about Euro Disney, was that critical. The consultants were asked by the consortium of bank lenders to provide an additional perspective on the problems of Euro Disney and to make recommendations to Eisner and Disney management on what should be done.

In the 10 years since Eisner and his senior management team had arrived, they had turned Disney into a company with annual revenues of $8.5 billion, compared with $1 billion in 1984. For Eisner, his track record was impeccable. "From the time they came in, they had never made a single misstep, never a mistake, never a failure," according to a former Disney executive. "There was a tendency to believe that everything they touched would be perfect." Eisner was particularly proud of the success of the immensely profitable Tokyo Disneyland, which had more visitors in 1993 than even the two parks in California and Florida. Based on the company's success in the United States and Japan, Eisner had vowed to make Euro Disney, located outside of Paris, the most lavish project that Disney had ever built. Eisner was obsessed with maintaining Disney's reputation for quality and he listened carefully to the designers who convinced them that Euro Disney would have to brim with detail to compete with the great monuments and cathedrals of Europe. Eisner believed that Europeans, unlike the Japanese, would not accept carbon copies. Construction of the park alone (excluding the hotels) was approaching $2.8 billion. In developing Euro Disney, Eisner had learned from some of the mistakes made on other projects. For example, in Southern California, Disney let other companies build the hotels to house visitors and in Japan, Disney merely collected royalties from the park rather than having an equity ownership stake.

In preparing for the meeting with the consultants, Eisner was shuffling through some of the papers on his desk. An article in that week's French news magazine *Le Point* quoted Eisner as saying that Euro Disney might be shut down if Disney failed to reach an agreement with its creditor banks on a financial rescue plan by March 31. The company's annual report for 1993 said that Euro Disney was the company's ". . . first real financial disappointment" since Eisner had taken over in 1984. Eisner's defense had been to publicly blame the performance on external factors including the severe European recession, high interest rates, and the strong French franc. Eisner picked up the financials from the comparable periods from the initial two years' operations of Euro Disney (Exhibit 1) and then quickly, after reviewing the numbers, put them down. The situation was deteriorating quickly, he thought. Eisner then turned to the attendance figures, which were also trending downward (Exhibit 2).

REVIEW OF PROJECTIONS/THE INITIAL PLAN

Eisner walked to his bookshelf from which he took down a bound copy of the initial 30-year business plan for Euro Disney. The plan was done in the typical detailed and methodical Disney fashion. The table of contents was exhaustive, appearing to cover virtually every detail. Over 200 locations in Europe were examined before selecting the site just outside Paris, with Paris being Europe's biggest magnet for tourism. A huge potential population could get to Euro Disney quickly (see Exhibit 3).

European vacation habits were also studied. Whereas Americans average 2 to 3 weeks' vacation, French and Germans typically have 5 weeks' vacation. Longer vacations

This case was prepared by James L. Bauer, Vice President, Consumer Market Management at Chemical Bank and doctoral candidate, Pace University Lubin School of Business under the direction of Dr. Warren J. Keegan, Professor of International Business and Marketing and Director of the Institute for Global Business Strategy as a basis for class discussion rather than to illustrate either effective or ineffective business leadership and managment. © 1998 by Dr. Warren J. Keegan.

EXHIBIT 1   Euro Disney P&L

	1992–1993 Six Months Ending Sept 30	
	1993	**1992**
Revenues (French francs)	1.8 billion	3.1 billion
Profit/(Loss)	(1.1 billion)	0.7 billion

EXHIBIT 2   Annual Attendance Figures

	Years Ending April (Initial Opening in April 1991)	
	1993	**1992**
Attendance	9.5 million	10.5 million

EXHIBIT 3 European Population Proximity
to Euro Disney

Population (Millions)	Time to Euro Disney
17	2-hour drive
41	4-hour drive
109	6-hour drive
310	2-hour flight

should translate into being able to spend more time at Euro Disney.

The French government was spending hundreds of millions of dollars to provide rail access and other infrastructure improvements. Within 35 minutes, potential visitors could get to the park from downtown Paris. The opening of the Channel Tunnel in 1993 would make the trip from London 3 hours and 10 minutes.

While the weather in France was not as warm as that in California or Florida, waiting areas and moving sidewalks would be covered to protect visitors from wind, rain, and cold. Tokyo Disney had been built in a climate similar to Euro Disney and the company had learned a lot about how to build and run a park in a climate that was colder and wetter than those of Florida and California.

The attractions themselves would be similar to those found in the American parks, with some modifications to increase their appeal to Europeans. Discoveryland, for example, would have attractions based on Frenchman Jules Verne's science fiction; a theater with a 360-degree screen would feature a movie on European history. The park would have two official languages, English and French; a multilingual staff would be on hand to assist Dutch, German, Italian, and Spanish visitors. Basically, however, Euro Disney's strategy was to transplant the American park. Robert Fitzpatrick, a U.S. citizen with extensive ties to France and the chairperson of Euro Disney, felt "it would have been silly to take Mickey Mouse and try to do surgery to create a transmogrified hybrid, half French and half American."

Other aspects of the American parks would also be transferred to France. These include Main Street U.S.A. and Frontierland, as well as Michael Jackson's Captain EO 3-D movie. Like the American parks, wine and other alcoholic beverages would not be served.

Fitzpatrick's greatest fear was ". . . that we will be too successful" and that too many people would come at peak times, forcing the park to shut its gates.

Eisner turned to the financing plan, which had been prepared by chief financial officer (CFO) Gary Wilson, a man known as a tough negotiator with a knack for creating complex, highly leveraged financing packages that placed the risk for many projects outside of Disney while keeping much of the upside potential for the company. Wilson had subsequently left Disney to become chief executive officer (CEO) of the parent company of Northwest Airlines.

The plan had set up a finance company to own the park and lease it back to an operating company. Under the plan, Disney held a 17 percent stake in the company, which was to provide tax losses and borrow capital at relatively low rates. Disney was to manage the resort for large fees and royalties, while owning 49 percent of the equity in the operating company, Euro Disney SCA. The remaining shares were sold to the public, largely to small individual European investors. A total of $3.5 billion in construction loans was raised from dozens of banks eager to finance the project.

Euro Disney was just the cornerstone of a huge real estate development planned by Disney in the area. Initially, the area was to have 5,200 hotel rooms, more than are available in the entire city of Cannes. The number of rooms was expected to triple after a second theme park opened in the area. Subsequent phases of the plan also included office space that would rival the size of France's largest office complex, La Defense, in Paris. Other plans showed shopping malls, golf courses, apartments, and vacation homes. Key to the plan's financial success was that Euro Disney would tightly control the design and build almost everything itself and then sell off the completed properties at a large profit.

THE JAPANESE EXPERIENCE

Eisner put the book down and picked up another file that contained an assessment of the incredible success of Tokyo Disneyland. Seeking to determine if there were any parallels between the Japanese and European experiences, he had commissioned a study of why the Japanese venture was doing so well.

Tokyo Disneyland had been open about 11 years and had been drawing larger crowds than the U.S. parks. Located less than 10 miles from Tokyo, the park drew over 16 million visitors from throughout Asia in 1993. Tokyo Disneyland is a near replica of the American original. Most of the signs are in English, with only occasional Japanese; the Japanese flag is never seen but variations on the Stars and Stripes appear throughout the park. In the file, Eisner found a study written by Masako Notoji, a Tokyo University professor, who studied the hold that Tokyo Disneyland has over Japanese people. Notoji wrote that the "Japanese who visit Tokyo Disneyland are enjoying their own Japanese dream, not the American dream. In part, this is because the park is so sanitized and precise in how it depicts an unthreatening, fantasy America that it has become totally Japanese, just the way that Japanese want it to be." It has been compared to the Japanese garden, which is a controlled and confined version of nature that becomes more satisfying and perfect than nature itself. The Japanese Disneyland, some say, outdoes the American parks because it is probably cleaner due to the Japanese obsession with cleanliness.

Notoji's report also noted that Tokyo Disneyland opened in 1983, a period in which the Japanese economy was especially strong. During that time period, the United States was perceived as a model of an affluent society. At the same time, as a result of its growing affluence, Japan was starting to feel part of world culture. Tokyo Disneyland became a symbol for many people of Japan's entry into world culture.

In commenting on the differences between Tokyo and France, Notoji's research hypothesized that "... the fakeness of (Tokyo) Disneyland is not evident because (the Japanese) only had fantasy images of these things before" while "Europeans see the fakeness because they have their own real castles and many of the Disney characters come from European folk tales."

Eisner's secretary announced that the consulting team had arrived and that the meeting would be held in his conference room. The meeting started with Eisner explaining the assignment and the short time frames in which solutions had to be developed.

EURO DISNEY PROBLEMS

In early February, a team of consultants returned to Eisner's office with the first phase of their study completed. Given the size and complexity of the problems that they expected to find, the study had been divided into three phases. The first phase was a top-level assessment of the problems that they had uncovered in the initial month of the study, without any recommendations as to what should be done. The second phase was to identify the most critical problems that needed to be addressed immediately and to develop action plans. The third phase was to identify the remaining, less critical problems, and develop recommended plans of action.

The consultants' report identified six critical major problem areas that they felt had contributed to the problems. The team felt that, even though not all of the problems could be rectified, it was critical that Disney management understand the fundamental problems so that they could fix the problems at Euro Disney and not repeat the same mistakes again should they expand to other countries. The six critical problem areas were

1. Management hubris
2. Cultural differences
3. Environmental and location factors
4. French labor issues
5. Financing and the initial business plan
6. Competition from U.S. Disney parks

Management Hubris

The first issue addressing the way in which Disney management had approached the development of the project and tactical errors made by members of the management team was the most sensitive. Because of the sensitivity of this subject, the consulting firm had brought in the head of their European practice, based in Paris, to analyze the problem and make the presentation. Extensive interviews had been conducted with members of the Disney management teams, both in the United States and in France; academicians who have studied French and American culture;

and executives of the European banks that had made many of the construction loans as well as workers at the park.

"The initial premise of Euro Disney in the mid-1980s was that there was no limit to the European public's appetite for American imports given the success of Big Macs, Coke, and Hollywood movies," the presentation started off. That initial assumption totally failed to take into consideration the fact that "the French flatter themselves that they are more resistant to American cultural imperialism." The "hermetically sealed world of the theme park did not give the French an ability to put their own mark on the park. Disney was exporting the American management system, experience and values with a management style that was brash, frequently insensitive, and often overbearing." The Americans were overly ambitious and always sure that it would work because they were Disney, and it had always worked in the past. By starting off on this premise, Euro Disney quickly became known as a "cultural Chernobyl" and it created hostility from the French people. The initial arrogance of American management further demoralized the workforce, creating a spiraling effect that cut down on the number of French visitors.

Much of this arrogance, the report continued, created tension and hostility among the management team. The first general manager, Robert Fitzpatrick, an American, spoke French and was married to a French woman; however, he was distrusted by some American as well as French executives. Management, unfamiliar with the French construction industry, had made a number of critical mistakes including selecting the wrong local contractors, some of whom went bankrupt. Fortunately, Fitzpatrick had already been replaced with a French native.

Cultural Differences/Marketing Issues

The firm's senior marketing strategist presented the second part of the report, which focused on cultural and marketing differences between the U.S. and European markets.

The first phase of the analysis had uncovered a number of obvious problems, some of which had already been rectified. The purpose in identifying these problems, the consultants said, was to be able to be sensitive and to identify other, possibly more subtle cultural and marketing problems.

While attendance was initially strong at the park, the length of the average stay was considerably different than at the U.S. parks. Europeans stayed in Euro Disney an average of 2 days and 1 night, arriving early in the morning of the first day and checking out early the next day. By comparison, the average length of the visit in the United States was 4 days. In large part, this was because the American parks in Florida and California had multiple parks in the immediate areas, while there was only one park at Euro Disney.

Attendance at the park was also highly seasonal, with peaks during the summer months when European children had school vacations and troughs during nonvacation periods. Unlike American parents who would take their children out of school for vacations, European parents were reluctant to do this. Europeans were also accustomed to taking one or more longer vacations, while Americans favored short mini-vacations.

Revenues from food were also significantly lower at Euro Disney compared with the other parks, the report found. Three of the reasons that had been identified just after the park had opened were related to misunderstandings about European lifestyles. The initial thinking was that Europeans did not generally eat a big breakfast and, as a result, restaurants were planned to seat only a small number of breakfast guests. This proved incorrect, with large numbers of people showing up for fairly substantial breakfasts. This problem was corrected by changing the menus as well as providing expanded seating for breakfast through the expansion of cafeteria facilities. While the park offered fast-food meals, they were priced too high, restraining the demand. This problem, too, had been taken care of by reducing the prices at the fast-food restaurants. At the U.S. parks, alcohol was not served, in keeping with the family-oriented values. The decision not to serve alcohol at Euro Disney failed to account for the fact that alcohol is viewed as a normal part of daily life and a regular beverage with meals. This error, too, was rectified after it was discovered.

Revenues from souvenir shop sales were also considerably below those in the other parks, particularly Tokyo Disneyland. In Japan, great value was placed on purchasing a souvenir from the park and giving the souvenir as a gift to friends and family upon one's return home. Europeans were far less interested in purchasing souvenirs.

In the initial design of the project, it was assumed that Europeans would be like Americans in terms of transportation around the park and from the hotels to the park attractions. In the United States, a variety of trains, boats, and tramways carried visitors from the hotels to the park. Although it was possible to walk, most Americans chose to ride. Europeans, on the other hand, chose to walk rather than ride, leaving the vehicles significantly underutilized. While not directly affecting revenue, the capital as well as ongoing costs for this transportation were considerable.

It was also assumed, given the automobile ownership statistics in Europe, that the majority of visitors would drive their own cars to Euro Disney and that a relatively small number of tourists would arrive by bus. Parking facilities were built accordingly, as were facilities for bus drivers who would transport passengers to the park. Once again, the initial planning vastly underestimated the proportion of visitors who would arrive by bus as part of school, community, or other groups. Facilities for bus drivers to park their buses and rest were also inadequate. This, too, was a problem that was initially solved.

The consultant concluded this portion of the presentation by saying that these were just a few examples of problems that resulted from a misunderstanding of the differences between the U.S. and Japanese parks that had already been identified. Most likely, he said, there were a number of other similar problems that needed to be identified and fixed.

Environmental and Location Factors

Next to speak was a team that included experts from an environmental planning firm. This presentation would be brief, since the problems that they identified were virtually impossible to correct at this stage in the project.

They initially noted that given the location in middle to northern Europe and the fact that there were only about six months of temperate weather when it was truly pleasant to be outside, the park was clearly sited in a location that did not encourage visitors on a year-round basis. Although accommodations were made (including the covered sidewalks), the fact that off-season visits had to be heavily discounted and promoted to groups to get even reasonable attendance still represented a major problem that needed to be corrected. Whether through pricing changes or the development of other attractions or other marketing and promotional vehicles, attendance in the off-peak months had to be increased.

The second problem that they identified, the location east of Paris rather than to the west, was also something that could not be rectified. It was reported that this was again related to overconfidence on the part of the initial planning team, which thought that even though most Parisians who would visit the park currently live west of the city, the longer-term population growth would be in the east. Consequently, it was felt that the park should be built in the east. Again, they noted, Disney executives disregarded the initial advice of the French.

French Labor Issues

Next to speak was a European labor economist. This problem, which stemmed from differences in the United States and Europe, could potentially be solved. Disney did not understand the differences in U.S. versus European labor laws, he said. In the United States, given the cyclicality and seasonality of the attendance at the parks, U.S. workers were scheduled based on the day of the week and time of year. This provided U.S. management with a high degree of flexibility and economy in staffing the park to meet peak visitor demand. French labor laws, however, did not provide this kind of flexibility and, as a result, management could not operate Euro Disney as efficiently and labor costs were significantly higher than the U.S. parks.

Financing and the Initial Business Plan

The consulting team had hired a major global investment banking concern to review the plan, identify the problems, and develop a restructuring plan.

The firm's senior managing director spoke: "Financing and the assumptions of the initial business plan is the area that has created the greatest problems for the park; its restructuring is most critical to the ability of the venture to continue operating and become profitable and, as a result, is the most important problem that needed to be addressed short term."

His presentation identified the following problem areas:

1. The initial plan was highly optimistic and extraordinarily complex. There was little room for error in this plan, which was based on overleveraged financial scenarios that depended on the office parks and hotels surrounding the park to pay off, rather than the park itself.

    In addition to the plan being highly leveraged, significant cost overruns in the construction of the park further increased the start-up costs, making the achievement of the promised returns even more unlikely.

    Disney itself had imposed on arbitrary deadline of March 31 to develop a refinancing package with the creditor banks, further putting pressure on developing a credible and viable restructuring plan. A separate team was already at work to develop such a restructuring plan.

2. The initial plan was presented as financially low risk; shares were largely sold to individual investors with little tolerance for risk.

    The plan was constructed in the mid-1980s, a period of high-flying free-market financing in the United States. European investors did not understand these kinds of deals and propositions.

3. A severe European recession, a drop in the French real estate market, and revaluation of European currencies against the French franc severely undercut all of the assumptions on which the plan was depending in order to succeed.

4. Euro Disney management, faced with the problem of trying to achieve an unrealistic plan, had made serious errors in pricing.

    Among the mistakes were charging $42.25/day for admission to the park compared with a $30 daily fee for the U.S. and Tokyo parks. Hotel prices were set similarly, with a room costing $340, equivalent to a top hotel room in Paris. Inside the park, food prices were also too high.

Competition from U.S. Disney Parks

Finally, given the strengthening of the European currencies against the French franc and U.S. dollar, it was often less expensive for Europeans to travel to the United States, especially Florida. Not only did their currencies buy more, but there were other attractions surrounding Orlando and the weather was warm and sunny year around. In addition, the U.S. park provided the real experience compared with the European simulation.

WHAT TO DO?

The consultants' phase-one report was concluded. As these problems were identified, teams had already been formed to develop potential solutions to the problems that could be solved. The investment bankers were already examining restructuring options. While it was critical to enable the park to remain open beyond the March 31 deadline, the long-term issues appeared to be in the area of marketing. In particular, park attendance and revenues per visitor needed to be increased while providing value and meeting Europeans' expectations about the Euro Disney experience.

The meeting adjourned after the group had agreed that phase two of the consultants' report, identifying action plans for the most critical issues, would be presented on March 15.

DISCUSSION QUESTIONS

1. What did Disney do wrong in its planning for Euro Disney?
2. What recommendations would you make to Disney to deal with the problems of Euro Disney?
3. What lessons can we learn from Disney's problems with Euro Disney?

Euro Disney (B)

THE FIRST BIENNIUM: "MELTDOWN AT THE CULTURAL CHERNOBYL"

In the 24 months since it first opened in 1992, the Euro Disney theme park suffered from the confluence of a number of environmental and internal problems. On the one hand, Euro Disney was adversely affected by an untimely European recession and a strong French franc, which, when combined with the park's high admission prices, conspired to keep European tourists from visiting the park and from spending money once they got there. Also, the financial performance of the park was greatly restrained by a massive debt burden. This debt was largely due to the cost overruns incurred in building the park combined with a slump in the French property market, which had left Euro Disney with a number of hotels—each built with borrowed money—that it had originally hoped to sell once the park

---

This case was prepared by Paul D. Ellis, Assistant Professor, The Hong Kong Polytechnic University. Used with permission.

became operational. In all, the interest charges for fiscal year (FY) 1993 came to around US$1 million per day.

Although the parent company, Walt Disney Company, was quick to blame the poor performance of its French subsidiary on the adverse conditions in the European environment, in reality these uncontrollable problems were exacerbated by the arrogant attitude and cultural naiveté of the American management. Inspired by their record financial performance during the 1980s, the Disney team had led itself to believe that it had perfected the recipe for success. In striving to apply this formula in the European market, however, Disney succeeded only in alienating its French stakeholders, namely the creditor banks, the minority shareholders, the labor unions, and, most importantly, the general public.

To its credit, Disney responded proactively and decisively once its mistakes had been recognized. To counter the perception of management hubris, Walt Disney actively promoted Europeans into the top management team. Robert Fitzpatrick, the French-speaking American chairman of Euro Disney SCA, was replaced by Philippe Bourguignon, a Frenchman who had spent 10 years working in the United States. The new chairman initiated a number of measures aimed at repositioning the theme park as a less expensive and more efficiently run resort. The admission price charged to locals was lowered and the park's stores had the number of lines of merchandise reduced from 30,000 to 17,000. In the Euro Disney hotels, labor-saving magnetic cards replaced meal vouchers, and the number of food items offered was slashed from 5,400 to 2,000. Moreover, a central purchasing department replaced the separate arrangements each hotel had had with its own suppliers. Finally, staff in 950 administrative posts, equivalent to 8.6 percent of the total workforce, were laid off in late 1993.

At the same time, environmental conditions in the European market were improving. Not only was the European economy coming out of recession, but the opening of the Channel Tunnel, combined with the 50th anniversary of the Normandy Invasion, augured well for the tourist season of 1994.

Yet, despite these measures and environmental changes, Euro Disney's future was never darker. Attendance figures recorded for FY 1994 were only 8.8 million, the lowest since the park had opened, while total revenue from the park and the five hotels fell 21 percent to FFr1.16 billion. As one French analyst observed with perspicacity and clarity: "They're getting fewer visitors at a lower price; that's definitely no good at all."

Why had the number of visitors fallen? Largely because of circulating rumors that Euro Disney was about to be closed down. As far back as the end of 1993, Euro Disney's financial situation had deteriorated so much that the usually upbeat Michael Eisner, who had earlier labeled Euro Disney "probably the best thing we ever built," distanced himself from the prodigal subsidiary by stating in his annual report to Walt Disney shareholders:

We certainly are interested in aiding Euro Disney SCA, the public company that bears our name and reputation. We will deal in good faith. . . . But in doing so, I promise all shareholders of the Walt Disney company that we will take no action to endanger the health of Disney itself.

Statements such as these were no doubt intended to communicate Walt Disney's reluctance to bear the brunt of the growing financial burden of the theme park.[1] By distancing itself from its subsidiary, Disney hoped to counter the widespread perception among Euro Disney's other stakeholders that it had cut a "sweet deal" in structuring its relationship with the theme park. Back in 1989, when Euro Disney SCA had been floated, Walt Disney had purchased 49 percent of the new company's shares for FFr10 each. In contrast, public shareholders paid FFr72 and later, when the theme park had opened in 1992, share prices had soared to FFr164.

In all, Walt Disney had arranged US$4 billion to finance the park, of which they had contributed only US$170 million (for a 49 percent equity stake) while the public had paid $1 billion (for the remaining 51 percent). The rest of the start-up capital (nearly $3 billion) had been borrowed. Also included in the initial deal was a management fee of 3 percent of gross revenues, an increasing "incentive management fee" of 30 to 50 percent of pretax cash flow, and royalties of 5 percent and 10 percent on food and admission, respectively. This meant that the parent company could make money even while Euro Disney was running at a loss. Indeed, analysts predicted that the profit per visitor to Euro Disney would actually decrease as attendance went up due to the proportion of fees that was to be repatriated to Walt Disney.

However, when Euro Disney's debt reached FFr20 billion, this no-lose deal for Walt Disney meant that banks would no longer lend money to the French subsidiary without a guarantee from the parent company. Thus, Euro Disney became an Achilles' heel to the parent company, giving Walt Disney its first quarterly net loss (in September 1993) since Michael Eisner had become chairman in 1984.

In the end, things had come to a head as Euro Disney simply ran out of cash. Walt Disney provided emergency funds, but it also imposed a deadline for a restructuring of the subsidiary's financial arrangements: Walt Disney had no intention of injecting further funds beyond the end of March 1994. Euro Disney's fate was sealed, and its stakeholders were compelled to come up with a rescue plan that either eliminated some of the crippling interest burden, converted

---

[1] *The Economist* suggested on 5 February 1994 that Michael Eisner was scaremongering in order to push down Euro Disney's share price to minimize the amount Walt Disney would have to pay out the event of a rights issue. In hindsight, it appears that this may have indeed been the motivation for his comments.

debt into equity, or raised funds by some other means. The question was, who would pay how much and when?

THE RESCUE PLAN

A number of issues affected the restructuring activities and influenced the bargaining power of the major stakeholders. On one side of the equation, Euro Disney's 63 creditor banks and bondholders agreed that Walt Disney should carry much of the burden for the bailout, reflecting its relationship with the French company. However, Walt Disney's legal relationship was with Euro Disney SCA, the operating company, and not with the beleaguered theme park itself, which was owned by a finance company that leased the park back to the operating company. (Disney had just a 17 percent stake in the finance company.) Nevertheless, the banks argued that the park was Disney's "creation and responsibility"—after all, Euro Disney's top management had been put in place by Walt Disney—and, consequently, called for "an asymmetrical sharing of the pain."

On the other side of the equation, Walt Disney wanted the banks to write down some of their debt or to convert the debt into equity. Although it appeared that Disney was not bargaining from a position of strength, the parent company did have the option of putting Euro Disney into bankruptcy, a position from which it could dictate the terms of the restructuring.

However, although Michael Eisner had hinted at closing the park, there were a number of good reasons why Disney probably would not exercise this option, not the least of which would be the impact on Disney's already tarnished corporate image in France. Conversely, some of the French banks, including the recently privatized Banque Nationale de Paris, were concerned about the risk of substantial losses and the consequent effect on their credit ratings. Similarly, other stakeholders (such as the French government) also stood to lose if the theme park closed and the 40,000 jobs that were indirectly related to the park were eliminated. Thus, there was some speculation that the state-owned Caisse de Depots and Consignations, which was Euro Disney's largest creditor with FFr4.4 billion in loans, might be compelled to lower its interest rates. However, despite the common interest in keeping Euro Disney afloat (Exhibit 1), drafting a rescue plan that would satisfy all the stakeholders seemed problematic.

Just prior to the March 31 deadline, Euro Disney was at its lowest point financially, with debts now approaching FFr24 billion. Curiously, a glimmer of hope was to be found across the Atlantic in the growing interest of U.S. "vulture" funds, which had begun purchasing Euro Disney debt at around 60 percent of face value. These secondary debt–market transactions reflected growing speculation that the debt would eventually be worth substantially more than what it was being purchased for.

Finally, 2 weeks ahead of schedule, a rescue plan was announced. In essence, the plan contained two elements. First, the plan comprised a deferment of interest and royalty payments. Specifically, the creditor banks forgave 18 months of interest payments and postponed principal payments for a period of 3 years. This reflected a saving to Euro Disney of FFr1.9 billion. Conversely, Walt Disney said it would eliminate management fees (worth FFr450 million per year) and royalties on sales of tickets and merchandise for a period of 5 years. It would, however, still receive an *incentive* fee based on Euro Disney profits. Finally, Disney agreed to purchase some of the park's underutilized assets for FFr1.4 billion and lease them back on terms favorable to Euro Disney.

The second part of the plan called for a rights issue to raise funds, which would be used to eliminate debt. This issue worked by giving existing shareholders the right to purchase a number of shares at below-market prices (FFr10) in the same proportion as their present equity stake. In this case, shareholders were to be permitted to subscribe to seven new shares for every two shares held. This meant that Disney would end up paying just under FFr3 billion for 49 percent of the offering.

The rights issue was approved by a meeting of shareholders on 8 June 1994. (Getting shareholder approval was a mere formality given the size of Walt Disney's holdings.) Euro Disney's share price immediately fell, reflecting the dilutive nature of the issue. Nevertheless, the rights issue succeeded in raising a total of FFr5.95 billion, which enabled Euro Disney to reduce its debt burden by 23 percent to FFr16.1 billion.

In evaluating the efficacy of the rescue plan, it is worth noting how the major stakeholders fared in the exercise. First, who were the winners? Although the plan called for the parent company to substantially increase its financial

EXHIBIT 1	Euro Disney's Stakeholders and Their Financial Interests
Walt Disney Co.	Total outlay of US$350 million (~FFr2.1 billion): based on initial outlay of $170 million for 49% equity and the subsequent injection of emergency funds
Public shareholders	Initial outlay of US$1 billion (~FFr6.4 billion) for subscribed shares
63 Creditor banks	FFr14 billion in loans
French government	Provided US$750 million (~FFr4.4 billion) in low-interest loans, built road and rail links to the park, and sold Disneyland at low prices
Bondholders	FFr4 billion of convertible bonds

stake in Euro Disney—an additional US$750 million on top of the $350 million already spent—Walt Disney benefited from the plan because the fees it deferred would have been lost if the park had closed down. Moreover, the concessions they made served to improve their tarnished corporate image in the French market. The banks were pleased with the deal because they did not end up owning or managing the park's assets, while Euro Disney's bondholders were happy just to be excluded from the plan. Finally, it is safe to assume that the labor unions and the French government also benefited from the bailout.

The only clear losers in the rescue plan were the minority shareholders. With 770 million shares now in the market—about four times the original number—Euro Disney's earnings per share inevitably fell, as did the company's share price. On the day the rights issue was announced, Euro Disney's market capitalization dipped 8 percent to FFr34 per share, and by the end of the month, shares were worth just FFr12.9. However, things were about to get worse before they got better, and within 2 months Euro Disney's share price had dropped to just FFr7.55 (Exhibit 2).

Despite the drop in its share price, the magnitude of the devaluation of Euro Disney's market capitalization was minimized by the timely appearance of a new player in the market. In the spring of 1994, Prince Al-Waleed bin Talal bin Abdulaziz Al Saud, the 37-year-old nephew of Saudi Arabia's King Fahd, announced his intention to purchase a significant equity stake in the company. By mid-October, the prince had acquired 74.6 million shares, reflecting a 24.6 percent equity stake (acquired for around US$350 million). Some of these shares had been purchased from Walt Disney, whose stake in the company had consequently been reduced from 49 percent to 39 percent.

THE SECOND BIENNIUM: EURO DISNEY GETS A REPRIEVE

The rescue plan effectively gave Euro Disney a 3- to 5-year reprieve from its interest and royalty charges. However, implicit in this reprieve was the mandate to make Euro Disney a profitable company as soon as possible, and Philippe

Bourguignon and his staff wasted little time in enacting a revamped marketing strategy geared to this objective.

Perhaps the most significant marketing change made was the renaming of the theme park itself. The name "Euro Disney" had been chosen in a period of pre-1992 unification hype. However, events in the past few years had seen some commentators come to equate Euro Disney with Euro Disaster. Consequently, and to reflect the new lease on life that had been given to it by the rescue plan, Euro Disney renamed the theme park "Disneyland Paris" to capitalize on its proximity to the French capital, the world's top tourist destination. (Euro Disney SCA would remain the name of the operating company.) By a fortuitous twist of fate, the newly renamed park received some timely publicity when Michael Jackson and Lisa Marie Presley visited Disneyland Paris on their honeymoon.

At the end of 1994 a 22 percent reduction in admission prices for the 1995 peak season was announced (Exhibit 3). Simultaneously, further efficiency measures were introduced. The park's total workforce had now been reduced to 12,000 from 17,000, of which 4,000 staff were employed on a seasonal basis. Moreover, new trainees were now required to undergo 6 to 12 months of training. Previously, new staff had received only one day of training. Also, negotiations with labor unions were under way to make staffing arrangements more flexible, in line with fluctuating attendance patterns. This meant that staff would now work longer hours on weekends and during the summer months when demand was greatest.

Other changes included the decentralization of decision-making authority to "small world" units consisting of 30 to 50 staff, with each unit given responsibility for achieving management targets and improving visitor satisfaction. Managers of these autonomous units would received performance-based bonuses whereas other staff, or "cast members," would receive nonfinancial rewards, such as better promotion prospects.

At the end of FY 1995 the cumulative effect of these changes in strategy and the rescue plan were evident. Not only did the park receive a record attendance of 10.7 million visitors (Exhibit 4) but Euro Disney SCA also recorded its

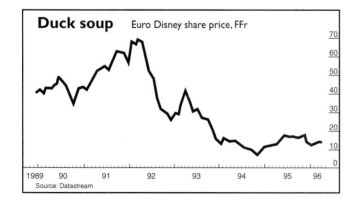

EXHIBIT 2   Euro Disney's Share Price

EXHIBIT 3	Admission Price Changes	
	Adult Price (FFr)	
	Peak (1 April–1 October)	**Off-peak**
Old price	250	175–225
1995 price	195	150

EXHIBIT 4	Annual Attendance Figures
(FY ending 30 September)	
1993	9.8 million
1994	8.8 million
1995	10.7 million

first-ever profit (Exhibit 5). However, it is sobering to note that the reported profit of FFr114 million is overstated because of the deferred royalty and interest payments and Euro Disney's buyback of 2.7 million convertible bonds. Profit before exceptional items was only FFr2 million.

Although the figures for 1995 indicated that Euro Disney SCA had turned the corner, much remained to be done in the next few years before the long-term viability of the venture could be established. Although Disneyland Paris has become Europe's number one paid tourist destination, there is a clear need to increase attendance even further. Philippe Bourguignon estimated that the park needs 12.5 million visitors per year to break even once royalty demands and interest payments resume in 1998. This figure, which before 1995 seemed an impossible target, even now appears highly optimistic.

Such an attendance target seems even more unlikely when the rapidly rising level of competition within the European amusement park industry is taken into consideration. While U.S. Disney parks posed a competitive threat in the early 1990s, the appearance of a number of new theme parks in Europe, such as Spain's Port Aventura, which opened in May 1995, and Germany's Warner Brothers Movie World, is likely to present a greater threat in the late 1990s. Despite high barriers to entry, many new parks are being built while established parks are investing in new attractions. Much of this demand-driven investment activity has been stimulated directly by the marketing appeals of

Euro Disney. In 1993, an estimated 58 million people spent around US$1.5 billion on Europe's theme parks. As the managing director of the United Kingdom's Thorpe Park observed, "We enjoyed 1993 on the back of Disney's promotional budget, but it's a tough and competitive business."

Indeed, with around 30 to 40 amusement parks, Western Europe is fast coming to resemble the North American market where Disney is the dominant player among a crowd of competitors (including Six Flags, Universal Studios, and Sea World). However, unlike North America, where there typically are clusters of parks in close proximity in places such as Orlando and Southern California (thus creating an incentive for visitors to stay a week or more in each locale), in Europe the amusement parks are scattered across the continent.

In addition to the direct competition from parks such as Alton Towers, the United Kingdom's largest theme park, Disneyland Paris also competes indirectly with other entertainment-based attractions such as roller-coaster parks, including Blackpool's Pleasure Beach and Goteborg's Liseberg. Furthermore, a new competitive threat is also emerging in the form of computer-based interactive entertainment, which has led to the establishment of a number of tourist attractions such as Sega's new Virtual World Center, located in London's popular Trocadero complex.

Competition in the amusement park industry is perhaps most evident in the introduction of new rides and attractions. For example, Euro Disney's record-breaking attendance figures for 1995 were positively influenced by the opening of Space Mountain, a roller coaster ride based on Jules Verne's book, *From the Earth to the Moon*. Across the Channel, Alton Towers also enjoyed record attendances in 1995 based largely on the crowd-pulling power of two newly opened rides, Nemesis and Energiser, while in Barcelona the Tussaud's-owned Port Aventura promotes its Dragon Khan roller coaster as being the first to turn thrill seekers upside down eight times.

THE THIRD BIENNIUM: WHAT TO DO?

In seeking to increase the attendance of Disneyland Paris and ensure the sustained profitability of the company beyond 1998, Philippe Bourguignon must deal with a number of issues.

1. How should the park differentiate itself from the competitive threat posed by the growing number of European amusement parks?
2. What target marketing strategy should be pursued in the face of the changing competitive environment?
3. What branding-strategy decisions are relevant?
4. What can be done to make better use of underutilized resources (such as the hotels) while increasing the profitability of well-patronized facilities?

EXHIBIT 5	Euro Disney Profit and Loss	
(FY Ending 30 September)		
	Revenue	**Profit (Loss)**
1993	4.9 billion	(5.3 billion)
1994	4.1 billion	(1.8 billion)
1995	4.8 billion	114 million

SOURCES: "Mickey Goes to the Bank," *The Economist,* 16 September 1989, pp. 78–79; "Introducing Walt d'Isigny," *The*

Economist, 11 April 1992, p. 53; "The Future of the Past," *New Statesman and Society,* 29 May 1992, pp. 31–31; "The Not-So-Magic Kingdom," *The Economist,* 26 September 1992, pp. 87–88; "Disney Records Loss on Charge for Europe Park," *The Wall Street Journal,* 11 November 1993, p. A3; "Disney's Eisner Gives 'D' Grade to Euro Disney," *The Wall Street Journal,* 30 December 1993, p. A2; "Marketing Changes Boost Euro Disney as Debt-Restructuring Talks Approach," *The Wall Street Journal,* 13 January 1994, p. A3; "Restructuring of Euro Disney Hits Bond Snag," *The Wall Street Journal,* 1 February 1994, p. A11; "Meltdown at the Cultural Chernobyl," *The Economist,* 5 February 1994, pp. 65–66; "Euro Disney Mulls Renaming Park to Highlight Paris," *The Wall Street Journal,* 13 September 1994, p. A14; "Big Stakes in a 'Small World,' " *The Financial Times (London),* 13 January 1995, p. 12; "Theme Parks Expect Thrills and Spills," *The Financial Times (London),* 1 May 1995, p. 2; "A Faint Squeak from Euro Mickey," *The Economist,* 29 July 1995, p. 44; "Bourguignon, Into the Black and off for a Break in Tahiti," *The Financial Times (London),* 31 July 1995, p. 7; "Investors Sing the Theme Song: The Park Market Is Becoming Increasingly Crowded," *The Financial Times (London),* 16 August 1995, p. 15; "Step Right Up, Monsieur," *The New York Times,* 23 August 1995, p. 1, C1; "Euro Disney Makes Communication Its Theme," *The Financial Times (International),* 16 November 1995, p. 20; "Euro Disney Posts First Annual Profit, Stock Slides 14%," *The Wall Street Journal,* 16 November 1995, p. A15; "The Kingdom Inside a Republic," *The Economist,* 13 April 1996, pp. 68–69.

Coca-Cola: Universal Appeal?

On April 15, 1996, Douglas N. Daft, the President of the Middle and Far East Group for Coca-Cola Company was in a quandary. He had just come back from a senior executive committee meeting where the main focus was on the concern over the additional investment in India and China, two countries that reported directly to him. He was baffled by the concern the committee was placing on funding these new investments. Coca-Cola's strategy had always been to take risks in emerging markets. It had always understood the need to be first in new markets to gain the competitive advantage. Even in tough markets, Coca-Cola ultimately wins market share. For instance, during apartheid in South Africa, the company stayed in the country by maintaining a presence through independent bottlers while Pepsi left the country. Coke now dominates the market.

Daft could not understand the committee's reluctance to go ahead with these investments. China's market potential was vast. With a population of 1.2 billion and per capita consumption of only four (meaning each person in China consumed only four 8-ounce servings of a company beverage per year), the opportunities were infinite (see Exhibit 1). The investment slated for China was to build five additional plants in 1996 and two more in 1997, which would bring the total number of plants to 23. A recent survey done by the company indicated that Coke and Sprite were the two leading soft drink brands in China. In addition, China's gallon sales grew by 30 percent last year.

India's market potential was similar to China's. Its population of 936 million and per capita consumption of two also made it a desirable market to be in. Although gallon sales were up 21 percent over 1995, there was a concern about antimultinational sentiment. The company already had a large, visible presence there, and given the negative attitude toward large multinationals, the committee felt further investment might not be a financially prudent decision at that time.

Daft quickly got on the phone to John Farrell, head of the China Division, and Andrew Angle, head of the Southeast and West Asia Division, to discuss this new turn of events. Information needed to be gathered, and things need to be hammered out before going back to committee with his recommendations. What were the political and economic risks of these two countries and how could it affect Coca-Cola? If Coca-Cola chose not to increase its investment in these countries, would it be missing out on an opportunity to further establish itself in these markets and to gain market share?

Coke articulated its vision in its annual report: "We have become mindful of one undeniable fact—the average body requires at least 64 ounces of liquid every day just to survive, and our beverages currently account for not even two of these ounces. For every person on this planet, consuming at least 64 ounces is not an option; but choosing where those ounces come from is." Daft's concerns addressed this vision.

BOTTLING

During the 1980s, Coca-Cola aggressively acquired smaller family-owned bottlers in the United States. Between 1980 and 1984, bottlers representing 50 percent of the company's volume underwent a change of ownership. Small, family-owned bottlers were purchased by either the company or large regional bottlers. This was done in order to control bottlers so that the company had the ability to do nationwide advertising, knowing that their bottlers would do the complementary promotional activities, as well as aggressive discounting when needed.

During the 1990s, Coke began the implementation of a program consolidation and company investment in

This case was prepared by Donna Cristo, doctoral candidate, Pace University, Lubin School of Business.

EXHIBIT 1	Per Capita Consumption and Market Populations	
Per Capita[a]	**Markets**	**Population (in Millions)**
179	Argentina	35
292	Australia	18
169	Benelux/Denmark	31
122	Brazil	162
181	Canada	29
248	Chile	14
4	China	1,221
107	Colombia	35
30	Egypt	63
71	France	58
201	Germany	82
114	Great Britain	56
125	Hungary	10
2	India	936
8	Indonesia	198
232	Israel	6
87	Italy	58
136	Japan	125
71	Korea	45
322	Mexico	94
45	Morocco	27
256	Norway	4
105	Philippines	68
65	Romania	23
6	Russia	147
147	South Africa	41
179	Spain	40
60	Thailand	59
343	United States	263
60	Zimbabwe	11

[a] 8-ounce servings of company beverages per person per year (excludes products distributed by Coca-Cola Foods).

bottling operations in the rest of the world. Currently, Coke is consolidating its bottlers in markets overseas.

Today, Coca-Cola is investing heavily in bottling operations in order to maximize the strength and efficiency of production, distribution, and marketing. Their strategy is to get involved in the bottling business so that it fuels continued growth of their syrup business. The company has three criteria for making a bottling investment:

1. The company needs to move quickly in an emerging market
2. When an existing bottler lacks the resources to meet the company's objectives
3. To help ensure long-term strategic alignment with key bottling partners

BRAND EQUITY

The Coca-Cola trademark is invaluable. If all of the company's assets burned to the ground today, it would have no trouble borrowing the money to rebuild, based on the strength of its trademark alone. Its brand is pervasive around the world. Exhibit 2 indicates how strong the brand Coca-Cola is in specified markets. The company's strategy for sustaining its brand image is the **three Ps:**

1. Pervasive **Penetration** in the marketplace
2. Offering consumers the best **Price** relative to value
3. Making Coca-Cola the **Preferred** beverage everywhere

In addition, Coca-Cola is finding new ways of building relevant value into Coke and all its other brands by further differentiating them, making them unique and distinctive. Three years ago, the company abandoned the use of entrusting all advertising and marketing to one single agency. Now, agencies are selected on the basis of their particular expertise in enhancing a particular brand; this year, agency compensation is being tied to the results their ads produce.

Moreover, Coca-Cola is reigniting the symbols that encapsulate the essence of its brand—the Dynamic Ribbon device, the contour bottle for Coke, the Coca-Cola script, the color red, and the dimpled bottle for Sprite. The new contour bottle, which was launched in April 1994, is credited with increasing sales by 500 million cases globally in 1994. Through June 1995, volume increases for Coke were approaching 45 percent in the United States, 23 percent in Japan, and 30 percent in Spain. In addition, it is currently linking its brands with one-of-a-kind events and activities such as the Olympic Games in 1996 and doing more in-store promotions and displays, especially in the U.S. market where growth is considered slow.

Coca-Cola's commitment to building and sustaining its brand image is indicated by the amount of money it spends on marketing. For instance, in 1995, the company spent $3.8 billion for marketing. Ad spending, which is still considered one of the best tools for building brand equity, was $1.3 billion. Its major rival, PepsiCo, spent more on advertising, at $1.8 billion but had to allocate these funds for its restaurant and snack-food segments as well.

FINANCIALS

Coca-Cola is the largest and most profitable soft-drink company in the world. Over a 10-year period, revenues have grown at a compound growth rate of 11.9 percent. By 1995, worldwide revenues exceeded $18 billion, and net income was a little under $3 billion (see Exhibit 3). Its operating income margin outpaced its major competitor, PepsiCo, significantly. While PepsiCo's beverage segment operating margin was 10 percent for 1995, Coca-Cola's was 23 percent. Its superior performance is further indicated

EXHIBIT 2	How Strong Is Brand Coca-Cola?		
	Market Leader	*Leadership Margin[a]*	*Second Place*
Australia	Coca-Cola	3.9:1	Diet Coke
Belgium	Coca-Cola	7.7:1	Coca-Cola light
Brazil	Coca-Cola	3.3:1	Brazilian brand
Chile	Coca-Cola	4.6:1	Fanta
France	Coca-Cola	4.3:1	French brand
Germany	Coca-Cola	3.1:1	Fanta
Great Britain	Coca-Cola	1.9:1	Diet Coke
Greece	Coca-Cola	3.8:1	Fanta
Italy	Coca-Cola	3.1:1	Fanta
Japan	Coca-Cola	2.3:1	Fanta
Korea	Coca-Cola	2.1:1	Korean brand
Norway	Coca-Cola	3.3:1	Coca-Cola light
South Africa	Coca-Cola	4.1:1	Sparletta
Spain	Coca-Cola	3.0:1	Spanish brand
Sweden	Coca-Cola	3.8:1	Fanta

Share of soft drink sales.

[a]Over second-place brand.

Source: Company data/store audit data.

by its return on equity, which was 56 percent in 1995, and its market year-end price of $74.25 at the end of 1995, which showed an appreciation of 44 percent.

Coca-Cola's strong financial performance over the last 5 years has been due primarily to increased expansion overseas, especially in the company's bottling and canning operations. In fact, international operations account for the majority of Coca-Cola's revenues and operating profits: In 1995, the company derived 71 percent of its revenues and 82 percent of its operating profit outside the United States

EXHIBIT 3	Consolidated Statements of Income			
Year Ended December 31 (In Millions Except Per-Share Data)	*1995*	*1994*	*1993*
Net Operating Revenues	$18,018	$16,181	$13,963
Cost of goods sold	6,940	6,168	5,160
Gross Profit	11,078	10,013	8,803
Selling, administrative, and general expenses	6,986	6,297	5,695
Operating Income	4,092	3,716	3,108
Interest income	245	181	144
Interest expense	272	199	168
Equity income	169	134	91
Other income (deductions)—net	20	(104)	(2)
Gain on issuance of stock by Coca-Cola Amatil	74	—	12
Income Before Income Taxes and Change in Accounting Principle	4,328	3,728	3,185
Income taxes	1,342	1,174	997
Income Before Change in Accounting Principle	2,986	2,554	2,188
Transition effect of change in accounting for postemployment benefits	—	—	(12)
Net Income	$2,986	$2,554	$2,176
Income per Share			
Before change in accounting principle	$2.37	$1.98	$1.68
Transition effect of change in accounting for postemployment benefits	—	—	(.01)
Net Income per Share	$2.37	$1.98	$1.67
Average Shares Outstanding	1,262	1,290	1,302

(see Exhibits 4 and 5). Coke operates in 200 countries and employs 32,000 people worldwide.

CURRENT INDUSTRY OUTLOOK AND TRENDS

The U.S. soft-drink market is considered mature, growing at approximately 3 percent to 4 percent annually. This is down considerably from the 1985 growth rate of 6.5 percent. In 1994, domestic retail sales were $52 billion, up 2.6 percent, year to year. Coca-Cola had 41 percent of the retail market and Pepsi had 31 percent. Coca-Cola's growth outpaced the industry at 7 percent and accounted for 80 percent of the U.S. soft drink's industry growth last year.

Although there is increased competition from other beverage choices, soft drinks remain the beverage of choice among U.S. consumers, accounting for more than one of every four drinks consumed. Colas continue to dominate the soft drink category but are slowly losing market share. They were 66 percent of all soft drinks consumed in 1994, down from 70 percent in 1990. International markets appear to mirror this trend.

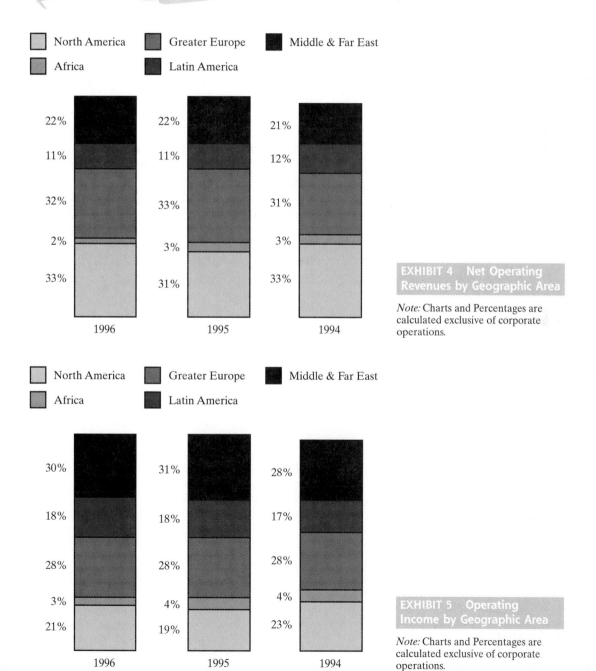

EXHIBIT 4   Net Operating Revenues by Geographic Area

Note: Charts and Percentages are calculated exclusive of corporate operations.

EXHIBIT 5   Operating Income by Geographic Area

Note: Charts and Percentages are calculated exclusive of corporate operations.

The international market has been the high growth segment in the beverage industry, growing at 8 percent to 10 percent annually.[1] In 1996, Coke sales grew at 8 percent, and it had 47 percent of the world market. Growth rates varied considerably around the world. Some emerging markets grew phenomenally. For example, last year China grew at 32 percent and Brazil grew at 52 percent. In 1997, worldwide growth was expected to be 6 percent to 7 percent for soft drinks. The highest growth was expected from developing Asian countries, including China, India, Korea, and Indonesia. Moreover, continued growth from South America was expected. Internationally, Coke outsells Pepsi three to one.

COMPETITION

Coca-Cola's major competitor is PepsiCo (see Exhibit 6). PepsiCo has three segments: beverage (35 percent of total revenues), snack foods (28 percent), and restaurants (37 percent). Over a 10-year period, revenues have grown at a compound rate of 15 percent. In 1995, $1.6 billion was generated from $30.4 billion of revenues, representing a net income margin of 5 percent (see Exhibit 7). Its growth has been fueled by the success of its beverage and snack-foods segments.

PepsiCo's beverage income was $10.5 billion for 1995, and it generated $1.3 billion in operating profit, representing a 10 percent margin. Although overall beverage revenue and operating income were up 9 percent and 8 percent, respectively, its significant revenue growth came from overseas, at 13 percent. Yet, international revenue and operating profit accounted for only 34 percent of total beverage revenue and 12 percent of total beverage operating profits (see Exhibit 8).

To gain more market share internationally, Pepsi is unveiling a comeback plan called "Project Blue," which is expected to cost $500 million. It calls for revamping manufacturing and distribution to get a consistent-tasting drink around the globe, as well as an overhaul of marketing and advertising. The most risky part of the program calls for giving up the red, white, and blue can in favor of an electric blue one. In addition, Pepsi-Cola plans to establish new freshness standards and quality controls. Currently, Coke outsells Pepsi three to one overseas; however, Pepsi predicts that with its new marketing plan it will be able to close the gap to 2 to 1 by the year 2000. According to *The Economist,* this could be a risky strategy, considering the fact that Pepsi has spent decades convincing consumers that Pepsi in a red, white, and blue can is cool to drink. Image is a delicate thing. By changing the color of its can, it may appear to consumers that Pepsi-Cola is trying too hard to convince them to drink their brand, and thus, this plan may come off as just another blatantly obvious gimmick.[2]

INTERNATIONAL MARKETS

Coca-Cola's worldwide philosophy has been:

We understand that as a practical matter our universe is infinite, and that we, ourselves, are the key variable in just how much of it we can capture.[3]

Coca-Cola always sees 64 daily ounces of opportunity. It currently has 2 percent of the world's daily consumption of 64 ounces of liquid. In emerging markets, its potential remains high, as 60 percent of the world's population live in markets where the average person consumes less than 10 servings of Coca-Cola products per year.

For decades, Coca-Cola has had an established position in foreign markets. The first foreign office was started in 1926, and by the 1940s and 1950s, Coke was already entrenched overseas. In 1950, *Time* magazine wrote, "Coke's peaceful near conquest of the world is one of the remarkable phenomena of the age. It has put itself always within an arm's length of desire."[4]

EXHIBIT 6 U.S. Soft Drink Market Share (Percent)						
	1989	*1990*	*1991*	*1992*	*1993*	*1994*
Coca-Cola	40.1	40.4	40.7	40.4	40.4	40.7
PepsiCo	31.8	31.8	31.5	31.3	30.9	30.9
Dr. Pepper/7Up[a]	9.9	9.9	10.6	11.2	11.4	11.6
Cadbury Schweppes	5.0	5.0	5.0	5.0	4.9	4.8
National Beverage	2.2	2.1	2.1	2.0	1.9	2.0
Royal Crown	2.7	2.6	2.4	2.3	2.2	2.0

[a]Cadbury Schweppes acquired Dr. Pepper/7Up on March 2, 1995.

Source: S&P Industry Surveys, August 24, 1995, p. F26.

[1] Timothy J. Muris, David T. Scheffman, and Pablo T. Spiller, *Strategy, Structure, and Antitrust in the Carbonated Soft Drink Industry.* (Westport, CT: Quorum Books, 1993).

[2] "Turning Pepsi Blue," *The Economist,* 13 April 1996, p. 15.
[3] Coca-Cola Annual Report, 1995.
[4] Beverage World, *Coke's First 100 Years* (KY: Keller International Publishing Corporation, 1986).

EXHIBIT 7   PepsiCo Consolidated Statement of Income

(In Millions Except Per-Share Amounts)
PepsiCo, Inc. and Subsidiaries
Fiscal years ended December 30, 1995, December 31, 1994, and December 25, 1993

	1995 (52 Weeks)	1994 (53 Weeks)	1993 (52 Weeks)
Net Sales	$30,421	$28,472	$25,021
Costs and Expenses, Net			
Cost of sales	14,886	13,715	11,946
Selling, general, and administrative expenses	11,712	11,244	9,864
Amortization of intangible assets	316	312	304
Impairment of long-lived assets	520	—	—
Operating Profit	2,987	3,201	2,907
Gain on stock offering by an unconsolidated affiliate	—	18	—
Interest expense	(682)	(645)	(573)
Interest income	127	90	89
Income Before Income Taxes and Cumulative Effect of Accounting Changes	2,432	2,664	2,423
Provision for Income Taxes	826	880	835
Income Before Cumulative Effect of Accounting Changes	1,606	1,784	1,588
Cumulative Effect of Accounting Changes			
Postemployment benefits (net of income tax benefit of $29)	—	(55)	—
Pension assets (net of income tax expense of $15)	—	23	—
Net Income	$1,606	$1,752	$1,588
Income (Charge) Per Share			
Before cumulative effect of accounting changes	$2.00	$2.22	$1.96
Cumulative effect of accounting changes			
Postemployment benefits	—	(0.07)	—
Pension assets	—	0.03	—
Net Income Per Share	$2.00	$2.18	$1.96
Average shares outstanding	804	804	810

EXHIBIT 8   PepsiCo Beverage Revenue and Operating Income

				% Growth Rates	
($ in Millions)	1995	1994	1993	1995	1994
Net Sales					
U.S.	$6,977	$6,541	$5,918	7	11
International	3,571	3,146	2,720	14	16
	$10,548	$9,687	$8,638	9	12
Operating Profit					
Reported					
U.S.	$1,145	$1,022	$937	12	9
International	164	195	172	(16)	13
	$1,309	$1,217	$1,109	8	10
Ongoing[a]					
U.S.	$1,145	$1,022	$937	12	9
International	226	195	172	16	13
	$1,371	$1,217	$1,109	13	10

[a]1995 excluded the initial, noncash charge upon adoption of SFAS 121.

Today, the international segment has grown so much that it now contributes 71 percent to total revenue. Because of the importance of international markets to Coca-Cola's future growth, it has eliminated its prior structure of two groups—international and domestic—and formed five operating groups: North America, Latin America, Greater Europe, the Middle and Far East, and Africa. The breakdown of unit case volume by group is found in Exhibit 9. As indicated by the pie chart, North America, which includes the United States and Canada, accounted for the largest, at 32 percent, and Latin America accounted for 24 percent of sales. Greater Europe and the Middle and Far East accounted for 21 percent and 18 percent, respectively. Africa trails at only 5 percent.

The hottest battles between Coca-Cola and PepsiCo will be in international markets, especially emerging ones. First-mover advantages can be crucial in the international soft-drink war. The strategic challenge is to establish greater brand awareness and preference through advertising on a scale similar to that of the domestic market. Another challenge is to make their brands as accessible and ubiquitous as they are in the United States. This is not often easy, and the effort often requires the direct intervention of the country managers (CMs) to secure improvements in the efficiency, cooperation, and competitive aggressiveness of overseas bottlers. For example, in 1995, Coca-Cola acquired bottling interests in Italy and Venezuela and took steps to consolidate its system in Germany. Although Coca-Cola controls the wealthy markets of Greater Europe, PepsiCo has been more successful in emerging markets such as India, the Arab

nations of the Middle East, and Russia. Entry into new markets has often required creative maneuvering and increasingly flexible accommodations by the CMs.

As the war heats up between Coca-Cola and PepsiCo, both CMs will be forced to take more risks. Pepsi is a company going global 50 years late and cannot afford to follow the leader, Coca-Cola, but must alter the market as indicated by its "Project Blue" plan. Moreover, PepsiCo has rejuvenated the Pepsi Challenge for overseas markets. In 1994, PepsiCo launched its first challenge internationally in Mexico, one of Pepsi's largest markets. The result was that 55 percent preferred Pepsi over Coke. In addition, PepsiCo plans to stage these challenges worldwide in such markets as Singapore, Malaysia, and Portugal. PepsiCo's international commitment is both long term and aggressive, as indicated by its approval of a $2 billion investment plan over 5 years for the international beverage segment, starting in 1994.

Of course, Coca-Cola does not take these aggressive moves sitting down. Coca-Cola will fight back, as it did with the Pepsi Challenge, by slashing prices, purchasing bottlers, and creating slick ads and promotions.

DAFT'S REPORT TO THE COMMITTEE

Douglas Daft recently met with John Farrell, who was responsible for China, and Andrew Angle, who was responsible for India. Both Farrell and Angle wished to go ahead with the investments in their respective countries. However, Douglas Daft was not sure he had enough information on the political and economic risks of each country to make an informed decision. Thus, he asked Farrell and Angle to update him on the political and economic status of their respective countries. After he read their reports, he would make his recommendations to the senior executive committee. Their reports are reproduced in Appendices I and II.

DISCUSSION QUESTIONS

1. What is Coca-Cola's international strategy?
2. What competitive advantages does Coca-Cola have over its major rival, PepsiCo?
3. What are the pros and cons of Coca-Cola's investing further in India's market?
4. What are the pros and cons of Coca-Cola's investing further in China's market?
5. What should Douglas Daft recommend to the senior executive committee concerning further investment in the emerging markets of China and India? Why?

APPENDIX I

The India Report by Andrew Angle, Southeast and West Asia Division

In 1994, India's economy grew at 6 percent; 8 million new jobs were created, and there was $818 million of U.S. direct investment. For all these positive signs, however, it appears

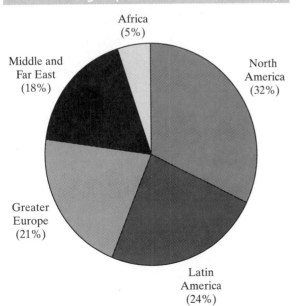

EXHIBIT 9   1995 Worldwide Unit Case Volume by Region (Worldwide Total: 12.7 Billion)

Africa (5%)

Middle and Far East (18%)

North America (32%)

Greater Europe (21%)

Latin America (24%)

that there has been a backlash against the economic reforms started 5 years ago. Why? First, for the 190 million Indians who live below the poverty line, 5 years of economic reforms have not improved their standard of living. Millions of poor believe that only the elite have benefited from economic liberalization. Second, soaring short-term interest rates, coupled with competition from foreigners, have hurt local businesses and caused enthusiasm for further economic change to wane. Now that foreign companies can increase their investment to 51 percent, up from 40 percent, in most industries and even 100 percent in others, some locals worry that foreigners will run roughshod over them.

Third, the Hindu right, led by the Bharatiya Janata Party (BJP), is divided over just what kind of foreign investment should be allowed. The BJP has adopted a much-used phrase—"microchips, not potato chips"—to describe what sort of investment should be allowed.[5] Thus, it appears that the BJP is against big American consumer brands such as PepsiCo, McDonald's, Colgate, and even ourselves, and they are the ones protesting against the multinationals. Pepsi's KFC braved protests and saw one of its outlets briefly closed. Most of the antimultinational sentiment has been against American companies, which bear the brunt of Indian worries about cultural imperialism. In contrast, Japanese and German companies encounter few such problems.

Last, these antimultinational demonstrations are being allowed to continue due to the upcoming democratic elections, which will begin on April 27 and finish on May 7. The existing Indian government, led by Prime Minister P. V. Narasimha Rao, dismisses these protests against foreign companies as grumblings of fringe groups. In truth, Rao and his government face stiff competition from the BJP and do not want to alienate voters by seeming to be pro foreign. Therefore, the existing government does little to defend these companies in the eyes of the public.

India's legal system, though it may be slow, provides some recourse against failure to perform in contracts. For instance, India backed away from a $2.8 billion power project with Enron, an American company. Negotiations are resuming primarily because Enron has a cast-iron case for compensation.

However, the most fundamental problem is that a backlash has set in before India has taken the most painful changes. The government has not touched sacrosanct labor laws that make it virtually impossible for any company employing more than 20 workers to lay anyone off. In addition, India must come up with a policy to deal with the state sector. About 200 of the country's 220 centrally owned companies are chronic money losers. Heavy borrowing by government companies—$60 billion from the central government alone—drives up interest rates.

Regardless of who wins the upcoming election—Rao's government, the BJP, or the Left–Front National Front, they will not turn back reforms already taken place. Some foreign investors have turned bullish on India, pouring $1.2 billion in the Bombay exchange for the first 4 months of 1996. Some companies such as McDonald's, Baskin–Robbins, and PepsiCo are moving ahead with investments despite the difficulties. The risk is that India's reforms will not be quick enough to appease the growing discontent among its large population. Moreover, there are many examples of foreign investors who have already had great success in China, but there are relatively few in India.

APPENDIX II

The China Report by John Farrell, China Division

According to a *Business Week* article entitled "Rethinking China":

> In stunningly short order, a powerful China has emerged. As an economic force, it is entering and altering the global marketplace—and in some cases—writing its own rules.[6]

China had a $35 billion trade surplus with the United States last year, whereas its own markets remain closed in sectors where U.S. businesses are competitive. Moreover, China is notorious as one of the world's greatest rip-off artists and bent on strong-arming U.S. and European companies into transferring jobs and technology as the cost for entering its markets. Although China has cleaned up some intellectual property abuses, piracy remains rampant, and the toll on U.S. businesses is growing. Trade officials estimate that bootlegging in China cost U.S. business nearly $2.5 billion in lost sales last year, far exceeding the $866 million in 1994.

Tax preferences for foreign investors have been scaled back, and there currently is a proposal to change the tax system in a way that puts foreign businesses at a disadvantage to local ones. In addition, foreign companies in China must grapple with changing central government rules, grasping local officials and capricious local business partners. The central government is cracking down on joint ventures that provincial officials used to wave through. In addition, contracts are not always enforceable in Chinese courts.

However, there is growing evidence that firms that are prepared to shrug off such obstacles and build a business presence in China will be rewarded. The playing field may be tilted against foreign companies, but domestic rivals are barely up and running. In the more open climate, domestic companies already competing are not able to rely so heavily on their connections, privileged information, and crony networks. Thus, the battle for China's markets has

---

[5] Sharon Moshavi, "Get the 'Foreign Devils,' " *Business Week,* 23 October 1995, pp. 48–50.

[6] Joyce Barathan, Stan Crock, and Bruce Einhom, "Rethinking China," *Business Week,* 4 March 1996, pp. 57–58.

been and will continue to be played out by foreigners for the time being.

This is especially true in the fast-moving consumer-goods markets in which gross margins average 18 percent to 25 percent, partly due to the fact that the Chinese love a good brand. Just as in the United States, Procter & Gamble fights Unilever for Chinese consumers. Many multinationals contend that transferring technology is largely risk free. Many pioneers in China have reaped rewards without creating new competitors. Yet, China's effort to milk more out of foreigners means few secrets are really safe. The demands on multinationals to help make Chinese industry competitive are unrelenting. For example, Microsoft, under threat of having its software banned, codeveloped a Chinese version of Windows 95 with a local partner and agreed to aid efforts to develop a Chinese software industry.

To keep control of China's economy, Communist leaders are retreating on many risky economic policies, which means no major reform of state enterprises or the banking system—both seen as crucial to completing the transformation of China's economic system. There are two reasons. First, to control economic growth and its resulting inflation, Vice Premier Zhu Rongji engineered an austerity program in 1993 to curb inflation; it worked. Growth in 1995 slowed to about 10 percent from 12.6 percent, a year earlier, while retail price increases eased from 21.7 percent in 1994 to 15 percent in 1995. Second, the central government fears that the poor inland provinces are falling too far behind. Many of its 700 million peasants live in near-feudal conditions, and

100 million have flooded into cities looking for work. The government fears that high unemployment will only fuel crime and corruption, which is already on the rise.

This recentralization is an attempt to enable the central government to set the pace of economic development rather than cede the power to the coastal provinces. The most needed reforms are in the state sector, which is one of the biggest drags on the economy. However, because state-owned factories employ 50 percent of the urban population, the leadership will not let them go bust. Yet, the state's companies churn out goods that nobody wants and then demand loans from the state banks, ultimately causing more inflation.

Nevertheless, other economic reforms are accelerating, such as a convertible currency tied to outside financial markets and regulations to protect intellectual property rights. The best hope for major reform is for China to enter into the World Trade Organization (WTO) because as a member, China would be forced over a designated period of time to liberalize its economy by dropping many trade barriers. However, chances of China's entering are slim. China would like to enter with developing-country status, which would allow it to protect domestic industries from foreign competition, but the United States would like China to enter on terms similar to those of other industrial nations.

The bottom line is that China's already large economy is set to double in the next 8 years, making it the world's sixth-largest economy, and those companies anxious to get access to China's riches are willing to take the risks.

The Education of an Expat

Upon returning to the United States after 10 years of working with Siemens in Germany, Tom Miller was asked to recap his impressions for a training program for international business personnel at his new company. During his tenure in Germany, he had observed hundreds of small differences and several major differences between German

and American attitudes. Although these attitudes do not apply to every German nor to every American, they should be considered in business and social situations. He identified 11 of the most important differences in a memo to his colleagues, which is reprinted here.

This case was written by Mr. Tom Miller, President of Carl Zeiss, Inc. It is intended as a basis for class discussion rather than to illustrate either effective or ineffective handling of a management situation. Copyright 2000 by Dr. Warren J. Keegan.

TO: Associates

FROM: Tom Miller

SUBJECT: The Cultural Differences—My Experience

I have had a number of meetings since coming to Zeiss in which I have been asked to comment on some cultural differences that I observed between the American style of work and the German style of work during my delegation in Eriangen with Siemens. Therefore, I thought I would put my thoughts in writing so they could be shared as part of our attempt to build a "learning organization."

As this could easily be a book, I will only highlight the differences that stand out most clearly. There are literally hundreds of small differences that I do not have the time or desire to mention here. In addition, as with all generalizations, this is a dangerous assessment. There is a high statistical fluctuation among individuals and so many of my comments may not apply to an individual situation. I am also not an expert here. So take care, these are my opinions only.

My last comment before I begin is that I was absolutely shocked by how large the cultural differences were between the working environment in Germany and in the United States. My 10 years of previous experience working with Germans in the United States led me to the false belief that the Germans were not all that different from the Americans. This is probably because the Germans I interacted with were trying to act "American." The differences are there, and they are not small.

I will categorize my comments into the following topics:

1. Attitude toward work and the separation between work and life
2. Homogeneity and the tolerance of individuality
3. The role of humor
4. Directness versus politeness
5. The show of emotion
6. Intelligence versus "street smarts"
7. Past versus future orientation
8. The need to place blame
9. The respect for authority
10. The team versus the individual
11. The role of the ego

The foregoing topics are listed in no particular order. It is only my attempt to bring some order to a jumble of impressions.

1. Attitude toward work/separation between between work and life:

   One of the first most striking observations of the workforce I managed in Germany was their attitude toward work itself. This is one of great pride but also seriousness. The German word *Ernst,* which does not directly translate into English, is an attitude that can be found in American employees but is not a dominant trait. In addition, the Germans I knew tended to have a much more distinct separation between their work life and their private life. Americans tend to blend these two together with personal relationships extending into the office environment and beyond. I heard one German express it with the short phrase, *"Arbett ist Arbett und Schnaps ist Schnaps,"* which I took to mean that the mixture of work and pleasure is something that does not naturally go together.

Many Americans on the other hand, tend to believe that their work is their life. Often times there is a very small distinction between the two and social gatherings may be based upon business contacts and many social events are really nothing more than informal opportunities to discuss business.

The German attitude toward work might make an American believe, at first Impression, that the work environment is a sterile, humorless, and dry place to be. While this is only true to a certain extent, what is more interesting is that not much more is expected by the average German worker of his workplace (this attitude is definitely changing with the younger generation of German workers). In other words, work is not supposed to be fun—it is only supposed to be work!

This positive aspect of this, however, is that when times are less pleasant and when the tasks are more boring, mundane, tedious, or distasteful, the German workforce seems to be much more willing to endure without complaint. The separation between work and life means that if work is unpleasant, it is only a temporary and maybe even expected unpleasantness. A demotivated German workforce will produce more than a demotivated American workforce.

To an American, since work is life, the unpleasantness is clearly unacceptable as no one wants to have an unpleasant life. As in most of these categories, on the balance there is no net advantage or disadvantage to this cultural difference. It is simply a difference that has to be recognized and worked around.

2. Homogeneity and the tolerance of individuality:

The Germans seem to regard social and cultural homogeneity as something that is highly desirable. Although this became apparent to me in discussions with my neighbors (where it was clearly indicated to me exactly how I should maintain my garden, how I should clean the street in front of my house, and where I should park my car, etc.). It was also apparent in the workplace. While we can all see how the American legal system certainly has created many more rules and regulations and bureaucracy than currently exists in Germany, the German social system has a great deal more spoken and unspoken rules of behavior that need to be strictly obeyed.

My impression was that there was much less tolerance for a lack of conformity. People who exhibited odd or eccentric behaviors were spoken about in a very negative way. It was as if it were impossible to rationalize the fact that even a person who appears or behaves differently could still be very productive. This may be easily explained by the history of the two cultures. America is a land of immigrants, all of who come from widely divergent cultures and backgrounds. Thus, Americans have been historically forced to live with more divergent forms of behavior and cultural inconsistency.

Once again, this has its positive and negative apsects. When the need for conformity is high and it is important to uniformly implement a procedure, it may be easier to do so in the German culture. In contrast however, individual ideas and behaviors that may be highly unusual or unique may be suppressed. And, as we know, such contributions may be an important wellspring of creativity.

3. The role of humor:

The Germans are seen by the Americans (as is indicated by the many jokes about this trait) as a very serious and almost humorless people. While my experience is contrary to this, it is true that Americans place a much higher value on the role of humor in the day-to-day workplace.

Germans will often find Americans cracking jokes and laughing during the most serious and difficult of discussions. The German reaction may be to take this to indicate a lack of commitment or seriousness on the part of the Americans but nothing can be further from the truth. Americans simply place a very high value on having fun in the workplace (see theme 1). An individual who can dissolve tension through the use of humor, creating in the process a more relaxed work environment (and one that is more fun), is thought to possess a desirable trait.

Once again this relaxed attitude is very often misinterpreted by the German and can lead to some serious tensions and difficulties in communication. Much of the joking of Americans is black humor and serves an important role in characterizing the underlying seriousness of the issue (although cloaked in humor). Thus, there are instances where some of the joking of Americans during a meeting is actually intended to be taken seriously and may be intended to push forward a difficult discussion. This type of joking will often be misinterpreted by the Germans present at such a meeting. In addition, I have seen Germans become frustrated by the Americans' lack of seriousness toward an issue that they believed should be treated with a tough, unsmiling attitude.

I believe theme 5 in this report conveys one of the underlying reasons for this cultural difference.

4. Directness versus politeness:

Early during my time in Eriangen, I had the opportunity to take part in a seminar in Feidefing (the Siemens management training center) and found myself embroiled in a heated argument with a young female manager from another German Bereich. The topic was her perception of Americans as a dishonest people. She had spent 6 months working in the United States and came back with the single strong impression that Americans were incapable of conveying the truth in their dealings with others. She said that Americans would never directly express what they truly thought about a person or situation and that their actions were often in direct contradiction to the attitude that they openly expressed in meetings. The examples she gave me to support her arguments indicated a clear misinterpretation of what was being said in the situations with which she was confronted.

The basic problem is that Americans will couch their criticism in such polite terms that often the message is simply missed by the Germans. The language barriers make this cultural misinterpretation even more likely to occur.

On the other hand, to the Americans, the Germans seem so brutally direct and confrontational that, if we were not to excuse the fact that they are Germans and, therefore, somehow different, the Americans would normally take great offense at what is being said.

I must say I found many of the tougher meetings in Germany to be distinctly uncomfortable and even stressful simply from the directness of the language being used. Such open attacks on people, situations, and problems would never be tolerated in an American meeting and would be interpreted as a total breakdown in relations and even an indication of open warfare. It is the direct attacks on the individuals themselves that Americans find so uncomfortable.

Once again there are no defined advantages or disadvantages to this cultural difference. If the subtleties of the American polite way of expressing problems would be correctly understood (as they are by most Americans) there would be no misinterpretation of the seriousness of a situation or actions of an individual. On the other hand, to a German, it will seem that the problems are being glossed over or avoided.

3

The direct approach of the German style, while more efficient, can be incredibly stressful to the majority of the Americans. The result may that the Americans simply stop listening and become more focused on the style of the interaction rather than the content.

It is also important to understand that there are American regional differences here as well. As someone born and brought up in the Northeast, I tend to be much less polite and much more direct than my counterparts from the Midwest and the West Coast. Even though my individual and personal characteristics make me, in some ways, more "German," I still could not always overcome my very stressful and adverse reaction to the direct German confrontational approach in discussions even after 3 years in Germany.

5. Show of emotions:

This topic is related to the preceding one in that the outward manifestation of a reaction an idea or incident may be severely misinterpreted by the other party.

Although Americans may be seen as more emotional, I found that this trait was unidirectional and counterbalanced by an even greater show of emotion on the German side. Americans are very willing to display what may be termed the positive emotions such as those of enthusiasm, happiness, excitement, surprise, and delight. However, Americans are extremely reluctant to show what might be considered the negative emotions such as anger, fear, resentment, disappointment, or disgust.

Interestingly enough, I found that the Germans are much more willing to openly display emotions on this other side of the scale (the so-called negative emotions listed earlier). This may have a great deal to do with the "directness versus politeness" theme. The Americans may deem it to be less polite to show open disgust at the behavior of another rather than to mask that emotion. In addition, emotional control is a prized trait among Americans. The ability to show no emotion at all during a stressful situation and to remain relaxed is considered to be a positive attribute. To "stay cool," "never let them see you sweat," "keep your head while all about you are losing theirs," etc. are all expressions in the language that demonstrate this value. Once again, when a German is expressing his anger over a situation very openly, directly, and confrontationally, the American will often sit silent and passive. This is partially out of the desire on the part of the American to show control (which means he is winning the confrontation) and partially because we simply do not know how to react to such direct displays of seemingly negative emotions.

Once again, there is no net advantage or disadvantage to this cultural difference. My belief is that, if everyone would show a bit more emotion throughout the emotional range we would have a more direct and understandable means of communication. Unfortunately, some of the positive emotions may seem silly to the Germans while the negative emotions are simply unacceptable to the Americans. That there is little overlap between acceptable displays of emotions is a cultural problem that must be clearly understood by both parties.

6. Intelligence versus street smarts:

To me this category is the most interesting of all of the differences that I have observed. However, I have read very little about it in the articles and books I have reviewed citing the cultural differences between Germans and Americans.

The German hero or cultural icon is often a man of great intellect and breeding. Well educated, extremely well spoken with a very precise elocution, intensely logical and rational, these are attributes that can be assigned to a large number of German cultural heroes. The German philosophers, poets, scientists, and musicians are serious men of awesome intellectual standing.

Americans, on the other hand, often look down at intellectuals. They are the butt of jokes, called names and made fun of ("professor long-hair," "nerd," "four-eyes," "geeks," etc.). The American hero is smart without being intelligent. He is able to make a simple analysis of very complex situations, reach a conclusion, and act upon it without a very long intellectual process. Even our most revered philosophers and poets possess a more "down-home" country wisdom than raw intellect (Mark Twain, Will Rogers, and Robert Frost spring to mind).

In many American movies the villain is very often portrayed as someone who is much more intelligent while the hero may be seen as being somewhat dumb and ill-educated. Even in movies where the villain is a foreigner (often German or Russian), the foe is better trained, more highly educated, more refined in taste and breeding, and probably of a higher raw IQ. However, the American hero always wins in these films because his street smarts and common sense are more highly prized than intelligence and education.

This distinction leads to some of the most interesting and difficult cultural misinterpretations that I have experienced. I would summarize it with the following phrase: The German tries to make the simple look hard, and the American tries to make the difficult look easy.

During a presentation or discussion of any topic, the German presenter will show openly the detailed analysis that has gone into making his pronouncements. All data will be gathered and displayed. Different scenarios will be put forward, quickly analyzed, and then tossed aside. The presentation can be highly complex with many more charts and graphs of greater analytical detail shown and expected for any given problem. It is obvious that the presenter wishes to demonstrate both the technical complexity of the problem at hand as well as his own highly intellectual approach in solving the problem.

The American, on the other hand, will attempt to make the most complicated problem extremely simple. He will often hide much of the analysis that may have gone into solving the problem and try to present the solution as something that is so intuitively obvious that anyone with a little common sense would easily reach the same conclusion—without any work or thought whatsoever. It is also thought that such detail is uninteresting as the conclusions are so intuitively obvious.

Both sides are, of course, lying. The American has often done much more work than is presented and will attempt to make the analysis look almost so simple that a child could have reached it. Looking behind many German presentations, we find that the analysis may not have been as detailed and iron-clad as has been presented. But the attempt is made to show that there is such in-depth research that is impossible to find a single data point or detail that has not been intensively analyzed or discussed.

The difficulty with these two styles is that the Americans often believe that the German has over-analyzed the problem and has missed very obvious points due to the need for such deep detail. The American expression, "He missed the forest due to the trees" captures this thought. They may also become bored by a long discussion of the analysis and lose attention waiting for the conclusion that they would have presented immediately at the beginning of the presentation.

But worse is the German tendency to believe that all Americans are sloppy, tend not to do their homework, and that the relaxed style of presentation means that they are coming to conclusions without the needed analysis or backup. A great difficulty for the German is to be able to distinguish between those Americans whose relaxed style masks a large amount of analysis and homework versus those Americans who use this trait to hide the fact that they (as suspected) have done too little analysis. The fact that a presentation may appear sloppy has little to do with whether the conclusions that are drawn are based upon sloppy research or a very in-depth analysis.

This difficulty leads to the situation in which Germans listening to an American presenting a problem will more intensively question the underlying analytical detail. The American often does not come prepared to present such detail (even where it exists) as they believe that no one would really want such a boring presentation of dry data. In addition, the constant questioning may be interpreted by the American as indicative of a lack of trust and may create resentment. Frankly, now having seen both sides, I understand easily why this situation often occurs and even find myself now acting "German" as I more intensively question American presentations.

7. Past versus future orientation:

One of my American bosses used to say that it was easy to tell the difference between an American and a German presentation: The American presentation would begin with an analysis of the events of this morning and would immediately leap to future pronouncements and outlook. The German presentation would start in the time of the Roman conquest, with an in-depth analysis of all historical events from that time to the present day, before he could possibly start to talk about the future plans of action. This trait may indeed be connected with the intelligence versus street smarts theme and leads to the same result; that Americans will often become extremely bored by German presentations and find themselves unable to wait through a lengthy review of the past in order to get what they consider to be the only thing that's relevant—what we do next.

8. The need to place blame:

This theme is a bit one-sided and something that I, to this day, don't clearly understand. If a group of Americans are confronted with a difficult situation, obviously as a result of a mistake by a team or individual, they will often gloss over the reason for the problem or who is responsible for the mistake. The mistake will often be discussed by using the word *we* ("We have made an error in our anaylsis," "We have misinterpreted the situation," "We did not see this problem coming," etc.). Everyone in the room is aware of who has caused the problem or who has made the mistake but often it is not openly and clearly stated.

In many German meetings that I have attended, there is the need to clearly place blame on a responsible individual before the problem can be analyzed. I have often been very frustrated by trying to use an American approach and could not stop the discussion of who is to blame or who is responsible or how the problem occurred so that we could move forward with an action-oriented solution. Often, I simply gave up and sat back to let the placement of blame occur so that we could move forward. This trait is, to an American, very difficult to understand and I can see no advantage to it. Once again, this may be due to my own personal cultural bias.

9. The role of authority:

This is also a difference that was easy to discern after only a short time in Germany. Authority plays a distinctly different role in decision making and actions than in an American corporate culture.

My experience as a manager in Germany was, at first, very confusing. I often found that mere suggestions, ideas, or comments that I would casually make in conversations would be interpreted as something I have dictated to the organization and that needs to be carried out to the letter. I would often question the individuals as to why they are implementing some action only to find that I was responsible (that I had made some offhand comment during a discussion, which was then taken literally and without question as a command to implemented).

At the same time, I was not seen in Germany as being a strong manager. One criticism of my performance by my employees was that I was not tough enough (this contrasts with my reputation in the United States). Upon discussion with my employees, we discovered that there was often a huge misinterpretation between things I believed I was communicating in a very strong and direct manner versus those that they took to be possible ideas or suggestions to consider.

An example of this cultural difference is in the use of the words *must* and *should.* Although these two words can be directly translated from English to German and they are even cognates of each other, their uses are very different. The German manager will often use the word *must* in conveying direction to his employees. The American manager restricts the use of the word *must* to employees who have shown the inability to think for themselves or act on their own. The strong use of the word *must* is, thus, interpreted by the American employee as almost a reprimand. My use of *sollen* in Germany was, therefore, not taken strongly enough.

I believe the root cause of this confusion is the desire for the German employee to have a manager with a very direct style. Although these attributes are also desirable in the United States, the ways in which they are expressed are very different. Combine this with the greater need of the American for personal freedom and one can have real confusion. The tough German manager will seem (to an American) to be almost dictatorial. The tough American manager will seem (to a German) decisive but not as forceful.

There is one last observation on this issue that I cannot explain. In the United States, the lower levels of the organization have much less respect for authority and are much more apt to disobey a command and not follow procedures than their "same level" counterparts in Germany. However, the upper levels of the organization in the United States have a greater obedience to authority than their "same level" counterparts in Germany. I often saw an attitude in Germany where relatively high levels of the organization felt that they could disregard the directions of their superiors. This would not occur to the same extent in the United States. This may be due to the greater feeling of job security in Germany, which increases the higher one goes in the organization. In the United States, to some extent, job security decreases the higher one rises in the organization. This may explain the level-dependent differences in the degree of conformity to authority in the two organizations.

10. Team versus the individual:

As working in teams is now both a trend and a tactic used in all companies in the attempt to increase productivity, I can say that I saw stylistic differences in teamwork between German and American teams but no real functional differences. On the surface, German teams seemed to function less well. There is more dissentions, open confrontation, and inability or reluctance to openly cooperate. I first misinterpreted this as a German inability to work well in teams and was very angered by it. It was only after my return to the United States that I saw this in a different perspective.

American teams, on the surface, seem to function much better. There is a great deal more harmony and a great deal more willingness to cooperate and to suppress dissenting opinions for the common good of the team. However, often this is simply a manifestation of the American politeness mentioned before. More often than in Germany I found that, after the meeting, the Americans feel less bound by the team decision and often more willing to break from the conformity

7

of the team decision and go their own way. Therefore, while the German team may take much longer to reach a similar conclusion, and while they may find themselves facing much more difficulties in working together, it also allows them to hammer out differences more openly (and often more painfully) during team meetings, which may result in a higher conformity after the team decision is made. The American lack of respect for authorities (even the authority of the team), coupled with the increased emphasis on the individual, may lead to the superficial appearance of better teamwork but the actual fact of less cooperation and more dissention.

The foregoing will also mean that Americans integrated in a German team will find themselves frustrated by the appearance of a total lack of commitment to team spirit and not understand that this is simply the cultural difference of as more confrontational working style.

One last team issue that I often encountered was the reaction of the team to new ideas. In an American team meeting, a new idea is greeted as something good—just because it is new. It will then be discussed and, if a flaw if found in it through discussion, it will be discarded.

In Germany, a new idea is often viewed as intrisically bad. Looked upon negatively from the very beginning, the idea must fight for survival. If it survives the attack, it may then be considered.

The result of the different approaches to ideas is that Germans have the tendency to kill ideas at birth and may lose a few good ideas. The Americans will have the tendency to attempt to implement ideas that are not analyzed critically and will often allow the survival of too many bad ideas.

11. Show of ego:

One last and almost trivial comment is the fact that Americans are much more willing than Germans to brag and openly take credit for work they have done. I found myself being embarrassed by the American display, of "me," "me," "me," and "I have done this" and "I have done that" during a presentation. I have the feeling that this is offensive to many German audiences and certainly something for Americans to watch for (myself included).

Summary:

As I originally stated, I was shocked by the magnitude of cultural difference between Germans and Americans when I first went to Eriangen. I was blissfully ignorant of the degree of difficulties that an American might have managing in a German environment. I would highly recommend a much more intense preparation period before such a delegation. Hopefully, through better preparation, my mistakes could be avoided and greater productivity would result.

Tom Miller

DISCUSSION QUESTIONS

1. Are Miller's experiences valuable as a training tool for expats?
2. How should this information be utilized in his new company's training program?
3. What are the major differences in culture between the Germans and the Americans?
4. Argue both pro and con that global cultural differences are declining.
5. Do these 11 differences relate to marketing and, if so, how?

CHAPTER 5

Global Customers

"The Chinese leadership is trying to demonstrate that a country can have a powerful modern economy without allowing its people the individual freedoms that the Western World calls 'human rights.' The entire Asian Model is based on a variant of this proposition: that it is possible to become as strong as the Western world without embracing its permissive ways."

—JAMES FALLOWS
Author

CHAPTER CONTENTS

In many ways, consumers around the world are becoming more alike. Almost everywhere in the world, one is never far from a McDonald's, Coca-Cola, and MTV. Several market segments, like the very wealthy, teenagers, and technocrats, even transcend national borders. Yet, despite the decreasing importance of geography as a basis of distinguishing consumers, the average consumers are different around the world. For example, as marketers in the clothing industry know, "Even underwear has national characteristics."

From a marketing perspective, up-to-date economic, demographic, and cultural information must be analyzed to either introduce new products or to develop existing markets. Chapter 2 discussed economic development on a broad basis while Chapter 3 addressed macrocultural considerations. Segmentation is further discussed in Chapter 7. This chapter presents a broad overview of the markets of the world on a regional basis. It describes the characteristics of the major regional markets and includes an extended analysis of the Japanese market. *Warning:* Regional markets, although sharing many characteristics, can be segmented in many ways and always contain segments that are quite distinctive. The following descriptions are meant to be only broad guidelines and each potential market must be thoroughly analyzed. For example, Carrefour recently entered the Indonesian market with a European hypermarche, which has been very successful in serving the emerging middle class of Jakarta. Carrefour would never have opened in Indonesia if its marketing research focused on country data in the aggregate. Its market is the high-income segment, not the country average.

◆ REGIONAL MARKET CHARACTERISTICS

There are various ways of dividing the countries of the world into different regional markets. In effect, defining regional markets is an exercise in clustering countries so that similarities within clusters and differences between clusters will be maximized. A simple approach to clustering is to simply use one's judgment regarding important or relevant criteria. For the most recent information about a country, check the Web sites for the individual countries and also check with the U.S. Department of Commerce. Of course, on-site visits are the best way to gain information. One useful publication is *Doing Business Around the World* by Dun & Bradstreet. (See the box "Sources of Marketing Information for Specific Countries.") In the section that follows, national markets are clustered judgmentally on the basis of geographic proximity. A brief survey of each region is presented; Japan is the subject of a more in-depth analysis.

WESTERN EUROPE

Western Europe, which is physically less than the size of Australia, generated nearly 32 percent of global income in 2000. The region has 23 countries (15 EU and 3 EEA countries, plus Switzerland, the Channel Islands, Gibraltar, Greenland, and Malta) and a total population approaching 460 million. Populations range from 278,000 in Iceland to 83.3 million in Germany.

The countries of Western Europe are among the most prosperous in the world, although income is unevenly distributed in the region. For example, the average per capita annual income in Portugal of $10,797 is 30 percent that of Switzerland's $36,479. Even though there are differences in income and obvious differences in language and culture, the once varied societies of Western Europe have grown remarkably alike. Although there are differences in family and work patterns, they tend to be moving in the same direction. For example, the proportion of women between ages 25 and 34 in the labor force has doubled in the past 30 to 40 years.

The objective of the EU member countries is to harmonize national laws and regulations so that goods, services, people, and eventually money can flow freely across national boundaries. December 31, 1992, marked the dawn of the new economic era in Europe. The EU is attempting to shake up Europe's cartel mentality by handing down rules of competition patterned after American antitrust law. The EU is encouraging the development of a community-wide labor pool; improvements to highway and rail networks are now being coordinated.

The European Monetary System (EMS) is already operating with a European Currency Unit (ECU) or "Euro" as its basis. The ECU exists on paper and in computers, based on a basket of "weighted" currencies. Many companies price their EU supplies and products with the Euro, in preparation for the complete conversion scheduled for 2002. (See section in Chapter 4.) Table 5-1 summarizes the changes that will affect marketers in this region. The marketing challenge is to develop strategies to take advantage of opportunities in one of the largest, most stable, and wealthiest markets in the world. Corporations must determine to what extent they can treat the region as one entity and how to change organizational structures to best take advantage of a unified Europe. Table 5-2 shows how the *Fortune* Global 500 companies are distributed in the EU and other major regional markets.

TABLE 5-1	Marketing Strategies in the European Community		
	Changes Affecting Strategies	***Threats to Marketers' Planning***	***Management's Strategic Options***
Product Strategies	Harmonization in product standards, testing, and certification process	Untimeliness of directives Rules of origin	Consolidate production Obtain marketing economies
	Common patenting and branding	Local content rules	Shift from brand to benefit segmentation
	Harmonization in packaging, labeling, and processing requirements	Differences in marketing research	Standardize packaging and labeling where possible
Pricing Strategies	More competitive environment	Parallel importing Different taxation of goods	Exploit different excise and value-added taxes
	Withdrawal of restrictions to foreign products	Less freedom in setting transfer prices	Understand price elasticity of consumer demand
	Antimonopoly measures		High-margin products
	Widening of the public procurement market		Introduce visible low-cost brand
Promotion Strategies	Common guidelines on TV broadcasting	Restrictions on alcohol and tobacco advertising	Coordinate components of promotional mix
	Deregulation of national broadcasting monopolies	Limits on foreign TV production	Exploit advantage of pan-European media
	Uniform standards for TV commercials	Differences in permitted promotional techniques	Position the product according to local markets
Distribution Strategies	Simplification of transit documents and procedures	Increase in distributors' margins	Consolidate manufacturing facilities
	Elimination of customs formalities	Lack of direct-marketing infrastructure	Centralize distribution
		Restrictions in the use of computer databases	Develop nontraditional channels (direct marketing, telemarketing)

Source: G. Guido, "Implementing a Pan-European Marketing Strategy," *Long Range Planning* (October 1991): 32.

A cultural aspect that greatly affects marketing throughout Western Europe, especially in packaging and advertising, is language. The main languages of the region are English, German, French, and Spanish while the major religion is based on Christianity.

EASTERN AND CENTRAL EUROPE

Eastern and Central Europe include the Balkan countries (Albania, Bosnia-Herzegovina, Bulgaria, Croatia, Macedonia, Montenegro, Romania, Slovenia, and Yugoslavia), the Baltic countries (Estonia, Latvia, and Lithuania), the Commonwealth of Independent States (the former USSR), the Czech and Slovak Republics, Hungary, and Poland. In the early 1990s, extraordinary political and economic reforms swept the region and focused attention on more open markets with over 338 million persons. The former Soviet bloc countries accounted for 6.9 percent of world GDP in 1990 and per capita GNP was $3,665. In 2000, the same countries accounted for 5.5 percent of world population and only 2.5 percent of world GNP with per capita GNP of $2,219. With wage rates much lower than those in Spain, Portugal, and Greece, Eastern and Central Europe represent attractive potential locations for low-cost manufacturing and, given their increasing wealth, are important developing markets.

Today, the differences in economic development vary widely between the countries. Europe's version of economic tigers, Poland ($3,937 per capita GNP), Hungary ($4,429),

TABLE 5-2 How Global Are Various Industries?				
Selected Industries	**Number in Industry**	**United States and Canada**	**EU**	**Japan**	**Non-Triad**
Aerospace	9	7	2	0	0
Banks	63	14	30	9	10
Beverage	5	4	1	0	0
Chemicals	14	2	9	2	1
Computers	11	8	0	3	0
Electronics	25	8	6	8	3
Energy	5	3	1	0	1
Engineering	10	2	2	6	0
Food	10	6	2	0	2
Food and Drugstore	30	12	12	2	4
Forest and Paper	7	4	2	1	0
General Merchandise	13	7	3	3	0
Industrial and Farm Equipment	10	2	5	2	1
Insurance	54	18	16	13	7
Mail Delivery	8	3	3	2	0
Metals	9	1	3	4	1
Motor Vehicles and Parts	24	6	9	8	1
Petro Refining	27	8	6	3	10
Pharmaceuticals	13	8	3	0	2
Specialty Retailers	13	10	3	0	0
Telecommunications	20	10	7	2	1
Trading	19	0	3	11	5
Utilities	19	8	5	5	1
Wholesalers	10	8	2	0	0

Source: The *Fortune* Global 500, *Fortune,* 2 August 1999, pp. F-15–F-21.

and the Czech Republic ($4,957), and the Slovak Republic ($3,593), each adopted radical economic policies, which appear to have been quite successful. The per capita income of each of these four countries places them in the upper-middle income category. Conversely, Armenia, Azerbaijan, Kyrgyz Republic, and Tajikistan, all former republics of the Soviet Union, are still low-income countries. The Russian Federation, for example, accounted for only 1 percent of world GNP in 2000, approximately 60 percent less than that of Mexico. GNP per capita in the Russian Federation was only $2,329, compared to the Mexican level of $3,943. Clearly, Russia in 2000 was a small player in the world market sweepstakes, yet the potential for growth and development in Russia is enormous. Marketing is undoubtedly a key to achieving the economic development of countries in Central and Eastern Europe. It may take several decades for marketing to reach a level of sophistication comparable to Western Europe in some of these countries but change is accelerating and marketing in many of these countries is quite advanced. Many people in these countries, especially the younger people, have "unlearned" the past ways of life and are quickly learning about democracy and capitalism. Countries in these regions need to develop their infrastructures and move beyond capricious legal and contractual frameworks. A business culture needs to be developed as well as a mechanism for forecasting demand. In research that was done with companies in Poland, researchers found that only 38 percent of companies have established a separate marketing department; that the incidence of marketing departments was higher among larger companies and those that export; and

◆ BOX 5-1 ◆

SOURCES OF MARKETING INFORMATION
FOR SPECIFIC COUNTRIES

In *Doing Business Around the World* by Dun & Bradstreet, 42 countries are profiled. Each section contains basic geographic, economic, and business data. Specifically pertinent to marketing are the following sections: age breakdown, religious societal influences on business, cultural tips, protection of intellectual property rights, and cultural notes. For example, the cultural note for Argentina (page 10) contains information that might prove valuable to advertisers and food marketers: Argentina's natural wealth has attracted immigrants from all over the world. Rags-to-riches stories were common, and the phrase "wealthy as an Argentine" entered the world's vocabulary in the late 1800s. Immigrants arrived from England, Ireland, Germany, Poland, and Russia. The parents of Argentine President Carlos Menem came from Syria. Aside from Spain, the major country of origin for Argentines was Italy. As a result, the Spanish spoken in Argentina is heavily influenced by Italian. While it is comprehensible to most Spanish speakers, it is quite unlike the Spanish spoken elsewhere. For South Africa (page 346), it notes that South Africans are big sports fans, and sports are always a good topic of conversation. Rugby is the most popular team sport among white South Africans. After rugby, the most popular sports in South Africa are football (soccer), squash, tennis, and golf. Jogging and bicycling are also very popular, as is swimming (many homes have swimming pools). The Afrikaners have an indigenous sport called *jukskei,* which is analogous to throwing horseshoes. This information would be helpful in determining sports sponsorship programs.

SOURCE: Terri Morrison, Wayne A. Conaway, and Joseph J. Douress, *Doing Business Around the World,* (Englewood Cliffs, NJ: Prentice Hall, 1997).

that industrial companies were spearheading the adoption of separate marketing departments.[1]

Consumer products require minimal adaptation for sales in Eastern European markets. Many Eastern bloc consumers are familiar with Western brand names and view them as being of higher quality than domestic products. Vast improvements have been made in the infrastructure in Central Europe but, unfortunately, the distribution infrastructure in Eastern Europe is weak. Underdeveloped wholesalers, lack of proper warehousing, and the monetary situation still are deterrents to doing business in the CIS. In the countryside, insufficient, poorly lit, and unattractive retail space still exists, which makes shopping frustrating.

Culturally, the most common language is Russian. The major religions are Eastern Orthodox and Roman Catholic. Potato chips, a product that has only begun production in this region since the downfall of the Soviet Union in 1991, have experienced tremendous growth. Estrella, a Swedish brand of potato chips that is produced by the Jacob Suchard division of Kraft in Lithuania and distributed throughout the region, has six different languages on the package: English, Lithuanian, Latvian, Russian, Ukranian, and Estonian.

NORTH AMERICA

North America includes The United States, Canada, and Mexico. In 2000, the combined population of 407 million people and a GNP surpassing $9,254 billion in this region are similar to that of the EU. The United States is a concentration of wealth and income in a single national economic and political environment that presents unique marketing

---

[1] David Shipley and Krzysztof Fonfara, " Organizing for Marketing Among Polish Companies," *European Journal of Marketing,* 27, no. 11/12 (1993): 60–79.

characteristics. The United States, with 276 million people, had a per capita GNP of $29,953. The U.S. market offers the combination of high per capita income, large population, vast space, and plentiful natural resources. High product ownership levels are associated with a high income and relatively high receptivity to innovations and new ideas both in consumer and industrial products. The United States and Canada are the home country (Table 5-2) of more global industry leaders than any other country in the world. For example, North American companies are the dominant producers in the beverage, computer, software, aerospace, entertainment, medical equipment, and specialty retailing industries.

Foreign companies are attracted to this sizable market. The U.S. market is as large as all of Western Europe and twice as large as the Japanese market. Another distinctive feature is the arm's-length relationship between business and government. This results in greater opportunities for market access than is true in most other countries of the world. Elsewhere, closer partnerships between government and business often hamper the marketing efforts of foreign suppliers.

Canada, with a population of 31 million and a 2000 per capita GNP of $19,183, is moving ahead in cooperation with the private sector to create a national industrial policy. Canada's smokestack industries are just beginning to cope with the restructuring that U.S. companies have been going through for more than a decade. Exports represent approximately over 30 percent of Canada's GNP, more than those of any major industrial country and about the same percentage as Germany. The bulk of Canada's exports are unprocessed natural resources, which are vulnerable to low-cost Latin American rivals. An effort is under way to develop innovation-based competitive advantages. The federal and provincial governments will need to align their policies to support this strategic objective.

Over $300 billion in goods and services flow between Canada and the United States—the biggest trading relationship between any two nations. Canada takes 22 percent of American exports and the United States buys nearly 80 percent of Canada's exports. Table 5-3 summarizes the top 5 U.S. export and import partners. Americans have more invested in Canada than any other foreign land. Many American companies, including General Electric and IBM, use their Canadian operations as major global suppliers for some product lines. The auto market enables U.S. automakers to gain greater economies of scale in North America.

Geographically, Mexico is part of North America but because of its Spanish heritage is often included in data for Latin and/or Central America. Economically, Mexico is

TABLE 5-3 U.S. Merchandise Trade Partners			
	(US$ in Billions)		
Import Sources	*1993*	*1995*	*1997*
Canada	$111	$144	$168
Japan	107	124	122
Mexico	39	62	74
China	32	46	63
Germany	29	37	43
Export Markets			
Canada	$100	$127	$152
Mexico	42	46	71
Japan	48	64	66
United Kingdom	26	29	36
Korea	15	25	25

Source: U.S. Statistical Abstract, 118th Edition, 1998, Table 1323.

rapidly changing. When adjusted for population growth, the Mexican economy only grew at an average rate of 0.1 percent per year from 1985 to 1995. Mexico joined NAFTA in 1993. Presently, its net growth rate is 2.6 percent for 1997 to 2000 and should continue to benefit from its alliance in NAFTA. Inflation dropped from a high of 160 percent a year to less than 16 percent in 1997. Since the mid-1980s, more than three quarters of Mexico's state-owned companies have been privatized. Companies that want to manufacture in Mexico can set up a wholly owned subsidiary, a joint venture, or a *maquiladora* program. The *maquiladora* allows manufacturing, assembly, or processing plants to import materials, components, and equipment duty free; in return, they use inexpensive Mexican labor to assemble the product. When the completed product is exported to the United States, the manufacturer pays duty only on the value added in Mexico.

The official languages of the region are English, Spanish, and French. After English, the second language in the United States is Spanish, and in Canada it is French.

ASIA-PACIFIC

The Asia-Pacific region consists of all the countries of Asia except for the Middle East, Australia, and New Zealand. Although both North and South America also border on the Pacific, they are not considered part of the Pacific region.

In terms of population, the 30-country Asian-Pacific region is a colossus, with approximately 52 percent of the world's population. However, the region accounted for only 25 percent of global income in 2000. Fifty-eight percent of the region's income was concentrated in Japan, which has only 5 percent of the region's population. The former four economic "tigers" of East Asia—South Korea, Taiwan, Singapore, and Hong Kong—have forged the fastest industrial revolutions the world has ever seen and now rank among the high-income nations of the world. Behind them are another four countries—Thailand, Malaysia, Indonesia, and China—which are poised to repeat the gains of the first set of "tigers." Originally, Indonesia and Thailand were considered tigers but have not boded well due to the Asian Flu and/or internal disorder. China, with a population of 1.27 billion potential consumers, is a country no marketer can afford to ignore although not all foreign companies are making a profit there presently. Table 5-4 contains statistics on Asia-Pacific countries; note in particular the GNP growth rates of the former tigers.

TABLE 5-4	Asia-Pacific Comparison 2000 Data			
Country	GNP ($ Billion)	Population (Million)	GNP per Capita ($)	GNP Growth Rate 1997–2000 (%)
Japan	4,427	127	34,796	1.1
China	1,179	1,268	930	8.9
Korea	521	47	10,992	5.0
India	430	1,015	424	2.5
Australia	407	19	21,239	1.2
Taiwan	362	22	16,370	0.0
Indonesia	248	211	1,176	4.2
Hong Kong	188	7	27,463	1.4
Thailand	177	63	2,822	4.7
Singapore	120	3	36,484	4.7
Malaysia	111	23	4,746	3.3
New Zealand	60	4	15,376	–0.4
Total	8,230	2,809	2,930	—

Source: Warren J. Keegan, *Global Income and Population: 2000 Edition and Projections to 2010 and 2020.* Institute for Global Business Strategy, Pace University, New York, NY.

Culturally, the major languages are Mandarin Chinese and Hindi but there are hundreds of languages and dialects throughout Asia. In Indonesia alone, there are about 365 separate languages and dialects spoken. In Hong Kong, since the colony reverted to Chinese rule, the English language is less favored, which is a subtle but important fact that has marketing implications. In terms of religions, the region has many different religions ranging from Buddhism to Hindu, Confucianism, Taoism, and Shintoism.

Although it is difficult to make generalizations about marketing in Asia given the diversity of cultures, several cultural values directly affect marketing (Table 5-5).

China

1 Million Billion of 6 Billion

China, with a population surpassing 1.27 billion, is the largest populated country in the world with approximately 15 percent of the world's population. This fact alone attracts many marketers. "Imagine if we just sold one package of X to every individual" is the motivating factor for many multinational companies to enter this market. In addition to its size, China is a rapidly developing economy that has been growing at approximately 10 percent annually. The GNP in 2000 was $1.2 billion but, on a per capita basis, this translates to $930 and varies widely from the coastal provinces in which the highly industrialized provinces of Guangzhou and Shanghai are located to the agricultural interior. The economic increases are the result of a gradual conversion from a communist economic system to a free market system. The changes occurring in terms of consumer purchases among the growing number of families with increasing income are noteworthy. Sales of home computers costing around $600 for a local brand grew 80 percent in 1998.[2]

TABLE 5-5 Traditional Western and Asian Cultural and Marketing Values

Cultural Values	
Classical Western	*Traditional Asian*
• Nuclear family, self, or immediate family	• Extended family, blood/kinship/work groups
• Beliefs in competition, challenge, self-expression	• Beliefs in harmony, cooperation, avoiding confrontation
• Personal responsibility, independence	• Shared responsibility, interdependence
• Doing one's own thing	• Public self and "face"
• Resentment of authority	• Respect for authority
• Primacy given more to youth and change	• Age and seniority important, value tradition
• Control by "guilt" and conscience	• Control by "shame" and "loss of face"

Marketing Values	
• Brand segmentation; personal choice and self-expression through brand	• Popular famous brands; confidence in brand and corporate names
• Presenters/testimonials important but more to draw attention to brands	• Imitation, emulation, use of presenters as role models in ads
• Seeding and diffusion from leading edge	• Rapid adoption of successful brands
• Belief in "understatement" of wealth	• Display of wealth and status
• Environmentalism	• Confidence in technology

Source: George Fields, Hitaka Katahira, and Jerry Wind, *Leveraging Japan: Marketing to the New Asia.* (New York: Jossey-Bass, 2000). Copyright © 2000. Reprinted by permission of Jossey-Bass, Inc., a subsidiary of John Wiley & Sons, Inc.

---

[2] Leslie Chang, "Chinese Consumers Are New Market for PCs," *The Wall Street Journal,* 19 August 1999, p. A-14.

China is one of the largest trading partners of the United States. Imports by the United States are heavily skewed to electrical machinery, toys/games, power-generation machinery, and apparel. Total U.S. imports from China were valued at $36 billion annually. This sharply contrasts to the top U.S. exports to China, aircraft, power-generation machinery, electrical machinery, and fertilizer, which only total $9 billion annually.

Besides importing, many foreign companies have made direct investments in China; however, they have met with varying degrees of success. An increasing number of companies are leaving and only about one third are profitable. The Freightliner subsidiary of DaimlerChrysler pulled out after investing money for three years without producing a single vehicle.[3] Yet, many foreign car companies are continuing to manufacture in China (Figure 5-1).

Japan

Population density and geographic isolation are the two crucial, immutable factors that cannot be overstated when discussing Japan as a world market. It is interesting that although Japan's territory occupies only 0.28 percent of the world total, and its population makes up only 2.1 percent of the world total, Japan generates 15 percent of the world's GNP. Japan's per capita GNP in 2000 totaled, $34,796 compared to China's $930. Recently, Japan's economy has been suffering an internal economic crisis and the impact of the Asian Flu. Japan has many internal economic policy issues to resolve and, until that is done, growth forecasts predict only a 1.5 percent rate of growth in the GNP.

Seventy-two percent of Japan's land area is mountainous. Residential areas represent only 3 percent of the land area, and industrial areas occupy another 1.4 percent of land. Tokyo, with a population of 8 million people, is one of the most densely crowded cities in the world. Not surprisingly, land prices are among the highest in the world. Mastering the Japanese market takes flexibility, ambition, and a long-term commitment. Japan has changed from being a closed market to one that is just tough. The major barriers to entry in Japan are the nontariff barriers of expense, custom and tradition, practice, and preference. For example, buying or renting space for retail operations or any kind of operation is very expensive in Japan. The high cost of real estate has been a major

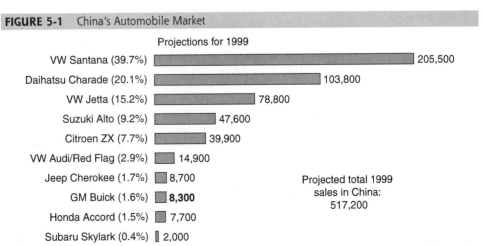

FIGURE 5-1   China's Automobile Market

Projections for 1999

VW Santana (39.7%)	205,500
Daihatsu Charade (20.1%)	103,800
VW Jetta (15.2%)	78,800
Suzuki Alto (9.2%)	47,600
Citroen ZX (7.7%)	39,900
VW Audi/Red Flag (2.9%)	14,900
Jeep Cherokee (1.7%)	8,700
GM Buick (1.6%)	**8,300**
Honda Accord (1.5%)	7,700
Subaru Skylark (0.4%)	2,000

Projected total 1999 sales in China: 517,200

Sources: GM Shanghai; Automotive Resources Asia Ltd., in The *Wall Street Journal,* 26 October 1999, p. A-18.

---

[3] Craig S. Smith, "Multinationals Rethink Chinese Joint Ventures," *The Wall Street Journal,* 26 October 1999, p. A-18.

financial obstacle to foreign automobile companies that need to create a dealer organization in Japan as part of a marketing strategy.

Any organization wishing to compete in Japan must be committed to providing top-quality products and services. In all cases, marketing strategies and plans must be tailored to Japanese tastes and practices. The Japanese particularly enjoy luxury products such as designer clothes and account for nearly half of the world's sales of these luxury items.[4] Countless visits and socializing with distributors are necessary to build trust. All competitors in Japan must understand the *keiretsu* system of tightly knit corporate alliances if they are to thrive.

What is striking about Japan is how different and at the same time how similar it is to Western countries. Many of these factors are quite well known but many myths about the Japanese consumer also exist. Table 5-6 illustrates some of the differences between Japan and the United States in culture, tradition, and behavior and Table 5-7 explores some myths that are specific to marketing. All of the differences begin with the fundamental cultural orientation in Japan, which emphasizes the group or the nation, and in the United States, which celebrates the individual.

Culturally, the major language is Japanese and Buddhism and Shintoism are the major religions.

Singapore

In fewer than three decades, Singapore has transformed itself from a British colony to a vibrant, 240-square-mile industrial power. Economically, it has been relatively unscathed by the Asian Flu. Singapore has an extremely efficient infrastructure—the port of Singapore is the world's second largest container port (Hong Kong ranks first)—and

TABLE 5-6	Comparisons and Contrasts in Culture, Tradition, and Behavior Between Japan and the United States	
	Japan	***United States***
Myth/hero emphasis	Group	Individual
Attitude	Self-denial, dependence	Self-expression, independence
Emphasis	Obligations	Rights
Style	Cooperation	Competition
Assumptions	Interdependence	Independence
View of self	Organization man	Individual with a skill
Cultural attitude 1	We are unique	Everyone is just like us
Cultural attitude 2	Willing to borrow/adopt/adapt	"Not invented here" syndrome
Organizational goal 1 (jobs/employment)	Share of market	Profitability, financial success
Organizational goal 2	World markets	National markets
Organizational goal 3	Quality, customer value	Production, financial return
Worker identification	Company	Craft, function
Management	Generalist	Specialist
Trust in	Feeling	Thinking
Governmental business relations	Cooperation	Separation
Financial structure (debt:equity)	80:20	40:60
Key stakeholders	Employees	Stockholders
Key values and goals	Perfection, harmony, consensus	Freedom, success, winning

The author is indebted to Chikara Higashi, member of the Japanese Diet and president, Recia, Tokyo, for assistance in preparing this table.

---

[4] "A Land Fit for Consumers," *The Economist*, 27 November 1999, p. 16.

TABLE 5-7   Marketing Myths versus Reality in Japan

Myth	Reality
Customers buy based on relationships and rarely shop around.	Japanese customers shop around for deals and sometimes even more than their peers in New York and London.
Japanese customers equate price with quality.	Japanese customers increasingly seek value.
Japanese customers are fiercely nationalistic.	Japanese customers are standing in line for good-quality foreign products.
Japanese customers are conservative and only purchase well-known Japanese brands.	Consumers are willing to experiment with new domestic and foreign brands.
Japanese customers only shop face-to-face.	Japanese customers are driving rapid growth in direct-mail and Internet sales.
Japanese distribution channels are impossible to crack.	New distribution channels and relaxed regulations are making the Japanese market easier to crack.
Japanese firms place long-term relationships with other companies above all other considerations.	In a value-conscious environment, companies are placing the value of business relationships above stability and harmony.

Source: George Fields, Hitaka Katahira, and Jerry Wind, *Leveraging Japan: Marketing to the New Asia.* (New York: Jossey-Bass, 2000).

a standard of living exceeding Japan. The country's GNP was $187 billion and GNP per capita was $36,484 in 2000. Singapore's 3 million citizens have played a critical role in the country's economic achievements by readily accepting the notion that "the country with the most knowledge will win" in global competition. It is ranked second in the world for economic freedom. Excellent training programs and a 97 percent literacy rate help explain why Singapore has more engineers per capita than the United States. Given full employment and economic growth, Singapore is recruiting high-tech workers in other countries. Approximately 5,000 foreign companies have offices in Singapore.

Singapore is closely tied with its neighbors, as more than a third of its imports are re-exported to other Asian countries. Singapore's efforts to fashion a civil society have gained the country some notoriety; crime is nearly nonexistent, thanks to the government's severe treatment of criminals, and chewing gum sales are prohibited as they lead to litter.

Culturally, the major languages are English, Mandarin, Malay, and Tamil.

India

With a population of approaching 1 billion and a GNP of $430 billion, India's per capita GNP of $424 in 2000 was one of the lowest in the region. Some population experts predict that India will overtake China, which still has a one-child policy, as the world's largest country by the middle of this century. Income within the country is polarized. India has hundreds of millions of poor people. Many of these people, an estimated 204 million or 22 percent of the population, are so poor that they are undernourished.[5] But India also has a "plethora of talented technical graduates" who are fueling the growth of the software industry in India. Given this talent, the low salaries vis-à-vis the United States and the expansion of real-time communications links, many U.S. companies have sourced or opened offices in India for software development and export. The software industry in India has experienced a growth rate of 55 to 60 percent per year for the past several years and this growth is expected to continue.[6] By 2008, the information technology sector is expected to be a $100 billion industry in India.[7]

---

[5] "The Hungry Are Always with Us," *The Economist,* 16 October 1999, p. 49.
[6] "India—Software Industry—an Update," 1999 FT Asia Intelligence Wire.
[7] Eric W. Pfeiffer, "From India to America," *Forbes,* 23 August 1999, pp. 21–24.

Another growing industry in India is filmmaking, commonly referred to as "Bollywood." Although filmmaking is a $750 million business per year, it is not officially recognized by the Indian government as an industry. The Indian industry produces approximately 750 films per year, thus making it one of world's leaders in film production. Most of these films are produced for the local market but many are broadcast over Asia via satellite television stations such as Star TV out of Hong Kong and Zee Telefilms. (Rupert Murdoch, owner of Star TV, has been involved in joint ventures with Zee Telefims.) Given the magnitude of the filmmaking industry, it is only a matter of time before multinational entertainment companies become involved in India.

Yet there have been ominous reminders recently that the political environment is still unstable. In 1998, following the detonation of five nuclear bombs, the United States invoked economic sanctions against India. This is a vivid reminder that the political situation in the area, especially with neighboring Pakistan, can be quite tenuous.

Culturally, the major languages are Hindu, Bengali, and English. The major religion is Hindu.

Oceania

Australia and New Zealand are island economies in the Asia region that were settled by Europeans. The two countries enjoy a special relationship because of their British heritage, but there is no apparent desire in either country to merge governments. Although both countries cooperate closely in many areas, there are also many differences in outlook, culture, and character. Citizens of each country do move freely into the other. There are no barriers or border restrictions on trade between the two countries. The combined population is 23 million, or 0.3 percent of the world total. The per capita income level in both countries is relatively high, $21,239 in Australia and $15,376 in New Zealand. The region accounts for 1.4 percent of global income. Australia has a population of 19 million. The country's midsized economy ($407 billion in 2000) is very dependent on trading conditions in Asia and world markets for its major exports of low value-added agricultural and mineral products. The ratio of exports to GNP is 17 percent, the same as for imports. Asia is Australia's largest market; 20 percent of exports go to Japan, 16 percents go to the ASEAN countries, and 9 percent goes to South Korea.

The domestic marketing environment in Australia is characterized by product and marketing mix strategies comparable to those found in Triad markets. A major challenge facing all marketers in Australia is the fact that the eight major cities are widely dispersed across a vast continent. This presents distribution and communication considerations that tend to increase national marketing costs.

New Zealand is a small, developed country with a population of 4 million and a land area approximately the size of Japan or the United Kingdom. Forty years ago, the country had the world's third highest per capita GNP. In 2000, GNP per capita was $15,376, passed in the last decade by Hong Kong, Singapore, and Taiwan in the Pacific region. The principal cause of the decline in the relative wealth of New Zealand was the country's failure to respond quickly enough to the decline in prices for agricultural commodities, which make up over 60 percent of its exports. In spite of the country's decline in relative GNP per capita, it remains one of the world's most beautiful countries with its magnificent mountains, glaciers, and fjords, its spectacular coastline, and its beautiful temperate climate. No global marketer should miss a visit to New Zealand, especially if he or she likes to travel by motorcycle. The country is, I am happy to report from personal experience riding a BMW K75 and a BMW F650, one of the world's great motorcycle travel destinations for the touring and sport rider.

English is the major language and Christianity is the major religion.

LATIN AMERICA

Latin America, with 7 percent of the world's wealth and 9.5 percent of its population, is a developing region. Average per capita income ranged from a high of $9,720 in Argentina—a high-income country—to a low of $307 in Haiti, one of the lowest in the world. The region includes the Caribbean, and Central and South America. Economically, Mexico is considered part of North America. Latin America is home to more than 510 million people—a population greater than Western Europe or the combined regions of Central and Eastern Europe. The allure of the Latin American market has been its considerable size and huge resource base.

After decades of stagnation, crippling inflation, increasing foreign debt, protectionism, and bloated government payrolls, the countries of Latin America have shown a startling change. Balanced budgets are a priority, and privatization is under way. All of the countries of Latin America, except for Cuba and Haiti now have democratically elected governments. In Venezuela, however, the number of people who do not get enough to eat has quadrupled over the last 20 years. As a percentage, Venezuela has more malnourished people than China.[8] Free markets, open economies, and deregulation have begun to replace the policies of the past in most countries.

Latin America is rapidly moving to eliminate barriers to trade and investment. In many countries, tariffs that sometimes reached as much as 100 percent or more have been lowered to 10 to 20 percent. As noted earlier in Chapter 3, Latin American countries have also focused on developing subregional common markets. These initiatives are seen as precursors to freer trade with the United States. Many observers envision a free trade area throughout the hemisphere.

Chile's export-driven success makes it a role model for the rest of Latin America as well as Central and Eastern Europe. The world-class wines produced in Chile's vineyards enjoy favor among price-conscious consumers around the world, and Chilean sea bass can be found in fish markets in Europe, Asia, and North America. With inflation held to single digits, unemployment hovering at about 6 percent, and a modest budget surplus, Chile is pointing the way toward changes in economic thinking in other emerging markets. Chile also boasts an impressive record in privatization and it pioneered debt-for-equity swaps as a way of retiring part of its foreign debt. Long-term foreign investment by the United States, Spain, and Canada alone in 1996 totaled an enviable $3 billion. This was the first time since 1974 that the mining sector was not the principal recipient of foreign direct investment (FDI). It has been replaced by investment in services, which totaled $2.3 billion.

Brazil is an example of a country that has recently made tremendous strides in developing its market. Brazil, with a population of 171 million, is the fifth largest country in the world and its land mass makes it the fifth largest in terms of area. Economically, it has 2.6 percent of the world's GNP, which equates to $4,986 per person. Starting in the early 1990s, Brazil began to privatize, reduced its tariffs, and reigned in its hyperinflation. As a result, foreign direct investment has poured in. Although there has been an increase in unemployment, many consumers have benefited from the economic growth. When Telefonica, the Spanish telecommunications company, entered the market, it drove down the prices of cellular phones from approximately $1,000 to $150. This now puts cellular phones in the reach of millions of Brazilians who once could only dream of such conveniences.

Latin American reforms show a broad shift away from the policy of protectionism toward recognition of the benefits of market forces and the advantages of participating

---

[8] "The Hungry Are Always with Us."

fully in the global economy. Global corporations are watching developments closely. They are encouraged by import liberalization, the prospects for lower tariffs within subregional trading groups, and the potential for establishing more efficient regional production.

Culturally, the major languages are Spanish and Portuguese and the major religion is Roman Catholic Christianity.

MIDDLE EAST

The Middle East includes 16 countries: Afghanistan, Cyprus, Bahrain, Egypt, Iran, Iraq, Israel, Jordan, Kuwait, Lebanon, Oman, Qatar, Saudi Arabia, Syria, the United Arab Emirates, and Yemen. The region accounted for 1.9 percent of 2000 world GNP and has a total population of approximately 260 million with an average annual per capita income of $2,831 in those countries where GNP data are available.

The majority of the population is Arab, followed by a large percentage of Persians and a small percentage of Israelis. Persians and Arabs share the same religion, beliefs, and Islamic traditions, making the population 95 percent Muslim and 5 percent Christian and Jewish. Despite this apparent homogeneity, diversity exists within each country and within religious groups.

Business in the Middle East is driven by the price of oil. Seven of the countries have high oil revenue: Bahrain, Iraq, Iran, Kuwait, Oman, Qatar, and Saudi Arabia. These economies hold more than 75 percent of the free world oil reserves. Oil revenues have widened the gap between poor and rich nations in the Middle East, and the disparities contribute to political and social instability in the area. Saudi Arabia remains the most important market in this region. The country is a monarchy with 16 million people. Saudi Arabia alone has 25 percent of the world's known oil reserves.

In the past, the region was characterized by pan-Arabism, a form of nationalism and loyalty that transcended borders and amounted to anti-Western dogma. During the Persian Gulf War, this pan-Arabism weakened somewhat. To defeat Iraq, the Gulf Arabs and their allies broke many of their unwritten rules, including accepting help from the United States, a traditional ally of Israel. Some observers interpret this change as a harbinger of new market opportunities in the region. Another positive sign was the July 1994 peace declaration by Israel and Jordan that may pave the way for a free trade area in the Middle East.

The Middle East does not have a single societal type with a typical belief, behavior, and tradition. Each capital and major city in the Middle East has a variety of social groups that can be differentiated on the basis of religion, social classes, educational fields, and degree of wealth. In general, Middle Easterners are warm, friendly, and clannish. Tribal pride and generosity toward guests are basic beliefs. Decision making is by consensus, and seniority has more weight than educational expertise. Life of the individual centers on the family. Authority comes with age, and power is related to family size and seniority. In business relations, Middle Easterners prefer to act through trusted third parties and they also prefer oral communications.

Connection is a key word in conducting business. Well-connected people find their progress is made much faster. Bargaining is a Middle Eastern art, and the visiting businessperson must be prepared for some old-fashioned haggling. Establishing a personal rapport, mutual trust, and respect is essentially the most important factor leading to a successful business relationship. Decisions are usually not made by correspondence or telephone. The Arab businessperson does business with the individual, not with the company. Most social customs are based on the Arab male-dominated society. Women are usually not part of the business or entertainment scene for traditional Muslim Arabs.

Some conversation subjects should be avoided, as they are considered an invasion of privacy. For example:

1. Avoid bringing up subjects of business before getting to know your Arab host. This is considered rude.
2. It is taboo to ask questions or make comments concerning a man's wife or female children.
3. Avoid pursuing the subjects of politics or religion.
4. Avoid any discussion of Israel.[9]

AFRICA

The African continent is an enormous landmass: The United States would fit into Africa about three and a half times. It is not really possible to treat Africa as a single economic unit. The continent is divided into three distinct areas: the Republic of South Africa, North Africa, and sub-Saharan Africa located between the Sahara Desert in the north and the Zambezi River in the south. The market is large, with over 730 million people. Africa, with 1.3 percent of the world's wealth and 11.9 percent of its population, is a developing region with an average per capita annual income of $536.

The Republic of South Africa has a GNP of $125 billion, almost 50 percent of the total GNP of Africa south of the Sahara. Income per capita is $2,902. The income, however, is very disproportionate as 24 percent of the population live below the poverty line.[10] South Africa suffers from the same problems as the rest of the continent: slow growth, big families, and low investment. The gold and other mineral mines, which generate almost 45 percent of South Africa's exports, are subject to worldwide gold prices and are winding down. Unemployment is approximately 30 percent and another 11 percent are underemployed. Sanctions, official and unofficial, restricted South African growth for years. With the elimination of apartheid and the removal of sanctions in 1992, trade and tourism have improved. Foreign banks started lending again. In sub-Saharan Africa, South Africa is an economic colossus with considerable promise but also with significant political risk.

Nigeria is the largest nation of Africa with a population of 128 million in 2000 and a GNP of $38 billion. In spite of the fact that it is a major supplier of oil to the world, Nigeria's per capita income was only $299 in 2000 and the country is only about one third the size of the Republic of South Africa economically. Almost 30 percent of Nigeria's population lives below the poverty line, which is defined as $1 per person per day.[11] The stability of Nigeria's general economic situation is highly dependent on the international oil market. Doing business in Nigeria is difficult, to say the least: The country's government is one of the most incompetent, inefficient, and corrupt in the world.

Several countries in sub-Saharan Africa have exhibited tremendous declines in GNP during the later part of the twentieth century. This decline is reflected in the number of undernourished people in the region. In Somalia, almost 75 percent of the population is malnourished. In Congo, Mozambique, Eriterea, and Ethiopia, over 50 percent do not have enough to eat.[12] Economically, Sierra Leone has declined 8 percent, Congo declined 12.5 percent, and Angola has declined 10 percent from 1990 to

---

[9] Philip R. Harris and Robert T. Moran, *Managing Cultural Differences*, 3rd ed. (Houston: Gulf Publishing Company, 1991): 506.
[10] "Africa: Bleak Prospects in Consumer Markets," Crossborder Monitor On-line Service, The Economist Intelligence Unit Limited (1998).
[11] "Africa: Bleak Prospects in Consumer Markets."
[12] "The Hungry Are Always with Us."

1996. In addition to economic problems, the greatest problems facing sub-Saharan Africa is the spread of AIDS. In the countries suffering epidemic proportions of AIDS, life expectancy has decreased seven years on the average.[13]

In North Africa, the 78 million Arabs are differentiated politically and economically. They are richer and more developed, with many of the countries benefiting from large oil resources.

The challenge to marketing in the low-income markets of Africa is not to stimulate demand for products but to identify the most important needs of the society and develop products that fit these needs. There is much opportunity for creativity in developing unique products that fit the needs of the people of the developing countries.

Culturally, the countries of Africa are very different from each other. In addition to the myriad of indigenous cultures, the culture and religion of former colonizers are also evident.

◆ MARKETING IN TRANSITIONAL ECONOMIES AND LESS DEVELOPED COUNTRIES

The shortage of goods and services is the central problem of transitional economies (those converting from a command economy to a free market economy) and less developed countries (LDC). Marketing is a discipline that guides the process of identifying and fulfilling the needs and wants of people. Clearly, marketing is needed and much desired by consumers in these countries.

Certain baseline characteristics present marketing challenges: (1) low per capita income ($4,000 and under), (2) high inflation (10 to 30 percent annually), (3) wide income distribution gap, (4) high levels of taxation, import duties, and other bureaucratic hurdles, (5) a lack of marketing awareness with the presence of a black market, (6) fragmented communications and distribution channels, and (7) inadequate distribution and logistics infrastructure.[14]

Despite these difficulties, long-term opportunities can be nurtured. Today, Nike produces and sells only a small portion of its output in China, but when the firm refers to China as a "2 billion foot market," it clearly has the future in mind. Greater competitive pressures will force firms to reevaluate their strategies and look ever further for new markets. Even some fast-growing companies in transitional economies (TEs) and LDC are initiating business in countries that lag behind them. Several companies from South Korea, itself a less developed country not long ago (e.g., Lucky-Goldstar), are entering these markets as they have experience producing goods at a lower unit cost. Emerging markets can be lost through indifference and preemptive foreign competition. In deciding whether to enter an LDC, one study suggested the following:

- Look beyond per capita GNP. The per capita figures may hide the existence of a sizable middle class in that market. India, for example, has a huge middle-class market that is hidden by the country's average statistics.
- Consider LDCs collectively rather than singly. One market may not be appealing; however, there may be broader possibilities with neighboring countries.
- Weigh the benefits and costs of being the first firm to offer a product or service in an LDC. Governments of LDCs often bestow tax subsidies or other special

---

[13] "Unshapely World, Too Old or Too Young," The Economist, 25 September 1999, p. 56.
[14] Rajeev Batra, "Executive Insights: Marketing Issues and Challenges in Transitional Economies," *Journal of International Marketing*, 5, no. 4 (1997): 95–114.

treatment on companies that set up operations. Entering a successful LDC is an opportunity to get in on the ground floor of a significant market opportunity.

• Set realistic deadlines for results. Due to different legal, political, or social forces, events may move slowly.[15]

Despite the serious economic difficulties now facing LDCs in Southeast Asia, Latin America, Africa, and Eastern Europe, many of these nations will evolve into attractive markets. Marketing's role in the LDCs is to focus resources on the task of creating and delivering products that best serve the needs of the people. Basic marketing concepts can be applied so that products are designed that fit the needs and incomes in the LDC market. Appropriate marketing communications techniques can also be applied to accelerate acceptance of these products. Marketing can be the link that relates resources to opportunity and facilitates need satisfaction on the consumer's terms.

◆ GLOBAL BUYERS

Each buyer is unique, and all buyers go through a similar process in making a purchase decision. Thus, although buyers in different countries and world regions will go through a similar process in making their purchase decisions, they will make different purchases since they will respond to the unique economic, social and cultural, political and governmental, environmental, competitive, and personal factors that influence buyer decisions.

CUSTOMER VALUE AND THE VALUE EQUATION

For any organization operating anywhere in the world, the essence of marketing is to surpass the competition at the task of creating perceived value for customers. The value equation is a guide to this task:

$$V = B/P$$

where

V = value
B = benefits
P = price

The marketing mix is integral to the equation because benefits are a combination of the product, promotion, and distribution. As a general rule, value as perceived by the customer—the variable to the left of the equal sign—can be increased in two basic ways. The numerator can be increased by improving benefits associated with the product itself, distribution, or communications. Alternatively, value can be increased by reducing price. (With certain categories of differentiated goods, including designer clothing and other luxury products, higher price is associated with increased value.) Companies using price as a competitive weapon may enjoy an ample supply of low-wage labor or access to cheap raw materials. Companies can also reduce prices if costs are low due to efficiencies in manufacturing. If a company is able to offer both superior product, distribution, or promotion benefits and lower prices relative to the competition, it enjoys an extremely advantageous position. This is precisely how Toyota, Nissan, and other Japanese automakers made significant gains in the American market in the 1980s. They offered cars that were higher in quality and lower in price than those made by Chrysler, Ford, and General

---

[15] Donald G. Halper and H. Chang Moon, "Striving for First-Rate Markets in Third-World Nations, " *Management Review* (May 1990): 20–21.

Motors. Needless to say, to become a market success, a product must come up to a threshold of acceptable quality.

The current equivalent of the early Japanese entrants in the U.S. market is Hyundai, which lists for $7,500 new. The car suffered from an early reputation for poor quality. Hyundai appears determined to improve quality and gain a foothold in the U.S. market. The corporate image depresses the product's perceived value, so Hyundai must increase value to a competitive level by lowering its price. Even if Hyundai is successful in raising quality to world standards, the company will be forced to offer its marque at a discount because the perception of quality will lag the actual improvement of quality. The same is true for Samsung in the computer monitor market: It will continue to sell at a discount to Sony even after it equals Sony's quality because image always lags reality of product quality.

The upside of the value equation is that when a company's perceived value is high, it can charge more than the competition for the same product. Toyota and General Motors (GM) produce the Toyota Corolla and the GM Prizm in a joint venture in California. Identical cars get Toyota and GM nameplates at the end of the assembly line. The Toyota Corolla sells for $1,000 more than the GM Prizm because of the greater perceived value of a Toyota. The perception is so powerful that stories of the superior quality of the Corolla versus the Prizm have been heard from numerous sources in the United States. This is a dramatic example of one company's positive brand equity and the other's inferiority in comparative brand equity.

The bottom line on the value equation is that you can succeed in a market only if you have perceived value that is equal to or greater than that of your competitors. If you are new and unknown, your best entry strategy is to enter the market with an offer that customers will find hard to refuse: Offer quality and features that equal or exceed that of your competition at a lower price. The price will get your prospect's attention, and the quality and features will keep it. Over time, as you become known, you can raise your prices to a level that is consistent with your perceived value.

DIFFUSION THEORY[16]

The process that buyers go through is summarized in diffusion theory, a marketing universal. Hundreds of studies have described the process by which an individual adopts a new idea. Sociologist Everett Rogers reviewed these studies and discovered a pattern of remarkably similar findings. In his book, *Diffusion of Innovations,* Rogers distilled the research into three concepts that are extremely useful to global marketers: the adoption process, characteristics of innovations, and adopter categories.

An innovation is something new. When applied to a product, new can mean different things. In an absolute sense, once a product has been introduced anywhere in the world, it is no longer an innovation because it is no longer new to the world. Relatively speaking, however, a product already introduced in one market may be an innovation elsewhere because it is new and different for the market being targeted. Global marketing often entails just such product introductions. Managers find themselves marketing products that may be, simultaneously, innovations in some markets and mature or declining products in other markets.

The Adoption Process

One of the basic elements of Rogers's diffusion theory is the concept of an adoption process—the mental stages through which an individual passes from the time of his or her first knowledge of an innovation to the time of product adoption or purchase.

---

[16] This section draws from Everett M. Rogers, *Diffusion of Innovations* (New York: Free Press, 1962).

Rogers suggests that an individual passes through five different stages in proceeding from first knowledge of a product to the final adoption or purchase of that product:

1. *Awareness.* In the first stage, the customer becomes aware for the first time of the product or innovation. Studies have shown that at this stage impersonal sources of information such as mass-media advertising are most important. An important early communication objective in global marketing is to create awareness of a new product through general exposure to advertising messages.
2. *Interest.* During this stage, the customer is interested enough to learn more. The customer has focused his or her attention on communications relating to the product and will engage in research activities and seek out additional information.
3. *Evaluation.* In this stage, the individual mentally assesses the product's benefits in relation to present and anticipated future needs and, based on this judgment, decides whether or not to try it.
4. *Trial.* Most customers will not purchase expensive products without the "hands-on" experience marketers call *trial*. A good example of a product trial that does not involve purchase is the automobile test drive. For health care products and other inexpensive consumer packaged goods, trial often involves actual purchase. Marketers frequently induce trial by distributing free samples. For inexpensive products, an initial single purchase is defined as trial.
5. *Adoption.* At this point, the individual either makes an initial purchase (in the case of the more expensive product) or continues to purchase—adopts and exhibits brand loyalty to—the less expensive product. Studies show that, as a person moves from the evaluation through trial to adoption, personal sources of information are more important than impersonal sources. It is during these stages that sales representatives and word of mouth become major persuasive forces affecting the decision to buy.

Adopter Categories

Adopter categories are classifications of individuals within a market on the basis of their innovativeness. The hundreds of studies of the diffusion of innovation demonstrate that adoption is a social phenomenon that is characterized by normal distributions, as shown in Figure 5-2.

Five categories have been assigned to the segments of this normal distribution. The first 2.5 percent of people to purchase a product are defined as innovators. The next 13.5 percent are defined as early adopters, the next 34 percent as the early majority, the next 34 percent as the late majority, and the final 16 percent as laggards. Studies show that innovators tend to be venturesome, more cosmopolitan in their social relationships, and wealthier than those who adopt later. Earlier adopters are the most influential people in their communities, even more than the innovators. Thus, the early adopters are a critical group in the adoption process, and they have a great influence on the majority, who make

FIGURE 5-2   Adopter Categories

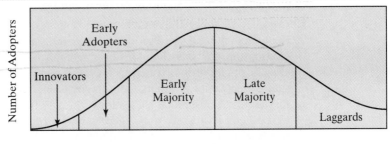

up the bulk of the adopters of any product. Several characteristics of early adopters stand out. First, they tend to be younger, have higher social status, and are in a more favorable financial position than later adopters. They must be responsive to mass-media information sources and must learn about innovations from these sources because they cannot simply copy the behavior of earlier adopters.

One of the major reasons for the normal distribution of adopter categories is the interaction effect, that is, the process through which individuals who have adopted an innovation influence others. Adoption of a new idea or product is the result of human interaction in a social system. If the first adopter of an innovation or new product discusses it with two other people, and each of these two adopters passes the new idea along to two other people, and so on, the resulting distribution yields a normal shape when plotted.

From the point of view of the marketing manager, steps taken to persuade innovators and early adopters to purchase a product are critical. These groups must make the first move and are the basis for the eventual penetration of a product into a new market because, over time, the majority will copy their behavior.

Characteristics of Innovations

In addition to describing the product adoption process, Rogers also identifies five major factors affecting the rate at which innovations are adopted:

1. *Relative advantage.* How does a new product compare with existing products or methods in the eyes of customers? The perceived relative advantage of a new product versus existing products is a major influence on the rate of adoption. If a product has a substantial relative advantage vis-à-vis the competition, it is likely to gain quick acceptance. When compact disc (CD) players were first introduced in the early 1980s, industry observers predicted that only audiophiles would care enough about digital sound—and have the money—to purchase them. However, the sonic advantages of CDs compared to LPs were obvious to the mass market; as prices for CD players plummeted, the 12-inch black vinyl LP was rendered virtually extinct in less than a decade.

   However, many innovations have unsuccessfully challenged the dominance of CDs and none have succeeded. A rule of thumb for venture investors in innovations is that the innovation must be at least 10 times better than the established product in order to succeed in an existing category. Digital audio tape (DAT) and new CD formats have failed to date because they have not cleared the 10-times-better hurdle.

2. *Compatibility.* This refers to the extent to which a product is consistent with existing values and past experiences of adopters. The history of innovations in international marketing is replete with failures caused by the lack of compatibility of new products in the target market. For example, the first consumer videocassette recorder (VCR), the Sony Betamax, ultimately failed because it could record for only one hour. Most buyers wanted to record movies and sports events; they shunned the Betamax in favor of VHS-format VCRs that could record 4 hours of programming.

3. *Complexity.* This is the degree to which an innovation or new product is difficult to understand and use. Product complexity is a factor that can slow down the rate of adoption, particularly in developing-country markets with low rates of literacy. Dozens of global companies are developing new, interactive, multimedia consumer electronics products. Complexity is a key design issue; it is a standing joke that in most households, VCR clocks flash 12:00 because users do not know how to set them. To achieve mass success, new products will have to be as simple to use as slipping a prerecorded videocassette into a VCR.

4. *Divisibility*. Can a product be tried and used on a limited basis without great expense? Wide discrepancies in income levels around the globe result in major differences in preferred purchase quantities, serving sizes, and product portions. CPC International's Hellmann's mayonnaise was simply not selling in U.S.-sized jars in Latin America. Sales took off after the company placed the mayonnaise in small plastic packets. The plastic packets were within the food budgets of local consumers, and they required no refrigeration—another plus.

5. *Communicability*. This is the degree to which benefits of an innovation or the value of a product may be communicated to a potential market. A new digital cassette recorder from Philips is off to a slow start, in part because advertisements have failed to clearly communicate the fact that the product can make CD-quality recordings using new cassette technology while still playing older analog tapes.

Diffusion of New Products

The diffusion of new products in various countries offers many challenges to the marketer as different countries respond in significantly different ways to a given new product. In their research, Tellefsen and Takada found that new products diffuse more slowly in the United States than in Asia or Europe, and that even within Europe, the diffusion rates vary from country to country. They noted that the order of introduction was also important, that the first country to receive a new product tends to have a slower diffusion rate than subsequent countries. Other considerations are the cultural context, cosmopolitanism, mobility, individualism, and uncertainty avoidance of the population.[17]

Diffusion of Innovations in Pacific Rim Countries

In a cross-national comparison of the United States, Japan, South Korea, and Taiwan, Takada and Jain present evidence that different country characteristics—in particular, culture and communication patterns—affect diffusion processes for room air conditioners, washing machines, and calculators.[18] Proceeding from the observation that Japan, South Korea, and Taiwan are high-context cultures with relatively homogeneous populations whereas the United States is a low-context, heterogeneous culture, Takada and Jain surmised that faster rates of diffusion would be found in Asia compared with the United States. A second hypothesis supported by the research was that adoption would proceed more quickly in markets in which innovations were introduced relatively late. Presumably, the lag time would give potential consumers more opportunity to assess the relative advantages, compatibility, and other product attributes. Takada and Jain's research has important marketing implications. They note:

> If a marketing manager plans to enter the newly industrializing countries (NICs) or other Asia markets with a product that has proved to be successful in the home market, the product's diffusion processes are likely to be much faster than in the home market.[19]

◆ THE GLOBAL MARKETING PLAN

Each country in the world is sovereign and unique, but there are similarities among countries in the same region or in countries at the same stage of development that make both the regional and the market stage approaches sound bases for marketing planning.

---

[17] Thomas Tellefsen and Hirokazu Takada, "The Relationship Between Mass Media Availability and the Multicountry Diffusion of Consumer Products," *Journal of International Marketing* 7, no. 1 (1999): 77–96.

[18] Hirokazu Takada and Dipak Jain, "Cross-National Analysis of Diffusion of Consumer Durable Goods in Pacific Rim Countries," *Journal of Marketing,* 55 (April 1991): 48–53.

[19] Ibid, p. 50.

In this chapter, the organization of material is around geographic regions. It could just as well be organized around stages of economic development, or a company may organize its plan by product or function. Further details of marketing plans and international organizational structure can be found in Chapter 17.

Summary

Perhaps the most striking fact about world markets and buyers is that for the first time in modern history, the entire world is growing. According to World Bank estimates, every world region including Africa will grow, and for the most part the poor countries will grow faster than the rich. This will provide new opportunities for marketers who, despite increasing globalization, need to look at the characteristics of each new market they plan to enter or expand.

Discussion Questions

1. What are the major characteristics of the world's regional markets? Which region is the fastest growing? Why? How does this region rate as an area for expanding marketing efforts?
2. What is the significance of the value equation for global marketers?
3. Do you agree with James Fallows's characterization of the "Asian model" in the opening chapter quote? Is it possible to achieve high income levels without political democracy?
4. In the United States, consumers often find products imported from Canada with packaging information in English and French, which meets Canadian packaging requirements. Given the large number of Spanish speakers in the United States, should Spanish be added by marketers to U.S. packaging?

Suggested Readings

Anderson, Kym, and Richard Blackhurst, Eds. *Regional Integration and the Global Trading System.* New York: Harvester/Wheatsheaf, 1993.

Axline, W. Andrew. *The Political Economy of Regional Cooperation.* London: Pinter, 1994.

Europa World Year Book, London: Europa Publications Limited.

Fields, George, Hotaka Katahira, and Jerry Wind. *Leveraging Japan: Marketing to the New Asia.* New York: Jossey-Bass, 2000.

Healey, Nigel M. "The Transition Economies of Central and Eastern Europe: A Political, Economic, Social and Technological Analysis." *The Columbia Journal of World Business,* 29 (Spring 1994): 62–70.

Koch-Weser, Caio. "Economic Reform and Regional Cooperation: A Development Agenda for the Middle East and North Africa." *Middle East Policy,* 2, no. 2 (1993): 28–36.

Kurus, Bilson. "The ASEAN Triad: National Interest, Consensus-Seeking, and Economic Cooperation." *Contemporary Southeast Asia,* 16 (March 1995): 404–420.

Mascarehas, B. "The Founding of Specialist Firms in a Global Fragmenting Industry." *Strategic Management Journal,* 27 (First Quarter 1996): 27–42.

Miyoshi, Masao. "A Borderless World? From Colonialism to Transnationalism and the Decline of the Nation-State." *Critical Inquiry,* 19 (Summer 1994): 726–751.

Ohmae, Kenichi. *The End of the Nation State: The Rise of Regional Economies.* New York: Free Press, 1995.

Rao, C. P., and Srivatsa Seshadri. "Industrial Buyers' Expectations of Supplier Attributes Across Developing Countries: Implications for Marketing Strategies." *The International Executive,* 38 (September/October 1996): 671–689.

Robson, Peter, and Ian Wooton. "The Transnational Enterprise and Regional Economic Integration." *Journal of Common Market Studies,* 31 (March 1993): 71–90.

Savitskie, Katrina. "Entering the Chinese Market: The Risks and Discounted Rewards." *Journal of International Marketing,* 7, no. 3 (1999): 126–128.

Steenkamp, Jan-Benedict E. M., Frendel ter Hofstede, and Michael Wedel. "A Cross-National Investigation into the Individual and National Cultural Antecedents of Consumer Innovativeness." *Journal of Marketing,* 63, no. 2 (1999): 55–69.

Sunje, Aziz. "Selling to Newly Emerging Markets." *Journal of International Marketing,* 7, no. 2 (1999): 93–96.

Tyler, Gus. "The Nation-State vs. the Global Economy." *Challenge,* 36 (March 1993): 26–32.

World Factbook, Washington, DC: Central Intelligence Agency of U.S. Government.

Global Marketing Information Systems and Research

"To survive in this new globally competitive world, we had to modernize. Information technology is the glue for everything we do."

—James Wogsland
Vice Chairman, Caterpillar

"Nothing changes more constantly than the past; for the past that influences our lives does not consist of what happened, but of what men believe happened."

—Gerald W. Johnston

Information, or useful data, is the raw material of executive action. The global marketer is faced with a dual problem in acquiring the information needed for decision making. In high-income countries, the amount of information available far exceeds the absorptive capacity of an individual or an organization. The information problem is superabundance, not scarcity. Although advanced countries all over the world are in the middle of an information explosion, there is a lack of information available on the market characteristics of less developed countries.

Thus, the global marketer is faced with the problem of information abundance and information scarcity. The global marketer must know where to go to obtain information, the subject areas that should be covered, and the different ways that information can be acquired. Acquired information must be processed in an efficient and useful way. The technical term for the process of information acquisition is *scanning*. This chapter presents an information acquisition model for global marketing as well as an outline of the global marketing research process. Once acquired, information must be processed in an efficient and effective way. The chapter concludes with a discussion of how to manage the marketing information collection system and the marketing research effort.

For example, K.M.S. "Titoo" Ahuwalia is the president of ORG-MARG, the largest marketing research company in India. His client list reads like a "Who's Who" of global companies: Avon Products, Gillette, Coca-Cola, and Unilever. And, as Titoo is fond of telling them, they are finding that "India is different." India is the second most populous nation on earth, with a middle class comprised of more than 200 million people. Despite increasing affluence, however, centuries-old cultural traditions and customs still prevail. As a result, consumer behavior sometimes confounds Western expectations. Despite the fact that summer temperatures frequently reach triple digits, only 2 percent of urban dwellers use deodorant. Instead, Indians bathe twice daily. Only 1 percent of households have air conditioners, and a recent Gallup survey revealed that only 1 percent intended to buy an air conditioner in the near future. The virtues of frugality once preached by Gandhi remain uppermost in the minds of many; smokers refill disposable lighters, and women recycle old sheets instead of spending money on sanitary napkins. Likewise, in a country where food is believed to shape personality and mood and hot breakfasts are thought to be a source of energy, Kellogg has had little luck winning converts to cold cereal.

For marketers hoping to achieve success in India and other emerging markets, information about buyer behavior and the overall business environment is vital to effective managerial decision making. When researching any market, marketers must know where to go to obtain information, what subject areas to investigate and information to look for, the different ways information can be acquired, and the various analytical approaches that will yield important insights and understanding. Obviously, India's 16 languages, 200 dialects, and low level of urbanization create special research challenges. However, similar challenges are likely to present themselves wherever the marketer goes.

It is the marketer's good fortune that, since the mid-1990s, a veritable cornucopia of market information has become available on the Internet. A few keystrokes can yield literally hundreds of articles, research findings, and Web sites that offer a wealth of information about particular country markets. Even so, marketers need to study several important topics in order to make the most of modern information technology. First, they need to understand the importance of information technology and marketing information systems as strategic assets. Second, they need a framework for information scanning and opportunity identification. Third, they should have a general understanding of the formal market research process. Finally, they should know how to manage the marketing information collection system and the marketing research effort. These topics are the focus of this chapter.

◆ OVERVIEW OF GLOBAL MARKETING INFORMATION SYSTEMS

The purpose of a marketing information system (MIS) is to provide managers and other decision makers with a continuous flow of information about markets, customers, competitors, and company operations. A MIS should provide a means for gathering, analyzing, classifying, storing, retrieving, and reporting relevant data about customers, markets, channels, sales, and competitors. A company's MIS should also cover important aspects of a company's external environment. For example, companies in any industry need to pay close attention to government regulations, mergers, acquisitions, and alliances. Acquisitions such as VNU NV, the Dutch media company, that was a recent purchase of Nielsen Media Research at $2.5 billion, allow it to maintain or enhance its leadership positions.[1] As suggested by the quote from James Wogsland of Caterpillar at

---

[1] Nikhil Deogun, "Made in U.S.A.: Deals From Europe Hit Record," *The Wall Street Journal,* 25 October 1999, p. C1.

◆ BOX 6-1 ◆

BENETTON'S INFORMATION SYSTEM

In the fashion business, the company that gets preferred styles and colors to market in the shortest time gains an edge over competitors. Luciano Benetton, founder of the Italian company that bears his name, notes, "Benetton's market is, for reasons of product and target, very dynamic, evolving rapidly." The company's information system includes relational databases and a network for electronic data interchange. Benetton managers rely heavily on inbound data generated at the point of purchase; data about each sales transaction are instantly transmitted via satellite to headquarters from cash registers at the company's 7,000 stores around the world. Analysts sift through the data to identify trends, which are conveyed to manufacturing.

Most of Benetton's knitwear is produced as undyed "grey goods"; garments are dyed in batches in accordance with the fashion trends identified by the MIS. Benetton's system helps cut inventory carrying costs and reduce the number of slow-selling items that must be marked down. The company's staff of field agents uses a tracking system to follow the movement of outbound merchandise. The system shows whether a particular item is in production, in a warehouse, or in transit. In Benetton's state-of-the-art, $57 million distribution center, computer-controlled robots sort, store, and retrieve up to 12,000 bar-coded boxes of merchandise each day.

The MIS even helps the designer team work more efficiently. Before the MIS was installed, designers had to personally visit the warehouse to review samples of clothing from previous seasons. With the new system, all clothing items are photographed and the images digitized and sorted on a laser disc connected to a personal computer. A designer sitting at the computer can request any item from seasonal collections dating back several years, and it will be displayed on screen.

Taken as a whole, Benetton's MIS has slashed the amount of time required to design and ship knitwear from 6 months to a matter of weeks. Reorders from any Benetton stores can be filled in 13 to 27 days. Still, Luciano Benetton is not satisfied. He hopes to go beyond data processing and use information technology as a tool for motivating employees. Explains MIS manager Bruno Zuccaro, "He says it's not enough to know what we sold, but we need to know what we should have sold and that we lost *X* dollars by not realizing our potential."

SOURCES: Michael M. Phillips, "Retailers Rely on High-Tech Distribution," *The Wall Street Journal,"* 12 December 1996, p. A2; Janette Martin, "Benetton's IS Instinct," *Datamation,* 1 July 1989, pp. 68-15–68-16.

the beginning of this chapter, global competition intensifies the need for an effective MIS. In addition to Caterpillar, Mitsui, Toyota, ABB, Federal Express, Grand Metropolitan PLC, Ford, and Texas Instruments are among the companies with global operations that have invested in sophisticated electronic data interchange (EDI) systems to improve intracompany information sharing. The Internet has also dramatically expanded our ability to access up-to-date information.

Poor operating results can often be traced to insufficient data and information about events both inside and outside the company. For example, when a new management team was installed at the American unit of Adidas AG, the German-headquartered athletic shoe marketer, data were not even available on normal inventory turnover rates. A new reporting system revealed that rivals Reebok and Nike turned inventories five times per year, compared with twice a year at Adidas. This information was used to tighten the marketing focus on the best-selling Adidas products. Benetton SpA's use of its MIS as a strategic competitive tool is described in the box "Benetton's Information System."

Colgate-Palmolive Company recently succeeded in standardizing its disparate and frequently incompatible electronic mail systems at locations around the globe. The process was tedious, but Colgate executives realized that a global messaging system would increase employee productivity. As a result, employees in 165 countries can now easily exchange messages and files; electronic mail traffic almost doubled in a three-year period after the system was fully implemented. An undertaking of this magnitude required the full support of senior management inside and outside the marketing function and integration into the strategic planning process.

Indeed, it is no easy task to organize, implement, and monitor global marketing information and research strategies and programs. Moreover, these are not simply marketing issues; they are organizational imperatives. These tasks must be coordinated in a coherent manner that contributes to the overall strategic direction of the organization. The MIS and research function must provide relevant information in a timely, cost-efficient, and actionable manner.

The past few years have seen dramatic changes in worldwide political and economic events. Increased global economic integration between countries, the demise of communism, volatile currency exchange rates, and other factors are driving the demand for access to credible worldwide business and political information. Today's economic and political environments require worldwide news information on a daily basis. Geocentric global companies generally have intelligence systems that meet these challenges. Typically, the strategic planning or market research departments staff these systems. They distribute information to senior management and to managers throughout the organization.

A more detailed discussion of the workings of an intracompany MIS is beyond the scope of this book. The discussion that follows focuses on the subject agenda, scanning modes, and information sources characteristic of a global information system that is oriented toward the external environment.

INFORMATION SUBJECT AGENDA

A starting point for a global MIS is a list of subjects about which information is desired. The resulting subject agenda should be tailored to the specific needs and objectives of the company. The general framework suggested in Table 6-1 consists of six broad information areas. The framework satisfies two essential criteria. First, it comprises all the information subject areas relevant to a company with global operations. Second, the categories in the framework are mutually exclusive: Any kind of information encompassed by the framework can be correctly placed in one and only one category. The basic elements of the external environment—economic, social and cultural, legal and regulatory, and financial factors—will undoubtedly be on the information agenda of most companies, as shown in the table.

TABLE 6-1 Six Subject Agenda Categories for a Global Business Intelligence System	
Category	*Coverage*
1. Markets	Demand estimates, consumer behavior, products, channels, communication media availability and cost, and market responsiveness
2. Competition	Corporate, business, and functional strategies and plans
3. Foreign exchange	Balance of payments, interest rates, attractiveness of country currency, expectations of analysts
4. Prescriptive information	Laws, regulations, rulings concerning taxes, earnings, dividends in both host countries and home country
5. Resource information	Availability of human, financial, information, and physical resources
6. General conditions	Overall review of sociocultural, political, technological environments

SCANNING MODES: SURVEILLANCE AND SEARCH

Once the subject agenda has been determined, the next step is the actual collection of information. This can be accomplished using surveillance and search.

In the surveillance mode, the marketer engages in informal information gathering. Globally oriented marketers are constantly on the lookout for information about potential opportunities and threats in various parts of the world. They want to know everything about the industry, the business, the marketplace, and consumers. This passion shows up in the way they keep their ears and eyes tuned for clues, rumors, nuggets of information, and insights from other people's experiences. Browsing through newspapers and magazines and surfing the Internet are ways to ensure exposure to information on a regular basis. Global marketers may also develop a habit of watching news programs and commercials from around the world via satellite. This type of general exposure to information is known as *viewing*. If a particular news story has special relevance for a company—for example, entry of a new player into a global industry, say, Samsung into automobiles—marketers in the automobile and related industries and all competitors of Samsung will pay special attention, tracking the story as it develops. This is known as *monitoring*.

The search mode is characterized by more formal activity. Search is characterized by the deliberate seeking out of specific information. Search often involves investigation, a relatively limited and informal type of search. Investigation often involves seeking out books or articles in trade publications or searching the Internet on a particular topic or issue. Search may also consist of research, a formally organized effort to acquire specific information for a specific purpose. This type of formal, organized research is described later in the chapter.

One study found that nearly 75 percent of the information acquired by headquarters executives at U.S. global companies comes from surveillance as opposed to search. However, the viewing mode generated only 13 percent of important external information, whereas monitoring generated 60 percent. Two factors contribute to the paucity of information generated by viewing. One is the limited extent to which executives are exposed to information that is not included in a clearly defined subject agenda. The other is the limited receptivity of the typical executive to information outside this agenda. Every executive limits his or her exposure to information that will not have a high probability of being relevant to the job or company. This is rational: A person can absorb only a minute fraction of the data available to him or her. Exposure to and retention of information stimuli must be selective. Nevertheless, it is vital that the organization as a whole be receptive to information not explicitly recognized as important. Some organizations suffer from a variation of the NIH (not invented here) syndrome. If the information they are viewing has not been generated by their company, it is summarily missed. To be effective, a scanning system must ensure that the organization is viewing areas where developments that could be important to the company might occur. Innovations in information technology have increased the speed with which information is transmitted and simultaneously shortened the life of its usefulness to the company. Advances in technology have also placed new demands on the global firm in terms of shrinking reaction times to acquired information. In some instances, the creation of a full-time scanning unit with responsibility for guiding and stimulating the process of acquiring and disseminating strategic information may be advisable.

Of all the changes in recent years affecting the availability of information, perhaps none is more apparent than the explosion of documentary and electronic information. An overabundance of information has created a major problem for anyone attempting to stay abreast of key developments in multiple national markets. Today, executives are overwhelmed with documentary information. However, too few companies employ a formal system for coordinating scanning activities. This situation results in considerable duplication of effort. For example, it is not uncommon for members of an entire management group to read a single publication covering a particular subject area despite the fact that several other excellent publications covering the same area may be available.

Wherever you are located, you can benefit from reading foreign publications. *The Economist, The Financial Times,* and *The Wall Street Journal*'s regional editions are good broad-based sources. Also, review the Web site recommendations throughout and at the end of the chapter.

VISIT THE WEB SITES
www.economist.com
www.ft.com
www.wsj.com

The best way to identify unnecessary duplication is to carry out an audit of reading activity by asking each person involved to list the publications he or she reads regularly. A consolidation of the lists will reveal the surveillance coverage. Often the scope of the group will be limited to a handful of publications to the exclusion of other worthwhile ones. A good remedy for this situation is consultation with outside experts regarding the availability and quality of publications in relevant fields or subject areas.

Over all, then, the global organization is faced with the following needs:

- An efficient, effective system that will scan and digest published sources and technical journals in the headquarters country as well as all countries in which the company has operations or customers.
- Daily scanning, translating, digesting, abstracting, and electronic input of information into a market intelligence system. Despite the advances in global information, its translation and electronic input are mostly manual. This will continue for the next few years, particularly in developing countries.
- Expanding information coverage to other regions of the world.

◆ SOURCES OF MARKET INFORMATION

HUMAN SOURCES

Although scanning is a vital source of information, research has shown that headquarters executives of global companies obtain as much as two thirds of the information they need from personal sources. A great deal of external information comes from executives based abroad in company subsidiaries, affiliates, and branches. These executives are likely to have established communication with distributors, consumers, customers, suppliers, and government officials. Indeed, a striking feature of the global corporation—and a major source of competitive strength—is the role executives abroad play in acquiring and disseminating information about the world environment. Headquarters executives generally acknowledge that company executives overseas are the people who know best what is going on in their areas. The following is a typical comment of headquarters executives:

> Our principal sources are internal. We have a very well informed and able overseas group. The local people have a double advantage. They know the local scene and they know our business. Therefore, they are an excellent source. They know what we are interested in learning, and because of their local knowledge they are able to effectively cover available information from all sources.

The information issue exposes one of the key weaknesses of a domestic company: Although more attractive opportunities may be present outside existing areas of operation, they will likely go unnoticed by inside sources in a domestic company because the scanning horizon tends to end at the home-country border. Similarly, a company with only limited geographical operations may be at risk because internal sources abroad tend to scan only information about their own countries or region.

Other important information sources are friends, acquaintances, professional colleagues, consultants, and prospective new employees. The latter are particularly important if they have worked for competitors. Sometimes, information-related ethical and legal issues arise when a person changes jobs. When J. Ignacio Lopez de Arriortua, head of purchasing at General Motors (GM), accepted a job as production chief with Volkswagen (VW), GM charged that Mr. Lopez had taken important documents and computer files when he moved to VW. Although he was acquitted by a German court, the resulting publicity was a source of embarrassment to Volkswagen.

It is hard to overstate the importance of travel and contact for building rapport and personal relationships. Moreover, one study found that three quarters of the information acquired from human sources is gained in face-to-face conversation. Why? Some information is too sensitive to transmit in any other way. For example, highly placed government employees could find their careers compromised if they are identified as information sources. In such cases, the most secure way of transmitting information is face-to-face rather than in writing. Information that includes estimates of future developments or even appraisals of the significance of current happenings is often considered too uncertain to commit to writing. Commenting on this point, one executive said:

> People are reluctant to commit themselves in writing to highly "iffy" things. They are not cowards or overly cautious; they simply know that you are bound to be wrong in trying to predict the future, and they prefer to not have their names associated with documents that will someday look foolish.

The great importance of face-to-face communication lies also in the dynamics of personal interaction. Personal contact provides an occasion for executives to get together for a long enough time to permit communication in some depth. Face-to-face discussion also exposes highly significant forms of nonverbal communication, as discussed in Chapter 3. One executive described the value of face-to-face contact in these terms:

> If you really want to find out about an area, you must see people personally. There is no comparison between written reports and actually sitting down with someone and talking. A personal meeting is worth a thousand written reports.

DOCUMENTARY SOURCES

One of the most important developments in global marketing research is the extraordinary expansion in the quantity and quality of documentary sources of information. The information explosion is an explosion in the availability of documentary information not only in print but increasingly on-line and on the Internet and the intranet for company-restricted information. The two broad categories of documentary information are published public information and unpublished private documents. The former is available on the Internet, and the latter is available on the intranet or company password-restricted-access networks created by organizations for their own employees.

The vast quantities of published documentary information that are available create a unique challenge: how to find the exact information you want. One of the fast-growing industries in the world are companies that gather, analyze, and organize data from multiple sources, which they then make available to clients.

INTERNET SOURCES

The range and depth of information available on the Internet are vast and growing every day. Companies, governments, nongovernmental organizations, market research companies, data assemblers and packagers, security analysts, news gathering organizations, universities, and university faculty to mention just a few are all sources that can be accessed on-line. The Internet is a unique information source: It combines the three basic information source types: human, documentary (published and private), and direct perception.

An e-mail communication may be personal or impersonal. A document may be text only, or it may include pictures and music. The pictures may be still or full-motion video or animation. The document may be combined with music.

With the ever expanding bandwidth of transmission media, the ever increasing speed of processors that organize and transmit information, and the ever expanding universe of senders and receivers of information, the Internet is clearly a revolutionary development in global marketing research.

A number of electronic resources have been developed in recent years. These include the National Trade Data Base, which is available on CD-ROM from the Department of Commerce. The GateWaze company in Manchester, Massachusetts, has developed PC software called "The World Trader" to help small firms find opportunities in export markets. Similarly, the Port Authority of New York developed a program called "Export to Win" to help small business owners learn about exporting. In addition, the Internet and other interactive information services feature bulletin boards where a great deal of information about various world markets is exchanged. Another on-line source is the EIU (Economist Intelligence Unit), which is maintained by *The Economist*.

> **VISIT THE WEB SITE**
> http://store.eiu.com

Yet, some things never change. The information explosion is a Janus-faced monster. There is more and more information, but the sheer quantity of information makes it more and more difficult to find what you are looking for. The challenge is to develop search strategies and skills that ensure that you get the information you need to better understand global markets, customers, and competition.

DIRECT PERCEPTION

Direct sensory perception provides a vital background for the information that comes from human and documentary sources. Direct perception gets all the senses involved. It means seeing, feeling, hearing, smelling, or tasting for oneself to find out what is going on in a particular country rather than getting secondhand information by hearing or reading about a particular issue. Some information is easily available from other sources but requires sensory experience to sink in.

Often, the background information or context one gets from observing a situation can help fill in the "big picture." For example, Niall FitzGerald, cochairman of Unilever, relates a story about the disastrous rollout in the United Kingdom of Persil Power, a laundry powder with "an extra scrubbing chemical." Unfortunately, the chemical worked too well and ate through clothing. When trying to determine a solution for the problem, FitzGerald asked the 30 Unilever executives how many did their own laundry. No one responded. "There we were, trying to figure out why customers wouldn't buy our soap and we didn't even know the first thing about how it was used."[2] The les-

---

[2] Deborah Orr, "A Giant Awakens." *Forbes,* January 25, 1999, p. 52.

son he learned from this scenario was to never lose sight of your customer. Company recruits at Hindustan Lever are asked to spend six weeks living with a family in a remote Indian village.[3]

The chief executive of a small U.S. company that manufactures an electronic device for controlling corrosion had a similar experience. After spending much time in Japan, the executive managed to book several orders for the device. Following an initial burst of success, Japanese orders dropped off; for one thing, the executive was told the packaging was too plain. "We couldn't understand why we needed a five-color label and a custom-made box for this device, which goes under the hood of a car or in the boiler room of a utility company," the executive said. While waiting for the bullet train in Japan one day, the executive's local distributor purchased a cheap watch at the station and had it elegantly wrapped. The distributor asked the American executive to guess the value of the watch, based on the packaging. Despite everything he had heard and read about the Japanese obsession with quality, it was the first time the American understood that in Japan, "a book is judged by the cover." As a result, the company revamped its packaging, seeing to such details as ensuring that strips of tape used to seal the boxes were cut to precisely the same length.[4]

Toyota relied heavily on direct perception when redesigning its flagship luxury car, the Lexus LS 400, for the 1995 model year. The chief engineer of Lexus and a five-person team came to the United States to get firsthand direct observation data on the market. They stayed in luxury hotels to gain an understanding of the level of service Lexus customers demanded. Design team members visited customers' homes and took notes on preferences for such things as furniture, paintings, and even briefcases. As Ron Brown, a U.S.-based product planning manager for Lexus, recalled, "It's like if you just bought a new washer-dryer, and the Kenmore people called and said they wanted to bring a bunch of people out to watch you wash your clothes."[5] One thing the team discovered was that the coat hooks in the first generation LS 400 were too small. The Japanese thought a coat hook was, literally, for hanging a coat. In reality, Lexus owners regularly hang their dry cleaning in the car. The hook was redesigned. "You can get five coat hangers on it. But now it's big enough that you wouldn't want it out all the time, so it retracts," says Brown.[6]

Euro Disney had been experiencing marketing and financial difficulties. Consumers were not flocking to the site and the consumers who visited were not very satisfied. One issue was the sale of alcohol within the park. Disney had a no-alcohol policy but it wasn't until a vice president who was sent to France to solve the problem realized, after living in France for several months, that wine with meals is the norm in France. Not serving wine was "an affront" to local customers. Based on his experience of living in the country, he worked diligently to have the policy changed.[7]

As these examples show, cultural and language differences require firsthand visits to important markets to "get the lay of the land." Travel should be seen not only as a tool for management control of existing operations but also as a vital and indispensable tool in information scanning.

◆ FORMAL MARKETING RESEARCH

Information is a critical ingredient in formulating and implementing a successful marketing strategy. As described earlier, a MIS should produce a continuous flow of information. Marketing research, on the other hand, is the project-specific, systematic gathering

---

[3] Ibid, p. 53.
[4] Nilly Landau, "Face to Face Marketing Is Best," *International Business* (June 1994): 64.
[5] James R. Healy, "Toyota Strives for New Look, Same Edge," *USA Today,* 13 October 1994, pp. 1B–2B.
[6] Ibid.
[7] J. Stewart Black and Hal B. Gregersen, "The Right Way to Manage Expats," *Harvard Business Review* (March–April 1999): 56.

of data in the search scanning mode. There are two ways to conduct marketing research. One is to design and implement a study with in-house staff. The other is to use an outside firm specializing in marketing research. The importance of the global market to research firms has increased considerably in recent years. For example, ACNielsen Company's 1998 revenues from non-U.S. research totaled $1.4 billion, over 70 percent of total revenue. (Marketing research companies are ranked in Table 6-2 according to revenues generated outside the United States.) ACNielsen with a combination of wholly owned subsidiaries and affiliates has offices in 80 countries and customers in more than 100 countries. If your company is in need of a research company in another country, the Green Book published by the New York Chapter of the American Marketing Association lists hundreds of companies around the world.

Web addresses for several of the market research firms identified in Table 6-2 include:

www.acnielsen.com
www.greenbook.com
www.tyn.geis.com
www.imshealth.com
www.sofresfsa.com
www.research-int.com
www.casro.org[8]

Table 6-3 shows the 10 largest global markets for measured market research in total and on a per capita basis. Except for Australia and Brazil, all the countries listed are in the Triad. The spending on a per capita basis ranges from a low of $1.46 in Brazil to $25.54 in the United Kingdom.

The process of collecting data and converting it into useful information can be divided into five basic steps: identifying the research problem, developing a research plan, collecting data, analyzing data, and presenting the research findings. Each step is discussed here. An overview of the international marketing research process is shown in Figure 6-1.

TABLE 6-2 Research Companies Ranked by Non-U.S. Revenue			
Rank	*Non-U.S. Research Revenue*	*Worldwide Research Revenue*	
1998 *Ad Organization*	*1998*	*1998*	*% of Total*
1. ACNielsen Corp. (U.S.)	$1,035.0	$1,425.4	72.6
2. IMS Health (U.K./U.S.)	671.7	1,084.0	62.0
3. Research International USA (Kantar Group)	290.3	335.2	86.6
4. NFO Worldwide (U.S.)	270.0	450.0	60.0
5. Gartner Group (U.S.)	183.0	494.7	37.0
6. Millward Brown Intl. (Kantar Group) (U.S.)	154.6	233.8	66.1
7. Video Research (Japan)	149.0	149.0	100.0
8. United Information Group (U.K.)	123.0	182.0	67.6
9. Information Resources (U.S.)	114.3	511.3	22.4
10. VNU Marketing Information Services	85.0	428.0	19.9

Source: Data from *Advertising Age,* 24 May 1999, p. 32.

---

[8] The Council of American Survey Research Organizations (CASRO) is a trade association for American-based research companies.

TABLE 6-3 10 Largest Markets by Country, in Value[a] of Marketing Research Data		
Country	*1998 Total Value*	*Per Capita Spending*
United States	$4,935.1	$17.90
United Kingdom	1,525.0	24.54
Germany	1,326.1	15.92
France	906.1	15.23
Japan	893.7	7.03
Italy`	414.7	7.17
Australia	285.0	14.84
Spain	274.2	6.92
The Netherlands	259.1	16.30
Brazil	250.0	1.46
Total	11,069.0	

[a] In millions of U.S. dollars.

Source: Adapted from *Marketing News,* 3 July 2000, p. 16. Data from ESOMAR.

STEP 1: IDENTIFYING THE RESEARCH PROBLEM

The following story illustrates the first step in the formal marketing research process.

The vice presidents of finance and marketing of a shoe company were traveling around the world to estimate the market potential for their products. They arrived in a very poor country and both immediately noticed that none of the local citizens were wearing shoes. The finance vice president said, "We might as well get back on the plane. There is no market for shoes in this country." The vice president of marketing replied, "What an opportunity! Everyone in this country is a potential customer!"

The potential market for shoes was enormous in the eyes of the marketing executive. To formally confirm his instinct, some research would be required. As this story shows, research is often undertaken after a problem or opportunity has presented itself. Perhaps a competitor is making inroads in one or more important markets around the world, or, as in the story just recounted, a company may wish to determine whether a particular country or regional market provides good growth potential. It is a truism of market research that "a problem well defined is a problem half solved." Thus, regardless of what situation sets the research effort in motion, the first two questions a marketer should ask are, "What information do I need?" and "Why do I need this information?"

The research problem often involves assessing the nature of the market opportunity, a phase that is also known as presearch. This, in turn, depends in part on whether the market that is the focus of the research effort can be classified as existing or potential. Existing markets are those in which client needs for secondary information are already being served. In many countries, data about the size of existing markets—in terms of dollar volume and unit sales—are readily available. In countries in which such data are not available, such as Cuba, a company must first estimate the market size, the level of demand, or the rate of product purchase or consumption. A second research objective in existing markets may be assessment of the company's overall competitiveness in terms of product appeal, price, distribution, and promotional coverage and effectiveness. Researchers may be able to pinpoint a weakness in the competitor's product or identify an unserved market segment.

Potential markets can be further subdivided into latent and incipient markets. A latent market is, in essence, an undiscovered segment. It is a market in which demand would materialize if an appropriate product were made available. In a latent market, demand is zero before the product is offered. In the case of existing markets, the main

FIGURE 6-1 The International Marketing Reeesearch Process

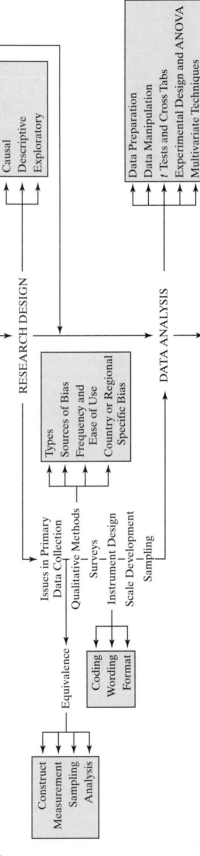

Source: V. Kumar, *International Marketing Research* (Upper Saddle River, NJ: Prentice Hall, 2000), p. 54.

research challenge is to understand the extent to which competition fully meets customer needs. With latent markets, initial success is not based on a company's competitiveness. Rather, it depends on the prime mover advantage—a company's ability to uncover the opportunity and launch a marketing program that taps the latent demand. Sometimes traditional marketing research is not an effective means for doing this. As Peter Drucker has pointed out, the failure of American companies to successfully commercialize fax machines—an American innovation—can be traced to research that indicated no potential demand for such a product. The problem, in Drucker's view, stems from the typical survey question for a product targeted at a latent market. Suppose a researcher asks, "Would you buy a telephone accessory that costs upward of $1,500 and enables you to send, for $1 a page, the same letter the post office delivers for 25 cents?" On the basis of economics alone, the respondent most likely will answer, "No."

Drucker explains that the reason Japanese companies are the leading sellers of fax machines today is that their understanding of the market was not based on survey research. Instead, they reviewed the early days of mainframe computers, photocopy machines, cellular telephones, and other information and communications products. The Japanese realized that, judging only by the initial economics of buying and using these new products, the prospects of market acceptance were low. Yet, each of these products had become a huge success after people began to use them. This realization prompted the Japanese to focus on the market for the benefits provided by fax machines rather than the market for the machines themselves. By looking at the success of courier services such as Federal Express, the Japanese realized that, in essence, the fax machine market already existed.

Incipient demand is demand that will emerge if a particular economic, technological, political, or sociocultural trend continues. If a company offers a product to meet incipient demand before the trends have taken root, it will have little market response. After the trends have had a chance to unfold, the incipient demand will become latent, and later, existing demand. This can be illustrated by the impact of rising income on demand for automobiles and other expensive consumer durables. As per capita income rises in a country, the demand for automobiles will also rise. Therefore, if a company can predict a country's future rate of income growth, it can also predict the growth rate of its automobile market. Figure 6-2 illustrates the relationship between automobile ownership and gross domestic product (GDP) per capita. The slope of the growth curve turns sharply upward at the $3,500 income per capita level, and levels off at about $20,000. Other factors influence the demand for automobiles. U.S. ownership is about 800 vehicles per 1,000 as compared to France, Germany, and Japan, where ownership is around 550 per 1,000. U.S. ownership is 45 percent higher than that in Japan even though Japanese income per capita is 15 percent higher than that in the United States. Cheap land and gasoline and a dispersal of the population over a vastly larger territory explain the higher U.S. automobile ownership.

STEP 2: DEVELOPING A RESEARCH PLAN

After defining the problem to be studied or the question to be answered, the marketer must address a new set of questions. What is this information worth to me in dollars (or yen, etc.)? What will we gain by collecting these data? What would be the cost of not getting the data that could be converted into useful information? Research requires the investment of both money and managerial time, and it is necessary to perform a cost-benefit analysis before proceeding further.

In some instances, a company may pursue the same course of action no matter what the research reveals. Even when more information is needed to ensure a high-quality

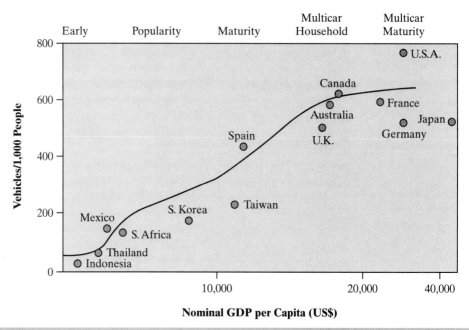

THE WORLD THAT AUTOMAKERS SERVE IN PRODUCT PLANNING

FIGURE 6-2 Automobile Ownership and GDP per Capita

Source: Toyota Annual Report, 1996, p. 5.

decision, a realistic estimate of a formal study may reveal that the cost to perform research is simply too high. As discussed in the next section, a great deal of potentially useful data already exists; utilizing such data instead of commissioning a major study can result in significant savings. In any event, during the planning step, methodologies, budgets, and time parameters are all spelled out. Only when the plan is completed should the next step be undertaken.

STEP 3: COLLECTING DATA

Are data available in company files, a library, industry or trade journals, or on-line? When is the information needed? Marketers must address these issues as they proceed to the data collection step of the research. Using readily available data saves both money and time. A formal market study can cost hundreds of thousands of dollars and take many months to complete with no guarantee that the same conditions are still relevant.

Secondary Data

A low-cost approach to marketing research and data collection begins with desk research. Personal files, company or public libraries, on-line databases, government records, and trade associations are just a few of the data sources that can be tapped with minimal effort and often at no cost. Data from these sources already exist. Table 6-4 shows how specific free data based on U.S. Customs data can be. Such data are known as secondary data because they were not gathered for the specific project at hand. Syndicated studies published by research companies are another source of secondary data and information. The Cambridge Information Group publishes Findex, a directory of more than 13,000 reports and studies covering 90 industries. The Economist Intelligence Unit's EIU Country Data is another valuable source of information both in print and

TABLE 6-4   Example U.S. Customs Data

Lens Blanks (Other Than for Spectacles) Not Optically Worked, of Glass, (Optical Elements)
U.S. Imports for Consumption: June 1998 and 1998 Year-to-Date
(Customs Value, in Thousands of Dollars)
(Units of Quantity: Number)

	June 1998		*1998 YTD*	
Country	*Quantity*	*Value*	*Quantity*	*Value*
World Total	65,814	141	998,244	940
Brazil	—	—	694,544	76
Canada	—	—	150	2
Germany	—	—	2,661	37
Japan	29,609	99	197,217	670
Malaysia	35,955	24	102,297	66
Singapore	—	—	300	2
Switzerland	31	3	31	3
United Kingdom	219	15	1,044	83

Sources: www.ita.doc.gov/. . . /Imports/70/701400.html and www.ita.doc.gov/industry/ot . . . atest-Month/
Imports/70/701400.html.

on-line. Another on-line example is the Global Market Information Database (GMID). It contains information on 330 consumer products in 49 countries such as the market for alcohol beverages in China. The cost of this report is contingent upon the various modules that are purchased and costs several thousands of dollars. It is available in many university libraries.

Primary Data and Survey Research

When data are not available through published statistics or studies, direct collection is necessary. Primary data pertain to the particular problem identified in step 1. Survey research, interviews, and focus groups are some of the tools used to collect primary market data. Personal interviews—with individuals or groups—allow researchers to ask "why" and then explore answers. A focus group is a group interview led by a trained moderator who facilitates discussion of a product concept, advertisement, social trend, or other topic. For example, the Coca-Cola Company convened focus groups in Japan, England, and the United States to explore potential consumer reaction to a prototype 12-ounce contoured aluminum soft-drink can. Coke was particularly anxious to counteract competition from private-label colas in key markets. In England, for example, Sainsbury's store-brand cola had an 18 percent market share[9] and Virgin Cola was a major competitor. There are, however, cultural differences that must be considered when using focus groups. In Asia, young people tend to defer to elders, and lower-level executives to higher-level executives when they are in the same group. In Latin America, respondents tend to overstate their enthusiasm and Asians tend to show diffidence.[10]

In some instances, product characteristics dictate a particular country location for primary data collection. For example, Case Corporation recently needed input from farmers about cab design on a new generation of tractors. Case markets tractors in North America, Europe, and Australia, but the prototypes it had developed were too expensive

---

[9] Karen Benezra, "Coke Queries on Contour Can," *Brandweek,* 7 November 1994, p. 4.
[10] Herschell Gordon Lewis and Carol Nelson, *Advertising Age Handbook of Advertising* (Chicago: NTC Business Books, 1998), p. 167.

and fragile to ship. Working in conjunction with an Iowa-based marketing research company, Case invited 40 farmers to an engineering facility near Chicago for interviews and reactions to instrument and control mockups. The visiting farmers were also asked to examine tractors made by Case's competitors and evaluate them on more than 100 different design elements. Case personnel from France and Germany were on hand to assist as interpreters.[11]

Survey research often involves obtaining data from customers or some other designated group by means of a questionnaire. Surveys can be designed to generate quantitative data ("How often would you buy?"), qualitative data ("Why would you buy?"), or both. Survey research generally involves administering a questionnaire by mail, by telephone, or in person. Many good marketing research textbooks provide details on questionnaire design and administration. A good questionnaire has three main characteristics:

1. It is simple.
2. It is easy for respondents to answer and for the interviewer to record.
3. It keeps the interview to the point and obtains desired information.

An important survey issue in global marketing is potential bias due to the cultural background of the persons designing the questionnaire. For example, a survey designed and administered in the United States may be inappropriate in non-Western cultures, even if it is carefully translated.[12] Sometimes bias is introduced when a survey is sponsored by a company that has a financial stake in the outcome and plans to publicize the results. For example, American Express joined with the French tourist bureau in producing a study that, among other things, covered the personality of the French people. The report ostensibly showed that, contrary to a long-standing stereotype, the French are not "unfriendly" to foreigners. However, the survey respondents were people who already had traveled to France on pleasure trips in the previous two years—a fact that likely biased the result.

Sampling

Sampling is the selection of a subset or group from a population that is representative of the entire population. The two basic sampling procedures are probability sampling and non-probability sampling. In a probability sample, each unit chosen has a known chance of being included in the sample. There are five types of probability sampling: random, stratified, systematic, cluster, and multistage. In a non-probability sample, the chance that any unit will be included in the sample is unknown. The four types of non-probability sampling are: convenience, judgmental, quota, and snowball.

Four considerations for using a probability sample are: the target population must be specified; the method of selection must be determined; the sample size must be determined; and non-responses must be addressed.

Three key characteristics of a probability sample determine the sample size:

1. The permissible sampling error that can be allowed (e)
2. The desired confidence in the sample results. In a statistical sense, the confidence is expressed in terms of the number of chances in 100 tries that the results obtained could be due to chance. Confidence is usually desired at the 99 percent level and is expressed as three standard errors (t).
3. The amount of variation in the characteristic being measured. This is known as the standard deviation (s).

---

[11] Jonathan Reed, "Unique Approach to International Research," *Agri Marketing* (March 1995): 10–13.
[12] Geert Hofstede and Michael Harris Bond, "The Confucius Connection: From Cultural Roots to Economic Growth," *Organizational Dynamics* (Spring 1988): 15.

The formula for sample size is

$$n = \frac{(t_2)\,(s_2)}{e_2}$$

where

- n = sample size
- t = confidence limit expressed in standard errors (three standard errors = 99 percent confidence = 2.57, 95% level = 1.96)
- s = standard deviation
- e = error limit

The important characteristic of this formula from the point of view of international marketers is that the sample size, n, is not a function of the size of the universe. Thus, a probability sample in Tanzania requires the same sample size as one in the United States if the standard deviation in the two populations is the same. This fact underlines the scale economies of marketing research in larger markets. For example, if we assume a 95 percent confidence level, a standard deviation of .5, and an error limit of ±5 percent, the sample size required for a random sample of a universe is 392.

$$N = \frac{(1.960)\,(.5)}{.05^2} = 392$$

The sample size of 392 does not vary with the size of the total population: In other words, the sample size for China with a population of 1.2 billion people is no larger than the sample required for, say, American Samoa with a population of 70,000.

Non-probability sampling can be used in the exploratory stage, in pretesting, in dealing with a homogeneous population, when the researchers lack statistical information, and when operation ease is vital. Although the cost and work of developing a statistical sample are eliminated, there is a chance that hidden biases and uncertainties may appear that cannot be eliminated by increasing the sample size.

A quota sample, a non-probability technique, is designed by taking known characteristics of the universe and including respondents in the sample in the same proportion as they occur in the known characteristic universe. For example, a population may be divided in six categories according to income as shown in Table 6-5.

If it is assumed that income is the characteristic that adequately differentiates the population for study purposes, then a quota sample would include respondents of different income levels in the same proportion as they occur in the population, that is, 15 percent with monthly earnings from 10 to 20, and so on.

In one convenience sample comparing consumer shopping attitudes in the United States, Jordan, Singapore, and Turkey, data for the latter three countries were gathered from samples recruited by an acquaintance of the researcher. Although data gathered in this way are not subject to statistical inference, they may be adequate to address the problem defined in step 1. In this study, for example, the researchers were able to identify a clear trend toward cultural convergence in shopping attitudes and customs

TABLE 6-5 Income Category Examples						
Percent of population	10%	15%	25%	25%	15%	10%
Earnings per month (in local currency (LC))	0–10	10–20	20–40	40–60	60–70	70–100

that cut across modern industrial countries, emerging industrial countries, and developing countries.[13]

STEP 4: ANALYZING RESEARCH DATA

Demand Pattern Analysis

Industrial growth patterns provide an insight into market demand. Because they generally reveal consumption patterns, production patterns are helpful in assessing market opportunities. Additionally, trends in manufacturing production indicate potential markets for companies that supply manufacturing inputs. At the early stages of growth in a country, when per capita incomes are low, manufacturing centers on such necessities as food and beverages, textiles, and other forms of light industry. As incomes rise, the relative importance of these industries declines as heavy industry begins to develop. As incomes continue to rise, service industries rise to overtake manufacturing in importance.

Income Elasticity Measurements

Income elasticity describes the relationship between demand for a good and changes in income. Income elasticity studies of consumer products show that necessities such as food and clothing are characterized by inelastic demand. Stated differently, expenditures on products in these categories increase but at a slower percentage rate than do increases in income. This is the corollary of Engel's law, which states that as incomes rise, smaller proportions of total income are spent on food. Demand for durable consumer goods such as furniture and appliances tends to be income elastic, increasing relatively faster than increases in income.

Market Estimation by Analogy

Estimating market size with available data presents challenging analytic tasks. When data are unavailable, as is frequently the case in both less developed and industrialized countries, resourceful techniques are required. One resourceful technique is estimation by analogy. There are two ways to use this technique. One way is to make cross-sectional comparisons, and the other is to displace a time series in time. The first method, cross-sectional comparisons, amounts simply to positing the assumption that there is an analogy between the relationship of a factor and demand for a particular product or commodity in two countries. This can best be explained as follows:

Let

X_A = demand for product X in country A

Y_A = factor that correlates with demand for product X in country A, data from country A

X_B = demand for product X in country B

Y_B = factor that correlates with demand for product X in country A, data from country B

If we assume that:

$$\frac{X_A}{Y_A} = \frac{X_B}{Y_B}$$

and if X_A, Y_A, and Y_B are known, we can solve for X_B as follows:

$$X_B = \frac{(X_A)\,(Y_B)}{Y_A}$$

---

[13] Eugene H. Fram and Riad Ajami, "Globalization of Markets and Shopping Stress: Cross-Country Comparisons," *Business Horizons* (January–February 1994): 17–23.

Basically, estimation by analogy amounts to the use of a single-factor index with a correlation value obtained from one country applied to a target market. This is a very simple method of analysis, but in many cases it is an extremely useful, rough estimating device whenever data are available in at least one potentially analogous market for product sales of consumption and a single correlation factor.

Displacing time is a useful method of market analysis when data are available for two markets at different levels of development. This method is based on the assumption that an analogy between markets exists in different time periods or, put another way, that the markets in question are going through the same stages of market development. The method amounts to assuming that the demand level for product X in country A in time period 1 was at the same stage as demand in time period 2 in country B. This can be illustrated as follows:

Let

X_{A1} = demand for product X in country A during time period 1
Y_{A1} = factor associated with demand for product X in country A during time period 1
X_{B2} = demand for product X in country B during time period 2
Y_{B2} = factor or factors correlating with demand for product X in country A and data from country B for time period 2

Assume that

$$\frac{X_{A1}}{Y_{A1}} = \frac{X_{B2}}{Y_{B2}}$$

If X_{A1}, Y_{A1}, and Y_{B2} are known, we can solve for X_{B2} as follows:

$$X_B = \frac{(X_{A1})(Y_{B2})}{Y_{A1}}$$

The time displacement method requires a marketer to estimate when two markets are at similar stages of development. For example, the market for Polaroid instant cameras in Russia in the mid-1990s might be comparable to the instant camera market in the United States in the mid-1960s. By obtaining data on the factors associated with demand for instant cameras in the United States in 1964 and in Russia in 1994, as well as actual U.S. demand in 1964, one could estimate the potential in Russia at the present time. However, because videocassette recorders (VCRs) and digital cameras were not available in the United States in the mid-1960s, this analogy is seriously flawed. Indeed, for the Polaroid camera, there is no market today that is analogous to markets anywhere in the world in the 1960s and 1970s because the competing electronic imaging technologies of today were not available then.

Several issues should be kept in mind in using estimation by analogy.

1. Are the two countries for which the analogy is assumed really similar? To answer this question with regard to a consumer product, the analyst must understand the similarities and differences in the cultural systems in the two countries. If the market for an industrial product is under study, an understanding of the respective national technology bases is required.
2. Have technological and social developments resulted in a situation in which demand for a particular product or commodity will leapfrog previous patterns, skipping entire growth patterns that occurred in more developed countries? For example, washing machine sales in Europe leapfrogged the pattern of sales in the United States.

3. If there are differences among the availability, price, quality, and other variables associated with the product in the two markets, potential demand in a target market will not develop into actual sales of a product because the market conditions are not comparable.

Cluster Analysis

The objective of cluster analysis is to group variables into clusters that maximize within-group similarities and between-group differences. Cluster analysis is well suited to global marketing research because similarities and differences can be established between local, national, and regional markets of the world.

Analyzing Results

Because there are numerous analysis techniques and different assumptions may be used, the net conclusions that may be drawn from market research may vary significantly. Two companies studying the same country or market segment can and often do reach different decisions accordingly. For example, the estimates of on-line shopping revenue for 1999 varied from $3.9 billion by the Direct Marketing Association to $36 billion by the Boston Consulting Group.[14]

STEP 5: PRESENTING THE FINDINGS

The report based on the marketing research must be useful to managers as input to the decision-making process. Whether the report is presented in written form, orally, or electronically via videotape, it must relate clearly to the problem or opportunity identified in step 1. Many managers are uncomfortable with research jargon and complex quantitative analysis. Results should be clearly stated and provide a basis for managerial action. Otherwise, the report may end up on the shelf where it will gather dust and serve as a reminder of wasted time and money. As the data provided by a corporate information system and marketing research become increasingly available on a worldwide basis, it becomes possible to analyze marketing expenditure effectiveness across national boundaries. Managers can then decide where they are achieving the greatest marginal effectiveness for their marketing expenditures and can adjust expenditures accordingly.

◆ CURRENT ISSUES IN GLOBAL MARKETING RESEARCH

Marketers engaged in global research face special problems and conditions that differentiate their task from that of the domestic market researcher. First, instead of analyzing a single national market, the global market researcher must analyze many national markets, each of which has unique characteristics that must be recognized in analysis. As noted earlier, for many countries, the availability of data is limited.

Second, the small markets around the world pose a special problem for the researcher. The relatively low profit potential in smaller markets permits only a modest marketing research expenditure. Therefore, the global researcher must devise techniques and methods that keep expenditures in line with the market's profit potential. In smaller markets, there is pressure on the researcher to discover economic and demographic relationships that permit estimates of demand based on a minimum of information. It may also be necessary to use inexpensive survey research that sacrifices some elegance or statistical rigor to achieve results within the constraints of the smaller marketing research budget.

Another frequently encountered problem in developing countries is that data may be inflated or deflated, either inadvertently or for political expediency. For example, a Middle Eastern country deliberately revised its balance of trade in a chemical product

---

[14] Nua Internet Surveys, "Online Shopping Revenue Estimates," *Marketing News* 3 July 2000, p. 20.

◆ BOX 6-2 ◆

MARKET RESEARCH IN DEVELOPING COUNTRIES

Nestlé demonstrates how understanding the market can lead to success. It successfully positioned its Maggi brand noodles as a between-meal snack food rather than a pasta meal item. Nestlé also caters to the Indian preference for local brands; although Nescafé is the company's flagship global coffee brand in many countries, Nestlé created chicory-flavored Sunrise especially for the Indian market. Nestlé managers have also learned that the 20 million wealthy households in its core target market exhibit a value orientation traditionally associated with mass markets. Nestlé has responded by keeping prices down: more than half of the products it sells in India cost less than 25 rupees—about 70 cents.

The tobacco industry is also learning about India. Sixty percent of Indian men smoke, although many perfer the native *bidi,* which is hand-rolled with a leaf outer wrapper rather than paper. As Darryl Jayson, economist

at the Tobacco Merchants Association (TMA), noted recently, "Many companies, local and international, are hoping that these bidi-smokers move up to cigarettes as India becomes more affluent." Although Western brands enjoy high levels of awareness, the government taxes make up 70 percent of the retail price of a single pack. As a result, premium European brands such as Dunhill cost $4 per pack, whereas Indian brands from Indian Tobacco Company and other local manufacturers sell for 50¢ to $1.50. Taste is an issue facing American tobacco companies; Indian smokers perfer Virginia blend tobaccos, while the typical American smoke uses oriental and burley blends. The TMA's Jayson says, "Indian smokers perceive U.S. cigarettes as roasted and harsh. I think it is very difficult to change the smoking habits of the Indians. It may take up to 20 years to bring about the change."

SOURCES: Miriam Jordan, "Marketing Gurus Say: In India, Think Cheap, Lose the Cold Cereal." *The Wall Street Journal,* 11 October 1996, p. A7; O. P. Malik, "The World's Tobacco Marketers Think 20 Million Indians Can't Be Wrong." *Brandweek,* 9 October 1995, pp. 46, 48; Malik, "The Great Indian Brand Bazaar," *Brandweek,* 5 June 1995, pp. 31–32.

by adding 1,000 tons to its consumption statistics in an attempt to encourage foreign investors to install domestic production facilities. In Russia, Goskomstat, the state agency that measures the economy, generates mountains of misleading statistics. Real GDP may be 40 percent higher than the official numbers because much of the economic activity in Russia's transitional economy is "off the books" due to high taxes and confusing laws.[15] Although market research in developing countries may have its challenges, the results are often well worth the effort as the examples in the box "Market Research in Developing Countries" demonstrate.

Another problem is that the comparability of international statistics varies greatly. An absence of standard data-gathering techniques contributes to the problem. In Germany, for example, consumer expenditures are estimated largely on the basis of turnover tax receipts, whereas in the United Kingdom, data from tax receipts are used in conjunction with data from household surveys and production sources.

Even with standard data-gathering techniques, definitions differ around the world. In some cases, these differences are minor; in others, they are quite significant. Germany, for example, classifies television set purchases as expenditures for "recreation and entertainment," whereas the same expenditure falls into the "furniture, furnishings, and household equipment" classification in the United States.

Survey data have similar comparability problems. When PepsiCo International—a typical user of global research—reviewed its data, it found a considerable lack of comparability in a number of major areas. Table 6-6 shows how age categories were developed

---

[15] Claudia Rosett, "Figures Never Lie but They Seldom Tell the Truth about the Russian Economy," *The Wall Street Journal,* 1 July 1994, p. A-6.

TABLE 6-6	Age Classification from Consumer Surveys, Major Markets					
Mexico	*Venezuela*	*Argentina*	*Germany*	*Spain*	*Italy*	*Philippines*
14–18	10–14	14–18	14–19	15–24	13–20	14–18
19–25	15–24	19–24	20–29	25–34	21–25	19–25
26–35	25–43	25–34	30–39	35–44	26–35	26–35
36–45	35–44	35–44	40–49	45–54	36–45	36–50
46+	45+	45–65	50+	55–64	46–60	
				65+		

Source: Pepsico International.

in seven countries surveyed by PepsiCo. PepsiCo's headquarters marketing research group pointed out that findings in one country could be compared with those in another only if data were reported in standard five-year intervals. Without this standardization, comparability was not possible. The marketing research group recommended, therefore, that standard five-year intervals be required in all reporting to headquarters but that any other intervals deemed useful for local purposes be allowed. Thus, for the purposes of local analysis, ages 14 to 19 might be a more pertinent "youth" classification in one country, whereas ages 14 to 24 might be a more useful definition of the same segment in another country.

PepsiCo also found that local market definitions of consumption differed so greatly that it was unable to make intermarket comparisons of brand share figures. Representative definitions of consumption are shown in Table 6-7.

Finally, global consumer research is inhibited by people's reluctance to talk to strangers, greater difficulty in locating people, and fewer telephones. Both industrial and consumer research services are less developed, although the cost of these services is much lower than in a high-wage country.

HEADQUARTERS CONTROL OF GLOBAL MARKETING RESEARCH

An important issue for the global company is where to locate control of the organization's research capability. The difference between a multinational, polycentric company and a global, geocentric company on this issue is significant. In the multinational, responsibility for research is delegated to the operating subsidiary. The global company delegates responsibility for research to operating subsidiaries but retains overall responsibility and control of research as a headquarters function. In practice, this means that the global company will, as in the PepsiCo example, ensure that research is designed and executed so as to yield comparable data.

Comparability requires that scales, questions, and research methodology be standardized. To achieve this, the company must inject a level of control and review of mar-

TABLE 6-7	Definition of Consumption Used by PepsiCo Market Researcher
Mexico	Count of number of occasions product was consumed on day prior to interview.
Venezuela	Count of number of occasions product was consumed on day prior to interview.
Argentina	Count of number of drinks consumed on day prior to interview.
Germany	Count of number of respondents consuming "daily or almost daily."
Spain	Count of number of drinks consumed "at least once a week."
Italy	Count of number of respondents consuming product on day prior to interview.
Philippines	Count of number of glasses of product consumed on day prior to interview.

keting research at the global level. The director of worldwide marketing research must respond to local conditions as he or she searches for a research program that can be implemented on a global basis. It is most likely that the marketing director will end up with a number of marketing programs tailored to clusters of countries that exhibit within-group similarities. The agenda of a coordinated worldwide research program might look like that in Table 6-8.

The director of worldwide research should not simply direct the efforts of country research managers. His or her job is to ensure that the corporation achieves maximum results worldwide from the total allocation of its research resources. Achieving this requires that personnel in each country are aware of research being carried out in the rest of the world and involved in influencing the design of their own in-country research as well as the overall research program. Ultimately, the director of worldwide research must be responsible for the overall research design and program. It is his or her job to take inputs from the entire world and produce a coordinated research strategy that generates the information needed to achieve global sales and profit objectives.

THE MARKETING INFORMATION SYSTEM AS A STRATEGIC ASSET

The advent of the transnational enterprise means that boundaries between the firm and the outside world are dissolving. Marketing has historically been responsible for managing many of the relationships across that boundary. The boundary between marketing and other functions is also dissolving, implying that the traditional notion of marketing as a distinct functional area within the firm is giving way to a new model. The process of marketing decision making is also changing. This is due largely to the changing role of information from a support tool to information as a wealth-generating, strategic asset.

Some firms are experimenting with "flatter" organizational structures, with less hierarchical, less centralized decision-making structures. Such organizations facilitate the exchange and flow of information between otherwise noncommunicative departments. The more information intensive the firm, the greater the degree to which marketing is involved in activities traditionally associated with other functional areas. In such firms, there is parallel processing of information.

Information intensity in the firm impacts market attractiveness, competitive position, and organizational structure. The greater a company's information intensity, the more the traditional product/market boundaries shift. In essence, companies increasingly face new sources of competition from other firms in historically noncompetitive industries, particularly if those firms are also information intensive. The most obvious and dramatic example is the emergence of the superindustry, combining telecommunications, computers, financial services, and retailing into what is essentially an information industry. Such diverse firms as AT&T, IBM, Merrill Lynch, Citicorp, and Sears now find themselves in direct competition with each other. They offer essentially the same products, although not as a result of diversification. Rather, the new competition reflects

TABLE 6-8 Worldwide Marketing Research Plan			
Research Objective	*Country Cluster A*	*Country Cluster B*	*Country Cluster C*
Identify market potential			X
Appraise competitive intentions		X	X
Evaluate product appeal	X	X	X
Study market response to price	X		
Appraise distribution channels	X	X	X

a natural extension and redefinition of traditional product lines and marketing activities. Today, when a company speaks of value added, it is less likely to be referring to unique product features. Rather, the emphasis is on the information exchanged as part of customer transactions—much of which cuts across traditional product lines.

◆ AN INTEGRATED APPROACH TO INFORMATION COLLECTION[16]

Coordinated organization activity is required to maintain surveillance of those aspects of the environment about which the organization wishes to stay informed. The goal of this activity, which may be termed *organized intelligence,* is to systematize the collecting and analysis of competitive intelligence to serve the needs of the organization as a whole. Organizing for intelligence requires more than gathering and disseminating good intelligence. Many companies that simply assign an analyst to the task of gathering, analyzing, and disseminating intelligence encounter problems in getting managers to use the output, in gaining credibility for the output and its function, and in establishing the relevance of the output for users.

The role of organized competitive intelligence in shaping strategy will depend on its ability to supplement, rather than replace, the informal activities of employees, especially those of top management. One obstacle to a fully integrated marketing information system encompassing both formal and informal information-gathering techniques is that monitoring activities are not usually fully integrated with the decision-making process. If the information is not used, the monitoring effort will invariably fail to increase a company's competitiveness. Michael Porter's influential work on competitive strategy, together with increasing global competitive pressures and loss of market dominance by many American companies, has helped bring environmental scanning into a new focus. The emphasis has been on competitive intelligence rather than on broader environmental scanning. When considering the possibility of establishing an organized intelligence system, a company may want to review the following questions.

WHEN DOES A COMPANY NEED ORGANIZED INTELLIGENCE?

1. Are top executives well informed about the competitive conditions in the market, or do they typically grumble about lack of sufficient knowledge?
2. Do proposals and presentations by middle management show an intimate knowledge of competitors and other industry players? Do these managers seem to know more than what has been published in trade literature?
3. Do managers in one department or division know of intelligence activities in other units? Do they share intelligence regularly?
4. How many times during the last six months was management surprised by developments in the marketplace? How many decisions yielded less than satisfactory results, and what percentage was caused by lack of accurate assessment of competitive response?
5. Has competitive pressure increased in the industry in question? Does management feel comfortable about its state of familiarity with foreign competitors?
6. How much does the company spend on on-line databases? How many users know about the availability of the system and how to access it?
7. Do users of information suffer from overload of data but underload of good analysis and estimates of implications to the company?

---

[16] This section is adapted from Benjamin Gilad, "The Role of Organized Competitive Intelligence in Corporate Strategy," *The Columbia Journal of World Business,* 24, no. 4 (1989): 29–36.

Summary

Information is one of the most basic ingredients of a successful marketing strategy. The global marketer must scan the world for information about opportunities and threats and make information available via a management information system. Scanning can be accomplished by keeping in touch with an area of interest via surveillance or by actively seeking out information via search. Information can be obtained from human and documentary sources or from direct perception.

Formal research is often required before decisions can be made regarding specific problems or opportunities. After developing a research plan, data are collected using either primary or secondary sources. A number of techniques are available for analyzing data, including demand pattern analysis, income elasticity measurements, estimation by analogy, comparative analysis, and cluster analysis. Research findings must be presented clearly to facilitate decision making. Global marketing research presents a number of challenges. First is the simple fact that research on a number of markets may be required, some of which are so small that only modest research expenditures can be made. Secondary data from some countries may be distorted; also, comparability may be an issue. A final issue is how much control headquarters will have over research and the overall management of the organization's information system.

Discussion Questions

1. What is the major source of information for headquarters executives of global companies?
2. What are the different modes of information acquisition? Which is the most important for gathering strategic information?
3. Assume that you have been asked by the president of your organization to devise a systematic approach to scanning. The president does not want to be surprised by major market or competitive developments. What would you recommend?
4. Outline the basic steps of the marketing research process.
5. What is the difference between existing, latent, and incipient demand? How might these differences affect the design of a marketing research project?
6. Describe some of the analytical techniques used by global marketers. When is it appropriate to use each technique?
7. How does the Internet affect market information systems?

Suggested Readings

Adler, Lee. "Managing Marketing Research in the Diversified Multinational Corporation." In Edward M. Mazze, Ed. *Marketing in Turbulent Times and Marketing: The Challenges and Opportunities—Combined Proceedings.* Chicago: American Marketing Association (1975): 305–308.

Cavusgil, S. Tamer. "Qualitative Insights into Company Experiences in International Marketing Research." *Journal of Business and Industrial Marketing* (Summer 1987): 41–54.

Crossen, Cynthia. *Tainted Truth: The Manipulation of Fact in America.* Upper Saddle River, NJ: Simon & Schuster, 1994.

Czinkota, M. R., and I. A. Ronkainen. "Market Research for Your Export Operations, Part I." *International Trade Forum,* 3 (1994): 22–33.

Czinkota, M. R., and I. A. Ronkainen. "Market Research for Your Export Operations, Part II." *International Trade Forum,* 31, no. 1 (1995): 16–21.

Davenport, Thomas H., Michael Hammer, and Tauno J. Metsisto. "How Executives Can Shape Their Company's Information Systems." *Harvard Business Review,* 67 (March/April 1989): 130–134.

Davidson, Lawrence S. "Knowing the Unknowable." *Business Horizons,* 32 (September/October 1989): 2–8.

Douglas, Susan P., C. Samuel Craig, and Warren J. Keegan. "Approaches to Assessing International Marketing Opportunities for Small- and Medium-Sized Companies." *Columbia Journal of World Business* (Fall 1982): 2–30.

Gilad, Benjamin. "The Role of Organized Competitive Intelligence in Corporate Strategy." *Columbia Journal of World Business* (Winter 1989): 29–35.

Glazer, Rashi. "Marketing in an Information-Intensive Environment: Strategic Implications of Knowledge as an Asset." *Journal of Marketing* (October 1991): 1–19.

Green, Robert, and Eric Langeard. "A Cross-National Comparison of Consumer Habits and Innovator Characteristics." *Journal of Marketing* (July 1975): 34–41.

Keegan, Warren J. "Scanning the International Business Environment: A Study of the Informational Acquisition Process," Doctoral Dissertation, Harvard Business School (1967).

Kelly, John M. *How to Check Out Your Competition: A Complete Plan for Investigating Your Market.* New York: Wiley, 1987.

King, W. R., and V. Sethi. "Developing Transnational Information Systems: A Case Study." *Omega* (January 1993): 53–59.

Kravis, Irving B., Zoltan Kenessey, Alan Heston, and Robert Summers. *A System of International Comparisons of Gross Product and Purchasing Power.* Baltimore: Johns Hopkins University Press, 1975.

Lindberg, Bertil C. "International Comparison of Growth in Demand for a New Durable Consumer Product." *Journal of Marketing Research* (August 1982): 364–371.

Moyer, Reed. "International Market Analysis." *Journal of Marketing Research* (November 1968): 353–360.

Mullen, Michael R. "Diagnosing Measurement Equivalence in Cross-National Research." *Journal of International Business Studies,* 26 (Third Quarter 1995): 573–596.

Naumann, Earl, Donald W. Jackson, Jr., and William G. Wolfe. "Comparing U.S. and Japanese Market Research Firms." *California Management Review,* 36 (Summer 1994): 49–69.

Panigrahi, Bragaban, Ranjita Misra, and Stephen E. Calrish. "Perceptions of Indian Business Organizations toward Formal Marketing Research." *The International Executive,* 38 (September/October 1996): 613–632.

Sethi, S. Prakash. "Comparative Cluster Analysis for World Markets." *Journal of Marketing Research,* 8 (August 1971): 350.

Sharer, Kevin. "Top Management's Intelligence Needs: An Executive's View of Competitive Intelligence." *Competitive Intelligence Review* (Spring 1991): 3–5.

Stanat, Ruth. "Tracking Your Global Competition." *Competitive Intelligence Review* (Spring 1991): 17–19.

Steenkamp, Jan-Benedict E. M. "Assessing Measurement Invariance in Cross-National Consumer Research." *Journal of Consumer Research,* 25, no 1 (1998): 78–91.

Vogel, R. H. "Uses of Managerial Perceptions in Clustering Countries." *Journal of International Business Studies* (Spring 1976): 91–100.

Wasilewski, Nikolai. "Dimensions of Environmental Scanning Systems in Multinational Enterprises." Pace University, Working Papers no. 3 (May 1993).

CHAPTER 7

Segmentation, Targeting, and Positioning

"What is reasonable is real; that which is real is reasonable."

—GEORG WILHELM FRIEDRICH HEGEL
Philosophy of Right (1821)

CHAPTER CONTENTS

Cigarettes are one of the most widely distributed and profitable global consumer products.[1] However, as the number of smokers in high-income countries declines due to heightened antismoking sentiment and health concerns, tobacco industry giants such as Britain's B.A.T. Industries PLC and America's Philip Morris Company have set their sights on new market opportunities. In particular, tobacco companies are targeting smokers in developing countries such as China, Thailand, India, and Russia. These are nations in which a combination of forces—rising incomes in some countries and challenging economic conditions in others, smoking's fashionableness, and the status assigned to Western cigarette brands—interacts to expand the smoking market and brand share of the leading global brands. Moreover, because many women in these countries view smoking as a symbol of their improving status in society, the tobacco companies are aggressively targeting women.

The actions taken by managers at Philip Morris, B.A.T., and other tobacco companies are examples of market segmentation and targeting. Market segmentation represents an effort to identify and categorize groups of customers and countries according to various characteristics. Targeting is the process of evaluating the segments and focusing marketing efforts on a country, region, or group of people that has significant potential to respond. Such targeting reflects the reality that a company should identify

---

[1] Richard J. Barnet and John Cavanagh, *Global Dreams: Imperial Corporations and the New World Order* (New York: Simon and Schuster, 1994), p. 184.

those consumers it can reach most effectively and efficiently. Segmentation, targeting, and positioning are all examined in this chapter.

◆ GLOBAL MARKET SEGMENTATION

Market segmentation is

> the process of subdividing a market into distinct subsets of customers that behave in the same way or have similar needs. Each subset may conceivably be chosen as a market target to be reached with a distinctive marketing strategy. The process begins with a basis of segmentation—a product-specific factor that reflects differences in customers' requirements or responsiveness to marketing variables (possibilities are purchase behavior, usage, benefits sought, intentions, preference, or loyalty).[2]

Global market segmentation is the process of dividing the world market into distinct subsets of customers that behave in the same way or have similar needs, or, as one author put it, it is "the process of identifying specific segments—whether they be country groups or individual consumer groups—of potential customers with homogeneous attributes who are likely to exhibit similar buying behavior."[3] Interest in global market segmentation dates back several decades. In the late 1960s, one observer suggested that the European market could be divided into three broad categories—international sophisticate, semisophisticate, and provincial—solely on the basis of consumers' presumed receptivity to a common advertising approach.[4] Another writer suggested that some themes (e.g., the desire to be beautiful, the desire to be healthy and free of pain, the love of mother and child) were universal and could be used in advertising around the globe.[5]

In the 1980s, Professor Theodore Levitt advanced the thesis that consumers in different countries increasingly seek variety and that the same new segments are likely to show up in multiple national markets. Thus, ethnic or regional foods such as sushi, Greek salad, or hamburgers might be in demand anywhere in the world. Levitt described this trend as the "pluralization of consumption" and "segment simultaneity" that provides an opportunity for marketers to pursue a segment on a global scale.[6]

Today, global companies (and the advertising agencies that serve them) are likely to segment world markets according to one or more key criteria: geography, demographics (including national income and size of population), psychographics (values, attitudes, and lifestyles), behavioral characteristics, and benefits sought. It is also possible to cluster different national markets in terms of their environments (e.g., the presence or absence of government regulation in a particular industry) to establish groupings. Another powerful tool for global segmentation is horizontal segmentation by user category.

GEOGRAPHIC SEGMENTATION

Geographic segmentation is dividing the world into geographic subsets. The advantage of geography is proximity: Markets in geographic segments are closer to each other and easier to visit on the same trip or to call on during the same time window. Geographic

---

[2] Peter D. Bennett (Ed.), *Dictionary of Marketing Terms,* 2nd ed. (Chicago: American Marketing Association, 1995), pp. 165–166.

[3] Salah S. Hassan and Lea Prevel Katsanis, "Identification of Global Consumer Segments: A Behavioral Framework," *Journal of International Consumer Marketing,* 3, no. 2 (1992): 17.

[4] John K. Ryans, Jr., "Is It Too Soon to Put a Tiger in Every Tank?" *Columbia Journal of World Business* (March–April 1969): 73.

[5] Arthur C. Fatt, "The Danger of 'Local' International Advertising," *Journal of Marketing* (January 1967).

[6] Theodore Levitt, "The Globalization of Markets," *Harvard Business Review* (May/June 1983): 92–102.

segmentation also has major limitations: The mere fact that markets are in the same world geographic region does not meant that they are similar. Japan and Vietnam are both in East Asia, but one is a high-income, postindustrial society and the other is an emerging, less developed, preindustrial society. The differences in the markets in these two countries overwhelm their similarities. Simon found in his sample of "hidden champions" that geography was ranked lowest as a basis for market segmentation (see Figure 7-1).

DEMOGRAPHIC SEGMENTATION

Demographic segmentation is based on measurable characteristics of populations such as age, gender, income, education, and occupation. A number of demographic trends—aging population, fewer children, more women working outside the home, and higher incomes and living standards—suggest the emergence of global segments.

For most consumer and industrial products, national income is the single most important segmentation variable and indicator of market potential. Annual per capita income varies widely in world markets, from a low of $81 in the Congo to a high of $38,587 in Luxembourg. The World Bank segments countries into high income, upper middle income, lower middle income, and low income. These categories are used in "Global Income and Population" in the Appendix of this book.

The U.S. market, with per capita income of $29,953, more than $8.3 trillion in 2000 national income, and a population of more than 275 million people, is enormous. Little wonder, then, that Americans are a favorite target market! Despite having comparable per capita incomes, other industrialized countries are nevertheless quite small in terms of total annual income. In Sweden, for example, per capita gross national product (GNP) is $24,487; however, Sweden's smaller population of 9 million means that annual national income is only about $220 billion. About 73 percent of world GNP is located in the Triad. Thus, by segmenting in terms of a single demographic variable—income—a company could reach the most affluent markets by targeting three regions: the European Union, North America, and Japan.

Many global companies also realize that for products with a low enough price—for example, cigarettes, soft drinks, and some packaged goods—population is a more important segmentation variable than income. Thus, China and India, with respective populations of 1.3 billion and 1.0 billion, might represent attractive target markets. In a country such as China, where per capita GNP is only $930, the marketing challenge is to successfully serve the existing mass market for inexpensive consumer products. Procter & Gamble, Unilever, Kao, Johnson & Johnson, and other packaged-goods companies are

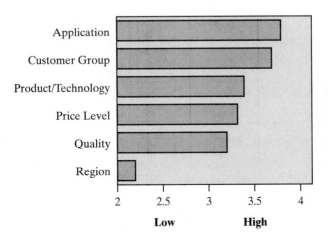

FIGURE 7-1 Importance of Market Definition Criteria

Source: Hermann Simon, *Hidden Champions: Lessons from 500 of the World's Best Unknown Companies* (Boston, MA: Harvard Business school Press, 1996), p. 45. Copyright © 1996 by Harvard Business School Publishing Corporation. Reprinted by permission of Harvard Business School Press.

targeting and developing the China market, lured in part by the possibility that as many as 100 million Chinese customers are affluent enough to spend, say, 14 cents for a single-use pouch of shampoo.[7]

Segmenting decisions can be complicated by the fact that the national income figures such as those cited previously for China and India are averages. There are also large, fast-growing, high-income segments in both of these countries. In India, for example, 100 million people can be classified as "upper middle class," with average incomes of more than $1,400. Pinning down a demographic segment may require additional information; India's middle class has been estimated to be as low as a few million and as high as 250 million to 300 million people. If *middle class* is defined as "persons who own a refrigerator," the figure would be 30 million people. If television ownership were used as a benchmark, the middle class would be 100 million to 125 million people.[8] The important lesson for global marketers is to beware of the misleading effect of averages, which distort the true market conditions in emerging markets.

Note also that the average income figures quoted here do not reflect the standard of living in these countries. In order to really understand the standard of living in a country, it is necessary to determine the purchasing power of the local currency. In low-income countries, the actual purchasing power of the local currency is much higher than that implied by exchange values. In India, for example, the authors' colleague recently returned from a trip during which he received a slight cut on his forehead from a taxi trunk lid. He decided to visit a doctor to get a tetanus shot and, because he knew that malaria was a hazard in India, he requested a prescription and a one-month supply of malaria pills. He did this, and the bill from the doctor for the shot, the pills, and the prescription was 30 rupees or US $1.00.

Age is another useful demographic variable. One global segment based on demographics is global teenagers—young people between the ages of 12 and 19. Teens, by virtue of their interest in fashion, music, and a youthful lifestyle, exhibit consumption behavior that is remarkably consistent across borders. Young consumers may not yet have conformed to cultural norms—indeed, they may be rebelling against them. This fact, combined with shared universal needs, desires, and fantasies (for name brands, novelty, entertainment, and trendy and image-oriented products), make it possible to reach the global teen segment with a unified marketing program. This segment is attractive both in terms of its size (about 1.3 billion) and its multibillion-dollar purchasing power. Coca-Cola, Benetton, Swatch, and Sony are some of the companies pursuing the global teenage segment. The global telecommunications revolution is a critical driving force behind the emergence of this segment. Global media such as MTV are perfect vehicles for reaching this segment. Satellites such as AsiaSatI are beaming Western programming and commercials to millions of viewers in China, India, and other countries.

Another global segment is the so-called elite: older, more affluent consumers who are well traveled and have the money to spend on prestigious products with an image of exclusivity. This segment's needs and wants are spread over various product categories: durable goods (luxury automobiles); nondurables (upscale beverages such as rare wines and champagne); and financial services (American Express gold and platinum cards). Technological change in telecommunications makes it easier to reach the global elite segment. Global telemarketing is a viable option today as AT&T International 800 services are available in more than 40 countries. Increased reliance on cata-

---

[7] Valerie Reitman, "Enticed by Visions of Enormous Numbers, More Western Marketers Move into China," *The Wall Street Journal,* 12 July 1993, pp. B1, B6.

[8] John Bussey, "India's Market Reform Requires Perspective," *The Wall Street Journal,* 8 May 1994, p. A1. See also Miriam Jordan, "In India, Luxury Is Within Reach of Many," *The Wall Street Journal,* 17 October 1995, p. A1.

log marketing by upscale retailers such as Harrods, Laura Ashley, and Ferragamo has also yielded impressive results.

PSYCHOGRAPHIC SEGMENTATION

Psychographic segmentation involves grouping people in terms of their attitudes, values, and lifestyles. Data are obtained from questionnaires that require respondents to indicate the extent to which they agree or disagree with a series of statements. In the United States, psychographics is primarily associated with SRI International, a market research organization whose original VALS and updated VALS 2 analyses of U.S. consumers are widely known.

Porsche AG, the German sports-car maker, turned to psychographics after watching worldwide sales decline from 50,000 units in 1986 to about 14,000 in 1993. Its U.S. subsidiary, Porsche Cars North America, already had a clear demographic profile of its customers: 40+-year-old male college graduates whose annual income exceeded $200,000. A psychographic study showed that, demographics aside, Porsche buyers could be divided into five distinct categories (see Table 7-1). Top Guns, for example, buy Porsches and expect to be noticed; for Proud Patrons and Fantasists, on the other hand, such conspicuous consumption is irrelevant. Porsche will use the profiles to develop advertising tailored to each type. Notes Richard Ford, Porsche vice president of sales and marketing, "We were selling to people whose profiles were diametrically opposed. You wouldn't want to tell an elitist how good he looks in the car or how fast he could go." Results have been promising; Porsche's U.S. sales improved nearly 50 percent in 1994.[9]

One early application of psychographics outside the United States focused on value orientations of consumers in the United Kingdom, France, and Germany. Although the study was limited in scope, the researcher concluded that "the underlying values structures in each country appeared to bear sufficient similarity to warrant a common overall communications strategy."[10] SRI International has recently conducted psychographic analyses of the Japanese market; broader-scope studies have been undertaken by several global advertising agencies, including Backer, Spielvogel & Bates Worldwide (BSB), D'arcy Massius Benton & Bowles (DMBB), and Young & Rubicam (Y&R).[11] These

TABLE 7-1	Psychographic Profiles of Porsche's American Customers	
Category	*% of All Owners*	*Description*
Top Guns	27%	Driven and ambitious; care about power and control; expect to be noticed
Elitists	24%	Old money; a car—even an expensive one—is just a car, not an extension of one's personality
Proud Patrons	23%	Ownership is what counts; a car is a trophy, a reward for working hard; being noticed doesn't matter
Bon Vivants	17%	Cosmopolitan jet setters and thrill seekers; car heightens excitement
Fantasists	9%	Car represents a form of escape; don't care about impressing others; may even feel guilty about owning car

---

[9] Alex Taylor III, "Porsche Slices Up Its Buyers," *Fortune,* 16 January 1995, p. 24.

[10] Alfred S. Boote, "Psychographic Segmentation in Europe," *Journal of Advertising Research,* 22, no. 6, (December 1982–January 1983): 25.

[11] The following discussion is adapted from Rebecca Piirto, *Beyond Mind Games: The Marketing Power of Psychographics* (Ithaca, NY: American Demographics Books, 1991).

analyses offer a detailed understanding of various segments, including the global teenager and global elite discussed earlier.

Backer Spielvogel & Bates's Global Scan

Global Scan is a study that encompasses 18 countries, mostly located in the Triad. To identify attitudes that could help explain and predict purchase behavior for different product categories, the researchers studied consumer attitudes and values, as well as media viewership/readership, buying patterns, and product use. The survey attempts to identify both country-specific and global attitudinal attributes; sample statements are "The harder you push, the farther you get," and "I never have enough time or money." Combining all the country data yielded a segmentation study known as Target Scan, a description of five global psychographic segments that BSB claims represent 95 percent of the adult populations in the 18 countries surveyed (see Figure 7-2). BSB has labeled the segments as Strivers, Achievers, Pressured, Traditionals, and Adapters.

> *Strivers (26 percent).* This segment consists of young people with a median age of 31 who live hectic, on-the-go lives. Driven to achieve success, they are materialistic pleasure seekers for whom time and money are in short supply.
>
> *Achievers (22 percent).* Older than the Strivers, the affluent, assertive Achievers are upwardly mobile and already have attained a good measure of success. Achievers are status-conscious consumers for whom quality is important.
>
> *Pressured (13 percent).* The Pressured segment, largely comprised of women, cuts across age groups and is characterized by constant financial and family pressures. Life's problems overwhelm the members of this segment.
>
> *Adapters (18 percent).* This segment is composed of older people who are content with their lives and who manage to maintain their values while keeping open minds when faced with change.
>
> *Traditionals (16 percent).* This segment is "rooted to the past" and clings to the country's heritage and cultural values.

Global Scan is a helpful tool for identifying consumer similarities across national boundaries, as well as highlighting differences between segments in different countries. For example, in the United States, the 75 million baby boomers help swell the ranks of Strivers and Achievers to nearly half the population. In Germany, on the other hand, the

FIGURE 7-2 BSB's Global Scan Segmentation Study

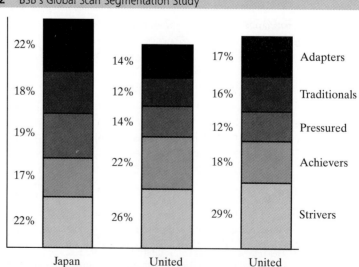

Striver segment is older and comprises a smaller proportion of the population. Global Scan has also pinpointed important differences between Americans and Canadians, who are often considered to be part of the same geographic segment of North America.

Similarly, Global Scan revealed marked differences between the circumstances in which Strivers find themselves in different countries. In the United States, Strivers are chronically short of both time and money, whereas Japanese Strivers have ample monetary resources. These differences translate directly into different preferences: U.S. Strivers buy cars that are fun, stylish, and represent a good value; Japanese Strivers view cars as an extension of their homes and will accessorize them with lavish features—curtains and high-end stereo systems, for example. This implies that different advertising appeals would be necessary when targeting Strivers in the two countries.

D'arcy Massius Benton & Bowles's Euroconsumer Study

DMBB's research team focused on Europe and produced a 15-country study titled "The Euroconsumer: Marketing Myth or Cultural Certainty?" The researchers identified four lifestyle groups: Successful Idealists, Affluent Materialists, Comfortable Belongers, and Disaffected Survivors. The first two groups represent the elite, the latter two, mainstream European consumers.

> *Successful Idealists.* Comprising from 5 to 20 percent of the population, this segment consists of persons who have achieved professional and material success while maintaining commitment to abstract or socially responsible ideals.
>
> *Affluent Materialists.* These status-conscious "up-and-comers," many of whom are business professionals, use conspicuous consumption to communicate their success to others.
>
> *Comfortable Belongers.* Comprising one quarter to one half of a country's population, this group, like Global Scan's Adapters and Traditionals, is conservative and most comfortable with the familiar. Belongers are content with the comfort of home, family, friends, and community.
>
> *Disaffected Survivors.* Lacking power and affluence, this segment harbors little hope for upward mobility and tends to be either resentful or resigned. This segment is concentrated in high-crime, urban inner city neighborhoods. Despite Disaffected Survivors' lack of societal status, their attitudes nevertheless tend to affect the rest of society.

DMBB has also recently completed a psychographic profile of the Russian market. The study divides Russians into five categories, based on their outlook, behavior, and openness to Western products. The categories include *kuptsy,* Cossacks, students, business executives, and "Russian Souls." Members of the largest group, the *kuptsy* (the label comes from the Russian word for *merchant*), theoretically prefer Russian products but look down on mass-produced goods of inferior quality. *Kuptsy* are most likely to admire automobiles and stereo equipment from countries with good reputations for engineering, such as Germany and Scandinavia. Nigel Clarke, the author of the study, notes that segmentation and targeting are appropriate in Russia, despite the fact that its broad consumer market is still in its infancy. "If you're dealing with a market as different as Russia is, even if you want to go 'broad,' it's best to think: 'Which group would go most for my brand? Where is my natural center of gravity?' "[12]

Young & Rubicam's Cross-Cultural Consumer Characterizations (4Cs)

Young & Rubicam's 4Cs is a 20-country psychographic segmentation study focusing on goals, motivations, and values that help to determine consumer choice. The research is based on the assumption that "there are underlying psychological processes involved

---

[12] Stuart Elliot, "Figuring Out the Russian Consumer," *The New York Times,* 1 April 1992, pp. C1, C19.

in human behavior that are culture-free and so basic that they can be found all over the globe."[13]

Three overall groupings can be further subdivided into a total of seven segments: Constrained (Resigned Poor and Struggling Poor), Middle Majority (Mainstreamers, Aspirers, and Succeeders), and Innovators (Transitionals and Reformers). The goals, motivations, and values of these segments range from "survival," "given up," and "subsistence" (Resigned Poor) to "social betterment," "social conscience," and "social altruism" (Reformers). Table 7-2 shows some of the attitudinal, work, lifestyle, and purchase behavior characteristics of the seven groups.

Combining the 4Cs data for a particular country with other data permits Y&R to predict product and category purchase behavior for the various segments. Yet, as noted previously in the discussion of Global Scan, marketers at global companies that are Y&R clients are cautioned not to assume that they can develop one strategy or one commercial to be used to reach a particular segment across cultures. As a Y&R staffer notes, "As you get closer to the executional level, you need to be acutely sensitive to cultural differences. But at the origin, it's of enormous benefit to be able to think about people who share common values across cultures."[14]

BEHAVIOR SEGMENTATION

Behavior segmentation focuses on whether people buy and use a product, as well as how often and how much they use it. Consumers can be categorized in terms of usage rates—

TABLE 7-2   Y&R's 4Cs

Attitudes	Work	Lifestyle	Purchase Behavior
Resigned Poor			
Unhappy	Labor	Shut-in	Staples
Distrustful	Unskilled	Television	Price
Struggling Poor			
Unhappy	Labor	Sports	Price
Dissatisfied	Craftsmen	Television	Discount stores
Mainstreamers			
Happy	Craftsmen	Family	Habit
Belong	Teaching	Gardening	Brand loyal
Aspirers			
Unhappy	Sales	Trendy sports	Conspicuous consumption
Ambitious	White collar	Fashion magazines	Credit
Succeeders			
Happy	Managerial	Travel	Luxury
Industrious	Professional	Dining out	Quality
Transitionals			
Rebellious	Student	Arts/crafts	Impulse
Liberal	Health field	Special-interest magazines	Unique products
Reformers			
Inner growth	Professional	Reading	Ecology
Improve world	Entrepreneur	Cultural events	Homemade/grown

[13] Piirto, *Beyond Mind Games,* p. 161.
[14] Ibid., p. 165.

for example, heavy, medium, light, and nonuser. Consumers can also be segmented according to user status: potential users, nonusers, ex-users, regulars, first-timers, and users of competitors' products. Although bottled water may be considered a luxury product in some high-income markets, Nestlé is marketing bottled water in Pakistan where there is a huge market of nonusers who, despite their low income, are willing to pay 18 rupees a bottle for clean water because of the widespread presence of arsenic poisoning in well water and the pollution of surface water. Tobacco companies are targeting China because the Chinese are heavy smokers.

Financial institutions have to consider many different pieces of information regarding consumer behavior toward saving and spending money. Japan has the highest number of cash dispensers, 1,115 per 1 million population, followed by Switzerland, Canada, and the United States where the average is slightly higher than 600. The average dollar amount withdrawn also varies considerably. In Japan, the average withdrawal is $289. This is followed by Switzerland at $187 and Italy at $185. The United States is far down the list with $68 as the average withdrawal. Japanese people tend to carry around a lot more cash than people in other countries.[15]

BENEFIT SEGMENTATION

Global benefit segmentation focuses on the numerator of the value equation—the B in $V = B/P$. This approach can achieve excellent results by virtue of marketers' superior understanding of the problem a product solves or the benefit it offers, regardless of geography. For example, Nestlé discovered that cat owners' attitudes toward feeding their pets are the same everywhere. In response, a pan-European campaign was created for Friskies dry cat food. The appeal was that dry cat food better suits a cat's universally recognized independent nature.

VERTICAL VERSUS HORIZONTAL SEGMENTATION

Vertical segmentation is based on product category or modality and price points. For example, in medical imaging there is X-ray, computed axial tomography (CAT) scan, magnetic resonance imaging (MRI), and so on. Each modality has its own price points. These price points were the traditional way of segmenting the medical imaging market. One company decided to take a different approach and segment the same market by the health care delivery system: national research and teaching hospitals, government hospitals, and so on. It then rolled out a campaign that was regional, national, and finally global, which was tailored for each different type of health care delivery. This horizontal segmentation approach worked as well in markets outside the home-country launch market as it did in the home country.[16]

◆ GLOBAL TARGETING

As discussed earlier, segmenting is the process by which marketers identify groups of consumers with similar wants and needs. Targeting is the act of evaluating and comparing the identified groups and then selecting one or more of them as the prospect(s) with the highest potential. A marketing mix is then devised that will provide the organization with the best return on sales while simultaneously creating the maximum amount of value to consumers.

---

[15] "Holes in the Wall," *The Economist,* 6 March 1999, p. 99.

[16] Interview with Nicholas F. Rossiello, Vice President Marketing and Sales, AFP Imaging Corporation, Elmsford, NY, October 30, 1996.

CRITERIA FOR TARGETING

The three basic criteria for assessing opportunity in global target markets are the same as in single-country targeting: current size of the segment and anticipated growth potential; competition; and compatibility with the company's overall objectives and the feasibility of successfully reaching a designated target.

Current Segment Size and Growth Potential

Is the market segment currently large enough that it presents a company with the opportunity to make a profit? If it is not large enough or profitable enough today, does it have high growth potential so that it is attractive in terms of a company's long-term strategy? Indeed, one of the advantages of targeting a market segment globally is that, whereas the segment in a single-country market might be too small, even a narrow segment can be served profitably with a standardized product if the segment exists in several countries.[17] The billion-plus members of the global "MTV Generation" constitute a huge market that, by virtue of its size, is extremely attractive to many companies.

China represents an individual geographic market that offers attractive opportunities in many industries. Consider the growth opportunity in financial services, for example. There are currently only about 3 million credit cards in circulation, mostly used by businesses. Low product saturation levels are also found for personal computers; there is one computer for every 1,250 people. The ratio in the United States is approaching one computer for every two people. The opportunity for automobile manufacturers is even greater. China has 1.2 million passenger cars, one car for every 20,000 Chinese. Even with the market in China growing at an annual rate of 33 percent, a tremendous potential market still exists.

Potential Competition

A market or market segment characterized by strong competition may be a segment to avoid or one in which to utilize a different strategy. Often a local brand may present competition to the entering multinational. In Peru, Inca Kola is as popular as Coca-Cola. In India, Thumbs Cola is a major brand. In the Siberian city of Krasnoyarsk, Crazy Cola has a 48 percent share of the market.[18] The multinational might try more or different promotions or may acquire the local company or form an alliance with it.

Kodak's position as the undisputed leader in the $2.4 billion U.S. color film market did not deter Fuji from launching a competitive offensive. In addition to offering traditional types of 35mm film at prices below Kodak's, Fuji quickly made inroads by introducing a number of new film products targeted at the "advanced amateur" segment that Kodak had neglected. Despite its early successes, after nearly two decades of effort, Fuji's U.S. market share has been in the 10 to 16 percent range. Part of the problem is Kodak's distribution clout: Kodak is well entrenched in supermarket and drugstore chains, where Fuji must also jostle with other newcomers such as Konica and Polaroid. In addition, Kodak has agreements with dozens of American amusement parks guaranteeing that only Kodak film will be sold on the premises. Fuji is also developing its market in Europe, where Kodak commands "only" 40 percent of the color film market. Fuji currently enjoys 25 percent of the European market, compared with 10 percent a decade ago. Meanwhile, Kodak has spent half a billion dollars in Japan, the world's second-largest market for photographic supplies; its market share there currently stands at about 10 percent.[19]

---

[17] Michael E. Porter, "The Strategic Role of International Marketing," *The Journal of Consumer Marketing,* 3, no. 2 (Spring 1986): 21.

[18] Betsy McKay, "Siberian Soft Drink Queen Outmarkets Coke and Pepsi," *The Wall Street Journal,* 23 August, 1999, p. B1.

[19] Clare Ansberry, "Uphill Battle: Eastman Kodak Co. Has Arduous Struggle to Regain Lost Edge," *The Wall Street Journal,* 2 April 1987, pp. 1, 12.

Compatibility and Feasibility

If a global target market is judged to be large enough, and if strong competitors are either absent or not deemed to represent insurmountable obstacles, then the final consideration is whether a company can and should target that market. In many cases, reaching global market segments requires considerable resources such as expenditures for distribution and travel by company personnel. Another question is whether the pursuit of a particular segment is compatible with the company's overall goals and established sources of competitive advantage. Although Pepsi was firmly entrenched in the Russian market, having entered in 1972, Coke waited 15 years to make its first move in Russia and 20 years before it decided to make major investments. At the time of Coke's entry, Pepsi had 100 percent of the Russian cola market. This would appear to be a difficult position to challenge, but because of the size of the Coke investment and the skillful execution of its investment moves in Russia, by 1996 Coke's market share had reached 50 percent.[20]

SELECTING A GLOBAL TARGET MARKET STRATEGY

If, after evaluating the identified segments in terms of the three criteria presented earlier, a decision is made to proceed, an appropriate targeting strategy must be developed. There are three basic categories of target marketing strategies: standardized marketing, concentrated marketing, and differentiated marketing.

Standardized Global Marketing

Standardized global marketing is analogous to mass marketing in a single country. It involves creating the same marketing mix for a broad market of potential buyers. This strategy calls for extensive distribution in the maximum number of retail outlets. The appeal of standardized global marketing is clear: greater sales volume, lower production costs, and greater profitability. The same is true of standardized global communications: lower production costs and, if done well, higher quality and greater effectiveness of marketing communications.

Coca-Cola, one of the world's most global brands, uses the appeal of youthful fun in its global advertising. Its sponsorship program is global and is adapted to events that are popular in specific countries such as soccer in other parts of the world versus football in the United States.

Concentrated Global Marketing

The second global targeting strategy involves devising a marketing mix to reach a single segment of the global market. In cosmetics, this approach has been used successfully by the House of Lauder, Chanel, and other cosmetics houses that target the upscale, prestige segment of the market. This is the strategy employed by the hidden champions of global marketing: companies that most people have never heard of that have adopted strategies of concentrated marketing on a global scale. These companies define their markets narrowly. They go for global depth rather than national breadth. For example, Winterhalter (a German company) is a hidden champion in the dishwasher market, but the company has never sold a dishwasher to a consumer. It has also never sold a dishwasher to a hospital, school, company, or any other organization. It focuses exclusively on dishwashers for hotels and restaurants. It offers dishwashers, water conditioners, detergents, and service. Jüergen Winterhalter commented in reference to the company's narrow market definition: "This narrowing of our market definition was the most important strategic decision we ever made. It is the very foundation of our success in the past decade."[21]

---

[20] Interview with Oleg Smirnoff, former marketing manager, PepsiCola International, New York, October 31, 1996.

[21] Hermann Simon, *Hidden Champions: Lessons from 500 of the World's Best Unknown Companies* (Boston: Harvard Business School Press, 1996), p. 54.

Differentiated Global Marketing

The third target marketing strategy is a variation of concentrated global marketing. It entails targeting two or more distinct market segments with different marketing mixes. This strategy allows a company to achieve wider market coverage. For example, in the segment of sports-utility vehicles (SUV), Rover has a $50,000+ Range Rover at the high end of the market; a scaled-down version, the Land Rover Discoverer, is priced at under $35,000, which competes directly with the Jeep Grand Cherokee. These are two different segments, and Rover has a concentrated strategy for each.

One of the world masters of differentiated global marketing is SMH, the Swiss Watch Company. SMH offers watches ranging from the Swatch fashion accessory watch at $50 worldwide to the $100,000+ Blancpain. Although the research and development (R&D) and manufacturing at SMH are integrated and serve the entire product line, each SMH brand is managed by a completely separate organization that targets a concentrated, narrow segment in the global market.

In the cosmetics industry, Unilever NV and Cosmair Inc. pursue differentiated global marketing strategies by targeting both ends of the perfume market. Unilever targets the luxury market with Calvin Klein and Elizabeth Taylor's Passion; Wind Song and Brut are its mass-market brands. Cosmair sells Tresnor and Giorgio Armani Gio to the upper end of the market and Gloria Vanderbilt to the lower end. Mass marketer Procter & Gamble (P&G), known for its Old Spice and Incognito brands, also embarked on this strategy with its 1991 acquisition of Revlon's EuroCos, marketers of Hugo Boss for men and Laura Biagiotti's Roma perfume. Now, P&G is launching a new prestige fragrance, Venezia, in the United States and nine European countries.[22]

◆ GLOBAL PRODUCT POSITIONING

Positioning is the location of your product in the mind of your customer. Thus, one of the most powerful tools of marketing is not something that a marketer can do to the product or to any element of the marketing mix: Positioning is what happens in the mind of the customer. The position that a product occupies in the mind of a customer depends on a host of variables, many of which are controlled by the marketer.

After the global market has been segmented and one or more segments have been targeted, it is essential to plan a way to reach the target(s). To achieve this task, marketers use positioning. In today's global market environment, many companies find it increasingly important to have a unified global positioning strategy. For example, Chase Manhattan Bank launched a $75 million global advertising campaign geared to the theme "profit from experience." According to Aubrey Hawes, a vice president and corporate director of marketing for the bank, Chase's business and private banking clients "span the globe and travel the globe. They can only know one Chase in their minds, so why should we try to confuse them?"

Can global positioning work for all products? One study suggests that global positioning is most effective for product categories that approach either end of a "high-touch/high-tech" continuum.[23] Both ends of the continuum are characterized by high levels of customer involvement and by a shared "language" among consumers.

---

[22] Gabriella Stern, "Procter Senses Opportunity in Posh Perfume," *The Wall Street Journal*, 9 July 1993, pp. B1, B5.

[23] See Teresa J. Domzal and Lynette Unger, "Emerging Positioning Strategies in Global Marketing," *Journal of Consumer Marketing*, 4, no. 4 (Fall 1987): 26–27.

GLOBAL MARKETING IN ACTION—TARGETING ADVENTURE SEEKERS WITH AN AMERICAN CLASSIC

Over the past decades, savvy export marketing has enabled Harley-Davidson to dramatically increase worldwide sales of its heavyweight motorcycles. Export sales increased from 3,000 motorcycles in 1983 to 32,000 units for the 1999 model year. By 1999, non-U.S. sales exceeded $537 million, up from $400 million in 1996, and $115 million in 1989. From Australia to Germany to Mexico City, Harley enthusiasts are paying the equivalent of up to $25,000 to own an American-built classic. In many countries, dealers must put would-be buyers on a six-month waiting list because of high demand.

Harley's international success comes after years of neglecting overseas markets. Early on, the company was basically involved in export selling, symbolized by its underdeveloped dealer network. Moreover, print advertising simply used word-for-word translations of the U.S. ads. By the late 1980s, after recruiting dealers in the important Japanese and European markets, company executives discovered a basic principle of global marketing. "As the saying goes, we needed to think global but act local," says Jerry G. Wilke, vice president for worldwide marketing. Harley began to adapt its international marketing, making it more responsive to local conditions.

In Japan, for example, Harley's rugged image and high quality helped make it the best-selling imported motorcycle. Still, Toshifumi Okui, president of Harley's Japanese division, was not satisfied. He worried that the tag line from the U.S. ads, "One steady constant in an increasingly screwed-up world," did not connect with Japanese riders. Okui finally convinced Milwaukee to allow him to launch a Japan-only advertising campaign, juxtaposing images from both Japan and America, such

as American cyclists passing a rickshaw carrying a geisha. After learning that riders in Tokyo consider fashion and customized bikes to be essential, Harley opened two stores specializing in clothes and bike accessories. Today, Japan is Harley-Davidson's largest market outside of the United States.

Harley discovered that in Europe an "evening out" means something different than it does in America. The company sponsored a rally in France, where beer and live rock music were available until midnight. Recalls Wilke, "People asked us why we were ending the rally just as the evening was starting. So I had to go persuade the band to keep playing and reopen the bar until 3 or 4 A.M." Still, rallies are less common in Europe than in the United States, so Harley encourages its dealers to hold open houses at their dealerships.

While biking through Europe, Wilke also learned that German bikers often travel at speeds exceeding 100 miles per hour. This required the company to investigate design changes to create a smoother ride at autobahn speeds. Harley's German marketing effort also caused it to begin focusing on accessories to increase rider protection.

Despite high levels of demand, the company intentionally limits production increases in order to uphold Harley's recent improvements in quality and to keep the product supply limited in relation to demand. Harley is still careful to make home-country customers a higher priority than those living abroad; thus, only 18 percent of its production goes outside the North American Division. The Harley shortage seems to suit company executives just fine. Notes Harley's James H. Patterson, "Enough motorcycles is too many motorcycles."

SOURCES: Harley-Davidson Annual Report 1999; Kevin Kelly and Karen Lowry Miller, "The Rumble Heard Round the World: Harleys," *Business Week,* 24 May 1993, pp. 58, 60; Robert L. Rose, "Vrooming Back: After Nearly Stalling, Harley-Davidson Finds New Crowd of Riders," *The Wall Street Journal,* 31 August 1990, pp. A1, A6; John Holusha, "How Harley Outfoxed Japan with Exports," *The New York Times,* 12 August 1990, p. F5; Robert C. Reid, "How Harley Beat Back the Japanese," *Fortune,* 25 September 1989, p. 155; Harley-Davidson 1996 Annual Report.

HIGH-TECH POSITIONING

Personal computers, video and stereo equipment, and automobiles are examples of product categories in which high-tech positioning has proven effective. Such products are frequently purchased on the basis of concrete product features, although image may also be important. Buyers typically already possess or wish to acquire considerable technical information. High-tech products may be divided into three categories: technical products, special-interest products, and demonstrable products.

Technical Products

Computers, chemicals, tires, and financial services are just a sample of the product categories whose buyers have specialized needs, require a great deal of product information, and share a common "language." Computer buyers in Russia and the United States are equally knowledgeable about microprocessors, 20-gigabyte hard drives, modems, and RAM (random access memory). Marketing communications for high-tech products should be informative and emphasize features.

Special-Interest Products

Although less technical and more leisure or recreation oriented, special-interest products also are characterized by a shared experience and high involvement among users. Again, the common language and symbols associated with such products can transcend language and cultural barriers. Fuji bicycles, Adidas sports equipment, and Canon cameras are examples of successful global special-interest products.

HIGH-TOUCH POSITIONING

Marketing of high-touch products requires less emphasis on specialized information and more emphasis on image. Like high-tech products, however, high-touch categories are highly involving for consumers. Buyers of high-touch products also share a common language and set of symbols relating to themes of wealth, materialism, and romance. The three categories of high-touch products are products that solve a common problem, global village products, and products with a universal theme.

Products That Solve a Common Problem

At the other end of the price spectrum from high tech, products in this category provide benefits linked to "life's little moments." Ads that show friends talking over a cup of coffee in a cafe or quenching thirst with a soft drink during a day at the beach put the product at the center of everyday life and communicate the benefit offered in a way that is understood worldwide.

Global Village Products

Chanel fragrances, designer fashions, mineral water, and pizza are all examples of products whose positioning is strongly cosmopolitan in nature. Fragrances and fashions have traveled as a result of growing worldwide interest in high-quality, highly visible, high-priced products that often enhance social status. However, the lower-priced food products just mentioned show that the global village category encompasses a broad price spectrum.

In global markets, products may have a global appeal by virtue of their country of origin. The "American-ness" of Levis, Marlboro, and Harley-Davidson enhances their appeal to cosmopolitans around the world. In consumer electronics, Sony is a name synonymous with vaunted Japanese quality; in automobiles, Mercedes is the embodiment of legendary German engineering.

Products That Use Universal Themes

As noted earlier, some advertising themes and product appeals are thought to be basic enough that they are truly transnational. Additional themes are materialism (keyed to images of well-being or status), heroism (themes include rugged individuals or self-sacrifice), play (leisure/recreation), and procreation (images of courtship and romance).

It should be noted that some products can be positioned in more than one way, within either the high-tech or high-touch poles of the continuum. A BMW car, for example, could simultaneously be classified as technical and special interest. To reinforce, the high-touch aspect, BMW publishes *BMW Magazine* for BMW owners. In addition to articles on the technical characteristics of the car, the magazine has lifestyle articles and advertisements for luxury products such as expensive watches, and jewelry.

> **VISIT THE WEB SITE**
> www.bmw.com

Summary

The global environment must be analyzed before a company pursues expansion into new geographic markets. Through global market segmentation, the similarities and differences of potential buying customers can be identified and grouped. Demographics, psychographics, behavioral characteristics, and benefits sought are common attributes used to segment world markets. After marketers have identified segments, the next step is targeting. The identified groups are evaluated and compared; the prospect(s) with the greatest potential is selected from them. The groups are evaluated on the basis of several factors: segment size and growth potential, competition, and compatibility and feasibility. After evaluating the identified segments, marketers must decide on an appropriate targeting strategy. The three basic categories of global target marketing strategies are standardized marketing, concentrated marketing, and differentiated marketing. Finally, companies must plan a way to reach their chosen target market(s) by determining the best positioning for their product offerings. Here, marketers devise an appropriate marketing mix to fix the product in the mind of the potential buyers in the target market. High-tech and high-touch positioning are two strategies that can work well for a global product.

Discussion Questions

1. What is a global market segment? Pick a market that you know something about, and describe the global segments for this market.
2. Identify the major geographic and demographic segments in global markets.
3. Amazon.com has been an early winner in the on-line book business. Which market segments has Amazon served? Are the Amazon target market segments in the United States and the rest of the world identical?
4. Smoking is on the decline in high-income countries where the combination of higher life expectancy, education, income, and legal action has created a powerful antismoking campaign. Global tobacco companies are shifting their focus from high-income to emerging markets where the combination of rising income and the absence of antismoking campaigns is leading to ever-increasing demand for cigarettes. Is this shift in focus by the global tobacco companies ethical? What, if anything, should residents in high-income countries do about the rise in smoking in emerging markets?

Suggested Readings

Alster, Judith, and Holly Gallo. "Corporate Strategies for Global Competitive Advantage." Reader's Digest Association Conference Board, Working Papers no. 996, 1992.

Garland, Barbara C., and Marti J. Rhea. "American Consumers: Profile of an Import Preference Segment." *Akron Business and Economic Review,* 19, no. 2 (1988): 20–29.

Green, Paul E., and Abba M. Krieger. "Segmenting Markets with Conjoint Analysis." *Journal of Marketing,* 55, no. 4 (October 1991): 20–31.

Hassan, Salah S., and Roger D. Blackwell. *Global Marketing.* Orlando, FL: The Dryden Press, 1994.

Ter Hofstede, Frenkel, Jan-Benedict E. M. Steenkamp, and Michel Wedel. "International Market Segmentation Based on Consumer-Product Relations." *Journal of Marketing Research,* 36, no. 1 (1999): 1–17.

Hout, Thomas, Michael E. Porter, and Eeleen Rudden. "How Global Companies Win Out." *Harvard Business Review* (September/October 1982): 98–108.

Miles, Gregory L. "Think Global, Go Intermodal." *International Business* (March 1993): 61.

Morwitz, Vicki G., and David Schmittlein. "Using Segmentation to Improve Sales Forecasts Based on Purchase Intent: Which 'Intenders' Actually Buy?" *Journal of Marketing Research,* 29, no. 4 (November 1992): 391–405.

Pawle, John. "Mining the International Consumer." *Journal of the Market Research Society,* 41, no. 1 (1999): 19–32.

Piirto, Rebecca. *Beyond Mind Games: The Marketing Power of Psychographics.* Ithaca, NY: American Demographics Books, 1991.

Prokesch, S. E. "Competing on Customer Service: An Interview with British Airways' Sir Colin Marshall." *Harvard Business Review* (November/December 1995): 100–116.

Raju, P. S. "Consumer Behavior in Global Markets: The A-B-C-D Paradigm and Its Application to Eastern Europe and the Third World." *Journal of Consumer Marketing,* 12, no. 5 (1995): 37–56.

Simon, Herman. *Hidden Champions: Lessons from 500 of the World's Best Unknown Companies.* Boston, MA: Harvard Business School Press, 1996.

Sonnenberg, Frank K. *Marketing to Win: Strategies for Building Competitive Advantage in Service Industries.* New York: HarperBusiness, 1990.

Taylor, William. "Message and Muscle: An Interview with Swatch Titan Nicolas Hayek." *Harvard Business Review,* 71 (March–April 1993): 99–110.

Trout, Jack, and Steve Rivkin. *The New Positioning: The Latest on the World's #1 Business Strategy.* New York: McGraw-Hill, 1996.

Wolfe, Bonnie Heineman. "Finding the International Niche: A 'How to' for American Small Business." *Business Horizons,* 34, no. 2 (1991): 13–17.

Womack, James P., Daniel T. Jones, and Daniel Roos. *The Machine That Changed the World.* New York: Harper-Collins, 1990.

◆◆◆ Part III Cases

Oriflame

INTRODUCTION

This case will give you a general overview of the Swedish cosmetic company, Oriflame International S.A., with concentration on the impressive development of Oriflame's entry into Eastern and Central Europe. A special focus will be directed toward Oriflame's operations in Poland.

COMPANY PROFILE

Oriflame was founded in Sweden in 1967 by brothers Jonas and Robert af Jochnick and Bengt Hellsten. In 1972, the parent company, Oriflame International S.A. (OISA), Luxembourg, was established. In 1982, OISA became listed on the London Stock Exchange.

Oriflame's specific market concept, which involves direct sales, also allowed for rapid market development outside the Nordic area. The company is currently represented in 42 countries in Europe, the Far East, Australia, and the Americas.

In 1987, the mail-order operation was expanded following the introduction of the Vevay brand name. In 1992, the natural cosmetics company Fleur de Santé became affiliated with the group. ACO Hud was acquired in 1992 and is Sweden's best-known brand name in skin care products. The products are retailed through Swedish, Norwegian, and Icelandic pharmacies.

Oriflame develops and produces its own naturally based products in its manufacturing plant in Ireland where the group's research laboratories are also located.

Oriflame Eastern Europe S.A. (ORESA), which is managed from Brussels, was established in 1990 with the objective of penetrating Eastern European markets.

In 1994, direct sales accounted for 83 percent of the group's sales (ORESA and OISA). Oriflame is represented by sales companies in 42 countries, of which 29 are wholly owned and mainly located in Europe. Oriflame has licensees operating in an additional 13 countries. The organizational structure of a country sales company is shown in Exhibit 1.

THE MARKET

The market for cosmetic products is developing positively with recent growth averaging around 4 percent per year by volume, although, as with other consumer industries, growth in 1992–1993 decreased as a consequence of the general economic recession.

This case was written by Nathalie Rouvier and Vahid Bafandi under the supervision of Professor Dominique Xardel, ESSEC, Cergy Pontoise, France. It is intended as a basis for class discussion rather than to illustrate either effective or ineffective handling of management situations. © D. Xardel 1998. Used by permission.

The company has experienced steady growth in sales since the start in 1967 with, in June 1994, sales totaling $230 million for the group. The increase has been particularly significant in Europe with the establishment of new operations in Central and Eastern Europe. This growth is also explained by the fact that people are becoming more discerning about how they buy things. Many people find visiting a department store tiresome and impersonal. The current trends are returning to personal service, care, and attention. Combine that with Oriflame's commitment to offering value for money with a full 100 percent money back guarantee and the current sales growth is explained.

In addition to Europe, major growth has come from South and Central America. Oriflame's operations on the South American continent are directed from Chile, where the success of the local operation continues.

The global market for cosmetics and toiletries (C&T) is mature, and growth through the year 2000 is projected to reach the modest rate of 3 percent annually. Europe accounts for 37 percent of overall sales and is the major single market for C&T products. The growth rate in the region is among the strongest of any in the world when the results from Eastern Europe are considered. By contrast, the U.S. market is saturated and growth is slow.

In the global market for C&T, skin care is a large sector in most countries, except in the United States where skin care is less developed than in Europe in terms of user penetration. One key trend is the launch of products that are marketed as having benefits to the skin which are not just cosmetic. This trend can be seen across the cosmetic markets and indicates that demand is becoming more sophisticated. It usually involves a close association with health benefits. These therapeutic cosmetics, "cosmeceuticals," are expected to become a major growth area in the skin care market. The cosmetics industry has been very active in the development of such products in recent years, spending heavily on research and development (R&D) and often transferring medical research to cosmetic products.

Although there is a continuous search for innovation in the C&T sector, the lack of legal protection in such forms as patents adds a factor of increased risk and hinders the potential for return on capital.

Pan-European sales of skin care lines increased by 8 to 10 percent during 1992. The growth trend continues in the area of antiaging products, with the quality demands on effective long-lasting moisturizers rising. The public's increasing concern about environmental pollution and the link to the harmful effects of the sun's ultraviolet rays is also of great interest to the industry.

Body care products continue to perform well in Europe, but market penetration levels are relatively low compared to the sun care market.

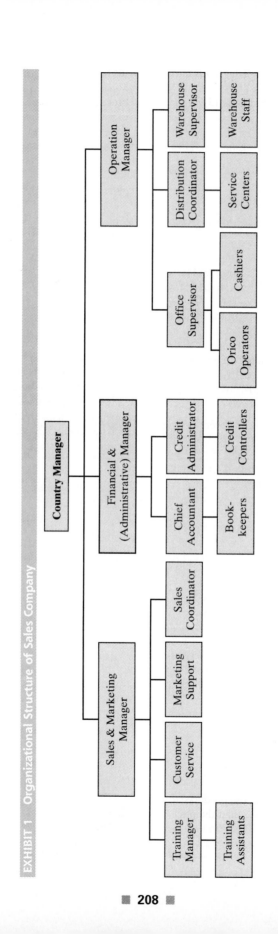

EXHIBIT 1 Organizational Structure of Sales Company

Cosmetics sold through direct-selling methods make up the following percentages of the following markets: Sweden (20), United Kingdom (15), Finland (13), France (7), Denmark (11), Eastern Europe (11), Spain (7), Holland (6), Norway (4), other (13).

Over all, direct sales of cosmetics account for 10 to 15 percent of the entire cosmetics market.

THE DIRECT-SELLING INDUSTRY

Direct selling, which was already a substantial industry in the United States by 1920, is defined by the Direct Selling Association as follows:

The selling of consumer goods direct to private individuals, in their homes and places of work, through transactions initiated and concluded by a salesperson. Direct selling has several advantages over shop retailing, not only for the customer, but also for the manufacturer. The customer can pick up the products at a service center or have them delivered at home. The manufacturer does not have to support advertising costs to attract its customers. The distributors play a double role, being both customers and sales people in the recruitment of new customers.

In July 1994, the World Federation of Direct Selling Association indicated that direct selling was a $60 billion industry in the world, with 30 million people involved in this activity each year. As an example, the United States counted 5 million to 7 million people in direct selling and Japan more than 2 million. Most people who sell direct do it not only because they like the products and want to increase their income, but also because it is a good opportunity for them to develop an independent activity. Direct sales is now a global activity, with many new players competing with traditional companies.

Most of today's successful direct selling companies use a sales system called Network Marketing or Multilevel Marketing. An article in *The Wall Street Journal* described Network Marketing in the following way:

Network marketing is a sales system which totally omits the stores. Networks sell all kinds of products: from pens or toothpaste to computers, cars, and even houses. These products are usually 15–50 percent cheaper than those purchased in the stores. By the end of this century, we will be buying 50–60 percent of all the products and services in this way.

The rules are about the same everywhere. An authorized distributor delivers the company's products directly to the customer's house. His first clients are his family and friends. A distributor buys the products at a price which is 20–30 percent cheaper than the price the customer will later pay for them. The difference is where his profit is. If he wants to make more, he recruits new sales agents. Depending on the number of people he recruits and on the volume of goods he and the recruits buy, he receives a commission and a bonus. Sometimes it can be a prize, a nice trip abroad, sometimes even a retirement pension. Those who recruit the biggest number of new agents make the most. The company also makes money because it has no such costs as rent or a lease. It would have to pay for all of this if it sold its goods in the stores.

Oriflame is one of the main direct-sales companies in many of its markets and the largest direct-sales company in Scandinavia and in Central and Eastern Europe.

ORIFLAME

Direct Selling

Conventional selling involves moving a product through a hierarchy of middlemen from the manufacturer to the end customer. All these middlemen—wholesalers, retailers, and jobbers—earn a profit from handling the product. In a direct-selling environment, these positions are not necessary and profits are instead shared among the distributors. These cost cuttings also give Oriflame the possibility to sell a higher-quality product at lower, more competitive prices.

Oriflame's responsibility in the markets in which it operates is to package the products and handle the financing and data processing, warehousing, shipping, and marketing, as well as creating training programs and materials to support the independent distributors.

The Oriflame distributors offer unique, value-added services such as cosmetics consultancy in their customers' homes or offices. It is company policy that prospective customers (1) are not subject to "pressure selling" nor are they obliged to purchase; (2) receive free skin analysis and personalized advice on proper skin care; and (3) are offered free ongoing after-sales service.

Oriflame has 300,000 distributors worldwide. Distributors usually have other jobs; thus, their involvement with Oriflame is sometimes only a hobby. Historically, distributors have been paid strictly on commission, and their primary sales tool has been sales catalogs provided by Oriflame. (More than 12 million catalogs in 17 languages are distributed every year.)

Oriflame's selling method consists of selling a wide range of the highest-quality cosmetics to consumers on a person-to-person basis, backed by a unique, multilevel marketing plan.

Distributors get their catalogs every 2 to 4 weeks and use them to sell to friends, relatives, and colleagues—normally, their primary customer base. Distributors order products they sell from the catalogs, receive bundled shipments from Oriflame, and then pass products on to individual customers.

Oriflame is now implementing and expanding a new (for them) marketing method. This involves the distributor's building up a sales network and receiving a bonus or commission on the sales made by each individual recruited to be a distributor, as well as on the sales made by the recruits. This system, often called multilevel marketing, can offer career opportunities for current "hobbyists" because the system permits "main source" levels of income. The method has worked most successfully for Oriflame in Latin American and several Eastern European countries. Distributors in these countries often enjoy incomes well above national averages. Catalogs are an integral part of this system, but are issued less frequently. Over time, Oriflame will adapt this method for use in its traditional Western European markets.

Oriflame has never been successful in the German and U.S. markets despite several start-up attempts. Direct sales accounted for 83 percent of Oriflame's sales in 1994 compared with 70 percent in 1994. It has been decided by the board of directors that Oriflame's future direction will be in the field of direct selling. This is where the company has its highest potential. (See appendix "The Marketing Plan: An Overview" for further explanations of the marketing plan.)

Other Activities

Mail order at Oriflame can be divided into two types. The first is by direct customer purchase of specially selected products appearing in sales catalogs that are distributed 10 to 12 times a year. This method is referred to as the *positive option*.

The second category of mail-order sales is based on the book club type of system. Subscribers/members/customers are offered specially composed packages through a brochure. The parcel is sent to the customers unless they actively inform the company that they do not wish to receive it (*negative option*).

The mail-order market accounts for around 5 percent of the total cosmetics market. The market is expanding, especially in the Nordic area. The activities in Eastern Europe have a major potential as the time is right for this concept and strong development is anticipated generally. The market as a whole is subject to tough competition from companies such as Yves Rocher.

The mail-order market within the Oriflame group is composed of Oriflame's operation in Denmark—Vevay's cosmetic club and Fleur de Santé's natural cosmetics. In 1992, the mail-order operations were combined to form a division within the Oriflame group.

The mail-order operations started in Denmark in 1978 with Oriflame's cosmetics club. Today, Oriflame in Denmark has around 100,000 members and sales of around $8 million.

Vevay was founded in Sweden in 1987. Since then, operations have expanded to Norway, Finland, and Denmark and during 1993 ORESA started up its own operations in Poland, Hungary, and the Czech Republic. Vevay has around 120,000 members and sales of around $4 million.

Fleur de Santé has been an associate company of Oriflame since May 1992 (36 percent ownership). The company, located in Malmo, has a turnover of around $15 million in Sweden, Norway, and Finland. In August 1992, Oriflame acquired the distribution rights for Fleur de Santé in Eastern Europe. A company was started in the Czech Republic in February 1993.

Mail order in 1994 accounted for 7 percent of total Oriflame sales.

ACO

The ACO company evolved from the Swedish pharmacy operations, and the name ACO dates back to 1939. In connection with the nationalization of Swedish pharmacies in 1972, ACO was transferred to the government-owned pharmaceuticals company, Kabi Vitrum. Oriflame acquired ACO on January 1, 1992.

ACO's main market is Sweden, where the products are sold through pharmacies. ACO is the best-known brand name for skin care products in Sweden. Its main products are creams, lotions, sun care products, and hand care products.

The ACO products exist within the low and average price ranges, whereas the Nordic Light products compete with exclusive prestige brands.

The growth in sales during the year has mainly been through new products or recently introduced products as well as sun care products. Sales increased to $24 million. ACO accounted for 10 percent of total Oriflame sales.

Manufacturing

At the end of 1977, Oriflame's board of directors decided to build a production plant on the outskirts of Dublin, Ireland. The plant was completed 2 years later, in July 1979, following extensive project work, including transfers of technology from former subcontractors. The building covered 2,800 square meters for production, research laboratories, and quality control. Extensions were made in 1980, 1989, 1991–1992, and 1992–1993. The current extensions now have been completed and have increased the capacity for filling from 22 million to approximately 40 million units. This, of course, includes the ACO equipment transferred from Stockholm. In 1993, the factory covered 11,000 square meters for production, research laboratories, and quality control. The plant is one of Europe's most modern cosmetic manufacturing units and is well equipped with high-technology production equipment.

All Oriflame products undergo strict physical, chemical, and microbiological control before reaching the customer. The objective is that the customer should be able to rely on the product to provide long-term quality, regardless of how it was purchased.

In order to attain this objective, all deliveries of raw materials and packaging are tested according to strict specification before they enter the production process. An overriding priority is to offer consumer products that meet the highest safety and quality standards. The water used is tested daily to guarantee a high degree of microbiological purity.

Research and product development in the Dublin plant is actively concentrated on developing new cosmetic formulations in line with the market demands and expec-

EXHIBIT 2

	1994 ($ Thousands)	1993 ($ Thousands)
Sales	232,137	192,406
Operating profit	36,192	31,431
Profit before tax	37,206	31,556
Profit after tax	28,676	23,522
Capital expenditure	20,349	13,822
Profit margin %	16	16.4
Equity/assets ratio (%)	57	55
Return on net capital employed (%)	32	36
Gearing (%)	14	31
Employees	1,328	1,148

Exchange rate $ = 1.56

tations. In production and development, products and packaging are tested continuously for microbiological stability and quality of packaging. The production philosophy, including packaging, is to concentrate on new consumer demands such as biodegradability, recycling, and the absence of animal raw materials.

The Research and Development Department has generated over 100 new products for Oriflame, Vevay, Fleur de Santé, and ACO in 1994.

Oriflame Results

In 1993 and 1994, the Oriflame Group results are shown in Exhibit 2.

ORIFLAME EASTERN EUROPE

Decision to Start

When Oriflame decided, in 1990, to create Oriflame Eastern Europe, Jonas af Jochnick called back to Europe a young Swedish manager, Sven Mattsson, who at the time was managing director for the operations in the Philippines. The year before, af Jochnick had resigned from his position as Oriflame chairman in order to devote more time to look at new marketing opportunities, particularly in Eastern Europe. Af Jochnick, together with Mattsson and a secretary, opened an office in Brussels for the new company, ORESA. The objective was to exploit business opportunities for the direct selling of cosmetic products in Eastern Europe, with initial emphasis on Czechoslovakia, Hungary, and Poland. In Eastern Europe, Oriflame targets for the later stage of its development were Bulgaria, Romania, the Soviet Union, and Yugoslavia.

On July 10, 1990, af Jochnick was appointed Chairman of ORESA. In a letter to Oriflame shareholders, he wrote:

The opening up of the Eastern European markets offers new and exciting opportunities to establish business activities in these countries. There is a strong am-

bition and commitment by the new democratically elected governments in some of these countries to develop their markets along the lines of Western-style market economies, and legislation is being proposed or passed in a number of Eastern European countries to encourage foreign investment.

In particular the Directors of ORESA believe that opportunities exist for companies:

1) which are active in the consumer goods areas;
2) which are prepared to re-invest cash and profits in the local markets and which are in a position to wait a considerable period before remitting profits;
3) with the resources to establish or invest in local manufacture;
4) which are willing to invest in the development and professional training of local nationals as future management.

Currently there is a high degree of uncertainty as to where and how quickly these opportunities will develop since definite legal frameworks have not yet been established in all the countries in Eastern Europe. It is therefore impossible to predict with any degree of certainty what financial returns can be expected or the timing of such returns.

Investment in these countries must instead be based on the belief that the recent political changes are irreversible and that there will remain a strong commitment to develop these economies with policies based on Western economic principles. I believe that for the companies which take the initiative early and take a long-term view, future reward and returns should far exceed what can be expected from mature markets in the West.

The initial objective of ORESA was to establish sales organizations in Czechoslovakia, Hungary, and Poland, using the well-proven direct-selling techniques already used by the company in its existing markets. The techniques seemed particularly well suited to these countries due to the highly undeveloped retail distribution networks found there at that time.

ORESA was also examining the possibility of entering into joint venture arrangements with existing cosmetic manufacturers in each of these countries to enable products to be sourced locally. In the longer term, manufacturing for export of cosmetic products in Eastern Europe was envisaged.

The Development 1990–1994 (Exhibit 3)

The first country that Oriflame entered was Czechoslovakia. Eliska Wescia, a woman of Czech origin living in Malmö, was made an offer to return to Prague. She accepted and first sales were made in December 1990. A 100-square-meter office was opened and after 3 months, $300,000 worth of sales were already made. Sales were growing so fast that

EXHIBIT 3 Sales Statistics

Country: Czech Republic	Start: December 1990			
	1991	*1992*	*1993*	*1994*
Total sales (USS thousands)	4,526	12,684	12,758	13,700
Active file count	2,320	7,629	12,494	18,804
Activity %/month (average)	74%	81%	68%	61%
Sales/active/month (USS average)	490	138	125	112
No. of employees	9	33	51	61
Office space (square meters)	300	300	450	600
Warehouse space (square meters)	600	660	700	1,000
No. of service centers		16	17	21
Advertising spending (USS in thousands)		15	378	400

Country: Slovakia	Start: January 1993		*1993*	*1994*
Total sales (USS in thousands)			3,197	6,400
Active file count			3,795	9,090
Activity %/month (average)			66%	59%
Sales/active/month (USS average)			180	90
No. of employees			10	30
Office space (square meters)			280	550
Warehouse space (square meters)			0	600
No. of service centers			0	6
Advertising spending (USS in thousands)			23.5	89

Note: Czechoslovakia split into two nations—the Czech Republic and Slovakia—January 1, 1993. During 1993 and most of 1994, warehousing was handled by Czech sales company fulfillment.

Country: Hungary	Start: May 1991			
	1991	*1992*	*1993*	*1994*
Total sales (USS in thousands)	1,400	6,500	9,500	13,500
Active file count	3,602	13,442	18,933	23,285
Activity %/month (average)	65%	62%	53%	50%
Sales/active/month (USS average)	133	100	81	93
No. of employees	14	35	60	75
Office space (square meters)	60	180	280	400
Warehouse space (square meters)	50	700	1,200	1,200
No. of service centers	0	1	4	9
Advertising spending (USS in thousands)	0	20	275	250

Country: Turkey	Start: April 1992			
	1991	*1992*	*1993*	*1994*
Total sales (USS in thousands)		1,278	9,933	12,900
Active file count		2,523	16,224	28,550
Active %/month (average)		83.7%	61.7%	47.4%
Sales/active/month (USS average)		289	167	98
No. of employees		11	37	74
Office space (square meters)		350	450	750
Warehouse space (square meters)		100	800	1,500
No. of service centers		1	4	9
Advertising spending (USS in thousands)		8.7	44.4	70.3

EXHIBIT 3 *(Continued)*

Country: Greece	Start: May 1993			
	1991	*1992*	*1993*	*1994*
Total sales (USS in thousands)			554	1,845
Active file count			819	3,048
Activity %/month (average)			89%	66%
Sales/active/month (USS average)			218	196
No. of employees			11	26
Office space (square meters)			280	480
Warehouse space (square meters)			200	300
No. of service centers			1	3
Advertising spending (USS in thousands)			22	50

Country: Bulgaria	Start: August 1994			
	1991	*1992*	*1993*	*1994*
Total sales (USS in thousands)				810
Active file count				2,450
Activity %/month (average)				93%
Sales/active/month (USS average)				200
No. of employees				15
Office space (square meters)				400
Warehouse space (square meters)				600
No. of service centers				0
Advertising spending (USS in thousands)				2

the company had to stop recruiting for a while to establish a warehouse and find new office facilities. In 1994, Oriflame had a 600-square-meter office in Prague with a 1,000-square-meter warehouse, and 15 service centers spread over the country.

In Poland, the company recruited the first 12 distributors in March 1991. They ordered, among themselves, $20,000 in the first 2 weeks and are still today among the leaders in the Polish network. A Polish citizen who had spent 2 years in Iran and who was fluent in English was recruited as country manager.

In Hungary, where competitors like Avon and Amway were already established, Sven Mattsson was general manager of Oriflame until the company found a Swede with a Hungarian background, Thomas Grünwald, to assume responsibility for Hungary in May 1991, which was when the first Oriflame products were sold. At the beginning, sales did not develop as fast as in Poland and Czechoslovakia. However, 3 years later, sales were developing faster in Hungary (plus 38 percent) than in the Czech Republic (plus 15 percent) or in Poland, which had only a small increase. Mattsson says, "This can partly be explained by the fact that Oriflame naturally offers the best service level within the capital region. Approximately 25 percent of the Hungarian population lives in the Budapest area, a figure which is much higher then the other bordering countries.

Local management has also been very successful in working with leaders of the network." In 1994, Oriflame had 75 employees in Hungary.

In April 1992, Oriflame started operations in Turkey. The company had great hopes for this more Western market where well-trained managers were available and where everything seemed to be a lot smoother and easier, in spite of a lot of red tape and bureaucracy. This was nothing compared with what the company had experienced in Eastern Europe up to now. The initial investment was paid back after 3 months of operations. In December 1992, Oriflame sales were $450,000. Turkish distributors appeared to be entrepreneurial and cooperative. The operations have been greatly helped by the country's well-developed infrastructure (banking, telecommunications, etc.). Oriflame's high expectations were not met in 1994 because of the economic crisis Turkey faced during the year. In March, the dollar value moved from 14,000 to 40,000 Turkish liras over a few days. Sales dropped 40 percent below forecast, but Sven Mattsson remained optimistic about the medium and long-term future. In January 1995, Oriflame Turkey opened a new 1,200-square-meter office and a 2,000-square-meter warehouse near the Istanbul airport.

In May 1993, Oriflame started its sales in Greece, a member country of the European Union with no import duties. Oriflame had to pay 12 percent duties for the Czech

Republic and from 10 to 50 percent for Hungary and 20 percent for Turkey. In 1994, Oriflame Greece showed profit.

In Bulgaria, Oriflame opened a 400-square-meter office and a 600-square-meter warehouse in August 1994. Success was immediate, and the company experienced its biggest initial growth, with distributors placing an average monthly order of $250 in this country where the average income is only about $80 per month.

In Russia, Ukraine, and Latvia, ORESA has, since 1991, sold its products wholesale to retail outlets as high inflation, inadequate banking systems, and a relatively undeveloped infrastructure has made it difficult to use the traditional Oriflame concept of selling through distributors. However, the company is now ready to adopt direct sales there, implementing the same Marketing Plan as in other Eastern European countries. A Swedish manager, Fredrik Ekman, moved to Moscow in October 1993.

From 1991 to 1995, ORESA increased its staff and office facilities in Brussels. In 1995, the head office was staffed by 30 people, ensuring centralized functions such as Operations and Marketing, Finance, Supply, Business Development, and Legal Affairs (see Exhibit 4).

In 1995, ORESA planned to open sales companies in Romania and Lithuania. A relaunch of Oriflame's activities in Germany took place during the course of 1995. Oriflame Germany is being managed from Brussels.

A 10,000-square-meter ultramodern manufacturing plant, located in Warsaw, was due to start operating in mid-1995. This involved a total investment of approximately 20 million U.S. dollars.

As Sven Mattsson likes to say, "Our initial aim was to start with Czechoslovakia and then to follow with Poland and Hungary and other markets according to our success in established markets, but also according to available management resources. Our ambition is to become market leaders, both in the direct selling industry as well as the cosmetic industry and to capitalize on all the advantages which result from being the first on a market."

ORIFLAME IN POLAND

Decision to Start

In December 1990, Edward Zieba, who had worked for a state chemical company in Poland and who had spent 3 years in Iran with a construction company, was recruited by Oriflame with the objective of starting operations in Warsaw. During that month, he had long discussions at the Brussels headquarters of ORESA and visited the Oriflame production plant in Ireland and the emerging sales company in Czechoslovakia. During the first months of 1991, Zieba became very skeptical about the development of Oriflame in Poland with direct-selling techniques and a multilevel approach, which had never been used in his country.

"I really thought at that time that it could not possibly work in Poland. Our mentality is too different and what we have lived through over past decades left little hope of implementing such methods with success. I had accepted the job because I treated it as something new and exciting, but I was very doubtful," commented Zieba to the case writer during his visit to Oriflame Warsaw in May 1994.

Oriflame started its operation in Poland in March 1991. At that time, Zieba gathered some 20 of his friends with their spouses for a cozy party during which he did not speak about Oriflame but only displayed some products on a table in the kitchen. After a while, all of those gathered there started asking questions. At the end of the

EXHIBIT 4 Oriflame Eastern Europe Organization

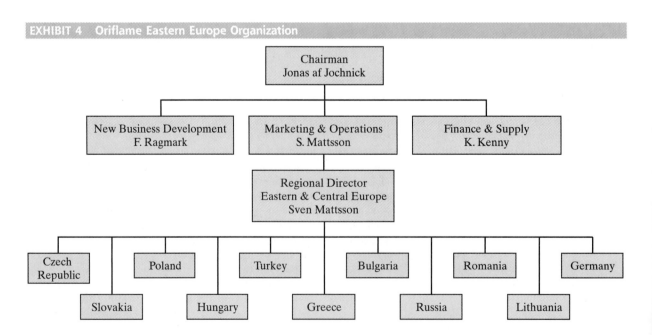

evening, he gave a few samples to those interested (all of them) while briefly explaining the opportunity of the Oriflame marketing plan. Although the quality of the products was fully recognized, each of the guests appeared concerned about the selling method. Three years later, in 1994, eight of them were selling Oriflame products as their only professional activity and were at the epicenter of several different networks of thousands of distributors.

Products and Pricing

Initially, a selection of 100 items was offered. One year later, the number increased to 150. Oriflame cosmetics are gentle but effective. They are produced from nonirritant, natural plant extracts and protect the skin against the harmful effects of pollution and stress. Oriflame products link the best of nature with the best of science to achieve the highest quality.

A first product selection was made by the Marketing Department in Brussels and one of Zieba's first assignments was to propose local pricing. Oriflame generally sells in local currency. At a later stage, free choice was given with regard to new introductions and discontinuations. Our intention was and still is to offer the most comprehensive range of skin care, color and fragrance products in the Polish market. The first months clearly showed that consumer habits differ in many areas from what we are used to in western countries.

Since conception, product price positioning has been one of the most important issues and intensive market studies are continuously carried out in this area. "It is necessary to keep on top of a rapidly changing economic environment. At an early stage it was decided to offer very competitive prices in order to attract millions of new customers rather than selling a limited number of items with traditionally high margins."

Merchandise Support

Twice a year, Oriflame issues 380,000 copies of its catalog, showing 250 products classified in the following categories: skin care, body care, family favorites, color, cosmetics, women's fragrance, and men's fragrance. Prices are not printed in the catalog but on a separate loose sheet. Oriflame prints all its catalogs in Sweden, using the same catalog in nine different countries. Translation and typesetting of the texts is made in each country before the printing. One of the difficulties the company has to face is product sales forecasts, which have to be made 15 months in advance.

Three catalogs, a product guide, information on the marketing plan, samples, and some real products are all in the starter kit that any new distributor has to buy at the cost of $28 in order to start their business. Additional catalogs can be acquired at cost by the distributors. The company decided that the catalogs should always pass through the distributors and would never be sent directly by the company to a prospective consumer.

We see a catalogue as a major marketing tool and there is a lot of effort going into the preparation of every issue. I do not think that one can not over estimate its impact on the company image, product awareness, and finally on sales. We are still investing considerable amounts of money into it and experimenting with its look and content. It is one of the best investments.

Operations

When Oriflame started operating in Warsaw from a rented villa, people were lining up for hours in the street to buy some of the first product range. Rapidly, 70 percent of the products were out of stock, and the company decided to stop recruiting new distributors for 3 months. That time was used to reorganize all distribution procedures and open some service centers.

In March 1992, Oriflame Poland purchased Kamelia, a cooperative that produced cosmetic products in Ursus, a suburb of Warsaw, later followed by the installation of packaging facilities in the old factory. By April 1992, Bozona Karpinska had joined the company as operations manager in charge of distributors, warehouses, and customer service.

In 1993, 12 service centers were opened, most of them in rented villas throughout the country, to allow distributors to come and pick up the merchandise. In 1994, Oriflame had created a total of 18 centers, 10 of which were company owned; the others were on an agreement basis with different entrepreneurs. A new warehouse has been completed along with new pick-and-pack facilities for a few thousand orders per day.

In 1994, Oriflame Poland employed 150 people, all of them of Polish origin. The distribution network counted over 50,000 registered members.

By 1995, Oriflame was selling a range of 200 products, 60 percent of which were filled and packed in Ursus, with the remaining 40 percent coming from the factory in Ireland.

On January 31, 1995, a daily newspaper published in Warsaw printed an article that said: "Swedish company Oriflame was the first direct selling company in our market (1991). According to Oriflame management, the speed of turnover growth and network development in Poland is the most remarkable in the 27 years history of the company."

Advertising and Public Relations

In 1993, it became evident that Oriflame was aiming toward a mass market with its sales volume and, therefore, the company decided to invest into both advertising and public relations (PR) activities to strengthen its brand awareness. The first successful advertising campaign was run in the autumn of 1993, followed by spring and autumn of 1994. The media used were mainly public TV and all segments of women's magazines. The advertising budget for 1994 was almost $700,000, of which 70 percent was spent on TV.

Below-the-line activities included not only traditional PR but also exhibitions and company promotional days in all major cities in the country, with an estimated audience of 300,000. Frequent contacts with the press resulted in broad media coverage, with little negative comment.

The Oriflame Distributors

When a new distributor registers with Oriflame, he or she can generally place orders on credit up to US$500, the average order being $100. Given the state of the bank system, which was still very poor in 1994, distributors' cash payment facilities are organized in all service centers across the country.

In December 1994, Oriflame Poland had built a network of 50,000 active distributors (placing orders at least once during the preceding 3 months) plus 30,000 nonactive distributors (no orders in the last 3 months). One distributor, Jerzy Ruggier, a student at Warsaw University, explains: "I know that I have to create a place for my job. I learned responsibility. It is important for me to sell high-quality products, to be honest, and not to break the rules. It is a way to start a small business and to help people to understand the new laws and taxes." Another distributor, Joanna Szablinska, had set an objective for herself: "I wanted to become a Sapphire Director and buy a new car, an Alpha Romeo. Oriflame is a way of socializing, something which gives you the opportunity to learn how to make safe contacts with other people and buy some luxury in different forms."

Of the 573 distributors who have reached the director level and beyond, 90 percent of them devoted all their working time to Oriflame. Another several hundred are making a living that is far beyond average standards in Poland. The Oriflame network consists of some 75 percent of women and 25 percent of men, the majority being 25 to 35 years old. Bert Wozciech, after 3 years as area manager for Benetton in Poland, joined Oriflame as training manager for the whole network. Since 1993, he has organized training sessions for the directors. Every Monday at 4:30 P.M. in Warsaw, he conducted, in a lawyers' club, a seminar on motivation, which was free of charge and open to any active or prospective distributor who wished to attend.

In May 1994, Edward Zieba commented on the Oriflame situation in Poland:

We want to intensify our support because we do not only want to do business but also develop social life and the individual distributor. We do not want to give only more money to the distributors, we want to develop a club, to make the distributors more able to meet other people and belong to something special. . . .

The years of rapid growth are over but I am convinced that in 3 years from now we will have at least 100,000 active distributors.

Competition

In 1994, it was estimated that over a million Poles were working for different networks in direct-selling, multinational companies such as Avon, Amway, Zepter, Oriflame, Herbalife, and so on. Two of them, Amway and Zepter, were described as follows:

Amway, one of the world's largest and most dynamic direct-sales companies, has been active in Poland since 1992. Although Amway came to our market relatively late, it now boasts the largest network of sales agents. In the opinion of the Amway bosses, Poland is their best market, both in terms of the number of distributors and in terms of sales. In the world, Amway has more than 2 million distributors, who sell about 400 of the company's own products and a few thousand products manufactured by other firms from which Amway has acquired selling rights. Its total annual sales amount in 1994 was $4 billion. In Poland, the monthly turnover is about $30 million zloty. In 1992–1993, Amway managed to build a network of 100,000 distributors. An Amway executive stated: "Poland is our best market in both sales and number of distributors in relation to its population." Amway distributors are not employees of the company but are independent entrepreneurs who have their own businesses. So far, Amway in Poland sells about 20 products: laundry detergents, dishwashing liquids, care cosmetics, and personal hygiene products. The big advantage of the Amway products is that they can be returned even after they are taken out of the packaging.

Amway is not just cosmetics. It is also the author of a television serial, *Bliznes Start*. This program talks not only about the basics of entrepreneurship and a free market

EXHIBIT 5 Sales Statistics				
Country: Poland	*1991*	*1992*	*1993*	*1994*
Total sales (in US$ thousands)	2,250	21,566	35,390	37,180
Active file count	1,782	24,101	38,925	45,020
Activity % /month (average)	84	65	58	53
Sales/active/month (US$ average)	355	288	161	118
No. of employees	14	81	130	154
Office space (in square meters)	130	600	800	1,000
Warehouse space (in square meters)	100	900	1100	2,400
No. of service centers	0	2	14	18
Advertising spending (in US$ thousands)	0	20	320	700

economy, it also presents people—Polish businessmen.

In Sweden, Amway differs from its Swedish competitor in that, at the moment, it has no plans to start production. The only products Amway buys from Polish companies are advertising gadgets: bags, balloons, and so forth. Total sales for 1994 were estimated to be $28 million.

Zepter is a Swiss-Austrian firm, which for the past year has been selling kitchen utensils. The demonstrations of its products take place in private homes. Using the products purchased by the owner of the house, the person making the presentation demonstrates the advantages of using the Zepter pots and pans, which are expensive by Polish standards. Zepter products can also be purchased by installments. One becomes the owner of the chrome-nickel pots, pans, and silverware or 24-carat gold-plated coffee set only after the last installment is paid. In 1993, Zepter had 25,000 distributors in Poland but, as the company's representative assures us, sales grow monthly.

Oriflame Manufacturing in Poland

The high demand for natural skin care and makeup products in Poland inclined the Oriflame corporate management to make the investment at Ursus. "We see Poland as a very big and important market for our products, a market which is still growing. We believe it is a prudent decision to broaden our activities here by building an ultramodern factory," said Jonas af Jochnick, the company's founder and president, during a press conference at Oriflame headquarters.

The $20 million manufacturing plant was due to start operating during 1995. It is a state-of-the-art production equipment and complete research and laboratory facility, which will make it the most modern cosmetics factory in Poland. Products will be made from the same ingredients and under the same strict quality control as in all other Oriflame plants. All production processes will be environmentally safe.

Poland is the second country where Oriflame cosmetics will be manufactured. Part of the production will be exported to neighboring countries. More than 300 people will be employed full time once the new plant is operational.

KEY FACTORS IN ORIFLAME'S SUCCESS

Looking back over the years from 1990 onward and the development of Oriflame in Eastern European markets, Sven Mattsson identified these key factors to the company's success.

Local management. Since the beginning, in 1990, Oriflame developed a local management policy. Sending expatriates to do the job, even if they had a solid knowledge and experience of both the company's products and the local culture, was never considered as an appropriate solution. In each country, the company recruits a local manager and staff, spending a lot of time during interviews explaining the nature and spirit of the

free market economy, the direct-selling method, and the Oriflame marketing plan.

Marketing plan. The marketing plan itself is considered one of the main assets of the company. Support, guidance, and training were supplied from Brussels, with staff spending a great amount of effort and time helping local markets. The marketing plan, called "The Success Plan," was the same for each country, with minor adaptations where required.

Mattsson summarizes the Oriflame concept, "Oriflame considers itself as a company offering two kinds of products. First, a concrete one, originating from the product range of 200 products displayed in a catalog with a pricing policy that favored volume rather than margins. Second, a more intangible product, which originated from the business opportunity offered to each distributor to develop their own business."

PR and advertising. Investing in PR has always been considered important. This is especially true of former communist countries who have long forgotten the knowledge and practice of a free market economy. Oriflame was spending approximately $45,000 per year in each country for PR and is planning to increase it in the coming years. A considerable amount was invested in "above the line" advertising to capitalize on the relative inexperience of media purchasing during 1991 to 1993. "Oriflame has reached 80 percent awareness in Poland, Czech Republic, and Hungary, which is definitely partly due to successful advertising campaigns during the past years," says Mattsson. Oriflame used a mix of TV commercials, printed advertisements, and billboards.

Product and price. Out of the range of approximately 200 products, the company manufactures about 65 percent; the remaining 35 percent come from subcontractors. Oriflame cosmetics are made from pure, natural ingredients. As Jonas af Jochnick explained, "The company is dedicated to ensuring that our customers receive the highest-quality products at reasonable prices each time they purchase Oriflame cosmetics." According to Mattsson, "Our aim is to have our products priced below our international competitors and at the same time be considered as an alternative to cheap local products."

Distribution. In order to facilitate the distributor's activity, the company has created in each country several service centers. This further improves the lead time between order and delivery. In 1994, Poland had 18 service centers; the Czech Republic and Slovakia, 20; Hungary, 9; Turkey, 9; and Greece, 3. The aim has been to give a 48-hour service turnaround throughout the country, with a 24-hour service in the capitals. "Our distribution strategy has proven to be very successful. As in all areas of life today, speed and accuracy are very important and this is especially true for direct selling."

STRATEGIC ISSUES

After 4 years of activity in Eastern Europe, results have been well beyond early expectations. Sven Mattsson is now facing various issues that will influence the recommendations he will make to Jonas af Jochnick and the ORESA board for the future.

How far should the company go to increase its service to the distributors who, of course, appreciate very much having products available as fast as possible? Moving the products faster always means higher costs. How much value should be attributed to distributor convenience? Should inventory of the whole Oriflame product range be kept at each service center?

Should the company invest in advertising campaigns? How important is the advertising for a direct-selling company to keep the awareness high? Is it worthwhile continuing when the increased media prices are taken into consideration?

Should the company enlarge its product range with noncosmetic products to increase sales and possibly to attract new distributors?

A few countries into which Oriflame is considering expanding and where it is conducting marketing research still have high inflation rates. What kind of specific pricing and product policy would the company need to implement in order to ensure a minimum risk for its investment?

Should the company go for local management or expatriates? What kind of management is needed for starting up a new, more distant sales company? What kind of management is required when the company enters into a more mature stage?

APPENDIX: THE MARKETING PLAN: AN OVERVIEW

To become an Oriflame distributor, a candidate should be sponsored by an existing registered Oriflame distributor. Products are sold directly to the consumer by independent distributors who are not employed by Oriflame.

There are no exclusive territories or franchises available under the Oriflame policy. Any distributor is free to conduct his or her business in any area of the country.

No distributor shall sell, demonstrate, or display Oriflame products in any retail outlet.

Oriflame recommends a markup of 30 percent on all products purchased at distributor price. The distributor's income is based on a monthly accumulation of points. All products are assigned two sets of numbers: bonus points (BP), which normally remains a constant number, and business volume (BV), which is a monetary value that changes if prices change. In general, the value of the BV equals the distributor price (DP), excluding value-added tax (VAT).

The total BP of all the products a distributor buys and sells during the course of a month will determine the distributor's performance discount percentage. The monthly performance discount is based not only on his or her own business volume, but also on the business volume generated by any distributors who have been sponsored by him or her. (See Exhibit 6.)

The monthly performance of discount is added to the 30 percent markup, the maximum being 21 percent, equivalent to 10,000 BP per month. Distributors can also earn a further 1 percent or 4 percent bonus if they meet certain criteria. Cash awards from $3,000 to $20,000 can be earned when reaching the higher titles in the marketing plan.

If a customer is not satisfied, the products are replaced or refunded through the "100% customer satisfaction guarantee."

The available credit per order is $500. All outstanding payments must be made before a next order is placed, or within 30 days from the date of invoice. Payments can be made at the Oriflame head office, at some Oriflame service centers, at the post office, or by bank transfer. Orders can be made at service centers or by mail or fax by using a distributor order form.

EXHIBIT 6

Monthly BP	Monthly Performance Discount Percentage of BV
10,000+	21%
6,600–9,900	18%
4,000–6,599	15%
2,400–3,999	12%
1,200–2,399	9%
600–1,199	6%
200–599	3%

Swatch Watch U.S.A.: Creative Marketing Strategy

"Vision is the art of seeing things invisible."
—JONATHAN SWIFT

INTRODUCTION

As speaker after speaker paid tribute to the extraordinary skills that had earned him the award of "Marketing Executive of the Year," Max Imgruth, president of Swatch Watch U.S.A., grew more and more uneasy. Fully confident that the product that changed the watch industry forever, the Swatch watch, would enjoy continued success, Imgruth nonetheless felt the need to change gears. The competition, which was at first slow to react, had begun to implement strategies that stood to erode Swatch's position. Gazing from his privileged place on the dais, Imgruth saw an audience that was content to rehash past successes for a night, which was nice, but not at all his style.

Imgruth had recently guided his company through a fast paced and, some would say, controversial diversification program. Having already achieved spectacular success with the Swatch watch, Imgruth spearheaded a plan to establish Swatch as a total fashion enterprise. This move was accompanied by a good deal of skepticism from colleague and competitor alike. His next objective was to make sure that this year's #1 marketing executive did not become one of the decade's more memorable disappointments.[1]

BACKGROUND—THE SWISS WATCH INDUSTRY

1985 was a good year for the Swiss watch industry. The number of finished watches shipped abroad rose 41 percent to 25.1 million and the value of watch exports increased by 12.2 percent. Luxury watches still comprised the backbone of the Swiss watch trade, accounting for only 2.1 percent of total shipments but 41.8 percent of total earnings. In 1985, the Swiss raised their share of the world market to 10 percent by volume (number of units sold) and 45 percent by value (Exhibits 1–3). For the first time in 15 years, an increase in employment was registered as 1,000 new jobs were created. The industry's good performance in 1985, combined

with a strong year in 1984, gave every indication that the Swiss watch industry was back on its feet after struggling for much of the previous decade.

The comeback had been led by the success of Swatch (a blend of Swiss and watch). Over 10 million of its brightly colored, plastic wristwatches were sold worldwide in 1984–1985. Success had been most notable in the United States, where Swatch's latest move was the launching of a diversification program aimed at making the company a total fashion enterprise.

Whether or not this expansion of the Swatch product line proved successful remained to be seen. What was certain, on the other hand, is that the Swatch watch had given new life (and increased market share) to an industry that was recently engaged in a very difficult struggle with Asian competitors. What was also clear is that Swatch's willingness to break with convention, especially in the area of marketing strategy, gave it a head start in what had become a vast new market—the low-priced watch as a fashion accessory.

Some might say that the Swatch watch was just another in a long line of Swiss successes. In the 1950s, few other industries enjoyed the domination known by the Swiss watch industry. In that decade, the Swiss possessed an estimated 80 percent share of the (non-Communist) world watch market. Production was centered in the Jura region where snowed-in farming families, doubling as skilled watchmakers, supplemented their incomes by assembling mechanical watch parts during the winter months. At the industry's peak in 1956, there were 2,332 such *maisons*. Two large watchmaking groups, Allgemeine Schweitzer Uhren AG (Asuag) and Societe Suisse pour l'Industrie Horlogere (SSIH), controlled most of the Swiss brands at this time.

The Swiss remained industry leaders until the mid-1970s when the mass production of electronic watches changed the watch industry forever. The most important difference between an electronic watch and a mechanical watch is that the former is much easier to manufacture. A mechanical watch is an intricate piece of machinery whose assembly necessitates a highly skilled workforce. The electronic watch is typically composed of microchips and printed units and lends itself well to mass production and automated processes. After having ruled supreme over the watch industry for decades, the Swiss suddenly found themselves faced with strong competition from Japan and such low wage producers as Hong Kong, Singapore, Taiwan, and Korea. These newcomers produced inexpensive watches

This case was prepared by Charles Anderer, case writer and research associate, under the supervision of Warren J. Keegan, Professor of International Business and Marketing, as part of the Leading Edge Case Study Project, Center for International Business Studies, Pace University. This project was funded in part from a grant from the United States Department of Education. © 1986, Pace University.

[1] This situation is fictional. Its purpose is to highlight the issues faced by the company described herein.

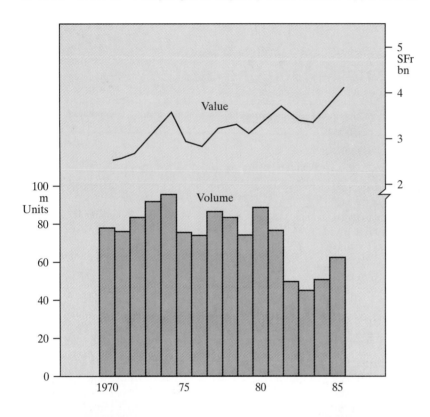

EXHIBIT 1 It's All in the Price Swiss Watch Production

Note: Including unassembled movements

Source: Federation of the Swiss Watch industry.

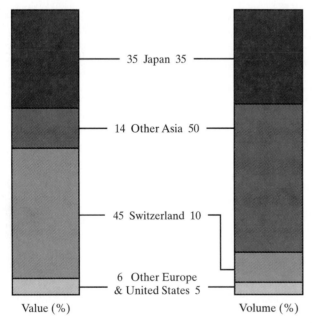

EXHIBIT 2 World Watch Production, 1985, by Country (estimates)

Source: Federation of the Swiss Watch industry.

with digital faces that were more accurate than mechanical watches.

Even though it was the Swiss who introduced the first electronic quartz watch in 1968, they were slow to accept the importance of the new technology. Hindsight suggests that small and fragmented producers had a vested interest in keeping things as they were—the new technology was still unproven in the marketplace and the Swiss proposition was secure. In any event, the Swiss were late and reluctant entrants into a new market whose rules were different. In

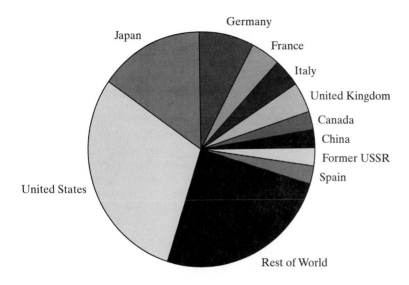

Germany
Japan
France
Italy
United Kingdom
Canada
China
Former USSR
Spain
United States
Rest of World

EXHIBIT 3 Swiss Watch Exports, 1985, by Destination

Note: Including unassembled movements

Source: Federation of the Swiss Watch Industry.

the 1970s, for example, watches were introduced to mass outlets such as department stores and supermarkets. This was nothing short of blasphemous to the proud Swiss who required their watches to be sold in approved watch and jewelry stores. The Swiss continued to produce watches whose styles were no longer in touch with consumer demands, and they displayed a noticeable lack of marketing creativity. In reality, the Swiss had ceased to be leaders in the watch industry. The Swiss luxury watch market was still healthy, but they had lost a huge amount of market share at the lower end of the market. In 1974 Swiss watch exports still accounted for 60 percent of the world's total. By 1979, the Swiss represented about a third of the world's watch exports. Economic recession and a sharp rise in the value of the Swiss franc played a part in the industry's problems. Most observers, however, now attribute the decline of the Swiss watch industry to too many years of unqualified success that gave it an aura of invincibility. As one watch executive put it:

> Just imagine the situation in the early post-war years when the Swiss were the only people making and selling watches; the industry had a waiting list of months; and selling prices were set to enable even inefficient firms to survive. The more efficient ones were making enormous profits. Why would any manager in his senses want to change things?[2]

As Switzerland entered the 1980s, the structure of its watchmaking industry, which had more or less retained its form since the late eighteenth century, finally began to adapt to the electronic age. This meant rationalization of production, automation, concentration, and the corollary of fewer jobs. Between 1980 and 1983, production of watches dropped by 50 percent. By 1983, only 686 *maisons*

[2] *Management Today,* December 1980.

remained and overall employment stood at about 40,000 jobs, down from 90,000 in the early 1970s.

THE MERGER OF ASUAG-SSIH

The merger of Asuag, whose flagship brand is Longines, and SSIH, whose best known brand is now Swatch but also boasts Omega and Tissot, was Switzerland's first response to the Asian challenge. The new group was granted a financial package worth $310 million, representing the largest rescue scheme in the history of Swiss banking. Heavy reorganization took place in both groups, especially SSIH which had lost $77 million in the year ending March 31, 1981. Most of SSIH's management was sacked and control of the watch division was transferred to Ernst Thomke, a rank outsider to the industry, who possessed both a medical doctor's degree and an advanced degree in chemistry.

The merger, as it turns out, was a sensible move because Asuag was far better technologically equipped to face the 1980s than SSIH, having already made a substantial commitment to the research and development of electronic watches. SSIH, for its part, possessed the better known brand names. (In the summer of 1985, Asuag-SSIH was renamed the Swiss Corporation for Microelectronics and Watchmaking Industries, SMH in short.)

Dr. Thomke made two important, tradition-breaking decisions in his first year. The first was to sell Swiss watch movements all over the world instead of restricting such sales to Switzerland, a move that allowed Asuag-SSIH to improve its technological base through increased production. The second was to recapture the lower end of the watch market by developing a product that was inexpensive to manufacture, low-priced, durable, technically advanced and stylish. The result was the Swatch watch, which was especially successful in the United States, with total retail sales increasing from $3 million in 1983 to $150 million in 1985.

PRODUCT DESCRIPTION

The Swatch is a lightweight (3/4 ounce), shock-proof, water-resistant (up to 100 feet), electronic watch with a plastic band that uses a quartz analog (with dial and hands) movement. It is manufactured by robots and sealed by lasers in a state of the art factory in Switzerland. The watch is comprised of only 51 components (the average is 91), which lends itself well to the thin look that is currently in vogue, and is manufactured off a single assembly line (the Japanese use three). What most distinguishes the product is its design and its departure from convention. A wide variety of faces have been used and even glow in the dark and scented bands (banana, raspberry, and mint) have been tried. Battery life is estimated to be three years, and the watch retails from $30 to $35, which represents a substantial markup on cost.

THE SWATCH MARKETING STRATEGY

Central to the marketing strategy of the Swatch watch is the notion of the watch as a fashion accessory. This is a novel approach in that it is typically used as a selling point for gold and diamond-studded watches at the higher end of the market. Watches in the $30 to $35 range normally compete on the basis of price, performance or, in the case of digitals in the late 1970s and early 1980s, on accessory features such as a stopwatch and/or calculator. Swatch, on the other hand, describes its target market as "fashion-oriented 12- to 24-year-olds."

One trend that worked in Swatch's favor from the start is that, during the period 1976–1986, more and more people bought watches. No longer was the watch primarily a gift item and no longer was it only the rich who owned more than one. In 1976, 240 watches per 1,000 inhabitants were sold in America. Ten years later the figure was 425 watches per 1,000 inhabitants. About 90 percent of sales were composed of inexpensive electronic watches of various styles and brands.[3]

Of course, Swatch never would have been able to take advantage of this trend without a sound marketing strategy. According to Imgruth, his company's strategy is divided into three elements: design, distribution, and production.

1. **Design.** An essential feature of the fashion oriented approach is a constant variety of product lines whose designs suit seasonal fashions. According to Imgruth, the company has "a clear product concept based on four directions: young and trendy; active and sporty; cool and clean high style; and classic. These four lines are available at all times. There are 12 small-faced models, and 12 larger ones. Every face is only out a restricted amount of time, sometimes only three months, sometimes 12 months, depending on the design concept of the watch." Each

line is given a distinct theme such as the "Cosmic Western" group which was described as a combination of Buck Rodgers and the Wild, Wild West. New models are introduced four times a year, the seasons being spring/summer/fall/holiday (see Exhibit 4). In addition, special versions of the Swatch Watch such as the $100 diamond-studded Limelight and limited edition art watches are added periodically. Generally speaking, the trendier the design, the shorter it will remain available; the more classic the design, the longer it will remain on the market. Says Imgruth: "This is done on purpose, to create collecting and spur multiple ownership."[4] Advertising media are chosen based on the product concept. There are four campaigns running simultaneously, each geared to a specific element of the four-tiered product mix.

2. **Distribution.** Distribution was originally limited to fashion outlets and now includes upscale department stores such as Bloomingdale's, Saks Fifth Avenue, Macy's, and so on. Such stores never used to handle Swiss watches and still only account for 10 percent of all watches sold. Imgruth scrupulously avoids distributing through drugstores and mass merchandisers such as Sears and JCPenney, even though these are the usual paths for watches priced under $100. Distribution is limited to 5,000 locations in the United States, although Imgruth claims that 5,000 more would love to sell his products. As one Swatch executive puts it: "You have to control distribution and not flood the market, or people lose their hunger for the product."[5]

3. **Production.** The production process described previously makes the design strategy possible. The flexibility that Swatch enjoys is unknown elsewhere in the industry. Design changes for other watchmakers typically require a substantial capital investment whereas Swatch can make changes without adding cost. Such flexibility is absolutely essential because of Swatch's product strategy. Without it, design runs of three months would be out of the question.

SWATCH MARKETING STRATEGY IN ACTION

In view of the fact that Swatch's strategy is unorthodox, it is not at all surprising that its marketing executives would look out of place in most corporate boardrooms. All advertising, marketing, and promotion activities are handled by 27-year-old Steve Rechtschaffner, vice president/marketing, and Nancy Kadner, director of advertising, 31. Rechtschaffner, a former member of the U.S. Ski Team and self-described workaholic who recently overcame a bout with thyroid

---

[3] *The Economist*, May 17, 1986

[4] *Marketing and Media Decisions,* Spring/1985.
[5] *Sales and Marketing Management,* March 11, 1985.

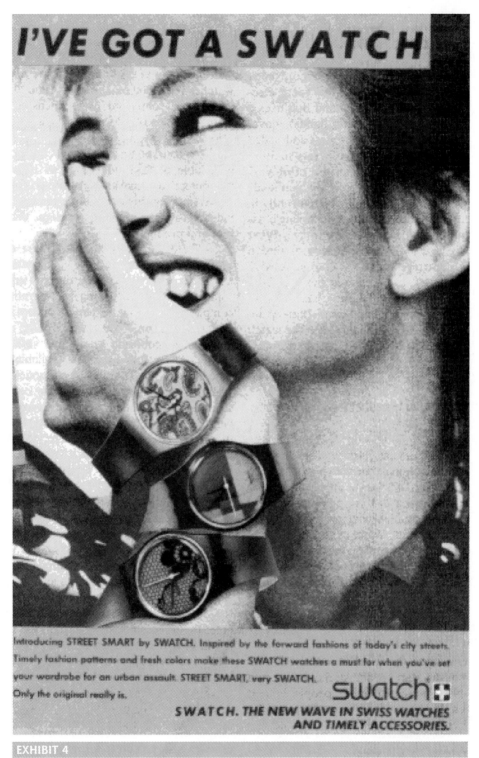

I'VE GOT A SWATCH

Introducing STREET SMART by SWATCH. Inspired by the forward fashions of today's city streets. Timely fashion patterns and fresh colors make these SWATCH watches a must for when you've set your wardrobe for an urban assault. STREET SMART, very SWATCH. Only the original really is.

swatch

SWATCH. THE NEW WAVE IN SWISS WATCHES AND TIMELY ACCESSORIES.

EXHIBIT 4

Source: Company records.

cancer, has no formal business education. He began his career by forming his own sports promotion business. As for Kadner, prior to her work at Swatch she spent over 4 years in the marketing department at MTV.

Rechtschaffner and Kadner are the creative forces behind Swatch's novel marketing strategy. Before Swatch entered the market, watches priced under $50 competed on the basis of price or performance. To gain an appreciation of just how different the Swatch strategy is, a glance at a typical advertisement for a low-priced watch would suffice. Normally, the watch is placed against a background in the hope that the right message is communicated. Timex developed one of the more creative performance-oriented campaigns in the early 1980s when it strapped a watch to an auto tire and proclaimed that the product "Takes a lickin' and keeps on tickin'." Others have not been so imaginative. For example, it is not uncommon to see digital watch advertisements where product features are simply listed next to a black and white photograph of the watch.

Swatch, for its part, has taken roads previously untraveled by watch producers. It employs the use of colorful (and often humorous) print ads, multi-page advertising inserts in magazines such as *Vogue* and *Rolling Stone,* concert and event sponsorship, and the use of music videos and MTV.

A good example of the Swatch strategy in action is its use of a rap music group and a graffiti artist to promote and develop its products. In September 1984, Swatch sponsored the World Breakdancing Championships. One of the participating rap music groups, the Fat Boys, was hired to do a commercial on MTV on which its lead singer, the Human Beat Box, incessantly chants "BrrrSWATCHUM ha ha ha SWATCHUM." In addition, Swatch wanted an artist to help promote the breakdancing championships so it hired Keith Haring, New York's best known graffiti artist. The result was a four-watch-series called the Keith Haring Swatch.

The Haring watches were promoted under the banner of "Great Modern Art That Tells Time." Swatch produced 9,999 of each edition. Each watch is numbered and, in Imgruth's words, is "a collectible piece of art, a distinctive fashion accessory, and a sturdy timepiece." The watches were introduced in separate months, the first being released in December, followed by new editions in April, May, and June.

THE COMPETITION

The under $50 watch segment is the most competive in the watch industry in terms of the number of companies involved. Based on 1984 watch sales, this segment of the watch market also was responsible for the large majority of all U.S. watch sales (see Exhibit 5).

Because the Swatch watch was such a novelty at its introduction, the company had free reign over the plastic fashion watch market (some have called it "cheap chic")

for well over a year. The picture has now changed considerably as strong competitors in the under $50 segment such as Casio, Timex, Lorus, Armitron, and Parker Watch have entered the fray. In addition to imitating some of the very styling and advertising techniques that Swatch employs (Exhibit 6), the new competition has targeted drug stores and mass retail outlets, the very areas Swatch has shied away from, as their primary points of distribution.

While it remained to be seen if the new entries could match Swatch's creativity and design flexibility (one Swatch insider said that technology-conscious Casio's bid to enter the fashion watch market was "like John Deere getting into sportscars"), the new array of low-cost watches was certain to exert downward pressure on retail prices. Lorus' initial line of plastic watches sold for $19.95 at full markup, Timex's Fun Timers sold for $17.95 and Casio's ColorBurst line started at $19.95. Most drug retailers feel prices will eventually fall to the $12 to $14 range.[6]

Swatch has also had to concern itself with the sale of phony Swatch watches and unlicensed sales. In October 1985, 5,000 fakes were uncovered by U.S. Customs and Asuag-SSIH quickly sued three Swiss imitators. There is also a thriving "gray market" in which unlicensed traders exploit price differences between the United States and Europe (the watch sells at a lower price in Europe). Swatch elected to buy up all such watches in 1985, spending an estimated $500,000 in order to maximize control over the sale of its products.

THE NEXT STEP: SWATCH AS A TOTAL FASHION ENTERPRISE

It was perhaps with an eye to an increasingly competitive environment that Swatch embarked on a fast-paced diversification program in late 1985. The company created over 470 "Swatch Shops" within major department stores nationwide selling, in addition to watches, a new ready-to-wear line called "Funwear" and an accessories line called "Fungear" (see Exhibit 7).

Swatch will continue to employ the same strategies that it uses to sell its watches. The new product groups are aimed at the same fashion-oriented 12- to 24-year-olds who are the target market for Swatch. Funwear is described as "a bright and whimsical line of unisex casual wear including shorts, T-shirts, tank tops, slip-on pants, big shirts, and beachwear." Each collection has a theme that ties in with a Swatch watch theme. Swatch's own marketing and design people will introduce new collections every eight weeks, and prices range between $10 and $50. Fungear is a collection of leather and rubber knapsacks, belts, bags, and the jacketpack, which is a backpack containing a windbreaker and a hood. Prices range from $10 to $65.

Swatch offers more than just the preceding two product lines. There are Swatch Shields, which are described

EXHIBIT 5	1984 Watch Sales by Price	
	Under $10	29%
	$10–$50	52
	Over $50	19

Source: Timex.

[6] *Drug Store News,* May 27, 1985.

EXHIBIT 6

as high-fashion sunglasses; Swatch Guards, small, colorful devices that cover watch faces; Swatch Chums, which are eyeglass holders; and umbrellas and sweats that feature current watch designs. Swatch also imports and markets pens, notebooks, address books, key rings, and safety razors.

The Swatch drive to open shops within major department stores is based on management's conviction that products should be sold in a total Swatch environment—an environment that has the Swatch "personality." The company president, Max Imgruth, has predicted that ready-to-wear and accessories will represent from 30 percent to 40 percent of total 1986 sales. In the long term, he expects the new product lines to account for the majority of Swatch sales.

OTHER EXAMPLES OF BRAND TRANSFER

There are several examples of companies that have attempted, for better or worse, to build on the success of its first product by using its brand name on other, not necessarily related products. One of the more infamous examples is that of Bill Blass, who put his name on chocolates only to see the idea fail miserably. Another example of failure is that of Nike, which unsuccesfully expanded its collection of footwear to runningwear and leisurewear. A Nike spokesman looking back at that experience notes: "When you're tremendously successful in one area, there's a tendency to develop an arrogance about your ability to transfer the value of a brand name."[7]

On the other side of the coin, there was the example of Conran's, which successfully expanded from a producer of home furnishings to a retailer of everything from towels to desk lamps. Like Swatch, Conran's started out catering to the needs of young people and, when expansion took place, stayed with the same target market. Another point in Swatch's favor was its Swatch Shops, which spared the company from having its new product lines being placed on shelves next to competitors who had the advantage of an established image as quality producers of ready-to-wear. In order to keep its shops and continue to avoid head-to-head competition with more established companies, Swatch had

---

[7] *Forbes*, January 27, 1986.

to remain a trend-setting, creative company. In this way they could avoid the fate of Bill Blass chocolates, which were sometimes found placed next to boxes of Godiva chocolates, leaving the consumer with what might be a choice easily made.

DISCUSSION QUESTIONS

1. Swatch is a unique success story. Why has the company been so successful? Was it important that the Swiss watch industry recapture the lower end of the market? Why? Why not?
2. Do you see any parallels between the decline of the Swiss watch industry and other Western industries?
3. Evaluate the cultural dimension of the Swatch story, taking into account such practices as the willingness to bring in people from other industries, to delegate authority to younger executives, and to employ new media such as rock concerts and music videos.
4. Swatch created a new market—can they continue to expand that market? What must they do to defend their position in this market?
5. What do you think of Swatch's chances for success as a total fashion enterprise? Do you agree with management's extension of the Swatch brand name to other products? Why? Why not?
6. Swatch is a classic example of marketing success through creativity. What lessons can be learned from their experience?

Smart Car

In 1998, DaimlerChrysler introduced a new car, a new brand, and a new look with new technology in nine EU countries. It is named "Smart" and is certainly distinctive looking. (See Exhibit 1.)

The Smart car is only 2,500 mm long, 1,515 mm wide, and 1,529 mm high. It seats two adults or one adult and two children. The Smart car weights 720 kg, has a 22-liter gas tank, and gets 100 kilometers per 4.8 liters. It is always two-toned in color. It has a frame called the Tridion Safety Cell, which comes in anthracite or silver color, and removable panels, which can be changed in less than an hour, in such colors as mad red, hello yellow, jack black, aqua orange,

scodic blue, and boomerang blue, green, or orange. The optional leather seats are papaya colored. If you are thinking that the interchangeable panels and the wild colors remind you of a Swatch watch, you are correct, as the Swatch watch was the initial inspiration for developing this car. In the

EXHIBIT 1

Source: http://www.smart.com.

SOURCES: "Daimler-Benz Buys Out Rest of Swatch Smart Car Venture," *The Wall Street Journal,* 5 November 1998, p. A17; William Diem, "Daimler's Tiny Smart Car Falters After a Fast Start," *The New York Times,* 3 March 1998, p. 12:1; DaimlerChrysler 1998 Annual Report. Michael Harvey, "Street-Wise Orphan Assumes Cult Status," *Financial Times,* 29 May 1999, p. XXII.

early stages of the project when Daimler-Benz and SMH (maker of the Swatch watch) formed a joint venture, the car was called a "Swatchmobile."

The Swatchmobile concept was based on Nicolas Hayek's (Chairman of SMH) conviction that consumers become emotionally attached to cars just as they do to watches. His vision was of high safety, ecology, and a very consumer-friendly area to sit in. Like the Swatch, the Swatchmobile was to be affordable, durable, and stylish. Hayek noted that safety would be a key selling point, declaring, "This car will have the crash security of a Mercedes." Furthermore, the car was to emit almost no pollutants, thanks to its electric engine. The car would also be capable of gasoline-powered operation, using a highly efficient, miniaturized engine. Hayek predicted worldwide sales would reach 1 million units, with the United States accounting for about half the market.

In 1998, shortly after the introduction, the joint venture between SMH and Daimler-Benz ended when Daimler-Benz bought out SMH's stake. Hayak was "disillusioned" with Daimler-Benz, and Daimler-Benz found Hayak difficult to work with.

To date, Smart car has two major criticisms: safety and price. Despite development of a crash management system that "enables smaller cars to be just as safe as larger ones," during its first winter (1999) on the road, there were reports of several accidents. In response, the company developed "Trust Plus," a software package that will cut power if the wheels start to slip.

As for the price, it originally sold for $10,500. After a period of disappointing sales in Italy and France, the price was reduced to $9,300. Although many buyers of the Smart car have high incomes or already own two cars, they are concerned about the price-value relationship.

DISCUSSION QUESTIONS

1. What do you think of the market potential of the Smart car? Comment on the original premise that a car could be the by-product of the joint-venture of a automobile manufacturer and a nonautomotive marketer.
2. Is the Smart car an international or a global product? Do you agree with the European-only launch? Why? Why not?
3. Identify target markets where you would introduce this car. What sequence of countries would you recommend for the introduction?
4. How would you position the Smart car in the target markets?
5. Who are the Smart car's major competitors? How are these products differentiated?
6. Should the price, assuming it would still make a profit, be reduced?

VISIT THE WEB SITE

www.smart.com

(Note: The first screen of the Web site asks the viewer to select a country. The nine choices are D, CH, A, I, F, E, B, L, or NL. Can you identify each country?)

Entry and Expansion Strategies: Marketing and Sourcing

"No nation is ever ruined by trade."

—BENJAMIN FRANKLIN, 1706–1790
Thoughts on Commercial Subjects

CHAPTER CONTENTS

When a company decides to go international, it faces a host of decisions. Which countries should it enter and in what sequence? What criteria should be used to select entry markets: proximity, stage of development, geographic region, cultural and linguistic criteria, the competitive situation, or other factors? How should it enter new markets? Directly via "green fields" expansion, directly through acquisition of a local established company, or indirectly using agents or representatives? Should the new market be supplied with imported product from the home or third countries or locally manufactured product? This chapter addresses these questions and examines various strategies that a company can utilize to "go international" starting with exporting and advancing to foreign direct investment. These options are not mutually exclusive and may be used concurrently. The impact of the Internet on entry and expansion strategies is discussed in Chapter 16.

The automobile industry provides a good example. In which countries can a company obtain parts necessary for production? In which countries and through which channels should the automobiles be sold? Should production be relocated or expanded to another country?

Manufacturers can achieve competitive advantage by shifting production among different sites. It is little wonder that most of the world's leading automakers have set their sights on Brazil and China. Both countries are big emerging markets; they boast the biggest populations in their respective regions as well as rapidly growing economies. Nearly 2 million vehicles were sold in Brazil in 1996, and analysts forecast sales of

♦ BOX 8-1 ♦

BIG EMERGING AUTO MARKETS

Like Brazil, China holds huge opportunities for auto-makers. The total vehicle market is expected to increase from 1.6 million units in 1996 to 2.7 million by the turn of the century. Volkswagen (VW) is currently the biggest player in the China market; the 200,000 Santana passenger cars produced each year by VW's joint venture with Shanghai Automotive Industry Corporation (SAIC) represent half of the market. VW also produces its Jetta model in Changchun in partnership with First Auto Works (FAW). Chrysler's joint venture with Beijing Auto Works has been producing Jeep Cherokees since the early 1980s. New investment plans are announced on a regular basis; for example, GM launched a joint venture with SAIC in 1997 valued at more than $1.5 billion. The venture is slated to produce Buick sedans for government officials.

Despite the general euphoria about China, a variety of obstacles and pitfalls await those hoping to develop the market. The Chinese government does not permit foreign companies to have majority stakes in joint ventures and reserves the right to set production levels and prices. The rhetoric from government officials can send chills down a car executive's spine. Recently, for example, an FAW official told a state newspaper, "We shouldn't be the appendage of the foreign automobile industry anymore. What the South Koreans and Japanese could achieve, so the Chinese can also manage." The business

landscape is littered with stalled projects; in 1997, for example, Peugeot was forced to abandon a joint venture in Guangzhou; Mercedes-Benz considered canceling its planned $1 billion joint venture with Nanfang South China Motor Corporation to build minivans and engines. The deal had been a triumph for Mercedes, which had bested both Chrysler and GM for the contract in 1995. Two years later, however, the venture was at a standstill, and Jurgen Hubbert, a member of the Daimler-Benz board, had some sobering advice for anyone considering business in China: "Whenever you're finalizing a project, you are really just starting."

The competitive environment in Brazil is also uniquely challenging. For example, in 1987, Ford and VW established a joint venture called Autolatina. Internal rivalries bogged down that venture; by 1994, the partnership was dissolved. Meanwhile, as Ford prepared to build its own capacity, it supplied the market with imports. In 1996, however, the Brazilian government suddenly boosted tariffs on car imports to 70 percent from 20 percent. Ford had no choice but to supply Brazilian dealers with a mixed bag of vehicles from a variety of sources—a move that alienated the dealers and tarnished Ford's reputation. Even though the new Fiesta is a much needed hit with car buyers, production delays allowed Fiat to reach the market first with its Palio.

SOURCES: Michelle Maynard, "Big Three Beef Up in Brazil," *USA Today*, 7 July 1997, pp. 1B, 2B; James Harding, "Long March to Mass Market," *Financial Times,* 25 June 25 1997, p. 13; James Cox, "Chinese Auto Industry Stumbles," *USA Today,* 16 December 1996, p. 9B; Matt Moffett, "Bruised in Brazil: Ford Slips as Market Blooms," *The Wall Street Journal,* 13 December 1996, p. A10; John Templeman, "How Mercedes Trumped Chrysler in China," *Business Week,* 31 July 1995, pp. 50–51.

3 million units by 2000. Brazil represents Volkswagen AG's largest market outside of Germany; VW of Brazil operates seven plants, including a lean-production truck plant in Resende, that produces nearly half a million vehicles annually. Fiat, Brazil's number-two producer, has spent $1 billion to increase production; its rugged new Palio "world car" has been a hot seller since its introduction in 1996. American producers are also in the market. General Motors (GM) produces Blazers in São José dos Campos; GM has earmarked $1.25 billion for three new plants, including a $600 million state-of-the-art small car works in the southern Brazil city of Rio Grande do Sul. Ford has invested more than $1 billion in a plant in São Bernardo do Campo that produces Fiesta subcompacts and the new Ka minicar. Chrysler has a production facility in Campo Largo and also participates in a small-displacement engine manufacturing joint venture with BMW. Surprisingly, Japan's automakers have been relatively slow to develop the market; Toyota is a minor player, and Honda's $100 million plant produces only 15,000 Civics each year.

The presence of VW, Fiat, GM, and other automakers in Brazil illustrates the fact that every firm, at various points in its history, faces a broad range of strategy alternatives. In far too many cases, companies fail to appreciate the range of alternatives open to them and, therefore, employ only one strategy—often to their grave disadvantage. The same companies also fail to consider the strategy alternatives open to their competitors and thereby set themselves up to be victims of the dreaded "Titanic" syndrome—the thud in the night that comes without warning and sinks the ship.

Some companies are making the decision to go global for the first time; other companies seek to expand their share of world markets. Companies in either situation face the same basic sourcing issues introduced in the previous chapter. Companies must also address issues of marketing and value chain management before deciding to enter or expand their share of global markets by means of licensing, joint ventures or minority ownership, and majority or 100 percent ownership. These decisions are affected by issues of investment and control as well as a company's attitude toward risk.

◆ DECISION CRITERIA FOR INTERNATIONAL BUSINESS

Before doing any business internationally through sourcing, exporting, investing, or a combination of these strategies, the company must look at conditions in the potential country to analyze what the advantages, disadvantages, and costs will be and whether it is worth the risk.

POLITICAL RISK

Political risk, or the risk of a change in government policy that would adversely impact a company's ability to operate effectively and profitably, is a deterrent to expanding internationally. The lower the level of political risk, the more likely it is that a company will invest in a country or market. The difficulty of assessing political risk is inversely proportional to a country's stage of economic development: All other things being equal, the less developed a country, the more difficult it is to predict political risk. The political risk of the Triad countries, for example, is quite limited as compared to a less developed preindustrial country in Africa, Latin America, or Asia. In general, there is an inverse relationship between political risk and the stage of development of a country. The higher the level of income per capita, the lower the level of political risk.

McDonald's in war-torn Belgrade, Yugoslavia, had to change its marketing strategy to survive and minimize its American origins, which were the basis of physical attacks. A Serbian cap was added to the Golden Arch logo, the basement was turned into an air-raid shelter, prices were lowered, and free hamburgers were distributed to anti-NATO demonstrators. Needless to say, McDonald's corporate headquarters had little to say about these tactics but local management is quite happy and proud of their achievement.[1]

MARKET ACCESS

A key factor in locating production facilities is market access. If a country or a region limits market access because of local content laws, balance-of-payments problems, or any other reason, it may be necessary to establish a production facility within the country itself. The Japanese automobile companies invested in U.S. plant capacity because of concerns about market access. By producing cars in the United States, they have a source of supply that is not exposed to the threat of tariff or nontariff barriers. In the 1950s and 1960s, U.S. companies created production capacity abroad to ensure continued access to markets that had been established with supply exported from U.S. plants.

---

[1] Katarina Kratovac, "At Least One U.S. Icon Survives in Belgrade," *Marketing News,* 11 October 1999, p. 29.

FACTOR COSTS AND CONDITIONS

Factor costs are land, labor, and capital costs (remember Economics 101!). Labor includes the cost of workers at every level: manufacturing and production, professional and technical, and management. Basic manufacturing direct labor costs today range from $0.50 per hour in the typical less developed country (LDC) to $6 to $20 or more per hour in the typical developed country. Table 8-1 shows indexes of hourly compensation costs for production workers in manufacturing for selected countries and regions. Note that, compared to the United States, manufacturing compensation costs are higher in Western European countries despite a recent decline, and Asia's emerging countries have increased relative to the United States since 1980.

Notice in Table 8-1 that German hourly compensation costs for production workers in manufacturing are 155 percent of those in the United States, whereas those in Mexico are only 10 percent of those in the United States. For Volkswagen (VW), if wages were the sole criteria for making a decision, the wage differential between Mexico and Germany would dictate a Mexican manufacturing facility that builds Golf and Jetta models destined for the United States. Do lower wage rates demand that a company relocate its manufacturing to the low-wage country? Hardly. In Germany, VW Chairman

TABLE 8-1   Indexes of Hourly Compensation Costs for Production Workers in Manufacturing for Selected Countries: 1980, 1990, 1995, and 1997

[**United States = 100.** Compensation costs include all pay made directly to the worker—pay for time worked and not worked (e.g., leave, except sick leave), other direct pay, employer expenditures for legally required insurance programs and contractual and private benefit plans, and for some countries, other labor taxes. Data adjusted for exchange rates. Area averages are trade-weighted to account for difference in countries' relative importance to U.S. trade in manufactured goods. The trade weights used are the sum of U.S. imports of manufactured products for consumption (customs value) and U.S. domestic exports of manufactured products (f.a.s. value); see source for detail.]

Area or Country	*1980*	*1990*	*1995*	*1997*	*European Union Area or Country*	*1980*	*1990*	*1995*	*1997*
United States	100	100	100	100	Austria	90	119	147	120
Total[a]	67	83	95	84	Belgium	133	129	155	125
OECD[b]	77	94	103	90	Denmark	110	120	140	121
Europe	102	118	129	112	Finland	83	141	140	118
					France	91	102	116	99
Asian NIESC	12	25	37	36	Germany	125	147	187	155
Canada	88	106	93	81	Greece	38	45	53	NA
Mexico	22	11	9	10	Ireland	60	79	79	74
Australia	86	88	88	88	Italy	83	119	94	92
Hong Kong[c]	15	21	28	30	Luxembourg	121	110	136	NA
Israel	38	57	61	66	Netherlands	122	123	140	113
Japan	56	86	139	106	Portugal	21	25	31	29
Korea, South	10	25	42	40	Spain	60	76	75	67
New Zealand	54	56	59	60	Sweden	127	140	125	122
Singapore	15	25	43	45	United Kingdom	77	85	80	85
Sri Lanka	2	2	3	NA					
Taiwan	10	26	34	32					

NA = Not available.

[a] The 28 foreign economies for which 1997 data are available.

[b] Canada, Mexico, Australia, Japan, New Zealand, and the European countries.

[c] Newly Industrialized Economies Hong Kong, South Korea, Singapore, and Taiwan.

Source: U.S. Department of Labor, Bureau of Labor Statistics, 1998.

Ferdinand Piech is trying to improve his company's competitiveness by convincing unions to allow flexible work schedules. For example, during peak demand, employees would work six-day weeks; when demand slows, factories would produce cars only three days per week.

Moreover, wages are only one of the costs of production and, many times, a small percentage of the total cost associated with the product. Many other considerations enter into the sourcing decision, such as management's aspirations. For example, SMH assembles all of the watches it sells, and it builds most of the components for the watches it assembles. It manufactures in Switzerland, the highest-income country in the world. SMH's Hayek decided that he wanted to manufacture in Switzerland in spite of the fact that a secretary in Switzerland makes more money than a chief engineer in Thailand. He did this by making a commitment to drive wage costs down to less than 10 percent of total costs. At this level, wages rates are no longer a significant factor in competitiveness. As Hayek puts it, he does not care if his competitor's workers work for free! He will still win in a competitive marketplace because his value is so much greater.[2]

The other factors of production are land, materials, and capital. The cost of these factors depends on their availability and relative abundance. Often, the differences in factor costs will offset each other so that, on balance, companies have a "level field" in the competitive arena. For example, the United States has abundant land and Germany has abundant capital. These advantages partially offset each other. When this is the case, the critical factor is management, professional, and worker team effectiveness.

World factor costs that affect manufacturing can be divided into three tiers. The first tier consists of the industrialized countries where factor costs are tending to equalize. The second tier consists of the industrializing countries—for example, Singapore and other Pacific Rim countries—that offer significant factor costs savings as well as an increasingly developed infrastructure and political stability, making them extremely attractive manufacturing locations. The third tier includes Russia and other countries that have not yet become significant locations for manufacturing activity. Third-tier countries present the combination of lower factor costs (especially wages) offset by limited infrastructure development and greater political uncertainty.

The application of advanced computer controls and other new manufacturing technologies has reduced the proportion of labor relative to capital for many businesses. In formulating a sourcing strategy, company managers and executives should also recognize the declining importance of direct manufacturing labor as a percentage of total product cost. The most advanced global companies are no longer blindly chasing cheap labor manufacturing locations because direct labor may be a very small percentage of total. As a result, it may not be worthwhile to incur the costs and risks of establishing a manufacturing activity in a distant location. The experience of the Arrow Shirt Company also illustrates several issues relating to factor costs. During the 1980s, Arrow sourced 15 percent of its dress shirts from the Far East at a cost savings of $15 per dozen compared to U.S.-manufactured shirts. Arrow decided to phase out imports after spending $15 million to automate its U.S. plants. Productivity increased 25 percent and Arrow is no longer at the mercy of a 12-month lead time between ordering and delivery; U.S.-sourced shirts can be ordered a mere three months in advance—a critical issue in the fashion industry. Interestingly, the Arrow experience illustrates how the decision to source at home rather than abroad does not automatically defuse the political issue of exporting jobs: After automating, Arrow laid off 400 U.S. workers and closed four factories.[3]

[2] William Taylor, "Message and Muscle: An Interview with Swatch Titan Nicolas Hayek," *Harvard Business Review* (March–April 1993): 99–110.

[3] Cynthia Mitchell, "Coming Home: Some Firms Resume Manufacturing in U.S. after Foreign Fiascoes," *The Wall Street Journal,* 14 October 1986, p. 1.

Many companies have been chagrined to discover that today's cheap factor costs can disappear as the law of supply and demand drives up wages and land prices. Shirt-makers like Arrow began sourcing in Japan in the 1950s. As wages and real estate costs increased, production was shifted to Hong Kong and then to Taiwan and Korea. During the 1970s and 1980s, production kept shifting to China, Indonesia, Thailand, Malaysia, Bangladesh, and Singapore. In recent years, shirt production has shifted from the Far East to Costa Rica, the Dominican Republic, Guatemala, Honduras, and Puerto Rico. In addition to low wages, these countries offer tax incentives under the 1983 Caribbean Basin Initiative agreement.[4]

SHIPPING CONSIDERATIONS

In general, the greater the distance between the product source and the target market, the greater the time delay for delivery and the higher the transportation cost. However, innovation and new transportation technologies are cutting both time and dollar costs. To facilitate global delivery, transportation companies such as CSX Corporation are forming alliances and becoming an important part of industry value systems. Manufacturers can take advantage of intermodal services that allow containers to be transferred between rail, boat, air, and truck carriers. Today, transportation expenses for U.S. exports and imports represent approximately 5 percent of total costs. In Europe, the advent of the single market means fewer border controls, which greatly speeds up delivery times and lowers costs.

Acer, a Taiwanese company and the seventh largest producer of computers, practices what it calls the "fast-food business model." Like a Big Mac at McDonald's, the final product is assembled just before the purchase. Acer divides computer components into two types, perishable and nonperishable. The nonperishable components such as housings, keyboards, and floppy disks are manufactured in Taiwan and shipped by sea to their 39 regional business units (RBUs). Perishables, such as drives, which are constantly being upgraded, are manufactured as needed and air shipped to the RBUs where the final product is assembled. Using this logistics strategy eliminates the minimum one- to-two-month time lag for shipping goods by sea and costly inventory expense and provides consumers with the latest product.

COUNTRY INFRASTRUCTURE

In order to present an attractive setting for a manufacturing operation, it is important that the country's infrastructure be sufficiently developed to support a manufacturing operation. The required infrastructure will vary from company to company, but minimally it will include power, transportation and roads, communications, service and component suppliers, a labor pool, civil order, and effective governance. In addition, a country must offer reliable access to foreign exchange for the purchase of necessary material and components from abroad as well as a physically secure setting where work can be done and product can be shipped to customers.

A country may have cheap labor, but does it have the necessary supporting services or infrastructure to support a manufacturing activity? Many developing countries offer these conditions, yet there are also many other countries that do not, such as Lebanon, Uganda, and El Salvador. One of the challenges of doing business in the Russian or Chinese market is an infrastructure that is woefully inadequate to handle the increased volume of shipments.

---

[4] Peter C. T. Elsworth, "Can Colors and Stripes Rescue Shirt Makers from a Slump?" *The New York Times,* 17 March 1991, Sec. 3, p. 5.

FOREIGN EXCHANGE

In deciding where to locate a manufacturing activity, the cost of production supplied by a country source will be determined in part by the prevailing foreign exchange rate for the country's currency. Exchange rates are so volatile today that many companies pursue global sourcing strategies as a way of limiting exchange-related risk. At any point in time, what has been an attractive location for production may become much less attractive due to exchange rate fluctuation. For example, the financial crisis in Russia in 1998 saw the ruble drop from 6 to the U.S. dollar to 25 rubles to the dollar. The prudent company will incorporate exchange volatility into its planning assumptions and be prepared to prosper under a variety of exchange rate relationships.

The dramatic shifts in price levels of commodities and currencies are a major characteristic of the world economy today. Such volatility argues for a sourcing strategy that provides alternative country options for supplying markets. Thus, if the dollar, the yen, or the mark becomes seriously overvalued, a company with production capacity in other locations can achieve competitive advantage by shifting production among different sites.

CREATING A PRODUCT-MARKET PROFILE

The first step in choosing export markets is to establish the key factors influencing sales and profitability of the product in question. If a company is getting started for the first time in exporting, its product-market profile will most likely be based on its experience in the home market, which may or may not be relevant to the individual export markets being considered. The basic questions to be answered can be summarized as the nine Ws:

1. Who buys our product?
2. Who does not buy our product?
3. What need or function does our product serve?
4. What problem does our product solve?
5. What are customers currently buying to satisfy the need and/or solve the problem for which our product is targeted?
6. What price are they paying for the products they are currently buying?
7. When is our product purchased?
8. Where is our product purchased?
9. Why is our product purchased?

Any company must answer these critical questions if it is going to be successful in export markets. Each answer provides an input into decisions concerning the four Ps. Remember, the general rule in marketing is that, if a company wants to penetrate an existing market, it must offer more value than its competitors—better benefits, lower prices, or both. This applies to export marketing as well as marketing in the home country.

MARKET SELECTION CRITERIA

Once a company has created a product-market profile, the next step in choosing an export market is to appraise each possible market. Six criteria should be assessed: (1) market potential, (2) market access, (3) shipping costs, (4) potential competition, (5) service requirements, and (6) product fit.

1. Market Potential

What is the basic market potential for the product? To answer this question, secondary information is a good place to start. Valuable sources were discussed in Chapter 6, "Global Marketing Information Systems and Research." In the United States, the federal government has numerous publications available, compiled by the Central Intelligence Agency (CIA) and various other agencies and organizations.

The cost of assembling sales literature, catalogs, and technical bulletins should also be considered in comparison to market potential and profitability. This cost is particularly important in selling highly technical products.

2. Market Access

This aspect of market selection concerns the entire set of national controls that applies to imported merchandise and any restrictions that the home-country government might have. It includes such items as export license, import duties, import restrictions or quotas, foreign exchange regulations, and preference arrangements. Because this information is quite detailed, it is best to directly consult the trade bureaus of countries that are being considered.

3. Shipping Costs and Time

Preparation and shipping costs can affect the market potential for a product. If a similar product is already being manufactured in the target market, shipping costs may render the imported product uncompetitive. If it takes months for the product to reach the target market and the product competes in a rapidly changing category such as computers, alternative transportation strategies should be considered. It is important to investigate alternative modes of shipping as well as ways to differentiate a product to offset the price disadvantage.

4. Potential Competition

Using a country's commercial representatives abroad can also be valuable. When contacting country representatives abroad, it is important to provide as much specific information as possible. If a manufacturer simply says, "I make lawn mowers. Is there a market for them in your territory?," the representative cannot provide much helpful information. If, on the other hand, the manufacturer provides the following information: (1) sizes of lawn mowers manufactured, (2) descriptive brochures indicating features and advantages, and (3) estimated cost insurance freight (C.I.F.) and retail price in the target market, then the commercial representative could provide a very useful report based on a comparison of the company's product with market needs and offerings.

5. Service Requirements

If service is required for the product, can it be delivered at a cost that is consistent with the size of the market?

6. Product Fit

With information on market potential, cost of access to the market, and local competition, the final step is to decide how well a company's product fits the market in question. In general, a product fits a market if it satisfies the criteria discussed previously and is profitable.

Table 8-2 presents a market selection framework that incorporates the information elements just discussed. Suppose a company has identified China, Russia, and Mexico as potential export markets. The table shows the countries arranged in declining rank by market size. At first glance, China might appear to hold the greatest potential simply on the basis of population and GNP. Although it is true that population and GNP are major factors in assessing market potential, there are other important issues to be considered.

First, the competitive advantage of our hypothetical firm is 0.1 in China, 0.2 in Russia, and 0.5 in Mexico. Multiplying the market size and competitive advantage index yields a market potential of 10 in China, 8.4 in Russia, and 22.0 in Mexico.

The next stage in the analysis requires an assessment of the relevant market access considerations. In Table 8-2, all these conditions or terms are reduced to an index number,

Market Population	Market GNP	Market Size Index	Competitive Advantage		Market Potential	Terms of Access		Export Potential
China (1.2 billion)	1,042	100	0.10	=	10.0	0.20	=	2.00
Russia (150 million)	440	42	0.20	=	8.4	0.60	=	5.04
Mexico (96 million)	456	44	0.50	=	22.0	0.90	=	19.80

TABLE 8-2 Market Selection Framework

which is 0.2 for China, 0.6 for Russia, and 0.9 for Mexico. In other words, the market access considerations are more favorable in Mexico than in Russia, perhaps due to NAFTA. Multiplying the market potential and the market access considerations index shows that Mexico, despite its small size, holds far greater potential than China or Russia. In this example, a company with limited resources would want to begin its export marketing program in Mexico because it offers the highest export market potential when a market size, competitive advantage, and terms of access are considered. The market selection framework can, of course, be expanded to include additional criteria such as political risk, growth potential, and so on.

VISITS TO THE POTENTIAL MARKET

After the research effort has zeroed in on potential markets, there is no substitute for a personal visit to size up the market firsthand and begin the development of an actual export marketing plan. A market visit should do several things. First, it should confirm (or contradict) assumptions regarding market potential. A second major purpose is to gather additional data necessary to reach the final go/no-go decision.

One way to visit a potential market is through a trade show. (See Chapter 15 on promotion for more information about international trade shows or a state or federally sponsored trade mission.) Hundreds of trade fairs—usually organized around a product, a group of products, or activity—are held in major markets. For example, U.S. trade centers alone hold 60 product shows annually in major cities abroad.

By attending trade shows and missions, company representatives can conduct market assessment, develop or expand markets, find distributors or agents, and locate potential end users (i.e., engage in direct selling). Perhaps most important, by attending a trade show, it is possible to learn a great deal about competitors' technology, pricing, and the depth of their market penetration. For example, while walking around the exhibit hall, one can gather literature about products that often contains strategically useful technological information. Over all, company managers or sales personnel should be able to get a good general impression of competitors in the marketplace while at the same time trying to sell their own company's product.

◆ ENTRY AND EXPANSION DECISION MODEL

A decision model for entry and expansion in new markets is shown in Table 8-3.

The first issue that an expanding firm must address is whether to export or produce locally. In many emerging markets, this issue is resolved by a national policy that requires local production. Any company wishing to enter the market of such a country must source locally. In high-income countries, local production is normally not required, so the choice is up to the company.

Assuming that the choice is up to the company, the trade-offs for local versus regional or global production are cost, quality, delivery, and customer value. Costs include labor, materials, capital, land, and transportation. Scale economies are an important factor in determining cost: For every product, there is some minimum volume required

TABLE 8-3 International Market Entry and Expansion Decision Model

1. Sourcing: Home, third, or host country?
   Cost, market access, country of origin factors
2. In-country or in-region marketing organization?
   Cost, market impact assessment. If choice is to establish own organization, must decide who to appoint to key positions
3. Selection, training, and motivation of local distributors and agents
4. Marketing mix strategy: Goals and objectives in sales, earnings, and share of market; positioning; marketing mix strategy
5. Strategy implementation

to justify the investment required to establish a production site. If the product is heavy, transportation costs are greater and provide an incentive to locate production closer to the customer. Offsetting transportation costs are scale economies that result from spreading fixed costs over a greater production volume.

If a company decides to source locally, it has a choice of buying, building, or renting its own manufacturing plant or signing a local contract manufacturer. A contract manufacturer may be in a position to add production to an existing plant with less investment than the manufacturer would require to achieve the same volume of production. If this is the case, the contract manufacturer is in a position to quote an attractive price.

◆ EXPORTING

In Germany, exporting is a way of life for the Mittlestand, 2.5 million small and mid-sized companies that generate two thirds of Germany's gross national product (GNP) and account for 30 percent of exports. For companies such as steelmaker J. N. Eberle; Trumpf, a machine tool manufacturer; and J. Eberspächer, which makes auto exhaust systems, exports account for as much as 40 percent of sales. For other companies the share is even higher. For example, Mattah Hohner has 85 percent of the world mouth organ and accordion market.

Mittelstand owner-managers target global niche markets and prosper by focusing on quality, and innovation, and investing heavily in research and development. For example, the chief executive of G. W. Barth, a company that manufactures cocoa-bean roasting machines, invested nearly $2 million in infrared technology that reduced temperature variances. The company's global market share stands at 70 percent—a threefold increase in a 10-year period—as Ghirardelli Chocolate, Hershey Foods, and other companies have snapped up Barth's roasters. At ABM Baumüller, a $40 million manufacturer of motors and other components for cranes, a major investment in technology allows the company to tailor products to customer needs by means of flexible manufacturing. New automated production equipment was installed—at a cost of $20 million—that allows changeover to different products in a matter of seconds. The story is repeated throughout Germany; as a result, in industry after industry, the Mittelstand are world-class exporters.[5]

The success of the Mittelstand serves as a reminder of the impact exporting can have on a country's economy. It also demonstrates the difference between export selling and export marketing. Export selling does not involve tailoring the product, the price, or the promotional material to suit the requirements of global markets. The only marketing mix element that differs is the place—that is, the country where the product is sold. This

---

[5] Gail E. Schares and John Templeman, "Think Small: The Export Lessons to Be Learned from Germany's Midsize Companies," *Business Week,* 4 November 1994, pp. 58–60+.

◆ BOX 8-2 ◆

GERMANY'S MITTELSTAND

Part of the Mittelstand's success can also be attributed to Germany's export infrastructure. Diplomats, bankers, and other officials around the world are constantly on the lookout for opportunities; information about promising deals is conveyed back to Germany. Meanwhile, representatives from trade associations, export trading companies, and banks assist exporters with documentation and other issues. Some banks have special Mittelstand departments to provide export financing and assist companies in obtaining insurance.

The current business environment both outside and inside Germany is presenting difficult challenges to the Mittelstand. In response to the 1992–1993 recession in Europe, several countries—notably Great Britain, Italy, and Sweden—devalued their currencies. This move brought down prices on exports from those countries

and made Germany's exports correspondingly less price competitive. Meanwhile, German unions have won wage hikes for workers, and the mark's continued strength puts additional upward pressure on export prices. Mittelstand owners are taking steps to ensure their own survival, but a lack of organization has limited their political influence in Bonn. Germany's banks have tightened loan terms, resulting in a credit crunch. Many companies are going public to raise capital, but venture capital can be hard to find. Professional managers are being hired to assist the owners. Some companies may even move production out of Germany. Melitta, for example, began assembling home coffeemakers in Portugal in 1995. For companies in which money is tight, licensing production is an economical alternative.

SOURCES: Matt Marshall, "Timid Lending Hits Germany's Exporters," *The Wall Street Journal*, 21 November 1995, p. A14; Karen Lowry Miller, "The Mittelstand Takes a Stand," *Business Week,* 10 April 1995, pp. 54–55; Gail E. Schares and John Templeman, "Think Small: The Export Lessons to Be Learned from Germany's Midsize Companies," *Business Week,* 4 November 1994, pp. 58–60.

selling approach may work for some products or services; for unique products with little or no international competition, such an approach is possible. Similarly, companies new to exporting may initially experience success with selling. Even today, the managerial mind-set in many companies still favors export selling. However, as companies mature in the global marketplace or as new competitors enter the picture, it becomes necessary to engage in export marketing.

Exporting is just one strategy for a company that has decided to go international. Other options are licensing, franchising, joint ventures, and foreign direct investment when it is an option for foreign companies (see Figure 8-1). In global marketing, the issue of customer value is inextricably tied to the sourcing decision. If customers are nationalistic, they may put a positive value on the feature "made in the home country." Such preferences must be identified using market research and factored in to solve for value in the equation. Global companies succeed by convincing customers in world markets that it is their brand that signifies value and quality, not the country or origin. A successful global company can source its product from any location: The customers trust the brand and don't care about the country of origin.

EXPORTING DECISION CRITERIA

Export marketing targets the customer in the context of the total market environment. The export marketer does not take the domestic product "as is" and simply sell it to international customers. To the export marketer, the product offered in the home market is a starting point. It is modified as needed to meet the preferences of international target markets. Mittelstand companies such as ABM Baumüller exemplify this approach. Similarly, the export marketer sets prices to fit the marketing strategy and does not merely

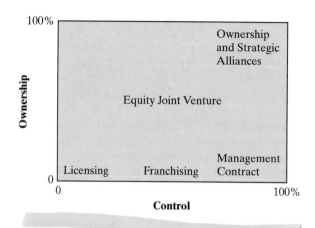

FIGURE 8-1 Ownership and Control

extend home-country pricing to the target market. Charges incurred in export preparation, transportation, and financing must be taken into account in determining prices. Finally, the export marketer also adjusts strategies and plans for communications and distribution to fit the market. In other words, effective communication about product features or uses to buyers in export markets may require creating brochures with different copy, photographs, or artwork. As the vice president of sales and marketing of one manufacturer noted, "We have to approach the international market with marketing literature as opposed to sales literature."

Export marketing is the integrated marketing of goods and services that are destined for customers in international markets. Export marketing requires

1. An understanding of the target market environment
2. The use of marketing research and the identification of market potential
3. Decisions concerning product design, pricing, distribution and channels, advertising, and communications—the marketing mix

Research has shown that exporting, in and of itself, is essentially a developmental process that can be divided into the following distinct stages.[6]

1. The firm is unwilling to export; it will not even fill an unsolicited export order. This may be due to perceived lack of time ("too busy to fill the order") or to apathy or ignorance.
2. The firm fills unsolicited export orders but does not pursue unsolicited orders. Such a firm would be an export seller.
3. The firm explores the feasibility of exporting (this stage may bypass stage 2).
4. The firm exports to one or more markets on a trial basis.
5. The firm is an experienced exporter to one or more markets.
6. After this success, the firm pursues country- or region-focused marketing based on certain criteria (e.g., all countries where English is spoken, all countries where it is not necessary to transport by water).
7. The firm evaluates global market potential before screening for the best target markets to include in its marketing strategy and plan. All markets—domestic and international—are regarded as equally worthy of consideration. At this point,

---

[6] This section relies heavily on Warren J. Bilkey, "Attempted Integration of the Literature of the Export Behavior of Firms," *Journal of International Business Studies,* 9 (Spring–Summer 1978): 33–46. The stages are based on Rogers' adaption process. See Everett M. Rodgers, *Diffusion of Innovation* (New York: Free Press, 1962).

other environmental factors may come into play and the marketer might want to explore joint ventures or foreign direct investment opportunities to maximize international opportunities.

The probability that a firm will advance from one stage to the next depends on different factors. Moving from stage 2 to stage 3 depends on management's attitude toward the attractiveness of exporting and its confidence in the firm's ability to compete internationally. However, commitment is the most important aspect of a company's international orientation. Before a firm can reach stage 4, it must receive and respond to unsolicited export orders. The quality and dynamism of management are important factors that can lead to such orders. Success in stage 4 can lead a firm to stages 5 and 6. A company that reaches stage 7 is a mature, geocentric enterprise that is relating global resources to global opportunity. To reach this stage requires management with vision and commitment.

One recent study noted that export procedural expertise and sufficient corporate resources are required for successful exporting. An interesting finding was that even the most experienced exporters express a lack of confidence in their knowledge about shipping arrangements, payment procedures, and regulations. The study also showed that, although profitability is an important expected benefit of exporting, other advantages include increased flexibility and resiliency and improved ability to deal with sales fluctuations in the home market. Whereas research generally supports the proposition that the probability of being an exporter increases with firm size, it is less clear that export intensity—the ratio of export sales to total sales—is positively correlated with firm size. Table 8-4 summarizes some of the export-related problems that a company typically faces.[7]

The decision to engage in export marketing should be based on a number of criteria, including potential market size, competitor activities, and overall marketing mix issues such as price, distribution, and promotion. The next step is the choice of one or more export markets to target. The selection process should begin with a product-market profile or plan.

TABLE 8-4 Export-Related Problems	
Logistics	**Servicing Exports**
1. Arranging transportation	12. Providing parts availability
2. Transport rate determination	13. Providing repair service
3. Handling documentation	14. Providing technical advice
4. Obtaining financial information	15. Providing warehousing
5. Distribution coordination	**Sales Promotion**
6. Packaging	16. Advertising
7. Obtaining insurance	17. Sales effort
	18. Marketing information
Legal Procedure	**Foreign Market Intelligence**
8. Government red tape	19. Locating markets
9. Product liability	20. Trade restrictions
10. Licensing	21. Competition overseas
11. Customers/duty	

---

[7] Masaaki Kotabe and Michael R. Czinkota, "State Government Promotion of Manufacturing Exports: A Gap Analysis," *Journal of International Business Studies,* 23, no. 4 (Fourth Quarter 1992): 637–658.

Market data are also available from export census documents compiled by the Department of Commerce on the basis of Shipper's Export Declarations (known as "exdecs" or SEDs, these must be filled out for any export valued at $1,500 or more). Another important source of market data is the Foreign Commercial Service. Web sites for the individual countries also provide much valuable information and contacts.

Whatever source of information is used, the ultimate goal is to determine the major factors affecting demand for a product. Then, using the tools and techniques described in Chapter 7 on targeting and segmentation, and available data, it is possible to arrive at a rough estimate of total potential demand for the product in one or more particular international markets. National income is often a good starting indicator on which to base demand estimates. A caveat, however, is income distribution within the country. India, with a population of 1 billion people, shows a per capita GNP of $424; however, 10 percent of the population or 100 million people are considered middle class and can afford most consumer goods. A market of 100 million customers should not be ignored. Additional statistical measures will considerably sharpen the estimate of total demand. For example, when estimating the demand for automobile tires, data on the total number of cars registered in any country in the world should be easy to obtain. These data, combined with data on gasoline consumption, should permit estimation of the total mileage driven in the target market. When this figure is combined with tire life predictions, it is a straightforward matter to calculate demand estimates.

ORGANIZING FOR EXPORTING

Manufacturers interested in export marketing have two broad considerations: organizing in the home country and organizing in the target market country. The issues and approaches that relate to organizing are discussed next.

Organizing in the Manufacturer's Country

Home-country issues involve deciding whether to assign export responsibility inside the company or work with an external organization specializing in a product or geographic area.

In-House Export Organization   Most companies handle export operations within their own organization. Depending on the company's size, responsibilities may be incorporated into an employee's domestic job description. Alternatively, these responsibilities may be handled as part of a separate division or organizational structure.

The possible arrangements for handling exports include the following:

1. As a part-time activity performed by domestic employees
2. Through an export partner affiliated with the domestic marketing structure that takes possession of the goods before they leave the country
3. Through an export department that is independent of the domestic marketing structure
4. Through an export department within an international division
5. For multidivisional companies, each of the foregoing possibilities exists within each division

A company that assigns a sufficiently high priority to its export business will establish an in-house organization. It then faces the question of how to organize effectively. This depends on two things: the company's appraisal of the opportunities in export marketing and its strategy for allocating resources to markets on a global basis. It may be possible for a company to make export responsibility part of a domestic employee's job description. The advantage of this arrangement is obvious: It is a low-cost arrangement requiring no additional personnel. However, this approach can work only under two conditions. First, the domestic employee assigned to the task must be thoroughly competent in terms of product/customer knowledge. Second, that competence must be applicable to the target international market(s). The key issue underlying the second condition is the extent to which the target export market is different from the domestic market. If customer circumstances and characteristics are similar, the requirements for specialized regional knowledge are reduced.

External Independent Export Organizations   If a company chooses not to perform its own marketing and promotion in-house, there are numerous export services providers from which to choose. These include export trading companies (ETCs), export management companies (EMCs), export merchants, export brokers, combination export managers, manufacturers' export representatives or commission agents, and export distributors. A typical EMC acts as the export department for several unrelated companies that lack export experience. EMCs perform a variety of services, including marketing research, channel selection, financing and shipping arrangements, and documentation. According to one recent survey of U.S.-based EMCs, the most important activities for export success are gathering marketing information, communicating with markets, setting prices, and ensuring parts availability. The same survey ranked export activities in terms of degree of difficulty; analyzing political risk, sales force management, setting pricing, and obtaining financial information were deemed most difficult to accomplish. One of the study's conclusions was that the U.S. government should do a better job of helping EMCs and their clients analyze the political risk associated with foreign markets.[8]

Organizing in the Market Country

In addition to deciding whether to rely on in-house or external export specialists in the home country, a company must also make arrangements to distribute the product in the target market country. The basic decision that every exporting organization faces is: To what extent do we rely on direct market representation as opposed to representation by independent intermediaries?

Direct Representation   There are two major advantages to direct representation by a company's own employees in a market: control and communications. Direct representation allows decisions concerning program development, resource allocation, and price changes to be implemented unilaterally. Moreover, when a product is not yet established in a market, special efforts are necessary to achieve sales. The advantage of direct representation is that these special efforts are ensured by the marketer's investment. The other great advantage to direct representation is that the possibilities for feedback and information from the market are much greater. This information can vastly improve export marketing decisions concerning product, price, communications, and distribution.

Direct representation does not mean that the exporter is selling directly to the consumer or customer. In most cases, direct representation involves selling to wholesalers or retailers. For example, the major automobile exporters in Germany and Japan rely on direct representation in the U.S. market in the form of their distributing agencies, which are owned and controlled by the manufacturing organization. The distributing agencies sell products to franchised dealers.

Independent Representation   In smaller markets, it is usually not feasible to establish direct representation because the low sales volume does not justify the cost. Even in larger markets, a small manufacturer usually lacks adequate sales volume to justify the cost of direct representation; therefore, use of an independent distributor is an effective method of sales distribution. Finding good distributors can be the key to export success.

---

[8] Donald G. Howard, "The Role of Export Management Companies in Global Partners Capital Investment Marketing," *Journal of Global Marketing*, 8, no. 1 (1994): 95–110.

Indirect or independent representation generally handles numerous other products for different companies. In many cases, there is simply not enough incentive for independents to invest significant time and money in representing a product.

Piggyback Marketing   Piggyback marketing is an innovation in international distribution that has received much attention in recent years. This is an arrangement whereby one manufacturer obtains distribution of products through another's distribution channels. Both parties can benefit: The active distribution partner makes fuller use of its distribution system capacity and thereby increases the revenues generated by the system. The manufacturer using the piggyback arrangement does so at a cost that is much lower than that required for any direct arrangement. Successful piggyback marketing requires that the combined product lines be complementary. They must appeal to the same customer, and they must not be competitive with each other. If these requirements are met, the piggyback arrangement can be a very effective way of fully utilizing an international channel system to the advantage of both parties. A case in point is the Kauai Kookie Kompany, whose owners observed Japanese tourists stocking up on cookies before returning home from Hawaii. Now the cookies are sold in a piggyback arrangement with travel agencies in Japan. The cookies can be purchased from a catalog after travelers have returned home, thus reducing the amount of baggage.[9]

◆ ADDITIONAL INTERNATIONAL ALTERNATIVES

SOURCING

The opposite of exporting is obviously importing. In fact, the United States imports more goods than it exports, and this trend appears to be increasing over the years. In analyzing the import statistics, imports can be subdivided into two categories: goods that are purchased ready-made and goods that a foreign company has a voice in their design and packing. These latter goods are referred to as *sourced goods* and merit different marketing considerations than goods that are solely imported.

Sourced goods can be found in both consumer and industrial goods. Nike doesn't make any athletic shoes. It does not own any manufacturing facilities. All its shoes are sourced in other countries, primarily in Asia. Turk, an industrial company known for its antennae, doesn't produce a single antenna. The antenna are all sourced in other countries under the specifications of Turk. How and why does a company select to employ this strategy?

There are no simple rules to guide sourcing decisions. Indeed, the sourcing decision is one of the most complex and important decisions faced by a global company. As shown in Table 8-5, six factors must be taken into account in the sourcing decision.

TABLE 8-5   Sourcing Decision Factors
1. Factor costs and conditions
2. Logistics (time required to fill orders, security and safety, and transportation costs)
3. Country infrastructure
4. Political risk
5. Market access (tariff and nontariff barriers to trade)
6. Exchange rate, availability, and convertibility of local money

---

[9] Jack G. Kaikati, "Don't Crack the Japanese Distribution System—Just Circumvent It," *Columbia Journal of World Business,* 28, no. 2 (Summer 1993): 41.

LICENSING

Licensing can be defined as a contractual arrangement whereby one company (the licensor) makes an asset available to another company (the licensee) in exchange for royalties, license fees, or some other form of compensation.[10] The licensed asset may be a patent, trade secret, or company name. Licensing is a form of global market entry and an expansion strategy with considerable appeal. A company with advanced technology, know-how, or a strong brand image can use licensing agreements to supplement its bottom-line profitability with little initial investment. Licensing can offer an attractive return on investment for the life of the agreement, providing the necessary performance clauses are in the contract. The only cost is the cost of signing the agreement and of policing its implementation.

Of course, anything so easily attained has its disadvantages and risks. The principal disadvantage of licensing is that it can be a very limited form of participation. When licensing technology or know-how, what a company does not know can put it at risk. Potential returns from marketing and manufacturing may be lost, and the agreement may have a short life if the licensee develops its own know-how and capability to stay abreast of technology in the licensed product area. Even more distressing, licensees have a troublesome way of turning themselves into competitors or industry leaders. This is especially true because licensing enables a company to borrow—leverage and exploit—another company's resources. In Japan, for example, Meiji Milk produced and marketed Lady Borden premium ice cream under a licensing agreement with Borden, Inc. Meiji learned important skills in dairy product processing, and, as the expiration dates of the licensing contracts drew near, rolled out its own premium ice cream brands.[11]

Perhaps the most famous U.S. licensing fiasco dates back to the mid-1950s, when Sony cofounder Masaru Ibuka obtained a licensing agreement for the transistor from AT&T's Bell Laboratories. Ibuka dreamed of using transistors to make small, battery-powered radios. Bell engineers informed Ibuka that it was impossible to manufacture transistors that could handle the high frequencies required for a radio; they advised him to try making hearing aids. Undeterred, Ibuka presented the challenge to his Japanese engineers, who spent many months improving high-frequency output. Sony was not the first company to unveil a transistor radio; an American-built product, the Regency, featured transistors from Texas Instruments and a colorful plastic case. However, it was Sony's high quality, distinctive approach to styling, and marketing savvy that ultimately translated into worldwide success.

Conversely, the failure to seize an opportunity to license can also lead to dire consequences. In the mid-1980s, Apple Computer chairman John Sculley decided against licensing Apple's famed operating system. Such a move would have allowed other computer manufacturers to produce Macintosh-compatible units. Meanwhile, Microsoft's growing world dominance in computer operating systems and applications got a boost from Windows, which featured a Mac-like graphical interface. Apple belatedly reversed direction and licensed its operating system, first to Power Computing Corporation in December 1994 and then to IBM and Motorola. The Mac clones have been very popular; Power Computing shipped 170,000 Macintosh clones in 1996, and in 1997 the Mac clones had captured over 25 percent of the Mac market. Despite these actions, the global market share for Macintosh and Mac clones has slipped below 5 percent. Apple's failure to license its technology in the pre-Windows era ultimately cost the company over

---

[10] Franklin Root, *Entry Strategies for International Markets* (New York: Lexington Books, 1994), p. 107.
[11] Yumiko Ono, "Borden's Breakup with Meiji Milk Shows How a Japanese Partnership Can Curdle," *The Wall Street Journal*, 21 February 1991, p. B1.

✦ BOX 8-3 ✦

POKEMON IN THE UNITED STATES

It started in Japan. A cartoon character that engaged in Japanese role-playing was presented in a simplistic animated style. And it became popular in Japan. Very popular. In Japan, Nintendo, owner of Pokemon (whose name means "pocket monster"), first introduced the video game. This was followed by toys, comic books, and trading cards. Finally, the Pokemon television show was introduced. In Japan, 50 percent of children watch the Pokemon television show. Given its tremendous success in Japan, the marketing question became "Could this popularity be transferred to the United States?"

Currently, Pokemon is a licensing success story in the United States. Despite initial hesitancy on the part of Nintendo, it was licensed to 4 Kids Entertainment, Inc. of New York. In the United States, 4 Kids decided to use the reverse introduction sequence of product introduction. The U.S. effort started with the television show and

then expanded with 90 different licensing agreements including 4 million video games. Merchandise sales were estimated at a billion dollars in 1999. The Pokemon cartoon was the 1998–1999 season's top children's show in the United States.

The show is also being shown in Canada, Australia, New Zealand, England, Mexico, and Latin America. The U.S. owners, however, spend considerable money to "westernize" the programs. Besides the translation to English, they have had to adjust for the wide usage of puns in the Japanese version, replace all Japanese writing, and even modify some of the characters.

From a financial perspective, licensing can be quite lucrative. The licensor receives between 5 and 15 percent of retail sales. The licensing agent receives 20 to 50 percent of the licensor's fees. Clearly, international licensing opportunities are not to be ignored.

SOURCES: Laurel Graeber, "Masters of the Universe, Youth Division," *The New York Times*, 29 August 1999, Sec. 13, p. 4. John Lippman, "Pokemon's Invincible Champion," *The Wall Street Journal*, 16 August 1999, p. B1.

$125 billion dollars (the market capitalization of Microsoft, the company that won the operating system war).

As the Borden and transistor stories make clear, companies may find that the upfront, easy money obtained from licensing turns out to be a very expensive source of revenue. To prevent a licensor/competitor from gaining unilateral benefit, licensing agreements should provide for a cross-technology exchange between all parties. At the absolute minimum, any company that plans to remain in business must ensure that its license agreements provide for full cross-licensing—that is, the licensee shares its developments with the licensor. Overall, the licensing strategy must ensure ongoing competitive advantage. For example, license arrangements can create export market opportunities and open the door to low-risk manufacturing relationships. They can also speed diffusion of new products or technologies.

When companies do decide to license, they should sign agreements that anticipate more extensive market participation in the future. Insofar as is possible, a company should keep options and paths open for other forms of market participation. One path is a joint venture with the licensee.

Trademarks can be an important part of the creation and protection of opportunities for lucrative licenses.[12] Image-oriented companies such as Coca-Cola and Disney, as well as designers such as Pierre Cardin, license their trademarked names and logos to overseas producers of clothing, toys, and watches. Business is booming: The top-tier names are expanding their fee income by 15 percent a year and more. When licensing a

---

[12] Private communication to Warren J. Keegan from E. M. Lang, President, REFAC Technology Development Corporation, 122 East 42nd Street, New York, NY.

trademark, the challenge is to maintain and enhance the brand equity of the marque. This means that licensees must be carefully selected and supervised. A bad licensee can seriously depreciate the value of a marque by turning out merchandise or services that do not meet up to the standard of the marque.

Franchising is a form of licensing. It is the practice whereby a company permits its name, logo, cultural design, and operations to be used in establishing a new firm or store. (See Chapter 13 for greater discussion of franchising.)

INVESTMENT: JOINT VENTURES

A joint venture with a local partner represents a more extensive form of participation in foreign markets than either exporting or licensing. The advantages of this strategy include the sharing of risk and the ability to combine different value chain strengths—for example, international marketing capability and manufacturing. One company might have in-depth knowledge of a local market, an extensive distribution system, or access to low-cost labor or raw materials. Such a company might link up with a foreign partner possessing considerable know-how in the area of technology, manufacturing, and process applications. Companies that lack sufficient capital resources might seek partners to jointly finance a project. Finally, a joint venture may be the only way to enter a country or region if government bid award practices routinely favor local companies or if laws prohibit foreign control but permit joint ventures.

Because of these clear advantages, especially in emerging markets, the conventional wisdom is that a joint venture is the only way to go. Not all agree with this "wisdom." In China, according to Wilfried Vanhonacker, the situation is changing rapidly, and today companies should think beyond the equity joint venture (EJV) with a well-connected local partner and consider the alternative of a wholly foreign-owned enterprise (WFOE). In China, EJVs and WFOEs are substantially the same in terms of taxation and corporate liability. They operate under similar rules and regulations. There are some technical differences, but the bottom line is that the WFOEs take less time to establish than EJVs and do not require a board of directors.

Today, there is a shift on the part of foreign investors in China from the EJV to the WFOE. The reasons are fundamental: Investors achieve greater flexibility and control with a WFOE, and the government is becoming more concerned about what a company brings to the country in terms of jobs, technology, and know-how than it is about how its deals are structured.

In China, as everywhere, each case must be decided on its merits. Two questions must be answered in every case: What does each partner bring to the deal, and what are the interests and capabilities of the partners going forward? The fact is that joint ventures are hard to sustain even in stable environments because the partners to a joint venture have different capabilities, resources, visions, and interests. In fast-growing and fast-changing environments, it is much more difficult to sustain joint ventures. In China, for example, access to markets has been hindered by what foreign investors thought was the essential success factor in China: *guanxi* (relationships). In fact, what many investors have discovered is that China is a big country and the scope of their partner's *guanxi* is limited. Many investors have discovered to their disappointment that their partner lacked the *guanxi* needed to move forward. A WFOE can retain agents and advisors to assist it in acquiring the land, materials, approvals, and services that it needs to do business in China.[13]

Some major joint venture alliances are outlined in Table 8-6.

---

[13] For an excellent brief supporting the WFOE in China, see Wilfried Vanhonacker, "Entering China: An Unconventional Approach," *Harvard Business Review* (March–April 1997): 130–140.

TABLE 8-6 Market Entry and Expansion by Joint Venture	
Companies Involved	*Purpose of Joint Venture*
GM, Toyota	New United Motors Manufacturing, Inc. (NUMMI)— a jointly operated plant in Freemont, California
Ford, Mazda	Joint operation of a plant in Flat Rock, Michigan
AT&T, NEC	AT&T provides CAD technology in exchange for NEC's advanced logic chips
AT&T, Mitsubishi Electric	AT&T manufactures and markets Mitsubishi's memory chips in exchange for the technology used to design them
Texas Instruments, Kobe Steel	Joint effort making logic semiconductors in Japan
IBM, Siemens AG	Joint research in advanced semiconductor chips
James River Corp., Oy Nokia AB Cragnotti and Partners Capital Investment	Jamont, a European-based paper products venture

Source: Adapted from Bernard Wysocki, "Global Reach: Cross-Border Alliances Become Favorite Way to Crack New Markets," *The Wall Street Journal*, 26 March 1990, pp. A1, A12.

It is possible to use a joint venture as a source of supply for third-country markets. This must be carefully thought out in advance. One of the main reasons for joint venture "divorce" is disagreement about third-country markets in which partners face each other as actual or potential competitors. To avoid this, it is essential to work out a plan for approaching third-country markets as part of the venture agreement.

The disadvantages of joint venturing can be significant. Joint venture partners must share rewards as well as risks. The main disadvantage of this global expansion strategy is that a company incurs very significant costs associated with control and coordination issues that arise when working with a partner. Also, as noted earlier with licensing, a dynamic joint venture partner can evolve into a stronger competitor. In some instances, country-specific restrictions limit the share of capital help by foreign companies. Cross-cultural differences in managerial attitudes and behavior can present formidable challenges as well.

James River's European joint venture, Jamont, brought together 13 companies from 10 countries. Major problems included computer systems and measures of production efficiency; Jamont uses committees to solve these and other problems as they arise. For example, agreement had to be reached on a standardized table napkin size; for some country markets, 30 by 30 centimeters was the norm; for others, 35 by 35 centimeters was preferred.[14]

Difficulties such as those outlined previously are so serious that, according to one study of 170 multinational firms, more than one third of 1,100 joint ventures were unstable, ending in "divorce" or a significant increase in the U.S. firm's power over its partner.[15] Another researcher found that 65 joint ventures with Japanese companies were either liquidated or transferred to the Japanese interest in 1976. This was up from 6 in 1972, a 600 percent increase. The most fundamental problem was the different benefits that each side expected to receive.[16]

---

[14] James Guyon, "A Joint-Venture Papermaker Casts Net Across Europe," *The Wall Street Journal*, 7 December 1992, p. B6.

[15] Lawrence G. Franko, "Joint Venture Divorce in the Multinational Company," *Columbia Journal of World Business* (May–June 1971): 13–22.

[16] W. Wright, "Joint Venture Problems in Japan," *Columbia Journal of World Business* (Spring 1979): 25–31. See also W. Wright and C. S. Russell, "Joint Venture in Developing Countries: Reality and Responses," *Columbia Journal of World Business* (Summer 1975): 74–80.

In an alliance the real payoff is from learning skills from the partner rather than just getting products to sell while avoiding investment. Yet, compared to American and European firms, Japanese and Korean firms seem to excel in their ability to leverage new knowledge that comes out of a joint venture. For example, Toyota learned many new things from its partnership with GM—about U.S. supply and transportation and managing American workers—that have been subsequently applied at its Camry plant in Kentucky. However, some American managers involved in the venture complained that the manufacturing expertise they gained was not applied broadly throughout GM. To the extent that this complaint has validity, GM has missed opportunities to leverage new learning. Still, many companies have achieved great successes pursuing joint ventures. Gillette, for example, has used this strategy to introduce its shaving products in the Middle East and Africa.

INVESTMENT: OWNERSHIP AND CONTROL

Another key variable in the location decision is the vision and values of company leadership. Some chief executives are obsessed with manufacturing in their home country. Nicolas Hayek is head of the Swiss Corporation for Microelectronics and Watchmaking (SMH), the company best known for its line of inexpensive Swatch watches. SMH's chief executive has presided over a spectacular comeback—the revitalization of the Swiss watch industry. Swatch has become a pop culture phenomenon, with sales approaching 1 billion watches. The flagship brand on the high end is Omega, whose models carry prices ranging from $700 to $20,000. SMH recently acquired Blancpain, a niche producer of luxury mechanical watches that retail for $200,000 and up. Hayek has demonstrated that, by embracing the fantasy and imagination of childhood and youth, a person can build mass-market products in countries such as Switzerland or the United States. The Swatch story is a triumph of engineering as well as a triumph of the imagination.

The sourcing decision highlights three roles for marketing in a global competitive strategy. The first relates to the configuration of marketing. Although many marketing activities must be performed in every country, advantage can be gained by concentrating some of the marketing activities in a single location. Service, for example, must be dispersed to every country. Training, however, might be at least partially concentrated in a single location for the world. A second role for marketing is the coordination of marketing activities across countries to leverage a company's know-how. This integration can take many forms, including the transfer of relevant experience across national boundaries in areas such as global account management and the use of similar approaches or methods for marketing research, product positioning, or other marketing activities. A third critical role of marketing is its role in tapping opportunities in product development and research and development (R&D). The development of Canon's AE-1 camera is a case in point. Research provided the information on market requirements that enabled Canon to develop a world product. Canon was able to develop a physically uniform product that required fewer parts, far less engineering, lower inventories, and longer production runs. Such advantages would have been lacking if Canon had developed separate camera models that were adapted to the unique conditions in each national market.

As for the form of cooperation and control, there are many, ranging from the management contract to wholly owned subsidiaries and global strategic partnerships. The issues that these alternatives raise are control and ownership. As shown in Table 8-7, the second issue that must be addressed in international marketing strategy is whether to establish an in-country or in-region marketing organization. This decision will be resolved by an assessment of the cost of creating such an organization compared to the expected impact of an in-country marketing organization on market share, sales, and earnings.

TABLE 8-7	International Market Entry and Expansion Decision Model

1. Sourcing: Home, third, or host country?
   Cost, market access, country of origin factors
2. In-country or in-region marketing organization?
   Cost, market impact assessment. If choice is to establish own organization, must decide who to appoint to key positions
3. Selection, training, and motivation of local distributors and agents
4. Marketing mix strategy: Goals and objectives in sales, earnings, and share of market; positioning; marketing mix strategy
5. Strategy implementation

The next task is the selection, training, and motivation of agents, distributors, and representatives. If it is decided to not establish an in-country marketing organization, the agent(s) or distributor(s) selected will be the in-country marketing organization. The fourth task is to formulate marketing mix and positioning strategy and, finally, to implement the strategy. This will be done by the organization itself if it has created an in-country marketing organization, and by the company in cooperation with an agent or distributor if it has not.

There are many options that vary the amount of ownership and investment and the degree of control of country marketing. Although it is possible to have ownership without control and control without ownership, greater ownership is normally linked with greater control (see Figure 8-1 on page 240). Companies with wholly owned affiliates or subsidiaries have complete control over every aspect of the affiliates' operations: strategy and structure, human resources, financial strategy and policy, marketing strategy and policy, and so on.

In the equity joint venture (EJV), this is not the case. The shared ownership of this type of company gives control to each of the owners. Licensing and franchising require little investment, but they may be part of agreements that give the licensor or franchisor considerable control over the business.

OWNERSHIP/INVESTMENT

After companies gain experience outside the home country via exporting or licensing and joint ventures, the time comes for many companies when a more extensive form of participation in global markets is wanted. The desire for control and ownership of operations outside the home country drives the decision to invest. Foreign direct investment (FDI) figures record investment flows as companies invest in or acquire plant, equipment, or other assets outside the home country. By definition, direct investment presumes that the investor has control or significant influence over the investment, as opposed to portfolio investment, in which it is assumed that the investor does not have significant influence or control. The operational definition of direct investment is ownership of 20 percent or more of the equity of a company. Companies, in addition to producing products, are products in themselves and it appears that many major international companies are on a shopping spree. While the United States had been the leader in overseas purchases, European companies have purchased many U.S. companies and these transactions carry large price tags. Vodafone, British Petroleum, and Scottish Power, which are all U.K. companies, have acquired AirTouch Communications, Amaco, and PacifiCorp, respectively. These three deals alone are valued at over $133 billion.[17] Conversely,

---

[17] Nikhil Deogun, "Made in U.S.A.: Deals from Europe Hit Record," *The Wall Street Journal,* 25 October 1999, p. C1.

Kodak, because of its stagnant sales in the U.S. market, is investing $1 billion in China in an effort to preempt Fuji, which controls more than 40 percent of the market, from expanding. By producing locally, Kodak would circumvent the 60 percent tariff on imported film. China is the world's third largest film market after the United States and Japan. Kodak currently has approximately 30 percent of the market. Lucky Film Co., a local producer, has 20 percent of the market.[18]

The most extensive form of participation in global markets is 100 percent ownership, which may be achieved by start-up or acquisition. (In China this is now referred to as the wholly foreign-owned enterprise or WFOE.) Ownership requires the greatest commitment of capital and managerial effort and offers the fullest means of participating in a market. Companies may move from licensing or joint venture strategies to ownership in order to achieve faster expansion in a market, greater control, or higher profits. In 1991, for example, Ralston Purina ended a 20-year joint venture with a Japanese company to start its own pet-food subsidiary. Monsanto Company and Bayer AG, the German pharmaceutical company, are two other companies that have also recently disbanded partnerships in favor of wholly owned subsidiaries in Japan.[19] In many countries, government restrictions may prevent majority or 100 percent ownership by foreign companies.

Large-scale direct expansion by means of establishing new facilities can be expensive and require a major commitment of managerial time and energy. Alternatively, acquisition is an instantaneous—and sometimes less expensive—approach to market entry. Although full ownership can yield the additional advantage of avoiding communication and conflict-of-interest problems that may arise with a joint venture or coproduction partner, acquisitions still present the demanding and challenging task of integrating the acquired company into the worldwide organization and coordinating activities.

Table 8-8 lists some additional examples, grouped by industry, of companies that have pursued global expansion via acquisition.

The decision to invest abroad—whether by expansion or acquisition—sometimes clashes with short-term profitability goals. This is an especially important issue for publicly held companies. Despite these challenges, there is an increasing trend toward foreign investment by companies. The market value of U.S. direct investment abroad and of foreign direct investment in the United States exceeds 1 trillion.

Several of the advantages of joint venture alliances also apply to ownership, including access to markets and avoidance of tariff or quota barriers. Like joint ventures, ownership also permits important technology experience transfers and provides a company with access to new manufacturing techniques. For example, the Stanley Works, a

TABLE 8-8 Market Entry and Expansion by Acquisition		
Product Category/Industry	*Acquiring Company*	*Target*
Automotive	DaimlerBenz	Chrysler
Pharmaceutical	Rhone-Poulenc	Hoechst
Tobacco	British American Tobacco	Zurich
Oil	BP Amoco	Arco
Communications	Vodafone	Mannesmann AirTouch

[18] William M. Bulkeley and Craig S. Smith, " Kodak to Invest in China in a Bid to Improve Its Strategic Position," *The Wall Street Journal,* 24 March 1998, p. B4.
[19] Ono, "Borden's Breakup with Meiji Milk."

toolmaker with headquarters in New Britain, Connecticut, has bought more than a dozen companies since 1986, among them Taiwan's National Hand Tool/Chiro company, a socket wrench manufacturer and developer of a cold-forming process that speeds up production and reduces waste. Stanley is now using the technology in the manufacture of other tools. Chairman Richard H. Ayers sees such global cross-fertilization and blended technology as a key benefit of globalization.[20]

The alternatives discussed earlier—licensing, joint ventures, and ownership—are in fact points along a continuum of alternative strategies or tools for global market entry and expansion. The overall design of a company's global strategy may call for combinations of exporting/importing, licensing, joint ventures, and ownership among different operating units. Such is the case in Japan for Borden, Inc.; it is ending licensing and joint venture arrangements for branded food products and setting up its own production, distribution, and marketing capabilities for dairy products. Meanwhile, in nonfood products, Borden has maintained joint venture relationships with Japanese partners in flexible packaging and foundry materials.[21]

A firm may decide to enter into a joint venture or coproduction agreement for purposes of manufacturing and may either market the products manufactured under this agreement in a wholly owned marketing subsidiary or sell the products from the coproduction facility to an outside marketing organization. Joint ventures may be 50-50 partnerships or minority or majority partnerships. Majority ownership may range anywhere from 51 percent to 100 percent.

INVESTMENT IN DEVELOPING COUNTRIES

Investment in developing nations grew rapidly in the 1990s. The appeal of the developing economies is their rapid growth, expanding purchasing power, and expanding markets. Major flows of investment have been directed toward emerging markets in Asia, the Americas, the Middle East, and Africa. Table 8-9 shows the sources of recent investment into Brazil.

Foreign investments may take the form of minority or majority shares in joint ventures, minority or majority equity stakes in another company, or, as in the case of Sandoz and Gerber, outright acquisition. A company may choose to use a combination of these entry strategies by acquiring one company, buying an equity stake in another, and operating a joint venture with a third. In recent years, for example, UPS

TABLE 8-9	Foreign Direct Investment in Brazil (Cumulative through June 30, 1995)
Country	*Amount (in Billions)*
United States	$190.0
Germany	7.1
Great Britain	5.2
Japan	4.5
Switzerland	3.6

Source: Diana Jean Schemo, "Brazil's Economic Samba," *The New York Times,* 7 September 1996, p. C1.

---

[20] Louis Uchitelle, "The Stanley Works Goes Global," *The New York Times,* 23 July 1989, sec. 3, pp. 1, 10.
[21] Borden, Inc. Annual Report, 1990, p. 13.

has made more than 16 acquisitions in Europe and has also expanded its transportation hubs.

◆ MARKETING STRATEGY ALTERNATIVES

Regardless of the entry form selected, companies must decide on their marketing strategy for each market. Broadly, the alternatives are to use independent agents and distributors or to establish a company-owned marketing subsidiary. These alternatives trade off ownership and investment with control, as shown in Figure 8-2.

The advantage of the agent/distributor option is the fact that it requires little investment. It is a pay-as-you-go option. The disadvantage of this option is that it does not create a company presence in the market and it does not give a company control over its marketing effort. In addition, agents and distributors are not necessarily a no-investment option. If the manufacturer has deep pockets, any termination of an agency or distributorship agreement may lead to a claim by the agent or distributor for lost profits and damages. A written contract with a no-cause termination clause is no guarantee of protection from an agent/distributor lawsuit because agents and distributors may press claims on the grounds of a breach of good faith.

In many countries, companies combine the company-owned marketing subsidiary with agents and distributors. This option gives the company local presence and control of the marketing effort and, where cost-effective, takes advantage of distributor and agent capabilities. The local presence of the company can provide a much better communications link with the regional and world headquarters and, if it is well executed, ensure that the company's effort reflects the fullest potential of the company's ability to execute a global strategy with local responsiveness.

With a local subsidiary presence, a company can focus on formulating and executing marketing strategies and plans that work. In China, Procter & Gamble (P&G) operates with a combination of joint ventures and its own company presence, with P&G marketing executives directing the company's China strategy. This approach has enabled P&G to increase its share of the urban shampoo market to 60 percent as compared to 9 percent for Unilever. P&G has invested heavily in market research, advertising, and distribution, and in creating its own command presence in the market. As a result of these initiatives, Head & Shoulders, P&G's brand, is China's fastest growing hair care brand.[22]

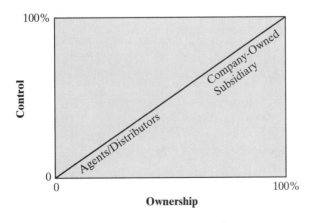

FIGURE 8-2   Marketing Strategy Alternatives

---

[22] The Procter & Gamble Company, 1995 Annual Report, p. 10.

FIVE MARKET EXPANSION STRATEGIES[23]

Companies must decide whether to expand by seeking new markets in existing countries or, alternatively, seeking new country markets for already identified and served market segments. These two dimensions in combination produce four strategic options, as shown in Table 8-10. Strategy 1 concentrates on a few segments in a few countries. This is typically a starting point for most companies. It matches company resources and market investment needs. Unless a company is large and endowed with ample resources, this strategy may be the only realistic way to begin.

In strategy 2, country concentration and segment diversification, a company serves many markets in a few countries. This strategy was implemented by many European companies that remained in Europe and sought growth by expanding into new markets. It is also the approach of the American companies that decide to diversify in the U.S. market as opposed to going international with existing products or creating new global products. According to the U.S. Department of Commerce, more than 80 percent of American companies that export limit their sales to five or fewer markets. This means the majority of American companies are pursuing strategy 1 or 2.

Strategy 3, country diversification and market segment concentration, is the classic global strategy whereby a company seeks out the world market for a product. The appeal of this strategy is that by serving the world customer, a company can achieve a greater accumulated volume and lower costs than any competitor and, therefore, have an unassailable competitive advantage. This is the strategy of the well-managed business that serves a distinct need and customer category.

Strategy 4, country and segment diversification, is the corporate strategy of a global, multibusiness company such as Matsushita. Over all, Matsushita is multicountry in scope and its various business units and groups serve multiple segments. Thus, at the level of corporate strategy, Matsushita may be said to be pursuing strategy 4. At the operating business level, however, managers of individual units must focus on the needs of the world customer in their particular global market. In Table 8-10, this is strategy 3—country diversification and market segment concentration. An increasing number of companies all over the world are beginning to see the importance of market share not only in the home or domestic market but also in the world market. Success in overseas markets can boost a company's total volume and lower its cost position.

TABLE 8-10   Market Expansion Strategies

		Market	
		Concentration	Diversification
Country	Concentration	1. Narrow focus	2. Country focus
	Diversification	3. Country diversification	4. Global diversification

---

[23] This section draws on Ayal and J. Zif, "Market Expansion Strategies in Multinational Marketing," *Journal of Marketing*, 43 (Spring 1979): 84–94, and "Competitive Market Choice Strategies in Multinational Marketing," *Columbia Journal of World Business* (Fall 1978): 72–81.

ALTERNATIVE STRATEGIES: STAGES OF DEVELOPMENT MODEL

Table 8-11 lists the stages in the evolution of the global corporation, from domestic to international, multinational, global, and transnational. As discussed in previous chapters, the differences between the stages can be quite significant. Unfortunately, there is little general agreement about the usage of each term. The terminology suggested here conforms to current usage by leading scholars. However, it should be noted that executives, journalists, and others who are not familiar with the scholarly literature may use the terms in quite different ways.

Bartlett and Ghoshal provide an excellent discussion of three industries—branded packaged goods, consumer electronics, and telecommunications switching—in which individual competitors have exemplified the different stages at various times in their corporate histories. For example, P&G, General Electric (GE), and Ericsson were stage 2 international companies. For many years, Unilever, Philips, and International Telephone and Telegraph (ITT) were stage 3 multinationals. The stage 4 global companies included in the study were all from Japan: Kao, Matsushita, and NEC.[24]

As you can see in Table 8-12, orientation does not change as a company moves from domestic to international. The difference between the domestic and the international company is that the international is doing business in many countries. Like the domestic company, it is ethnocentric and home-country oriented. However, the stage 2 international company sees extension market opportunities outside the home country and extends marketing programs to exploit those opportunities. The first change in orientation occurs as a company moves to stage 3, multinational. At this point, its orientation shifts from ethnocentric to polycentric. The difference is quite important. The stage 2 ethnocentric company seeks to extend its products and practices to foreign countries. It sees similarities outside the home country but is relatively blind to differences. The stage 3 multinational is the opposite: It sees the differences and is relatively blind to similarities. The focus of the stage 3 multinational is on adapting to what is different in a country. Figure 8-3 outlines the different orientations of management.

TABLE 8-11	Stages of Development of the Transnational Corporation
	1. Domestic
	2. International
	3. Multinational
	4. Global
	5. Transnational

TABLE 8-12   Stages of Development I

Stage & Company	1 Domestic	2 International	3 Multinational	4 Global	5 Transnational
Strategy	Domestic	International	Multidomestic	Global	Global
Model	NA	Coordinated federation	Decentralized federation	Centralized hub	Integrated network
View of world	Home country	Extension markets	National markets	Global markets or resources	Global markets and resources
Orientation	Ethnocentric	Ethnocentric	Polycentric	Mixed	Geocentric

NA = not available.

[24] See Christopher A. Bartlett and Sumantra Ghoshal, *Managing Across Borders: The Transnational Solution* (Boston: Harvard Business School Press, 1989).

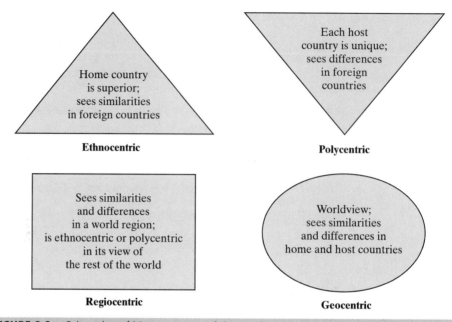

FIGURE 8-3 Orientation of Management and Companies

The stage 4 global company is a limited form of the transnational. Management's orientation is either on global markets or global resources but not on both. For example, Harley-Davidson is focused on global markets but not on global resources. The company has no interest in conducting R&D, design, engineering, or manufacturing outside of the United States. Until recently, the same was true for BMW and Mercedes. Both companies marketed globally but limited R&D, engineering, design, and manufacturing activity to Germany. Mercedes now plans to double its purchases from outside suppliers and to build more than 10 percent of its vehicles outside Germany. Notes Mercedes chairman, Helmut Werner, "The fundamental problem of German exports is that we are producing in a country with a hard currency and selling in countries with soft currencies."[25] When a company moves from stage 4 to stage 5, its orientation encompasses both global markets and global resources.

Table 8-13 illustrates some of the other differences in companies at the different stages. Special mention must be made of some of the distinctive qualities of stage 4 companies that pursue integrated global strategies. Key assets are dispersed, specialized, and interdependent. A transnational automobile company—Toyota, for example—makes engines and transmissions in various countries and ships these components to assembly plants located in each of the world regions. Specialized design labs might be located in different countries and work together on the same project. The role of country units changes dramatically as a company moves across the stages of development. In the stage 2 international company, the role of the country unit is to adapt and leverage the competence of the parent or home-country unit. In the stage 5 transnational, the role of each country is to contribute to the company worldwide. In the international and multinational, the responsibility of the marketing organization is to realize the potential of the individual national markets. In the transnational, the responsibility of the marketing unit

---

[25] Audrey Choi, "For Mercedes, Going Global Means Being Less German," *The Wall Street Journal*, 27 April 1995, p. B4.

TABLE 8-13   Stages of Development II

Stage and Company	Organization Characteristics				
	1 Domestic	*2 International*	*3 Multinational*	*4 Global*	*5 Transnational*
Key assets	Located in home country	Core centralized others dispersed	Decentralized and self-sufficient	All in home country except marketing or sourcing	Dispersed interdependent and specialized
Role of country units	Single country	Adapting and leveraging competencies	Exploiting local opportunities	Marketing or sourcing	Contributions to company worldwide
Knowledge	Home country	Created at center and transferred	Retained within operating units	Marketing or sourcing developed jointly and shared	All functions developed jointly and shared

is to realize the potential of the national market and, if possible, to contribute to the success of marketing efforts worldwide by sharing successful innovations and ideas with the entire organization.

As shown in Table 8-14 each of the stages has its strengths. The international company's strength is its ability to exploit the parent company's knowledge and capabilities outside the home country. In the telecommunications industry, Ericsson gained a competitive edge over NEC and ITT by pursuing this approach. The multinational's strength is its ability to adapt and respond to national differences. Unilever's local responsiveness was well suited to the packaged goods industry. Thus, in many markets, the company outperformed both Kao and P&G. The global company leverages internal skills and resources by taking advantage of global markets or global resources. In consumer electronics, Matsushita's ability to serve global markets from world-scale plants caused great woes for Philips and GE. (In fact, GE's Jack Welch decided to exit the business altogether.)[26] The transnational combines the strengths of each of the earlier stages by serving global markets using global resources and leveraging global learning and experience.

TABLE 8-14   Stages of Development III

Strengths at Each Level

International
  Ability to exploit the parent company's knowledge and capabilities through worldwide diffusion of products
Multinational
  Flexible ability to respond to national differences
Global
  Global market or supplier reach, which leverages the home-country organization, skills, and resources
Transnational
  Combines the strengths of each of the preceding stages in an integrated network, which leverages worldwide learning and experience

---

[26] For an excellent in-depth treatment of GE, see Noel Tichy and Stratford Sherman, *Control Your Destiny or Someone Else Will* (New York: HarperBusiness, 1994).

In stage 3, the most frequently preferred sourcing arrangement is local manufacture. In stage 5, product sourcing is based on an analysis that takes into account cost, delivery, and all other factors affecting competitiveness and profitability. This analysis produces a sourcing plan that maximizes both competitive effectiveness and profitability. When a company is in stage 2, key jobs go to home-country nationals in both the subsidiaries and the headquarters. In stage 3, key jobs in host countries go to country nationals, whereas headquarters management positions are usually held by home-country nationals. In stage 5, the best person is selected for all management positions regardless of nationality. Research and development (R&D) in stage 2 is conducted in the home country; in stage 3, R&D becomes decentralized and fragmented. By the time a company reaches stage 5, research is part of an integrated worldwide R&D plan and is typically decentralized. The transnational company in stage 5 can take advantage of resources as well as respond to local aspirations to produce a worldwide decentralized R&D program.

Table 8-15 shows an example of how Fleetguard, Inc., a wholly owned subsidiary of Cummins Engine Company, evolved over an 11-year period.

On occasion, the best marketing and management efforts fail when trying to expand into foreign markets. In this case, it is equally important to know when to pull out.

TABLE 8-15   The Evolution of Fleetguard, Inc.

Strategic Dimension	Stage 2 International Years 1–4	Stage 3 Multinational Years 5–8	Stage 5 Transnational Years 9–11
Management assumptions	70% Ethnocentrism	80% Polycentrism	60% Polycentrism
	30% Polycentrism	20% Ethnocentrism	40% Geocentrism
Design	Extension	75% Decentralized	80% Integration
		25% Extension	20% Decentralized
Structure	Regional	Regional	20% Matrix
			80% Regional
Planning process	Bottom-up	Bottom-up	20% Interactive
			80% Bottom-up
Decision making	70% Decentralized	80% Decentralized	20% Centralized
	30% Centralized	20% Centralized	80% Decentralized
Marketing process	Not standardized	Partially standardized	Standardized
Marketing programs	Standardized	30% Unique	Unique
		70% Standardized	
Product sourcing	Export	Construct plant	60% Local manufacture
		Export	40% Export
Human resources			
Key job nationality			
Country management	Home country	Host country	Host country
HQ management	NA	Host country	Best person
R&D, product development	Home country	60% Home country	70% Integrated
		40% Decentralized	30% Decentralized
Control/measurement	50% Home standardized	60% Decentralized	75% Decentralized
	50% Decentralized	40% Home standardized	25% Integrated

NA = not available.

Source: This example was provided by Jon Adamson.

Summary

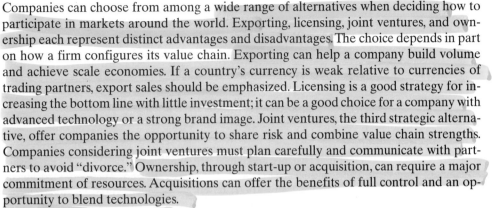

Companies can choose from among a wide range of alternatives when deciding how to participate in markets around the world. Exporting, licensing, joint ventures, and ownership each represent distinct advantages and disadvantages. The choice depends in part on how a firm configures its value chain. Exporting can help a company build volume and achieve scale economies. If a country's currency is weak relative to currencies of trading partners, export sales should be emphasized. Licensing is a good strategy for increasing the bottom line with little investment; it can be a good choice for a company with advanced technology or a strong brand image. Joint ventures, the third strategic alternative, offer companies the opportunity to share risk and combine value chain strengths. Companies considering joint ventures must plan carefully and communicate with partners to avoid "divorce." Ownership, through start-up or acquisition, can require a major commitment of resources. Acquisitions can offer the benefits of full control and an opportunity to blend technologies.

Market expansion strategies can be represented in matrix form to assist managers in thinking through the various alternatives. The options include country and market concentration, country concentration and market diversification, country diversification and market concentration, and country and market diversification. The preferred expansion strategy will be a reflection of a company's stage of development. An international company will use exporting and licensing to exploit headquarters knowledge through worldwide diffusion of products. Multinational companies will respond to local differences using acquisitions and manufacturing start-ups in various countries. Global companies will either export products around the globe from world-scale plants or will rely on the world for resources. The stage 5 transnational combines the strengths of these three stages into an integrated network to leverage worldwide learning.

This chapter provides an overview of export marketing and the decisions company personnel have to make to become successful exporters. Governments exert a strong influence on exports, through support programs, regulations, nontariff barriers, and tariff classifications.

In choosing export markets, companies must assess market potential, market access, shipping costs, competition, product fit, and service requirements. It is definitely a good idea to visit a potential market before developing an export program. Market access considerations are particularly important for the exporter and the importer. Exporters must understand how tariffs and duties affect the prices that must be paid by the importers. Successful exporting entails organizational decisions (e.g., regarding internal or external expertise) in both the manufacturer's country and the market country.

Exporters and importers must also have a thorough understanding of international financial instruments, especially letters of credit. Barter and countertrade are methods of making sales to customers who do not have access to hard currency but are prepared to make payment in some form other than money.

Discussion Questions

1. What are the alternative tools or strategies for expanding internationally? What are the major advantages and disadvantages of each strategy?
2. The president of XYZ Manufacturing Company of Buffalo, New York, comes to you with a license offer from a company in Osaka. In return for sharing the company's patents and know-how, the Japanese company will pay a license fee of 5 percent of the ex-factory price of all products sold based on the U.S. company's license. The president wants your advice. What would you tell him?

3. What are the differences among companies at the international, multinational, global, and transnational stages of development? Find examples of companies that fit the characteristics of each of these types.
4. Why is exporting from the United States dominated by large companies? What, if anything, could be done to increase exports from smaller companies?
5. What six criteria should be assessed when evaluating potential export markets?
6. What does it take to be a successful exporter?
7. Which strategic options for market entry or expansion would a small company be likely to pursue? A large company?

Suggested Readings

Agarwal, Sanjeev. "Socio-Cultural Distance and the Choice of Joint Venture: A Contingency Perspective." *Journal of International Marketing,* 2, no. 2 (1994): 63–80.

Al-Khalifa, Ali K., and S. Eggert Peterson. "The Partner Selection Process in International Joint Ventures," *European Journal of Marketing,* 33, no. 11/12 (1999).

Ali, Abbas J., and Robert C. Camp. "The Relevance of Firm Size and International Business Experience to Market Entry Strategies." *Journal of Global Marketing,* 6, no. 4 (1993): 91–112.

Atuahene-Gime, Kwaku. "International Licensing of Technology: An Empirical Study of the Differences between Licensee and Non-Licensee Firms." *Journal of International Marketing,* 1, no. 2 (1993): 71–88.

Aulakh, P., and M. Kotabe. "Antecedents and Performance Implications of Channel Integration in Foreign Markets." *Journal of International Business Studies,* 28 (First Quarter 1997): 145–175.

Azsomer, Aysegel, and S. Tamer Cavusgil. "A Dynamic Analysis of Market Entry Rates in Global Industry," *European Journal of Marketing,* 33, no.11/12 (1999).

Bello, D. C., and R. Lohtia. "Export Channel Design: The Use of Foreign Distributors and Agents." *Journal of the Academy of Marketing Science,* 23, no. 2 (1995): 83–93.

Bonaccorsi, Andrea. "What Do We Know About Exporting by Small Italian Exporting Firms?" *Journal of International Marketing,* 1, no. 3 (1993): 49–76.

Cavusgil, S. Tamer, Shaoming Zou, and G. M. Naidu. "Product and Promotion Adaptation in Export Ventures: An Empirical Investigation." *Journal of International Business Studies,* 24, no. 3 (Third Quarter 1993): 449–464.

Das, M. "Successful and Unsuccessful Exporters from Developing Countries." *European Journal of Marketing,* 28, no. 12 (1994): 19–33.

Dow, Douglas. "A Note on Psychological Distance and Export Market Selection." *Journal of International Marketing,* 8, no. 1 (2000): 51–64.

Hamel, Gary, and C. K. Prahalad. "Do You Really Have a Global Strategy?" *Harvard Business Review* (July–August 1985): 139–148.

Harrigan, Kathryn Rudie. "Joint Ventures and Global Strategies." *Columbia Journal of World Business* (Summer 1984): 7–16.

Hill, Charles W. L., Peter Hwang, and W. Chan Kim. "An Eclectic Theory of the Choice of International Entry Mode." *Strategic Management Journal,* 11, no. 2 (1990): 117–128.

Howard, Donald G. "The Role of Export Management Companies in Global Marketing." *Journal of Global Marketing,* 8, no. 1 (1994): 95–110.

Katsikeas, Constantine S. "Perceived Export Problems and Export Involvement: The Case of Greek Exporting Manufacturers." *Journal of Global Marketing,* 7, no. 4 (1994): 95–110.

Kim, C. K., and J. Y. Chung. "Brand Popularity, Country Image and Market Share: An Empirical Study." *Journal of International Business Studies,* 28, no. 2 (1997): 361–386.

Kogut, Bruce. "Designing Global Strategies: Comparative and Competitive Value-Added Chains." *Sloan Management Review* (Summer 1985): 17–27.

Kotabe, Masaaki, and Michael R. Czinkota. "State Government Promotion of Manufacturing Exports: A Gap Analysis." *Journal of International Business Studies,* 23, no. 4 (Fourth Quarter 1992): 637–658.

Leonidou, Leonidas C. "Empirical Research on Export Barriers: Review, Assessment, and Synthesis." *Journal of International Marketing,* 3, no. 1 (1995): 29–44.

Leonidou, L. C., and C. S. Katsikeas. "The Export Development Process: An Integrative Review of Empirical Models." *Journal of International Business Studies,* 27 (September 1996): 517.

Madhok, Anoop. "Revisiting Multinational Firms' Tolerance for Joint Ventures: A Trust-Based Approach." *Journal of International Business Studies,* 26, no. 1 (First Quarter 1995): 117–138.

McCaffrey, Roger A., and Thomas A. Meyer. *An Executive's Guide to Licensing.* Homewood, IL: Dow Jones–Irwin, 1989.

McDougall, Patricia. "New Venture Strategies: An Empirical Identification of Eight 'Archetypes' of Competitive Strategies for Entry," *Strategic Management Journal,* 11, no. 6 (October 1990): 447–467.

Mahone, Charlie E., Jr. "Penetrating Export Markets: The Role of Firm Size." *Journal of Global Marketing,* 7, no. 3 (1994): 133–148.

Morrison, Allen J., and Kendall Roth. "A Taxonomy of Business-Level Strategies in Global Industries." *Strategic Management Journal,* 13, no. 6 (September 1992): 399–417.

Murray, Janet Y., Masaaki Kotabe, and Albert Wildt. "Strategic and Financial Performance Implications of Global Sourcing Strategy: A Contingency Analysis." *Journal of International Business Studies,* 26, no. 1 (1995): 181–202.

Osland, Gregory E. "Successful Operating Strategies in the Performance of U.S.–China Joint Ventures." *Journal of International Marketing,* 32, no. 4 (1994): 53–78.

Perlmutter, Howard V., and David A. Heenan. "How Multinational Should Your Top Managers Be?" *Harvard Business Review* (November/December, 1974): 121–132.

Quelch, John A., and James E. Austin. "Should Multinationals Invest in Africa?" *Sloan Management Review,* 4, no. 3 (Spring 1993): 107–119.

Raval, Dinker, and Bala Subramanian. "Product Cycle and International Product Life Cycle: Economic and Marketing Perspectives." *Business Journal,* 12, nos. 1 and 2 (1997): 48–51.

Robertson, Thomas S. "How to Reduce Market Penetration Cycle Times." *Sloan Management Review,* (Fall 1993): 87–96.

Robock, Stefan H. "The Export Myopia of U.S. Multinationals: An Overlooked Opportunity for Creating U.S. Manufacturing Jobs." *Columbia Journal of World Business,* 28, no. 2 (Summer 1993): 24–32.

Root, Franklin R. *Entry Strategies for International Markets.* New York: Lexington Books, 1994.

Rossen, Philip J., and Stan D. Reid, Eds. *Managing Export Entry and Expansion.* New York: Praeger, 1987.

Rynning, Marjo-Riitta, and Otto Andersen. "Structural and Behavioral Predictors of Export Adoption: A Norwegian Study." *Journal of International Marketing,* 2, no. 1 (1994): 73–90.

Schoemaker, Paul J. H. "How to Link Strategic Vision to Core Capabilities." *Sloan Management Review,* 34, no. 1 (Fall 1992): 67–81.

Seringhaus, F. H. Rolf. "Export Promotion in Developing Countries: Status and Prospects." *Journal of Global Marketing,* 6, no. 4 (1993): 7–32.

Singer, Thomas Owen, and Michael R. Czinkota. "Factors Associated with Effective Use of Export Assistance." *Journal of International Marketing,* 2, no. 1 (1994): 53–72.

Solberg, Carl Arthur. "Educator Insights: Standardization or Adaptation of the International Marketing Mix." *Journal of International Marketing,* 8, no. 1 (2000): 78–98.

Swamidass, Paul M. "Import Sourcing Dynamics: An Integrative Perspective." *Journal of International Business Studies,* 24, no. 4 (Fourth Quarter 1993): 671–692.

Terpstra, Vern, and Chow-Ming Joseph Yu. "Export Trading Companies: An American Trade Failure?" *Journal of Global Marketing,* 6, no. 3 (1992): 29–54.

U.S. Department of Commerce. *A Basic Guide to Exporting.* Washington, DC: U.S. Department of Commerce, 1981).

Vanhonacker, Wilfried. "Entering China: An Unconventional Approach." *Harvard Business Review,* 75 (March/April 1997): 130–140.

Van Wolferen, Karel G. "The Japan Problem." *Foreign Affairs* (Winter 1986): 288–303.

Wichmann, H. J. "Private and Public Trading Companies within the Pacific Rim Nations." *Journal of Small Business* (January 1997): 62–65.

Yavas, Ugur, Dogan Eroglu, and Sevgin Eroglu. "Sources and Management of Conflict: The Case of Saudi–U.S. Joint Ventures." *Journal of International Marketing,* 2, no. 3 (1994): 61–82.

Yip, George S. "Global Strategy as a Factor in Japanese Success." *The International Executive,* 38, no. 1 (January/February 1996): 145–167.

Cooperative Strategies and Global Strategic Partnerships

CHAPTER 9

"Alliances are a big part of this game [of global competition] . . . They are critical to win on a global basis . . . the least attractive way to try to win on a global basis is to think you can take on the world by yourself."

—JACK WELCH
CEO, General Electric Corporation

"Business growth and expansion in different parts of the world will increasingly have to be based on alliances, partnerships, joint ventures and all kinds of relations with organizations located in other political jurisdictions."

PETER DRUCKER
Author

"Alliances as a broad-based strategy will only ensure a company's mediocrity, not its international leadership."

—MICHAEL PORTER
Professor, Harvard Business School

CHAPTER CONTENTS

What does a car, household appliance, personal computer, a beer, a deodorizer, and a travel company have in common? In Japan, the answer is a brand. Five major companies (Toyota Motor, Matsushita Electric, Asahi Breweries, and Kao) have formed a marketing alliance to share the brand name "WiLL."[1]

---

[1] Yumiko Ono, "In Japan, a New Brand Has Five Parents," *The Wall Street Journal,* 8 October 1999, p. B1.

> **VISIT THE WEB SITES**
> www.asahibeer.com
> www.kao.com

Their purpose is to create a new, modern image that would appeal to consumers in their late twenties and early thirties. This age segment is composed of approximately 8 million consumers who want to express their own preferences and are cynical of traditional, conservative brands.

Airlines offer an excellent example of global strategic partnerships. Table 9-1 lists the world's top airlines and the world's top airline fleets. United Airlines, the largest commercial airline in the world, has agreements with fourteen airlines: Air Canada, Air New Zealand, All Nippon, Ansett Australia, Austria, British Midland, Lauda Air, Lufthansa, Mexican, SAS, Singapore, Thai, Tyrolean, and Varig airlines. This alliance is known as the Star Alliance, whose motto is "The Airline Network for Earth."

> **VISIT THE WEB SITE**
> www.star-alliance.com

TABLE 9-1 Top 25 Airlines / Top 25 Airline Fleets

Rank	Airline	1997 No. of RPK[a]	Rank	Airline	No. of Aircraft
1	United	195,372	1	American	641
2	American	172,166	2	FedEx	616
3	Delta	160,398	3	United	575
4	Northwest	115,898	4	Delta	559
5	British Airways	98,405	5	Northwest	406
6	Japan Airlines	79,063	6	US Airways	352
7	Continental	77,081	7	Continental	327
8	Lufthansa	68,267	8	British Airways	268
9	US Airways	66,901	9	Southwest	261
10	Air France	63,812	10	Lufthansa	217
11	Qantas	59,199	11	UPS	208
12	KLM	55,418	12	Mesa Air Group	185
13	Singapore	55,388	13	TWA	185
14	All Nippon	51,219	14	Air France	182
15	Southwest	45,623	15	Air Canada	155
16	TWA	40,470	16	SAS	147
17	Korean	40,190	17	Alitalia	144
18	Cathay Pacific	38,962	18	All Nippon	136
19	Air Canada	36,866	19	Japan Airlines	134
20	Alitalia	36,002	20	Iberia	124
21	Thai Intl	31,154	21	Continental Express	121
22	Iberia	27,679	22	Korean	117
23	Swissair	27,522	23	KLM	114
24	America West	26,072	24	Aeroflot Russian	113
25	Canadian	25,784	25	Airborne	106

[a] Revenue passenger kilometers

Source: Air Transport World; 1 July 1998.

In previous chapters, we reviewed the range of options—exporting, licensing, joint ventures, and ownership—traditionally used by companies wishing either to enter global markets for the first time or expand their activities beyond present levels. However, recent changes in the political, economic, sociocultural, and technological environments of the global firm have combined to change the relative importance of those strategies. Trade barriers have fallen, markets have globalized, consumer needs and wants have converged, product life cycles have shortened, and new communications technologies and trends have emerged. Although these developments provide unprecedented market opportunities, there are strong strategic implications for the global organization and new challenges for the global marketer.

Like the airline example cited previously, such strategies will undoubtedly incorporate—or may even be structured around—a variety of collaborations. Once thought of as only joint ventures with the more dominant party reaping most of the benefits (or losses) of the partnership, cross-border alliances are taking on surprising new configurations and even more surprising players. Why would any firm—global or otherwise—seek to collaborate with another firm, be it local or foreign? Why do executives decide to pursue competitive collaboration with other firms, some of which are rivals?

Every company faces a business environment characterized by unprecedented degrees of dynamism, turbulence, and unpredictability. Today's firm must be equipped to respond to mounting economic and political pressures. Reaction time has been sharply cut by advances in technology. The firm of tomorrow must be ready to do whatever it takes to ensure that it is creating a unique value for customers and that it has a competitive advantage.

As suggested in the opening chapter quotations, there appears to be less than agreement by major strategic thinkers on the wisdom of cooperation. This chapter will address the fundamental issue: whether to cooperate and when to cooperate. It will focus on global strategic partnerships, the Japanese *keiretsu*, and various other types of cooperation strategies that may be an important element of the success of the global firm.

◆ THE NATURE OF GLOBAL STRATEGIC PARTNERSHIPS

The terminology used to describe the new forms of cooperation strategies varies widely. The phrases *collaborative agreements, strategic alliances, strategic international alliances,* and *global strategic partnerships* (GSPs) are frequently used to refer to linkages between companies to jointly pursue a common goal. A broad spectrum of interfirm agreements, including joint ventures, can be covered by this terminology. However, the strategic alliances discussed in this chapter exhibit three characteristics.[2]

1. The participants remain independent subsequent to the formation of the alliance.
2. The participants share the benefits of the alliance as well as control over the performance of assigned tasks.
3. The participants make ongoing contributions in technology, products, and other key strategic areas.

According to estimates, the number of strategic alliances has been growing at a rate of 20 to 30 percent since the mid-1980s. The upward trend for GSPs comes in part at the expense of traditional cross-border mergers and acquisitions.

Roland Smith, chairman of British Aerospace, offers a straightforward reason why a firm would enter into a GSP: "A partnership is one of the quickest and cheapest ways

---

[2] Michael A. Yoshino and U. Srinivasa Rangan, *Strategic Alliances: An Entrepreneurial Approach to Globalization* (Boston: Harvard Business School Press, 1995), p. 5. For an alternative description, see Riad Ajami and Dara Khambata, "Global Strategic Alliances: The New Transnationals," *Journal of Global Marketing, 5,* no. ½ (1991): 55–59.

to develop a global strategy."[3] Like traditional joint ventures, GSPs have some disadvantages. Each partner must be willing to sacrifice some control, and there are potential risks associated with strengthening a competitor from another country. Despite these drawbacks, GSPs are attractive for several reasons. First, high product development costs may force a company to seek partners; this was part of the rationale for Boeing's partnership with a Japanese consortium to develop a new jet aircraft, the 777. Second, the technology requirements of many contemporary products mean that an individual company may lack the skills, capital, or know-how to go it alone.[4] Third, partnerships may be the best means of securing access to national and regional markets. Fourth, partnerships provide important learning opportunities; in fact, one expert regards GSPs as a "race to learn." Professor Gary Hamel of the London Business School has observed that the partner that proves to be the fastest learner can ultimately dominate the relationship.[5]

GSPs and joint ventures differ in significant ways. Traditional joint ventures are basically alliances focusing on a single national market or a specific problem. A true global strategic partnership is different.[6] It is distinguished by the following six attributes:

1. Two or more companies develop a joint long-term strategy aimed at achieving world leadership by pursuing cost leadership, differentiation, or a combination of the two and by creating a variety, needs, or access-based position or a combination of the three.
2. The relationship is reciprocal. Each partner possesses specific strengths that it shares with the others; learning must take place on all sides.
3. The partners' vision and efforts are truly global, extending beyond home countries and home regions to the rest of the world.
4. If the relationship is organized along horizontal lines, continual transfer of resources laterally between partners is required, with technology sharing and resource pooling representing norms.
5. If the relationship is along vertical lines, both parties to the relationship must understand their core strengths and be able to defend their competitive position against the possibility of either a forward or backward integration move by their vertical partner, and they must work together to create a unique value for the customers of the downstream partner in the value chain.
6. When competing in markets excluded from the partnership, the participants retain their national and ideological identities.

The Iridium program described in the box "Iridium: Anatomy of a Marketing Failure" embodied several prerequisites that experts believe are the hallmarks of good alliances. First, Motorola formed an alliance to exploit a unique strength, namely, its leadership in wireless communications. Second, the Iridium alliance partners possessed unique strengths of their own. Third, it was unlikely that any of the partners has the ability or the desire to acquire Motorola's unique strength. Finally, rather than focusing on a particular market or product, Iridium was an alliance based on skills, know-how, and technology.[7] However, when all was said and done, Iridium failed. The lesson is that getting all of the alliance elements aligned is of no use if the product does not offer a unique value. Iridium was overtaken by cellular and by alternative and more realistic satellite projects.

As James Brian Quinn, Professor Emeritus at the Tuck School, pointed out, Nike, the largest producer of athletic footwear in the world, does not manufacture a single

---

[3] Jeremy Main, "Making Global Alliances Work," *Fortune,* 17 December 1990, p. 121.
[4] Kenichi Ohmae, "The Global Logic of Strategic Alliances," *Harvard Business Review* (March–April 1989): 145.
[5] Main, "Making Global Alliances Work," p. 122.
[6] Howard Perlmutter and David Heenan, "Cooperate to Compete Globally," *Harvard Business Review* (March–April 1986): 137.
[7] Adapted from Michel Robert, *Strategy Pure and Simple: How Winning CEOs Outthink Their Competition* (New York: McGraw-Hill, 1993).

◆ BOX 9-1 ◆

IRIDIUM: ANATOMY OF A MARKETING FAILURE

In the spectrum of companies operating in the global marketplace, there are winners and there are losers. Iridium, which thought it had the resources and strategy to be a leader in the telecommunications industry, ended up as one of the most expensive marketing failures in history. Although marketing alone is rarely the sole cause of failure, in the case of Iridium, the fundamental and critical reason for failure was the total lack of marketing analysis and realistic marketing planning.

The Iridium project cost an estimated $5 billion in 1998. Its business consisted of a global satellite network of 66 satellites and the manufacture of digital phones and chips. The company was a consortium with many diverse partners from around the world. Motorola, a major investor, provided product systems and financing, and owned 18 percent of Iridium.

Iridium was supposed to revolutionize the telecommunications industry. Its unique feature was that it could provide service anywhere in the world. The primary target was international business travelers, a market estimated to be about eight million.

What actually happened? The Iridium phone was described by users as a "brick-like device." It weighed 500g versus 120g for most cell phones, and required several attachments. Instructions for using the phone were difficult to understand. The phone cost $3,000 and air time ranged from $3 to $7 per minute.

Iridium spent $140 million in media to launch the product. Their slogan was "Anytime, anywhere." Unfortunately, this slogan was referring only to their worldwide service—the phone could not be used inside buildings or moving cars. Their advertisements appeared in *The Wall Street Journal, Fortune,* other business publications and airline magazines. A direct mail campaign in numerous international markets and employing 20 different languages was utilized. The advertising campaign generated over one million sales leads. Unfortunately, the company bungled this effort by not adequately following up on these leads.

As if all these conditions weren't enough to condemn the product to failure, the first samples of the product were late in delivery and experienced software problems. The product had not been properly tested, there was not guarantee for the security of the system, and only 25,000 users could be serviced at one time.

Iridium is an example of technology in search of a market. From the beginning, the project was driven by a technological vision that ignored both the competition and the consumer. In the end, it failed because it failed to create a unique value in a competitive marketplace.

SOURCES: Leslie Cauley, "Iridium's Downfall: The Marketing Took a Back Seat to Science," *The Wall Street Journal,* 18 August, 1999, p. A1; Christopher Rice, "Iridium: Born on a Beach but Lost in Space," *Financial Times,* 20 August, 1999, p. 16.

shoe; Gallo, the largest wine company on earth, does not grow a single grape; and Boeing, the preeminent aircraft manufacturer, makes little more than cockpits and wings.[8] While outsourcing manufacturing for many companies might be a tactical response dedicated to some immediate cost savings, it is clear that Nike, Gallo, and Boeing put significant thought into establishing their supply chains, and that they could view their supplier arrangements as strategic. In fact, Nike's ability to outsource its manufacturing to multiple low-cost producers in the Far East has been a critical component of its success. Although these vertical arrangements may be critically important to the success of the firm, they are not alliances unless the partners are linked in a long-term relationship. If they are not, then they are simply supply agreements.

Nike and many other companies have faced a growing consumer concern about the working conditions in supplier companies. Essentially, even though the legal link between the supplier and buyer is limited to the purchase agreement, consumers have insisted that the buyer be held responsible for working conditions in the supplier company.

---

[8] James Brian Quinn, "Strategic Outsourcing," *Sloan Management Review* (Summer 1994).

An example of a strategic relationship of partners along vertical lines is in lean manufacturing; for example, the assembler of an automobile relies on suppliers to not only build but to also design key components of the automobile. This kind of cooperation can lead to shorter design cycles, superior quality, and lower cost but it will not occur unless there is a mutual commitment to work together and a confidence on both sides that the two parties will not invade each other's domain. This kind of cooperation can strengthen the competitive advantage of each of the partners by enabling them to identify and concentrate on their core strengths.

Another example of a strategic relationship is a university that contracts with a hospitality company to provide management services for lodging and meal service at a training center. The hospitality company provides superior service as compared to what the university could do itself, and thereby enables the university to be a more effective competitor in its market. The relationship is strategic because it enables the company to create greater value for its customers.

◆ SUCCESS FACTORS

Assuming that a proposed alliance meets the six prerequisites just outlined, it is necessary to consider the following six basic factors that are deemed to have significant impact on the success of GSPs:[9]

1. *Mission.* Successful GSPs create win-win situations, in which participants pursue objectives on the basis of mutual need or advantage.
2. *Strategy.* A company may establish separate GSPs with different partners; strategy must be thought out up front to avoid conflicts.
3. *Governance.* Discussion and consensus must be the norms. Partners must be viewed as equals.
4. *Culture.* Personal chemistry is important, as is the successful development of a shared set of values. The failure of a partnership between Britain's General Electric Company and Siemens A. G. was blamed in part on the fact that the former was run by finance-oriented executives and the latter by engineers.
5. *Organization.* Innovative structures and designs may be needed to offset the complexity of multicountry management.
6. *Management.* GSPs invariably involve a different type of decision making. Potentially divisive issues must be identified in advance and clear, unitary lines of authority established that will result in commitment by all partners.

Companies forming GSPs must keep these factors in mind. Moreover, successful collaborators will be guided by the following four principles:

1. Despite the fact that partners are pursuing mutual goals in some areas, partners must remember that they are competitors in others.
2. Harmony is not the most important measure of success; some conflict is to be expected.
3. All employees, engineers, and managers must understand where cooperation ends and competitive compromise begins.
4. As noted earlier, learning from partners is critically important.[10]

---

[9] Perlmutter and Heenan, "Cooperate to Compete Globally," p. 137.
[10] Gary Hamel, Yves L. Doz, and C. K. Prahalad, "Collaborate with Your Competitors—and Win," *Harvard Business Review* (January–February 1989): 134.

The issue of learning deserves special attention. One team of researchers notes the following:

> The challenge is to share enough skills to create advantage vis-à-vis companies outside the alliance while preventing a wholesale transfer of core skills to the partner. This is a very thin line to walk. Companies must carefully select what skills and technologies they pass to their partners. They must develop safeguards against unintended, informal transfers of information. The goal is to limit the transparency of their operations.[11]

◆ ALLIANCES BETWEEN MANUFACTURERS AND MARKETERS

Many companies have decided to source their product from suppliers. Although many companies source in lower-wage countries, even domestic companies are outsourcing tasks to achieve greater efficiency. They contract out the manufacturing or service activities in the value chain to companies that can supply product at a lower cost than is possible with manufacturing in-house.

These companies may find themselves at a disadvantage in GSPs with a supplier, especially if the latter's manufacturing skills are the attractive quality. Unfortunately for the marketer, a company's manufacturing excellence represents a multifaceted competence that is not easily transferred. The higher-income country managers and engineers must also learn to be more receptive and attentive—they must overcome the "not-invented-here" syndrome and begin to think of themselves as students, not teachers. At the same time, they must learn to be less eager to show off proprietary lab and engineering successes. To limit transparency, some companies involved in GSPs establish a collaboration section. Much like a corporate communications department, this department is designed to serve as a gatekeeper through which requests for access to people and information must be channeled. Such gatekeeping serves an important control function that guards against unintended transfers.

A report by McKinsey and Company shed additional light on the specific problems of alliances between Western and Japanese firms.[12] Often, problems between partners had less to do with objective levels of performance than with a feeling of mutual disillusionment and missed opportunity. The study identified four common problem areas in alliances gone wrong. The first problem was that each partner had a different dream; the Japanese partner saw itself emerging from the alliance as a leader in its business or entering new sectors and building a new basis for the future, while the Western partner sought relatively quick and risk-free financial returns. Said one Japanese manager, "Our partner came in looking for a return. They got it. Now they complain that they didn't build a business. But that isn't what they set out to create."[13]

A second area of concern is the balance between partners. Each must contribute to the alliance, and each must depend on the other to a degree that justifies participation in the alliance. The most attractive partner in the short run is likely to be a company that is already established and competent in the business with the need to master, say, some new technological skills. The best long-term partner, however, is likely to be a less competent player or even one from outside the industry.

Another common cause of problems is frictional loss, caused by differences in management philosophy, expectations, and approaches. All functions within the alliance may be affected, and performance is likely to suffer as a consequence. Speaking of his Japanese counterpart, a Western businessperson said, "Our partner just wanted to go

---
[11] Ibid., p. 136.
[12] Kevin K. Jones and Walter E. Schill, "Allying for Advantage," *The McKinsey Quarterly,* no. 3 (1991): 73–101.
[13] Ibid.

ahead and invest without considering whether there would be a return or not." The Japanese partner stated that "the foreign partner took so long to decide on obvious points that we were always too slow."[14] Such differences often cause much frustration and time-consuming debates, which stifle decision making.

Finally, the study found that short-term goals can result in the foreign partner's limiting the number of people allocated to the joint venture. Those involved in the venture may perform only two- or three-year assignments. The result is corporate amnesia; that is, little or no corporate memory is built up on how to compete in Japan. The original goals of the venture will be lost as each new group of managers takes their turn. When taken collectively, these four problems will almost always ensure that the Japanese partner will be the only one in it for the long haul.

CASE EXAMPLES OF PARTNERSHIPS

CFM International/GE/Snecma—A Success Story

Commercial Fan Moteur (CFM) International, a partnership between General Electric's (GE's) jet engine division and Snecma, a government-owned French aerospace company, is a frequently cited example of a successful GSP. GE was motivated in part by the desire to gain access to the European market so it could sell engines to Airbus Industrie; also, the $800 million in development costs was more than GE could risk on its own. While GE focused on system design and high-tech work, the French side handled fans, boosters, and other components. The partnership resulted in the development of a highly successful new engine that, to date, has generated tens of billions of dollars in sales to 125 different customers.

The alliance got off to a strong start because of the personal chemistry between two top executives, GE's Gerhard Neumann and the late General René Ravaud of Snecma. The partnership thrives despite each side's differing views regarding governance, management, and organization. Brian Rowe, senior vice president of GE's engine group, has noted that the French like to bring in senior executives from outside the industry, whereas GE prefers to bring in experienced people from within the organization. Also, the French prefer to approach problem solving with copious amounts of data, whereas Americans may take a more intuitive approach.[15] Still, senior executives from both sides involved in the partnership have been delegated substantial responsibility.

AT&T/Olivetti—A Failure

In theory, the partnership in the mid-1980s between AT&T and Italy's Olivetti appeared to be a winner: The collective mission was to capture a major share of the global market for information processing and communications.[16] Olivetti had what appeared to be a strong presence in the European office equipment market; AT&T executives, having just presided over the divestiture of their company's regional telephone units, had set their sights on overseas growth, with Europe as the starting point. AT&T promised its partner $260 million and access to microprocessor and telecommunications technology. The partnership called for AT&T to sell Olivetti's personal computers in the United States; Olivetti, in turn, would sell AT&T computers and switching equipment in Europe. Underpinning the alliance was the expectation that synergies would result from the pairing of companies from different industries—communications and computers.

Unfortunately, that vision was nothing more than a hope: There was no real strength in Olivetti in the computer market, and Olivetti had no experience or capability in communications equipment. Tensions ran high when sales did not reach expected levels.

---

[14] Ibid.
[15] Bernard Wysocki, "Global Reach: Cross Border Alliances Become Favorite Way to Crack New Markets," *The Wall Street Journal*, 26 March 1990, p. A12.
[16] Perlmutter and Heenan, "Cooperate to Compete Globally," p. 145.

AT&T group executive Robert Kavner cited communication and cultural differences as being important factors leading to the breakdown of the alliance. "I don't think we or Olivetti spent enough time understanding behavior patterns," Kavner said. "We knew the culture was different but we never really penetrated. We would get angry, and they would get upset."[17] In 1989, AT&T cashed in its Olivetti stake for a share in the parent company Compagnie Industriali Riunite S.p.A. (CIR). In 1993, citing a decline in CIR's value, AT&T sold its remaining stake.

Boeing/Japan—A Controversy

GSPs have been the target of criticism in some circles. Critics warn that employees of a company that become reliant on outside suppliers for critical components will lose expertise and experience erosion of their engineering skills. Such criticism is often directed at GSPs involving U.S. and Japanese firms. For example, a proposed alliance between Boeing and a Japanese consortium to build a new fuel-efficient airliner, the 7J7, generated a great deal of controversy. The project's $4 billion price tag was too high for Boeing to shoulder alone. The Japanese were to contribute between $1 billion and $2 billion; in return, they would get a chance to learn manufacturing and marketing techniques from Boeing. Although the 7J7 project was shelved in 1988, a new wide-body aircraft, the 777, was developed with about 20 percent of the work subcontracted out to Mitsubishi, Fuji, and Kawasaki.[18]

Critics envision a scenario in which the Japanese use what they learn to build their own aircraft and compete directly with Boeing in the future—a disturbing thought because Boeing is a major exporter to world markets. One team of researchers has developed a framework outlining the stages that a company can go through as it becomes increasingly dependent on partnerships.[19]

Stage One: Outsourcing of assembly for inexpensive labor
Stage Two: Outsourcing of low-value components to reduce product price
Stage Three: Growing levels of value-added components move abroad
Stage Four: Manufacturing skills, designs, and functionally related technologies move abroad
Stage Five: Disciplines related to quality, precision manufacturing, testing, and future avenues of product derivatives leave
Stage Six: Core skills surrounding components, miniaturization, and complex systems integration move abroad
Stage Seven: Competitor learns the entire spectrum of skills related to the underlying core competence

The next stage is obvious: The partner now has the complete manufacturing skill set and capability and may decide to push for forward integration, that is, to move closer to the customer by introducing its own brand into the marketplace.

◆ INTERNATIONAL PARTNERSHIPS IN DEVELOPING COUNTRIES

Central and Eastern Europe, Asia, Mexico, and Central and South America offer exciting opportunities for firms seeking to enter gigantic and largely untapped markets. An obvious strategic alternative for entering these markets is the strategic alliance. Like the early joint ventures between American and Japanese firms, potential partners will trade

[17] Wysocki, "Global Reach," p. A12.
[18] John Holusha, "Pushing the Envelope at Boeing," *The New York Times,* 10 November 1991, sec. 3, pp. 1, 6.
[19] David Lei and John W. Slocum, Jr., "Global Strategy, Competence-Building and Strategic Alliances," *California Management Review* (Fall 1992): 81–97.

market access for know-how, but the question of whether alliances are the best way to go to gain market access must be carefully evaluated.

In China, multinational companies are required to take local partners and many are doing quite well. Presently, the top 200 joint ventures in China are growing at an average compound annual growth rate of 38 percent at an 8 percent after-tax margin.[20] Although investment spending is understandable in developing countries, many multinational companies have taken a long-term strategy too far and are rethinking their joint venture efforts in China. Rick Yan states, "If you're not making money in China now, there's little chance you will without changing your strategy."[21] He concludes that companies who tolerate poor short-term results in the mistaken belief that such results are a trade-off for future probability should reexamine their strategies. Yan found that success is more a matter of managerial capacity, critical mass scale, and product portfolio than length of stay. Coca-Cola has been successful while Pepsi-Cola is not. When regulations were eased, Coca-Cola sought equity stakes and management control in its joint ventures. Pepsi failed to do this until much later. It is not enough to have a local partner—marketing and management are also critical.

A Central European market with interesting potential is Hungary. Hungary already has the most liberal financial and commercial system in the region. It has also provided investment incentives to Westerners, especially in high-tech industries. This former communist economy has its share of problems. Digital's recent joint venture agreement with the Hungarian Research Institute for Physics and the state-supervised computer systems design firm Szamalk is a case in point. Though the venture was formed so Digital will be able to sell and service its equipment in Hungary, the underlying importance of the venture was to stop the cloning of Digital's computers by Central European firms.

◆ COOPERATIVE STRATEGIES IN JAPAN: *KEIRETSU*

Japan's *keiretsu* represent a special category of cooperative strategy. A *keiretsu* is an interbusiness alliance or enterprise group that, in the words of one observer, "resembles a fighting clan in which business families join together to vie for market share."[22] *Keiretsu* exist in a broad spectrum of markets, including the capital market, primary goods markets, and component parts markets.[23] *Keiretsu* relationships are often cemented by bank ownership of large blocks of stock as well as cross-ownership of stock between a company and its buyers and nonfinancial suppliers. Furthermore, *keiretsu* executives can legally sit on each other's boards, as well as share information and coordinate prices in closed-door meetings of "presidents' councils." Thus, *keiretsu* are essentially cartels that have the government's blessing.

Some observers have disputed charges that *keiretsu* have an impact on market relationships in Japan, claiming instead that the groups primarily serve a social function. Others acknowledge the past significance of preferential trading patterns associated with *keiretsu* but assert that the latter's influence is now weakening. It is beyond the scope of this chapter to address these issues in detail, but there can be no doubt that, for companies competing with the Japanese or wishing to enter the Japanese market, a general understanding of *keiretsu* is crucial. Imagine, for example, what it would mean in the United States if an automaker (e.g., General Motors [GM]), an electrical products company

---

[20] Richard Yan, "Short-Term Results: The Litmus Test for Success in China," Harvard Business Review (September-October 1998): 70.

[21] Ibid., pp. 61–75.

[22] Robert L. Cutts, "Capitalism in Japan: Cartels and Keiretsu," Harvard Business Review (July–August 1992): 49.

[23] Michael L. Gerlach, "Twilight of the Keiretsu? A Critical Assessment," *Journal of Japanese Studies,* 18, no. 1 (Winter 1992): 79.

(GE), a steelmaker (USX), and a computer firm (IBM) were interconnected rather than separate firms. Global competition in the era of *keiretsu* means competition exists not only among products but between different systems of corporate governance and industrial organization.[24]

As the hypothetical example from America suggests, some of Japan's biggest and best-known companies are at the center of *keiretsu*. For example, Mitsui Group and Mitsubishi Group are organized around big trading companies. These two, together with the Sumitomo, Fuyo, Sanwa, and DKB groups, make up the "big six" *keiretsu*. Each group strives for a strong position in each major sector of the Japanese economy. Annual revenues in each group are in the hundreds of billions of dollars.[25] In absolute terms, *keiretsu* constituted less than 0.01 percent of all Japanese companies. However, they accounted for an astonishing 78 percent of the market valuation of shares on the Tokyo Stock Exchange, a third of Japan's business capital, and approximately one quarter of its sales.[26] These alliances can effectively block foreign suppliers from entering the market and result in higher prices to Japanese consumers, while at the same time resulting in corporate stability, risk sharing, and long-term employment. The Mitsubishi Group's *keiretsu* structure is shown in detail in Figure 9-1.

In addition to the big six, several other *keiretsu* have formed, bringing new configurations to the basic forms described previously. Vertical supply and distribution *keiretsu* are alliances between manufacturers and retailers. For example, Matsushita controls a chain of 25,000 National stores in Japan, through which it sells its Panasonic, Technics, and Quasar brands. About half of Matsushita's domestic sales are generated through the National chain, 50 to 80 percent of whose inventory consists of Matsushita's brands. Japan's other major consumer electronics manufacturers, including Toshiba and Hitachi, have similar alliances (Sony's chain of stores is much smaller and weaker by comparison). All are fierce competitors in the Japanese market.[27]

Another type of manufacturing *keiretsu* outside the big six consists of vertical hierarchical alliances between assembly companies and suppliers and component manufacturers. Intergroup operations and systems are closely integrated, with suppliers receiving long-term contracts. Toyota, for example, has a network of about 175 primary and 4,000 secondary suppliers. One supplier is Koito; Toyota owns about one fifth of Koito's shares and buys about half of its production. The net result of this arrangement is that Toyota produces about 25 percent of the sales value of its cars, compared with 50 percent for GM. Manufacturing *keiretsu* show the gains that can result from an optimal balance of supplier and buyer power. Because Toyota buys a given component from several suppliers (some are in the *keiretsu,* some are independent), discipline is imposed down the network. Also, since Toyota's suppliers do not work exclusively for Toyota, they have an incentive to be flexible and adaptable.[28]

The practices described here lead to the question of whether or not *keiretsu* violate antitrust laws. As many observers have noted, the Japanese government frequently puts the interests of producers ahead of the interests of consumers. In fact, the *keiretsu* were formed in the early 1950s as regroupings of four large conglomerates—*zaibatsu*—that dominated the Japanese economy until 1945. They were dissolved after the occupational forces introduced antitrust as part of the reconstruction. Today, Japan's Fair Trade Commission appears to favor harmony rather than pursuing anticompetitive behavior. As a

[24] Ronald J. Gilson and Mark J. Roe, "Understanding the Japanese Keiretsu: Overlaps Between Corporate Governance and Industrial Organization," *The Yale Law Journal,* 102, no. 4 (January 1993): 883.

[25] Clyde V. Prestowitz, Jr. *Trading Places: How We Are Giving Our Future to Japan and How to Reclaim It* (New York: Basic Books, 1989), p. 296.

[26] Carla Rappoport, "Why Japan Keeps on Winning," *Fortune* (July 15, 1991): 76.

[27] The importance of the chain stores is eroding due to increasing sales at mass merchandisers not under the manufacturers' control.

[28] "Japanology, Inc.—Survey," *The Economist,* 6 March 1993, p. 15.

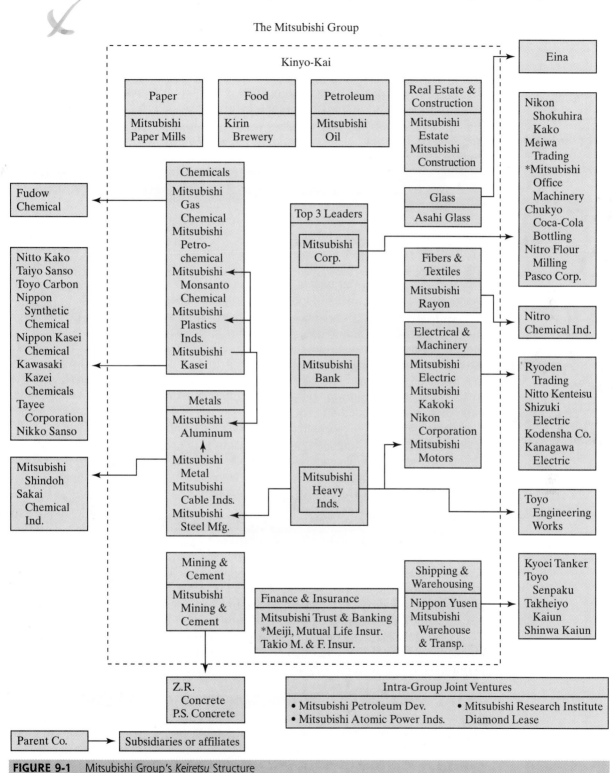

FIGURE 9-1   Mitsubishi Group's *Keiretsu* Structure

Source: Courtesy of the Mitsubishi Group, from Collins & Doorley *Teaming Up for the '90s* (Copyright Deloitte & Touche, New York, 1991).

result, the U.S. Federal Trade Commission has launched several investigations of price fixing, price discrimination, and exclusive supply arrangements. Hitachi, Canon, and other Japanese companies have also been accused of restricting the availability of high-tech products in the U.S. market. The Justice Department has considered prosecuting the U.S. subsidiaries of Japanese companies if the parent company is found guilty of unfair trade practices in the Japanese market.[29]

◆ BEYOND STRATEGIC ALLIANCES

The relationship enterprise is said to be the next stage of evolution of the strategic alliance. Groupings of firms in different industries and countries will be held together by common goals that encourage them to act almost as a single firm.

More than the simple strategic alliances we know today, relationship enterprises will be superalliances among global giants, with revenues approaching $1 trillion. They would be able to draw on extensive cash resources, circumvent antitrust barriers, and, with home bases in all major markets, enjoy the political advantage of being a "local" firm almost anywhere. This type of alliance is not driven simply by technological change but by the political necessity of having multiple home bases.

Another perspective on the future of cooperative strategies envisions the emergence of the virtual corporation. (The term *virtual* is borrowed from computer science; some computers feature virtual memory that allows them to function as though they have more storage capacity than is actually built into their memory chips.) As described in a *Business Week* cover story, the virtual corporation "will seem to be a single entity with vast capabilities but will really be the result of numerous collaborations assembled only when they're needed."[30]

On a global level, the virtual corporation could combine the twin competencies of cost-effectiveness and responsiveness; thus, it could pursue the "think global, act local" philosophy with ease. This reflects the trend toward mass customization. The same forces that are driving the formation of the digital *keiretsu*—high-speed communication networks, for example—are embodied in the virtual corporation. As noted by Davidow and Malone, "The success of a virtual corporation will depend on its ability to gather and integrate a massive flow of information throughout its organizational components and intelligently act upon that information."[31]

Why has the virtual corporation suddenly burst onto the scene? Previously, firms lacked the technology to facilitate this type of data management. Today, distributed databases, networks, and open systems make possible the kinds of data flows required for the virtual corporation. In particular, these data flows permit supply-chain management. Ford provides an interesting example of how technology is improving information flows among the far-flung operations of a single company. Ford's $6 billion world car—known as the Mercury Mystique and Ford Contour in the United States and the Mondeo in Europe—was developed using an international communications network linking computer workstations of designers and engineers on three continents.[32]

One of the hallmarks of the virtual corporation will be the production of virtual products—products that practically exist before they are manufactured. As described by Davidow and Malone, the concept, design, and manufacture of virtual products are stored in the minds of cooperating teams, in computers, and in flexible production lines.[33]

---

[29] Rappoport, "Why Japan Keeps on Winning," p. 84.

[30] John Byrne, "The Virtual Corporation," *Business Week,* 8 February 1993, p. 103.

[31] William H. Davidow and Michael S. Malone, *The Virtual Corporation: Structuring and Revitalizing the Corporation for the 21st Century* (New York: HarperBusiness, 1993), p. 59.

[32] Julie Edelson Halpert, "One Car, Worldwide, with Strings Pulled from Michigan," *The New York Times,* 29 August 1993, sec. 3, p. 7.

[33] Davidow and Malone, *The Virtual Corporation,* p. 4.

Summary

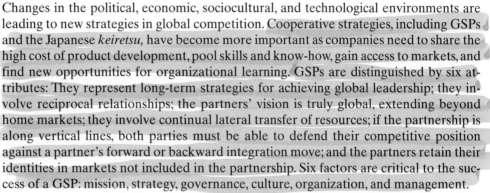

Changes in the political, economic, sociocultural, and technological environments are leading to new strategies in global competition. Cooperative strategies, including GSPs and the Japanese *keiretsu,* have become more important as companies need to share the high cost of product development, pool skills and know-how, gain access to markets, and find new opportunities for organizational learning. GSPs are distinguished by six attributes: They represent long-term strategies for achieving global leadership; they involve reciprocal relationships; the partners' vision is truly global, extending beyond home markets; they involve continual lateral transfer of resources; if the partnership is along vertical lines, both parties must be able to defend their competitive position against a partner's forward or backward integration move; and the partners retain their identities in markets not included in the partnership. Six factors are critical to the success of a GSP: mission, strategy, governance, culture, organization, and management.

Keiretsu have had enormous significance for the success of Japanese companies, both in Japan and the rest of the world. In the United States, the dawning of the digital age is resulting in *keiretsu*-style alliances among companies in the computer, telecommunications, and entertainment industries. At the same time, some alliances are resulting in the creation of the virtual corporation, an organization that exists solely in the network of linkages among partners.

Discussion Questions

1. What are six attributes that distinguish GSPs from traditional joint ventures? How could these benefit marketing?
2. What six basic factors affect the success of GSPs?
3. What are *keiretsu?* How does this form of industrial structure affect companies that compete with Japan or that are trying to enter the Japanese market?
4. Describe what is meant by a virtual corporation.
5. The opening chapter quotations present opposing views about the value and wisdom of strategic alliances. With which do you agree? Why? Can these views be integrated and reconciled, or is it necessary to take sides?

Suggested Readings

Adler, Paul S. "Time-and-Motion Regained." *Harvard Business Review,* 71, no. 1 (January/February 1993): 97–108.

Adler, Paul S., and Robert E. Cole. "Designed for Learning: A Tale of Two Auto Plants." *Sloan Management Review,* 34, no. 3 (Spring 1993): 85–94.

Bleeke, Joel, and David Ernst. "Is Your Strategic Alliance Really a Sale?" *Harvard Business Review,* 73, no. 1 (January/February 1995): 97–105.

Blodgett, Linda Longfellow. "Research Notes and Communications Factors in the Instability of International Joint Ventures: An Event Historical Analysis." *Strategic Management Journal,* 13, no. 6 (September 1992): 475–481.

Contractor, Farok, and Peter Lorange. *Cooperative Strategies in International Business.* Cambridge, MA: Ballinger, 1987.

Davidow, William H., and Michael S. Malone. *The Virtual Corporation.* New York: HarperBusiness, 1993.

Dyer, Jeffrey H., and William G. Ouchi. "Japanese-Style Partnerships: Giving Companies a Competitive Edge." *Sloan Management Review* (Fall 1993): 51–63.

Enen, Jack. *Venturing Abroad: International Business Expansion Via Joint Ventures.* Blue Ridge Summit, PA: Liberty Hall Press, 1991.

Erdmann, Peter B. "When Businesses Cross International Borders: Strategic Alliances and Their Alternatives." *Columbia Journal of World Business,* 28, no. 2 (Summer 1993): 107–108.

Fedor, Kenneth J., and William B. Werther, Jr. "Making Sense of Cultural Factors in International Alliances." *Organizational Dynamics,* 24, no. 4 (Spring 1995): 33–48.

Flanagan, Patrick. "Strategic Alliances Keep Customers Plugged In." *Management Review,* 82, no. 3 (March 1993): 24–26.

Frey, S. C. J., and M. M. Schlosser. "ABB and Ford: Creating Value through Cooperation." *Sloan Management Review* (Fall 1993): 65–72.

Fruin, Mark. *The Japanese Enterprise System.* Oxford: Oxford University Press, 1992.

Gates, Stephen. *Strategic Alliances: Guidelines for Successful Management.* New York: Conference Board, 1993.

Gerlach, Michael L. *Alliance Capitalism: The Social Organization of Japanese Business.* Berkeley: University of California Press, 1992.

Gomes-Casseres, Benjamin. "Joint Ventures in the Face of Global Competition." *Sloan Management Review,* 30, no. 3 (Spring 1989): 17–26.

Haigh, Robert W. "Building a Strategic Alliance—The Hermosillo Experience as a Ford–Mazda Proving Ground." *Columbia Journal of World Business,* 27, no. 1 (Spring 1992): 60–74.

Hamel, Gary, Yves L. Doz, and C. K. Prahalad. "Collaborate with Your Competitors—and Win." *Harvard Business Review,* 67, no. 1 (January/February 1989): 133–139.

Johnston, Gerald A. "The Yin and the Yang: Cooperation and Competition in International Business." *Executive Speeches,* 7, no. 6 (June/July 1993): 15–17.

Ketelhohn, Werner. "What Do We Mean by Cooperative Advantage?" *European Management Journal,* 11, no. 1 (March 1993): 30–37.

Klein, Saul, and Jehiel Zif. "Global Versus Local Strategic Alliances." *Journal of Global Marketing,* 8, no. 1 (1994): 51–72.

Kodama, Fumio. "Technology Fusion and the New R&D." *Harvard Business Review,* 70, no. 4 (July/August 1992): 70–78.

Kruytbosch, Carla. "Let's Make a Deal." *International Business,* 6, no. 3 (March 1993): 92–96.

Lawrence, Paul, and Charalambos Vlachoutsicos. "Joint Ventures in Russia: Put the Locals in Charge." *Harvard Business Review,* 71, no. 1 (January/February 1993): 44–51.

Lei, David. "Offensive and Defensive Uses of Alliances." *Long Range Planning,* 25, no. 6 (December 1992): 10–17.

Lei, David, and John W. Slocum, Jr. "Global Strategy, Competence-Building and Strategic Alliances." *California Management Review,* 35, no. 1 (Fall 1992): 81–97.

Lewis, Jordan D. "Competitive Alliances Redefine Companies." *Management Review,* 80, no. 4 (April 1991): 14–18.

Lorange, Peter. "Interactive Strategic Alliances and Partnerships." *Long Range Planning,* 29, no. 4 (1996): 581–584.

Lorange, Peter, and Johan Roos. "Why Some Strategic Alliances Succeed and Others Fail." *Journal of Business Strategy,* 12, no. 1 (January/February 1991): 25–30.

Luo, Yadong. "Evaluating the Performance of Strategic Alliances in China." *Long Range Planning,* 29, no. 4 (1996): 534–542.

Michelet, Robert, and Rosemary Remacle. "Forming Successful Strategic Marketing Alliances in Europe." *Journal of European Business,* 4, no. 1 (September/October 1992): 11–15.

Mowery, David C., and David J. Teece. "Japan's Growing Capabilities in Industrial Technology: Implications for US Managers and Policymakers." *California Management Review,* 35, no. 2 (1993): 9–34.

Murray, Edwin A., Jr., and John F. Mahon. "Strategic Alliances: Gateway to the New Europe?" *Long Range Planning,* 26, no. 4 (August 1993): 102–111.

Newman, Victor, and Kazem Chaharbaghi. "Strategic Alliances in Fast-Moving Markets." *Long Range Planning,* 29, no. 6 (1996): 850–856.

Niland, Powell. "Case Study—US–Japanese Joint Venture: New United Motor Manufacturing, Inc. (NUMMI)." *Planning Review,* 17, no. 1 (January/February 1989): 40–45.

Ohmae, Kenichi. "The Global Logic of Strategic Alliances." *Harvard Business Review,* 67 (March/April 1989): 143–154.

Pant, P. Narayan, and Vasant G. Rajadhyaksha. "Partnership with an Asian Family Business—What Every Multinational Corporation Should Know." *Long Range Planning,* 29, no. 6 (1996): 812–820.

Perlmutter, H. V., and D. A. Heenan. "Cooperate to Compete Globally." *Harvard Business Review* (March/April 1986): 136–152.

Raval, Dinker and Bala Subramanian. "Strategic Alliances for Reentry into Abandoned Markets: A Case Study of Coca-Cola in India." *Journal of Global Competitiveness,* 4, no. 1 (1996): 142–150.

Robert, Michel. "The Do's and Don'ts of Strategic Alliances." *Journal of Business Strategy,* 13, no. 2 (March/April 1992): 50–53.

Robert, Michel. *Strategy Pure and Simple: How Winning CEOs Outthink Their Competition.* New York: McGraw-Hill, 1993.

Spencer, William J., and Peter Grindley. "SEMATECH After Five Years." *California Management Review* (Summer 1993): 9–35.

Thakar, Manab, and Luis Ma. R. Calingo. "Strategic Thinking Is Hip, but Does It Make a Difference?" *Business Horizons,* 35, no. 5 (September/October 1992): 47–54.

Voss, Bristol. "Strategic Federations Frequently Falter in Far East." *Journal of Business Strategy,* 14, no. 4 (July/August 1993): 6.

Wever, Kirsten S., and Christopher S. Allen. "Is Germany a Model for Managers?" *Harvard Business Review,* 70, no. 5 (September/October 1992): 36–43.

Yoshida, Kosaku. "New Economic Principles in America—Competition and Cooperation: A Comparative Study of the U.S. and Japan." *Columbia Journal of World Business,* 26, no. 4 (Winter 1992): 30–44.

Yoshino, Michael Y., and U. Srinivasa Rangan. *Strategic Alliances: An Entrepreneurial Approach to Globalization.* Boston: Harvard Business School Press, 1995.

CHAPTER 10

Competitive Analysis and Strategy

"The best strategy is always to be very strong, first generally then at the decisive point . . . there is no more imperative and no simpler law for strategy than to keep the forces concentrated."

—CARL VON CLAUSEWITZ, 1780–1831
Vom Kriege, Book III, Chapter XI,
"Assembly of Forces in Space," (1832–1837)

From its home base in Sweden, IKEA has become the world's largest furniture retailer doing $8.5 billion in annual sales in 1998–1999. With 150 stores in 29 countries, the company's success reflects founder Ingvar Kamprad's vision of selling a wide range of stylish, functional home furnishings at prices so low that the majority of people can afford to buy them. The store exteriors are painted bright blue and yellow—Sweden's national colors. Shoppers view furniture on the main floor in scores of realistic settings arranged throughout cavernous showrooms. In a departure from standard industry practice, IKEA's furniture bears names such as "Ivar" and "Sten" instead of model numbers. At IKEA, shopping is very much a self-service activity; after browsing and writing down the names of desired items, shoppers pick up their furniture on the lower level. There they find boxes containing the furniture in kit form; one of the cornerstones of IKEA's strategy is having customers take their purchases home in their own vehicles and assemble the furniture themselves. The lower level of a typical IKEA store also contains a restaurant, a grocery store called the Swede Shop, a supervised play area for children, and a baby care room.

The bottom line for IKEA is that the company creates a unique value for customers: Instead of salespersons, a limited number of display items, and a catalog from which to order, IKEA offers informative displays and product information for everything it sells. In a traditional furniture store, you place an order and wait weeks or months for delivery. At IKEA, you make a purchase and take it with you. Traditional furniture is assembled and ready to use. IKEA furniture is sold in kit form ready to assemble. The traditional store offers salespersons or consultants, assembled and ready to use product, delivery, and higher prices. IKEA offers rock-bottom prices.

IKEA is focused on the young customer or the young at heart: The core market is the customer with a limited budget who appreciates IKEA's product line, displays, and prices. Because IKEA knows the needs and wants of this market segment, it has been successful in serving customers not only in Sweden where the company was founded but also globally. IKEA's success in crossing borders has been instrumental in changing furniture retailing from a multidomestic industry to a global one.

> **VISIT THE WEB SITE**
> www.ikea.com

The essence of global marketing strategy is in successfully relating the strengths of an organization to its environment. As the horizons of marketers have expanded from domestic to global markets, so too have the horizons of competitors. The reality in almost every industry today—including home furnishings—is global competition. This fact of life puts an organization under increasing pressure to master techniques for conducting industry analysis, competitor analysis, understanding competitive advantage at both the industry and national levels, and developing and maintaining competitive advantage. These topics are covered in detail in this chapter.

◆ INDUSTRY ANALYSIS FORCES INFLUENCING COMPETITION

A useful way of gaining insight into the nature of competition is through industry analysis. As a working definition, an industry can be defined as a group of firms that produce products that are close substitutes for each other. In any industry, competition works to drive down the rate of return on invested capital toward the rate that would be earned in the economist's perfectly competitive industry. Rates of return that are greater than this so-called competitive rate will stimulate an inflow of capital either from new entrants or from existing competitors making additional investment. Rates of return below this competitive rate will result in withdrawal from the industry and a decline in the levels of activity and competition.

According to Michael E. Porter of Harvard University, a leading theorist of competitive strategy, there are five forces influencing competition in an industry (see Figure 10-1):

FIGURE 10-1 Forces Influencing Competition in an Industry

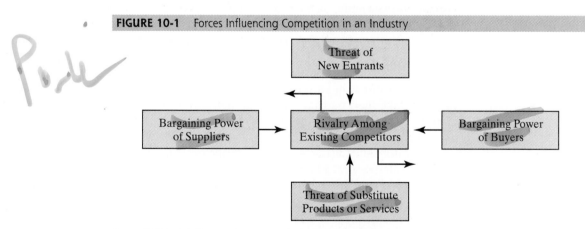

Source: Michael E. Porter, *Competitive Strategy* (New York: Free Press, 1980), p. 4. Copyright © 1980, 1998 by The Free Press. Adapted with permission of The Free Press, a division of Simon & Schuster.

the threat of new entrants; the threat of substitute products or services; the bargaining power of suppliers; the bargaining power of buyers; and the competitive rivalry between current members of the industry. In industries such as soft drinks, pharmaceuticals, and cosmetics, a favorable combination of the five forces has resulted in attractive returns for competitors. However, pressure from any of the forces can reduce or limit profitability, as evidenced by the recent fortunes of some competitors in the personal computer (PC) and semiconductor industries. A discussion of each of the five forces follows.

THREAT OF NEW ENTRANTS

New entrants to an industry bring new capacity, a desire to gain market share and position, and, very often, new approaches to serving customer needs. The decision to become a new entrant in an industry is often accompanied by a major commitment of resources. New players push prices downward and squeeze margins, resulting in reduced industry profitability. Porter describes eight major sources of barriers to entry, the presence or absence of which determines the extent of the threat of new industry entrants.[1]

The first barrier, economies of scale, refers to the decline in per unit product costs as the absolute volume of production per period increases. Although the concept of scale economies is frequently associated with manufacturing, it is also applicable to research and development (R&D), general administration, marketing, and other business functions. Honda's efficiency at engine R&D, for example, results from the wide range of products it produces that feature gasoline-powered engines. When existing firms in an industry achieve significant economies of scale, it becomes difficult for potential new entrants to be competitive.

Product differentiation, the second major entry barrier, is the extent of a product's perceived uniqueness—in other words, whether or not it is a commodity. High levels of product differentiation and brand loyalty, whether the result of physical product attributes or effective marketing communication, "raise the bar" for would-be industry entrants. For example, managers at Monsanto's G. D. Searle subsidiary achieved differentiation and erected a barrier in the artificial sweetener industry by insisting that the Nutrasweet logo and brand mark—a red-and-white swirl—appear on diet soft-drink cans and bottles.[2]

A third entry barrier relates to capital requirements. Capital is required not only for manufacturing facilities (fixed capital) but also for financing R&D, advertising, field sales and service, customer credit, and inventories (working capital). The enormous capital requirements in such industries as pharmaceuticals, mainframe computers, chemicals, and mineral extraction present formidable entry barriers.

A fourth barrier to entry are one-time switching costs caused by the need to change suppliers and products. These might include retraining, ancillary equipment costs, the cost of evaluating a new source, and so on. The perceived cost to customers of switching to a new competitor's product may present an insurmountable obstacle preventing industry newcomers from achieving success. For example, Microsoft's huge installed base of PC operating systems and applications presents a formidable entry barrier.

A fifth barrier to entry is access to distribution channels. To the extent that channels are full, expensive to enter, or unavailable, the cost of entry is substantially increased because a new entrant must create and establish new channels. Most foreign companies have encountered this barrier in Japan. This is not a so-called nontariff barrier, or a barrier designed to discriminate against foreign firms—it applies to *any* firm, domestic or foreign, seeking market entry.

Government policy is frequently a major entry barrier. In some cases, the government will restrict competitive entry. This is true in a number of industries, especially those

[1] Michael E. Porter, *Competitive Strategy* (New York: Free Press, 1980), pp. 7–33.
[2] Eben Shapiro, "Nutrasweet's Bitter Fight," *The New York Times,* 19 November 1989, p. C4.

in the low, lower-middle, and upper-middle income countries that have been designated as national industries by their respective governments. Japan's postwar industrialization strategy was based on a policy of preserving and protecting national industries in their development and growth phases. In many cases, the Japanese companies in these protected industries have gone on to become major world competitors in their industries. Komatsu, for example, was a weak local company when Caterpillar announced its interest in entering the Japanese market. Komatsu was given two years of protection by the Japanese government, and today it is the number-two earth-moving equipment company in the world. China is following a policy today of requiring foreign investors in many industries to join with local partners in their Chinese investments. In telecommunications, for example, it is not possible to invest in China without a partner.

Established firms may also enjoy cost advantages independent of the scale economies that present barriers to entry. Access to raw materials, favorable locations, and government subsidies are several examples.

Finally, expected competitor response can be a major entry barrier. If new entrants expect existing competitors to respond strongly to entry, their expectations about the rewards of entry will certainly be affected. A potential competitor's belief that entry into an industry or market will be an unpleasant experience may serve as a strong deterrent. Bruce Henderson, former president of the Boston Consulting Group, used the term *brinkmanship* to describe a recommended approach for deterring competitive entry. Brinkmanship occurs when industry leaders convince potential competitors that any market entry effort will be countered with vigorous and unpleasant responses.

G. D. Searle used brinkmanship—especially price cuts—to deter competitors from entering the low-calorie artificial sweetener market as Nutrasweet's patents expired. At the end of 1989, Systse T. Kuipers, a marketing manager at Holland Sweetener Company, complained that "it is a bloody fight and everybody's losing money. [Nutrasweet managers] go for the last kilo even if they have to give the product away." In Kuipers's view, G. D. Searle's tactic of deep price cuts on Nutrasweet had "the sole intent of chasing competitors out of the marketplace."[3] In fact, several European producers have already abandoned the business, proof that G. D. Searle's policy of brinkmanship was an effective competitive response to the threat of new entrants.

THREAT OF SUBSTITUTE PRODUCTS

A second force influencing competition in an industry is the threat of substitute products. The availability of substitute products places limits on the prices market leaders can charge in an industry; high prices may induce buyers to switch to the substitute.

For example, Barnes & Noble watched the upstart Amazon create a new product: the on-line bookstore. Customers could now order from millions of books and have them delivered to their doors in a matter of days. For a segment of the book market, local bookstores with only a few thousand books and a Starbucks Coffee facility were not necessary. Since it started in 1995, Amazon.com has grown to over $1.6 billion, expanded its product line into CDs and videos, diversified into pet and drug supplies to name but two areas, and served 17 million customers in 160 countries. Amazon.com is growing at the rate of 169 percent while Barnes & Noble is only growing at 16 percent. Apparently, the virtual bookstore is an extremely successful replacement for a traditional format.

VISIT THE WEB SITES

www.Amazon.com
www.barnesandnoble.com

---

[3] Ibid.

BARGAINING POWER OF SUPPLIERS

If suppliers have enough leverage over industry firms, they can raise prices high enough to significantly influence the profitability of the industry. Several factors influence supplier bargaining power:

1. Suppliers will have the advantage if they are large and relatively few in number.
2. When the suppliers' products or services are important inputs to user firms, are highly differentiated, or carry switching costs, the suppliers will have considerable leverage over buyers.
3. Suppliers will also enjoy bargaining power if their business is not threatened by alternative products.
4. The willingness and ability of suppliers to develop their own products and brand names if they are unable to get satisfactory terms from industry buyers will influence their power.

A good example of the bargaining power of suppliers is OPEC, which controls the price of oil. In the 1970s and again in 2000, gasoline prices were significantly raised. At one point in time gasoline prices at the pumps had increased about 33 percent in six months. Since there is no alternative, customers are forced to pay the higher prices.

BARGAINING POWER OF BUYERS

The ultimate aim of industrial customers is to pay the lowest possible price to obtain the products or services that they use as inputs. Usually, therefore, the buyers' best interests are served if they can drive down profitability in the supplier industry. The following are conditions under which buyers can exert power over suppliers:

1. When they purchase in such large quantities that supplier firms depend on the buyers' business for survival.
2. When the supplier's products are viewed as commodities—that is, as standard or undifferentiated—buyers are likely to bargain hard for low prices because many supplier firms can meet their needs.
3. When the supplier industry's products or services represent a significant portion of the buying firms' costs.
4. When the buyer is willing to achieve backward vertical integration.

RIVALRY AMONG COMPETITORS

Rivalry among firms refers to all the actions taken by firms in the industry to improve their positions and gain advantage over each other. Rivalry manifests itself in price competition, advertising battles, product positioning, and attempts at differentiation. To the extent that rivalry among firms forces companies to innovate and/or rationalize costs, it can be a positive force. To the extent that it drives down prices and, therefore, profitability, it creates instability and negatively influences the attractiveness of the industry. Several factors can create intense rivalry:

1. Once an industry becomes mature, firms focus on market share and how it can be gained at the expense of others.
2. Industries characterized by high fixed costs are always under pressure to keep production at full capacity to cover the fixed costs. Once the industry accumulates excess capacity, the drive to fill capacity will push prices—and profitability—down.

3. A lack of differentiation or an absence of switching costs encourages buyers to treat the products or services as commodities and shop for the best prices. Again, there is downward pressure on prices and profitability.

4. Firms with high strategic stakes in achieving success in an industry generally are destabilizing because they may be willing to accept unreasonably low profit margins to establish themselves, hold position, or expand.

◆ GLOBAL COMPETITION AND NATIONAL COMPETITIVE ADVANTAGE[4]

An inevitable consequence of the expansion of global marketing activity is the growth of competition on a global basis. In industry after industry, global competition is a critical factor affecting success. In some industries, global companies have virtually excluded all other companies from their markets. An example is the detergent industry, in which three companies—Colgate, Unilever, and Procter & Gamble (P&G)—dominate an increasing number of detergent markets worldwide, including Latin America and the Pacific Rim. Because many companies can make a quality detergent, global brand-name muscle and marketing skills have become the sources of global competitive advantage that overwhelm local competition in market after market.[5]

Based on recent changes in the way business is done around the world, Michael Porter urges global companies not to lose sight of "local things—knowledge, relationships and motivation that distant rivals cannot match."[6] (See discussion under "Related and Supporting Industries" later in this chapter.)

The automobile industry has also become fiercely competitive on a global basis. Part of the reason for the initial success of foreign automakers in the United States was the reluctance or inability of U.S. manufacturers to design and manufacture high-quality, inexpensive small cars. The resistance of U.S. manufacturers was based on the economics of car production: the bigger the car, the higher the list price. Under this formula, small cars meant smaller unit profits. Therefore, U.S. manufacturers resisted the growing preference of U.S. customers for smaller cars—a classic case of ethnocentrism and marketing myopia. Meanwhile, European and Japanese manufacturers' product lines have always included cars smaller than those made in the United States. In Europe and Japan, market conditions were much different than in America: less space, high taxes on engine displacement and on fuel, and greater market interest in functional design and engineering innovations. First Volkswagen and then Japanese automakers such as Nissan and Toyota discovered a growing demand for their cars in the U.S. market. It is noteworthy that many significant innovations and technical advances—including radial tires, antilock brakes, and fuel injection—also came from Europe and Japan. Airbags are a notable exception.

Another major innovation in the auto industry, which has since spread to all industries, is the revolutionary innovation of lean manufacturing first introduced at Toyota. This radically different way of designing and building an automobile dramatically reduced costs and increased quality. Lean manufacturing was invented in Japan and gave the Japanese automobile companies a knockout advantage in world markets: lower costs and higher quality. Indeed, lean manufacturing has replaced mass production in the same way that mass production replaced craft production, and for the same reasons: It

---

[4] This section draws heavily on Michael E. Porter, *The Competitive Advantage of Nations* (New York: Free Press, 1990), Chaps. 3 and 4, pp. 179–273.

[5] See Joseph Kahn, "Cleaning Up: P&G Viewed China as a National Market and Is Conquering It," *The Wall Street Journal,* 12 September 1995, pp. A1, A6.

[6] Michael E. Porter, "Cluster and the New Economics of Competition," *Harvard Business Review, 76,* no. 6 (November–December 1998): 77–90.

raised the bar on quality and dramatically reduced costs. Today, companies that have not mastered the art and science of lean manufacturing are no longer in the auto business.

The effect of global competition has been highly beneficial to consumers around the world. In the two examples cited—detergents and automobiles—consumers have benefited. In Central America, detergent prices have fallen and quality has risen as a result of global competition. In the United States, for example, foreign companies have provided consumers with the automobile products, performance, and price characteristics they wanted. If smaller, lower-priced imported cars had not been available, it is unlikely that Detroit manufacturers would have provided a comparable product as quickly. What is true for automobiles in the United States is true for every product class around the world. Global competition expands the range of products and increases the likelihood that consumers will get what they want.

The downside of global competition is its impact on the producers of goods and services. When a company offers consumers in other countries a better product at a lower price, this company takes customers away from domestic suppliers. Unless the domestic supplier can create new values and find new customers, the jobs and livelihoods of the domestic supplier's employees are threatened. The social effects of these influences often prompt political responses that destabilize the business environment. Both business and government policy makers are trying to better understand the factors that make a specific nation a better (or worse) place for a company in a specific industry. Businesses want to understand how to choose locations for their activities that give them a competitive advantage. Governments want to know whether they should intervene in the business environment and, if so, how.

The following section addresses a number of questions. Why is a particular nation a good home base for specific industries? Why, for example, is the United States the home base for the leading competitors in PCs, software, credit cards, and movies? Why is Germany the home of so many world leaders in printing presses, chemicals, and luxury cars? Why are so many leading pharmaceutical, chocolate/confectionery, and trading companies located in Switzerland? Why are the world leaders in consumer electronics home based in Japan?

According to Michael E. Porter, the presence or absence of particular attributes in individual countries influences industry development. Porter describes these attributes—factor conditions, demand conditions, related and supporting industry, and firm structure and rivalry—in terms of a national diamond (see Figure 10-2). The diamond shapes the environment in which firms compete in their global industries.

FACTOR CONDITIONS

The phrase *factor conditions* refers to a country's endowment of resources. Factor resources may have been created or inherited and are divided into five categories: human, physical, knowledge, capital, and infrastructure.

Human Resources

The quantity of workers available, the skills possessed by these workers, wage levels, and the overall work ethic of the workforce together constitute a nation's human resource factors. Countries with a plentiful supply of low-wage labor have an obvious advantage in the current production of labor-intensive products; however, in most manufacturing industries of the developed world, the cost of manual labor is rapidly becoming a smaller and smaller factor. Presently, labor averages about one eighth or less of total costs.[7] Any cost advantage will disappear if wages increase and production moves to

---

[7] Peter F. Drucker, *Management Challenges for the 21st Century* (New York: HarperBusiness, 1999): 99.

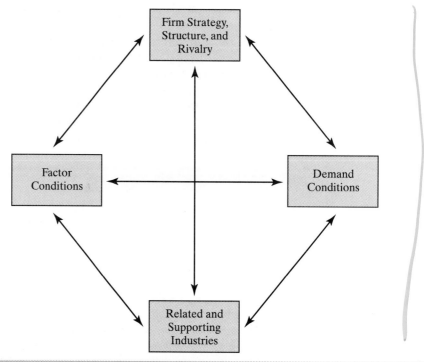

FIGURE 10-2 Determinants of National Advantage

Source: Michael E. Porter, *The Competitive Advantage of Nations* (New York: Free Press, 1990), p. 72. Copyright © 1990, 1998 by Michael E. Porter. Reprinted with permission of The Free Press, a division of Simon & Schuster.

another country. However, low-wage countries may be at a disadvantage when it comes to the production of sophisticated products requiring highly skilled workers capable of working without extensive supervision.

Physical Resources
The availability, quantity, quality, and cost of land, water, minerals, and other natural resources determine a country's physical resources. A country's size and location are also included in this category because proximity to markets and sources of supply, as well as transportation costs, are strategic considerations. These factors are obviously important advantages or disadvantages to industries dependent on natural resources.

Knowledge Resources
The availability within a nation of a significant population with scientific, technical, and market-related knowledge means a nation is endowed with knowledge resources. The presence of these factors is usually a function of the educational orientation of the society as well as the number of research facilities and universities—both government and private—operating in the country. These factors are important to success in sophisticated products and services and to doing business in sophisticated markets. This factor relates directly to Germany's leadership in chemicals; for some 150 years, Germany has been home to top university chemistry programs, advanced scientific journals, and apprenticeship programs.

Capital Resources
Countries vary in the availability, amount, cost, and types of capital available to the country's industries. The nation's savings rate, interest rates, tax laws, and government

deficits all affect the availability of capital. The advantage to industries with low capital costs versus those located in nations with relatively high costs is sometimes decisive. Firms paying high capital costs are frequently unable to stay in a market in which the competition comes from a nation with low capital costs. The firms with the low cost of capital can keep their prices low and force the firms paying high costs to either accept low returns on investment or leave the industry. The globalization of world capital markets is changing the manner in which capital is deployed. Investors can now send their capital to nations or markets with the best risk/return profile. Global firms will increasingly be following capital to the best places rather than operating in nations where capital is scarce or expensive.

Infrastructure Resources

Infrastructure includes a nation's banking system, health care system, transportation system, and communications system, as well as the availability and cost of using these systems. More sophisticated industries are more dependent on advanced infrastructures for success.

BASIC VERSUS ADVANCED FACTORS

Factors can be further classified as either basic factors, such as natural resources and labor, or advanced factors, such as highly educated personnel and modern data communications infrastructure. Basic factors do not lead to sustainable international competitive advantage. For example, cheap labor is a transient national advantage that erodes as a nation's economy improves and average national income increases relative to other countries. Advanced factors, which lead to sustainable competitive advantage, are scarcer and require sustained investment. For example, the existence of a labor force of trained artisans offers Italy a basis of sustained competitive advantage in the Italian tile industry.

GENERALIZED VERSUS SPECIALIZED FACTORS

Another categorization of factors differentiates between generalized factors, such as a suitable highway system, and specialized factors, such as focused educational systems. Generalized factors are precedents required for competitive advantage; however, sustainable advantage requires the development of specialized factors. For example, the competitive advantage of the Japanese robotics industry is fueled by extensive university robotics courses and programs that graduate robotics skilled trainees of the highest caliber.

Competitive advantage may also be created indirectly by nations that have selective factor disadvantages. For example, the absence of suitable labor may force firms to develop forms of mechanization that give the nation's firms an advantage. Scarcity of raw materials may motivate firms to develop new materials. For example, Japan, faced with scarce raw materials, developed an industrial ceramics industry that leads the world in innovation.

DEMAND CONDITIONS

The nature of home-market demand conditions for the firm's or industry's products and services is important because it determines the rate and nature of improvement and innovation by the firms in the nation. These are the factors that either train firms for world-class competition or fail to adequately prepare them to compete in the global marketplace. Three characteristics of home demand are particularly important to the creation of competitive advantage: (1) the composition of home demand, (2) the size and pattern of growth of home demand, and (3) the means by which a nation's home demand pulls the nation's products and services into foreign markets.

The composition of home demand determines how firms perceive, interpret, and respond to buyer needs. Competitive advantage can be achieved when the home demand sets the quality standard and gives local firms a better picture of buyer needs, at an earlier time, than is available to foreign rivals. This advantage is enhanced when home buyers pressure the nation's firms to innovate quickly and frequently. The basis for advantage is the fact that the nation's firms can stay ahead of the market when firms are more sensitive to and more responsive to home demand and when that demand, in turn, reflects or anticipates world demand.

The size and pattern of growth of home demand are important only if the composition of the home demand is sophisticated and anticipates foreign demand. Large home markets offer opportunities to achieve economies of scale and learning while dealing with familiar, comfortable markets. There is less apprehension about investing in large-scale production facilities and expensive R&D programs when the home market is sufficient to absorb the increased capacity. If the home demand accurately reflects or anticipates foreign demand, and if the firms do not become content with serving the home market, the existence of large-scale facilities and programs will be an advantage in global competition.

Rapid home-market growth is another incentive to invest in and adopt new technologies faster, and to build large, efficient facilities. The best example of this is Japan, where rapid home-market growth provided the incentive for Japanese firms to invest heavily in modern, automated facilities. Early home demand, especially if it anticipates international demand, gives local firms the advantage of getting established in an industry sooner than foreign rivals. Equally important is early market saturation, which puts pressure on a company to expand into international markets and innovate. Market saturation is especially important if it coincides with rapid growth in foreign markets.

The means by which a nation's products and services are pushed or pulled into foreign countries is the third aspect of demand conditions. The issue here is whether a nation's people and businesses go abroad and then demand the nation's products and services in those second countries. For example, when the U.S. auto companies set up operations in foreign countries, the U.S. auto parts industry followed. The same is true for the Japanese auto industry. When the Japanese auto companies set up operations in the United States, Japanese parts suppliers followed their customers. Similarly, when overseas demand for the services of U.S. engineering firms skyrocketed after World War II, those firms in turn established demand for U.S. heavy construction equipment. This provided an impetus for Caterpillar to establish foreign operations.

A related issue is whether foreigners come to a nation for training, pleasure, business, or research. After returning home, they are likely to demand the products and services with which they became familiar while abroad. Similar effects can result from professional, scientific, and political relationships between nations. Those involved in the relationships begin to demand the products and services of the recognized leaders.

It is the interplay of demand conditions that contributes to competitive advantage. Of special importance are those conditions that lead to initial and continuing incentives to invest and innovate and to continuing competition in increasingly sophisticated markets.

RELATED AND SUPPORTING INDUSTRIES

A nation has an advantage when it is home to internationally competitive industries in fields that are related to, or in direct support of, other industries. Internationally competitive supplier industries provide inputs to downstream industries that are likely to be internationally competitive in terms of technological innovation, price, and quality. Access is a function of proximity both in terms of physical distance and cultural similarity. It is not the inputs themselves that give advantage. It is the contact and coordination with the suppliers that allow the firm the opportunity to structure the value chain so that linkages with suppliers are optimized. These opportunities may not be available to foreign firms.

Similar advantages accrue when there are internationally competitive and related industries in a nation that coordinate and share value chain activities. These centers of competitive advantage are known as *clusters*. Clusters are geographic concentrations of interconnected companies and institutions in a particular field, which constitute a critical mass. Opportunities for sharing between computer hardware manufacturers and software developers provide a clear example of clusters. Related industries also create pull-through opportunities as described earlier. Sales of U.S. computers abroad have created demand for software from Microsoft and other U.S. companies. Porter notes that the development of the Swiss pharmaceuticals industry can be attributed in part to Switzerland's large synthetic dye industry; the discovery of the therapeutic effects of dyes in turn led to the development of pharmaceutical companies.[8]

Other clusters are the leather fashion in Italy, chemicals, home appliances and household furniture in Germany, wood products in Portugal, and flower growing in the Netherlands. Multinational companies such as Nestlé are incorporating this concept when establishing locations for their various businesses. They have relocated their headquarters for bottle water to France and moved the Rowntree Mackintosh confectionery division to York, England.

FIRM STRATEGY, STRUCTURE, AND RIVALRY

Differences in management styles, organizational skills, and strategic perspectives create advantages and disadvantages for firms competing in different types of industries, as do differences in the intensity of domestic rivalry. In Germany, for example, company structure and management style tend to be hierarchical. Managers tend to come from technical backgrounds and to be most successful when dealing with industries that demand highly disciplined structures, such as chemicals and precision machinery. Italian firms, however, tend to look like, and be run like, small family businesses that stress customized rather than standardized products, niche markets, and substantial flexibility in meeting market demands.

Capital markets and attitudes toward investments are important components of national environments. For example, the majority of shares of U.S. publicly held companies are owned by institutional investors such as mutual funds and pension plans. These investors will buy and sell shares to reduce risk and increase return rather than get involved in an individual company's operations. These very mobile investors drive managers to operate with a short-term focus on quarterly and annual results. This fluid capital market structure will provide funds for new growth industries and rapidly expanding markets in which there are expectations of early returns. On the other hand, U.S. capital markets do not encourage more mature industries in which return on investment is lower and patient searching for innovations is required. Many other countries have an opposite orientation. For example, in Japan, banks are allowed to take equity stakes in the companies to which they loan money and provide other profitable banking services. These banks take a longer-term view than stock markets and are less concerned about short-term results.

Perhaps the most powerful influence on competitive advantage comes from domestic rivalry. Domestic rivalry keeps an industry dynamic and creates continual pressure to improve and innovate. Local rivalry forces firms to develop new products, improve existing ones, lower costs and prices, develop new technologies, and improve quality and service. Rivalry with foreign firms lacks this intensity. Domestic rivals have to fight each

---

[8] Porter, "Clusters and the New Economics of Competition," pp. 77–90.

other not just for market share but also for employee talent, R&D breakthroughs, and prestige in the home market. Eventually, strong domestic rivalry will push firms to seek international markets to support expansions in scale and R&D investments, as Japan amply demonstrates. The absence of significant domestic rivalry will create complacency in the home firms and eventually cause them to become noncompetitive in the world markets.

It is not the number of domestic rivals that is important; rather, it is the intensity of the competition and the quality of the competitors that make the difference. It is also important that there be a fairly high rate of new business formations to create new competitors and safeguard against the older companies becoming comfortable with their market positions and products and services. As noted earlier in the discussion of the forces shaping industry competition, new entrants bring new perspectives and new methods. They frequently define and serve new market segments that established companies have failed to recognize.

There are two final external variables to consider in the evaluation of national competitive advantage: chance and government.

OTHER FORCES ACTING ON THE DIAMOND

Two additional elements of Porter's model to consider in the evaluation of national competitive advantage are chance and government. In addition, there are nonmarket forces that are part of the environment and that should be considered as an expansion of or supplement to government and chance.

Chance

Chance events play a role in shaping the competitive environment. Chance events are occurrences that are beyond the control of firms, industries, and usually governments. Included in this category are such things as wars and their aftermath, major technological breakthroughs, sudden dramatic shifts in factor or input cost (e.g., the oil crises), dramatic swings in exchange rates, and so on.

Chance events are important because they create major discontinuities in technologies that allow nations and firms that were not competitive to leapfrog over old competitors and become competitive—even leaders—in the changed industry. For example, the development of microelectronics allowed many Japanese firms to overtake American and German firms in industries that had been based on electromechanical technologies—areas traditionally dominated by the Americans and Germans.

From a systemic perspective, the role of chance events lies in the fact that they alter conditions in the diamond shown in Figure 10-2. The nation with the most favorable diamond, however, will be the one most likely to take advantage of these events and convert them into competitive advantage. For example, Canadian researchers were the first to isolate insulin, but they could not convert this breakthrough into an internationally competitive product. Firms in the United States and Denmark were able to do that because of their respective national diamonds.

Government

Although it is often argued that government is a major determinant of national competitive advantage, the fact is that government is not a determinant but rather an influence on determinants. Government influences determinants by virtue of its role as a buyer of products and services and by its role as a maker of policies on labor, education, capital formation, natural resources, and product standards. It also influences determinants by its role as a regulator of commerce, for example, by telling banks and telephone companies what they can and cannot do.

By reinforcing positive determinants of competitive advantage in an industry, government can improve the competitive position of the nation's firms. Governments devise legal systems that influence competitive advantage by means of tariff and non-tariff barriers and laws requiring local content and labor. The Yen's decline over the past decade was due in part to a deliberate policy to strengthen Japanese exports and stem imports. In other words, government can improve or lessen competitive advantage but cannot create it.

OTHER NONMARKET FACTORS

In addition to government and chance, there are other nonmarket forces that affect the strategy system. The nonmarket forces include, in addition to government, interest groups, activists, and the public. These nonmarket forces are part of a noneconomic strategy system that operates on the basis of social, political, and legal forces that interact in the nonmarket environment of the firm.[9] An understanding of these forces is especially complicated and critical to the success of global strategies that are implemented in many different countries and cultures. The nonmarket environment differs from the market environment in many ways. For example, the market environment is principally one involving economic exchange, whereas the nonmarket environment includes regulatory bodies, interest groups, and others whose interest may not be driven by economic motives and often involve political motives. For example, in some countries, environmental groups have promoted regulations that dramatically increase capital and operating costs for businesses that operate manufacturing plants. In the pharmaceutical industry, religious groups have impeded progress in genetic research. Competing companies operating in different national or geographic markets that do not have these limitations or costs have a competitive advantage.

The System of Determinants

It is important to view the determinants of national competitive advantage as an interactive system in which activity in any one of the four points of the diamond impacts on all the others and vice versa. This interplay between the determinants is depicted in Figure 10-3. The interaction of all of the forces is presented in Figure 10-4.

SINGLE OR DOUBLE DIAMOND?

Other researchers have challenged Porter's thesis that a firm's home-base country is the main source of core competencies and innovation. For example, Professor Alan Rugman of the University of Toronto argues that the success of companies based in small economies such as Canada and New Zealand stems from the diamonds found in a particular host country or countries. For example, a company based in a European Union (EU) nation may rely on the national diamond of one of the 14 other EU members. Similarly, one impact of the North American Free Trade Agreement (NAFTA) on Canadian firms is to make the U.S. diamond relevant to competency creation. Rugman argues that, in such cases, the distinction between the home nation and host nation becomes blurred. He proposes that Canadian managers must look to a double diamond depicted in Figure 10-5 and assess the attributes of both Canada and the United States when formulating corporate strategy.[10]

---

[9] David P. Baron, "The Nonmarket Strategy System," *Sloan Management Review,* 37, no. 1 (Fall 1995): 73–85.
[10] See Alan M. Rugman and Alain Verbeke, "Foreign Subsidiaries and Multinational Strategic Management: An Extension and Correction of Porter's Single Diamond Framework," *Management International Review,* 33, no. 2 (Special Issue 1993): 71–84.

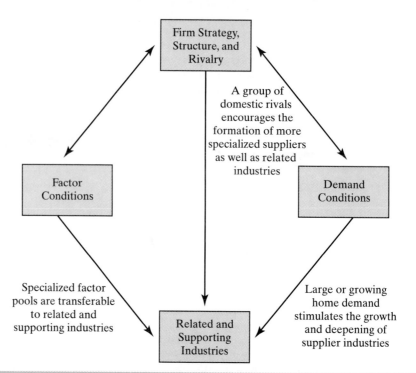

FIGURE 10-3   Influences on the Development of Related and Supporting Industries

Source: Michael E. Porter, *The Competitive Advantage of Nations* (New York: Free Press, 1990), p. 139. Copyright © 1990, 1998 by Michael E. Porter. Reprinted with permission of The Free Press, a division of Simon & Schuster.

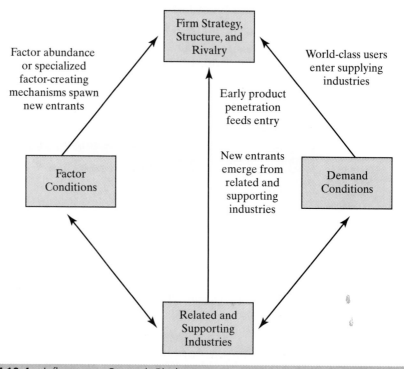

FIGURE 10-4   Influences on Domestic Rivalry

Source: Michael E. Porter, *The Competitive Advantage of Nations* (New York: Free Press, 1990), p. 141. Copyright © 1990, 1998 by Michael E. Porter. Reprinted with permission of The Free Press, a division of Simon & Schuster.

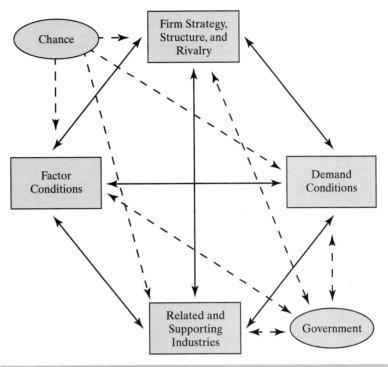

FIGURE 10-5   The Complete System

Source: Michael E. Porter, *The Competitive Advantage of Nations* (New York: Free Press, 1990), p. 127.
Copyright © 1990, 1998 by Michael E. Porter. Reprinted with permission of The Free Press, a division
of Simon & Schuster.

◆ COMPETITIVE ADVANTAGE AND STRATEGIC MODELS

Strategy is integrated action in pursuit of competitive advantage.[11] Successful strategy
requires an understanding of the unique value that will be the source of the firm's competitive advantage. Firms ultimately succeed because of their ability to carry out specific activities or groups of activities better than their competitors. These activities
enable the firm to create unique value for their customers. It is this value that is central
to achieving and sustaining competitive advantage. This unique value must be something
that competitors will not be able to easily match. The uniqueness and magnitude of the
customer value created by a firm's strategy are ultimately determined by customer perception. Operating results such as sales and profits are measures that depend on the
level of psychological value created for customers: the greater the perceived consumer
value, the stronger the competitive advantage, and the better the strategy. A firm may
market a better mousetrap, but the ultimate success of the product depends on customers deciding for themselves whether to buy it. Value is like beauty—it is in the eye
of the beholder. In sum, competitive advantage is achieved by creating more value than
the competition, and value is defined by customer perception.

Two different models of competitive advantage have received considerable attention.
The first offers generic strategies, which are four alternative positions that organizations
can seek in order to offer superior value and achieve competitive advantage. According
to the second model, the generic strategies alone do not explain the astonishing success

[11] See George Day, *Market Driven Strategy: Processes for Creating Value* (New York: Free Press, 1990).

IKEA COST FOCUSED

IKEA, the Swedish furniture company described in the chapter introduction, is an example of the cost focus strategy. Notes George Bradley, president of Levitz Furniture in Boca Raton, Florida, "[IKEA] has really made a splash. They're going to capture their niche in every city they go into." Of course, such a strategy can be risky. As Bradley explains, "Their market is finite because it is so narrow. If you don't want contemporary, knock-down furniture, it's not for you. So it takes a certain customer to buy it. And remember, fashions change." The issue of sustainability is central to this strategy concept. As noted, cost leadership is a sustainable source of competitive advantage only if barriers exist that prevent competitors from achieving the same low costs. Sustained differentiation depends on continued perceived value and the absence of imitation by competitors. Several factors determine whether focus can be sustained as a source of competitive advantage. First, a cost focus is sustainable if a firm's competitors are defining their target markets more broadly. A focuser does not try to be all things to all people: Competitors may diminish their advantage by trying to satisfy the needs of a broader market segment—a strategy that, by definition, means a blunter focus. Second, a firm's differentiation focus advantage is sustainable only if competitors cannot define the segment even more narrowly. Also, focus can be sustained if competitors cannot overcome barriers that prevent imitation of the focus strategy, and if consumers in the target segment do not migrate to other segments that the focuser does not serve.

IKEA's approach to the furniture business has enabled it to rack up impressive growth in an industry in which overall sales have been flat. Sourcing furniture from more than 2,330 suppliers in 64 countries helps the company maintain its low-cost position.

IKEA's international growth has been quite successful but probably would not have been possible if the company had gone public according to its founder, Ingvar Kamprad. He does not feel a need to show constant profits and, therefore, can take more investment risks. During the 1990s, IKEA opened several stores in Central and Eastern Europe (Poland is one of its fastest-growing markets) and has since expanded into Russia where it plans to open a total of 10 outlets. Because many consumers in those regions have relatively low purchasing power, the stores offer a smaller selection of goods; some furniture was designed specifically for the cramped living styles typical in former Soviet bloc countries. Kamprad firmly believes in long-term investment and states: "It will take twenty-five years to furnish Russia." He believes that investment in Russia would not have been possible if the company had been a public company, which often suffers from a need to show short-term profits. Throughout Europe, IKEA benefits from the perception that Sweden is the source of high-quality products. The United Kingdom represents the fastest-growing market in Europe; IKEA's London store has achieved annual sales growth of 20 percent. Germany currently accounts for more than one quarter

of many Japanese companies in recent years. A more recent model, based on the concept of strategic intent, proposes four different sources of competitive advantage. Both models are discussed next.

GENERIC STRATEGIES FOR CREATING COMPETITIVE ADVANTAGE

In addition to the five forces model of industry competition, Porter developed a framework of so-called generic business strategies based on two sources of competitive advantage: low cost and differentiation. Figure 10-6 shows that the combination of these two sources with the scope of the target market served (narrow or broad) or product mix width (narrow or wide) yields four generic strategies: cost leadership, product differentiation, focused differentiation, and cost focus.

Generic strategies aiming at the achievement of competitive advantage demand that the firm make choices. The choices are the position it seeks to attain from which to offer unique value (based on cost or differentiation) and the market scope or product mix width within which competitive advantage will be attained.[12] The nature of the

---

[12] Porter, *The Competitive Advantage of Nations*, p. 12.

of IKEA's total revenues. IKEA has also opened two stores in China but is having difficulty securing local suppliers and positioning for one store that is located in a shopping mall.

Industry observers predict the United States will eventually be IKEA's largest market (presently it accounts for 15 percent of IKEA's volume). The company opened its first U.S. store in Philadelphia in 1985; today, IKEA has 14 outlets in major metropolitan areas. Notes Jeff Young, chief operating officer of Lexington Furniture Industries, "IKEA is on the way to becoming the Wal-Mart stores of the home-furnishing industry. If you're in this business, you'd better take a look." Some American customers, however, are irked to find popular items are sometimes out of stock. Another problem is the long lines resulting from the company's no-frills approach. Complained one shopper, "Great idea, poor execution. The quality of much of what they sell is good, but the hassles make you question whether it's worth it."

Goran Carstedt, president of IKEA North America, responds to such criticism by referring to the company's mission. "If we offered more services, our prices would go up," he explains. "Our customers understand our philosophy, which calls for each of us to do a little in order to save a lot. They value our low prices. And almost all of them say they will come back again." To keep them coming back, IKEA is spending between $25 million and $35 million on advertising to get its message across. Although it is a common industry practice to rely heavily on newspaper and radio advertising, two thirds of IKEA's North American advertising budget is allocated for TV. John Sitnik, an executive at IKEA's U.S. Inc., says, "We distanced ourselves from the other furniture stores. We decided TV is something we can own."

For more information,

> **VISIT THE WEB SITE**
> www.Ikea.com

SOURCES: Tim Burt, "Ikea Chief Breaks Silence to Tell Home Truths," *The Financial Times,* 18 August 1998, p. 17; Tim Burt, "Ikea's Expansion Includes Move into Russia," *The Financial Times,* 22 July 1998, p. 16; George Nichols, "Ikea Will Never Be Listed," *The Financial Times,* 23 March 1999, p. 29; Loretta Roach, "IKEA: Furnishing the World," *Discount Merchandiser* (October 1994): 46, 48; "Furnishing the World," *The Economist,* 19 November 1994, pp. 79–80; Jack Burton, "Rearranging the Furniture," *International Management* (September 1991): 58–61; Ela Schwartz, "The Swedish Invasion," *Discount Merchandiser* (July 1990): 52, 56; Lisa Marie Petersen, "The 1992 Client Media All-Stars: John Sitnik, IKEA," *Mediaweek,* 12 December 1992, p. 25; Michael E. Porter, *The Competitive Advantage of Nations* (New York: Free Press, 1990), p. 158.

choice between positions and market scope is a gamble and involves risk. By choosing a given generic strategy, a firm always risks making the wrong choice.

BROAD MARKET STRATEGIES

Cost-Leadership Advantage

When the unique value delivered by a firm is based on its position as the industry's low-cost producer, in broadly defined markets or across a wide mix of products, a cost-leadership advantage occurs. This strategy has become increasingly popular in recent years as a result of the popularization of the experience curve concept. A firm that bases its competitive strategy on overall cost leadership must construct the most efficient facilities (in terms of scale or technology) and obtain the largest share of market so that its cost per unit is the lowest in the industry. These advantages, in turn, give the producer a substantial lead in terms of experience with building the product. Experience then leads to more refinements of the entire process of production, delivery, and service, which lead to further cost reductions.

Whatever its source, cost-leadership advantage can be the basis for offering lower prices (and more value) to customers in the late, more competitive stages of the product

Competitive Scope	Lower Cost	Differentiation
Broad Target	Cost Leadership	Differentiation
Narrow Target	Cost Focus	Focused Differentiation
	Competitive Advantage	

FIGURE 10-6 Generic Competitive Strategies

Source: Michael E. Porter, *The Competitive Advantage of Nations* (New York: Free Press, 1990), p. 39. Copyright © 1990, 1998 by Michael E. Porter. Reprinted with permission of The Free Press, a division of Simon & Schuster Inc.

life cycle. In Japan, companies in a range of industries—35 mm cameras, consumer electronics and entertainment equipment, motorcycles, and automobiles—have achieved cost leadership on a worldwide basis. Cost leadership, however, is a sustainable source of competitive advantage only if barriers exist that prevent competitors from achieving the same low costs. In an era of process reengineering and increasing technological improvements in manufacturing, manufacturers constantly leapfrog over one another in pursuit of lower costs. At one time, for example, IBM enjoyed the low-cost advantage in the production of computer printers. Then the Japanese took the same technology and, after reducing production costs and improving product reliability, gained the low-cost advantage. IBM fought back with a highly automated printer plant in North Carolina, where the number of component parts was slashed by more than 50 percent and robots were used to snap many components into place. Despite these changes, IBM ultimately chose to exit the business and the plant was sold.

Differentiation

When a firm's product delivers unique value because of an actual or perceived uniqueness in a broad market, it is said to have a differentiation advantage. This can be an extremely effective strategy for defending market position and obtaining above-average financial returns; unique products often command premium price. Examples of successful differentiation include Maytag in large home appliances, Nike in athletic shoes, and almost any successful branded consumer product. Among motorcycle manufacturers, Harley-Davidson stands out as the market leader in the U.S. market but must adjust its marketing strategy in various countries depending on the local competition. Figure 10-7 shows Harley-Davidson's market share in its three geographical divisions.

NARROW TARGET STRATEGIES

The preceding discussion of cost leadership and differentiation considered only the impact on broad markets. By contrast, strategies to achieve a narrow-focus advantage target a narrowly defined market or customer. This advantage is based on an ability to create more customer value for a narrowly targeted segment and results from a better understanding of customer needs and wants. A narrow-focus strategy can be combined with either cost- or differentiation-advantage strategies. In other words, whereas cost focus means offering a narrow target market low prices, a firm pursuing focused differentiation will offer a narrow target market the perception of product uniqueness at a premium price.

North American 651 + cc Motorcycle Registrations
(Units in Thousands)

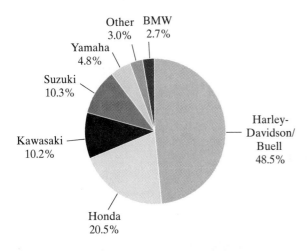

Asia/Pacific 651 + cc Motorcycle Registrations
(Units in Thousands)

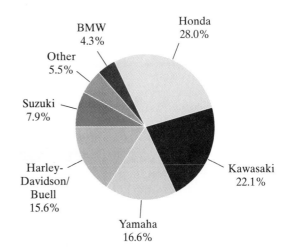

European 651 + cc Motorcycle Registrations
(Units in Thousands)

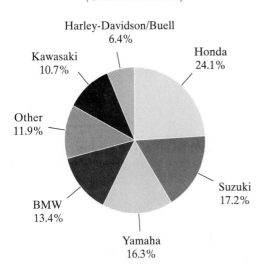

FIGURE 10-7   Harley-Davidson's Competitive Environment

Source: Harley-Davidson Annual Report.

Focused Differentiation

The German Mittelstand companies have been extremely successful pursuing focused differentiation strategies backed by a strong export effort. The world of high-end audio equipment offers another example of focused differentiation. A few hundred companies, in the United States and elsewhere, make speakers and amplifiers and related hi-fi gear that cost thousands of dollars per component. Although audio components as a whole represent a $21 billion market worldwide, annual sales in the high-end segment are only $1 billion. In Japan alone, discriminating audiophiles purchase $200 million in high-end audio equipment each year—much of it American made. Also, the American companies are learning more about their overseas customers and building relationships with distributors outside the United States.[13]

---

[13] Jared Sandberg, "High-End Audio Entices Music Lovers," *The Wall Street Journal,* 12 February 1993, p. B1.

Cost Focus

The final strategy is cost focus, when a firm's lower-cost position enables it to offer a narrow target market lower prices than the competition. In the shipbuilding industry, for example, Polish and Chinese shipyards offer simple, standard vessel types at low prices that reflect low production costs.[14]

◆ STRATEGIC POSITIONS

Strategic positions that provide competitive advantage are based on the activities that a firm chooses to perform and on where it chooses to perform them.[15] From these positions, a firm can deliver unique value to its customers. A position is based on a set of activities that combine to create unique value for a market. Porter has identified three classifications for strategic positions.[16] A firm may choose to develop one or a combination of these positions as the basis of its competitive advantage. The three positions and the related generic strategy are shown in Table 10-1.

VARIETY-BASED POSITIONING

Variety-based positioning is based on a firm's decision to carry out a limited number of activities related to delivering a limited product or service. This type of position is built by a firm, such as Southwest Airlines, that chooses to deliver value to its customers by limiting its product offering (point-to-point service, no baggage transfer service, no seat reservations, no meals, etc.) in order to minimize its prices and maximize its reliability and efficiency. Another example is GIVI, an Italian company that makes luggage for motorcycles. GIVI's product is unique in design, integration, and fabrication. It is premium priced, but given its unique design and quality, it is a value winner in the motorcycle luggage marketplace. The company is successfully expanding from its European variety-based position to a world variety-based position.

NEEDS-BASED POSITIONING

Needs-based positioning occurs when a company attempts to deliver value to a specific customer segment by carrying out activities to satisfy a comparatively broad set of needs

TABLE 10-1	Strategic Positions		
Position		**Examples**	**Generic Strategy**
1. Variety based		Vanguard	Cost leadership
Producing a subset of an		Bic	
industry's product or service		Jiffy Lube	
2. Customer needs based		Citibank	Differentiation
		Bessemer Trust	
		IKEA	
3. Customer access based		CARmike Cinemas	Segmentation
Segmenting customers who			
are accessible in different ways			

---

[14] Porter, *The Competitive Advantage of Nations*, p. 39.

[15] Not to be confused with positioning, marketing action which focuses on efforts to position a product or company in the minds of consumers and customers.

[16] Michael Porter, "What Is Strategy," *Harvard Business Review* (November–December 1996): 65–67.

of these customers. This position is well developed by firms such as IKEA, which offers everything the young (or young at heart), budget-conscious consumer might need to furnish an apartment or home. Another example of a company with a clear positioning strategy is Purdue Pharma, the world leader in narcotic analgesics for severe pain. Purdue has focused on a need, alleviation of pain, and developed an integrated program for addressing this need. It has developed products that offer more relief with fewer side effects. In addition to focusing on the need, Purdue has created the world's best-trained field sales force to call on doctors to answer their questions on how to effectively use Purdue's products. It has also been able to get its products listed on the formulary of hospitals and managed care organizations and government agencies. All of these activities are driven by the company's focus on the need to alleviate pain.

ACCESS-BASED POSITIONING

The ability of a firm to uniquely or preferentially reach a specific market is an access-based position. For example, international management recruitment firms, such as Korn Ferry International, establish relationships with executives and track them throughout their careers. They know where these executives are located and help their clients get to them. Access consideration can be a critical knockout factor. The first level of all international expansion is about access. Global marketing strategy must deal with barriers to access to national markets that are typically created by governmental authorities. Access to national markets is restricted by regulations, tariffs, distance, and a host of nontariff barriers, which include ways of doing business and openness to new entrants. As a prerequisite to international expansion, firms must develop the ability to carry out the activities that deal with these barriers to access. However, developing the ability to operate in many national markets does not necessarily confer global competitive advantage on a firm. This is not the same as access-based positioning, which refers to the advantage that can be gained by preferential access or control of access to customers. In order to gain competitive advantage in the target market, the entrant must establish a perceived unique value to its customers. If other competitors can gain access or are already established in the market, it is not enough to merely be present in a market. The annals of international business failures are replete with examples of companies that did not understand this message. They believed that all they needed to do was to show up. When the market told them that they had a competitive disadvantage, they simply packed up and retreated. Renault did this in the U.S. automobile market in the 1960s, and Federal Express did it again in the express delivery market in Europe in the 1980s. FedEx has regrouped and restrategized its European entry, whereas Renault's setback in the United States sent it back to Europe, where its position today was as a regional player in a global industry. It has never attempted to reenter the U.S. market, but with its operations in Brazil and its control of Nissan, it is today a global player in a global industry.

WHICH POSITION TO TAKE?

All real strategies are a combination of all three positions: Every winning strategy is based on a combination of doing the right thing (activity based), meeting a need (needs based), and on access. Nevertheless, it is valuable and useful to identify the principal thrust of a strategy: activity, need, or access. Company winners are ones that have established a strategic position that focuses on the decisive point and is, at the same time, everywhere very strong. This is the von Clausewitz maximum: The best strategy is to be very strong, first generally, and then at the decisive point.

◆ COMPETITIVE INNOVATION AND STRATEGIC INTENT

An alternative framework for understanding competitive advantage focuses on competitiveness as a function of the pace at which a company implants new advantages deep within its organization. This framework identifies strategic intent, growing out of ambition and obsession with winning, as the means for achieving competitive advantage. Writing in the *Harvard Business Review,* Hamel and Prahalad note:

> Few competitive advantages are long lasting. Keeping score of existing advantages is not the same as building new advantages. The essence of strategy lies in creating tomorrow's competitive advantages faster than competitors mimic the ones you possess today. An organization's capacity to improve existing skills and learn new ones is the most defensible competitive advantage of all.[17]

This approach is founded on the principles of W. E. Deming, who stressed that a company must commit itself to continuing improvement in order to be a winner in a competitive struggle. For years, Deming's message fell on deaf ears in the United States, whereas the Japanese heeded his message and benefited tremendously. Japan's most prestigious business award is named after him. Finally, however, U.S. manufacturers are starting to respond.

The significance of Hamel and Prahalad's framework becomes evident when comparing Caterpillar and Komatsu. As noted earlier, Caterpillar is a classic example of differentiation: The company became the largest manufacturer of earth-moving equipment in the world because it was fanatic about quality and service. Caterpillar's success as a global marketer has enabled it to achieve a 35 percent share of the worldwide market for earth-moving equipment, more than half of which represents sales to developing countries. The differentiation advantage was achieved with product durability, global spare parts service (including guaranteed parts delivery anywhere in the world within 48 hours), and a strong network of loyal dealers.

Caterpillar has faced a very challenging set of environmental forces. Many of Caterpillar's plants were closed by a lengthy strike in the early 1980s; a worldwide recession at the same time caused a downturn in the construction industry. This hurt companies that were Caterpillar customers. In addition, the strong dollar gave a cost advantage to foreign rivals.

Compounding Caterpillar's problems was a new competitive threat from Japan. Komatsu was the world's number-two construction equipment company and had been competing with Caterpillar in the Japanese market for years. Komatsu's products were generally acknowledged to offer a lower level of quality. The rivalry took on a new dimension after Komatsu adopted the slogan *Maru-c,* meaning "encircle Caterpillar." Emphasizing quality and taking advantage of low labor costs and the strong dollar, Komatsu surpassed Caterpillar in earth-moving equipment sales in Japan and made serious inroads in the United States and other markets. Yet, the company continued to develop new sources of competitive advantage even after it achieved world-class quality. For example, new-product development cycles were shortened, and manufacturing was rationalized. Caterpillar struggled to sustain its competitive advantage because many customers found that Komatsu's combination of quality, durability, and lower price created compelling value. Yet even as recession and a strong yen put new pres-

---

[17] Gary Hamel and C. K. Prahalad, "Strategic Intent," *Harvard Business Review* (May–June 1989): 69. See also Gary Hamel and C. K. Prahalad, "The Core Competence of the Corporation," *Harvard Business Review* (May–June 1990): 79–91.

sure on Komatsu, the company sought new opportunities by diversifying into machine tools and robots.[18]

The Komatsu/Caterpillar saga is just one example of how global competitive battles are shaped by more than the pursuit of generic strategies. Many firms have gained competitive advantage by disadvantaging rivals through competitive innovation, defined by Hamel and Prahalad as "the art of containing competitive risks within manageable proportions." They identify four successful approaches utilized by Japanese competitors: building layers of advantage, searching for loose bricks, changing the rules of engagement, and collaborating.

LAYERS OF ADVANTAGE

A company faces less risk in competitive encounters if it has a wide portfolio of advantages. Successful companies steadily build such portfolios by establishing layers of advantage on top of one another. Komatsu is an excellent example of this approach. Another is the TV industry in Japan. By 1970, Japan was not only the world's largest producer of black-and-white TV sets but was also well on its way to becoming the leader in producing color sets. The main competitive advantage for such companies as Matsushita at that time was low labor costs.

Because they realized that their cost advantage could be temporary, the Japanese also added additional layers of quality and reliability advantages by building plants large enough to serve world markets. Much of this output did not carry the manufacturer's brand name. For example, Matsushita Electric sold products to other companies such as RCA that marketed them under their own brand names. Matsushita was pursuing a simple idea: A product sold was a product sold, no matter whose label it carried.[19]

In order to build the next layer of advantage, the Japanese spent the 1970s investing heavily in marketing channels and Japanese brand names to gain recognition. This strategy added yet another layer of competitive advantage: the global brand franchise—that is, a global customer base. By the late 1970s, channels and brand awareness were established well enough to support the introduction of new products that could benefit from global marketing—videocassette recorders (VCRs) and photocopy machines, for example. Finally, many companies have invested in regional manufacturing so their products can be differentiated and better adapted to customer needs in individual markets.

The process of building layers illustrates how a company can move along the value chain to strengthen competitive advantage. The Japanese began with manufacturing (an upstream value activity) and moved on to marketing (a downstream value activity) and then back upstream to basic R&D. All of these sources of competitive advantage represent mutually desirable layers that are accumulated over time.

LOOSE BRICKS

A second approach takes advantage of the loose bricks left in the defensive walls of competitors whose attention is narrowly focused on a market segment or a geographic area. For example, Caterpillar's attention was focused elsewhere when Komatsu made its first entry into the Eastern European market. A similar chain of events occurred in the global motorcycle industry. For many years, Harley-Davidson focused its efforts on large motorcycles. Thus, it was not concerned when Honda first entered the U.S. motorcycle market with exports of bikes with small (50 cc) engines. Managers at Harley

---

[18] Robert L. Rose and Masayoshi Kanabayashi, "Komatsu Throttles Back on Construction Equipment," *The Wall Street Journal*, 13 May 1992, p. B4.

[19] James Lardner, *Fast Forward: Hollywood, The Japanese, and the VCR Wars* (New York: New American Library, 1987), p. 135.

were not aware of—or did not appreciate the significance of—Honda's involvement with racing larger bikes in Europe. But Honda used this approach to gain important experience in large-displacement engine design and technology. Harley was caught off guard, and by 1983, Honda had more than 50 percent of the U.S. market share in motorcycles with 700 cc engines or larger.

That same year, import quotas were imposed on large motorcycles imported into the United States. Even though the quotas helped save Harley from extinction, Honda was already using its core competence in engines to diversify. It created engines for other products, starting with cars. The first Honda Civic models were powered by overhead cam motorcycle engines. Today, Honda boasts a wide product mix that includes lawn mowers, outboard marine motors, welders, and generators—in short, anything powered by a gasoline engine. This approach, as noted earlier, allows Honda to enjoy significant scale economies in R&D and production. Harley-Davidson eventually reshaped itself by dramatically improving product quality and has successfully won back much of its lost market share.

CHANGING THE RULES

A third approach involves changing the so-called rules of engagement and refusing to play by the rules set by industry leaders. For example, in the copier market, IBM and Kodak imitated the marketing strategies used by market leader Xerox. Meanwhile, Canon, a Japanese challenger, wrote a new rule book.

Whereas Xerox built a wide range of copiers, Canon built standardized machines and components, reducing manufacturing costs. Whereas Xerox employed a huge direct sales force, Canon chose to distribute through office-product dealers. Canon also designed serviceability, as well as reliability, into its products so that it could rely on dealers for service rather than incurring the expense required to create a national service network. Canon further decided to sell rather than lease its machines, freeing the company from the burden of financing the lease base. In another major departure, Canon targeted its copiers at secretaries and department managers rather than at the heads of corporate duplicating operations.[20]

Canon introduced the first full-color copiers and the first copiers with connectivity—the ability to print images from such sources as video camcorders and computers. The results have been impressive; in 1994, Canon's share of the U.S. color copier market was 64 percent. In both 1988 and 1992, Canon was granted more U.S. patents than any other company in the world. The Canon example shows how an innovative marketing strategy—with fresh approaches to the product, pricing, distribution, and selling—can lead to overall competitive advantage in the marketplace.

COLLABORATING

A final source of competitive advantage is using know-how developed by other companies. Such collaboration may take the form of licensing agreements, joint ventures, and partnerships. History has shown that the Japanese have excelled at using the collaborating strategy to achieve industry leadership. One of the legendary licensing agreements of modern business history is Sony's licensing of transistor technology from AT&T's Western Electric subsidiary in the 1950s for $25,000. This agreement gave Sony access to the transistor and allowed the company to become a world leader. Building on its initial successes in the manufacturing and marketing of portable radios, Sony has grown into a superb global marketer whose name is synonymous with a wide assortment

---

[20] Hamel and Prahalad, "Strategic Intent," p. 69.

of high-quality consumer electronics products. More recent examples of Japanese collaboration are found in the aircraft industry. Today, Mitsubishi Heavy Industries Ltd. and other Japanese companies manufacture airplanes under license to American firms and also work as subcontractors for aircraft parts and systems. Many observers fear that the future of the American aircraft industry may be jeopardized as the Japanese gain technological expertise. Various examples of collaborative advantage are discussed in detail in the next section.

Hamel and Prahalad have continued to refine and develop the concept of strategic intent since it was first introduced in their groundbreaking 1989 article. Recently, the authors outlined five broad categories of resource leverage that managers can use to achieve their aspirations: concentrating resources on strategic goals via convergence and focus; accumulating resources more efficiently via extracting and borrowing; complementing one resource with another by blending and balancing; and conserving resources by recycling, co-opting, and shielding.[21]

HYPERCOMPETITION?

In his book, Professor Richard D'Aveni suggests that the Porter strategy frameworks fail to adequately address the dynamics of competition in the 21st century.[22] D'Aveni notes that, in today's business environment, market stability is undermined by short product life cycles, short product design cycles, new technologies, and globalization. The result is an escalation and acceleration of competitive forces. In light of these changes, D'Aveni believes the goal of strategy has shifted from sustaining to disrupting advantages. The limitation of the Porter models, D'Aveni argues, is that they provide a snapshot of competition at a given point in time. In other words, they are static models.

Acknowledging that Hamel and Prahalad broke new ground in recognizing that few advantages are sustainable, D'Aveni aims to build on their work to shape "a truly dynamic approach to the creation and destruction of traditional advantages." D'Aveni uses the term *hypercompetition* to describe a dynamic, competitive world in which no action or advantage can be sustained for long. In such a world, D'Aveni argues, everything changes because of the dynamic maneuvering and strategic interactions by hypercompetitive firms such as Microsoft and Gillette. According to D'Aveni's model, competition unfolds in a series of dynamic strategic interactions in four arenas: cost versus quality, timing and know-how, entry barriers, and deep pockets. Each of these arenas is "continuously destroyed and recreated by the dynamic maneuvering of hypercompetitive firms." According to D'Aveni, the only source of a truly sustainable competitive advantage is a company's ability to manage its dynamic strategic interactions with competitors' frequent movements that maintain a relative position of strength in each of the four arenas. The irony and paradox of this model is that, in order to achieve a sustainable advantage, companies must seek a series of unsustainable advantages! D'Aveni is in agreement with Peter Drucker, who has long counseled that the role of marketing is innovation and the creation of new markets. Innovation begins with abandonment of the old and obsolete. In Drucker's words, "Innovative organizations spend neither time nor resources on defending yesterday. Systematic abandonment of yesterday alone can transfer the resources . . . for work on the new."[23]

---

[21] Gary Hamel and C. K. Prahalad, "Strategy as Stretch and Leverage," *Harvard Business Review* (March–April 1993): 75–84.

[22] Richard D'Aveni, *Hypercompetition: Managing the Dynamics of Strategic Maneuvering* (New York: Free Press, 1994).

[23] Peter Drucker, "On the Profession of Management," Harvard Business Review Book Series (Boston, MA: Harvard Business School Publishing, 1988), p. 12.

D'Aveni urges managers to reconsider and reevaluate the use of what he believes are old strategic tools and maxims. He warns of the dangers of commitment to a given strategy or course of action. The flexible, unpredictable player may have an advantage over the inflexible, committed opponent. D'Aveni notes that, in hypercompetition, pursuit of generic strategies results in short-term advantage at best. The winning companies are the ones that successfully move up the ladder of escalating competition, not the ones that lock into a fixed position. D'Aveni also is critical of the five forces model. The best entry barrier, he argues, is maintaining the initiative, not mounting a defensive attempt to exclude new entrants.

ISO-9000

Another strategy to achieve competitive advantage is the incorporation of ISO-9000 criteria in product development and manufacturing policies, although service companies are finding innovative ways to apply the criteria to their businesses.

In 1987, the International Organization for Standardization (ISO) published a series of five international product and service quality standards. This publication was titled "Quality Management and Quality Assurance Standards—Guidelines for Selection and Use" and is commonly referred to as ISO-9000 Standards. The standards were originally designed with the intent to achieve conformity and congruence for two-party applications through normal supplier-customer relationships in a wide range of industries on either a contractual or noncontractual basis. This has now moved to another level whereby third-party assessment and certification of a supplier's processes is required by some customers. Basically, the application of ISO-9000 standards allows a supplier to direct and control the operations that determine the acceptability of a product or service being supplied. ISO-9000 standards represent the common denominator of business quality that is accepted internationally. In the United States, the standards are referred to as the ANSI/ASQC-Q 90 series.

The two major advantages of ISO-9000 registration and certification occur in domestic advantage and international advantage. Domestically, it provides (1) competitive advantage over suppliers who are not certified, (2) a focus on continuous improvement, (3) media awareness, and (4) customer perception.[24] Internationally, having ISO-9000 certification eases entry into export markets and as part of product liability defense if it should become necessary. The ISO-9000 standards are widely accepted by EC members and serve as a "method of ensuring its citizens of the quality of goods freely moving within the EC."[25] Approximately 15 percent of all products and services that are sold in the EC are currently regulated by ISO-9000 standards.

Summary

In this chapter, we focus on factors helping industries and countries achieve competitive advantage. According to Porter's five forces model, industry competition is a function of the threat of new entrants, the threat of substitutes, the bargaining power of suppliers and buyers, and rivalry among existing competitors. Porter's strategic positions can be used by managers to understand how to combine activities to create unique value, the source of competitive advantage.

Hamel and Prahalad have proposed an alternative framework for pursuing competitive advantage, growing out of a firm's strategic intent and use of competitive innovation. A firm can build layers of advantage, search for loose bricks in a competitor's defensive

---

[24] John T. Rabbitt and Peter A. Bergh, *The ISO 9000 Book* (White Plains, NY: Quality Resources 1994).
[25] Ibid.

walls, change the rules of engagement, or collaborate with competitors and utilize their technology and know-how. This framework is not necessarily inconsistent with the positions proposed by Porter. The concepts proposed by Hamel and Prahalad, as well as D'Aveni, stress the dynamic environment. Strategic positions have shorter lives than in the past and may have to be supplemented or abandoned faster than ever before.

Today, many companies are discovering that industry competition is changing from a purely domestic to a global phenomenon. Thus, competitive analysis must also be carried out on a global scale. Global marketers must also have an understanding of national sources of competitive advantage. Porter has described four determinants of national advantage. Factor conditions include human, physical, knowledge, capital, and infrastructure resources. Demand conditions include the composition, size, and growth pattern of home demand. The rate of home-market growth and the means by which a nation's products are pulled into foreign markets also affect demand conditions. The final two determinants are the presence of related and supporting industries and the nature of firm strategy, structure, and rivalry. Porter notes that chance and government also influence a nation's competitive advantage.

Discussion Questions

1. How can a company measure its competitive advantage? How does a firm know if it is gaining or losing competitive advantage?
2. Outline Porter's five forces model of industry competition. How are the various barriers of entry relevant to global marketing?
3. Identify three strategic positions. Pick a successful company that you know or have read about, and identify that company's strategic position.
4. Give an example of a company that illustrates each of the four generic strategies that can lead to competitive advantage: overall cost leadership, cost focus, differentiation, and focused differentiation.
5. What are the three strategic positions identified by Michael Porter? Identify a company example for each position.
6. What is the relationship, if any, between Porter's four generic strategies and his three strategic positions?
7. Briefly describe Hamel and Prahalad's framework for competitive advantage.
8. How can a nation achieve competitive advantage?
9. Do you agree with D'Aveni that no action or strategic advantage can be sustained for long? Why? Why not?
10. What is ISO-9000 and how would it benefit a company?

Suggested Readings

Abegglen, James C., and George Stalk, Jr. Kaisha: *The Japanese Corporation.* New York: Basic Books, 1985.

Baron, David P. "The Nonmarket Strategy System," *Sloan Management Review,* 37 (Fall 1995): 73–85.

Bartmess, Andrew, and Keith Cerny. "Building Competitive Advantage through a Global Network of Capabilities." *California Management Review,* 35, no. 2 (Winter 1993): 78–103.

Calantone, Roger J., and C. Anthony Di Benedetto. "Defensive Marketing in Globally Competitive Industrial Markets." *Columbia Journal of World Business,* 23, no. 3 (Fall 1988): 3–14.

Cravens, David W., H. Kirk Downey, and Paul Lauritano. "Global Competition in the Commercial Aircraft Industry: Positioning for Advantage by the Triad Nations." *Columbia Journal of World Business,* 26, no. 4 (Winter 1992): 46–58.

D'Aveni, Richard. *Hypercompetition: Managing the Dynamics of Strategic Maneuvering.* New York: Free Press, 1994.

Day, George S. *Market Driven Strategy: Processes for Creating Value.* New York: Free Press, 1990.

Dertouzos, Michael L., Richard K. Lester, and Robert M. Solow. *Made in America: Regaining the Competitive Edge.* New York: HarperCollins, 1989.

Egelhoff, William G. "Great Strategy or Great Strategy Implementation—Two Ways of Competing in Global Markets." *Sloan Management Review,* 34, no. 2 (Winter 1993): 37–50.

Garsombke, Diane J. "International Competitor Analysis." *Planning Review,* 17, no. 3 (May/June 1989): 42–47.

Ghosal, Sumantra, and D. Eleanor Westney. "Organizing Competitor Analysis Systems." *Strategic Management Journal,* 12, no. 1 (January 1991): 17–31.

"Global Competition: Confront Your Rivals on Their Home Turf." *Harvard Business Review,* 71, no. 3 (May/June 1993): 10.

Grove, Andrew S. *Only the Paranoid Survive.* New York: Doubleday, 1996.

Halberstam, David. *The Reckoning.* New York: William Morrow, 1986.

Hamel, Gary, and C. K. Prahalad. "The Core Competence of the Corporation." *Harvard Business Review,* 68 (May/June 1990): 79–93.

Hamel, Gary, and C. K. Prahalad. "Strategic Intent." *Harvard Business Review,* 67 (May/June 1989): 63–76.

Hamel, Gary, and C. K. Prahalad. "Strategy as Stretch and Leverage." *Harvard Business Review,* 71, no. 2 (March/April 1993): 75–85.

Harrigan, Kathryn Rudie. "A World-Class Company Is One Whose Customers Cannot Be Won Away by Competitors: Internationalizing Strategic Management." *Journal of Business Administration,* 21, no. 12 (1992–93): 251–264.

Hillis, W. Daniel, Daniel F. Burton, Robert B. Costello, et al. "Technology Policy: Is America on the Right Track?" *Harvard Business Review,* 70, no. 3 (May/June 1992): 140–157.

Jacquemin, Alexis. "The International Dimension of European Competition Policy." *Journal of Common Market Studies,* 31, no. 1 (March 1993): 91–101.

Li, Jiatao, and Stephen Guisinger. "How Well Do Foreign Firms Compete in the United States?" *Business Horizons,* 34, no. 6 (November/December 1991): 49–53.

Lorange, Peter, and Johan Roos. "Why Some Strategic Alliances Succeed and Others Fail." *Journal of Business Strategy,* 12, no. 1 (January/February 1991): 25–30.

Mascarenhas, Briance. "Order of Entry and Performance in International Markets." *Strategic Management Journal,* 13, no. 7 (October 1992): 499–510.

Moore, Geoffrey A. *Crossing the Chasm: Marketing and Selling Technology Products to Mainstream Customers.* New York: HarperBusiness, 1991.

Moore, Geoffrey A. *Inside the Tornado: Marketing Strategies From Silicon Valley's Cutting Edge.* New York: HarperBusiness, 1995.

Moore, James F. *The Death of Competition: Leadership and Strategy in the Age of Business Ecosystems.* New York: HarperBusiness, 1996.

Morrison, Allen J., and Kendall Roth. "A Taxonomy of Business-Level Strategies in Global Industries." *Strategic Management Journal,* 13, no. 6 (September 1992): 399–417.

Ohmae, Kenichi. *Triad Power.* New York: Free Press, 1985.

Pearson, Andrall E. "Corporate Redemption and the Seven Deadly Sins." *Harvard Business Review,* 70, no. 3 (May/June 1992): 65–75.

Peters, Tom. "Rethinking Scale." *California Management Review,* 35, no. 1 (Fall 1992): 7–29.

Porter, Michael E. *Competition in Global Industries.* Boston: Harvard Business School Press, 1986.

Porter, Michael E. *Competitive Advantage: Creating and Sustaining Superior Performance.* New York: Free Press, 1985.

Porter, Michael E. *The Competitive Advantage of Nations.* New York: Free Press, 1990.

Porter, Michael E. *Competitive Strategy.* New York: Free Press, 1980.

Porter, Michael E. "What Is Strategy?" *Harvard Business Review* (November/December 1996): 60–78.

Robert, Michel M. "Attack Competitors by Changing the Game Rules." *Journal of Business Strategy,* 12, no. 5 (September/October 1991): 53–56.

Rugman, Alan M., and Alain Verbeke. "Foreign Subsidiaries and Multinational Strategic Management: An Extension and Correction of Porter's Single Diamond Framework." *Management International Review,* 33, no. 2 (Special Issue 1993/2): 71–84.

Schill, Ronald L., and David N. McArthur. "Redefining the Strategic Competitive Unit: Towards a New Global Marketing Paradigm?" *International Marketing Review,* 9, no. 3 (1992): 5–24.

Schoemaker, Paul J. H. "How to Link Strategic Vision to Core Capabilities." *Sloan Management Review,* 34, no. 1 (Fall 1992): 67–81.

Williams, Jeffrey R. "How Sustainable Is Your Competitive Advantage?" *California Management Review,* 34, no. 3 (Spring 1992): 29–51.

Womack, James P., Daniel T. Jones, and Daniel Roos. *The Machine That Changed the World.* New York: HarperCollins, 1990.

Yip, George S. *Total Global Strategy: Managing for Worldwide Competitive Advantage.* Upper Saddle River, NJ: Prentice Hall, 1995.

◆◆◆ **Part IV Cases**

Odysseus, Inc. (The Decision to Go "International")

She faced him waiting. And Odysseus came, debating inwardly what he should do; embrace this
beauty's knees in supplication or stand apart and use honeyed speech, inquire the way to town and
beg some clothing? In his swift reckoning, he thought it best to trust in words to please her—and keep
away; he might anger the girl, touching her knees.

—HOMER

The Odyssey, Book Six, "The Princess
at the River," Robert Fitzgerald Trans.

In early 1991, Mr. Donald R. Odysseus, president of the Odysseus Manufacturing Company of Kansas City, Kansas, was actively considering the possibilities of major expansion of the firm's currently limited international activities and the form and scale such expansion might take.

Odysseus was founded in 1926 by Edward Odysseus as a small machine shop. By 1991, the head office and production facilities of the company were located in a 500,000-square-foot modern factory on a 30-acre site near the original location. Odysseus products were sold throughout the United States and Canada. In 1990, net sales were over $83,800,000 while after-tax profits were about $4,835,000. In early 1990, Odysseus employed just over 1,000 people, and its stock was held by 1,000 shareholders. (The company's 1990 income statement and balance sheet are given in Exhibits 1 and 2.)

Odysseus produced a line of coupling and clutches including flange, compression, gear type, flex pin, and flexible disc couplings, and overrunning and multiple disc clutches.

In all, the company manufactured about 600 different sizes and types of its eight standard items. The company's single most important product was the Odysseus Flexible Coupling, which its research department had developed in 1985 and which, produced in about 70 different sizes and combinations, now accounted for one third of Odysseus's sales. Odysseus held patents throughout the world on its flexible coupling as well as several other devices. By 1991, Odysseus had carved itself a secure niche in the clutch and couplings market, despite the competition in this market of larger firms with widely diversified product lines.

EXHIBIT 1   Consolidated Income Statement, Year Ending December 31, 1990 (in $ thousands)

Income		
Net sales	$84,700	
Royalties, interest, and other income	174	
	$84,874	$84,874
Costs and expenses		
Cost of goods sold	$54,019	
Depreciation	1,773	
Selling, administrative, and general expense	18,845	
Interest on long-term debt	219	
	$74,856	$74,856
Income before income taxes		10,018
Federal taxes on income (estimated)		5,157
Net income		$4,861

EXHIBIT 2   Balance Sheet, December 31, 1990 (in $ thousands)

Assets		
Cash	5,667	
Marketable securities	3,688	
Accounts receivable	6,399	
Inventories	25,578	
Total current assets	41,332	41,332
Investments and other assets		1,351
Property, plant, and equipment (net)		23,177
Total assets		65,860
Liabilities		
Accounts payable	2,015	
Dividends payable	745	
Accruals	3,394	
Federal income tax liability (estimated)	3,752	
Installment on long-term debt	277	
Total current liabilities	10,183	10,183
Long term debt (20-year 6 7/8% notes, final maturity 1987)		5,051
Preferred stock		6,370
Common stock and retained earnings		44,256
Total liabilities		65,860

Odysseus was not dependent on any single customer or industry. Sales were made through distributors to original equipment manufacturers for use in small motor drives for a wide range of products including machine tools, test gear, conveyors, farm implements, mining equipment, hoisting equipment, cranes, shovels, and so on. No more than 10 percent of its output went to any single industry; its largest single customer took less than 4 percent of production. Speaking generally, Odysseus couplings and clutches were used more by small- and medium-sized producers of general-purpose equipment than by large manufacturers of highly automated machines. Odysseus's sales manager believed that demand for the company's couplings and clutches would benefit from continuation of a long-term trend toward increased installation of labor-saving equipment in medium enterprises. This trend and the breadth of its market had provided some protection against cyclical fluctuations in business activities. During the period 1977 to 1990, sales had increased from $32 million to over $84 million; the largest annual decline during the period had been 8 percent, while in the most recent recession year sales had actually increased by 5 percent.

The company's commercial objective was to operate as a specialist in a product field in which its patents and distinctive skills would give it a strong competitive position. In the past, the company had experimented with various products outside its coupling and clutch line; it had tried to make components for egg-candling machinery, among other things. The investment in these products was initially considered a means of more efficiently utilizing the company's forging and machining capacity, but the firm had not been particularly successful. The Odysseus management had come to the conclusion that it should concentrate its efforts on its line of couplings and clutches; and in 1991, Mr. Odysseus stated the company's corporate objectives explicitly as being a coupling and clutch manufacturer. New investments were made to develop better products within this field, and to open new markets for Odysseus products.

Odysseus's production and assembly facilities were located in its modern factory near Kansas City, Kansas. The site offered ample room for expansion and was well located for both rail and highway transportation. The company maintained warehousing facilities in Boston, Jersey City, Atlanta, Columbus, Ohio, and Oakland, California. The scale economies stemming from concentrating production in one factory can be seen from the following examples. One of the company's largest selling items, product K-2A (a flexible coupling component) produced in lots of 750, cost $5.19 each; in lots of 1,200, $4.22 each. The incremental 450 units produced after the initial 750, therefore, cost only $2.6 each. Put differently, on this particular product, a 50 percent cost saving could be realized on the marginal production from the 750-unit level to the 1,200-unit level. Although specific cost savings from higher volume varied among its products, a fundamental characteristic of Odysseus's cost structure was that marginal cost typically

was significantly less than average cost and that important economies of scale could be obtained by achieving larger lot sizes and longer production runs.

Odysseus's cost structure was, of course, dictated by its manufacturing process. In the first of three major steps in the manufacture of couplings or clutches, steel bars or tubing were cut and forged. Apart from the unit cost reductions stemming from more complete utilization of the existing forging facilities, economies of scale in this department were limited. Second, the forged steel pieces were machined to close tolerances in the machine shop. Here costs varied significantly with lot sizes. For most products, the choice among two or three alternative methods of production depended on the lot size. If a large lot size were indicated, special-purpose automatic machines with large setup costs and lower variable unit costs were used. Smaller lot sizes were produced on general-purpose turret and engine lathes where setup time was less but unit costs were higher.

Typically, production of smaller lot sizes was more labor intensive than the larger runs. For example, one operator running three automatic machines could perform all the boring and cutting operations on 300 2½-inch coupling flange units in an hour. The same output on general-purpose lathes and boring machines would require about six person-hours. To set up the automatic machines required a day and a half, however, while the lathes could be set up in about two hours. Furthermore, the burden charge on the automatics was considerably higher. On the other hand, the cost of the third step, assembly, did not vary under different lot sizes. (Exhibit 3 presents a breakdown of the costs of some representative components.)

Mr. Odysseus regarded Odysseus's U.S. and Canadian market position as a strong one. The patented Odysseus

EXHIBIT 3 Typical Variation of Production Costs with Lot Sizes Product N-15Cl		
Operation	*Lots of 150*	*Lots of 400*
I. Foundry	$51.67	$51.67
II. Machine Shop		
1. Boring	55.67	32.69
2. Turning	14.17	11.43
3. Facing	19.79	16.25
4. Drilling	32.23	26.30
5. Turning	18.95	15.41
6. Facing	19.95	14.76
7. Finishing	18.76	18.76
8. Finishing	17.95	18.24
III. Assembly	7.96	7.96
	257.10	$213.49

Product L-36G:
    Lots of 3: $108.6 each
    Lots of 4: $90.6 each

Flexible Coupling possessed unique characteristics that no other coupling device duplicated, and many other Odysseus products served special functions not performed by competitive devices. Of course, other coupling and clutch systems competed with Odysseus, but no single company could be said to compete directly by introducing an identical product line. Mr. Odysseus estimated that Odysseus accounted for roughly 10 percent of total sales of its products in the American market and that was ample room for Odysseus to expand its sales in this domestic market as the total market grew and through an increase in its share of industry sales. Odysseus products were sold by distributors who generally, but not always, carried the entire line of Odysseus couplings and clutches. These distributor organizations were complemented by a 45-person Odysseus sales force.

In 1990, export sales were $1,353,862, on which the company made a $161,174 operating profit. Although export sales had never been actively solicited, a small but steady stream of orders for export trickled into the Kansas City sales office. These orders were always filled expeditiously, but the active exploitation of export markets was considered too difficult in view of the barriers of language, custom, and currency. Furthermore, although he recognized that foreign wages were increasing more rapidly than those in the United States, Mr. Odysseus had always believed that Odysseus could not compete in export markets because its costs in Kansas City were too high. Also, tariffs imposed on Odysseus products by foreign governments were typically 10 percent ad valorem or higher.

Odysseus sold all products on flat price basis (FOB warehouse) to all customers. In competing with other suppliers of similar products, Odysseus stressed delivery time, quality, service, and merchandising, but not price.

In its management's view, improvements in its products or in delivery or service promised more than temporary competitive advantage. Price-cutting moves, in contrast, would likely be matched by competitors the same day. No added sales would be gained, and total revenues would be cut. The company's export pricing policy was identical to its domestic policy. This meant that the foreign importer paid the U.S. free-on-board (FOB) price plus freight and import duties.

Along with filling orders, Odysseus's activities outside the United States and Canada consisted of a licensing agreement with an English coupling manufacturer. In 1985, on a vacation trip in England, where Odysseus's vice president in charge of engineering had spent his youth, he met the chairperson of Siren Ltd. of Manchester. Siren, a manufacturer of related equipment with sales of $14.6 million in 1984, was anxious to diversify by adding other power transmission products. Consequently, Siren became interested in several Odysseus patents, particularly those on the Odysseus Flexible Coupling. In late 1985, Odysseus granted the English concern an exclusive 15-year license to manufacture and sell all present and future Odysseus products in the United Kingdom. The licensing arrangement specifically defined

the United Kingdom to include England, Scotland, Wales, and Northern Ireland. Siren was granted also a nonexclusive license to sell products produced from Odysseus patents in all other countries except the United States, Canada, Mexico, and France. The terms of the license agreement stipulated a 1.5 percent royalty on the ex-factory sales price of all products in which devices manufactured from Odysseus patents were incorporated. The 1990 royalty income from Siren amounted to $128,939 and was expected to rise to $161,174 in 1991.

Mr. Odysseus had noted Siren's success with considerable interest. The royalty payments were a welcome addition to Odysseus income, especially since they had not necessitated any additional investment. Mr. Odysseus felt that the licensee was receiving very generous profits from this deal, as Siren had almost tripled its sales (which by 1990 were equivalent to $35.5 million) during its five-year association with Odysseus and its equity had appreciated many times the total royalties of about $483,522 that Odysseus had received.

During the five years Odysseus and Siren had worked together, however, the English firm had made it understood that in general it considered its territory to be the Eastern Hemisphere, while Odysseus's was in the Western Hemisphere. Siren was especially interested in the German market for couplings and clutches and was a licensee of a German brake shoe manufacturer.

In addition, Odysseus had a licensing agreement on the same terms (1.5 percent royalty) with Scylla, S.A. Scylla was a medium-sized French manufacturer of clutches and complementary lines located near Paris. The company was financially sound and well headed by a young and aggressive management team. Scylla had been granted an exclusive license in France and a nonexclusive license in Belgium to sell products incorporating Odysseus-patented devices. Odysseus had entered the agreement during 1989 for an initial period of 10 years. Royalty income in 1990, the first full year of operation in France, had totaled roughly $32,200. Odysseus expected a doubling of this figure in 1991.

In February 1991, M. Scylla, the president of the French firm, had proposed to Mr. Odysseus a closer association of their two companies. M. Scylla was anxious to expand his operations and needed capital to do this. He, therefore, proposed that Odysseus form a joint venture with Scylla. According to the terms of the proposal, Odysseus would bring $645,000 into the joint venture, paid in cash, while Scylla would provide a 40,000-square-foot plant, equipment, a national distribution system, and managerial personnel. Scylla S.A. would cease to exist as a corporate entity; its expanded organization and plant would become Scylla Odysseus, S.A. (SOSA). The original owners of Scylla, S.A. (the Scylla family) would own 60 percent of SOSA, and their return would be in the form of dividends plus salaries of members of the Scylla family employed by SOSA. Odysseus would own 40 percent of SOSA and, for tax reasons, would receive fees and royalties rather than dividends totaling 5 percent of the ex-factory price of all products incorporating Odysseus patents.

Mr. Odysseus thought that he should give this proposal serious attention. The French market for couplings looked very attractive. Moreover, the geographical location of SOSA within the European Community would make it possible to supply the even larger German market from the SOSA plant near Paris. M. Scylla had indicated that he considered Germany a primary target for future expansion.

So far, Odysseus had not actively pursued business leads in Germany in spite of several inquiries about licensing from German companies. Odysseus even had the possibility of acquiring an existing German manufacturer of couplings, Charybdis Metallfabrik GmbH (CMF) of Kassel. Mr. Odysseus had learned that CMF's aging owner-managers were anxious to sell their equity interest in the company but would stay on in managerial capacity. Odysseus's British licensee, Siren, had made it clear, however, that although it had no sizable business in Germany, it considered this market to be in Siren's sales territory and a move into Germany by Odysseus without Siren an "unfriendly act." In the light of Odysseus's growing royalty income from Siren, Mr. Odysseus did not want to antagonize the British licensee.

Mr. Odysseus had no ready means of precisely quantifying the market potential for clutches and couplings in Germany and in France. He knew, however, that the total market for Odysseus's "type L" couplings in the United States was $72.5 million in 1990, or 14 percent of the U.S. market. Odysseus assumed that the coupling market in France was correlated with sales of durable equipment in France, which were 12 percent of the U.S. total. The French type-L coupling market, therefore, would be $8.7 million a year, of which SOSA should expect to capture 14 percent, or $1,218,000. Similarly in Germany, durable equipment sales were 20 percent of those in the United States. The type-L coupling market could, therefore, be expected to be about $14.5 million, of which a company using Odysseus patents and know-how should obtain between 10 percent and 15 percent. Sales of comparable lines by both Scylla, S.A. and CMF appeared to justify these estimates; Scylla had sold $870,000 of a device closely comparable to the type-L coupling, or 10 percent of the assumed French market, and CMF had sold $1,160,000 of virtually the same device, or 8 percent of the assumed German market.

In 1991, the European market with its accelerating pace of industrial development and mechanization appeared to offer great opportunities for Odysseus. Mr. Odysseus was therefore most anxious to capitalize on these opportunities, presumably by manufacturing in Europe in cooperation with a European firm. He saw three reasons why Odysseus should expand its foreign operations.

First, the corporate objectives of focusing on a single line of products sold in as large a market as possible—the policy of area instead of products diversification—dictated expansion into markets outside the United States and Can-

ada. The nature of the demand for Odysseus's products appeared to limit near-term sales potential in less developed areas but especially in Europe. Odysseus couplings and clutches appeared to find ready acceptance. Proof of this seemed to be contained in Siren's success in the United Kingdom.

Second, an important improvement on the Odysseus multiple disc clutch had been the result of European research. Mr. Odysseus felt that by becoming an active participant in the European market, the company could obtain valuable recent innovations that would be important to its competitive position in the United States. There was considerable activity in the clutch and coupling field in Europe, and Mr. Odysseus wanted to be in touch with the latest developments in the industry.

Third, Mr. Odysseus was seriously worried about the trend of costs in his Kansas City plant. He had heard that a French firm was planning to invest in a manufacturing plant in Mexico where wages were 16 percent of those in the United States. How could Odysseus compete against this kind of cost advantage? Ultimately, Odysseus might have to follow the lead of U.S. watch and bicycle firms and perform much of its manufacturing abroad and import parts, or even finished products, into the United States. At the present time, Mr. Odysseus felt that there was some reluctance on the part of American manufacturers to buy foreign couplings and clutches, and foreign competition was virtually nil in this market in 1991. But Mr. Odysseus was worried about the future and wanted to preserve Odysseus's competitive position by assuring a foreign source of supply. Also, the company would be in a better position to withstand exorbitant demands from the local labor union if it possessed alternative manufacturing facilities.

Before definitely deciding whether Odysseus should become more deeply involved in foreign operations, Mr. Odysseus wanted to review the ways this might be done. First, Odysseus could establish foreign markets by expanding export sales. Mr. Odysseus believed, however, that Odysseus's costs might be too high for it to compete successfully on this basis. Second, the company could enter into additional licensing agreements. This it had done with Siren in England and Scylla in France, but there was a definite ceiling on the possible profit potential from exclusive use of this method. Third, the company could enter joint ventures with a firm already established in foreign markets. Presumably, Odysseus would supply capital and know-how and the foreign firms would supply personnel (both local managerial skill and a labor force), market outlets, and familiarity with the local business climate. This approach appeared particularly promising to Mr. Odysseus. Finally, the company could establish wholly owned foreign subsidiaries. Mr. Odysseus saw formidable barriers to such action, since Odysseus lacked managerial skill in foreign operations. They were unfamiliar with foreign markets and business practices. They did not have executives to spare from the Kansas City operations who might learn the intricacies of foreign business, and the development of wholly owned operations from scratch would require significant investment of time and money.

As he reflected on these issues, he looked at a set of tables on global income and population, productivity, wages, exports/imports, and trade and investment (Exhibits 4-9 on the following pages) and decided to attempt to comprehend what, if any, significance the data in these tables had for Odysseus. Mr. Odysseus recognized that certain deep-seated ideas of his tended to make him predisposed toward active development of overseas business. These included a view that his business should not shrink from difficult tasks—organizations, he believed, couldn't stand still—the choice was one of moving forward or falling backward. He considered "taking the plunge" into less familiar areas and learning from the experience was generally preferable to long-extended and expensive inquiry before taking action. Nonetheless, he wanted to be sure that the most basic issues related to expansion overseas by Odysseus were thought through before firm decisions were made.

EXHIBIT 4   Global Income and Population, 1992

Global Income and Population	GNP ($ billion)	GNP per Capita ($)	GNP	1992 Population (million)	% of World Population
Country Summary					
World Total	21,427.1	3,905	100.0	5,486.98	100.0
High Income	17,110.0	20,906	79.9	818.44	14.9
Triad Total	16,573.6	21,127	77.3	784.49	14.3
United States and Canada	6,379.1	22,540	29.8	283.01	5.2
Japan	3,403.8	27,233	15.9	124.99	2.3
European Economic Area	6,790.7	18,037	31.7	376.49	6.9
Other High Income	536.4	15,800	2.5	33.95	0.6
Upper-Middle Income	2,469.4	2,708	11.5	912.03	16.6
Lower-Middle Income	1,318.2	668	6.2	1,974.37	36.0
Low Income and Unavailable Data	529.5	307	2.5	1,782.13	32.5
Expansion of High-Income Countries[a]	17,110.0	20,906	79.9	818.44	14.9
GNP per Capita >$12,000					
United States	5,799.9	22,657	27.1	255.99	4.7
Canada	579.2	21,433	2.7	27.02	0.5
Japan	3,403.8	27,233	15.9	124.99	2.3
EC	5,851.4	17,717	27.3	330.26	6.0
Belgium	159.0	15,848	0.7	10.04	0.2
Denmark	118.3	23,008	0.6	5.19	0.1
France	1,148.7	20,186	5.4	56.91	1.0
Germany	1,642.3	21,328	7.7	77.00	1.4
Italy	1,017.8	17,603	4.7	57.82	1.1
Luxembourg	11.8	31,172	0.1	0.38	0.0
Netherlands	268.7	17,820	1.3	15.08	0.3
Portugal	53.8	5,123	0.3	10.50	0.2
Spain	456.4	11,514	2.1	39.64	0.7
United Kingdom	974.5	16,886	4.5	57.71	1.1
EFTA	843.2	25,883	3.9	32.58	0.6
Austria	153.3	20,012	0.7	7.66	0.1
Finland	139.3	27,763	0.7	5.02	0.1
Iceland	5.7	21,652	0.0	0.26	0.0
Norway	104.4	24,381	0.5	4.28	0.1
Sweden	211.1	24,536	1.0	8.60	0.2
Switzerland	229.5	33,971	1.1	6.76	0.1
Asia	114.7	13,138	0.5	8.73	0.2
Hong Kong	76.3	12,845	0.4	5.94	0.1
Singapore	38.4	13,763	0.2	2.79	0.1

EXHIBIT 4 (cont.)

Global Income and Population	GNP ($ billion)	GNP per Capita ($)	GNP	1992 Population (million)	% of World Population
Caribbean	2.9	16,771	0.0	0.17	0.0
Bermuda	1.4	24,365	0.0	0.06	0.0
Virgin Islands, U.S.	1.4	12,798	0.0	0.11	0.0
Oceania	353.8	16,865	1.7	20.98	0.4
Australia	309.4	17,662	1.4	17.52	0.3
New Zealand	44.4	12,834	0.2	3.46	0.1
Oil-Producing Countries	65.0	15,977	0.3	4.07	0.1
Kuwait (est.)	35.3	15,136	0.2	2.33	0.0
United Arab Emirates	29.7	17,107	0.1	1.74	0.0

[a]Does not show all countries for a particular region.

EXHIBIT 5 Productivity and Investment in the World Economy, 1971–1990 (Thousands of 1980 Dollars)	1971–75	1976–80	1981–85	1986–90
Gross Product per Worker				
Developed market economies	20.2	22.2	23.0	25.8
Eastern Europe and USSR	6.0	7.3	8.2	9.2
Developing Countries of which:	1.5	1.7	1.8	1.9
Africa	1.8	2.0	1.8	1.8
Asia, exluding West Asia	0.6	0.8	0.9	1.2
Latin America and Caribbean	5.4	6.0	5.9	5.8
World	5.5	6.0	6.2	6.6
Investment per Worker				
Developed market economies	5.1	5.2	5.1	6.2
Eastern Europe and USSR	1.9	2.3	2.3	2.4
Developing Countries of which:	0.3	0.4	0.5	0.5
Africa	0.4	0.5	0.4	0.3
Asia, exluding West Asia	0.2	0.2	0.3	0.4
Latin America and Caribbean	1.2	1.5	1.1	0.9
World	1.4	1.5	1.5	1.6

Source: World Economic Survey 1992; United Nations.

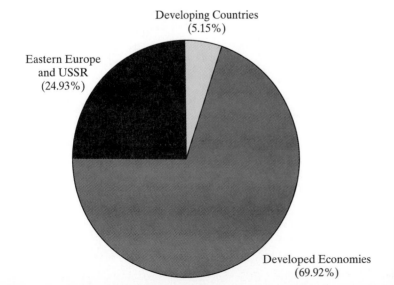

Developing Countries (5.15%)

Eastern Europe and USSR (24.93%)

Developed Economies (69.92%)

EXHIBIT 6 Gross Output per Worker, 1986–1990 (as a Percentage of World Total)

Source: Prepared by author.

EXHIBIT 7   Hourly Compensation Costs—Industrial Structure

Indexes of Hourly Compensation Costs for Production Workers in Manufacturing Selected Countries: 1975 to 1989 [United States = 100. Compensation costs include pay for time worked, other direct pay, employer expenditures for legally required insurance programs, and contractual and private benefits plan, and for some countries, other labor taxes. Data adjusted for exchange rates. Area averages are trade-weighted to account for difference in countries' relative importance to U.S. trade in manufactured goods. The trade weights used are the sum of U.S. imports of manufactured products for consumption (customs value) and U.S. domestic exports of manufactured products (x.a.s. value) in 1986; see source for detail.]

Area or Country	1975	1980	1985	1987	1988	1989
United States	100	100	100	100	100	100
Total[a]	62	70	54	75	82	82
OECD[b]	75	83	85	91	99	97
Europe[c]	82	103	63	101	105	100
Asian newly ind. economies[d]	6	12	13	16	19	23
Canada	91	85	83	89	98	103
Brazil	14	14	9	10	11	12
Mexico[e]	31	30	16	12	14	16
Australia	67	66	63	70	81	85
Hong Kong[f]	12	15	13	16	17	19
Israel	35	39	31	47	55	54
Japan	48	57	50	81	92	88
South Korea	6	10	10	13	16	25
New Zealand	50	54	34	51	59	55
Singapore	13	15	19	17	19	22
Sri Lanka	4	2	2	2	NA	NA
China: Taiwan	6	10	12	17	20	25
Austria[f]	68	87	56	98	101	95
Belgium	101	133	69	112	112	106
Denmark	99	111	63	109	115	106
Finland[g]	72	84	62	100	113	116
France	71	91	58	93	94	89
Germany[h]	100	125	74	126	131	123
Greece	27	38	26	34	36	38
Ireland	47	60	45	60	70	66
Italy	73	81	56	91	93	92
Luxembourg	100	122	59	97	100	NA
Netherlands	103	123	69	116	117	109
Norway	107	119	82	129	136	131
Portugal	25	21	12	19	19	19
Spain	41	61	37	59	64	64
Sweden	113	127	75	113	121	122
Switzerland	96	113	75	127	130	117
United Kingdom	52	76	49	67	76	73

NA = not available.

[a] The 27 foreign economies for which 1989 data are available.

[b] Canada, Australia, Japan, New Zealand, and the 16 European countries for which 1989 data are available.

[c] The 16 European countries for which 1989 data are available.

[d] Hong Kong, Singapore, South Korea, and China: Taiwan.

[e] Average of selected manufacturing industries.

[f] Excludes workers in establishments considered handicraft manufacturers (including all printing and publishing and miscellaneous manufacturing in Austria).

[g] Includes workers in mining and electrical power plants.

[h] Data refer to September.

Source: Bureau of Labor Statistics, Report 787, August 1990. Extracted from *Statistical Abstract of the United States 1991*, p. 851.

EXHIBIT 8 20 Leading Exporters and Importers in World Merchandise Trade in 1990 ($ million and Percentages)

Imports (CIF)	1990	'90/'89	Exports (FOB)	1990	'90/'89
1. United States [1]	516,987	4.88	1. Germany [2]	410,104	20.18
2. Germany [2]	346,153	28.35	2. United States [1]	393,592	8.19
3. Japan [3]	235,368	12.23	3. Japan [3]	287,581	4.98
4. France [5]	234,426	21.47	4. France [4]	216,580	20.73
5. United Kingdom [4]	222,777	12.67	5. United Kingdom [5]	185,160	21.54
6. Italy [6]	181,984	18.94	6. Italy [6]	170,348	21.20
7. Netherlands [8]	126,098	20.86	7. Netherlands [8]	131,802	22.22
8. Canada [7]	124,422	3.87	8. Canada [7]	131,665	9.50
9. Belgium [9]	119,971	21.83	9. Belgium [9]	118,156	18.14
10. Spain [11]	87,696	22.70	10. Hong Kong [10]	82,160	12.33
11. Hong Kong [10]	82,474	14.30	11. Korea [11]	64,956	4.21
12. Korea [13]	69,640	13.61	12. Switzerland [14]	63,784	23.79
13. Switzerland [12]	58,194	−16.49	13. China, P.R. [12]	60,920	18.00
14. Sweden [16]	54,435	11.15	14. Sweden [13]	57,574	11.69
15. China, P.R. [15]	52,275	−10.31	15. Spain [16]	55,642	25.06
16. Singapore [14]	49,667	−18.44	16. Singapore [15]	52,752	18.11
17. Austria [18]	49,146	26.08	17. Austria [18]	41,265	29.34
18. Australia [17]	42,032	−6.46	18. Australia [17]	39,837	5.78
19. Thailand [20]	33,379	29.52	19. Denmark [19]	35,065	24.76
20. Denmark [19]	31,760	19.00	20. Norway [20]	34,030	25.75

Note: Figures in brackets indicate rank in 1989.

DISCUSSION QUESTIONS

1. Should Odysseus expand international business operations?
2. Rightly or wrongly, Odysseus management has decided in the affirmative. What form should these operations take? What *scope* will be required for Odysseus's international activities to achieve success? Possible forms, which in turn may be combined, include (a) exporting, (b) licensing, (c) joint ventures, and (d) wholly owned subsidiaries, either by starting them from scratch or by acquiring one or more existing companies. This decision should take into account Odysseus's capabilities (as determined, for example, by its products, its capital and labor strength, and its marketing and research needs) as well as the industry's competitive requirements and foreign conditions, such as trade and business barriers, the number and sizes of countries to be covered, and political and business risk.
3. Evaluate the arrangement with Siren, particularly the following questions:
   a. What assumptions were in Mr. Odysseus's mind when he concluded the licensing arrangement with Siren?
   b. Do you consider it a success?
   c. How does the timing of this arrangement fit into Odysseus's overall business strategy?
4. Evaluate the Scylla, S.A. proposal and the Charybdis possibility.
5. Recommend a global strategic plan to Mr. Odysseus.

EXHIBIT 9 Trade and Investment Exports and Imports of the World to and from the Areas Listed (in US$ Millions)

Exports (FOB) Imports (CIF)

	1988	*1989*	*1990*	*1988*	*1989*	*1990*
Areas						
IFS World Total (US$ Bi)	2,699.3	2,913.8	3,325.0	2,774.8	3,009.4	3,455.0
DOTS World Total	2,693.4	2,912.8	3,339.6	2,773.8	3,002.2	3,450.6
Ind. Countries (US$ Bi)	1,958	2,118	2,449	2,016.1	2,160.9	2,500.1
Developing Countries	689,839	744,726	835,509	746,592	832,674	935,954
Africa	64,507	65,103	73,846	66,131	74,466	86,196
Asia	342,136	381,836	433,172	362,822	403,131	456,448
Europe[a]	80,139	83,095	95,105	84,684	85,714	86,086
Middle East	99,008	100,572	105,801	103,082	124,568	150,387
Western Hemisphere[b]	104,048	114,120	127,585	129,874	144,794	156,837
USSR and selected other countries n.i.e.[c]	81,676	86,095	73,905	78,319	78,997	68,476
Memorandum Items						
EEC (US$ Bi)	1,043	1,125	1,357	1,058	1,122	1,359
Triad** (US$ Bi)	1,740	1,881	2,182	1,780	1,909	2,208
Oil-Exporting Countries	96,543	98,488	108,864	132,497	160,121	195,419
Nonoil Developing Countries	593,296	646,238	726,646	614,095	672,553	740,535
Annual Percent Change						
World	14.4	8.1	14.7	14.6	8.2	14.9
Industrial Countries	13.2	8.2	15.7	14.9	7.2	15.7
Developing Countries	18.1	8.0	12.2	14.1	11.5	12.4
Africa	12.1	0.9	13.4	5.9	12.6	15.8
Asia	29.0	11.6	13.4	22.5	11.1	13.2
Europe	5.7	3.7	14.5	11.4	1.2	0.4
Middle East	7.4	1.6	5.2	–3.1	20.8	20.7
Western Hemisphere	11.4	9.7	11.8	15.1	11.5	8.3
USSR and selected other countries n.i.e.	14.8	5.4	–14.1	8.5	0.9	–13.2

[a] Defined as: Albania, Bulgaria, Cuba, East Germany, the Mongolian Republic, North Korea, Czechoslovakia, and the USSR, which are not included in the world trade table published in the IFS.

[b] Latin America, Greenland, Netherland Antilles, and other not spec. DOTS = Direction of Trade Statistics, IFS = International Financial Statistics.

[c] In the absence of a more suitable term that would conveniently cover the countries included in the third category (Europe), they are referred to as USSR and selected other countries n.i.e.

Metro Corporation: Technology Licensing Negotiation

Details of negotiations between Metro Corporation and Impecina Construcciones S.A. of Peru, for the licensing of Petroleum Tank Technology follow.

THE LICENSOR FIRM

Metro Corporation is a diversified steel rolling, fabricating, and construction company based in the Midwest and considers itself to be in a mature industry. Innovations are few and far between. With transport and tariff barriers, and the support given by many governments to their own companies, exporting as a means of doing foreign business is rather limited. Similarly, given the large investment, modest return, and political sensitivity of the industry, direct foreign investment is all but a closed option. In a global strategic sense then, Metro Corporation has far more frequently focused on licensing as a market entry method, with technologies confined to (1) processes and engineering peripheral to the basic steel-making process, for example, mining methods, coke oven door designs, galvanizing, and so on, and (2) applications of steel in construction and other industries, for example, petroleum tank design, welding methods, thermoadhesion, and so on.

All Metro's licensing is handled by its international division, International Construction and Engineering (ICE), which is beginning to develop a reputation in Western Europe and South America as a good source for specialized construction technology.

THE PROPOSED LICENSEE

Impecina, a private firm, is the largest construction company in Peru and operates throughout Latin America. Impecina has a broad range of interests including residential and commercial buildings, hydraulic works, transportation, and maritime works. Employing several thousand personnel, engineers, and technicians, its sales had doubled in the last five years. It was still primarily a Peruvian business with most turnover in Peru, but was in the process of expanding into Colombia, the North African Mediterranean countries, and Argentina, Brazil, and Venezuela. Impecina has advanced computer capacity with a large IBM and other computers at their branches. In oil-storage tanks, Impecina experience was limited to the smaller fixed-cone roof designs under 150-feet diameter.

This case was prepared by Professor Farok Contractor as a basis for class discussion rather than to illustrate either effective or ineffective handling of an administrative situation. © by Farok J. Contractor. Used with permission.

THE TECHNOLOGY

National Tank Inc., a fabrication division of Metro, had developed a computerized design procedure for floating-roof oil-storage tanks, which minimized the use of steel within American Petroleum Institute or any other oil industry standards. Particularly for the larger tanks, for instance, 150-feet diameter and above, this would confer upon the bidding contractor a significant cost advantage. National Tank had spent one labor-year at a direct cost of $225,000 to write the computer program alone. Patents were involved in an incidental manner, only for the seals on the floating roof. Metro had not bothered to file for this patent except in the United States.

THE MARKET

Peru's indigenous oil output is very low, but it imports and refines annually 50 million tons mostly for domestic demand. Following the escalation of oil prices and tightening of supplies in 1973, the Peruvian government determinedly set about to formulate a program to augment Peru's oil-storage capacity. Impecina's representatives at a preliminary meeting with ICE in U.S. headquarters said their government planned $200 million expenditures on oil-storage facilities over the next 3 years (mostly in large-sized tanks). Of this, Impecina's "ambition" was to capture a one-third market share. That this appeared to be a credible target was illustrated by their existing 30 percent share of the fixed-cone type under 150-feet diameter. Additionally, they estimated private-sector construction value over the next three years to total $40 million.

Approximately half of a storage system's construction cost goes for the tank alone, the remainder being excavation, foundation, piping, instrumentation, and other ancillary equipment, all of which Impecina's engineers were very familiar with.

Neighboring Colombia was building a 12 million ton refinery, but the tank installation plans of other South American nations were not known, according to the Impecina representative.

Each of Impecina's competitors in Peru for this business was affiliated with a prominent company: Umbertomas with Jefferson Inc. in the United States, Zapa with Philadelphia Iron & Steel, Cosmas with Peoria-Duluth Construction Inc., and so on. Thus, association with Metro would help Impecina in bidding.

THE FIRST MEETING

National Tank had in the past year bid jointly with Impecina on a project in southern Peru. Though that bid was unsuccessful, Impecina had learned about Metro's computerized design capabilities and initiated a formal first round of negotiations, which were to lead to a licensing agreement. The meeting took place in the United States. Two Impecina executives of subdirector rank were accompanied by an American consultant. Metro was represented by the vice president of ICE, the ICE attorney, and an executive from National Tank.

Minutes of this meeting show it was exploratory. Both genuine and rhetorical questions were asked. Important information and perceptions were exchanged and the groundwork laid for concluding negotiations. Following is a bare summary of important issues from the somewhat circular discussion:

1. **Licensee Market Coverage:** Impecina tried to represent itself as essentially a Peruvian firm. It reviewed its government expenditure plans and its hoped-for market share. Yet through the meeting, there kept cropping up the issue of the license also covering Libya, Algeria, Morocco, Colombia, Argentina, Brazil, and Venezuela.

2. **Exclusivity:** For Peru, Metro negotiators had no difficulty conceding exclusivity. They mentioned that granting exclusivity to a licensee for any territory was agreeable in principle, provided a minimum performance guarantee was given. At this, the question was deferred for future discussion. At one point a Metro executive remarked, "We could give Impecina a nonexclusive—and say, for example, we wouldn't give another (licensee) a license for one year (in those nations)," proposing the idea of a trial period for Impecina to generate business in a territory.

3. **Agreement Life:** Impecina very quickly agreed to a 10-year term, payment in U.S. dollars, and other minor issues.

4. **Trade Name:** The Impecina negotiators placed great emphasis on their ability to use Metro's name in bidding, explaining how their competition in Peru had technical collaboration with three U.S. companies (as noted previously). "Did that mean Metro's National Tank Division could compete with Impecina in Peru?" they were asked rhetorically. (Actually both sides seem to have tacitly agreed that it was not possible for Metro to do business directly in Peru.)

5. **Licensee Market Size:** Attention turned to the dollar value of the future large (floating-roof) tank market in Peru. Impecina threw out an estimate of $200 million government expenditures and $40 million private-sector spending, over the coming three years, of which they targeted a one-third share. Later, a lower market-size estimate of $150 million (government *and* private) with a share of $50 million received by Impecina over three years was arrived at (memories are not clear on how the estimates were revised). "Will Impecina guarantee us they will obtain one-third of the market?" brought the response "That's an optimistic figure that we hope we can realize." Impecina offered as evidence their existing one-third share of the "fixed roof under 150 feet" market, an impressive achievement.

6. **Product Mix Covered by License:** It became clear that Impecina wanted floating-roof technology for *all* sizes, *and* fixed roof over 100-feet diameter. They suggested the agreement cover tanks over 100 feet in size. Impecina was asked if it would pay on all tanks (of any size) to simplify royalty calculation and monitoring. After considerable discussion, Metro seems to have acceded to Impecina's proposal (to cover both types, only over 100 feet) based on consensus over three points.
   a. The competition probably does not pay (its licensors) on small tanks and, therefore, Impecina would be at a disadvantage if it had to pay on small tanks also.
   b. The market in floating-roof tanks was usually over 100 feet.
   c. Impecina claimed that customers normally dictate the dimensions of the tanks, so Impecina cannot vary them in order to avoid paying a royalty to Metro.

7. **Compensation Formula:** Metro proposed an initial lump-sum payment (in two installments, one when the agreement is signed, the second on delivery of the computer program and designs), *plus* engineers and executives for bid assistance on a per diem rate, *plus* a royalty on successful bids based on the barrel capacity installed by Impecina. Impecina's American consultant countered with the idea of royalties on a sliding scale, lower with larger-capacity tanks, indicating talk about "1 million barrel capacity tanks." The (rhetorical?) question about Peru's oil capacity seems to have brought the discussion down to earth and veered it off on a tangent, while both sides mentally regrouped.

   On returning to this topic, Impecina executives ventured that as a rule of thumb their profit markup on a turnkey job was 6 percent. (However, on excluding the more price-sensitive portions such as excavation, piping, and ancillary equipment, which typically constitute half the value, Impecina conceded that on the tank alone they might mark up as much as 12 percent, although they kept insisting 5 to 6 percent was enough.)

   Impecina executives later offered only royalties (preferably sliding) *and* per diem fees for bid assistance from Metro executives and engineers.

   Metro countered by pointing out that per diem fees of $225 plus travel costs amounted at best to recovering costs, not profit.

   The compensation design question was left at this stage, deferred for later negotiation, the broad outlines having been laid. Metro's starting formal offer, which would mention specific numbers, was to be telexed to Lima in a week.

8. ***The Royalty Basis:*** Metro entertained the idea that Impecina engineers were very familiar with excavation, piping, wiring, and other ancillary equipment. Metro was transferring technology *for the tank alone,* which typically comprised half of overall installed value.

9. ***Government Intervention:*** Toward the end of the discussions, Impecina brought up the question of the Peruvian government having to approve of the agreement. This led to their retreat from the idea of a 10-year term agreed to earlier, and Impecina then mentioned five years. No agreement was reached. (Incidentally, Peru had in the last two years passed legislation indicating a "guideline" of five years for foreign licenses.)

INTERNAL DISCUSSION IN METRO LEADING TO THE FORMAL OFFER

The advantages derived by the licensee would be acquisition of floating-roof technology, time and money saved in attempting to generate the computerized design procedure in house, somewhat of a cost and efficiency advantage in bidding on larger tanks, and finally the use of Metro's name.

It was estimated that National Tank had spent $225,000 (one labor-year = two executives for six months, plus other costs) in developing the computer program. Additionally, it may cost $40,000 (three quarters of a labor-year) to convert the program into Spanish, the metric system, and adapt it to the material availability and labor cost factors peculiar to Peru. Simultaneously, there would be semiformal instruction of Impecina engineers in the use of the program, petroleum industry codes, and Metro fabrication methods. All this had to be done before the licensee would be ready for a single bid.

It was visualized that Metro would then assist Impecina for two labor-weeks for each bid preparation, and four labor-weeks on successful receipt of a contract award. Additionally, if Metro's specialized construction equipment were used, three labor-months of on-site training would be needed.

As the licensee's personnel moved along their learning curve, assistance of the type just described would diminish until it was no longer needed after a few successful bids.

Additional considerations that went into a determination of the initial offer:

1. Metro obligations (and sunk costs) in development and conversion were fairly determinate, whereas their obligations to assist Impecina in bidding depended on the technical sophistication and absorptive capacity of the licensee's engineers, their success rate in bidding, and so on.

2. If Impecina's market estimates were used, over the next three years, they would generate large tank orders worth $50 million, on which they would make a profit of $3 million (at 6 percent on $50 million or 12 percent on half the amount).

3. The market beyond three years was an unknown.

4. Exclusive rights might be given to Impecina in Peru and Colombia, with perhaps ICE reserving the right of conversion to nonexclusive if minimum market share was not captured.

5. While Impecina's multinational expansion plans were unknown, their business in the other nations was too small to justify granting them exclusivity. They may be satisfied with a vague promise of future consideration as an exclusive licensee in those territories.

6. Metro would agree to a term of 10 years. It was felt that Impecina computer and engineering capability was strong enough so they would not need Metro assistance after a few bids.

Surprisingly, the discussions reveal no explicit consideration given to the idea that Impecina may emerge some day as a multinational competitor.

In view of the uncertainty about how successful the licensee would actually be in securing orders, the uncertainty surrounding the Peruvian government's attitude, a safe strategy seemed to be to try and get as large a front-end fee as possible. Almost arbitrarily, a figure of $400,000 was thrown up. (This was roughly 150 percent of the development costs plus the initial costs of transferring the technology to the licensee.) There would be sufficient margin for negotiations and to cover uncertainties. In order that the licensee's competitiveness not be diminished by the large lump-sum fee, a formula as described later may be devised whereby the first five years' royalties could be reduced.

THE FORMAL OFFER

The formal offer communicated in a telex a week later called for the following payment terms:

- $400,000 lump-sum fee payable in two installments.
- A 2 percent royalty on any tanks constructed of a size over 100 feet in diameter, with up to one half of royalties owed in each of the first 5 years reduced by an amount up to $40,000 each year, without carryovers from year to year. The royalty percentage would apply to the total contract value less excavation, foundation, dikes, piping, instrumentation, and pumps.
- Agreement life of 10 years.
- Metro to provide services to Impecina described earlier in consideration of the lump-sum and royalty fees.
- For additional services, as described earlier, Metro would provide on request personnel paid up to $225 per day, plus travel and living costs while

away from their place of business. The per diem rates would be subject to escalation based on a representative cost index. There would be a ceiling placed on the number of labor-days Impecina could request in any year.

- All payments to be made in U.S. dollars, net, after all local withholding, and other taxes.
- Impecina would receive exclusive rights for Peru and Colombia only, and nonexclusive rights for Morocco, Libya, Algeria, Argentina, Venezuela, and Brazil. These could be converted to an exclusive basis on demonstration of sufficient business in the future. For Peru and Colombia, Metro reserves the right to treat the agreement as nonexclusive if Impecina fails to get at least 30 percent of installed capacity of a type covered by the agreement.
- Impecina would have the right to sublicense only to any of its controlled subsidiaries.
- Impecina would supply free of charge to ICE all improvements made by it on the technology during the term of the agreement.
- Impecina would be entitled to advertise its association with Metro in assigned territories on prior approval of ICE as to wording, form, and content.

THE FINAL AGREEMENT

ICE executives report that the Peruvians "did not bat an eyelid" at their demands, and that an agreement was soon reached in a matter of weeks. The only significant change was Metro agreeing to take a lump sum of $300,000 (still a large margin over costs). In return, the provision for reducing one half of the royalties up to $40,000 per year was *dropped*. The final agreement called for a straight 2 percent royalty payment (on tank value alone, as before). Other changes were minor: Impecina to continue to receive benefit of further R&D; ICE to provide at cost a construction engineer if specialized welding equipment was used; the per diem fee fixed at $200 per day (indexed by an average hourly wage escalation factor used by the U.S. Department of Labor); and the $300,000 lump-sum fee to be paid in installments over the first year.

In other respects such as territory, royalty rate, exclusivity, travel allowances, and so on, the agreement conformed with Metro's initial offer.

AN UPSET

The Peruvian government disallowed a 10-year agreement life. By then, both parties had gone too far to want

to reopen the entire negotiations and Metro appears to have resigned itself to an agreement life of five years, with a further extension of another five years subject to mutual consent. Given Impecina's in-house engineering and computer capability, extension of the agreement life was a very open question.

DISCUSSION QUESTIONS

Analyze the negotiations from each party's perspective:

1. List what each party is offering and what it hopes to receive.
2. Identify the elements in each list that are "musts" and those where flexibility may be shown, and state why.
3. Describe negotiating tactics or ploys each party used or could have used.
4. Compute net cash flows for each party under several scenarios. For example:
   a. Licensee fails to get a single order.
   b. Licensee gets one-third market share in Peru for three years, no orders thereafter, and no orders in any other nation.
   c. Licensee gets one-third share in Peru for ten years and half again as much in business in other nations, and so forth.
5. Compute the share of net present value of profits that each of the two parties will capture under various market scenarios.
6. What do you think of the rule of thumb, encountered in licensing literature, that licensors should settle for roughly one quarter to one half of the licensee's incremental profit?
7. a. Are sunk costs relevant here?
   b. What, if any, are the opportunity costs?
   c. In computing the licensor's cash flows, remember that in addition to the direct costs of implementing an agreement, there are sometimes substantial indirect costs. What are they? How would you apply the licensor's development costs to this exercise?
8. Why did the licensee accept the offer (with small changes) without "batting an eyelid"? (Hint: Calculate break-even sales for both parties.)
9. Should the licensor have threatened to pull out when the government limited the agreement life to five years? (Hint: Recalculate question 5 under a five-year limit.)
10. Do you think the licensee knew this all along?
11. Discuss the role of government intervention in licensing negotiations in general.

A.S. Norlight

In the middle of March 1992, Mrs. Anne Solbakken (CEO, and a major shareholder of Norlight—a privately owned corporation) had problems hiding her temper when she confronted her marketing manager, Mr. Ole Olsen. "This is a real mess!" she said, referring to a letter received that same morning from the company's Italian agent, Mr. Antonio di Napoli. Mr. di Napoli had in fact informed A.S. Norlight that he terminated the contract they had signed less than a year ago, and demanded Lira 500 million in indemnities.

This was not all. Their representative in Newcastle, GB-Light, had insisted on further changes of the present products in order to satisfy the requirements of the British market. According to Mr. Tore Bu, Norlight's financial officer, and Mr. Knut Johansen, the company's technical manager, the costs of complying with GB-Light's request would lead to a price increase that would virtually eliminate Norlight in the British market.

Fortunately, Norlight had a very good position in the home market, with about 30 percent market share and annual sales approaching NOK 60 million. This should enable them to sustain the costs incurred during the introduction period in new markets. In Norway, they were well entrenched in the market, had excellent relations to the distribution channels, and were technologically well ahead of their competitors. Return on sales had been close to 5 percent during each of the last four years, and annual net profit after taxes had been above NOK 1 million during the same period.

Their main competitor in the domestic market—it had actually developed into quite a rivalry—was A.S. Lite-Tech, also a Norwegian company, but companies from Germany and Sweden also held considerable market shares. However, it was quite typical for this industry worldwide that the domestic companies held an edge. The major reasons for this were the local design and technical standards, the great number of contractors and the peculiarities of the channels of distribution in each market.

Norlight's export ventures had come about in response to the Single Market Act, and expected increased competition from foreign competitors. After some discussion with representatives of the Norwegian Export Council, and having done some basic research on the marketing opportunities, it was decided to approach the following EC countries: Great Britain, Denmark, Italy, France, and Germany. The markets of Great Britain and Italy were considered to be the most promising, and Mr. Olsen was assigned the task of looking into the opportunities. A primary concern was to find the best possible candidates to work with—either an agent or a distributor.

After some investigation—partly through small advertisements in trade magazines, partly with the assistance of the local representatives of the Export Council—they ended up with a long list of candidates in each country, most of which seemed quite serious and capable. It was the most diverse types of companies, ranging from one-man operations to large, established import firms.

Mrs. Solbakken expressed some doubts as to what kind of company they ideally should tie up with. A large and well introduced import company with an established network of wholesalers and customers would perhaps be best suited, but such a company might be too big for Norlight. Norlight would only be a small and insignificant supplier to such a company. On the other hand, a "one-man operation" would be advantageous if that person would give all his attention to the Norlight products. After endless discussions, Mrs. Solbakken favored trying both alternatives.

THE BRITISH MARKET

In the United Kingdom Norlight negotiated with a company well introduced in this type of business, GB-Light Ltd. in Newcastle-upon-Tyne. This company had been importing electrical fixtures and equipment ever since the early 1960s, and had developed a large network of retailers mostly in the North East region of England. The company was chosen primarily because Mr. Jones, their managing director, immediately established a pleasant working relationship both with Mrs. Solbakken and Mr. Olsen, and because the company had excellent financial results and a very solid reputation. Yearly sales were about UK£ 14 million and the sales staff numbered 18 to 20 people.

The contract negotiations were a new and unexpected experience for both Mrs. Solbakken and Mr. Olsen. In the introductory phases they had met with Mr. Jones alone. He gave a refreshing impression of a professional manager, quite unlike the stereotyped picture of a British manager. When they later met in Newcastle to discuss the final details of the agency agreement, Mr. Jones was joined by three other men: Mr. P. Holloway, Mr. Jones' partner in GB-Light, Mr. A. G. Ressing, the sales manager, and Sir John Lawson, the company lawyer. The four were all equipped with a 10-page standard contract, which they would like to use as a starting point

This case was written by carl Arthur Solberg and Hermann Kopp at the Norwegian Management Institute. Although the background of the story is real, facts and names have been changed to disguise the company.

for the discussions. Sir John politely presented the details of the contract to the two representatives of Norlight.

Mrs. Solbakken was quite astounded. This was very different from the relaxed meetings they had previously had with Mr. Jones. During these meetings they had discussed things like commission and sales volume, and had reached a general agreement on these issues. The Norlight representatives believed the contract negotiations would be a mere formalization of this discussion. Instead they were met with a long range of new demands. Accordingly, Norlight was now expected to:

- Develop an English version of their product catalog, manuals, and service instructions.
- Transfer for one week in Newcastle a product engineer in order to train the sales and service people involved in the project.
- Send GB-Light within three weeks a complete set of demos at no cost.
- Stock sufficient spare parts and the most popular models in a warehouse in Newcastle.
- Guarantee maximum delivery to be no more than one month.
- Authorize GB-Light to grant price discounts, accept returns, and extend credit beyond four months when necessary.
- Contribute at least UK£ 20,000 to the introductory advertising campaign, and pay 25 percent of any future advertising campaigns.

Mrs. Solbakken did not find any clause in the suggested contract that really committed GB-Light in any significant way, and she and Mr. Olsen had a hard time introducing such terms as:

- Minimum sales the first year UK£ 200,000 to be increased to UK£ 400,000 in the third year.
- A guarantee that GB-Light would not extend credit or pursue sales to customers who had exhibited a notoriously bad credit record.
- Changes in prices and terms of payment should be submitted to Norlight for approval.

In order to accept such "concessions," the GB-Light negotiators demanded a new clause entitling their company to a compensation of UK£ 20,000 if any of Norlight's commitments were breached. This was a bitter pill to swallow, but was accepted because Mrs. Solbakken and Mr. Olsen felt confident that Norlight could comply, and because the British representatives seemed quite stubborn on this if they were to accept Norlight's requirements.

Back in Norway, the Norlight organization immediately began their preparations to fulfill their commitments. The brochures and manuals were translated, and the company's development manager was sent to Newcastle to train GB-Light's sales and service people. Arrange-ments were also made to rent storage space and the demo models were shipped. Finally UK£ 20,000 were transferred to GB-Light's account in Barclay's Bank. A rough calculation indicated that by now NOK 500,000 had been spent on the introduction.

Mr. Bu, the financial officer, persuaded the local bank to extend the company's line of credit, and submitted a request for support from the Export Council. The council was generally prepared to cover part of the costs for translation, initial training, and advertising expenses.

THE ITALIAN MARKET

The Italian experience was quite different. Mr. Olsen received a telephone call from Mr. Antonio di Napoli. He was at the Oslo airport, had just landed, and was just starting a two-week holiday with his family. He referred to the ads about representation, and was prepared to stop by Norlight anytime during his visit to discuss the prospects of working together.

Mr. di Napoli arrived at Norlight's headquarters the next morning. He was a charming and knowledgeable man who could refer to a long list of references in Italy. He was an experienced salesman and had worked in the electro fixtures industry for several decades. He knew the dealers better than his own cousins. After a visit to the factory, he expressed great interest in being Norlight's agent in Italy. At the end of a couple of hours of discussion, they agreed in principle on the main points of a representation agreement. The contract would be signed before Mr. di Napoli returned to Italy, about two weeks later. This would give Norlight's management a chance to check some of his references.

All references recommended Mr. di Napoli, and they also double checked with the Milan office of the Norwegian Export Council. Mrs. Solbakken and Mr. Olsen were confident that they had found the right man for the job, but Mr. Bu was somewhat reserved. "We haven't even considered the names on the list of candidates we already have," he said. He was overruled by the two others, who were very impressed with Mr. di Napoli, not least his mastery of English which they considered unusual in Italy.

A contract was signed, and the major terms were:

- Mr. di Napoli would get exclusive rights for all of Norlight's products in Italy.
- He was committed to sell for at least Lira 200 million in the first full year of operations, increasing to Lira 500 million the following year and reaching Lira 1 billion in the fourth year.
- His commission would be 10 percent on total sales.
- The two parties would seek to develop a good spirit of cooperation.

No mention was made of advertising expenditures. In fact, Mr. di Napoli did not place any importance on advertising. "What matters," he said, "is a good network of personal contacts. Then the rest comes by itself!" Mr. di Napoli even agreed to return to Norway soon in order to get required technical training, and he was prepared to cover the travel costs himself.

BUSINESS AS USUAL?

After half a year of operations, the status of Norlight's export efforts could be summed up as follows:

In the United Kingdom trial orders started to come in already two weeks after the first "introductory months" (when all the preparatory work was done). GB-Light had in fact presented the products at a local trade fair near Newcastle, and received some noticeable interest from one dealer. However, Mr. Jones reported that in order to push the sales, they had to grant substantial discounts, between 12 and 15 percent. Mr. Olsen was not in doubt: "We have to go along with these requirements, otherwise we will not get our products out to the dealers, and then nobody will use them." This made sense, but the other officers of the company were reluctant. Mr. Bu exclaimed: "Who do they think they are? We've already put more than half a million kroners in this venture and now they are asking for discounts!" However, they agreed to allow GB-Light to grant a 5 to 7 percent discount to select customers.

The reaction from Mr. Jones was one of qualified acceptance. After some weeks he returned with a request for "minor product alterations," as he put it. "Our dealers find it difficult to achieve preference for your products as they now stand and at the price you quote . . . etc. . . . .etc." He finally suggested some changes in the design of the products.

Mr. Johansen was furious. "We have had endless discussion with our British representative on just about every tiny issue of our products, and of our marketing program, but so far they haven't achieved a single major sale. In Italy we don't meet any such objections. Both prices and products are being accepted as they are, and Antonio has been successful with about 20 dealers. I think we should look for a new distributor in the United Kingdom. I'm fed up with all their 'minor product alterations.' It only adds to our production costs!"

In Italy, things developed nicely. There was an endless stream of orders, initial trial orders, that later reached considerable numbers. In fact, next year's sales target had already been exceeded. Norlight was very happy and executed the orders as they came in. "We certainly have found the right representative in Italy," Mrs. Solbakken said one morning.

However, next week, Mr. Bu entered her office and presented last quarter's figures. It turned out that only 10 percent of all the invoices that were due from the Italian customers had been paid. "I don't like this," he grunted, "I wonder what kind of customers our friend Antonio is selling to?" "I can't understand this," Mr. Olsen said, "last week Antonio reassured me that our customer base was very solid, and based on his references, I find it hard to doubt what he's saying." "That's fine, Ole," the financial officer countered, "but I think that when 12 out of 14 invoices have not been paid in time—and we've granted liberal credit terms—then it's time to review our credit policies towards our Italian customers!"

Mr. Olsen conceded that something should be done and agreed to write a letter to Mr. di Napoli airing Norlight's concerns. The situation did not improve when they received a message two days later from Banco di Milano that Stella Lucia, their biggest account so far in Italy, had filed for bankruptcy. An inquiry to the Export Council revealed that several of Mr. di Napoli's customers did not exhibit the world's best track record concerning timely payments. In his report the trade officer in Milan added that this is not unusual in Italy, and that Norlight would have to be patient if they wanted to retrieve their accounts receivable. Mr. Olsen, nevertheless, tried to be very polite when writing his letter (Exhibit 1).

"Gentlemen," she said, "we have tried for one year to enter two export markets. The results so far are not satisfactory. We are, of course, newcomers, but what we are experiencing now exceeds any expectation of bad luck. The efforts that we have put into these two markets cannot be quantified, but we spent at least NOK 700,000 in the United Kingdom, and our customers in Italy owe us more than Lira 150 million, plus of course Antonio's demand for indemnity. And if this was not enough, I'm sorry to tell you that our business in Norway has suffered. We have not paid enough attention to our domestic business and our market share and profits have been eroding. I think time has come to reassess our strategy. This should be done before we discuss how to proceed with Antonio and GB-Light. I look forward to your comments!"

EXHIBIT 1   The Response, However, Was Not Very Pleasant (Exhibit 2)

Ytterfjord
Norway

Tel (476)330780
Fax (476)330770

Mr. Antonio di Napoli
Villa di Lucia
Genoa
Italy

March 2, 1992

Dear Antonio,

We have just received the news of Stella Lucia's bankruptcy, and would like to ask you to do anything in your power to minimize our loss. We have also experienced that some of your other customers are not paying our invoices on time, and this is clearly not acceptable.

So far we have liberally paid your commission and intend to do so in the future, but we are forced to suggest some new routines:

1. All new customers should pay by Letter of Credit, and established customers who do not meet their obligations in time should be required to do the same. This, naturally, is until we get to know them better.

2. We will not transfer any commission on sales before payment has been received from the customer.

I trust you understand this and look forward to hearing from you in the near future.

Sincerely,

Ole Olsen
Sales Manager

EXHIBIT 2   Mrs. Solbakken Immediately Called a Management Meeting

Antonio di Napoli
Genoa
Italy

Tel. (371)6590034
Telex 78560 agent i

Norlight A/S
POB 13
Ytterfjord
Norway

<u>Att. Ole Olsen</u>

Re terms of payment

I have received your letter of March 2, 1992, and can inform you that I do not see how I can work under the conditions stated in your letter. I thought that I had to do with professional business people, but your suggestions on commission payments and L/C suggest to me that we will have problems in getting along in the future.

I will therefore by April 1, 1992, end our relationship, and will demand that you pay a fee of Lira 500 million in indemnities.

Sincerely yours,

Antonio di Napoli

Ascom Hasler Mailing Systems Inc.: Competing in the Shadow of a Giant

INTRODUCTION

On a beautiful fall day in New England at the end of the millennium, Michael Allocca, president of Ascom Hasler Mailing Systems Inc., was struggling with the question of how to move his company beyond its position as one of the three dwarfs of the postage meter industry. Although his company had achieved the greatest share gain of any competitor in the United States between 1985 and 1997, he was not complacent. He was number three in the U.S. market, and number one still had more than 85 percent of the total market.

Moreover, there were technological, market, and regulatory changes occurring that opened up entry possibilities for new entrants who had in effect been blocked from entry to the industry for the past half-century and longer.

Globalization had come to the sleepy postage meter industry with a vengeance, and Mr. Allocca was worried. He knew that he needed a strategy to improve his position, and questioned in his own mind whether he had one. He remembered the famous Von Clausewitz maxim: "the best strategy is to be everywhere very strong, first generally and then at the decisive point." Easy to say, he thought, but how could he be strong as a dwarf in the industry? And, furthermore, what was the decisive point?

HISTORY AND EVOLUTION OF THE U.S. POSTAGE METER INDUSTRY

In 1920, Arthur Pitney and Walter Bowes received approval from the United States Post Office to market a device they had invented, which they called a postage meter. The postage meter was a complex mechanical device that provided the secure storing of fund information, the dispensing of postage, and the printing of indicia on envelopes or tape. It was a convenient replacement for the postage stamp in higher-volume mail applications. Pitney Bowes, Inc. was born, and a manufacturing and corporate facility was established in Stamford, Connecticut. At about the same time, similar companies were independently established in

This case was prepared by Michael A. Allocca, President and CEO, Ascom Hasler Inc. and Doctoral Candidate at Lubin School of Business, Pace University, New York under the supervision of Warren J. Keegan, Professor of International Business and Marketing and Director of the Institute for Global Business Strategy, as a basis for class discussion rather than to illustrate either effective or ineffective handling of a business situation. © 2000 Dr. Warren J. Keegan. Used with permission.

Europe. Today there are four major players globally. Pitney Bowes (PB), remaining the largest by far, has three European counterparts.

Since its beginning, PB has aggressively defended its market share. Today, after the infiltration by three foreign competitors, it still retains about 85 percent of the U.S. market. It has very effectively used its portfolio of over 3,000 patents as a weapon and barrier to the entry of other competitors. In 1959, the U.S. Justice Department challenged PB's monopoly. As part of the consent decree that resulted, PB was required to license its patents, royalty free. This and other constraints were lifted late in the 1960s; however, it still offers its patents for a royalty fee to avoid further confrontation with the Justice Department and the U.S. Postal Service (USPS).

While there has been substantial growth in electronic communications, facsimile, and other substitutes for the postal service, mail continues to grow and to be a cost-effective, major source of information transfer in the United States. Each year the USPS delivers over 100 billion pieces of mail through over 38,000 post offices, to over 130 million delivery points. The USPS handles 41 percent of the world's mail volume, over 630 million pieces every day. The next largest postal service market is in Japan, which handles 6 percent of the world's mail volume. With its budget of over $50 billion, and over 750,000 career employees, if the USPS were in the *Fortune* 500, it would be ranked number eight.

While they have some presence in most developed countries around the globe, all postage meter manufacturers concentrate their efforts in five main markets: the United States, Canada, France, Germany, and the United Kingdom.

THE MAJOR PLAYERS

A significant measure of U.S. market share is the division of the installed base of postage meters on rental, published quarterly by the USPS. Exhibit 1 is an indication of recent trends.

PITNEY BOWES

Pitney Bowes, clearly the world leader in the manufacture and sale of mailing equipment, in 1998 had total revenues that exceeded $4.2 billion. Revenue from the sales and financing of mailing equipment, related supplies and services, and postage meters exceeded $2.7 billion. The remaining revenue comes primarily from its Office Solutions business, which includes the sale, financing, rental, and service of reprographic and facsimile equipment and related supplies and facilities management services.

EXHIBIT 1

	1985		1990		1995		1998	
	Units	%	Units	%	Units	%	Units	%
PB	956,987	91.6	1,156,585	88.6	1,303,106	85.8	1,399,156	82.9
Neopost	52,077	5.0	67,277	5.1	87,912	5.8	123,367	7.3
Ascom	21,007	2.0	64,018	4.9	104,412	6.9	118,774	7.0
Postalia	15,227	1.4	15,227	1.4	23,363	1.5	46,497	2.8
Totals	**1,045,298**	**100**	**1,303,107**	**100**	**1,518,793**	**100**	**1,687,794**	**100**

Figures represent installed meters at year-end.

PB's historically strong financial performance is based on the foundation of its postage meter rental base and equipment leasing business. *Fortune* magazine, in its April 27, 1998 issue, ranked PB number one in the Office Equipment Industry Group for Net Operating Profit Margin, Return on Stockholder's Equity, 3-Year Total Return, and 10-year Total Return.

In its mailing equipment business, PB offers the most comprehensive product line, including postage meter machines, letter folders, inserters, openers, addressing machines, and PC-based mailing and shipping systems. It offers more "one-stop-shopping" opportunities than any of its competitors. It prides itself on being a product innovator and uses its huge patent portfolio to defend its inventions and to provide an entry barrier to would-be encroachers in its highly valued and protected market. PB ranked among the top 200 recipients of U.S. patents for 13 years in a row. In 1998, it spent over $100 million in research and development, and was awarded 124 patents, with 44 percent more than in 1997, its highest year ever. PB has a precedent for effectively using its patent clout when each of its foreign competitors attempted to introduce electronic postage meters into the market.

When competitors introduced new products into PB's home market, its strong technology base allowed it to respond quickly. It did so when Neopost introduced the first electronic postage meter, when Ascom Hasler introduced the first modular machines, and when Francotyp-Postalia introduced the first digital-printing meters. It is trying to do so again, as two California start-ups introduced the first Web-based postage systems.

A primary ingredient in PB's formula for domination of the U.S. market has been its direct-sales organization, consisting of over 100 branch offices and thousands of sales and service representatives distributed throughout the country. In 1998, it mounted a new distribution initiative to address the fast-growing SOHO (Small Office, Home Office) market, with the creation of its "Office Direct" business unit. It will provide channels for PB's future Web-based products and lower ticket items that cannot support direct sales. Channels include telemarketing, direct-mail marketing, television, the Internet, and retail office-supply store chains.

For the first time in its history, PB has boldly turned to an "outsider" (Brother of Japan) for the development and production of a core product, risking the potential creation of a formidable future competitor. It did so to produce a stand-alone meter product with very low cost to target a new market of very low-mail-volume users. It is using direct marketing and, again for the first time, TV advertising to convince these low-mail-volume users to switch from stamps to a cost-effective postage meter.

PB very effectively uses its wholly owned subsidiary, Pitney Bowes Credit Corporation, to lease its mailing systems products. Once "captured," a customer is continually revisited for lease renewal.

NEOPOST

Neopost, based in Paris, France, started in the mailing equipment business at about the same time as PB. Its U.S. subsidiary began in 1933 as Friden, a California-based calculator company. It later expanded into the mailing equipment business, becoming the second U.S. supplier. It was later merged with Roneo, a British company that had been in the mailing equipment business since the 1930s. Neopost manufactures in France and in the United Kingdom.

The company prides itself on being a technical innovator in its new products. Friden had the distinction, in 1979, of introducing the first electronic postage meter, before PB. At the time of the decertification of mechanical meters by the USPS, Neopost had mostly electronic meters in the U.S. market and was, therefore, less negatively impacted than its competitors. It has a full product-line offering, manufacturing a line of letter folders and inserters and OEM'ing PC-based mail/shipping management systems to round out its product line. It was quick to develop a digital thermal transfer meter after Francotyp-Postalia, and also got an early start in developing Internet-based postage-evidencing products.

Neopost USA has its headquarters in Union City, California, where it employs about 250 people. It distributes its products through 22 direct field offices in major markets and over 150 independent dealers. Total U.S. employment is over 1,300. Like PB, it also has its own subsidiary that provides equipment leasing to its customers.

ASCOM HASLER MAILING SYSTEMS

Ascom A.G. (Ascom), a $2 billion corporation headquartered in Bern, Switzerland, focuses two thirds of its business in the telecommunications market in the areas of carrier access, PBX, paging, defense and security systems, and terminals. The remaining third of its business is in an area it calls "Service Automation," which includes cash-handling systems, payphone systems, transport revenue systems (ticketing), and mailing systems (Ascom Hasler Mailing Systems [AHMS]). For at least the past 10 years, Ascom has experienced difficulty in its core business due to the privatization of the Swiss Telecom industry, which began to privatize and open its market to foreign competitors in the late 1980s. As a result, AHMS took a back seat to the needs of Ascom's telecom core business.

In recent years, its core telecommunications business has also suffered from an acquisition that resulted in a significant cash drain on the company before it failed. Investments in its noncore companies were minimized while it struggled to return its core business to profitability. As a result, AHMS fell behind all of its competitors in new product offerings. In fact, in the mid-1990s, it found itself without a low-end meter product when its mechanical model was decertified by the USPS, and it had no electronic model to replace it.

Ascom Hasler can trace its origin back to the same era as PB, although it has been in the United States only since the early 1980s. Unlike its three competitors, it distributes exclusively through a network of independent dealers in the United States. It has no direct sales offices in the United States and the core of its product line consists of a range of electronic mailing machines manufactured in Bern that still print mechanically, most of which have been installed recently to replace the USPS decertified mechanical machines. These machines are vulnerable to a further decertification by the USPS, which will ultimately require that all meters in service print digital, encrypted indicia. It is the only manufacturer that has not yet introduced a digital-printing postage meter. It is also the only manufacturer that has not announced plans to market a PC-based postage product.

Over half of AHMS's business is in the United States. Their U.S. organization consists primarily of customer and distribution support. In the past few years, an engineering organization has been formed at its headquarters in Shelton, Connecticut, to develop software-based products for global markets and to support development efforts in Bern, Switzerland. Engineering and manufacture of the company's core postage meter products are performed in Bern. Ascom uses a third party to lease its products.

FRANCOTYP-POSTALIA

Francotyp-Postalia, Inc. (FP) entered the U.S. market in 1961. It is a subsidiary of Francotyp-Postalia, A.G., of Berlin, Germany. The parent started in 1923 as a manufacturer of special machinery and office machines and as electric equipment wholesalers. It markets its mailing products in 86 countries. The U.S. subsidiary, primarily a distributor, is located in Lisle, Illinois, and employs about 100 people. The German-based mailing equipment manufacturer, while a major player in its home market, has not made a noticeable impact on the market in the United States. Until recently its product line was extremely limited, causing it to market relabeled products manufactured by Neopost in England. Until the mid-1990s, FP was the only manufacturer that was not able to offer postage meter resetting by phone. At that time, FP appeared to mount a new initiative when it built a new, modem manufacturing facility in East Berlin and launched an extensive new-product development effort. FP was the first manufacturer to introduce a postage meter named "Conquest," which printed variable information digitally using a dot-matrix print head and thermal transfer technology. The introduction of Conquest, and later a higher-mail-volume machine using inkjet technology to print indicia, placed FP on a new market-share growth curve, making it the fastest-growing meter supplier in the United States.

In July 1998, FP entered into a strategic partnership with E-Stamp, a start-up company pioneering on-line postage.

FP has two direct sales offices in the United States but uses independent mailing and office equipment dealers as its main distribution network to sell and service its products. It uses a third party to lease its products.

THE PRODUCTS

Early meters were totally mechanical and utilized an electric motor to drive a rotary drum containing a print die of the indicia. When cost-effective electronics and microprocessors became available in the mid-1970s, they were utilized in postage meter design to provide keyboard input, display, calculation, and control. A motor-driven print drum was still used to deliver the indicia to the envelope or tape. The transition from mechanical to electronic/software devices proved to be a challenge for all manufacturers.

In addition to postage meters, manufacturers also produce mailing machines that allow for the automatic feeding, sealing, and stacking of mail at various speeds. Postage meters are mounted on these machines to perform the printing of postage indicia within the mail feeding-stacking process. In this configuration, the meter is rented and owned by the manufacturer (by U.S. postal regulation), while the mailing machine is sold. Other peripheral products, including postal scales that compute postage rates based upon weight, folders, inserters, and mail openers, as well as PC-based mail management systems are manufactured or sourced from OEM suppliers in an effort to provide a complete product line.

AN AGGRESSIVE USPS CHANGES ORIENTATION

A congressional hearing in 1967 concluded that despite a huge growth in mail volume, with the exception of the zip code, the mail was being handled the same way it was 100 years ago. Years of mismanagement, labor problems, poor control of operations, and transportation facilities resulted in a post office that was inefficient and piling up debt. Its heavily subsidized rates bore little relationship to its costs.

In 1969, Congress passed the Postal Service Act, removing the Postmaster General from the President's Cabinet, and creating a self-supporting postal corporation wholly owned by the federal government. The Post Office Department became the United States Postal Service (USPS), an independent establishment of the executive branch of the U.S. government. Operational authority transferred from the Congress to the USPS executive management and the board of governors. Despite this new orientation, the USPS continued to face mounting financial and competitive pressures. Substitutes for mail, including facsimile and electronic messaging, and funds transfer threatened to reduce the volume of mail. Private companies, such as Federal Express, dominated the market for urgent delivery of mail and packages.

On May 5, 1992, Marvin Runyon became the 70th Postmaster General of the United States. Unlike several of his predecessors, Runyon was not a postal career employee. Following a 37-year career with Ford, he became CEO of Nissan, U.S.A. In 1988, he left Nissan to take the top job at the Tennessee Valley Authority, where he was responsible for a major turnaround of the organization, achieving cumulative savings and efficiency improvements of $1.8 billion and stable rates for the first time in 20 years.

Runyon wasted no time in implementing similar cost-cutting changes at the USPS. Within six months, he built a leaner management structure, improved customer service, and increased efficiency that resulted from 47,000 voluntary employee retirements. His actions essentially eliminated a $2 billion deficit the USPS faced in 1993 and set records for on-time performance and customer satisfaction.

In 1993, Runyon targeted the postage meter as a device subject to tampering, claiming that losses to the USPS exceed $100 million annually. Meter manufacturers were criticized for not incorporating state-of-the-art technology, particularly microprocessors, making the devices inherently more tamper-proof. The new technology was not embraced because previous USPS administrations discouraged its use, and the rental business model favored the lower-cost, longer-life attributes of the simpler mechanical meters. As part of Runyon's initiative, the USPS started a campaign to "decertify" mechanical meters and demand that they be removed from the market and be replaced by safer, electronic meters. For postage meter manufacturers this meant that their existing, profitable rental base of meters would have to be replaced and recapitalized at great cost. Compared to their mechanical counterparts, electronic meters are significantly more costly to design, produce, and maintain, and have much shorter life cycles, both factors having negative impact on the meter rental financial model.

USPS decertification schedule announced in May 1996:

- *June 1, 1996:* Placements of new mechanical meters would no longer be allowed.

- *March 1, 1997:* Mechanical meters used by firms processing mail for a fee would have to be removed from service.
- *December 31, 1998:* Mechanical meters mounted on machines that automatically feed, seal, and stack mail would have to be removed from service. This resulted in a one-time windfall for manufacturers whose customers were required to upgrade their automatic machines to handle the newly mandated electronic meters.
- *March 1, 1999:* All remaining mechanical meters (*stand-alone meters*), would have to be removed from service.

The new, financially oriented USPS openly encouraged the use of new technologies, promising an expedient certification process. At the same time, it used its power to start a process that would lead to the decertification and phasing out of all mechanical meters by March 31, 1999. It also aggressively took over the funds that manufacturers were holding in trust for its customers to allow for the resetting of postage meters by phone. Manufacturers lost the interest on those funds, which they claimed helped cover costs of operating the system. PB sued the USPS for breach of contract and settled in mid-1999 for $52 million. It is expected that the other manufacturers affected will follow PB's lead.

TECHNOLOGY-DRIVEN CHANGES

Today, growth in the use of computers for electronic funds transfers (EFT) has led to the development of technologies to ensure the safety of such transfers. Microelectronics, software, and communications technologies provide systems that are virtually impossible to infiltrate. Elaborate systems that encrypted data before transmission were developed to ensure security.

Working closely with Carnegie Mellon University in its Information-Based Indicia Program, the USPS defined its own criteria for a system that would result in the secure printing of postage indicia. The system, developed and announced by the USPS in May 1995, is based upon encrypted Information Based Indicia (IBI). The IBI contains the following information: readable postage amount, mail class, date, device ID number, and town or licensing post office; in addition, a two-dimensional bar code that encodes the readable information as well as a digital signature (for security management), and delivery point code. Unlike the indicia produced by a die mounted on a rotary drum, each printed indicia is unique, making counterfeiting virtually impossible.

Much of the new technology is covered by PBs' patent portfolio. On June 10, 1999, PB announced that it had filed suit against E-Stamp, a new market entry, charging that E-Stamp was infringing on PB patents. At the same time, PB announced that it was involved in "discussions" with other marketers of computer-based postal products, to grant patent licenses for use of PB-developed technology.

NEW MARKET ENTRIES AND THE INTERNET

The USPS, as a regulator, had always been a barrier to new entrants into the postage meter business. In its new image, it has encouraged and openly promoted new entrants, and encouraged the use of new technology not requiring huge capital investments. As a result, two new, serious players have entered the market, providing a software alternative to postage stamps to a new segment of the market: the small office and the home (SOHO) having Internet access.

E-Stamp, a California start-up, developed a system entitled E-Stamp Internet Postage that allows a user to access the Internet and download postage funds into a secure device interfaced to the user's existing PC and printer. The secure device is rented to the user for a monthly fee. The user can draw funds from the secure device to print postal indicia developed on the PC, directly on envelopes, labels, or documents on an existing off-the-shelf PC printer. E-Stamp has received financing from Microsoft Corporation, AT&T Ventures, Compaq Computer Corporation, and FP. Its management team includes computer industry veterans from Microsoft and Oracle. In the summer of 1999, its products were approved by the USPS and the company announced its intentions to go public.

Stamps.com, also a California start-up, developed a system called Stamps.com Internet Postage that utilizes the Internet, but does not require a secure device to interface with the user's PC. Instead, it allows users to print the USPS-approved indicia on envelopes, labels, or documents directly as it is transmitted over the Internet. Printing is accomplished on the user's existing off-the-shelf PC printer. Stamps.com will charge a premium of about 10 percent for postage, which the company claims is significantly less than the 18 to 25 percent levied by traditional postage meter systems. Stamps.com's business venture partners include Intel and AOL. In the summer of 1999, its products were approved by the USPS and the company went public.

While there are two on-line-postage products that have received the final approval of the USPS, there are also three additional products on test:

1. *PC Stamp*, a stand-alone product offered by Neopost.
2. *Postage Plus,* an on-line product offered by Neopost.
3. *Click-stamp,* a stand-alone product offered by PB (PB is also expected to offer an on-line product shortly).

WHAT TO DO

Mr. Allocca looked again at the beautiful New England landscape. He knew that the clock was ticking, and that things would never be the same for the postage meter industry. He knew that he needed a strategy, and that it had to address both the competition and the need to create a unique value. As he saw the situation, there were four options:

1. Convince its parent company, Ascom, to significantly increase its investment in new-product development, manufacturing, and marketing. To be effective in the required time frame might require a total restructuring of the organization worldwide.
2. Establish a partnership with a competitor, or competitors, or perhaps the USPS, to address the imbalance in the marketplace caused by the dominance of the industry giant.
3. Phase out the company's postage meter business in favor of a related business in which a competitive advantage could reasonably be realized. Perhaps a source of opportunity could be the growing population of shipments over the Internet. Use of funds from the postage meter rental base could help to fund a new venture.
4. Ascom could divest itself of the mailing business and concentrate on its core telecommunications business. Perhaps a sale to a competitor would be a possibility.

Which option would you choose? Would you develop another?

DISCUSSION QUESTIONS

1. Analyze the attractiveness of the U.S. postage meter mailing equipment industry for:
   - Pitney Bowes
   - PB's three foreign competitors
   - An increasingly profit-oriented USPS
   - New Internet-based market entries
2. Develop a SWOT analysis for each of the players listed in question 1.
3. What key issues must be considered in the development of a go-forward business strategy for each of the players listed in question 1?
4. Develop a scenario of how the industry structure might change over the next five years.
5. Which one of the options identified by Mr. Allocca would you choose? Why?
6. Formulate your recommended strategy for Ascom Hasler Inc. and Ascom A.G.

CHAPTER 11

Product Decisions

The prospects for American car manufacturers in Europe would appear to be good if they will meet the conditions and requirements of these various countries but to attempt to do so on the lines on which business is done in America would make it a fruitless task.
—JAMES COUZENS, 1907–
Officer of the Ford Motor Company

CONTENTS

Ste. Suisse Microelectronique et d'Horlogerie S.A. (SMH) is best known as the corporate home of the Swatch watch. A truly global brand, the Swatch name is synonymous with innovative watch designs that, in the early 1980s, virtually reinvented the watch as a moderately priced, durable fashion accessory. Trend-conscious consumers snapped up 100 million of the colorful watches between 1983 and 1993. During the same period, the Swiss share of the global timepiece market rose from 15 percent to more than 50 percent, in large measure because of Swatch.

The fabulous Swatch, which sold for $40 around the world for the first decade (1986–1996) and which now sells for $50 around the world, is designed in the Swatch Design Lab in Milan, headed by Franco Bosisio who also runs SMH Italy. Why? Because Northern Italy is one of the design centers of the world, and people who are interested in design want to come there. In addition, they also value the chance to interact with Alessandro Mendini, the lab's art director and a major figure in European styling.

SMH was created to save the fragmented and wounded Swiss watch industry. The Swiss banks were ready to pull the plug and let Asian companies take over the global watch industry. One man, Nicolas Hayek, convinced the banks that he had a better idea: Form SMH to take over some of the most celebrated luxury brands and launch the Swatch. SMH is much more than the Swatch company: It is also a leader in the luxury watch category in which the Swiss know no peer in the world. *Swiss Made* is synonymous with value and luxury in the world of watches. SMH has nine major global brands: Blancpain, Omega, Longines, Rado, Tissot, Certina, Hamilton, Swatch, and Flik Flak. Marketing in SMH is radically decentralized, but production is not. The brand managers have total authority over design, marketing, and communications, but they play a limited role in manufacturing and assembly.

The Blancpain (since the 18th century there has never been a quartz Blancpain and there never will be) is a mechanical watch that sells for over $100,000, and the Omega brand retails price from $1,000 to $50,000. When SMH was formed, Omega was a wreck. The key to success in luxury is exclusivity: The maximum number of luxury watches that you can sell worldwide and still be a luxury watch is 600,000. Omega got greedy and responded to calls from dealers for lower-priced watches. At one point, Omega was making over 2,000 models. No one knew what the brand stood for. Under SMH, the number of models was cut back to 130, and Omega has been repositioned as an elite watch for people who achieve.

In 1991, SMH chairman Nicolas Hayek announced the signing of a contract with Volkswagen to develop a battery-powered "Swatch car." At the time, Hayek said his goal was to build "an ecologically inoffensive, high-quality city car for two people" that would sell for about $6,400. Two years later, the alliance with Volkswagen was dissolved; Hayek claimed it was because of disagreement on the concept of the car (Volkswagen officials said low profit projections were the problem). In the spring of 1994, Hayek announced that he had lined up a new joint venture partner. The Mercedes-Benz unit of Daimler-Benz AG would invest 750 million deutsche marks in a new factory in Hambach—Saargemuend, France. Although a prototype was unveiled in Stuttgart in March, test models were not scheduled to be available until the 1996 Olympics in Atlanta. Swatch spent $40 million to be an official sponsor of the 1996 games.

The focus of this chapter is the product, probably the most crucial element of a marketing program. To a very important degree, a company's products define its business. Every aspect of the enterprise—including pricing, communication, and distribution policies—must fit the product. A firm's customers and competitors are determined by the products it offers. Research and development (R&D) requirements will depend in part on the technologies of a company's products and in part—as is clear from the Swatch example—on the vision of its managers and executives. The challenge facing a company with global horizons is to develop product policies and strategies that are sensitive to market needs, competition, and company resources on a global scale. Product policy must strike a balance between the payoff from adapting products to local market preferences and the competitive advantages that come from concentrating company resources on a limited number of standardized products.

This chapter examines the major dimensions of global product decisions. First, basic product concepts are explored. The diversity of preferences and needs in global markets is then underlined by an examination of product saturation levels. Product design criteria are identified and attitudes toward foreign products are explored. The next section outlines strategic alternatives available to global marketers. Finally, new-product issues in global marketing are discussed.

◆ BASIC CONCEPTS

We begin our introduction to global product decisions by briefly reviewing product concepts typically covered in a basic marketing course. All basic product concepts are fully applicable to global marketing. Additional concepts that apply specifically to global marketing are also discussed.

PRODUCTS: DEFINITION AND CLASSIFICATION

What is a product? On the surface, this seems like a simple question with an obvious answer. A product can be defined in terms of its tangible, physical attributes—such as weight, dimensions, and materials. Thus, an automobile could be defined as 3,000 pounds of metal or plastic, measuring 190" long, 75" wide, and 59" high. However, any description limited to physical attributes gives an incomplete account of the benefits a product provides. At a minimum, car buyers expect an automobile to provide safe, comfortable transportation, which derives from physical features such as air bags and adjustable seats. However, marketers cannot ignore status, mystique, and other intangible product attributes that a particular model of automobile may provide. Indeed, major segments of the auto market are developed around these intangible attributes.

Similarly, Harley-Davidson riders get much more than basic transportation from their beloved "hogs." The Harley is a recreational product: Even people who ride their Harleys to work are riding because it is a form of recreation. The motorcycle in low-income countries is a form of transportation. Clearly, there is a literal world of difference between the need served by a motorcycle to the recreational rider and the rider who is using the motorcycle as a form of transportation. Some companies such as Harley are focused on the recreational rider (Harley also sells to the police market) whereas others, such as Honda, sell to recreational riders and to the basic transportation market. Harley, however, focuses on a broad spectrum of needs: needs for status, fun, affiliation with the Harley legend and history and with Harley riders both past and present, and the feeling that riders experience on a Harley. Harley is a luxury brand: expensive, exclusive, and special. Harley-Davidson is selling a social and personal experience. The Harley has a unique sound and feel. It is a brand that has evolved over time with a genetic link to its origins. The Harley is an American bike that celebrates the romance, adventure, and camaraderie of travel. When you buy a Harley, you are eligible to become a member of the Harley Owners Group (HOG). As a HOG member, you will meet other Harley owners and share the fun and pleasure of motorcycling with others.

Honda is an example of an activity-based strategy company: If you can power it with a motor, Honda will make it, from 50 to 5000cc, from a few hundred dollars to $75,000 dollars, from the transportation market in the developing world to the recreation market in any country.

A product, then, can be defined as a collection of physical, psychological, service, and symbolic attributes that collectively yield satisfaction, or benefits, to a buyer or user.

A number of frameworks for classifying products have been developed. A frequently used classification is based on users and distinguishes between consumer and industrial goods. Both types of goods, in turn, can be further classified on the basis of other criteria, such as how they are purchased (convenience, preference, shopping, and specialty goods) and their life span (durable, nondurable, and disposable).[1] These and other classification frameworks developed for domestic marketing are fully applicable to global marketing.

PRODUCTS: LOCAL, NATIONAL, INTERNATIONAL, AND GLOBAL

Many companies find that, as a result of expanding existing businesses or acquiring a new business, they have products for sale in a single national market. For example, Kraft Foods at one time found itself in the chewing gum business in France, the ice cream business in Brazil, and the pasta business in Italy. Although each of these unrelated businesses

---

[1] For a more detailed discussion, see Warren Keegan, Sandra Moriarty, and Thomas Duncan, *Marketing,* 2nd ed. (Upper Saddle River, NJ: Prentice Hall), 1994, Ch. 10.

was, in isolation, quite profitable, the scale of each was too small to justify heavy expenditures on R&D, let alone marketing, production, and financial management from international headquarters. An important question regarding any product is whether it has the potential for expansion into other markets. The answer will depend on the company's goals and objectives and on perceptions of opportunity.

Managers run the risk of committing two types of errors regarding product decisions in global marketing. One error is to fall victim to the "not invented here" (NIH) syndrome, ignoring product decisions made by subsidiary or affiliate managers. Managers who behave in this way are essentially abandoning any effort to leverage product policy outside the home-country market. The other error has been to impose product decision policy on all affiliate companies on the assumption that what is right for customers in the home market must also be right for customers everywhere. German carmaker Volkswagen A. G. has learned the consequences of this latter error; VW saw its position in the U.S. import market erode from leader to also-ran. One industry observer summed up the company's main mistake this way: "Up to now Volkswagen has thought that what works in Germany should work in the United States." Volkswagen recently opened a design studio in Los Angeles, hoping to become better attuned to the tastes of American car buyers.[2] Today, Volkswagen is making a comeback in global markets by creating global cars on from basic platforms.

The four product categories in the local-to-global continuum—local, national, international, and global—are described in the following sections.

Local Products

A local product is available in a portion of a national market. In the United States, the term *regional product* is synonymous with local product. These products may be new products that a company is introducing using a rollout strategy, or a product that is distributed exclusively in that region. Originally, Cape Cod Potato Chips was a local product in the New England market. The company was later purchased by Frito-Lay and distribution was expanded to other regions of the United States.

National Products

A national product is one that, in the context of a particular company, is offered in a single national market. Sometimes national products appear when a global company caters to the needs and preferences of particular country markets. For example, Coca-Cola developed a noncarbonated, ginseng-flavored beverage for sale only in Japan and a yellow, carbonated flavored drink called Pasturina to compete with Peru's favorite soft drink, Inca Cola. After years of failing to dislodge Inca Cola, Coke followed the old strategic maxim, "if you can't beat them, buy them," and acquired Inca Cola.

Similarly, Sony and other Japanese consumer electronics companies produce a variety of products that are not sold outside of Japan. The reason: Japanese consumers have a seemingly insatiable appetite for electronic gadgets. One recent example is Casio's 16,000 yen ($155) Can-Tele, a television in a beer can, with a one-inch screen. It is designed to fit in an automobile drink holder. Also, there is Sony's Uka LaLa, a desktop speaker system designed to work with Walkman and Discman portable music players.[3]

Such examples notwithstanding, there are several reasons why national products—even those that are quite profitable—may represent a substantial opportunity cost to a company. First, the existence of a single national business does not provide an oppor-

---

[2] Steven Greenhouse, "Carl Hahn's East German Homecoming," *The New York Times,* 23 September 1990, sec. 3, p. 6.

[3] David P. Hamilton, "Wacky Electronic Gear Again Fills Japanese Stores," *The Wall Street Journal,* 4 May 1994, p. B1.

◆ BOX 11-1 ◆

PRIVATE-LABEL "DAVIDS" FIGHT GLOBAL BRAND "GOLIATHS"

While many differences separate consumers in different parts of the world, there is one characteristic that consumers everywhere seem to share: a preference for low-priced, high-quality, private-label products, rather than better-known—and more expensive—brands. In some places, the move toward private labels is just beginning. In others, private labels have been dominant for years.

In some of the world's markets, consumer preference for private labels—often encouraged by local companies—undermines hard-fought efforts by American companies to open markets to imports. In 1992, for example, after prolonged trade negotiations, Dole, Tropicana, and other American beverage makers finally were able to sell their orange juice brands in Japan. At about the same time the American products appeared on store shelves, the Daiei supermarket chain launched its own Savings private-label brand. Daiei's private-label products include juice made from Brazilian oranges and priced 40 percent less than American brands; pints of premium ice cream that sell for 299 yen, half the price of Lady Borden; and canned coffee drinks priced 30 percent less than Coca-Cola's Georgia brand. Competitive imitation helps sell the Savings brands; Daiei buys the ice cream from the same supplier as Borden and packages it in rectangular cartons similar to Lady Borden's.

In the United Kingdom, grocery store operating profit margins are as high as 8 percent, whereas those in the United States are a meager 1 percent. The reason? Private labels. Moreover, private labels account for 36 percent of total grocery sales in Britain, compared with 14 percent in the United States. The success of private labels in Britain is due partly to much less national advertising, thereby preventing brand loyalty among consumers. In particular, the BBC's refusal to carry advertising means that TV advertising—a key strategy for building brands and brand loyalty—is much less important than in the United States. Industry structure is also a factor: The grocery business in Britain is much less fragmented than in the United States. Britain's five largest chains—including J. Sainsbury PLC, Safeway, and Tesco—command nearly two thirds of the grocery business; in the United States, Safeway and other major chains account for about one fifth of grocery sales. Well-known brands are feeling the heat: Sainsbury's Gio lemon-lime soft drink competes directly with 7-UP and Sprite; its Novon laundry detergent outsells brands from global giants Procter & Gamble and Unilever PLC.

The story is much the same in Canada. In the early 1980s, David A. Nichols, head of the Toronto-based Loblaw Cos. Ltd., created a private-label brand called President's Choice. Today, the upscale PC products are found not only throughout Canada but in many U.S. grocery stores as well. Savvy marketing and advertising help differentiate the line: Unending puffery and hyperbole ("decadent" cookies, peanut butter that is "too good to be true," "the ultimate" frozen pizza), fancy labels, and exotic names ensure consumer attention and interest. Coca-Cola and PepsiCo are now faced with a soft-drink market share in Canada in which the share of private labels has grown from 5 percent in 1990 to as high as 25 percent in 1993.

SOURCES: E. S. Browning, "Europeans Witness Proliferation of Private Labels," *The Wall Street Journal,* 20 October 1992, p. B1; Yumiko Ono, "The Rising Sun Shines on Private Labels," *The Wall Street Journal,* 26 April 1993, pp. B1, B6; Richard Gibson, "Pitch, Panache Buoy Fancy Private Label," *The Wall Street Journal,* 27 January 1994, p. B1; Eleena De Lisser and Kevin Helliker, "Private Labels Reign in British Groceries," *The Wall Street Journal,* 3 March 1994, p. B4.

tunity to develop and utilize global leverage from headquarters in marketing, R&D, and production. Second, the local product does not allow for the transfer and application of experience gained in one market to other markets. One of the major tools available to the multicountry marketer is comparative analysis. By definition, single-country marketers cannot avail themselves of this tool. A third shortcoming of single-country product is the lack of transferability of managerial expertise acquired in the single-product area. Managers who gain experience with a local product can utilize their product experience only in the one market in which the product is sold. Similarly, any manager coming from outside the market in which the single product is sold will lack experience in the single-product business. For these reasons, purely national products should generally be viewed as less attractive than products with international or global potential.

International Products

International products are offered in multinational, regional markets. The classic international product is the Euro product, offered throughout Europe but not in the rest of the world. Renault was for many years a Euro product. When Renault entered the Brazilian market, it became a multiregional company. Most recently, Renault invested in Nissan and has taken control of the company. The combination of Renault in Europe and Latin America, and Nissan in Asia, the Americas, Europe, the Middle East and Africa, has catapulted Renault from a multiregional to a global position. Renault is an example of how a company can move overnight through investment or acquisition from an international to a global position.

Global Products and Global Brands

Global products are offered in global markets. A truly global product is offered in the Triad, in every world region, and in countries at every stage of development. Some global products were designed to meet the needs of a global market; others were designed to meet the needs of a national market but also, happily, meet the needs of a global market.

Note that a product is not a brand. For example, portable personal sound systems or personal stereos are a category of global product; Sony is a global brand. A global brand, like a national or international brand, is a symbol about which customers have beliefs or perceptions. Many companies, including Sony, make personal stereos. Sony created the category more than 10 years ago, when it introduced the Walkman. It is important to understand that global brands must be created by marketers; a global brand name can be used as an umbrella for introducing new products. Although Sony, as noted previously, markets a number of local products, the company also has a stellar track record both as a global brand and a manufacturer of global products.

Figure 11-1 identifies the qualities of a global brand: It has the same name as is the case for Coke, Sony, BMW, Harley-Davidson, and so on; or it may be the same meaning in different languages, as is true of Unilever's Snuggle (United States) fabric softener, which carries a cuddly teddy bear logo and the local translation of a meaning identical or similar to the meaning of *snuggle* in American English. A global brand has a similar image, similar positioning, and is guided by the same strategic principles. However, the marketing mix for a global brand may vary from country to country. That means that the product, price, promotion, and place (channels of distribution) may vary from country to country. Indeed, if one tracks the examples—Marlboro, Coke, Sony, Mercedes, and Avon—one will indeed find that the marketing mix for these products varies from country to country. The Mercedes, which is exclusively a luxury car in the United States, is also a strong competitor in the taxi market in Europe. Avon, which is a premium-priced and packaged cosmetic line in Japan, is popularly priced in the rest of the world. In spite of these variations in marketing mix, each of these products is a world or global brand.

- Guided by the Same Strategic Principles
- Same Name, Similar Image
- Similar Positioning
- Marketing Mix May Vary
  Product
  Price
  Promotion
  Place

Examples: Marlboro, Coke, Sony, Avon, Mercedes, BMW, Volvo

FIGURE 11-1 Global Brands

A global product differs from a global brand in one important respect: It does not carry the same name and image from country to country. Like the global brand, however, it is guided by the same strategic principles, is similarly positioned, and may have a marketing mix that varies from country to country. Whenever a company finds itself with global products, it faces an issue: Should the global product be turned into a global brand? This requires that the name and image of the product be standardized. The two biggest examples of this move were the shift from Standard Oil's many different local brands to Exxon, and Nissan's decision to drop the Datsun marque in the United States and adopt various model names for Nissan's worldwide product line. Table 11-1 shows the numerous marques that Nissan utilizes.

Table 11-2 shows the world's most valuable brands as defined by Interbrand, an international brand consultancy and part of Omnicom. Of the top 20 brands in the world, 14 brands are classified as U.S. companies. Japan has two brands and Finland, Germany, Switzerland, and Sweden have one brand each, thus showing that U.S. companies, or maybe the image of the United States, is propelling globalization. When viewed by category, technology-based industries have nine brand names whereas the other 11 brands, except for automobiles with three of the top brands, are quite diversified. (Now is a good time to review Porter's cluster analysis in Chapter 10.)

When an industry globalizes, companies are under pressure to develop global products. A major driver for the globalization of products is the cost of product R&D. As competition intensifies, companies discover that they can reduce the cost of R&D for a product by developing a global product design. Even products such as automobiles, which must meet national safety and pollution standards, are under pressure to become global: With a global product, companies can offer an adaptation of a global design instead of a unique national design in each country.

Mars, Inc. confronted the global brand issue with its chocolate-covered caramel bar that sold under a variety of national brand names, such as Snickers in the United States and Marathon in the United Kingdom. Mars decided to transform the candy bar—a global product—into a global brand. This decision entailed some risk, such as the possibility that consumers in the United Kingdom would associate the name Snickers with *knickers,* British slang for a woman's undergarment. Mars also changed the name of its successful European chocolate biscuit from Raider to Twix, the same name used in the United States. In both instances, a single brand name gives Mars the opportunity to leverage all of its product communications across national boundaries. In doing this, managers must now think globally about the positioning of Snickers and Twix, something that they were not obliged to do when the candy products were marketed under different national brand names.

Coke is arguably the quintessential global product and global brand. Coke's positioning and strategy are the same in all countries; it projects a global image of fun, good times, and enjoyment. Coke is "the real thing." There is only one Coke. It is unique. It is a brilliant example of marketing differentiation. The essence of discrimination is to show the difference between your products and other competing products and services.

This positioning is a considerable accomplishment when you consider the fact that Coke is a low/no-tech product. It is flavored, carbonated, sweetened water in a plastic, glass, or metal container. The company's strategy is to make sure that the product is within arm's reach of desire. However, the marketing mix for Coke varies. The product itself is adapted to suit local tastes; for example, Coke increases the sweetness of its beverages in the Middle East, where customers prefer a sweeter drink. Also, prices may vary to suit local competitive conditions, and the channels of distribution may differ. However, the basic, underlying, strategic principles that guide the management of the brand are the same worldwide. Only an ideologue would insist that a global product cannot be adapted

TABLE 11-1 Nissan Marques in Various Markets

Model Type	Japan	North America	Europe	Southeast Asia	Latin America and Caribbean	Middle East	Oceania	Africa
G50	Infiniti Q45	(Infiniti) Q45	—	—	Infiniti	—	Infiniti	—
JY32	—	(Infiniti) J30	—	—	—	—	—	—
Y30 Y31 Y33	Cedric/ Gloria	—	—	Gong Jue[b] (China)	Cedric	Cedric Gloria (Kuwait)	—	Cedric
Z32	Fairlady Z	300ZX	300ZX	—	300ZX	—	300ZX	—
A32	Cefiro	(Infiniti) I30	Maxima QX, QX (UK)	Cefiro Feng Du[b] (China)	Maxima	Maxima	Maxima	Maxima
A32	—	Maxima	—	—	—	—	—	—
U13	—	Altima	—	Altima (Taiwan, Philippines) Bluebird (Asia) Lan Liao[b] (China)	Bluebird	Bluebird	Bluebird	Bluebird
U14	Bluebird	—	—	—	—	—	—	—
P10	—	(Infiniti) G20	Primera	Primera (Taiwan)	—	—	—	—
P11	Primera	—	Primera[a]	—	—	—	—	—
S14	Silvia	240SX	200SX	200SX	200SX	—	200SX (Australia)	200SX
B13	—	Sentra Coupe (Canada)	—	Sentra (Philippines)	Sentra (Mexican made) Tsuru (Mexico)	—	—	—
B14	Sunny	Sentra (sedan)	—	Sunny Sentra (Philippines, Malaysia, Taiwan) Yiang Guang[b] (China)	Sentra	Sunny (sedan)	—	Sunny (sedan)
B14	Lucino	200SX (Coupe)	—	—	Lucino (Mexico)	—	—	—
N14	—	—	—	—	—	—	Pulsar (Australia) Sentra (New Zealand)	Sentra (South Africa)
N15	Pulsar	—	Almera	Pulsar (Singapore, Brunei)	Almera	—	Pulsar	—
K11	March	—	Micra	March (Taiwan, Singapore)	—	—	Micra (Australia)	—

Model Type	Japan	North America	Europe	Southeast Asia	Latin America and Caribbean	Middle East	Oceania	Africa
W10	Avenir (New Zealand)	—	Primera Wagon	—	—	—	Avenir	—
Y10	Sunny California AD Wagon	—	Sunny Wagon	AD Wagon AD Resort (Thailand, Taiwan, Malaysia, Philippines)	AD Wagon Tubame (Mexico)	—	Sentra Wagon (New Zealand)	AD Wagon
Y10	AD Van	—	Sunny Van	—	—	—	—	—
260 Y60	Safari	—	Patrol Patrol GR	Patrol Tu Le[b] (China)	Patrol	Patrol	Patrol	Patrol
R50 WD21	Terrano	Pathfinder	—	Terrano (Indonesia) Xiao Xuan Feng[b] (China)	Pathfinder Terrano	Pathfinder	Pathfinder (Australia New Zealand)	Pathfinder
R20	Mistral	—	Terrano II	—	Terrano II	—	—	—
V40	—	Quest	—	Quest (Taiwan)	Quest	—	—	—
D21	Datsun	Nissan Truck Nissan Hard Body (Canada)	Pickup	Nissan Pickup Pathfinder (Philippines) Hard Body (Taiwan) Pi Ka[b] (China) Big M (Thailand)	Nissan Pickup	Nissan Pickup	Navara	Nissan Pickup 1 Tonner (South Africa)
H41 F23	Atlas	—	Cabstar	Cabstar Jing Wang[b] (Taiwan) Ka Xing[b] (China)	Cabstar/ Atlas	Cabstar	—	Cabstar
E24	Caravan/ Homy	—	Urvan	Urvan Jia Ben[b] (China)	Urvan	Urvan	—	Urvan
GC22	—	—	—	Fu Man Duo[b] (Taiwan)	—	—	—	—
C23	Serena	—	Serena/ Vanette Cargo	Serena	Vanette Serena	—	Serena (Australia)	—
W40	Civilian	—	—	Civilian Bi Lian[b] (China)	Civilian	Civilian	Civilian (Australia)	Civilian

Notes: Besides the aforementioned, there are some more area-specific model names used in other countries.

[a]Sales start from October 1996.

[b]These are transliterations of local product names written in Chinese characters.

TABLE 11-2	The World's 20 Most Valuable Brands		
Rank	**Brand Name**	**Industry**	**Country**
1	Coca-Cola	Beverage	United States
2	Microsoft	Software	United States
3	IBM	Computers	United States
4	General Electric	Diversified	United States
5	Ford	Automobiles	United States
6	Disney	Entertainment	United States
7	Intel	Computers	United States
8	McDonald's	Food	United States
9	AT&T	Telecommunications	United States
10	Marlboro	Tobacco	United States
11	Nokia	Telecommunications	Finland
12	Mercedes	Automobiles	Germany
13	Nescafé	Beverages	Switzerland
14	Hewlett-Packard	Computers	United States
15	Gillette	Personal Care	United States
16	Kodak	Imaging	United States
17	Ericsson	Telecommunications	Sweden
18	Sony	Electronics	Japan
19	Amex	Financial Services	United States
20	Toyota	Automobiles	Japan

Source: Interbrand, www.interbrand.com.

to meet local preferences; certainly, no company building a global brand needs to limit itself to absolute marketing mix uniformity. The issue is not exact uniformity but rather offering essentially the same value. As discussed in the next few chapters, other elements of the marketing mix—for example, price, communications appeal and media strategy, and distribution channels—may also vary.

In comparing the experiences of two food companies in China, one, Nestlé, has been very successful while the other, Kraft, is struggling. Kraft attempted to sell Tang and dairy products such as cheese and yogurt. Tang, despite initial success, has lost share to an emerging local brand, Jianlibao, a carbonated orange-flavored drink.[4] And, dairy products are not traditionally part of the Chinese diet. In fact, many Chinese are lactose intolerant. Additionally, there is little refrigeration in many parts of the country. Conversely, Nestlé has concentrated on its global brands, such as Nescafé and Kit Kat, while developing instant noodles, mineral water, and a health drink.

Global marketers should systematically identify and assess opportunities for developing global brands. Creating a global brand requires a different type of marketing effort—including up-front creative vision—than that required to create one or more national brands. On the other hand, the ongoing effort to maintain brand awareness is less for a leading global brand than it is for a collection of local brands. What criteria do marketers use to decide whether to establish global brands? One expert has argued that the decision must be "determined by bottom-up consumer-driven considerations, not by top-down manufacturer-driven business convenience."[5] A major determinant of suc-

---

[4] Rick Yan, "Short-Term Results: The Litmus Test for Success in China," *Harvard Business Review* (September–October 1998): 67.
[5] A. E. Pitcher, "The Role of Branding in International Advertising," *International Journal of Advertising,* no. 4 (1985): 244.

cess will be whether the marketing effort is starting from scratch with a "blank slate," or whether the task is to reposition or rename an existing local brand in an attempt to create a global brand. Starting with a blank slate is vastly easier than repositioning existing brands. Still, Mars and many companies have succeeded in transforming local brands into international or global brands. Today, there are thousands of global brands, and every day the list grows longer.

◆ PRODUCT POSITIONING

Product positioning is a communications strategy based on the notion of mental "space": *Positioning* refers to the act of locating a brand in customers' minds over and against other products in terms of product attributes and benefits that the brand does and does not offer. The word *positioning*, first formally used in 1969 by Ries and Trout in an article that appeared in *Industrial Marketing*, describes a strategy for "staking out turf" or "filling a slot" in the minds of target customers.[6]

Several general strategies have been suggested for positioning products: positioning by attribute or benefit, quality/price, use or application, and use/user.[7] Two additional strategies, high-tech and high-touch, have been suggested for global products.

ATTRIBUTE OR BENEFIT

A frequently used positioning strategy exploits a particular product attribute, benefit, or feature. In global marketing, the fact that a product is imported can itself represent a benefit positioning. Economy, reliability, and durability are other frequently used attribute/benefit positions. Volvo automobiles are known for solid construction that offer safety in the event of a crash. In the ongoing credit card wars, VISA's advertising focuses on the benefit of worldwide merchant acceptance.

QUALITY/PRICE

This strategy can be thought of in terms of a continuum from high fashion/quality and high price to good value (rather than low quality) at a low price.[8] The American Express Card, for example, has traditionally been positioned as an upscale card whose prestige justifies higher annual fees than VISA or MasterCard. The Discover card is at the other end of the continuum. Discover's value position results from no annual fee and a cash rebate to cardholders each year.

Marketers of imported vodkas such as Absolut, Finlandia, and Stolichnaya Cristall have successfully positioned their brands as premium products at double the price of "ordinary" vodka. For example, ads for Stolichnaya Russian vodka hail it as "the most distinctive vodka in the world." Vodkas also play up their national origins, demonstrating how price/quality can also be used in conjunction with other positions such as benefit/attribute. Marketers sometimes use the phrase *transformation advertising* to describe advertising that seeks to change the experience of buying and using a product—in other words, the product benefit.[9] Presumably, the experience of buying and consuming Stolichnaya Cristall is a higher-quality experience than that of, say, buying and consuming a less expensive brand such as Popov.

[6] Al Ries and Jack Trout, *Positioning: The Battle for Your Mind* (New York: Warner Books, 1982), p. 44.
[7] David A. Aaker and J. Gary Shansby, "Positioning Your Product," *Business Horizons* (May–June 1982): 56–62.
[8] Ibid., p. 57.
[9] William Wells, John Burnett, and Sandra Moriarty, *Advertising: Principles and Practices* (Upper Saddle River, NJ: Prentice Hall, 1989), p. 207.

USE/USER

Positioning can also be achieved by describing how a product is used or associating a product with a user or class of users the same way in every market. For example, Benetton uses the same positioning for its clothing when it targets the global youth market. Marlboro's extraordinary success as a global brand is due in part to the product's association with cowboys—the archetypal symbol of rugged independence, freedom, space, and Americana—and transformation advertising that targets urban smokers. As Clive Chajet, a corporate and brand identity expert, explains, "The cowboy is as enduring an icon as you can have. And the stronger your brand image, regardless of the environment in which you compete, the better off you are."[10]

Why choose Marlboro instead of another brand? Smoking Marlboro is a way of getting in touch with a powerful urge to be free and independent. Lack of physical space may be a reflection of the Marlboro user's own sense of "macho-ness" or a symbol of freedom and independence. The message is reinforced in advertising with an image carefully calculated to appeal to the universal human desire for those things and urges smokers to "join that rugged, independent cowboy in the Old West!" The advertising succeeds because it is very well done and, evidently, addresses a deep, powerful need that is found around the globe.[11] Not surprisingly, Marlboro is the most popular cigarette brand in the former Soviet Union.

Honda used the slogan "You meet the nicest people on a Honda" to attract a new segment of first-time American motorcycle buyers in the 1960s. More recently, Harley-Davidson has successfully broadened its image to reach a new class of motorcycle enthusiasts: aging baby boomer professionals who wanted to adopt an outlaw persona on weekends. An ad for the upscale Range Rover showing the sports-utility vehicle on a mountaintop has the headline, "The real reason many CEOs are unavailable for comment."

In today's global market environment, many companies find it increasingly important to have a unified global positioning strategy. For example, Chase Manhattan Bank launched a $75 million global advertising campaign geared to the theme "Profit from experience." According to Aubrey Hawes, a vice president and corporate director of marketing for the bank, Chase's business and private banking clients "span the globe and travel the globe. They can only know one Chase in their minds, so why should we try to confuse them?"[12]

Can global positioning work for all products? One study suggests that global positioning is most effective for product categories that approach either end of a "high-touch/high-tech" continuum.[13] Both ends of the continuum are characterized by high levels of customer involvement and by a shared language among consumers.

HIGH-TECH POSITIONING

Personal computers, video and stereo equipment, and automobiles are product categories for which high-tech positioning has proven effective. Such products are frequently purchased on the basis of physical product features, although image may also be important. Buyers typically already possess—or wish to acquire—considerable technical information. High-tech products may be divided into three categories: technical products, special-interest products, and demonstrable products.

---

[10] Stuart Elliot, "Uncle Sam Is No Match for the Marlboro Man," *The New York Times,* 27 August 1995, sec. 3, p. 11.

[11] Jagdish N. Sheth, *Winning Back Your Market* (New York: Wiley, 1985), p. 158.

[12] Gary Levin, "Ads Going Global," *Advertising Age,* 22 July 1991, p. 42.

[13] The following discussion is adapted from Teresa J. Domzal and Lynette Unger, "Emerging Positioning Strategies in Global Marketing," *Journal of Consumer Marketing* (Fall 1987): 27–37.

Computers, chemicals, tires, and financial services are technical products in the sense that buyers have specialized needs, require a great deal of product information, and share a common language. Computer buyers in Russia and the United States are equally knowledgeable about Pentium microprocessors, hard drives, and random access memory (RAM) requirements. Marketing communications for high-tech products should be informative and emphasize features.

Special-interest products also are characterized by a shared experience and high involvement among users, although they are less technical and more leisure or recreation oriented. Again, the common language and symbols associated with such products can transcend language and cultural barriers. Fuji bicycles, Adidas and Nike sports equipment, Canon cameras, and Sega video game players are examples of successful global special-interest products.

HIGH-TOUCH POSITIONING

Marketing of high-touch products requires less emphasis on specialized information and more emphasis on image. Like high-tech products, however, high-touch categories are highly involving for consumers. Buyers of high-touch products also share a common language and set of symbols relating to themes of wealth, materialism, and romance. There are three categories of high-touch products: products that solve a common problem, global village products, and products with a universal theme. At the other end of the price spectrum from high-tech, high-touch products that can solve a problem often provide benefits linked to "life's little moments." Ads that show friends talking over a cup of coffee in a cafe or quenching thirst with a soft drink during a day at the beach put the product at the center of everyday life and communicate the benefit offered in a way that is understood worldwide. Upscale fragrances and designer fashions are examples of products whose positioning is strongly cosmopolitan in nature. Fragrances and fashions have traveled as a result of growing worldwide interest in high-quality, highly visible, high-priced products that often enhance social status.

Products may have a global appeal by virtue of their country of origin. The Americanness of Levi's, Marlboro, McDonald's, and Harley-Davidson enhances their appeal to cosmopolitans around the world and offers opportunities for benefit positioning. In consumer electronics, Sony is a name synonymous with vaunted Japanese quality; in automobiles, Mercedes is the embodiment of legendary German engineering.

Some products can be positioned in more than one way, within either the high-tech or high-touch poles of the continuum. A sophisticated camera, for example, could simultaneously be classified as technical and special interest. Other products may be positioned in a bipolar fashion, that is, as both high-tech and high-touch. For example, Bang & Olufsen consumer electronics products, by virtue of their design elegance, are perceived as both high-tech and high-touch.

◆ PRODUCT SATURATION LEVELS IN GLOBAL MARKETS

Many factors determine a product's market potential. In general, product saturation levels, or the percentage of potential buyers or households who own a particular product, increase as national income per capita increases. However, for markets in which income is sufficient to enable consumers to buy a particular product, other factors must be considered. For example, the sale of air conditioners is explained by income and climate. In a low-income country, many people cannot afford an air conditioner no matter how hot it is. Affluent people in a northern climate can easily afford an air conditioner but have no need for one.

During the 1960s, the ownership of electric vacuum cleaners in the European Common Market ranged from a high of 95 percent of households in the Netherlands to a low of 7 percent of households in Italy. The differences in ownership of this appliance in Europe are explained only partially by income. A much more important factor in explaining ownership levels is the type of floor covering used in the homes of the country. Almost every home in the Netherlands contains rugs, whereas in Italy the use of rugs is uncommon. This illustrates the importance of need in determining the sales potential for a product. Thus, in addition to attitudes toward cleanliness, the presence or absence of a particular companion product is very significant for electric vacuum cleaners. If Italians had more carpets covering their floors, the saturation level for vacuum cleaners would be higher.

The existence of wide disparities in the demand for a product from one market to the next is an indication of the possible potential for that product in the low-saturation-level market. For example, a major new-product category in the United States in the early 1980s was mousse, a hair grooming product for women that is more flexible than stiff, dry hair spray. This product, known as a gel in France, had been available in France and Europe for 25 years prior to its introduction in the United States. The success of the product in Europe was a clear signal of market potential. Indeed, it is more than likely that this opportunity could have been tapped earlier. Every company should have an active global scanning system to identify potential market opportunities based on demand disparities.

◆ PRODUCT DESIGN CONSIDERATIONS

Product design is a key factor in determining success in global marketing. Should a company adapt product design for various national markets or offer a single design to the global market? In some instances, making a design change may increase sales. However, the benefits of such potential sales increases must be weighed against the cost of changing a product's design and testing it in the market. Global marketers need to consider four factors when making product design decisions: preferences, cost, laws and regulations, and compatibility.

PREFERENCES

There are marked and important differences in preferences around the world for factors such as color and taste. Marketers who ignore preferences do so at their own peril. In the 1960s, for example, Italy's Olivetti Corporation had gained considerable distinction in Europe for its award-winning modern consumer typewriter designs; Olivetti typewriters had been displayed at the Museum of Modern Art in New York City. Although critically acclaimed, Olivetti's designs did not enjoy commercial success in the United States. The U.S. consumer wanted a heavy, bulky typewriter that was ugly by modern European design standards. Bulk and weight were considered prima facie evidence of quality by American consumers, and Olivetti was, therefore, forced to adapt its award-winning design in the United States.

Sometimes, a product design that is successful in one world region does meet with success in the rest of the world. BMW and Mercedes dominate the luxury car market in Europe and are strong competitors in the rest of the world, with exactly the same design. In effect, these companies have a world design. The other global luxury car manufacturers are Japanese, and they have expressed their flattery and appreciation for the appeal of the BMW and Mercedes look by styling cars that are influenced by the BMW and Mercedes line and design philosophy. If imitation is the most sincere form of flattery, BMW and Mercedes have been honored by their competition.

COST

In approaching the issue of product design, company managers must consider cost factors broadly. Of course, the actual cost of producing the product will create a cost floor. Other design-related costs—whether incurred by the manufacturer or the end user—must also be considered. Earlier in this chapter, we noted that the cost of repair services varies around the world and has an impact on product design. Another example of how labor cost affects product decisions is seen in the contrasting approaches to aircraft design adopted by the British and the Americans. The British approach, which resulted in the Comet, was to place the engine inside the wing. This design meant lower wind resistance and, therefore, greater fuel economy. A disadvantage of the design was less accessible engines than externally mounted ones, meaning they were more time consuming to maintain and repair. The American approach to the question of engine location was to hang the engines from the wings at the expense of efficiency and fuel economy to gain a more accessible engine and, therefore, to reduce the amount of time required for engine maintenance and repair. Both approaches to engine location were rational. The British approach took into account the relatively lower cost of the labor required for engine repair, and the American approach took into account the relatively high cost of labor for engine repair in the United States.

LAWS AND REGULATIONS

Compliance with laws and regulations in different countries has a direct impact on product design decisions, frequently leading to product design adaptations that increase costs. This may be seen especially clearly in Europe, where one impetus for the creation of the single market was to dismantle regulatory and legal barriers—particularly in the areas of technical standards and health and safety standards—that prevented pan-European sales of standardized products. In the food industry, for example, there were 200 legal and regulatory barriers to cross-border trade within the European Union (EU) in 10 food categories. Among these were prohibitions or taxes on products with certain ingredients, and different packaging and labeling laws. Experts predict that the removal of such barriers will reduce the need to adapt product designs and will result in the creation of standardized Euro-products.[14]

COMPATIBILITY

The last product design issue that must be addressed by company managers is product compatibility with the environment in which it is used. A simple thing such as failing to translate the user's manual into various languages can hurt sales of American-made home appliances built in America outside the United States. Also, electrical systems range from 50 to 230 volts and from 50 to 60 cycles. This means that the design of any product powered by electricity must be compatible with the power system in the country of use.

Manufacturers of televisions and video equipment find that the world is a very incompatible place for reasons besides those related to electricity. Three different TV broadcast and video systems are found in the world today: the U.S. NTSC system, the French SECAM system, and the German PAL system. Companies that are targeting global markets design multisystem TVs and VCRs that allow users to simply flip a switch for proper operation with any system. Companies that are not aiming for the global market design products that comply with a single type of technical requirements.

---

[14] John Quelch, Robert Buzzell, and Eric Salama, *The Marketing Challenge of Europe 1992* (Reading, MA: Addison-Wesley, 1991), p. 71.

Cell phones manufactures encounter the GSM standard which has been adapted in Europe and in many other countries. However, the United States has three different cell technologies, and Japan has yet another CCU Standard.

Measuring systems do not demand compatibility, but the absence of compatibility in measuring systems can create product resistance. The lack of compatibility is a particular danger for the United States, which is the only nonmetric country in the world. Products calibrated in inches and pounds are at a competitive disadvantage in metric markets. When companies integrate their worldwide manufacturing and design activity, the metric-English measuring system conflict requires expensive conversion and harmonization efforts.

LABELING AND INSTRUCTIONS

Product labeling and instructions must comply with national law and regulation. For example, there are very precise labeling requirements for prescription drugs and poisons. In addition, however, labeling can provide valuable consumer information on nutrition, for example. Finally, many products require operating and installation instructions.

In which languages should labeling and instructions be printed? One approach to this issue is to print labels and instructions in languages that are used in all of the major markets for the product. The use of multiple languages on labels and instructions simplifies inventory control: The same packaging can be used for multiple markets. The savings from simplicity must be weighed against the cost of longer instruction booklets and more space on labels for information.

◆ ATTITUDES TOWARD COUNTRY OF ORIGIN

One of the facts of life in global marketing is the existence of stereotyped attitudes toward foreign products. Stereotyped attitudes may either favor or hinder the marketer's efforts. On the positive side, as one marketing expert pointed out, "German is synonymous with quality engineering, Italian is synonymous with style, and French is synonymous with chic."[15] However, no country has a monopoly on a favorable foreign reputation for its products or a universally inferior reputation. Similarly, individual citizens in a given country are likely to differ in terms of both the importance they ascribe to a product's country of origin and their perceptions of different countries. A recent Gallup poll showed that, among Americans, people 61 years of age or older were most likely to be influenced by a product's country of origin (see Table 11-3).

The reputation of a particular country may vary around the world; a particular country's reputation can change over time. Studies conducted during the 1970s and 1980s indicated that the "Made in U.S.A." image lost ground when compared with the "Made in Japan" image. Today, however, American companies and American brands are finding renewed acceptance in Europe, Japan, and elsewhere. For example, Jeep Cherokee sports-utility vehicles, Lands' End clothing, and even Budweiser beer are being successfully marketed in Europe with strong American themes.

Country image is not uniform. Swiss watches are preferred in Europe by an overwhelming margin, but in Japan customers prefer Japanese watches. In the United States, the preference for Swiss-made watches varies from region to region.

Country stereotyping can present a considerable disadvantage to a competitor in a given market. Because of this, global marketers should consider shifting production locations to exploit country-specific advantages. One recent study investigated the rela-

---

[15] Dana Milbank, "Made in America Becomes a Boast in Europe," *The Wall Street Journal,* 19 January 1994, p. B1.

TABLE 11-3	Influence of Country of Manufacture on Consumer Purchase Decisions	
Age	**Percentage**	
18–30	19%	
31–45	35%	
46–60	29%	
61+	50%	

Source: Gallup poll conducted for the International Mass Retail Association.

tionship between a product's country of origin and American consumer perceptions of risk. Specifically, the study compared perceptions of two product categories—microwave ovens and blue jeans—produced in the United States, Mexico, and Taiwan. Over all, the study found a significant consumer bias in favor of U.S.-made microwaves and jeans. However, the study also showed no difference in perceived risk between microwave ovens in terms of "Made in U.S.A." and "Made in Taiwan." On the other hand, respondents indicated a higher perceived risk for jeans manufactured in Taiwan compared with those from the United States. Comparison of the two product categories for the United States and Mexico showed a negative country-of-origin bias for Mexican-made products. Finally, the survey indicated a significantly higher perceived risk for a Mexican microwave oven compared to one made in Taiwan; there was no significant difference between Mexico and Taiwan in terms of perceived risk in purchasing jeans.[16]

Of course, customers in Mexico and Taiwan exhibit country-of-origin biases of their own. One new enterprise in Brazil, which supplied a sensitive scientific instrument to the oil-drilling industry, discovered that its Mexican customers would not accept scientific instruments manufactured in Brazil. To overcome the prejudice in Mexico against instruments from Brazil, the company was forced to export the components for its instruments to Switzerland, where they were assembled and the finished product stamped "Made in Switzerland." Only then did the company achieve satisfactory sales levels in Mexico.

If a country's manufacturers produce quality products that are nonetheless perceived as being of low quality, there are two alternatives. One is to attempt to hide or disguise the foreign origin of the product. Package, label, and product design can minimize evidence of foreign sourcing. A brand policy of using local names will contribute to a domestic identity. The other alternative is to continue the foreign identification of the product and attempt to change consumer or customer attitudes toward the product. Over time, as consumers experience higher quality, the perception will change and adjust. It is a fact of life that perceptions of quality often lag behind reality.

In some market segments, foreign products have a substantial advantage over their domestic counterparts simply because they are foreign. This appears to be the case with beer in the United States. In one study, subjects who were asked to indicate taste preference for beer in a blind test indicated a preference for domestic beers over imports. The same subjects were then asked to indicate preference ratings for beers in an open test with labels attached. In this test, the subjects preferred imported beer. Today, many Americans still seem to have a taste for imported beers. According to *Impact,* a beverage industry newsletter, imports account for 5 percent of U.S. beer sales by volume.

It is a happy situation for the global marketer when foreign origin has a positive influence on perceptions of quality. One way to reinforce foreign preference is by charging a premium price for the foreign product to take advantage of consumer tendencies

---

[16] Jerome Witt and C. P. Rao, "The Impact of Global Sourcing on Consumers: Country-of-Origin Effects on Perceived Risk," *Journal of Global Marketing,* 6, no. 3 (1992): 105–128.

to associate price and quality. The relative position of imported beer in the U.S. premium-priced beer market is an excellent example of this positioning strategy. Similarly, Anheuser-Busch is enjoying great success with its Budweiser brand in Europe. In Britain, where it is positioned as a superpremium beer, a six-pack of Bud sells for the equivalent of $7—about twice the U.S. price.

◆ GEOGRAPHIC EXPANSION—STRATEGIC ALTERNATIVES

Companies can grow in three different ways. The traditional methods of market expansion—further penetration of existing markets to increase market share and extension of the product line into new-product market areas in a single national market—are both available in domestic operations. In addition, a company can expand by extending its existing operations into new countries and areas of the world. The latter method, geographic expansion, is one of the major opportunities of global marketing. To pursue geographic expansion effectively, a framework for considering alternatives is required. When a company has a product/market base, it can select from five strategic alternatives to extend this base into other geographic markets, or it can create a new product designed for global markets. Four alternatives are shown in Figure 11-2.

STRATEGY 1: PRODUCT/COMMUNICATION EXTENSION (DUAL EXTENSION)

Many companies employ product/communication extension as a strategy for pursuing opportunities outside the home market. Under the right conditions, this is the easiest product marketing strategy and, in many instances, the most profitable one as well. Companies pursuing this strategy sell exactly the same product, with the same advertising and promotional appeals as used in the home country, in some or all world-market countries or segments. Note that this strategy is utilized by companies in stages 2, 4, and 5. The critical difference is one of execution and mind-set. In the stage 2 company, the dual extension strategy grows out of an ethnocentric orientation; the stage 2 company is making the assumption that all markets are alike. A company in stage 4 or 5 does not make such assumptions; the company's geocentric orientation allows it to thoroughly understand its markets and consciously take advantage of similarities in world markets.

Some marketers have learned the hard way that the dual extension approach does not work in every market. When Campbell Soup tried to sell its tomato soup in the

FIGURE 11-2 Global Product Planning Strategic Alternatives

	Same Product	Different Product
Different Communications	Strategy 2: Product Extension, Communications Adaptation *Example:* Bicycles and motorcycles	Strategy 4: Dual Adaptation *Example:* Greeting cards
Same Communications	Strategy 1: Dual Extension *Example:* Applications software	Strategy 3: Product Adaptation, Communication Extension *Example:* Electrical products

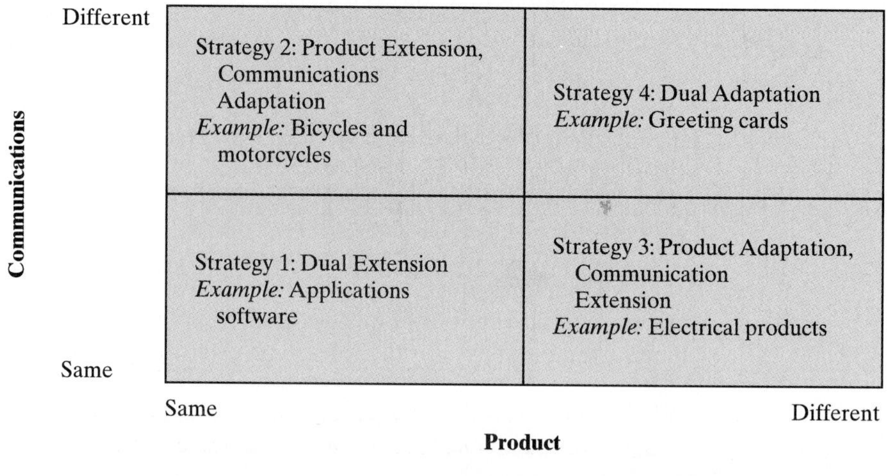

United Kingdom, it discovered, after substantial losses, that the English prefer a more bitter taste than Americans. Happily, Campbell learned its lesson and subsequently succeeded in Japan by offering seven soup varieties—for example, corn potage—designed specifically for the Japanese markets. Another U.S. company spent several million dollars in an unsuccessful effort to capture the British cake mix market. It offered fancy U.S.-style cake mixes with frosting. After the product was launched, the company discovered that the British consume their cake at tea time. The cake they prefer is dry, spongy, and suitable for being picked up with the left hand while the right manages a cup of tea. A second U.S. company hoping to sell cake mixes in the United Kingdom assembled a panel of housewives and asked them to bake their favorite cake. Having learned about British cake preferences through this study, the company created a dry, spongy cake mix product and acquired a major share of the British market.

Philip Morris once attempted to take advantage of the fact that its U.S. TV advertising reached a sizable Canadian audience in border areas. Canadian smokers prefer a straight Virginia cigarette, in contrast to American smokers, who prefer cigarettes made from blended tobacco. Philip Morris managers chose to ignore market research indicating that Canadians would not accept a blended cigarette. The managers went ahead with marketing programs designed to extend retail distribution of U.S. blended brands in the Canadian border areas served by U.S. television. Not surprisingly, the Canadian preference for straight, nonblended cigarettes remained unchanged. American-style cigarettes sold right up to the border but no farther. Philip Morris had to withdraw its U.S. brands.

In the early 1960s, CPC International hoped to pursue a product extension strategy with Knorr dehydrated soups in the United States. Dehydrated soups dominate the soup market in Europe, and CPC managers believed they had a market opportunity in the United States. However, a faulty marketing research design led to erroneous conclusions concerning market potential for this product. CPC International based its decision to go ahead with Knorr on reports of taste panel comparisons of Knorr dehydrated soups with popular canned soups. The results of these panel tests indicated a strong preference for the Knorr product. Unfortunately, these taste panel tests did not simulate the actual market environment for soup, which includes not only eating but also preparation. Dry soups require 15 to 20 minutes cooking time, whereas canned soups offer the benefit of heat and serve. The preparation difference is a critical factor in influencing soup purchases, and it resulted in another failure of the extension strategy. In this case, it was only partial extension: Flavors were adapted, but the basic form of the product was extended. The failure was not absolute. The product has been a failure in relation to the original expectations, but it has been a success in the United States in its category (dry soups). However, the category market share remains small compared to Europe.

The product/communication extension strategy has an enormous appeal to global companies because of the cost savings associated with this approach. The two most obvious sources of savings are manufacturing economies of scale and elimination of duplicate product R&D costs. Also important are the substantial economies associated with standardization of marketing communications. For a company with worldwide operations, the cost of preparing separate print and TV ads for each market can be enormous. Although these cost savings are important, they should not distract executives from the more important objective of maximum profit performance, which may require the use of an adaptation or invention strategy. As we have seen, product extension, in spite of its immediate cost savings, may in fact result in market failure.

STRATEGY 2: PRODUCT EXTENSION/COMMUNICATION ADAPTATION

When a product fills a different need, appeals to a different segment, or serves a different function under conditions of use that are the same or similar to those in the domestic market, the only adjustment that may be required is in marketing communications. Bicycles and motor scooters are examples of products that have been marketed with this approach. They satisfy recreational needs in the United States but serve as basic or urban transportation in many other countries. Similarly, outboard marine motors are usually sold to a recreation market in the high-income countries, whereas the same motors in most lower-income countries are mainly sold to fishing and transportation fleets. Another example is the U.S. farm machinery company that decided to market its U.S. line of home lawn and garden power equipment in less developed countries (LDCs) as agricultural implements. The equipment was ideally suited to the needs of farmers in many LDCs. Equally important was the lower price: almost a third less than competing equipment especially designed for small-acreage farming, and offered for sale by competing foreign manufacturers.

As these examples show, the product extension/communication adaptation strategy—either by design or by accident—results in product transformation. The same physical product ends up serving a different function or use than that for which it was originally designed or created. There are many examples of food product transformation. The classic example is Perrier. Whereas mineral water has long been advertised and consumed in Europe as a staple with healthful qualities, Perrier became a success in America only after it was marketed as the chic beverage to order in restaurants and bars instead of a cocktail.[17]

The appeal of the product extension/communication adaptation strategy is its relatively low cost of implementation. Because the product in this strategy is unchanged, R&D, tooling, manufacturing setup, and inventory costs associated with additions to the product line are avoided. The only costs of this approach are in identifying different product functions and revising marketing communications (including advertising, sales promotion, and point-of-sale material) around the newly identified function.

STRATEGY 3: PRODUCT ADAPTATION/COMMUNICATION EXTENSION

A third approach to global product planning is to extend, without change, the basic home-market communications strategy while adapting the product to local use or preference conditions. Note that this strategy (and the one that follows) may be utilized by both stage 3 and stage 4 companies. The critical difference is, as noted earlier, one of execution and mind-set. In the stage 3 company, the product adaptation strategy grows out of a polycentric orientation; the stage 3 company assumes that all markets are different. By contrast, the geocentric orientation of managers and executives in a stage 4 global company has sensitized them to actual, rather than assumed, differences between markets.

Exxon adheres to this third strategy: It adapts its gasoline formulations to meet the weather conditions prevailing in different markets while extending the basic communications appeal, "Put a tiger in your tank," without change. Similarly, Pioneer Hi-Bred International markets different varieties of seed corn that produce optimum yield under different soil conditions and also provide different types and levels of drought and insect resistance. There are many other examples of products that have been adjusted to perform the same function around the globe under different environmental conditions. Soap and detergent manufacturers have adjusted their product formulations to meet local water and washing equipment conditions with no change in their basic communications approach. Household appliances have been scaled to sizes appropriate to different use environments, and clothing has been adapted to meet fashion criteria. Also, food products, by virtue of their potentially high degree of environmental sensitivity, are often

---

[17] In 1993, Perrier Group of America shifted to strategy 1 by bringing U.S. advertising more in line with the parent company's European approach.

adapted. Mueslix, for example, is the name of a mushlike European health cereal that is popular in Europe. Kellogg's brought the Mueslix name and product concept to the United States but completely changed the formulation and nature of the product.

STRATEGY 4: DUAL ADAPTATION

Sometimes, when comparing a new geographic market to the home market, marketers discover that environmental conditions or consumer preferences differ; the same may be true of the function a product serves or consumer receptivity to advertising appeals. In essence, this is a combination of the market conditions of strategies 2 and 3. In such a situation, a stage 4/5 company will utilize the strategy of product and communications adaptation. As is true about strategy 3, stage 3 companies will also use dual adaptation—regardless of whether the strategy is warranted by market conditions, preferences, function, or receptivity.

Unilever's experience with fabric softener in Europe exemplifies the classic multinational road to adaptation. For years, the product was sold in 10 countries under seven different brand names, with different bottles and marketing strategies. Unilever's decentralized structure meant that product and marketing decisions were left to country managers. They chose names that had local-language appeal and selected package designs to fit local tastes. Today, rival Procter & Gamble is introducing competitive products with a pan-European strategy of standardized products with single names, suggesting that the European market is more similar than Unilever assumed. In response, Unilever's European brand managers are attempting to move gradually toward standardization.[18]

Hallmark, American Greetings, and other U.S.-based greeting card manufacturers have faced genuine market condition and preference differences in Europe, where the function of a greeting card is to provide a space for the sender to write an individual message. In contrast, U.S. cards contain a prepared message, known in the greeting card industry as sentiment. In European stores, cards are handled frequently by customers, a practice that makes it necessary to wrap greeting cards in cellophane. Thus, American manufacturers pursuing an adjustment strategy have changed both their product and their marketing communications in response to this set of environmental differences.

Sometimes, a company will draw on all four of these strategies simultaneously when marketing a given product in different parts of the world. For example, H. J. Heinz utilizes a mix of strategies in its ketchup marketing. Whereas a dual extension strategy works in England, spicier, hotter formulations are also popular in Central Europe and Sweden. Recent ads in France featured a cowboy lassoing a bottle of ketchup and, thus, reminded consumers of the product's American heritage. Swedish ads conveyed a more cosmopolitan message; by promoting Heinz as "the taste of the big world" and featuring well-known landmarks such as the Eiffel Tower, the ads disguised the product's origins.[19]

STRATEGY 5: PRODUCT INVENTION

Adaptation strategies are effective approaches to international (stage 2) and multinational (stage 3) marketing, but they may not respond to global market opportunities. They do not respond to the situation in markets in which customers do not have the purchasing power to buy either the existing or adapted product. This latter situation applies to the LDCs of the world, which are home to roughly three quarters of the world's population. When potential customers have limited purchasing power, a company may need to develop an entirely new product, designed to satisfy the need or want at a price that

---

[18] E. S. Browning, "In Pursuit of the Elusive Euroconsumer," *The Wall Street Journal,* 23 April 1992, p. B2.
[19] Gabriella Stern, "Heinz Aims to Export Taste for Ketchup," *The Wall Street Journal,* 20 November 1992, pp. B1, B9.

is within the reach of the potential customer. Invention is a demanding but potentially rewarding product strategy for reaching mass markets in LDCs.

The winners in global competition are the companies that can develop products offering the most benefits, which in turn create the greatest value for buyers. In some instances, value is not defined in terms of performance but rather in terms of customer perception. The latter is as important for an expensive perfume or champagne as it is for an inexpensive soft drink. Product quality is essential—indeed, it is frequently a given—but it is also necessary to support the product quality with imaginative, value-creating advertising and marketing communications. Most industry experts believe that a global appeal and a global advertising campaign are more effective in creating the perception of value than a series of separate national campaigns.

Colgate pursued this strategy in developing Total, a toothpaste brand whose formulation, imagery, and ultimate consumer appeal were designed from the ground up to translate across national boundaries. The product was tested in six countries, each of which had a different cultural profile: the Philippines, Australia, Colombia, Greece, Portugal, and the United Kingdom. Total is now sold in nearly 100 countries. According to John Steel, senior vice president for global business development at Colgate, Total's success resulted from the application of a fundamental marketing principle: Consumers are the ones who make or break brands. "There ain't no consumers at 300 Park Avenue," he says, referring to company headquarters. Steel explains, "You get a lot more benefit and you can do a lot more with a global brand than you can a local brand. You can bring the best advertising talent from the world to a problem. You can bring the best research brains, the best leverage of your organization onto something that is truly global. Then all your R&D pays off, the huge packaging costs pay off, the advertising pays off, and you can leverage the organization all at once."[20]

How to Choose a Strategy

Most companies seek a product strategy that optimizes company profits over the long term. Which strategy for global markets best achieves this goal? There is, unfortunately, no general answer to this question. Rather, the answer depends on the specific product–market–company mix.

Recall from Chapter 3 that, in terms of cultural sensitivity, consumer products are more sensitive than industrial products. Another rule of thumb is that food products, especially those served at home, frequently exhibit the highest degree of cultural sensitivity. What this means to managers is that some products, by their nature, are likely to demand significant adaptation. Others require only partial adaptation, and still others are best left unchanged.

Companies differ in both their willingness and capability to identify and produce profitable product adaptations. Unfortunately, too many stage one and stage two companies are oblivious to the foregoing issues. One new-product expert has described three stages that a company must go through as follows:

1. *Cave dweller.* The primary motivation behind launching new products internationally is to dispose of excess production or increase plant-capacity utilization.
2. *Naive nationalist.* The company recognizes growth opportunities outside the domestic market. It realizes that cultures and markets differ from country to country, and as a result, it sees product adaptation as the only possible alternative.
3. *Globally sensitive.* This company views regions or the entire world as the competitive marketplace. New-product opportunities are evaluated across

---

[20] Pam Weisz, "Border Crossings: Brands Unify Image to Counter Cult of Culture," *Brandweek,* 31 October 1994, p. 24.

countries, with some standardization planned as well as some differentiation to accommodate cultural variances. New-product planning processes and control systems are reasonably standardized.[21]

To sum up, the choice of product and communications strategy in international marketing is a function of three key factors: (1) the product itself, defined in terms of the function or need it serves; (2) the market, defined in terms of the conditions under which the product is used, the preferences of potential customers, and the ability to buy the products in question; and (3) the costs of adaptation and manufacture to the company considering these product/communications approaches. Only after analysis of the product/market fit and of company capabilities and costs can executives choose the most profitable international strategy.

◆ NEW PRODUCTS IN GLOBAL MARKETING

What is a new product? Newness can be assessed in the context of the product itself, the organization, and the market. The product may be an entirely new invention or innovation—for example, the videocassette recorder (VCR) or the compact disc. It may be a line extension (a modification of an existing product) such as Diet Coke. Newness may also be organizational, as when a company acquires an already existing product with which it has no previous experience. Finally, an existing product that is not new to a company may be new to a particular market.

In today's dynamic, competitive market environment, many companies realize that continuous development and introduction of new products are keys to survival and growth. Which companies excel at these activities? Gary Reiner, a new-product specialist with the Boston Consulting Group, has compiled the following list: Honda, Compaq, Motorola, Canon, Boeing, Merck, Microsoft, Intel, and Toyota. One common characteristic: They are global companies that pursue opportunities in global markets in which competition is fierce, thus ensuring that new products will be world class. Other characteristics noted by Reiner are as follows:

1. They focus on one or only a few businesses.
2. Senior management is actively involved in defining and improving the product development process.
3. They have the ability to recruit and retain the best and the brightest people in their fields.
4. They understand that speed in bringing new products to market reinforces product quality.[22]

IDENTIFYING NEW-PRODUCT IDEAS

The starting point for an effective worldwide new-product program is an information system that seeks new-product ideas from all potentially useful sources and channels. Those ideas relevant to the company undergo screening at decision centers within the organization. There are many sources of new-product ideas, including customers, suppliers, competitors, company salespeople, distributors and agents, subsidiary executives, headquarters executives, documentary sources (for example, information service reports and publications), and, finally, actual firsthand observation of the market environment. Figure 11-3 shows how corporate spending on research and development varies by country.

---

[21] Thomas D. Kuczmarski, *Managing New Products: The Power of Innovation* (Upper Saddle River, NJ: Prentice Hall, 1992), p. 254.
[22] Gary Reiner, "Lessons from the World's Best Product Developers," *The Wall Street Journal,* 4 April 1990, p. A12.

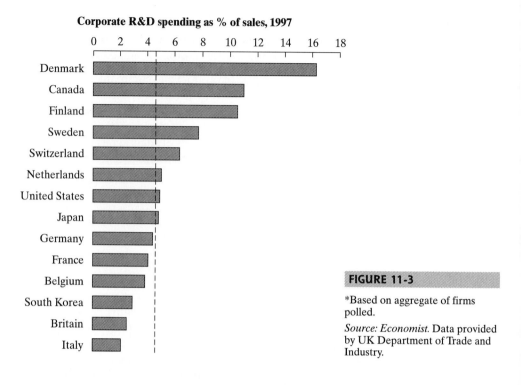

Corporate R&D spending as % of sales, 1997

FIGURE 11-3

*Based on aggregate of firms polled.

Source: Economist. Data provided by UK Department of Trade and Industry.

NEW-PRODUCT DEVELOPMENT LOCATION

A global company must make an important decision regarding new-product development. Should development activity be dispersed to different country/regional locations, or should new-product activities be concentrated in a single location? The advantage of concentration is that all of the new-product development people can interact daily on a face-to-face basis. There may also be cost efficiencies in a single location. The disadvantage of concentration is that it does not take advantage of global thinking and separates the developers from the ultimate consumer. Utilizing a dispersed strategy requires coordination of employees and the effective transfer of information between locations, and may result in duplicated efforts.

Regardless of which strategy a company selects, a high volume of information flow is required to scan adequately for new-product opportunities, and considerable effort is subsequently required to screen these opportunities to identify candidates for product development. An organizational design for addressing these requirements is a new-product department. The function of such a department is fourfold: (1) to ensure that all relevant information sources are continuously tapped for new-product ideas; (2) to screen these ideas to identify candidates for investigation; (3) to investigate and analyze selected new-product ideas; and (4) to ensure that the organization commits resources to the most likely new-product candidates and is continuously involved in an orderly program of new-product introduction and development on a worldwide basis.

With the enormous number of possible new products, most companies establish screening grids to focus on those ideas that are most appropriate for investigation. The following questions are relevant to this task:

1. How big is the market for this product at various prices?
2. Can we market the product through our existing structure? If not, what changes will be necessary and what costs will be required to make the changes?

3. Given estimates of potential demand for this product at specified prices with estimated levels of competition, can we source the product at a cost that will yield an adequate profit?
4. What are the likely competitive moves in response to our activity with this product?
5. Does this product fit our strategic development plan?
   a. Is the product consistent with our overall goals and objectives?
   b. Is the product consistent with our available resources?
   c. Is the product consistent with our management structure?
   d. Does the product have adequate global potential?

TESTING NEW PRODUCTS IN NATIONAL MARKETS

The major lesson of new-product introduction outside the home market has been that whenever a product interacts with human, mechanical, or chemical elements, there is the potential for a surprising and unexpected incompatibility. Since virtually every product matches this description, it is important to test a product under actual market conditions before proceeding with full-scale introduction. A test does not necessarily involve a full-scale test-marketing effort. It may simply involve observing the actual use of the product in the target market.

Failure to assess actual use conditions can lead to big surprises, as in the case of Singer sewing machines sold in African markets. These machines, manufactured in Scotland by Singer, were slightly redesigned by Scottish engineers. The location of a small bolt on the product's base was changed; the change had no effect on product performance but did save a few pennies per unit in manufacturing costs. Unfortunately, when the modified machine reached Africa, it was discovered that this small change was disastrous for product sales. The Scottish engineers did not take into account the fact that in Africa, it is customary for women to transport any bundle or load—including sewing machines—on their heads. The relocated bolt was positioned at exactly the place where head met machine for proper balance; since the sewing machines were no longer transportable, demand decreased substantially.

Summary

The product is the most important element of a marketing program. Global marketers face the challenge of formulating a coherent global product strategy for their companies. Product strategy requires an evaluation of the basic needs and conditions of use in the company's existing and proposed markets. Whenever possible, opportunities to market global products should be given precedence over opportunities to market local or international products. The same positioning and marketing approaches can be used with global brands such as Coca-Cola.

Marketers must consider four factors when designing products for global markets: preferences, costs, regulations, and compatibility. Attitudes toward a product's country of origin must also be taken into account. Five strategic alternatives are open to companies pursuing geographic expansion: product/communications extension; product extension/communications adaptation; product adaptation/communications extension; dual adaptation; and product invention. Global competition has created pressure on companies to excel at product development. There are different definitions of what constitutes a new product; the most difficult type of new-product launch is clearly one involving an entirely new product in a market in which a company has little or no experience. Successful global product launches require leverage. An organization must accumulate and disseminate knowledge concerning past practices—both successful and unsuccessful. Opportunities for comparative analysis further enhance the effectiveness of marketing planning activities within the global system.

Discussion Questions ■■■

1. What is the difference between a product and a brand?
2. What are the differences among a local, a national, an international, and a global product or brand? Cite examples.
3. What criteria should global marketers consider when making product design decisions?
4. How can buyer attitudes about a product's country of origin affect marketing strategy?
5. Identify several global brands. What are some of the reasons for the global success of the brands you chose?
6. Briefly describe various combinations of product/communication strategies available to global marketers. When is it appropriate to use each?

Suggested Readings ■■

Carpano, Claudio, and James J. Chrisman. "Performance Implications of International Product Strategies and the Integration of Marketing Activities." *Journal of International Marketing,* 3, no. 1 (1995): 9–28.

Chao, Paul. "Partitioning Country of Origin Effects: Consumer Evaluations of a Hybrid Product." *Journal of International Business Studies,* 24, no. 2 (Second Quarter 1993): 291–306.

Clark, Terry, and Daniel Rajaratnam, "International Services: Perspectives at Century's End," *Journal of Service Marketing,* 13, no. 4/5 (1999).

Du Preez, Johann P., Adamantios Diamantopoulos, and Bodo B. Schlegelmilch. "Product Standardization and Attribute Saliency: A Three-Product Empirical Comparison." *Journal of International Marketing,* 2, no. 1 (1994): 7–28.

Elliott, Gregory R., and Ross C. Cameron. "Consumer Perception of Product Quality and the Country-of-Origin Effect." *Journal of International Marketing,* 2, no. 2 (1994): 49–62.

Faulds, David J., Orlen Grunewald, and Denise Johnson. "A Cross National Investigation of the Relationship Between the Price and Quality of Consumer Products: 1970–1990." *Journal of Global Marketing,* 8, no. 1 (1994): 7–26.

Gronroos, Christian. "Internationalization Strategies for Services." *Journal of Service Marketing,* 13, no. 4/5 (1999).

Hamilton, Carl. *Absolut: Biography of a Bottle,* New York: Texere, 2000.

Hill, John S., and William L. James. "Product and Promotion Transfers in Consumer Goods Multinationals." *International Marketing Review,* 8, no. 2 (1991): 6–17.

Hill, John S., and Up Kwon. "Product Mixes in U.S. Multinationals: An Empirical Study." *Journal of Global Marketing,* 6, no. 3 (1992): 55–73.

Johansson, Johny K., Susan P. Douglas, and Ikuiiro Nonaka. "Assessing the Impact of Country of Origin on Product Evaluations: A New Methodologic

Prospective." *Journal of Marketing Research,* 12 (November 1985): 388–396.

Johansson, Johny K., Ilkka A. Ronkainen, and Michael R. Czinkota. "Negative Country-of-Origin Effects: The Case of the New Russia." *Journal of International Business Studies,* 25, no. 1 (First Quarter 1994): 157–176.

Johansson, Johny K., and Hans B. Thorelli. "International Product Positioning." *Journal of International Business Studies,* 16, no. 3 (Fall 1985): 57–76.

Keegan, Warren J., Sandra Moriarty, and Tom Duncan. *Marketing,* 2nd. ed. Upper Saddle River, NJ: Prentice Hall, 1995.

Kotabe, Masaaki. "Corporate Product Policy and Innovative Behavior of European and Japanese Multinational: An Empirical Investigation." *Journal of Marketing,* 54, no. 2 (April 1990): 19–33.

Kuczmarski, Thomas D. *Managing New Products: The Power of Innovation.* Upper Saddle River, NJ: Prentice Hall, 1992.

Macrae, Chris. *World Class Brands.* Reading, MA: Addison-Wesley, 1991.

Mathe, Herve, and Teo Forcht Dagi. "Harnessing Technology in Global Service Businesses." *Long Range Planning,* 29, no. 4 (1996): 449–461.

Moskowitz, Howard R., and Samuel Rabino. "Sensory Segmentation: An Organizing Principle for International Product Concept Generation." *Journal of Global Marketing,* 8, no. 1 (1994): 73–94.

Ogbuehi, Alphonso O., and Ralph A. Bellas Jr. "Decentralized R&D for Global Product Development: Strategic Implications for the Multinational Corporation." *International Marketing Review,* 9, no. 5 (1992): 60–70.

Papadopoulos, Nicolas, and Louise A. Heslop. *Product–Country Images: Impact and Role in International Marketing.* New York: International Business Press, 1993.

Prasad, V. Kanti, and G. M. Naidu. "Perspectives and Preparedness Regarding ISO-9000 International

Quality Standards." *Journal of International Marketing,* 2, no. 2 (1994): 81–98.

Quelch, John A., Robert Buzzell, and Eric Salama. *The Marketing Challenge of Europe 1992.* Reading, MA: Addison-Wesley, 1991.

Robinson, William T., and Claes Fornell. "Sources of Market Pioneer Advantages in Consumer Goods Industries." *Journal of Marketing Research* (August 1985): 305–317.

Rosenthal, Stephen R. *Effective Product Design and Development: How to Cut Lead Time and Increase Customer Satisfaction.* Homewood, IL: Business One Irwin, 1992.

Roth, Martin S. "Effects of Global Market Conditions on Brand Image Customization and Brand Performance." *Journal of Advertising,* 24 (Winter 1995): 55–77.

Samiee, Saeed. "Customer Evaluation of Products in a Global Market." *Journal of International Business Studies,* 25, no. 3 (Third Quarter 1994): 579–604.

Samiee, Saeed. "The Internationalization of Services; Trends, Obstacles and Issues," *Journal of Service Marketing,* 13, no. 4/5 (1999).

Tse, David K., and Gerald Gorn. "An Experiment on the Salience of Country-of-Origin in the Era of Global Brands." *Journal of International Marketing,* 1, no. 1 (1993): 57–76.

Tse, David K., and Wei-na Lee. "Removing Negative Country Images: Effects of Decomposition, Branding, and Product Experience." *Journal of International Marketing,* 1, no. 4 (1993): 25–48.

Ulgado, Francis M., and Moonku Lee. "Consumer Evaluations of Bi-National Products in the Global Market." *Journal of International Marketing,* 1, no. 3 (1993): 5–22.

Witt, Jerome, and C. P. Rao. "The Impact of Global Sourcing on Consumers: Country-of-Origin Effects on Perceived Risk." *Journal of Global Marketing,* 6, no. 3 (1992): 105–128.

Zou, Shaoming. "Global Product R&D and the Firm's Strategic Position." *Journal of International Marketing,* 7, no. 1 (1999): 57–77.

CHAPTER 12

Pricing Decisions

The real price of everything is the toil and trouble of acquiring it.

—ADAM SMITH
Wealth of Nations (1776)

CONTENTS

For many people, the phrase *black market* conjures up images of a shadowy, underground economy in which goods are bought and sold in back alleys without the knowledge of government authorities. For better or for worse, global marketing has a distinctive color on its palette: gray. Gray marketing is the distribution of trademarked products in a country by unauthorized persons. Sometimes, gray marketers bring a product produced in one country—French champagne, for example—into a second country market in competition with authorized importers. The gray marketers sell at prices that undercut those set by authorized importers. This practice, known as parallel importing, may flourish when a product is in short supply or when producers attempt to set high prices. This has happened with French champagne sold in the United States; it is also true of the European market for pharmaceuticals, in which prices vary widely from country to country. In the United Kingdom and the Netherlands, for example, parallel imports account for as much as 10 percent of the sales of some pharmaceutical brands.

With the introduction of the Euro, however, these discrepancies will be reduced as consumers can now easily compare prices in the EU Euro countries. Another trend that increases consumers' ability to comparison shop is the Internet. Table 12-1 shows the cost of a Dell laptop in selected EU countries. Why buy the computer in Belgium when

TABLE 12-1   Local Currency Versus the Euro

	Local Currency*	Euro
Austrian Schillings	37,825	2,749
Belgian Francs	115,200	2,856
Finnish Markkaa	15,354	2,582
French Francs	17,490	2,666
German Deutsche Marks	5,530	2,735
Irish Pounds	2,145	2,723
Italian Lire	4,720,656	2,436
Netherlands Guilders	6,230	2,827
Spanish Pesetas	419,576	2,522

*The before-tax prices of a popular laptop computer with 64MB of memory as seen on Web sites on 12/31/98.

Source: Data from Dell Computer Corporation sites, 31 December 1998.

the same computer is 15 percent cheaper in Italy? A consumer in Japan can pay the same price for an L.L. Bean shirt as the consumer in the United States. The only added costs will be shipping and currency exchange.

In any country, three basic factors determine the boundaries within which market prices should be set. The first is product cost, which establishes a price floor, or minimum price. Although it is certainly possible to price a product below the cost boundary, few firms can afford to do this for extended periods of time. Second, competitive prices for comparable products create a price ceiling, or upper boundary. International competition almost always puts pressure on the prices of domestic companies. A widespread effect of international trade is to lower prices. Indeed, one of the major benefits to a country of international business is the favorable impact of international competition on national price levels and, in turn, on a country's rate of inflation. Between the lower and upper boundaries for every product there is an optimum price, which is a function of the demand for the product as determined by the willingness and ability of customers to buy. As the gray marketing example illustrates, however, sometimes the optimum price can be affected by arbitrageurs, who exploit price differences in different countries.

The interplay of these factors is reflected in the pricing policies adopted by companies. With increasing globalization, there is greater competitive pressure on companies to restrain price increases. In a globalized industry, companies must compete with other companies from all over the world. Automobiles are a good example. In the United States, one of the most open and competitive automobile markets in the world, the fierce struggle for market share by American, European, Japanese, and Korean companies makes it difficult for any company to raise prices. If a manufacturer does raise prices, it is important to make sure that the increase does not put the company's product out of line with competitive alternatives. Notes John Ballard, chief executive officer (CEO) of a California-based engineering company, "We thought about price increases. But our research of competitors and what the market would bear told us it was not worth pursuing."[1]

---

[1] Lucinda Harper and Fred R. Bleakley, "Like Old Times: An Era of Low Inflation Changes the Calculus for Buyers and Sellers," *The Wall Street Journal,* 14 January 1994, p. A1.

◆ BASIC PRICING CONCEPTS

As CEO Ballard's experience shows, the global manager must develop pricing systems and pricing policies that address price floors, price ceilings, and optimum prices in each of the national markets in which his or her company operates. The following list identifies eight basic pricing considerations for marketing outside the home country.[2]

1. Does the price reflect the product's quality?
2. Is the price competitive?
3. Should the firm pursue market penetration, market skimming, or some other pricing objective?
4. What type of discount (trade, cash, quantity) and allowance (advertising, trade-off) should the firm offer its international customers?
5. Should prices differ by market segment?
6. What pricing options are available if the firm's costs increase or decrease? Is demand in the target market elastic or inelastic?
7. Are the firm's prices likely to be viewed by the host-country government as reasonable or exploitative?
8. Do the target country's dumping laws pose a problem?

The task of determining prices in global marketing is complicated by fluctuating exchange rates, which may bear only limited relationship to underlying costs. According to the concept of purchasing power parity, changes in domestic prices will be reflected in the exchange rate of the country's currency. Thus, in theory, fluctuating exchange rates should not present serious problems for the global marketer because a rise or decline in domestic price levels should be offset by an opposite rise or decline in the value of the home-country currency and vice versa. In the real world, however, exchange rates do not move in lockstep fashion with inflation. This means that global marketers are faced with difficult decisions about how to deal with windfalls resulting from favorable exchange rates, as well as losses due to unfavorable exchange rates.

A firm's pricing system and policies must also be consistent with other uniquely global constraints. Those responsible for global pricing decisions must take into account international transportation costs, middlemen in elongated international channels of distribution, and the demands of global accounts for equal price treatment regardless of location. In addition to the diversity of national markets in all three basic dimensions—cost, competition, and demand—the international executive is also confronted by conflicting governmental tax policies and claims as well as various types of price controls. These include dumping legislation, resale price maintenance legislation, price ceilings, and general reviews of price levels. For example, Procter & Gamble (P&G) encountered strict price controls in Venezuela in the late 1980s. Despite increases in the cost of raw materials, P&G was granted only about 50 percent of the price increases it requested; even then, months passed before permission to raise prices was forthcoming. As a result, by 1988 detergent prices in Venezuela were less than what they were in the United States.[3]

The textbook approach outlined earlier is used in part or in whole by most experienced global firms, but it must be noted that the inexperienced or part-time exporter does not usually go to all this effort to determine the best price for a product in international markets. Such a company will frequently use a much simpler approach to pricing, such as the cost-plus method explained later in this chapter. As managers gain experience and

---

[2] Adapted from "Price, Quotations, and Terms of Sale Are Key to Successful Exporting," *Business America* (October 4, 1993): 12.

[3] Alecia Swasy, "Foreign Formula: Procter & Gamble Fixes Aim on Tough Market: The Latin Americans," *The Wall Street Journal,* 15 June 1990, p. A7.

become more sophisticated in their approach, however, they realize that the factors identified previously should be considered when making pricing decisions.

There are other important internal organizational considerations besides cost. Within the typical corporation, there are many interest groups and, frequently, conflicting price objectives. Divisional vice presidents, regional executives, and country managers are each concerned about profitability at their respective organizational levels. Similarly, the director of international marketing seeks competitive prices in world markets. The controller and financial vice president are also concerned about profits. The manufacturing vice president seeks long runs for maximum manufacturing efficiency. The tax manager is concerned about compliance with government transfer pricing legislation, and company counsel is concerned about the antitrust implications of international pricing practices.

Compounding the problem is the rapidly changing global marketplace and the inaccurate and distorted nature of much of the available information regarding demand. In many parts of the world, external market information is distorted and inaccurate. It is often not possible to obtain the definitive and precise information that would be the basis of an optimal price. The same may be true about internal information. In Russia, for example, market research is a fairly new concept. Historically, detailed market information was not gathered or distributed. Also, managers at newly privatized factories are having difficulty setting prices because cost accounting data relating to manufacturing are frequently unavailable.

There are other problems. When attempting to estimate demand, for example, it is important to consider product appeal relative to competitive products. Although it is possible to arrive at such estimates after conducting market research, the effort can be costly and time consuming. Company managers and executives have to rely on intuition and experience. One way of improving the estimates of potential demand is to use analogy. As described in Chapter 6, this approach basically means extrapolating potential demand for target markets from actual sales in markets judged to be similar.

◆ ENVIRONMENTAL INFLUENCES ON PRICING DECISIONS

Global marketers must deal with a number of environmental considerations when making pricing decisions. Among these are currency fluctuations, inflation, government controls and subsidies, competitive behavior, and market demand. Some of these factors work in conjunction with others; for example, inflation may be accompanied by government controls. Each consideration is discussed in detail next.

CURRENCY FLUCTUATIONS

Fluctuating currency values are a fact of life in international business. The marketer must decide what to do about this fact. Are price adjustments appropriate when currencies strengthen or weaken? There are two extreme positions; one is to fix the price of products in country target markets. If this is done, any appreciation or depreciation of the value of the currency in the country of production will lead to gains or losses for the seller. The other extreme position is to fix the price of products in home-country currency. If this is done, any appreciation or depreciation of the home-country currency will result in price increases or decreases for customers with no immediate consequences for the seller.

In practice, companies rarely assume either of these extreme positions. Pricing decisions should be consistent with the company's overall business and marketing strategy: If the strategy is long term, then it makes no sense to give up market share in order to maintain export margins. When currency fluctuations result in appreciation in the value of the currency of a country that is an exporter, wise companies do two things: They accept that currency fluctuations may unfavorably impact operating margins, and

TABLE 12-2 Global Pricing Strategies	
When Domestic Currency Is Weak	**When Domestic Currency Is Strong**
1. Stress price benefits.	1. Engage in nonprice competition by improving quality, delivery, and after-sale service.
2. Expand product line and add more costly features.	2. Improve productivity and engage in cost reduction.
3. Shift sourcing to domestic market.	3. Shift sourcing outside home country.
4. Exploit market opportunities in all markets.	4. Give priority to exports to countries with stronger currencies.
5. Use full-costing approach but employ marginal-cost pricing to penetrate new or competitive markets.	5. Trim profit margins and use marginal-cost pricing.
6. Speed repatriation of foreign-earned income and collections.	6. Keep the foreign-earned income in host country; slow down collections.
7. Minimize expenditures in local or host-country currency.	7. Maximize expenditures in local or host-country currency.
8. Buy advertising, insurance, transportation, and other services in domestic market.	8. Buy needed services abroad and pay for them in local currencies.
9. Bill foreign customers in their own currency.	9. Bill foreign customers in the domestic currency.

Source: S. Tamer Cavusgil, "Pricing for Global Markets," *Columbia Journal of World Business,* 31, no. 4 (Winter 1996): 69. Copyright 1996. *Columbia Journal of World Business.* Reprinted with permission.

they double their efforts to reduce costs. In the short run, lower margins enable them to hold prices in target markets, and in the longer run, driving down costs enables them to improve operating margins.

For companies that are in a strong, competitive market position, price increases can be passed on to customers without significant decreases in sales volume. In more competitive market situations, companies in a strong-currency country will often absorb any price increase by maintaining international market prices at pre-revaluation levels. In actual practice, a manufacturer and its distributor may work together to maintain market share in international markets. Either party, or both, may choose to take a lower profit percentage. The distributor may also choose to purchase more product to achieve volume discounts; another alternative is to maintain leaner inventories if the manufacturer can provide just-in-time delivery. By using these approaches, it is possible to remain price competitive in markets in which currency devaluation in the importing country is a price consideration.

If a country's currency weakens relative to a trading partner's currency, a producer in a weak-currency country can cut export prices to hold market share or leave prices alone for healthier profit margins. The Euro is a good example. In the first 17 months after the launch of the Euro at the beginning of 1999, the currency lost nearly a quarter of its value. One option for the European Central Bank (ECB) was to raise interest rates to strengthen the Euro. While the Euro remains weak, Germany is enjoying an export boom.

The crisis that occurred with the Russian ruble in 1998 is another good example of how currency fluctuations can affect marketing. Prior to the devaluation of the ruble from January 1998 to June 1998, the market share for Russian shampoos, face care products, hair coloring, toothpaste, deodorants, and soaps in Russia was only 27 percent.

---

[4] Sabrina Tavernise, "Russians Want Beauty with Scent of Home," *The New York Times,* 29 July, 2000, p. C1-2.

- *Purpose:* To protect parties from unforeseen large swings in currencies.
- Exchange rate review is made quarterly to determine possible adjustments for the next period.
- Comparison basis is the three-month daily average and the initial average.

FIGURE 12-1 Exchange Rate Clauses

When the price of imported products rose dramatically, many Russian women switched to local products. By January to June 2000, the market share of local products rose to 44 percent and had forced some foreign producers out of the market.[4]

Table 12-2 provides a synopsis of pricing strategies to use when domestic currency is weak and when it is strong.

EXCHANGE RATE CLAUSES

Many sales are contracts to supply goods or services over time. When these contracts are between parties in two countries, the problem of exchange rate fluctuations and exchange risk must be addressed.

An exchange rate clause allows the buyer and seller to agree to supply and purchase at fixed prices in each company's national currency. If the exchange rate fluctuates within a specified range, say plus or minus 5 percent, the fluctuations do not affect the pricing agreement that is spelled out in the exchange rate clause. Small fluctuations in exchange rates are not a problem for most buyers and sellers. Exchange rate clauses are designed to protect both the buyer and the seller from unforeseen large swings in currencies. Figure 12-1 summarizes the key elements of an exchange rate clause. An example of an actual clause used by one U.S.-headquartered *Fortune* 100 company is shown in Figure 12-1.

The basic design of an exchange rate clause is straightforward: Review exchange rates periodically (this is determined by the parties; any interval is possible, but most

FIGURE 12-2 Actual Exchange Rate Clause

Initial base exchange rate per US$

Base U.S. Dollar	Italy Lira	Spain Peseta	Britain Pound	Germany Mark	Sweden Krona	Denmark Krone	Turkey Lira
$1 =	1,500	115	0.699	1.622	7.277	6.261	8,849.597
Product Price $5	7,500	575	3.495	8.11	36.385	31.305	44,247.985

Compare initial base to three-month daily average:

- If rate differences are greater than ±5%, adjust prices for the next three-month period.
- If greater than ±10%, open discussion/negotiation.

clauses specify a monthly or quarterly review), and compare the daily average during the review period and the initial base average. If the comparison produces exchange rate fluctuations that are outside the agreed range of fluctuation, an adjustment is made to align prices with the new exchange rate if the fluctuation is within some range (in the example in Figure 12-2, this range is specified as greater than ±5 percent). If the fluctuation is greater than some limit (10 percent in our example), the parties agree to discuss and negotiate new prices.

In other words, the clause accepts the foreign exchange market's effect on currency value, but only if it is within the range of 5 to 10 percent. Anything less than 5 percent does not affect pricing, and anything more than 10 percent opens up a renegotiation of prices.

PRICING IN AN INFLATIONARY ENVIRONMENT

Inflation, or a persistent upward change in price levels, is a worldwide phenomenon. Inflation requires periodic price adjustments. These adjustments are necessitated by rising costs that must be covered by increased selling prices. An essential requirement when pricing in an inflationary environment is the maintenance of operating profit margins. Regardless of cost accounting practices, if a company maintains its margins, it has effectively protected itself from the effects of inflation. To keep up with inflation in Peru, for example, Procter & Gamble has resorted to biweekly increases in detergent prices of 20 percent to 30 percent.[5]

Within the scope of this chapter, it is possible only to touch on the major accounting issues and conventions relating to price adjustments in international markets. In particular, it is worth noting that the traditional FIFO (first-in, first-out) costing method is hardly appropriate for an inflationary situation. A more appropriate accounting practice under conditions of rising prices is the LIFO (last-in, first-out) method, which takes the most recent raw material acquisition price and uses it as the basis for costing the product sold. In highly inflationary environments, historical approaches are less appropriate costing methods than replacement cost. The latter amounts to a next-in, first-out approach. Although this method does not conform to generally accepted accounting principles (GAAP), it is used to estimate future prices that will be paid for raw and component materials. These replacement costs can then be used to set prices. This approach is useful in managerial decision making, but it cannot be used in financial statements. Regardless of the accounting methods used, an essential requirement under inflationary conditions of any costing system is that it maintain gross and operating profit margins. Managerial actions can maintain these margins subject to the following constraints.

GOVERNMENT CONTROLS AND SUBSIDIES

If government action limits the freedom of management to adjust prices, the maintenance of margins is definitely compromised. Under certain conditions, government action is a real threat to the profitability of a subsidiary operation. In a country that is undergoing severe financial difficulties and is in the midst of a financial crisis (e.g., a foreign exchange shortage caused in part by runaway inflation), government officials are under pressure to take some type of action. This has been true in Brazil for many years. In some cases, governments will take expedient steps rather than getting at the underlying causes of inflation and foreign exchange shortages. Such steps might include the use of broad or selective price controls. When selective controls are imposed, foreign companies are more vulnerable to control than local businesses, particularly if

---

[5] Swasy, "Foreign Formula," p. 1.

the outsiders lack the political influence over government decision making possessed by local managers.

Government control can also take the form of prior cash deposit requirements imposed on importers. This is a requirement that a company has to tie up funds in the form of a non-interest-bearing deposit for a specified period of time if it wishes to import products. Such requirements clearly create an incentive for a company to minimize the price of the imported product; lower prices mean smaller deposits. Other government requirements that affect the pricing decision are profit transfer rules that restrict the conditions under which profits can be transferred out of a country. Under such rules, a high transfer price paid for imported goods by an affiliated company can be interpreted as a device for transferring profits out of a country.

Government subsidies can also force a company to make strategic use of sourcing to be price competitive. In Europe, government subsidies to the agricultural sector make it difficult for foreign marketers of processed food to compete on price when exporting to the European Union (EU). In the United States, some, but not all, agricultural sectors are subsidized. For example, U.S. poultry producers and processors are not subsidized, a situation that makes their prices noncompetitive in world markets. One midwestern chicken processor with European customers sourced its product in France for resale in the Netherlands. By doing so, the company took advantage of lower costs derived from subsidies and eliminated price escalation due to tariffs and duties.

COMPETITIVE BEHAVIOR

As noted at the beginning of this chapter, pricing decisions are bounded not only by cost and the nature of demand but also by competitive action. If competitors do not adjust their prices in response to rising costs, management—even if acutely aware of the effect of rising costs on operating margins—will be severely constrained in its ability to adjust prices accordingly. Conversely, if competitors are manufacturing or sourcing in a lower-cost country, it may be necessary to cut prices to stay competitive.

PRICE AND QUALITY RELATIONSHIPS

Is there a relationship between price and quality? Do you, in fact, get what you pay for? During the past several decades, studies conducted in the United States have indicated that the overall relationship between price and quality as measured by consumer testing organizations is quite weak. A recent four-country international study found a high degree of similarity with the results from the U.S. studies. The authors conclude that the lack of a strong price–quality relationship appears to be an international phenomenon.[6] This is not surprising when one recognizes that consumers make purchase decisions with limited information and rely more on product appearance and style and less on technical quality as measured by testing organizations.

◆ GLOBAL PRICING OBJECTIVES AND STRATEGIES

A number of different pricing strategies are available to global marketers. An overall goal must be to contribute to company sales and profit objectives worldwide. Customer-oriented strategies such as market skimming, penetration, and market holding can be used when consumer perceptions, as determined by the value equation, are used as a

---

[6] David J. Faulds, Orlen Grunewals, and Denise Johnson, "A Cross-National Investigation of the Relationship between the Price and Quality of Consumer Products, 1970–1990," *Journal of Global Marketing,* vol. 8, no. 1 (1994): 7–25.

guide. Global pricing can also be based on other external criteria such as the escalation in costs when goods are shipped long distances across national boundaries. The issue of global pricing can also be fully integrated in the product design process, an approach widely used by Japanese companies. Prices in global markets are not carved in stone; they must be evaluated at regular intervals and adjusted if necessary. Similarly, pricing objectives may vary, depending on a product's life-cycle stage and the country-specific competitive situation.

MARKET SKIMMING

The market skimming pricing strategy is a deliberate attempt to reach a market segment that is willing to pay a premium price for a product. In such instances, the product must create high value for buyers. This pricing strategy is often used in the introductory phase of the product life cycle, when both production capacity and competition are limited. By setting a deliberately high price, demand is limited to early adopters who are willing and able to pay the price. One goal of this pricing strategy is to maximize revenue on limited volume and to match demand to available supply. Another goal of market skimming pricing is to reinforce customers' perceptions of high product value. When this is done, the price is part of the total product positioning strategy.

When Sony first began selling Betamax videocassette recorders (VCRs) in the United States, it used a skimming strategy. Harvey Schein, who was president of Sony of America at the time, recalled the response to the $1,295 price tag.

> It was fantastic, really. When you have a new product that is as jazzy as a video-tape recorder, you really skim off the cream of the consuming public. The Beta-max was selling for over a thousand dollars. . . . But there were so many wealthy people who wanted to be the first in the neighborhood that it just went whoof—like a vacuum. It flew off the shelf.[7]

The initial success of the Betamax proved that consumers were willing to pay a high price for a piece of consumer electronics equipment that would allow them to watch their favorite television shows at any time of the day or night.

PENETRATION PRICING

Penetration pricing uses price as a competitive weapon to gain market position. The majority of companies using this type of pricing in international marketing are located in the Pacific Rim. Scale-efficient plants and low-cost labor allow these companies to blitz the market.

It should be noted that a first-time exporter is unlikely to use penetration pricing. The reason is simple: Penetration pricing often means that the product may be sold at a loss for a certain length of time. Companies that are new to exporting cannot absorb such losses. They are not likely to have the marketing system in place (including transportation, distribution, and sales organizations) that allows global companies such as Sony to make effective use of a penetration strategy. However, a company whose product is not patentable may wish to use penetration pricing to achieve market saturation before the product is copied by competitors.

When Sony developed the portable compact disc player, the cost per unit at initial sales volumes was estimated to exceed $600. Since this was a "no-go" price in the United States and other target markets, Akio Morita instructed management to price the unit

---

[7] James Lardner, *Fast Forward: Hollywood, The Japanese, and the VCR Wars* (New York: New American Library, 1987), p. 91.

in the $300 range to achieve penetration. Because Sony was a global marketer, the sales volume it expected to achieve in these markets led to scale economies and lower costs.

The Sony example illustrates the penetration approach to pricing as it is practiced by Japanese firms. As shown in Figure 12-3, the Japanese begin with market research and product characteristics. Up to this point, the processes are parallel in the United States and Japan. At the next step, the processes diverge. In Japan, the planned selling price minus the desired profit is calculated, resulting in a target cost figure. It is only at this point that design, engineering, and supplier pricing issues are dealt with; extensive consultation among all value-chain members is used to meet the target. Once the necessary negotiations and trade-offs have been settled, manufacturing begins, followed by continuous cost reduction. In the U.S. process, cost is typically determined after design, engineering, and marketing decisions have been made in sequential fashion; if the cost is too high, the process cycles back to square one—the design stage.[8]

FIGURE 12-3 How the Japanese Keep Costs Low

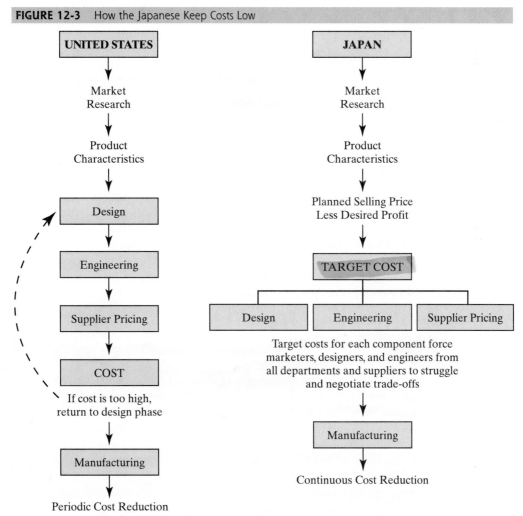

Source: Michel Robert, *Strategy Pure and Simple: How Winning CEOs Outthink Their Competition* (New York: McGraw-Hill, 1993), p. 115.

---

[8] Michel Robert, *Strategy Pure and Simple: How Winning CEOs Outthink Their Competition* (New York: McGraw-Hill, 1993), pp. 114–115.

MARKET HOLDING

The market holding strategy is frequently adopted by companies that want to maintain their share of the market. In single-country marketing, this strategy often involves reacting to price adjustments by competitors. For example, when one airline announces special bargain fares, most competing carriers must match the offer or risk losing passengers. In global marketing, currency fluctuations often trigger price adjustments.

Market holding strategies dictate that source-country currency appreciation will not be automatically passed on in the form of higher prices. If the competitive situation in market countries is price sensitive, manufacturers must absorb the cost of currency appreciation by accepting lower margins in order to maintain competitive prices in country markets.

A strong home currency and rising costs in the home country may also force a company to shift its sourcing to in-country or third-country manufacturing or licensing agreements, rather than exporting from the home country, to maintain market share. IKEA, the Swedish home furnishing company, sourced 50 percent of its products in the United States in 1992, compared with only 10 percent in 1989.[9]

Chrysler-Daimler and BMW built manufacturing and assembly plants in the United States to produce Mercedes and BMW sport-utility and two-seater sport car vehicles for the United States and the world market. This was a decision to invest in new locations for capacity expansion. Market holding means that a company must carefully examine all its costs to ensure that it will be able to remain competitive in target markets. In the case of the German automobile manufacturers, the expansion of production outside Germany meant that the companies were no longer tied exclusively to German costs in their manufacturing.

When the currency of a country weakens, it becomes more difficult to compete on price with imported product. However, a weak-currency country can be a windfall for a global company with production operations in a weak-currency country. When the Indonesian rupiah fell from 2,400 to 18,000 and then recovered to below 8,000 to the U.S. dollar during the Asian Flu of the late 1990s, global companies with production operations in Indonesia made windfall profits. Their costs in rupiah increased 100 percent but the value of their production in dollars or any "hard" currency increased by 300 to 700 percent. Thus, while the country was in a crisis, many of the global companies in Indonesia were having their best years ever.

COST PLUS/PRICE ESCALATION

Companies new to exporting frequently use a strategy known as cost-plus pricing to gain a toehold in the global marketplace. There are two cost-plus pricing methods: The older is the historical accounting cost method, which defines cost as the sum of all direct and indirect manufacturing and overhead costs. An approach used in recent years is known as the estimated future cost method.

Cost-plus pricing requires adding up all the costs required to get the product to where it must go, plus shipping and ancillary charges, and a profit percentage. The obvious advantage of using this method is its low threshold: It is relatively easy to arrive at a selling price, assuming that accounting costs are readily available. The disadvantage of using historical accounting costs to arrive at a price is that this approach completely ignores demand and competitive conditions in target markets. Therefore, historical accounting cost-plus prices will frequently be either too high or too low in the light of

[9] Joan E. Rigdon and Valerie Reitman, "Pricing Paradox: Consumers Still Find Imported Bargains Despite Weak Dollar," *The Wall Street Journal,* 7 October 1992, p. A6.

market and competitive conditions. If historical accounting cost-plus prices are right, it is only by chance.

However, novice exporters do not care—they are reactively responding to global market opportunities, not proactively seeking them. Experienced global marketers realize that nothing in the historical accounting cost-plus formula directly addresses the competitive and customer-value issues that must be considered in a rational pricing strategy.

Price escalation is the increase in a product's price as transportation, duty, and distributor margins are added to the factory price. Table 12-3 is a typical example of the kind of price escalation that can occur when a product is destined for international markets. In this example, a distributor of agricultural equipment in Kansas City is shipping a container load of farm implements to Tokyo, Japan. A shipment of product that costs ex-works $30,000 in Kansas City ends up having a total retail price in excess of US$50,000 in Tokyo—almost double the ex-works Kansas City price. (*Ex-works* and other trade terms are explained in Appendix 1 at the end of this chapter.)

Let us examine this shipment to see what happened. First, there is the total shipping charge of $5,453.07, which is 18 percent of the ex-works Kansas City price. The principal component of this shipping charge is a combination of land and ocean freight totaling $5,267.80. A currency adjustment factor (CAF) is charged due to the strength of the dollar relative to the yen. This figure will fluctuate as currency values change.

All import charges are assessed against the landed price of the shipment (cost, insurance, freight, or C.I.F. value). Note that there is no line item for duty in this example; no duties are charged on agricultural equipment sent to Japan. Duties may be charged in other countries. A nominal distributor markup of 10 percent ($3,652) actually represents 12 percent of the C.I.F. Yokohama price, because it is a markup not only on the ex-works price but on freight and value-added tax (VAT) as well. (It is assumed here that the distributor's markup includes the cost of transportation from the port to Tokyo.) Finally, a

TABLE 12-3   Price Escalation: A 20-Foot Container of Agricultural Equipment from Kansas City to Yokohama

Item			Percentage of FOB Price
Ex-works Kansas City		$30,000	100%
Container freight charges from Kansas City to Seattle	$1,475.00		
Terminal handling fee	350.00		
Ocean freight for 20-foot container	2,280.00		
Currency adjustment factor (CAF) (51% of ocean freight)	1,162.80		
Insurance (110% of C.I.F. value)	35.27		
Forwarding fee	150.00		18
Total shipping charges	5,453.07		
Total C.I.F. Yokohama value		35,453.07	
VAT (3% of C.I.F. value)		1,063.69	3
		36,516.76	
Distributor markup (10%)		3,651.67	12
		40,168.43	
Dealer markup (25%)		10,042.10	33
Total retail price		$50,210.53	166%

Note: This was loaded at the manufacturer's door, shipped by stack train to Seattle, and then via ocean freight to Yokohama. Total transit time from factory door to foreign port is about 28 days.

dealer markup of 25 percent adds up to $10,042—33 percent—of the C.I.F. Yokohama price. Like distributor markup, dealer markup is based on the total landed cost.

The net effect of this add-on accumulating process is a total retail price in Tokyo of $50,210, or 166 percent of the ex-works Kansas City price. This is price escalation. The example provided here is by no means an extreme case. Indeed, longer distribution channels, or channels that require a higher operating margin—as are typically found in export marketing—can contribute to price escalation. Because of the layered distribution system in Japan, the markups in Tokyo could easily result in a price that is 200 percent of the C.I.F. value.

The example of cost-plus pricing shows an approach that a beginning exporter might use to determine the C.I.F. price. Another cost-plus example is the export of household cleaning products from the United States to South America. The escalation of the U.S. C.I.F. price to the retail shelf in South America, with transportation, import duties and taxes, wholesaler and distributor margins, retail margins, and the VAT is in excess of 300 percent! This kind of escalation provides a major incentive to locate production closer to the customer to reduce and eliminate costs that are part of the export sourcing arrangement. Experienced global marketers view price as a major strategic variable that can help achieve marketing and business objectives.

USING SOURCING AS A STRATEGIC PRICING TOOL

The global marketer has several options when addressing the problem of price escalation described in the last section. The choices are dictated in part by product and market competition. Marketers of domestically manufactured finished products may be forced to switch to lower-income, lower-wage countries for the sourcing of certain components or even of finished goods to keep costs and prices competitive. The athletic footwear industry is an example of an industry in which the leading companies have opted for low-income, low-wage country sourcing of their production. Even companies such as the U.S. firm New Balance, which continues to manufacture athletic footwear in the United States, imports components from lower-income countries.

The low-wage strategy option should never become a formula, however. The problem with shifting production to a low-wage country is that it provides a one-time advantage. This is no substitute for ongoing innovation in creating value. High-income countries are the home of thriving manufacturing operations run by companies that have been creative in figuring out ways to drive down the cost of labor as a percentage of total costs and in creating a unique value. The Swiss watch industry, which owns the world's luxury watch business, did not achieve and maintain its preeminence by chasing cheap labor: It continues to succeed because it has focused on creating a unique value for its customers. Labor as a percent of the selling price in Swiss watches is so small that the price of labor is irrelevant in determining competitive advantage.

Another option is to source a finished product near or in target markets. Companies can enter into one of the arrangements discussed in Chapter 9, such as licensing, joint venture, or a technology transfer agreement. With this option, the company has a presence in the market it is trying to penetrate; price escalation due to high home country manufacturing costs and transportation charges is no longer an issue.

The third option is a thorough audit of the distribution structure in the target markets. A rationalization of the distribution structure can substantially reduce the total markups required to achieve distribution in international markets. Rationalization may include selecting new intermediaries, assigning new responsibilities to old intermediaries, or establishing direct-marketing operations. For example, Toys "Я" Us has invaded the Japanese toy market because it bypassed layers of distribution and adopted a warehouse style of selling similar to its U.S. approach. Toys "Я" Us has been viewed as a test case of the ability of Western retailers—discounters in particular—to change the rules of distribution.

◆ GRAY MARKET GOODS

Gray market goods are trademarked products that are exported from one country to another, where they are sold by unauthorized persons or organizations. Sometimes, gray marketers bring a product produced in one country—French champagne, for example—into a second-country market in competition with authorized importers. The gray marketers sell at prices that undercut those set by the legitimate importers. This practice, known as *parallel importing,* may flourish when a product is in short supply or when producers attempt to set high prices. This has happened with French champagne sold in the United States; it is also true of the European market for pharmaceuticals, where prices vary widely from country to country. In the United Kingdom and the Netherlands, for example, parallel imports account for as much as 10 percent of the sales of some pharmaceutical brands.

In another type of gray marketing, a company manufactures a product in the home-country market as well as in foreign markets. In this case, products manufactured abroad by the company's foreign affiliate for sales abroad are sometimes sold by a foreign distributor to gray marketers. The latter then bring the products into the producing company's home-country market, where they compete with domestically produced goods. For example, in the mid-1980s, Caterpillar's U.S. dealers found themselves competing with gray market construction equipment manufactured in Europe. The strong dollar had provided gray marketers with an opportunity to bring Caterpillar equipment into the United States at lower prices than domestically produced equipment. Even though the gray market goods carry the same trademarks as the domestically produced ones, they may differ in quality, ingredients, or some other way. Manufacturers may not honor warranties on some types of gray market imports such as cameras and consumer electronics equipments.[10]

As these examples show, the marketing opportunity that presents itself requires gray market goods to be priced lower than goods sold by authorized distributors or domestically produced goods. Clearly, buyers gain from lower prices and increased choice. In the United Kingdom alone, for example, total annual retail sales of gray market goods are estimated to be as high as $1.6 billion. A recent case in Europe resulted in a ruling that strengthened the rights of brand owners. Silhouette, an Austrian manufacturer of upscale sunglasses, sued the Hartlauer discount chain after the latter obtained thousands of pairs of sunglasses that Silhouette had intended for sale in Eastern Europe. The European Court of Justice found in favor of Silhouette. In clarifying a 1989 directive, the court ruled that stores cannot import branded goods from outside the EU and then sell them at discounted prices without permission of the brand owner. The *Financial Times* denounced the ruling as "bad for consumers, bad for competition, and bad for European economies.[11]

In the United States, gray market goods are subject to a 70-year-old law, the Tariff Act of 1930. Section 526 of the act expressly forbids importation of goods of foreign manufacture without the permission of the trademark owner. There are, however, several exceptions spelled out in the act; the U.S. Customs Service, which implements the

---

[10] James E. Inman, "Gray Marketing of Imported Trademarked Goods: Tariffs and Trademark Issues," *American Business Law Journal* (May 1993): 59–116; Paul Lansing and Joseph Gabriella, "Clarifying Gray Market Gray Areas," *American Business Law Journal* (September 1993): 313–337.

[11] Peggy Hollinger and Neil Buckley, "Grey Market Ruling Delights Brand Owners," *Financial Times,* 17 July 1998, p. 8.

◆ BOX 12-1 ◆

GRAY MARKETING

Another type of gray marketing occurs when a company manufactures a product in multiple locations—in the home-country market as well as in foreign markets. In this case, products manufactured abroad by the company's foreign affiliate for sale abroad are sometimes sold by a foreign distributor to gray marketers. The latter then bring the products into the producing company's home-country market, where they compete with domestically produced goods. Even though the gray market goods carry the same trademarks as the domestically produced ones, they often differ in quality, ingredients, or in some other way. For example, in the mid-1980s, Caterpillar's U.S. dealers found themselves competing with gray market construction equipment manufactured in Europe. The strong dollar had provided gray marketers with an opportunity to bring Caterpillar equipment into the United States at lower prices than domestically produced equipment.

As these examples show, the marketing opportunity that presents itself depends on gray market goods being priced lower than goods sold by authorized distributors or domestically produced goods. Clearly, buyers gain from lower prices and increased choice. However, gray market goods—especially cameras and consumer electronics equipment—may not be covered by manufacturers' warranties.

In the United States, gray market goods are subject to a 60-year-old law, the Tariff Act of 1930. Section 526 of the act expressly forbids importation of goods of foreign manufacture without the permission of the trademark owner. There are, however, several exceptions spelled out in the act; this provides the U.S. Customs Service, which implements the regulations, and the court system considerable leeway in decisions regarding gray market goods. For example, in 1988 the U.S. Supreme Court ruled that trademarked goods of foreign manufacture such as champagne could legally be imported and sold by gray marketers. In many instances, however, the Court's interpretation of the law differs from that of the Customs Service.

Because of problems associated with regulating gray markets, one legal expert has argued that, in the name of free markets and free trade, the U.S. Congress should repeal Section 526. In its place, a new law should require gray market goods to bear labels clearly explaining any differences between them and goods that come through authorized channels. Other experts believe that, instead of changing the laws, companies should develop proactive strategic responses to gray markets. One such strategy would be improved market segmentation and product differentiation to make gray market products less attractive; another would be to aggressively identify and terminate distributors that are involved in selling to gray marketers.

SOURCES: Per-Henrik Mansson, "Supreme Court Upholds Gray Market Champagne," *Wine Spectator,* 15 July 1988, p. 5; James E. Inman, "Gray Marketing of Imported Trademarked Goods: Tariffs and Trademark Issues," *American Business Law Journal* (May 1993): 59–116; Paul Lansing and Joseph Gabriella, "Clarifying Gray Market Gray Areas," *American Business Law Journal* (September 1993): 313–337.

regulation, and the court system have considerable leeway in decisions regarding gray market goods. For example, in 1988 the U.S. Supreme Court ruled that trademarked goods of foreign manufacture such as champagne could legally be imported and sold by gray marketers. In many instances, however, the court's interpretation of the law differs from that of the Customs Service.

Because of problems associated with regulating gray markets, one legal expert has argued that, in the name of free markets and free trade, the U.S. Congress should repeal Section 526. In its place, a new law should require gray market goods to bear labels clearly explaining any differences between them and goods that come through authorized channels. Other experts believe that, instead of changing the laws, companies should develop proactive strategic responses to gray markets. One such strategy would be improved market segmentation and product differentiation to make gray market products less attractive; another would be to aggressively identify and terminate distributors that are involved in selling to gray marketers.

◆ DUMPING

Dumping is an important global pricing strategy issue. GATT's 1979 Antidumping Code defined dumping as the sale of an imported product at a price lower than that normally charged in a domestic market or country of origin. In addition, many countries have their own policies and procedures for protecting national companies from dumping. The U.S. Antidumping Act of 1921, which is enforced by the U.S. Treasury, did not define dumping specifically but instead referred to unfair competition. However, Congress has defined dumping as an unfair trade practice that results in "injury, destruction, or prevention of the establishment of American industry." Under this definition, dumping occurs when imports sold in the U.S. market are priced either at levels that represent less than the cost of production plus an 8 percent profit margin or at levels below those prevailing in the producing country.

Dumping was a major issue in the Uruguay Round of GATT negotiations. Many countries disapproved of the U.S. system of antidumping laws, in part because the Commerce Department historically almost always ruled in favor of a U.S. company filing a complaint. Another issue was the fact that U.S. exporters were often targeted in antidumping investigations in countries with few formal rules for due process. The U.S. negotiators hoped to improve the ability of U.S. companies to defend their interests and understand the bases for rulings.

The result of the GATT negotiations was an Agreement on Interpretation of Article VI. From the U.S. point of view, one of the most significant changes between the agreement and the 1979 code is the addition of a standard of review that makes it harder to dispute U.S. antidumping determinations. There were also a number of procedural and methodological changes. In some instances, these have the effect of bringing regulations more in line with U.S. law. For example, in calculating fair price for a given product, any sales of the product at below-cost prices in the exporting country are not included in the calculations; inclusion of such sales would have the effect of exerting downward pressure on the fair price. The agreement also brought GATT standards into line with U.S. standards by prohibiting governments from penalizing differences between home-market and export-market prices of less than 2 percent.

As the nature of these issues and regulations suggests, some countries use dumping legislation as a legitimate device to protect local enterprise from predatory pricing practices by foreign companies. In other nations, they represent protectionism, a device for limiting foreign competition in a market. The rationale for dumping legislation is that dumping is harmful to the orderly development of enterprise within an economy. Few economists would object to long-run or continuous dumping. If this were done, it would be an opportunity for a country to take advantage of a low-cost source of a particular good and to specialize in other areas. However, continuous dumping rarely occurs; the sale of agricultural products at international prices, with farmers receiving subsidized higher prices, is an example of continuous dumping. The type of dumping practiced by most companies is sporadic and unpredictable and does not provide a reliable basis for national economic planning. Instead, it may hurt domestic enterprise.

Recently, there has been a shift in the countries bringing charges of dumping. In 1998, the United States, EU, Australia, and Canada brought approximately one third or 225 of the cases opened. This is down significantly from the late 1980s when these same countries accounted for four fifths of all cases.[12] The leading countries bringing suit were South Africa, the United States, India, the European Union, and Brazil.

---

[12] Guy de Jonquieres, "Poor Nations Starting More Dumping Cases," *Financial Times,* 6 May 1999, p. 5.

◆ BOX 12-2 ◆

THE CONTRARIAN VIEWS OF JAMES BOVARD

James Bovard might be considered the Ralph Nader of global marketing. He is a tireless advocate of unrestricted trade and a vocal critic of U.S. trade policy who campaigns to influence the views of policy makers and the general public. In his recent book, *The Myth of Fair Trade,* and in numerous articles and essays, Bovard argues that U.S. trade laws are hypocritical because they reduce rather than encourage competition. The result, he asserts, is higher prices for U.S. consumers. His positions and opinions on two trade issues, dumping and Super 301, are summarized next, along with a sampling of responses.

- *Dumping.* Bovard believes America's antidumping laws should be repealed. Calling dumping laws a relic of the fixed exchange rate era, he notes that the U.S. Commerce Department can convict a company of dumping on the basis of dumping margins (price differences) as small as one half of 1 percent, even though the dollar can experience double-digit fluctuations relative to other world currencies. Moreover, a dumping conviction can restrict a company's market access for 15 years, long after an offense has occurred. Bovard cautions that other nations may copy America's antidumping regulations, to the ultimate detriment of U.S. companies.

Although the Uruguay Round of GATT negotiations resulted in some changes addressing Bovard's specific concerns, the broader issue is still open. Should America's antidumping laws be repealed? Not according to Don E. Newquist, former chairman of the International Trade Commission. He argues that antidumping laws help preserve America's manufacturing and technology base. He warns that without the laws, foreign producers who are sheltered from import competition in their home markets

(e.g., Japanese companies) can use excess profits from domestic sales to subsidize low-cost exports to America. This could lead to market share losses, cash flow reductions, and even plant closings in the United States.

- *Super 301 and Section 301.* In March 1994, Bovard blasted the Clinton administration's decision to reinstate Super 301 to punish Japan for unfair trade practices. Super 301 was a 1988 trade provision that allowed the United States to single out individual nations as unfair traders and impose 100 percent tariffs on exports from those nations unless U.S. demands were granted. An earlier regulation, Section 301 of the Trade Act of 1974, allowed the U.S. government to investigate and retaliate against unfair trade barriers in other nations. Bovard's specific complaint about President Clinton's action was that both 301 provisions have been ineffective, and that threats of retaliation have brought results in only a handful of cases.

Bovard has also frequently argued that the United States is hypocritical when it comes to trade policy, citing numerous examples of U.S. trade practices over the past 20 years to support his claim. For example, in 1990, the United States initiated a case against Canada for limiting American beer imports, even though the United States imposes its own complicated regulations on Canadian beer imports. In 1989, the United States threatened Japan with Section 301 on the grounds that Motorola had not been granted a large enough geographic selling area. Bovard ascribed Motorola's sales problems in Japan to a simple lack of product adaptation; the company initially exported cellular phones designed for American frequencies; Japanese cellular phone exports to the United States are designed for U.S. frequencies.

SOURCES: James Bovard, "Trade Quotas Build New Chinese Wall," *The Wall Street Journal,* 10 January 1994, p. A12; Bovard, "A U.S. History of Trade Hypocrisy," *The Wall Street Journal,* 8 March 1994, p. A1.

Nearly 20 percent of the cases were brought against the EU or member countries followed by China and Korea.

One U.S. company, Smith Corona Corporation of New Canaan, Connecticut, filed an antidumping complaint against Brother Industries of Japan in 1974 and was involved in dumping-related litigation until the day it declared bankruptcy. One of the lessons from this saga is that it can take years to get relief from the International Trade Commission (ITC). Smith Corona had to refile its original complaint; the ITC finally found in its favor in 1980, ordering a 48.7 percent duty on imports of portable typewriters.

However, the duties only applied to typewriters; Brother responded by designing new products with chip-based memory functions. Because this new product was no longer classified as a typewriter—rather, it was a word processor—Brother effectively side-stepped the duties. Brother also began assembling typewriters and word processors from imported parts in a plant in Tennessee. This example shows to what lengths a company will go to get around dumping regulations; Brother used both product innovation and a new sourcing strategy. Finally, in an ironic twist, Brother turned the tables on Smith Corona by accusing the latter of dumping. The rationale: Many of Smith Corona's type-writers are imported from a plant in Singapore; Brother pointed to its own U.S. plant as evidence that it was the true U.S. producer.[13]

For a positive proof of dumping to occur in the United States, both price discrimi-nation and injury must be demonstrated. The existence of either one without the other is an insufficient condition to constitute dumping. Companies concerned with running afoul of antidumping legislation have developed a number of approaches for avoiding the dumping laws. One approach is to differentiate the product sold from that sold in the home market. An example of this is an auto accessory that one company packaged with a wrench and an instruction book, thereby changing the accessory to a tool. The tariff rate in the export market happened to be lower on tools, and the company also acquired im-munity from antidumping laws because the package was not comparable to competing goods in the target market. Another approach is to make non-price-competitive adjust-ments in arrangements with affiliates and distributors. For example, credit can be ex-tended and essentially have the same effect as a price reduction.

◆ TRANSFER PRICING

Transfer pricing refers to the pricing of goods and services bought and sold by operating units or divisions of a single company. In other words, transfer pricing concerns intra-corporate exchanges—transactions between buyers and sellers that have the same cor-porate parent. For example, Toyota subsidiaries sell to, and buy from, each other. The same is true of other companies operating globally. As companies expand and create de-centralized operations, profit centers become an increasingly important component in the overall corporate financial picture. Appropriate intracorporate transfer pricing systems and policies are required to ensure profitability at each level. When a company extends its operations across national boundaries, transfer pricing takes on new dimensions and complications. In determining transfer prices to subsidiaries, global companies must ad-dress a number of issues, including taxes, duties and tariffs, country profit transfer rules, conflicting objectives of joint venture partners, and government regulations.

There are three major alternative approaches to transfer pricing. The approach used will vary with the nature of the firm, products, markets, and the historical circumstances of each case. The alternatives are (1) cost-based transfer pricing, (2) market-based trans-fer pricing, and (3) negotiated prices.

COST-BASED TRANSFER PRICING

Because companies define costs differently, some companies using the cost-based ap-proach may arrive at transfer prices that reflect variable and fixed manufacturing costs only. Alternatively, transfer prices may be based on full costs, including overhead costs from marketing, research and development (R&D), and other functional areas. The way

---

[13] Eduardo Lachica, "Legal Swamp: Anti-Dumping Pleas Are Almost Useless, Smith Corona Finds," *The Wall Street Journal,* 18 June 1992, pp. A1, A8.

costs are defined may have an impact on tariffs and duties on sales to affiliates and subsidiaries by global companies.

Cost-plus pricing is a variation of the cost-based approach. Companies that follow the cost-plus pricing method are taking the position that profit must be shown for any product or service at every stage of movement through the corporate system. In such an instance, transfer prices may be set at a certain percentage of fixed costs, such as "110 percent of cost." While cost-plus pricing may result in a price that is completely unrelated to competitive or demand conditions in international markets, many exporters use this approach successfully.

MARKET-BASED TRANSFER PRICE

A market-based transfer price is derived from the price required to be competitive in the international market. The constraint on this price is cost. However, as noted previously, there is a considerable degree of variation in how costs are defined. Because costs generally decline with volume, a decision must be made regarding whether to price on the basis of current or planned volume levels. To use market-based transfer prices to enter a new market that is too small to support local manufacturing, third-country sourcing may be required. This enables a company to establish its name or franchise in the market without committing to a major capital investment.

NEGOTIATED TRANSFER PRICES

A third alternative is to allow the organization's affiliates to negotiate transfer prices among themselves. In some instances, the final transfer price may reflect costs and market prices, but this is not a requirement.[14] The gold standard of negotiated transfer prices is known as an arm's-length price: the price that two independent, unrelated entities would negotiate.

TAX REGULATIONS AND TRANSFER PRICES

Because the global corporation conducts business in a world with different corporate tax rates, there is an incentive to maximize system income in countries with the lowest tax rates and to minimize income in high-tax countries. Governments, naturally, are well aware of this situation. In recent years, many governments have tried to maximize national tax revenues by examining company returns and mandating reallocation of income and expenses.

Although a full treatment of tax issues is beyond the scope of this book, students should understand that a basic pricing question facing global marketers is, "What can a company do in the international pricing area in the light of current tax laws?" It is important to note that U.S. Treasury regulations do not have the weight of law until they are upheld by the courts. Global marketers must examine the regulations carefully, not only because they are the tax laws but because they guide the Internal Revenue Service (IRS) when it reviews transactions between related business organizations. In the United States, Section 482 of the tax code and the accompanying regulations are devoted to transfer pricing. The complete text of Section 482 appears in Appendix 2 at the end of this chapter.

Sales of Tangible and Intangible Property
Section 482 of the U.S. Treasury regulations deals with controlled intracompany transfers of raw materials and finished and intermediate goods, as well as intangibles such as

---

[14] Charles T. Horngren and George Foster, *Cost Accounting: A Managerial Approach* (Upper Saddle River, NJ: Prentice Hall, 1991), p. 856.

charges for the use of manufacturing technology. The general rule that applies to sales of tangible property is known as the arm's-length formula, defined as the prices that would have been charged in independent transactions between unrelated parties under similar circumstances. Three methods—listed next in order of priority—are spelled out in the regulations for establishing an arm's-length price. The regulations require that a company disprove the applicability of one method before utilizing a lower-priority one.

According to the comparable uncontrolled price method, uncontrolled sales (between unrelated seller and buyer) are considered comparable to controlled sales (sales between related parties) if the property and circumstances involved are identical or nearly identical to those in controlled sales. Frequently, no comparable uncontrolled sale is available to use as a reference. In such instances, it may be necessary to determine an applicable resale price, that is, the price at which property purchased in a controlled sale is resold by the buyer in an uncontrolled sale. Using this approach, which is sometimes referred to as retail price minus, an arm's-length price can be established by reducing the applicable resale price by an amount that reflects an appropriate markup. This is the resale price method of determining transfer prices. The third and lowest priority method is the cost-plus method. When the quest for an arm's-length price brings a global company to cost-plus pricing, it has come full circle to the basic transfer pricing methods described earlier.

Table 12-4 summarizes the results of recent studies comparing transfer pricing methods by country. As shown in the table, nearly half of U.S.-based companies doing business internationally use some form of cost-based transfer pricing.

Competitive Pricing

Because Section 482 places so much emphasis on arm's-length price, a manager at an American company who examines the regulations might wonder whether the spirit of these regulations permits pricing decisions to be made with regard to market and competitive factors. Clearly, if only the arm's-length standard is applied, a company may not be able to respond to competitive factors existing in every market, domestic and global. Fortunately, the regulations provide an opening for the company that seeks to be price competitive or to aggressively price U.S.-sourced products in its international operations. Many interpret the regulations to mean that it is proper for a company to reduce prices and increase marketing expenditures through a controlled affiliate to gain market share even when it would not do so in an arm's-length transaction with an independent distributor. This is because market position represents, in effect, an investment and an asset. A company would invest in such an asset only if it controlled the reseller—that is, if the reseller is a subsidiary. The regulations may also be interpreted as permitting a company to lower its transfer price for the purpose of entering a new market or meeting competition in an existing market either by instituting price reductions or by increased marketing efforts in the target markets. Companies must have and use this

TABLE 12-4 Transfer Pricing Methods for Selected Countries				
Methods	*United States*	*Canada*	*Japan*	*United Kingdom*
1. Cost based	46%	33%	41%	38%
2. Market price based	35%	37%	37%	31%
3. Negotiated	14%	26%	22%	20%
4. Other	5%	4%	0%	11%
	100%	100%	100%	100%

Source: Adapted from Charles T. Horngren and George Foster, *Cost Accounting: A Managerial Approach* (Upper Saddle River, NJ: Prentice Hall, 1991), p. 866.

latitude in making price decisions if they are to achieve significant success in international markets with U.S.-sourced goods.

Importance of Section 482 Regulations

Whatever the pricing rationale, it is important that executives and managers involved in international pricing policy decisions familiarize themselves with the Section 482 regulations. The pricing rationale must conform with the intention of these regulations. In an effort to develop more workable transfer pricing rules, the U.S. Internal Revenue Service (IRS) issued regulations calling for contemporaneous documentation that supports transfer price decisions. Such documentation will require participation of management and marketing personnel in transfer pricing decisions, as opposed to the tax department. Companies should be prepared to demonstrate that their pricing methods are the result of informed choice, not oversight.

It is true that U.S. Treasury regulations and IRS enforcement policy often seem perplexingly inscrutable. However, there is ample evidence that the government simply seeks to prevent tax avoidance and to ensure fair distribution of income from the operations of companies doing business internationally. Still, the government does not always succeed in its efforts to enforce Section 482 by reallocating income. In one recent court decision, Merck & Co. sued the U.S. government on the grounds that the IRS's allocation of 7 percent of the income from a wholly owned subsidiary to the parent company was "arbitrary, capricious, and unreasonable." The IRS had argued that Merck artificially shifted income to the subsidiary by sharing costs associated with research and development, marketing facilities, and management personnel. The court agreed with Merck and ordered the IRS to issue a tax refund.

As the Merck case demonstrates, even companies that make a conscientious effort to comply with the regulations and that document this effort may find themselves in tax court. Should a tax auditor raise questions, executives should be able to make a strong case for their decisions. Fortunately, consulting services are available to help managers deal with the arcane world of transfer pricing.

Transfer pricing to minimize tax liabilities can lead to unexpected and undesired distortions. A classic example is a major U.S. company with a decentralized, profit-centered organization that promoted and gave frequent and substantial salary increases to its divisional manager in Switzerland. The reason for the manager's rapid rise was his outstanding profit record. His stellar numbers were picked up by the company's performance appraisal control system, which in turn triggered the salary and promotion actions. The problem in this company was that the financial control system had not been adjusted to recognize that a Swiss tax haven profit center had been created. The manager's sky-high profits were simply the result of artificially low transfer pricing into the tax haven operations and artificially high transfer pricing out of the Swiss tax haven to operating subsidiaries. It took a team of outside consultants to discover the situation. In this case, the company's profit and loss records were a gross distortion of true operating results. The company had to adjust its control system and use different criteria to evaluate managerial performance in tax havens.

DUTY AND TARIFF CONSTRAINTS

Corporate costs and profits are also affected by import duties. The higher the duty rate, the more desirable a low transfer price. The high duty creates an incentive to reduce transfer prices to minimize the customs duty. As discussed in Chapter 8, duties in many industry sectors were substantially reduced or eliminated by the Uruguay Round of GATT negotiations. Many companies tend to downplay the influence of taxes when developing pricing policies. There are a number of reasons for this. First, some companies consider tax savings to be trivial in comparison with the earnings that can be obtained by concentrating on effective systems of motivation and corporate resource allocation. Second, management may consider any effort at systematic tax minimization to be unethical. Another argument is that a simple, consistent, and straightforward pricing policy minimizes the tax investigation problems that can develop if sharper pricing policies are pursued. According to this argument, the savings in executive time and the costs of outside counsel offset any additional taxes that might be paid using such an approach. Finally, after analyzing the worldwide trend toward harmonization of tax rates, many chief financial officers (CFOs) have concluded that any set of policies appropriate to a world characterized by wide differentials in tax rates will soon become obsolete. They have, therefore, concentrated on developing pricing policies that are appropriate for a world that is very rapidly evolving toward relatively similar tax rates.

JOINT VENTURES

Joint ventures present an incentive to set transfer prices at higher levels than would be used in sales to wholly owned affiliates because a company's share of the joint venture earnings is less than 100 percent. Any profits that occur in the joint venture must be shared. The increasing frequency of tax authority audits is an important reason for working out an agreement that will also be acceptable to the tax authorities. The tax authorities' criterion of arm's-length prices is probably most appropriate for the majority of joint ventures.

To avoid potential conflict, companies with joint ventures should work out pricing agreements in advance that are acceptable to both sides. The following are several considerations for joint venture transfer pricing:[15]

1. The way in which transfer prices will be adjusted in response to exchange rate changes.
2. Expected reductions in manufacturing costs arising from learning curve improvements and the way these will be reflected in transfer prices.
3. Shifts in the sourcing of products or components from parents to alternative sources.
4. The effects of competition on volume and overall margins.

◆ GLOBAL PRICING—THREE POLICY ALTERNATIVES

What pricing policy should a global company pursue? Viewed broadly, there are three alternative positions a company can take on worldwide pricing.

EXTENSION/ETHNOCENTRIC

The first can be called an extension/ethnocentric pricing policy. This policy requires that the price of an item be the same around the world and that the importer absorb freight and import duties. This approach has the advantage of extreme simplicity because no information on competitive or market conditions is required for implementation. The disadvantage of this approach is directly tied to its simplicity. Extension pricing does not respond to the competitive and market conditions of each national market and, therefore, neither maximizes the company's profits in each national market nor globally. The box, "Pricing Reeboks in India," gives an example of a company that is trying to maintain its image of high quality in global markets.

---

[15] Timothy M. Collins and Thomas L. Doorley, *Teaming Up for the 90s: A Guide to International Joint Ventures and Strategic Alliances* (Homewood, IL: Business One Irwin), 1991, pp. 212–213.

PRICING REEBOKS IN INDIA

When Reebok, the world's number two athletic shoe company, decided to enter India in 1995, it faced several basic marketing challenges. For one thing, Reebok was creating a market from scratch. Upscale sports shoes were virtually unknown, and the most expensive sneakers available at the time cost 1,000 rupees (about $23). Reebok officials also had to select a market entry mode. The decision was made to subcontract with four local suppliers, one of which became a joint venture partner. Only a limited number of distribution options were available. Bata, a Canadian company with global operations, was the sole shoe retailer with national coverage. American-style sports stores were unknown in India. To reinforce Reebok's high-tech brand image, company officials decided to establish their own retail infrastructure. There were two other crucial pieces of the puzzle: product and price. Should Reebok create a line of mass-market shoes specifically for India and priced at Rs 1,000? The alternative was to offer the same designs sold in other parts of the world and price them at Rs 2,500 ($58), a figure that represented the equivalent of a month's salary for a junior civil servant.

In the end, Reebok decided to offer Indian consumers about 60 models chosen from the company's global offerings. The decision was based in part on a desire to sustain Reebok's brand image of high quality. Management realized that the decision would limit the size of the market. Despite estimates that India's "middle class" was comprised of 300 million people, the number who could afford premium-priced products was estimated to be about 30 million. Reebok's least expensive shoes were priced at about Rs 2,000 per pair; for about the same amount of money, a farmer could buy a dairy cow or a homeowner could buy a new refrigerator. Nevertheless, customer response was very favorable, especially among middle-class youths. As Muktesh Pant, Reebok's regional manager, noted, "For Rs 2,000 to Rs 3,000, people feel they can really make a statement. It's cheaper than buying a new watch, for instance, if you want to make a splash at a party. And though our higher-priced shoes put us in competition with things like refrigerators and cows, the upside is that we're new being treated as a prestigious brand."

Reebok was also pleased to discover that demand was strong outside of key metropolitan markets such as Delhi, Mumbai, and Chennai. The cost of living is lower in small towns, so consumers have more disposable income to spend. In addition, inhabitants of rural areas have had less opportunity to travel abroad and therefore have not had the opportunity to shop for trendy brands elsewhere. Reebok now has about 100 branded franchise stores that sell about 300,000 pairs of athletic shoes in India each year. The company exports twice that number of Indian-made shoes to Europe and the United States. As Pant observed, "At first we were embarrassed about our pricing. But it has ended up serving us well."

> **VISIT THE WEB SITES**
> www.reebok.com
> www.bata.com

SOURCES: Mark Nicholson, "Where a Pair of Trainers Costs as Much as a Cow," *Financial Times,* 18 August 1998, p. 10.

ADAPTATION/POLYCENTRIC

The second pricing policy can be termed *adaptation/polycentric.* This policy permits subsidiary or affiliate managers to establish whatever price they feel is most desirable in their circumstances. Under such an approach, there is no control or firm requirement that prices be coordinated from one country to the next. The only constraint on this approach is in setting transfer prices within the corporate system. Such an approach is sensitive to local conditions, but it may create product arbitrage opportunities in cases in which disparities in local market prices exceed the transportation and duty cost separating markets.

When such a condition exists, there is an opportunity for the enterprising business manager to take advantage of these price disparities by buying in the lower-price market and selling in the higher-price market. There is also the problem that under such a policy, valuable knowledge and experience within the corporate system concerning effective pricing strategies are not applied to each local pricing decision. The strategies are not applied because the local managers are free to price in the way they feel is most desirable, and they may not be fully informed about company experience when they make their decision.

Letting each country unit make price decisions carries another disadvantage: It may send a signal to the rest of the world that is contrary to company interests. For example, drug companies must be extremely careful when setting prices for drugs sold to agencies in different countries. They are dealing with monopoly buyers in many countries, and these buyers have the resources and motivation to negotiate the lowest possible price. Without headquarters control, a small country might decide for various reasons to sell a drug at a low price that would be extremely disadvantageous and unwise for the company in the rest of the world. In the chemical industry, a price move anywhere in the world is known instantly all over the world. It is, therefore, important for pricing to be under the control of the headquarters organization.

INVENTION/GEOCENTRIC

The third approach to international pricing can be termed *invention/geocentric.* Using this approach, a company neither fixes a single price worldwide nor remains aloof from subsidiary pricing decisions but instead strikes an intermediate position. A company pursuing this approach works on the assumption that there are unique local market factors that should be recognized in arriving at a pricing decision. These factors include local costs, income levels, competition, and the local marketing strategy. Local costs plus a return on invested capital and personnel fix the price floor for the long term. However, for the short term, a company might decide to pursue a market penetration objective and price at less than the cost-plus return figure using export sourcing to establish a market. Another short-term objective might be to estimate the size of a market at a price that would be profitable given local sourcing and a certain scale of output. Instead of building facilities, the target market might first be supplied from existing higher-cost external supply sources. If the price and product are accepted by the market, the company can then build a local manufacturing facility to further develop the identified market opportunity in a profitable way. If the market opportunity does not materialize, the company can experiment with the product at other prices because it is not committed to a fixed sales volume by existing local manufacturing facilities.

Selecting a price that recognizes local competition is essential. Many international market efforts have floundered on this point. A major U.S. appliance manufacturer introduced its line of household appliances in Germany and, using U.S. sourcing, set price by simply marking up every item in its line by 28.5 percent. The result of this pricing method was a line that contained a mixture of underpriced and overpriced products. The overpriced products did not sell because better values were offered by local companies. The underpriced products sold very well, but they would have yielded greater profits at higher prices. What was needed was product line pricing, which took lower than normal margins in some products and higher margins in others to maximize the profitability of the full line.

For consumer products, local income levels are critical in the pricing decision. If the product is normally priced well above full manufacturing costs, the global marketer has the latitude to price below prevailing levels in low-income markets and, as a result, reduce the gross margin on the product. No business manager enjoys reducing margins; however, margins should be regarded as a guide to the ultimate objective, which is profitability. In some markets, income conditions may dictate that the maximum profitability will be obtained by sacrificing normal margins. The important point here is that in global marketing there is no such thing as a normal margin.

The final factor bearing on the price decision is the local marketing strategy and mix. Price must fit the other elements of the marketing program. For example, when it is decided to pursue a pull strategy that uses mass-media advertising and intensive distribution, the price selected must be consistent not only with income levels and competition but also with the costs and extensive advertising programs.

In addition to these local factors, the geocentric approach recognizes that headquarters price coordination is necessary in dealing with international accounts and product arbitrage (the purchase and sale of product in different markets to profit from price discrepancies). Finally, the geocentric approach consciously and systematically seeks to ensure that accumulated national pricing experience is leveraged and applied wherever relevant.

Of the three methods, only the geocentric approach lends itself to global competitive strategy. A global competitor will take into account global markets and global competitors in establishing prices. Prices will support global strategy objectives rather than the objective of maximizing performance in a single country.

ACTUAL PRICING PRACTICES

Samli and Jacobs studied the pricing practices of U.S. multinational firms.[16] Based on a mail survey, they concluded that 70 percent of the firms in their sample of the top 350 of the *Fortune* 500 largest industrial companies and the 100 largest U.S. multinational companies standardized their prices, whereas 30 percent used variable pricing in world markets. The survey raises two interesting questions. The first is: What are the actual pricing practices of companies operating globally? Are 70 percent of U.S. firms approaching global markets with standardized prices? As Samli and Jacobs suggest, if indeed this is true, it would appear that many companies should consider reviewing the pricing policies. What are the practices of non-U.S. firms? However, results of a mail survey on a subject as sensitive and complex as pricing must always be considered suspect.

The second question is: What should be the pricing policy of firms operating globally? As we outlined earlier, there are three options: extension/ethnocentric or standardized, adaptation/polycentric or localized, and invention/geocentric. Of the three, the third is clearly superior theoretically. It requires more information and integration between headquarters and subsidiaries than either of the other two approaches, but it is clearly superior in its ability to respond to both the customer's ability to pay and competitive pricing in each national market.

Summary

Pricing decisions are a critical element of the marketing mix that must reflect costs and competitive factors. There is no absolute maximum price, but for any customer, price must correspond to the customer's perceived value of the product. The aim of most marketing strategies is to set a price that corresponds to customers' perceptions of value in the product and at the same time does not "leave money on the table" (i.e., set a price that is lower than consumers are willing to pay for a product or service). Generally, a company must charge what a product is worth to the customer, cover all costs, and provide a margin for profit in the process. Pricing strategies include market skimming, market penetration, and market holding. Pricing decisions must also take into account the price escalation that occurs when products are shipped from one country to another.

International pricing is complicated by the fact that businesses must conform to different laws and different competitive situations in each country. Each company must examine the market, the competition, and its own costs and objectives and local and re-

[16] A. Coskun Samli and Laurence Jacobs, "Pricing Practices of American Multinational Firms: Standardization vs. Localization Dichotomy," *Journal of Global Marketing,* 8, no. 2 (1994): 51–73.

gional regulations and laws in setting prices that are consistent with the overall marketing strategy. Dumping—selling products in international markets at prices below those in the home country or below the cost of production—and parallel importing are two particularly contentious pricing issues. Company managers must also set transfer prices that are appropriate to company profitability objectives and that also conform to tax regulations in individual country markets.

Discussion Questions ▪▪

1. What are the three basic factors affecting price in any market? What considerations enter into the pricing decision?
2. Identify some of the environmental constraints on global pricing decisions.
3. What is dumping? Is it an important trade issue? Is dumping an attractive competitive price strategy for a company?
4. What is a transfer price? What is the difference, if any, between a transfer price and a regular price? What are three methods for determining transfer prices?
5. What are the three alternative approaches to global pricing? Which one would you recommend to a company that has global market aspirations?
6. If you were responsible for marketing computed axial tomography (CAT) scanners worldwide and your sourcing country (location of manufacture) was experiencing a strong and appreciating currency against almost all other world currencies, what options are available for adjusting prices to take into account the strong currency situation?

Suggested Readings ▪▪

Abdallah, Wagdy M. *International Transfer Pricing Policies: Decision Making Guidelines for Multinational Companies.* New York: Quorum Books, 1989.

Cannon, Hugh M., and Fred W. Morgan. "A Strategic Pricing Framework." *Journal of Business and Industrial Marketing,* 6, no. 3,4 (Summer/Fall 1991): 59–70.

Cavusgil, S. Tamer. "Pricing for Global Markets," *Columbia Journal of World Business,* 31, no. 4 (1996).

Coopers & Lybrand. *International Transfer Pricing.* Oxfordshire: CCH Editions Limited, 1993.

Eccles, Robert G. *The Transfer Pricing Problem: A Theory for Practice.* Lexington, MA: Lexington Books, 1985.

Faulds, David J., Orlen Grunewald, and Denise Johnson. "A Cross-National Investigation of the Relationship Between the Price and Quality of Consumer Products, 1970–1990." *Journal of Global Marketing,* 8, no. 1 (1994): 7–25.

Glicklich, Peter A., and Seth B. Goldstein. "New Transfer Pricing Regulations Adhere More Closely to an Arm's-Length Standard." *Journal of Taxation,* 78, no. 5 (May 1993): 306–314.

Lancioni, Richard, and John Gattorna. "Strategic Value Pricing: Its Role in International Business." *International Journal of Physical Distribution and Logistics,* 22, no. 6 (1992): 24–27.

Lew, Albert Y., Stella Cho, and Phoebe Yam. "Multinational Transfer Pricing: Implications for North American Firms," *The National Public Accountant,* 41, no. 8 (1996).

Marn, Michael V., and Robert L. Rosiello. "Managing Price, Gaining Profit." *Harvard Business Review,* 70, no. 5 (September/October 1992): 84–94.

McGowan, Karen M. "Dimensions of Price as a Marketing Universal: A Comparison of Japanese and U.S. Consumers." *Journal of International Marketing,* 6, no. 4 (1998): 49–63.

Myers, Matthew B. "The Pricing of Export Products: Why Aren't Managers Satisfied with the Results?" *Journal of World Business,* 32, no. 3 (1997): 277+.

Nagle, Thomas T. *The Strategy and Tactics of Pricing: A Guide to Profitable Decision Making.* Upper Saddle River, NJ: Prentice Hall, 1987.

Organization for Economic Cooperation and Development. *Tax Aspects of Transfer Pricing Within Multinational Enterprises: The United States Proposed Regulations.* Paris: OECD, 1993.

Paun, Dorothy A., Larry D. Compeau, and Shruv Grewal. "A Model of the Influence of Marketing Objectives on Pricing Strategies in International Countertrade." *Journal of Public Policy & Marketing,* 16 (Spring 1997): 69–82.

Robert, Michel. *Strategy Pure and Simple: How Winning CEOs Outthink Their Competition.* New York: McGraw-Hill, 1993.

Samiee, Saeed, and Patrik Anckar. "Currency Choice in Industrial Pricing: A Cross-National Evaluation." *Journal of Marketing,* 62, no. 3 (1998): 112–127.

Samli, A. Coskun, and Laurence Jacobs. "Pricing Practices of American Multinational Firms: Standardization vs.

Localization Dichotomy." *Journal of Global Marketing,* 8, no. 2 (1994): 51–74.

Seymour, Daniel T. *The Pricing Decision.* Chicago: Probus Publishing, 1989.

Simon, Hermann. "Pricing Opportunities—and How to Exploit Them." *Sloan Management Review,* 33, no. 2 (Winter 1992): 55–65.

Simon, Hermann, and Eckhard Kucher. "The European Pricing Time Bomb and How to Cope with It."

European Management Journal, 10, no. 2 (June 1992): 136–145.

Sinclair, Stuart. "A Guide to Global Pricing." *Journal of Business Strategy,* 14, no. 3 (1993): 16–19.

Williams, Jeffery R. "How Sustainable Is Your Competitive Advantage?" *California Management Review,* 34, no. 3 (Spring 1992): 29–51.

◆◆◆ **Appendix 1**

Trade Terms

A number of terms covering the conditions of the delivery are commonly used in international trade. The internationally accepted terms of trade are known as *Incoterms.* Every commercial transaction is based on a contract of sale, and the trade terms used in that contract have the important function of naming the exact point at which the ownership of merchandise is transferred from the seller to the buyer.

The simplest type of export sale is *ex-works* (manufacturer's location). Under this type of contract, the seller assists the buyer in obtaining an export license, but the buyer's responsibility ends there. At the other extreme, the easiest terms of sale for the buyer are *Delivered Duty Paid* (named place of destination), including duty and local transportation to his or her warehouse. Under this contract, the buyer's only responsibility is to obtain an import license if one is needed and to pass the customs entry at the seller's expense. Between these two terms, there are many expenses that accrue to the goods as they move from the place of manufacture to the buyer's warehouse. Following are some of the steps involved in moving goods from a factory to a buyer's warehouse:

1. Obtaining an export license if required (in the United States, nonstrategic goods are exported under a general license that requires no specific permit)
2. Obtaining a currency permit if required
3. Packing the goods for export
4. Transporting the goods to the place of departure (this would normally involve transport by truck or rail to a seaport or airport)
5. Preparing a land bill of lading
6. Completing necessary customs export papers
7. Preparing customs or consular invoices as required by the country of destination
8. Arranging for ocean freight and preparation
9. Obtaining marine insurance and certificate of the policy

Who carries out these steps? It depends on the terms of the sale. In the following paragraphs, some of the major terms are defined.

The following two terms are acceptable Incoterms for all modes of transportation:

> *Ex-works.* In this contract, the seller places goods at the disposal of the buyer at the time specified in the contract. The buyer takes delivery at the premises of the seller and bears all risks and expenses from that point on.
>
> *Delivered Duty Paid.* Under this contract, the seller undertakes to deliver the goods to the buyer at the place he or she names in the country of import with all costs, including duties, paid. The seller is responsible under this contract for getting the import license if one is required.

The following are acceptable Incoterms for sea and inland waterway transportation only:

> *FAS (Free Alongside Ship) Named Port of Shipment.* Under this contract, the seller must place goods alongside, or available to, the vessel or other mode of transportation and pay all charges up to that point. The seller's legal responsibility ends once he or she has obtained a clean wharfage receipt.
>
> *FOB (Free on Board).* In an FOB contract, the responsibility and liability of the seller does not end until the goods have actually been placed aboard a ship. Terms should preferably be "FOB ship (name port)." The term *FOB* is frequently misused in international sales. FOB means "goods must be loaded on board, and buyer pays freight." Since freight charges generally include loading the goods, in essence, a double payment is made; the buyer pays twice!
>
> *CIF (Cost, Insurance, Freight) Named Port of Importations.* Under this contract, as in the FOB contract, the risk of loss or damage to goods is transferred to the buyer once the goods have passed the ship's rail. However, the seller has to pay the expense of transportation for the goods up to the port of destination, including the expense of insurance.
>
> *CFR (Cost and Freight).* The terminology is the same as CIF except the seller is not responsible for risk or loss at any point outside the factory.

The following Incoterm is acceptable for air, rail shipments, and multimodal shipments:

> *FCA (Free Carrier) Named Place.* Seller fulfills obligations when he or she hands over goods cleared for exports to the carrier named by the buyer at the named place or point (e.g., airport, rail siding, or seller's factory).

◆◆◆ **Appendix 2**

Section 482, U.S. Internal Revenue Code

In any case of two or more organizations, trades, or businesses (whether or not incorporated, whether or not organized in the United States, and whether or not affiliated) owned or controlled directly or indirectly by the same interests, the Secretary may distribute, apportion, or allocate gross income, deductions, credits, or allowances between or among such organizations, trades, or businesses, if he determines that such distribution, apportionment, or allocation is necessary in order to prevent evasion of taxes or clearly to reflect the income of any of such organizations, trades, or businesses. In the case of any transfer (or license) of intangible property (within the meaning of section 936(h)(3)(B)), the income with respect to such transfer or license shall be commensurate with the income attributable to the intangible.

CHAPTER 13

Global Marketing Channels and Physical Distribution

Wherever the Roman conquers, there he dwells.
—LUCIUS ANNAEUS SENECA, 8 B.C.–A.D. 65
Moral Essays to Helvia on Consolation

CONTENTS

Hypermarkets are giant stores as big as four or more football fields. Part supermarket, part department store, they feature a wide array of product categories—groceries, toys, furniture, fast food, and financial services—all under one roof. Hypermarkets have flourished in Europe for more than three decades. Carrefour SA, a French company, opened the first hypermarket in 1962; with help from the French government, zoning laws ensured that competing stores would be kept from the vicinity. At the beginning of the 2000s, Carrefour and its chief rival, Euromarché SA, together had about 150 of France's nearly 1,000 hypermarkets; the giant stores account for about 20 percent of all retail sales and nearly one half of all grocery sales. Most of the European stores were established before competing outlets such as shopping malls and discount stores made the Atlantic crossing from America. Because the French government has severely limited Carrefour's expansion plans in France, Carrefour was forced to expand internationally and to grow its business through acquisitions. It is the world's fourth largest retailer with 43 percent of its sales coming from countries outside of France.[1] Carrefour has a strong presence in Asia where 39 of its 308 hypermarkets are located. It is scheduled to open its first store in Japan and will be the first foreign supermarket operator to do so.[2] It opened two hypermarkets

---

[1] *Hoover's Handbook of World Business 1999.*
[2] David Owen and Alexandra Harney, "Carrefour Expects First Store in Japan by 2001," *Financial Times,* 24 May 1999, p. 15.

◆ BOX 13-1 ◆

HYPERMARKETS

In the United States, retailing channels are quite diverse. In addition to long-entrenched shopping malls and discount stores, there are wholesale clubs such as Price Costco and Sam's Club, offering rock-bottom prices, plus "category killers" with wide selections such as Toys "Я" Us and Circuit City. Undeterred by such competitors, Euromarché opened its first American hypermarket in October 1984. Bigg's, in Cincinnati, was one and a half times the size of a football field, with 75 aisles, 40 checkout lanes, and 60,000 different items available at low prices. One shopper summed up the advantage of shopping at Bigg's: "I can buy bread, lunchmeat, and electrical equipment all at the same place." In February 1988, Carrefour opened its own U.S. hypermarket, a gigantic store in Philadelphia with 330,000 square feet of floor space. Not to be outdone, several American retailers soon followed suit. Wal-Mart opened several Hypermarket USA stores; Kmart called its version American Fare.

Before long, however, many of the big stores were floundering. The problem? Not surprisingly, many shoppers found the stores too big and too overwhelming. Moreover, the big scale changed the economics of profitable operation. For example, consultants for Kmart noted that its hypermarket near Atlanta could succeed only if it attracted four times as many shoppers as a regular discount department store and if the average transaction equaled $43—double the average for discount stores. Meanwhile, costs associated with running the huge stores translated into gross margins of around 8 percent—half the margin of the typical discount store. Last, but not least, Americans just did not take to mixing food and nonfood purchases in one location. As retail consultant Kurt Barnard noted, "One-stop shopping did not take hold easily. Working parents don't have time for their kids, let alone a shopping expedition that takes hours." The lesson from hypermarkets in the United States seems to be that bigger is not, in fact, better.

SOURCES: Laurie M. Grossman, "Hypermarkets: A Sure-Fire Hit Bombs," *The Wall Street Journal,* 25 June 1992, p. B1; Steven Greenhouse, " 'Hypermarkets' Come to U.S.," *The New York Times,* 7 February 1985, p. 29; Anthony Ramirez, "Will American Shoppers Think Bigger Is Really Better?" *The New York Times,* 1 April 1990, sec. 3, p. 11.

in the United States but has since closed them, due to lack of appeal of the hypermarket format in the United States.

Hypermarkets are just one of the many elements that constitute distribution channels around the globe. The American Marketing Association defines *channel of distribution* as "an organized network of agencies and institutions which, in combination, perform all the activities required to link producers with users to accomplish the marketing task."[3] Distribution is the physical flow of goods through channels; as suggested by the definition, channels are comprised of coordinated groups of individuals or firms that perform functions adding utility to a product or service. In addition to this chapter, Chapter 16 contains specific information on how the Internet is affecting marketing channels.

Distribution channels in markets around the world are among the most highly differentiated aspects of national marketing systems. On the opposite end of the spectrum from hypermarkets, for example, are small stores in Latin America called *pulperias.* The diversity of channels and the wide range of possible distribution strategies can present challenging problems to anyone designing a global marketing program. Smaller companies are often blocked by their inability to establish effective channel arrangements. In larger companies operating via country subsidiaries, channel strategy is the element of the marketing mix that headquarters understands the least. To a large extent, channels are an aspect of the marketing program that is locally led through the discretion of

---

[3] Peter D. Bennett, *Dictionary of Marketing Terms* (Chicago: American Marketing Association, 1988), p. 29.

the in-country marketing management group. Nevertheless, it is important for managers responsible for world marketing programs to understand the nature of international distribution channels. Channels and physical distribution are integral parts of the total marketing program and must be appropriate to the product design, price, and communications aspects of the total marketing program.

◆ CHANNEL OBJECTIVES AND CONSTRAINTS

The purpose of marketing channels is to create utility for customers. The major categories of channel utility are place (the availability of a product or service in a location that is convenient to a potential customer); time (the availability of a product or service when desired by a customer); form (the product is processed, prepared, and ready to use and in proper condition); and information (answers to questions and general communication about useful product features and benefits are available). Because these utilities can be a basic source of competitive advantage and product value, choosing a channel strategy is one of the key strategic decisions marketing management must make.

Coke's leadership position in world markets is based on its ability to put Coke "within an arm's reach of desire," which is, in marketing channel terminology, *place utility*. Successful marketing strategies creatively innovate in channel strategy: Dell's rise to the number-three position in the world computer industry is based on its innovative channel strategy: direct marketing and build to order (BTO). Dell customers love Dell's low prices and the ability to order the exact computer configuration they want. They do not miss the trip to the local computer store. The Dell strategy was developed in the United States and is now being successfully extended to world markets including China.

Channel decisions are important because of the number and nature of relationships that must be managed. Channel decisions typically involve long-term legal commitments and obligations to other firms and individuals. Such commitments are often extremely expensive to terminate or change. Even in cases in which there is no legal obligation, commitments may be backed by good faith and feelings of obligation, which are equally difficult to manage and painful to adjust. From the viewpoint of the marketer concerned with a single-country program, channel arrangements in different parts of the world are a valuable source of information and insight into possible new approaches for more effective channel strategies. (Of course, the same is true for the other elements of the marketing mix.) For example, self-service discount pricing in the United States was studied by retailers from Europe and Asia, who then introduced the self-service concept in their own countries. Governments and business executives all over the world have examined Japanese trading companies with great interest to learn from their success.

The starting point in selecting the most effective channel arrangement is a clear focus of the company's marketing effort on a target market and a determination of its needs and preferences. Where are the potential customers located? What are their information requirements? What are their preferences for service? How sensitive are they to price? Customer preference must be carefully determined because there is as much danger to the success of a marketing program in creating too much utility as there is in creating too little. Moreover, each market must be analyzed to determine the cost of providing channel services. What is appropriate in one country may not be effective in another.

For example, an international manufacturer of construction products that emphasized the speedy service provided by a sales force in radio-equipped station wagons made the mistake of offering too much service in the United States. The company prided itself on the fact that a maximum of two hours elapsed between the receipt of a customer order from a construction site and the actual delivery by a salesperson. The cost of this service was included in the prices the company charged. Although its service record was

━━━━━━━━━━━━━━━━━━━━━━━━━━━ ◆ BOX 13-2 ◆ ━━━━━━━━━━━━━━━━━━━━━━━━━━━━

A CASE OF WINE: ADDING UTILITY THROUGH DISTRIBUTION CHANNELS

Each year, wine and spirits worth more than $1 billion are exported from France, Germany, Italy, and other European countries to all parts of the world. Have you ever wondered how a case of wine finds its way from, say, France to your local liquor store? In fact, after leaving the winery, the wine may pass through the hands of brokers, freight forwarders, shipping agents, export agents, shippers, importers, wholesalers, and distributors before it finishes its journey at your local retailer.

In France, the structure of the wine industry is quite complex. An intermediary called a *négociant* plays an important role that varies according to region. *Négociants* sometimes act as brokers and have standing contracts to buy specified quantities of finished wine on behalf of various American importers. The *négociant* also functions somewhat like a banker, paying the producer as much as 25 percent in advance of delivery. *Négociants* may also buy grapes from growers to make their own wine, blending and bottling them under their own labels. Wine may be bottled and packed in cases by the producer or by the *négociant*.

Wine destined for France or other European markets travels by truck. If the wine is to be exported to the United States or Japan, a freight forwarder or shipping agent sends a truck to the winery to pick up the wine. For the largest producers, the simplest type of consolidation takes place at the winery itself; a truck carrying a 20- or 40-foot shipping container is backed up to the door of

the winery and loaded there for the ocean voyage. For smaller producers, the wines are picked up and then delivered to a warehouse. There the shipping agent consolidates various deliveries to fill a container for the shipping line of the importer's choosing.

Shipping dates and rates will vary depending on the availability of containers. In general, a 20-foot container can hold 800 cases of wine; a single 40-foot container can take up to 1,300 cases. The weight of the wine is a consideration when determining how many cases to ship in a given container. Not only do wine bottles vary in size (750-ml bottles are the most common, with 12 bottles in a case), but there is likely to be a difference in weight between two cases of different types of wine. For example, heavier bottles are required for champagne and other sparkling wines since the contents are under pressure; bottles of fine Bordeaux are packaged in wooden crates that weigh more than ordinary cardboard cartons.

Shipping wine is a challenging venture because of the volatile and perishable nature of the product. Proper storage and transportation are vital; light, heat, and temperature fluctuations are wine's worst enemies. Ideally, wine should be kept at a constant temperature near 55 degrees. To prevent improper shipping from ruining a shipment, temperature-controlled containers (known as reefers) are often used, even though they add about $3 per case to the cost of the shipment. To further protect

━━

outstanding, the company discovered that in the United States its products were at a serious competitive price disadvantage. Customers gave the company high marks for its service, but in terms of actual buying behavior, they preferred to buy from a competitor whose costs were much lower because of less speedy delivery service. The competitor passed these cost savings on to customers in the form of lower prices. In this particular example, price was more important than time utility to most U.S. customers. This situation did not apply to European markets, in which competition and customer preference made speedy delivery necessary.

Channel strategy in a global marketing program must fit the company's competitive position and overall marketing objectives in each national market. If a company wants to enter a competitive market, it has two basic choices:

1. Direct involvement (its own sales force, retail stores, etc.)
2. Indirect involvement (independent agents, distributors, wholesalers)

The first choice requires the company to establish company-owned or franchised outlets. The second choice requires incentives to independent channel agents that will induce them to promote the company's product. The process of shaping international

the wine, some importers avoid shipping during the hot summer months. Because ownership of the wine is transferred to the importer at the moment the wine leaves the French storage warehouse, it is important to insure the shipment. Wine shipments can even be insured against possible losses due to war and terrorism. The best importers arrange for proper warehouse storage even before taking title to the wines.

The trans-Atlantic trip for U.S.-bound wine takes a week or more. The port of entry depends on the location of the importer or wholesaler/distributor. The Port of New York is used when wines are destined for the East Coast. Wine bound for the nation's midsection often enters through Baltimore, Maryland, or Norfolk, Virginia. Ships going to a western destination may chart a course through the Gulf of Mexico on their way to Houston, Texas; wines bound for the Port of San Francisco pass through the Panama Canal. Once the wine enters the United States, it must clear U.S. Customs. Customs agents and the importer or wholesaler make sure the shipment meets all government regulations and that paperwork is properly prepared. The Bureau of Alcohol, Tobacco, and Firearms is the U.S. government agency with jurisdiction over wines and spirits.

After it has cleared Customs, the wine is then shipped to the wholesaler's warehouse. Again, the importance of temperature-controlled shipping comes into play. If the wholesaler is too busy to pick the container up immediately, it may sit on the dock for a week or more in warm weather; without refrigeration, the wine—and the importer's investment—might be lost. If the distributor is located in Chicago, the wine often enters the country in Baltimore and completes the next leg of the trip via rail. Sometimes trucks will bring a shipment of wine to the Midwest from the East Coast and return full of meat in order to make the trip cost-effective. After the wine has been unloaded at the warehouse, the distributor's sales staff arranges for the cases of wine to be delivered by truck or van to individual retailers.

There is as much variety among retail channels for wine as there is among wine producers. Outlets vary from "mom and pop" grocery stores to wine sections in large supermarkets to huge wine and liquor discounters, with considerable variety in between. In some stores, wine is stored and displayed haphazardly, often in sunny windows or near heating vents. Other stores go to great lengths to make sure that the wine is not ruined after its long journey in protective containers. One large retailer, Big Y in Northampton, Massachusetts, even goes so far as to keep the entire store at 55 degrees year round.

There are still other factors that have a major influence on sales. One is the marketing and merchandising skill of the retailer: Point-of-sale recommendation from an informed retailer is important in selling fine wines. Also, the industry press can have a huge impact on sales. A good rating in publications such as *Wine Spectator* or *The Wine Advocate* can make the difference between obscurity and a sellout in a particular wine. Often, savvy wine retailers will display a press clipping with a positive rating right on the bin of a certain wine so that customers can educate themselves as they shop.

channels to fit overall company objectives is constrained by several factors: customers, products, middlemen, and the environment. Important characteristics of each of these factors will be discussed briefly.

CUSTOMER CHARACTERISTICS

The characteristics of customers are an important influence on channel design. Their number, geographic distribution, income, shopping habits, and reactions to different selling methods all vary from country to country and, therefore, require different channel approaches. Remember, channels create utility for customers.

In general, regardless of the stage of market development, the need for multiple channel intermediaries increases as the number of customers increases. The converse is also true: The need for channel intermediaries decreases as the number of customers decreases. For example, if there are only 10 customers for an industrial product in each national market, these 10 customers must be directly contacted by either the manufacturer or an agent. For mass-market products bought by millions of customers, retail distribution outlets or mail-order distribution is required. In a country with a large number of low-volume retailers, it is usually cheaper to reach them via wholesalers. Direct selling that bypasses wholesale intermediaries may be the most cost-effective means of serving large-volume retailers. These generalizations apply to all countries, regardless of stage of development; however, individual country customs will vary. For example, Toys "Я" Us faced considerable opposition from Japanese toy manufacturers that refused to sell directly to the American company after it built its first stores in Japan.

PRODUCT CHARACTERISTICS

Certain product attributes such as degree of standardization, perishability, bulk, service requirements, and unit price have an important influence on channel design and strategy. Products with a high unit price, for example, are often sold through a company sales force because the selling cost of this expensive distribution method is a small part of the total sale price. Moreover, the high cost of such products is usually associated with complexity or with product features that must be explained in some detail, and this can be done most effectively by a controlled sales force. For example, mainframe computers are expensive, complicated products that require both explanation and applications analysis focused on the customer's needs. A company-trained salesperson or sales engineer is well suited to the task of creating information utility for computer buyers.

Mainframe computers, photocopiers, and other industrial products may require margins to cover the costs of expensive sales engineering. Other products require margins to provide a large monetary incentive to a direct sales force. In many parts of the world, cosmetics are sold door to door; company representatives call on potential customers. The reps must create customer awareness of the value of cosmetics and evoke a feeling of need for this value that leads to a sale. The sales activity must be paid for. Companies using direct distribution for consumer products rely on wide gross selling margins to generate the revenue necessary to compensate salespeople. Amway and Avon are two companies that have succeeded in extending their direct-sales systems globally.

Perishable products impose special form utility demands on channel members. Such products usually need relatively direct channels to ensure satisfactory condition at the time of customer purchase. In less developed countries, producers of vegetables, bread, and other food products typically sell their goods in public marketplaces. In developed countries, perishable food products are distributed by controlled sales forces, and stock is checked by these sales distributor organizations to ensure that it is fresh and ready for purchase.

In 1991, Andersen Consulting assisted the Moscow Bread Company in improving its ability to distribute bread in the Russian capital. For Russians, bread is truly the staff of life, with consumers queuing up daily to buy fresh loaves at numerous shops and kiosks. Unfortunately, distribution was often hampered by excessive paperwork that resulted in the delivery of stale bread; Andersen found that as much as one third of the bread produced was wasted. The consulting team arrived at a simple solution: plastic bags to keep the bread fresh. The team found that, although 95 percent of food is packaged in developed countries, the figure was only 2 percent in the former Soviet Union, where open-air markets are the norm. Russian consumers responded favorably to the change; not only did the bags guarantee freshness and extend the shelf life of the bread by 600 percent, the bags themselves created utility. In a country where such extras are virtually unknown, the bags constituted a reusable "gift."[4]

Bulky products usually require channel arrangements that minimize the shipping distances and the number of times products change hands between channel intermedi-

---

[4] "Case Study: Moscow Bread Company," Andersen Consulting, 1993.

aries before they reach the ultimate customer. Soft drinks and beer are examples of bulky products whose widespread availability is an important aspect of an effective marketing strategy.

MIDDLEMAN CHARACTERISTICS

Channel strategy must recognize the characteristics of existing middlemen. Middlemen are in business to maximize their own profit and not that of the manufacturer. They are notorious for cherry picking, that is, the practice of taking orders from manufacturers whose products and brands are in demand to avoid any real selling effort for a manufacturer's products that may require push. This is a rational response by the middleman, but it can present a serious obstacle to the manufacturer attempting to break into a market with a new product. The cherry picker is not interested in building a market for a new product. This is a problem for the expanding international company. Frequently, a manufacturer with a new product or a product with a limited market share is forced to set up some arrangement for bypassing the cherry-picking segment of the channel. In some cases, manufacturers will set up an expensive direct-distribution organization to obtain a share of the market. When they finally obtain a share of the target market, they may abandon the direct-distribution system for a more cost-effective intermediary system. The move does not mean that intermediaries are better than direct-distribution. It is simply a response by a manufacturer to cost considerations and the newly acquired attractiveness of the company's product to independent distributors.

An alternative method of dealing with the cherry-picking problem does not require setting up an expensive direct sales force. Rather, a company may decide to rely on a distributor's own sales force by subsidizing the cost of the sales representatives the distributor has assigned to the company's products. This approach has the advantage of holding down costs by tying missionary and support selling in with the distributor's existing sales management team and physical distribution system. With this approach, it is possible to place managed direct-selling support and distribution support behind a product at the expense of only one salesperson per selling area. The distributor's incentive for cooperating in this kind of arrangement is that he or she obtains a free sales representative for a new product with the potential to be a profitable addition to his or her line. This cooperative arrangement is ideally suited to getting a new export-sourced product into distribution in a market.

Selection and Care of Distributors and Agents

The selection of distributors and agents in a target market is a critically important task. A good commission agent or stocking distributor can make the difference between realizing zero performance and performance that exceeds 200 percent of what is expected. At any point in time, some of any company's agents and distributors will be excellent, others will be satisfactory, and still others will be unsatisfactory and in need of replacement.

To find a good distributor, a firm can begin with a list provided by the home country's Ministry of Trade or Department of Commerce. The local chamber of commerce in a country can also provide lists, as can local trade associations. It is a waste of time to try to screen the list by mail. Go to the country and talk to end users of the products you are selling and find out which distributors they prefer and why they prefer them or get this information from someone in the country who can do the research for you. If the product is a consumer product, go to the retail outlets and find out where consumers are buying products similar to your own and why. Two or three names will keep coming up. Go to these two or three and see which of them would be available to sign. Before signing, make sure there is someone in the organization who will be the key person for your product. The key person is someone who will make it a personal objective to achieve success with your product.

This is the critical difference between the successful distributor and the worthless distributor. There must be a personal, individual commitment to the product. The second and related requirement for successful distributors or agents is that they must be successful with the product. Success means that they can sell the product and make money on it. In any case, the product must be designed and priced to be competitive in the target market. The distributor can assist in this process by providing information about customer wants and the competition and by promoting the product he or she represents.

Agent/Distributor Performance

The RF Division of Harris Corporation achieved great success in international markets with its shortwave radios. One of the reasons for its success was the quality of agents in key markets and their commitment to the Harris product. They were attracted to Harris because the company made a product that was as good as or better than any other product on the market. Also, Harris offered commissions of 33 percent on all sales—at least 15 percent higher than commissions offered by any other competitor. This was certainly one of the single most important factors in ensuring Harris's success. The generous commission motivated the agents to sell Harris products and provided the financial resources to support a strong marketing effort. There was, of course, a trade-off: Harris prices were higher, but in their target markets, this price effect was more than offset by the effectiveness of the higher margins.

Termination

The only way to keep a good distributor or agent is to work closely with him or her to ensure that he or she is making money on the product. Any distributor who does not make money on a line will drop it. It is really quite simple. In general, if a distributor is not working out, it is wise to terminate the agreement and find another one. Few companies are large enough to convert a mediocre distributor or agent into an effective business representative. Therefore, the two most important clauses in the distributor contract are the performance and cancellation clauses. Make sure they are written in a way that will make it possible to terminate the agreement. There is a myth that it is expensive or even impossible to terminate distributor and agent agreements. Some of the most successful global marketers have terminated hundreds of agreements and know success is based on their willingness to terminate if a distributor or agent does not perform. The key factor is performance: Distributors who do not perform must either shape up or be replaced.

However, termination may result in legal adversity. In some countries, companies are exposed to courts that are blatantly corrupt. In Ecuador, for example, the courts have been handing down awards to terminated distributors of global companies that have been as high as 400 years of sales! Even if you have a termination clause, agents and distributors have rights in many jurisdictions that cannot be taken away by agreement. For example, say that your agreement gives you the right to terminate without cause with 90 days' notice. The agent, if the agreement is enforceable in New Jersey, can sue on the grounds that you have breached the good faith and fair dealing covenant of law in New Jersey. In other words, even though your agreement gave you the right to terminate, you can be sued in New Jersey on the grounds that, the agreement notwithstanding, you have breached the good faith and fair dealing covenant of law in New Jersey. This is a rule of law that holds that if a distributor is acting in good faith on the assumption that his or her appointment as a distributor is going to continue, he or she has a right to sue a manufacturer for damages if the agreement is terminated. Clearly, any agreement signed in New Jersey should be drafted with this covenant in mind. There is no substitute for the advice of qualified counsel when it comes to the preparation of agent/distributor agreements.

Another rule for agreements is that you should be able to read and understand the agreement. If you cannot, insist that your attorney redraft the agreement in understandable language. If you cannot understand the agreement, you may find that it will come to haunt you. Whether you are an agent or a manufacturer, you should know what your rights and obligations are under your agreements.

ENVIRONMENTAL CHARACTERISTICS

The general characteristics of the total environment are a major consideration in channel design. Because of the enormous variety of economic, social, and political environments internationally, there is a need to delegate a large degree of independence to local operating management or agents. A comparison of food distribution in countries at different stages of development illustrates how channels reflect and respond to underlying market conditions in a country. In the United States, several factors combine to make the supermarket or the self-service, one-stop food store the basic food retailing unit. These factors include high incomes, large-capacity refrigerator/freezer units, automobile ownership, acceptance of frozen and convenience foods, and attitudes toward food preparation. Many shoppers want to purchase a week's worth of groceries in one trip to the store. They have the money, ample storage space in the refrigerator, and the hauling capacity of the car to move this large quantity of food from the store to the home. The supermarket, because it is efficient, can fill the food shoppers' needs at lower prices than are found in butcher shops and other traditional full-service food stores. Additionally, supermarkets can offer more variety and a greater selection of merchandise than can smaller food stores, a fact that appeals to affluent consumers.

The trend continues even in countries with an already low density of stores. For example, in the United States, thousands of stores have disappeared in the past several years. Industry observers expect this trend of fewer grocery stores to continue in the future at varying rates in different countries.

◆ DISTRIBUTION CHANNELS: TERMINOLOGY AND STRUCTURE

Distribution channels are systems that link manufacturers to customers. Although channels for consumer products and industrial products are similar, there are also some distinct differences, as will be discussed. Consumer channels are designed to put products in the hands of people for their own use; industrial channels deliver products to manufacturers or organizations that use them in the production process or in day-to-day operations.

CONSUMER PRODUCTS

Figure 13-1 summarizes channel structure alternatives for consumer products. A consumer products manufacturer can sell to customers directly (using a door-to-door sales force), through mail-order selling (using a catalog or other printed materials), through manufacturer-owned or independent retailers, or the Internet. Of the first four direct alternatives, the mail-order business is the most widely used and the Internet is the fastest growing. Most companies use a combination of channels. For example, IKEA, the world's largest furniture retailer, relies primarily on its company-owned retail stores, but it also has a catalog that supports both the retail stores and the expanding on-line store as well as direct mail-order selling. IKEA, annually prints 38 editions of its catalog in 17 languages.

Door-to-Door Selling
Door-to-door selling is a relatively expensive form of distribution that, as noted earlier, requires high gross margins and can result in higher prices to the customer. In the United States, it is a form of selling that is mature. Certain items—frozen food, vacuum cleaners,

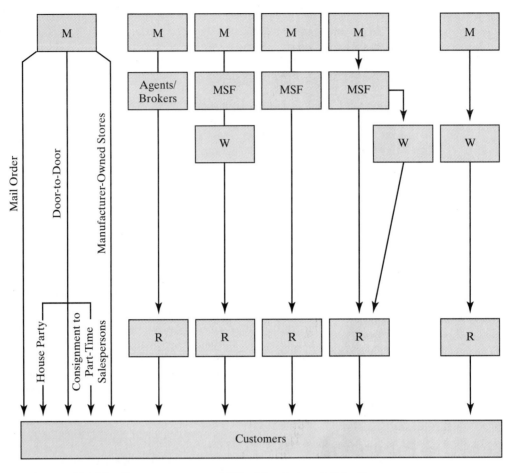

FIGURE 13-1 Marketing Channel Alternatives—Consumer Products

and cosmetics—continue to be sold in this manner. Door-to-door selling, however, is growing in popularity in many countries outside the United States. For example, over 10 percent of Amway's business comes from Japan, and Avon has successfully used this approach in more than 50 countries identified by company executives as having weak retail infrastructures. Also, they recognized that low levels of discretionary income translate into low levels of expenditures on cosmetics and toiletries. Thus, the role of the sales force is to communicate the benefits of cosmetics and build demand.

In such countries as China, Hungary, the Czech Republic, and Russia, home direct selling is the perfect channel strategy. In fact, Avon became the first company permitted to sell door-to-door in China. Since 1990, Avon has operated a joint venture with Guangzhou Cosmetics Factory in the province of Old Canton. Direct-sales companies are especially popular in China, where Amway is now the largest U.S.-based company. Amway Asia Pacific Ltd. (excluding Japan) has a network of approximately 600,000 distributors.

> **VISIT THE WEB SITE**
> www.avon.com

American automobile manufacturers attempting to penetrate the Japanese market are not faced with high tariffs. Rather, they are confronted with the fact that half the nation's cars are sold door-to-door. Toyota and its eight Japanese competitors maintain showrooms that are quite small compared to U.S. showrooms with sometimes only two models on display, but they employ more than 100,000 car salespeople. Unlike their American counterparts, many Japanese car buyers never visit dealerships. In fact, the close, long-term relationships between auto salespersons and the Japanese can be thought of as a consumer version of the *keiretsu* system discussed in Chapter 11. Car buyers expect numerous face-to-face meetings with a sales representative, during which trust is established. The relationship continues after the deal is closed; sales representatives send cards and continually seek to ensure the buyer's satisfaction. American rivals such as Ford, meanwhile, try to generate showroom traffic. Nobumasa Ogura, who manages a Ford dealership in Tokyo, says, "We need to come up with some ideas to sell more cars without door-to-door sales, but the reality is that we haven't come up with any."[5]

Manufacturer-Owned Store

A third direct-selling alternative is the manufacturer-owned store. For example, the Walt Disney Company owns stores that sell apparel, videos, toys, and other merchandise relating to the company's trademarked characters. Some companies establish one or a few retail outlets as a showcase or means of obtaining marketing intelligence rather than as a distribution strategy. If a manufacturer's product line is sufficiently broad to support a retail outlet, this form of distribution can be very attractive. The shoe store, for example, is a viable retail unit, and shoe manufacturers typically have established their own direct outlets as a major element in their distribution strategy, both at home and in important world markets. One of the first successful U.S.-based international companies, Singer, established a worldwide chain of company-owned and operated outlets to sell and service sewing machines.

Franchise Operations

Franchise operations are a contractual agreement between a franchiser and a franchisee whereby the franchiser grants the right to sell goods and/or services to a franchisee. The franchisee agrees to operate the business according to a plan defined by the franchiser and under a trade name owned by the franchiser.

Of course, the world's most famous franchises are fast-food chains (Table 13-1). A McDonald's restaurant can be found in over 120 countries. Almost half of McDonald's volume is derived from international sales. Being an icon of American culture, McDonald's has both benefited and suffered from this status. Over 50 percent of revenue is derived from international sales for KFC (formerly known as Kentucky Fried Chicken), Shakey's Pizza Parlor, East Side Mario's, and I Can't Believe It's Yogurt.

Combination Structures

The other channel structure alternatives for consumer products are various combinations of a manufacturer's sales force and wholesalers calling on retail outlets, which in turn sell to customers. In a given country at a particular point in time, various product classes will have characteristic distribution patterns associated with them. In Japan, for example, several layers of small wholesalers play an important role in the distribution of food. Attempts to bypass these apparently unnecessary units in the channel have failed because the cost to a manufacturer of providing their service (frequent, small deliveries to small grocery outlets) is greater than the margin they require. Channel patterns that appear to

---

[5] Valerie Reitman, "Toyota Calling: In Japan's Car Market, Big Three Face Rivals Who Go Door-to-Door," *The Wall Street Journal,* 28 September 1994, pp. A1, A6.

TABLE 13-1	Top 25 Food Franchises Abroad			
1997 International Sales Rank	*Chain*	*1997 International Sales ($000)*	*1997 International Share of Sales*	*1997 International % Sales Growth*
1	McDonald's	$16,513,000	49.09%	6.90%
2	KFC	4,330,000	51.98	0.70
3	Pizza Hut	2,525,000	34.95	1.10
4	Burger King	2,042,410	20.62	13.10
5	Tim Hortons	749,901	97.14	18.50
6	Domino's Pizza	680,000	21.51	36.00
7	Wendy's	625,000	11.95	25.00
8	Baskin-Robbins, USA	500,000	46.70	6.40
9	Subway Sandwiches	500,000	14.71	3.70
10	Hard Rock Cafe	425,000	61.15	25.70
11	Dairy Queen	370,000	12.11	8.80
12	Coco's	333,000	53.28	(12.50)
13	Dunkin' Donuts	286,136	13.97	0.20
14	Yogen Fruz/Paradise/Java	281,000	98.25	46.00
15	Planet Hollywood	267,000	47.51	167.00
16	T.G.I. Friday's	240,853	19.16	14.80
17	Shakey's Pizza Parlors	240,000	72.73	4.30
18	Churchs Chicken	149,125	20.60	(0.30)
19	Taco Bell	145,000	2.93	31.80
20	Popeyes Chicken & Biscuits	129,457	15.18	45.80
21	Big Boy	125,000	13.81	13.60
22	East Side Mario's	115,000	58.38	2.70
23	Arby's Restaurants	110,000	5.09	29.40
24	A&W Restaurants	109,000	27.74	18.50
25	Starbucks	100,615	10.48	43.70

Source: Restaurant Business (November 1998): 54–55.

be inefficient may reflect rational adjustment to costs and preferences in a market, or they may present an opportunity to the innovative global marketer to obtain competitive advantage by introducing more effective channel arrangements.

INDUSTRIAL PRODUCTS

Figure 13-2 summarizes marketing channel alternatives for the industrial product company. Three basic elements are involved: the manufacturer's sales force, distributors or agents, and wholesalers. A manufacturer can reach customers with its own sales force, or a sales force that calls on wholesalers who sell to customers, or a combination of these two arrangements. A manufacturer can sell directly to wholesalers without using a sales force, and wholesalers in turn can supply customers. Finally, a distributor or agent can call on wholesalers or customers for a manufacturer. B2B sales via the Internet are a new and rapidly growing option.

Distribution patterns vary from country to country. Before deciding which pattern to use and which wholesalers and agents to select, managers must study each country individually. In general, the larger the market, the more feasible it is for a manufacturer to use its own sales force. Kyocera Corporation of Kyoto, Japan, has successfully used its own sales force at home and in the United States to achieve leadership in the $1.2 billion global market for ceramic microchip covers. Company founder Kazuo Inamori

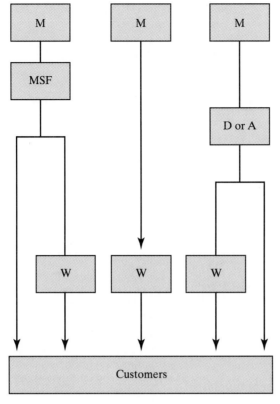

M = Manufacturer   MSF = Manufacturer's Sales Force
W = Wholesaler   D or A = Distributor or Agent

FIGURE 13-2 Marketing Channel Alternatives—Industrial Products

goes to great lengths to make sure the spiritual drive of Kyocera's unique corporate culture extends to all parts of the company, including the sales force.

GLOBAL RETAILING

Global retailing is any retailing activity that crosses national boundaries. Today, there is a growing interest among successful retailers to expand globally, but this is not a new phenomenon. For centuries, venturesome merchants have gone abroad both to obtain merchandise and ideas and to operate retail establishments. The development of trading company operations in Africa and Asia by British, French, Dutch, Belgian, and German retailing organizations progressed extensively during the 19th and early 20th centuries. International trading and retail store operation were two of the economic pillars of the colonial system of that era. The big change taking place in international retailing today involves the gradual dissolution of the colonial retailing structure and, in its place, the creation of international retailing organizations operating in the industrialized countries.

Retail stores can be divided into categories according to the amount of square feet of floor space, the level of service offered, and width and depth of product offerings. In practice, stores have many different names in different countries, and definitions based on selling area also vary. A variety of terms is used to refer to large stores, including *hypermarkets, mass merchandisers, discounters, supermarkets,* and *superstores.*

In general, countries in which the proportion of store numbers is low relative to their share of turnover are those that joined the supermarket revolution many years

---

◆ BOX 13-3 ◆

WHY DOESN'T THE UNITED STATES EXPORT MORE?

CHANNELS IN LESS DEVELOPED COUNTRIES

One of the conspicuous features of retail channels in less developed countries is the remarkable number of people engaged in selling very small quantities of merchandise. In Ethiopia and other East African countries, for example, an open window in the side of a building is likely to be a *souk*, a small walk-up store whose proprietor sells everything from toilet paper and playing cards to rice and eggs. To maximize sales, *souks* are strategically interspersed throughout neighborhood areas. The proprietors know what customers want and need. For example, early in the day they may sell incense and a paper cone with enough coffee for the morning coffee ceremony. In the evening, cigarettes and gum may be in demand, especially if the *souk* is located near a neighborhood nightclub. If a *souk* is closed, it is often possible to rouse the proprietor by knocking on the window, since the store also serves as the proprietor's domicile. Some *souk* owners will even provide "curb service" and bring items to a customer waiting in a car.

By comparison, government department stores in East Africa are less likely to display such a service orientation. Government stores may be stocked with mass quantities of items that are slow to sell. For example, the shelves may hold row after row of tinned tomatoes, even though fresh tomatoes are readily available year around in the market. Customers must go through several steps before actually taking possession of their purchases: determining what goods are available, making a purchase decision, moving to another area to pay, and finally, actually taking possession of the goods. This usually involves a substantial number of papers, seals, and stamps,

as well as interaction with two or three clerks. Clerk jobs are highly prized in countries where jobs are scarce; compared to the *souk* proprietor, who is willing to work from dawn to dusk, the government employee works from 9:00 A.M. to 5:00 P.M., with two hours off for lunch.

In Costa Rica, the privately owned *pulperia* is similar to the Western-style general store that was popular in the first part of the century. Customers enter the store, tell clerks what items are desired, and the clerks fetch the items—which may range from chicken feed to thumb tacks. A typical *pulperia* stocks staples such as sugar and flour in 50-kilo bags, which the proprietor resells in smaller portions. Most *pulperias* have a refrigeration unit so they can sell ice cream novelties; in areas where there is no electricity, the *pulperia* owner will use a generator to provide power for the refrigerator. *Pulperias* are serviced by a fleet of private wholesalers; on any given day, the soft-drink truck, the candy truck, or the staples truck may make deliveries. The *pulperia* serves as a central gathering place for the neighborhood and generally has a public telephone from which patrons can make calls for a fee. This attracts many people to the store in communities where there are few, if any, telephones.

Both the *souk* and the *pulperia* typically offer an informal system of credit. People who patronize these shops usually live in the neighborhood and are known to the proprietor. Often, the proprietor will extend credit if he or she knows that a customer has suffered a setback such as loss of a job or a death in the family. Informally, the proprietors of private retail shops fulfill the role of a lender, especially for people who do not have access to credit through regular financial institutions.

SOURCE: Private communication from Brian Larson of CARE Niger.

---

after it began. France, Belgium, Spain, Brazil, and Colombia are some of the countries in which supermarket retailing sprang up as large, modern, highly efficient units were built. In Italy, where worker-protective legislation limiting the opening of large supermarkets is a factor, large surface stores grew in popularity more gradually. They have more than half of the grocery market share today, up from only 25 percent several years ago. In other countries, supermarkets have existed for more than two decades. Some of the smaller units have been closed down, and new, very large stores have appeared in their place. Retailing is a two-way street. Many foreign companies either have stores in the United States or own U.S. chains. BI-LO, Tops, Stop and Shop, and Giant, popular grocery store chains on the east coast of the United States, are owned by Ahold USA, whose parent company is Royal Ahold of the Netherlands.

The large number of unsuccessful international retailing ventures suggests that anyone contemplating a move into international retailing should do so with a great deal of caution. Speaking of global opportunities for U.S.-based retailers, one industry analyst noted, "It's awfully hard to operate across the water. It's one thing to open up in Mexico and Canada, but the distribution hassles are just too big when it comes to exporting an entire store concept overseas."[6] The critical question for the would-be international retailer is, "What advantages do we have relative to local competition?" The answer will often be "nothing," when local laws governing retailing practice are taken into account. In such cases, there is no reason to expect highly profitable operations to develop from a venture into international retailing.

On the other hand, the answer may indicate that potential advantages do exist. Basically, a retailer has two things to offer consumers. One is the selection of goods at a price, and the second is the overall manner in which the goods are offered in the store setting. This includes such things as the store site, parking facilities, in-store setting, and customer service. JCPenney is expanding retailing operations internationally for both reasons. After touring several countries, JCPenney executives realized that retailers outside the United States often lack marketing sophistication in terms of displaying products, locating aisles to optimize customer traffic, and grouping products. For example, in Istanbul, Turkey, a visiting team noted that one store featured lingerie next to plumbing equipment. According to William R. Howell, Penney chairman and chief executive officer (CEO), Penney's advantage in such instances is its ability to "develop an environment that invites the customer to shop."[7]

◆ INTERNATIONAL CHANNEL INNOVATION

As noted at the beginning of this chapter, distribution channels around the world are highly differentiated. On the surface, it appears this differentiation can be explained only in terms of culture and the income level that exists in the market. However, the incidence and rate of innovation in retail channels can be explained in terms of the following four observations:

1. Innovation takes place only in the most highly developed systems. In general, channel agents in less developed systems will adapt developments already tried and tested in more highly developed systems.
2. The ability of a system to successfully adapt innovations is directly related to its level of economic development. Certain minimum levels of economic development are necessary to support anything beyond the most simple retailing methods.
3. When the economic environment is favorable to change, the process of adaptation may be either hindered or helped by local demographic/geographic factors, social mores, government action, competitive pressures, and infrastructure.
4. The process of adaptation can be greatly accelerated by the actions of aggressive individual firms.

Self-service—the provision for customers to handle and select merchandise themselves in a store with minimal assistance from sales personnel—is a major 20th-century channel innovation. It provides an excellent illustration of the postulates just outlined. Self-service was first introduced in the United States. The spread of self-service to other countries supports the hypothesis that the ability of a system to accept innovations is

---

[6] Neil King, Jr., "Kmart's Czech Invasion Lurches Along," *The Wall Street Journal,* 8 June 1993, p. A11.
[7] Bob Ortega, "Foreign Forays: Penney Pushes Abroad in Unusually Big Way as It Pursues Growth," *The Wall Street Journal,* 1 February 1994, pp. A1, A7.

directly related to the level of economic development in the system. Self-service was first introduced internationally into the most highly developed systems. It has spread to the countries at middle and lower stages of development but serves very small segments of the total market in these countries.

If a marketing system has reached a stage of development that will support a channel innovation, it is clear that the action of well-managed firms can contribute considerably to the diffusion of the channel innovation. The rapid growth of Benetton and McDonald's is a testament to the skill and competence of these firms as well as to the appeal of their products. In some instances, channel innovations are improved, refined, and expanded outside the home country. 7-Eleven stores in Japan, for example, are half the size of U.S. stores and carry one third the inventory, yet they ring up twice as much in sales. 7-Eleven Japan boasts a fourth-generation point-of-sale (POS) information system that is more sophisticated than the system used in the United States. (Note: 7-Eleven, the parent company, is Japanese-owned.) Conversely, in China, KFC (Kentucky Fried Chicken) outlets are twice the size of those in the United States due to the greater emphasis of eating in a restaurant rather than taking food out.[8]

Another Japanese 7-Eleven innovation is an in-store catalog, Shop America, that allows Japanese shoppers to order imported luxury products from companies such as Tiffany's and Cartier.[9]

◆ CHANNEL STRATEGY FOR NEW MARKET ENTRY

A global company expanding across national boundaries often finds itself in the position of entering a market for the first time. The company must use established channels, build its own channels, or abandon the market. Channel obstacles are often encountered when a company enters a competitive market in which brands and supply relationships are firmly established. As noted previously, there is little immediate incentive for an independent channel agent to take on a new product when established names are accepted in the market and are satisfying current demands. The global company seeking to enter such a market must either provide some incentive to channel agents or establish its own direct-distribution system. Each of these alternatives has its disadvantages.

A company may decide to provide special incentives to independent channel agents; however, this approach can be extremely expensive. The company might offer outright payments—either direct cash bonuses or contest awards—tied to sales performance. In competitive markets with sufficiently high prices, incentives could take the form of gross margin guarantees. Both incentive payments and margin guarantees are expensive. The incentive payments are directly expensive; the margin guarantees can be indirectly expensive because they affect the price to the consumer and the price competitiveness of a manufacturer's product.

Establishing direct distribution in a new market can also be expensive. Sales representatives and sales management must be hired and trained. The sales organization will inevitably be a heavy loser in its early stage of operation in a new market because it will not have sufficient volume to cover its overhead costs. Therefore, any company contemplating establishing a direct sales force, even one assigned to distributors, should be prepared to underwrite losses for this sales force for a reasonable period of time.

The expense of a direct sales force acts as a deterrent to establishing direct distribution in a new market. Nevertheless, it is often the most effective method. Indeed, in

[8] David J. Arnold and John A. Quelch, "New Strategies in Emerging Markets," *Sloan Management Review,* 40, 1 (1998): 7–20.

[9] James Sterngold, "New Japanese Lesson; Running a 7-11," *The New York Times,* 9 May 1991, p. C7.

many instances, direct distribution is the only feasible way for a company to establish itself in a new market. By using a sales force, the manufacturer can ensure aggressive sales activity and attention to its products. Sufficient resource commitment to sales activity, backed up by appropriate communications programs (including advertising), may in time allow a manufacturer with competitive products and prices to obtain a reasonable share of market. When market share objectives have been reached, the manufacturer may consider shifting from the direct sales force to reliance on independent intermediaries. This shift becomes a possibility when market share and market recognition make the manufacturer's brand attractive to independent intermediaries.

Kyocera achieved great success in the U.S. market by custom-tailoring ceramic chip housings to each customer's needs. Kyocera also has become legendary for its service among California's Silicon Valley chipmakers. Instead of following the electronics industry norm of using distributors for its products, Kyocera relies on a salaried sales force. Kyocera backs up its $100 million-per-year research and development (R&D) expenditures with sales forces in both the United States—50 direct salespersons at 12 direct-sales offices—and Japan that place unwavering emphasis on quality and customer service. Early on, Kyocera earned a reputation for answering customer questions overnight, whereas American suppliers often took weeks to respond. Employees would work around the clock to satisfy customer requests for samples. Another hallmark: No company is too small for Kyocera to serve. Jerry Crowley of Gazelle Microcircuits in Santa Clara reported, for example, that Kyocera salespeople began calling on him when he had only 11 employees. Gazelle has been buying custom chip packages from Kyocera ever since.

◆ PHYSICAL DISTRIBUTION AND LOGISTICS

The value chain and value system are conceptual tools that provide a framework for integrating various organizational activities, including physical distribution of goods (see Table 13-2). Physical distribution and logistics are the means by which products are made available to customers when and where they want them. Distribution issues include order processing, warehousing, inventory management, and transportation.

ORDER PROCESSING

Activities relating to order processing provide information inputs that are critical in fulfilling a customer's order. Order processing includes order entry, in which the order is actually entered into a company's information system; order handling, which involves locating, assembling, and moving products into distribution; and order delivery, the process by which products are made available to the customer.

WAREHOUSING

Warehouses are used to store goods until they are sold; another type of facility, the distribution center, is designed to efficiently receive goods from suppliers and then fill orders for individual stores. A company may have its own warehouses and distribution centers or pay a specialist to provide these facilities.

INVENTORY MANAGEMENT

Proper inventory management ensures that a company neither runs out of manufacturing components or finished goods nor incurs the expense and risk of carrying excessive stocks of these items.

TABLE 13-2	Distribution Functions in the Value Chain

Purchasing

Inbound Logistics

R&D
Assembly and manufacturing

Outbound Logistics

Marketing
    Information and research
    Target market selection
    Product policy and strategy
    Pricing policy and strategy

Distribution Policy and Strategy

Communications policy and strategy
    Messages, appeals
    Media strategy and plan
    Advertising plan
    Promotion plan
    Personal selling
    Direct-marketing plan
        Direct mail
        Telemarketing
Installation and testing service
Margin

TRANSPORTATION

Finally, transportation decisions concern which of five methods a company should use to move its products: rail, truck, air, water, or pipeline.

When contemplating market expansion outside the home country, management's inclination may be to configure these aspects of the value chain exactly as they are at home. However, this may not be the most effective solution because the organization may lack the necessary skill and experience to conduct all value-chain activities in target markets. A company with home-market competitive advantages in both upstream activities and downstream activities—manufacturing and distribution, for example—may be forced to reconfigure distribution activities to successfully enter new global markets. For example, Wal-Mart's expansion into Mexico has been hampered by the fact that most Mexican suppliers ship directly to stores rather than to retailer warehouses and distribution centers. Thus, Wal-Mart lacks the control that is the key to its low prices in the United States. Notes Sam Dunn, director of administration for Wal-Mart de Mexico, "The key to this market is distribution. The retailer who solves that will dominate."[10]

Among American companies, 3M does an excellent job of managing the physical distribution aspects of the value chain to support global market exports. Outbound logistics, for example, represent just one aspect of the company's overall global strategic plan to support burgeoning exports to Europe. In St. Paul, 3M's international distribution center receives more than 5,000 orders per week. In 1985, export orders took 11

---

[10] Bob Ortega, "Tough Sale: Wal-Mart Is Slowed by Problems of Price and Culture in Mexico," *The Wall Street Journal,* 28 July 1994, pp. A1, A5.

days to get through the center. By 1990, only 5.5 days were required; shipping mistakes were cut 71 percent, despite the fact that volume was up 89 percent. In Europe, meanwhile, 3M set up a distribution center in Breda, the Netherlands, to receive containers from Norfolk, Virginia, and other ports. Logistics managers convinced 3M to spend as much as $1 million per year for additional trucks to provide daily delivery service to each of 3M's 19 European subsidiaries. The outlay was approved after the managers demonstrated that savings could be achieved—due to lower inventories and faster deliveries—even if trucks were not filled to capacity.[11]

Laura Ashley, the global retailer of traditional English-style household linen and clothing for women, recently reconfigured its supply chain. The company has more than 300 company-owned retail stores around the world, supplying them with goods manufactured in 15 different countries. In the past, Laura Ashley's suppliers all sent goods to the company's distribution center in Wales. This meant that blouses manufactured in Hong Kong were first sent to Wales; blouses bound for the company's Tokyo store then had to be sent back to the Far East. Not surprisingly, this was not an effective arrangement; Laura Ashley stores were typically sold out of 20 percent of goods even though the company's warehouses were full. To cut costs and improve its inventory management, Laura Ashley has subcontracted physical distribution to FedEx's Business Logistics Service. FedEx's information system is tied in with the retail stores; when a Laura Ashley buyer orders blouses from Hong Kong, FedEx arranges shipment from the manufacturer directly to the stores.[12]

◆ CASE EXAMPLE: JAPAN

Japan has presented an especially difficult distribution challenge to foreign companies. Japanese distribution is a highly developed system that has evolved to satisfy the needs of the Japanese consumer. The total number of retail outlets in Japan—1.6 million stores—represents about 5 percent more stores than in the United States for a population that is half the size. Japan has 132 retail stores per 10,000 people, compared to 65 stores per 10,000 people in the United States. A correspondingly high number of intermediaries, including more than 400,000 wholesalers, is needed in Japan to service this fragmented system of outlets.[13] Some changes, albeit slowly, are occurring in distribution strategies in Japan. In response to the growing number of Japanese women who desire luxury products, are marrying later and living longer, theme shopping facilities are being developed. In Tokyo, VenusFort is a huge shopping center that attracts 120,000 visitors a day, most of whom are women. It is decorated with southern European ambiance and even has a "fake sky in which the sun rises and sets every hour."[14]

The categories of wholesalers and retailers in Japan are very finely divided. For example, meat stores in Japan do about 80 percent of their business in meat items. Similar specialization exists in other specialty stores as well. This kind of concentration is also true at the wholesale level. This very high degree of specialization in Japan is made possible by the clustering of various types of stores at major street intersections or stops along commuter rail lines.

There are, of course, many instances in which overseas firms have entered the Japanese market and have been able to overcome difficulties presented by the distribution

[11] Robert L. Rose, "Success Abroad: 3M, by Tiptoeing into Foreign Markets, Became a Big Exporter," *The Wall Street Journal,* 29 March 1991, p. A10.

[12] Stephanie Strom, "Logistics Steps onto Retail Battlefield," *The New York Times,* 3 November 1993, pp. D1, D2.

[13] Jack G. Kaikati, "Don't Crack the Japanese Distribution System—Just Circumvent It," *Columbia Journal of World Business* (Spring 1993): 38–41.

[14] "A Land Fit for Consumers," *The Economist,* 27 November 1999, p. 16.

system. Unfortunately, problems in coping with and adapting to Japanese distribution have also prevented a number of firms from achieving the success they might have had. Historically, foreign marketers in Japan make two basic mistakes. The first is their assumption that distribution problems can be solved the same way they would be in the West, that is, by going as directly as possible to the customer and, thus, cutting out the middleman. In Japan, because of the very fragmented nature of retailing, it is simply not cost-effective to go direct.

The second mistake often made is in treating the Japanese market at arm's length by selling to a trading company. The trading company may sell in low volumes to a very limited segment of the market, such as the luxury segment, with the result that there is usually limited interest on the part of the trading company. The experience is likely to be disappointing to all parties involved.

Successful distribution in Japan (or any other market) requires adaptation to the realities of the marketplace. In Japan, this means first and foremost adaptation to the reality of fragmented distribution. Second, it requires research into the market itself including customer needs and competitive products. Then a company must develop an overall marketing strategy that (1) positions the product vis-à-vis market segment identified according to need, price, and other issues; (2) positions the product against competitors; and (3) lays out a marketing plan—including a distribution plan—for achieving volume and share-of-market objectives.

DEVISING A JAPANESE DISTRIBUTION STRATEGY

In the 1970s, Shimaguchi and Rosenberg identified several considerations for any company formulating and implementing a Japanese distribution strategy. The first called for finding a Japanese partner, such as an import agent, to help navigate the unfamiliar waters. Import agents range in size from small local distributors to the giant *sogo-sosha* (general trading companies). The authors also advised companies to pursue a strategy of offering better quality, lower price, or a distinctive positioning as a foreign product. Foreigners are advised to prepare for a long-term effort and modest returns; nothing happens quickly in Japanese distribution, and patience is required. Finally, cultivate personal relationships in distribution. Loyalty and trust are important.[15]

These considerations are still relevant today; however, some recent studies have described ways to bypass the Japanese distribution quagmire by pursuing alternative distribution channels. For example, foreign companies may wish to follow the example of Toys "Я" Us and establish their own retail stores in Japan. Toys "Я" Us attempted to circumvent the multilayered wholesale system by buying direct from manufacturers. A second approach is to use direct-marketing techniques. Although telemarketing is relatively new and has proven more successful with business-to-business rather than consumer marketing, mail order in Japan has been experiencing 17 percent annual growth. L.L. Bean, with the help of the Internet, sells a substantial amount of merchandise in Japan despite the fact that it has never published a Japanese catalog. Door-to-door selling is a third alternative channel strategy in Japan that has been successfully pursued by Amway. Amway has established its own system of over one million independent distributors; most of the 190-plus products sold are imported from the United States. Finally, a company may wish to explore creative ways of piggybacking with other successful companies. For example, Shop America successfully launched a specialty catalog business by piggybacking with Japan's 7-Eleven convenience stores.[16]

---

[15] Mitsuaki Shimaguchi and Larry R. Rosenberg, " Demystifying Japanese Distribution," *Columbia Journal of World Business* (Spring 1979): 38–41.
[16] Kaikati, "Japanese Distribution System."

Summary

Channel decisions are difficult to manage globally because of the variation in channel structures from country to country. Nevertheless, certain patterns of change associated with market development offer the astute global marketer the opportunity to create channel innovations and gain competitive advantage. The characteristics of customers, products, middlemen, and environment all impact channel design and strategy. Consumer channels may be direct, via mail, door-to-door, the Internet, or direct factory/manufacturer outlets, or they may involve one or more levels of resellers. A combination of the manufacturer's sales force, agents/brokers, and wholesalers may also be used. Channels for industrial products are less varied, with the manufacturer's sales force, wholesalers, and dealers or agents being utilized.

In developed countries, retail channels are characterized by the substitution of capital for labor. This is evident in self-service stores, which offer a wide range of items at relatively low gross margins. The opposite is true in less developed countries with abundant labor. Such countries disguise their unemployment in inefficient retail and wholesale channels suited to the needs of consumers; such channels may have gross margins that are 50 percent lower than those in self-service stores in developed countries. A global marketer must either tailor the marketing program to these different types of channels or introduce new retail concepts.

Transportation and physical distribution issues are critically important in global marketing because of the geographical distances involved in sourcing products and serving customers in different parts of the world. Today, many companies are reconfiguring their supply chains to cut costs and improve efficiency.

Discussion Questions

1. In what ways can channel intermediaries create utility for buyers?
2. What factors influence the channel structures and strategies available to global marketers?
3. What is cherry-picking? What approaches can be used to deal with this problem?
4. Compare and contrast the typical channel structures for consumer products and industrial products.
5. Briefly discuss the global issues associated with physical distribution and transportation logistics. Cite one example of a company that is making efficiency improvements in its physical distribution.
6. What special distribution challenges exist in Japan? What is the best way for a non-Japanese company to deal with these challenges?

Suggested Readings

Alexander, Nicholas. *International Retailing.* Oxford, UK: Blackwell Business, 1997.

Allen, Randy L. "The Why and How of Global Retailing." *Business Quarterly,* 57, no. 4 (Summer 1993): 117–122.

Bauer, P. T. *West African Trade.* Cambridge: Cambridge University Press, 1954.

Bello, Daniel C., and Ritu Lohtia. "Export Channel Design: The Use of Foreign Distributors and Agents." *Journal of the Academy of Marketing Science,* 23, no. 2 (1995): 83–93.

Burns, David J., and John T. Brady. "Retail Ethics as Appraised by Future Business Personnel in Malaysia and the United States," *Journal of Consumer Affairs,* 30, no.1 (1996): p. 195+.

Carr, Mark, Arlene Hostrop, and Daniel O'Connor. "The New Era of Global Retailing." *Journal of Business Strategy,* 19, 3 (1998): 11–15.

Cavusgil, S. Tamer. "The Importance of Distributor Training at Caterpillar." *Industrial Marketing Management,* 19, no. 1 (February 1990): 1–9.

Fields, George. *From Bonsai to Levi's: An Insider's Surprising Account of How the Japanese Live.* New York: Macmillan, 1983.

Hanson, Ward. *Principles of Internet Marketing.* Cincinnatti: South Western College Publishing, 2000.

Hill, John S., Richard R. Still, and Unal O. Boya. "Managing the Multinational Sales Force." *International Marketing Review,* 8, no. 1 (1991): 19–31.

Kaikati, Jack G. "Don't Crack the Japanese Distribution System—Just Circumvent It." *Columbia Journal of World Business,* 28, no. 2 (Summer 1993): 34–45.

Kale, Sudhir, and Roger P. McIntyre. "Distribution Channel Relationships in Diverse Cultures." *International Marketing Review,* 8, no. 3 (1991): 311–345.

Klein, Saul, and Victor Roth. "Satisfaction with International Marketing Channels." *Journal of the Academy of Marketing Science,* 21, no. 1 (Winter 1993): 39–44.

Murphy, Paul R., James M. Daley, and Douglas R. Dalenberg. "Doing Business in Global Markets: Perspectives of International Freight Forwarders." *Journal of Global Marketing,* 6, no. 4 (1993): 53–68.

Olsen, Janeen E., and Kent L. Granzin. "Economic Development and Channel Structure: A Multinational Study." *Journal of Macromarketing,* 10, no. 2 (Fall 1990): 61–77.

Raguraman K., and Claire Chan. "The Development of Sea-Air Intermodal Transportation: An Assessment of Global Trends." *The Logistics and Transportation Review,* 30, no. 4 (December 1994): 379–396.

"Retail Marketing: International Perspectives." *The European Journal of Marketing,* 26, no. 8/9 (1992), special issue.

Sachdev, Harash J., Daniel C. Bello, and Bruce K. Pilling. "Control Mechanisms within Export Channels of Distribution." *Journal of Global Marketing,* 8, no. 2 (1994): 31–50.

Samiee, Saeed. "Retailing and Channel Considerations in Developing Countries: A Review and Research Proposition." *Journal of Business Research,* 27, no. 2 (June 1993): 103–129.

Sherwood, Charles, and Robert Bruns. "Solving International Transportation Problems." *Review of Business,* 14, no. 1 (Summer/Fall 1992): 25–30.

Stern, Louis W., and Adel L. El-Ansary. *Marketing Channels,* 4th ed. Upper Saddle River, NJ: Prentice Hall, 1992.

Weigand, Robert E. "Parallel Import Channels—Options for Preserving Territorial Integrity." *Columbia Journal of World Business,* 26, no. 1 (Spring 1991): 53–60.

CHAPTER 14

Global Advertising

Eighteen-year-olds in Paris have more in common with 18-year-olds in New York than with their own parents. They buy the same products, go to the same movies, listen to the same music, sip the same colas. Global advertising merely works on that premise.

—WILLIAM ROEDY
Director, MTV Europe

CONTENTS

Clearly, advertising, publicity, and other forms of communication are critical tools for the global marketer. Marketing communications—the promotion P of the marketing mix—refers to all forms of communication used by organizations to inform, remind, explain, persuade, and influence the attitudes and buying behavior of customers and other persons. The primary purpose of marketing communications is to tell customers about the benefits and values that a product or service offers. The elements of the promotion mix are advertising, public relations, personal selling, sales promotion, and direct marketing. The Internet, a medium that combines all of these components, will be discussed in Chapter 16. All of these elements can be utilized in global marketing, either alone or in varying combinations.

Numerous changes are occurring in advertising, such as the growth of the Internet and global television. This growth is reflected in the annual advertising expenditures. In 1998, world advertising expenditures exceeded $300 billion (Figure 14-1) and this amount is expected to approach $350 billion by 2001. The television market in the United States has stabilized and in Japan it has declined, but China and India are experiencing double-digit growth in advertising spending.

The environment in which marketing communications programs and strategies are implemented also varies from country to country. The challenge of effectively communicating across borders is one reason Nike, Nestlé, Microsoft, and other companies are embracing a concept known as integrated marketing communications (IMC). Adherents

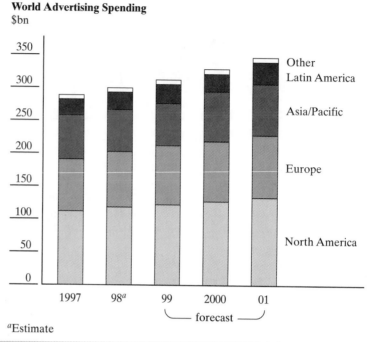

World Advertising Spending
$bn

FIGURE 14-1 World Advertising Spending

Source: The Economist, 2 January 1999, p. 88. © 1999 The Economist Newspaper Group, Inc. Reprinted with permission. Further reproduction prohibited. Data provided by Zenith Media.

of an IMC approach explicitly recognize that the various elements of a company's communication strategy must be carefully coordinated.[1] In this chapter, advertising will be examined from the perspective of the global marketer. Chapter 15 is devoted to the remaining elements of the promotion mix: public relations, personal selling, sales promotion, direct marketing, trade shows, and sponsorship.

> **VISIT THE WEB SITE**
> www.adageglobal.com

◆ GLOBAL ADVERTISING AND BRANDING

Advertising may be defined as any sponsored, paid message placed in a mass medium. Global advertising is the use of the same advertising appeals, messages, art, copy, photographs, stories, and video segments in multiple-country markets. A global company that has the ability to successfully transform a domestic campaign into a worldwide one, or to create a new global campaign from the ground up, has a critical advantage. There are powerful reasons to try to create an effective global campaign. The creative process will force a company to determine whether there is a global market for its product. The first company to find a global market for any product is always at an advantage over competitors making the same discovery later. The search for a global advertising campaign can be the cornerstone of the search for a coherent global strategy. Such a search should bring together everyone involved with the product to share information and leverage their experiences.

---

[1] Thomas R. Duncan and Stephen E. Everett, "Client Perception of Integrated Marketing Communications," *Journal of Advertising Research* (May–June 1993): 119–122.

Because advertising is often designed to add psychological value to a product or brand, it plays a more important communications role in marketing consumer products than in marketing industrial products. Frequently purchased, low-cost products generally require heavy advertising support to remind consumers about the product. Table 14-1 lists the top 15 global product categories by measured advertising spending. After automobiles, personal care and food rank as numbers two and three, respectively.

Not surprisingly, therefore, consumer products companies top the list of big global advertising spenders. Unilever, Procter & Gamble, Nestlé, and Coca-Cola each spent over $1 billion on advertising outside the United States. *Advertising Age*'s ranking of global marketers in terms of advertising expenditures outside the United States is shown in Table 14-2. Note that Asian and European companies spend more in their respective regions.

Table 14-3 shows the top 10 countries in the world by advertising expenditure. The United States and Japan top the list. Two companies, Coca-Cola and Colgate-Palmolive, spent substantial portions of their international budgets in Latin America, 29.9 percent and 44.8 percent, respectively. Nestlé and General Motors spent substantial portions of their budgets in Africa, the Middle East, and Canada. The trend in worldwide advertising expenditures is expected to continue.

There are several reasons for global advertising's growing popularity. Global campaigns attest to management's conviction that unified themes not only spur short-term sales but also help build long-term product identity and offer significant savings in production costs.[2] Regional trading centers such as Europe are experiencing an influx of internationalized brands as companies align themselves, buy up other companies, and get their pricing policies and production plans organized for a united region. From a marketing point of view, there is a great deal of activity going on that will make brands truly pan-European in a very short period of time. This phenomenon is accelerating the growth of global advertising.

TABLE 14-1   Top 15 Global Categories by Measured Ad Spending

Category	Measured Advertising 1998	Measured Advertising 1997	% Change	Rank
Automotive	$9,904.2	$9,711.9	2.0	1
Beer, wine, and liquor	633.9	553.4	14.6	11
Cell phones	307.1	252.5	21.6	15
Cigarettes	430.0	386.3	11.3	14
Cleaners	1,017.4	921.4	10.4	8
Computers, software, peripherals	697.7	683.2	2.1	10
Drugs	1,573.3	1,479.7	6.3	5
Electronics	1,352.7	1,552.3	−12.9	7
Entertainment and media	2,448.7	2,109.0	16.1	4
Fast-food restaurants	726.6	694.5	4.6	9
Food	5,224.9	4,868.5	7.3	3
Personal care	9,558.3	9,022.9	5.9	2
Retail	530.7	403.5	31.5	13
Soft drinks	1,377.3	1,265.6	8.8	6
Toys	591.7	575.4	2.8	12

Source: Advertising Age, www.adage.com/dataplace/archives/dp402.html.

---

[2] Ken Wells, "Selling to the World: Global Ad Campaigns after Many Missteps Finally Pay Dividends," *The Wall Street Journal,* 27 August 1992, p. A8.

TABLE 14-2	Top 25 Global Marketers			
Rank 1999	**Advertiser**	**Headquarters**	**Spending Outside the U.S. 1999**	**Country Count**
1	Unilever	Rotterdam/London	$3,110	66
2	Procter & Gamble Co.	Cincinnati	2,988	68
3	Nestlé	Vevey, Switzerland	1,580	67
4	Coca-Cola Co.	Atlanta	1,178	69
5	Ford Motor Co.	Dearborn, MI	1,150	51
6	General Motors Corp.	Detroit	1,148	43
7	L'Oreal	Paris	1,120	47
8	Volkswagen	Wolfsburg, Germany	1,009	33
9	Toyota Motor Corp.	Toyota City, Japan	1,007	44
10	PSA Peugeot Citroen	Paris	906	37
11	Sony Corp.	Tokyo	886	53
12	Mars Inc.	McLean, VA	841	37
13	Renault	Paris	809	31
14	Philip Morris Cos.	New York	767	49
15	Henkel	Duesseldorf	728	35
16	Nissan Motor Co.	Tokyo	657	39
17	McDonald's Corp.	Oak Brook, IL	649	54
18	Fiat	Turin, Italy	649	26
19	Danone Group	Paris	642	24
20	Ferrero	Perugia, Italy	603	34
21	Colgate-Palmolive Co.	New York	591	57
22	Deutsche Telekom	Bonn, Germany	578	5
23	DaimlerChrysler	Stuttgart, Germany	556	39
24	Reckitt Benckiser	Windsor, Berkshire, U.K.	543	39
25	Johnson & Johnson	New Brunswick, NJ	486	52

Source: Advertising Age, www.adageglobal.com/cgi-bin/pages.pl?link=438.

TABLE 14-3	Top Markets by Adverstising Expenditure
United States	Italy
Japan	Brazil
Germany	Spain
United Kingdom	Canada
France	

Source: Advertising Age, www.adageglobal.com/cgi-bin/pages.pl?link=425.

The potential for effective global advertising also increases as companies recognize and embrace new concepts such as product cultures. Companies realize that some market segments can be defined on the basis of global demography—youth culture, for example—rather than ethnic or national culture. Athletic shoes and other clothing products, for example, can be targeted to a worldwide segment of 18- to 25-year-old males. As noted in the quote at the beginning of this chapter, William Roedy, director of MTV Europe, sees clear implications of such product cultures for advertising. MTV is just one of the media vehicles that enable people virtually anywhere to see how the rest of the world lives and

◆ BOX 14-1 ◆

ADIDAS

The American athletic shoe companies are skilled global marketers. Reebok is the market leader in France, Spain, and England, but Nike is number one in many other European countries. Although advertising tag lines such as "Just Do It" and "Planet Reebok" are presented in English, other parts of the message are adapted to reflect cultural differences. In France, for example, violence in ads is unacceptable, so Reebok replaced boxing scenes with images of women running on a beach. Also, European participation in sports is lower than in America; accordingly, Europeans are less likely to visit sporting goods stores. In France, Reebok shoes are instead sold in nearly 1,000 traditional shoe stores.

Even in the face of such tough and growing competition, Adidas still enjoys high brand loyalty among older Europeans. The company recruits young people and pays them to wear Adidas shoes in public; they are also paid to work at sporting goods stores and promote Adidas products in other ways. Adidas also updated its image among younger European consumers by creating a new sport called Streetball. Ads airing on MTV Europe fea-

ture players outfitted in the company's Streetball apparel line. Unlike its American rivals, Adidas does not utilize a global ad campaign. For example, a 1995 campaign that ran outside the United States featured Emil Zatopke, a Czechoslovakian Olympic runner.

The company does, however, maintain a single advertising agency—London-based Leagas Delany—for all its global markets. Bruce Haines, the agency's chief executive, notes, "Adidas is structured by geographic territories and sports-based business units. We're anxious to make sure there's one hand writing one signature whatever the work, whatever the sport." In a move that indicated optimism about Adidas's future, in 1995 Dreyfus's group raised its stake to full ownership. Meanwhile, Adidas was hard at work on a revolutionary new barefootwear product. As Dreyfus said in an interview on CNN, "The idea is there is nothing better than the foot as an instrument for running. The only problem is abrasion. So they are very revolutionary shoes and it will have a huge campaign behind it after June [1996]."

SOURCES: Dagmar Mussey, "Adidas Strides on Its Own Path," *Advertising Age,* 13 February 1995, p. 6; Kevin Goldman, "Adidas Tries to Fill Its Rivals' Big Shoes," *The Wall Street Journal,* 17 March 1994, p. B5; Joseph Pereira, "Off and Running: Pushing U.S. Style, Nike and Reebok Sell Sneakers to Europe," *The Wall Street Journal,* 22 July 1993, pp. A1, A8; Stephen Barr, "Adidas on the Rebound," *CFO* (September 1991): 48–56; Igor Reichlin, "Where Nike and Reebok Have Plenty of Running Room," *Business Week,* 11 March 1991, pp. 56–60.

to learn about products that are popular in other cultures. Many human wants and desires are very similar if presented within recognizable experience situations. People everywhere want value, quality, and the latest technology made available and affordable; everyone everywhere wants to be loved and respected, gets hungry, and so on.[3]

Global advertising also offers companies economies of scale in advertising as well as improved access to distribution channels. In cases in which shelf space is at a premium, as with food products, a company has to convince retailers to carry its products rather than those of competitors. A global brand supported by global advertising may be very attractive because, from the retailer's standpoint, a global brand is less likely to languish on the shelves. Landor Associates, a company specializing in brand identity and design, recently determined that Coke has the number one brand-awareness and esteem position in the United States, number two in Japan, and number six in Europe. However, standardization is not always required or even advised. Nestlé's Nescafé is marketed as a global brand even though advertising messages and product formulation vary to suit cultural differences.

---

[3] Dean M. Peebles, "Executive Insights: Don't Write Off Global Advertising," *International Marketing Review,* 6, no. 1 (1989): 73–78.

◆ GLOBAL ADVERTISING CONTENT: THE EXTENSION VERSUS ADAPTATION DEBATE

Communication experts generally agree that the overall requirements of effective communication and persuasion are fixed and do not vary from country to country. The same thing is true of the components of the communication process: The marketer's or sender's message must be encoded, conveyed via the appropriate channel(s), and decoded by the customer or receiver. Communication takes place only when meaning is transferred. Four major difficulties can compromise an organization's attempt to communicate with customers in any location:

1. The message may not get through to the intended recipient. This problem may be the result of an advertiser's lack of knowledge about appropriate media for reaching certain types of audiences. For example, the effectiveness of television as a medium for reaching mass audiences will vary proportionately with the extent to which television viewing occurs within a country.
2. The message may reach the target audience but may not be understood or may even be misunderstood. This can be the result of an inadequate understanding of the target audience's level of sophistication or improper encoding.
3. The message may reach the target audience and may be understood but still may not induce the recipient to take the action desired by the sender. This could result from a lack of cultural knowledge about a target audience.
4. The effectiveness of the message can be impaired by noise. Noise in this case is an external influence such as competitive advertising, other sales personnel, and confusion at the receiving end, which can detract from the ultimate effectiveness of the communication.

The key question for global marketers is whether the specific advertising message and media strategy must be changed from region to region or country to country because of environmental requirements. Proponents of the "one world, one voice" approach to global advertising believe that the era of the global village is fast approaching, and that tastes and preferences are converging worldwide. According to the standardization argument, because people everywhere want the same products for the same reasons, companies can achieve great economies of scale by unifying advertising around the globe. Advertisers who follow the localized approach are skeptical of the global village argument. Even Coca-Cola, the most global brand in the world, records radio spots in 40 languages with 140 different music backgrounds.[4] Coca-Cola asserts that consumers still differ from country to country and must be reached by advertising tailored to their respective countries. Proponents of localization point out that most blunders occur because advertisers have failed to understand and adapt to foreign cultures. Nick Brien, managing director of Leo Burnett, explains the situation this way:

> As the potency of traditional media declines on a daily basis, brand building locally becomes more costly and international brand building becomes more cost effective. The challenge for advertisers and agencies is finding ads which work in different countries and cultures. At the same time as this global tendency, there is a growing local tendency. It's becoming increasingly important to understand the requirements of both.[5]

During the 1950s, the widespread opinion of advertising professionals was that effective international advertising required assigning responsibility for campaign prepa-

---

[4] The Coca-Cola Company 1999 Annual Report, p. 18.
[5] Meg Carter, "Think Globally, Act Locally," *Financial Times,* 30 June 1997, p. 12.

━━━

◆ BOX 14-2 ◆

GLOBAL CAMPAIGNS FOR GLOBAL PRODUCTS

Certain consumer products lend themselves to advertising extension. If a product appeals to the same need around the world, there is a possibility of extending the appeal to that need. The list of products "going global," once confined to a score of consumer and luxury goods, is growing. Global advertising is partly responsible for increased worldwide sales of disposable diapers, diamond watches, shampoos, and athletic shoes. Some longtime global advertisers are benefiting from fresh campaigns. Jeans marketer Levi Strauss & Company racked up record sales in Europe in 1991 on the strength of a campaign extended unchanged to Europeans, Latin Americans, and Australians. The basic issue is whether there is in fact a global market for the product. If the market is global, appeals can be standardized and extended. Soft drinks, Scotch whiskey, Swiss watches, and designer clothing are examples of product categories whose markets are truly global. For example, Seagram's recently ran a global campaign keyed to the theme line, "There will always be a Chivas Regal." The campaign ran in 34 countries and was translated into 15 languages. In 1991, Seagram's launched a global billboard campaign to enhance the universal appeal for Chivas. The theory: The rich all over will sip the brand, no matter where they made their fortune.

Gillette Company took a standardized "one product/one brand name/one strategy" global approach when it introduced the Sensor razor in 1990. The campaign slogan was "Gillette. The Best a Man Can Get," an appeal that was expected to cross boundaries with ease. Peter Hoffman, marketing vice president of the North Atlantic Shaving Group, noted in a press release: "We are blessed with a product category where we're able to market shaving systems across multinational boundaries as if they were one country. Gillette Sensor is the trigger for a total Gillette megabrand strategy which will revolutionize the entire shaving market." In the Japanese market, Gillette's standardized advertising campaign differs strikingly from that of arch-rival Schick. Prior to the Sensor launch, Gillette custom-made advertising for the Japanese market; now, except that the phrase, "The best a man can get," is translated into Japanese, the ads shown in Japan are the same as those shown in the United States and the rest of the world. Schick, meanwhile, uses Japanese actors in its ads.

━━

ration to a local agency. In the early 1960s, this idea of local delegation was repeatedly challenged. For example, Eric Elinder, head of a Swedish advertising agency, wrote: "Why should three artists in three different countries sit drawing the same electric iron and three copywriters write about what after all is largely the same copy for the same iron?"[6] Elinder argued that consumer differences between countries were diminishing and that he would more effectively serve a client's interest by putting top specialists to work devising a strong international campaign. The campaign would then be presented with insignificant modifications that mainly entailed translating the copy into language well suited for a particular country.

As the decade of the 1980s began, Pierre Liotard-Vogt, former CEO of Nestlé, expressed similar views in an interview with *Advertising Age*.

> *Advertising Age:* Are food tastes and preferences different in each of the countries in which you do business?
>
> *Liotard-Vogt:* The two countries where we are selling perhaps the most instant coffee are England and Japan. Before the war they didn't drink coffee in those countries, and I heard people say that it wasn't any use to try to sell instant coffee to the English because they drink only tea and still less to the Japanese because they drink green tea and they're not interested in anything else.

───────────

[6] Eric Elinder, "International Advertisers Must Devise Universal Ads, Dump Separate National Ones, Swedish Ad Man Avers," *Advertising Age,* 27 November 1961, p. 91.

When I was very young, I lived in England and at that time, if you spoke to an Englishman about eating spaghetti or pizza or anything like that, he would just look at you and think that the stuff was perhaps food for Italians. Now on the corner of every road in London you find pizzerias and spaghetti houses.

So I do not believe [preconceptions] about "national tastes." They are "habits," and they're not the same. If you bring the public a different food, even if it is unknown initially, when they get used to it, they will enjoy it too.

To a certain extent we know that in the north they like a coffee milder and a bit acid and less roasted; in the south, they like it very dark. So I can't say that taste differences don't exist. But to believe that those tastes are set and can't be changed is a mistake.[7]

The standardized-versus-localized debate picked up tremendous momentum after the publication in 1983 of Professor Ted Levitt's *Harvard Business Review* article titled "The Globalization of Markets," noted in earlier chapters. In contrast to the view expounded by Levitt and Liotard-Vogt, some recent scholarly research suggests that the trend is toward the increased use of localized international advertising. Kanso reached that conclusion in a study surveying two different groups of advertising managers—those taking localized approaches to overseas advertising and those taking standardized approaches.[8] Another finding was that managers who are attuned to cultural issues tended to prefer the localized approach, whereas managers less sensitive to cultural issues preferred a standardized approach. Bruce Steinberg, ad sales director for MTV Europe, has discovered that the people responsible for executing global campaigns locally can exhibit strong resistance to a global campaign. Steinberg sometimes has to visit as many as 20 marketing directors from the same company to get approval for a pan-European MTV ad.[9]

As Kanso correctly notes, the controversy over advertising approaches will probably continue for years to come. Localized and standardized advertising both have their place and both will continue to be used. Kanso's conclusion: What is needed for successful international advertising is a global commitment to local vision. In the final analysis, the decision of whether to use a global or localized campaign depends on recognition by managers of the trade-offs involved. On the one hand, a global campaign will result in the substantial benefits of cost savings, increased control, and the potential creative leverage of a global appeal. On the other hand, localized campaigns have the advantage of appeals that focus on the most important attributes of a product in each nation or culture. The question of when to use each approach depends on the product involved and a company's objectives in a particular market.

In Japan, for example, PepsiCo has achieved great success with a local campaign featuring "Pepsiman," a superhero action figure. Prior to 1996, the ads shown in Japan were the same global spots used throughout the rest of the world. However, in Japan's $24 billion soft-drink market, Pepsi trailed far behind Coca-Cola; Pepsi had a mere 3 percent market share compared with Coke's 30 percent share. The Pepsiman character was designed by local Japanese talent, but Industrial Light & Magic, the special-effects house owned by *Star Wars* creator George Lucas, was retained to give the TV spots a U.S.-style, high-tech edge. By breaking with its usual strategy of running global ads and increasing the ad budget by 50 percent over 1995, Pepsi's 1996 sales in Japan rose by 14 percent.[10]

McDonald's advertising has also enjoyed a surge of popularity in Japan, but for the opposite reason: McDonald's is including Japan in its global approach that invites con-

---

[7] "A Conversation with Nestlé's Pierre Liotard-Vogt," *Advertising Age,* 30 June 1980, p. 31.
[8] Ali Kanso, "International Advertising Strategies: Global Commitment to Local Vision," *Journal of Advertising Research* (January–February 1992): 10–14.
[9] Wells, "Selling to the World," p. A1.
[10] Yumiko Ono, "PepsiCo's Pitch in Japan Has New Twist," *The Wall Street Journal,* 23 May 1997, p. B10.

sumers to associate the restaurant with family members interacting in various situations. Starting in 1996, McDonald's campaign in Japan depicted various aspects of fatherhood. One spot showed a father and son bicycling home with burgers and fries; another showed a father driving a vanful of boisterous kids to McDonald's for milkshakes. The ads come at a time when many Japanese "salarymen" are reassessing the balance between work and family life. The campaign illustrates the use of localized global advertising; Japanese actors are used in the spots and local musicians composed music reminiscent of Japanese prime time TV shows.[11]

◆ SELECTING AN ADVERTISING AGENCY

Another global advertising issue companies face is whether to create ads in house, use an outside agency, or combine both strategies. For example, Chanel, Benetton, and Diesel rely on in-house marketing and advertising staffs for creative; Coca-Cola has its own agency, Edge Creative, but also uses the services of outside agencies such as Leo Burnett. When one or more outside agencies are used, they can serve product accounts on a multicountry or even global basis. It is possible to select a local agency in each national market or an agency with both domestic and overseas offices. In addition to Coca-Cola, Levi Strauss and Polaroid use local agencies. Today, however, there is a growing tendency for Western clients to designate global agencies for product accounts in order to support the integration of the marketing and advertising functions; Japan-based companies are less inclined to use this approach. Agencies are aware of this trend and are themselves pursuing international acquisitions and joint ventures to extend their geographic reach and their ability to serve clients on a global account basis. The 20 largest global advertising organizations ranked by 1998 gross income are shown in Table 14-4.

The organizations identified in Table 14-4 may include one or more core advertising agencies as well as units specializing in direct marketing, public relations, or research. The family tree of Adidas AG's advertising agency reflects the structure that is typical of agency ownership today: Leagas is owned by Abbott Mead Vickers/BBDO, which in turn is a unit of BBDO Worldwide, whose parent is the Omnicom Group. Also interesting to note is that the only three agencies to show declines were Japanese and that the declines were greater than 10 percent, the direct result of the Asian economic crisis. Total gross income in Japan fell 2.2 percent, 33.1 percent in Thailand, 33.9 percent in Malaysia, 39.1 percent in South Korea, and 68.1 percent in Indonesia.[12]

In selecting an advertising agency, the following issues should be considered:

- *Company organization.* Companies that are decentralized may want to leave the choice to the local subsidiary.
- *National responsiveness.* Is the global agency familiar with local culture and buying habits in a particular country, or should a local selection be made?
- *Area coverage.* Does the candidate agency cover all relevant markets?
- *Buyer perception.* What kind of brand image does the company want to project? If the product needs a strong local identification, it would be best to select a national agency.

It should be noted that advertising agencies in other countries may differ in their structure and strategies. In Japan, the advertising is much more concentrated than in the United States. There are two superagencies, Hakuhodo and Dentsu, while global agencies

---

[11] Yumiko Ono, "Japan Warms to McDonald's Doting Dad Ads," *The Wall Street Journal,* 8 May 1997, pp. B1, B12.

[12] R. Craig Endicott, "New York, NY, Once Again Is World's Leading Advertising Venue, as Its Agencies Generated $44.57 bil in 1998 Billings," *Advertising Age,* 19 April 1999, pp. 1+.

TABLE 14-4 World's Top 20 Advertising Organizations

Rank 1998	Ad Organization	Headquarters	Worldwide Gross Income 1998	% Change
1	Omnicom Group	New York	$4,812.0	12.0
2	Interpublic Group of Cos.	New York	4,304.5	13.1
3	WPP Group	London	4,156.8	14.9
4	Dentsu	Tokyo	1,786.0	−10.2
5	Young & Rubicam	New York	1,659.9	10.8
6	Havas Advertising	Paris	1,297.9	9.7
7	True North Communications	Chicago	1,242.3	3.1
8	Grey Advertising	New York	1,240.4	8.5
9	Leo Burnett Co.	Chicago	949.8	8.2
10	Publicis	New York	930.0	28.8
11	Snyder Communications	Bethesda, MD	904.2	29.1
12	MacManus Group	New York	859.2	2.0
13	Hakuhodo	Tokyo	734.8	−13.4
14	Saatchi & Saatchi	New York	682.1	7.5
15	Cordiant Communications Group	London	603.2	1.0
16	TMP Worldwide	New York	347.4	13.7
17	Asatsu-DK	Tokyo	343.4	−12.5
18	Carlson Marketing Group	Plymouth, MN	326.8	15.2
19	USWeb/CKS	Santa Clara	228.6	100.0
20	HA-Lo	Niles, IL	224.0	37.4

Source: Advertising Age, 19 April 1999.

only account for approximately 6 percent of billings. The Japanese place much more emphasis on media and it is not unusual for an agency to represent direct competitors.[13]

Despite an unmistakable trend toward using global agencies to support global marketing efforts, companies with geocentric orientations will adapt to the global market requirements and select the best agency or agencies accordingly. For example, Colgate recently acquired the Kolynos line of oral care products in Latin America; McCann-Erickson Worldwide will be responsible for that account even though Young & Rubicam has the bulk of Colgate's business elsewhere.[14] Western agencies still find markets such as South Korea and Japan very complex; similarly, Japanese and Korean agencies find it just as difficult to establish local agency presence in Western markets. Not surprisingly, as the Saturn unit of General Motors prepared for its 1997 entry into the Japanese market, it hired the Tokyo-based Dai-Ichi Kikaku as its agency.

◆ ADVERTISING APPEALS AND PRODUCT CHARACTERISTICS

Advertising must communicate appeals that are relevant and effective in the target market environment. Because products are frequently at different stages in their life cycle in various national markets, and because of the basic cultural, social, and economic differences that exist in markets, the most effective appeal for a product may vary from market to market. Yet, global marketers should attempt to identify situations in which

---

[13] George Fields, Hotaka Katahira, and Jerry Wind, *Leveraging Japan: Marketing to the New Asia* (1999) (manuscript).

[14] Sally Goll Beatty, "Young & Rubicam Is Only One for Colgate," *The Wall Street Journal,* 1 December 1995, p. B6.

(1) potential cost reductions exist because of the presence of economies of scale; (2) barriers to standardization such as cultural differences are not significant; and (3) products satisfy similar functional and emotional needs across different cultures.

Green, Cunningham, and Cunningham conducted a cross-cultural study to determine the extent to which consumers of different nationalities use the same criteria to evaluate two common consumer products: soft drinks and toothpaste. Their subjects were college students from the United States, France, India, and Brazil. Compared to France and India, the U.S. sample placed more emphasis on the subjective and less on functional product attributes, and the Brazilian sample appeared even more concerned with the subjective attributes than did the U.S. sample. The authors concluded that advertising messages should not use the same appeal for these countries if the advertiser is concerned with communicating the most important attributes of its product in each market.[15]

Effective advertising may also require developing different creative executions or presentations using a product's basic appeal or selling proposition as a point of departure. In other words, there can be differences between what one says and how one says it. If the creative execution in one key market is closely tied to a particular cultural attribute, the execution may have to be adapted to other markets. For example, the selling proposition for many products and services is fun or pleasure, and the creative presentation should show people having fun as appropriate for a country or culture.

Many Japanese advertisements puzzle foreign viewers. One commercial for Mita copies showed a building being demolished with only a mention of the brand name at the end. Tomatu Kishii, Dentsu senior creative director, notes "although it's not easy to find a connection between a copy machine and a building being demolished—since there is none—it is precisely this great disparity which, to the Japanese, imbues this commercial with impact and, to Westerners, makes it so difficult to appreciate."[16]

According to one recent survey, experienced advertising executives indicated that strong selling propositions can be transferred more than 50 percent of the time. An example of a selling proposal that transfers well is top quality. The promise of low price or of value for money regularly surmounts national barriers. In the same survey, most executives indicated that they did not believe that creative presentations traveled well. The obstacles are cultural barriers, communications barriers, legislative problems (for example, children cannot be used in France to merchandise products), competitive positions (the advertising strategy for a leading brand or product is normally quite different from that for a minor brand), and execution problems.

Food is the product category most likely to exhibit cultural sensitivity. Thus, marketers of food and food products must be alert to the need to localize their advertising. A good example of this is the recent effort by H. J. Heinz Company to develop the international market for ketchup. Heinz's strategy called for adapting both the product and advertising to target country tastes.[17] In Greece, for example, ads show ketchup pouring over pasta, eggs, and cuts of meat. In Japan, they instruct Japanese homemakers on using ketchup as an ingredient in Western-style food such as omelets, sausages, and pasta. Barry Tilley, London-based general manager of Heinz's Western Hemisphere trading division, says Heinz uses focus groups to determine what foreign consumers want in the way of taste and image. Americans like a relatively sweet ketchup, but Europeans prefer a spicier, more piquant variety. Significantly, Heinz's foreign marketing efforts are most successful when the company quickly adapts to local cultural preferences. In Sweden, the made-in-America theme is so muted in Heinz's ads that "Swedes don't realize Heinz is

15 Robert T. Green, William H. Cunningham, and Isabella C. M. Cunningham, "The Effectiveness of Standardized Global Advertising," *Journal of Advertising* (Summer 1975): 25–30.
16 *Nikkei Sangyo Shimbun,* 26 January 1999, p. 3.
17 Gary Levin, "Ads Going Global," *Advertising Age,* 22 July 1991, pp. 4, 42.

American. They think it is German because of the name," says Mr. Tilley. In contrast to this, American themes still work well in Germany. Kraft and Heinz are trying to outdo each other with ads featuring strong American images. In Heinz's latest TV ad, American football players in a restaurant become very angry when the 12 steaks they ordered arrive without ketchup. The ad ends happily, of course, with plenty of Heinz ketchup to go around.[18]

In general, the fewer the number of purchasers of a product, the less important advertising is as an element of the promotion mix. For example, successful marketing of expensive and technically complex industrial products generally requires a highly trained direct sales force. The more sophisticated and technically complicated an industrial product is, the more necessary this becomes. For such products, there is no point in letting national agencies duplicate each other's efforts. Advertising of industrial products—computers and telecommunications equipment, for example—does play an important role in setting the stage for the work of the sales force. A good advertising campaign can make it significantly easier for a salesperson to get in the door and, once inside, make the sale.

◆ CREATING ADVERTISING

ART DIRECTION

Art direction is concerned with visual presentation—the body language of print and broadcast advertising. Some forms of visual presentation are universally understood. Revlon, for example, has used a French producer to develop television commercials in English and Spanish for use in international markets. These commercials, which are filmed in Parisian settings, communicate the universal appeals and specific advantages of Revlon products. By producing its ads in France, Revlon obtains effective television commercials at a much lower price than it would have to pay for similar-length commercials produced in the United States. PepsiCo has used four basic commercials to communicate its advertising themes. The basic setting of young people having fun at a party or on a beach has been adapted to reflect the general physical environment and racial characteristics of North America, South America, Europe, Africa, and Asia. The music in these commercials has also been adapted to suit regional tastes, ranging from rock and roll in North America to bossa nova in Latin America to high life in Africa.

The international advertiser must make sure that visual executions are not inappropriately extended into markets. Benetton recently encountered a problem with its "United Colors of Benetton" campaign. The campaign appeared in 77 countries, primarily in print and on billboards. The art direction focused on striking, provocative interracial juxtapositions—a white hand and a black hand handcuffed together, for example. Another version of the campaign, depicting a black woman nursing a white baby, won advertising awards in France and Italy. However, because the image evoked the history of slavery in America, that particular creative execution was not used in the U.S. market.

COPY

Translating copy, or the written text of an advertisement, has been the subject of great debate in advertising circles. Copy should be relatively short and avoid slang or idioms. This is because other languages invariably take more space to convey the same message; thus, the increased use of pictures and illustrations. More and more European and Japanese advertisements are purely visual, conveying a specific message and invoking the company

---

[18] Gabriella Stern, "Heinz Aims to Export Taste for Ketchup," *The Wall Street Journal,* 20 November 1992, p. B1.

name.[19] Low literacy rates in many countries seriously compromise the use of print as a communications device and require greater creativity in the use of audio-oriented media.

It is important to recognize overlap in the use of languages in many areas of the world (e.g., the EU, Latin America, and North America). Capitalizing on this, global advertisers can realize economies of scale in producing advertising copy with the same language and message for these markets. Of course, the success of this approach will depend in part on avoiding unintended ambiguity in the ad copy. On the other hand, in some situations ad copy must be translated into the local language. Advertising slogans often present the most difficult translation problems. The challenge of encoding and decoding slogans and tag lines in different national and cultural contexts can lead to hilarious errors. For example, Kentucky Fried Chicken's "Finger-lickin' good" came out in Chinese as "eat your fingers off"; the Asian version of Pepsi's "Come Alive" copy line was rendered as a call to bring ancestors back from the grave.

Advertising executives may elect to prepare new copy for a foreign market in the language of the target country, or to translate the original copy into the target language. A third option is to leave some (or all) copy elements in the original (home-country) language. In choosing from among these alternatives, the advertiser must consider whether a translated message can be received and comprehended by the intended foreign audience. Anyone with a knowledge of foreign languages realizes that the ability to think in that language facilitates accurate communication. One must understand the connotations of words, phrases, and sentence structures, as well as their translated meaning, in order to be confident that a message will be understood correctly after it is received. The same principle applies to advertising, perhaps to an even greater degree. A copywriter who can think in the target language and understands the consumers in the target country will be able to create the most effective appeals, organize the ideas, and craft the specific language, especially if colloquialisms, idioms, and humor are involved. For example, in southern China, McDonald's is careful not to advertise prices with multiple occurrences of the number four. The reason is simple: In Cantonese, the pronunciation of the word *four* is similar to that of the word *death*.[20] In its efforts to develop a global brand image, Citicorp discovered that translations of its slogan "Citi Never Sleeps" conveyed the meaning that Citibank had a sleeping disorder such as insomnia. Company executives decided to retain the slogan but use English throughout the world.[21]

When formulating television and print advertising for use in high-income countries such as the United States, Canada, Japan, and the EU, the advertiser must recognize major style and content differences. Ads that strike viewers in some countries as irritating may not necessarily be perceived that way by viewers in other countries. American ads make frequent use of spokespersons and direct product comparisons and use logical arguments to try to appeal to the reason of audiences. Japanese advertising is more image oriented and appeals to audience sentiment. In Japan, what is most important frequently is not what is stated explicitly but, rather, what is implied. Nike's U.S. advertising is legendary for its irreverent, "in your face" style and relies heavily on celebrity sports endorsers such as Michael Jordan. In other parts of the world, where soccer is the top sport, some Nike ads are considered to be in poor taste and its pitchmen have less relevance. Nike has responded by adjusting its approach; notes Geoffrey Frost, director of global advertising, "We have to root ourselves in the passions of other countries. It's part of our growing up."[22]

[19] Vern Terpstra and Ravi Sarathy, *International Marketing* (Orlando, FL: The Dryden Press, 1991), p. 465.

[20] Jeanne Whalen, "McDonald's Cooks Worldwide Growth," *Advertising Age International* (July–August 1995): I4.

[21] Stephen E. Frank, "Citicorp's Big Account Is at Stake as It Seeks a Global Brand Name," *The Wall Street Journal,* 9 January 1997, p. B6.

[22] Roger Thurow, "Shtick Ball: In Global Drive, Nike Finds Its Brash Ways Don't Always Pay Off," *The Wall Street Journal,* 5 May 1997, p. A10.

♦ BOX 14-3 ♦

REGULATIONS OF TOBACCO ADVERTISING

CHINA

Effective October 31, 1994, the Chinese government banned all types of tobacco advertising. With a population of 1.2 billion people and having one out of every three smokers in the world, China is considered to be a massive potential market for cigarette manufacturers at a time when Western markets are shrinking. The ban—which prohibits advertising in the media and public places such as theaters and sporting events—was part of China's first Law of Advertisements. The law means that the green neon sign for R. J. Reynolds' (RJR's) Salem brand will be removed from the Shanghai airport, where freelance antismoking police are employed to collect fines from violators of the smoking ban.

CENTRAL AND EASTERN EUROPE

The recent flood of Western goods, from Mars candy bars and Winston cigarettes to Mercedes cars, has begun to cause some hard feelings in Russia. As one observer noted, hostility to Western advertising and sales goes back to the communist era, when the Soviets were afraid of being cheated in arms talks or trade agreements. Now that the Cold War is over, the animosity is manifesting itself at the consumer level. Advertising opponents are receiving help from the West: Late in 1993, TV spots advocating a ban on all types of cigarette advertising began appearing on most Russian channels. The ads were financed by Andrew Tobias, a Time columnist and financial guru, and Smoke-free Educational Services, a U.S. antismoking group.

A spokeswoman for RJR in Winston-Salem, North Carolina, said the company is simply fulfilling a need that was already there. The company was asked by the Russian government to help fill a demand after riots over a cigarette shortage several years ago. Still, many Russians believe Western tobacco companies spend heavily on ads in their country because they know there are enormous profits to be made from Russian smokers. As one Russian noted, "In most countries, tobacco advertising is banned. Is our health worth less than theirs? Please, President Yeltsin, put a stop to cigarette advertising."

There have been efforts in other countries such as Hungary and Romania to crack down on tobacco advertising with bans or partial bans, but the new laws tend to be so confusing and poorly enforced that marketers frequently ignore them. Nonetheless, some tobacco marketers have already prepared for growing restrictions on tobacco advertising by eliminating all mention of cigarettes and even the pack itself from their ads. As one example, Philip Morris's Marlboro ads are widely recognizable from just their red and white logo.

AUSTRALIA

In June 1994, the Philip Morris Company began legal action to overturn the Australian government's ban on cigarette advertising, contending that it infringes on the company's freedom of speech. Under legislation passed in 1992, tobacco advertising and sponsorship in Australia are being phased out and will be banned entirely by 1996,

CULTURAL CONSIDERATIONS

Knowledge of cultural diversity, especially the symbolism associated with cultural traits, is essential when creating advertising. Local country managers will be able to share important information, such as when to use caution in advertising creativity. Use of colors and man–woman relationships can often be stumbling blocks. For example, white in Asia is associated with death. In Japan, intimate scenes between men and women are considered to be in bad taste; they are outlawed in Saudi Arabia. Veteran adman John O'Toole offers the following insights to global advertisers:

> Transplanted American creative people always want to photograph European men kissing women's hands. But they seldom know that the nose must never touch the hand or that this rite is reserved solely for married women. And how do you know that the woman in the photograph is married? By the ring on her left hand, of course. Well, in Spain, Denmark, Holland, and Germany, Catholic women wear the wedding ring on the right hand.

except for international events such as Formula One racing. Philip Morris is trying to have the Commonwealth Tobacco Advertising Prohibition Act declared invalid. Vice president David Davies believes the act goes beyond preventing cigarette advertising and imposes a wide array of restrictions that infringe on basic rights. According to Davies, "The Philip Morris Australian subsidiary says the anti-tobacco laws breach the Australian Constitution's implied guarantee of freedom of communication, breaches the states and is beyond the powers of the federal Government."

EUROPEAN UNION

Portugal, Norway, and France have banned tobacco advertising altogether. However, print ads in France and Norway offer branded products such as Camel boots and Marlboro lighters. In the United Kingdom, voluntary restrictions have been in force since 1971; cigarette ads are barred from shop windows, TV, and movie theaters, but outside posters, billboards, and sponsorship of sporting events are allowed. In a 1997 speech, Queen Elizabeth called for a total ban. A Union-wide tobacco ad ban proposal was introduced in mid-1991 with the aim of fulfilling single-market rules of the Maastricht Treaty on European Union. Not surprisingly, the ban has been op-

posed by tobacco companies and advertising associations. The commission justified the ban, noting that various countries had or were considering restrictions on tobacco advertising and that there was a need for common rules on cross-border trade.

The hotly debated directive to ban tobacco advertising across the European Union (EU) is losing steam and was sent back to the negotiating table. Greece, a country that has opposed the ban, officially took over the EU presidency in January 1994 and set the agenda for the EU negotiations. A big campaign to save the tobacco directive is highly unlikely. EU members are coming to the conclusion that each country should handle the ban individually rather than blindly following the EU directive. For example, in January 1994, the Dutch prime minister pressed leaders at the Brussels European Council to withdraw the tobacco directive and allow countries to decide their own fates.

For R. J. Reynolds International, Philip Morris International, B.A.T., and other tobacco marketers, the receding threat of a pan-European ban on tobacco ads is welcome news. The industry spends between $600 million and $1 billion on advertising in the EU annually. An EU ban would have hurt them most in the countries where they compete with entrenched state tobacco monopolies, namely France, Italy, and Spain.

SOURCES: "Australia's Ad Ban Is Fought," *The New York Times,* 7 June 1994, p. 19; Marcus Brauchli, "China Passes Law in Move to Prohibit Ads for Tobacco," *The Wall Street Journal,* 31 October 1994, p. B10; Lili Cui, "Mass Media Boycott Tobacco Ads," *Beijing Review,* 6 June 1994, p. 8; Amy Haight, "EC Ad Ban May Go Up in Smoke," *Advertising Age,* 17 January 1994, p. 18; Steven Gutterman, "After the Russian Thaw, a New Big Chill to the West," *Advertising Age,* 24 January 1994, pp. 3, 44; "Tobacco Adverts: Fuming," *The Economist,* 5 February 1994, pp. 60–61.

When photographing a couple entering a restaurant or theater, you show the woman preceding the man, correct? No. Not in Germany and France. And this would be laughable in Japan. Having someone in a commercial hold up his hand with the back of it to you, the viewer, and the fingers moving toward him should communicate "come here." In Italy it means "good-bye."[23]

Tamotsu Kishii identified seven characteristics that distinguish Japanese from American creative strategy.

1. Indirect rather than direct forms of expression are preferred in the messages. This avoidance of directness in expression is pervasive in all types of communication among the Japanese, including their advertising. Many television ads do not mention what is desirable about the brand in use and let the audience judge for themselves.

---

[23] John O'Toole, *The Trouble with Advertising* (New York: Chelsea House, 1981), pp. 209–210.

2. There is often little relationship between ad content and the advertised product.
3. Only brief dialogue or narration is used in television commercials, with minimal explanatory content. In the Japanese culture, the more one talks, the less others will perceive him or her trustworthy or self-confident. A 30-second advertisement for young menswear shows five models in varying and seasonal attire, ending with a brief statement from the narrator: "Our life is a fashion show!"
4. Humor is used to create a bond of mutual feelings. Rather than slapstick, humorous dramatizations involve family members, neighbors, and office colleagues.
5. Famous celebrities appear as close acquaintances or everyday people.
6. Priority is placed on company trust rather than product quality. Japanese tend to believe that if the firm is large and has a good image, the quality of its products should also be outstanding.
7. The product name is impressed on the viewer with short, 15-second commercials.[24]

A recent survey of Japanese marketing and advertising executives identifies five primary approaches to advertising copy in Japan:

Connectors (30%)   Focuses on fostering personal bonds between the brand and consumer.

Product Pusher (19%)   Focuses on the product's strength. A short-term sales tactic.

Ubiquity Seeker (19%)   Desire to win awards and popular acclaim through integrated marketing activities.

Cut-Through (18%)   Use of celebrities, exaggerated product attributes and other memorable associations.

Entertainers (14%)   Feel that advertising should be entertaining or newsworthy.[25]

GLOBAL MEDIA CONSIDERATIONS

Marketers and their advertising agencies invest great amounts of time and money to develop the appropriate advertising appeals, but effective media must be selected to reach consumers with these advertising appeals. The creative task of developing appeals in turn should be informed by knowledge of the media channels that will be used to communicate the appeals.

Media Decisions

Although markets are becoming increasingly similar in industrial countries, media situations still vary to a great extent. The availability of television, newspapers, and other forms of electronic and print media varies around the world. The rapid increase of Internet users is also changing global advertising. This can have an impact on media decisions. Spending for on-line advertising by U.S. companies is expected to triple by 2004. This would place the spending ahead of advertising in the Yellow Pages and magazines and would rival advertising expenditures on radio.[26] For example, circulation figures of newspapers on a per capita basis cover a wide range. In Japan, where readership is high, there is one newspaper in circulation for every two people. There are approximately 65

---

[24] C. Anthony di Benedetto, Mariko Tamate, and Rajan Chandran, "Developing Creative Advertising Strategy for the Japanese Marketplace," *Journal of Advertising Research* (January/February 1992): 39–48. A number of recent studies have been devoted to comparing ad content in different parts of the world, including Mary C. Gilly, "Sex Roles in Advertising: A Comparison of Television Advertisements in Australia, Mexico, and the United States," *Journal of Marketing* (April 1988): 75–85; Marc G. Weinberger and Harlan E. Spotts, "A Situation View of Information Content in TV Advertising in the U.S. and U. K.," *Journal of Advertising*, 53 (January 1989): 89–94.

[25] Fields, Katahira, and Wind, *Leveraging Japan: Marketing to the New Asia.*

[26] Youchi Dreazen, "Net Is Expected to Rival Radio in Ad Spending by 2004," *The Wall Street Journal*, 12 August 1999, p. B12.

million newspapers in daily circulation in the United States, a per capita ratio of approximately one to four. The ratio is one paper to 10 to 20 people in Latin America and one to 200 persons in Nigeria and Sweden.

Even when media availability is high, its use as an advertising vehicle may be limited. For example, in Europe, television advertising either does not exist or is very limited, as in Denmark, Sweden, and Norway. The time allowed for advertising each day varies from 12 minutes in Finland to 80 in Italy, with 12 minutes per hour per channel allowed in France and 20 in Switzerland, Germany, and Austria. Regulations concerning content of commercials vary, and there are waiting periods of up to two years in several countries before an advertiser can obtain broadcast time. In Germany, advertising time slots are reserved and paid for one year in advance.

In Saudi Arabia, where all advertising is subject to censorship, regulations prohibit a long list of subject matter, including the following:

- Advertisements of horoscope or fortune-telling books, publications, or magazines are prohibited.
- Advertisements that frighten or disturb children are to be avoided.
- Use of preludes to advertisements that appear to indicate a news item or official statement is to be avoided.
- Use of comparative advertising claims is prohibited.
- Noncensored films cannot be advertised.
- Women may appear only in those commercials that relate to family affairs, and their appearance must be in a decent manner that ensures their feminine dignity.
- Female children under 6 years of age may appear in commercials provided that their roles are limited to a childhood-like activity.
- Women should wear a long, suitable dress that fully covers their body except face and palms. Sweatsuits or similar garments are not allowed.[27]

Media Vehicles and Expenditures

As with all marketing decisions, advertisers must choose between global or local media vehicles. Global media consist primarily of cable television such as MTV, ITN, and CNN, which are rapidly expanding, and regional editions of publications. An exploding new global advertising medium is the World Wide Web. Any company, organization, or individual can plant a flag on the Net, and if they are willing to create their Web site, they have established a global presence!

Local media vehicles vary by country and consist of television, radio, newspapers, transit, and outdoor. Table 14-5 shows a historical analysis of spending by medium in Japan. It shows that newspaper advertising expenditures have decreased by 10 percentage points while the direct marketing/outdoor/other category has increased by 11 percentage points, thus indicating that the media mix in each country warrants constant monitoring. By contrast, media spending in the EU in 1996 was newspapers, 39.3 percent; television, 31.2 percent; magazines, 18.8 percent; radio, 4.2 percent; outdoor, 5.1 percent; and cinema, 0.7 percent.[28] In Table 14-6, media spending in Japan is compared to media spending in the United Kingdom.

As might be expected, the largest per capita advertising expenditures occurred mostly in the highly developed countries of the world. The lowest per capita expenditures were in the less developed countries. The high-income countries spend roughly from 1.5 to 2.5 percent of their gross national product (GNP) on advertising. In the low-income

---

[27] National Trade Data Bank: The Export Connection, USDOC, International Trade Administration, Market Research Reports (October 2, 1992). See also Mushtag Luqmani, Ugur Yavas, and Zahir Quraeshi, "Advertising in Saudi Arabia: Content and Regulation," *International Marketing Review* 6, no. 1 (1989): 59–72.
[28] Advertising Association, "Survey of European Advertising Expenditures 1980–1996" (February 1998): 115.

Year	Newspaper %	Magazine %	Radio %	TV %	DM/Outdoor/ Others %	Export Ad %	Total %
TABLE 14-5 Historical Spending by Media in Japan (1976–1997)							
1976	31.2	5.6	4.8	36.0	23.4	2.3	100.0
1977	30.8	5.3	4.9	36.5	21.4	1.8	100.0
1978	30.9	5.2	4.9	36.7	21.6	1.8	100.0
1979	31.0	6.3	5.0	36.5	21.8	2.0	100.0
1980	32.1	6.6	5.2	34.0	21.0	2.6	100.0
1981	30.7	5.9	6.1	34.0	21.8	2.0	100.0
1982	30.2	5.2	6.1	34.5	21.8	2.5	100.0
1983	30.1	8.8	6.1	34.6	21.7	3.3	100.0
1984	30.0	6.4	6.1	35.4	21.8	2.5	100.0
1985	25.3	6.4	4.6	30.9	33.3	0.1	100.0
1986	25.1	6.6	4.5	29.9	33.9	0.1	100.0
1987	25.0	6.5	4.4	29.7	34.1	0.2	100.0
1988	25.6	6.7	4.3	29.8	33.5	0.2	100.0
1989	26.1	8.6	4.1	28.8	35.3	0.2	100.0
1990	24.4	8.7	4.2	28.8	35.6	0.2	100.0
1991	23.5	8.8	4.7	23.3	36.0	0.2	100.0
1992	22.3	6.7	4.3	30.3	36.2	0.2	100.0
1993	21.6	6.7	4.1	31.0	38.4	0.2	100.0
1994	21.7	6.7	3.9	31.0	35.6	0.3	100.0
1995	21.5	6.9	3.8	32.3	35.2	0.3	100.0
1996	21.6	7.0	3.8	33.1	34.2	0.3	100.0
1997	21.1	7.3	3.8	33.5	34.0	0.3	100.0

Source: George Fields, Hotaka Katahira, and Jerry Wind, *Leveraging Japan* (San Francisco: Jossey-Bass, 2000).

TABLE 14-6 Media Spending in Japan Versus United Kingdom

	% 1996	
	Japan	**United Kingdom**
Television	33%	36%
Newspapers	22%	38%
Magazines	7%	17%
Radio	4%	4%
Outdoor[a]	34%	5%
	100%	100%

[a] Includes direct mail and other in Japan only.

countries, expenditures range from less than 0.5 percent to 1 percent. The United States is by far the largest consumer of advertising in the world.

A key issue in advertising is that of which of the measured media—print, broadcast, transit, and so forth—to utilize. Print advertising continues to be the number one advertising vehicle in most countries. However, spending on print media in the United States has been declining. The use of newspapers for print advertising is so varied around the world as to almost defy description. In Mexico, an advertiser that can pay for a full-page ad may get the front page, whereas in India, paper shortages may require booking an ad six months in advance.

In some countries, especially those where the electronic media are government owned, television and radio stations can broadcast only a restricted number of advertising messages. In Saudi Arabia, no commercial television advertising was allowed prior to 1986; currently, ad content and visual presentation are restricted. In such countries, the proportion of advertising funds allocated to print is extremely high. In 1995, Russia's national Channel 1 banned all commercial advertising; the ban was subsequently lifted.

As ownership of television sets increases in other areas of the world, such as Southeast Asia, television advertising will become more important as a communication vehicle.

Worldwide, radio continues to be a less important advertising medium than print and television. As a proportion of total measured media advertising expenditures, radio trails considerably behind print, television, and direct advertising. However, in countries where advertising budgets are limited, radio's enormous reach can provide a cost-effective means of communicating with a large consumer market. Also, radio can be effective in countries where literacy rates are low. Radio accounted for more than 20 percent of the total measured media in only two countries, which were both less developed countries.

As countries add mass-transportation systems and build and improve their highway infrastructures, advertisers are utilizing more indoor and outdoor posters and billboards to reach the buying public. Transit advertising was recently introduced in Russia, where drab streetcars and buses have been emblazoned with the bright colors of Western brands.

Another issue facing advertising agencies is whether they will be compensated on a flat rate or on performance basis. In using the Internet, rates are either based on a flat rate per 1,000 banner ads or by the number of people who actually click onto a site. Tracking performance in the various markets around the world will not be easy, but major advertisers are pressing for it in the United States.

THE MILLENNIUM

What will advertising look like in this millennium? The advertising agency of the future will be very different. The major differences will be the increasing use of computers for all functional areas of the agency and in all markets. Computers will be the source of more timely market research, creatives who live in different countries will be able to work together on the same campaign. And as a global advertising medium, the number of Internet users around the world will increase. Agencies will have alliances around the world as advertising becomes more global and as consumers simultaneously become more global and more individualistic at the same time. There will be an increasing integretion of marketing analysis and strategy and creativity as the old divisions between marketing consulting and creative agencies give way to a new integration of these activities.

Summary ▪▪▪

Marketing communications—the promotion P of the marketing mix—includes advertising, public relations, sales promotion, and personal selling. Although marketers may identify opportunities for global advertising campaigns, local adaptation or distinct local campaigns may also be required. A powerful reason to try to create a global campaign is that the process forces a company to attempt to identify a global market for its product. In addition, the identification of global appeals and benefits forces a company to probe deeply to identify basic needs and buying motives. When creating advertising, care must be taken to ensure that the art direction and copy are appropriate for the intended audiences in target countries. Advertisers may place a single global agency in charge of worldwide advertising; it is also possible to use one or more agencies on a regional or local basis. Advertising intensity varies from country to country. The United States, for example, accounts for less than 25 percent of gross world product but almost 50 percent of world advertising expenditures. Media availability varies considerably from country to country. Television is the leading medium in many markets, but its availability for advertising is severely restricted or nonexistent in others.

Discussion Questions ■

1. In what ways can global brands and global advertising campaigns benefit a company?
2. How does the standardized-versus-localized debate apply to advertising?
3. When creating advertising for world markets, what issues must art directors and copywriters take into account?
4. How do the media options available to advertisers vary in different parts of the world? What can advertisers do to cope with media limitations in certain countries?

Suggested Readings ■

Alden, Dana L., Wayne D. Hoyer, and Chol Lee. "Identifying Global and Culture-Specific Dimensions of Humor in Advertising: A Multinational Analysis," *Journal of Marketing,* 57, no. 2 (April 1993): 64–75.

Andrews, J. Craig, Srinivas Durvasula, and Richard G. Netemeyer. "Testing the Cross-National Applicability of U.S. and Russian Advertising." *Journal of Advertising,* 23 (March 1994): 71–82.

Banerjee, Anish. "Transnational Advertising Development and Management: An Account Planning Approach and Process Framework." *International Journal of Advertising,* 13 (1994): 95–124.

Birch, Dawn, and Janelle McPhail. "Does Accent Matter in International Television Advertisements?" *International Journal of Advertising,* 18 (May 1999): 251+.

Duncan, Thomas R., and Stephen E. Everett. "Client Perception of Integrated Marketing Communications." *Journal of Advertising Research* (May/June 1993): 119–122.

Hanni, David A., John K. Rynas Jr., and Ivan R. Vernon. "Coordinating International Advertising—The Goodyear Case Revisited for Latin America." *Journal of International Marketing,* 3, no. 2 (1995): 83–98.

Harris, Greg. "International Advertising Standardization: What Do the Multinationals Actually Standardize?" *Journal of International Marketing,* 2, no. 4 (1994): 13–30.

Hiebert, Ray E. "Advertising and Public Relations in Transition from Communism: The Case of Hungary, 1989–1994." *Public Relations Review,* 20, no. 4 (Winter 1994): 357–372.

Hill, John S., and Alan T. Shao. "Agency Participants in Multicountry Advertising: A Preliminary Examination of Affiliate Characteristics and Environments." *Journal of International Marketing,* 2, no. 2 (1994): 29–48.

Johansson, Johny K. "The Sense of 'Nonsense': Japanese TV Advertising." *Journal of Advertising,* 23, no. 1 (March 1994): 17–26.

Leong, Siew Meng, Sween Hoon Ang, and Leng Lai Tham. "Increasing Brand Name Recall in Print Advertising among Asians." *Journal of Advertising,* 25, no. 2 (1996): 65–81.

Leslie, D. A. "Global Scan: The Globalization of Advertising Agencies, Concepts, and Campaigns." *Economic Geography,* 71, no. 4 (October 1995): 402–426.

Lewis, Herschell Gordon and Carol Nelson, *Advertising Age Handbook of Advertising* (Chicago: NTC Business Books, 1998), p. 200.

Lohtia, Ritu, Wesley J. Johnston, and Linda Aab. "Creating an Effective Print Advertisement for the China Market: Analysis and Advice." *Journal of Global Marketing,* 8, no. 2 (1994): 7–30.

Luqmani, Mushtag, Ugur Yavas, and Zahir Quraeshi. "Advertising in Saudi Arabia: Content and Regulation." *International Marketing Review,* 6, no. 1 (1989): 59–72.

McCullough, W. R. "Global Advertising Which Acts Local: The IBM Subtitles Campaign." *Journal of Advertising Research,* 36, no. 3 (1996): 11–15.

Mooij, Marieke K. De. *Advertising Worldwide: Concepts, Theories, and Practice of International, Multinational and Global Advertising,* 2nd ed. Upper Saddle River, NJ: Prentice Hall, 1994.

Mueller, Barbara. *International Advertising: Communicating Across Cultures.* Belmont, CA: Wadsworth Publishing Company, 1995.

Mueller, Barbara. "Standardization vs. Specialization: An Examination of Westernization in Japanese Advertising." *Journal of Advertising Research* (1991): 7–18.

Murphy, David. "Cross-Border Conflicts" *Marketing,* 11 February 1999, pp. 30–33.

Parameswaran, Ravi, and R. Mohan Pisharodi. "Facets of Country of Origin Image: An Empirical Assessment." *Journal of Advertising,* 23, no. 1 (March 1994): 43–56.

Roth, Martin S. "Depth versus Breadth Strategies for Global Brand Image Management." *Journal of Advertising,* 21, no. 2 (June 1992): 25–36.

Sanford, Douglas M. and Lynda Maddox, "Advertising Agency Management of Domestic and International Accounts," *International Marketing Review,* 16, no. 6 (1999).

Tansey, Richard, and Michael R. Hyman. "Dependency Theory and the Effects of Advertising by Foreign-Based Multinational Corporations in Latin America." *Journal of Advertising,* 23, no. 1 (March 1994): 27–42.

Taylor, Charles R., R. Dale Wilson, and Gordon E. Miracle. "The Effect of Brand Differentiating Messages on the Effectiveness of Korean Advertising." *Journal of International Marketing,* 2, no. 4 (1994): 31–52.

Wells, Ludmilla Gricenko. "Western Concepts, Russian Perspectives: Meanings of Advertising in the Former Soviet Union." *Journal of Advertising,* 23, no. 1 (March 1994): 83–95.

Zandpour, Fred. "Global Reach and Local Touch: Achieving Cultural Fitness in TV Advertising." *Journal of Advertising Research,* 34, no. 5 (September/October 1994): 35–63.

Zhou, Nan, and Russell W. Belk. "China's Advertising and the Export Marketing Curve: The First Decade." *Journal of Advertising Research,* 33, no. 6 (November–December 1993): 50–66.

CHAPTER 15

Global Promotion

Public Relations, Personal Selling, Sales Promotion, Direct Marketing, Trade Shows, and Sponsorship

Ideally, advertising aims at the goal of a programmed harmony among all human impulses and aspirations and endeavors. Using handicraft methods, it stretches out toward the ultimate electronic goal of a collective consciousness.
—MARSHALL McLUHAN, 1911–1980
Canadian communications theorist

CONTENTS

In Chapter 14 we focused on advertising, one of the forms of communication available to marketers. In this chapter, we focus on global promotion, which includes public relations (sometimes known as marketing publicity), personal selling, sales promotion, direct marketing, trade shows, and sponsorship.

◆ PUBLIC RELATIONS AND PUBLICITY

A company's public relations (PR) effort should foster goodwill and understanding among constituents both inside and outside the company. PR practitioners attempt to generate favorable publicity, which, by definition, is a nonpaid form of communication. (In the PR world, publicity is sometimes referred to as earned media, whereas advertising and promotions are known as unearned media.) PR personnel also play a key role in responding to unflattering media reports or controversies that arise because of company activities in different parts of the globe. In such instances, PR's job is to make sure that the company responds promptly and gets its side of the story told. The basic tools of PR include news releases, newsletters, press conferences, tours of plants and other company facilities, articles in trade or professional journals, company publications and brochures, TV and radio talk show appearances by company personnel, special events, and homepages on the Internet. As noted earlier, a company exerts complete control over the content of its advertising and pays for message placement in the media. However, the media typically receive far more press releases and other PR materials than they can use. Generally speaking, a company has little control over when, or if, a news story runs. The company cannot directly control the "spin," slant, or tone of the story. In addition to the examples discussed later, Table 15-1 summarizes several recent instances of global publicity involving well-known firms.

Indeed, even in the field of PR itself, there are often great differences between the theory and the practice. One specific area of discourse is the notion of PR as a "two-way symmetrical model" of communication that should occur between equal entities. This model holds that public relations efforts should be oriented toward social responsibility and problem solving and be characterized by dialogue and harmonization of interests. As such, the symmetrical model takes PR beyond an advocacy role that benefits the organization. A similar model developed in Austria known as "consensus-oriented public relations" supports the view that two-way symmetrical communication is more desirable and successful than asymmetrical PR. The two-way and consensus models are presumed to be especially effective in situations with a potential for conflict between differing parties. The issues pertaining to planning a hazardous waste landfill would be one example. However, as one expert has noted, implementation of these models remains problematic.[1]

PepsiCo made good use of integrated marketing communications when it undertook an ambitious global program to revamp the packaging of its flagship cola. To raise awareness of its new blue can, Pepsi leased a Concorde jet and painted it in the new blue color. Pepsi also garnered some "free ink" by spending $5 million to film an ad with two Russian cosmonauts holding a giant replica of the new can while orbiting the earth in the Mir space station. As Massimo d'Amore, PepsiCo's head of international marketing, told reporters, "Space is the ultimate frontier of global marketing. The cola wars have been fought all over the place, and it's time to take them to space." It remains to be seen whether this effort will pay off in terms of increased brand loyalty.

IBM spent about $5 million to stage a rematch of a 1996 chess game between Gary Kaparov and a computer called Deep Blue. The match, which took place in New York

TABLE 15-1 Examples of Global Publicity	
Company/Brand (Home Country)	***Nature of Publicity***
Bruno Magli (Italy)	Markets shoes allegedly worn by O. J. Simpson on the night Nicole Simpson was murdered; widespread attention in newsreels and print media estimated to be worth $100 million. Shoe sales increased 50 percent during trial.
Nike (United States)	Victims of Heaven's Gate suicide cult wore Nikes when they died.
Mitsubishi (Japan)	Charges of sexual harassment at a plant in Illinois received widespread media coverage.
McDonald's (United States)	Plaintiff in the longest civil trial in British history. McDonald's charged two vegetarian activists with libel after the two distributed pamphlets calling McDonald's a "multinational menace" that abused animals and workers. The defendants gained worldwide publicity for their cause.

[1] Karl Nessman, "Public Relations in Europe: A Comparison with the United States," *Public Relations Journal,* 21, no. 2 (Summer 1995): 155–158.

City, was hailed as one of the best publicity stunts in recent years. To build visibility and interest, IBM purchased full-page newspaper ads, sent out numerous press releases, established an Internet site, and purchased bus posters in Manhattan. The effort was a textbook study in integrated marketing communications; the match was widely covered by the world media. As Peter Harleman of Landor Associates, a corporate-identity firm, told *The Wall Street Journal,* "Money almost can't buy the advertising [IBM] is getting out of this." John Lister, of the Lister Butler brand identity consulting firm, agreed. "They're doing a tremendous job of leveraging the brand in this. Not only do they have the IBM name attached to virtually every news report about it, but they even branded their computer the corporate color, blue." Industry experts estimate that the match generated about $100 million in favorable earned media. IBM's Internet site provided live coverage and generated a million visits during a single match, a number which was believed to be a record for the World Wide Web at that time. The publicity was especially gratifying to IBM officials because its problems with its much-ballyhooed information system at the 1996 Olympics resulted in a great deal of negative news coverage.[2]

Sometimes publicity is generated when a company simply goes about the business of global marketing activities. Nike and other marketers have received a great deal of negative publicity regarding alleged sweatshop conditions in factories run by subcontractors. To date, Nike's public relations team has not done an effective job of counteracting the criticism by effectively communicating the positive economic impact Nike has had on the nations where its sneakers are manufactured. Volkswagen received a great deal of press coverage over a period of several months after its newly hired operations chief was accused of industrial espionage.

The ultimate test of an organization's understanding of the power and importance of public relations occurs during a time of environmental turbulence, especially a potential or actual crisis. When disaster strikes, a company or industry often finds itself thrust into the spotlight. A company's swift and effective handling of communications during such times can have significant implications. The best response is to be forthright and direct, reassuring the public and providing the media with accurate information.

Any company that is increasing its activities outside the home country can utilize PR personnel as boundary spanners between its stakeholders: the company and employees, unions, stockholders, customers, the media, financial analysts, governments, and suppliers. Many companies have their own in-house PR staff. Companies may choose to engage the services of an outside PR firm. Some PR firms are associated with advertising organizations; for example, Burston-Marsteller is a PR unit of Young & Rubicam, while Fleishman-Hillard is affiliated with D'Arcy Masius Benton & Bowles. Other PR firms, including the London-based Shandwick PLC and Edelman Public Relations Worldwide and Canada's Hill & Knowlton, are independent. Several independent PR firms in the United Kingdom, Germany, Italy, Spain, Austria, and the Netherlands have joined together in a network known as Globalink. The purpose of the network is to provide members with various forms of assistance such as press contacts, event planning, literature design, and suggestions for tailoring global campaigns to local needs in a particular country or region.[3]

THE GROWING ROLE OF PUBLIC RELATIONS IN GLOBAL MARKETING COMMUNICATIONS

Public relations professionals with international responsibility must go beyond media relations and serve as more than a company mouthpiece; they are called on to simulta-

---

[2] Bart Ziegler, "Checkmate! Deep Blue Is IBM Publicity Coup," *The Wall Street Journal,* 9 May 1997, p. B1.
[3] Joe Mullich, "European Firms Seek Alliances for Global PR," *Business Marketing,* 79 (August 1994): 4, 31.

neously build consensus and understanding, create trust and harmony, articulate and influence public opinion, anticipate conflicts, and resolve disputes.[4] As companies become more involved in global marketing and the globalization of industries continues, it is important that company management recognize the value of international public relations. One recent study found that, internationally, PR expenditures are growing an average of 20 percent annually. Fueled by soaring foreign investment, industry privatization, and a boom in initial public offerings (IPOs), PR expenditures in India are reported to be growing by 200 percent annually.

The number of international PR associations is growing as well. The new Austrian Public Relations Association is a case in point; many European PR trade associations are part of the Confédération Européenne des Relations Publiques and the International Public Relations Association. Another factor fueling the growth of international PR is increased governmental relations between countries. Governments and organizations are dealing with broad-based issues of mutual concern such as the environment and world peace. Finally, the technology-driven communication revolution that has ushered in the information age makes public relations a profession with truly global reach. Faxes, satellites, high-speed modems, and the Internet allow PR professionals to be in contact with media virtually anywhere in the world.

In spite of these technological advances, PR professionals must still build good personal working relationships with journalists and other media representatives as well as leaders of other primary constituencies. Therefore, strong interpersonal skills are needed. One of the most basic concepts of the practice of public relations is to know the audience. For the global PR practitioner, this means knowing the audiences in both the home country and the host country or countries. Specific skills needed include the ability to communicate in the language of the host country and familiarity with local customs. Obviously, a PR professional who is unable to speak the language of the host country will be unable to communicate directly with a huge portion of an essential audience. Likewise, the PR professional working outside the home country must be sensitive to nonverbal communication issues in order to maintain good working relationships with host-country nationals. Commenting on the complexity of the international PR professional's job, one expert notes that, in general, audiences are "increasingly more unfamiliar and more hostile, as well more organized and powerful . . . more demanding, more skeptical, and more diverse." International PR practitioners can play an important role as "bridges over the shrinking chasm of the global village."[5]

HOW PUBLIC RELATIONS PRACTICES DIFFER AROUND THE WORLD

Public relations practices in specific countries can be affected by cultural traditions, social and political contexts, and economic environments. As noted earlier, the mass media and the written word are important vehicles for information dissemination in many industrialized countries. In developing countries, however, the best way to communicate might be through the gongman, the town crier, the market square, or the chief's courts. In Ghana, dance, songs, and storytelling are important communication channels. In India, where half of the population cannot read, writing press releases will not be the most effective way to communicate.[6] In Turkey, the practice of PR is thriving in spite of that country's reputation for harsh treatment of political prisoners. Although the Turkish government

---

[4] Nessmann, "Public Relations in Europe," 151–160.

[5] Larissa A. Grunig, "Strategic Public Relations Constituencies on a Global Scale," *Public Relations Review,* 18, no. 2 (Summer 1992): 130.

[6] Carl Botan, "International Public Relations: Critique and Reformulation," *Public Relations Review,* 18, no. 2 (Summer 1992): 150–151.

still asserts absolute control as it has for generations, corporate PR and journalism are allowed to flourish so that Turkish organizations can compete globally.

Even in industrialized countries, there are some important differences between PR practices. In the United States, much of the news in a small, local newspaper is placed by means of the hometown news release. In Canada, on the other hand, large metropolitan population centers have combined with Canadian economic and climatic conditions to thwart the emergence of a local press. The dearth of small newspapers means that the practice of sending out hometown news releases is almost nonexistent.[7] In the United States, PR is increasingly viewed as a separate management function. In Europe, that perspective has not been widely accepted; PR professionals are viewed as part of the marketing function rather than distinct and separate specialists in a company. In Europe, fewer colleges and universities offer courses and degree programs in public relations than in the United States. Also, European coursework in PR is more theoretical; in the United States, PR programs are often part of mass communication or journalism schools and there is more emphasis on practical job skills.

A company that is ethnocentric in its approach to PR will extend home-country PR activities into host countries. The rationale behind this approach is that people everywhere are motivated and persuaded in much the same manner. Obviously, this approach does not take cultural considerations into account. A company adopting a polycentric approach to PR gives the host-country practitioner more leeway to incorporate local customs and practices into the PR effort. Although such an approach has the advantage of local responsiveness, the lack of global communication and coordination can lead to a PR disaster.[8]

In 1994, computer chip maker Intel showed a poor understanding of public relations basics after a college professor discovered a technical defect in the company's flagship Pentium chip. The professor, Thomas Nicely, contacted Intel and asked for a replacement chip, but his request was refused. Intel acknowledged that Pentium had a flaw but insisted it would cause a computing error only once in 27,000 years. Having received no satisfaction from the semiconductor giant—Intel commands an 80 percent share of the global semiconductor market—Nicely posted his complaint on the Internet. Word about the Pentium flaw and Intel's response spread quickly. Intel chief executive officer (CEO) Andrew Grove added fuel to the fire when he issued an apology via the Internet. Grove said, "No chip is ever perfect," and offered to replace defective chips if customers could prove they used computers to perform complicated mathematical calculations. Grove's lack of humility, coupled with revelations that the chip maker itself had been aware of the Pentium flaw for months, only worsened the public's perception of the company. After weeks of negative publicity around the world, Intel finally announced that new Pentium chips would be available to anyone who requested them. The furor eventually died down without permanent damage to Intel's reputation.[9]

◆ PERSONAL SELLING

Personal selling is two-way, personal communication between a company representative and a potential customer as well as back to the company. The salesperson's job is to correctly understand the buyer's needs, match those needs to the company's product(s), and then persuade the customer to buy. Effective personal selling in a salesperson's home country requires building a relationship with the customer; global marketing presents additional challenges because the buyer and seller may come from different national or cultural backgrounds. It is difficult to overstate the importance of a face-to-face, personal

---

[7] Malvin L. Sharpe, "The Impact of Social and Cultural Conditioning on Global Public Relations," *Public Relations Review,* 18, no. 2 (Summer 1992): 104–105.
[8] Botan, "International Public Relations," p. 155.
[9] Andrew S. Grove, *Only The Paranoid Survive* (New York: Bantam Doubleday Dell Publishing Group, 1996).

selling effort for industrial products in global markets. In 1993, a Malaysian developer, YTL Corp, sought bids on a $700 million contract for power-generation turbines. Siemens AG of Germany and General Electric (GE) were among the bidders. Datuk Francis Yeoh, managing director of YTL, requested meetings with top executives from both companies. "I wanted to look them in the eye to see if we can do business," Yeoh said. Siemens complied with the request; GE did not send an executive. Siemens was awarded the contract.[10]

The selling process is typically divided into several stages: prospecting, preapproaching, approaching, presenting, problem solving, handling objections, closing the sale, and following up. The relative importance of each stage can vary by country or region. Experienced American sales reps know that persistence is one tactic often required to win an order in the United States; however, persistence in the United States often means tenacity, as in "don't take 'no' for an answer." Persistence is also required if a global industrial marketing effort is to succeed; in some countries, however, persistence often means endurance, a willingness to patiently invest months or years before the effort results in an actual sale. For example, a company wishing to enter the Japanese market must be prepared for negotiations to take from 3 to 10 years.

Prospecting is the process of identifying potential purchasers and assessing their probability of purchase. If Ford wanted to sell vans in another country where they would be used as delivery vehicles, which businesses would need delivery vehicles? Which businesses have the financial resources to purchase such a van? Those businesses that match these two needs are better prospects than those who do not. Successful prospecting requires problem-solving techniques, which involve understanding and matching the customer's needs and the company's products in developing a sales presentation.

The purpose of the preapproach or problem solving stage is to gather information on a prospective customer's problem areas and tailor a presentation that demonstrates how the company's product can solve these specific problems. If a potential customer has a grocery business, their needs in a van would be different from a customer who owns a carpentry business. The sales representative would need to select the best models of Ford vans, collect the appropriate model specifications, and so on to prepare for an effective presentation.

The next two steps, the approach and the presentation, involve one or more meetings between seller and buyer. In global selling, it is absolutely essential for the salesperson to understand cultural norms and proper protocol. In some countries, the approach is drawn out as the buyer gets to know or takes the measure of the salesperson on a personal level with no mention of the pending deal. In such instances, the presentation comes only after rapport has been firmly established.

During the presentation, the salesperson must deal with objections. Objections may be of a business or personal nature. A common theme in sales training is the notion of active listening; naturally, in cross cultural selling, verbal and nonverbal communication barriers present special challenges for the salesperson. When objections are successfully overcome, the salesperson moves on to the close and asks for the order. A successful sale does not end there, however; the final step of the selling process involves following up with the customer to ensure his or her ongoing satisfaction with the purchase. For a description of a salesperson's experience see "Marketing an Industrial Product in Latin America" in Chapter 3.

◆ SALES PROMOTION

Sales promotion refers to any consumer or trade program of limited duration that adds tangible value to a product or brand. Sales promotion laws and usage vary around the world but may consist of any of the following: promotional pricing tactics, contests,

---

[10] Marcus W. Brauchli, "Looking East: Asia, on the Ascent, Is Learning to Say No to 'Arrogant' West," *The Wall Street Journal,* 13 April 1994, pp. A1, A8.

sweepstakes and games, premium and specialties, dealer loaders, merchandising materials, tie-ins and cross-promotions, packaging, trade shows (also known as exhibitions), and sponsorship. The EU, however, is working to harmonize promotional tactics across its member countries. It is considering "mutual recognition" that would allow a company to carry out promotional activities in another country as long as that tactic is legal in the company's home country. The tangible value created by the promotion may come in various forms, such as a price reduction or a "buy one, get one free" offer. The purpose of a sales promotion may be to stimulate customers to sample a product or to increase consumer demand. Trade promotions are designed to increase product availability in distribution channels.

The increasing popularity of sales promotion as a marketing communication tool outside the United States can be explained in terms of several strengths and advantages. Besides providing a tangible incentive to buyers, sales promotion also reduces the perceived risk buyers may associate with purchasing the product. From the point of view of the company, sales promotion provides accountability; the manager in charge of the promotion can immediately track the results of the promotion. Moreover, some consumer sales promotions, including sweepstakes and rebates, require buyers to fill out a form and mail it to the company. This allows a company to build up information in its database, which it can use when communicating with customers in the future.

Many international managers have learned about American-style promotion strategies and tactics by attending seminars such as those offered by the Promotional Marketing Association of America (PMAA). Sometimes, adaptation to country-specific conditions is required; for example, TV ads in France cannot have movie tie-ins. Ads must be designed to focus on the promotion rather than the movie. According to Joseph Potacki, who teaches a Basics of Promotion seminar for the PMAA, the biggest difference between promotion in the United States and in other countries pertains to couponing. In the United States, couponing accounts for 70 percent of consumer promotion spending. That percentage is much lower outside the United States. According to Potacki, "It is far less—or nonexistent—in most other countries simply because the cultures don't accept couponing." Potacki notes that couponing is gaining importance in countries such as the United Kingdom as retailers learn more about couponing.[11]

Despite efforts to harmonize regulations, sales promotion within the EU is still quite diverse, as shown in Table 15-2. Germany is the most strict while France and the United Kingdom are the most open. More important is the fact that several types of promotion techniques are under review by individual countries, thus warranting constant monitoring of regulations to assure that a company's promotions comply with local regulations.

Companies must take extreme care when designing a sales promotion. A 1992 promotion sponsored by Maytag Corporation's Hoover European Appliance Group was a smashing success that turned into a financial and public relations fiasco. Over a period of several months, Hoover offered free round-trip airline tickets to the United States and Europe to purchasers of vacuum cleaners or other Hoover appliances. The promotion was designed to take advantage of low-cost, "space available" tickets; executives hoped that the cost of the tickets would be offset by commissions paid to Hoover when customers rented cars or booked hotel rooms. Finally, it was expected that a percentage of customers who bought appliances would fail to meet certain eligibility requirements and, thus, be denied free tickets.

The number of people who actually qualified for the free tickets—more than 200,000 in all—far exceeded company forecasts, while the number of car rentals and hotel bookings was lower than expected. Hoover was swamped by the volume of inquiries; many customers were angered by long delays in responses to their requests for the tickets. The

---

[11] Leslie Ryan, "Sales Promotion: Made in America," *Brandweek,* 31 July 1995, p. 28.

TABLE 15-2	Sales Promotion in Select EU Countries				
Tactic	*Germany*	*France*	*U.K.*	*Netherlands*	*Belgium*
On-pack price reductions	Yes	Yes	Yes	Yes	Yes
In-pack gift	??	??	Yes	??	??
Extra product	??	Yes	Yes	??	??
Money-off vouchers	No	Yes	Yes	Yes	Yes
Free prize contest	No	Yes	Yes	No	No

KEY: Yes—legally allowed; ??—under review; No—not legally allowed

Source: U.K. Institute of Sales Promotion.

bottom line was that Hoover had failed to budget enough for the promotion, forcing Maytag CEO Leonard Hadley to take pretax charges of $72.6 million. In an effort to honor its commitment to Hoover customers, Maytag bought several thousand seats on various airlines. "The Hoover name in the United Kingdom is valuable, and this investment in our customer base there is essential to our future," Hadley said.

Hadley fired the president and director of marketing services at Hoover Europe and the vice president of marketing at Hoover UK. Fallout from the promotion became an ongoing PR nightmare, as headlines in the *London Daily Mail* trumpeted "Hoover Fiasco: Bosses Sacked" and "How Dumb Can You Get?" Meanwhile, complaints from angry Europeans poured into Maytag's Newton, Iowa, headquarters. A Hoover Holiday Pressure Group was rumored to have thousands of members; three people even traveled to Newton in an unsuccessful attempt to meet with CEO Hadley. By May 1995, Hadley was ready to throw in the towel: He decided to sell Hoover Europe to Italy's Candy SpA for $170 million. Hadley intends to refocus Maytag on the North American market.[12]

◆ DIRECT MARKETING

The use of direct marketing is growing rapidly in many parts of the world due to increased use of computer databases, credit cards, and toll-free numbers, as well as changing lifestyles. Direct marketing is a system of marketing that integrates ordinarily separate marketing mix elements to sell directly to both consumers and other businesses, bypassing retail stores and personal sales calls. It is used by virtually every consumer and business-to-business category from banks to airlines to nonprofit organizations. Because the customer responds directly to the company making the offer, international considerations that apply to communications, distribution, and sales have to be considered. Direct marketing uses a wide spectrum of media, including direct mail; telephone; broadcast, including television and radio; and print, including newspapers and magazines.

The usage of direct mail, the most popular type of direct marketing, varies around the world based on literacy rates, level of acceptance, infrastructure, and culture. In countries with low levels of literacy, a medium that requires reading is not effective. In other countries, the literacy rate may be high, but consumers are unfamiliar with direct mail and suspicious of products they cannot see.

The infrastructure of a country must be developed sufficiently to handle direct mail. The postal system must deliver mail on a timely basis and be free of corruption. In addition to physical infrastructure, a system for developing databases and retrieving

---

[12] Rick Jost, "Maytag Wrings out after Flopped Hoover Promotion," *The Des Moines Register,* 5 April 1993, p. 3B; Jost, "Mail Flying in from Britons Upset by Maytag Promotion," *The Des Moines Register,* 11 July 1994, p. B3.

◆ BOX 15-1 ◆

DIRECT MAIL IN MEXICO

Mexico is an often ignored market for direct mail, yet actually has a lot of potential. Recently, the country's 99 million plus consumers have been enjoying a gross national product (GNP) per capita real growth rate of approximately 6 percent, with GNP per capita of $US 3,943. Inflation is in check, and the North American Free Trade Agreement (NAFTA) has resulted in lower tariffs and more jobs.

To date, Mexicans receive very little direct mail, so they are not as jaded as consumers in the United States, who refer to direct mail as "junk mail." Mexicans love bargains and are brand conscious and brand loyal. An added benefit to marketers is that postage and fulfillment costs are low.

In a recent direct-mail campaign, an automobile financing company, Gruppo Financiero Serfin, distributed 8,000 pieces, had a 10 percent response rate, and converted 33 percent of respondents.

SOURCE: Steven Soricillo, "Mexico: Direct Mail Marketing across Our Border," *Direct Marketing* (August 1996): 39.

appropriate target names and the tracking results is necessary. In one former Soviet republic, merchants were resistant to having their name and address publicly listed in a telephone directory. They feared that the local "mafia" could readily use this information to extort protection money from these businesses.

Culture also plays a significant role in the decision to use direct mail. In Thailand, the local astrologer plays an important role in many business decisions. If the day that a direct-mail campaign is scheduled to begin is not auspicious, the marketer may delay the mailing until a more fortuitous day appears.

Database marketing uses extensive lists of prospects and relevant demographic and psychographic information to narrow target markets to serious prospects and then to customize an offer to the prospect's interests. This is essential not only for direct marketing but also for market research and personal selling. Lists can be created in house from the company's current customers, from responses to previous direct-marketing offers, or from telephone or membership directories. These lists may also be purchased from list brokers, companies that specialize in the acquisition and sale of lists of prospective customers.

◆ TRADE SHOWS AND EXHIBITIONS

Trade shows and exhibitions are other promotion vehicles that are increasingly important in the promotional mix, especially for industrial products and in the international marketplace. At two recent international packaging trade shows, the percentages of international companies were 33 percent and 40 percent.[13] International trade shows offer businesses the opportunity to identify and recruit importers/exporters and agents and to make contact with trade bureaus of foreign governments. They also offer an inexpensive and efficient way to meet potential customers from other countries. Trade shows differ from country to country. For example, in the United States printed material and promotion giveaways are much more common than in many other countries. Figure 15-1 is a general model for trade show performance, which suggests the variables that should influence the selection of shows, and the management of show performance.

---

[13] Aviv Shoham, "Performance in Trade Show and Exhibitions: A Synthesis and Directions for Future Research," *Journal of Global Marketing* (December 1999): 41–57.

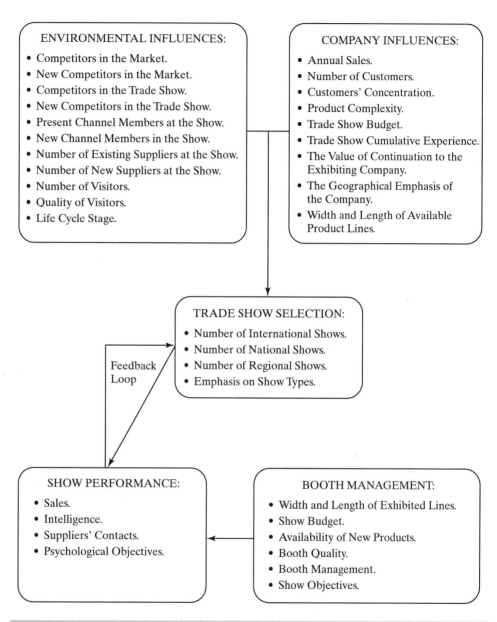

FIGURE 15-1 A General Model of Trade Show Performance

Source: Aviv Shoman, "Performance in Trade Show and Exhibitions: A Synthesis and Directions for Future Research," *Journal of Global Marketing* (December 1999): 51.

◆ SPONSORSHIP PROMOTION

Sponsorship serves purposes other than sales promotion. Sponsorship can be used to increase awareness and esteem, to build the brand identification, to enhance the brand's positioning and sales, and to circumvent advertising restrictions in some countries. Examples of global sponsorship are the Olympics, the World Cup in Soccer, the Grand Prix, and the Tour de France. An example of a regional sponsorship event is the Pan American Games while a local sponsorship event is the Vasaloppet Ski Race in Sweden or sumo wrestling in Japan. Table 15-3 shows how Coca-Cola varies its sponsorship programs around the world.

TABLE 15-3	Coca Cola Sponsorship Around the World
Canada	Leftie-Rightie Golf Match
	Annual Big Rock Games for Waiters,
	Waitresses, and Bartenders
Zambia	Soccer camp, squash tournament
Ghana	Soccer tournament
Malaysia	Youth participation in Malaysia World Cup
Ireland	Industry Challenge for Primary Schools contest
China	International breeding program to protect pandas

TABLE 15-4 Estimated 1999 Sponsorship Spending by Region	*Spending*	*% Total*	*% Change*
Total	US$ 19.2B	100	+11%
North America	7.6B	40	+12%
Europe	5.6B	29	+11%
Pacific Rim	3.4B	18	+ 4%
Central and South America	1.5B	8	+19%
Other	1.1B	5	+10%

Source: IEG.

Just as with media, the effectiveness of sponsorship varies across geographic regions (see Table 15-4) and should be taken into consideration when planning programs in individual countries or measuring program effectiveness.

Expenditures on sponsorship are rising (Table 15-4) and expected to continue to do so. Two causes for this trend are increases in corporate mergers and cause marketing. Many companies that are consolidating want to quickly increase awareness of the merger and to establish a new image. Cause marketing, which is the use of marketing funds to enhance a cause while acting as a good corporate citizen, is gaining popularity. In the United States, Clairol Professional Care Products supports AIDS research while Avon supports breast cancer research.

Sponsorship, however, does have its distractors. Many people claim the Olympics are overcommercialized and that sponsors "McDonaldize" local events. Needless to say, these people are in the minority given the wide acceptance of sponsorship, but some may generate negative publicity for the company.

Summary ■

Marketing communications—the promotion P of the marketing mix—includes advertising, public relations, personal selling, sales promotion, direct marketing, trade shows, and sponsorship. These techniques are important tools in global marketing. Public relations is an important tool in global marketing. Corporate communications must be designed to foster goodwill and provide accurate, timely information, especially in the event of a crisis.

Personal selling, or one-on-one communication, requires company representatives to be well versed in the culture of countries in which they do business. Behavior in each stage of the selling process may have to be appropriately tailored to individual country requirements. Sales promotions must also conform with regulations in each country market. An ill-designed promotion can result in unwanted publicity and lost customers.

Other, considerations for the international marketing mix are direct marketing, trade shows, sponsorship, and the Internet. Each technique is rapidly gaining acceptance around the world and can alter a company's marketing strategies for directly reaching the consumer.

Discussion Questions ■■■

1. What is the role of public relations in global marketing?
2. What is the role of sales promotion in the marketing mix? How do these roles differ for industrial and consumer products?
3. Does the role of promotion in the marketing mix vary from one country to the next for the same product?
4. How does personal selling differ in international markets?
5. What are four considerations in selecting a direct-mail strategy in a particular country?
6. What are four sources of databases?
7. What effect will the Internet have on global promotion?

Suggested Readings ■■

Botan, Carl. "International Public Relations: Critique and Reformulation." *Public Relations Review,* 18, no. 2 (Summer 1992): 149–159.

Bovet, Susan Fry. "Building an International Team." *Public Relations Journal* (August/September 1994): 26–28.

Cornwell, T. Bettina, and Isabelle Maignan. "An International Review of Sponsorship Research," *Journal of Advertising,* 27, no. 1 (1998): 1.

Dowling, Grahame R., Mark Uncles. "Do Customer Loyalty Programs Really Work?" *Sloan Management Review, 38,* no. 4 (1997): 71.

Easton, Simon, and Penny Mackie. "When Football Came Home: A Case History of the Sponsorship Activity at Euro '96." *International Journal of Advertising,* 17, no. 1 (1998): 99–114.

Epley, Joe S. "Public Relations in the Global Village: An American Perspective." *Public Relations Review,* 18, no. 2 (Summer 1992): 109–116.

Grunig, Larissa A. "Strategic Public Relations Constituencies on a Global Scale." *Public Relations Review,* 18, no. 2 (Summer 1992): 127–136.

Hiebert, Ray E. "Advertising and Public Relations in Transition from Communism: The Case of Hungary, 1989–1994," *Public Relations Review,* 20, no. 4 (Winter 1994): 357–372.

Honeycutt, Earl D., John B. Ford, and Lew Kurtzman, "Potential Problems and Solutions When Hiring and Training a Worldwide Sales Team," *Journal of Business & Industrial Marketing* (Winter 1996): 42+.

Josephs, Ray, and Juanita W. Josephs. "Public Relations, the U. K. Way." *Public Relations Journal* (April 1994): 14–18.

Kaynak, Erdener. "Sales Promotion Practices of Consumer Goods Companies in an Advanced Developing Country." *International Journal of Advertising,* 17, no. 2 (1998): 213–233.

Kruckeberg, Dean. "A Global Perspective on Public Relations Ethics: The Middle East." *Public Relations Review,* 22, no. 2 (Summer 1996): 181–189.

Kucukemiroglu, Orsay, Erdener Kaynak, and Sevgu Ayse Ozturk. "Sales and Promotion Practices of Consumer Goods Companies in an Advanced Developing Country," *International Journal of Advertising,* 17, no. 2 (1998): 213+.

Lewin, Jeffrey E., and Wesley J. Johnston. "International Salesforce Management: A Relationship Perspective," *Journal of Business & Industrial Marketing,* 12, no. 3–4 (Summer 1997): 232+.

Nessmann, Karl. "Public Relations in Europe: A Comparison with the United States." *Public Relations Journal,* 21, no. 2 (Summer 1995): 151–160.

Newsom, Doug, and Bob Carrell. "Professional Public Relations in India: Need Outstrips Supply." *Public Relations Journal,* 20, no. 2 (Summer 1994): 183–188.

Sharpe, Melvin L. "The Impact of Social and Cultural Conditioning on Global Public Relations." *Public Relations Review,* 18, no. 2 (Summer 1992): 103–107.

Shoham, Aviv. "Performance in Trade Shows and Exhibitions: A Synthesis and Directions for Future Research." *Journal of Global Marketing,* 12, no. 3 (1999): 41–57.

Stewart-Allen, Allyson L. "Cross-Border Conflicts of European Sales Promotions." *Marketing News,* 26 April 1999, p. 10.

Zavrl, Frani, and Dejan Vercic. "Performing Public Relations in Central and Eastern Europe." *International Public Relations Journal,* 18, no. 2 (1995): 21–23.

Global
e.marketing

Every *business is an information business.*

—PHILIP EVANS AND THOMAS S. WURSTER,
*Blown to Bits: How the New Economics
of Information Transforms Strategy* (2000)

CONTENTS

CONCEPTS AND DEFINITIONS

e.marketing	The integration of information technology (IT) and the Internet into marketing.
Internet	The largest computer network in the world, which links over 130 million people. By 2003, this number is projected to grow to 350 million users, split between North America—35 percent; Europe—30 percent; Asia Pacific—21 percent; South America— 9 percent; and the rest of the world—about 5 percent.[1]
Intranet	A computer network that links users in a single company or organization. Access to an intranet is limited to authorized users who are company or organization employees or members.

---

[1] Jerry Wind and Vijay Mahajan, "Digital Marketing," unpublished working paper, Wharton School, University of Pennsylvania, 1999, p. 7.

Extranet	A computer network that links authorized users. In contrast to the Internet, it is not open to the general public and, in contrast to the intranet, it is not limited to members of a single organization or company.
World Wide Web	Makes the Internet more accessible and easier to use by nonexperts. Technically it is a system of hypermedia linking text, graphics, sounds, and video on computers spread across the globe.
Portals	Context suppliers that attract millions of Web users with a wide swath of information, search services, e-mail, and chat rooms. Among the most important context providers are Internet on-line services such as America Online, Web browsers such as Netscape Communicator, and search engines such as Yahoo!
Web Browser	Software used to navigate the hyperlinks that make up the World Wide Web.
Virtual Reality	Imaginary "worlds" created by cutting edge computer technology. For example, wearing special headsets, consumers might get the impression of walking through a house and visualizing and experiencing the rooms before the house is actually built.
E-Commerce	Selling goods and services over the Internet, both business to consumer (B2C), consumer to consumer (C2C), and business to business (B2B). The latter is sometimes also referred to as *e-business*.

e.*marketing* is a term that can be used to label the potential of information technology (IT) and the Internet, and the impact on marketing. e.marketing is perhaps the single most important new development in technology in the entire history of marketing, particularly in its ability to leap over distance. It is clear that marketing is undergoing a revolution as a result of the explosion of information technology and the World Wide Web. In this chapter we will review the known and speculate about the unknown impact of the Web and information technology on global marketing.

In this chapter, we look at some of the basic elements of the new technological environment and discuss how the changes we are experiencing impact the way global marketing is conducted. The chapter opens by considering some of the key drivers of the ICT revolution, most importantly the Internet. Subsequently, we discuss the influence of these fundamental changes on competitive strategies. Finally, we consider the changes the technological environment brings to the configuration of the global value chain.

◆ THE DEATH OF DISTANCE

Distance was, in the premodern world, a variable of the greatest marketing significance. As the real estate maxim has it, the three rules of real estate valuation are location, location, location. In global marketing, strategies and practice reflected the importance of distance. The most important variable impacting trade behavior, for example, is distance. The primary trading partners of every county are the proximate neighbors: for the United States they are Canada and Mexico, for Canada and Mexico it is the United States. For France it is Germany, and for Germany it is France, and so on around the world. There has always been a positive correlation between trade and proximity. However, the internet is totally independent of distance. Electrons traveling at the speed of light get to anywhere in the world in the same time and at the same cost. If I send an e-mail, it does not make a difference in time or cost whether the mail is addressed to my next door neighbor or to someone halfway around the world. The same thing is true of a Web site: The location of the site does not affect the cost or speed of access.

For the first time in history, the world has become a level playing field. Anyone, anywhere in the world can communicate with anyone else in the world in real time with no premium charged for distance.

These long-standing historical patterns of trade are a reflection of the importance of physical distance in global marketing. The improvement of transportation and communications technologies has been a major driver pushing the world toward greater globalization. Costs have come down and service has improved steadily and dramatically since the end of World War II. The Internet and IT have been major new drivers of globalization since the beginning of the 1990s. A Web presence is instantly global. The global reach of credit card issuers, package delivery services, and the Internet has created a whole new level of possibilities for global retail and business-to-business marketing by even the smallest firms.

For example, until the Internet, the aftermarket for motorcycle accessories was fragmented by country. The only way an accessory would cross national boundaries was if the manufacturer set up marketing and distribution operations in overseas or foreign markets. Today, this is no longer necessary. *Motorcycle Consumer News,* a reader-sponsored magazine, which does not accept paid advertising, reviews new accessories and products for motorcyclists. For the past year, the magazine has included reviews of products that are marketed in other countries with the telephone number, and Web and e-mail addresses of the manufacturer. Readers of the magazine anywhere in the world can communicate directly with the supplier, who can receive payment via credit card with card authorization and ship anywhere in the world via express delivery. The dramatic decline in communications and shipping costs and the decline of both tariff and nontariff barriers to trade have opened up world markets to companies that were formerly too small to participate in world markets.

◆ COMMUNICATIONS

E-mail is a major new communications tool that supplements the fax and telephone to eliminate the barrier of distance. It is instant, cheap (free to most users), and insensitive to time zone. You can read e-mail when you wish regardless of time zone considerations. E-mail is a marketing communications tool that offers unprecedented power for one-on-one messages for both B2B and B2C communications. Remarkably, it has emerged as a universal communications tool in a mere five years.

◆ TARGETING THE INDIVIDUAL CUSTOMER: BEYOND SEGMENTATION

The aim of marketing segmentation has always been to create a unique value offer for as many customers as possible. Before the Internet, this meant, in practice, creating an offer for a segment of the market that was an aggregation of customers. Almost overnight, the World Wide Web has emerged as a powerful new tool for accomplishing what in the past was only a theoretical possibility in marketing: creating marketing programs that target a segment of one. With the Internet, that theoretical possibility has become a reality. Indeed, the whole notion of segmentation has to be reconsidered. Segmentation was a goal in marketing because it was too expensive to address the individual customer. With the available tools of the Internet and IT, it is now possible to respond to the individual customer regardless of where the customer is located.

◆ RELATIONSHIP MARKETING

Another major thrust of marketing in recent years has been relationship marketing. The Internet has opened up immense new possibilities for creating a relationship with global customers, potential customers, suppliers, and channel members. The end of segmentation means that marketers can now focus on delivering value to the individual customer. The best way to do this is to create a win-win relationship with the customer. The company should offer the customer a unique value, and serving the customer should be profitable for the company. The relationship should be mutually beneficial. Whenever the benefit is one sided, the relationship is threatened.

◆ INTERACTIVITY

Before the emergence of the Internet and IT, communications between companies and their customers were generally limited to one-way communications. Companies made offers, and customers voted in the marketplace. The possibility of an interactive relationship between customers and prospects has now emerged. This is particularly true for on-line retailers who can use customer purchase behavior information to uniquely tailor communications to their customers. A customer who purchases sun screen skin protection from an on-line retailer can be advised of other products that also provide sun protection.

◆ SPEED TO MARKET

Globalization has unfolded in stages. The first stage was the move of companies to make sure that their products were sold in global markets. Before the Internet and IT created a new world of instant global communications, the pace of information and company communications traveled slowly. Products were introduced in one country at a time or at best one region at a time. Today, that has changed.

The Web is causing the Hollywood movie industry to rethink its America-First policy. Take Mel Gibson's epic *Braveheart,* for example. It was released in the United States on May 24, 1995, and it crept around the world. Some countries, such as Portugal, waited seven months to see the movie.

When Mel Gibson returned to the screen with a new movie, *The Patriot,* on June 28, 2000, the studio rolled it out around the world in two months.

What happened? The Internet. As Warren Lieberfarb, president of Time Warner Inc.'s Warner Home Video put it, "The world is discovering movies on the weekend they open in the U.S."[2] One of the pressures for global releases of new films is the DVD version. Consumers are modifying DVD players to enable players to play DVD disks from anywhere in the world, defeating the effect of a regional coding system designed to stop consumers from playing DVD disks that were purchased from outside their region. When the DVD version of a film goes on sale in the United States, it can be played anywhere in the world on a modified player.

The solution to this problem is to move to a global release of new films. This offers a number of advantages. It helps movies that "bomb" in the United States because, when this happens, it has no effect on the international market, which makes an independent judgment on a new release. It also has opened up new costs savings since there is no time to develop expensive, customized marketing programs for each country. Studios are simply recycling art and photos from the U.S. campaign to create a global campaign with the same look around the world.

---

[2] "Web's Reach Forces Hollywood to Rethink America-First Policy," *The Wall Street Journal,* 12 June 2000, p. 1.

◆ LIVING IN AN AGE OF TECHNOLOGICAL DISCONTINUITIES

PRICE PLUNGES INDICATE SPEED OF TECHNOLOGICAL PROGRESS

So what are the drivers of the technology revolution we are witnessing? Arguably, the changes with the most dramatic impact on globalization occurred in two fields: transportation and communication. Dicken refers to these two areas as "enabling technologies."[3] In transportation, key advances have been made in air travel and the speedier loading and unloading of container shipments. On the communication side, the reduced cost of long-distance telecommunication is most remarkable. Today, a three-minute telephone call between New York and London costs about $0.30; in 1930 it would have cost about $250 when expressed in today's prices. That is an 83,333 percent decrease in prices in 70 years. (This is a reminder that when it comes to technology, prices decline instead of increase.) Market liberalization is expected to bring down international rates by as much as 80 percent over five years.[4] Cambridge Strategic Management predicts that by 2005, a transatlantic videophone call will cost only a "a few cents an hour."[5] Already, about two thirds of the world's new telephone subscriptions are for mobile phones and, in some developed countries, this share is as high as 75 percent.[6]

A second important cost reduction is the dizzying decline in the cost of computer-processing power: It now costs only 1 percent of what it did in the early 1970s. Expressed differently, "If cars had developed at the same pace as microprocessors . . . a typical car would now cost less than $5 and do more than 250,000 miles to the gallon."[7] These price reductions reflect the breathtaking speed of technological change; indeed, never before have such dramatic price falls been observed.

TECHNOLOGICAL CONVERGENCE AND THE UBIQUITY OF TECHNOLOGY

In information and communication technology, it is not only the improved speed and reliability of devices that have brought about the rapid technological change but also the convergence between the transmission of information and the processing of information. Moreover, it is expected that the next few years will witness a convergence of different types of information and communication technologies into one common Internet standard. Figure 16-1 illustrates this development.

A second development has been labeled technological ubiquity. Andersen Consulting describes it as "a world in which information technology is an integral part of everything we see and do in the workplace and at home."[8] Thus, every kitchen device, car, or exercise machine will be packed with easy-to-use electronics that will add value to the product, for example, by tailoring it to personal preferences, enabling remote communication, and so on.

EXPLOSIVE GROWTH OF THE INTERNET

Arguably, the Internet represents one of the most important drivers of the technological revolution because it has led to the development of an entirely new form of doing business called e-commerce or e-business. The history of the Internet can be traced back to 1969, when the U.S. Department of Defense introduced ARPANET. Apart from enabling access to remote computers, the network also permitted the transfer of electronic mes-

---

[3] P. Dicken, *Global Shift. The Internationalization of Economic Activity* (London: Paul Chapman Publishing, 1992): p. 103.
[4] "The World in 1998," *The Economist,* (London, 1997): 90.
[5] "Going Digital: How New Technology Is Changing Our Lives," *The Economist* (London, The Economist Newspaper Ltd., 1998): 19.
[6] "Economic Indicators," *The Economist,* 112.
[7] "Going Digital: How New Technology Is Changing Our Lives," *The Economist,* p. 19.
[8] "Technology Visioning Workshop" (Andersen Consulting, Sophia Antipolis, July 1999).

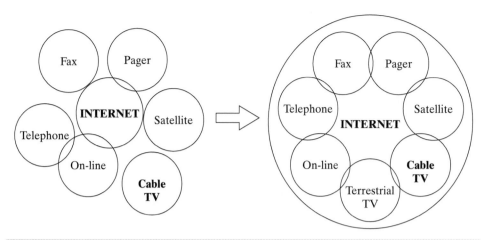

FIGURE 16-1   Convergence of Information and Communication Technologies

sages (e-mail).[9] At this stage, the users were restricted to a few military researchers. Although subsequent years witnessed an extension of users and the development of similar networks springing up from a cooperative effort among NASA, IBM, and MCI, the true breakthrough occurred as recently as 1992. In this year, Tim Berners-Lee at the Conseil Européen pour la Recherche Nucléaire (CERN), a European research institute in Switzerland, introduced the World Wide Web (WWW). For the first time, this protocol permitted the graphic representation of information in the Internet. In connection with Web browsers used to navigate the network of hyperlinks that make up the World Wide Web, this development is widely seen as the origin of the explosive growth of the Internet. Today, the World Wide Web is often used synonymously for the entire Internet, although the latter also hosts traditional Internet services such as Telnet, Gopher, and FTP.[10] Figure 16-2 shows the development of the Internet hosts over time, and Figure 16-3 depicts the geographical distribution of users.

Web access is still very much skewed toward developed countries. Moreover, a number of countries connected to the Internet offer only e-mail and are, consequently, cut off from the wealth of information available on the Web.[11] Despite the fact that current developments and growth rates, particularly in China and South America, will help ease the problem of geographically unequal access, there is still concern. Richard Jolly, author of the latest development report of the United Nations, notes that technology is a double-edged sword, opening new ways for many but also cutting off access for others.[12] In Bangladesh, for example, a computer costs eight times the average annual income.

Technological change as such, of course, is nothing new. What is remarkable today is the speed of change. For example, although it took some 38 and 25 years, respectively, for the radio and telephone to reach 50 million U.S. consumers, television only needed 13 years and cable television 10 years to reach the same threshold. The Internet with the World Wide Web achieved the same penetration level in less than 5 years (Figure 16-4). On a worldwide basis, the Internet has expanded by about 2,000 percent in the last decade and is doubling in size every 6 to 10 months.[13] By 2003, there are projected to be 350 million users, split between North America (35 percent), Europe (30 percent), Asia Pacific

[9] Robert Zakon, info.isoc.org/guest/Internet/History/HIT.html#Growth, 29 August 1999.

[10] John Browning, *Pocket Information Technology* (London: The Economist Books, 1997), pp. 97–99.

[11] Uwe Afemann, "Verschärfung bestehender Ungleichheiten," *Forum Wissenschaft,* Heft 1, (1996): 21–26.

[12] "UN-Entwicklungsbericht: Technik vergrößert Not vieler Menschen," *Kölner Stadt-Anzeiger,* 13 July 1999, p. 7.

[13] Donna L. Hoffmann and Thomas P. Novak, "Marketing in Hypermedia-Computer-Mediated Environments: Conceptual Foundations," *Journal of Marketing,* 60 (July 1996): 50–68.

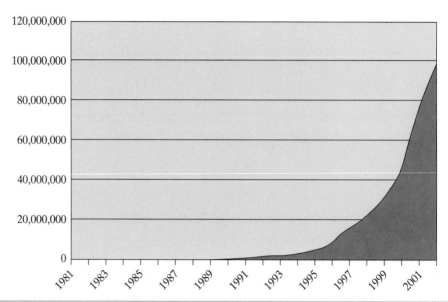

FIGURE 16-2 Development of Internet Hosts

Source: Adapted from www.mids.org/mapsale/data/trends/trends-199907/sld004.htm, 30 August 1999.

(21 percent), South America (9 percent), and the rest of the world (about 5 percent). Other forecasts expect the Internet to reach the 1 billion user mark by 2008; to appreciate the magnitude of this growth note that it took until 1999 for telephone users to reach the 1 billion mark.[14] Freeing Internet access from the confines of computer keyboards and enabling access via mobile phones, pagers, and so on will fuel this growth.

Another revolution, voice recognition technology, is just round the corner. Rendering keyboards largely superfluous and, thus, finally fulfilling the science fiction notion of

FIGURE 16-3 Geographical Distribution of Internet Users

Geographic Location (1998)

Region	Percentage
North America	57%
Europe	22%
Asia	17%
South America	3%
Africa	1%
Middle East	1%

Source: www.nua.ie/surveys/graphs_charts/1998graphs/location.html, 30 August 1999.

---

[14] Jerry Wind and Vijay Mahajan. "Digital Marketing," unpublished working paper, Wharton School, University of Pennsylvania 1999, p. 7.

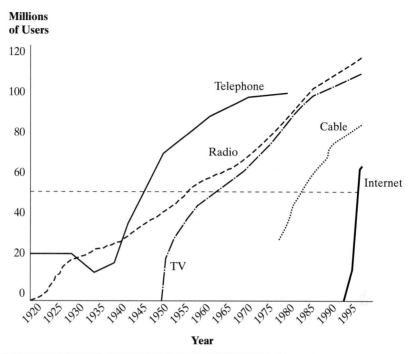

FIGURE 16-4 Uptake of Consumer Technologies

Source: Morgan Stanley, *The Internet Advertising Report.*

commanding a machine through the human voice, this technology will dramatically accelerate the use of computers and drive information and communication technology (ICT) into completely new applications: objects we talk to, drive with, touch, or wear.[15]

THE DEVELOPMENT OF E-COMMERCE

Technology, particularly information and communication technology (ICT), is more than merely an enabler. It has become the basis for an entirely new business model. Starting with electronic data exchange (EDI, i.e., the transfer of standardized data between corporations), the Internet has undergone a metamorphosis from a medium primarily used to advertise a product or service to an e-commerce platform combining information, transactions, dialogue, and exchange. In short, the Internet has given birth to an entirely new business model and opened completely novel opportunities for global marketing. The German-based consulting firm Roland Berger & Partner illustrates this development in Figure 16-5.

The scope for new developments arising from the new technologies is considerable. Consider the example of the well-known electronic bookseller Amazon.com. Using a virtual network that seamlessly connects suppliers and customers, the firm has changed the way in which books are traded. Over 30,000 associated Web sites are recommending the company for a commission and provide links to the Amazon site. Of course, Amazon not only offers books but also informs customers about new publications and encourages readers to post reviews of books they have read. Virtual chat rooms and meetings with authors also foster the formation of an Amazon community. More than half the business Amazon conducts is with loyal customers.

---

[15] "Special Report: Let's Talk," *Business Week,* 23 February 1998, pp. 44–56; and "Smitten with the Written Word," *Financial Times,* 12 February 1998, p. 21.

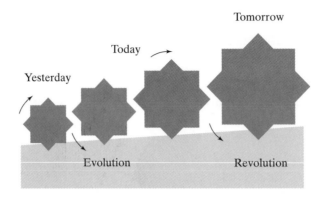

FIGURE 16-5 The Evolution of Electronic Commerce

Source: Roland Berger & Partner, *Erfolgsfaktoren im Electronic Commerce: Auszug aus den Ergebnissen der Studie,* Wien/ Frankfurt am Main, 1999, p. 12.

Further examples of companies that developed their business around the possibilities offered through e-commerce are Dell Computers, which shows growth rates that exceed those of conventional computer manufacturers by a factor of four, E*Trade, an on-line brokerage with annual growth rates of 200 percent, and eBay, which offers on-line auctions and has an annual transaction volume of more than $300 million. At eBay, customers provide the entire content, starting from the goods on offer up to the chat rooms in which they exchange background information on these goods.

Although most media attention has focused on consumer marketing on the Internet, more of Internet transactions are generated in the business-to-business field. Forester Research puts the relationship between business-to-business (B2B) and business-to-consumer (B2C) e-commerce at 5:1.[16]

Rapid technological change does not only affect high-tech companies that like to include an *e* in their name. Michael Hruby presents the example of sport shoes.[17] Thirty years ago, he argues, such shoes were inexpensive, made out of canvas, and came in two designs and three colors. Today, their high-tech descendants boast inflatable air bladders and gel inserts. They come in dozens of styles, colors, and materials, and, of course, are different for each sport. They are not athletic shoes any longer, they are equipment. And they are not cheap. Moreover, some of the household names in the business, such as Nike, do not produce a single shoe. Instead they use outsourcing to get the shoes manufactured in low-labor-cost countries and concentrate on what they can do best, that is, global marketing.

For a global marketer, rapid technological advances in general and the unprecedented speed of change in ICT in particular have resulted in numerous new challenges; virtual organizations, symbiotic relationships, electronic markets, new forms of co-option, blurring corporate boundaries, and flatter organizational hierarchies are among the most important.[18]

Although these challenges open entirely new business opportunities, they also represent fundamental threats to established organizations. Companies have to learn how to live with a high degree of volatility. John Stopford of the London Business School eloquently pointed to the reduced value of incumbency.[19] Companies that were success stories only a few years ago are now fighting to survive; Westinghouse or DEC spring to mind. On the other hand, there are companies that have appeared virtually overnight. In

---

[16] "E-Business: What Every CEO Needs to Know," *Business Week*, 22 March 1999, p. 10.

[17] Michael F. Hruby, *Technoleverage: Using the Power of Technology to Outperform the Competition* (New York: AMACOM, 1999).

[18] For an excellent in-depth analysis of these issues, see Arnold Picot, Ralf Reichwald, and Rolf T. Wigand, *Die grenzenlose Unternehmung: Information, Organisation und Management* (Wiesbaden: Gabler Verlag, 1996).

[19] John Stopford, "Global Strategies for the Information Age." Presentation at the 23rd EIBA Conference on Global Business in the Information Age, Stuttgart, 14–16 December 1997.

this context, the author coined the phrase *mushroom companies*.[20] A well-known characteristic of mushrooms is, of course, that they grow virtually overnight but then often disappear rather quickly. Consider Yahoo!, which provides the largest search engine on the Internet. Only a few years ago, Yahoo!'s cofounder, David Filo, was a relatively poor ex-student. Today, his on-line service leads the field in both traffic and advertising revenues. But while Internet search companies such as Yahoo!, Infoseek, Lycos, and Excite raised $170 million by going public in 1996, Internet search facilities have become a commodity. There are now hundreds of ways to find and retrieve information on the Web. The Internet search business, in which a number of engines compete for a pool of willing advertisers, may soon take some casualties. However, Yahoo! might well survive. It has three times the market share of any of its competitors and has the advantage of being the first kid on the block.

Another example is Netscape, which was founded in 1994 as Mosaic Communications. It offered the first version of its Internet navigator one year later and, at its peak in the first quarter of 1997, generated revenues in excess of $150 million per year. However, since October 1997, the company's stock has lost value on fears that it will be the big loser in its browser war with Microsoft's Internet Explorer.

Given these dramatic business histories, it is not surprising that Microsoft's CEO Bill Gates supposedly said, "We are always two years away from failure," and Intel's CEO Andy Grove coined the motto, "Only the paranoid survive."

◆ NEW TECHNOLOGIES CHANGE THE RULES OF COMPETITION

In addition to increasing volatility, the move from an industrial to a postindustrial e-economy also presents the global marketer with a new set of business rules. Long established principles, such as the emphasis of retailers on "location, location, location," are passé. Why should a busy executive spend her valuable time and fight traffic to buy some books or videos for her children in town? She can do the same in much greater comfort from home via the Web. Looking at the changing business principles forced by the new e-economy, Arvind Rangaswamy of Penn State University summarized the situation in Table 16-1.[21]

In a similar vein, Andersen Consulting stated that the new economy will force companies to adopt some new game plans.[22] Among the most important follow.

1. Secure a dominant market position as quickly as possible.
2. Form alliances based on their potential for market access and synergies.
3. Anticipate very high start-up investments.
4. Defend positions through an ongoing process of innovations.

We will look next at some of these issues in more depth.

IMPORTANCE OF DOMINANT MARKET POSITIONS

In the industrial environment, scale advantages have their limits. This is referred to as decreasing returns to scale. Although a large factory might be more cost-efficient than a small one, there is a point at which adding capacity at the same location will be

[20] Bodo B. Schlegelmilch and R. Sinkovics, "Marketing in the Information Age—Can We Plan for an Unpredictable Future?" *International Marketing Review,* 14, no. 3 (1998): 162–170.

[21] Arvind Rangaswamy, "Toward a Model of eBusiness Performance." Presentation at the American Marketing Association Summer Educators' Conference, San Francisco, 7–10 August 1999.

[22] Diane D. Wilson and Paul F. Nunes, eds., *eEconomy: Ein Spiel mit neuen Regeln.* Sonderteil eCommerce: Wege zum Erfolg in der elektronischen Wirtschaft, *Outlook:* Andersen Consulting, Heft 1, 1998, pp. 45–50.

TABLE 16-1 Evolution in Business Context and Strategies	
From ———————————————→	*To*
Market share	Strategic control
Technology as an enabler	Technology as a driver
Seller-centric market	Buyer-centric markets
Physical assets	Knowledge assets
Vertical integration based on size	Vertical integration based on speed
Decreasing return to scale	Increasing return to scale
Firm-centric marketing strategies	Network-centric marketing strategies

Source: Adapted from Arvind Rangaswamy, "Toward a Model of eBusiness Performance," Presentation at the American Marketing Association Summer Educators' Conference, San Francisco, 7–10 August 1999.

uneconomical. The cost of adding labor and material will exceed the added returns. This effect permits smaller competitors to compete against those with larger market shares, providing they can achieve production sizes that yield optimal efficiency. Under the new technological regime, the rule of decreasing returns to scale no longer holds universally. In many cases, the optimal output is not determined by the factory size but is based on the point of market saturation. This can be observed in markets in which fixed costs are much higher than variable costs. Examples are computer software or pharmaceutical products, which demand a high degree of intellectual factor input. The same holds for products or services that become more valuable when used by more people, that is, products that develop into a de facto standard and profit from the frequently mentioned *network effect*. Microsoft Office is an example that shows how useful it is to use the same product used by many other people. In all these cases, the returns achieved through increasing market shares do not diminish over time but grow in a reversal of the "law" of decreasing returns. Figures 16-6 and 16-7 illustrate the argument.

Being placed in such a technological environment, it is important for companies to gain market share quickly and, as Rangaswamy states, to achieve strategic control. This explains why America Online (AOL) distributes its disks through all sorts of available media (e.g., glued into journals and handed out at supermarkets). New subscribers are lured with irresistible trial offers. Netscape pursued a different strategy. It gave its prod-

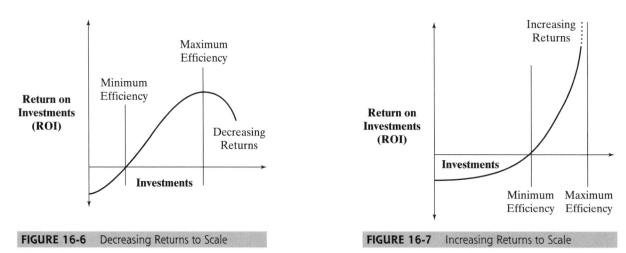

FIGURE 16-6 Decreasing Returns to Scale

FIGURE 16-7 Increasing Returns to Scale

Source: Diane D. Wilson and Paul F. Nunes, eds., *eEconomy: Ein Spiel mit neuen Regeln,* Sonderteil eCommerce: Wege zum Erfolg in der elektronischen Wirtschaft, *Outlook,* Andersen Consulting, Heft 1, 1998, p. 49.

◆ BOX 16-1 ◆

GLOBAL PERSPECTIVE

U.S. AIRLINES "HANDOFFS" RAISE SAFETY CONCERNS

A burgeoning practice of sharing or combining flights, known as *code-sharing,* allows airlines to create marketing alliances that give passengers almost seamless travel around the globe. But the scramble for partnerships into regions such as Asia and Africa—with some of the world's least safe airlines, has begun to trouble some airline executives and federal officials.

China Airlines of Taiwan, for example, is an American Airlines and Continental Airlines code-share partner. Airclaims Ltd. of London, which tracks airline accidents, lists three China Airlines crashes with 465 deaths in the past decade. And a 1996 Conde Nast survey listed China Airlines as having an accident rate throughout its existence of 11.43 fatal accidents per 1 million flights, compared with a 0.15 rate for American and a 0.29 rate for Continental.

A person flying from Dallas to Taipei tonight, for instance, would depart on American Flight 691 and transfer in San Francisco to American Flight 6123. At least that's what the ticket would say. But American Flight 6123, which leaves shortly after midnight, is really China Airlines Flight 3. American Airlines has been quietly working with the Taiwanese airline on safety in the past few months, officials said.

Under code-sharing, one airline buys a block of tickets on another airline's flight and lists the flight in reservation systems under its name, or code. The tickets will read as if the passengers are flying on a U.S. carrier, even though they actually transfer to a plane flown by another airline. Passengers are supposed to be notified, but many pay little attention until they show up at the gate and find themselves boarding a plane of a different color. Code-sharing is attractive for airlines because it increases feeder traffic on domestic routes and makes an airline's international reach seem much greater.

SOURCE: Adapted from: Don Phillips "U.S. Airlines 'Handoffs' Raise Safety Concerns: Foreign Partners Come Under Scrutiny," *The Washington Post,* March 7, 1999, Page A01.

uct away in the hope of earning money with follow-up deals. The new technological environment has increased the importance of achieving market share. Conversely, the global marketer can no longer afford to tolerate even small attacks from competitors and must be prepared for a vigorous defense of its market position.

IMPORTANCE OF STRATEGIC ALLIANCES

The postindustrial e-economy is more and more characterized by a dilution of traditional corporate structures and boundaries in favor of a move toward symbiotic alliances with external partners. Companies involve legally and economically independent firms to fulfill various tasks. Technology is important in this context, since the use of ICT leads to a reduction of transaction costs and, thus, promotes the market and alliances orientation of companies.[23] Videoconferencing, electronic data exchange, extranets, and other technologies offer companies involved in symbiotic alliances cost-efficient means of communication.

Three types of alliances can be distinguished. Vertical cooperation describes partnerships between companies active in different stages of the value chain, such as a collaboration between a manufacturer and a retailer in the marketing of an innovative product. Horizontal cooperation involves companies in the same industry, such as research and development cooperation of two or more microelectronic companies. Diagonal cooperation, finally, refers to situations in which companies from different industries collaborate.

---

[23] A. Picot, T. Ripperger, and B. Wolff, "The Fading Boundaries of the Firm," *Journal of Institutional and Theoretical Economics* (1996): 65–72.

While cooperation and alliances as such are not a new phenomenon, the changes in the technological environment have not only made cross-country alliances easier to manage but have also influenced the motivation behind the alliances. Besides the desire to increase efficiency, it is now primarily the desire to gain market access and market share that drives cooperation. The desire to utilize network effects and to achieve synergies in products and services, for example, was behind the cooperation between the American Broadcasting Company (ABC), the New York Times, and America Online (AOL). Indeed, the benefit of gaining access to its customers allowed AOL to bill the other two companies $1 billion.[24] Airlines can serve as another example of strategic alliances. E-commerce permits airlines to utilize their brand names in on-line reservations through so called "code-sharing." This, in turn, eventually results in higher market shares for the globally networked partner airlines.

IMPORTANCE OF ANTICIPATING HIGH START-UP INVESTMENTS

Increasing returns to scale in many e-based industries necessitate high start-up costs in order to achieve the desired market share. A substantial part of the investment must be committed for years before the revenues eventually exceed the costs. AOL, for example, had to invest $500 million per year into marketing and sales before it reached its current position as market leader.[25] Toys "Я" Us recently announced that it planned to update its Web site organized as a separate company in order to fight increasing Web competition in the toy industry. The anticipated costs for this Web site update are $80 million.[26] Many e-based companies need the backing of well-established, financially strong corporations or are forced to turn to the stock exchange to raise the required capital. The high stock market valuation of the so-called Internet stocks in comparison to the stocks of traditional companies shows that the market, contrary to its reputation as being too short-term oriented, is willing to take a long-term view. Table 16-2 illustrates this argument.

IMPORTANCE OF ONGOING INNOVATIONS

In the traditional technical environment, innovations were primarily a means to gain a few points of market share. It was a rare event that consumers changed allegiances in droves. Information about goods and services diffused relatively slowly and there were significant gaps between lead and lag countries in the adoption of technology.

In today's technological environment, the situation is drastically different. Not only has the diffusion speed increased significantly (70 percent of the computer industry's revenue, for example, comes from products that did not exist two years ago),[27] but the penalties for falling behind the latest world-class technological standard are quick and sharp. Consider WordPerfect, which for a long time was the world's leading word-processing package. When Microsoft Word offered a more up-to-date technological standard, WordPerfect suffered a drastic fall.

Increasing use of ICT is leading to greater efficiencies in all stages of the new-product development process. Many companies are encouraging their employees, customers, and suppliers to submit ideas for new products or improvements through interactive Web sites or e-mail. Toyota, for example, generated over 2 million suggestions for improvements from its employees alone.[28] After new ideas are generated, expert systems can be used in the evaluation of these ideas. At the design stage, computer-aided design (CAD) and

---

[24] Diane D. Wilson and Paul F. Nunes, eds., *eEconomy: Ein Spiel mit neuen Regeln.*
[25] Diane D. Wilson and Paul F. Nunes, eds., *eEconomy: Ein Spiel mit neuen Regeln.*
[26] "This Toy War Is No Game," *Business Week,* 9 August 1999, p. 54.
[27] "Going Digital: How New Technology Is Changing our Lives," p. 19.
[28] John O'Conner and Eamonn Galvin, *Marketing & Information Technology: The Strategy, Application and Implementation of IT in Marketing* (London: Pitman Publishing, 1997).

TABLE 16-2   Market Valuations

Company	*Digital Economy Valuations (1998)*		*Traditional Economy Valuations (1998)*		Company
Company	*Annual Revenues ($m)*	*Market Cap ($m)*	*Market Cap ($m)*	*Annual Revenues ($m)*	*Company*
AOL	2,600.0	149,800	149,800	14,700	Pfizer
Yahoo!	203.3	34,500	34,700	15,100	Allied Signal
eBay	47.4	24,000	24,300	18,400	J.P. Morgan
Amazon	610.0	23,000	23,000	15,500	Alcoa
Priceline	35.2	17,900	17,700	15,900	FedEx
@Home	48.0	16,800	16,900	26,300	Lockheed Martin
E*Trade	285.0	12,900	13,500	19,200	AMR
CMGI	91.5	11,200	11,400	8,300	Ingersoll Rand
RealNetworks	64.8	5,700	5,500	11,200	Toys "Я" Us

Sources: Fortune, 26 April and 24 May 1999; Hoover.com; Arvind Rangaswamy, "Toward a Model of eBusiness Performance," Presentation at the American Marketing Association Summer Educators' Conference, San Francisco, 7–10 August 1999.

design teams that work in parallel in different time zones substantially speed up this stage. ICT applications such as virtual reality further aid the development process. To achieve a better fit between product features and customer needs, customers are increasingly involved in the design of the product. Smart, a European automobile marque, for example, permits customers to design their own version of the car on the Web (Figure 16-8).

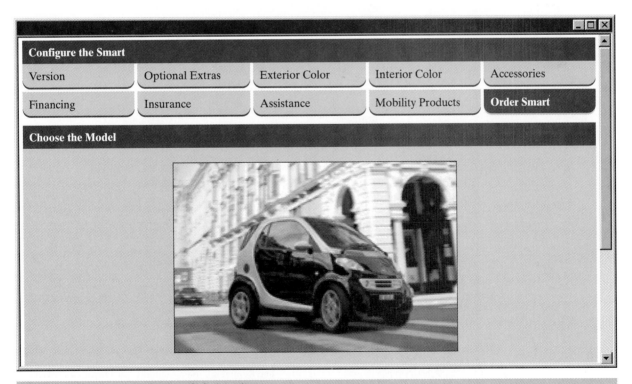

FIGURE 16-8   Customers Design Their Own Car

Source: Adapted from http://mitglied.tripod.de/~smartinfo/new2.htm, 20 August 1999.

Business and marketing analyses, running concurrently with the technical development of new-product ideas, may use ICT in the form of data mining to identify whether there is a likely demand for the new product from existing customers. Finally, simulated test markets again speed up the new-product development process. Such approaches use mathematical modeling of marketing mix data to gauge the likelihood of the new product's success and may render real-life test marketing superfluous.

◆ COMPONENTS OF THE ELECTRONIC VALUE CHAIN

For global marketers, one of the most dramatic and relevant effects of technological changes has been the "death of distance." As Frances Cairncross of the *Economist* put it: "The death of distance as a determinant of the cost of communications will probably be the single most important economic force shaping society in the first half of the [21st] century. It will alter, in ways that are only dimly imaginable, decisions about where people live and work, concepts of national borders, patterns of international trade. Its effects will be as pervasive as those of the discovery of electricity."[29] Some effects are already emerging in the shape of a reconfiguration of the value chain.[30] Figure 16-9 illustrates that ICT permits an organizational structure in which not all parts of the value chain need to be *physically* present in each country, although they may be viewed as *virtually* present from the perspective of suppliers and customers.

A major part of the attractiveness and dynamics of the new technological environment stems from the ability to "modularize," "segment," or "fragment" the value chain into small and distinct customer-oriented processes. ICT facilitates the coordination between these modules in largely nonhierarchical systems and increases the scope for outsourcing

FIGURE 16-9   Location of Value Chain Across Countries

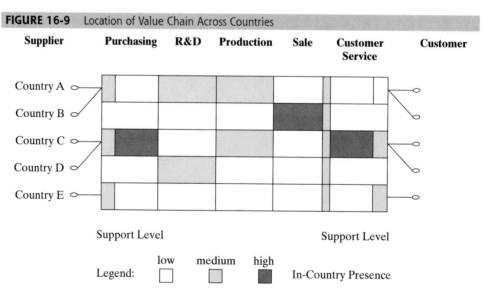

Source: Adapted from J. Griese, *Auswirkungen globaler Informations- und Kommunikationssysteme auf die Organisation weltweit tätiger Unternehmen,* in W. H. V. Staehle and P. Conrad (eds.) Managementforschung 2 (Berlin/New York: de Gruyter, 1992), p. 423.

---

[29] Frances Cairncross, "The Death of Distance," *Economist: Special Report on Telecommunications,* 30 September 1995, p. SS5.

[30] J. Griese, "Auswirkungen globaler Informations und Kommuniktionssysteme auf die Organisation weltweit tätiger Unternehmen." In *Managementforschung 2,* edited by W. H. V. Staehle and P. Conrad, Berlin: de Gruyter, 1992, pp. 163–175.

specific modules.[31] Closely related to the modularization within companies is the transformation of linear value chains into multidimensional networks. For the customer, it is often not transparent which part of a transaction is carried out by which particular member of the network. For example, the customer usually does not know which reservation system a travel agency uses to book a flight. Indeed, most often the customer does not care as long as the required goods or services are delivered as requested. What appears to emerge under the new technological regime is a network of specialists, which permits participants to focus on their respective core values. Figure 16-10 illustrates this point.

CONTEXT SUPPLIERS

Context suppliers, also called *portals,* support the use of the electronic channel both for customers and suppliers. Their key functions are to offer access to the channel and reduce the complexity of the electronic environment. Among the most important context providers are Internet on-line services such as America Online, Web browsers such as Netscape Communicator and Microsoft Explorer, or search engines such as Yahoo! and Lycos. In 1998, the top nine portals generated approximately 15 percent of all Internet traffic. However, their growth appears to be slowing down, and it has been estimated that by 2003, the Internet traffic flowing through the top nine portals will plateau at 20 percent.[32]

SALES AGENTS

Sales agents support suppliers primarily through offering high-quality address banks of potential customers. Metromail provides an example. It offers suppliers carefully sifted address banks of potential customers that typically contain a wealth of information about customer preferences, demographics, and other data. One of the latest services is referred to as the "firefly technique." It helps companies to target consumer groups and provide special product offerings based on profiles of musical and reading preferences.[33]

FIGURE 16-10   The Intermediaries as Networks of Specialists

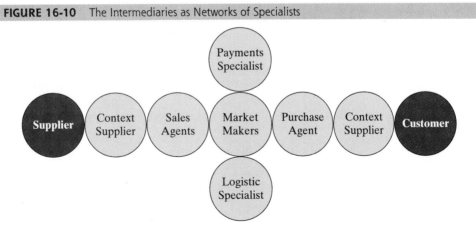

Source: Adapted from Paul F. Nunes and Brian S. Pappas, "Der Vermittler auf der Suche nach Reichtum und Glück," *Outlook,* Andersen Consulting, Heft 1, 1998, p. 55.

---

[31] Arnold Picot, Ralf Reichwald, and Rolf T. Wigand, *Die grenzenlose Unternehmung: Information, Organization und Management* (Wiesbaden: Gabler Verlag, 1996).

[32] "Portals Are Mortal After All," *Business Week,* 21 June 1999, pp. 66–67.

[33] E. Sivadas, Grewel R., and J. Kellaris, "The Internet as a Micro Marketing Tool: Targeting Consumers through Preferences Revealed in Music Newsgroup Usage," *Journal of Business Research,* 41, no. 3 (1998): 179–186.

◆ BOX 16-2 ◆

PENOP: SIGNING UP FOR E-COMMERCE

One of the last hurdles facing the introduction of e-commerce and a paperless business culture is the need for a signature on documents such as contracts, loans, and government-related forms. But PenOp, a British company, has achieved considerable success with its electronic signature technology that legally binds a handwritten digital signature to electronic documentation. PenOp now has 60,000 users worldwide, mostly in the United States, ranging from the Food and Drug Administration (FDA) and judges in Georgia to insurance salespeople. PenOp's software is linked to the personal computer either as an integral software kit or used via an electronic signature pad now commonly found on laptops, dedicated PC peripherals, and PalmPilots. When a manager writes his or her signature on the pad, PenOp notes 30 different physical aspects of the action, including pressure of the pen and its angle of elevation. The rhythm of the action is recorded 100 times per second, as well as the exact symmetry in the curves of the script. The signature's electronic profile is then automatically encrypted.

To deter fraud, the date and time of the event are also logged. "This element delivers evidential force to the signature," says Christopher Smithies, who founded the company with Jeremy Newman, "and can be used in future audit trails or forensic examinations." The software also includes a "ceremony box" to remind the writer that a legally binding act under common law is taking place. Even more important, PenOp's software prevents the content of that document from being altered after it has been signed. PenOp's chief financial officer, Robert Levin, says, "Our technology's security is much stronger than paper. . . . With paper, a buyer can subsequently repudiate an order for whatever reason, but with secure, irrefutable electronic signatures this isn't so easy."

In the United States it is estimated that 2.8 million signatures are written on paper every minute, and the total cost of printing and postage can cost $50 each. But using PenOp, the FDA has set up on-line drug trial forms that open the way to a completely electronic application process for pharmaceutical companies. In Gwinnett County,

PURCHASE AGENTS

On the customers' side, electronic purchase agents help the Internet shopper to find the desired goods or services. Auto-By-Tel, for example, is a service that helps customers find the right car for the right price. Similarly, search robots such as PriceSCAN permit consumers to find the best price on thousands of computer hardware and software products. Such programs automatically travel the Web and gather data from magazine ads and vendor catalogs. Web robots are also sometimes referred to as Web crawlers or spiders. Companies such as BizBots are developing a "real time 24 by 7 (24 hours a day, 7 days a week) automated market of markets" that link multiple sites in various business sectors (such as chemicals) to provide complete transparency for buyers and sellers.[34]

MARKET MAKERS

Market makers are mediators that bring together buyers and sellers and increase market efficiency. Typical examples are the numerous auction sites that have sprung up on the Web. According to its Web site, Onsale, for example, had more than 160,000 visitors per day and in excess of 1 million registered users.[35] And the need to innovate can also be felt in this part of the supply chain. eBay, with some 5.6 million registered users as the world's leading person-to-person on-line trading community, recently announced the availability of pagers featuring "eBay a-go-go," a new service that allows users to receive updates on

---

[34] Jerry Wind and Vijay Mahajan. "Digital Marketing," p. 6.
[35] www.ebay.com/index.html, cited 30 August 1999.
[36] www.ebay.com/index.html, cited 30 August 1999.

Georgia, where distances are large, judges who once had to be visited in person by police officers to sign off-hours arrest and home search warrants are now connected via PCs to local police stations. "A video conference link enables the judges to discuss the warrant and, if they're satisfied, sign it using the PenOp system, which no one at the police station can tamper with," says Mr. Levin. In Tennessee, the First American Bank offers insurance at its retail branches using PenOp software to verify signatures, and a local insurance company with a sales force of 7,000 uses it to collect signatures for policy application forms. American General Life and Accident, the insurer, has saved $2 to $3 million in costs, cut its error rate to nil, and accelerated the dispatch of policy certificates.

With the cost of peripheral digitizers falling from $200 to as little as $30 PenOp believes the market is ready to explode. "It's an end-solution that removes paper completely," says Mr. Levin. "We think it's the 'last mile' in enabling e-commerce." Recently, the software has been made compatible with Windows CE technology. In the United Kingdom, PenOp has been used at DSS offices in Liverpool to combat fraud based on impersonation. "When three dole claimants saw that they had to sign on a computer, they left quickly," says Mr. Smithies. PenOp also expects digitizers to become widespread for the checking of signatures on credit card transactions. "Credit card companies charge retailers more when no signature is involved in the transaction," says Mr. Smithies. "And, by contrast, identification via smart cards does not provide proof of intent. Ours does." Soon, PenOp will launch a second patented product that combines its technology with that of IriScan, a U.S. company. James Cambier, chief technology officer at IriScan, says his system will provide confirmation of the person's identity while PenOp will secure legal proof of intent by the author as well as the "bonding" of the signature to the document. In streamlining the signatory process, whether across the Internet, intranets, or extranets, PenOp believes it can remove an important and unnecessary bottleneck hindering the development of e-commerce.

SOURCE: Marcus Gibson, "Signing Up for E-commerce," *Financial Times,* 7 July 1999, p. XV.

their eBay auctions via pagers.[36] PlasticNet.com for plastics, Metals.com for steel, and various other sites bring together buyers and sellers in business-to-business markets.

PAYMENT AND LOGISTIC SPECIALISTS

Currently, one of the main stumbling blocks for the use of electronic markets continues to be the means of payment via the Internet. However, the development of efficient electronic payment systems is advancing rapidly. It is expected that by the year 2005, some 30 percent of all consumer payments will be based on digital payment systems.[37] In the meantime, traditional credit card companies such as VISA are managing the transfer of payments and the associated risks. The box "PenOP: Signing Up for E-Commerce" provides some insights on how a British company helps to overcome one of the last hurdles facing a paperless business culture, namely the need for a signature on documents.

Physical distribution via the Internet is only possible for software products or information services (e.g., investor, stock market, and database information). All other products have to be shipped via traditional channels. Nevertheless, the Internet and the Web offer a completely new view of the traditional distribution function. Although physical distribution was one of the core functions for the traditional retail/commerce systems, this aspect can be unbundled and outsourced using international distribution experts (e.g., UPS). Moreover, the logistic functions of warehouses get outsourced to logistic experts and software companies.

---

[37] Georg Kristoferitsch, *Digital Money, Electronic Cash, Smart Cards: Chancen und Risiken des Zahlungsverkehrs via Internet* (Wien: Überreuter, 1998).

Summary

The rapid advances in information technology are profoundly affecting the way global marketing is conducted. The global, instant reach of customers has not only opened up additional distribution and communication channels and enabled precise targeting (segment of one), customization, and interaction, but it has also given rise to fundamentally new business models. Technological changes have also empowered customers by proving more transparency, allowing them to propose their own prices, and offering a platform for dealing directly with each other at auction sites.[38] This chapter documented some of the paradigmatic changes in the technological environment and discussed the impact of these changes on established rules of competition. The need to reach a dominant market position in a very short time, the shift from firm-focused strategies to strategic alliances and networks, high start-up investment requirements, and the heightened importance of ongoing innovations are among the issues raised in this context. Finally, we have taken a closer look at the components of the electronic value chain to demonstrate the different roles global marketers can play in e-commerce.

Discussion Questions

1. What are the key players in an electronic value chain and which functions do they serve?
2. What are the main characteristics of consumers buying on the Internet and how do these differ from the characteristics of traditional consumers?
3. Which strategic marketing implications arise from the so-called "network effect"?
4. How can information and communication technology contribute to shorter new-product development cycles? Cite examples.
5. What are the implications of the described technological changes on
   (a) the organizational structure of corporate activities across countries
   and (b) the importance of organizational boundaries?
6. It has been argued that the Internet has given rise to new business models. Do you agree with this proposition? Please provide reasons why you do or do not support this notion.

Web Hot Spots

INTERNET TRENDS

This site gives the latest figures on the trends and growth of the Internet. It also shows you how many .com, .edu, .org, and others exist around the world.

www.mids.org/mapsale/data/trends/trends-199907/index.htm

BUILD A SMART

If you want to design your own frog-green and yellow Smart with exchangeable body panels, this is the place to go.

http://mitglied.tripod.de/ ~ smartinfo/new2.htm

SHOPPING AGENTS

Want to buy a new computer and use a shopping agent to find the lowest price? This is your site: eSmarts has done extensive testing on shopping agents for computers and rated them on a scale of one to five.

www.esmarts.com/computers/computers_shopping_agents.html

---

[38] For example, at Priceline.com.

ONSALE.COM

Onsale is one of the largest and oldest on-line auctions. It holds several large auctions each week with lots of merchandise, especially in computers, sports and fitness, home and office, and travel.

www.onsale.com

VIRTUALVINEYARD.COM

In case you are dying to buy a 1997 Pinot Noir from the Martinborough Vineyard in New Zealand and save some travel money, this is the way to shop. Apparently, the Pinot Noir is absolutely stunning and an indication of what can come out of New Zealand in a good vintage. Ripe, quite full bodied, and tasty.

www.virtualvin.com

Suggested Readings

Browning, John. *Pocket Information Technology.* London: The Economist Books, 1997.

Burke, Raymond R. "Virtual Shopping Breakthrough in Marketing Research," *Harvard Business Review* (March/April 1996): 120–131.

Cairncross, Frances. "The Death of Distance." *Economist: Special Report on Telecommunications,* 30 September 1995, p. SS5.

Carpenter, Phil. *eBrands.* Boston: Harvard Business School Press, 2000.

Deighton, John. "Commentary on Exploring the Implications of the Internet for Consumer Marketing." *Journal of the Academy of Marketing Science,* 24, no. 4 (1997): 347–351

Dempsey, Gery. "A Hands-On Guide for Multilingual Websites," *World Trade* (1999).

Dicksen, P. *Global Shift. The Internationalization of Economic Activity.* London: Paul Chapman Publishing, 1992.

Downes, Larry, and Chunka Mui. *Unleashing the Killer App: Digital Strategies for Market Dominance.* Boston: Harvard Business School Press, 1998.

Evans, Philip, and Thomas S. Wurster. *Blown to Bits.* Boston: Harvard Business School Press, 1999.

Gielgun, Ron. *How to Succeed in Internet Business by Employing Real-World Strategies.* Preview Publications, 1998.

"Going Digital: How New Technology Is Changing our Lives." In *The Economist.* London: The Economist Newspaper Ltd., 1998.

Griese, J. "Auswirkungen globaler Informations und Kommuniktionssysteme auf die Organisation weltweit tätiger Unternehmen." In *Managementforschung 2,* edited by W.h. V. Staehle and P. Conrad, pp. 163–175. Berlin: de Gruyter, 1992.

Hagel, John III, and Marc Singer. *Net Worth: Shaping Markets When Customers Make the Rules.* Boston: Harvard Business School Press, 1999.

Iansiti, Marco, and Alan MacCormack. "Developing Products on Internet Time," *Harvard Business Review* (September–October 1997): 108-117.

Komenar, Margo. *Electronic Marketing.* New York: John Wiley & Sons, Inc., 1996

McKenna, Regis. "Real-Time Marketing," *Harvard Business Review* (July/August 1995): 87–95.

Modahl, Mary. *Now or Never: How Companies Must Change Today to Win the Battle for Internet Consumers.* New York: HarperBusiness, 2000

Mougayar, Walid. *Opening Digital Markets: Battle Plans and Business Strategies for Internet Commerce.* Upper Saddle River, NJ: Prentice Hall, 1997.

Picot, Arnold, Ralf Reichwald, and Rolf T. Wigand. *Die grenzenlose Unternehmung: Information, Organisation und Management.* 2nd ed. Wiesbaden: Gabler Verlag, 1996.

Picot, A., T. Ripperger, and B. Wolff. "The Fading Boundaries of the Firm." *Journal of Institutional and Theoretical Economics* (1996): 65–72.

Rayport, Jeffrey F., and John J. Sviokla. "Exploiting the Virtual Value Chain," *Harvard Business Review* (November/December 1995): 75–85.

Römer, Marc. *Strategisches IT-Management in internationalen Unternehmungen.* Wiesbaden: Gabler, 1997.

Schlegelmilch, Bodo B., and R. Sinkovics. "Marketing in the Information Age—Can We Plan for an Unpredictable Future?" *International Marketing Review,* 14, no. 3 (1998): 162–170.

Schwartz, Evan I. *Digital Darwinism: Seven Breakthrough Business Strategies for Surviving in the Cutthroat Web Economy.* New York: Broadway Books, 1999.

Schwartz, Evan I. *Webonomics.* New York: Broadway Books, 1997.

Seybold, Patricia B. *customers.com: How to Create a Profitable Business Strategy for the Internet and Beyond.* New York: Times Books, 1998.

Silverstein, Barry. *Business-to-Business Internet Marketing: Proven Strategies for Increasing Profits Through Internet Direct Marketing.* Wilson Press, 1998.

Sivadas, E., R. Grewel, and J. Kellaris. "The Internet as a Micro Marketing Tool: Targeting Consumers through

Preferences Revealed in Music Newsgroup Usage." *Journal of Business Research,* 41, no. 3 (1998): 179–186.

Sterne, Jim. *Customer Service on the Internet: Building Relationships, Increasing Loyalty, and Staying Competitive.* New York: John Wiley & Sons, Inc., 1996.

Tomlinson, Richard. "Internet Free Europe," *Fortune,* 6 September 1999.

Wilson, Diane D., and Paul F. Nunes, eds. *eEconomy: Ein Piel mit neuen Regeln.* Sonderteil eCommerce: Wege zum Erfolg in der elektronischen Wirtschaft ed. vol. 1, *Outlook:* Anderson Consulting, 1998.

Yudkin, Marcia. *Marketing Online: Low-Cost, Hight-Yield Strategies for Small Businesses and Professionals.* New York: McGraw Hill, 1995.

◆◆◆ Part V Cases

CEAC–China

At the end of October 1995 the Board of Directors of CEAC held a meeting in Barcelona. With the company approaching its 50th anniversary, CEAC's directors were facing what could well be one of the most far-reaching decisions in the company's history: after almost two years of preliminary negotiations, they had to decide what action to take in China.

CEAC was an entirely Spanish, family-owned group of companies that had been founded in 1946 and was active in the closely related fields of vocational distance learning and publishing

The Group had significant international experience. Starting in Argentina in 1964, it had achieved a presence in practically all Spanish-speaking countries. Subsequently, it had extended its activities, either directly or indirectly, to other countries such as Switzerland, Sweden, France and Portugal.

In the early 1990s—after the fall of Communism— CEAC had commenced activities in the Polish and Hungarian markets and had also begun exploring its possibilities in Romania and Russia.

In April 1994, Juan Antonio Martí Castro, Group Managing Director and founder of the FECEA[1] Foundation, had taken part in a trade mission to China organized by the said Foundation.

The task of organizing the contacts that the delegates were to make in China had been entrusted to Manuel Vallejo, a Spanish citizen with almost ten years' experience in China. At the end of 1993 he had joined Taxon, a company with permanent head offices in Beijing, to act as a commercial and business consultant in China.

Thanks to Manuel Vallejo's perseverance and dedication, after a number of tentative and unfruitful contacts, a possible Chinese partner for CEAC had eventually been found: New World Publishing Co., a company belonging to the State-run Foreign Language Publications Bureau. After several months' negotiations, they had hammered out the financial and operational details of an agreement to set up a joint venture, which, curiously enough, would be formally set up as a consulting company: "Beijing New World–CEAC Consulting Co. Ltd."

By October 1995, the CEAC Group had invested around US$100,000 in trips, surveys and exploratory work

for the project. But now, if CEAC's Board of Directors decided to go ahead and sign the agreement negotiated with New World Publishing Co., they would most likely have to Invest a further US$300,000 at least.

Everyone present at the board meeting fully realized that the moment of truth had arrived and that if they approved the signing of the agreement with New World Publishing Co., they would be putting an end to the "sounding out and exploration" stage and embarking upon a course that would involve far more substantial commitments of financial, human and technological resources. In fact, the decision could significantly influence the CEAC Group's strategic development in the 21st century.

BACKGROUND

The CEAC Group originated in 1945, when Juan Martí-Salavedra took the initiative of writing a course to prepare students for the entrance exam to the Architectural Technicians' Colleges of Barcelona and Madrid. These courses were advertised in the press and the material was mailed to the student's home address and paid for, lesson by lesson, on delivery.

Those first mimeographed lessons bore the words "Centro de Estudios A.C." on the cover, which quite simply meant Architectural Technicians by Mail ("Aparejadores por Correspondencia").

Martí-Salavedra secured the help of his brother-in-law, and subsequently that of José Menal Ramón, who was somewhat younger than Martí, had a degree in business administration, and worked in a construction company. José Menal became Martí's chief collaborator and partner.[2]

They gradually developed other vocational distance learning courses. At first, these new courses were all on subjects connected with the building industry ("Draftsman," "Reinforced Concrete Technican," "Surveyor," etc.). Later on, they started offering sold-by-mail courses for other professions, such as machinist ("Milling Machine Operator," "Lathe Operator," etc.) and automobile repairman.

The procedure for developing courses in each new speciality was the same as for the building sector: they first produced a general course (e.g. "Automobile Repairs"). If this was a success, they would write other more highly specialized courses on the same subject (e.g. "Automobile Electrical Circuits," "Automobile Mechanics," "Bodyworks," etc.). They later went on to offer distance learning courses on hobbies and artistic subjects, such as "Drawing," "Oil Painting," and "Photography."

This case is from the Research Department at IESE. Prepared by Professor Lluís G. Renart and Francisco Parés, Lecturer, October 1996. Copyright © 1996, IESE. Used with permission. No part of this publication may be reproduced.

[1] FECEA (Fundació Empresa Catalunya Europa Amèrica; Catalonia-Europe-America Business Foundation) was created in 1989 by a group of businessmen to promote the internationalization of Catalan enterprises, mainly through training activities and trade missions.

---

[2] The CEAC Group was still owned by the Martí and Menal families in 1996.

Another significant development was the eventual separation of their two lines of business: producing and marketing vocational distance learning courses, on the one hand, and book and magazine publishing activities on the other. The latter were later consolidated in a new company: Grupo Editorial CEAC, S.A.

The growth of the company had been entirely self-financed.

"We have never taken bills to the bank for discount," declared Juan Martí Salavedra proudly in 1995. "We have confined ourselves to doing what we could finance out of our own resources, and if we could not finance something, we simply did not do it. This superbly sound financial position has always given us great peace of mind, and also liberty to experiment with new ideas and to embark upon entrepreneurial innovations and adventures, since if one of our new undertakings was unsuccessful, no damage was done. It was our own money, which we ourselves had generated and which, therefore, obviously did not have to be paid back to any financial institution."

SELLING PROCESS FOR DISTANCE LEARNING COURSES IN SPAIN, UP TO 1985

CEAC gradually developed distance learning courses in a number of different fields.[3] When CEAC first started up, students who signed up received one lesson a week by mail, paying cash on delivery (C.O.D.).

As early as 1955, the company management decided to offer—and, of course, by subsequently honour—a total guarantee on their courses. Under this guarantee, students who had completed a course—and had done all the exercises—and were not fully satisfied, would be entitled to a full refund of the amount they had paid and, moreover, to keep all the teaching materials they had received.

The selling process for a specific course began with advertisements in newspapers and magazines, or direct mail campaigns targeted at certain segments of potential customers, which were defined according to demographic criteria or the content of the course (see Exhibit 1 for two adverts published at the end of 1995).

Potential students sent CEAC a request for further information, using the coupon from the advert or the coupon and prepaid envelope included in the direct mail piece.

CEAC immediately sent them a full-colour glossy brochure of several pages. The brochure emphasized the impor-

---

[3] The breakdown of students by subject group in 1994 was as follows: Construction and Installation Technician (17.8% of students enrolled in 1994), Electronics (5.6%), Computer Systems (6.8%), Automobile (5.3%), Draftsman (3.7%), Accounting and Business Administration (13.8%), General Culture (21.7%), Film and Photography (3.3%), Beauty Care, Fashion and Tailoring/Dressmaking (8.7%), and Languages (4.5%). CEAC offered up to ten specific courses in each subject group.

tance of the subject of the course for the student's career and gave a detailed description of the teaching programme, which was divided up into a number of chapters or teaching units. It also explained how the course would be carried out with the help of a teacher-tutor and gave CEAC's guarantee of a refund should the student not be fully satisfied at the end of the course. The brochure came with a registration form, which gave the price of each complete course.

If the potential students were persuaded, they would register by completing and signing the registration form, and mailing it to CEAC. A few days later, they would receive a letter from CEAC, congratulating them on their decision and enclosing, the first lesson of the course, which was paid for on delivery. They would subsequently receive the rest of the course, lesson by lesson, paying for each one C.O.D., until the course had been completed.

From 1974 onward, still faithful to their guarantee, Juan Martí Salavedra and José Menal Ramón decided that students who enrolled on a course would receive all the relevant material In one go, immediately upon registration (all the teaching, units, evaluation tests and other material), although they would continue to pay for it month by month, against a simple reimbursement card mailed to them.

Should a potential student who had shown interest and received the brochure not register for the course, CEAC would send him/her up to seven reminder letters. It should be noted that at that time (1950s and 1960s) all contact with students was by mail.

INSTRUCTOR ATTENTION FOR ENROLLED STUDENTS

After the initial years, during which Juan Martí Salavedra or José Menal personally attended to students' queries and corrected their exercises and exams, CEAC engaged an ever-expanding team of collaborators to handle these tasks. Eventually, CEAC created a Studies Department to cover two broad areas of responsibility: the development of new courses, and attention to and monitoring of enrolled students.

The monitoring was done by an ample staff of teacher-tutors, specialists in their respective subjects. These tutors were responsible for correcting tests and giving students guidance, both on the content of the course and on study methods and any difficulties that might arise during the learning period. The average length of a course was 15 months, the shortest being 6 months and the longest 36 months.

Each teacher-tutor was responsible for a certain number of students, whose progress he would monitor until the course was concluded, at which time they received the appropriate CEAC diploma.

INITIAL INTERNATIONAL ACTIVITIES

In the early 1960s, by which time the company was quite well consolidated in Spain, CEAC management began to think about ways of selling their courses in other Spanish-

EXHIBIT 1   CEAC Advertisements Published in Spain at the End of 1995

speaking countries. In 1964, with the help of the Ibero-American Education Office (OEI) and UNESCO, they started promoting the courses in various Latin American markets, starting with Argentina.

They decided to share the business with local partners, one in each country. These partners were called "Licensees."

CEAC gave its Licensees the benefit of the teaching and business experience it had acquired in distance learning,

COMPUTER SYSTEMS
- Introduction to data processing
- Windows 3.1
- Windows 95
- Lotus 1-2-3 for Windows
- WP for Windows
- dBase for Windows
- Corel Draw
- DOS
- Programmer-Analyst. Basic

GEN. CULTURE
- School leaving certificate
- Childcare and pre-school education
- Psychology
- Entrance exams for Government Administration and Social Security auxiliary staff
- Study and speed reading techniques
- Guitar

DRAFTING
- General
- Mechanical
- Construction

ELECTRONICS
- Electronics and microelectronics
- Digital electronics

BUSINESS ADMINISTRATION
- Management and administration of small and medium-sized enterprises
- Taxation and tax consulting
- General Accounting
- Financial and accounts management
- Analytical accounts and budget control
- Balance sheet analysis and auditing
- Retail business management
- Marketing Sales Director
- Professional salesperson

IMAGE
- Photography
- Video

BEAUTY CARE AND FASHION
- Tailoring/Dressmaking, with cassettes
- Hairdressing
- Beauty care (with and without videotapes)
- Fashion design

CONSTRUCTION
- Skilled bricklayer
- Construction technician

INSTALLATION TECHNICIANS
- Plumbing
- Electrical installer: General, home and industrial installations
- Electrical technician
- Gardening (with and without videotapes)
- Kitchen design technician
- Air conditioning/heating
- Antenna installer
- Gas installer

AUTOMOBILES
- Automobile mechanic
- Motorbike mechanic
- Bodywork and painting
- Automobile electronics and electricity

CATERING
- Professional waiting

DRAWING, PAINTING AND DECORATION
- Humorous drawing
- Oil painting
- Decoration

LANGUAGES
- English
- English with videotape
- French
- German

With CEAC, YOU can learn.

Courses in Interior Decoration

You will learn at home, at your own pace, without set hours or transport problems.

Your teacher can be reached by phone to answer your queries.

With all the necessary material for you to practise right from the very first day.

You will obtain your CEAC diploma that will vouch for your professional training and knowledge.

902 102 103
24-hour information service
http:// www.ceac.com

Under the CEAC guarantee, your money will be refunded if you are not satisfied after completing the course.

CEAC has 50 years' experience. More than a million and a half students have trained through CEAC.

APPLY FOR INFORMATION free, with no obligation

Fill in this coupon in block letters and send it to CEAC c/Aragón, 472 08013 Barcelona.

You may also request more information by phone (902 102 103) or by INTERNET (http:// www.ceac.com)

Please send me information on the Course on ....

Full Name ....

Address: Street name: ....

Nº.................... Floor: .... Door Nº:.................... Post Code: ....

City: ....

Province: ....Tel: ....

Date of birth: .... Profession: ....

Ministry of Education and Science authorization nº 8039185 (Official Bulletin 3-6-83)

either by bringing the Licensee to Barcelona for training or by having Juan Martí Salavedra do it "on the spot."

The courses were designed and printed in Barcelona. The Licensee would buy this material at cost, plus an "industrial margin," and had one year in which to pay for it. The Licensee would then, at its own expense, take care of all marketing activities, as well as the support and monitoring of enrolled students. In addition to buying the courses from CEAC, the Licensee had to pay Barcelona a royalty of 10% on sales, to be settled once the Licensee had received payment from its students.

CEAC had to deal with certain "surmountable" problems, such as differences in terminology or in the words used for certain materials in the different Latin American countries. The real problem was finding Licensees who would put enough effort into the business and were capable of running it in a professional and responsible manner and were reliable as far as payments were concerned.

They also found that sudden, drastic devaluations of the local currency, or a scarcity of convertible currency, often led to situation where a Licensee was unable to pay its debts. However, in spite of these difficulties, CEAC at one time had up to 40,000 students enrolled with its Licensees in Argentina, Uruguay, Venezuela, Perú, Colombia, Bolivia, Costa Rica–Central America and Mexico. As Martí Salavedra admitted, "on the whole, it was very profitable for CEAC."

Outside of Spanish America, instead of negotiating and signing agreements with Licensees to sell the same courses as in Spain, CEAC opted to sell the translation and sales rights for its courses. This brought revenues from countries such as Switzerland, Sweden, France, Germany, Greece and Portugal. In some cases, a local firm would take on the job of translating, printing and selling the courses and monitoring students. The local firm would sell the courses together with its own courses—or courses acquired from other sources—under its own name on the domestic market, so that the students never actually saw the name CEAC or knew where the course came from. In some cases, CEAC reached an agreement to exchange courses. In this way, it also sold courses designed in other countries, duly translated and revised, in Spain and Spanish-speaking countries.

In the specific case of Portugal, an agreement was reached in 1965 with a local publishing company. The publisher would act as Licensee, although with certain special concessions, such as that CEAC would assist in translating its courses into Portuguese. The Portuguese Licensee set up a separate company called CETOP (Centro de Educación a Distancia de Portugal).

JUAN ANTONIO MARTÍ CASTRO JOINS THE COMPANY

In 1974, Juan Antonio Martí Castro, the only son among Juan Martí Salavedra's five children, obtained his degree in Business Administration at ESADE. He joined the company after graduation and over the following ten years held posts of increasing responsibility in the different departments of the companies belonging to the Group, whose activities by then extended beyond vocational distance learning (with some complementary activities in the field of direct classroom teaching) to publishing, graphic arts and bookbinding.

In 1985 Juan Antonio Martí Castro was appointed Chief Executive Officer of the CEAC Group, taking the reins from his father, who, having reached the age of 65, stayed on as President of the Group.[4]

By 1989 the conversion rate of "potential students" (those who had shown an interest in a specific course by replying to an advertisement or direct mail) into "fully enrolled students" had fallen quite considerably, to reach a low of around 10%, compared with 25–30% in the past. As a consequence, the advertising and promotional costs per fully enrolled student increased significantly. At the same time, "drop-out rates"[5] rose alarmingly.

In view of the situation, Juan Antonio Martí Castro took a number of decisions that radically changed the way CEAC conducted its marketing in Spain:

First of all, whereas previously the company had always promoted its courses through its own internal Advertising Department, they now started to use an outside advertising and direct marketing agency: Ogilvy & Mather Direct.

Secondly, and much more importantly, they started to build up a company sales force, which was gradually extended throughout Spain. The new sales force initiated a process of personal selling to potential students who answered the adverts or direct mail.

Under to the new sales procedure, potential students who had responded to an advert or direct mail were visited in their homes by a "cultural advisor" from CEAC, who personally gave them all the details of the course and encouraged them to sign up and enroll. If the customer was convinced, the "cultural advisor" himself would hand over all the material for the course, and at the same time prepare the official payment documents. The payment documents took the legal form of a hire purchase agreement. Payment was no longer made through cards submitted each month for payment in cash through the Post Office but by means of a monthly direct charge to a designated bank account. The

---

[4] They still held the same posts in 1996.

[5] The drop-out rate was calculated by dividing the total number of students who dropped out, i.e. who did not pay all the monthly installments for a particular course, by the total number of students registered on that course over a given period. The higher the drop-out rate, the heavier the loss for the company, as CEAC, in handing over all the course material on enrollment, effectively granted students credit, which they were supposed to repay month by month, using the reimbursement cards mailed to them.

student him or herself, or a parent, would therefore authorize the necessary standing order for monthly payments until the total cost of the course had been paid. This new system of collecting payment through the bank was much more formal and reliable than the earlier arrangement by mail.

Lastly, the company went to great lengths to renew and update the range of courses it offered, in part by revising and updating the courses it planned to keep, in part by discarding certain courses altogether and replacing them with totally new ones.

Similar efforts were being made in Latin America where, due to the general economic difficulties during the "lost decade" of the 80's, in 1995 CEAC had some 10,000 enrolled students.

IMPLEMENTING A NEW APPROACH TO INTERNATIONAL ACTIVITIES

Although the Licensee in Portugal had set up CETOP as a separate subsidiary, the company still had the mentality more of a book publisher than of a distance learning company.

Consequently, in 1990 CEAC took an unprecedented decision in its international expansion: it purchased 100% of CETOP and terminated its relationship with the Licensee. The name of the company was changed to, CEAC-Portugal and 49.9% of the new company was sold to another Portuguese publishing house (Pilátano Editora), which was already working with CEAC in the field of publishing. From then on, CEA–Spain took full responsibility for the management of the Portuguese firm and changed its operating policy: the subsidiary was to be an exact replica of the Barcelona head office, except that the courses would continue to be designed in Barcelona. But from now on the courses were to be translated, adapted and printed in Portugal. And, of course, all the marketing and everything to do with assisting and monitoring students was to be done there too.[6]

CEAC's management team then decided to adopt the Portuguese model as standard: from then on, no more Licensees would be appointed (although the existing ones would be kept).

This new way of operating meant setting up local subsidiaries in all new markets where CEAC planned to start selling its courses. CEAC–Spain would be the majority shareholder in these subsidiaries, but it was considered desirable to have a local partner as a minority shareholder in each country. As in Portugal, each local subsidiary would be an absolute replica of CEAC–Spain, except that all the courses would be designed in Barcelona.

This decision coincided in time with the fall of the Communist regimes in Central and Eastern Europe. Thanks to the experience it had acquired in Latin America and Portugal, CEAC was the first Western company in the field of vocational distance learning to start operations in these countries.

Poland:

In January 1990, a small trade mission of Spanish businessmen led by Josep Antoni Durán i Lleida—head of Unió Democràtica de Catalunya, a Catalan political party—visited Poland and held a meeting with Lech Walesa while he was still leader of Solidarity.

After this initial contact, CEAC management entered into collaboration with Mercé Soley, a secretary at the Spanish Embassy, who had been living in Poland for over 20 years and was married to a Polish citizen. Mercé Soley had set up an office offering services to Spanish companies.

In September 1990 they carried out the first, very tentative, market test, which consisted of placing advertisements in the press offering courses that had not yet been translated into Polish. It was soon discovered that there were hardly any requests for further information on vocational training courses. However, there was a lot of interest in the English Language course.

Consequently, after writing to the interested students to tell them that the course would be slightly delayed, within a month CEAC was established in Poland and was selling the English Language course. It was able to do this because the course it sold in Spain was not in fact a Spanish-English course but a progressive immersion course, written completely in English, so that it could be sold in Poland in virtually the same form.

What was intended to be just an initial market test, therefore, became the basis for setting up the new subsidiary in Warsaw.

CEAC invested some US$200,000 in the new subsidiary, including the subsequent translation of several courses into Polish. Initially, the subsidiary was managed by a Pole, a former high-ranking civil servant in the Polish Ministry of Education, who spoke Spanish. Unfortunately, after a period of successful growth in 1991 and 1992, sales levelled off in 1993 and began to fall in 1994. Accordingly, a new manager was appointed in 1995, a Spaniard, whose mission was to reorganize the company and set up—as in Spain—a team of "cultural advisors," who would personally follow up all requests for information about courses, with a view to clinching more sales.

At the end of 1995, CEAC management felt that Poland was potentially a reasonably attractive market, although not the "gold mine" they had originally thought. The market could perhaps stabilize at around 5,000 enrollments per year. Nevertheless, it should be pointed out that, in view of the low purchasing power of Polish consumers, CEAC was selling at an average price of around 50,000 pesetas per course.

Hungary:

Encouraged by the initial success in Poland, CEAC started to sell its courses in Hungary in 1991 and six courses were translated.

---

[6] The Portuguese subsidiary was expected to achieve a turnover of some 2 billion escudos (equivalent to some 1.6 billion pesetas) in 1996.

Unfortunately, after a promising start, the business quickly came to a standstill and in 1995 the company decided to end its activities in Hungary.

Russia:

In 1991–92, members of CEAC's management team contacted a State-run university that had some distance learning activities. However, the discussions were cut short after a strange dinner at which CEAC's managers felt it was being suggested that the project could not go ahead unless it had the "protection" of certain unsavoury-looking individuals among the guests.

Romania:

CEAC made contacts with a number of government institutions during 1994–95, but nothing came of them, so no courses were translated.

THE CEAC GROUP IN SPAIN AT THE END OF 1995

The CEAC Group was expected to close the 1995 financial year with a total turnover (all the companies throughout the world) of approximately 13 billion pesetas. Of this figure, 10.5 billion pesetas came from sales in Spain and 2.5 billion from CEAC Group activities outside Spain.[7]

a) Vocational Distance Training Activities

At the end of 1995, the CEAC Group was offering 58 different vocational distance learning courses. The total number of courses available was stable since whenever a new course was launched, one of the older courses was discontinued, in a process of constant renewal and updating.

The General Manager, Tomás Blay[8] estimated that by the end of 1995, 25,000 new students would have enrolled. Since the courses lasted an average of 15 months, the CEAC Group would at any one time be training some 32,000 students in Spain. The record year for enrollments was 1991, with 41,000 new student registrations.

The average price of a course was around 125,000 pesetas. (Prices ranged from 75,000 pesetas for a course lasting 6 months to 175,000 pesetas for a 36-month course, which included audio-visual material and videotapes.) The student could choose between a number of different payment options.

Each pupil was assigned a tutor, who was an expert in his/her subject and an employee of the company. The tutor could be consulted at any time, in person, by telephone, by letter, by fax or on the Internet. The exercises that the pupil had to do at the end of each teaching unit were reviewed by a teacher-reviewer, who was not an employee of the company and who passed the reviewed exercises on to the tutor. The reviewers were normally specialists in their subject who worked in the relevant sector.

The whole process of following up and monitoring the progress of each student was highly computerized, so that if any student failed to send in his exercises on time, he was automatically sent a reminder note.

On finishing the course, students had to take a final exam, also by correspondence. If they passed the exam, they received the appropriate CEAC diploma, which, although not officially recognized, was held in high regard by Spanish companies.

The profile of the students naturally varied according to the subject matter of the course. Overall, however, they were between 18 and 25 years old, of both sexes, of middle or lower-middle class families, and they tended—though not to any significant decree—to live in rural areas.

According to company management, the main *key success factors* in this vocational distance training activity in 1995 were the following:

a) Juan Martí Salavedra, Group President, insisted in 1995 that the company depended for its very existence, and always would depend, on the intrinsic quality of the courses, as well as on the quality of the constant monitoring, attention and support it gave to students.

Still sprightly at 75, Juan Martí Salavedra's face lit up when he said, with total conviction:

"Our primary goal has to be prestige based on the quality of our courses and the service we give our students. Over and above any consideration of money and profit, we must ensure that people think of CEAC first and foremost as a centre of learning. The student must always come first. Internally, we have to operate as a company, with an organization chart, budgets, and all sorts of economic and financial calculations. But we would fail in our mission if our students did not receive more than they expect from us. We must ensure that the students feel they are getting more than their money's worth. We must be caring and encouraging and convey warm-hearted understanding."

b) Juan Antonio Martí Castro, Chief Executive Officer, agreed with his father; then, following the different steps in the business process, he said that the next key success factor was creativity in the advertising message. The advertisements in the press and those sent by mail had to generate enough serious requests for further information.

c) The next key success factor, closely related to the previous one, was to accurately monitor the cost of a request for further information. CEAC had set up control systems and mechanisms that told them

---

[7] According to the "Official Census of Spanish Exporters—14th Edition," published by ICEX (Spanish Foreign Trade Institute), in 1993 CEAC, S.A. and Editorial CEAC, S.A. exported goods to the value of 58 and 159 million pesetas respectively, all under customs tariff 49.01—"Books, leaflets and similar printed matter, including loose sheets."

[8] Tomás Blay was a lawyer and IESE MBA.

exactly how many requests for information had been generated by each press advert or direct mail piece. Knowing the cost of each action in each medium, it was possible to calculate the "yield" or cost in pesetas of each request for information they received.

With this information it was possible to continuously adjust and fine-tune a wide range of variables, such as the advertising, message, the size of the reply coupon, whether a full-colour advert was more effective than a black-and-white one, the size of the press advert, etc.

d) Ultimately, the most important thing, was to effectively monitor and control the cost per new student enrolled. Juan Antonio Martí Castro emphasized that these two cost variables (the cost per request for information received and the cost per student enrolled) were not totally independent of each other, but were interrelated. For example, an advert for the guitar course published in the music magazine "Super Pop," which was read by youngsters, might generate a large number of requests for further information, but few actual enrollments. At the other extreme, adverts for certain vocational courses, such as the Tax and Fiscal Advisor course, which were inserted in more serious professional publications and targeted at a more adult audience, usually generated fewer requests for further information, but the rate of conversion into actual enrollments was higher. In summary, a whole range of variables was involved, such as the content of the course offered, the advertising medium, the average age of the readers, etc.

e) Another key factor was the quality of the sales team, which CEAC called the "network of cultural advisors." At the end of 1995, CEAC had a strong team of sales representatives, who visited prospective students in their homes to explain the content of the course they had shown an interest in, the teaching method, methods of payment, and other details. They also filled in the enrollment forms.

The team covered the whole of Spain and was made up of a sales manager, 8 area managers, 23 assistant area managers and some 170 cultural advisors. The cultural advisors worked full-time for the company; however, they were not actually on the company payroll, but acted as mercantile agents. They worked entirely on commission and none of their expenses were covered by the company. In spite of this, the turnover rate was relatively low and 120 of the 170 could be considered to be working permanently for the company.

f) The last key success factor was the payment default rate. In 1995, the company's internal accounts included a provision for unpaid debts of 11% of the total cross value of the enrollment fees.

g) As a result of the above-mentioned key success factors, the breakdown of the company's profit and loss account in Spain was as follows:

Gross sales	100% = average 125,000 pesetas per course
Cost of goods sold	6%
Marketing costs	22%
Sales force	20%
Personnel	10%
Bad debts	11%
Overheads	16%
Profits before tax	15%

Personnel expenses included the salaries of the tutors and the approximately 120 general administrative employees. Overheads included the variable compensation of the correctors of students' exercises and exams, together with depreciation and financial expenses.

b) Book Publishing Activities: Grupo Editorial CEAC, S.A.

This company published books. There were several trademarks or registered publishing names within the Group, such as Ediciones CEAC, Timun Mas and Vidorama. Each of them specialized in publishing a particular kind of book: technical books, children's and fantasy books, art books, etc.

In 1995 the Group was publishing around 250 new books per year, with a turnover of approximately 1.8 billion pesetas.

c) Other Business Activities

The CEAC Group held a substantial majority shareholding in Home English, S.A., a company that sold language courses by mail. In 1995 its turnover was expected to be around 3,000 million pesetas.

It also had a majority shareholding in a company that sold women's underwear, using direct selling methods.

Another group company was in partnership with the Caixa d'Estalvis i Pensions de Barcelona, Spain's largest savings bank. It had a team of some 500 female sales personnel, working under an agency agreement, who carried out cross-selling activities to persuade customers of La Caixa to buy a wider range of financial products and services from the bank.

Finally, other companies belonging to the CEAC Group were involved in a variety of industrial activities, such as printing and bookbinding, plastic lamination of published materials, etc.

BRIEF BACKGROUND ON THE PEOPLE'S REPUBLIC OF CHINA

Economic reforms had begun in China in 1978, after the death of Mao Tse-tung. The first regulations on foreign investment were issued in 1980. Step by step, foreign investment was authorized in the fields of oil prospecting and extraction, the hotel business, and light industry.

In 1990, after the Tiananmen Square incidents, the pace of foreign investment was to a certain extent frozen, to be resumed with great momentum after Deng Xiaoping's famous voyage and speech at Shenzhen in February 1992.

One of the main consequences was heavy investment in real estate and major infrastructure, and the first stirrings of activity on the stock exchanges. Even so, investment was still severely restricted in certain sectors, such as financial services (banking and insurance), the media (radio and television) and publishing. As in other countries, the defence and telecommunications industries were closed to foreign investment.

See Exhibit 2 for further information on China.

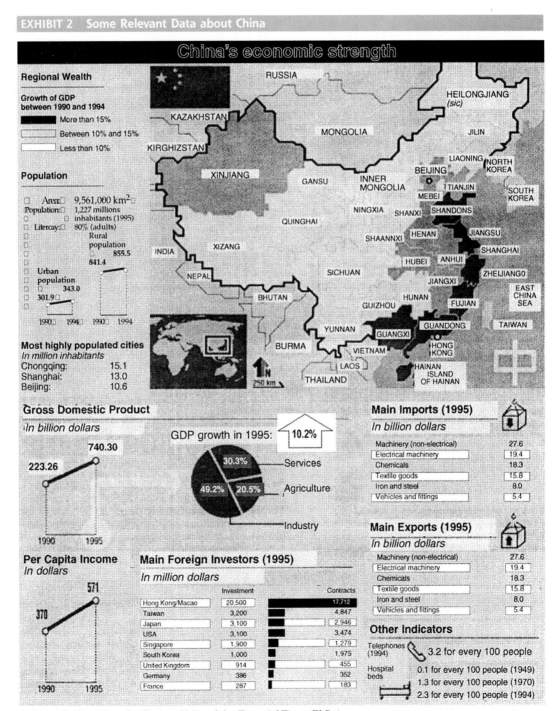

EXHIBIT 2   Some Relevant Data about China

Source: The Economist Intelligence Unit and the Financial Times, El País.

CEAC'S ACTIVITIES IN CHINA

In January 1994, the FECEA foundation charged Manuel Vallejo with the task of organizing the visits to be made by the members of a trade mission that was due to visit China from 14 to 25 April of that year. Manuel Vallejo was a Spanish citizen with considerable international experience, particularly in China (see Exhibit 3 for a summary of his career up to 1994), where he had just become a partner in the consultancy Taxon.

Juan Antonio Martí Castro had known Manuel Vallejo for more than 25 years. They had both studied at ESADE, although with a difference of two years.

At the beginning of 1994, Martí Castro was fully aware that CEAC had achieved its highest sales peak in Spain back in 1991 and was now suffering from a certain inertia in sales. In 1993, as a result of what some called the "post-Olympic shock," Spain's gross domestic product had fallen each quarter and the country had entered the deepest and longest-lasting recession since the oil crisis of the 1970s.

Moreover, the company's attempts to penetrate new markets, such as Poland or Hungary, had not worked out.

Martí Castro came to the conclusion that CEAC should opt for entering developing countries with large populations, where it could establish a "complete" sub-

---

EXHIBIT 3 Summary of Manuel Vallejo's Career up to 1994

Manuel Vallejo was born in Barcelona in 1950. He graduated in Business Administration and obtained his MBA at ESADE in 1972. He later took a Law degree at the University of Barcelona in 1980. Between 1972 and 1980 he worked for several different companies in Barcelona (Agrolimen, Matutano, Fincas Anzizu and Banco de la Pequeña y Mediana Empresa).

In 1980 he joined the Nutrexpa Group as Assistant General Manager for the business in Ecuador and set up the branch office in Peru.

In 1984 he worked as a consultant in Peru with MAC and on behalf of the World Bank. And in 1986 he was in Venezuela, representing a Catalan investment group, in the area of aluminium smelting and recycling.

In 1987, right after Spain and Portugal joined the European Community, he participated in the COM/A470 competitive examination and was included in the reserve list as apt for level A5 in DG1 of the European Community Commission. Until the end of 1988, whilst awaiting admission, he worked for the Economics and Enterprises Department of Barcelona City Hall.

In autumn 1988, the Nutrexpa Group offered him the post of resident General Manager in China, to start up a new joint venture in Tiajing that was to manufacture and launch their product, Cola Cao, on the Chinese market. Vallejo organized everything to do with installing the factory and personally took care of finding local raw materials, registering the trademark ("Gao La Gao"), creating the first television advertisements, appointing distributors, hiring personnel and organizing the accounting and financial structures.

The Cola Cao factory in China was officially inaugurated on 24 September 1990 by Juan Antonio Samaranch, the Chairman of the International Olympic Committee.

In April 1991, by which time the joint venture was producing, selling and generating income, Vallejo left China for Nutrexpa-Poland to attend to the vicissitudes of Cola Cao and their new branch in that country until the end of 1991.

In 1992, he opened the branch offices of Agrolimen in Hong Kong and Canton, while living in Hong Kong and travelling regularly to Canton to supervise the Panyu Confectionery Co. Ltd., a joint venture that manufactured TA TA chewing gum, the leading brand on the Chinese market. He took care of power relationships with the local partners and of product and trademark falsification problems there. His contract concluded at the end of 1992.

During 1993, he gave lectures at the Fuqua School of Business, Duke University, and at Davidson College in the United States, based on his experience in China and Poland.

In mid-1993, Vallejo joined Taxon Consultants in Beijing as Senior Consultant. Taxon was founded by a Chinese businessman with an MBA from the CEMI school (a business school created under the aupices of the European Foundation for Management Development). He began carrying out surveys of the Chinese market for Spanish companies in a variety of industries (hospital equipment, wine, electronic components, motorbike spare parts, veterinary products, construction machinery, chemicals and pigments, etc.).

At the beginning of 1994, he was commissioned by the FECEA foundation to organize the trade mission that was to take place during the second half of April 1994.

sidiary, i.e. one that was capable of operating just as CEAC did in Spain.

During Martí Castro's trip to China with the FECEA mission, Vallejo arranged for him to visit five State-run universities that already had a distance learning department or were active in that field, though in a very badly organized way. They all expressed an interest in exploring ways of collaborating with CEAC.

"My intuition told me that we would find a market there," affirmed Martí Castro. "Our incursions into some of the countries of Central and Eastern Europe were not too successful, but I felt that it would at least be worth our while to try out the Chinese market; this was relatively easy to do, with Manolo Vallejo working and living there for a good part of the year."

Therefore, in June 1994, after a few months' reflection, Martí Castro formally entrusted Vallejo with the task of carrying out studies and surveys of the potential market, and making contacts with a view to identifying, and possibly negotiating with, a prospective local partner. Vallejo would not be working exclusively for CEAC and would receive a fixed monthly retainer fee, plus a success fee, which would take the form of a small share in the capital of the hypothetical future CEAC subsidiary in China. The assignment was for an initial minimum period of fifteen months, renewable for a further length of time.

Vallejo started to work on the project in June 1994, with occasional help from his Chinese partner in Taxon. He was fully aware of the great difficulty of the undertaking:

"I knew that CEAC had two main activities: vocational distance training and book publishing. Both of these fields were subject to strict State and ideological control in China. CEAC's Chinese partner would therefore have to be institutionally sound and to have good connections. So I patiently went about visiting a number of colleges and universities in Beijing and Tianjing. I soon came to the conclusion that the universities would never be suitable partners for CEAC, for at least two reasons: a) because their standard response was that education in China could not be carried out by joint ventures, nor could it be done for profit. At most there could be some kind of institutional collaboration under a non-commercial legal arrangement. And b) because, naturally enough, the people I dealt with at the Chinese universities belonged to the academic world, not the business world. Some of them even disapproved of commercial activities. . . ."

Vallejo consequently decided to change his tactics and began to focus his efforts on the publishing world. But, once more, the contacts were unfruitful. One day he had dinner with a Colombian friend who worked as a translator and copy editor for the State-run firm New World Publishing Co., which belonged to the Foreign Language Publishing Group, formerly the International Publications Bureau of the Council of State. The Colombian friend very kindly offered to introduce Vallejo to some of the managers of New World Publishing Co.

"The first contact was fruitless, because the person we visited had no interest whatsoever in our proposal. However, the second interview, held on the same day, was with a real gentleman, who spoke exquisite Spanish and who, as he later told me, had agreed to receive me purely for the pleasure of speaking Spanish for a while. His name was Zheng Mou Da, and he turned out to be a lucky find for our project."

Vallejo told Zheng Mou Da about CEAC and its activities in Spain and other countries. The first meeting was followed by a series of interviews—two or three a month between July and December 1994—in which the two parties got to know each other better.

"Gradually, as we slowly built up a relationship of trust, Zheng Mou Da told me that the Chinese government was putting pressure on them to find new business opportunities. A publishing operation for Taiwan, for example. They also realized that they needed to improve their business administration skills. Their interest in CEAC was completely centered on book publishing activities. He also felt comfortable talking to the representative of a small Spanish publishing company, which did not have the same approach as the large American and German publishing groups. Later, he confessed that they had turned down proposals for collaboration with other large Western publishing groups."

In October 1994, Zheng Mou Da gave Manuel Vallejo a draft that outlined a possible operating agreement between CEAC and New World Publishing Co. This draft had, in principle, been approved by Zheng Mou Da's superiors. Vallejo analyzed the document, added his own comments and sent it to Martí Castro.

In November 1994, CEAC's CEO, accompanied by Esteve Julià, manager of the International Division, went to Beijing, where they had several meetings with Zheng. This was a preliminary direct contact, basically just so they could get to know each other, since Vallejo had stressed how important it was in China first and foremost to establish good personal relationships. It soon became clear that an atmosphere of trust and understanding had built up between Zheng Mou Da and Juan Antonio Martí Castro. Among the various issues that were dealt with, Martí Castro came to the conclusion that the Chinese expected CEAC, should an agreement be reached, to appoint one of its most experienced managers, one who had a thorough knowledge of the industry, to run the hypothetical future operation in China.

During these meetings, they also started to work out some of the details of a possible letter of intent.

Having made progress on both points, Martí Castro invited Zheng Mou Da to visit CEAC in Barcelona, alone, with some of his managers, so that they could see for themselves how the company worked. Their expenses, in Spain would be paid by CEAC.

In January 1995, Zheng Mou Da visited Barcelona with two of his executives (future members of the Board of Directors of the hypothetical joint venture), where, with the help of an interpreter hired locally by CEAC, they were given a comprehensive presentation of the company's activities. They were also received by the President of the Catalan Parliament and had dinner with the Chinese Consul in Barcelona. Vallejo had recommended that CEAC show that it was well connected and had good contacts. Finally, CEAC invited the visitors, accompanied by Vallejo, on a trip to Madrid and Granada, once the Protocol of Intentions had been signed. This document specified the objectives of a joint venture to be formed by the two parties and the financial and other contributions to be made by each partner. It was stipulated that 70% of the capital would be held by CEAC and 30% by New World Publishing Co. All of this tallied with the framework mandate that had previously been approved by Zheng Mou Da's superiors.

The contract, articles of association and operating procedures for the new joint venture were negotiated by Manuel Vallejo in Beijing between February and June 1995. At the halfway point, in April, Vallejo came to Barcelona to analyze the way the plan was progressing with Martí Castro and his whole management team.

By 25 June 1995, Zheng Mou Da and Vallejo had completed their work, in that they had prepared drafts of all the documents needed to set up the new joint venture and start operations. Now it was up to New World Publishing Co. to obtain approval from the relevant Chinese authorities.

Meanwhile, on the strength of the Protocol of Intentions signed in Barcelona, CEAC had applied for an ECIP loan [9] from the European Community, which was to be approved in September 1995, for the amount of 250,000 ecus (approximately 41 million pesetas).

Finally, at the beginning of October 1995, Zheng Mou Da informed them that everything had been approved and that New World Publishing Co. agreed to the contents of the draft documents. It was now up to the CEAC Group's Board of Directors to ratify the project. Then, if both parties agreed, the new joint venture would be set up under the name: *"Beijing New World CEAC Consulting Co. Ltd."*

---

[9] The European Community Investment Partners (ECIP) Programme was set up in 1988 within the political framework of the European Community to foster cooperation with developing countries. It is a financial instrument that offers a number of "facilities" or "windows" to support the successive phases of such ventures: identifying a business sector to invest in and a local business partner, carrying out a feasibility study, setting up a joint venture or expanding an existing joint venture, etc. Further information can be found in the book "Política comunitaria de cooperación para el desarrollo," Instituto de Cooperación para el Desarrollo, Madrid, 1992, pp. 207–216.

"THIS IS ALL VERY WELL, BUT . . . WHO AMONG THE CEAC MANAGEMENT TEAM WILL BE WILLING TO GO TO CHINA TO SET IT ALL UP?"

This was a question that Martí Castro had been asking himself for some months. After signing the Protocol of Intentions in Barcelona in January 1995, it was becoming more and more crucial and urgent to find an answer.

Martí Castro was convinced that he would need to send a high-ranking CEAC manager to China to head the joint venture as Managing Director. This post could not easily be occupied by Manuel Vallejo—not because of any lack of personal ability but because his consulting firm, Taxon, had other assignments to fulfill. Furthermore, although Vallejo had gradually become acquainted with the CEAC Group's business policy, he was far from having the intimate operational knowledge required to start up a subsidiary located so far away.

At the end of February 1995, Martí Castro was wondering whether he would have to resort to a head-hunting company to find a Managing Director for China from outside the CEAC Group. However, one day, while he was discussing some details of the China project quite informally, over lunch, with a group of managers, it suddenly occurred to him to say, more as a joke than as a serious proposition: ". . . Well, if any of you wants to go to Beijing to be in charge of this project, speak up. . . ."

Among the managers having lunch with Martí Castro was Jesús Flores, Director of the Data Processing Department of all the companies within the CEAC Group.[10] He recalled that moment:

> "I had made several trips to Portugal and had been to Poland a couple of times. Naturally, when the Chinese delegation led by Zheng Mou Da visited our company in Barcelona in January 1995, I had explained the Group's data processing systems to them. When Juan Antonio asked the question, I had to give an evasive answer at the time, but the truth is that, from that moment on, I started thinking about it. I saw it as a completely new challenge. After a few days of thinking it over to myself, I mentioned the idea at home. To my surprise, my wife Mireia agreed."

A few days later, Flores discussed the matter formally with Martí Castro, who thought it a marvelous idea. Thus, in April 1995, the "China project" was assigned to Flores, once certain details had been settled, such as his acceptance of the

---

[10] Flores was 36, married, with two children aged 4 and 6. He had graduated in Industrial Engineering in 1984. After working for 4 years in a computer services company, he had joined CEAC in 1989 as head of the Data Processing Department of Centro de Estudios CEAC, where he was responsible for a team of five. In 1991 he had been appointed Data Processing Director for all the CEAC Group companies, with a team of 18 people.

assignment for a term of three years, which was the time it was expected to take to start up the new company in China.

In July, husband and wife spent a fortnight in Beijing to sort out everything to do with living there, especially housing and schools for their children. When they saw that these matters could be satisfactorily settled their decision to go to China was confirmed, in spite of the fact that Mireia, who was an industrial engineer and a PDD graduate from IESE, would have to leave a good job.

During the following months, Flores gradually devoted more of his time to the China project and handed over responsibilities to his replacement at the head of the Data Processing Department. "During that time, I was in contact with Vallejo almost daily via the Internet."

MARKET SURVEY CARRIED OUT BY OGILVY & MATHER

In October 1995, Ogilvy & Mather carried out a market survey by conducting a series of focus groups in Yantai (Shandong). The aim was to get to know the initial reaction of the market, that is, of the potential CEAC students in China. The participants in the focus groups were asked about their educational needs, their opinions on vocational distance training in general, their reactions to the type of courses that New World-CEAC Consulting Co. would be offering both as regards content and as regards the system for monitoring students' progress by means of tutors, the exercises, the final exam, etc.

The opinions of about 50 participants were gathered. The following is a summary of the conclusions:

- The focus group participants did not consider what New World-CEAC was offering as "distance training." For them, "distance training" was something quite different, with much lower quality materials and content, and without any real monitoring of students at all. Distance learning was seen as archaic, and as a "poor relation" of the university, to the extent that the very words "distance learning" made them nervous and tense. They said: "Everything you have been showing us and telling us about is NOT distance training! It is something quite different much better!" It was therefore decided that New World-CEAC would offer "PERSONALIZED training" courses.
- The potential students expected to receive some sort of officially recognized certificate at the end of the course.
- Distance training, though of poorer quality, did exist in China in traditional subjects such as accounting, fashion design, English and medicine. However, there were no courses on subjects such as finance, marketing, automobile mechanics, air-conditioning systems or childcare.
- There was obviously a certain demand for courses—like the CEAC courses—that were not simply texts but a complete system for independent distance learning, taking the student through the material step by step, breaking it down into manageable chunks, high-

lighting the key features, so that ". . . pupils who are studying on their own do not feel that they are left to their own devices, given that they are accompanied by the text itself, the exercises and the teacher-tutor."
- The participants in the focus groups were also asked about the price they would be prepared to pay for a course of this type. The conclusion was that they would be prepared to pay up to 100 yuan for each monthly lesson or teaching unit, i.e. about 1,500 pesetas per month. This represented approximately 20% of the average official wage of New World-CEAC's target market, which was around 500 yuan per month.

If it sold its courses at this price, New World-CEAC would obtain income equivalent to about 30,000 pesetas for a complete course (1,500 pesetas per teaching unit × 20 monthly teaching units), whereas the average price of a course in Spain was around 125,000–130,000 pesetas. However, the economic effort made by the Chinese students would be relatively much greater, since the average CEAC client in Spain could pay for the whole course out of one month's wages, whereas in China they were willing to pay the equivalent of FOUR months' wages for a course!

This seemed to confirm the view expressed by Manuel Vallejo and the executives of Ogilvy & Mather that the average Chinese citizen earns little, but nevertheless has money to spend, perhaps partly from activities in the informal economy.
- Curiously, the participants were convinced that anything to do with education was a "local issue." They found it difficult to understand how anyone could possibly offer educational services from one city to another, or even across the whole country. They thought that . . . "a school in Beijing is designed to serve the citizens of Beijing."
- Finally, contrary to what they had found in certain formerly Communist countries of Central and Eastern Europe, it became apparent that in China people were anxious to do things, to improve themselves, to build a better future, to make money.

SALES FORECASTS AND QUANTIFICATION OF THE PROJECT

In October 1995, using the information gathered by Manuel Vallejo and bearing in mind the results of the focus groups and CEAC's experience in Spain and Poland, Jesús Flores prepared forecasts of enrollments and sales (see Exhibit 4).

Flores estimated that if the first adverts appeared in the press in September 1996, the company could expect around 1,504 student enrollments in the last four months of that year. In 1997, the first full year of operations, there would be 13,750 new enrollments, and 18,100 in 1998.

Flores then applied high drop-out rates. He assumed that only 45.7% of those who enrolled on a course would actually complete it. For example, of the first 280 students to enroll in October 1996 (see Exhibit 5), he assumed that

EXHIBIT 4   Forecasts Prepared by Jesús Flores in October 1995, on the Assumption that the New Joint Subsidiary in China Would Start Selling Vocational Distance Learning Courses in September 1996

1996

	January	February	March	April	May	June	July	August	September	October	November	December	Total
Print run (thousand units) of media used									8,000	8,000	8,000	8,000	32,000
Response rate from media adverts									0.04%	0.07%	0.09%	0.09%	0.07%
Number of requests for information									2,800	5,600	7,200	7,200	22,800
Conversion rate requests/enrollments									0%	5%	7%	10%	6.60%
Enrollments (new students)									0	280	504	720	1,504

1997

	January	February	March	April	May	June	July	August	September	October	November	December	Total
Print run (thousand units) of media used	10,000	10,000	10,000	11,500	11,500	11,500	11,500	11,500	13,000	13,000	13,000	13,000	139,500
Replies from media adverts	0.09%	0.09%	0.10%	0.10%	0.10%	0.10%	0.10%	0.10%	0.10%	0.10%	0.10%	0.10%	0.10%
Number of requests for information	9,000	9,000	10,000	11,500	11,500	11,500	11,500	11,500	13,000	13,000	13,000	13,000	137,500
Conversion rate requests/enrollments	10%	10%	10%	10%	10%	10%	10%	10%	10%	10%	10%	10%	10.0%
Enrollments (new students)	900	900	1,000	1,150	1,150	1,150	1,150	1,150	1,300	1,300	1,300	1,300	13,750

1998

	January	February	March	April	May	June	July	August	September	October	November	December	Total
Print run (thousand units) of media used	16,000	16,000	18,000	18,000	20,000	20,000	22,000	22,000	22,000	22,000	22,000	22,000	240,000
Response rate from media adverts	0.08%	0.08%	0.08%	0.08%	0.08%	0.08%	0.08%	0.07%	0.07%	0.07%	0.07%	0.07%	0.08%
Number of requests for information	12,800	12,800	14,400	14,400	16,000	16,000	17,600	15,400	15,400	15,400	15,400	15,400	181,000
Conversion rate requests/enrollments	10%	10%	10%	10%	10%	10%	10%	10%	10%	10%	10%	10%	10.00%
Enrollments (new students)	1,280	1,280	1,440	1,440	1,600	1,600	1,760	1,540	1,540	1,540	1,540	1,540	18,100

EXHIBIT 5 Forecasts of Revenue from Distance Training Courses in China, Prepared by Jesús Flores in October 1995

Revenue

1996 % of Drop-Outs/ Total Enrollments	January	February	March	April	May	June	July	August	September	October	November	December	Total
Students enrolled									0	280	504	720	1,504
Unit 1 3.44%									0	270	487	695	1,452
Unit 2 16.5 %										0	226	406	632
Unit 3 8.25%											0	207	207
Unit 4 4.81%												0	0
Total	0	0	0	0	0	0	0	0	0	550	1,216	2,029	3,796
Amount in RMB	0	0	0	0	0	0	0	0	0	53,936	119,209	198,815	371,960
Amount in Pesetas	0	0	0	0	0	0	0	0	0	784,770	1,734,493	2,892,762	5,412,025

Retail Price: 98RMB
1RMB = 14.55 ptas.

1997 % of Drop-Outs/ Total Enrollments	January	February	March	April	May	June	July	August	September	October	November	December	Total
Number of students enrolled	900	900	1,000	1,150	1,150	1,150	1,150	1,150	1,300	1,300	1,300	1,300	13,750
Unit 1 3.44%	869	869	966	1,110	1,110	1,110	1,110	1,110	1,255	1,255	1,255	1,255	13,277
Unit 2 16.50%	581	726	726	806	927	927	927	927	927	1,048	1,048	1,048	10,619
Unit 3 8.25%	373	533	666	666	740	851	851	851	851	851	962	962	9,154
Unit 4 4.81%	197	355	507	634	634	704	810	810	810	810	810	915	7,995
Unit 5 6.87%	0	184	331	472	590	590	656	754	754	754	754	754	6,593
Unit 6 7.90%		0	169	304	435	544	544	604	695	695	695	695	5,378
Unit 7 2.06%			0	166	298	426	532	532	592	680	680	680	4,587
Unit 8 4.47%				0	158	285	407	509	509	565	650	650	3,732
Unit 9 2.75%					0	154	277	396	495	495	550	632	2,997
Unit 10 3.09%						0	149	268	383	479	479	533	2,292
Unit 11 0.35%							0	149	267	382	478	478	1,754
Unit 12 1.03%								0	147	265	378	473	1,263
Unit 13 1.72%									0	145	260	372	776
Unit 14 2.06%										0	142	255	396
Unit 15 1.72%											0	139	139
Unit 16 2.06%												0	0
Total	2,920	3,566	4,364	5,308	6,043	6,741	7,413	8,060	8,985	9,723	10,440	11,140	84,702
Amount in RMB	315,313	385,111	471,277	573,316	652,605	728,025	800,598	870,485	970,331	1,050,131	1,127,552	1,203,125	9,147,869
Amount in Pesetas	4,358,416	5,323,197	6,514,229	7,924,654	9,020,629	10,063,127	11,066,271	12,032,273	13,412,404	14,515,431	15,585,593	16,630,200	126,446,423

Retail Price: 108RMB
1RMB = 13.82 Ptas.

EXHIBIT 5 (cont.)

Revenue

1998

	% of Drop-Outs/ Total Enrollments	January	February	March	April	May	June	July	August	September	October	November	December	Total
Number of students enrolled														
Unit 1	3.44%	1,280	1,280	1,440	1,440	1,600	1,600	1,760	1,540	1,540	1,540	1,540	1,540	18,100
Unit 2	16.50%	1,236	1,236	1,390	1,390	1,545	1,545	1,699	1,487	1,487	1,487	1,487	1,487	17,477
Unit 3	8.25%	1,048	1,032	1,032	1,161	1,161	1,290	1,290	1,419	1,242	1,242	1,242	1,242	14,400
Unit 4	4.81%	962	962	947	947	1,065	1,065	1,184	1,184	1,302	1,139	1,139	1,139	13,035
Unit 5	6.87%	915	915	915	901	901	1,014	1,014	1,127	1,127	1,239	1,084	1,084	12,239
Unit 6	7.90%	853	853	853	853	839	839	944	944	1,049	1,049	1,154	1,010	11,240
Unit 7	2.06%	695	785	785	785	785	773	773	870	870	966	966	1,063	10,117
Unit 8	4.47%	680	680	769	769	769	769	757	757	852	852	946	946	9,548
Unit 9	2.75%	650	650	650	735	735	735	735	723	723	814	814	904	8,867
Unit 10	3.09%	632	632	632	632	714	714	714	714	703	703	791	791	8,375
Unit 11	0.35%	612	612	612	612	612	692	692	692	692	682	682	767	7,962
Unit 12	1.03%	531	610	610	610	610	610	690	690	690	690	679	679	7,701
Unit 13	1.72%	473	525	604	604	604	604	604	683	683	683	683	672	7,422
Unit 14	2.06%	465	465	516	594	594	594	594	594	671	671	671	671	7,098
Unit 15	1.72%	364	455	455	506	581	581	581	581	581	657	657	657	6,659
Unit 16	2.06%	250	358	447	447	497	571	571	571	571	571	646	646	6,149
Unit 17	3.09%	136	245	350	438	438	487	560	560	560	560	560	633	5,525
Unit 18	0.28%	0	132	238	340	424	424	472	542	542	542	542	542	4,742
Unit 19	1.50%	0	0	132	237	339	423	423	470	541	541	541	541	4,188
Unit 20	1.00%	0	0	0	130	233	334	417	417	463	533	533	533	3,592
								330	413	413	459	527	527	3,029
Total		11,782	12,296	13,009	13,424	14,052	14,485	15,163	15,137	15,344	15,546	15,742	15,933	171,913
Amount in RMB		1,402,029	1,463,189	1,548,084	1,597,502	1,672,199	1,723,687	1,804,436	1,801,266	1,825,899	1,849,957	1,873,341	1,896,009	20,457,598
Amount in Pesetas		18,991,959	19,820,437	20,970,424	21,639,840	22,651,685	23,349,154	24,442,980	24,400,045	24,733,721	25,059,604	25,376,368	25,683,428	277,119,644

Retail Price: 119RMB

1RMB = 13.55 ptas.

a certain proportion would drop out each month, so that by May 1998—after 20 months—only 128 students would buy and pay for lesson No. 20 and so complete the course.

Assuming gradually increasing selling prices and a gradually decreasing Yuan/Peseta exchange rate, Flores estimated that total revenues from students would be around 5.4 million pesetas in 1996 (3 months); 126.4 million in 1997; and 277.1 million in 1998. By the end of 1998, New World-CEAC would be enrolling 1,540 new students per month. Taking into account the estimated "drop-out rates", by December 1998 the company would be selling 16,000 lessons or teaching units per month to students who had enrolled during the previous 20 months.

Flores used these sales figures to prepare the projected profit and loss accounts for 1996, 1997 and 1998 (see Exhibit 6).

According to these projections, the new subsidiary would lose around 14.4 million pesetas in 1996, but would earn 26.4 million pesetas before tax in 1997, and 72.8 million in 1998. In theory, these profits were to be shared between the partners in proportion to the capital each one of them had put in, i.e. 70% for CEAC and 30% for New World Publishing Co. However, CEAC's management felt that, for many years to come, all profits should be plowed back into the business.

The action plan specified that students would pay for their monthly lessons month by month. The lessons would be sent and paid for on delivery, or could be picked up and paid for in person at any of New World Publishing Co.'s 2,300 retail bookshops. The new company would initially launch three courses, English Language, Marketing, and Accounting, with a view to extending this number to six during the first full year of operations.

The formal accounting procedures were as follows: CEAC-Spain would supply Beijing New World-CEAC Consulting Co. Ltd. with business and teaching expertise in exchange for a 6% royalty on sales to students. New World Publishing Co., in cooperation with an adult education center, would take care of selling the courses and collecting payment. From these sales revenues it would deduct its translation, adaptation, printing, advertising and distribution expenses, as well as a commission for its services. The consulting company would then invoice New World Publishing Co. for the amount of this gross margin and from it deduct its own expenses (personnel, administration, communications, utilities, financing), plus the 6% royalty on sales payable to CEAC-Spain. The remainder, after tax, was the amount available, in theory, to self-finance the development of the joint venture or, even more theoretically, to be distributed to the partners in proportion to their shareholdings.

The accounting procedure was clearly rather complicated, since the idea was to specify and take into account the contributions and activities of each partner, allocating the costs incurred. There was a danger of disagreements in

EXHIBIT 6 Projected Profit and Loss Accounts in China for 1996, 1997, and 1998, Prepared by Jesús Flores in October 1995 (in thousands)

	1996			1997			1998		
	RMB	Ptas.	Percentage of Sales	RMB	Ptas.	Percentage of Sales	RMB	Ptas.	Percentage of Sales
Gross sales	372	5,412		9,148	126,446		20,458	277,120	
Taxes (VAT, consumption)	43	623		1,052	14,547		2,354	31,881	
Net sales	329	4,789	100	8,095	111,899	100	18,104	245,239	100
Cost of goods sold	86	1,253	26.16	2,219	30,672	27.41	4,526	61,310	25.00
Distribution costs	6	84	1.75	145	2,003	1.79	324	4,390	1.79
Sales commission	11	159	3.33	270	3,726	3.33	603	8,166	3.33
Marketing expenses	320	4,656	97.21	1,473	20,355	18.19	3,174	42,995	17.53
Cost of reviewing students exercises	3	38	0.80	132	1,824	1.63	295	3,997	1.63
Depreciation	35	507	10.59	100	1,376	1.23	208	2,820	1.15
Overheads (general expenses)	724	10,537	220.00	1,545	21,362	19.09	3,259	44,143	18.00
Office rental	70	1,019	21.27	140	1,935	1.73	280	3,793	1.55
Technology royalties	44	640	13.37	46	636	0.57	48	650	0.27
Profit before interest and tax	(969)	(14,104)	−294.48	2,026	28,011	25.03	5,387	72,974	29.76
Interest	(25)	(364)	−7.59	(115)	(1,590)	−1.42	(15)	(203)	−0.08
Profit before tax	(994)	(14,467)	−302.07	1,911	26,422	23.61	5,372	72,771	29.67

the future as to how it should be interpreted, but it seemed a workable system for publishing and selling CEAC's courses on the Chinese market, with royalties payable to the Spanish partner.

THE CEAC BOARD MEETING AT THE END OF OCTOBER 1995

In making their decision whether to sign the agreement with New World Publishing Co., the members of CEAC's Board of Directors[11] considered the following points in favour and against:

In Favour:

1. We have already invested around 100,000 dollars in the project. If we decide to back out now, this sum will have to be computed directly to losses.
2. Jesús Flores is willing to take charge of the project. It is very important that we have our man on the spot, managing the project.
3. We can also count on the continued collaboration of Manuel Vallejo as a consultant and as a member of the Board of Directors of the joint venture. Vallejo can back Flores in any "power relations" with the Chinese partners.
4. The ECIP loan has been approved by Brussels since September 1995. This means not only that CEAC-Spain will have to put up less capital of its own, but also—according to the rules governing ECIP loans—that if the project eventually fails, the entire loan will be written off.
5. Manuel Vallejo—who attended the meeting with a right to speak but not to vote—summed up his experience in the Chinese market: "If you want to get into China, you have to do it gradually, step by step. There is an old Chinese proverb that says you must cross a river slowly, feeling the stones under your feet. It will be a process of trial and error. Although at the moment we are not too sure about the project, the important thing is to be there, to start doing business, to start gaining the confidence of our local partner and the Chinese authorities. They must see that we mean business, that we are loyal, cooperative partners. If we do that, we may find that opportunities start to emerge, sometimes even unexpectedly and in surprising ways."
6. And, of course, for its sheer size the Chinese market is every entrepreneur's dream. More than 1.2 billion people, hungry for knowledge and for good-quality services. CEAC's vocational distance training courses would have practically no competition.

Against:

Other members of CEAC's Board of Directors raised the following points against the project:

1. My first objection is a question of priorities. China is very far away and possibly more remote, culturally and politically, to us in Spain than any other country. Why don't we give priority to the Central and East European countries for the time being? Once we have consolidated our position there, I would be in favour of setting ourselves more ambitious goals. Going to China now seems like too great a leap. We should take a more gradual approach.
2. I don't like the substance of the agreement. We will be too dependent on our local partner. We are effectively placing ourselves in the hands of New World Publishing Co., since they are the ones who do the invoicing and collect payment from the students.
3. If we give our approval, we had better prepare ourselves to invest at least another 300,000 dollars in the project. And what is worse, if we start the project and it does not work, it could turn into a bottomless pit. The bigger our investment becomes, the more difficult it will be to abandon it if things do not work out.
4. We know practically nothing about the market or the way it might react. We hardly know what advertising media we would use, or what the cost per newly enrolled student might be. In fact, we do not even know whether the Chinese will be remotely interested in the courses we sell in Spain. . . .
5. New World Publishing Co. is in the publishing business. We have an agreement with them to create a *consulting* company! As things stand, if we sign these documents, the only thing we would *really* be authorized to do in China would be to provide consultancy services in areas connected with publishing, such as photocomposition software and desktop publishing. *Nowhere is it clearly stated that this new subsidiary can sell vocational distance learning courses, because it is legally FORBIDDEN for a joint venture with a foreign partner to carry out educational activities.* We have known for months that what little vocational distance training there is in China is run by State-owned universities, in other words, non-profit public corporations, which, naturally, do not have any foreign shareholders. It is impossible to guess how many years we might have to wait for a change in the laws, in a Communist country like China!
6. Furthermore, the market research carried out through the focus groups in Yantai clearly indicates that students will expect to receive a diploma or certificate on completing their studies. Not even New World Publishing Co. is authorized to issue such certificates—and it never will be authorized, because it does not belong to the Ministry of Education but to the

---

[11] The Board had four members: Juan Martí, José Menal, and their sons Juan Antonio Martí Castro and Guillermo Menal.

Bureau of Publications. Our local partner is simply a publishing house, not a university or a school.

7. Manuel Vallejo warned: "We are entering virgin territory, taking the first steps in an environment so far unexplored by foreign companies. We must maintain a presence, until the laws that govern this industry in China start to change . . . assuming they do eventually change, as we all expect. We must trust and rely on our local partner. They are institutionally powerful, and they seem to be ready to take active steps to ensure that we are allowed to operate, maybe under some exception to current legislation, or by finding some unexpected way around it. Of course, everything will be under the absolute control of the Chinese, to the extent that they will even censor the text of the courses we sell. All things considered, we do not know with any precision what our starting point is, and there is no guarantees that we will ever reach our target destination . . . and we have even less idea where all this might lead."

Nokia and the Cellular Phone Industry

In the early spring of 1994, Mr. Jorma Ollila, CEO of the Nokia group, looked back on a successful year where his company's cellular phone sales had increased by more than 70 percent and his profits had more than doubled. In a growing market, the Finnish company had managed to increase its market share, moving up from a global market share of 13 percent in early 1992 to 20 percent at the end of 1993. Rapidly increasing development costs had forced many of Nokia's competitors to shut down or sell out to larger rivals. How could Nokia sustain its growth in such a turbulent industry? How could the management make decisions in light of such uncertainty?

EVOLUTION OF THE INDUSTRY

The mobile phone industry was born as a result of the need for professionals to contact others on the move. With only a restricted amount of the radio spectrum, it meant that an open broadcast system needed to squeeze every conversation out on the same limited bandwidth. The cellular breakthrough was achieved at AT&T's Bell laboratories in 1979, making it possible for the same tiny bandwidth to be used by thousands of individual, switched messages (see Appendix). By the beginning of 1993, cellular service was in place in more than 90 countries.

There were several categories of products on the market for wireless communication. Mobile communication was, beside cellular telephones, largely represented by pagers, with an estimated 50 million subscribers[1] worldwide in 1993. The pagers can, like the cellular phones, also receive short messages in both data and voice. Computer companies like Apple, AT&T, IBM, and AST Research introduced personal digital assistants (PDAs). These handheld, pen-based computers could send wireless facsimile and electronic mail and were expected to include voice communication eventually. The mode of communication used depended mainly on the complexity and urgency of the message. E-mail, pagers, computers, or facsimile did not provide instant confirmation that the message was received. This was possible only with the telephone.

The cellular telephone industry consisted, like the telecommunication industry, of production of phones, infrastructure, and operators of the infrastructure. Infrastructure refers to the transmitting towers, and the many categories of switching technology used to establish the connections. Motorola, Ericsson, and Nokia were manufacturers of both infrastructure and cellular phones. The interdependency between these two sectors is very tight, as a feature developed for handsets only is functional if the infrastructure can accommodate it (see Appendix). Operators of the cellular networks were often also those providing fixed wire telecommunication in a given area, although competitors were starting to make aggressive moves on that market. Well-known companies such as Sprint, AT&T, McCaw cellular, and most of the national operators in Europe were players in this arena.

The Nordic governments had chosen the NMT (Nordic Mobile Telephone) 450 analog standard in 1981, when this region became one of the first areas in the world to establish cellular services. Sparsely populated areas cost too much to connect by fixed wire, and this posed a further incentive for establishing cellular services. Unique to the Nordic countries were the roaming possibilities between the countries (see Appendix), creating a system covering the entire Nordic area. Cellular users roam as they move

This case was awarded the first prize in the 1995 European Foundation for Management Development Case Writing Competition in the category International Business. The case was submitted on March 26, 1995, by Jakob Fritz Hansen and Claus Groth-Andersen. Both were at the time masters students of the International Business Program at Copenhagen Business School, Denmark. The case was supervised by Dr. Heather Hazard of the Institute of International Economics and Management at Copenhagen Business School, Denmark.

Special thanks are due to Dianna Powell Ward of the Lubin School of Business, Pace University, New York, who edited the final version.

Used with permission.

---

[1] Motorola Annual Report 1993.

from the coverage of one service provider to another. The existence of roaming agreements between service providers/operators of different areas widen the geographic coverage provided to the users. By 1994 the fruits, resulting from an early move into cellular communication along with a common standard and a coherent set of roaming agreements, had begun to show: Penetration rates in this region, of up to 10 percent, were the highest in the world. The NMT-450, and the newer NMT-900 standard had also been adopted in many other countries, such as the Netherlands, France, Belgium, Spain, Austria, and Thailand, but roaming across borders was only possible within the Nordic NMT system due to the agreements existing between the governments in these countries.

Several producers of cellular telephones existed in the Nordic region. The dominant producers were Swedish L. M. Ericsson and Nokia Mobile Phones, headquartered in Finland. These were also the main providers of cellular infrastructure to the system. Other European producers of cellular telephones were Siemens, primarily focused on the German market, and Technophone Ltd., the main producer of cellular phones in the U.K. market. Several small, innovative companies were on the scene in the industry's infancy, like Storno and Cetelco, and major multinationals like Philips and Bosch were marketing phones under OEM agreements.

Before the implementation of the European digital standard, as described later, several analog standards prevailed in the area. There were seven noncompatible analog standards in Europe, led by the NMT-450 and NMT-900 standards, and the British developed TACS standard.

Most of the European telecommunications services were state owned, resulting in monopolistic situations with the effect of slowing the growth in cellular phones and services due to the high calling fees that were demanded. In 1993, the German penetration rate was as low as 2.47 percent due also to a poorly integrated cross-country coverage.

In the United States, commercial cellular telecommunications began in 1983, with the implementation of the AMPS (American Mobile Phone System) standard. The Federal Communications Commission (FCC) sets the rules for competition on the cellular communication scene in the United States, and has given licenses to several regional operators.

The American structure was based upon regionally competing companies/operators which have made the overall network differentiated and incoherent. Roaming possibilities were technically possible, but agreements between the operators uncommon. Furthermore, the U.S. antitrust laws complicated the rise of nationwide agreements between competing entities. The penetration rate in 1993 was approximately 6 percent, and the American manufacturer Motorola Inc. dominated this market. At this point, the innovator of the technology, AT&T, had only just started to manufacture cellular phones themselves.

Japan was the first country to license cellular service in 1981, but the development of a nationwide service was not achieved until 1984. This service was offered by the Nippon Telegraph and Telephone Corporation, who had a monopoly position on the Japanese market. After 1985, NTT was to be privatized over a five-year period and other private companies got access to providing cellular services. The structure was controlled by the government in such a way that NTT provided national services, and the competitors had their own regional area, in which NTT was the only other competitor. The structure caused a slow growth in subscribers because of the high connection prices, and a low level of geographical coverage. This manifested itself with a base of only 1.7 million subscribers in 1993.

The Asian-Pacific countries, except for Japan, had adopted diverse standards including NMT, TACS, and AMPS, and the Latin American countries had chosen the AMPS. Growth within the standards in these markets was relatively low compared to the other regions, with a subscriber base accounting only for approximately 10 percent of the worldwide number of both analog and digital subscribers in 1993.

In the middle of 1993, there were an estimated 27.3 million analog subscribers worldwide, where the United States counted for 48 percent, Europe 25 percent, and Asia-Pacific (including Japan) 15 percent.

Change in Technology

By 1991, the limitations of the analog standards were becoming critical due to the high growth in subscribers, prompting the emergence of the digital technologies. The analog standards had less capacity within a given frequency band and were also affected by wave interference, thereby easily absorbing noise.

The first standards employing digital technology were the pan-European GSM and the American TDMA. The new systems were based on digital transmission of signals (bits), eliminating noise in the transmission. Digital signals take up less bandwidth in the radio spectrum, allowing a given allotted channel range to carry more information—and as a result allowing more users on a system than the analog technology. The digital standards also made it possible to transmit facsimile and computer files at far higher speeds and higher quality, which opened up the prospects for these functions. The digital standards were, over a period of time, likely to replace the analog standards, but as has been the case with the analog technology, several different standards already existed within the digital technology. As a result, the global market was divided up into smaller segments according to which standards (both analog and digital) prevailed in the regional markets.

Some drastic changes occurred in the industry along with the technological shift. In the initial stage of the digital era, development costs rose sharply, as the knowledge required to develop a handset in a digital standard was far greater than the same effort in the analog field. Developing an analog handset took roughly 10 man-years of engineering, while, initially, a model in the new digital standards required 150 man-years, or 15 times the amount of work, posing far larger requirements for the size of the development team. The development of software was becoming an activity of importance, as much of the functionality of handsets and networks would now depend on this component.

A notable difference between the digital and analog technologies was an overall shift in the production process. While the analog standards were relatively low in knowledge content, they were harder to mass-produce. The digital standards required a lot of development, increasing fixed costs, but were better suited for mass production due to lower marginal costs. Moreover, the pace of development grew and the number of standards on the global market, as a whole, rose. As with the analog standards, having developed models in one of the digital standards increased a company's knowledge base for entering the next generation of standards, creating a springboard effect. Another factor necessitating scale was the constant shortening of the model life spans. The PLC curve (Exhibit 1) can be viewed as an aggregate of the sales of all the cellular phone models on the market at a point in time. It is made up of the life-span curves of the different models introduced over time.

The average market life of the various top models used to be over a year. In early 1994, a premium model marketed six months earlier, was already moving into the discount segment, having been replaced by a more sophisticated version.

Many of the small national producers were hit hard by this change in the structural environment. At the time when these firms had managed to develop a digital model,

the three large players were already promoting their second generation of terminals. Some of the small players disappeared, while others were bought out by rivals. Meanwhile, entrants were trying to acquire the competence to participate on the scene. A fierce battle was raging.

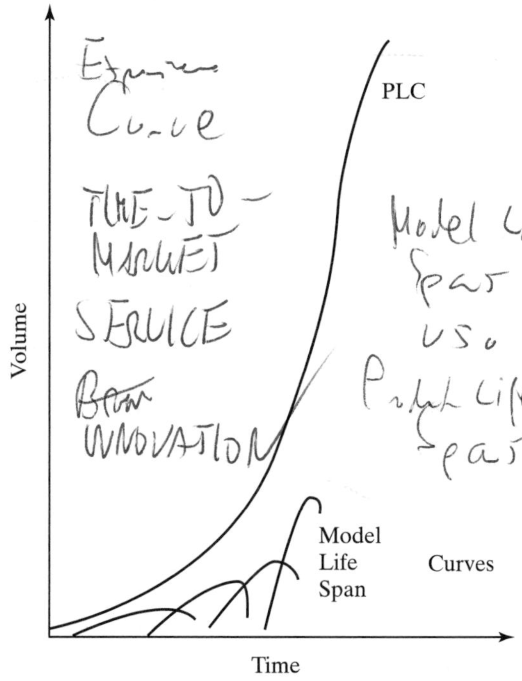

The Market Implications of the Technological Change

The large potential for economies of scale did not, however, result in a convergence of the many standards. The establishment of the standards had not been controlled by government intervention or voluntary international standards agreement, but rather resulted from innovations taking place in the individual markets, and this was still the case as the digital standards emerged.

Europe now had two digital standards, the Group Speciale Mobile (GSM), promoted by the European Union (EU) countries, and the DCS 1800 which is explained later. The argument for implementing a pan-European digital standard was to promote the development of the European telecommunication industry and provide other industries with improved communication and information possibilities. As was the case with the NMT, the GSM was designed as an open standard in a collaborative effort between governments and industry—and could thus be adopted by any producer capable of developing the technology. The GSM was meant by the EU to replace the existing analog standards and was supposed to reach 13 million subscribers by 1997, but the analog systems were cash cows for the operators, so their life span was projected to reach somewhat beyond the turn of the millennium.

The GSM roaming agreements stretched across borders, allowing, for example, the use of the GSM standard to communicate to/from all EU countries, and several nations on the periphery, where a base-station was in reach. The vision of the GSM system was technical compatibility combined with roaming agreements to provide access within the system. A system could conceivably also encompass two standards, if dual standard terminals were made and roaming was agreed upon between the two subsystems. The GSM networks in other areas of the world can be said to have used the same standard, but made up separate systems of roaming. To have access to cellular communication, it was necessary to have both a handset and a service agreement. In most cellular phones, the service agreement was identified by an electronic code stored in the handset, which would identify the caller and give her access to the network. For the GSM standard, this caller ID was stored on an electronic card the size of a credit card, which was inserted in the handset in order to make it operable. Thus, the same phones could be used, but they required separate service agreements (SIM cards). GSM had already been adopted by 62 countries at the end of 1993.

Another digital system, the Public Communication Network (PCN), came about due to the recognized problems of GSM capacity limitations in highly populated areas. PCNs, following the DCS-1800 standard, use a higher

EXHIBIT 1   PLC and Model Life Spans

operating frequency than the GSM standard, and each connection takes up only half the bandwidth, thereby ensuring higher capacity. Each base station covers an area of approximately 500 meter radius (or smaller). The capacity is greatly increased as each of the small cells is capable of carrying twice the connections of the larger one, while using only the same frequency width. Costs per connection were also expected to be much lower than for the larger radius systems, resulting over time in lower calling fees. Because of the shorter range required of the PCN terminals, battery time would increase significantly. In all, PCN was directed at the mass market, making quick reduction in unit costs possible, and thereby also lower prices. PCN systems were installed in the United Kingdom and Germany by the end of 1994.

In the United States, the FCC did not interfere in the implementation of the digital standards. The fight stood between the TDMA standard, which was largely provided by Swedish L. M. Ericsson, and the CDMA standard which was provided by Motorola. These two standards could exist side by side, but were not compatible. Implementation of digital standards in the United States was based upon a coexistence with the prevailing analog standards (quite the opposite of the European strategy of replacing the analog standards with the GSM system). PCN systems were also to be installed in the United States as a third digital standard.

The analog standards were still profitable and had excess capacity, which, together with the voluntary choice of transition to digital standards, had set the pace of digital implementation to be slower than that in Europe. Critics argued that this delay would be problematic for the evolution of international standards, where some (perhaps inferior) technologies get a head start, and thereby hamper the introduction of superior technologies.

In Japan, the analog systems were experiencing capacity overload, and implementation of a digital standard was expected in 1994. By that time, another two service providers had been licensed, but the licenses given to those other than NTT were still only regional, therefore, creating a poorly developed nationwide net for cellular services, with a low penetration rate as a result.

Market Growth and Expected Changes in Segments

The cellular phone market growth rates from 1991 to 1992 and 1992 to 1993 were 60 percent and 50 percent, respectively. The total number of subscribers amounted to 33 million by the end of 1993. Predictions on the total number of subscribers in the year 2000 range from 100 to 170 million, suggesting high compounded annual growth rates (see Exhibits 2 to 5).

Up to 1994, market predictions had been mostly understated. There was no doubt that the number of subscribers would rise sharply in the coming years, but the price level and, thus, the market size would be shaped by conditions about which there was great uncertainty. Aspects affecting growth were cost of the terminals, the pric-

---

EXHIBIT 2 Number of Cellular Phone Subscribers

	Millions of Subscribers		
	End 1988	*End 1992*	*End 1993*
Europe[a]	1.5	6.0	8.3
United States	1.6	NA	15.0
Japan	0.4[b]	0.9[c]	1.7
Asia-Pacific excluding Japan	NA	1.6	2.6
Latin America	NA	NA	1.1
Others	NA	NA	4.4
Total subscribers	4.1	22.1	33.1

[a] Including the European Economic Area and Switzerland.

[b] End 1989.

[c] Mid-1991.

Sources: International Herald Tribune, 27 April 1994; Motorola Annual Report 1993.

EXHIBIT 3 Changes in Segments (European Market)

Segment	*1994*	*1998*
Consumers	15%	40%
Business	80%	45%
Mobile data	5%	15%

Source: Nokia Mobile Phones.

EXHIBIT 4 Estimates of Cumulative Cellular Subscribers (Millions of Subscribers)

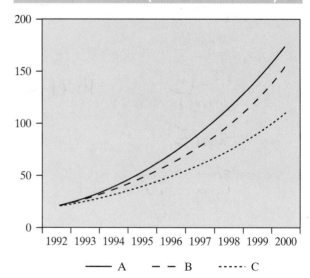

Sources: Affärsvärlden, nr. 46, 1991; *International Herald Tribune,* 27 April 1994; *Business Week,* October 4, 1993.

EXHIBIT 5	Development in Global Unit Sales of Cellular Handsets
Year	**Unit Sales**
1992	8.7 million
1993	11.0 million
1997	32.3 million[a]
2001	53.0 million[a]

[a] Estimates.

Source: Nokia.

ing of air time, versatility of the product, ease of use, and coverage of the service agreements.

Nokia Mobile Phones forecast the increased importance of the consumer and mobile data market segment.

The level of product differentiation was not high, although special features were used to a certain degree, aiming to attract the higher-priced business segment.

With investments made in the digital networks that had still not borne fruit, and a still low base of subscribers, operators deemed it necessary to boost sales in order to reach the degree of utilization that would ensure returns on their investments. This was often done by subsidizing the handsets when consumers signed up for service agreements. The retail promotions boosted demand from the op-erators to the producers. Ability to deliver was key to the operators so they pressured producers on delivery schedules rather than price.

The larger part of the sales derived from the United States and Europe, but other markets were rapidly starting to emerge. Eastern Europe and China and other Asian countries were starting to demand both infrastructure and handsets. Because of the economic growth in the regions, the demand for communications services was rising, and cellular technology was a cost-effective and speedy alternative to investing in a new fixed wire network.

NOKIA

Nokia started as a paper and pulp mill in 1865, where the first ground-wood mill was situated on the Nokia River in Finland.

In 1967, the company expanded by merging with large rubber and cable interests. Later on, through the 1970s and 1980s, Nokia added plastic, metal products, chemicals, and electronics to the group by acquisition. In 1994, Nokia consisted of five business groups: Consumer Electronics, Telecommunications, Cables & Machinery, Mobile Phones, and Other Operations (e.g., tires), but had over a relatively short period changed its focus toward telecommunications (see Exhibits 6 and 7), where it ranked as the ninth largest telecommunications equipment vendor globally. Total assets

EXHIBIT 6	Key Financial Statistics of the Nokia Group: 1989–1993				
Nokia Group M$	**1993**	**1992**	**1991**	**1990**	**1989**
Net sales	4,096	3,463	3,747	6,103	5,627
Costs and expenses	3,898	3,493	3,668	5,907	5,478
Earnings excluding tax, etc.	198	−30	79	196	149
Taxes/minorities, etc.	397	108	130	120	110
Net earnings	−199	−138	−51	76	39

Source: Nokia Annual Report 1993.

EXHIBIT 7	Nokia Group Operating Profit by Segment, 1989–1993				
Operating Profit Nokia Group M$	**1993**	**1992**	**1991**	**1990**	**1989**
Telecommunications	170	81			
Mobile Phones	164	83			
Consumer Electronics	−129	−149			
Electronic Groups total[a]	—	—	−56	144	57
Cables and Machinery	45	22	24	106	100
Basic Industries[b]	—	—	52	68	86
Other Operations	3	18	−43	−19	−2
Nokia Group	253	55	−23	299	241

[a] 1992–1993 Nokia tires and Noka power are included in the group "Other Operations."

[b] Nokia data were included in Electronic Groups in 1989–1990.

Source: Nokia Annual Report 1993.

of the Nokia group were $3.9 billion, with a debt to asset ratio of approximately 50 percent.

NOKIA MOBILE PHONES

Nokia Mobile Phones represented 26 percent of the group net sales, corresponding to $1.1 billion (see Exhibit 8). Research and development (R&D) expenditures were $50.3 million and $73.6 million in 1992 and 1993, respectively. The productivity within the cellular phone division increased dramatically after 1990, with an increase in sales per employee of 138 percent.

The firm was shaped by vigorous rivalry because Finland has one of Europe's most innovative and competitive markets in telecommunications, with some 52 communications providers in 1991.

In the beginning of the 1980s, the Nokia group started producing analog infrastructure and cellular phones for the NMT-450 standard. The small home market meant that Nokia had to export from day one in order to increase volume. Soon, the company was manufacturing multiple standards and had thus acquired a wide base of knowledge and scale at an early stage.

The firm's main objective was to satisfy its customers, and this was used as the guiding principle on which all activities were focused. An objective was to acquire 25 percent global market share in 1995 (see Exhibit 9), emphasizing expansion on all markets. The importance of not getting trapped producing low value-added commodity products,

and remaining flexible in order to produce cellular phones to many different standards, and being able to market them, was emphasized. Priority was placed on design, consumer adaptation, and user friendliness, including a focus on size and weight of the cellular phones.

The firm's strengths in fast development enabled them to be the first supplier of the GSM network in Europe and the first in the market with a commercial GSM portable phone. Furthermore, they delivered phones and network infrastructure to three of the world's four PCN systems. Nokia develops and markets all cellular infrastructure through Nokia Mobile Phones. In all, they had a broad, well-developed knowledge base built upon the competence gained from the many offered standards. Even so, Nokia recognized the necessity of increasing the development effort to meet future challenges.

The product range included all major analog and digital standards. They also had original equipment manufacturer (OEM) producer status for Philips, Hitachi, Swatch, and AT&T. The agreement with AT&T was made in April 1994 and valued by Nokia at $170 million a year. Joint ventures with Japanese cellular companies like Mitsui and Kansai in developing digital cellular phones for the Japanese market has improved access to this market. Nokia's global market share rose when they acquired the British cellular producer Technophone Ltd. in 1991.

Production facilities were situated in Finland, Germany, the United Kingdom, the United States, Hong Kong,

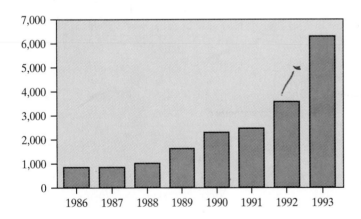

Source: Nokia Annual Report 1993.

EXHIBIT 9 Market Shares (and Ranks) of Incumbents of the Cellular Phone Industry, 1988, 1992, and 1993			
Market Shares	**May 1988**	**February 1992**	**End 1993**
Motorola, Inc.	12.8% (2)	22.0% (1)	36.0% (1)
Nokia	13.4% (1)	13.0% (2)	20.0% (2)
L. M. Ericsson	3.9% (9)	NA	10.0% (3)
Panasonic	NA	NA	4.0% (4)

Market shares for NEC not available, but are very small.

Sources: Keinala, Severi: Finnish High-Tech Industries & European Integration, 1989; Nokia, Motorola, and L. M. Ericsson.

and Korea. Even though the main costs of producing a phone derived from the components and development, there were still cost advantages to assembling handsets in low-wage countries. The attractiveness of these locations was often augmented by the availability of government subsidized loans.

Nokia was not vertically integrated. Semiconductors were bought mainly from AT&T, supplying also the essential Digital Systems Processor. Components were also bought from Motorola. Nokia focused on designing the electronic components themselves, and outsourced the manufacturing to other companies. They manufactured both cellular infrastructure and handsets providing the ability to offer complete packages to operators, as well as technological spillovers.

Distribution channels to consumer markets were, however, not yet well established. Nokia though had a relative advantage because of their Consumer Electronics Division, which had experience promoting products to the consumer segment, and which had established access to distributions channels. Brand identification was becoming increasingly important, with the transition toward the mass market. The firm was still struggling with a low degree of recognition, but expected to intensify marketing efforts.

A study made on this subject revealed that consumers had positive opinions of Sony's cellular phone, even though it was not yet marketed—where it became clear that the major players in the cellular phone industry did not enjoy nearly the same degree of recognition among the consumers. Nokia was often thought of as a Japanese brand, which caused a problem due to still lingering negative images of Japanese producers, especially in the U.S. market when up against an American firm. Nokia had furthermore formed numerous alliances and agreements with other firms such as Tandy Corporation in the United States in 1983, mainly to overcome some of the marketing hurdles. Nokia cellular telephones were sold under the names Nokia, Technophone, Mobira and, as mentioned, via numerous OEM deals. The terminals were sold through specialized stores, retail chains, and operators. Nokia's market share in GSM phones was higher than in analog phones. Sales in the United States increased 73 percent in 1993, yielding a 19 percent United States market share,[2] while European sales "only" doubled. The growth in cellular subscribers was smaller in these two regions in 1993, meaning that Nokia gained overall market share. The number of potential users of the digital TDMA standard in the United States was increasing with positive implications for Nokia's prospects.

Nokia believed open communication to be indispensable for setting mutual targets, and each employee bore responsibility in this respect. Knowledge is a capacity only when it is shared. The development of products employed the Concurrent Engineering Process. This meant that, when designing new products, the product development, marketing, sourcing, and production departments cooperated closely as a team, making the developing process faster and more cost-efficient, and cutting the product's time to market. Nokia's operations were based on decentralized structures and measured control. Fast change in the environment and technology brought opportunities which in turn provided the firm with the possibility to discover new abilities and resources within the organization. The company consisted of young, flexible, and cooperative employees, but the pressure on them was great, increasing the risk of organizational defects. They were, however, equipped with the strong fighting spirit expressed by the Finnish word *Sisu*.

NOKIA'S MAIN EXISTING AND POTENTIAL COMPETITORS

Motorola, Inc.

Motorola was founded in 1928 as Galvin Manufacturing Corporation and was the leading company in the cellular phone industry (see Exhibit 7). Furthermore, it held a strong position in the field of cellular infrastructure, wireless communications, semiconductors, and advanced electronic systems and services. Of the turnover in 1993, 54 percent was in wireless communications (including two-way radios, etc. Figures for cellular communications cannot be isolated. See Exhibit 10). The total assets were $13.5 billion, with a debt to assets ratio of 56 percent. They held a position as the third largest telecom equipment provider on a global scale.

Motorola focused on gaining market share, and set a goal of obtaining more than 50 percent of the global market for cellular terminals. Another important factor was the concept of constant renewal of technology and processes. Motorola stayed close to four closely coupled sectors including communications, components, computers, and control and constantly sought to create bridges between them. The company was characterized as a huge venture capital outfit, constantly spinning off technology and capital into new businesses. The R&D expenditures for the group were $1.5 billion in 1993. A prime example was Motorola's ambitious Iridium project, a low-orbit satellite system that was conceived with the objective of bringing wireless phone service to the world by 1998. By 1994, they had spent 8 years and $100 million backing the Iridium system. However, some analysts were skeptical of Iridium's profitability, as the average connection price would be $3 per minute, and handsets would cost approximately $3,000. Motorola aimed at 1 million subscribers for this system by 2002, 2 percent of the projected 200 million users of wireless telephony. The wireless connection charges in the United States were roughly one seventh of what Iridium intended to charge.

Motorola had a large home market, which was an advantage in the beginning when lag times between markets were still significant. Every time a new product was introduced, it could readily achieve higher volume in sales than

---

[2] Bibliographic Citation, HFD, 10 February 1992 and *The Wall Street Journal Europe,* 27 April 1994.

EXHIBIT 10 Key Financial Statistics for Motorola, 1989–1993					
Motorola, Inc. M$	*1993*	*1992*	*1991*	*1990*	*1989*
Net sales	16,963	13,303	11,341	10,855	9,620
Costs and expenses	15,438	12,503	10,728	10,219	8,974
Earnings before tax	1,525	800	613	666	646
Income taxes	503	224	159	167	148
Net earnings	1,022	453	454	499	498

Source: Motorola Annual Report 1993.

companies in smaller countries. With rapid internationalization, this advantage decreased in significance.

High competence at mass production was core to the strategy at Motorola. A quality program called *Six Sigma* had been introduced and aimed at only three to four mistakes per million processes (not per million units produced). Motorola produced cellular infrastructure equipment and competed in all major analog and digital standards and had delivered GSM infrastructure equipment to seven countries, and several U.S. operators had ordered the Motorola developed CDMA digital standard infrastructure. The company also produced the digital systems processor (DSP), crucial to the digital standard terminal, in contrast to other major cellular phone producers who had to obtain this component from suppliers. Moreover, the company held fundamental patents required for the GSM standard, but was not able to deliver the complete range of infrastructure for the GSM system due to a lack of the very sophisticated switching technology needed for the roaming function.[3] The takeover of the Danish company Storno in the early 1990s was a step to gain more know-how in this area.

Motorola had a wide distribution network covering most of the world. Its phones were sold through operators, mass merchants, specialty retailers, direct sales, and as original options on cars. The marketing activities stretched over more than 80 countries either under the Motorola name or as parts of OEM agreements with companies such as Bosch and Pioneer. Motorola lacked experience in consumer marketing and focused mainly on production and market shares.

Motorola opted for a policy of decentralization. Organizational boundaries were broken down, and cooperation between personnel and management was promoted. The result was an atmosphere of informality, where people contacted each other across the former boundaries, creating flexibility and a better flow of information. This resulted in an increase in productivity (sales per employee) of 126 percent between 1986 and 1993.

L. M. Ericsson

L. M. Ericsson was founded in 1876 as a producer of wire-based network equipment. The company, with assets of $8.1 billion manufactured equipment for both wired and mobile communication and also produced advanced electronic defense systems (see Exhibit 11 for key financials). Ericsson was positioned as number five on the ranking of global telecommunications providers.

Net sales of cellular telephones was $325 million[4] in 1992, and increased 2.5 times in 1993. Within cellular communications the company controlled a leading 40 percent of the world market for traditional analog cellular infrastructure, and had been able to acquire 60 percent of the surging market for digital cellular infrastructure equipment.

The objective of L. M. Ericsson was to keep its strong position in the cellular business, and to gain a part of the expected future growth in the industry, especially within infrastructure equipment, and an important factor in realizing these goals was product development, a cornerstone at Ericsson. Concurrent Engineering was an important feature in achieving an effectively short cycle from a product's initial development stage to the market launch. The importance of R&D was emphasized by its budget of $1.3 billion in 1993.

The firm produced semiconductors and also had suppliers such as General Electrics and Analog Devices from which the crucial Digital Systems Processor was acquired. Ericsson focused on small production batches, having traditions in ordinary telecommunications and phones. On the cellular side, they concentrated on minor batches of advanced units.

The home market of Ericsson was rather small, necessitating exports in order to get volume in sales. This forced the company to be internationally oriented at an early stage, and it already had an integrated distribution network around the world due to sales of ordinary telecommunication equipment. Ericsson was also into several partnerships around the world, such as with Alcatel and NEC and with Nokia in China. Heavy spending on advertising in foreign markets provided the firm with a degree of brand recognition in most markets.

At Ericsson, human capabilities took on a central role. Motivation of employees through personal responsibility, and a high degree of freedom at work combined with cooperation and also a degree of independence, explained some of the success of the project-oriented organization.

---

[3] Switches are a central part of the brain, which is called MTX.

[4] *Business Week,* 4 October 1993.

EXHIBIT 11	Key Financial Statistics for L. M. Ericsson, 1989–1993				
L. M. Ericsson M$	1993	1992	1991	1990	1989
Net sales	7,630	6,770	8,395	7,702	6,130
Costs and expenses	7,207	6,492	8,019	6,883	5,424
Earnings before tax	423	278	376	818	576
Tax/minorities	82	210	216	NA	NA
Net earnings	341	68	160	NA	NA

Source: Ericsson Annual Reports 1993–1994.

The Japanese Competitors

Japan had about 20 companies selling cellular phones in 1991.[5] Some had their own production, of which Matsushita (using the brand name Panasonic) and NEC were the only ones with significant sales of cellular phones outside Japan, though they were still operating at a rather small scale compared to Motorola, Nokia, and Ericsson (see Exhibit 7). Others had signed OEM agreements with major producers outside Japan such as Motorola and Nokia. The best known in this category were Sony, Pioneer, and Hitachi.

The Japanese were trying to establish themselves in the fast-growing cellular phone market. They were attracted by the high future potential in the consumer segment, especially because of the high knowledge they possessed in this area due to their consumer electronics. They were regarded as having an advantage in this area.

The Japanese home market was large, providing potential for high volume. The consumer electronics market, however, was usually characterized by being protected by import restrictions with fierce competition raging between a large number of national companies. These companies had access to low cost capital, due to the favorable financial environment created by the culture, encompassing longer perspectives, higher savings, and high degrees of intercorporate lending. The Japanese share owners were traditionally less focused on high and immediate returns.

The Japanese generally had competence in large-scale, low-priced, high-quality production, and a comprehensive distribution network all over the world, which they coupled with strong brand names. This was particularly exhibited by their position on the consumer electronics market. However, the speed of development and the many existing cellular standards did not favor the use of reverse engineering, which was a commonly used method of development.

By 1994, Matsushita had not yet launched a globally competitive cellular terminal for the digital systems. With the industry environment current at that time, the Japanese had some difficulty entering the scene. The companies also lacked knowledge in cellular infrastructure.

FUTURE EXPECTATIONS IN THE INDUSTRY

In 1994, the industry was in turbulence, but this was expected to calm down with product standardization. A prediction of when this would happen and which standard would become dominant was not possible due to the many possibilities of further systems' innovations.

Development could also slow down within certain standards as technologies stabilized, as was predicted to happen with the GSM not far beyond 1994. This has provided firms like the Korean company Maxon with an opportunity to enter the field. Maxon planned to produce low price GSM phones to be marketed in Europe and other regions employing the GSM standard. In 1994, the highly innovative firms still had an edge over late entrants, in handset technology and in their ability to cover multiple standards. Two tendencies were predicted: short-term high innovation and turbulence, and medium-term maturity.

The major future objective of Nokia was to protect and expand its position. This required awareness of changes in the environment and a continuous accumulation of resources and capabilities inside the organization in order to establish the capacity needed to cope with the expected growth in the cellular phone market.

APPENDIX: HOW DOES CELLULAR COMMUNICATION WORK?

An illustrative example is used to explain the functioning of the cellular technology.

Discerning between the terms *system* and *standard* is important in order to comprehend the different solutions to cellular communications offered on the market. A system, in the context of this case, is understood to be the network within which a personal service agreement and terminal can be used. This, in other words, is defined by the extent of the existing roaming (see later) agreements and whether the same terminal is compatible with the whole system. A standard defines the specific technology used for the contact to take place. In order for a terminal to be used, it must be compatible in standard and the user must have a service agreement with an operator within the system.

A person moving down the highway dials a number on a cellular handset. The handset sends a signal, with a range of 10 to 30 km, that is received by a base station (Tower), as shown by A in Exhibit 12. The base station has to use the

---

[5] *The Economist,* 13 April 1991, pp. 62–64.

same technological standard as the phone does. The base station with the best contact to the cellular phone is chosen by the network and the signal passes through the public fixed wire network to the MTX (Mobile Telephone Exchange, [B]). The MTX is the *brain* in the system, constantly keeping track of the cellular phone on stand-by, in order to track its position. The MTX sends the signal back through the fixed public network, which, if the call is to a stationary phone, connects the call to the dialed number (C in exhibit). If the dialed number is to another cellular telephone, the MTX locates the other terminal (the MTX tracks this, if the terminal is on standby and within range of a base station) and sends the signal to the base station—through the fixed network (D)—closest to the receiving terminal, and final contact is made (E). The second cellular phone does not have to be covered by the same service provider as the one calling. If the two service providers are different, the MTX of the first service provider will simply connect through the fixed network to the MTX of the second.

The people using cellular phones are often moving from one area (cell) to another during a conversation. The MTX ensures that seamless contact is sustained by switching the transmission from one base station to another; this is referred to as the hand-off function. The MTX will typically serve the base stations in one area. As the user moves into another area, her conversation is "handed off" to the MTX serving that area and this capability is referred to as roaming, and provides the user with a wider area of use for her terminal.

The question of channel allocation and terminal identification also needs to be addressed. The telephone calling is registered through a signal with an access code, in order to bill the calling fee to the owner. The cellular system is closed, meaning that a terminal will not be recognized and serviced without the access code. Each operator is licensed to use a portion of the frequency band allocated for the total system/standard in a given area. This frequency portion is able to carry a certain number of simultaneous contacts. The frequency used for transmission is chosen individually for each separate call by the MTX. Each base station can utilize the whole allocated frequency band. The MTX only has to ensure that adjacent towers do not transmit two separate contacts using the same frequency, as this would cause interference between the signals.

As the systems work now, the interconnect problem, using the public fixed wire lines, affects the prices charged by the operators. The national monopolies can use discriminatory pricing on the connections used by the external cellular operators. To overcome this problem, there are examples of operators that intend to use parabolic antennae between the base stations, in order to avoid using the fixed wire network (at least when the contact is cellular to cellular).

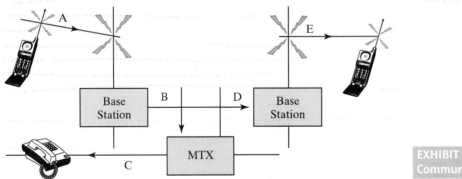

EXHIBIT 12 Cellular Communications Illustrated

The Launch of GSM Cellular Telephones in South Africa

Driving to Jan Smuts Airport for yet another flight to Cape Town, Vodacom's Managing Director, Alan Knott-Craig contemplated the year ahead in anticipation of tomorrow's

This case was prepared by Professor Steve Burgess of The School of Economic and Business Studies at the University of the Witwatersrand as the basis for class discussion rather than to illustrate either effective or ineffective handling of an administrative situation.

management strategy meeting. South Africa's cellular industry had not only recorded the world's fastest launch of a GSM cellular subscriber base but had also become the world's fastest-growing cellular market and the second largest GSM cellular subscriber base in the world in just one year. Such an achievement, during the transition to Mandela and De Klerk's new South Africa, surprised industry experts around the world. Solid market leaders with a 65 percent estimated share, Knott-Craig's team would be contemplating the next phase of market growth and competitive strategy.

THE CELLULAR COMMUNICATIONS INDUSTRY

South Africa's cellular communications industry consisted of four main players: network operators, service providers, dealers, and equipment manufacturers.

Network Operators

Vodacom and Mobile Telephone Networks (MTN) were awarded the first two network operator licenses by the government regulator. The licenses empowered each operator to set up and operate the network infrastructure necessary to provide national GSM digital cellular coverage. Although Europe's GSM digital cellular standard was more expensive than the analogue cellular standard most common to the United States, Britain, and other countries, GSM's many advanced capabilities such as fax and data transmission were leading to growing acceptance as a global standard. After many debates, the South African government specified the GSM standard. Vodacom and MTN were assigned separate frequencies for transmission and reception from the available radio frequency band. Some frequencies were reserved for a potential third network in the future.

The ownership of both network operators included international firms, government or quasi-governmental bodies, and local black business consortia. Vodacom's relationship to Telkom, the state-owned, fixed-wire telephone monopoly, almost assured it of appointment as the first network operator.

Licenses were awarded to both Vodacom and MTN on September 30, 1993 and they began building network infrastructure. However, due to the certainty that Vodacom or Telkom would be awarded at least one of the licenses, MTN began building network infrastructure later and was well behind on April 1, 1994 when the test period began for a limited number of subscribers. Although MTN had made gains by the official launch date of June 1, 1994, it was clear that Vodacom remained ahead in many important geographic coverage areas.

The regulator leveled the playing field by requiring both network operators to allow "roaming" during the test period and the first 3 months of normal operations. Roaming allowed an MTN subscriber to place calls in an area where only Vodacom base stations existed or where MTN base stations were operating at capacity when a subscriber call was placed. Similarly, Vodacom callers could place calls using MTN infrastructure if Vodacom coverage was not available. The two networks agreed to cease roaming ahead of schedule in August 1994, except for emergency calls. Subscribers from either network could make a "112" emergency call on any network—even from phones without the Subscriber Identity Module (SIM) card inserted in the cellular phone. The SIM card was a *smart card* containing an integrated circuit chip to identify the caller at network-level for billing and administrative purposes.

The regulator allowed the network operators to set up and manage their own distribution channel. Following the international trend, both network operators appointed service providers.

Service Providers

Service providers marketed network services and provided the bulk of customer care. Exclusive service providers acted on behalf of one network—dual service providers represented both—but in all cases a client wishing to subscribe to a cellular network was required to sign a contract with one of the network operators' appointed service providers. The South African Cellular Service Providers Association (SACSPA) was established to promote the interests of service providers and provided a forum for cooperating on matters of common concern such as fraud and bad debt. Both network operators encouraged service providers to become SACSPA members.

Service providers were responsible for the sale of handsets, car kits and other cellular equipment, airtime subscriptions, account billing and collection, and ongoing client service. Customers did not have any direct relationship with the network operators. The network operators billed service providers for total calls made by each subscriber (airtime) less a discount of approximately 25 percent to 30 percent (depending on the number of subscribers enrolled by the service provider and a loyalty bonus) plus a monthly subscription fee, which varied according to the tariff the customer chose. Certain incentive payments also were paid. Connection bonuses were paid for net new subscriptions signed by a service provider. Although these subsidies were confidential, the media regularly speculated that subsidies ranged from R500 to R2,000. Most media sources indicated that service providers used the subsidies to lower the price of cellular handsets. The loyalty bonuses were designed to entice dual service providers to concentrate business with one network and varied according to the proportion of a service provider's total subscribers using a particular network.

Network operators received and transmitted customer calls. Every time a cell phone was turned on, the Vodacom system would record the nearest base station(s). This allowed the placement of a call from any telephone or cellphone to interconnect into the appropriate switches for ultimate transmission to the cell user. Thus, a particular call might utilize not only Vodacom's equipment, but also equipment of Telkom. Vodacom's network equipment recorded the SIM card number, the number called, the cellular handset IMEI identification number, the starting and ending time of the call and the type of call for every call as part of a call data record (CDR). The network operators downloaded the resulting CDRs, and reports concerning calls, to service providers on multiple occasions during the day via node-to-node links. Data were formatted to be readable by the service providers' billing systems.

Service providers received the CDR transmissions and other reports for use with internal accounting and management software—the most important component being the billing system. Billing systems performed the mission-critical function of allocating CDRs to subscribers so subscribers were billed for calls placed. In addition, some billing systems offered integrated application processing capabilities that included issuance, activation, and deactivation of handsets and SIM cards on the network as well as performance of certain record-keeping in customer care centers. The software used was complicated and most service providers procured the EPPIX billing system marketed by a U.K. firm that specialized in cellular billing systems. Other service providers formed strategic alliances with overseas service providers and adapted the partner's administrative systems and business strategies to the local market. A few service providers developed local administrative and billing systems. There was little standardization of billing systems and even EPPIX installations could be configured quite differently. Vodacom's own information technology division was headquartered in Cape Town.

There was little doubt that all service providers had experienced administrative and financial difficulties that were exacerbated by the short notice many had received concerning their appointments. As a result, some service providers did not have billing systems up and running when the test period began.

Service providers were hard hit by the faster than expected growth, especially the financial management and management information departments. It was obvious that many were having difficulties getting costs under control. The first-year results announced by the two publicly traded service providers showed signs of the severe trading conditions. Knott-Craig had heard rumors that the published results were typical, perhaps better, than many privately held service providers, and he had heard the reverse. In any case, the persistent rumors that smaller service providers would not last 6 months had not been fulfilled, and the industry ended the first year with 17 service providers—the same number that had begun the year.

Vodacom owned a service provider—VODAC. MTN's major shareholders controlled another service provider, M-TEL. Suspicions of favoritism to these service providers tainted relationships with some service providers. The network operators' licenses did not require them to use service providers, but Vodacom believed that service providers had been proven to speed market penetration around the world and the firm had committed to contracts with 11 service providers.

Dealers

Service providers often appointed dealers to sell airtime subscriptions on their behalf. Vodacom had gained an early competitive advantage when Teljoy and Vodac signed dealer agreements with certain major retail outlets and dealers. This had resulted in fast growth. Teljoy, the leading national TV rental chain with shops located in top retail sites, had become the world's second largest GSM cellular service provider and captured over one third of the South African market, largely as a result of its retail presence and extensive advertising prior to and during the launch of cellular. Teljoy had been advertising heavily in advance of the launch of national satellite TV in recent months.

Many dealers had come and gone during the first year. For some, this was an intentional strategy to take advantage of short-term opportunities created by the explosive launch. Others were undercapitalized, and service provider billing system problems allegedly held up incentive payments far too long to allow dealer survival in many cases.

International and local fraud syndicates had penetrated the dealer network, and the police had made many arrests. Service providers often used the full connection bonus payment and other promotional funds to subsidize the price of equipment sold on longer-term airtime subscriber contracts—often comparing the sale of R2,500 phones for little or nothing to the sale of razors below cost to promote usage of blades.

Posing as legitimate clients, fraud teams either bought cellular phones at the low, subsidized prices or stole them and exported them to other GSM countries. Theft of airtime represented a far greater hazard. Many "phone shops" had been discovered in urban areas where local and international phone calls were sold at reduced rates. Call charges exceeding many thousands of Rands were sometimes completed before service providers became aware of the problem. Customers were reporting their cell phones stolen from restaurants, cafés, and even from their bedside tables while they slept.

Fraud team links to African and Asian drug syndicates had been reported in the press. A "phone shop" could quickly run up a R10,000 bill on a stolen SIM card in a weekend, offsetting the total monthly airtime (calls) revenue of more than 65 average subscribers. SACSPA had shared police evidence concerning the infiltration of the country by international fraud syndicates in anticipation of the 1995 Rugby World Cup (which South Africa later won). A classic tournament watched by billions around the world, this was the first time the World Cup had been held in one country and experts wondered if the police force was up to the challenge of international fraud teams.

Regulation

The Postmaster General was the official regulator of the telecommunications industry. Pallo Jordan, Minister of Posts, Telecommunications, and Broadcasting, was responsible for the government's overall communications strategy. The minister was rethinking telecommunications policy, and an extensive Green Paper had been circulated for discussion to the South African public and all interested parties. The continuation of Telkom's fixed wire telephone monopoly was debated in the Green Paper but seemed unlikely to change. The regulator had approved a number of Vodacom tariff plans. Service providers could not charge more than the regulated call tariffs, although they were free to discount any tariff.

Knott-Craig was conscious that the Vodacom and Telkom cultures were different due to the nature of the businesses but felt that certain aspects of culture were shared. He was particularly pleased that he could draw on Telkom and Vodafone technical expertise and business experience when required. However, the impression that Vodacom received special favors, either from Telkom or the Regulator, were a constant source of irritation that Knott-Craig was tired of denying. He also tired of rejecting allegations that Vodacom favored Vodac or Teljoy over other service providers.

EQUIPMENT MANUFACTURERS

Equipment manufacturers participated in the industry in two ways: by supplying cellular base stations and infrastructure to network operators and by supplying cellular handsets and accessories to service providers and dealers. Nokia, Ericsson, Alcatel, Siemens, Panasonic, and Motorola were among the leading brands participating in the latter. Vodacom sourced base stations from Siemens and Alcatel while MTN's network standardized on Ericsson equipment.

Service providers felt that the equipment manufacturers were becoming problematic. Consumer dissatisfaction with manufacturers was a serious problem, according to the SACSPA. Some manufacturers were taking up to 6 months to repair handsets under warranty, and this necessitated significant investments in loan phones. No doubt, Motorola's decision to appoint major retailers as distributors would affect service providers, even though retailers would require a service provider to connect their subscribers to a network operator.

There was also a constant threat of stock shortages as new countries adopted the GSM standard. Many manufacturers shipped stock only after receiving a letter of credit and then shipped amounts less than those ordered by the major service providers. News of a Chinese consortium beginning the manufacture of GSM handsets had appeared in the South African business press. Manufacturers also were organized in a trade association, the CTMIA.

THE BUSINESS ENVIRONMENT

South Africa's cellular industry received a baptism of fire in its first year. Violence racked the country in the run-up to President Nelson Mandela's election on April 29, 1994. When the government announced that two network operators would be appointed, the appointment of a second network operator became highly politicized, delaying the appointment of a second network operator.

The first half of 1994 had been politically turbulent. There were constant rumors right-wing or left-wing forces would attempt to sabotage the elections or overthrow the government if Nelson Mandela's African National Congress (ANC) won. Many skilled people were leaving the country and, paradoxically, many were returning. Some political parties spoke of privatizing state-run monopolies, such as Telkom, and the parastatals controlling the trans-

portation, iron and steel, and electrical distribution industries. Although these bodies represented a comparatively high percentage of GNP compared to other countries, ANC supporters such as the labor unions and the Communist Party of South Africa voiced disapproval of privatization schemes. Some political parties were advocating that reconstruction and development required nothing less than a centrally planned Marxist/Leninist economy.

Cellular telephony was viewed with suspicion by many parties who viewed the proposed launch as a thinly disguised attempt to keep the control of telecommunications in the hands of the white minority. Thus, even though both licenses were awarded on September 30, 1993, an agreement was reached with the African National Congress only on October 22, 1993. Equipment purchases and service provider appointments could only begin thereafter. South Africa traditionally comes to a standstill during the mid-December to mid-January Christmas break, and this created additional problems. Some service providers had been appointed as late as a few weeks prior to the April 1994 rollout to a limited subscriber base for testing.

Both licenses required the network operators to subsidize cellular telephony in the historically disadvantaged communities. Both networks had initiated projects in this regard and appointed black-owned service providers. In addition, Vodacom and MTN were to engage in economic activities outside their mainstream business to the value of R1 billion to the government at the end of five years. Attempts to increase the historically disadvantaged population's access to telecommunications resulted in Vodacom's telephone shop, which was designed to house up to 10 cellular pay telephones. The shops also created much needed jobs. MTN could take credit for the invention of the world's first working GSM cellular pay phone in a similar project.

The Market

South Africa blends First and Third World characteristics. First World shopping malls and business areas and Third World squatter shacks often coexist within kilometers. Urbanized areas generally have high economic activity and income, but rural areas are much poorer. Exhibit 1 highlights some indicators of human and economic development.

Knott-Craig was concerned about the escalating violence in the country during early 1995. Violent crime had reached the levels experienced prior to the election in some areas, and the police were clearly experiencing difficulty in combating crime. Security had positive and negative impacts on cellular telephone usage. Security was a popular reason for buying a cellular phone and promotions featuring on-call security services by Autopage Cellular and Teljoy both seemed to have done well. However, it was far too early for reliable usage statistics to be available for subscribers interested in security.

The Government of National Unity was exceeding the expectations many held prior to the election. President Mandela was especially popular. However, ANC's Reconstruction and Development Programme was moving more

EXHIBIT 1   Selected Development Statistics for Selected Countries

	Population in 1992 in Millions	Gross Domestic Product in 1992 in $US Million	Energy Use per Capita in 1992 (per Capita Kilograms)	Telephone Main Lines in 1990 (in Thousands)	Access to Safe Drinking Water (%)	Crude Birthrate in 1992 (per 1,000 Population)	Human Development Index
United States	255.4	5,920,199	7,662	136,337		16	.925
New Zealand	3.4	41,304	4,284	1,469	97	17	.907
Korea	43.7	296,136	2,569	13,276	93	16	.859
Chile	13.6	41,203	837	861	87	23	.848
Mexico	85.0	329,011	1,525	5,355	89	28	.804
South Africa	39.8	103,651	2,487	3,315		31	.650
Indonesia	184.3	126,364	303	1,069	34	25	.586
Kenya	25.7	6,884	223	183	49	37	.434
Pakistan	119.3	41,904	92	843	72	40	.393

Source: The World Bank. *World Development Report 1994: Infrastructure for Development.* New York: Oxford, 1994; except for Human Development Index, excerpted from United Nations Development Program, *Human Development Report 1994.* New York: Oxford.

slowly than expected, and President Mandela had recently ordered his cabinet to pursue economic growth with increased vigor. The school system was a particular worry for many people with school-aged children, and there was a perception that managerial and professional people with kids were leaving the country in record numbers, although official emigration statistics did not confirm this perception. There was a possibility that the stringent exchange controls placed on emigrating people may have had some impact on how many people actually reported immigration.

MARKETING

Achieving competitive advantage required careful analysis on the network operator and service provider tier. The nature of government regulation often made it difficult to differentiate a business in meaningful ways from one's competitor.

Product

Network coverage, that is, the area in which calls could be placed and received by cellular users, was a common way to differentiate cellular networks. With the exception of a difficult period of oversubscription during August and September 1994, Vodacom felt that its network covered a far larger area and boasted superior quality. Network quality was measured by counting calls dropped (disconnected due to some network problem) and consumer complaints about the quality of the audio transmission. Although MTN's network started building months after Vodacom, it was clear that MTN would catch up to Vodacom within the short term.

Promotion

The coverage advantage had been the focus of Vodacom's major selling effort masterminded by GM Joan Joffe and was a major reason that two out of three subscribers had chosen Vodacom. The award-winning Launch of GSM Cellular Telephone in South Africa TV advertisement focused on this coverage advantage. The R21 million measured ad spending placed the combined TV, press, and radio spending in the top 20 South African companies' ad spending for 1994—just behind MTN's R23 million. Service providers also promoted network brands in their own advertising and both networks enjoyed widespread brand awareness. Exact figures were unavailable but the combined advertising spend of the service providers probably exceeded R20 million.

Joffe was particularly proud of the recent promotions connected to Vodacom's sponsorship of the Rugby World Cup. Adverts had high recognition and had received high liking and noting scores. Market research indicated that the TV advertisements were particularly well liked and Vodacom's share of purchase intent had increased significantly. Joffe could not say whether this was due to MTN's ongoing coverage problems or the promotional campaigns but believed it might be due to both.

MTN's advertising also had been very effective. Featuring a unique and humorous monotonic delivery by a male gravelly-voiced announcer, the TV and radio ad shared the advantages of having the magic of MTN's mobile communications at one's disposal. MTN positioned its brand as "the better connection" and achieved high recognition and branding. The innovative use of an MTN airship also aided brand recognition.

Pricing

Government regulation affected pricing strategies most. Consumers generally judged two costs when considering adopting cellular telephony. Initial one-time costs included the cost of the cellular handset and any accessories (such as a hands-free car kit), the cost of the SIM card (R65.00), and the cost of activating the SIM card on the network (the connection fee R125.00). Ongoing costs included the monthly

subscription (R125.00) and call charges (R1.10 per minute during peak hours and R.65 during off-peak hours). The average user received a monthly bill of R250 to R300.

Call charge tariffs, monthly subscription fees, SIM card charges and connection fees were regulated, and both network operators charged the same amounts. Network operators could ask for new tariffs to be approved but the other network was also free to apply to use the same new tariff immediately. Service providers were allowed to discount call tariffs in order to gain business. However, a discount of even 10 percent of the call tariff would be reduced directly from the service provider's 25 percent to 30 percent of the total call charge—thus, a 10 percent discount could result in almost a 40 percent reduction in sales revenue at the service provider tier. SACSPA felt that such discounting would seriously jeopardize the long-term survival of the service provider tier, and there was some question as to how discounts could be applied without infringing on the network requirements for approval of new tariffs by the regulator. Indeed, one firm that was alleged to discount tariffs ran into financial trouble almost immediately. Some service providers were cleverly bundling packages with added-value emergency services and other augmented product offers that were clearly legal.

Both networks subsidized the cost of handsets. Initial subsidies did not affect the price of handsets significantly but, as competition heated up at the end of the first year, subsidies had increased to a very significant level.[1] The large subsidies allowed service providers to sell low-end R1,500 handsets for almost nothing and to sell top-range handsets for as little as R2,000.00. Indeed, Autopage had

---

[1]The end of the first year was important because many new subscribers who signed one-year contracts in the first few months of the cellular launch had paid more than R3,000 for handsets that had much limited functionality when compared to the handsets selling at the end of the year. It did not make commercial sense for the network operators to subsidize these subscribers to move from one service provider to another simply to get a better handset with the new contract.

bought up the total available stock of a new Alcatel handset that was offered with an added-value emergency services package free of charge to qualifying applicants. Free phones fueled rapid growth but also created the problems noted earlier.

Distribution

The service provider distribution model was a cause of some concern. Vodafone was experimenting with a direct-to-market approach in the United Kingdom. The U.S. model featured network operators and dealers. In the U.S. model, dealers were marketing agents and the networks took total responsibility for the billing and customer service functions. Both approaches had been successful.

Most industry experts would attribute Vodacom's commanding market share to its superior network coverage and quality and its exclusive presence in leading retail outlets. Teljoy sold cellular subscriptions through its retail outlets located in most shopping mall locations across the country. In addition, exclusive service providers—primarily Teljoy and Vodac—had tied up exclusive dealerships with major retailers, office supply outlets, and dealers. MTN had also tied up exclusive agreements, but Knott-Craig was confident he had won the early rounds of this fight as he approached a traffic jam on the R24.

THE CURRENT SITUATION

As he thought about tomorrow's strategy meeting, Knott-Craig became frustrated at the traffic jam ahead. It was not normally so crowded at this time of day on the R24 and, as he changed from the CD to hear the traffic report on Radio 702, tomorrow's strategy meeting continued to dominate his thinking. The industry had exceeded forecasts of 100,000 subscribers and achieved 350,000 in its first year.

He sensed that new problems would require very different solutions to the past. It seemed certain that explosive growth would not be repeated but that the industry could achieve 1 million subscribers by the end of the first three years. It seemed certain that the quality of new subscribers (as measured by average airtime and bad debt) would deteriorate as cellular usage expanded. New subscriptions had declined dramatically since both networks had reduced connection bonuses on April 1, 1995. Balancing the desirability for growth against the profitability required to satisfy shareholders and to make the RDP payment was not going to be easy.

Technologically, Knott-Craig planned for Vodacom to stay ahead. MTN had recently announced a host of value-added network services that allowed users to use a cellular phone as a pager or to call for a host of services, such as legal advice. Both networks had launched fax and data services and paging services at about the same time. Caller identification would also be available soon on both networks.

Teljoy had already taken the initiative to launch a 112 emergency service enhancement using the 911 number popularized by an American TV series shown on South

African TV. Fax services were to be enhanced shortly. A fax would then be held similarly to voice mail to be retrieved later when desirable.

The traffic jam cleared as he passed a minor motor car accident on the freeway, and Knott-Craig could see the airport in the distance. He would arrive on time.

Harley-Davidson Motor Co., Inc.: Defending a Piece of the Domestic Pie

INTRODUCTION

Throughout the 20th century, motorcycles have been produced by a host of American companies. Names such as Indian, Yale, Pope, and Minnesota can be found in the graveyard of defunct American motorcycle producers. Today, only one company in the United States is a manufacturer of motorcycles—Harley-Davidson. Founded in 1903 by William S. Harley and a trio of Davidsons, Harley-Davidson was for many years the unchallenged leader in American motorcycle sales. The company's success was due to a combination of factors—innovative engineering and product design and a company image that inspired fierce loyalty on the part of its customers. In fact, few American manufacturers have ever boasted a product as ingrained in the country's folklore as Harley-Davidson. Be it in movies such as *The Wild One* or *Easy Rider,* or in real life with motorcycle gangs like the Hell's Angels, the Harley-Davidson trademark has always evoked an image that is, for better or worse, distinctly American. Seen in this light, it is not so surprising that the first far-reaching piece of protectionist legislation of the Reagan presidency was granted in favor of none other than Harley-Davidson, the only remaining American manufacturer of motorcycles.

On April 1, 1983, the President heeded the recommendations of the International Trade Commission (ITC) that a five-year tariff relief program be accorded Harley-Davidson. The ruling culminated a six-year effort on the part of Harley for governmental help. Predictably, the company felt it had been vindicated by the Reagan administration. Vaughn Beals, chairman and CEO of Harley-Davidson had this to say: "The President's courageous action demonstrates his support for the concept that free trade must also be fair trade. The administration's decision, on the merits of the case, tells our trading partners that the U.S. fully supports the concept of free trade, but that does not mean that our government will tolerate unfair competition."

BACKGROUND TO THE TARIFF RULING

In the 1950s, Harley-Davidson possessed a share of the American market of anywhere from 60 percent to 70 percent. It produced powerful, uniquely styled motorcycles that inspired an unusually high degree of brand loyalty. It was in this decade that other American motorcycle makers ceased to exist. Harley was totally unprepared for what it would call the "Japanese invasion" of the 1960s. The Japanese were able to produce quality merchandise for cheaper prices because of their size and efficient production techniques. These companies were also willing to spend huge amounts on advertising and they successfully introduced millions of Americans (and Europeans) to the joys of motorcycling.

Harley-Davidson, for its part, was bogged down with an image problem that was largely of its own making. For years it had catered to the rough hewn biker because he was, after all, Harley's most loyal customer. This strategy did not at all mesh with the spirit of the 1960s most typified by Honda's, "You meet the nicest people on a Honda" campaign. Unable to capitalize on this huge new market for motorcycles (sales increased by 35 percent in 1962 and by an average of 18 percent for 10 years afterward), Harley watched its market share drop precipitously. In 1970, it claimed a mere 5 percent of the American market (see Exhibit 1 for current data).

AMF–Harley-Davidson

In 1969, Harley-Davidson was bought by AMF, a recreational equipment conglomerate. AMF proceeded to manage the company in a way that "only portfolio theory can embrace."[1] Product lines that were deemed unprofitable were dropped instead of improved and very little money was directed to shore up Harley's position. By 1976, the company offered only four models to consumers, whereas the four big Japanese producers routinely offered 20 to 25 models. Harley's only remaining strength was in large bikes (700cc and up), and here too they would lose a huge amount of market share. In 1972, Harley-Davidson sold 99.6 percent of the heavy bikes purchased in America. By 1975, this figure was down to 44.4 percent (see Exhibit 2 for current data).

The company's initial reaction to these results was to accuse the Japanese of "dumping" their products at unfairly low prices and of copying some of the Harley-Davidson big

This case was prepared by Charles J. Anderer, research associate, under the supervision of Warren J. Keegan, Professor of International Business and Marketing, as part of the International Business Case Study Project, Center for International Business Studies, Pace University. This project was funded in part by a grant from the United States Department of Education. © 1986 by the Board of Trustees of Pace University.

---

[1] *Business Marketing* (August 1984).

EXHIBIT 1	New Motorcycle Registrations 10 Leading Brands by Market Share, 1979–1984											
	1984		**1983**		**1982**		**1981**		**1980**		**1979**	
Make	*Rank*	*Mrkt. Share*	*Rank*	*Mrkt. Share*	*Rank*	*Mrkt. Share*	*Rank*	*Mrkt. Share*	*Rank*	*Mrkt. Share*	*Rank*	*Mrkt. Share*
Honda	1	57.7%	1	54.8%	1	45.1%	1	39.1%	1	39.5%	1	39.7%
Yamaha	2	18.6	2	19.0	2	22.2	2	24.9	2	23.5	2	23.0
Suzuki	3	10.0	3	11.8	3	14.2	4	13.6	4	14.9	4	13.3
Kawasaki	4	8.9	4	9.8	4	12.7	3	15.7	3	15.4	3	14.7
Harley-Davidson	5	3.7	5	3.3	5	3.5	5	5.0	5	4.7	5	6.1
BMW	6	0.6	6	0.6	6	0.5	7	0.4	7	0.4	6	0.7
Husqvarna	7	0.2	7	0.3	8	0.2	9	0.2	9	0.2	10	0.3
Moto Guzzi	8	0.1	9	0.1	10	0.1	—	—	—	—	—	—
Can Am	9	[a]	—	—	9	0.1	10	0.1	10	0.1	—	—
Vespa	10	[a]	8	0.1	7	0.3	6	0.5	6	0.8	7	0.7
Triumph	10	—	10	[a]	—	—	8	0.2	8	0.3	8	0.6
Hodaka	—	—	—	—	—	—	—	—	—	—	9	0.3

[a] Less than 0.05%.

R. L. Polk new registrations include the three most current model years. Some off-highway motorcycle and all-terrain vehicle new registrations are included.

California new off-highway motorcycle and ATV registrations have been added to 1983 and prior year new registrations, so that comparisons can be made with 1984 and subsequent years that include California off-highway registrations.

New York new registrations were not available from October 1983 through December 1984.

Oklahoma new registrations are not available.

Source: New Motorcycle Registrations, R. L. Polk & Co., Detroit, Michigan.

EXHIBIT 2	New Registration of 700+cc Motorcycles and Market Share Breakdown					
	Registrations			**Market Share**		
	1984	*1983*	*% Change*	*1984*	*1983*	*% Change*
Harley-Davidson 700+cc	28,354	25,342	+11.9	15.5	12.3	+3.2
Honda 700+cc	79,337	103,794	−23.6	43.2	50.6	−7.4
Kawasaki 700+cc	24,262	23,398	+3.7	13.2	11.4	+1.8
Suzuki 700+cc	15,797	17,179	−8.1	8.6	8.4	+0.2
Yamaha 700+cc	31,420	31,159	+0.8	17.1	15.2	+1.9
BMW 700+cc	3,617	3,257	+11.1	2.0	1.6	+0.4
Other 700+cc	668	1,018	−34.4	0.4	0.5	−0.1
Grand Total 700+cc	183,455	205,147	−10.6	100.0	100.0	—

Data include 699cc "Tariff Busters."

Source: R. L. Polk.

bike models. A petition for some form of protection was unsuccessfully submitted to the government in 1977. At the same time, Harley did very little to extricate itself from its poor market position. The company experienced a gradual decline both in terms of share and product performance. "Quality went to hell and labor relations went to pot," CEO Beals would later say. Harley continued to emphasize the emotional appeal of its machines rather than stress their performance features: "No other motorcycle arouses the same pride, passion, even fanaticism," proclaimed one ad.[2] Later, they would direct much of their energies toward the Japanese, giving their seal of approval to T-shirts bearing the message "I'd rather eat worms than ride a Honda."[3]

[2] *Business Week,* 21 August 1983.
[3] *Fortune,* 16 May 1983.

Leveraged Buyout (1981)

Perhaps the most important development of the past decade was the leveraged buyout of Harley-Davidson in 1981 led by Vaughn Beals himself. Beals has since established himself as a charismatic and dedicated manager. In fact, company literature describes him as providing the perfect blend of technical expertise and management skill required to spearhead the "new" Harley-Davidson's aggressive revitalization programs. The most important feature of the buyout, beyond putting Mr. Beals in charge, was that it got the company away from the short-term mentality that characterized the AMF years. Freed from the duty to annually present its performance to a group of dividend-hungry shareholders, management has been able to concentrate on spending the necessary funds to put Harley on its feet again.

The Tariff Ruling (1983)

Essential to the rebirth of Harley-Davidson, argued Beals, was a tariff program that would allow time for its program to prove successful. Particularly annoying to Beals was the way in which each Japanese company would slash its prices whenever its inventories built up due to faulty demand assessments or a general economic slowdown. This practice irked Harley to no end because its products were more expensive to begin with. The recession years of 1981 to 1982 were very bad for Harley. The company, teetering near the edge of bankruptcy, decided to once again petition for help from Washington. This time, it got some.

The five-year tariff, which went into effect April 15, 1983, provided an additional 45 percent tariff (on top of the existing 4.4 percent) on motorcycles having an engine displacement of 700cc or more, in the first year, with reductions to 35, 20, 15, and 10 percent respectively, in the four succeeding years. European imports are effectively excluded from the surcharge through tariff-rate quotas, which provide that only motorcycle exporters of significant size (i.e., X number of units exported) have to absorb the surcharge cost.

Without getting involved in a debate on the merits of free trade versus protectionism, two basic arguments on this ruling have been advanced. First, free trade purists would argue that the tariff is unfair because it protects an inefficient producer of motorcycles. Harley-Davidson is inefficient, they would say, because it has shown itself incapable of offering the consumer anything but overpriced bikes of second-rate quality. The proof of this lies in the vote of the customers in the marketplace. On the other hand, Harley-Davidson argues that the ruling is necessary because the government has a duty to protect its only remaining producer of motorcycles, who, in addition to competing in an unfair environment, has showed itself to be more than willing to make the financial commitment to improve, but needs time to do so.

THE "NEW" HARLEY-DAVIDSON (1981–1985)

Operational Improvements

The most remarkable aspect of Harley's new approach is how heavily it borrows from the Japanese. Today, the company stresses employee involvement, uses "just-in-time" inventory and manufacturing principles, and manages all of its processes statistically. This, from a company that had said the Japanese owed their success to unfair practices and the copying of Harley's own models. Intelligently, Harley-Davidson has admitted that there might be something to the Japanese approach after all. Says Thomas A. Gelb, Vice President/Operations: "Initially, our management attributed the price and quality differences of Japanese motorcycles to culture, wage rates, and illegal trade practices such as dumping. Only after extensive research did it become apparent that a large part of the competitive edge they enjoyed was achieved through a truly different manufacturing approach, using improved and more efficient manufacturing techniques.

"One of the first examples of Harley-Davidson's willingness to adopt innovative manufacturing techniques is in the employee involvement area. Harley-Davidson was the second U.S. manufacturing company to implement Quality Circles—back in 1978. At this point, over half of the company's employees in Wisconsin are active participants in this program. This employee involvement and participation program permits employees to contribute their ideas, do hands-on problem solving, and improve the efficiency and quality of their work. Doors that were previously closed to employees are now being opened. For example, company policy now requires that employees be consulted in the planning of any changes to an employee's workplace or layout, or where equipment or process changes are being considered. Rapport and morale are up. Grievances have been cut in half; absenteeism has been reduced by 44 percent, and a job security committee (with representatives of both labor and senior management) meets regularly.

"The second area of Harley-Davidson leadership is the 'Just-in-Time' manufacturing program. Since JIT is based on large numbers of small parts runs, it is critical that machine set-up times be held to an absolute minimum. This was one of the first hurdles that was attacked. Set-up reduction is being approached aggressively and, to date, has resulted in an average of 75 percent reduction in the set-up times of the machines to which the process has been applied. These reductions have not been achieved through major capital investments, but rather, through team efforts. Usage of JIT has also helped reduce floor space requirements by 40 percent, required movement through the complete production process by 62 percent.

"In the Statistical Process Control (SPC) area, Harley-Davidson is proving daily the premise that a continual improvement in quality reduces overall operating costs. Essentially, SPC uses statistics to identify variations in a 'process' (be it in the office, shop, or field) and thus pinpoints items that need tighter controls and improvement.

"These three areas—Statistical Process Control, Just-in-Time manufacturing, and Employee Involvement—are producing dramatic quality and efficiency results, such as:

- 50 percent reduction in reject rates;
- 40 percent reduction in warranty costs;

- 300 percent increase in defect-free vehicles received by dealers since 1982;
- Consumers rating quality and reliability as "excellent" increased by 25 percent from 1982 to 1984 (Diagnostic Research Inc. study);
- Increasing inventory turns from 4.5 turns in 1982 to 16 turns in 1984;
- Improving productivity by 19.8 percent per employee, from 1982 to 1984."

Development of a Quality Product Line

Harley-Davidson has increased the number of models it offers to the consumer to 12 from the lowpoint of 4 in 1976 (see Exhibit 3). More importantly, the new Harleys have been praised more for their performance than for their trademark. Since the buyout in 1981, Harley-Davidson has spent two-and-a-half times the national average for manufacturing companies on research and development, resulting in numerous product improvements. The single most notable achievement has been the introduction of the Evolution engine, the product of five years of intensive engineering development. The Evolution engine features all new major components using the latest design techniques and advanced materials. The result is an engine that produces 15 percent more usable torque and 10 percent more horsepower, while using 10 percent less fuel. The engine is designed for high reliability and durability with a minimum of scheduled maintenance, making it simpler and less expensive to operate and maintain.

EXHIBIT 3	Harley-Davidson 1986 Model Year Price List	
Model Code	**Model Name**	**Retail Price**
FLHTC Lib.	Electra Glide Lib.	$10,474.00
FLHTC	Electra Glide Classic	10,224.00
FLHT	Electra Glide	9,624.00
FXRD	Grand Touring Sport Glide	9,474.00
FXRT	Sport Glide	8,749.00
FXST-C	Softail Custom	9,499.00
FXST	Softail	8,949.00
FXWG	Wide Glide	8,899.00
FXRS Lib.	Low Rider Lib.	8,849.00
FXRS	Low Rider	8,499.00
FXRS	Low Rider Special	8,649.00
FXR	Super Glide	7,549.00
XLH Lib.	Sportster 1100 Lib.	5,699.00
XLH	Sportster 1100	5,399.00
XLH	Sportster	4,545.00
XLH	Sportster 883	4,195.00

Note: All Harley-Davidsons have an engine displacement of 1340cc with the exception of the XLH models, which range from 883cc to 1100cc.

Product Innovations

Harley-Davidson has also succeeded in introducing a host of product innovations:

1. 1984 introduction of a patent-pending "anti-dive" air suspension system that keeps the front end of the motorcycle stable during a hard stop to increase braking efficiency and safety for the rider.
2. Application of elastomer-isolated engines to reduce the vibration previously associated with Harley-Davidson engines.
3. Introduction of a new-design, smooth shifting, five-speed transmission.
4. The first application in the motorcycle industry of solid-state electronic ignition (in 1979) to improve performance and reliability, followed by the first computer-controlled ignition system in 1983.
5. Changes in chassis design and steering geometries to improve handling and increase rider comfort and safety, including introduction of computer-designed frames in 1981.

These improvements have not gone unnoticed by long-time Harley customers. Motorcycle gangs and police forces alike have returned to buying Harleys. Michael O'Farrell, president of the Oakland Hell's Angel chapter remarked in a recent article in *The New York Times:* "It's amazing, the difference. (The motorcycles) don't beat you to death any more and your kidneys are still intact."

Development of a New Harley Image

Management has strived to make a break with the past by changing the company's image. Rather than continuing to cultivate the impression that Harley-Davidson represents quality because it is the motorcycle of choice for law-breaker and lawman alike, the company now portrays doctors, lawyers, craftsmen, and foremen as being the "real" Harley riders. In an attempt to differentiate itself from others in the crowded big bike sector (which remains Harley's meal ticket), the company cites market research data, which indicates that the Harley rider is generally more educated and has a higher income and a more responsible job than Japanese motorcycle owners:

- 44 percent of Harley purchasers have attended college, versus 34 percent to 39 percent for the owners of Japanese imports.
- Only 11 percent of Harley owners *do not* have a high school diploma, versus 18 percent for Honda and 30 percent for Kawasaki owners.
- Harley purchasers have significantly higher incomes than the owners of Japanese machines. A full 28 percent of Harley purchasers earn more than $35,000, compared with 11 percent of Kawasaki owners. At incomes from $25,000 to $35,000, the contrast is even sharper—35 percent of Harley purchasers earn in this range, with only 12 percent to 14 percent of the owners of Japanese motorcycles earning at this level.

Reactions from Harley Dealers and Riders

Harley-Davidson's efforts to improve its product have not at all been in vain, those familiar with the company will tell you. In Harley's New York City showroom a dealer points to a handful of bikes and says that this is all that is left from the 1985 stock. In general, the mood is upbeat concerning Harley-Davidson: "Here in New York City, at least, management's commitment to quality is showing up both in sales figures and performance. Vaughn Beals is the Lee Iacocca of the motorcycle industry."

In suburban White Plains, 42-year-old Richie Pierce, a long-time cycling enthusiast, sells both Harley-Davidsons and Suzukis. Pierce fully acknowledges all that Harley has done to improve itself, yet he says that Harleys and Suzukis, or any other Japanese bike for that matter, should never be compared. "The Harley is, and always has been, an image bike. Japanese bikes are performance bikes. Even with the tariff Harleys sell at a premium. This is because Harley-Davidsons are prestige bikes. As for performance, Harleys just don't match up. The Japanese can easily outspend them and it shows up in the type of motorcycles they produce."

Even though there is a significant difference in performance, Pierce feels there will always be a market for Harleys: "I own three bikes and one of them is a Harley. There is something about Harley-Davidson that sets them apart from other bikes. The Japanese have tried to copy the Harley look but it just doesn't work. That's why it is so much easier to resell a Harley than a Japanese bike. If you're going to buy performance, why buy used performance? Harleys have an inimitable style and that's what keeps them going. Besides, the government would never let the only American motorcycle company left go down the tubes."

Harley-Davidsons do indeed seem to have that special something that other bikes lack. When asked to review one of Harleys large touring bikes, the FLTC, for the magazine *Cycle Guide,* Marc Cook came back with these remarks: "The Harley makes me giggle. Out on the highway, with little else to do but watch the white line, the FLTC makes me laugh out loud inside my helmet. And I'm not entirely sure why. Perhaps it's the seductive rhythm of the engine pulses, or the way that massive vee-twin never seems to run out of torque. Or it could be the uncanny directional stability of the big 'Hog.' Maybe it's the response of the young ladies at the local Haagen-Dazs. But, really, I don't think any of these is the answer. The truth is, the Harley flat surprises me. It works so well on the open road—in spite of its rough edges and idiosyncrasies—that I have a hard time *not* watching the scenery."

HARLEY'S POSTTARIFF PERFORMANCE

In spite of the preceding improvements, Harley-Davidson has yet to return to profitability. The company is certainly in better shape compared to 1981–1982 and yet management doesn't forsee any substantial profits before 1987.

Demand for motorcycles has yet to bounce back from the recessionary levels of 1982. A glimpse at new motorcycle wholesale sales data reveals that sales in the big bike segment have declined sharply since 1981 (see Exhibit 4). As for Harley, its sales have actually decreased since the pretariff era. There have, however, been gains made in terms of market share. In 1984, Harley's share of the big bike segment increased 3.2 percent, from 12.3 percent to 15.5 percent. Harley-Davidson has also succeeded in reducing the gap between itself and Honda, the leader in the heavyweight segment. On the other hand, Harley-Davidson's overall share of the American market has actually decreased since 1981, from 5 percent to 3.7 percent.

The impact of the tariff on the Japanese has been offset, in part, by Honda and Kawasaki, who both have production facilities in the United States. According to Beals, this has enabled the Japanese to sidestep the tariff: "The Japanese have managed to duck the tariff on about two-thirds of the vehicles that should have been subject to it, by stepping up their U.S. final assembly operations and through the introduction of 699cc motorcycles which fall just below the 700cc tariff limit." On the other hand, statistics show dramatic decreases both in the number of Japanese-produced motorcycles entering the United States since 1982 and in the number of Japanese-produced motorcycles with an engine displacement larger than 790cc (see Exhibits 5 and 6).

International Sales/Global Strategy

Harley-Davidson, although it has made some key changes in the areas of operations, design, and product image, has chosen to remain an essentially domestic company. This point is underscored by the fact that, in 1984, Japanese motorcycle manufacturers exported 660,484 units to the United States, while a mere 1,046 Harleys made their way to Japan. European export figures are similarly low. Is the passion American Harley owners feel for their machines exportable? Alfred E. Eckes, chairman of the ITC, hopes as much. Eckes wrote in his tariff ruling that "as exports become more competitive with the depreciation of the dollar, it is reasonable to think that Harley . . . will participate again in export sales."

The difference in size between Harley-Davidson and the four Japanese companies means that it will continue to operate with severe technological and cost disadvantages in relation to its competitors. Tariff or no tariff, the Japanese were able to produce 4,026,307 motorcycles in 1984, or one hundred times as many units as Harley-Davidson produced. The only other surviving small motorcycle maker is BMW and it does so with the benefit of the technological and production experience gained through its large automobile division.

When the tariff on large displacement motorcycles expires in 1988, Harley-Davidson's fate will be determined by the marketplace. What remains to be seen is if its reputation and history, combined with some noticeable improvements

EXHIBIT 4   New Motorcycle Wholesale Sales by Major Brands, 1980–1984

				Units									
				Model Type			Engine Type		Displacement Size (cc)				
	Wholesale $ Volume ($000's)	Est. Retail $ Volume ($000's)	Total Units	On-Highway	Off-Highway	Dual Purpose	Two Stroke	Four Stroke	Under 1 25cc	125– 349cc	350– 449cc	450– 749cc	750cc and Up
1980	$1,702,130	$2,136,866	1,156,843	711,295	332,753	112,795	314,854	841,989	322,294	263,336	133,069	182,202	255,942
(% of Total Units)			(100.0%)	(61.4%)	(28.9%)	(9.7%)	(27.2%)	(72.8%)	(27.9%)	(22.8%)	(11.5%)	(15.7%)	(22.1%)
1981	$1,861,821	$2,236,790	1,137,918	669,062	391,599	77,257	271,633	866,285	270,743	301,357	78,476	225,589	261,753
(% of Total Units)			(100.0%)	(58.8%)	(34.4%)	(6.8%)	(23.9%)	(76.1%)	(23.8%)	(26.5%)	(6.9%)	(19.8%)	(23.0%)
1982	$1,600,070	$1,993,127	1,018,840	495,521	476,419	46,900	286,529	732,311	307,713	342,283	28,223	117,519	223,102
(% of Total Units)			(100.0%)	(48.6%)	(46.8%)	(4.6%)	(28.1%)	(71.9%)	(30.2%)	(33.6%)	(2.7%)	(11.6%)	(21.9%)
1983	$1,985,979	$2,468,186	1,241,808	539,040	641,758	61,010	294,256	947,552	294,711	507,960	25,873	215,026	198,238
(% of Total Units)			(100.0%)	(43.4%)	(51.7%)	(4.9%)	(23.7%)	(76.3%)	(23.7%)	(40.9%)	(2.1%)	(17.3%)	(16.0%)
1984	$2,270,332	$2,816,370	1,310,240	446,968	802,530	60,742	220,833	1,089,407	251,365	634,403	37,280	227,286	159,906
(% of Total Units)			(100.0%)	(34.1%)	(61.3%)	(4.6%)	(16.9%)	(83.1%)	(19.2%)	(48.4%)	(2.8%)	(17.4%)	(12.2%)

Model Type Definition: *On-Highway* motorcycles are those certified by the manufacturer as being in compliance with the Federal Motor Vehicle Safety Standards, and designed primarily for use on public roads. Includes scooters. Excludes mopeds and nopeds (limited speed motor-driven cycles under 50cc that are not generally defined by state as mopeds). *Off-Highway* motorcycles are those that are not certified by the manufacturer as being in compliance with the Federal Motor Vehicle Safety Standards. Includes three- and four-wheel all-terrain vehicles (ATVs) and off-highway competition motorcycles. *Dual Purpose* motorcycles are certified by the manufacturer as being in compliance with the Federal Motor Vehicle Safety Standards, and designed with the capacity for use on public roads as well as off-highway recreational use.

Source: Manufacturers Shipment Reporting System, Annual Statistical Report, 1980–1984 Motorcycle Industry Council, Inc., Costa Mesa, California. Includes wholesale shipments to dealers by Harley-Davidson, Honda, Kawasaki, Suzuki, and Yamaha.

EXHIBIT 5	U.S. Motorcycle Imports by Country 1978–1984						
	1978	*1979*	*1980*	*1981*	*1982*	*1983*	*1984*
Japan							
Units	882,038	848,959	1,072,856	1,032,520	897,861	522,573	417,825
$ Value	$741,232,155	$825,909,951	$1,091,699,966	$1,270,949,357	$1,079,362,753	$666,284,854	$482,238,238
European Countries							
Units	50,623[a]	33,824[a]	40,455[a]	21,112[a]	16,100[a]	13,597[a]	17,397[a]
$ Value	$54,297,847	$40,121,247	$44,199,496	$39,213,065	$27,977,592[a]	$29,266,634	$38,296,805
All Others							
Units	2,825[a]	3,969[a]	6,905[a]	2,081[a]	3,242[a]	4,043[a]	6,198[a]
$ Value	$1,737,985	$4,258,537	$6,036,560	$3,624,403	$2,827,574	$1,633,326	$2,851,599
Total							
Units	935,486[a]	886,752[a]	1,120,216[a]	1,056,713[a]	917,203[a]	540,213[a]	441,420[a]
$ Value	$797,267,987	$870,289,735	$1,141,936,022	$1,313,786,825	$1,110,167,919	$697,184,814	$523,386,642

Dollar Value = Dutiable value for 1978–1979 and C.I.F. value for 1980 and subsequent years. All-terrain vehicles not included.

[a] Excludes estimated imports of mopeds (motorized bicycles) as follows:
1978—350,027 units, $90,470,166
1979—129,663 units, $36,775,715
1980—182,037 units, $61,714,528
1981—66,779 units, $23,097,891
1982—18,145 units, $4,384,230
1983—21,645 units, $5,471,009
1984—32,889 units, $8,900,146

Source: U.S. Department of Commerce, Domestic and International Business Administration; *U.S. Motorcycle Imports,* Werner C. Single, Foreign Trade Services, West New York, New Jersey.

over the last five years, will enable it to survive on its own in the face of stiff competition from companies much larger than itself.

(*Note:* See Appendix for the reaction of Mr. Vaughn Beals, Chief Executive Officer of Harley-Davidson Motor Company, to this case study.)

DISCUSSION QUESTIONS

1. Do you consider Harley-Davidson to be the victim of unfair competitive practices or of its own lack of strategic vision?
2. How does the size difference between Harley-Davidson and its Japanese competitors affect Harley-Davidson's ability to compete?
3. What are the basic strategic alternatives for Harley-Davidson? What do you recommend? Why?

APPENDIX[4]

AMF–Harley-Davidson

Contrary to your statement, AMF was most generous in their investment in Harley-Davidson. In the period from

[4] Letter to Warren J. Keegan from Vaughn L. Beals, Jr., Chairman of the Board and Chief Executive Officer, Concerning the Harley-Davidson, Inc., Case Study. Dated December 13, 1985.

1969 to 1975 (prior to my association), they invested very heavily in facility expansion and in new product development. Most, if not all, the new product development effort was wasted.

From the period 1975 to 1981, they also met the vast majority of our capital needs. That is not to say it wasn't a subject of annual debate, but there was only one major capital program that they refused (and in hind-sight that wasn't a bad decision).

The Japanese copying of Harley styling did not commence until after we filed the dumping suit in 1977 and received the decision in 1978. It was in the late 1970s that the Japanese started to copy our styling (Yamaha first), and it took them until early in 1981 for them to copy our V-engine format (again Yamaha). In fact, the time from the ITC decision to copying correlates almost perfectly with the time to modify their products.

Rest assured, we have not given our seal of approval to nasty t-shirts. To the contrary, we undertook a trademark license program three or four years ago. While this was partially motivated by a need to protect our trademarks by vigorously defending them, it also served the key purpose of cleaning up the offensive t-shirts, etc. which were emblazoned with Harley trademarks. We didn't believe then, and we don't believe now, that insulting the rider of a competitive product is a good way to convince him to switch to your product. Unfortunately, there are still a large number

EXHIBIT 6 U.S. Motorcycle Imports by Engine Displacement, 1978–1984

	1978	1979	1980	1981	1982	1983	1984
Under 191cc							
Units	410,260[a]	390,900[a]	418,829[a]	313,944[a]	312,891[a]	175,212[a]	191,856[a]
$ Value	$163,144,748	$173,583,756	$189,667,483	$154,771,771	$152,019,038	$94,634,569	$97,761,171
191–490cc							
Units	203,659	166,768	316,596	249,586	182,948	75,321	67,792
$ Value	$173,111,295	$167,195,874	$307,104,651	$259,816,032	$198,421,920	$82,609,565	$78,049,993
491–790cc							
Units	226,584	224,984	240,604	369,142	298,182	215,975	141,716
$ Value	$301,554,886	$326,914,082	$372,062,671	$639,025,333	$532,150,565	$362,771,480	$256,491,632
Over 790cc							
Units	76,182	93,222	127,518	120,224	119,625	65,093	34,828
$ Value	$153,575,906	$198,020,881	$266,590,704	$258,903,692	$226,188,672	$153,545,173	$88,441,983
Unspecified							
Units	18,801	10,878	16,669	3,817	3,557	8,612	5,228
$ Value	$5,881,152	$4,575,142	$6,510,513	$1,269,997	$1,387,633	$3,624,017	$2,641,863
Total							
Units	935,486[a]	886,752[a]	1,120,216[a]	1,056,713[a]	917,203[a]	540,213[a]	441,420[a]
$ Value	$797,267,987	$870,289,735	$1,141,936,022	$1,313,786,825	$1,110,167,919	$697,184,814	$523,386,642

Dollar Value = Dutiable value for 1978–1979 and C.I.F. value for 1980–1984. All-terrain vehicles not included.

[a] Excludes estimated imports of mopeds (motorized bicycles) as follows:
  1978—350,027 units, $90,470,166
  1979—129,663 units, $36,775,715
  1980—182,037 units, $61,714,528
  1981—66,779 units, $23,097,891
  1982—18,145 units, $4,384,230
  1983—21,645 units, $5,471,009
  1984—32,889 units, $8,900,146

Source: U.S. Department of Commerce, Domestic and International Business Administration; *U.S. Motorcycle Imports,* Werner C. Single, Foreign Trade Services, West New York, New Jersey.

of offensive t-shirts out there, but far less of them are now displayed at our dealers and only rarely do they use our logo and then illegally.

As part of our program to combat this, we have seized merchandise under court order where trademark violations are involved.

Leveraged Buyout (1981)

Your statement, "putting Mr. Beals in charge," etc. is misleading. I was Deputy Group Executive (no. 2 responsible for the Motorcycle Group) from 1975 through 1977. From 1977 to 1981, I was Group Executive with full responsibility for the Motorcycle Group and became CEO in June 1981. Basically, I have directed the organization since November 1977.

The Tariff Ruling (1983)

You referenced "faulty demand assessments" by the Japanese as a cause for price reductions. Unquestionably from time to time they, like Harley, misjudged the market. The facts surrounding our complaint in September, 1982 were

that the Japanese had *increased* production substantially (if I recall correctly, it was like 20 percent) at a time when the world market for motorcycles had been depressed for the better part of two years.

Published Japanese production data only shows the segment from above 250cc. However, because of the dominance of the U.S. in the world market for these larger displacement motorcycles, it isn't a great leap of logic to correlate this with increases in the heavyweight (700cc and up) category.

Harley's Posttariff Performance

Harley returned to profitability in 1983 and has remained so since. The company was profitable in every year from the depression through 1980. In fact, 1979 and 1980 were years of record profit for the Motor Company. While these years were records for Harley, they were not outstandingly high in an absolute sense for a couple of reasons. During the late 1970s we were making extraordinarily heavy investments in new product development which was reducing earnings; secondly, our basic cost structure prevented us from being high earners in competition against the Japanese who were steadily driving their prices down.

In 1981 and 1982, we had record losses, but by downsizing, we were able to return the total corporation to profitability in 1983 and improve that a bit in 1984. Through October 1985, we were a bit ahead of last year.

Our contract business, which is wholly performed at the York plant, has grown significantly since 1982 in both revenue and profit. This has been a vital contributor to the profitability of the company. In the future, the benefits of an extensive cost reduction program plus manufacturing productivity improvements will bring us pretty close to cost parity with the Japanese on our basic motorcycle business. Even despite record losses in 1982, we generated a small positive cash flow as a result of our downsizing of the company and our very tight control of raw material and work-in-process. We have maintained a positive operating cash flow (prior to principal repayment) in 1983, 1984, and 1985.

You indicated in the same paragraph that "Harley sales have actually decreased since the pre-tariff era." In discussing sales it is important to distinguish between retail and wholesale sales. Since retail inventories vary from time to time, the focus should be on *retail* sales. We measure these by daily reports from our dealers whom we audit several times per year. Occasionally, there are discrepancies between our estimated retail sales and reported registrations. In most cases, we believe our data is more reliable than that published by Polk.

In this context, our U.S. retail sales were as follows:

(000) Units

1981	1982	1983	1984
41.0	31.2	26.3	31.5

You commented on the decrease of Harley's market share in the total market. That is correct, but the data is grossly distorted by the tremendous growth of three and four wheeler (balloon tire) off-road bikes plus scooters. We recently extracted this information from registration data with the results shown in Exhibit 7.

Let me reemphasize the data is for the first nine months of each of those years. This study was just completed and that happened to be our frame of interest.

As you can see, there has been a significant drop in the total motorcycle market. In this environment, Harley's share has been increasing significantly. I believe this reflects the greater commitment of Harley riders to the sport, as well as the fact that the destruction of used motorcycle values by Japanese pricing practices in the last three or four years has removed many of them from the market. We expect the demographics (which are very favorable to motorcycling and Harley-Davidson), combined with a firming up of Japanese prices when they liquidate their excess inventories, to reverse this downward trend in two-wheelers. When that happens, I would not expect Harley's market share to hold the current levels. In short, we believe our share improves in a shrinking market and worsens in an expanding market.

International Sales—Global Strategy

I don't believe that Harley is operating with severe technological disadvantages versus our competitors today. This is verified by the fact that we have been first to market with many innovations (belt drive, computer ignition, true anti-dive suspension, vibration isolation, etc.). Except for the last year, we have also been able to dominate dirt track racing. We temporarily lost first position in 1984 and 1985 as a result of a massive investment by Honda (probably 10 times Harley's investment). By the end of the 1985 season, we showed the ability to beat them on many occasions. With some updating to our race engine, we expect to be fully competitive in 1986 or 1987 at the latest.

While the above may represent the claims of a proud CEO, I believe a quick reading of the last couple of years of motorcycle press reviews of our product will provide third-party judgment as to our technical ability.

We clearly are at a cost disadvantage versus our competitors. Our entire manufacturing strategy, and more recently our cost reduction strategy, has been aimed at eliminating this disadvantage. Our objective is to attain cost parity, which we think is achievable.

It is interesting to observe, when you look at market share, that Honda is clearly our only competitor of significance. Now all of Honda's heavyweights are assembled in

EXHIBIT 7	Total Motorcycle[a] Registrations Nine Months Total U.S. (000) Units						
1978	1979	1980	1981	1982	1983	1984	1985
671	722	699	667	536	534	458	366
Harley Volume (000) Units							
44.7	48.0	35.6	37.5	28.6	23.7	25.2	25.6
H-D Market Share (000) Units							
6.7%	6.6%	5.1%	5.6%	5.3%	4.4%	5.5%	7.0%

[a] This includes all displacements, but excludes three and four wheel all-terrain vehicles as well as scooters.

the United States. We believe that Honda's labor rates in their chassis plant are now higher than those in our chassis plant. With the opening of a new motorcycle engine plant in Ohio, we expect to see increasing U.S. content in Honda's heavyweight motorcycles. Thus, relatively soon we will both be using U.S. employees and paying comparable rates to manufacture the bulk of our products. Thus, the game with our critical competitor degenerates to who can manage best. Today, we would acknowledge their lead, but we don't believe it is necessary or appropriate to concede them the race in the long run.

The premise for your third paragraph is that the tariffs have helped Harley in the marketplace. I would strongly argue that. All the tariffs have done is to force the Japanese to finally liquidate their excess inventories in the U.S. They are still way in excess of current needs, despite the fact that they have been substantially discounting the old product. In a recent analysis I conducted, I picked one heavyweight model of each of our four competitors and contrasted the original suggested retail price (in 1981 or 1982) to the current price of the same *new* motorcycle of the same model year. (A quick check will confirm that you can still buy 3- and 4-year-old new motorcycles at Japanese stores.) This showed a range from 48 percent to 52 percent price reduction—in itself, an interesting consistency in pricing practices.

Harley's share increase in its heavyweight market and the entire two-wheel market (as shown above) has been accomplished in an environment of heavy discounting. Our large displacement motorcycles (FX designation), which represent the largest of our three generic product lines and also the most profitable, are priced two to three times above comparable competitive models. Despite this, our unit volume and share from this segment of our business is slowly but steadily increasing. (Effectively, we're selling Mercedes versus Fords.)

Additionally, the Japanese have succeeded in evading virtually all tariff payments. All Honda and Kawasaki heavyweight motorcycles are now *assembled* in the United States; previously Kawasaki was virtually out of U.S. assembly. Nearly all 750cc displacements (half of the heavyweight volume prior to the tariffs) have been downsized to 695 to 699cc to evade the tariff. Thus, as a practical matter, only Suzuki and Yamaha, who do not have U.S. assembly facilities, have been paying tariff and then only on their motorcycles of 1,000cc displacement and above. Since the special tariff provides for a few thousand (7,000 to 8,000, if I recall correctly) of tariff-free imports, my guess is that this has covered the vast majority of imported Yamahas and Suzukis.

A final comment—an International Trade Commission report on the first year after the tariffs reported a 2 percent *reduction* in the average retail price of heavyweight motorcycles despite the 45 percent tariff increase. Realize, when reading that number, that this included the period during which Kawasaki, in particular, and Honda to a lesser extent, were moving assembly on-shore.

That finishes the comments on your specific draft. All in all, I thought it was a very good effort. I hope the above will clarify a few points.

To the above let me add the following—some thoughts I had while reading your case study:

1. ***Lightweights:*** Harley was not asleep at the switch on lightweights. If you go back in time, Harley has been in the scooter business (in the 1960s), mopeds, lightweights, etc. The company bought a 50% interest in Aermacchi, an Italian lightweight motorcycle manufacturer, many years ago and purchased the balance of that interest in the mid- to late 1960s. They made a good motorcycle, but basically could not remain competitive with the Japanese. Market scale was the difference. We had a plant in Italy making 25,000 motorcycles with 500 people as contrasted to a Honda plant making 985,000 motorcycles with 1,400 people.

   Undoubtedly, we were too late in discovering that difference or we would have taken action earlier. However, the capital investment in tooling up for that large Honda scale production plus the investment in developing the distribution system to sell that many products was orders of magnitude beyond the ability of Harley-Davidson as a private company, and I suspect would not have been even possible under AMF ownership. Frankly, I think that's an area where the industrial/banking relationships in Japan make high risk taking possible. A book published a couple of years ago on Honda reported on the tremendous increases in investment and the resultant volume increases during some of those periods. Frankly, I don't believe that is possible in the United States in today's capital markets.

2. ***Product Quality:*** I think it would be helpful to elaborate on Harley's quality/product situation in the early 1970s.

   From 1969 to approximately 1973, the first four years of AMF ownership, the company's unit volume increased by three to four times and revenues quadrupled. At the beginning of that period you had a small manufacturing company in which each functional head was a family member who had run that function for literally decades. Systems were appropriate to a closely held family company that had a fairly stable volume history. Manufacturing was characterized by craftsmen knowing what to do without reference to drawings.

   The tremendous growth imposed upon the company in that state in the early 1970s caused utter chaos. They converted from a craftsman to a production line environment, and the systems utterly failed to keep the company under control. The ultimate result was terrible quality and worse labor relations. The whole thing came unglued in 1974 with a 100-day plus strike. As a result, management was changed and the rebuilding process which is still going on was initiated.

A new group executive was brought in in early 1974. (I'm not sure whether this was before or during the strike.) His first effort was to quickly get manufacturing under control. He then started a major effort in 1975 to expand the Engineering Department staff and facilities and to totally redesign the product line. As a practical matter, the last major piece of that program was completed in June of 1985 when we introduced our last new engine.

When those efforts were well underway in the late 1970s, we then turned our attention to improving quality and then productivity. Briefly then the 1975 to 1980 period could be defined as "getting the product line modernized" and the 1980 to 1985 period getting manufacturing pointed in the right direction.

As I noted above, the catch-up game in product development is behind us. The manufacturing improvements now have their own momentum and require little input from senior management. The current focus in the last year has been on strengthening the dealer network. We are already starting with a network that we believe is the most effective and most profitable (albeit the smallest).

With our catch-up work well along in the engineering and manufacturing area, we deemed it appropriate about a year ago to really kick off a major effort to further strengthen our dealer network. This is aimed at making them better businessmen and improving their ability to close on sales. As a result, we expanded the sales force by about 50% and have started to invest more heavily in their training and later in dealer training.

3. *Contract Business:* There has been a legacy of contract business at the York plant for some years. This represented only 2 to 3 percent of sales in 1982, but now it is between 15 and 17 percent. This provides a source of profit, but more importantly a source of jobs to absorb people freed up by productivity improvements in the motorcycle business. We are aggressively trying to expand that business at York and to develop a similar ability to successfully perform contract business in our Wisconsin operations. It is our expectation that this business will represent a quarter to a third of our business in three or four years, thus, also giving us some degree of internal diversification.

By adopting various Japanese manufacturing methods in our motorcycle business, we are improving our position relative to the Japanese, but we are not there yet. However, when these methods are applied in domestic markets (which all of our contract business represents), they give us an extremely great

competitive advantage which has been directly responsible for our rapid growth in this area.

4. *Parts and Accessories:* The company has had a successful parts and accessories business for many years. In late 1976, we established this as a separate division, ultimately giving it its own president, administrative staff, etc. As a result it grew very rapidly in the late 1970s. Shortly after buying the company, in an effort to reduce our overhead, we consolidated it back into the Marketing organization. As a result of that and having to "cherry pick" some of our best people out of that area, we lost ground. About a year ago, we again spun it off as a separate entity to give it greater senior management focus.

As in most companies, the parts business is extremely profitable. Because of the stability of Harley's designs as opposed to the Japanese and also because of the very large population of older Harleys in the field (most of the Japanese motorcycles don't last beyond three or four years due to high repair costs in the context of a decreasing new price), Harley represents a prime target for aftermarket competitors. A couple of years ago, we introduced a second-tier product line (Eagle Iron) to combat this. These products are sourced in the orient (as are our aftermarket competitors' parts) rather than the United States, as are most of our OEM parts. This new product line is growing rapidly, and we expect it to recapture a significant part of the lost parts business today.

We also have tried to become "the" motorcycle store for rider apparel, helmets, etc. as a way of developing floor traffic. Large numbers of our dealers have set up apparel boutiques which are achieving this purpose as well as generating considerable profitability for the individual dealerships.

5. *Recreational versus Transportation Vehicles:* In viewing Harley-Davidson's position in the motorcycle industry, it is important to distinguish between a motorcycle as a recreational vehicle and a transportation device. In the U.S., motorcycles are toys. While they are occasionally used for transportation, it is rare indeed to find someone whose sole means of transport is a motorcycle.

By contrast, in many less developed countries, a motorcycle is the first step above a bicycle. Classically, motorcycle sales drop as the economy strengthens and people move into small automobiles. Only after they satisfy their need for four-wheel transportation do they then come back to motorcycles as toys.

As you know, Harley's displacement range until last June started from 1,000cc and up; today, we start at 883cc and go up. In the 1960s and 1970s, we offered a wide variety of smaller displacement motorcycles from 50cc to 350cc. As noted above, we could not remain cost competitive in that area. Frankly, we never expect to be able to reenter that market.

We do believe, however, that we can go down in displacement range successfully to about 500cc. Our Nova project was conceived to produce a V-4 that would be competitive with 750cc (the bottom half of the heavyweight market which is defined as 700cc plus) and a two-cylinder version would give us a 400 or 500cc motorcycle. Fortunately, the volumes in these larger displacement ranges (500cc and above) are such that we do not feel we will be at a great disadvantage with the Japanese. Their giant production numbers all relate to their small displacement vehicles sold in developing countries. Otherwise, our manufacturing scale is about the same.

Benetton Group SpA: Raising Consciousness and Controversy with Global Advertising

Benetton Group SpA, the Italy-based global clothing retailer, seems to have fallen on hard times. Until recently, financial results were excellent: Worldwide sales of Benetton's brightly colored knitware and contemporary clothing doubled between 1988 and 1993 to 2.75 trillion lire ($1.63 billion). In 1993 alone, sales were up about 10 percent, and net income increased by 13 percent. The strong showing in 1993 was due in part to the devaluation of the Italian lire, which enabled Benetton to cut prices for its clothing around the world.

By contrast, 1994 results were discouraging. Sales were flat at $1.69 billion, operating profits fell 5 percent, to $245 million, and margins narrowed to 13.9 percent down from 14.7 percent during the three-year period 1991–1993. The sales slump was surprising in view of the fact that Benetton had opened stores in China, Eastern Europe, and India, and extended the brand into new categories such as footwear and cosmetics. Some industry observers believed that Benetton's wounds were self-inflicted. According to this view, 1994's results represented the backlash from Benetton's highly controversial global advertising campaigns, now several years old, keyed to the theme "The United Colors of Benetton."

SOURCES: John Rossant, "The Faded Colors of Benetton," *Business Week,* 10 April 1995, p. 87, 90; Peter Gumbel, "Benetton Is Stung by Blacklash over Ad," *The Wall Street Journal,* 4 March 1994, p. A8; Gary Levin, "Benetton Ad Lays Bare the Bloody Toll of War," *Advertising Age,* 21 February 1994; Judith Graham, "Benetton 'Colors' the Race Issue," *Advertising Age,* 11 September 1989: 3; Kim Foltz, "Campaign on Harmony Backfires for Benetton," *The New York Times,* 20 November 1989, p. 32; Dennis Rodkin, "How Colorful Can Ads Get?" *Mother Jones* (January 1990): 52; Stuart Elliott, "Benetton Stirs More Controversy," *The New York Times,* 23 July 1991, p. 19; Gary Levin, "Benetton Brouhaha," *Advertising Age,* 17 February 1992, p. 62; Teri Agins, "Shrinkage of Stores and Customers in U.S., Causes Italy's Benetton to Alter Its Tactics," *The Wall Street Journal,* 24 June 1992, pp. B1, B10.

EXHIBIT 1   United Colors of Benetton

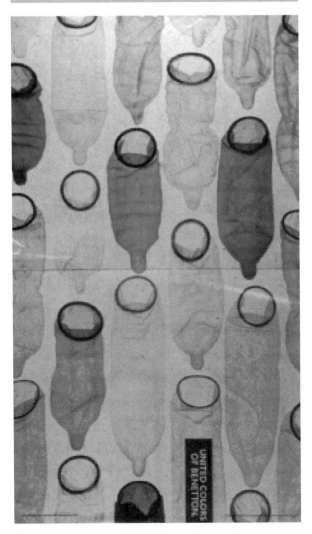

Concept: O. Toscani, Spring 1991. Photo: Theresa Frare. Reprinted by permission.

EXHIBIT 2   United Colors of Benetton

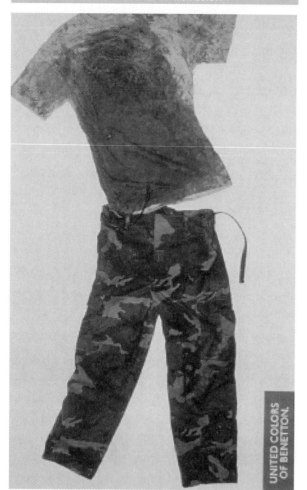

Spring 1994. Photo: O. Toscani. Reprinted by permission.

Various executions of the ads, in magazines and on posters and billboards, featured provocative, even shocking photos designed to focus public attention on social and political issues such as the environment, terrorism, racial issues, and sexually transmitted diseases. The creative concept of the ads reflected the views of Oliviero Toscani, creative director and chief photographer for Benetton. "I have found out that advertising is the richest and most powerful medium existing today. Therefore, I feel responsible to do more than say, 'Our sweater is pretty,' " he told *The New York Times.* Noted Vittorio Rava, worldwide advertising manager, "We believe our advertising needs to shock, otherwise people will not remember it."

One of the first ads to stir controversy depicted a white hand and a black hand joined by handcuffs; another showed an angelic white child embracing a black child whose hair was unmistakably styled to resemble the horns of a devil.

An ad with a picture of a black woman nursing a white baby appeared in 77 countries; while not used in the United States and the United Kingdom, the ad won awards in France and Italy. In the fall of 1991, several U.S. magazine publishers refused to carry some of the ads; one depicted a nun kissing a priest. A picture of a newborn baby covered with bloody placenta was also rejected. According to Benetton's Ravo, "We didn't envision a political idea when we started this 'Colors' strategy five years ago, but now, with racist problems becoming more important in every country it has become political on its own."

With its next series of ads, Benetton began using images associated with sexuality. As Peter Fressola, director of communications, explained the message strategy, "We're saying there are two important issues to be addressed, and they are overpopulation and sexually transmitted diseases such as AIDS. I think it is time to take the gloves off and put on the rubbers and address these issues." In an interview with *Advertising Age,* Mr. Toscani explained, "Everybody uses emotion to sell a product. We want to show, in this case, human realities that we are aware of." The ads broke new ground for the images they presented: A man dying of AIDS surrounded by his family; a montage of multicolored condoms; a group of people with the initials "HIV" stamped on their arms; test tubes filled with blood labeled with the names of world leaders.

In France, the HIV ad caused a great deal of controversy. One man who was dying of AIDS ran an ad with a picture of his own face above a tagline that read "during the agony, the sales continue." In the United States, where the number of Benetton stores had been slowly dwindling, the ads were poorly received by many customers and Benetton retailers. The manager of a Benetton store in Biloxi, Mississippi, received telephone calls from people who said they refused to shop at stores selling products from a "sick" company. In Florida, one franchisee closed a dozen Benetton locations, noting, "It is not our function as retailers to raise the consciousness of people. I've had long, hard fights with Italy over the advertising." In an effort to help mollify its American licensees, Benetton began providing them with local ads featuring clothing instead of social issues. At the national level, however, Benetton continued the controversial ads. When asked about the possible negative impact of customer boycotts, Luciano Benetton, president of the company's U.S. division, said, "It's silly to change direction because someone in the market thinks it's not right. We are sincere, and we are consistent in pursuing it this way."

In the spring of 1994, it appeared that Benetton had finally gone too far. A new $15 million ad campaign that ran in 25 countries featured a picture of the bloody uniform of a Croatian soldier who had died in the Bosnian civil war. While Benetton executives had come to expect criticism, they were unprepared for the latest reaction. The company was accused of exploiting the war for the sake of profit. In France, many of the offending posters were pulled down or covered with grafitti reading "Boycott

Benetton" and "This is blood for money." The French minister for humanitarian affairs even made a public announcement discouraging people from buying Benetton sweaters; he called for his fellow citizens to "pull [the sweaters] off people who are going to wear them." In some parts of Germany and Switzerland, the company's products were banned. Some media reports in Europe questioned the authenticity of the uniform, alleging it did not belong to the fallen soldier named in the ad. The Vatican newspaper charged Benetton with "advertising terrorism."

Mr. Benetton acknowledged that "this is not what a corporate communications campaign should do. It should create interest." Still, he vowed the company would continue "to search for new facts and new emotions" to include in its ads. Indeed, when the Sarajevo daily newspaper *Oslo bodhenie* ("Liberation") requested posters of the ad to put up around the city, Benetton supplied 10,000 copies.

In France, however, a court ordered the company to pay $32,000 to French HIV victims; a German court banned several of the most controversial ads.

DISCUSSION QUESTIONS

1. What is your personal reaction to the controversial Benetton ads?
2. Do you believe Benetton is "sincere" in its campaign, or is the company just exploiting human misery?
3. There is a saying in the marketing world that "there is no such thing as bad publicity." Does that apply in the Benetton case?
4. From a marketing (as opposed to personal) point of view, advise Benetton on its campaign. Should the company continue, expand, change, or terminate the campaign?

CHAPTER

17

Leading, Organizing, and Monitoring the Global Marketing Effort

It seems incredible, and yet it has happened a hundred times, that troops have been divided and separated merely through a mysterious feeling of conventional manner, without any clear perception of the reason.

—CARL VON CLAUSEWITZ, 1780–1831
Vom Kriege (1832–1837) Book III,
Chapter XI, "Assembly of Forces in Space"

Leadership in this new landscape is not about controlling decision making. We don't have time anymore to control decision making. It's about creating the right environment. It's about enablement, empowerment. It is about setting guidelines and boundaries and parameters and setting the people free.

CARLETON "CARLY" S. FIORINA
Commencement Address, Massachusetts
Institute of Technology, June 2, 2000

CONTENTS

This chapter focuses on the integration of each element of the marketing mix into a total plan that addresses expected opportunities and threats in the global marketing environment. Bill Gates of Microsoft, Rupert Murdoch of the News Corporation, Jack Welch of General Electric (GE), Richard Branson of Virgin, Percy Barnavik of ABB, and Hank Greenburgh of AIG are just a few of the global leaders who by their example and the success of their organizations illustrate the critical role of leadership in a global firm. Leaders must be capable of articulating a coherent global vision and strategy that integrates local responsiveness, global efficiency, and leverage. The challenge is to direct the efforts and creativity of everyone in the company toward a global effort that best utilizes organizational resources to exploit global opportunities.

◆ LEADERSHIP

Global marketing demands exceptional leadership. As we have said throughout this book, the hallmark of a global company is the capacity to formulate and implement global strategies that leverage worldwide learning, respond fully to local needs and wants, and draw on all of the talent and energy of every member of the organization. This is a heroic task requiring global vision and a sensitivity to local needs. Members of each operating unit must address their immediate responsibilities and at the same time cooperate with functional, product, and country experts in different locations.

As Carly Fiorina put it so eloquently in her MIT commencement address:

> Leadership is not about hierarchy or title or status: it is about having influence and mastering change. Leadership is not about bragging rights or battles or even the accumulation of wealth; it's about connecting and engaging at multiple levels. It's about challenging minds and capturing hearts. Leadership in this new era is about empowering others to decide for themselves. Leadership is about empowering others to reach their full potential. Leaders can no longer view strategy and execution as abstract concepts, but must realize that both elements are ultimately about people.[1]

TEAMS

The practice of using self-directed work teams to respond to competitive challenges is becoming more widespread. Reports vary as to how widely teams are being used today. One study found that 47 percent of *Fortune* 1000 companies used teams with at least some of their employees. With the increased usage of e-mail, team members can even be located on different continents.

Jon Katzenbach and Douglas Smith believe "teams will become the primary unit of performance in high-performance organizations."[2] The implementation of self-directed work teams is another example of the need for organizational innovation to maintain competitiveness. They represent another corporate response to the need to flatten the organization, to reduce costs and overheads, and to be more responsive.

Companies are looking to reduce bureaucracy and hierarchy to improve responsiveness and to reduce costs. As Tom Peters put it, "You can't survive, let alone thrive, in a time-competitive world with a six- to eight-layer organization structure. The time-obsessed organization is flat—no barriers among functions, no borders with the outside."[3]

Philip J. Quigley, president and chief executive officer (CEO) of Pacific Bell, sees two kinds of organizations: the large, powerful, yet cumbersome organization that is like an elephant; and the agile, quick, but weaker, small organization that is like a rabbit. Neither, however, is completely suited to compete in today's competitive global marketplace. Quigley's answer is a new form of organization, the rabbiphant, which combines the strength and agility of the two present types of organizations.[4]

---

[1] Carleton "Carly" S. Fiorina, Commencement Address, Massachusetts Institute of Technology, Cambridge, MA, June 2, 2000.

[2] Jon R. Katzenbach and Douglas K. Smith, "The Discipline of Teams," *Harvard Business Review* (March–April 1993): 119.

[3] Tom Peters, "Time Obsessed Competition," *Management Review* (September 1990): 18.

[4] Philip J. Quigley, "The Coming of the Rabbiphant: Toward Decentralized Corporations," *Vital Speeches,* 15 June 1990, p. 535.

MIND-SET

A major role of top management is to instill important values necessary for success in a global marketplace throughout their organization. One critical value vital to an effective global organization is to have the proper mind-set for both the leadership and the organization. Gupta and Govindarajan suggest that the following be reviewed:[5]

Composition of the board of directors—mix of nationalities, international experience, language skills.

Choice of locations for board meetings.

Background of the chief executive, executive committee, and business unit managers in terms of international experience and language skills.

Distribution of time spent by the chief executive in various regions.

Choice of locations for business unit headquarters.

Proportion of middle and senior managers who are members of cross-border teams.

Executive career ladders that reward international experience.

Performance measurement and incentive system that motivate senior managers to optimize not only local but also global performance.

◆ ORGANIZATION

The goal in organizing for global marketing is to find a structure that enables the company to respond to relevant market environment differences while ensuring the diffusion of corporate knowledge and experience from national markets throughout the entire corporate system. The pull between the value of centralized knowledge and coordination and the need for individualized response to the local situation creates a constant tension in the global marketing organization. A key issue in global organization is how to achieve balance between autonomy and integration. Subsidiaries need autonomy in order to adapt to their local environment. However, the business as a whole needs integration to implement global strategy.[6]

When management at a domestic company decides to pursue international expansion, the issue of how to organize arises immediately. Who should be responsible for this expansion? Should product divisions operate directly or should an international division be established? Should individual country subsidiaries report directly to the company president or should a special corporate officer be appointed to take full-time responsibility for international activities? Once the first decision of how to organize initial international operations has been reached, a growing company is faced with a number of reappraisal points during the development of its international business activities. Should a company abandon its international division and, if so, what alternative structure should be adopted? Should an area or regional headquarters be formed? What should be the relationship of staff executives at corporate, regional, and subsidiary offices? Specifically, how should the marketing function be organized? To what extent should regional and corporate marketing executives become involved in subsidiary marketing management?

It is important to recognize that there is no single correct organizational structure for global marketing. Even within an industry, worldwide companies have developed very different strategic and organizational responses to changes in their environments.

---

[5] Anil K. Gupta and Vijay Govindarajan, "Success Is All in the Mindset," Controlling the Global Organisation (Part Five of Ten) *Financial Times Mastering Global Business*, p. 2.

[6] George S. Yip, *Total Global Strategy* (Upper Saddle River, NJ: Prentice Hall, 1992), p. 179.

Still, it is possible to make some generalizations. Leading-edge global competitors share one key organizational design characteristic: Their corporate structure is simple and flat, rather than tall and complex. The message is clear: The world is complicated enough; there is no need to add to the confusion with a complex internal structuring. Simple structures increase the speed and clarity of communication and allow the concentration of organizational energy and valuable resources on learning, rather than on controlling, monitoring, and reporting.[7] According to David Whitwam, CEO of Whirlpool, "You must create an organization whose people are adept at exchanging ideas, processes, and systems across borders, people who are absolutely free of the 'not-invented-here' syndrome, people who are constantly working together to identify the best global opportunities and the biggest global problems facing the organization."[8]

A geographically dispersed company cannot limit its knowledge to product, function, and the home territory. Company personnel must acquire knowledge of the complex set of social, political, economic, and institutional arrangements that exist within each international market. Most companies, after initial ad hoc arrangements—for example, all foreign subsidiaries reporting to a designated vice president or to the president—establish an international division to manage their geographically dispersed new business. It is clear, however, that the international division in the multiproduct company is an unstable organizational arrangement. As a company grows, this initial organizational structure frequently gives way to various alternative structures.[9]

In today's fast-changing, competitive global environment, corporations are having to find new and more creative ways to organize. New forms of flexibility, efficiency, and responsiveness are required to meet the market demands. The need to be cost-effective, to be customer driven, to deliver the best quality, and to deliver that quality quickly are some of today's market realities.

Several authors have described new organizational designs that represent responses to the competitive environment of the 21st century. These designs acknowledge the need to find more responsive and flexible structures, to flatten the organization, and to employ teams. There is also the recognition of the need to develop networks, to develop stronger relationships among participants, and to exploit technology. They also reflect an evolution in approaches to organizational effectiveness. At the beginning of the twentieth century, Fredrick Taylor claimed that all managers had to see the world the same way. Then came the contingency theorists who said that effective organizations design themselves to match their conditions. These two basic theories are reflected in today's popular management writings. As Henry Mintzberg has observed, "To Michael Porter, effectiveness resides in strategy, while to Tom Peters it is the operations that count—executing any strategy with excellence."[10] Successful companies, the real global winners, must have both: good strategies and good execution.

PATTERNS OF INTERNATIONAL ORGANIZATIONAL DEVELOPMENT

Organizations vary in terms of the size and potential of targeted global markets and local management competence in different country markets. Conflicting pressures may arise from the need for product and technical knowledge, functional expertise in marketing, finance, and operations, and area and country knowledge. Because the con-

---

[7] Vladimir Pucik, "Globalization and Human Resource Management." In V. Pucik, N. Tichy, and C. Barnett, Eds. *Globalizing Management: Creating and Leading the Competitive Organization* (New York: Wiley, 1992), p. 70.

[8] Regina Fazio Maruca, "The Right Way to Go Global: An Interview with Whirlpool CEO David Whitwam," *Harvard Business Review* (March–April 1994): 136–137.

[9] John M. Stopford and Louis T. Wells, *Managing the Multinational Enterprise* (New York: Basic Books, 1972).

[10] Henry Mintzberg, "The Effective Organization: Forces and Forms," *Sloan Management Review* (Winter 1991): 54–55.

stellation of pressures that shape organizations is never exactly the same, no two organizations pass through organizational stages in exactly the same way, nor do they arrive at precisely the same organizational pattern. Nevertheless, some general patterns have developed.

Most companies undertake initial foreign expansion with an organization similar to that in Figures 17-1 and 17-2. When a company is organized on this basis, foreign subsidiaries report directly to the company president or other designated company officer, who carries out his or her responsibilities without assistance from a headquarters staff group. This is a typical initial arrangement for companies getting started in international marketing operations.

INTERNATIONAL DIVISION STRUCTURE

As a company's international business grows, the complexity of coordinating and directing this activity extends beyond the scope of a single person. Pressure is created to assemble a staff group that will take responsibility for coordination and direction of the growing international activities of the organization. Eventually, this pressure leads to the creation of the international division, as illustrated in Figures 17-3 and 17-4.

Four factors contribute to the establishment of an international division. First, top management's commitment to global operations has increased enough to justify an organizational unit headed by a senior manager. Second, the complexity of international operations requires a single organization unit whose management has sufficient authority to make its own determination on important issues such as which market entry strategy to employ. Third, an international division is frequently formed when the firm has recognized the need for internal specialists to deal with the special demands of global operations. A fourth contributing factor arises when management exhibits the desire to develop the ability to scan the global horizon for opportunities and competitive threats rather than simply respond to situations that are presented to the company.

FIGURE 17-1 Functional Corporate Structure, Domestic Corporate Staff Orientation, Preinternational Division

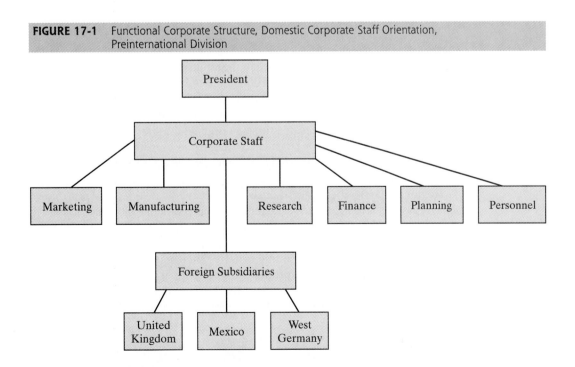

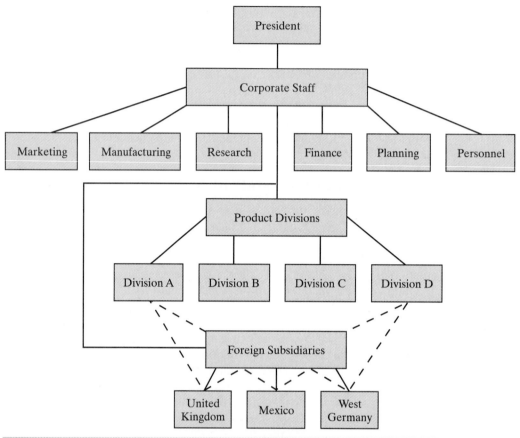

FIGURE 17-2 Divisional Corporate Structure, Domestically Oriented Product Division Staff, Preinternational Division

REGIONAL MANAGEMENT CENTERS

Another stage of organizational evolution is the emergence of an area or regional head-quarters as a management layer between the country organization and the international division headquarters. This division is illustrated in Figures 17-5 and 17-6. When business is conducted in a single region that is characterized by similarities in economic, social, geographic, and political conditions, there is both justification and need for a management center. The center coordinates decisions on pricing, sourcing, and other matters. Executives at the regional center also participate in the planning and control of each country's operations with an eye toward applying company knowledge and optimal utilization of corporate resources on a regional basis.

Regional management can offer a company several advantages. First, many regional managers agree that an on-the-scene regional management unit makes sense when there is a real need for coordinated, pan-regional decision making. Coordinated regional planning and control is becoming necessary as the national subsidiary continues to lose its relevance as an independent operating unit. Regional management can probably achieve the best balance of geographic, product, and functional considerations required to implement corporate objectives effectively. By shifting operations and decision making to the region, the company is better able to maintain an insider advantage.[11]

---

[11] See Allen J. Morrison, David A. Ricks, and Kendall Roth, "Globalization versus Regionalization: Which Way for the Multinational?" *Organizational Dynamics* (Winter 1991): 25.

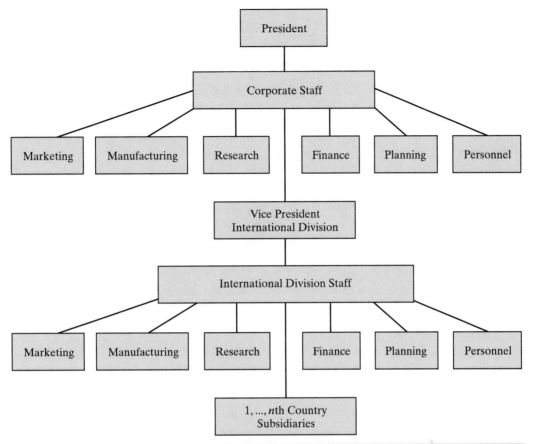

FIGURE 17-3 Functional Corporate Structure, Domestic Corporate Staff Orientation, International Division

A major disadvantage of a regional center is its cost. Even a two-person office could cost in excess of $600,000 per year. The scale of regional management must be in line with scale of operations in a region. A regional headquarters is premature whenever the size of the operations it manages is inadequate to cover the costs of the additional layer of management. Thus, the basic issue with regard to the regional headquarters is, "Does it contribute enough to organizational effectiveness to justify its cost and the complexity of another layer of management?"

GEOGRAPHIC STRUCTURE

The geographic structure involves the assignment of operational responsibility for geographic areas of the world to line managers. The corporate headquarters retains responsibility for worldwide planning and control, and each area of the world—including the "home" or base market—is organizationally equal. For the company with French origins, France is simply another geographic market under this organizational arrangement. The most common appearance of this structure is in companies with closely related product lines that are sold in similar end-use markets around the world. For example, the major international oil companies utilize the geographic structure, which is illustrated in Figure 17-7.

GLOBAL PRODUCT DIVISION STRUCTURE

When an organization assigns worldwide product responsibility to its product divisions, the product divisions must decide whether to rely on an international division, thereby

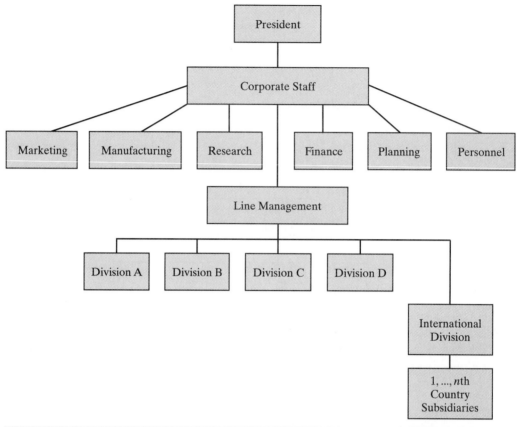

FIGURE 17-4 Divisional Corporate Structure, Domestically Oriented Corporate Staff, Domestically Oriented Product Divisions, International Division

dividing their world into domestic and foreign, or to rely on an area structure with each region of the world organizationally treated on an equal basis. In most cases in which a divisional company shifts from a corporate international division to worldwide product divisions, there are two stages in the internationalization of the product divisions. The first stage occurs when international responsibility is shifted from a corporate international division to the product division international departments. The second occurs when the product divisions themselves shift international responsibility from international departments within the divisions to the total divisional organization. In effect, this shift is the utilization of a geographic structure within each product division. The worldwide product division with an international department is illustrated in Figure 17-8. The product structure works best when a company's product line is widely diversified, when products go into a variety of end-use markets, and when a relatively high-technological capability is required.

THE MATRIX STRUCTURE

The most sophisticated organizational arrangement brings to bear four basic competencies on a worldwide basis. These competencies are as follows:

1. *Geographic knowledge.* An understanding of the basic economic, social, cultural, political, and governmental market and competitive dimensions of a country is

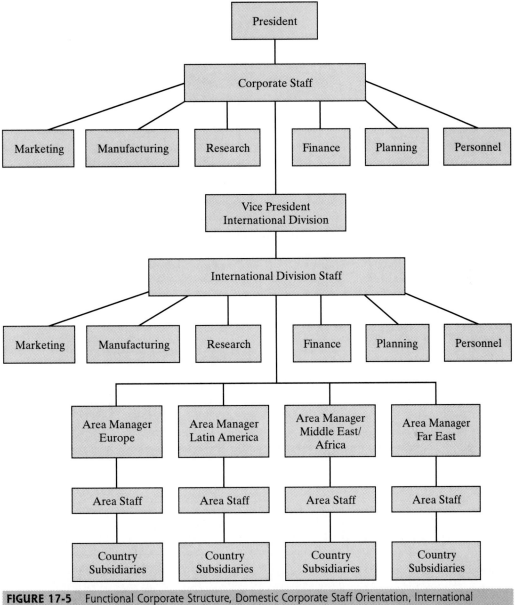

FIGURE 17-5   Functional Corporate Structure, Domestic Corporate Staff Orientation, International Division, Area Divisions

essential. The country subsidiary is the major structural device employed today to enable the corporation to acquire geographic knowledge.

2. *Product knowledge and know-how.* Product managers with a worldwide responsibility can achieve this level of competence on a global basis. Another way of achieving global product competence is simply to duplicate product management organizations in domestic and international divisions, achieving high competence in both organizational units.

3. *Functional competence in such fields as finance, production, and especially marketing.* Corporate functional staff with worldwide responsibility contributes to the development of functional competence on a global basis. In a handful of companies,

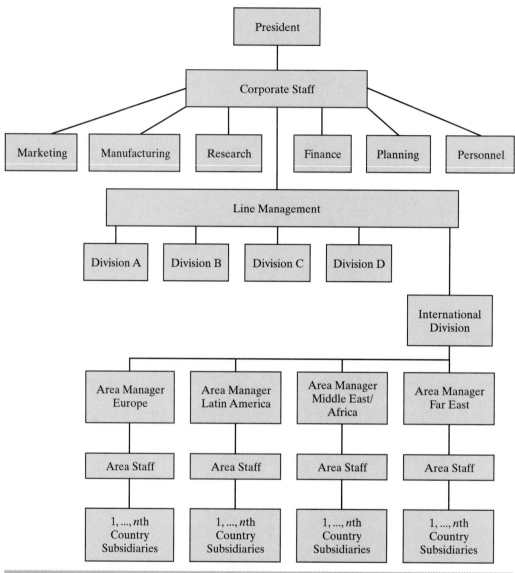

FIGURE 17-6 Divisional Corporate Structure, Domestically Oriented Corporate Staff, International Division, Area Subdivisions

the appointment of country subsidiary functional managers is reviewed by the corporate functional manager who is responsible for the development of his or her functional activity in the organization on a global basis.

What has emerged in a growing number of companies is a dotted-line relationship among corporate, regional, and country staff. The dotted-line relationship ranges from nothing more than advice offered by corporate or regional staff to regional country staff to a much "heavier" line relationship in which staff activities of a lower organizational level are directed and approved by higher-level staff. The relationship of staff organizations can become a source of tension and conflict in an organization if top management does not create a climate that encourages organizational integration. Headquarters staff wants to extend its control or influence over the activities of lower-level staff.

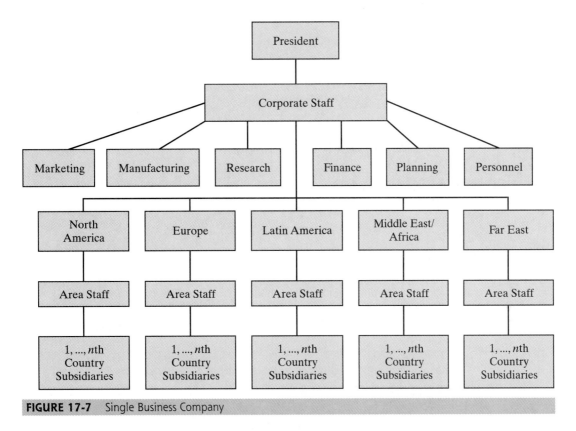

FIGURE 17-7 Single Business Company

For example, in marketing research, unless there is coordination of research design and activity, the international headquarters is unable to compare one market with another. If line management, instead of recognizing the potential contribution of an integrated worldwide staff, wishes to operate as autonomously as possible, the influence of corporate staff is perceived as undesirable. In such a situation, the stronger party wins. This can be avoided if the level of management to which both line and staff report creates a climate and structure that expect and require the cooperation of line and staff and that recognize that each has responsibility for important aspects of the management of international markets.

4. *A knowledge of the customer or industry and its needs.* In certain large and very sophisticated international companies, staff with a responsibility for serving industries on a global basis exists to assist the line managers in the country organizations in their efforts to penetrate specific customer markets.

In the fully developed, large-scale international company, product, function, area, and customer know-how are simultaneously focused on the organization's worldwide marketing objectives. This type of total competence is a matrix organization. In the matrix organization, the task of management is to achieve an organizational balance that brings together different perspectives and skills to accomplish the organization's objectives. Under this arrangement, instead of designating national organizations or product divisions as profit centers, both are responsible for profitability: the national organization for country profits and the product divisions for national and worldwide product profitability. Figure 17-9 illustrates the matrix organization.

This organization chart starts with a bottom section that represents a single-country responsibility level, moves to representing the area or international level, and finally

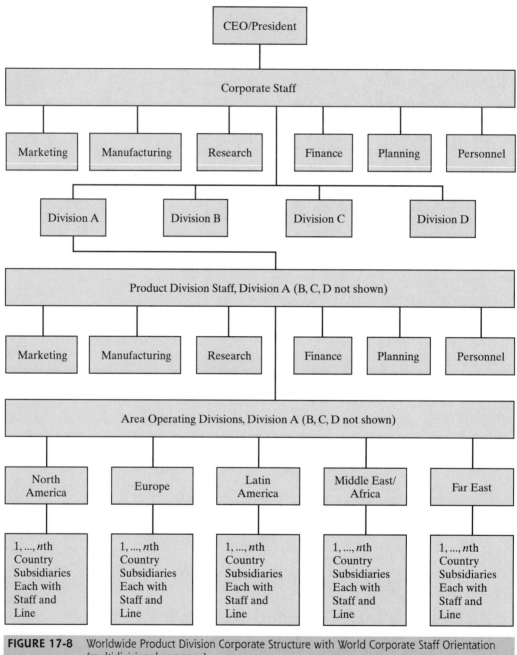

FIGURE 17-8 Worldwide Product Division Corporate Structure with World Corporate Staff Orientation (multidivisional company)

moves to representing global responsibility from the product divisions to the corporate staff, to the chief executive at the top of the structure.

The key to successful matrix management is the extent to which managers in the organization are able to resolve conflicts and achieve integration of organization programs and plans. Thus, the mere adoption of a matrix design or structure does not create a matrix organization. The matrix organization requires a fundamental change in management behavior, organizational culture, and technical systems. In a matrix, influence is based on technical competence and interpersonal sensitivity, not on formal authority.

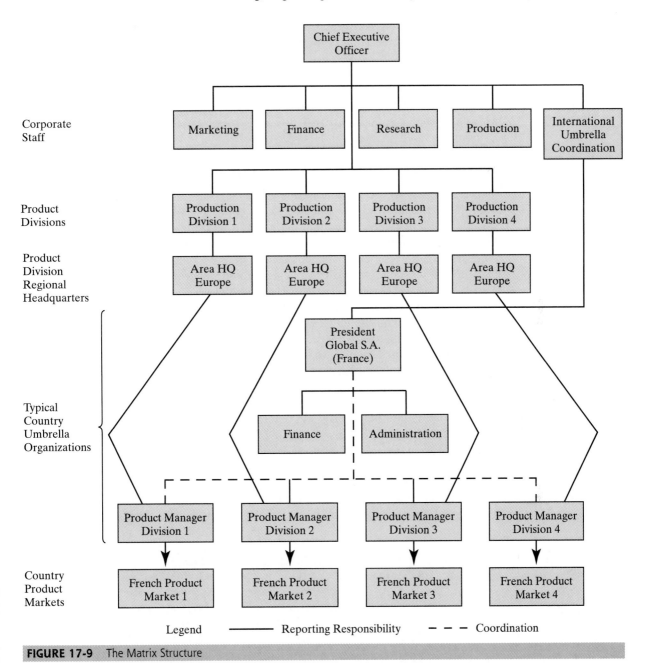

FIGURE 17-9   The Matrix Structure

In a matrix culture, managers recognize the absolute need to resolve issues and choices at the lowest possible level and do not rely on higher authority.

RELATIONSHIP AMONG STRUCTURE, FOREIGN PRODUCT DIVERSIFICATION, AND SIZE

John Stopford and Louis T. Wells, Jr., have hypothesized the relationship among structure, foreign product diversification (defined as sales of a firm outside its major product line expressed as a percentage of the total sales), and size. This formulation posits that when size abroad grows, the emergence of an area division develops so that whenever size abroad is 50 percent of total size or more, several area divisions will probably be adopted. On the other hand, as foreign product diversification increases, the likelihood that product divisions will operate on a worldwide basis increases. In a company in which there is both worldwide product diversity and large-scale business abroad as a percentage of total business, foreign operation will tend to move toward the matrix structure. Companies with limited foreign product diversification (under 10 percent) and limited size as a percentage of total size will utilize the international structure. This formulation is summarized schematically in Figure 17-10.

ORGANIZATIONAL STRUCTURE AND NATIONAL ORIGIN

Before 1960, the American multidivisional structure was rarely found outside the United States. This structure was introduced in the United States as early as 1921 by Alfred P. Sloan at General Motors. The multidivisional structure in the United States had three distinctive characteristics. First, profit responsibility for operating decisions was assigned to general managers of self-contained business units. Second, there was a corporate headquarters that was concerned with strategic planning, appraisal, and the allocation of resources among the business divisions. Third, executives at the corporate headquarters were separated from operations and were psychologically committed to the whole organization rather than the individual businesses.[12] During the 1960s, European enterprises underwent a period of unprecedented reorganization. Essentially, they adopted the American divisional structure. Today, at the overall level, there is little difference between European and American organizations.

The organizational structure of Japanese and other Asian companies is quite different from the U.S. model. Japanese organizations, for example, rely on generalists as opposed to functional specialists and make greater use of project teams to design and manufacture products. They also form much closer relationships with suppliers than do American companies, are in a different relationship to sources of capital, and have a fundamentally different governance structure than U.S. companies. The success of Japanese companies has recommended their organizational structure and design for careful evaluation, and many non-Japanese companies have successfully adopted Japanese organizational design features.

FIGURE 17-10 The Relationship Among Structure, Foreign Product Diversification, and Size Abroad (as a % of total size)

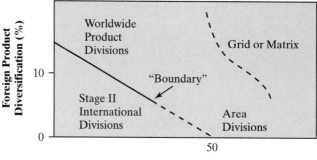

Source: Adapted from John M. Stopford and Louis T. Wells, Jr., *Managing the Multinational Enterprise* (New York: Basic Books, 1972).

---

[12] Lawrence G. Franko, "The Move Toward a Multidivisional Structure in European Organizations," *Administrative Science Quarterly,* vol. 19, no. 4 (December 1974): 493–506.

STRUCTURING FOR GLOBAL BRANDS

P. Hankinson and G. Hankinson conclude that the organizational structure necessary for global brands requires a much greater emphasis on integrating and/or "globalizing" the marketing process at a worldwide level[13] as well as promoting and embedding within the corporate culture inter- and intra- organizational cooperation. They identified eight new organizational arrangements to support global brand management:

> *Global Co-ordinations Groups:* Similar to discussion groups but with the focus on implementation. They are task oriented and instrumental in the establishment of a corporate culture.
>
> *Strategic Planning Groups:* These involve multidisciplinary or cross-functional brand management teams whose purpose is to implement centrally developed policies and strategies with a local focus.
>
> *Lead Country Concept:* Different countries take leadership responsibility for a particular brand or aspect of marketing policy. In the case of Mars Candy, Snickers is led from Germany, M&Ms from Holland, Twix from France, and Galaxy and Bounty from the United Kingdom.
>
> *Global Brand Managers:* This position is at a high level of seniority and functions in the role of brand champion.
>
> *Starbursts:* As new products and services are developed, the entrepreneurial enterprise is spun off from the parent company and is encouraged to grow into a separate subsidiary. An example is Thermo Electron.
>
> *Cluster Organizations:* Individual members may work on different enterprises within the company as and when their particular skills are required. General Electric and Volvo are examples.
>
> *Strategic Alliances, Joint Ventures, Mergers and Acquisitions:* These structures form a continuum and collectively are termed *hybrid, interorganizational relationships.* Examples are Hewlett-Packard and Matsushita.
>
> *Network Structures:* Although known in various forms, at the heart of each structure is the fundamental principle that a number of different organizations, companies, and individuals work together on a common business project.

Implications for Changing Organizational Structure

Based on their research, Hankinson and Hankinson identified the following eight implications for management in global companies.

1. Declining profitability and shareholder value are greater motivators of change than increasing economic turbulence.
2. A charismatic or transformation style of leadership is helpful.
3. Those who implement change need a firm grasp on *all* aspects of the business.
4. A correct balance between long-term strategic objectives and short-term attention to shareholder value.
5. "Loose-tight" balance. (The balance of power shifts back and forth from the headquarters to the regional offices.)
6. Employees need to learn to behave differently and a learning culture helps to achieve this.

---

[13] Philippa Hankinson, and Graham Hankinson, "The Role of Organizational Structure in Successful Global Brand Management: A Case Study of the Pierre Smirnoff Company," *The Journal of Brand Management,* 6, no. 1 (1998): 29–43.

7. Knowing when the strategic imperative is strong enough to require changes to the organizational structure.
8. A loose organizational structure requires a common understanding of the measures of success.

GETTING OFF THE REORGANIZATION MERRY-GO-ROUND

Bartlett studied 10 U.S.-based multinational corporations (MNCs) that, according to the theory outlined earlier, should have moved from the international division to the worldwide product division, area, or matrix structure but did not.[14] He found that these successful companies avoided the myth of the ideal organizational structure and instead concentrated on building and maintaining a complex decision-making, resource-transfer, and information-sharing process. For example, Corning Glass Works' TV tube marketing strategy required local decision making for service and delivery and global decision making for pricing.

The successful companies, Bartlett found, developed in three stages. The first was to recognize the diversity of the world. In other words, the companies made the transition from ethnocentric and polycentric orientations to a geocentric orientation. The second stage involved building channels of communication between managers in various parts of the organization. An example of a communications channel-building move might be a world meeting of executives at a conference center where, for the first time, executives in the companies' businesses from all over the world get a chance to meet each other and to learn about the business strategies of their counterparts in other countries and businesses.

In the third stage, the company develops norms and values within the organization to support shared decisions and corporate (as opposed to country or product) perspectives. The highest value is placed on corporate goals and cooperative effort as opposed to parochial interests and adversarial relationships. Many Japanese companies fit this description perfectly, which is why they have been so successful.

The important task of top management is to eliminate a one-dimensional approach to decisions and encourage the development of multiple management perspectives and an organization that will sense and respond to a complex and fast-changing world. By thinking in terms of changing behavior rather than changing structural design, companies can free themselves from the static nature and limitations of the structural diagram and instead can focus on achieving the best possible results with available resources.

◆ GLOBAL MARKETING MANAGEMENT AUDIT

Global marketing presents formidable problems to managers responsible for marketing control. Each national market is different from every other market. Distance and differences in language, custom, and practices create communications problems. As noted earlier in the chapter, in larger companies, the size of operations and number of country subsidiaries often result in the creation of an intermediate headquarters. This adds an organizational level to the control system. This section reviews global marketing control practices, compares these practices with domestic marketing control, and identifies the major factors that influence the design of a global control system.

In the managerial literature, control is defined as the process by which managers ensure that resources are used effectively and efficiently in the accomplishment of organizational objectives. Control activities are directed toward marketing programs and

---

[14] Christopher A. Bartlett, "MNCs: Get Off the Reorganization Merry-Go-Round," *Harvard Business Review* (March–April 1983): 138–146.

other programs and projects initiated by the planning process. Data measures and evaluations generated by the control process in the form of a global audit are also a major input to the planning process.

THE GLOBAL MARKETING AUDIT

A global marketing audit can be defined as a comprehensive, systematic, and periodic examination of a company's or business unit's marketing environment, objectives, strategies, programs, policies, and activities, which is conducted with the objective of identifying existing and potential problems and opportunities and recommending a plan of action to improve a company's marketing performance.

The global marketing audit is a tool for evaluating and improving a company's global marketing operations. The audit is an effort to assess effectiveness and efficiency of marketing strategies, practices, policies, and procedures vis-à-vis the firm's opportunities, objectives, and resources.

A full marketing audit has two basic characteristics. The first is that it is formal and systematic. Asking questions at random as they occur to the questioner may bring about useful insights, but this is not a marketing audit. The effectiveness of an audit normally increases to the extent that it involves a sequence of orderly diagnostic steps, as is the case in the conduct of a public accounting audit.

The second characteristic of a marketing audit is that it is conducted annually. Most companies in trouble are well on their way to disaster before the trouble is fully apparent. It is, therefore, important that the audit be conducted periodically—even when there are no apparent problems or difficulties inherent in the company's operations.

The audit may be broad or it may be a narrowly focused assessment. A full marketing audit is comprehensive. It reviews the company's marketing environment, competition, objectives, strategies, organization, systems, procedures, and practices in every area of the marketing mix including product, pricing, distribution, communications, customer service, and research strategy and policy.

Audits are either independent or internal. An independent marketing audit is conducted by someone who is free from influence of the organization being audited. The independent audit may or may not be objective: It is quite possible to influence a consultant or professional firm that you are paying. The company that wants a truly independent audit should discuss with the independent auditor the importance of objectivity. A potential limitation of an independent marketing audit is the lack of understanding of the industry by the auditor. In many industries, there is no substitute for experience, because if you do not have it, you are simply not going to see the subtle clues that any pro would easily recognize. On the other hand, the independent auditor may see obvious indications that the experienced pro may be unable to see.

An internal or self-audit may be quite valuable because it is conducted by the company's marketing personnel who understand the industry. However, it may lack the objectivity of an independent audit. Because of the strengths and limitations of the two types of audit, we recommend that both be conducted periodically for the same scope and time period, and that the results be compared. The comparison may lead to insights on how to strengthen the performance of the marketing team.

Setting Objectives and Scope of the Audit

The first step of an audit is a meeting between company executives and the auditor to agree on objectives, coverage, depth, data sources, report format, and time period for the audit.

Gathering Data One of the major tasks in conducting an audit is data collection. A detailed plan of interviews, secondary research, review of internal documents, and so forth is required. This effort usually involves an auditing team.

A basic rule in data collection is not to rely solely on the opinion of people being audited for data. In auditing a sales organization, it is absolutely essential to talk to field sales personnel as well as sales management; and, of course, no audit is complete without direct contact with customers and suppliers.

Creative auditing techniques should be encouraged and explored by the auditing team. For example, if you are auditing an organization and you want to determine whether the chief executive or operating officer of the organization unit is really in touch with the organization and all of its activities, send an auditor into the mailroom. Find out if the chief executive has ever visited the mailroom. If he or she has never been there, it tells you volumes about the management style and the degree of hands-on management in the organization. If an organization has developed an elaborate marketing incentive program that is purported to generate results with customers, an audit should involve customer contact to find out if indeed the program is actually having any impact. For example, you can be certain that 99 percent of the material that is associated with frequent flier plans is never read or noted by fliers who have got better things to do with their time than read complicated rules and announcements.

Analyzing the Data   A library is filled with data, but, just like the marketing audit, unless that data is properly analyzed it is useless. In fact, many companies assume that just gathering data is sufficient to the process ("Hey—look at this 100-page report I did!") or that the more data the better. Despite the abundance of information available about the marketing environment, this abundance does not directly provide value in making decisions.

When a marketing audit involves international markets, the data should be analyzed by both local employees who are familiar with the specific implications of the data and also by headquarters staff who are aware of corporate strategic issues and similar experiences in other countries.

Preparing and Presenting the Report   After data collection and analysis, the next step is the preparation and presentation of the audit report. This presentation should restate the objectives and scope of the audit, present the main findings, and present major recommendations and conclusions as well as major headings for further study and investigation.

Components of the Marketing Audit

There are six major components of a full global marketing audit:

1. Marketing environment audit
2. Marketing strategy audit
3. Marketing organization audit
4. Marketing systems audit
5. Marketing productivity audit
6. Marketing function audit

Problems, Pitfalls, and Potential of the Global Marketing Audit

The marketing audit presents a number of problems and pitfalls. Setting objectives can be a pitfall, if indeed the objectives are blind to a major problem. It is important for the auditor to be open to expand or shift objectives and priorities while in the conduct of the audit itself.

Similarly, new data sources may appear during the course of an audit, and the auditor should be open to such sources. The approach of the auditor should simultaneously be systematic, following a predetermined outline, and perceptive and open to new directions and sources that appear in the course of the audit investigation.

Report Presentation   One of the biggest problems in marketing auditing is that the executive who commissions the audit may have higher expectations about what the audit will do for the company than the actual results seem to offer. An audit is valuable even if it does not offer major new directions or panaceas. It is important for all concerned to recognize that improvements at the margin are what truly make a difference between success and mediocrity. In major league baseball, the difference between a batter with a .350 batting average (3.5 hits out of 10 times at bat) and a .250 (2.5 hits out of 10 times at bat) is the difference between a major league hitter and someone who is not even good enough for the minor leagues. Major league marketers understand this fact and recognize it in the audit. Do not look for dramatic revolutionary findings or panaceas. Accept and recognize that improvement at the margin is the winner's game in global marketing.

Global marketers, even more than their domestic counterparts, need marketing audits to assess far-flung efforts in highly diverse environments. The global marketing audit should be at the top of the list of programs for strategic excellence and implementation excellence for the winning global company.

Planning and control are intertwined and interdependent. With the information from the global marketing audit, the planning process can begin and result in a more effective document. The planning process can be divided into two related phases. Strategic planning is the selection of opportunities defined in terms of products and markets, and the commitment of resources, both human and financial, to achieve these objectives. Operational planning is the process in which strategic market objectives and resource commitments to these objectives are translated into specific projects and programs. The relationship among strategic planning, operational planning, and control is illustrated in Figure 17-11.

For companies with global operations, marketing control presents additional challenges. The rate of environmental change in a global company is a dimension of each of the national markets in which it operates. At the beginning of this book, we examined these environments; each is changing at a different rate, and each exhibits unique characteristics. The multiplicity of national environments challenges the global marketing control system with much greater environmental heterogeneity and, therefore, greater complexity in its control. Finally, global marketing can create special communications problems associated with the great distance between markets and headquarters and differences among managers in languages, customs, and practices.

When company management decides that it wants to develop a global strategy, it is essential that control of the subsidiary operations of the company shifts from the subsidiary to the headquarters. The subsidiary will continue to make vital inputs into the strategic planning process, but the control of the strategy must shift from subsidiary to headquarters. This involves a shift in the balance of power in the organization and may result in strong resistance to change. In many companies, a tradition of subsidiary autonomy and self-sufficiency limits the influence of headquarters. Three types of mechanisms are available to help headquarters acquire control: (1) data management mechanisms, (2) managers' management mechanisms that shift the perception of self-interest from subsidiary autonomy to global business performance, and (3) conflict resolution mechanisms that resolve conflicts triggered by necessary trade-offs.

PLANNING AND BUDGETING

Planning and budgeting are two basic tools of monitoring the global marketing effort. Planning involves expressing planned sales, profit objectives, and expenditures on marketing programs in unit and money terms and these are translated into a budget. The budget spells out the financial objectives and necessary expenditures to achieve these objectives. Monitoring consists of measuring actual sales and expenditures. In the case of no variance or a favorable variance between actual and budget, no action is usually taken. An unfavorable variance—lower unit sales than planned, for example—acts as a

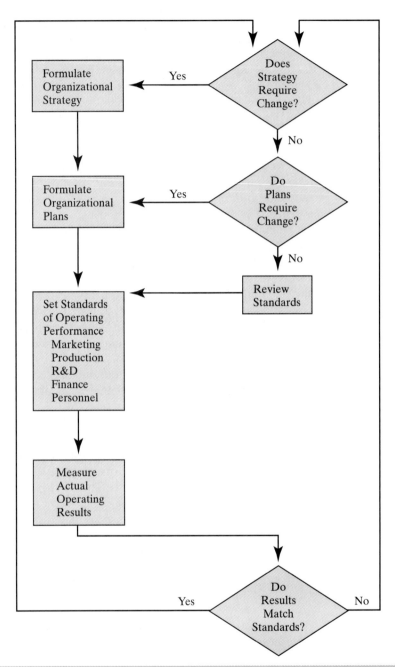

FIGURE 17-11   Relationship of Strategic Control and Planning

red flag that attracts the attention of line and staff executives at regional and international headquarters. They will investigate and attempt to determine the cause of the unfavorable variance and what might be done to improve performance.

EVALUATING PERFORMANCE

In evaluating performance, actual performance is compared with budgeted performance, as described in the previous section. Thus, the key question is, "How is the budget established?" Most companies in both domestic and global operations place heavy reliance on two standards: last year's actual performance and some kind of industry average or historical norm. A more normative approach is for headquarters to develop an estimate of the kind of growth that would be desirable and attainable in each national market. This estimate can be based on company studies of national markets.

Larger companies may have sufficient business volume to justify staff product specialists at corporate headquarters who follow the performance of products worldwide. They have staff responsibility for their product from its introduction to its termination. Normally, a new product is first introduced in the largest and most sophisticated markets and then sequentially introduced in smaller and less developed markets. As a result, the company's products are typically at different stages of the product life cycle in different markets. A major responsibility of staff specialists is to ensure that lessons learned in more advanced markets are applied to the management of their products in smaller, less developed markets. Wherever possible, the specialists try to avoid making the same mistake twice, and they try to capitalize on what they have learned and apply it elsewhere. They also ensure that useful ideas from markets at similar stages of development are fully applied. Smaller companies focus on key products in key markets. Key products are those that are important to the company's sales, profit objectives, and competitive position. They are frequently new products that require close attention in their introductory stage in a market. If any budget variances develop with a key product, headquarters intervenes directly to learn about the nature of the problem and to assist local management in dealing with the problem.

INFLUENCES ON MARKETING PLANS AND BUDGETS

In preparing a budget or plan, the following factors are important.

Market Potential
How large is the potential market for the product being planned? In every domestic market, management must address this question in formulating a product plan. A company that introduces a product in more than one national market must answer this question for each market.

Competition
A marketing plan or budget must be prepared in light of the competitive level in the market. The more entrenched the competition, the more difficult it is to achieve market share and the more likely a competitive reaction will occur to any move that promises significant success in the target market. Competitive moves are particularly important as a variable in international market planning because many companies are moving from strong competitive positions in their base markets to foreign markets in which they have a minor position and must compete against entrenched companies. Domestic market standards and expectations of marketing performance are based on experience in markets in which the company has a major position. These standards and expectations are simply not relevant to a market in which the company is in a minor position trying to break into the market.

Impact of Substitute Products
One of the sources of competition for a product in a market is the frequent existence of substitute products. As a product is moved into markets at different stages of development, improbable substitute products often emerge. For example, in Colombia, a major source of competition for manufactured boxes and other packaging products is woven bags and wood boxes made in the handicraft sector of the economy. Marketing officials of multinational companies in the packaging industry in Columbia report that the

garage operator producing a handmade product is very difficult competition because of low costs of materials and labor.

Process

The manner in which targets are communicated to subsidiary management is as important as the way in which they are derived. One of the most sophisticated methods used today is the so-called indicative planning method. Headquarters' estimates of regional potential are disaggregated and communicated to subsidiary management as guidance. The subsidiaries are in no way bound by guidance. They are expected to produce their own plan, taking into account the headquarters guidance that is based on global data, and their own data from the market, including a detailed review of customers, competitors, and other relevant market developments. This method produces excellent results because it combines a global perspective and estimate with specific country marketing plans that are developed from the objective to the program by the country management teams themselves.

Headquarters, in providing guidance, does not need to understand a market in depth. For example, it is not necessary that the headquarters of a manufacturer of electrical products know how to sell electric motors to a French buyer. What headquarters can do is gather data on the expected expansion in generating capacity in France and use experience tables drawn from world studies that indicate what each megawatt of additional generating capacity will mean in terms of the growth in demand in France for electrical motors. The estimate of total market potential together with information on the competitiveness of the French subsidiary can be the basis for a guidance in terms of expected sales and earnings in France. The guidance may not be accepted by the French subsidiary. If the indicative planning method is used properly, the subsidiary educates the headquarters if its guidance is unrealistic. If headquarters does a good job, it will select an attainable but ambitious target. If the subsidiary does not see how it can achieve the headquarters goal, discussion and headquarters involvement in the planning process will either lead to a plan that will achieve the guidance objective or it will result in a revision of the guidance by headquarters.

Share of Market

Another principal measure of marketing performance is share of market. This is a valuable measure because it provides a comparison of company performance with that of other competitors in the market. Companies that do not obtain this measure, even if it is an estimate, are flying blind. In larger markets, data are reported for subsidiaries and, where significant sales are involved, on a product-by-product basis. Share-of-market data in larger markets are often obtained from independent market audit groups. In smaller markets, share-of-market data are often not available because the market is not large enough to justify the development of an independent commercial marketing audit service. In smaller markets, it is possible for a country manager or agent to hide a deteriorating market position or share of market behind absolute gains in sales and earnings.

Informal Control Methods

In addition to budgeting, informal control methods play an important role. The main informal control method is the transfer of people from one market to another. When people are transferred, they take with them their experience in previous markets, which will normally include some standards for marketing performance. When investigating a new market that has lower standards than a previous market, the investigation will lead to revised standards or to discovery of why there is a difference. Another valuable informal control device is face-to-face contact between subsidiary staff and headquarters staff as well as contact among subsidiary staff. These contacts provide an opportunity for an exchange of information and judgments that can be a valuable input to the planning and control process. Annual meetings that bring together staff from a region of the world often result in informal inputs to the process of setting standards.

Summary

To respond to the opportunities and threats in the global marketing environment, a firm must have a global vision and strategy. By providing leadership, organizing a global effort, and establishing control procedures, a firm can exploit global opportunities. Leaders must have the vision, in addition to the technical resources, to build global competencies. In organizing the global marketing effort, a structure that enables the company to respond to relevant differences in international market environments and enables the company to extend valuable corporate knowledge is the goal. A balance between autonomy and integration must be established. Within this organization, firms must establish core competencies to be competitive. For global marketing control practices to be effective, differences from purely domestic control must be recognized and implemented in planning and control practices.

Discussion Questions

1. What are the major variables influencing control in a global company?
2. What is the major complaint of managers in subsidiary companies about the control practices of headquarters?
3. What is a global marketing audit?
4. What kind of planning problems develop in the headquarters of a global company?
5. What are the problems in planning at the country or subsidiary level in a global company?
6. How would you advise a company manufacturing a line of construction equipment to organize its business on a global scale?

Suggested Readings

Bartlett, Christopher A., and Sumantra Ghoshal. *Managing Across Borders: The Transnational Solution.* Boston: Harvard Business School Press, 1989.

Bennis, Warren. *Organizing Genius: The Secrets of Creative Collaboration.* Reading, MA: Addison-Wesley, 1997.

Cho, Namshin. "How Samsung Organized for Innovation." *Long Range Planning,* 29, no. 6 (1996): 783–796.

Cohen, Susan G. "Designing Effective Self-Managing Work Teams." *CEO Publication—University of Southern California* (1993): G93–9.

Deshpande, Rohit. "Corporate Culture and Market Orientation: Comparing Indian and Japanese Firms." *Journal of International-Marketing,* 7, no. 4 (1999): 111–128.

Doremus, Paul N., William W. Keller, Louis W. Pauly, and Simon Reich. *The Myth of the Global Corporation.* Princeton, NJ: Princeton University Press, 1998.

Egelhoff, W. G. *Exploring the Limits of Transnationalism, Fordham University. Report 90-6-2* (September 1990).

Epstein, M. J., and J. F. Manzoni. *The Balanced Scorecard and Tableau De Bord: A Global Perspective on Translating Strategy into Action.* Fontainebleau: INSEAD, The European Institute of Business Administration,1997.

Gerlach, Michael L. *Alliance Capitalism: The Social Organization of Japanese Business.* Berkeley and Los Angeles: University of California Press, 1992.

Ghoshal, Sumantra, and Christopher A. Bartlett. *The Individualized Corporation.* New York: HarperBusiness, 1997.

Gorchels, Linda, Thani Jambulingam, and Timothy W. Aurand. "Executive Insights: International Marketing Manager: A comparison of Japanese, German, and U.S. Perceptions." *Journal of International Marketing,* 7, no. 1 (1999): 97–106.

Hammer, Michael, and James Champy. *Reengineering the Corporation.* New York: HarperCollins, 1993.

Heenan, David, and Warren Bennis. *Co-Leaders: The Power of Great Partnerships.* New York: John Wiley & Sons. 1999.

Johansson, Johny K., and Ikujiro Nonaka. *Relentless, The Japanese Way of Marketing.* New York: Harper-Business, 1997.

Kaplan, Robert S., and David P. Norton. *The Balanced Scorecard: Translating Strategy into Action.* Boston: Harvard Business School Press. 1996.

Kashani, Kamran. "Beware the Pitfalls of Global Marketing." *Harvard Business Review,* 67, no. 5 (September/October 1989): 91–98.

Katzenbach, Jon R., and Douglas K. Smith. "The Discipline of Teams." *Harvard Business Review* (March/April 1993): 111-121.

Katzenbach, Jon R., and Douglas K. Smith. *The Wisdom of Teams: Creating the High Performance Organization.* Boston: Harvard Business School Press, 1993.

Kogut, Bruce, and Udo Zander. "What Forms DD? Coordination, Identity, and Learning." *Organization Science,* 7 (September–October 1996): 502–518.

Krugman, Paul. "Competitiveness: A Dangerous Obsession." *Foreign Affairs,* 73, no. 2 (March/April 1994): 28–44.

Kuniyasu, Sakai. "The Feudal World of Japanese Manufacturing." *Harvard Business Review* (November/December 1990): 38–49.

Maruca, Regina Fazio. "The Right Way to Go Global: An Interview with Whirlpool CEO David Whitwam." *Harvard Business Review,* 72, no. 2 (March–April 1994): 134–145.

McDonald, Malcolm, and Warren J. Keegan. *Marketing Plans That Work: How to Prepare Them, How to Use Them.* Newton, MA: Butterworth Heinemann, 1997.

Mintzberg, Henry. "The Effective Organization: Forces and Forms." *Sloan Management Review* (Winter 1991).

Moore, James F. *The Death of Competition: Leadership and Strategy in the Age of Business Ecosystems.* New York: HarperBusiness, 1996.

Morrison, Allen J., David A. Ricks, and Kendall Roth. "Globalization versus Regionalization: Which Way for the Multinational?" *Organizational Dynamics* (Winter 1991): 7–30.

Pillai, Rajnandini, Terri Scandura, and Ethlyn Williams. "Leadership and Organizational Justice: Similarities and Differences Across Cultures." *Journal of International Business Studies,* 30, no. 4 (1999): 763.

Prahalad, C. K., and Gary Hamel. "The Core Competence of the Corporation." *Harvard Business Review,* 68 (May–June 1990): 79–93.

Schill, Ronald L., and David N. McArthur. "Redefining the Strategic Competitive Unit: Towards a New Global Marketing Paradigm?" *International Marketing Review,* 9, no. 3 (1992): 5–24.

Stevenson, Howard H., and Jeffrey L. Cruikshank. *Do Lunch or Be Lunch: The Power of Predictability in Creating Your Future.* Boston: Harvard Business School Press, 1997.

Womack, James P., and Daniel T. Jones. *Lean Thinking: Banish Waste and Create Wealth in Your Corporation.* New York: Simon & Schuster, 1996.

Yip, George S. *Total Global Strategy.* Upper Saddle River, NJ: Prentice Hall, 1992.

CHAPTER

18

The Future of
Global Marketing

*We describe our emerging culture by an awkward but descriptive name: "boundaryless."
It is the soul of our integrated diversity and at the heart of everything we do well. It is
the small-company culture we've been after for all these years.*

*E-business is the final nail in the coffin for bureaucracy at GE. The utter transparency
it brings about is a perfect fit for our boundaryless culture and means everyone in the
organization has total access to everything worth knowing.[1]*

—JOHN F. WELCH, JR.
*Chairman of the Board and Chief Executive
Officer, General Electric Company*

CONTENTS

The world economy has undergone revolutionary changes during the past 50 years.
Perhaps the greatest and most profound change is the emergence of global markets,
global competitors, and winners and losers in global competition.

◆ SIX MAJOR CHANGES

The changes continue. Six major changes that will continue well into this century are
listed next.

1. *World growth.* Many of the poor countries of the world, which have always been
   poor, are getting richer faster than the rich countries of the world, which are also
   getting richer. Most of the world is in a stage of economic growth. The geographic
   exception to this world growth is Africa south of the Sahara where many countries are economically stagnant or in economic decline.
2. *The world economy dominates.* The world economy is the dominant economic unit.
   The macroeconomics of the nation-state no longer control economic outcomes in

---

[1] GE Annual Report, 1999, p. 7.

countries, and even the large superpower countries such as the United States can no longer dictate to poorer countries how they should behave.

3. *End of the so-called trade-cycle decision rule.* The old trade-cycle model, which implied to a generation of managers that as a product matures, the location of production must shift to low-wage countries, has been clarified. The location of production is not dictated exclusively by wage levels. Wages are simply one element of the cost equation. For any product in which labor is less than, say, 15 percent to 20 percent of total costs, the location of production of mature products may be anywhere in the world. Factors such as transportation costs, availability of skilled labor, market responsiveness, and market access and high levels of innovation in product design and manufacturability may all indicate that the best location for production is a high-income, high-wage country.

4. *Free markets rule the world.* The 75-year "contest" between capitalism and communism is over. The clear success of the capitalist market-driven system over the communist centrally controlled model has led to the collapse of communism as a model for the organization of economic activity and as an ideology. Markets are in control of the allocation of resources all over the world with the exception of the two autocratic national anachronisms, Cuba and North Korea.

5. *Accelerating growth of global markets.* Global markets will grow at rates that were once thought impossible. The engine behind this accelerating growth is the high rate of growth in both the high- and low-income countries. The high-income county growth leadership has shifted from Japan to the United States. Low- and lower-middle-income country growth leadership has been concentrated in Southeast Asia and southern Asia with China as a unique, high-growth, large country in the region and the world, and Singapore, Taiwan, and South Korea at the vanguard of the small countries in the region. The driving forces of this growth are technology, deregulation, global integration, and the triumph of marketing.

6. *The rise of the Internet and information technology.* As Jack Welch, CEO of GE suggests in the quotation at the beginning of this chapter, e-business is revolutionizing the way the world does business. We are now seeing the payoff for the huge investments in information technology over the past two decades. These investments are transforming the strategy and structure of every company in the world.

WORLD GROWTH

The first change is that most of the world's poor countries are getting richer. The emergence of the newly rich countries from among the ranks of the formerly less developed group breaks the long monopoly of Western Europe, the United States, Canada, and Japan on the rich-nation status. These countries are proving that it is not necessary to be European, North American (north of the Rio Grande), or Japanese to be rich. Countries such as Singapore and Hong Kong are already high-income countries; eastern Asia in particular is home to many countries that have been growing at annual rates of 7 percent or higher. A 7 percent real growth rate will double real income in a decade. The emerging rich countries include smaller countries such as South Korea as well as the largest countries in the world, China and India, which have begun to develop a middle class.

The exception to this growth in the emerging markets is Africa south of the Sahara, where the promise of economic progress has been set back by incompetent leadership and fundamentally by widespread ignorance, poverty, and disease. With the exception of South Africa, the economic progress in Africa south of the Sahara has been disappointing and discouraging.

Nevertheless, with the exception of Africa, for the first time in the history of the world, there is the very real likelihood of a much broader global prosperity in the first half of this century.

The population within the developed economies of the world is continuing to gray (see Table 18-1). The change from 1995 to the year 2050 will be quite dramatic. In 1995 nine countries had between 14.0 and 17.5 percent of their populations over the age of 65. In 2050 in the six countries of Spain, Hong Kong, Italy, Greece, Japan, and Germany, 30.0 percent or more of their populations will be over the age of 65. What impact will this graying shift have on marketing? Certainly, it will impact medical markets, but not all opportunities will be in medicines and adult diapers. The older populations are living more active, healthier lives and will be a major market for goods and services across a broad spectrum of consumer products.

Hand in hand with older populations, the birthrate in the high-income countries is collapsing. In fact, Peter Drucker claims that this is the most important, single, new certainty for the future of business.[2] In Japan and many European countries, the number of births has dropped to below population equilibrium level. The combination of low birthrates and wealth will drive a continuation of the global movement of people from poor, undeveloped countries to the rich, developed countries.

THE WORLD ECONOMY DOMINATES

The second major change is the emergence of the world economy as the dominant economic unit. Companies and countries that recognize this fact have the greatest chance of success. The United States is still a superpower, but it is no longer in a position to tell other successful nations how to behave in matters of internal affairs. As the poor countries grow richer, they assume that their values are responsible for their success, and they do not listen to lectures from their less successful former world leaders. Indeed, they start giving the lectures. Wealth creates the foundation for political and military power and the basis for an assumption of moral superiority. The attitude of politicians and businesspeople

TABLE 18-1 Persons Aged over 65			
	1995 *(% of total)*		2050 (Prj.) *(% of total)*
Sweden	17.5[a]	Spain	34.6
Norway	16.0[a]	Hong Kong	34.5
Germany	16.0[a]	Italy	34.3
United Kingdom	15.7[a]	Greece	31.4
Switzerland	15.7[a]	Japan	30.2
Belgium	15.7[a]	Germany	30.0
Denmark	15.4[a]	Austria	26.4
Greece	15.2[a]	Slovenia	26.3
France	15.1	Portugal	25.9
Austria	15.0[a]	Netherlands	25.6
Japan	14.0[a]	Switzerland	25.3
United States	12.7	Belgium	24.8

[a] 1994

Source: Japan 1988 An International Comparison Keizai Koho Center, p. 13. Data from *Labour Force Statistics 1975–1995* (Paris: OECD, 1997); and *The Sex and Age Distribution of the World Population* (UN, 1994).

---

[2] Peter Drucker, *Management Challenges for the 21st Century,* (New York: HarperBusiness, 1999), p. 44.

from rich countries and from countries that are successfully developing is that if we are rich or fast growing, we must be doing something right. The United States has long lectured the world from the pulpit of its economic success, and Southeast Asia was quick to join in with lectures on Asian values when it was growing at 7 percent plus per annum.

The "Asian Flu" that began in 1997 and continued into 1998 (the sudden collapse of currency values, employment, and economic output and the realization that many of the companies of the region were insolvent because of their dollar-denominated debt), which infected Southeast Asia, did not impact only the economic well-being of countries in Asia. It clearly threatened the growth rate and economic well-being of the rest of the world, including the high-income countries. It also underlined the vulnerability of smaller countries to currency fluctuations and capital outflows and the urgent need for economic and political reform at the national, regional, and global levels. Most of the countries that were hit by the Asian Flu in 1997 to 1998 have resumed economic growth. In Indonesia, the crisis led to the emergence of a popular movement for more democratic expression and a move from the autocratic rule of the Suharto regime to an elected head of state.

TRADE-CYCLE MODEL CLARIFIED

The trade-cycle model, which suggested to many managers that as a product matures, its production location would shift to lower-income countries, has been clarified. In the early 21st century, it is clear that product maturity is a concept that must be carefully defined in a dynamic world. The automobile is a mature product in the sense that growth has leveled in all of the high-income countries of the world. Does this mean that it is standardized? Far from it, the automobile is a highly differentiated, incredibly complicated, increasingly sophisticated, high-value product, and the way cars are designed and manufactured has been revolutionized. The result is that automobiles continue to be designed, manufactured, and assembled in high-income countries. The reason is simple: Labor is a factor in the production cost of an automobile, but as a percentage of total cost, it is not high enough to determine the location of all automobile production. Automobiles today are produced in countries at every stage of development, but 98 percent of world production is from high- and upper-middle-income countries.

In the 1980s, the Swiss banks concluded that Switzerland was finished in the low end of the watch business. One man, Nicolas Hayek, disagreed. He formed the company Swatch and demonstrated that in spite of the high wage costs in Switzerland, the country could compete in world watch markets not only in the luxury watch segment but also in the low-priced segment of fashion accessory watches. The Swiss understand the watch business, and they have been creative innovators in the design, manufacturability, and marketing of watches. All luxury watches, which account for a small percentage of volume in units but more than half of the value of world watch production, are made in Europe, and over 95 percent of European luxury watch production is in Switzerland.

In the meantime, there are mature products that have become relatively standardized in their manufacture and continue to require a relatively high percentage of labor to produce. These products today are made almost exclusively in lower-income countries. A good example of a product in this mature category is athletic footwear. The entire industry has shifted its production to low-income countries, and no company has been able to reverse this trend. This has offered employment opportunity for the lower-income countries and a challenge for the higher-income countries to shift labor to other industries in which the cost of labor is not such a significant factor in the production location decision.

Changes in global competition are bringing companies into more direct competition with economic rivals in other parts of the world than was the case in the past. Yes-

IS COMPETITIVENESS A DANGEROUS OBSESSION?

Stanford University economist Paul Krugman wants every student of international trade to reflect carefully on the following proposition:

Today, America is part of a truly global economy. To maintain our standard of living, America must learn to compete in an ever tougher world marketplace. That's why high productivity and product quality have become essential. We can only be competitive in the new global economy if we forge a new partnership between government and business.

To many, this proposition will sound reasonable. In style and substance, it echoes assertions being made in the 1990s by such well-known figures as economist Lester Thurow, presidential advisor Ira Magaziner, and U.S. Secretary of Labor Robert Reich. Krugman, however, says that the proposition is "baloney." In his words, it represents "the rhetoric of competitiveness," in which the United States is likened to a large corporation such as General Motors (GM). According to the rhetoric of competitiveness, America—like GM—is suffering because of global competition, and the nation's standard of living has stagnated as a result.

In numerous articles and a recent book, Krugman offers a painstaking analysis of what he believes to be a mistakenly held proposition. In sorting out the salient issues, Krugman's reasoning flies in the face of positions held by Thurow, Magaziner, Reich, and others; Krugman calls these individuals strategic traders and policy entrepreneurs. Surprisingly, Krugman's critiques are not based on partisan politics; he himself is a liberal. His complaint is that fundamental economic concepts—especially comparative advantage—are being misinterpreted, misapplied, or ignored altogether in the name of public policy.

First, Krugman disputes the assertion that America is "part of a truly global economy." The reason: Approximately 90 percent of the goods and services produced in the United States are for domestic consumption; only 10 percent are destined for world markets. Indeed, 70 percent of the U.S. economy is based on services, and services are less likely than manufactured products to be marketed abroad. Thus, despite all the talk about global integration, the global economy is not as interconnected as people might think.

Next, Krugman attacks the notion that America itself "competes in the global marketplace." Krugman argues that Japan, the United States, and other nations of the world are not in competition with each other in the sense that, say, Coca-Cola and PepsiCo or Reebok and Nike are. Few Coca-Cola employees buy Pepsi products, and vice versa. Thus, a company is not like a nation: No company sells 90 percent of its output to its own employees. In the "cola wars," PepsiCo can only win by taking customers away from Coca-Cola. The same cannot be said of nations, Krugman asserts. The world's major industrial nations can be successful without causing harm to each other because they are not just competitors; trading partners also represent export markets and sources of imports. In other words, every potential problem also presents opportunities, and those opportunities may outweigh the problems.

Third, Krugman objects to linking the issue of higher U.S. productivity with international trade. Contrary to the message coming out of Washington, the fact that productivity improvement rates in other nations exceed those in the United States does not make the United States less competitive or lessen Americans' standard of living. Krugman asserts quite simply that America needs to be productive to produce more. That may sound tautological, but it is a plain and simple economic truth that would be valid even if the United States did not engage in international trade. In his writings, Krugman reviews the basics of comparative advantage to demonstrate that, in fact, no special problems are created for a country that is less productive than its trading partners.

Finally, Krugman argues that the issues relating to the rhetoric of competitiveness are not simply academic ones. If the strategic traders' rhetoric of competitiveness message is heeded, the results could have far-reaching, undesirable consequences. First, it could lead to wasteful government spending in a misguided effort to enhance competitiveness. In the interest of competitiveness, government support might be directed at manufacturing. Yet it is the service sector, which is not a major part of international trade, where productivity is lagging. Second, it could lead to protectionism and trade wars. Finally, it could lead to poor public policy decisions in a variety of areas—health care, for example—that are unrelated to trade.

SOURCES: Paul Krugman, "A Country Is Not a Company," *Harvard Business Review,* 74, no. 1 (January–February 1996): 40–44; Paul Krugman, "Competitiveness: A Dangerous Obsession," *Foreign Affairs* (March–April 1994): 28–44; Paul Krugman, "Competitiveness: Does It Matter?" *Fortune,* 7 March 1994, p. 109; Paul Krugman, *Peddling Prosperity: Economic Sense and Nonsense in the Age of Diminished Expectations* (New York: W. W. Norton & Co., 1994).

terday's global forces were founded on exports of products and services not available to competing nations. In the past, countries would export agricultural products others could not grow, raw materials others did not have, and high-tech products others could not build. Today, companies in the same industries in different countries and regions compete ferociously with each other in manufactured goods, agricultural products, natural resources, and services.

THE TRIUMPH OF MARKETS

After almost a century of debate in the world about the merits of markets and marketing versus a state-controlled system of allocating resources and controlling production, the capitalist/marketing model has clearly won. Markets are king the world around, with the exception of Cuba and North Korea. The big issue today is whether economic democracy (the market allocation of resources, one dollar, yen, or rupiah/one vote) must be combined with political democracy. This debate will continue. What is no longer debated is the global emergence of the acceptance of markets and marketing.

THE RISE OF GLOBAL MARKETS

The fifth trend that will change the future of global marketing is the rise of global market segments. Today, more than ever before, there are global segment opportunities. In category after category, global efforts succeed. For example, the soft-drink industry was first successful in reaching a global cola segment and has now moved to address the fast-growing fruit-and-flavor segment.

There are global segments for luxury cars, wine and spirits, every type of medical and industrial product, teenagers, senior citizens, and enthusiasts of every stripe and type, from scuba divers to snowboarders.

The rapidly growing diffusion of Internet access combined with the rapidly expanding bandwidth and capacity of the global Internet itself will play a major role in supporting the growth of global markets and global marketing. Amazon.com can reach customers in Taiwan and Tokyo just as easily as it can reach customers in Boston. Customers anywhere in the world are only a click away from the book of their choice. With express mail service, customers are only two days away from delivery wherever they live, and with credit cards they can pay for goods and services in any currency.

These are the new economic realities. The rich are getting richer, the poor in many countries are getting richer faster, and the world economy is becoming more and more integrated. This means new opportunities and new challenges for companies and countries.

What is the future for the average consumer? The possibilities are unlimited. How about high-tech "pets" to care for the elderly? Matsushita Electric has developed "pets," which record the number of times their owners talk to them or hold them. This information is transmitted to an agency that monitors these elderly. The pet "can respond to a greeting, engage in simple conversation and even express remorse when scolded."[3] In every field, from medicine and health care to transportation to information technology to entertainment to retailing, there will continue to be revolutionary changes.

THE RISE OF THE INTERNET AND INFORMATION TECHNOLOGY

The sixth and perhaps the most significant of all of the changes impacting global marketing is the rise of the Internet and information technology (IT). Marketing, for the first time in history, can address the individual customer. Before the Internet, the smallest marketing segment was a group or cluster of customers with similar needs. Today,

---

[3] Alexandra Nusbaum. "Japan Plans a High-Tech Breed of 'Pets' to Care for the Elderly," *Financial Times*, 13 April 1999, p. 16.

marketing has the tools to address the segment of one, the individual customer and his or her needs.

This capability is available to address markets from local to global. In addition, companies can for the first time really focus on the customer. Today, small companies can act like large companies, and large, giant companies can act like small companies. This is energizing every sector of the global economy, especially in the high-income countries that have the resources to invest in IT. In addition to e-commerce, the Internet revolution is creating a new medium for information, entertainment, communication, and advertising and a new e-commerce retail segment.

◆ CAREERS IN GLOBAL MARKETING

There has never been a better time to prepare for a career in global marketing. Now that you are completing this book, the author would like to offer a few suggestions on how to jump-start your global marketing career.

First, remember that times have changed. Until very recently, one sure way to put your career at risk in many companies (especially U.S. companies) was to go overseas. There was nothing wrong with being overseas per se, but the problem for careers was that management did not recognize the value of global experience and turned to executives who were close at hand when making promotions. "Out of sight, out of mind" seemed to be the operative phrase.

Today, this is changing. Global experience counts. Only the truly lost do not recognize that we are in a global market with global competition, and those with global experience have a definite advantage. Top U.S. executives with international experience include Samir F. Gibara, president and chief executive officer (CEO) of Goodyear Tire & Rubber; Michael Hawley, president and chief operating officer (COO) of Gillette; Harry Bowman, chairman, president, and CEO of Outboard Marine; Lucio A. Noto, chairman and CEO of Mobil; and Raymond G. Viault, vice chairman of General Mills.[4] According to Cendant International, the most frequent locations for international employees are the United States, United Kingdom, Mexico, Canada, Singapore, Saudi Arabia, Germany, France, China, and Japan.[5]

Ray Viault was a vice president of General Foods in charge of the Maxwell House Coffee Division. When Philip Morris acquired General Foods, it kept Viault on as president of the Maxwell House division. Later, when Philip Morris acquired Jacob Suchard, the Zurich-based chocolate and coffee company, it chose Viault as the new CEO of the acquired company. Viault was able to take his grounding in the U.S. coffee market to Europe and did an outstanding job of leading the global marketing effort of Jacob Suchard. Following this assignment, Viault returned to the United States to become a vice chairman of General Mills.

How do you establish a career in global marketing? There are two broad paths:

1. Go directly into a job outside your home country or into a headquarters job in a global company.
2. Get experience with a company in an industry that prepares you for promotion to a job with multicountry responsibility or to an assignment outside your home country.

For many the second choice is better than the first. There is no substitute for solid experience in a company in an industry. Your best opportunity to get solid experience

---

[4] Joann S. Lublin, "An Overseas Stint Can Be a Ticket to the Top," *The Wall Street Journal,* 29 January 1996, p. B1.
[5] Sherrie Zhan, "Smooth Moves: Lowering Expatriate Angst," *World Trade* (July 1999): 63.

may be in your home country. You speak the language, understand the culture, and are trained in business and marketing. You are ready to learn.

Another option is to get this basic experience in a different country. The advantage of this move is that you will learn a new culture and language and broaden your international experience while you learn about a company and industry.

Summary

The future of global marketing will reflect five major changes in world growth but with some major new directions. The growth of Southeast Asia has been interrupted. That region now offers exceptional risk and reward equations for global marketers who are willing to make a bet on the long-term potential of the region. The cost of market entry has dropped as dramatically as the decline in values of national currencies. For companies with a stomach for risk, there is an opportunity to invest, building market positions in countries that most experts believe will soon return to long-term growth. In the meantime, other world regions will continue to grow, and world wealth will become more evenly distributed.

The trade cycle has not eliminated manufacturing as a source of employment and income in the high-income countries. By investing in capital equipment and by designing products for manufacturability, rich countries have proven that they can continue to successfully compete as manufacturing locations.

Global markets will continue to grow in importance as global marketers continue their quest to identify and serve global segments. This growth will enhance and expand the value of global experience for managers and executives worldwide.

Finally, marketing is at the threshold of a new and exciting era: e-business, e-commerce, and e-marketing. For the first time in history, marketers have the tools to address the needs of the individual customer.

Discussion Questions

1. Do you believe that economic democracy (free markets) will inevitably lead to political democracy? Why? Why not?
2. Why did markets and marketing win out in the competition with communism?
3. Is the trade cycle relevant to companies today? Why? Why not?
4. How has the Internet changed marketing?

Suggested Readings

Baetz, Mark C., and Christopher Bart. "Developing Mission Statements Which Work." *Long Range Planning,* 29, no. 4 (1996): 526–533.

Collins, James C., and Jerry I. Porras. "Building a Visionary Company." *California Management Review,* 37, no. 2 (Winter 1995): 80–100.

Doyle, Peter. "Marketing in the New Millennium." *European Journal of Marketing,* 29, no. 13 (1995): 23–41.

Drucker, Peter. *Management Challenges for the 21st Century.* New York: HarperBusiness, 1999.

McKenna, R. *Real Time: Preparing for the Age of the Never Satisfied Customer.* Boston: Harvard Business School Press, 1997.

McRae, Hamish. *The World in 2020: Power, Culture, and Prosperity.* Boston: Harvard Business School Press, 1994.

Stevenson, H. H., and J. L. Cruikshank. *Do Lunch or Be Lunch: The Power of Predictability in Creating Your Future.* Boston: Harvard Business School Press, 1997.

◆◆◆ **Part VI Cases**

Kodak Versus Fuji
The Battle for Global Market Share

As retail America undergoes a dramatic change with the constant consolidation of companies, management must strive to maintain a competitive advantage or risk being acquired. The worldwide success of Wal-Mart has led many to diversify and heed the adage that "bigger is indeed better." An example in the global grocery industry is the Ahold Group (Netherlands) which now operates in more than 17 countries including its recent acquisition of New York-based Pathmark. In the U.S. grocery industry, the merger between Albertson's and American Stores, and the U.S. drug chain landscape has rapidly changed over the last two years with only four major players left standing: CVS, Rite Aid, Walgreen's, and Eckerd.

As the retail community shrinks, retailers put greater emphasis on their suppliers for quality products at a competitive price that enables them to make healthy margins to attract consumers. If one manufacturer cannot supply the necessary ingredients, retailers will look for other alternatives. This environment has provided an opportunity to shake up an otherwise mature and stable industry, the photographic industry, and has paved the way for a viable competitor to Kodak, such as Fuji Photo Film U.S.A. The phenomenon has contributed to Fuji making significant inroads into Kodak's once commanding U.S. market share in particular and to its global share in general.

This case study shows the evolution of the Kodak-Fuji relationship, specifically from Kodak's perspective. The case study will attempt to show how Kodak has fallen from its lofty position and how it has developed strategies to rectify the situation. H. Donald Hopkins provided the groundwork for this revised case study in his original work "Kodak vs. Fuji: A Case of Japanese-American Strategic Interaction." The follow-up study examines this relationship, with respect to market share battles (both globally and domestically), sponsorship battles, court battles, and the photographic industry in general.

The relationship between Kodak and Fuji had always been adversarial, as competitors naturally are; however, the relationship took a very serious turn in May 1995, when Kodak filed a Section 301 petition under U.S. trade law. The petition claimed that Kodak's 7 to 10 percent market share in Japan was not a result of consumer choice and marketing efforts but rather a result of four principal Japanese

wholesalers, backed by the Japanese government, that are exclusive Fujifilm supporters.

As a result, the World Trade Organization, which eventually presided over the court decision, announced on January 30, 1998, a "sweeping rejection of Kodak's complaints"[1] about the film market in Japan.

At present, with the court battles behind them, it appears that Kodak and Fuji can now pool their efforts to grow the photographic and imaging business as they did with their shared effort, along with Canon, Minolta, and Nikon, in releasing the Advanced Photo System in 1996. These types of efforts are necessary to stave off the real competition to photography, the computer-savvy consumer who demands digital imaging.

KODAK AND FUJI . . . NOT A PRETTY PICTURE

"How can Kodak possibly sit on its hands and allow this to happen?" pondered Alex Henderson, an analyst at Prudential Securities, Inc. in New York, as quoted in an article in the *Rochester Democrat & Chronicle*. "You can't have your nearest competitor growing at this volume and not deal with it."[2] Analysts stated that for the first time in Kodak's 113-year history, it could no longer take its home market for granted. Over the last decade, while the U.S.-based Eastman Kodak Company was sleeping, the Japanese firm Fuji Photo Film opened its first film-production plant in the United States, cut prices, marketed aggressively, and stole valuable market share.

Kodak maintains that it will not engage in a price war to win customers back due to potential profit erosion. The inroads that Fuji has made in the U.S. market will certainly continue to build its momentum. "They (Kodak) are competing against an extremely determined, extremely proficient and extremely well-financed company in Fuji," says Michael Ellman, who tracks Kodak for Schroder & Company.[3] What then, begs the question, is Kodak to do? Many analysts are demanding that Kodak's CEO George Fisher take drastic action to cut costs, reduce debt, and right Kodak's sinking ship.

THE CHANGING CUSTOMER

The dynamics within the photo industry have changed dramatically within the past 15 years. Once upon a time, the film industry within the United States was basically stable and predictable, with industry leader Eastman Kodak, a

---

This case was prepared by Thomas C. Finnerty, Doctoral Candidate at the Lubin School of Business, Pace University, under the supervision of Warren J. Keegan as a basis for class discussion rather than to illustrate either effective or ineffective handling of a business situation. © 2000 Dr. Warren J. Keegan.

---

[1] *Edelman Public Relations Press Release,* 30 January 1998.
[2] *Rochester Democrat & Chronicle,* 16 September 1997, p. 9.
[3] Ibid.

U.S.-based company headquartered in Rochester, New York, holding a commanding share of the industry, hovering between 80 to 90 percent.[4] No competitors even had a double-digit percentage of the amateur photo market and many consumers automatically equated Kodak with film. Competitors were left to fight for the scraps off Kodak's table and the pickings were slim.

Then, beginning in 1984, the general photographic market and particularly Kodak noticed a subtle change in consumer attitude. Kodak still retains its enviable and commanding share of the market, but the market-savvy consumers of the new millennium now have more choices and do not automatically equate film with Kodak alone. Three major functions have eroded consumer brand loyalty and allegiance to Kodak these past 15 years.

First, American consumers are more accepting of foreign-based products, although they enjoy preaching the virtues of "buying American." They celebrate their patriotic freedom by waving the American flag at picnics on the Fourth of July. However, it is not uncommon for some guests to drive to the Independence Day celebration in a Mercedes Benz (German) automobile, while listening to music on a Sony (Japanese) radio/disc player. In addition, while waiting for their all-American burgers to cook, many Americans are reaching into the ice chest to find Bass (English) Ale, along with Perrier (French) bottled water.

A January 1999 study showed that the United States recorded its single largest trade deficit month ever at $17 billion dollars.[5] Imports outweighed exports. Unless protectionist legislation is initiated and passed, U.S. consumers will continue to purchase what they perceive is the best deal (be it domestic or foreign) for their money.

Second, consumers have found a bona fide competitor to Kodak in the name of Fujifilm. Clearly, Fuji has emerged from a minor player in the early 1980s to take a solid number-two position within the U.S. market and has caught the attention, as well as the wrath, of Kodak. Third, the landscape within retail America has changed dramatically in the past five years. The success of Wal-Mart has taught retailers that diversification, scrambled marketing, and "one-stop" shopping are important to consumers. As consolidation sweeps the nation in mass merchants, food, and drug accounts, retailers realize they must maintain their competitive advantage or close shop. To survive, they are squeezing manufacturers for quality products at competitive prices to capture profit margins for expansion within the industry. This environment has provided an opportunity for Fuji to prosper in an otherwise stable and mature photographic industry.

Today an all-out war has emerged. While Kodak and Fuji fight for market share, the real winner and benefactor is the consumer. "Retailers and consumers will be the big winners in this struggle for market share among the big players," says one retailer. "We are going to get more incentives to sell merchandise and the consumer is going to see a lot more new product at lower prices."[6] Kodak and Fuji deny they are engaging in a price war, but for each move Fuji makes, Kodak counters with a vengeance. "Smack them until they figure it out," is how Eric Steenburgh, Kodak's assistant chief operating officer, describes its strategy toward Fuji.[7]

TODAY'S PICTURE

The amateur photo market's estimated worth is $14.2 billion. Film sales generate 20 percent or $2.84 billion (Exhibit 1). Within film sales, 35-millimeter film commands 80.2 percent or $2.27 billion dollars (Exhibit 2). While unit film sales showed a moderate 2 percent growth rate, the real shining stars within this segment, which continues to exhibit strong growth, are the one-time-use cameras (OTUC), which are considered film within the industry. Unit sales grew at 23 percent in 1997 and a 20 percent annual growth rate is expected to continue (Exhibit 3).

THE NEW PLAYERS

While Kodak and Fuji are familiar competitors, they have to be aware as new competition enters the picture. In 1997, digital imaging accounted for 6.4 percent or just under $1 billion in the amateur photo market (Exhibit 1). As technology inevitably increases and prices drop, the consumer may prefer digital imaging. A recent Salomon Smith Barney report on imaging stated that the digital camera market in

EXHIBIT 1 1997 Amateur Photo Market		
Segment	*Percentage*	*Dollars*
Photoprocessing	43.50	$6,177,000,000
Film Sales	20.00	$2,840,000,000
Conventional Cameras	9.70	$1,377,400,000
Digital Imaging	6.40	$908,800,000
Portrait Studios	5.50	$781,000,000
Frames	3.30	$468,600,000
Photo Accessories	3.20	$454,400,000
Albums	2.50	$355,000,000
Camera Repair	1.00	$142,000,000
Consumables	0.90	$127,800,000
Video Camcorders	0.70	$99,400,000
Video Accessories	0.50	$71,000,000
Other	2.80	$397,600,000
	100.00	$14,200,000,000

Source: 1997 Photo Marketing Association (PMA) figures.

---

[4] Photo Marketing Association Industry figures.
[5] *USA Today,* 19 March 1999, Source: U.S. Commerce Department.

[6] *Supermarket Business* (February 1999): 47.
[7] *The Wall Street Journal,* 18 November 1998.

EXHIBIT 2   Total Film Sales, 1997

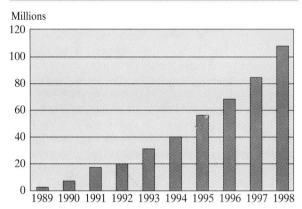

Source: Photo Marketing Association.

EXHIBIT 3   1997 One-Time-Use Camera Sales Up 23 Percent

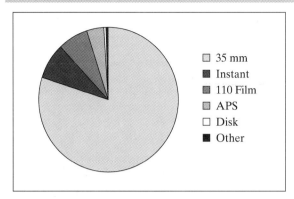

Source: PMA Marketing Research.

the United States will be 12.7 million units by 2002, which is larger than the current conventional lens shutter business in the United States. The report also states that the average price of a digital camera in 2002 will be about $168. Digital cameras are being mainstreamed quickly.

Nontraditional competitors such as Sony, Casio, and Hewlett-Packard are entering the industry with digital cameras and printers. To combat these threats, Kodak and Fuji each have manufactured digital cameras and printers of their own to stay competitive as "film companies" in the 21st century. To capture this technological consumer, both Kodak (Kodak/AOL "You've Got Pictures") and Fuji (Fuji.Net) have instituted cutting-edge services to allow customers to order prints directly over the Internet.

THE GLOBAL MARKET SHARE BATTLES

Traditionally, Kodak and Fuji have battled it out in the overseas film markets. In 1995, it was estimated that Kodak

had a 44 percent global share while Fuji had 33 percent.[8] Today the global share has changed as the U.S. market and Asian markets have shifted. Experts estimate that both Kodak and Fuji were neck in neck, with roughly a third of the market each. Alex Henderson, managing director of technology research at Prudential Securities, Inc. in New York, has been watching the two companies since 1985. Henderson believes that Fuji will overtake Kodak by 2001. "When that happens," says Henderson, "Kodak will go from being Coke to being Pepsi."[9]

In a letter to Kodak employees, Fisher and top management stated, "Competitors are making bold claims. They claim they will dominate the future of this business. We speak for the tens of thousands of people who work for Kodak when we say, 'Not on our watch'."[10]

THE U.S. MARKET SHARE BATTLES

Eastman Kodak has a commanding, yet declining, 70 percent of the U.S. market share. Fujifilm has approximately 17 percent of U.S. market share. Other minor players in the U.S. market include private-label brands, which constitute 7 percent. Agfa of Germany and Konica of Japan each have less than 2 percent market share.

THE PRICE WARS

Domestically speaking, Kodak and Fuji traditionally enjoyed healthy margins and treated the market as a mutually profitable duopoly. Then in the spring of 1996, Fuji cut prices on film by 10 percent to 15 percent after Costco Wholesalers decided to go exclusively with Kodak. Fuji had excess inventory of 2.5 million rolls of film. They distributed the heavily discounted film to other retailers to avoid losses from film expiration. This began a correlation between price cutting and market share.

As Fuji's market share grew incrementally in 1997 at Kodak's expense, Kodak initially stated that it would not engage in a price war. Fisher stated in 1997 that: "Our challenge is to figure out ways to introduce some exciting new products. That's a better way to fight an intense battle like the one we're in."[11] Later in the year he said, "We do not intend to continue to lose share at the rate we lost over the summer months."[12] Kodak stated that it did not intend to engage in a price war, and for good reason. Jonathan Rosenzweig, an analyst at Salomon Smith Barney, figures that "for every 1 percent cut in Kodak film prices, a 1 percent drop in earnings per share results."

Consumer reaction surprised the industry. Once consumers tried Fuji, they found they liked the product as long as it was priced lower than Kodak. By 1998 the hectic pace of competition between Fuji and Kodak seemed to slow

---

[8] *Fortune,* 1 May 1995.
[9] *The Wall Street Journal,* 18 November 1998.
[10] *Rochester Democrat & Chronicle,* 16 September 1997, p. 9.
[11] Ibid.
[12] *Business Week,* 20 October 1997, p. 124.

down, with the exception of value packs. "Spurring sales this year was the fact that the category in general got more price competitive, with both Kodak and Fuji sharpening their prices, particularly in promoted prices," states Jerry Quindlan, Kodak's vice president and general manager of Mass and Wholesale Clubs. "I would not call it a price war, however; it is really just sharpening prices. Our average price did not go down that much, but we did get more aggressive to protect market share."[13]

SPONSORSHIP BATTLES

The rivalry between Kodak and Fuji does not stop on the grocery or camera specialty shelves. This rivalry has heated up in the sponsorship arena as well. In his visit to Pace University's Lubin School of Business on April 28, 1999, Herb Baer, director of Marketing, Consumer Film and Quick-Snaps at Fuji, stated, "Fujifilm sponsored the 1984 Los Angeles Olympic Games and this sponsorship really helped put Fuji on the map." As the story goes, Peter Ueberroth, the Olympic organizer for the U.S. Olympic Games, visited Rochester and asked Kodak to be the exclusive film sponsor. Kodak refused the $1 million deal (far below its $4 million asking price). Ueberroth called Fuji and Fuji agreed on the spot. Fuji, a relatively small player in those days, still benefits from this agreement.

Kodak did not sit idle during the actual airing of the Olympic Games. It initiated a legal ambush to divert attention away from Fuji. "While Fuji was a worldwide sponsor of the Olympics, its competitor, Kodak, became a 'sponsor' of ABC television's broadcasts of the games and the 'official film' supplier to the U.S. track team."[14] Fuji returned the 1984 favor to Kodak during the 1988 Olympics and, thus, began the sponsorship and ambush marketing that continues today.

COURT BATTLES

Ironically, Kodak and Fuji each command roughly the same market share in their home-country markets: 70 percent. While Fuji has recently made significant strides in the U.S. market to gain approximately 17 percent, Kodak hovers around 7 to 9 percent in the Japanese market (see Exhibit 4).

The main differences between the U.S. and Japanese markets are the existing systems to distribute film, paper, and supplies to end users. In the United States, film manufacturers sell directly to retailers and photofinishers. In Japan, distributors mediate between the two parties. Fuji has close ties to the four principal distributors, while Kodak claims that these strong relationships prevent distribution of other brands.

Furthermore, Kodak states that Tokyo-based Fuji has hundreds of exclusive deals with photofinishing labs and

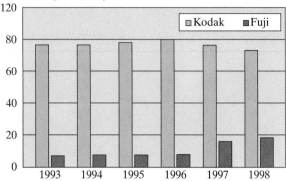

EXHIBIT 4 U.S. Market Street

Unit Sales (In mllions)

Source: Information Resources, Inc. ending 6/21/98.

that the Japanese government is backing the entire system in order to impede Kodak's success in the Japanese market. Exhibit 5 illustrates how the Japanese distribution system typically works.

On May 18, 1995, the Eastman Kodak Company asked the United States Trade Representative (USTR), the U.S. government official responsible for negotiating international trade disputes, to investigate whether the government of Japan had allowed anticompetitive practices to deny Kodak opportunities to sell film and color paper in Japan.

Kodak asked for this investigation under Section 301 of the U.S. Trade Act, a law that requires the USTR to determine whether trade practices by a foreign country are unreasonable and discriminate against U.S. exporters.

In a news conference in Tokyo in July, Kodak's Ira Wolf said that "We understand the risks inherent in going ahead with a 301 case, especially given the feelings of the average Japanese consumer about 301. But we decided there was no alternative . . . The Office of the Trade and Investment Ombudsman (Japan) is too weak and the Geneva-based World Trade Organization does not cover competition policy."[15]

Both companies claimed that injustices occurred in their respective market. Fisher said, "While Fuji competes with Kodak on a global basis, it makes virtually all of its profits in Japan, using those proceeds to finance low-price sales outside Japan."[16] He also said, "The Japan market, a large percentage, maybe 70 percent, is closed to us. And as a result, Fuji is allowed to have a profit sanctuary and amass a great deal of money, which they use to buy market share in Europe and in the United States."[17]

Fisher added, "All we are seeking is the opportunity to compete in an open market. We want resolution, not retaliation. Nor do we want market share targets. We want an

---

[13] *Supermarket Business* (February 1999): 47.

[14] R. Fannin, "Gold Rings of Smoke Rings?" *Marketing and Media Decisions,* 23 (September 1988): 64–70.

[15] *Kyodo News Service,* 26 July, 1995.

[16] *International Trade Reporter, BNA Inc.,* 7 June 1995.

[17] *Moneyline,* 2 August 1995.

EXHIBIT 5   The Japanese Film Distribution System

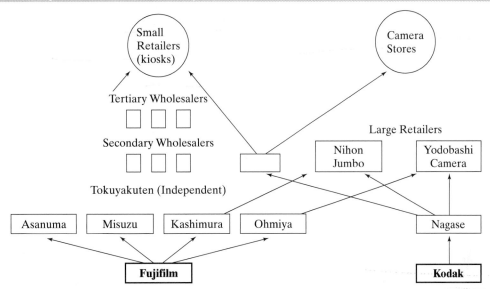

Source: Professor David P. Baron, *The Kodak-Fujifilm Trade Dispute, S-P-17,* Graduate School of Business, Stanford University, July 1998, p. 7.

end to illegal market barriers . . . Kodak sells world-class products. If given a chance, we believe that our products can compete successfully in any market. We have not had that chance in Japan."[18]

Fuji rebutted in a 588-page defense entitled, *Rewriting History, Kodak's Revisionist Account of the Japanese Consumer Photographic Market.* In the rebuttal, it cited that Kodak's problems in Japan stemmed from mismanagement and other factors, not unfair trade. Fujifilm president Minoru Ohnishi called Kodak's allegations a violation of business ethics and said that Kodak "shamelessly made false allegations" against Fujifilm.

Fuji drew upon some powerful quotes that people were making about the case. Some included, "The combined sales of these Eastman Kodak subsidiaries in Japan in 1994 was $1.2 billion, and Eastman Kodak is 43rd on the list of the largest foreign companies. Whatever its complaints, Eastman Kodak has a major position in the Japanese market. It has not been closed out."[19]

Another convincing statement came from former Kodak president Kay Whitmore. He stated, "I think there is no further barrier in the Japanese market for Kodak to proceed with its business in Japan. If there should be something, it would be only due to Kodak's own insufficient effort in the Japanese market."[20]

After nearly two and one half years of court rulings, the World Trade Organization in Geneva issued a "sweep-ing rejection of Kodak's complaints" about the film market in Japan. Fuji Photo Film U.S.A., Inc. President Osamu Inoue said, "The World Trade Organization failed to find even minimal evidence to support the U.S. case . . . After today, there can longer be doubt: imported film is widely available and competitively priced in Japan."[21]

THE EASTMAN KODAK COMPANY

For generations, employment at the Eastman Kodak Company meant job security. Rochester, New York's biggest and most paternalistic employer gave a sense that Kodak would never relinquish its U.S. market dominance to "foreign competition."

Kodak opened photography to the masses with inexpensive cameras and easy-to-use film. Kodak's name is one of the most recognized brand names in consumer goods in the world. Its slogan of "you push the button, we do the rest," enabled people to take the worry out of a complicated, scientific process and make photography accessible to nearly everyone who wanted to take pictures.

Kodak has been characterized as the leader in photography, an industry that has gone from rudimentary glass plates to cutting-edge digital images. Yet, Kodak realizes that for all of its historical success throughout the world, it must now increasingly include digital technology into the product mix to stay at the forefront of the photographic and imaging industry.

The climate at Kodak over the past few years has been well documented. Wall Street has been nervous due in part

[18] Eastman Kodak Company Press Release, 27 July 1996.
[19] James C. Abegglen and Peter S. Kirby, Gemini Consulting, *The Wall Street Journal Europe,* 4 March 1996.
[20] *Chemical Industry Journal* (Japan), 4 October 1990.
[21] *Edelman Public Relations Press Release,* 30 January 1998.

to soft sales in the United States, which stemmed from the battles with Fuji and a botched launch of the New Advanced Photo System. Massive layoffs (16,000), the strong U.S. dollar—meaning exports become less profitable and imports become more profitable for Kodak competitors—and sluggish growth in emerging markets have all contributed to Kodak's decline in market share. "We went from 20 percent growth to about 7 percent," says CEO George Fisher glumly.[22]

When Kodak hired Fisher in December 1993, he was hailed as the leader that would bring back the highest levels of success that recently had eluded Kodak. Indeed, Fisher has pared down costs, shed debt, sold off businesses not related to photography, and refocused goals, but analysts say that Kodak was slow to react when it could see the writing on the wall. According to Eugene Glazer, a *Fortis* Advisers analyst who never changed his mind that Kodak was in a mature business that couldn't grow: "Fisher moved too slowly and didn't instill a sense of urgency."[23]

Profits and sales at Kodak have been eroding throughout the 1990s. In 1998, sales were $13.4 billion as compared to $18.9 billion in 1990 (see Exhibit 6). Kodak's market share in 35-millimeter film has dropped; film prices have declined an average of 8 percent, which cuts into Kodak's profitability. The company is at risk of losing the title of world leader in the photographic industry. However, Kodak posted a net profit for the first quarter of 1999, bolstered by steady film sales growth in China and Brazil as well as in low-end digital cameras in the United States.[24]

Nielsen data indicate that film sales in the U.S. market rose 10 percent in the first quarter of 1999, as compared to the first quarter of 1998. Unit sales have increased even though neither Kodak nor Fuji Photo Film dropped prices in 1999. "They're all finally realizing that it is marketing, not price, that makes the difference," Ulysses Yannas, an analyst with Mercer, Bokert, Buckman & Reid, said.[25]

Perhaps George Fisher's vision is taking hold. He has been successful in attracting new talent to Kodak's close-knit Rochester community. He appointed Daniel Carp, a 27-year Kodak sales veteran in Canada, Latin America, and London, as president and chief operating officer in December 1996. Carp fully realizes the changing industry as well as emerging markets. To help foster change, Kodak admitted that they had to set up shop where the talent is. To that end, they have software operations in the Silicon Valley and marketing offices in Atlanta.

In the restructuring of Kodak, four main segments have emerged:

1. *The Consumer Imaging Segment:* traditional films, papers, processing, photofinishing, photographic chemicals, cameras (including one-time use), and the Advanced Photo System.
2. *The Kodak Professional Segment:* traditional films, papers, digital cameras, printers, scanners, and chemicals.
3. *The Health Imaging Segment:* medical films, chemicals, and processing equipment as well as services.
4. *Other (Digital and Applied Imaging) Imaging Segment:* motion pictures, audiovisual equipment, certain digital cameras, printers, microfilm products, application software, scanners, and other equipment.

While these segments serve the advanced countries of the world and keep Kodak current with competitors, Kodak recognizes that there are untapped consumers in emerging markets, such as China. In an interview with Carp in the February 1999 issue of *Photo Marketing,* Carp explained, "In terms of strategy, it's evolving just as we predicted. We are building plants that will make world-class products to supply the domestic market. . . . The second part is to build a team to get the word out to consumers that photography is fun. . . . The third part is to build the infrastructure so it's a good experience for the consumer."[26]

| EXHIBIT 6   1998 Kodak Annual Report |

Fiscal Year-End: December

Income Statement ($mil)

	1998	*1997*	*1996*	*1995*
Sales	13,406	14,538	15,968	14,980
Cost of Goods Sold	7,293	8,130	8,326	7,962
SG & A Expense	3,303	6,432	5,438	5,093
Net Income	1,390	5	1,288	1,252
EPS Primary ($)	4.30	0.01	3.82	3.67
EPS Fully Diluted ($)	4.24	0.01	3.82	3.67

Assets ($mil)

	1998	*1997*	*1996*	*1995*
Cash	457	728	1,777	1,764
Receivables	2,527	2,271	2,738	3,145
Inventories	1,424	1,252	1,575	1,660
Current Assets	5,599	5,475	6,965	7,309
Total Assets	14,733	13,145	14,438	14,477

Equity ($mil)

	1998	*1997*	*1996*	*1995*
Common Stock Equity	3,988	3,161	4,734	5,121
Shares Outstanding (mil.)	323.3	323.1	331.8	345.9

[22] "Why Kodak Still Isn't Fixed," *Fortune,* 11 May 1998.
[23] Ibid.
[24] Claudia Deutsch, *The New York Times,* 17 April 1999.
[25] Ibid.
[26] *Photo Marketing* (February 1999): 55.

EXHIBIT 7	Ratio of Households to Rolls of Film Consumed			
Countries	Japan United States	Australia Canada Korea France Germany United Kingdom	Italy Mexico Brazil Thailand	Indonesia China Russia India
Number of households in these regions	145,000,000	114,000,000	92,000,000	607,000,000
Average rolls of film consumed per household year	8.2	4.6	2.2	.5
Total rolls of film	1,189,000,000	524,400,000	202,400,000	303,500,000

Source: Kodak Annual Report 1998.

Kodak believes that the future of photography, in addition to advancing technology, is in getting more people to take pictures. To that end, it states in its 1998 annual report: "What if households in developing markets shot a full roll of Kodak film each year? The gain would be immense."[27]

FUJI PHOTO FILM CO., LTD.

Fuji Photo Film Co., Ltd. was founded in 1934 and is headquartered in Tokyo, Japan. If one person can claim to be the architect of Fuji's growth, it's Minoru Ohnishi. At the age of 55, he took over the company in 1980, making him Fuji's youngest president ever. It was under Ohnishi's reign that salespeople were encouraged to spend time with distributors and build relationships. As Japanese insiders say, "One cup of sake means 100,000 yen (of business)."

Fuji Photo Film has always prided itself on having the technology to produce superior products to drive sales. The company has consistently spent 7 percent of sales on research and development to maintain a competitive advantage. Because of this investment, Fuji was able to introduce faster film with brighter colors (400 speed, 1600 speed), which is what the professional and serious amateur photographers were asking for in the 1970s. In 1986, Fuji was the first to introduce one-time-use cameras. By the time Kodak caught up with the technology, Fuji established a lead in one-time-use cameras that Kodak never experienced with traditional film.

This attention to detail and ability to occasionally outpace Kodak technologically has endeared Fuji to the professional market and served as a stepping-stone to build creditability in the larger amateur market. Originally, Fuji started out in the U.S. market in 1965 as a private-brand supplier. In 1972, Fuji began to market film under its brand name and, after remaining a very small player in the shadow of Kodak in the United States, Fuji's initial success came with the sponsorship of the 1984 Olympic Games in Los Angeles. Every year since, Fuji has been slowly and quietly progressing in the U.S. market. "The fact that Fuji has made inroads in the U.S. has surprised even Kodak," says Sugaya Aiko, an analyst at Kleinwort Benson in Tokyo. "That is one reason why they are fighting back in every other market."[28]

"Fuji's greatest strength is that they always make sure that consumers are ready to buy their new products, and they actually get the products to the consumers," says Toby Williams, an analyst at SBC Warburg in Tokyo.[29]

As a company, Fuji Photo Film has three core business systems:

1. *Imaging System:* color films, motion picture film, cameras, magnetic audiovisual media, electronic imaging, and equipment.
2. *Photofinishing System:* photofinishing equipment, paper, and chemicals.
3. *Information System:* graphic systems, medical diagnostic systems, office automation systems, industrial materials, and data-recording media.

Fuji's long-term strategy in the United States is to produce locally but compete globally. "Globalization through localization" translates to producing as much film and paper on U.S. soil as possible to avoid troublesome trade disputes, become more responsive to demanding U.S. accounts needs, and keep overall costs to a minimum. In 1987, Fuji produced just 3.5 percent of its goods outside of Japan; today the figure is roughly 40 percent, with manufacturing plants in the United States, the Netherlands, Germany, France, and the People's Republic of China.[30]

Like Kodak, Fuji has to stay competitive with Silicon Valley to produce state-of-the-art digital products. To that

---

[27] Eastman Kodak Annual Report 1998.

[28] *Asia Week,* 5 July 1996.
[29] *Fortune,* 11 May 1998.
[30] Fuji Photo Film Co., Ltd. 1998, p. 16.

end, Fuji established FUJIFILM Software (California), Inc. in October 1998.

Fuji is one of the leanest Japanese companies. In the past 10 years, Fuji's sales have almost doubled, yet the number of staff in Japan remains almost flat. Fuji's worldwide output per employee is $285,000, while Kodak's—even after extensive layoffs—is $155,000. It is this type of drive that has maintained Fuji's double-digit sales growth each year for the last decade (see Exhibit 8).

Still Fuji's drive to lead the industry has not come without a price. "As a company Fuji has been so obsessed with building its brand, improving product quality, and investing in research and development and marketing that it has neglected areas like profitability," says Sugaya Aiko of Kleinwort Benson. "Payouts have been far lower than Kodak because they focused too much on long-term goals," according to Sugaya.[31]

With world-class product quality in the balance for both Kodak and Fuji, both are poised to battle it out for global dominance. "There are two giants in this field and each wants to be bigger than the other," according to Su-gaya. "You'd have to spend billions of dollars on research and development, marketing and distribution and even then, there's no guarantee you could catch up with these two."[32]

CONCLUSION

Based on Kodak's 1999 first-quarter earnings, it is too early to predict Kodak's status. However, Fujifilm is a formidable opponent. To Kodak's surprise, statistics indicate that those consumers who have tried Fuji stay with it as long as there is a price advantage.

Generally speaking, the industry, Kodak and Fuji included, does not want to lower price for fear that it will turn this industry into a commodity business. Healthy margins are desirable for everyone involved in the industry at the consumers' expense. The formula of $V = B/P$ clearly is crystallized as consumers enjoy an increased value. For the past two years the benefits remained constant, but prices have dropped. The longevity of this trend is a major concern.

Domestically, new products such as the Advanced Photo System, digital cameras, and Internet services are the keys to increasing usage, which will invigorate this mature market. Increased advertising and educated consumers will also drive sales for everyone involved.

From a global perspective, Kodak and Fuji are vying for hegemony in another battle, this time in emerging markets, specifically in China. Both are poised to implement strategies that will give them market share in this vast region of the world. Generally speaking, Kodak will concentrate on push marketing, market share, and cross promotion with its photoprocessing network, while Fuji will focus on innovative new products, price advantages over Kodak, and research and development.

EXHIBIT 8 Fuji Photo Film Co. Ltd. 1998 Annual Report

Fiscal Year-End: March 31
(Assumes Y132 = U.S.$1, 3/31/98)
Income Statement ($mil)

	1998	1997	1996
Sales	10,439	9,485	8,219
Income before taxes	1,230	1,214	993
Net income	672	646	552
Per share of common stock			
Net income	1.31	1.25	1.07
Cash dividends	0.17	0.16	0.15
R&D expenses	613	575	554
Acquisition of fixed assets	854	737	571
Depreciation	589	558	519
Total assets at year-end	16,148	15,041	13,991
Total shareholders' equity	10,837	10,188	9,488
Number of employees	36,580	33,154	29,903

DISCUSSION QUESTIONS

1. How can Kodak protect its strategic advantage from competitors, especially Fuji?
2. How can Kodak anticipate market changes faster and react accordingly?
3. What are Fuji's chances for future growth?
4. What are some disadvantages that Fuji has to overcome?
5. Should both Kodak and Fuji be concerned over digital integration into the silver halide industry?

[31] *Asia Week*, 5 July 1996.

[32] Ibid.

Parker Pen Co. (A)
International Marketing Strategy Review

> *It is circumstance and proper timing that give an action its character*
> *and make it either good or bad.*
> —AGESILAUS

INTRODUCTION

The meeting at sunny Palm Beach concluded with nary a whimper of dissent from its participants. After years of being run as a completely decentralized company whose managers in all corners of the world enjoyed a high degree of flexibility, Parker Pen Co., of Janesville, Wisconsin, was forced to reexamine itself. The company had enjoyed decade after decade of success until the early 1980s. By this time, Parker faced strong competitive threats and a deteriorating internal situation. A new management team was brought in from outside the company—an unprecedented step for what had been until then an essentially family-run business. At the March 1984 Palm Beach meeting, this new group of decision makers would outline a course of action that would hopefully set Parker back on a path to success.

The men behind the new strategy were supremely confident of its chances for success—and with good reason. Each was recognized as a highly skilled practitioner of international business and their combined extensive experience gave them an air of invincibility. They had been recruited from larger companies, had left high-paying, rewarding jobs, and each had come to Janesville with a grand sense of purpose. For decades, Parker had been a dominant player in the pen industry. In the early 1980s, however, the company had seen its market share dwindle to a mere 6 percent and, in 1982, net income plunged a whopping 60 percent.

To reverse this decline, Parker recruited James Peterson, an executive vice president at R. J. Reynolds, as the new president and CEO. Peterson hired Manville Smith as president of the writing instruments group at Parker. Smith, who was born in Ecuador and had a broad international background, came from 3M where he had been appointed division president at the tender age of 30. Richard Swart was vice president/marketing of the writing instruments

group. He spent 11 years at the advertising agency BBDO and was an expert on marketing planning and theory. Jack Marks was head of writing instruments advertising. Marks came to Parker from Gillette, where, among other things, he assisted in the worldwide marketing of Paper Mate pens. Rounding out the team was Carlos Del Nero, manager of global marketing planning, who brought with him considerable international experience at Fisher-Price. Each of these men was convinced that Parker would right itself by following the plan they unveiled at Palm Beach.

A BRIEF HISTORY OF PARKER PEN
The "Rolls Royce" of the Pen Industry

The Parker name has been identified with pens since 1888 when George S. Parker delighted ink-splotched pen users everywhere by introducing a leakproof fountain model called the Parker Lucky Curve. Parker Pen would eventually blossom into America's, if not the world's, largest and best-known pen maker. Parker's products, which would eventually include ballpoint pens, felt-tip pens, desk sets, mechanical pencils, inks, leads, erasers, and, of course, the fountain pen, were also known for their high price tags. In 1921, for example, Parker introduced the Duofold pen. The Duofold, even though it was comparable to other $3 pens on the market, was extravagantly priced at $7. Parker was able to charge a premium price because of its reputation for quality and style, and its skill in positioning products in the top price segment.

Parker's position as America's leading pen maker was solidified during the years when the pen was mainly viewed as a gift item. High school and college graduates in the 1940s and 1950s, for example, were quite likely to receive a Parker "51" fountain pen (priced at $12.50) commemorating their achievement. Indeed, it was with a "51" that General Douglas MacArthur signed the Japanese Peace Treaty in 1945. Parker's stylish products and high profile name would keep it at the top of the pen market until the late sixties when American competitors A.T. Cross and Sheaffer, as well as a few foreign brands, knocked them out of first place once and for all.

Of course, Parker would not have lost its hold on the market had it not made some oversights along the way. In addition to a more competitive environment, Parker failed to come to terms with a fundamental change in the pen market—the development of the disposable, ballpoint market. When Parker unveiled the $25 "75" pen in 1963, it showed that it remained committed to supplying high-priced pens to the upper end of the market. As the 1960s wore on, a clear trend toward cheap ballpoint and soft-tip pens developed. Meanwhile, Parker's only ultimately successful addition to its product range in the late sixties was the "75" Classic line, yet another high-priced pen.

A Brief Flirtation with Low-Priced Pens

Parker did, however, make an effort to compete in the lower price segment of the market in the late 1960s only to see it fail. In an attempt to capitalize on the trend toward inexpensive pens, Parker introduced the T-Ball Jotter, priced at $1.98. The success of the Jotter led it to move even further down the price ladder when it acquired Eversharp. Whereas the Jotter had given Parker reason to believe it could make the shift from pricy pens to cheap pens with little or no difficulty, the Eversharp experience proved to be different. George Parker, a grandnephew of the company's founder and president of Parker at the time, stated the reasons for the Eversharp failure, as well as its consequences:

> All the market research surveys said go lower, go lower, go lower, that's where the business is. So I said, 'Go lower? Fine. But we don't know how.' We bought Eversharp and tried to run it ourselves, and we couldn't do it. Our people just couldn't think in terms of big units, and they didn't know how to sell people on the lower-priced end of the business—grocers, supermarkets, rack jobbers. The result was, Bic and Paper Mate were cleaning up in the lower-priced end, Cross in the high, and Parker was getting squeezed in the middle. Volume was going up, but our costs went up faster, and our profits were squeezed.[1]

The 1970s: The Illusion of Success

Despite the difficulties Parker encountered when it left its niche in the upper end of the pen market, the company experienced a healthy period of growth and profitability for most of the 1970s. Demand for its products remained strong, and its worldwide markets expanded significantly due to a rise in consumer income and increasing literacy rates in much of the Third World. Parker also chose to diversify during this decade, and its most noteworthy acquisition, Manpower, Inc., proved to be a very strong asset. In 1975, when it acquired Manpower, a temporary-help firm, Parker was the slightly more profitable of the two. With the boom in temporary services in the late seventies and early eighties, however, Manpower eclipsed Parker in sales and earnings and eventually subsidized its parent company during down periods.

Why did Parker fall from its position of leadership in the writing instrument market? There were many reasons, and one of the most important was the weakening of the

U.S. dollars. At its peak, Parker accounted for half of all U.S. exports of writing instruments and 80 percent of its total sales came from 154 foreign countries. Parker was especially strong in Europe, most particularly in the United Kingdom. When sales in the strong European currencies were translated into dollars, Parker earned huge profits.

The downside of a weak dollar, however, was that it gave Parker the illusion that it was a well-run company. In fact, throughout the 1970s, Parker was a model of inefficiency. Manufacturing facilities were dated and inefficient. Production was so erratic that the marketing department often had no idea what type of pens they would be selling from year to year or even month to month. Under the leadership of George Parker, nothing was done by company headquarters to update these facilities or to develop new products. As a result, subsidiaries and distributors around the world saw fit to develop their own products. By the end of George Parker's reign, the company's product line included 500 writing instruments.

That distant subsidiaries would have the leeway to make such decisions was not at all unusual at Parker, for it had long been known as one of the most globally decentralized companies in the world. Decentralization, in fact, was something that Parker took pride in and considered to be vital to its success as a multinational. Yet it was this very concept that Peterson and his new management team would hold to be responsible for much of what ailed Parker Pen.

PARKER'S GLOBAL OPERATIONS BEFORE PETERSON

In addition to having a hand in manufacturing and product-line decisions, Parker's subsidiaries developed their own marketing strategies. More than 40 different advertising agencies promoted Parker pens in all the corners of the globe. When Peterson came to Parker, he was proudly informed that the company was a "federation" of autonomous geographical units. The downside to the "federation" concept, Peterson thought, was that home country management often lacked the information needed to make and coordinate basic business decisions. Control was so completely decentralized that Parker didn't even know how many pens it was selling by the time Peterson and his group arrived.

On the other hand, decentralization obviously had its positive aspects, most noticeably in the field of advertising. Pens mean different things to different people. Whereas Europeans are more likely to choose a pen based on its style and feel, a consumer from a lesser-developed country in the seventies viewed the pen as nothing less than a badge of literacy. In addition, tastes varied widely from country to country. The French, for example, remained attached to the fountain pen. Scandinavians, for their part, showed a marked preference for the ballpoint. The logic behind having so many different advertising agencies was that, even if it appeared to be somewhat inefficient, in the end the company was better off from a sales standpoint.

---

[1] *Forbes,* 1 October 1973.

Some of the individual advertising agencies were able to devise excellent, imaginative campaigns that struck a responsive chord among their local audiences. One example was the Lowe Howard-Spink agency in London. The Parker U.K. division became the company's most profitable during the tenure of the Lowe agency. An example of its creativity is an ad entitled "Rediscover the lost art of the insult." Gracing the ad is a picture of a dead plumber, on his back, with a giant Parker pen protruding from his heart. Part of the text is as follows:

Do you know plumbers who never turn up?

Hairdressers who missed their vocations as butchers?

Drycleaners who make your stains disappear—and your clothes with them?

Today, we at Parker give you the chance to get your own back.

Not only are we offering a beautiful new pen called the Laque which owes its deep lustre to a Chinese technique 2000 years old, but we are attempting to revive something that went out when the telephone came in.

The well-armed, witty, malicious dart.[2]

---

[2] *Ad Age,* 2 June 1986.

Although the Parker U.K. division was a success, however, the company's general inefficiencies, loss of market share, and lack of strategic direction were finally revealed in the early 1980s with the rise of the U.S. dollar. Parker's financial decline was even more precipitous than the dollar's increase. When the huge 1982 losses were registered, Peterson was brought in from R. J. Reynolds to try and turn things around for Parker. He decided that every aspect of the company needed to be closely examined, not the least of which was Parker's decentralization of global operations.

DISCUSSION QUESTIONS (A)

1. What would you do if you were in James Peterson's shoes in January 1982?
2. What changes, if any, would you make in Parker's marketing strategy?
3. Which aspects of Parker's structure would you discard? Which would you keep?
4. Assume that you are James Peterson and you have just hired a new management team composed of highly qualified executives from outside companies. You and your new team are convinced that you have the solution to Parker's problems but there are many holdovers who disagree with you. How would you implement your plan? To what extent would you incorporate the views of Parker management into your plan?

Parker Pen Co. (B)
Parker Goes Global

> *We will be creating more news in the next two years than we have in the past ten.*
> —JAMES PETERSON
> *July 1982*

James Peterson relished the chance to be the top man at Parker Pen. He spent 24 years at Pillsbury and had a taste of what it was like to be at the helm of a corporation when he rose to the rank of president, the number two power spot in the company. At R. J. Reynolds, he was an executive vice president—an influential position, to be sure, but not one that afforded him the freedom of movement that he would have liked. When he was brought to Parker in January 1982, Peterson, then 54, had finally had the chance to run a company. All the theories he held to be true would be tested. All the lessons he had learned after some 30 years of practical business experience—much of it in international operations—would now be applied.

His years at R. J. Reynolds had convinced him of the superiority of global marketing, which he understood to mean standardized product and promotion strategies the whole world over. This view made him unalterably opposed to the loose structure that had characterized Parker Pen before his arrival. In the opinion of Peterson, there was absolutely no way that any company operating in the modern world would be able to survive such disarray. That a subsidiary thousands of miles away could decide not only what products it would manufacture but also how they would market them ran counter to everything Peterson believed.

Peterson quickly moved to remold Parker Pen in his own image. In addition to too much decentralization, Peterson thought Parker lacked "a good enunciation of business philosophy." According to Peterson, "every good company has to have one." In order to correct this problem, Peterson devised an eight-point statement of his management philosophy and had it translated into more than 40 languages and sent in letter form to Parker managers all over the world. The statement contained such phrases as, "There is no substitute for quality," and, "Like most managers, I don't like surprises." The letters concluded by saying: "As I get to meet each of you in the months ahead, I will be discussing this business philosophy with you and asking you how you have used it."[1]

THE DISMANTLING OF DECENTRALIZATION: FROM 40 AGENCIES TO 1

The core of Peterson's revitalization efforts would be directed at dismantling the geographical organization that Parker had evolved into over the years. He slashed the product line from 500 to the 100 most profitable items. The manufacturing function was consolidated, greatly reducing the number of units produced overseas. As for what products would be manufactured, that was to be strictly decided by the management team at the Janesville headquarters. Of course, the manufacturing facilities themselves would have to be updated, for no longer could the production department be allowed to dictate to marketing executives exactly what kind of products it would be selling. None of these measures in and of themselves was startling—each addressed problems that needed to be corrected. However, when Peterson decided to get rid of Parker's 40-odd advertising agencies in favor of one "world-class agency," more than a few eyebrows were raised.

The logic behind the decision to go with one advertising agency (Ogilvy & Mather) was consistent with Peterson's desire to make Parker Pen a global marketing corporation. With one agency instead of 40, not only could money be saved, but strategies could be coordinated on a global scale. One problem, however, was that formerly productive agencies such as Lowe Howard-Spink in London were fired. This had a devastating effect on morale at Parker U.K., the company's most profitable subsidiary which had in effect been subsidizing the same American division that was now telling it how to advertise.

"THE WORLD'S NO. 1 PEN COMPANY"

Even though Parker had experienced many problems before Peterson arrived, the company was still very proud of its tradition as a leading producer of "quality writing instruments." Of course, this pride was sometimes translated into overblown statements such as, "Parker is the world's No. 1 pen company." This indeed was the party line at Parker even though it was paid little more than lip service. When Manville Smith arrived in 1982, he commissioned a study to see just how important Parker was. His findings shocked him: Parker had only a 6 percent share of the global pen market and it didn't even attempt to par-

ticipate in a segment that was responsible for 65 percent of all sales of pens in the world—that is, pens that sold for less than $3.

The new management team wanted to make Parker more than just a fictitious number-one company. In order to recapture market share, Parker would have to participate in the lower end of the market—the same area that George Parker himself had so hastily abandoned in the late 1960s. A new $15 million state-of-the-art plant would be built whose main function would be to manufacture the Vector, a roller-ball pen selling for $2.98. The Vector was Manville Smith's pet project. Using a new automated line at Parker's new plant, Smith calculated that the Vector could be produced for 27 cents per unit and therefore generate huge profits for the company. After the Vector, Smith planned to plunge even deeper into the low-price market with the Itala, an even cheaper model that would be Parker's first disposable pen.

THE FIRST RUMBLINGS OF DISSENT: GEORGE PARKER

Although George Parker was still formally the chairman of Parker Pen, he was expected to lead a quiet, charmed life in Marco Island, Florida, and never to be heard from again. In fact, George Parker was paying very close attention to the new developments in the company that bore his name, and he was none too happy. As his earlier remarks might suggest, he was scornful of a strict market research approach to the pen business. He also took pride in Parker Pen's autonomous federation system that provided a high degree of flexibility to the company's many subsidiaries. Even more disturbing to him was the planned foray into the lower depths of the marketplace, as he might put it. Cheap pens were beneath Parker Pen, in his opinion, and nothing could be more disgraceful than a disposable pen bearing his name. What were they manufacturing anyway, garbage bags?

Compounding George Parker's displeasure was his sincere dislike for James Peterson, whom he dubbed "motormouth." To him, Peterson was the embodiment of everything that was wrong with the new Parker Pen. The grandnephew of the company's founder still had many well-placed friends in the company, and his constant criticism of the new management team probably did little to aid their cause.

PROBLEMS: FINANCIAL LOSSES, SMITH GETS FIRED, ONE WORLD MARKETING FAILS

Despite all the complaints from George Parker, Peterson's major problems lay elsewhere. The strong dollar that had exposed so many of his company's weaknesses got even stronger. Recession was a worldwide plague. The costs of new plant development were not absorbed by profits and the company lost $13.6 million in fiscal 1983 (as shown in Exhibit 1). Still, Peterson had the luxury of time on his side,

---

[1] *Ad Age,* 26 July 1982.

EXHIBIT 1 Parker Pen Co. Selected Operating Results

Year Ended Feb. 28	Revenues (Millions)	Net Income	Earnings	Dividends (Per Share)	Range
1985	$843.7	$5.4	$0.32	$0.52	21–13
1984	708.8	11.8	0.70	0.52	21–12
1983	635.3	d13.6	d0.80	0.52	17–11
1982	679.1	15.7	0.92	0.50	24–14
1981	723.2	37.7	2.23	0.44	26–14

d = Deficit.

Balance sheet as of June 30, 1985:
   Current assets: $284.5 million
   Current liabilities: $239.5 million
   Current ratio: 1.1-to-1
   Long-term debt: $27.1 million
   Common shares: 17,635,000
   Book value: $7.65

Source: Annual reports.

since he had little more than one full year under his belt. One more year like 1983, however, and he was gone.

In Peterson's opinion, only a full-fledged global marketing effort could save Parker. At the March 1984 Palm Beach meeting, it was decided that Parker would participate "in every viable segment of the writing instrument business." In addition, it was declared that, "The concept of marketing by centralized direction has been discussed and consensus was reached." The management team, filled with a sense of purpose, then set out to achieve its lofty goals.

There remained one major problem: Parker's new plant was proving to be a failure. The plant was not functional for the 1983 Christmas season, costing the company millions of dollars in sales. Even as Peterson and his group were working round-the-clock to see its strategy through, the computer-automated plant which was supposed to spearhead Parker's drive into the lower end of the market, broke down repeatedly. With automation having failed, the company was forced to hire labor again and its costs skyrocketed. Manville Smith, who had placed his name next to the fully automated Vector project, was fired by Peterson as a result.

Smith's departure was important because he was the only member of the management team that held out for local advertising flexibility. Smith had worked closely with Ogilvy & Mather (O & M) on Parker's first worldwide advertising campaign. At Smith's urging O & M devised a campaign that allowed for some degree of local flexibility. When Smith left, however, Peterson took over the advertising reins and pushed very hard for "one-look" advertising and the results were disastrous.

The fashion in which Peterson promoted his advertising policy was enough to alienate once and for all those remaining managers that supported his efforts. A procla-

mation issued from the Janesville office and sent across the globe headquarters stated that: "Advertising for Parker pens [no matter model or mode] will be based on a common creative strategy and positioning. . . . The worldwide advertising theme, 'Make your mark with a Parker,' has been adopted. . . . [It] will utilize similar graphic layout and photography. It will utilize an agreed-upon typeface. It will utilize the approved Parker logo/graphic design. It will be adapted from centrally supplied materials."

The new advertising campaign was indeed rigidly controlled. Subsidiaries were sent their materials and told to get on with it. Managers abroad were seen as simple implementers of the global marketing strategy with little or no input. The problem was that many of them realized right away that the new advertising campaign wouldn't work in their markets. In fact, the campaign really didn't work anywhere. Jack Marks would later qualify it as "lowest common denominator advertising" that "tried to say something to everybody, and didn't say anything to anybody."

The last to admit failure was Peterson himself, who ignored all evidence and tried to move forward with a second wave of global advertising in January of 1985, this time for the Vector, which had finally made it off the production line. By this time, however, Peterson's position was terminally weakened. Production problems persisted, morale was low, resentment of the management team was high and reaction to yet another generic campaign was so negative that Peterson felt compelled to resign.

POSTSCRIPT: "GLOBAL MARKETING IS DEAD"

The successor to Peterson as CEO was Mitchell Fromstein, president of what once was Parker's Manpower subsidiary.

Since it was purchased in 1975 by Parker, Manpower continued to grow to the point where it was far more profitable than its parent and, indeed, subsidized it for several years. Manpower would wind up taking over Parker, finally selling it to a group of British investors in 1986.

Fromstein was an implacable foe of Peterson's. Manpower was as international as Parker Pen, and Fromstein had his own views as to how an international business should be run. When he assumed control of Parker in January 1985, he gathered the company's country managers in Janesville and told them: "Global marketing is dead. You're free again."[2]

DISCUSSION QUESTIONS (B)

1. Why did Peterson's global strategy fail?
2. What lessons can be drawn from the decline and fall of Parker Pen?

———————
[2] *Ad Age*, 2 June 1986.

Parker Pen Co. (C)

*Global Marketing Strategy: An Interview with Dr. Dennis Thomas[1]
of the Berol Corporation[2]*

Charles Anderer[3]: I would first like to thank you for taking the time to share your views on global marketing and Parker Pen in this interview.

Dennis Thomas: It's my pleasure.

CA: I would like to start out by asking you a question about an article that we both have read.[4] Do you agree with the notion that the big issue today is not whether to go global but how to tailor the global marketing concept to each business?

DT: If it's an either-or proposition, I am broadly in agreement with the proposition. I believe that there are relatively few major markets where the local conditions are so self-contained, so capable of being kept self-contained, and so different, either for cultural or other kinds of reasons, that the underlying, increasing level of similarity that is coming into most major marketplaces, as opposed to the nuances of necessary local difference, cannot form the bedrock of acceptable product offerings, positionings and what you have. Also, the economies of scale and the relative size of self-contained markets, in and of themselves, are of decreasing appeal other than for a small business which chooses to remain small. But in many industries and many marketplaces, the products which adequately serve market needs increasingly have within them either outright commodities or commodity-like ingredients if they are likely to be products that are positioned in a marketplace over a period of decades rather than over a few fash-

ion cycles of a few months or a few years. . . . The real question is: What is the appropriate international scale for the business and what is the appropriate international scale for the underlying marketplace?

CA: What forces do you see behind the increasing similarities of markets? Telecommunications is one that comes to mind.

DT: Sure. We are much more aware, whether we are conscious of it or not, of what other parts of the world look like. . . . Broadly speaking, people behave as consumers who may be appealed to in the same kinds of ways. Whether they are at level two or level four of a Maslow hierarchy or any kind of structure you would like to adopt, we are becoming more steadily accepting of the fact that they are likely to go through the same kinds of progressions. The form that a status need may take in one society as opposed to another may be somewhat different, but status needs exist in both. How well developed they are, whether people may exercise them, how many people, in what kinds of ways, and what they will be looking for—those are all to my mind subsidiary kinds of questions, but you know it's going to be there.

You do, also, have the fact of increasing international communities. People travel, they go from one culture and from one history to another. The world is becoming more interrelated, either directly through people transfer or indirectly through visual transfer, on a much more regular basis. Something that has already happened in Tokyo will be there for you to see on the 6 o'clock news. It sounds as though it's a long way between that phenomenon and whether or not you can sell the same pen in Japan and the United States. But I don't think it's as far-fetched as many have historically supposed when you stop and think about it.

There is no reason why the intervention of water should be a cutoff point between groups of people and their often similar characteristics.

———————
[1] President, The Berol Corporation, Danbury, Connecticut.
[2] The Berol Corporation manufactures a variety of office products including a wide range of writing instruments.
[3] Case writer and researcher, the Leading Edge Case Study Project, Lubin Graduate School of Business, Pace University.
[4] J. A. Quelch and E. J. Hoff, "Customizing Global Marketing," *Harvard Business Review* (May–June 1986): 59–68.

CA: When you look at recent developments in the global business arena such as Rupert Murdoch's bid to establish a global communications empire and the growing concentration of the world's advertising agencies as evidenced by the rash of mergers and acquisitions which culminated with Saatchi & Saatchi's purchase of Ted Bates Worldwide, do you see an irreversible trend toward the globalization of business and, if so, what do you make of it?

DT: There probably is a trend and, certainly, the existence of a large number of international unifiers in various forms of communication is going to make it more possible for companies to entertain the notion of doing business internationally. Whether, however, businesses will look for over-homogenization and try to bring it about to make their own lives easier or simply to see a reflection of their own set of values cast on a worldwide stage remains to be seen. That's an area where I'm a little puzzled and, perhaps, a little concerned at this point in time. There are important shades, colors, and nuances in individual countries or regions or cultures whether those cultures happen to coincide or not with international boundaries. I am also not so sure that there won't be an encouragement or an enticement to make Parker pen type mistakes.

The economic incentive to homogenize the world is indeed very strong. It is also probably the natural route for the northern hemisphere in particular to counter demographics and broad scale cultural differences. There is more appeal to continue to do as you have done particularly if [the firm] has evolved to a "higher level." To look to do the same thing somewhere else is somehow more appealing than to go back two or three paces and start over in an emerging country or society and be successful doing the things you did ten or fifteen years ago.

Pure volume and demographic growth is likely to be much more concentrated in the southern hemisphere and the far east over the next twenty years or so. However, there are more concerns about political and societal stability in those kinds of arenas. They are more prone to political and economic volatility than they once were and they are no longer easy to colonize in the economic sense. They're more likely to pinch whatever technology they need, start their own businesses, and kick you out than used to be the case. You can't sit back and control the world from New York or London or Frankfurt as once you could. It's a more unruly place, therefore, we prefer to deal with safer and more secure boundaries which are spread across the northern hemisphere with digressions into the south when we consider it relatively safe. The trend that you've identified is partly a response to this way of thinking and that's how you can make the economic case for continuing to do what you are doing.

CA: In addition to making developing nations more technologically sophisticated, what are the broader implications of worldwide availability of and easy access to advanced technologies?

DT: Since there is more access to technology and much less in the way of protection and security around technologies and, because of the sheer length of life of many technologies and many basic product categories, the opportunity for capital substitution in place of human substitution has to a large extent already taken place. Therefore, there is a more even access to the various forms of production advantage—whether it be economies of scale, optimum size of plant and configuration, or an optimum form of technology. Quite simply, the thresholds for entry into many kinds of industries are not that great. And, certainly, the ability to maintain exclusivity or erect boundaries is nowhere near what it used to be. You cannot keep people out.

CA: Static demographics and markets, worldwide technological parity and converging product quality make it more important than ever to have a handle on your costs and to be efficient. Are we moving toward the day when only the largest and most highly efficient firms can afford to compete internationally?

DT: Yes. Unless you set out to be, and deliberately restrain your ambitions to very clearly identified and defensible niches of one kind or another. It's a very, I think, competent strategist and manager who can make a success of a totally niche-based strategy. Not many people can do that. Most companies simply cannot afford to.

I think you can afford to internationally extend some of the segmentation that you have already domestically achieved. For example, if you've got a particular product portfolio that has appeal in a certain market segment that you've historically concentrated on within your domestic base, it is sometimes easier to transfer that segmentation geographically than to add other segments to it domestically. By the same token, it is perhaps easier to extend yourself horizontally than to move vertically. Certainly to move up. It may not be easier to move down, as many people point out when evaluating Parker Pen's strategy.

I don't think that many people operating in product fields where differentiation is possible yet not, for very long, sustainable either in terms of an individual product or a product category could follow a niche-based strategy. It's only the real late arrival to a market that, by default, has to pursue such a strategy. For the other players, I think there has to be a combination of capability to operate at the low-cost end and forms of niche-differentiation either in terms of market boundaries (segmentation) or in terms of product characteristics. Although the latter, as I say, are more difficult to sustain over time.

CA: Besides the problem of moving down the product line in the case of Parker Pen, many observers felt that the company's drastic shift from a largely decentralized organization to the more tightly controlled version that is necessary when implementing a classic global marketing strategy automatically ruled out the strategy's chances for success because it resulted in too much loss of employee morale on the local level. Do you see this as a problem in any company undergoing that same shift from a decentralized to a centralized organization?

DT: A lot depends on how you do it. The time scale that you negotiate to achieve [the strategic shift] with, either with your board or with your stockholders as opposed to with your managers, goes a long way toward determining success or failure. To achieve some of those things in terms of internal human scale often requires a longer commitment than might be available in terms of an external financial scale. There is probably an underlying sentiment that says, satisfy those external audiences and see if you can't sit on top of the internal ones . . . and, yes, if these guys don't like it, presumably there are others that are prepared to operate within that kind of a changed culture.

But I believe that, in Parker's instance, they probably put an impossible time scale on themselves to achieve the desired degree of change in acceptable human terms without precipitating unnecessary turnover. You see, a certain amount of turnover is not only to be expected but is probably necessary because the kinds of values and skills that you've looked for and rewarded in the truly decentralized operation may not be as valid or as useful in the more integrated approach. Particularly if you give the pendulum a big yank and a swing towards the other end you can expect the sheer momentum to throw people off from side to side. It's really a question of how many people did you lose that you didn't want to or that, at the end of the day, you couldn't afford to? This is more the measure of success or failure in implementing that kind of strategy.

And, finally, by what audacity do you believe that your insights, analytical abilities, creative talents, administrative skills and business acumen combine to make such a decision failure-proof? For the decision to come from an individual or a very small group of individuals, some of whom might be very new to that industry and to that marketplace . . . you've got to have a lot of reasons to justify having self-confidence in that small a pool of talent than what might have been available out of a goodly proportion of your previously successful decentralized managers. But if you have a French operation, for example, that had been losing money for quite a period of time or about whose management you have questions concerning their capability, you would have those questions whether the company was centralized or decentralized. The question is: How flexible are some of those domestic managers? They may learn, grow, and develop in some extraordinary ways by being exposed to the international world. So it's not that they're always right and the center is always wrong either.

CA: It seems as if Parker not only gave itself very little time to accomplish its transition from decentralization to centralization but that it also engaged in draconian measures on the operational side. I speak here of dropping all 40 of its advertising agencies in favor of a single "world class" agency. Can a single agency hope to be all things to

all people or, in the case of Parker, do the job more effectively than a multitude of agencies?

DT: It depends on the advertising program that they come up with, which in turn depends on the degree of internationalism within the agency. I think one of the difficulties is that, historically at least, some of the worldwide agencies have been strongly oriented to their home countries—that is, wherever they started—be it the United States or Japan. There is a substantial difference between an American agency operating in France and a French agency, that has been fused to an American agency through acquisition, operating in France. Some advertising agencies, just like some multinationals, are unmistakably ethnocentric.

It's also a question of the extent to which certain appeals in relation to a product themselves are international. Some products lend themselves to a high degree of uniformity in terms of what it is that they will do and in terms of what it is that will appeal in relation to what they do. From one country to the next, you may well be able to have very easy local adaptation as long as you avoid some of the major cultural pitfalls. If, for example, there are visual symbols that are somewhat obscene in certain cultures and perfectly okay in others and you screen for those adequately, you may be able to get away with a high degree of uniformity. If you can, then I would think that the proportional level of local resistance would be that much lower. The question is whether local management thinks the program will work in terms of its market segment.

CA: Can a pen in the Parker price range that was generally moderate to expensive be successfully marketed in uniform fashion from country to country?

DT: Let's try and pick it apart a little bit. You might have some elements of appeal in terms of a relatively uniform visual configuration. Whether that product performs as a fountain pen or a ballpoint or a felt-tip or a roller ball—that's easily variable from the inside out. You can have a common external configuration with a fair variety of tip, and therefore, performance variation coming out of it. So you could have an element of design uniformity that, given a fair degree of demand in whatever geographically international market segment you are targeting, should not compromise the product's appeal to different people.

The higher up you go in terms of price, the closer you get to a piece of personal jewelry or adornment, and the easier it is to market the product uniformly. In the higher segments it is purely an issue of cosmetics—whether the product, which you would want to be slim and elegant no matter the country, would be better in silver for that market or in gold for this market—these are second order questions. The real question is: Do people regard personal adornment with writing instruments as a way of expressing a level of achievement and status in their local community? If the answer is yes, then you can very easily market that product on an international scale. An interesting example might be Dunhill. Admittedly, their success has been on a limited international scale. Still, it is interesting to think how a tobacco seller gets into writing instruments and the fact that the same Dunhill pens are available in world-class cosmopolitan cities. This is a good example of a totally uniform product and presentation on an international scale in a particularly narrow market segment.

At the other end of the scale, you go right down to the commodity product and the same argument prevails for slightly different reasons. If what you are interested in is a very basic writing instrument to make a mark on paper you have two choices: Do you want to be able to make that mark and subsequently to change it, in which case you go predominantly for a wood-case pencil, or, do you want to be able to make it and have a certain amount of longevity associated with it, in which case you go for a ballpoint pen? These products are fairly basic, straightforward, and, I would say, uniform. As long as you take into account the lower, if not the lowest, common denominator in terms of writing surface and your ballpoint is able to operate on lower-quality paper as opposed to the finest bond, you can probably make, sell, and present the same product in India as you can in Ghana or in Peru because the basic consumer's need is uniform on a worldwide basis.

CA: Let's switch from marketing the product to producing it. As you know, Parker was beset by production woes before and after it marketed its products globally. How important is the production process in the pen industry in general and how far do you think faulty production went toward the undermining of its global marketing plan?

DT: Reliable consistency is important in that industry as in most. In Parker's instance, I think the very marked contrast between the new Parker and the old Parker in terms of production had as much of a disruptive effect as anything else. Secondly, I believe that very often people coming into any industry new, or relatively new, tend to shortchange the need to understanding manufacturing and technological processes. Such understanding enables managers to know with confidence what kinds of future commitments they can make and expect to meet. Historically, company takeover or turnaround specialists don't usually have strong personal background or interest in the manufacturing function. They tend to have spent their time in either marketing or finance rather than in manufacturing, so that function gets shortchanged.

I would suspect that the new Parker management didn't have the ability to look at the projections for the rationalization and re-equipment program and say: "Come on guys, you say you can do that in 15 months. Where is your Kentucky Windage Factor? Where are the critical delivery bottlenecks? How reliable are those suppliers? What has been their track record in terms of on-time delivery? What allowance has been made for debugging? Do we have people experienced with that kind of equipment? Are we getting equipment that's new to the suppliers as well as new to our own production people? In which case, you should probably build a safety factor into the debugging period rather than just the shortest possible time to get it done." I'm probably beginning to sound like a cracked record, but it points out the need to know what is realistic and achieveable. This is never going to be satisfactory, but at least you know how much time things should be taking and then how much you're compromising, as opposed to how much you don't know you're overpromising to yourself or to other people.

Appendix

Global Income and Population 2000 and Projections to 2010 and 2020

CONTENTS

"Global Income and Population 2000," the seventh in a series by the Institute, is a report of the gross national product (GNP) and Population for every country in the world in 2000 with a projection to the year 2010 and 2020. GNP is the value of all of the goods and services produced by a country. This value is reported as a monetary value in U.S. dollars based on the value of the national currency at the foreign exchange rate. Where data are available they are also reported as purchasing power, an estimate of value of a national currency in goods and services in the country of currency issue. For the U.S. dollar, the exchange value and purchasing power are identical. For all other currencies, the exchange value and purchasing power are different. Data sources include the World Bank and Warren Keegan Associates, Inc. estimates.

The countries of the world are divided into five economic categories: High-Income Countries (GNP per capita ≥ \$9,656), Upper-Middle-Income Countries (GNP per capita ≥ \$3,126 but <\$9,655), Lower-Middle-Income Countries (GNP per capita ≥ \$786 but <\$3,125), Low-Income Countries (GNP per capita <\$785), and Unavailable Data Countries.

The publication contains several reports: a world market summary for 2000, a world market summary for 2000 with purchasing power parity (PPP), a 2000 summary by trade groups, 2000 listing by income category, 2000 alphabetical listing by country, projections for 2010 and 2020 sorted by 2000 income category, country top 10 listings of GNP, population and GNP per capita for the years 2000, 2010, and 2020, global purchasing power for 2000, and country top 10 listing by PPP for 2000.

HOW TO READ THE TABLES

The United States, for example, has a 2000 GNP of \$8,259,358 million, GNP per capita, of \$29,953, and accounts for 27 percent of the world's GNP. When adjusted for purchasing power, the United States accounts for 22 percent of the world's GNP with PPP. Population for the United States is 276 million, which is 4.5 percent of the world's population. The real growth in GNP for the United States during the 1997–2000 period was 2.7 percent. Projections are based on Warren Keegan Associates future growth rate estimates. The forecast for U.S. GNP in 2010 is \$11,763,698 million and \$39,005 per capita.

Dollar figures are based on national currency amounts converted to U.S. dollars at official exchange rates for comparison across economics, although an alternative rate is used when the official exchange rate is judged to diverge by an exceptionally large margin from the rate effectively applied to internationally traded products. An Atlas method of conversion is used in which the conversion factor averages the exchange rates for a given year and the two preceding years, adjusted for differences in rates of inflation between the country and the G-7 countries.

GNP per capita in U.S. dollars does not translate into equivalent purchasing power. For example, GNP per capita in China using the exchange rate method is \$930 but GNP per capita in purchasing power (PPP) in China is worth \$4,472. In other words the purchasing power of the Chinese yuan is 480 percent greater than its exchange value. This difference reflects the relatively low cost of housing, food, services, and so on in China as compared to the United States.

The Low-Income countries share of 2000 world purchasing power is 7 percent versus 3 percent share of world GNP. The High-Income countries, on the other hand, have 80 percent of world GNP but only 58 percent of world purchasing power.

NOTES

GNP real growth rate, 1997–2000, is the average annual percentage change in a country's real GNP per capita.

Population growth rate, 1997–2000, is the average annual percentage change in a country's population. It is the sum of births and immigrants minus the sum of deaths and emigrants in a year.

Projections to 2010 and 2020 are based on Warren Keegan Associates projected growth rates; 2000 income and population data are estimates based on World Bank data and Warren Keegan Associates, Inc. estimates and adjustments.

Andorra, Aruba, Bermuda, Cayman Islands, Eritrea, Faeroe Islands, French Guiana, Gibraltar, Greenland, Isle of Man, Marshall Islands, Northern Mariana Islands, San Marino, and West Bank and Gaza were excluded from this report due to lack of GNP and population figures.

ACKNOWLEDGMENTS

Special thanks are due to my research assistants Nikhil Aggarwal, Thoma Sillery, and Ginevra Felt, and all of my former research assistants who have painstakingly constructed the software architecture for this report. My research associate, Dorothy Minkus-McKenna, provided skillful and invaluable editing. I would also like to acknowledge the continuing support and encouragement of Deans Arthur Centonze and Peter Hoefer, the outstanding leadership and encouragement of Stephen Blank, Director of the Center for International Business, and my Center for International Business, Professor Lawrence Bridwell, Chair of the International Business Department, Professor Martin Topol, Chair of the Marketing Department, Professor James Gould, Graduate Marketing Program Chair, and Professors Michael Szenberg and Surendra Kaushik, Director and Associate Director of the Center for Applied Research, all of the Lubin School of Business, Pace University.

Dr. Warren J. Keegan

Global Income and Population: 2000 (U.S. Dollars)

Market	GNP (millions)	% of World GNP	GNP per Capita	Population (000)	% of World Population	GNP (PPP) (millions)	% of World GNP (PPP)
World	30,251,491	100.00%	4,931	6,134,466	100.00%	38,016,773	100.00%
High income	24,280,533	80.26%	24,693	983,284	16.03%	21,967,247	57.78%
Triad (Total)	21,632,194	71.51%	26,606	813,057	13.25%	19,387,896	51.00%
United States	8,259,358	27.30%	29,953	275,746	4.50%	8,259,358	21.73%
Canada	602,158	1.99%	19,183	31,390	0.51%	650,121	1.71%
Japan	4,427,104	14.63%	34,796	127,229	2.07%	2,971,197	7.82%
EU	8,343,574,	27.58%	22,033	378,691	6.17%	7,507,220	19.75%
Upper middle income	2,010,621	6.65%	4,476	449,162	7.32%	2,820,655	7.42%
Lower middle income	3,150,490	10.41%	1,303	2,418,156	39.42%	10,439,973	27.46%
Low income	809,846	2.68%	355	2,283,863	37.23%	2,788,897	7.34%

Global Income and Population: 2010 (U.S. Dollars)

Market	GNP (millions)	% of World GNP	GNP per Capita	Population (000)	% of World Population	GNP (PPP) (millions)	% of World GNP (PPP)
World	41,619,938	100.00%	5,778	7,203,265	100.00%	52,076,285	100.00%
High income	32,383,735	77.81%	30,778	1,052,164	14.61%	25,946,025	49.82%
Triad (Total)	28,532,101	68.55%	33,105	861,867	11.96%	22,174,983	42.58%
United States	11,763,698	28.26%	39,005	301,592	4.19%	8,095,733	15.55%
Canada	833,131	2.00%	23,556	35,367	0.49%	901,688	1.73%
Japan	5,137,835	12.34%	38,802	132,411	1.84%	3,449,690	6.62%
EU	10,797,437	25.94%	27,510	392,497	5.45%	9,727,872	18.68%
Upper middle income	4,097,717	9.85%	4,799	853,801	11.85%	5,966,480	11.46%
Lower middle income	3,911,223	9.40%	1,551	2,522,028	35.01%	15,841,961	30.42%
Low income	1,227,263	2.95%	442	2,775,272	38.53%	4,321,819	8.30%

Global Income And Population: 2020 (U.S. Dollars)

Market	GNP (millions)	% of World GNP	GNP per Capita	Population (000)	% of World Population	GNP (PPP) (millions)	% of World GNP (PPP)
World	56,536,056	100.00%	6,658	8,492,006	100.00%	75,104,053	100.00%
High income	42,856,183	75.80%	37,089	1,155,487	13.61%	34,364,807	45.76%
Triad (Total)	37,114,271	65.65%	40,389	918,918	10.82%	28,451,879	37.88%
United States	15,809,426	27.96%	48,405	326,607	3.85%	10,464,772	13.93%
Canada	1,119,659	1.98%	28,098	39,848	0.47%	1,214,338	1.62%
Japan	6,262,992	11.08%	45,449	137,804	1.62%	4,207,792	5.60%
EU	13,922,194	24.63%	33,575	414,659	4.88%	12,564,977	16.73%
Upper middle income	6,217,912	11.00%	5,423	1,146,537	13.50%	9,969,818	13.27%
Lower middle income	5,615,567	9.93%	2,048	2,741,647	32.29%	24,213,358	32.24%
Low income	1,846,393	3.27%	535	3,448,335	40.61%	6,556,069	8.73%

Trade Groups: Income—Population: 2000 (U.S. Dollars)

Trade Groups	GNP (millions)	% of World GNP	Population (000)	% of World Population	GNP per Capita	GNP (PPP) (millions)
World Totals	30,251,491	100.00%	6,134,466	100.00%	4,841	38,016,773
Trade Group Total	26,617,844	87.99%	2,669,799	43.52%	9,970	28,000,352
NAFTA	9,254,029	30.59%	406,672	6.63%	22,756	9,497,152
EU	8,343,574	27.58%	378,691	6.17%	22,033	7,507,220
Japan and Tigers	5,907,076	19.53%	293,043	4.78%	20,158	5,047,241
Mercosur	1,332,406	4.40%	231,926	3.78%	5,745	1,527,859
ASEAN	780,021	2.58%	522,865	8.52%	1,492	2,138,297
Andean Group	283,769	0.94%	113,399	1.85%	2,502	621,667
GCC	200,487	0.66%	30,956	0.50%	6,477	308,149
SADCC	174,541	0.58%	208,368	3.40%	838	356,350
AMU	95,625	0.32%	78,134	1.27%	1,224	278,177
ACC	95,297	0.32%	114,019	1.86%	836	304,524
ECOWAS	76,722	0.25%	238,550	3.89%	322	256,378
CACM	56,601	0.19%	35,811	0.58%	1,581	114,487
CARICOM	17,696	0.06%	17,365	0.28%	1,019	42,851

Note:

ACC = Arab Cooperation Council, (Egypt, Arab Rep., Iraq, Jordan, Yemen)

AMU = Arab Maghreb Union, (Algeria, Libya, Mauritania, Morocco, Tunisia)

Andean Group = Bolivia, Colombia, Ecuador, Peru, Venezuela

ASEAN = Association Of Southeast Asian Nations (Brunei, Cambodia, Indonesia, Laos, Malaysia, Myanmar, Philippines, Singapore, Thailand, Vietnam)

CARICOM = Caribbean Community and Common Market (Antigua and Barbuda, Bahamas, Barbados, Belize, Dominica, Grenada, Guyana, Haiti, Jamaica, Montserrat, St. Kitts and Nevis, St. Lucia, St. Vincent and the Grenadines, Suriname, Trinidad and Tobago)

ECOWAS = Economic Community of West African States (Benin, Burkina Faso, Cape Verde, Cote d'Ivoire, Gambia, Ghana, Guinea, Guinea-Bissau, Liberia, Mali, Mauritania, Niger, Nigeria, Senegal, Sierra Leone, Togo)

EU = European Union (Austria, Belgium, Denmark, Finland, France, Germany, Greece, Ireland, Italy, Luxembourg, Netherlands, Portugal, Spain, Sweden, United Kingdom)

GCC = Cooperation Council for the Arab States of the Gulf (Bahrain, Kuwait, Oman, Qatar, Saudi Arabia, United Arab Emirates)

Japan and Tigers = Hong Kong, Japan, Malaysia, Singapore, South Korea (Republic of), Taiwan and Thailand (this is not an official trade group but is listed for comparison purposes)

Mercosur = Southern Cone Common Market (Argentina, Brazil, Paraguay, Uruguay with Chile as an associate member)

NAFTA = North American Free Trade Area (United States, Canada, Mexico)

SADCC = South African Development Coordination Conference (Angola, Botswana, Congo, Lesotho, Malawi, Mauritius, Mozambique, Namibia, Seychelles, South Africa, Swaziland, Tanzania, Zambia, Zimbabwe)

SICA = Central American Integration System (Costa Rica, El Salvador, Guatemala, Honduras, Nicaragua)

Triad = United States, Canada, Japan and EU

Trade Groups: Income—Population: 2010 (U.S. Dollars)

Trade Groups	GNP (millions)	% of World GNP	Population (000)	% of World Population	GNP per Capita	GNP (PPP) (millions)
World Totals	41,619,938	100.00%	7,207,845	100.00%	5,623	52,076,725
Trade Group Totals	34,552,720	83.02%	3,127,315	43.39%	11,049	33,867,195
NAFTA	12,148,772	29.19%	459,488	6.37%	26,440	9,960,246
EU	10,797,437	25.94%	392,497	5.45%	27,510	9,727,872
Japan and Tigers	7,256,790	17.44%	320,829	4.45%	22,619	6,214,481
Mercosur	1,953,157	4.69%	270,922	3.76%	7,209	2,272,234
ASEAN	955,013	2.29%	629,549	8.73%	1,517	2,403,184
Andean Group	436,809	1.05%	130,724	1.81%	3,341	923,387
GCC	269,114	0.65%	40,131	0.56%	6,706	417,922
SADCC	245,446	0.59%	272,769	3.78%	900	499,952
ACC	141,091	0.34%	150,081	2.08%	940	469,638
AMU	128,772	0.31%	98,085	1.36%	1,313	375,677
ECOWAS	101,574	0.24%	295,509	4.10%	344	355,318
CACM	94,599	0.23%	46,246	0.64%	2,046	189,924
CARICOM	24,146	0.06%	20,485	0.28%	1,179	57,360

Trade Groups: Income—Population: 2020 (U.S. Dollars)

Trade Groups	GNP (millions)	% of World GNP	Population (000)	% of World Population	GNP per Capita	GNP (PPP) (millions)
World Totals	56,536,056	100.00%	8,504,642	100.00%	6,508	76,994,660
Trade Group Totals	45,995,251	81.36%	3,713,401	43.66%	12,386	46,438,189
NAFTA	15,866,529	28.06%	515,817	6.07%	30,760	13,109,817
EU	13,789,622	24.39%	414,659	4.88%	33,255	12,442,042
Japan and Tigers	9,912,619	17.53%	350,407	4.12%	28,289	8,852,042
Mercosur	2,746,972	4.86%	313,534	3.69%	8,761	3,235,093
ASEAN	1,541,446	2.73%	758,266	8.92%	2,033	3,923,024
Andean Group	663,696	1.17%	170,096	2.00%	3,902	1,441,049
GCC	359,140	0.64%	51,173	0.60%	7,018	563,577
SADCC	351,771	0.62%	352,052	4.14%	999	721,223
ACC	228,031	0.40%	195,919	2.30%	1,164	752,305
ECOWAS	183,522	0.32%	387,583	4.56%	474	524,262
AMU	171,429	0.30%	120,459	1.42%	1,423	501,507
CACM	147,862	0.26%	59,232	0.70%	2,496	296,069
CARICOM	32,612	0.06%	24,204	0.28%	1,347	76,179

2000 Income Category List (U.S. Dollars)

Category	1997–2000 Growth Rates					Year 2000						
	Pop	GNP	GNP per Capita	Population (000)	% of World Pop	GNP (millions)	% of World GNP	GNP (PPP) (millions)	% of World GNP (PPP)	GNP per Capita	GNP per Capita (PPP)
High-Income Countries, GNP/Capita ≥ $9,656				**983,284**	**16.04%**	**24,280,533**	**80.27%**	**21,967,247**	**57.78%**	**24,693**	**22,341**
Argentina	1.30%	4.50%	3.20%	37,087	0.60%	360,472	1.19%	355,545	0.94%	9,720	9,587
Australia	1.40%	3.40%	2.00%	19,207	0.31%	407,949	1.35%	386,141	1.02%	21,239	20,104
Austria	0.60%	2.40%	1.80%	8,218	0.13%	212,469	0.70%	179,046	0.47%	25,854	21,787
Belgium	0.30%	2.40%	2.10%	10,282	0.17%	255,828	0.85%	234,068	0.62%	24,881	22,765
Canada	1.20%	3.30%	2.10%	31,390	0.51%	602,158	1.99%	650,121	1.71%	19,183	20,711
Cyprus	1.20%	5.00%	3.80%	777	0.01%	8,944	0.03%	na	na	11,518	na
Denmark	0.20%	2.80%	2.60%	5,348	0.09%	181,253	0.60%	125,963	0.33%	33,894	23,555
Finland	0.40%	4.00%	3.60%	5,202	0.08%	120,100	0.40%	94,719	0.25%	23,088	18,208
France	0.50%	2.50%	2.00%	59,491	0.97%	1,446,515	4.78%	1,282,677	3.37%	24,315	21,561
Germany	0.50%	2.50%	2.00%	83,308	1.36%	2,127,086	7.03%	1,688,783	4.44%	25,533	20,272
Greece	0.50%	2.60%	2.10%	10,681	0.17%	123,350	0.41%	128,228	0.34%	11,549	12,006
Hong Kong	1.30%	3.00%	1.70%	6,880	0.11%	188,936	0.62%	169,255	0.45%	27,463	24,602
Iceland	1.10%	3.00%	1.90%	278	0.00%	na	na	5,555	0.01%	na	19,954
Ireland	0.10%	6.00%	5.90%	3,727	0.06%	74,331	0.25%	74,591	0.20%	19,942	20,012
Israel	2.70%	6.00%	3.30%	6,414	0.10%	103,178	0.34%	102,638	0.27%	16,085	16,001
Italy	0.10%	2.00%	1.90%	57,869	0.94%	1,168,771	3.86%	1,196,590	3.15%	20,197	20,678
Japan	0.40%	1.50%	1.10%	127,229	2.08%	4,427,104	14.64%	2,971,197	7.82%	34,796	23,353
Korea, Rep.	0.90%	3.50%	2.60%	47,385	0.77%	520,855	1.72%	692,451	1.82%	10,992	14,613
Kuwait	1.50%	2.90%	1.40%	1,687	0.03%	59,455	0.20%	99,038	0.26%	35,242	58,705
Luxembourg	1.10%	2.50%	1.40%	440	0.01%	16,977	0.06%	15,711	0.04%	38,587	35,708
Netherlands	0.60%	3.00%	2.40%	15,890	0.26%	384,534	1.27%	338,145	0.89%	24,200	21,281
New Zealand	1.00%	2.40%	1.40%	3,944	0.06%	60,649	0.20%	63,251	0.17%	15,376	16,035
Norway	0.50%	3.50%	3.00%	4,470	0.07%	170,188	0.56%	115,368	0.30%	38,070	25,807
Portugal	0.00%	3.60%	3.60%	9,975	0.16%	107,701	0.36%	138,853	0.37%	10,797	13,920
Qatar	3.00%	3.00%	0.00%	849	0.01%	na	na	na	0.02%	na	9,934
Singapore	1.80%	4.50%	2.70%	3,294	0.05%	120,177	0.40%	94,367	0.25%	36,484	28,648
Slovenia	0.15%	3.00%	2.85%	1,980	0.03%	20,716	0.07%	na	na	10,463	na
Spain	0.20%	3.00%	2.80%	39,559	0.65%	544,944	1.80%	606,697	1.60%	13,775	15,336
Sweden	0.60%	2.40%	1.80%	8,982	0.15%	219,950	0.73%	164,051	0.43%	24,487	18,264
Switzerland	0.80%	2.30%	1.50%	7,259	0.12%	264,820	0.88%	175,841	0.46%	36,479	24,222

Taiwan (Rep. of China)	0.85%	5.50%	4.65%	22,113	0.36%	362,000	1.20%	276,567	0.73%	16,370	12,507
United Arab Emirates	4.00%	3.00%	-1.00%	2,970	0.05%	na	na	31,198	0.08%	na	10,506
United Kingdom	0.30%	2.80%	2.50%	59,720	0.97%	1,359,764	4.50%	1,239,099	3.26%	22,769	20,748
United States	0.90%	3.60%	2.70%	275,746	4.50%	8,259,358	27.30%	8,259,358	21.73	29,953	29,953
Upper-Middle-Income GNP/Capita ($3,126–$9,655)				**449,162**	**7.33%**	**2,010,621**	**6.65%**	**2,820,655**	**7.42%**	**4,476**	**6,280**
Antigua and Barbuda	0.40%	3.00%	2.60%	67	0.00%	515	0.00%	na	na	7,685	na
Bahrain	3.10%	3.60%	0.50%	677	0.01%	5,580	0.02%	8,898	0.02%	8,236	13,134
Barbados	0.50%	0.70%	0.20%	268	0.00%	na	na	2,668	0.01%	na	9,947
Brazil	1.60%	3.40%	1.80%	170,661	2.78%	850,852	2.81%	944,838	2.49%	4,986	5,536
Chile	1.60%	6.00%	4.40%	15,335	0.25%	89,280	0.30%	184,557	0.49%	5,822	12,035
Czech Republic	0.00%	2.60%	2.60%	10,273	0.17%	50,924	0.17%	99,369	0.26%	4,957	9,673
Croatia	0.20%	na	na	4,768	0.08%	21,072	0.07%	na	na	4,419	na
Gabon	2.90%	3.80%	0.90%	1,245	0.02%	4,465	0.01%	na	na	3,585	na
Grenada	0.20%	3.20%	3.00%	97	0.00%	314	0.00%	na	na	3,241	na
Hungary	0.20%	3.00%	2.80%	10,064	0.16%	44,571	0.15%	66,138	0.17%	4,429	6,572
Malaysia	2.30%	2.30%	0.00%	23,333	0.38%	110,739	0.37%	247,559	0.65%	4,746	10,610
Mauritius	0.90%	4.40%	3.50%	1,190	0.02%	4,864	0.02%	17,783	0.05%	4,088	14,946
Mexico	1.70%	5.00%	3.30%	99,536	1.62%	392,513	1.30%	587,673	1.55%	3,943	5,904
Malta	0.80%	5.70%	4.90%	384	0.01%	3,687	0.01%	na	na	9,599	na
Panama	1.90%	4.07%	2.17%	2,868	0.05%	9,180	0.03%	18,208	0.05%	3,200	6,348
Poland	0.40%	5.00%	4.60%	38,882	0.63%	153,066	0.51%	255,454	0.67%	3,937	6,570
Saudi Arabia	2.30%	3.00%	0.70%	22,183	0.36%	135,453	0.45%	144,357	0.38%	6,106	6,508
Slovak Republic	0.30%	3.00%	2.70%	5,432	0.09%	19,515	0.06%	19,608	0.05%	3,593	3,610
St. Kitts and Nevis	0.00%	4.50%	4.50%	41	0.00%	287	0.00%	473	0.00%	7,081	11,671
Seychelles	1.20%	4.00%	2.80%	82	0.00%	556	0.00%	na	na	6,822	na
Trinidad and Tobago	0.90%	2.00%	1.10%	1,339	0.02%	5,655	0.02%	11,354	0.03%	4,224	8,482
Uruguay	0.60%	3.00%	2.40%	3,335	0.05%	21,924	0.07%	25,385	0.07%	6,574	7,612
Venezuela	2.40%	5.00%	2.60%	24,314	0.40%	84,969	0.28%	170,108	0.45%	3,495	6,996
St. Lucia	1.40%	5.00%	3.60%	163	0.00%	641	0.00%	na	na	3,924	na
Lower-Middle-Income GNP/Capita ($786–$3,125)				**2,418,156**	**39.44%**	**3,150,490**	**10.42%**	**10,439,973**	**27.46%**	**1,303**	**4,317**
Albania	1.00%	2.20%	1.20%	3,344	0.05%	2,685	0.01%	na	na	803	na
Algeria	2.40%	3.10%	0.70%	31,388	0.51%	42,698	0.14%	136,350	0.36%	1,360	4,344
Belarus	0.40%	2.00%	1.60%	10,267	0.17%	18,928	0.06%	32,480	0.09%	1,844	3,164
Belize	2.50%	6.00%	3.50%	250	0.00%	622	0.00%	1,189	0.00%	2,488	4,758

Category	1997–2000 Growth Rates			Population (000)	% of World Pop	GNP (millions)	% of World GNP	Year 2000			
	Pop	GNP	GNP per Capita					GNP (PPP) (millions)	% of World GNP (PPP)	GNP per Capita	GNP per Capita (PPP)
Bolivia	2.30%	3.90%	1.60%	8,340	0.14%	8,241	0.03%	20,763	0.05%	988	2,490
Botswana	2.90%	5.20%	2.30%	1,656	0.03%	5,085	0.02%	8,654	0.02%	3,071	5,227
Bulgaria	0.00%	1.00%	1.00%	8,139	0.13%	9,160	0.03%	34,152	0.09%	1,125	4,196
Cape Verde	2.00%	4.70%	2.70%	429	0.01%	432	0.00%	752	0.00%	1,006	1,752
China	1.20%	7.00%	5.80%	1,268,121	20.68%	1,179,345	3.90%	5,671,304	14.92%	930	4,472
Colombia	1.80%	4.00%	2.20%	42,368	0.69%	99,763	0.33%	268,934	0.71%	2,355	6,348
Costa Rica	2.30%	5.00%	2.70%	3,654	0.06%	9,978	0.03%	21,918	0.06%	2,730	5,998
Dominica	0.00%	4.50%	4.50%	75	0.00%	231	0.00%	na	na	3,091	na
Dominican Republic	2.00%	4.80%	2.80%	8,578	0.14%	16,212	0.05%	35,939	0.09%	1,890	4,190
Ecuador	2.30%	2.90%	0.60%	12,742	0.21%	19,301	0.06%	50,367	0.13%	1,515	3,953
Egypt, Arab Rep.	2.20%	4.50%	2.30%	64,042	1.04%	83,097	0.27%	254,583	0.67%	1,298	3,975
El Salvador	1.80%	6.00%	4.20%	6,309	0.10%	12,391	0.04%	17,653	0.05%	1,964	2,798
Equatorial Guinea	2.50%	12.10%	9.60%	452	0.01%	690	0.00%	na	na	1,526	na
Estonia	0.00%	4.30%	4.30%	1,410	0.02%	4,169	0.01%	5,463	0.01%	2,956	3,873
Fiji	1.10%	2.50%	1.40%	852	0.01%	2,057	0.01%	4,661	0.01%	2,414	5,469
Guatemala	2.80%	6.00%	3.20%	11,361	0.19%	18,397	0.06%	35,904	0.09%	1,619	3,160
Guyana	0.60%	1.50%	0.90%	871	0.01%	981	0.00%	3,715	0.01%	1,127	4,265
Iran, Islamic Rep.	3.10%	2.70%	-0.40%	63,901	1.04%	130,742	0.43%	354,811	0.93%	2,046	5,553
Indonesia	1.60%	0.00%	-1.60%	210,785	3.44%	247,846	0.82%	983,923	2.59%	1,176	4,668
Jamaica	0.90%	4.00%	3.10%	2,624	0.04%	4,104	0.01%	9,241	0.02%	1,564	3,522
Jordan	4.50%	5.00%	0.50%	5,107	0.08%	7,394	0.02%	18,743	0.05%	1,448	3,670
Kiribati	2.10%	1.50%	-0.60%	88	0.00%	76	0.00%	na	na	859	na
Kazakstan	0.50%	2.00%	1.50%	15,565	0.25%	17,441	0.06%	32,769	0.09%	1,120	2,105
Lebanon	2.30%	2.00%	-0.30%	4,387	0.07%	17,710	0.06%	na	na	4,037	na
Latvia	0.20%	1.00%	0.80%	2,385	0.04%	4,439	0.01%	5,835	0.02%	1,861	2,447
Lithuania	0.50%	3.40%	2.90%	3,695	0.06%	7,526	0.02%	10,590	0.03%	2,037	2,866
Macedonia, FYR	0.70%	na	na	2,039	0.03%	2,045	0.01%	na	na	1,003	na
Micronesia, Fed. Sts.	2.40%	3.00%	0.60%	118	0.00%	203	0.00%	na	na	1,715	na
Maldives	3.10%	7.00%	3.90%	276	0.00%	352	0.00%	926	0.00%	1,272	3,351
Morocco	2.00%	2.80%	0.80%	28,811	0.47%	32,693	0.11%	88,774	0.23%	1,135	3,081
Namibia	2.70%	5.40%	2.70%	1,753	0.03%	3,445	0.01%	6,745	0.02%	1,965	3,848
Papua New Guinea	2.20%	4.30%	2.10%	4,819	0.08%	4,346	0.01%	11,778	0.03%	902	2,444

Paraguay	2.70%	4.50%	1.80%	5,508	0.09%	9,877	0.03%	17,533	0.05%	1,793	3,183
Peru	2.00%	5.00%	3.00%	25,635	0.42%	71,495	0.24%	111,495	0.29%	2,789	4,349
Philippines	2.30%	4.50%	2.20%	78,718	1.28%	89,835	0.30%	216,603	0.57%	1,141	2,752
Romania	0.00%	4.00%	4.00%	22,284	0.36%	34,418	0.11%	98,626	0.26%	1,544	4,426
Russian Federation	0.30%	3.50%	3.20%	146,866	2.40%	342,008	1.13%	438,382	1.15%	2,329	2,985
Sao Tome and Principe	2.10%	0.70%	-1.40%	180	0.00%	199	0.00%	na	na	1,104	na
St. Vincent and the Grenadines	0.80%	4.50%	3.70%	114	0.00%	287	0.00%	na	na	2,509	na
Solomon Islands	2.50%	5.00%	2.50%	443	0.01%	378	0.00%	868	0.00%	854	1,959
South Africa	2.30%	3.20%	0.90%	43,089	0.70%	125,054	0.41%	193,924	0.51%	2,902	4,501
Sri Lanka	1.30%	4.50%	3.20%	19,285	0.31%	16,789	0.06%	71,607	0.19%	871	3,713
Suriname	0.30%	4.00%	3.70%	416	0.01%	666	0.00%	899	0.00%	1,602	2,161
Swaziland	3.00%	3.80%	0.80%	1,050	0.02%	1,421	0.00%	2,504	0.01%	1,354	2,385
Syrian Arab Republic	3.00%	4.00%	1.00%	16,229	0.26%	18,198	0.06%	88,078	0.23%	1,121	5,427
Thailand	1.30%	0.50%	-0.80%	62,810	1.02%	177,265	0.59%	595,845	1.57%	2,822	9,486
Tonga	0.90%	2.00%	1.10%	99	0.00%	198	0.00%	na	na	2,003	na
Tunisia	2.10%	3.10%	1.00%	9,693	0.16%	19,141	0.06%	49,196	0.13%	1,975	5,075
Turkey	1.90%	5.00%	3.10%	67,250	1.10%	207,213	0.69%	384,728	1.01%	3,081	5,721
Uzbekistan	2.30%	3.00%	0.70%	25,116	0.41%	20,820	0.07%	40,091	0.11%	829	1,596
Vanuatu	2.70%	2.00%	-0.70%	191	0.00%	209	0.00%	320	0.00%	1,095	1,672
Western Samoa	3.10%	3.00%	-0.10%	180	0.00%	199	0.00%	357	0.00%	1,104	1,980
				2,283,863	**37.25%**	**809,846**	**2.68%**	**2,788,897**	**7.34%**	**355**	**1,221**
Low-Income GNP/Capita $785 or Less											
Angola	3.00%	-10.00%	-13.00%	12,852	0.21%	3,196	0.01%	8,248	0.02%	249	642
Armenia	1.20%	-10.70%	-11.90%	3,890	0.06%	1,248	0.00%	4,746	0.01%	321	1,220
Azerbaijan	1.20%	-16.00%	-17.20%	7,807	0.13%	2,562	0.01%	4,517	0.01%	328	579
Bangladesh	2.00%	3.30%	1.30%	129,663	2.11%	47,489	0.16%	194,670	0.51%	366	1,501
Benin	2.80%	1.70%	-1.10%	6,315	0.10%	2,221	0.01%	10,463	0.03%	352	1,657
Bhutan	2.60%	2.00%	-0.60%	803	0.01%	348	0.00%	967	0.00%	433	1,204
Burkina Faso	2.80%	0.80%	-2.00%	11,246	0.18%	2,447	0.01%	8,092	0.02%	218	720
Burundi	2.80%	-5.90%	-8.70%	6,910	0.11%	789	0.00%	2,823	0.01%	114	408
Cameroon	2.90%	-3.30%	-6.20%	15,140	0.25%	7,691	0.03%	23,320	0.06%	508	1,540
Central African Republic	2.10%	-1.00%	-3.10%	3,638	0.06%	973	0.00%	3,325	0.01%	268	914
Cambodia	2.70%	2.70%	0.00%	11,352	0.19%	3,297	0.01%	na	na	290	na
Chad	2.50%	1.00%	-1.50%	7,839	0.13%	1,622	0.01%	4,935	0.01%	207	630
Comoros	2.80%	-3.10%	-5.90%	559	0.01%	177	0.00%	551	0.00%	316	984

2000 Income Category List (U.S. Dollars) (cont.)

Category	1997–2000 Growth Rates			Year 2000							
	Pop	GNP	GNP per Capita	Population (000)	% of World Pop	GNP (millions)	% of World GNP	GNP (PPP) (millions)	% of World GNP (PPP)	GNP per Capita	GNP per Capita (PPP)
Congo	3.10%	-12.50%	-15.60%	58,856	0.96%	4,775	0.02%	43,385	0.11%	81	737
Cote d'Ivoire	na	0.90%	na	15,484	0.25%	9,698	0.03%	22,114	0.06%	626	1,428
Eritrea	2.60%	2.90%	0.30%	4,075	0.07%	904	0.00%	na	na	222	na
Ethiopia	2.60%	2.20%	-0.40%	63,781	1.04%	6,766	0.02%	28,701	0.08%	106	450
Gambia, The	3.90%	-0.60%	-4.50%	1,313	0.02%	393	0.00%	985	0.00%	299	750
Georgia	0.20%	-14.90%	-15.10%	5,411	0.09%	3,253	0.01%	3,571	0.01%	601	660
Ghana	2.90%	1.40%	-1.50%	19,481	0.32%	7,042	0.02%	36,313	0.10%	361	1,864
Guinea–Bissau	1.90%	1.00%	-0.90%	1,214	0.02%	259	0.00%	903	0.00%	213	744
Guinea	2.80%	2.70%	-0.10%	7,474	0.12%	4,000	0.01%	na	na	535	na
Haiti	2.00%	-4.40%	-6.40%	7,974	0.13%	2,451	0.01%	5,185	0.01%	307	650
Honduras	3.00%	1.00%	-2.00%	6,522	0.11%	4,707	0.02%	11,259	0.03%	722	1,726
India	1.90%	4.30%	2.40%	1,015,287	16.56%	430,096	1.42%	1,608,186	4.23%	424	1,584
Kenya	2.51%	-0.30%	-2.81%	31,083	0.51%	9,934	0.03%	36,646	0.10%	320	1,179
Kyrgyz Republic	1.10%	-9.70%	-10.80%	4,747	0.08%	1,256	0.00%	4,907	0.01%	265	1,034
Lesotho	2.40%	2.50%	0.10%	2,150	0.04%	1,370	0.00%	3,885	0.01%	637	1,807
Lao PDR	3.00%	3.90%	0.90%	5,237	0.09%	1,966	0.01%	na	na	375	na
Madagascar	3.00%	-1.60%	-4.60%	15,370	0.25%	3,279	0.01%	7,855	0.02%	213	511
Malawi	3.00%	0.80%	-2.20%	11,131	0.18%	2,538	0.01%	7,585	0.02%	228	681
Mali	2.80%	0.30%	-2.50%	11,179	0.18%	2,492	0.01%	5,417	0.01%	223	485
Mauritania	2.40%	1.50%	-0.90%	2,674	0.04%	1,093	0.00%	3,857	0.01%	409	1,442
Moldova	0.40%	2.00%	1.60%	4,286	0.07%	1,285	0.00%	na	na	300	na
Mongolia	2.50%	-1.40%	-3.90%	2,698	0.04%	943	0.00%	4,425	0.01%	350	1,640
Mozambique	1.80%	2.60%	0.80%	17,804	0.29%	2,779	0.01%	14,639	0.04%	156	822

Country											
Nepal	2.50%	2.20%	-0.30%	24,037	0.39%	5,267	0.02%	27,704	0.07%	219	1,153
Nicaragua	3.10%	1.60%	-1.50%	5,096	0.08%	1,949	0.01%	9,546	0.03%	382	1,873
Niger	3.20%	-1.90%	-5.10%	10,833	0.18%	1,729	0.01%	6,188	0.02%	160	571
Nigeria	2.90%	0.70%	-2.20%	128,454	2.10%	38,416	0.13%	140,218	0.37%	299	1,092
Pakistan	2.90%	2.00%	-0.90%	138,334	2.26%	66,219	0.22%	300,850	0.79%	479	2,175
Rwanda	0.60%	-5.70%	-6.30%	8,329	0.14%	1,551	0.01%	3,046	0.01%	186	366
Senegal	2.80%	0.00%	-2.80%	9,494	0.15%	4,427	0.01%	14,813	0.04%	466	1,560
Sierra Leone	1.60%	-5.70%	-7.30%	5,113	0.08%	681	0.00%	1,933	0.01%	133	378
Sudan	2.20%	3.70%	1.50%	29,435	0.48%	9,982	0.03%	na	na	339	na
Tajikistan	2.40%	-16.10%	-18.50%	6,348	0.10%	1,192	0.00%	2,178	0.01%	188	343
Tanzania	3.00%	0.90%	-2.10%	34,220	0.56%	7,583	0.03%	19,696	0.05%	222	576
Togo	3.00%	-1.20%	-4.20%	4,748	0.08%	1,395	0.00%	4,329	0.01%	294	912
Turkmenistan	3.20%	-14.60%	-17.80%	5,149	0.08%	1,764	0.01%	na	na	343	na
Uganda	3.00%	4.40%	1.40%	22,266	0.36%	7,470	0.02%	34,914	0.09%	336	1,568
Ukraine	0.10%	-12.60%	-12.70%	50,243	0.82%	32,793	0.11%	62,558	0.16%	653	1,245
Vietnam	2.30%	6.10%	3.80%	81,646	1.33%	28,896	0.10%	na	na	354	na
Yemen, Rep.	4.10%	-1.50%	-5.60%	18,236	0.30%	4,806	0.02%	na	na	264	na
Zaire	3.10%	-5.30%	-8.40%	48,194	0.79%	4,512	0.01%	15,146	0.04%	94	314
Zambia	2.60%	-0.90%	-3.50%	10,259	0.17%	3,563	0.01%	7,901	0.02%	347	770
Zimbabwe	2.70%	-0.70%	-3.40%	12,278	0.20%	8,311	0.03%	21,403	0.06%	677	1,743

Category	2001–2010 WKA Forecast			Year 2010							
	Pop	GNP	GNP per Capita	Population (000)	% of World Pop	GNP (millions)	% of World GNP	GNP (PPP) (millions)	% of World GNP (PPP)	GNP per Capita	GNP per Capita (PPP)
High-Income Countries, GNP/Capita ≥$9,656				1,052,164	14.61%	32,383,735	77.81%	25,946,025	49.82%	30,778	24,660
Argentina	1.20%	3.00%	1.80%	42,200	0.59%	559,803	1.35%	554,352	1.06%	13,266	13,136
Australia	1.30%	2.50%	1.20%	22,072	0.31%	569,916	1.37%	540,913	1.04%	25,821	24,507
Austria	0.50%	2.20%	1.70%	8,725	0.12%	269,336	0.65%	227,207	0.44%	30,870	26,042
Bahamas, The	1.50%	1.50%	0.00%	356	0.00%	na	na	4,406	0.01%	na	12,367
Belgium	0.30%	2.20%	1.90%	10,595	0.15%	324,301	0.78%	296,899	0.57%	30,610	28,024
Canada	1.20%	3.00%	1.80%	35,367	0.49%	833,131	2.00%	901,688	1.73%	23,556	25,495
Denmark	0.20%	2.75%	2.55%	5,456	0.08%	238,900	0.57%	166,109	0.32%	43,790	30,448
Finland	0.50%	3.50%	3.00%	5,414	0.08%	177,778	0.43%	140,402	0.27%	32,838	25,934
France	0.50%	2.75%	2.25%	62,533	0.87%	1,851,661	4.45%	1,643,537	3.16%	29,611	26,283
Germany	0.40%	2.40%	2.00%	87,569	1.22%	2,722,849	6.54%	2,163,895	4.16%	31,094	24,711
Greece	0.50%	2.20%	1.70%	11,227	0.16%	159,445	0.38%	165,921	0.32%	14,202	14,779
Hong Kong	1.20%	4.00%	2.80%	7,828	0.11%	253,914	0.61%	227,953	0.44%	32,436	29,119
Iceland	1.00%	2.90%	1.90%	311	0.00%	na	na	7,480	0.01%	na	24,086
Ireland	0.20%	4.00%	3.80%	3,765	0.05%	133,116	0.32%	133,655	0.26%	35,359	35,502
Israel	2.60%	4.00%	1.40%	8,373	0.12%	184,776	0.44%	185,359	0.36%	22,069	22,139
Italy	0.20%	2.20%	2.00%	58,450	0.81%	1,424,726	3.42%	1,458,908	2.80%	24,375	24,960
Japan	0.40%	2.00%	1.60%	132,411	1.84%	5,137,835	12.34%	3,449,690	6.62%	38,802	26,053
Korea, Rep.	0.80%	4.50%	3.70%	51,826	0.72%	734,718	1.77%	978,981	1.88%	14,177	18,890
Kuwait	1.00%	2.70%	1.70%	1,958	0.03%	79,130	0.19%	132,081	0.25%	40,416	67,462
Luxembourg	1.00%	2.50%	1.50%	491	0.01%	21,733	0.05%	20,141	0.04%	44,277	41,034
Netherlands	0.50%	2.90%	2.40%	16,869	0.23%	516,782	1.24%	455,075	0.87%	30,635	26,977
New Zealand	0.90%	2.30%	1.40%	4,357	0.06%	76,882	0.18%	80,289	0.15%	17,645	18,427
Norway	0.40%	3.20%	2.80%	4,699	0.07%	240,067	0.58%	162,973	0.31%	51,089	34,683
Portugal	0.20%	3.50%	3.30%	9,975	0.14%	153,397	0.37%	197,766	0.38%	15,378	19,826
Qatar	4.30%	3.00%	-1.30%	1,141	0.02%	na	na	11,335	0.02%	na	9,934
Singapore	1.70%	3.75%	2.05%	3,937	0.05%	186,631	0.45%	147,232	0.28%	47,401	37,394
Spain	2.00%	2.90%	0.90%	40,358	0.56%	732,359	1.76%	815,794	1.57%	18,147	20,214
St. Kitts and Nevis	2.00%	3.00%	1.00%	41	0.00%	445	0.00%	734	0.00%	10,996	18,124
Sweden	0.60%	2.30%	1.70%	9,536	0.13%	278,820	0.67%	208,178	0.40%	29,238	21,830
Switzerland	0.70%	2.20%	1.50%	7,862	0.11%	332,435	0.80%	220,996	0.42%	42,286	28,111

	(1)	(2)	(3)	(4)	(5)	(6)	(7)	(8)	(9)	(10)	(11)	(12)
Taiwan (Rep. of China)	0.80%	4.50%	0.80%	3.70%	24,066	0.33%	618,348	1.49%	474,190	0.91%	25,694	19,704
United Arab Emirates	3.00%	3.00%	3.00%	0.00%	4,396	0.06%	na	na	41,765	0.08%	na	9,501
United Kingdom	0.30%	2.60%	2.30%	2.30%	61,536	0.85%	1,792,234	4.31%	1,634,383	3.14%	29,125	26,560
United States	0.80%	3.00%	0.80%	2.20%	301,592	4.19%	11,763,698	28.26%	8,095,733	15.55%	39,005	29,420
Upper-Middle-Income Countries, GNP/Capita ($3,126–$9,655)					853,801	47.42%	4,097,717	9.85%	5,966,480	11.46%	4,799	6,988
Bahrain	3.00%	3.50%	3.00%	0.50%	919	0.01%	7,947	0.02%	12,693	0.02%	8,644	13,806
Barbados	0.40%	2.00%	0.40%	1.60%	282	0.00%	na	na	3,287	0.01%	na	11,659
Belize	2.40%	3.00%	2.40%	0.60%	320	0.00%	1,113	0.00%	2,147	0.00%	3,480	6,712
Botswana	2.80%	3.00%	2.80%	0.20%	2,204	0.03%	8,443	0.02%	14,458	0.03%	3,831	6,561
Brazil	1.50%	3.00%	1.50%	1.50%	200,019	2.78%	1,188,665	2.86%	1,323,647	2.54%	5,943	6,618
Chile	1.50%	4.00%	1.50%	2.50%	17,973	0.25%	159,887	0.38%	332,716	0.64%	8,896	18,512
Costa Rica	2.20%	4.00%	2.20%	1.80%	4,588	0.06%	16,253	0.04%	35,914	0.07%	3,543	7,829
Czech Republic	0.10%	3.00%	0.10%	2.90%	10,273	0.14%	65,826	0.16%	128,447	0.25%	6,408	12,503
Estonia	0.10%	3.50%	0.10%	3.40%	1,410	0.02%	6,351	0.02%	8,321	0.02%	4,503	5,900
Hungary	0.00%	3.00%	0.00%	3.00%	10,267	0.14%	59,900	0.14%	88,933	0.17%	5,834	8,662
Malaysia	2.20%	4.75%	2.20%	2.55%	29,290	0.41%	139,014	0.33%	310,767	0.60%	4,746	10,610
Mauritius	0.80%	1.50%	0.80%	0.70%	1,301	0.02%	7,480	0.02%	27,428	0.05%	5,748	21,077
Mexico	1.50%	4.00%	1.50%	2.50%	117,812	1.64%	639,362	1.54%	962,385	1.85%	5,427	8,169
Oman	3.60%	4.50%	3.60%	0.90%	3,870	0.05%	na	na	25,741	0.05%	na	6,652
Panama	1.70%	3.00%	1.70%	1.30%	3,463	0.05%	13,686	0.03%	27,252	0.05%	3,952	7,871
Peru	1.90%	3.50%	1.90%	1.60%	31,249	0.43%	116,457	0.28%	182,654	0.35%	3,727	5,845
Poland	0.50%	4.00%	0.50%	3.50%	40,466	0.56%	249,328	0.60%	416,838	0.80%	6,161	10,301
Russian Federation	0.40%	3.25%	0.40%	2.85%	151,331	2.10%	482,437	1.16%	618,955	1.19%	3,188	4,090
Saudi Arabia	2.20%	3.00%	2.20%	0.80%	27,847	0.39%	182,038	0.44%	194,308	0.37%	6,537	6,978
Slovak Republic	0.40%	2.00%	0.40%	1.60%	5,597	0.08%	26,226	0.06%	26,372	0.05%	4,686	4,712
South Africa	2.00%	3.50%	2.00%	1.50%	54,091	0.75%	171,354	0.41%	266,256	0.51%	3,168	4,922
Trinidad and Tobago	0.80%	2.00%	0.80%	1.20%	1,464	0.02%	6,893	0.02%	13,853	0.03%	4,708	9,462
Turkey	1.80%	4.50%	1.80%	2.70%	81,177	1.13%	337,529	0.81%	630,206	1.21%	4,158	7,763
Uruguay	0.70%	2.50%	0.70%	1.80%	3,541	0.05%	29,464	0.07%	34,164	0.07%	8,322	9,649
Venezuela	2.40%	4.50%	2.40%	2.10%	30,821	0.43%	138,406	0.33%	278,740	0.54%	4,491	9,044
Lower-Middle-Income Countries, GNP/Capita ($786–$3,125)					2,522,028	35.01%	3,911,223	9.40%	15,841,961	30.42%	1,551	6,281
Algeria	2.00%	3.00%	2.00%	1.00%	39,789	0.55%	57,942	0.14%	185,331	0.36%	1,456	4,658
Belarus	0.50%	3.00%	0.50%	2.50%	10,685	0.15%	23,073	0.06%	39,618	0.08%	2,159	3,708

| Category | 2001–2010 WKA Forecast | | | Year 2010 | | | | | | | |
	Pop	GNP	GNP per Capita	Population (000)	% of World Pop	GNP (millions)	% of World GNP	GNP (PPP) (millions)	% of World GNP (PPP)	GNP per Capita	GNP per Capita (PPP)
Bolivia	2.10%	3.80%	1.70%	10,469	0.15%	12,082	0.03%	30,548	0.06%	1,154	2,918
Bulgaria	0.10%	2.00%	1.90%	8,139	0.11%	10,118	0.02%	37,725	0.07%	1,243	4,635
Cape Verde	1.90%	3.50%	1.60%	523	0.01%	683	0.00%	1,196	0.00%	1,306	2,286
China	1.20%	5.50%	4.30%	1,428,781	19.84%	2,319,949	5.57%	11,229,094	21.56%	1,624	7,859
Colombia	1.80%	3.90%	2.10%	50,643	0.70%	147,673	0.35%	399,607	0.77%	2,916	7,891
Dominican Republic	2.70%	3.00%	0.30%	10,456	0.15%	25,908	0.06%	57,742	0.11%	2,478	5,522
Ecuador	2.20%	2.80%	0.60%	15,996	0.22%	25,688	0.06%	67,125	0.13%	1,606	4,196
Egypt, Arab Rep.	2.10%	4.00%	1.90%	79,611	1.11%	129,047	0.31%	397,278	0.76%	1,621	4,990
El Salvador	1.70%	4.00%	2.30%	7,542	0.10%	22,190	0.05%	31,840	0.06%	2,942	4,222
Fiji	1.00%	2.50%	1.50%	951	0.01%	2,635	0.01%	5,977	0.01%	2,771	6,287
Guatemala	2.70%	3.75%	1.05%	14,974	0.21%	32,946	0.08%	64,844	0.12%	2,200	4,330
Guyana	0.50%	1.40%	0.90%	925	0.01%	1,139	0.00%	4,314	0.01%	1,232	4,665
Indonesia	1.50%	4.50%	3.00%	247,045	3.43%	247,846	0.60%	981,407	1.88%	1,003	3,973
Iran, Islamic Rep.	3.00%	3.50%	0.50%	86,715	1.20%	170,655	0.41%	462,570	0.89%	1,968	5,334
Jamaica	0.90%	2.00%	1.10%	2,869	0.04%	6,075	0.01%	13,716	0.03%	2,117	4,780
Jordan	4.00%	4.00%	0.00%	7,931	0.11%	12,044	0.03%	30,595	0.06%	1,519	3,858
Kazakstan	0.60%	2.75%	2.15%	16,361	0.23%	21,260	0.05%	39,975	0.08%	1,299	2,443
Latvia	0.30%	2.00%	1.70%	2,433	0.03%	4,903	0.01%	6,447	0.01%	2,015	2,649
Lesotho	2.30%	4.00%	1.70%	2,725	0.04%	2,695	0.01%	7,721	0.01%	989	2,833
Lithuania	0.60%	3.00%	2.40%	3,884	0.05%	10,514	0.03%	14,816	0.03%	2,707	3,815
Maldives	3.00%	4.00%	1.00%	375	0.01%	692	0.00%	1,843	0.00%	1,844	4,913
Morocco	1.90%	2.60%	0.70%	35,121	0.49%	43,091	0.10%	117,191	0.23%	1,227	3,337
Namibia	2.60%	4.00%	1.40%	2,288	0.03%	5,829	0.01%	11,492	0.02%	2,548	5,023
Papua New Guinea	2.10%	3.50%	1.40%	5,990	0.08%	6,622	0.02%	18,024	0.03%	1,105	3,009
Paraguay	2.50%	4.00%	1.50%	7,190	0.10%	15,339	0.04%	27,355	0.05%	2,133	3,805
Philippines	2.10%	4.00%	1.90%	98,817	1.37%	139,551	0.34%	338,110	0.65%	1,412	3,422
Romania	0.20%	3.00%	2.80%	22,284	0.31%	50,946	0.12%	145,991	0.28%	2,286	6,551
Solomon Islands	2.20%	4.00%	1.80%	567	0.01%	616	0.00%	1,422	0.00%	1,086	2,508
Sri Lanka	2.00%	4.00%	2.00%	21,944	0.30%	26,072	0.06%	111,647	0.21%	1,188	5,088
Suriname	2.10%	3.50%	1.40%	428	0.01%	986	0.00%	1,331	0.00%	2,301	3,108
Swaziland	2.90%	4.00%	1.10%	1,411	0.02%	2,063	0.00%	3,645	0.01%	1,462	2,583

Country											
Syrian Arab Republic	2.90%	3.50%	0.60%	21,810	0.30%	26,937	0.06%	130,753	0.25%	1,235	5,995
Thailand	1.20%	5.00%	3.80%	71,470	0.99%	186,330	0.45%	625,669	1.20%	2,607	8,754
Tunisia	2.00%	3.10%	1.10%	11,932	0.17%	25,975	0.06%	66,897	0.13%	2,177	5,606
Ukraine	0.20%	2.50%	2.30%	50,748	0.70%	39,974	0.10%	76,273	0.15%	788	1,503
Uzbekistan	2.20%	3.30%	1.10%	31,528	0.44%	27,980	0.07%	53,964	0.10%	887	1,712
Vanuatu	2.60%	2.50%	-0.10%	250	0.00%	255	0.00%	389	0.00%	1,023	1,558
Western Samoa	3.00%	2.80%	-0.20%	245	0.00%	268	0.00%	480	0.00%	1,093	1,960
Low-Income Countries, GNP/Capita $785 or Less				2,775,272	38.53%	1,227,263	2.95%	4,321,819	8.30%	442	1,557
Angola	2.50%	2.00%	-0.50%	17,272	0.24%	5,206	0.01%	13,511	0.03%	301	782
Armenia	1.10%	3.00%	1.90%	4,383	0.06%	2,236	0.01%	8,546	0.02%	510	1,950
Azerbaijan	1.10%	3.00%	1.90%	8,796	0.12%	3,793	0.01%	6,708	0.01%	431	763
Bangladesh	1.90%	3.30%	1.40%	158,058	2.19%	72,350	0.17%	297,891	0.57%	458	1,885
Benin	2.70%	3.00%	0.30%	8,323	0.12%	3,977	0.01%	18,897	0.04%	478	2,270
Bhutan	2.50%	4.00%	1.50%	1,038	0.01%	623	0.00%	1,746	0.00%	601	1,682
Burkina Faso	2.70%	3.50%	0.80%	14,823	0.21%	3,764	0.01%	12,501	0.02%	254	843
Burundi	2.80%	3.00%	0.20%	9,107	0.13%	962	0.00%	3,433	0.01%	106	377
Cameroon	2.80%	2.90%	0.10%	20,150	0.28%	10,138	0.02%	30,728	0.06%	503	1,525
Central African Republic	2.10%	2.50%	0.40%	4,478	0.06%	1,198	0.00%	4,094	0.01%	268	914
Chad	2.40%	3.50%	1.10%	10,035	0.14%	2,617	0.01%	8,008	0.02%	261	798
Comoros	2.70%	3.00%	0.30%	737	0.01%	226	0.00%	704	0.00%	306	955
Congo	3.00%	3.20%	0.20%	79,869	1.11%	5,380	0.01%	48,597	0.09%	67	608
Ethiopia	2.50%	4.00%	1.50%	82,445	1.14%	11,587	0.03%	49,512	0.10%	141	601
Gambia, The	3.80%	3.00%	-0.80%	1,925	0.03%	456	0.00%	1,133	0.00%	237	589
Georgia	0.30%	2.00%	1.70%	5,520	0.08%	3,594	0.01%	3,945	0.01%	651	715
Ghana	2.70%	3.50%	0.80%	25,928	0.36%	10,831	0.03%	56,089	0.11%	418	2,163
Guinea-Bissau	1.80%	3.00%	1.20%	1,465	0.02%	405	0.00%	1,422	0.00%	277	971
Haiti	1.90%	2.00%	0.10%	9,720	0.13%	2,988	0.01%	6,321	0.01%	307	650
Honduras	2.90%	3.40%	0.50%	8,765	0.12%	6,640	0.02%	15,904	0.03%	758	1,815
India	1.80%	4.75%	2.95%	1,225,550	17.01%	700,581	1.68%	2,634,298	5.06%	572	2,149
Kenya	2.51%	4.00%	1.49%	39,828	0.55%	17,790	0.04%	66,172	0.13%	447	1,661
Kyrgyz Republic	1.00%	2.00%	1.00%	5,296	0.07%	1,401	0.00%	5,474	0.01%	265	1,034
Madagascar	2.90%	3.00%	0.10%	20,656	0.29%	4,198	0.01%	10,040	0.02%	203	486
Malawi	2.90%	4.00%	1.10%	14,959	0.21%	4,993	0.01%	15,089	0.03%	334	1,009
Mali	2.70%	3.50%	0.80%	14,734	0.20%	4,060	0.01%	8,876	0.02%	276	602
Mauritania	2.30%	3.00%	0.70%	3,389	0.05%	1,763	0.00%	6,258	0.01%	520	1,846

Projection to 2010 (U.S. Dollars) (Cont.)

Category	2001–2010 WKA Forecast			Year 2010							
	Pop	GNP	GNP per Capita	Population (000)	% of World Pop	GNP (millions)	% of World GNP	GNP (PPP) (millions)	% of World GNP (PPP)	GNP per Capita	GNP per Capita (PPP)
Mongolia	2.40%	3.50%	1.10%	3,453	0.05%	1,536	0.00%	7,251	0.01%	445	2,100
Mozambique	1.70%	4.00%	2.30%	21,281	0.30%	4,658	0.01%	24,683	0.05%	219	1,160
Nepal	2.40%	4.00%	1.60%	30,770	0.43%	8,498	0.02%	44,956	0.09%	276	1,461
Nicaragua	3.00%	3.90%	0.90%	6,915	0.10%	2,884	0.01%	14,169	0.03%	417	2,049
Niger	3.10%	3.90%	0.80%	14,844	0.21%	2,559	0.01%	9,182	0.02%	172	619
Nigeria	2.80%	3.00%	0.20%	170,963	2.37%	56,864	0.14%	208,194	0.40%	333	1,218
Pakistan	2.80%	3.50%	0.70%	184,112	2.56%	106,791	0.26%	487,857	0.94%	580	2,650
Rwanda	0.80%	3.00%	2.20%	8,843	0.12%	2,296	0.01%	4,517	0.01%	260	511
Senegal	2.70%	4.00%	1.30%	12,513	0.17%	6,553	0.02%	21,998	0.04%	524	1,758
Sierra Leone	1.50%	3.00%	1.50%	5,993	0.08%	872	0.00%	2,478	0.00%	145	414
Tajikistan	2.30%	3.00%	0.70%	8,047	0.11%	1,564	0.00%	2,860	0.01%	194	355
Tanzania	2.90%	4.00%	1.10%	45,989	0.64%	11,225	0.03%	29,239	0.06%	244	636
Togo	2.90%	3.50%	0.60%	6,381	0.09%	2,272	0.01%	7,092	0.01%	356	1,111
Uganda	2.90%	4.00%	1.10%	29,923	0.42%	13,378	0.03%	63,059	0.12%	447	2,107
Zaire	3.00%	3.20%	0.20%	65,400	0.91%	6,123	0.01%	20,553	0.04%	94	314
Zambia	2.50%	2.60%	0.10%	13,261	0.18%	4,343	0.01%	9,617	0.02%	328	725
Zimbabwe	2.60%	2.90%	0.30%	16,026	0.22%	10,954	0.03%	28,217	0.05%	684	1,761

Category	2001–2020 WKA Forecast			Year 2020							
	Pop	GNP	GNP per Capita	Population (000)	% of World Pop	GNP (millions)	% of World GNP	GNP (PPP) (millions)	% of World GNP (PPP)	GNP per Capita	GNP per Capita (PPP)
High-Income Countries, GNP/Capita ≥$9,656				1,155,487	13.61%	42,856,183	75.80%	34,364,807	45.76%	37,089	29,741
Argentina	1.20%	3.00%	2.80%	47,546	0.56%	752,328	1.33%	746,567	0.99%	15,823	15,702
Australia	1.30%	2.50%	1.70%	25,115	0.30%	729,541	1.29%	693,469	0.92%	29,048	27,611
Austria	0.50%	2.20%	1.70%	9,171	0.11%	334,814	0.59%	282,678	0.38%	36,508	30,823
Bahamas, The	1.50%	1.50%	8.50%	413	0.00%	na	na	5,113	0.01%	na	12,367
Belgium	0.30%	2.20%	1.90%	10,917	0.13%	403,141	0.71%	369,284	0.49%	36,928	33,827
Canada	1.20%	3.00%	1.80%	39,848	0.47%	1,119,659	1.98%	1,214,338	1.62%	28,098	30,474
Chile	1.50%	4.00%	3.50%	20,859	0.25%	236,672	0.42%	494,279	0.66%	11,346	23,697
Denmark	0.20%	2.75%	2.30%	5,566	0.07%	313,353	0.55%	217,985	0.29%	56,301	39,166
Finland	0.50%	3.50%	3.00%	5,691	0.07%	250,773	0.44%	198,338	0.26%	44,068	34,853
France	0.50%	2.75%	1.90%	65,731	0.77%	2,428,733	4.30%	2,158,109	2.87%	36,950	32,833
Germany	0.40%	2.40%	2.00%	91,135	1.07%	3,451,622	6.11%	2,745,207	3.66%	37,874	30,122
Greece	0.50%	2.20%	1.60%	11,801	0.14%	198,208	0.35%	206,430	0.27%	16,796	17,493
Hong Kong	1.20%	4.00%	3.80%	8,820	0.10%	375,855	0.66%	338,518	0.45%	42,614	38,381
Iceland	1.00%	2.90%	1.90%	343	0.00%	na	na	9,974	0.01%	na	29,074
Ireland	0.20%	4.00%	4.30%	3,841	0.05%	197,045	0.35%	197,987	0.26%	51,304	51,550
Israel	2.60%	4.00%	2.40%	10,823	0.13%	273,513	0.48%	275,339	0.37%	25,272	25,441
Italy	0.20%	2.20%	1.70%	59,630	0.70%	1,771,088	3.13%	1,814,290	2.42%	29,701	30,426
Japan	0.40%	2.00%	2.00%	137,804	1.62%	6,262,992	11.08%	4,207,792	5.60%	45,449	30,535
Korea, Rep.	0.80%	4.50%	4.70%	56,125	0.66%	1,140,994	2.02%	1,524,639	2.03%	20,330	27,165
Kuwait	1.00%	2.70%	1.70%	2,163	0.03%	103,287	0.18%	172,689	0.23%	47,758	79,849
Luxembourg	1.00%	2.50%	1.50%	542	0.01%	27,820	0.05%	25,820	0.03%	51,310	47,622
Netherlands	0.50%	2.90%	2.40%	17,732	0.21%	687,798	1.22%	606,377	0.81%	38,789	34,197
New Zealand	0.90%	2.30%	1.70%	4,766	0.06%	96,512	0.17%	100,913	0.13%	20,252	21,176
Norway	0.40%	3.20%	2.80%	4,890	0.06%	328,950	0.58%	223,555	0.30%	67,265	45,713
Portugal	0.20%	3.50%	3.30%	10,176	0.12%	216,382	0.38%	279,147	0.37%	21,264	27,431
Singapore	1.70%	3.75%	3.30%	4,660	0.05%	269,690	0.48%	213,472	0.28%	57,870	45,807
Spain	2.00%	2.90%	0.90%	49,196	0.58%	974,715	1.72%	1,087,662	1.45%	19,813	22,109
St. Kitts and Nevis	2.00%	3.00%	2.40%	49	0.00%	599	0.00%	989	0.00%	12,123	20,020
Sweden	0.60%	2.30%	1.70%	10,124	0.12%	350,010	0.62%	261,592	0.35%	34,572	25,839
Switzerland	0.70%	2.20%	1.50%	8,430	0.10%	413,253	0.73%	275,005	0.37%	49,024	32,624

| Category | 2001–2020 WKA Forecast | | | Year 2020 | | | | | | | |
	Pop	GNP	GNP per Capita	Population (000)	% of World Pop	GNP (millions)	% of World GNP	GNP (PPP) (millions)	% of World GNP (PPP)	GNP per Capita	GNP per Capita (PPP)
Taiwan (Rep. of China)	0.80%	4.50%	4.20%	26,062	0.31%	960,276	1.70%	738,491	0.98%	36,845	28,336
United Arab Emirates	3.00%	3.00%	0.00%	5,908	0.07%	na	na	56,129	0.07%	na	9,501
United Kingdom	0.30%	2.60%	2.30%	63,407	0.75%	2,316,692	4.10%	2,114,071	2.81%	36,537	33,341
United States	0.80%	3.00%	1.80%	326,607	3.85%	15,809,426	27.96%	10,464,772	13.93%	48,405	35,117
Uruguay	0.70%	2.50%	1.80%	3,796	0.04%	37,716	0.07%	43,786	0.06%	9,935	11,533
Upper-Middle-Income Countries, GNP/Capita ($3,126–$9,655)				1,146,537	13.50%	6,217,912	11.00%	9,969,818	13.27%	5,423	8,696
Bahrain	3.00%	3.50%	0.50%	1,236	0.01%	11,210	0.02%	17,930	0.02%	9,073	14,512
Barbados	0.40%	2.00%	0.10%	293	0.00%	na	na	4,009	0.01%	na	13,664
Belize	2.40%	3.00%	2.60%	405	0.00%	1,496	0.00%	2,889	0.00%	3,690	7,125
Botswana	2.80%	3.00%	1.90%	2,904	0.03%	11,346	0.02%	19,441	0.03%	3,906	6,694
Brazil	1.50%	3.00%	2.40%	232,130	2.73%	1,597,467	2.83%	1,782,761	2.37%	6,882	7,680
Colombia	1.80%	3.90%	2.10%	60,533	0.71%	216,500	0.38%	587,987	0.78%	3,577	9,713
Costa Rica	2.20%	4.00%	2.30%	5,703	0.07%	24,059	0.04%	53,365	0.07%	4,219	9,358
Czech Republic	0.10%	3.00%	2.90%	10,376	0.12%	88,464	0.16%	172,670	0.23%	8,526	16,641
El Salvador	1.70%	4.00%	3.30%	8,926	0.11%	32,847	0.06%	47,308	0.06%	3,680	5,300
Estonia	0.10%	3.50%	3.90%	1,425	0.02%	8,958	0.02%	11,742	0.02%	6,288	8,242
Fiji	1.00%	2.50%	1.50%	1,050	0.01%	3,373	0.01%	7,665	0.01%	3,212	7,298
Hungary	0.00%	3.00%	3.00%	10,267	0.12%	80,501	0.14%	119,518	0.16%	7,841	11,641
Lithuania	0.60%	3.00%	2.90%	4,123	0.05%	14,130	0.02%	19,939	0.03%	3,427	4,836
Malaysia	2.20%	4.75%	3.70%	36,411	0.43%	221,105	0.39%	496,936	0.66%	6,072	13,648
Mauritius	0.80%	1.50%	3.20%	1,409	0.02%	8,681	0.02%	31,849	0.04%	6,160	22,599
Mexico	1.50%	4.00%	1.70%	136,726	1.61%	946,412	1.67%	1,429,710	1.90%	6,922	10,457
Namibia	2.60%	4.00%	2.40%	2,958	0.03%	8,629	0.02%	17,071	0.02%	2,918	5,772
Oman	3.60%	4.50%	0.90%	5,512	0.06%	na	na	40,099	0.05%	na	7,275
Panama	1.70%	3.00%	1.80%	4,098	0.05%	18,392	0.03%	36,703	0.05%	4,488	8,956
Peru	1.90%	3.50%	2.60%	37,721	0.44%	164,274	0.29%	258,409	0.34%	4,355	6,851
Poland	0.50%	4.00%	4.40%	42,535	0.50%	369,067	0.65%	618,061	0.82%	8,677	14,531
Qatar	4.30%	3.00%	–1.30%	1,738	0.02%	na	na	15,151	0.02%	na	8,715
Romania	0.20%	3.00%	3.80%	22,734	0.27%	68,468	0.12%	196,306	0.26%	3,012	8,635

Country											
Russian Federation	0.40%	3.25%	3.00%	157,495	1.85%	664,264	1.17%	853,176	1.14%	4,218	5,417
Saudi Arabia	2.20%	3.00%	0.80%	34,617	0.41%	244,643	0.43%	261,580	0.35%	7,067	7,556
Slovak Republic	0.40%	2.00%	3.60%	5,825	0.07%	31,969	0.06%	32,168	0.04%	5,489	5,523
South Africa	2.00%	3.50%	1.50%	65,937	0.78%	241,711	0.43%	376,671	0.50%	3,666	5,713
Thailand	1.20%	5.00%	3.80%	80,525	0.95%	303,512	0.54%	1,023,583	1.36%	3,769	12.711
Trinidad and Tobago	0.80%	2.00%	1.20%	1,586	0.02%	8,403	0.01%	16,903	0.02%	5,300	10,661
Turkey	1.80%	4.50%	3.70%	97,031	1.14%	524,172	0.93%	983,252	1.31%	5,402	10,133
Venezuela	2.40%	4.50%	2.00%	39,070	0.46%	214,940	0.38%	434,966	0.58%	5,501	11,133
Lower-Middle-Income Countries, GNP/Capita ($786–$3,125)				2,741,647	32.29%	5,615,567	9.93%	24,213,358	32.24	2,048	8,832
Algeria	2.00%	3.00%	1.00%	48,502	0.57%	77,870	0.14%	249,554	0.33%	1,605	5,145
Belarus	0.50%	3.00%	2.50%	11,232	0.13%	31,008	0.05%	53,308	0.07%	2,761	4,746
Bolivia	2.10%	3.80%	1.70%	12,887	0.15%	17,544	0.03%	44,509	0.06%	1,361	3,454
Bulgaria	0.10%	2.00%	1.90%	8,220	0.10%	12,334	0.02%	45,995	0.06%	1,500	5,595
Cape Verde	1.90%	3.50%	2.70%	632	0.01%	964	0.00%	1,693	0.00%	1,526	2,680
China	1.20%	5.50%	6.80%	1,609,796	18.96%	3,962,808	7.01%	19,274,936	25.66%	2,462	11,974
Dominican Republic	2.70%	3.00%	0.30%	13,649	0.16%	34,819	0.06%	77,662	0.10%	2,551	5,690
Ecuador	2.20%	2.80%	0.60%	19,884	0.23%	33,858	0.06%	88,587	0.12%	1,703	4,455
Egypt, Arab Rep.	2.10%	4.00%	0.90%	98,001	1.15%	191,021	0.34%	590,329	0.79%	1,949	6,024
Guatemala	2.70%	3.75%	2.30%	19,546	0.23%	47,608	0.08%	93,959	0.13%	2,436	4,807
Guyana	0.50%	1.40%	0.90%	972	0.01%	1,309	0.00%	4,960	0.01%	1,346	5,102
Honduras	2.90%	3.40%	0.50%	11,666	0.14%	9,277	0.02%	22,250	0.03%	795	1,907
Indonesia	1.50%	4.50%	3.90%	286,706	3.38%	384,897	0.68%	1,530,671	2.04%	1,342	5,339
Iran, Islamic Rep.	3.00%	3.50%	-0.20%	116,537	1.37%	240,726	0.43%	653,447	0.87%	2,066	5,607
Jamaica	0.90%	2.00%	3.00%	3,138	0.04%	7,405	0.01%	16,736	0.02%	2,359	5,332
Jordan	4.00%	4.00%	0.00%	11,740	0.14%	17,828	0.03%	45,288	0.06%	1,519	3,858
Kazakstan	0.60%	2.75%	2.40%	17,370	0.20%	27,886	0.05%	52,499	0.07%	1,605	3,022
Latvia	0.30%	2.00%	1.70%	2,507	0.03%	5,977	0.01%	7,862	0.01%	2,384	3,136
Lesotho	2.30%	4.00%	2.70%	3,421	0.04%	3,989	0.01%	11,471	0.02%	1,166	3,353
Maldives	3.00%	4.00%	2.00%	504	0.01%	1,024	0.00%	2,736	0.00%	2,031	5,427
Morocco	1.90%	2.60%	0.70%	42,394	0.50%	55,701	0.10%	151,681	0.20%	1,314	3,578
Papua New Guinea	2.10%	3.50%	2.10%	7,374	0.09%	9,340	0.02%	25,497	0.03%	1,267	3,458
Paraguay	2.50%	4.00%	1.50%	9,203	0.11%	22,705	0.04%	40,639	0.05%	2,467	4,416
Philippines	2.10%	4.00%	2.40%	121,643	1.43%	206,569	0.37%	502,408	0.67%	1,698	4,130
Solomon Islands	2.20%	4.00%	1.80%	705	0.01%	912	0.00%	2,113	0.00%	1,293	2,998
Sri Lanka	2.00%	4.00%	2.00%	26,749	0.31%	38,593	0.07%	165,901	0.22%	1,443	6,202

Category	2001–2020 WKA Forecast			Year 2020							
	Pop	GNP	GNP per Capita	Population (000)	% of World Pop	GNP (millions)	% of World GNP	GNP (PPP) (millions)	% of World GNP (PPP)	GNP per Capita	GNP per Capita (PPP)
Suriname	2.10%	3.50%	1.90%	527	0.01%	1,390	0.00%	1,884	0.00%	2,637	3,572
Swaziland	2.90%	4.00%	1.10%	1,878	0.02%	3,054	0.01%	5,411	0.01%	1,627	2,882
Syrian Arab Republic	2.90%	3.50%	1.10%	29,028	0.34%	37,998	0.07%	184,751	0.25%	1,309	6,365
Tunisia	2.00%	3.10%	1.10%	14,545	0.17%	35,248	0.06%	90,974	0.12%	2,423	6,255
Ukraine	0.20%	2.50%	2.30%	51,772	0.61%	51,170	0.09%	97,679	0.13%	988	1,887
Uzbekistan	2.20%	3.30%	1.10%	39,193	0.46%	38,712	0.07%	74,838	0.10%	988	1,909
Vanuatu	2.60%	2.50%	–0.10%	323	0.00%	327	0.00%	498	0.00%	1,013	1,543
Western Samoa	3.00%	2.80%	–0.20%	329	0.00%	353	0.00%	632	0.00%	1,072	1,921
Low-Income Countries, GNP/Capita $785 or Less				**3,448,335**	**40.61%**	**1,846,393**	**3.27%**	**6,556,069**	**8.73%**	**535**	**1,901**
Angola	2.50%	2.00%	1.50%	22,109	0.26%	6,346	0.01%	16,450	0.02%	287	744
Armenia	1.10%	3.00%	3.90%	4,890	0.06%	3,004	0.01%	11,508	0.02%	614	2,354
Azerbaijan	1.10%	3.00%	1.90%	9,813	0.12%	5,097	0.01%	9,033	0.01%	519	921
Bangladesh	1.90%	3.30%	2.10%	190,792	2.25%	100,102	0.18%	413,218	0.55%	525	2,166
Benin	2.70%	3.00%	1.30%	10,865	0.13%	5,344	0.01%	25,416	0.03%	492	2,339
Bhutan	2.50%	4.00%	2.50%	1,329	0.02%	923	0.00%	2,594	0.00%	694	1,953
Burkina Faso	2.70%	3.50%	1.50%	19,349	0.23%	5,309	0.01%	17,671	0.02%	274	913
Burundi	2.80%	3.00%	0.30%	12,004	0.14%	1,293	0.00%	4,616	0.01%	108	385
Cameroon	2.80%	2.90%	0.00%	26,558	0.31%	13,492	0.02%	40,908	0.05%	508	1,540
Central African Republic	2.10%	2.50%	0.40%	5,513	0.06%	1,534	0.00%	5,244	0.01%	278	951
Chad	2.40%	3.50%	2.30%	12,720	0.15%	3,691	0.01%	11,325	0.02%	290	890
Comoros	2.70%	3.00%	0.30%	963	0.01%	304	0.00%	947	0.00%	315	984

Congo	3.00%	3.20%	0.00%	107,338	1.26%	7,372	0.01%	66,629	0.09%	69	621
Ethiopia	2.50%	4.00%	2.00%	105,537	1.24%	17,152	0.03%	73,555	0.10%	163	697
Gambia, The	3.80%	3.00%	-2.30%	2,795	0.03%	613	0.00%	1,518	0.00%	219	543
Georgia	0.30%	2.00%	1.70%	5,688	0.07%	4,381	0.01%	4,811	0.01%	770	846
Ghana	2.70%	3.50%	1.30%	33,844	0.40%	15,279	0.03%	79,284	0.11%	451	2,343
Guinea-Bissau	1.80%	3.00%	2.20%	1,751	0.02%	545	0.00%	1,915	0.00%	311	1,094
Haiti	1.90%	2.00%	0.00%	11,733	0.14%	3,642	0.01%	7,707	0.01%	310	657
India	1.80%	4.75%	3.20%	1,464,902	17.25%	1,114,291	1.97%	4,211,203	5.61%	761	2,875
Kenya	2.51%	4.00%	3.49%	51,033	0.60%	26,334	0.05%	98,303	0.13%	516	1,926
Kyrgyz Republic	1.00%	2.00%	1.00%	5,850	0.07%	1,708	0.00%	6,680	0.01%	292	1,142
Madagascar	2.90%	3.00%	-1.30%	27,492	0.32%	5,642	0.01%	13,497	0.02%	205	491
Malawi	2.90%	4.00%	2.10%	19,910	0.23%	7,390	0.01%	22,403	0.03%	371	1,125
Mali	2.70%	3.50%	1.30%	19,232	0.23%	5,727	0.01%	12,547	0.02%	298	652
Mauritania	2.30%	3.00%	1.70%	4,254	0.05%	2,369	0.00%	8,423	0.01%	557	1,980
Mongolia	2.40%	3.50%	1.60%	4,377	0.05%	2,167	0.00%	10,254	0.01%	495	2,342
Mozambique	1.70%	4.00%	3.30%	25,189	0.30%	6,894	0.01%	36,674	0.05%	274	1,456
Nepal	2.40%	4.00%	2.40%	39,005	0.46%	12,579	0.02%	66,792	0.09%	322	1,712
Nicaragua	3.00%	3.90%	0.90%	9,293	0.11%	4,229	0.01%	20,826	0.03%	455	2,241
Niger	3.10%	3.90%	0.80%	20,143	0.24%	3,751	0.01%	13,494	0.02%	186	670
Nigeria	2.80%	3.00%	1.10%	225,338	2.65%	76,421	0.14%	279,948	0.37%	339	1,242
Pakistan	2.80%	3.50%	1.20%	242,669	2.86%	150,639	0.27%	689,474	0.92%	621	2,841
Rwanda	0.80%	3.00%	2.70%	9,576	0.11%	3,086	0.01%	6,081	0.01%	322	635
Senegal	2.70%	4.00%	1.30%	16,333	0.19%	9,700	0.02%	32,672	0.04%	594	2,000
Sierra Leone	1.50%	3.00%	1.50%	6,955	0.08%	1,171	0.00%	3,338	0.00%	168	480
Tajikistan	2.30%	3.00%	0.70%	10,101	0.12%	2,102	0.00%	3,849	0.01%	208	381
Tanzania	2.90%	4.00%	1.10%	61,207	0.72%	16,616	0.03%	43,413	0.06%	271	709
Togo	2.90%	3.50%	1.10%	8,492	0.10%	3,204	0.01%	10,021	0.01%	377	1,180
Uganda	2.90%	4.00%	1.10%,	39,826	0.47%	19,803	0.04%	93,629	0.12%	497	2,351
Zaire	3.00%	3.20%	-1.00%	87,892	1.03%	8,390	0.01%	28,179	0.04%	95	321
Zambia	2.50%	2.60%	0.00%	16,975	0.20%	5,614	0.01%	12,434	0.02%	331	733
Zimbabwe	2.60%	2.90%	0.30%	20,715	0.24%	14,579	0.03%	37,584	0.05%	704	1,814

Country Income Category Movement (U.S. Dollars)

Year 2000 to 2010

Country	2000 GNP per Capita	2010 GNP per Capita	From	To
Botswana	3,071	3,831	Lower middle	Upper middle income
Costa Rica	2,730	3,543	Lower middle	Upper middle income
Estonia	2,956	4,503	Lower middle	Upper middle income
Lesotho	637	989	Low	Lower middle
Peru	2,789	3,727	Lower middle	Upper middle income
Russian Federation	2,329	3,188	Lower middle	Upper middle income
South Africa	2,902	3,168	Lower middle	Upper middle income
St. Kitts and Nevis	7,081	10,996	Upper middle	High
Turkey	3,081	4,158	Lower middle	Upper middle income
Ukraine	653	788	Low	Lower middle

Year 2010 to 2020

Country	2010 GNP per Capita	2020 GNP per Capita	From	To
Chile	8,896	12,486	Upper middle	High income
Colombia	2,916	3,577	Lower middle	Upper middle income
El Salvador	2,942	4,049	Lower middle	Upper middle income
Fiji	2,771	3,212	Lower middle	Upper middle income
Honduras	758	795	Low	Lower middle income
Indonesia	1,003	1,342	Lower middle	Lower middle income
Lithuania	2,707	3,597	Lower middle	Upper middle income
Namibia	2,548	3,211	Lower middle	Upper middle income
Romania	2,286	3,317	Lower middle	Upper middle income
Seychelles	8,963	11,333	Upper middle	High income
Thailand	2,607	3,769	Lower middle	Upper middle income
Uruguay	8,322	9,935	Upper middle	High income

2000 Alphabetical Listing (U.S. Dollars)

Country	1990–1997 Growth Rate (%) Pop	GNP	GNP per Capita	Year 2000 Population (000)	% of World Pop	GNP (millions)	% of World GNP	GNP per Capita	GNP per Capita (PPP)	GNP (PPP) (millions)	% of World GNP (PPP)
Afghanistan	2.90%	na	na	27,201	0.44%	na	na	na	na	na	na
Albania	0.20%	2.20%	2.00%	3,344	0.05%	2,685	0.01%	803	na	na	na
Algeria	2.30%	−1.60%	−3.90%	31,388	0.51%	42,698	0.14%	1,360	4,344	136,350	0.36%
American Samoa	3.90%	na	na	70	0.00%	na	na	na	na	na	na
Andorra	3.10%	na	na	70	0.00%	na	na	na	na	na	na
Angola	3.30%	−10.00%	−13.30%	12,852	0.21%	3,196	0.01%	249	642	8,248	0.02%
Antigua and Barbuda	0.50%	1.80%	1.30%	67	0.00%	515	0.00%	7,685	na	na	na
Argentina	1.30%	4.20%	2.90%	37,087	0.60%	360,472	1.19%	9,720	9,587	355,545	0.94%
Armenia	0.90%	−10.70%	−11.60%	3,890	0.06%	1,248	0.00%	321	1,220	4,746	0.01%
Aruba	4.40%	−0.60%	−5.00%	101	0.00%	na	na	na	na	na	na
Australia	1.20%	2.40%	1.20%	19,207	0.31%	407,949	1.35%	21,239	20,104	386,141	1.02%
Austria	0.60%	1.10%	0.50%	8,218	0.13%	212,469	0.70%	25,854	21,787	179,046	0.47%
Azerbaijan	0.90%	−16.00%	−16.90%	7,807	0.13%	2,562	0.01%	328	579	4,517	0.01%
Bahamas, The	1.70%	−2.00%	−3.70%	304	0.00%	na	na	na	12,183	3,703	0.01%
Bahrain	3.00%	2.60%	−0.40%	677	0.01%	5,580	0.02%	8,236	13,134	8,898	0.02%
Bangladesh	1.60%	3.30%	1.70%	129,663	2.11%	47,489	0.16%	366	1,501	194,670	0.51%
Barbados	0.40%	−0.90%	−1.30%	268	0.00%	na	na	na	9,947	2,668	0.01%
Belarus	0.00%	−5.60%	−5.60%	10,267	0.17%	18,928	0.06%	1,844	3,164	32,480	0.09%
Belgium	0.30%	1.30%	1.00%	10,282	0.17%	255,828	0.85%	24,881	22,765	234,068	0.62%
Belize	2.80%	0.30%	−2.50%	250	0.00%	622	0.00%	2,488	4,758	1,189	0.00%
Benin	2.90%	1.70%	−1.20%	6,315	0.10%	2,221	0.01%	352	1,657	10,463	0.03%
Bermuda	0.50%	na	na	64	0.00%	na	na	na	na	na	na
Bhutan	2.90%	2.00%	−0.90%	803	0.01%	348	0.00%	433	1,204	967	0.00%
Bolivia	2.40%	2.00%	−0.40%	8,340	0.14%	8,241	0.03%	988	2,490	20,763	0.05%
Bosnia and Herzegovina	−9.10%	na	na	1,762	0.03%	na	na	na	na	na	na
Botswana	2.60%	1.30%	−1.30%	1,656	0.03%	5,085	0.02%	3,071	5,227	8,654	0.02%
Brazil	1.40%	1.90%	0.50%	170,661	2.78%	850,852	2.81%	4,986	5,536	944,838	2.49%
Brunei	2.60%	−2.10%	−4.70%	333	0.01%	na	na	na	na	na	na
Bulgaria	−0.70%	−2.00%	−1.30%	8,139	0.13%	9,160	0.03%	1,125	4,196	34,152	0.09%
Burkina Faso	2.40%	0.80%	−1.60%	11,246	0.18%	2,447	0.01%	218	720	8,092	0.02%
Burundi	2.40%	−5.90%	−8.30%	6,910	0.11%	789	0.00%	114	408	2,823	0.01%

2000 Alphabetical Listing (U.S. Dollars) (Cont.)

| Country | 1990–1997 Growth Rate (%) | | | Year 2000 | | | | | | | |
	Pop	GNP	GNP per Capita	Population (000)	% of World Pop	GNP (millions)	% of World GNP	GNP per Capita	GNP per Capita (PPP)	GNP (PPP) (millions)	% of World GNP (PPP)
Cambodia	2.70%	2.70%	0.00%	11,352	0.19%	3,297	0.01%	290	na	na	na
Cameroon	2.80%	−3.30%	−6.10%	15,140	0.25%	7,691	0.03%	508	1,540	23,320	0.06%
Canada	1.20%	0.80%	−0.40%	31,390	0.51%	602,158	1.99%	19,183	20,711	650,121	1.71%
Cape Verde	2.30%	1.00%	−1.30%	429	0.01%	432	0.00%	1,006	1,752	752	0.00%
Cayman Islands	na	na	na	na	na	na	na	na	na	na	na
Central African Republic	2.10%	−1.00%	−3.10%	3,638	0.06%	973	0.00%	268	914	3,325	0.01%
Chad	3.10%	1.00%	−2.10%	7,839	0.13%	1,622	0.01%	207	630	4,935	0.01%
Channel Islands	0.60%	na	na	151	0.00%	na	na	na	na	na	na
Chile	1.60%	6.40%	4.80%	15,335	0.25%	89,280	0.30%	5,822	12,035	184,557	0.49%
China	1.10%	10.00%	8.90%	1,268,121	20.67%	1,179,345	3.90%	930	4,472	5,671,304	14.92%
Colombia	1.90%	2.60%	0.70%	42,368	0.69%	99,763	0.33%	2,355	6,348	268,934	0.71%
Comoros	2.60%	−3.10%	−5.70%	559	0.01%	177	0.00%	316	984	551	0.00%
Congo	6.00%	−12.50%	−18.50%	58,856	0.96%	4,775	0.02%	81	737	43,385	0.11%
Costa Rica	1.80%	2.30%	0.50%	3,654	0.06%	9,978	0.03%	2,730	5,998	21,918	0.06%
Cote d'Ivoire	2.90%	0.90%	−2.00%	15,484	0.25%	9,698	0.03%	626	1,428	22,114	0.06%
Croatia	0.00%	2.70%	2.70%	4,768	0.08%	21,072	0.07%	4,419	na	na	na
Cuba	0.60%	na	na	11,259	0.18%	na	na	na	na	na	na
Cyprus	1.30%	2.60%	1.30%	777	0.01%	8,944	0.03%	11,518	na	na	na
Czech Republic	−0.10%	−0.30%	−0.20%	10,273	0.17%	50,924	0.17%	4,957	9,673	99,369	0.26%
Denmark	0.40%	2.50%	2.10%	5,348	0.09%	181,253	0.60%	33,894	23,555	125,963	0.33%
Djibouti	3.00%	na	na	695	0.01%	na	na	na	na	na	na
Dominica	0.30%	0.70%	0.40%	75	0.00%	231	0.00%	3,091	na	na	na
Dominican Republic	1.90%	3.50%	1.60%	8,578	0.14%	16,212	0.05%	1,890	4,190	35,939	0.09%
Ecuador	2.20%	0.90%	−1.30%	12,742	0.21%	19,301	0.06%	1,515	3,953	50,367	0.13%
Egypt, Arab Rep.	2.00%	2.80%	0.80%	64,042	1.04%	83,097	0.27%	1,298	3,975	254,583	0.67%
El Salvador	2.10%	3.50%	1.40%	6,309	0.10%	12,391	0.04%	1,964	2,798	17,653	0.05%
Equatorial Guinea	2.50%	12.10%	9.60%	452	0.01%	690	0.00%	1,526	na	na	na
Eritrea	2.60%	2.90%	0.30%	4,075	0.07%	904	0.00%	222	na	na	na
Estonia	−1.10%	−2.80%	−1.70%	1,410	0.02%	4,169	0.01%	2,956	3,873	5,463	0.01%
Ethiopia	2.20%	2.20%	0.00%	63,781	1.04%	6,766	0.02%	106	450	28,701	0.08%
Faeroe Islands	na	na	na	na	na	na	na	na	na	na	na

Country											
Fiji	1.50%	0.40%	-1.10%	852	0.01%	2,057	0.01%	2,414	5,469	4,661	0.01%
Finland	0.40%	0.90%	0.50%	5,202	0.08%	120,100	0.40%	23,088	18,208	94,719	0.25%
France	0.50%	1.00%	0.50%	59,491	0.97%	1,446,515	4.78%	24,315	21,561	1,282,677	3.37%
French Guiana	1.90%	na	na	na	na	na	na	na	na	na	na
French Polynesia	na	na	na	237	0.00%	na	na	na	na	na	na
Gabon	2.60%	-0.10%	-2.70%	1,245	0.02%	4,465	0.01%	3,585	na	na	na
Gambia, The	3.60%	-0.60%	-4.20%	1,313	0.02%	393	0.00%	299	750	985	0.00%
Georgia	-0.10%	-14.90%	-14.80%	5,411	0.09%	3,253	0.01%	601	660	3,571	0.01%
Germany	0.50%	0.70%	0.20%	83,308	1.36%	2,127,086	7.03%	25,533	20,272	1,688,783	4.44%
Ghana	2.70%	1.40%	-1.30%	19,481	0.32%	7,042	0.02%	361	1,864	36,313	0.10%
Greece	0.50%	1.00%	0.50%	10,681	0.17%	123,350	0.41%	11,549	12,006	128,228	0.34%
Greenland	0.10%	na	na	56	0.00%	na	na	na	na	na	na
Grenada	0.30%	1.30%	1.00%	97	0.00%	314	0.00%	3,241	na	na	na
Guadeloupe	1.30%	na	na	444	0.01%	na	na	na	na	na	na
Guam	1.20%	na	na	151	0.00%	na	na	na	na	na	na
Guatemala	2.60%	1.50%	-1.10%	11,361	0.19%	18,397	0.06%	1,619	3,160	35,904	0.09%
Guinea	2.60%	2.70%	0.10%	7,474	0.12%	4,000	0.01%	535	na	na	na
Guinea-Bissau	2.20%	1.00%	-1.20%	1,214	0.02%	259	0.00%	213	744	903	0.00%
Guyana	0.90%	12.90%	12.00%	871	0.01%	981	0.00%	1,127	4,265	3,715	0.01%
Haiti	2.10%	-4.40%	-6.50%	7,974	0.13%	2,451	0.01%	307	650	5,185	0.01%
Honduras	2.90%	1.00%	-1.90%	6,522	0.11%	4,707	0.02%	722	1,726	11,259	0.03%
Hong Kong	1.90%	3.30%	1.40%	6,880	0.11%	188,936	0.62%	27,463	24,602	169,255	0.45%
Hungary	-0.30%	0.20%	0.50%	10,064	0.16%	44,571	0.15%	4,429	6,572	66,138	0.17%
Iceland	0.90%	0.40%	-0.50%	278	0.00%	na	na	na	19,954	5,555	0.01%
India	1.80%	4.30%	2.50%	1,015,287	16.55%	430,096	1.42%	424	1,584	1,608,186	4.23%
Indonesia	1.70%	5.90%	4.20%	210,785	3.44%	247,846	0.82%	1,176	4,668	983,923	2.59%
Iran, Islamic Rep.	1.60%	1.90%	0.30%	63,901	1.04%	130,742	0.43%	2,046	5,553	354,811	0.93%
Iraq	2.70%	na	na	23,665	0.39%	na	na	na	na	na	na
Ireland	0.60%	5.60%	5.00%	3,727	0.06%	74,331	0.25%	19,942	20,012	74,591	0.20%
Israel	3.20%	2.60%	-0.60%	6,414	0.10%	103,178	0.34%	16,085	16,001	102,638	0.27%
Italy	0.20%	1.00%	0.80%	57,869	0.94%	1,168,771	3.86%	20,197	20,678	1,196,590	3.15%
Jamaica	0.90%	0.80%	-0.10%	2,624	0.04%	4,104	0.01%	1,564	3,522	9,241	0.02%
Japan	0.30%	1.40%	1.10%	127,229	2.07%	4,427,104	14.63%	34,796	23,353	2,971,197	7.82%
Jordan	4.80%	2.80%	-2.00%	5,107	0.08%	7,394	0.02%	1,448	3,670	18,743	0.05%
Kazakstan	-0.50%	-7.40%	-6.90%	15,565	0.25%	17,441	0.06%	1,120	2,105	32,769	0.09%
Kenya	2.80%	-0.30%	-3.10%	31,083	0.51%	9,934	0.03%	320	1,179	36,646	0.10%
Kiribati	2.00%	-0.60%	-2.60%	88	0.00%	76	0.00%	859	na	na	na
Korea, Dem. Rep.	1.60%	na	na	24,010	0.39%	na	na	na	na	na	na
Korea, Rep.	1.00%	6.00%	5.00%	47,385	0.77%	520,855	1.72%	10,992	14,613	692,451	1.82%

Country	1990–1997 Growth Rate (%)			Year 2000							
	Pop	GNP	GNP per Capita	Population (000)	% of World Pop	GNP (millions)	% of World GNP	GNP per Capita	GNP per Capita (PPP)	GNP (PPP) (millions)	% of World GNP (PPP)
Kuwait	−2.30%	17.50%	19.80%	1,687	0.03%	59,455	0.20%	35,242	58,705	99,038	0.26%
Kyrgyz Republic	0.80%	−9.70%	−10.50%	4,747	0.08%	1,256	0.00%	265	1,034	4,907	0.01%
Lao PDR	2.60%	3.90%	1.30%	5,237	0.09%	1,966	0.01%	375	na	na	na
Latvia	−1.10%	−7.30%	−6.20%	2,385	0.04%	4,439	0.01%	1,861	2,447	5,835	0.02%
Lebanon	1.90%	4.90%	3.00%	4,387	0.07%	17,710	0.06%	4,037	na	na	na
Lesotho	2.20%	2.50%	0.30%	2,150	0.04%	1,370	0.00%	637	1,807	3,885	0.01%
Liberia	2.40%	na	na	3,099	0.05%	na	na	na	na	na	na
Libya	2.30%	na	na	5,568	0.09%	na	na	na	na	na	na
Liechtenstein	na	na	na	na	na	na	na	na	na	na	na
Lithuania	−0.10%	−7.10%	−7.00%	3,695	0.06%	7,526	0.02%	2,037	2,866	10,590	0.03%
Luxembourg	1.40%	0.20%	−1.20%	440	0.01%	16,977	0.06%	38,587	35,708	15,711	0.04%
Macao	2.60%	na	na	484	0.01%	na	na	na	na	na	na
Macedonia, FYR	0.70%	−2.10%	−2.80%	2,039	0.03%	2,045	0.01%	1,003	na	na	na
Madagascar	2.80%	−1.60%	−4.40%	15,370	0.25%	3,279	0.01%	213	511	7,855	0.02%
Malawi	2.70%	0.80%	−1.90%	11,131	0.18%	2,538	0.01%	228	681	7,585	0.02%
Malaysia	2.50%	5.80%	3.30%	23,333	0.38%	110,739	0.37%	4,746	10,610	247,559	0.65%
Maldives	2.60%	4.30%	1.70%	276	0.00%	352	0.00%	1,272	3,351	926	0.00%
Mali	2.80%	0.30%	−2.50%	11,179	0.18%	2,492	0.01%	223	485	5,417	0.01%
Malta	0.80%	3.00%	2.20%	384	0.01%	3,687	0.01%	9,599	na	na	na
Marshall Islands	na	na	na	na	na	na	na	na	na	na	na
Martinique	1.30%	na	na	409	0.01%	na	na	na	na	na	na
Mauritania	2.80%	1.50%	−1.30%	2,674	0.04%	1,093	0.00%	409	1,442	3,857	0.01%
Mauritius	1.20%	3.70%	2.50%	1,190	0.02%	4,864	0.02%	4,088	14,946	17,783	0.05%
Mayotte	na	na	na	na	na	na	na	na	na	na	na
Mexico	1.80%	0.20%	−1.60%	99,536	1.62%	392,513	1.30%	3,943	5,904	587,673	1.55%
Micronesia, Fed. Sts.	2.10%	−1.80%	−3.90%	118	0.00%	203	0.00%	1,715	na	na	na
Moldova	−0.20%	−10.80%	−10.60%	4,286	0.07%	1,285	0.00%	300	na	na	na
Monaco	na	na	na	na	na	na	na	na	na	na	na
Mongolia	2.00%	−1.40%	−3.40%	2,698	0.04%	943	0.00%	350	1,640	4,425	0.01%
Morocco	1.80%	0.20%	−1.60%	28,811	0.47%	32,693	0.11%	1,135	3,081	88,774	0.23%
Mozambique	2.30%	2.60%	0.30%	17,804	0.29%	2,779	0.01%	156	822	14,639	0.04%
Myanmar	1.10%	na	na	45,357	0.74%	na	na	na	na	na	na

Namibia	2.60%	1.10%	-1.50%	1,753	0.03%	3,445	0.01%	1,965	3,848	6,745	0.02%
Nepal	2.50%	2.20%	-0.30%	24,037	0.39%	5,267	0.02%	219	1,153	27,704	0.07%
Netherlands	0.60%	1.90%	1.30%	15,890	0.26%	384,534	1.27%	24,200	21,281	338,145	0.89%
Netherlands Antilles	1.50%	na	na	220	0.00%	na	na	na	na	na	na
New Caledonia	2.60%	na	na	218	0.00%	na	na	na	na	na	na
New Zealand	1.60%	1.20%	-0.40%	3,944	0.06%	60,649	0.20%	15,376	16,035	63,251	0.17%
Nicaragua	2.90%	1.60%	-1.30%	5,096	0.08%	1,949	0.01%	382	1,873	9,546	0.03%
Niger	3.40%	-1.90%	-5.30%	10,833	0.18%	1,729	0.01%	160	571	6,188	0.02%
Nigeria	2.90%	0.70%	-2.20%	128,454	2.09%	38,416	0.13%	299	1,092	140,218	0.37%
Northern Mariana Islands	na	na	na	na	na	na	na	na	na	na	na
Norway	0.50%	3.80%	3.30%	4,470	0.07%	170,188	0.56%	38,070	25,807	115,368	0.30%
Oman	4.70%	-0.40%	-5.10%	2,589	0.04%	na	na	na	6,265	16,223	0.04%
Pakistan	2.50%	2.00%	-0.50%	138,334	2.26%	66,219	0.22%	479	2,175	300,850	0.79%
Panama	1.80%	3.00%	1.20%	2,868	0.05%	9,180	0.03%	3,200	6,348	18,208	0.05%
Papua New Guinea	2.30%	2.50%	0.20%	4,819	0.08%	4,346	0.01%	902	2,444	11,778	0.03%
Paraguay	2.70%	0.00%	-2.70%	5,508	0.09%	9,877	0.03%	1,793	3,183	17,533	0.05%
Peru	1.70%	4.60%	2.90%	25,635	0.42%	71,495	0.24%	2,789	4,349	111,495	0.29%
Philippines	2.30%	1.60%	-0.70%	78,718	1.28%	89,835	0.30%	1,141	2,752	216,603	0.57%
Poland	0.20%	4.20%	4.00%	38,882	0.63%	153,066	0.51%	3,937	6,570	255,454	0.67%
Portugal	0.10%	2.00%	1.90%	9,975	0.16%	107,701	0.36%	10,797	13,920	138,853	0.37%
Puerto Rico	1.10%	na	na	3,955	0.06%	na	na	na	na	na	na
Qatar	5.60%	-5.30%	-10.90%	849	0.01%	na	na	na	9,934	8,434	0.02%
Reunion	1.70%	na	na	713	0.01%	na	na	na	na	na	na
Romania	-0.40%	-0.10%	0.30%	22,284	0.36%	34,418	0.11%	1,544	4,426	98,626	0.26%
Russian Federation	-0.10%	-7.90%	-7.80%	146,866	2.39%	342,008	1.13%	2,329	2,985	438,382	1.15%
Rwanda	1.80%	-5.70%	-7.50%	8,329	0.14%	1,551	0.01%	186	366	3,046	0.01%
Sao Tome and Principe	2.70%	0.70%	-2.00%	180	0.00%	199	0.00%	1,104	na	na	na
Saudi Arabia	3.40%	-2.50%	-5.90%	22,183	0.36%	135,453	0.45%	6,106	6,508	144,357	0.38%
Senegal	2.60%	0.00%	-2.60%	9,494	0.15%	4,427	0.01%	466	1,560	14,813	0.04%
Seychelles	1.50%	1.70%	0.20%	82	0.00%	556	0.00%	6,822	na	na	na
Sierra Leone	2.50%	-5.70%	-8.20%	5,113	0.08%	681	0.00%	133	378	1,933	0.01%
Singapore	2.00%	6.70%	4.70%	3,294	0.05%	120,177	0.40%	36,484	28,648	94,367	0.25%
Slovak Republic	0.30%	0.30%	0.00%	5,432	0.09%	19,515	0.06%	3,593	3,610	19,608	0.05%
Slovenia	-0.10%	4.20%	4.30%	1,980	0.03%	20,716	0.07%	10,463	na	na	na
Solomon Islands	3.20%	1.00%	-2.20%	443	0.01%	378	0.00%	854	1,959	868	0.00%
Somalia	1.70%	na	na	9,230	0.15%	na	na	na	na	na	na
South Africa	2.00%	-0.20%	-2.20%	43,089	0.70%	125,054	0.41%	2,902	4,501	193,924	0.51%
Spain	0.20%	1.30%	1.10%	39,559	0.64%	544,944	1.80%	13,775	15,336	606,697	1.60%

2000 Alphabetical Listing (U.S. Dollars) (Cont.)

Country	1990–1997 Growth Rate (%) Pop	GNP	GNP per Capita	Year 2000 Population (000)	% of World Pop	GNP (millions)	% of World GNP	GNP per Capita	GNP per Capita (PPP)	GNP (PPP) (millions)	% of World GNP (PPP)
Sri Lanka	1.30%	4.00%	2.70%	19,285	0.31%	16,789	0.06%	871	3,713	71,607	0.19%
St. Kitts and Nevis	-0.40%	4.00%	4.40%	41	0.00%	287	0.00%	7,081	11,671	473	0.00%
St. Lucia	0.90%	2.80%	1.90%	163	0.00%	641	0.00%	3,924	na	na	na
St. Vincent and the Grenadines	0.70%	1.80%	1.10%	114	0.00%	287	0.00%	2,509	na	na	na
Sudan	2.00%	3.70%	1.70%	29,435	0.48%	9,982	0.03%	339	na	na	na
Suriname	0.30%	-0.50%	-0.80%	416	0.01%	666	0.00%	1,602	2,161	899	0.00%
Swaziland	3.10%	-0.60%	-3.70%	1,050	0.02%	1,421	0.00%	1,354	2,385	2,504	0.01%
Sweden	0.50%	0.20%	-0.30%	8,982	0.15%	219,950	0.73%	24,487	18,264	164,051	0.43%
Switzerland	0.80%	-0.50%	-1.30%	7,259	0.12%	264,820	0.88%	36,479	24,222	175,841	0.46%
Syrian Arab Republic	2.90%	3.30%	0.40%	16,229	0.26%	18,198	0.06%	1,121	5,427	88,078	0.23%
Taiwan (Rep. of China)	0.00%	0.00%	0.00%	22,113	0.36%	362,000	1.20%	16,370	12,507	276,567	0.73%
Tajikistan	1.80%	-16.10%	-17.90%	6,348	0.10%	1,192	0.00%	188	343	2,178	0.01%
Tanzania	3.00%	0.90%	-2.10%	34,220	0.56%	7,583	0.03%	222	576	19,696	0.05%
Thailand	1.20%	5.90%	4.70%	62,810	1.02%	177,265	0.59%	2,822	9,486	595,845	1.57%
Togo	3.00%	-1.20%	-4.20%	4,748	0.08%	1,395	0.00%	294	912	4,329	0.01%
Tonga	0.30%	1.40%	1.10%	99	0.00%	198	0.00%	2,003	na	na	na
Trinidad and Tobago	0.80%	0.50%	-0.30%	1,339	0.02%	5,655	0.02%	4,224	8,482	11,354	0.03%
Tunisia	1.70%	2.00%	0.30%	9,693	0.16%	19,141	0.06%	1,975	5,075	49,196	0.13%
Turkey	1.80%	2.30%	0.50%	67,250	1.10%	207,213	0.68%	3,081	5,721	384,728	1.01%
Turkmenistan	3.40%	-14.60%	-18.00%	5,149	0.08%	1,764	0.01%	343	na	na	na
Uganda	3.10%	4.40%	1.30%	22,266	0.36%	7,470	0.02%	336	1,568	34,914	0.09%
Ukraine	-0.30%	-12.60%	-12.30%	50,243	0.82%	32,793	0.11%	653	1,245	62,558	0.16%
United Arab Emirates	4.80%	-3.80%	-8.60%	2,970	0.05%	na	na	na	10,506	31,198	0.08%

United Kingdom	0.40%	1.90%	1.50%	59,720	0.97%	1,359,764	4.49%	22,769	20,748	1,239,099	3.26%
United States	1.00%	1.70%	0.70%	275,746	4.50%	8,259,358	27.30%	29,953	29,953	8,259,358	21.73%
Uruguay	0.70%	3.50%	2.80%	3,335	0.05%	21,924	0.07%	6,574	7,612	25,385	0.07%
Uzbekistan	2.00%	−5.60%	−7.60%	25,116	0.41%	20,820	0.07%	829	1,596	40,091	0.11%
Vanuatu	2.60%	−3.50%	−6.10%	191	0.00%	209	0.00%	1,095	1,672	320	0.00%
Venezuela	2.20%	−0.20%	−2.40%	24,314	0.40%	84,969	0.28%	3,495	6,996	170,108	0.45%
Vietnam	2.10%	6.10%	4.00%	81,646	1.33%	28,896	0.10%	354	na	na	na
Virgin Islands (U.S.)	1.60%	na	na	123	0.00%	na	na	na	na	na	na
West Bank and Gaza	5.10%	na	na	2,984	0.05%	na	na	na	na	na	na
Western Samoa	1.20%	0.70%	−0.50%	180	0.00%	199	0.00%	1,104	1,980	357	0.00%
Yemen, Rep.	4.30%	−1.50%	−5.80%	18,236	0.30%	4,806	0.02%	264	na	na	na
Yugoslavia, FR (Serbia/ Montenegro)	0.10%	na	na	10,646	0.17%	na	na	na	na	na	na
Zaire	3.20%	−5.30%	−8.50%	48,194	0.79%	4,512	0.01%	94	314	15,146	0.04%
Zambia	2.80%	−0.90%	−3.70%	10,259	0.17%	3,563	0.01%	347	770	7,901	0.02%
Zimbabwe	2.30%	−0.70%	−3.00%	12,278	0.20%	8,311	0.03%	677	1,743	21,403	0.06%
World Total				**6,134,466**	**100%**	**30,251,491**	**100%**	**4,931**	**6,197**	**38,016,773**	**100%**

Top 10 in 2000 (U.S. Dollars)

GNP	GNP (millions)	% of World GNP
World Total	**30,251,491**	**100.00%**
Top 10 Total	**21,965,897**	**72.61%**
Rest of World	**8,285,594**	**27.39%**
United States	8,259,358	**27.30%**
Japan	4,427,104	**14.63%**
Germany	2,127,086	**7.03%**
France	1,446,515	**4.78%**
United Kingdom	1,359,764	**4.49%**
China	1,179,345	**3.90%**
Italy	1,168,771	**3.86%**
Brazil	850,852	**2.81%**
Canada	602,158	**1.99%**
Spain	544,944	**1.80%**

Population	Population (000)	% of World Pop
World Total	**6,134,466**	**100.00%**
Top 10 Total	**3,611,145**	**58.87%**
Rest of World	**2,523,321**	**41.13%**
China	1,268,121	**20.67%**
India	1,015,287	**16.55%**
United States	275,746	**4.50%**
Indonesia	210,785	**3.44%**
Brazil	170,661	**2.78%**
Russian Federation	146,866	**2.39%**
Pakistan	138,334	**2.26%**
Bangladesh	129,663	**2.11%**
Nigeria	128,454	**2.09%**
Japan	127,229	**2.07%**

GNP per Capita

Country	GNP per Capita	% of Luxembourg
Luxembourg	38,587	100.00%
Norway	38,070	98.66%
Singapore	36,484	94.55%
Switzerland	36,479	94.54%
Kuwait	35,242	91.33%
Japan	34,796	90.18%
Denmark	33,894	87.84%
United States	29,953	77.62%
Hong Kong	27,463	71.17%
Austria	25,854	67.00%

Top 10 GNP (PPP)

Country	GNP (PPP) (millions)
United States	8,259,358
China	5,671,304
Japan	2,971,197
Germany	1,688,783
India	1,608,186
France	1,282,677
United Kingdom	1,239,099
Italy	1,196,590
Indonesia	983,923
Brazil	944,838

Top 10 GNP per Capita (PPP)

Country	GNP per Capita (PPP)
Luxembourg	35,708
United States	29,953
Singapore	28,648
Norway	25,807
Hong Kong	24,602
Switzerland	24,222
Denmark	23,555
Japan	23,353
Belgium	22,765
Austria	21,787

Top 10 GNP: 2000

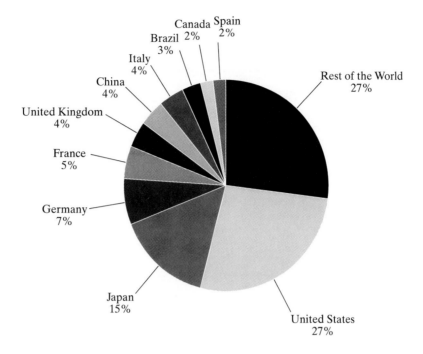

Top 10 Population: 2000

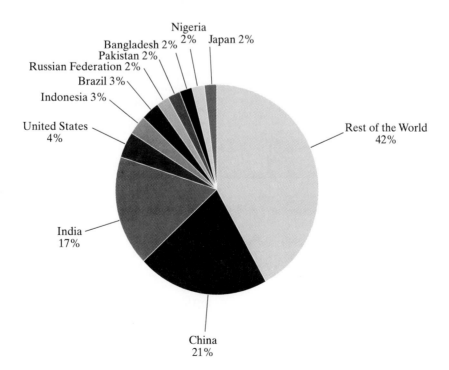

Top 10 GNP per Capita: 2000

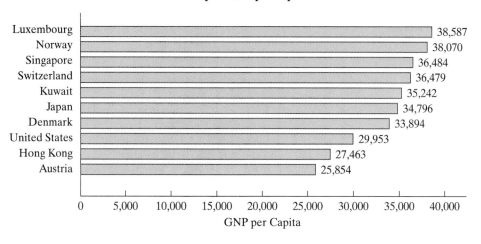

Country	GNP per Capita
Luxembourg	38,587
Norway	38,070
Singapore	36,484
Switzerland	36,479
Kuwait	35,242
Japan	34,796
Denmark	33,894
United States	29,953
Hong Kong	27,463
Austria	25,854

Top 10 in 2010

GNP	GNP (millions)	% of World GNP	Population	Population (000)	% of World Population
World	41,619,938	100.00%	World	7,203,265	100.00%
Top 10	29,769,466	71.53%	Top 10	4,199,863	58.30%
Rest of the World	11,850,471	28.47%	Rest of the World	3,003,402	41.70%
United States	11,763,698	28.26%	China	1,428,781	19.84%
Japan	5,137,835	12.34%	India	1,225,550	17.01%
Germany	2,722,849	6.54%	United States	301,592	4.19%
China	2,319,949	5.57%	Indonesia	247,045	3.43%
France	1,851,661	4.45%	Brazil	200,019	2.78%
United Kingdom	1,792,234	4.31%	Pakistan	184,112	2.56%
Italy	1,424,726	3.42%	Nigeria	170.963	2.37%
Brazil	1,188,665	2.86%	Bangladesh	158,058	2.19%
Canada	833,131	2.00%	Russian Federation	151,331	2.10%
Korea, Rep.	734,718	1.77%	Japan	132,411	1.84%

GNP per Capita		
Country	*GNP per Capita*	*% of Norway*
Norway	51,089	100.00%
Singapore	47,401	92.78%
Luxembourg	44,277	86.67%
Denmark	43,790	85.71%
Switzerland	42.286	82.77%
Kuwait	40,416	79.11%
Japan	38,802	75.95%
United States	39,005	76.35%
Ireland	35,359	69.21%
Finland	32,838	64.28%

Top 10 GNP: 2010

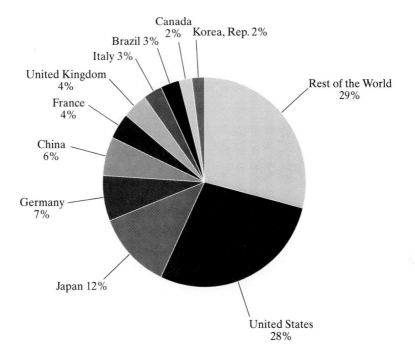

Top 10 GNP per Capita: 2010

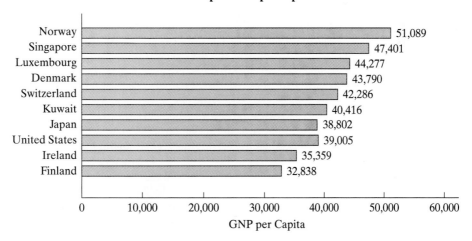

Top 10 in 2020

GNP	GNP (millions)	% of World GNP
World	56,536,056	100.00%
Top 10	40,975,773	72.48%
Rest of the World	15,560,283	27.52%
United States	15,809,426	27.96%
Japan	6,262,992	11.08%
China	3,962,808	7.01%
Germany	3,451,622	6.11%
France	2,428,733	4.30%
United Kingdom	2,316,692	4.10%
Italy	1,771,088	3.13%
Brazil	1,597,467	2.83%
Korea, Rep.	1,140,994	2.02%
India	1,114,291	1.97%

Population	Population (000)	% of World Pop
World	8,492,006	100.00%
Top 10	4,873,160	57.39%
Rest of the World	3,618,846	42.61%
China	1,609,796	18.96%
India	1,464.902	17.25%
United States	326,607	3.85%
Indonesia	286,706	3.38%
Pakistan	242,669	2.86%
Brazil	232,130	2.73%
Nigeria	225,338	2.65%
Bangladesh	190,792	2.25%
Russian Federation	157,495	1.85%
Mexico	136,726	1.61%

Country	GNP per Capita	% of Norway
Norway	67,265	100.00%
Singapore	57,870	86.03%
Denmark	56,301	83.70%
Ireland	51,304	76.27%
Luxembourg	51,310	76.28%
Switzerland	49,024	72.88%
Kuwait	47,758	71.00%
Japan	45,449	67.57%
Finland	44,068	65.51%
Hong Kong	42,614	63.35%

Top 10 GNP: 2020

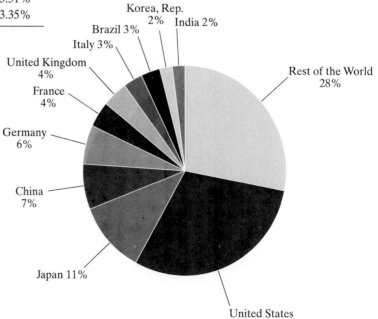

Top 10 Population: 2020

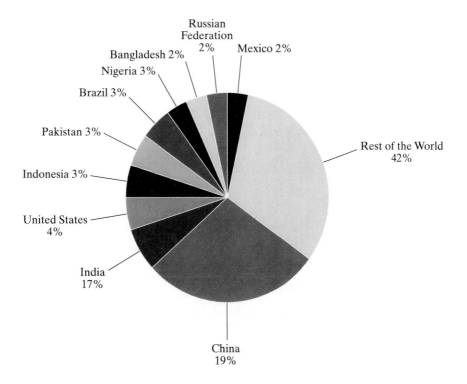

Top 10 GNP per Capita: 2020

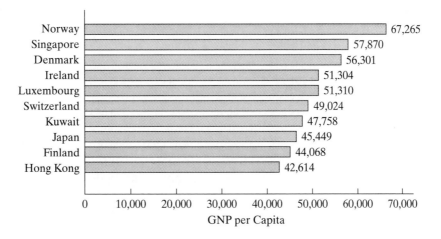

2000: Big Emerging Markets[a] (BEMs) (U.S. Dollars)

Market	GNP (millions)	% of World GNP	GNP per Capita	Population (000)	% of World Population	GNP (PPP) (millions)	% of World GNP (PPP)
BEM (Total)	5,360,256	17.7%	1,689	3,173,940	51.7%	12,562,231	33.0%
China Economic Area (Total)	1,730,280	5.7%	1,334	1,297,114	21.1%	6,117,126	16.1%
China	1,179,345	3.9%	930	1,268,121	20.7%	5,671,304	14.9%
Taiwan (Rep. of China)	362,000	1.2%	16,370	22,113	0.4%	276,567	0.7%
Hong Kong	188,936	0.6%	27,463	6,880	0.1%	169,255	0.4%
Brazil	850,852	2.8%	4,986	170,661	2.8%	944,838	2.5%
Korea, Rep.	520,855	1.7%	10,992	47,385	0.8%	692,451	1.8%
India	430,096	1.4%	424	1,015,287	16.6%	1,608,186	4.2%
Mexico	392,513	1.3%	3,943	99,536	1.6%	587,673	1.5%
Argentina	360,472	1.2%	9,720	37,087	0.6%	355,545	0.9%
Russian Federation	342,008	1.1%	2,329	146,866	2.4%	438,382	1.2%
Indonesia	247,846	0.8%	1,176	210,785	3.4%	983,923	2.6%
Turkey	207,213	0.7%	3,081	67,250	1.1%	384,728	1.0%
Poland	153,066	0.5%	3,937	38,882	0.6%	255,454	0.7%
South Africa	125,054	0.4%	2,902	43,089	0.7%	193,924	0.5%

[a] Countries with 2000 GNP of more than $100 billion, which we believe will grow at rates that exceed the world average and are well positioned to become high- or higher-income countries in the new millennium. These countries are at very different stages of development ranging from India, which is a low-income country, to Taiwan and Korea, which are high-income countries. As a group we believe that the BEMs will increase their share of world income.

2010: Big Emerging Markets (BEMs) (U.S. Dollars)

Market	GNP (millions)	% of World GNP	GNP per Capita	Population (000)	% of World Population	GNP (PPP) (millions)	% of World GNP (PPP)
BEM (Total)	8,503,833	20.43%	2,316	3,672,192	51.0%	21,298,562	40.90%
China Economic Area (Total)	3,192,211	7.67%	2,185	1,460,676	20.3%	11,931,237	22.91%
China	2,319,949	5.57%	1,624	1,428,781	19.8%	11,229,094	21.6%
Taiwan (Rep. of China)	618,348	1.49%	25,694	24,066	0.3%	474,190	0.9%
Hong Kong	253,914	0.61%	32,436	7,828	0.1%	227,953	0.4%
Brazil	1,188,665	2.86%	5,943	200,019	2.8%	1,323,647	2.5%
Korea, Rep.	734,718	1.77%	14,177	51,826	0.7%	978,981	1.9%
India	700,581	1.68%	572	1,225,550	17.0%	2,634,298	5.1%
Mexico	639,362	1.54%	5,427	117,812	1.6%	962,385	1.8%
Argentina	559,803	1.35%	13,266	42,200	0.6%	554,352	1.1%
Russian Federation	482,437	1.16%	3,188	151,331	2.1%	618,955	1.2%
Turkey	337,529	0.81%	4,158	81,177	1.1%	630,206	1.2%
Poland	249,328	0.60%	6,161	40,466	0.6%	416,838	0.8%
Indonesia	247,846	0.60%	1,003	247,045	3.4%	981,407	1.9%
South Africa	171,354	0.41%	3,168	54,091	0.8%	266,256	0.5%

2020: Big Emerging Markets (BEMs) (U.S. Dollars)

Market	GNP (millions)	GNP per Capita	% of World GNP	Population (000)	% of World Population	GNP (PPP) (millions)	% of World GNP (PPP)
BEM (Total)	13,034,542	3,080	23.06%	4,231,811	49.8%	34,408,655	45.8%
China Economic Area (Total)	6,896,406	3,675	12.20%	1,876,808	22.1%	22,134,706	29.5%
China	3,962,808	2,462	7.01%	1,609,796	19.0%	19,274,936	25.7%
Taiwan (Rep. of China)	960,276	36,845	1.70%	26,062	0.3%	738,491	1.0%
Hong Kong	375,855	42,614	0.66%	8,820	0.1%	338,518	0.5%
Brazil	1,597,467	6,882	2.83%	232,130	2.7%	1,782,761	2.4%
Korea, Rep.	1,140,994	20,330	2.02%	56,125	0.7%	1,524,639	2.0%
India	1,114,291	761	1.97%	1,464,902	17.3%	4,211,203	5.6%
Mexico	946,412	6,922	1.67%	136,726	1.6%	1,429,710	1.9%
Argentina	752,328	15,823	1.33%	47,546	0.6%	746,567	1.0%
Russian Federation	664,264	4,218	1.17%	157,495	1.9%	853,176	1.1%
Turkey	524,172	5,402	0.93%	97,031	1.1%	983,252	1.3%
Indonesia	384,897	1,342	0.68%	286,706	3.4%	1,530,671	2.0%
South Africa	241,711	3,666	0.43%	65,937	0.8%	376,671	0.5%
Poland	369,067	8,677	0.65%	42,535	0.5%	618,061	0.8%

Name Index

A

Aab, Linda, 426
Aaker, David A., 339
Abdallah, Wagdy M., 381
Abegglen, James C., 89, 303, 545
Adams, Richard, 112
Adamson, John, 258
Adelman, Irma, 40–41
Adler, Lee, 189
Adler, Paul S., 275
Afemann, Uwe, 445
Agarwal, Sanjeev, 260
Agesilaus, 549
Agins, Teri, 505
Ahuwalia, K. M. S. "Titoo," 166
Aiko, Sugaya, 547, 548
Ajami, Riad, 182, 264
Albright, Katherine, 106, 113
Alden, Dana L., 426
Alexander, Nicholas, 405
Ali, Abbas J., 260
Allen, Christopher S., 276
Allen, John M., Jr., 109
Allen, Randy L., 405
Allocca, Michael, 323
Alster, Judith, 205
Ambrose, St., 91
Amine, Lyn S., 113
Anckar, Patrik, 381
Anderer, Charles J., 219, 494, 549, 554–557
Andersen, Otto, 261
Anderson, Kym, 164
Andrews, J. Craig, 426
Ang, Sween Hoon, 426
Angle, Andrew, 124, 130–131
El-Ansary, Adel L., 406
Ansberry, Clare, 200
Ardrey, William J., 65
Armani, Giorgio, 202
Arnold, David J., 400
Atuahene-Gime, Kwaku, 260
Aulakh, P., 260
Aurand, Timothy W., 531
Austin, James E., 261
Axline, W. Andrew, 164

Ayers, Richard H., 252
Azsomer, Ayesegl, 260

B

Baer, Herb, 544
Baetz, Mark C., 540
Bafandi, Vahid, 207
Bagley, Jennifer M., 113
Bahree, Bhushan, 52
Bailey, James, 13
Baker, R. Garrity, 99
Ballard, John, 357–358
Banerjee, Anish, 426
Barathan, Joyce, 131
Barnard, Kurt, 386
Barnavik, Percy, 509
Barnet, Richard J., 21, 191
Barnett, C., 512
Baron, David P., 289, 303, 545
Barr, Stephen, 411
Bart, Christopher, 540
Bartlett, Christopher A., 255, 524, 531
Bartmess, Andrew, 303
Bassiry, G. R., 21
Basu, K., 113
Batra, Rajeev, 158
Bauer, James L., 115
Bauer, Peter T., 44, 405
Beals, Vaughn L., Jr., 494–496, 498, 500–501
Beatty, Sally Goll, 416
Bega, Lou, 1
Belk, Russell W., 427
Bell, Daniel, 37
Bellas, Ralph A., Jr., 354
Bello, Daniel C., 260, 405, 406
Benedict, Ruth, 71, 73, 89
Benetton, Luciano, 167, 506–507
Benezra, Karen, 179
Bennett, Peter D., 192, 386
Bennis, Warren, 531
Berbeke, Alain, 289
Bergh, Peter A., 302
Berners-Lee, Tim, 445
Biagiotti, Laura, 202

Bilkey, Warren J., 240
Bingaman, Anne, 104
Birch, Dawn, 426
Black, J. Stewart, 173
Blackhurst, Richard, 164
Blackwell, Roger D., 205
Blass, Bill, 227
Blay, Tomás, 467
Bleakley, Fred R., 357
Bleeke, Joel, 275
Blodgett, Linda Longfellow, 275
Boddewyn, Jean J., 54
Bonaccorsi, Andrea, 260
Bond, Michael Harris, 68, 78, 90, 180
Bonvillian, Gary, 74, 88
Boote, Alfred S., 195
Borrus, Amy, 106
Bosisio, Franco, 329
Boss, Hugo, 202
Botan, Carl, 431, 439
Bourgeois, Jacques C., 84
Bourguignon, Philippe, 120, 122–123
Bovard, James, 372
Bovet, Susan Fry, 439
Bowes, Walter, 323
Bowman, Harry, 539
Boya, Unal O., 406
Bradley, George, 292
Bradshaw, Della, 87
Brady, John T., 405
Braithwaite, John, 113
Branson, Richard, 509
Brauchli, Marcus W., 421, 433
Brien, Nick, 412
Brodsky, Ira, 266
Browder, Seanna, 84
Browning, E. S., 333, 349
Browning, John, 445, 459
Bruns, Robert, 406
Bu, Tore, 318–320
Buckley, Neil, 369
Bulkeley, William M., 251
Burgess, Steven M., 21
Burke, Raymond R., 459
Burnett, John, 339
Burns, David J., 405
Burt, Tim, 293

Subject Index